Taxation for Decision Makers

2019 EDITION

Shirley Dennis-Escoffier

and

Karen A. Fortin

WILEY

EDITORIAL DIRECTOR	Michael McDonald
EXECUTIVE EDITOR	Lise Johnson
SENIOR EDITORIAL MANAGER	Leah Michael
EDITORIAL MANAGER	Judy Howarth
CONTENT MANAGEMENT DIRECTOR	Lisa Wojcik
CONTENT MANAGER	Nichole Urban
SENIOR CONTENT SPECIALIST	Nicole Repasky
PRODUCTION EDITOR	Bharathy Surya Prakash
COVER PHOTO CREDIT	© Adam Gault/Getty Images

This book was set in 10/12 TimesLTStd-Roman by SPi Global, Chennai and printed and bound by Quad/Graphics.

This book was previously published by Pearson Education, Inc.

ISBN: 978-1-119-49728-8 (PBK)
ISBN: 978-1-119-49726-4 (EVALC)
Serial Record: ISSN 2006209815

The inside back cover will contain printing identification and country of origin if omitted from this page. In addition, if the ISBN on the back cover differs from the ISBN on this page, the one on the back cover is correct.

V10009206_040819

To the memory of Marty Escoffier who was always ready with a willing hand to help, a word of encouragement as deadlines neared, and a sense of humor that never failed to make us laugh when we needed it most. His presence has been missed as we have worked on this revision.

Shirley Dennis-Escoffier and Karen A. Fortin

Brief Table of Contents

Table of Contents

PART II Income, Expenses, and Individual Taxes

3 Determining Gross Income 108

4 Employee Compensation 153

PART IV Property Dispositions

8 Property Dispositions 354

PART V Business Taxation

10 Taxation of Corporations 452

11 Sole Proprietorships and Flow-Through Entities 501

PART VI Wealth Taxation

Preface

FOCUS

This text is designed for a one-semester introductory tax course at either the undergraduate or graduate level. It is ideal for an MBA course or any program emphasizing a decision-making approach. This text introduces all tax topics on the CPA exam in only 12 chapters.

COMPREHENSIVE YET CLEAR AND CONCISE

This text covers basic taxation of all taxable entities—individuals, corporations, S corporations, partnerships, and fiduciary entities, emphasizing a balance between concepts and details. Tax concepts and applications are presented in a clear, concise, student-friendly writing style with sufficient technical detail to provide a foundation for future practice in taxation and consulting while not overwhelming the student with seldom-encountered details.

WHAT'S NEW THIS EDITION

The Tax Cuts and Jobs Act passed by Congress in December 2017 is the most significant change to tax law in more than thirty years. This text has been completely updated for all changes made by this Act as well as the Bipartisan Budget Act of 2018 and all other new pronouncements issued in the first several months of 2018. Because the CPA exam will not be testing on the new law until 2019, examples and problems on 2017 law are still included in this text in addition to the new law effective in 2018.

In addition to updating all chapters for changes to the tax law, Chapter 1 was modified to introduce the changes made to the taxation of corporations and flow-through businesses. The decision-making focus of this text is introduced in this first chapter through simple problems on the choice of business form.

Chapter 2 now includes a discussion of the legislative process involved in passing the Tax Cuts and Jobs Act. New tax forms are now introduced in several chapters of the text. A complete set of filled-in forms for a C corporation, partnership, S corporation, and sole proprietorship are also included on the companion website for this text.

Finally, the authors went over the text line-by-line, not only to update it, but to improve readability.

TAX PLANNING

TAX PLANNING

The importance of tax planning is emphasized throughout the text. Margin icons are woven into each chapter to highlight planning opportunities. Tax planning strategies are introduced early in Chapter 2 along with the impact of taxes on cash flow.

LEARNING OBJECTIVES

Each chapter begins with learning objectives for that specific chapter as well as a basic introduction to the included topics, emphasizing why decision makers need to understand these topics. Each chapter is organized by learning objective making is easy to identify relevant topics.

SETTING THE STAGE—AN INTRODUCTORY CASE

Each chapter opens with a case that focuses on one or more key issues within the chapter to promote critical analysis and decision-making skills. The case is then revisited at the end of the chapter with a suggested solution to stimulate further class discussion.

EXAMPLES

Rigorous topics are tackled through numerous simple but realistic examples.

Example 1.1

When Alex Rodriguez, the former Texas Rangers shortstop, lived in Texas (a state with no individual income tax), he owed more than $271,000 to California (which assesses a nonresident income tax) for games he played in that state during baseball season. It was estimated that if the Rangers had played all their games at home, A-Rod's state tax bill could have been reduced by more than half a million dollars a year. When A-Rod switched to the New York Yankees, his state and local tax burden increased dramatically. On the $155 million that A-Rod was to be paid over his seven-year contract, he was expected to owe $3.57 million to New York City and an additional $6.19 million to the State of New York for income taxes. His tax burden increased further when he renegotiated his contract in a deal worth $275 million over ten years.

KEY CASES

Key Cases bring real world applications into the classroom.

KEY CASES *In 2008, actor Wesley Snipes was sentenced to 3 years in prison for willfully failing to file tax returns for years 1999–2004, a period in which he earned more than $38 million. Following an unsuccessful appeal, he served his sentence in a medium-security prison in Pennsylvania.*

In December 2014, Representative Michael Grimm, who had just been re-elected to his third term in Congress, resigned from Congress after agreeing to plead guilty to felony tax fraud. The indictment alleged that he kept two sets of records for a restaurant he previously owned concealing more than $1 million in gross receipts and underreporting his employees' wages to avoid federal and state taxes. He faced up to 30 months in prison.

EXPANDED TOPICS

The *Expanded Topics* section included at the end of Chapters 3, 4, 6, 11, and 12 contains more advanced topics for instructors who wish to challenge their students. These advanced discussions relate to the other material within the chapters, but which our adopters and reviewers have indicated could be omitted to allow more time for the more critical material.

SUMMARY

Each chapter closes with a *Summary* of the most important topics introduced in the chapter, reinforcing important concepts for students.

KEY TERMS

A list of *Key Terms* is included at the end of each chapter. They appear in bold print and are keyed to the first page on which the term is discussed.

TEST YOURSELF

Each chapter includes a *Test Yourself* section of five multiple-choice questions for students to assess their understanding of topics covered in the chapter. Answers to these questions follow the end-of-chapter materials.

PROBLEM ASSIGNMENTS

More than 60 problems are included at the end of each chapter. *Check Your Understanding* includes a wide variety of noncomputational questions that review the topics included in the chapter. *Crunch the Numbers* presents quantitative problems covering the computational aspects of chapter materials. Comprehensive problems integrate topics covered in several different chapters.

DEVELOP PLANNING SKILLS

Develop Planning Skills problems give students the opportunity to test their knowledge in planning situations. The tax planning suggestions integrated throughout the text continually remind students of the importance of developing appropriate planning strategies.

THINK OUTSIDE THE TEXT

For instructors wishing to challenge their students, *Think Outside the Text* questions develop critical thinking skills by requiring students to expand their thinking beyond the material covered in the chapter.

IDENTIFY THE ISSUES

Identify the Issues includes short scenarios designed to challenge the students to identify issues and formulate research questions. These scenarios, however, do not provide enough information to enable students to develop definitive solutions but are designed to help students practice the issue-identification step in the research process, a step that many new tax students consider the most difficult.

DEVELOP RESEARCH SKILLS

Develop Research Skills requires students to research the relevant authorities and present possible solutions. These can be solved using a subscription-based tax service or free Internet sources. Citations to relevant Internal Revenue Code sections, cases, and rulings are included only in the Instructor's Manual along with solutions to these research problems, allowing each instructor to decide what, if any, hints should be given to students when a problem is assigned.

FILL-IN THE FORMS

Most of the chapters have problems that require completion of one of more tax forms in a *Fill-in the Forms* section. Some of these are very basic and may simply require completion of forms for earlier problems—usually one or two forms—and will assist in familiarizing the student with basic tax forms. There are, however, several chapters that have more comprehensive problems that require completion of a number of forms. These will present a challenge to the student and lend themselves to completion in small groups. These include returns for individuals and the four types of business entities covered. All or parts of these problems may be assigned when the instructor feels the students are ready for additional challenges presented in translating tax knowledge to form completion. The solutions for these problems are only included in the Instructor's Manual.

CHAPTER APPENDICES

End-of-chapter appendices introduce topics not typically covered in a first tax course including corporate reorganizations and taxation of nonprofit entities. These materials are placed in chapter appendices to allow instructors the flexibility to include or omit them as deemed appropriate.

SAMPLE TAX RETURNS

Sample Filled-In Tax Returns are on the companion website for this text for easy access and updating. There are completed returns for a C corporation, S corporation, partnership, and a self-employed individual.

UP-TO-DATE

This text has been completely updated for all recent legislation and for all IRS pronouncements available as of April 2018.

ORGANIZATION

This text is ideal for schools with only one required tax course. Its 12 chapters can be covered in one semester, with time for assessments, eliminating the need to omit chapters. The text emphasizes tax planning to stimulate students' thinking in terms of the effect taxation has on decisions for both individuals and entities.

There are two introductory chapters in Part I. The first chapter includes a brief introduction to the different types of taxes and introduces Adams Smith's Canons of Taxation that can be used throughout the text to evaluate specific tax legislation. To emphasize to students the decision-making focus of this text, the first chapter introduces simple problems on the choice of business entity and provides an easily understood background for the more complex material to follow. The second chapter covers tax compliance issues, an introduction to tax planning, and the basics of tax research. A sample research problem (with sources included in an appendix) is included that can be used to guide students in performing basic tax research at any time during the course.

Part II has three chapters that cover income and expenses, as well as other topics needed for individual return preparation. Chapter 3 answers the question, "What is income?" by exploring the various facets of taxable and nontaxable income for entities as well as individuals. Chapter 4 introduces an example of a dual planning orientation (the two sides to any transaction) with the discussion of employee compensation, a subject often relegated to the end of a text where, unfortunately, many students are never introduced to it. This topic provides an opportunity for students to view transactions from an individual employee's perspective (maximizing employee benefits while minimizing taxable income) and the employer's perspective (designing an optimum compensation plans that combines salary and benefits to attract valuable employees). The chapter provides a broader view of income by including the perspective of the entity making the payments.

Chapter 5 includes deductions for individuals and the additional related information on credits and tax rates necessary to complete an individual tax return. This allows the assignment and completion of basic individual tax returns early in the term.

The focus in Parts III and IV turns primarily to business-related subjects covering general business expenses in Chapter 6 and then capital recovery through depreciation, depletion, and amortization in Chapter 7. Chapters 8 and 9 present discussions of taxable and nontaxable property dispositions, respectively.

With the completion of Chapters 6 through 9, the student is ready to apply the information to the basic business entities starting in Part V with the regular corporation in Chapter 10. The specifics of the sole proprietorship and the basic flow-through entities of partnerships and S corporations and their relationship to their owners are included in Chapter 11.

Part VI includes an introduction to wealth transfer taxes—estate and gift taxes. It also includes a discussion of income taxation of estates and trusts, the tax effects on beneficiaries, and the kiddie tax.

YOUR COURSE YOUR WAY

The organization of the text is designed primarily to respond to our adopters who have indicated that many students' interest in taxation is delayed until they are introduced to the provisions affecting their own current or potential taxation. Chapters 3 through 5 now contain the primary information relevant to individual taxation (excluding property transactions) for instructors who prefer introducing individual taxation prior to taxation of entities. Alternatively, Chapter 3, selected topics from Chapter 4, and Chapter 6 may be covered in sequence with topics unique to individuals tackled later in the term along with entity taxation. The flexibility of this text makes it easy to change the sequence of chapters as well as the topics within the chapters. Sections of the chapters are easily identifiable allowing instructors to pick and choose those they deem more important for classroom coverage. We have emphasized the readability of the text so that instructors feel comfortable simply assigning sections to be read by students outside of the class while spending their limited classroom time on more complex topics. This text also works particularly well for instructors who use a flipped-classroom approach to their course.

SUPPLEMENTS

Supplements include an author-prepared Solutions Manual, a separate Instructor's Manual with solutions to the Research and Tax Return Problems, an extensive Test Bank, and PowerPoint slides.

COMMENTS AND SUGGESTIONS

We realize that it is almost impossible for a text to be completely free of technical errors or to include every relevant topic. We welcome comments and suggestions on how we can improve the next edition. Please email your comments and suggestions to sdennis@miami.edu.

ACKNOWLEDGMENTS

We wish to acknowledge and thank Jacklyn Collins, Diana Falsetta, Saira Fida, and Mario Perez, at the University of Miami, for their suggestions. We are grateful to the entire Wiley team for their assistance.

SHIRLEY DENNIS-ESCOFFIER AND KAREN A. FORTIN

About the Authors

Shirley Dennis-Escoffier is an associate professor at the University of Miami, where she teaches both graduate and undergraduate tax classes. She received her Ph.D. from the University of Miami and returned to UM after teaching at the University of Hawaii and California State University in Hayward. She is a Certified Public Accountant licensed to practice in Florida. She is a Past President of the American Taxation Association and remains actively involved in the association receiving the Outstanding Service Award. She is also involved with the American Institute of Certified Public Accountants. She has received several teaching awards including the University of Miami Excellence in Teaching Award and the Masters in Taxation Excellence in Teaching Award. She has published numerous articles in tax and accounting journals and is the recipient of an Ernst and Young Foundation tax research grant.

Karen A. Fortin retired from her position as Professor of Accounting and Taxation at the University of Baltimore, where she had been Department Chair and taught graduate and undergraduate tax classes in both the Business School and the Law School. She received her Ph.D. from the University of South Carolina and held teaching positions at the University of Wisconsin–Milwaukee and the University of Miami. She was a Wisconsin Certified Public Accountant and a recipient of a Sells Award. During her teaching years, she was active in the American Taxation Association and the American Accounting Association as an editor, reviewer, and chairperson for numerous events. As a member of the AICPA she served on several committees and task forces. She has published numerous articles in tax and accounting journals and has co-authored and edited a number of textbooks. When not working on the textbook revision, she volunteers at the local hospital and travels extensively.

Introduction to Taxation and Its Environment

PART I

CHAPTER 1 An Introduction to Taxation

CHAPTER OUTLINE

LEARNING OBJECTIVES

After completing this chapter, you should be able to:

1.1 Explain the basic types of taxes and the bases on which they are levied by various governmental units.

1.2 Compare the effects of progressive, proportional, and regressive tax systems on taxpayers' incomes.

1.3 Explain the characteristics of a good tax system using characteristics of equity, economy, certainty, and convenience.

1.4 Describe the components of the basic income tax model and understand how the tax due is calculated.

1.5 Identify the most common business entities recognized by the U.S. tax system and explain the basic differences in ownership and their effects on entity taxation.

This chapter presents an overview of the various types of taxation, the basic concepts important to the evaluation and understanding of taxation, and an introduction to alternate business forms and taxable entities. These serve as a backdrop to the more detailed provisions of income tax law that follow in subsequent chapters. This chapter is not concerned with specific numbers or their origin, as the majority of these numbers change with each filing year. Their specific applications will be discussed in subsequent chapters. Instead, the focus is on developing a broad understanding of how the U.S. income tax system works.

This first part begins with some background information on the various forms of taxation (income, consumption, wealth, and wealth transfer taxes). It is followed by a discussion of the effects of various tax rate structures (progressive, proportional, and regressive), examples of each type, and their effects. It ends with a brief description of Adam Smith's Canons of Taxation (equity, economy, certainty, and convenience), which provide the framework for assessing what constitutes a "good" tax.

An introductory discussion of federal income taxation follows and introduces the three types of taxable persons—individuals, C corporations, and fiduciaries—the ultimate payers of all income taxes. The basic tax model is introduced and the concepts of gross income, taxable income, tax rates, gross tax liability, and tax credits are presented in the context of the tax model.

The final section ends with a discussion of the various business entities that are subject to federal income taxes, including sole proprietorships, partnerships, C corporations, and S corporations. The individual owner of a sole proprietorship is taxed on the business's income. Partnerships and S corporations are conduit or flow-through entities that pass their income (and loss) items through to their owners for taxation at the owner level. A C corporation's income is subject to double taxation, first at the entity level by the corporate income tax and then a second time when distributed to shareholders as dividends. A table comparing the basic attributes of each of these entities completes this chapter.

SETTING THE STAGE—AN INTRODUCTORY CASE

Wing Hue, an engineer from China with U.S. residency status, recently obtained permanent employment with a U.S. consulting firm. Before coming to the United States, Hue developed a totally new system of gears for bicycles. He obtained a patent on his gear design and plans to solicit several venture capitalists for funds to begin manufacturing and marketing the gears as a venture separate from his consulting work. He believes his gear design would be attractive to both bicycle manufacturers and repair shops as replacements for existing gears.

As a student in China, Hue never had sufficient income to pay taxes. He understands that as a U.S. resident, he is subject to a variety of taxes. He is particularly interested in how his gear manufacturing enterprise will be taxed. He asks you for a brief explanation of the potential taxes that he faces as an employee and as an entrepreneur. We will return to this case at the end of this chapter.

1.1 AN INTRODUCTION TO TAXES

1.1.1 WHAT IS A TAX?

A tax is a forced payment made to a governmental unit that is unrelated to the value of goods or services received. Taxes are not voluntary. When income exceeds an allowable minimum, income taxes are assessed on that excess income by the federal government, and possibly, by certain state and/or local governments.[1] Many states (and other smaller governmental units) require the sellers of certain consumer goods or services to collect sales taxes on these purchases. Failure to collect and remit these taxes to the appropriate governmental unit, subjects the responsible persons to civil, or even criminal, penalties.

The owners of real property are responsible for property taxes levied annually by the local government, based on the assessed value on that property. A bill is sent to the owner for these property taxes and, if unpaid, the government may seize the property.

There are hidden taxes as well. Hidden taxes are those taxes paid on a taxable purchase but not specifically itemized as part of the purchase price. When we buy gasoline for our automobiles, there are significant taxes imbedded in the pump price. The same is true for many other items, such as cigarettes and alcoholic beverages. Nevertheless, if we want that particular good (legally, that is), we pay the hidden tax.

Taxes are not levied as punishment (as are fines for speeding), nor are they levied as payment for government goods or services (such as garbage collection fees). Although we may benefit from governmental activities paid for by these taxes, there is generally no direct connection between the benefit a taxpayer receives and the taxes paid. Property taxes to support local schools are based on the value of the property owned and are unrelated to the owner's school-age children (if any) who benefit from free public education. Thus, taxes are often called forced extractions. You must pay them, but you may have no direct benefit from them.

[1] Individuals are assessed federal income taxes only if their income exceeds their allowable deductions (including their standard or itemized deductions).

For a number of years, there has been a realization that the current income tax system is no longer workable due to its complexity. Its primary goal is no longer to meet the revenue needs of the government's basic functions, but has evolved into an engine that fosters the economic and social goals lawmakers deem appropriate. As our government has grown, so have the laws governing the determination of taxable income and taxes owed. Although there have been many calls for simplifying the tax system, it is necessary to have a basic understanding of the current tax system and its potential alternatives, before developing a new tax system to either replace or supplement the current federal system.

To begin this introductory study of the income tax system, certain basic tax concepts, alternative types of taxes, and the types of tax rates that can be applied to a taxable base are introduced. Adam Smith's canons of taxation, developed many years ago, provide a foundation for assessing whether a tax is indeed a good tax. Once an understanding of these concepts is integrated with an understanding of the current income tax laws, one can intelligently participate in discussions about reforming our current tax system.

1.1.2 EVOLUTION OF THE FEDERAL INCOME TAX

The federal income tax is the most significant tax assessed by the U.S. government. What was once an initially simple concept of taxing income, has expanded over the years into an exceedingly complicated system. Although there had been a federal income tax during the Civil War, the federal income tax system as we know it today did not begin until 1913 when the 16th Amendment to the U.S. Constitution was ratified. The 16th Amendment gave Congress the power to lay and collect taxes "on income, from whatever source derived," without the previous requirement that all direct taxes be imposed based on population. This first federal income tax law enacted in 1913 consisted of only 16 pages and required only a simple individual income tax return.

Each time the income tax statutes were revised between 1913 and 1939, an entire set of new provisions replaced the existing law. In 1939 this procedure changed, and the income tax laws were codified as the **Internal Revenue Code**. Amendments and revisions were then made to the specific sections of the Code, rather than replacing the old law with an entirely new set of statutes.

In 1954, there was another major overhaul of the tax laws. In this 1954 recodification, the income, estate, gift, and excise tax laws were incorporated into the *Internal Revenue Code of 1954*. There were many significant tax law changes between then and 1986, each amending the *Internal Revenue Code of 1954*. Because the Tax Reform Act of 1986 was so extensive, the Code was renamed the *Internal Revenue Code of 1986*. Any current changes to the tax laws are now amendments to the *Internal Revenue Code of 1986*.

A number of factors influence the federal tax laws, but probably the makeup of Congress is the most important. The political parties have different views of the level of taxation relative to the services that should be provided by the federal government. In general, the Democratic and Republican Parties disagree on whether the federal government or the state and local governments are best able to serve the public interest. Individual states or regions have particular interests that their elected representatives espouse and bargain to achieve. This often leads to rather strange results; for example, the federal government successfully sued the tobacco industry for the harm done by cigarette smoking while maintaining subsidy programs for tobacco farmers.

Washington is full of lobbyists who try to influence representatives and senators to sponsor or vote for legislation favorable to their particular industries. This influence is manifested in two ways. First, industries contribute substantial monies to election campaigns, pouring the greatest amount of money into the campaigns of persons they believe will support their positions—incumbent or not. Second, many lobbyists and political action committees (PACs) have extremely large staffs available to research various technical issues. They can funnel this research, often slanted in their desired direction, to the various members of Congress. It is not unusual for a lobbyist to have provided the basic text of a tax law introduced in Congress.

The attempt to satisfy the many constituencies of our elected representatives has led to a collection of tax laws that have become more and more complex. This has significantly increased the compliance burden on taxpayers as well as Internal Revenue Service (IRS) administration. In spite of many calls for simplification, Congress continues to pass additional tax provisions, adding complexity to the system, without revisiting or deleting existing provisions.

Both political parties provide tax breaks to their constituents referred to as **tax expenditures**. Tax expenditures can take the form of special exclusions, deductions, credits or preferential rates for specific activities. These tax expenditures result in a reduction in the revenue that would be collected under a more comprehensive income tax. Although many of these tax expenditures are viewed positively because they can stimulate the economy, the dispute among politicians is usually over how to pay for them. They can usually be paid for in one of three ways: (1) reducing spending, (2) adding to the budget deficit, or (3) raising other tax revenue to offset the cost of the tax expenditures. Although politicians say they want to cut spending, they have been very ineffective in doing so. They usually add to the budget deficit or increase taxes. This dilemma has led to an alternative way to minimize the cost of tax expenditures by making them temporary rather than permanent. A tax expenditure expected to expire in only a few years, needs to raise far less revenue to pay for it than making the expenditure permanent. Unfortunately, the uncertainly surrounding the extension of some of these provisions makes tax planning difficult so that much of any expected economic stimulus is negated by this uncertainly.

The elections in November 2016 gave the Republican Party control of the House of Representatives, the Senate, and the White House. This gave them their best opportunity in some time to enact change. In December 2017, Congress passed the Tax Cuts and Jobs Act which permanently reduced corporate tax rates from a high of 35 percent to a flat rate of 21 percent. Individual tax rates were also slightly reduced, but only temporarily. These cuts were paid for by placing new limits on some deductions, completely eliminating other deductions, and adding over $1.4 trillion to the budget deficit. The legislative process through which tax proposals become law is discussed in the next chapter.

Although this text is primarily about the federal income tax, a basic understanding of other taxes will be helpful before we begin exploring the federal income tax in more detail.

1.1.3 STATE AND LOCAL INCOME TAXES

While most students are aware of the federal income tax, not all are familiar with state and local income taxes. The increasing importance of these taxes is reflected in the growth of state and local tax (SALT) practices in public accounting. Most states (and some local governments) impose corporate and/or personal (individual) income taxes on both residents and nonresidents.[2] States, however, normally tax nonresidents only on income from business activities or property located within that state.

[2] States not imposing a corporate income tax or other form of business tax include Nevada, South Dakota, and Wyoming. Alaska, Florida, Nevada, South Dakota, Texas, Washington, and Wyoming do not impose individual income taxes. Additionally, some states only tax certain types of interest and dividend income.

Example 1.1

When Alex Rodriguez, the former Texas Rangers shortstop, lived in Texas (a state with no individual income tax), he owed more than $271,000 to California (for nonresident income tax) for games he played there during baseball season. It was estimated that if the Rangers had played all their games at home, A-Rod's state tax bill would have been reduced by more than half a million dollars a year.[3] When A-Rod became a New York Yankee, his state and local tax burden increased dramatically. On the $155 million that A-Rod was to be paid over his seven-year contract, he was expected to owe $3.57 million to New York City and an additional $6.19 million to the State of New York for income taxes.[4] His tax burden increased further when he renegotiated his contract for $275 million over ten years.

The state in which a corporation is organized has the right to impose an income tax on that corporation under the residency principle. Alternatively, the source principle allows taxation of a business that has an economic connection to a state (derives income from assets or activities located within a state). When a resident corporation of one state derives income from business activities in another state, double taxation could result. To minimize this, states that levy an income tax on its resident businesses usually allow them to claim a credit for some or all of the income taxes paid to other states. The type and degree of connection between a business and a state necessary for the state to impose a tax is referred to as **nexus**.

Example 1.2

Corian Corporation manufactures equipment for sale nationwide. Corian's corporate headquarters and production facilities are located in Florida. Corian has regional sales offices in New York, Illinois, and California. Corian has nexus in Florida, New York, Illinois, and California due to the presence of employees and business property in those states.

In place of the income tax, some states impose a **franchise tax**. A franchise tax is an excise tax based on the right to do business or own property in the state. Whether the tax is called an income tax or a franchise tax, the tax is usually determined based on corporate income.[5]

Most states piggyback their computation of state taxable income on the federal income tax system by beginning with individual or corporate federal taxable income. Piggybacking on the federal system is particularly problematical, however, when Congress amends the tax law resulting in reduced taxable income (for example, by increasing or accelerating deductions). To minimize the potential impact on state tax revenues, many states adopt a fixed version of federal tax law by computing state taxable income as determined under the federal tax rules in effect as of a specific date. This allows state legislatures time to study the impact of changes on state revenue before adopting them. Although most states eventually adopt the federal changes, considerable delays are common.

When a corporation has nexus in several states, each state taxes only a percentage of the corporation's income based on the business allocated to that state. Although computations differ from state to state, many states use a three-factor allocation formula based on sales, payroll costs, and tangible property. Some states place more weight on the sales factor, while others weigh these factors equally.[6]

[3] Mark Hyman, "Why the 'Jock Tax' Doesn't Play Fair," Business Week, July 7, 2003, p. 37.

[4] Dan Kadison, "$10M is Ballpark for Taxman," The New York Post, February 17, 2004, p. 4.

[5] A few states impose their franchise tax on a corporation's stock value or net worth, either in addition to or instead of a tax on corporate income if it results in a higher tax.

[6] Because of the variation in allocation formulas between states, some corporations may have more than 100 percent of their total taxable income subject to state income taxes.

Example 1.3

Southeastern Corporation does business and has nexus in States X and Y. Its sales, payroll costs, and tangible property located in each state are:

	Sales	Payroll	Property
State X	$800,000	$315,000	$540,000
State Y	800,000	135,000	360,000
Total	$1,600,000	$450,000	$900,000

Based on these dollar figures, the percentages for the three factors are as follows:[7]

	Sales	Payroll	Property	Total
State X	50%	70%	60%	180%
State Y	50%	30%	40%	120%
Total	100%	100%	100%	

If each factor is weighted equally, the apportionment formula computes the average of the three factors so that the apportionment percentage for State X is 60 percent (180%/3) and the apportionment percentage for State Y is 40 percent (120%/3). Southeastern Corporation allocates 60 percent of its income to State X and 40 percent to State Y.

Nonbusiness income, such as interest, dividends, rent and royalties, is taxed in only one state—the state in which the corporation is domiciled or the state in which the underlying property is located or used.[8]

Income tax planning for multistate corporations usually involves shifting income from high-tax states to low-tax states by shifting assets from one state to another or by outsourcing some functions to eliminate or move nexus from a particular state. Businesses that are expanding or relocating facilities should measure the impact this will have on the amount of income apportioned to the state. For example, a corporation with plans to expand its facilities should avoid a high tax-rate state that uses an apportionment formula that weights property and payroll factors more heavily. The expansion of plant and the addition of employees can increase the percentage of total income subject to state tax.

1.1.4 EMPLOYMENT TAXES

Employment taxes include those specified under the Federal Insurance Contributions Act (FICA) along with federal and state unemployment taxes. The **FICA tax** has two components: Social Security and Medicare. Social Security pays monthly retirement benefits (also survivor and disability benefits) to qualified individuals. The 6.2 percent Social Security tax applies to salaries and wages up to an annual maximum of $128,400 for 2018. The Medicare tax pays for medical insurance for individuals who are elderly or disabled. The 1.45 percent Medicare portion of the FICA tax applies to all salary and wages without limit. Thus, an employer pays 7.65 percent FICA tax on each employee's wages up to $128,400 and 1.45 percent on compensation above $128,400.

[7] The percentage for each factor is determined by dividing the dollar amount of the item attributable to that state by the total dollar amount for that factor. For example, payroll for State X is $315,000. Dividing $315,000 by the total payroll costs of $450,000 means 70 percent of all payroll costs were incurred in State X.

[8] The corporation's domicile is the principal place from which the business is managed or directed, not necessarily the state of incorporation.

In addition to the employer FICA tax, employees pay a matching FICA tax. Employers withhold the employee portion of the FICA tax from the employee's salary or wages and forward it to the federal government (along with any income tax withheld).

Example 1.4

Maria is an employee of Marlin Corporation. In 2018, Maria received a salary of $130,000. Marlin Corporation paid a Social Security tax of $7,960.80 ($128,400 limit × 6.2%) plus a Medicare tax of $1,885 ($130,000 × 1.45%) for a total FICA tax of $9,845.80. Marlin Corporation withheld $7,960.80 from Maria's pay for her share of Social Security tax and $1,885 for her Medicare tax. Marlin Corporation also withheld income tax based on Maria's W-4 form that indicated her filing status (single). Marlin Corporation forwards both the employer's and employee's share of FICA tax to the federal government, as well as any income tax withheld for Maria.

Self-employed individuals (such as independent contractors, sole proprietors and partners) must pay the self-employment tax that includes both the employer and employee share of FICA tax, as discussed in detail in Chapter 4.

In addition to FICA taxes, employers are also required to pay federal and state unemployment taxes. These taxes fund temporary unemployment benefits for employees terminated from their jobs without cause. The rate under the Federal Unemployment Tax Act (FUTA) is 6 percent on the first $7,000 of wages. The state rates vary widely but the federal government allows a credit of up to 5.4 percent for state unemployment taxes the employer pays. Unemployment taxes are usually only paid by the employer and not the employee. Self-employed individuals are not eligible to collect unemployment benefits so they do not pay unemployment taxes for themselves; they pay unemployment taxes only for their employees.

1.1.5 WEALTH TAXES

Wealth taxes are based on the taxable entity's total wealth or the value of specific types of property. The most common wealth tax is the **real property tax**. This **ad valorem** tax is levied on individuals and businesses that own real property—land and buildings—and is assessed on the fair market value of the property. Local taxing jurisdictions rely heavily on the real property tax for the support of schools, police and fire protection, and other services furnished by the local municipality. The federal government generally does not levy any form of wealth tax, leaving the various forms of wealth taxes to the state or local governments.

To determine the rate at which the real property taxes will be levied, the municipality "works backward." The total budget is determined along with the total assessed valuation for all property subject to the tax. A mill levy (a "mill" is one-tenth of one cent) is then determined based on the total assessed value of the property to raise the revenue required by the budget. The mill levy is applied to each individual property within the district to determine its separate property tax.

Example 1.5

A municipality's budget is $1,000,000 and the total assessed value of all the property subject to the property tax is $200,000,000. To raise the required $1,000,000, a five-mill levy is required per $1 of assessed value ($1,000,000/$200,000,000 = $.005). When this mill levy is applied to a piece of property with an assessed value of $100,000, the owner would pay $500 ($.005 × $100,000) in real property taxes.

Other forms of wealth taxes include the personal property tax, the tangible property tax, and the intangible property tax. These taxes are collected annually on property owned as of a certain date based on a predetermined fixed rate applied to the fair market value of the property. Personal property or tangible property taxes are more likely to be levied on the value of a business's inventory and/or operating assets. Individuals may not always escape this tax, however, as a number of states base a part of the cost of obtaining automobile registrations or license plates on the value of the auto as an ad valorem tax.

Some states levy intangible taxes on the value of receivables, stocks, bonds, and other forms of investment instruments owned by businesses and individuals. Intangible taxes are based on a fixed tax rate times the fair market value of the intangible assets owned as of a specific date.

Two major problems related to wealth taxes have lessened government reliance on them as a source of revenue: the difficulty in establishing fair market value annually and the taxpayer's ability to "hide" personal property. The market value of many types of personal property (tangible or intangible) is not verifiable, leading to significant undervaluation by taxpayers. Moreover, the government may not know who owns a specific asset unless there is a way to trace or detect ownership. Thus, most local governments rely heavily on real property taxes rather than other types of personal property taxes, as real estate is much harder to hide. Through the assessment system, taxes are thought to be levied on a more uniform basis across the value of the properties.[9]

Based on ability to pay, wealth taxes would seem to be a sound source of tax revenue. Many items, however, such as a personal residence, do not produce direct income, and the owner may have little or no disposable income with which to pay the tax—a major problem for the elderly or others on fixed incomes when real property taxes increase.

1.1.6 WEALTH TRANSFER TAXES

Wealth transfer taxes are levied when all or part of an individual's wealth is transferred to another person. Since 1916, the United States has had an **estate tax**, a wealth transfer tax that applies to transfers of property as a result of the owner's death. A second wealth transfer tax, the **gift tax**, was enacted in 1932. The gift tax is imposed on a donor who makes a gratuitous lifetime transfer of property.[10] To avoid double taxation on these transfers, the recipient is not subject to income tax on gifted or inherited property.

Since 1976, the federal estate and gift taxes have been unified. Gift transfer taxes are levied based on a person's transfers during his or her lifetime with the final estate tax based on transfers at death. The tax is assessed on the fair market value of the property transferred. To ease the administrative burden, an *annual* gift exclusion (currently \$15,000 per recipient per year) prevents smaller gifts from being subject to the transfer tax.[11] Additionally, unlimited transfers to a spouse and qualified charities (during lifetime and at death) escape taxation. A unified gift and estate *lifetime* credit (equivalent to the tax on a transfer of \$11.18 million in 2018) assures that a certain base amount of wealth can be transferred to others (including children, grandchildren, other relatives, and friends) through lifetime gifts or transfers at death free of a transfer tax.

---

[9] Ideally, there would be an annual valuation process, but in reality, property assessments may increase or decrease based on indices only, or are otherwise revised only when a property is sold.

[10] Chapter 12 contains a more detailed discussion of wealth transfer taxes.

[11] If a taxpayer's annual gifts to an individual recipient do not exceed \$15,000, the donor is not required to file a gift tax return. A husband and wife can combine their \$15,000 annual exclusions through gift splitting to jointly give up to \$30,000 to each recipient annually.

Example 1.6

In 2018, Marleen gave $50,000 to a qualified charity. She also gave each of her five grandchildren 700 shares of stock valued at $10,000 on their birthdays. The charitable gift is not subject to the gift tax. The birthday gifts are also free of the gift tax (and Marleen does not have to file a gift tax return) as they do not exceed each grandchild's $15,000 annual gift tax exclusion. If Marlee gives an additional $10,000 to each grandchild this year, she now exceeds the annual gift exclusion ($10,000 + $10,000 − $15,000 = $5,000 taxable gift to each) and would have to file a gift tax return for 2018. This notifies the government that she is using some of her lifetime unified credit.

Marleen's gifts remain free of any gift tax until her total taxable gifts exhaust her unified credit that is equal to the tax on total taxable gifts of $11.18 million (the current lifetime exclusion). The grandchildren have no tax consequences on the receipt of the gifts because gifts are not subject to income taxes. They will, however, be subject to income tax on future dividends received or realized gains on any stock sales.

With the integration of the gift and estate taxes, any unified credit not used for lifetime gifts can be used for transfers made by the decedent's estate. Thus, the decedent's estate escapes taxation unless his or her total lifetime taxable gifts plus taxable transfers at death exceed the lifetime exclusion.[12]

A number of states levy inheritance taxes rather than estate taxes. The inheritance tax is based on a person's right to receive property upon the death of another. The tax rates and amount excluded from taxation vary with the relationship of the heir to the decedent and the value of the property received. The estate normally pays the inheritance tax, but the tax paid reduces the total value of the property transferred to the heir. In addition to an inheritance or estate tax, many states also levy a gift tax.

1.1.7 CONSUMPTION TAXES

Consumption taxes may take many forms, but the **sales tax** is the most common form in the United States. Most states levy sales taxes on some or all of the goods and services purchased, although certain items considered necessities may be exempt from tax. For example, food, clothing, prescriptions, and many services may be excluded from the sales tax while items not considered necessities such as restaurant meals, rental cars, and hotel rooms are taxed. Purchases of inventory for resale are usually exempt from sales tax because the inventory will be taxed when sold; however, purchases for use in a business are taxable as a final sale.

The retailer is responsible for collecting and remitting sales taxes to the appropriate state and local tax authority. Because the determination of items subject to sales tax varies greatly from state to state, multistate retailers must determine not only the appropriate sales tax rates (which may vary within a zip code due to local sales taxes) but also determine which items are subject to tax in each location.

The concept of nexus is as important in determining the sales tax as it is for an income tax. A state cannot require an out-of-state business to collect sales tax unless it has nexus with the state. The exact definition for sales tax nexus may differ from that of income tax nexus. A business may have nexus in a state for sales taxes but not for income taxes or vice versa. For example, employees from out-of-state who solicit sales within a state may create sales tax nexus but not income tax nexus.

Each state that imposes a sales tax also imposes a companion use tax. A **use tax** is imposed on property to be used in one state but purchased in another state if no sales tax was paid in the

[12] The lifetime exclusion for taxable transfers is $11,180,000 for 2018 ($5,490,000 for 2017). Chapter 12 has a more complete discussion of the annual and lifetime exclusions for taxable transfers.

state of purchase. A use tax is self-assessed and usually at the same rate as the sales tax. Without a use tax, there is an incentive to purchase from out-of-state businesses not required to collect a state sales tax to the detriment of in-state businesses.

Example 1.7

JX Corporation operates in a state with a 6 percent sales and use tax. JX purchases office supplies over the Internet from an out-of-state supplier for $2,000. JX pays no sales tax. If JX purchased these supplies from the local office supply store, it would have to pay a sales tax of $120 ($2,000 × 6%). JX should file a use tax return and pay the $120 use tax to its state because the supplies will be used within the state.

Most states have difficulty collecting use taxes from individuals (except for automobiles that require registration with the state). Collection from businesses is much easier to enforce because most states regularly audit in-state businesses for compliance with sales and use tax laws.

One benefit of a consumption tax like the sales tax is that it encourages savings—considered a necessity for continued investment and economic growth. A person can avoid the sales tax by not purchasing certain goods for consumption; income that is not consumed is available for savings. The income tax not only taxes income whether consumed or saved, but taxes the income earned on savings, further discouraging savings.

Other types of consumption taxes include excise taxes, value-added taxes, and turnover taxes—although only the excise tax is in common use in this country. An excise tax is another form of sales tax and the only sales tax levied by the federal government. Excises are generally levied on taxable goods for which there is a low elasticity of demand or on goods whose use the government wishes to discourage, such as tobacco products and alcoholic beverages. This latter group of excises is generally referred to as "sin" taxes.[13] Other excises offset some of the costs incurred by the government for certain services, for example, the tax on airline tickets helps pay for the system of air traffic controllers.

The **value-added tax (VAT)**, in use in most of the developed countries of the world, has not been adopted in the United States. It is a type of sales tax that is added to a product or service based on the value added at specific points in the production or service process. Although there are several methods for calculating the value-added tax, it basically works as described in the following example.

Example 1.8

A business buys parts to manufacture a widget. The parts cost $400, to which a 10 percent value-added tax is added by the seller—a total cost of $440. The business assembles the parts into a widget and sells the assembled widget for $800 plus a 10 percent value-added tax of $80—the purchaser's total purchase price is $880. The business, however, remits only $40 of the tax to the government—the total $80 VAT less a credit for the $40 VAT paid to the supplier of the purchased parts. The government collects the other $40 from the parts supplier. The consumer pays the full tax on the product to the last business in the business chain. The tax collected at each step is based on the difference in the price paid for the goods coming in and the price received when leaving.

[13] The indirect costs incurred from the consumption of these products must be borne by the government; that is, treating persons for lung cancer and alcoholism is the justification for taxing these products at rates that are designed to discourage their use.

Some features of a VAT differentiate it from a sales tax. First, it is generally included directly in the selling price at the consumer level. Second, the VAT is not levied on goods exported to other countries. Businesses that export goods to other countries receive refunds of the VAT paid on exported goods. When the United States exports goods to a foreign country in competition with another exporting country that levies a value-added tax (instead of a corporate income tax), the United States may be at a competitive disadvantage. All other costs being equal, the U.S. firm will have to charge more than the other exporter to make the same profit because it receives no rebate of income taxes while the foreign exporter receives a rebate of its value-added taxes.[14]

The turnover tax, another consumption tax, is a sales tax levied at each step of a business chain—both wholesale and retail—but with no rebates or credits for prior taxes paid. Thus, if one firm handles all the steps in a manufacturing process from raw materials to finished goods, the tax is levied only once, when the product is sold to the consumer. If, however, that same product's manufacturing process is handled by two or three firms, the tax is levied and collected each time the items move from one manufacturer to the other—driving up its costs relative to the manufacturer that is able to complete the various manufacturing steps.

1.1.8 TARIFFS AND DUTIES

Tariffs are taxes levied on goods and materials brought into a country, usually for one of two reasons: (1) A foreign business sells goods to the purchasers in the destination country at prices that may be below production costs in an attempt to capture a market and put the local operations out of business. (2) A local business's operating costs are higher than those costs for the same product produced in the foreign jurisdiction.[15]

Import duties are similar to tariffs as they are taxes on goods brought into a country and levied by the destination country. When persons travel abroad, they are permitted to purchase a certain amount of goods and bring them back "duty free." When the duty-free allowance is exceeded, the government levies a tax on the excess. This encourages the purchase of goods at home by making imported goods more expensive. Export duties are taxes levied on goods that are leaving the country of origin. These taxes discourage producers from selling their goods abroad by making them more expensive. In this way, they are available for purchase in the country of origin at lower prices.

1.2 TYPES OF TAX RATE SYSTEMS

1.2.1 THE PROGRESSIVE TAX RATE SYSTEM

The current federal income tax system is a **progressive tax system**—one in which the tax rates increase as income increases. The progressive tax system is based on the fundamental belief that taxpayers with higher levels of income should pay a greater proportion of the taxes necessary to support the government. This is known as the "ability to pay" or the "wherewithal to pay" concept. Most taxpayers probably believe that a progressive system is a fair tax system in that they agree that people who have more should contribute more to the country's welfare through taxes. There is, however, nothing that makes a progressive tax system inherently fairer—the fairness of a tax is a value judgment that varies from person to person.

The U.S. income tax rate structure has always been progressive with initial rates in 1913 of 1 percent to 7 percent. In 1945, to fund the war, the top rate increased to 94 percent.[16] In 1985, there were 15 tax brackets from a low of 11 percent to a high of 50 percent. In an attempt to

[14] Foreign firms that sell goods within the United States may be subject to U.S. income taxes, but they may be levied at rates significantly different from those faced by comparable U.S. firms. Taxation of foreign corporations is discussed in Chapter 3.
[15] The tariffs on foreign steel introduced by the George W. Bush administration are examples of taxes levied because of the concern that foreign countries were "dumping" steel here at prices below their costs.
[16] See www.taxpolicycenter.org/statistics/historical-top-tax-rate.

simplify the tax system, the Tax Reform Act of 1986 drastically reduced the number of brackets as well as the rates. However, the top rate and the number of rates have continued to change either to raise revenue to balance the budget or to provide a tax cut when budget surpluses were predicted.

The current federal tax rates range from 10 percent to 37 percent. The range of income subject to a specific tax rate is known as a tax bracket. As the taxpayers' income exceeds a specific bracket, income within that next bracket is subject to the increased percentage rate. Table 1.1 shows the tax rates on ordinary income for single individuals and married couples filing a joint return for 2018. The brackets to which these rates apply are adjusted annually for inflation.

Table 1.1 Ordinary Income Tax Rates for 2018

Tax rates	Taxable income for single individuals	Taxable income for married filing a joint return
10%	$0–$9,525	$0–$19,050
12%	$9,526–$38,700	$19,051–$77,400
22%	$38,701–$82,500	$77,401–$165,000
24%	$82,501–$157,500	$165,001–$315,000
32%	$157,501–$200,000	$315,001–$400,000
35%	$200,001–$500,000	$400,001–$600,000
37%	Over $500,000	Over $600,000

As an individual's income increases through this progressive tax rate schedule, the lower tax rates continue to apply to the amount of income in each of the lower tax brackets. As a result, the first $9,525 of income of all single individuals is taxed at only the 10 percent rate—even individuals whose total taxable income exceeds $500,000.

Two types of income are subject to lower tax rates: dividend income and long-term capital gains. Dividend income is taxed at a lower rate because a corporation pays tax on earned income but is not allowed a deduction for dividends paid to its shareholders. Shareholders' dividend income is effectively subject to a second tax at the shareholder level. To minimize the impact of this double taxation, the dividend income of individual shareholders is taxed at lower tax rates as shown in Table 1.2.

Table 1.2 Tax Rates for Dividend Income and Long-term Capital Gains

Tax rates for dividend income and long-term capital gains	Taxable income for single individuals	Taxable income for married filing a joint return
0%	$0–$38,600	$0–$77,200
15%	$38,601–$425,800	$77,201–$479,000
20%	Over $425,800	Over $479,000

To encourage long-term investment, individuals owning investments (such as stock) for more than 12 months are taxed at lower rates when sold. Table 1.2 provides the long-term capital gain tax rates which are the same rates that apply to dividend income. Short-term capital gains (those that do not meet the more-than-one-year holding period) are taxed at an individual's ordinary income tax rate.

Prior to 2018, corporations also faced progressive tax rates consisting of four nominal tax rates of 15%, 25%, 34% and 35% and two surtaxes applied at different income levels. Unlike individuals, corporations that had taxable incomes above certain levels did not keep the benefit of the lower tax rates on income below these levels. A five percent surtax eliminated the benefit of the 15 percent and 25 percent brackets on income below $75,000 and a three percent surtax eliminated the benefit of the 34 percent rate on income below $10,000,000. The tax brackets for corporations for tax years prior to 2018, including both nominal rates and surtaxes, are shown in Table 1.3. Corporations also had no special long-term capital gains tax rates; their capital gains

Table 1.3 Corporate Tax Rates Before 2018

Taxable income	Tax rate
0–$50,000	15%
$50,001–$75,000	25%
$75,001–$100,000	34%
$100,001–$335,000	39% (34% nominal rate + 5% surtax)
$335,001–$10,000,000	34%
$10,000,001–$15,000,000	35%
$15,000,001–$18,333,333	38% (35% nominal rate + 3% surtax)
Over $18,333,333	35%

were taxed using the same rates as their ordinary income. Beginning in 2018, corporations pay a flat tax rate of 21 percent on all taxable income.

There are several other important tax rate concepts in a progressive tax rate system. An **average tax rate** is determined by dividing the taxpayer's tax liability by taxable income. For example, a single individual with $250,000 of taxable income and a tax liability of $63,189 pays a 35 percent tax rate on the last $50,000 of income above the $200,000 starting point for the 35 percent tax bracket but has an average tax rate of only 25.28 percent ($63,189/$250,000). In highlighting the tax effects on different groups of taxpayers, the average tax rate is often used to compare the percentage of taxes paid on taxable earned income.

The **marginal tax rate** is the tax rate that applies to the next dollar of taxable income (or deduction).

Example 1.9

Sarah is single with taxable income of $120,000 that puts her in the 24 percent marginal tax bracket. If she earns an additional $10,000 in ordinary income, her taxable income increases to $130,000 and she will pay an additional $2,400 ($10,000 × 24% marginal tax rate) in income tax. If, instead, she has $10,000 of additional deductions, her taxable income decreases to $110,000, she will save $2,400 in income taxes.

As a taxpayer moves from one tax bracket to another, the marginal tax rate moves from one rate to the next. For decision purposes, the marginal tax rate is the most relevant rate for tax planning. Basic tax planning strategies that use the marginal tax rate are discussed in Chapter 2.[17]

In a progressive individual income tax system, the marginal tax rate is always higher than the average tax rate. The average rate may approach the highest marginal rate, but there is always some income that was taxed at a lower rate preventing the average rate from equaling the marginal rate for individuals.

1.2.2 PROPORTIONAL "FLAT" TAX RATE

One alternative to a progressive system of taxation is a proportional or flat tax system. A **proportional tax system** requires all income to be taxed at the same rate regardless of the amount or type of the taxpayer's income. Thus, marginal and average tax rates would be identical over all ranges of income.

Beginning in 2018, corporations are taxed at a flat rate of 21 percent on their taxable income. The state sales tax is another common example of a proportional tax; the tax paid is a fixed percentage of the amount spent.

[17] A third tax rate, the effective tax rate, divides the taxes paid by an individual's economic income (both taxable and nontaxable).

1.2.3 REGRESSIVE TAXES

A **regressive tax system** is one in which taxpayers pay a decreasing proportion of their income as their incomes increase. As the taxpayer's income goes from one bracket to another, his or her average tax on total income decreases, as does the marginal tax rate.

The only regressive taxes that taxpayers are subject to at the federal level are FICA and unemployment taxes. The 6.2 percent Social Security portion of the FICA tax only applies to salaries and wages up to a maximum of $128,400.[18] The 1.45 percent Medicare portion of the FICA tax applies to all salary and wages without limit and is a proportional tax.[19] As a taxpayer's salary or wage exceeds the Social Security maximum, the rate drops to 0 (zero) percent for additional wages and the 6.2 percent average tax rate begins to decrease for an employee as shown below:

Wages	Social security tax @ 6.2%	Average %
$75,000	$4,650.00	6.2%
$200,000	$7,960.80	4.0%

The Medicare portion, however, is proportional.

Wages	Medicare tax @ 1.45%	Average %
$75,000	$1,087.50	1.45%
$200,000	$2,900.00	1.45%

The FUTA tax also is regressive because the unemployment rate of 6 percent only applies to the first $7,000 of an employee's wages. When the employee's wages exceed this amount, no further unemployment taxes are collected and the average rate falls below 6 percent, similar to the average Social Security portion of the FICA tax rate.

1.3 CHARACTERISTICS OF A GOOD TAX

Raising revenue is only one of the many goals of taxation. The tax laws foster many economic and social goals such as wealth redistribution, price stability, economic growth, full employment, home ownership, charitable activities, and environmental preservation. For example, the government encourages contributions to charities through the charitable contribution deduction. If the charitable organizations did not exist, the government would have to undertake many of the activities the charities provide. Thus, the tax law is used to achieve this social objective.

In 1776, Adam Smith proposed the concepts known as the four **canons of taxation**, *equity, convenience, certainty,* and *economy* in *The Wealth of Nations*.[20] To this day, these concepts are still valid for determining whether a tax should be considered a good tax. No one since Adam Smith has come up with a more widely accepted criteria for judging a tax, although other criteria have been added.

[18] The ceiling was $127,200 for 2017 and $118,500 for 2016.

[19] Employers also pay FICA taxes in addition to that withheld from employees so that the total Social Security rate is 12.4 percent (6.2% employer rate + 6.2% employee rate) and the Medicare rate is 2.9 percent (1.45% × 2). Self-employed individuals, however, must pay both the employer's and employee's share (referred to as the self-employment tax), resulting in a combined rate of 15.3 percent on the first $128,400 of self-employment income and 2.9 percent on the excess. An additional 0.9 percent Medicare surtax is only assessed on the taxpayer and not assessed on businesses. The detailed computations of the additional Medicare surtax are discussed in Chapter 5.

[20] Smith's 1776 work was originally titled *An Inquiry Into the Nature and Causes of the Wealth of Nations* but was shortened into *The Wealth of Nations* (New York: Dutton, 1910).

1.3.1 EQUITY

Equity is probably the most difficult of the four canons on which to achieve consensus. When is a tax equitable? How a person answers that question depends on that person's perspective, background, and view of society. A person who works very hard and earns an extremely good living, may not view the progressive tax system as equitable when 37 percent or more of any additional earned income is taken away in taxes. On the other hand, someone supporting a large family on a meager income may not believe that paying any taxes, when basic necessities cannot be purchased, is an equitable tax system.

The basic idea of equity is that persons with similar incomes should face similar taxes on that income. There is a major problem in determining when persons have similar incomes, however.

In the current U.S. system, most capital assets held by individuals for more than 12 months are taxed at rates significantly lower than the maximum tax rate for salary or wages income. Consider Taxpayers A and B who are in the same marginal tax bracket because of equal salaries. They each earn an additional \$20,000—Taxpayer A by working overtime and Taxpayer B by selling stock resulting in a \$20,000 long-term capital gain. Taxpayer A pays tax at the ordinary income tax rate on his additional wages while Taxpayer B benefits from the lower capital gains tax rate on his extra income by selling an investment asset. Is this equitable? Should equivalent incomes be taxed equally?

Capital gains tax rates on the disposition of capital assets held for a minimum period of time have traditionally been taxed at rates lower than regular income tax rates for several reasons. First, there is no inflation adjustment for capital gains; yet often the capital gain is an inflation gain rather than a real gain. If inflation is very high, the taxpayer may indeed have a loss when constant dollars are considered, but he or she will still be subject to the capital gains tax. Lower capital gains rates encourage investors to move money from unprofitable investments into more profitable ones. When capital gains rates are high, taxpayers tend to keep their appreciated but no-longer-profitable assets to avoid the tax. (This is called the *lock-in effect* of capital gains taxes.) In each of the situations described above, there are arguments for both sides of the equity issue.

Equity would also require persons with higher-incomes to pay a greater proportion of that income in taxes than lower-income persons—a concept referred to as *the ability to pay,* that is the basis for a progressive tax rate system. As a person's income increases, he or she is assumed to need a smaller percentage of that income for basic living and other expenses and, thus, is in a better position to pay a greater share of that income in taxes. There are difficulties with this concept of equity, however.

Compare two families: one family consists of a husband and wife and one healthy child with \$50,000 in annual income; the other consists of a husband and wife with six children, two of whom have significant handicaps, but with an annual income of \$60,000. When focusing only on the dollar amount of income, equity would tell us that the second family should pay a greater percentage of their income than the first—but which family really has the better ability to pay the tax? The U.S. tax system relieves some of the extra tax burden on the second family through the medical expense deduction and child care credits—but this also complicates the system.

Tax policy struggles to achieve fairness. Differing notions of fairness, however, guarantee that this goal remains elusive. The fairness debate revolves around two very different concepts of what is equitable or fair. **Horizontal equity**, one of the key principles of tax fairness, asserts that persons in similar circumstances should face similar tax burdens. The difficult part is determining when different taxpayers are in similar circumstances.

Example 1.10

Susan rents a condominium for \$2,500 per month. Barry pays \$2,500 per month on the mortgage for his condominium in the same building. Both Susan and Barry are single, have no dependents, and have annual incomes of \$75,000. Susan cannot deduct any portion of her rent, but Barry can deduct the interest and taxes portion of his mortgage payment. In this case, the goal of horizontal equity gives way to the objective of encouraging home ownership.

The other major fairness concept is vertical equity. **Vertical equity** asserts that persons with higher incomes should pay not only more tax but also higher percentages of their income as tax. Underlying this is the economic theory that income has diminishing marginal utility. In other words, as a person's income rises, each dollar is worth less to that person. As a result, higher rates are necessary to obtain approximately comparable sacrifices from all taxpayers. Although this has long been a feature of the U.S. tax system (as evidenced by the progressive tax rates), it remains controversial, especially among those subject to the higher tax rates.

Example 1.11

Bill and Susan, married with two children, have taxable income of $75,000. Shelly and John, also married with two children, have taxable income of $150,000. Because their income is twice that of Bill and Susan, vertical equity would require that Shelley and John pay more than twice the income tax that Bill and Susan pay.

There is no one answer as to what truly constitutes an equitable tax system. As we try to make the tax system appear to be more equitable, more complexity is introduced into that system. The simplest system of all would be a single rate of tax applied to all increases in a person's wealth (including that used for consumption, the economists' definition of income); yet, this probably will never be considered because it would not be perceived as fair.

1.3.2 ECONOMY

A tax meets the criterion of economy when the amount of revenue it raises is at an optimum level after the costs of administration and compliance are considered. The costs of a tax are not just limited to the costs incurred for tax administration and collection. Certain taxes impose an enormous burden on the taxpayer for compliance. More than half the individual taxpayers in the United States use some form of tax preparer to assist in preparing their tax returns. Many businesses have their own tax departments with no other responsibility than to ensure that all federal, state, and local income, employment, and property taxes are paid in a timely manner.

Compare a state income tax to a state sales tax based on the concept of economy. A sales tax is collected at the point of retail purchase and remitted by the retailer to the state. The purchaser simply pays the added tax to the retailer when the good or service is purchased. To comply with state income tax requirements, taxpayers generally cannot use the information from their federal tax returns without a number of adjustments. Thus, the taxpayer must pay a preparer or spend additional time preparing the state income tax return. The state must use procedures similar to the federal government to check for accuracy and compliance to the laws applicable to these returns. The state must conduct many more audits on individual taxpayers to audit the same percentage of returns as the number of audits conducted on retailers remitting sales taxes. Thus, administrative costs are much higher for the income tax. Yet, in many states, the income tax is a revenue source secondary to the sales tax. Based on economy, a national sales tax has great appeal.

Economy is also related to the concept of simplicity. The simpler a tax system is, the less costly is administration and compliance. One of the major thrusts of the American Institute of CPAs (AICPA) has been to simplify the tax system. Tax professionals realize that the current system is so complex that even a reasonably well-educated person and his or her tax advisor can readily fall into tax traps because of many obscure and complex provisions. When tax professionals make errors because of the complexity of the law, they may still be held liable for these mistakes—and the cost to the professional may be significant.

1.3.3 CERTAINTY

Certainty is also a canon related to simplicity. Certainty would dictate that a taxpayer know with reasonable accuracy the tax consequences of a transaction at the time the transaction takes place. Unfortunately, U.S. tax laws are continually changing. It is not uncommon today for a change in the tax laws to be effective from the date proposed, rather than from the date passed. This practice imposes an uncertain environment on the taxpayer who is contemplating a transaction that could be affected by a tax law change. He or she does not know if the law will be passed—thus, he or she cannot know if the transaction will be affected. Certainty would dictate that tax laws change as little as necessary so that the outcome of a particular transaction could be predicted with reasonable accuracy.

Example 1.12

The Tax Cuts and Jobs Act (TCJA) that was passed in December 2017 made most changes effective as of January 1, 2018. Changes to the bonus depreciation provision, however, were retroactive to September 27, 2017, the date when the changes were first proposed. The effective date for this provision was made retroactive because equipment manufacturers were concerned that if the special tax provision was available only for equipment purchased in 2018, customers would not purchase any equipment in the last quarter of 2017.

Although the reduction in the corporate tax rate was a permanent change, many of the provisions in the TCJA are temporary and will expire in a few years. These temporary provisions include not only the bonus depreciation provision but also the reduction in individual tax rates. It is unknown whether Congress will extend the lower individual tax rates when they expire.

1.3.4 CONVENIENCE

The last canon of convenience states that a convenient tax is one that would be readily determined and paid with little effort. Consider again the difference between paying a sales tax and an income tax. A sales tax is paid each time a taxed purchase is made. Most people do not consider that they are paying a tax in addition to making a purchase of some good or service. Although the withholding of income taxes from salaries offers a measure of convenience, the myriad of forms and schedules that must be filed to reconcile the actual tax liability with withholding does not always meet the test of convenience. The requirements for estimated tax payments for significant amounts of income from other than salaries and wages simply may be educated guesses, particularly when income is expected to be passed through by partnerships and S corporations. Underestimating these estimated payments based on unknown information places an enormous burden on the taxpayer and may result in underpayment penalties.

1.4 THE TAXING UNITS AND THE BASIC INCOME TAX MODEL

There are only three types of persons[21] subject to income taxation in the United States: the individual, the C corporation,[22] and the fiduciary. An individual is a male or female person subject to the tax. A **C corporation** is a business entity formed under state law on which the income tax is levied directly. A fiduciary, either an estate or a trust, may be subject to income taxes.

[21] Any entity subject to the income tax is a taxable person; the term "individual" is reserved exclusively for a man, woman, or child subject to an income tax.

[22] The term "C" or "regular corporation" (called "C" corporation because its governing tax rules are contained in Internal Revenue Code subchapter C) is used to distinguish it from a subchapter S (or simply "S") corporation (whose rules are contained in IRC subchapter S), which is a flow-through entity.

In most cases, however, fiduciary income passes through to income beneficiaries who include it in their income and are responsible for the taxes.[23] The **fiduciary** is a modified "flow-through" entity because the entity is taxed only on income retained by the estate or the trust; the income distributed to the recipients is taxed only to the recipients.

Individual taxpayers (including married persons filing jointly) and corporate taxpayers pay the bulk of all income taxes collected. The corporation is the basic business unit, but it is only one of the forms in which a business can operate. In addition to the C or regular corporate form, a business may be organized as a sole proprietorship, a partnership, a limited liability company (LLC), or an S corporation. The income taxes on these businesses are not usually paid by the businesses; instead, at the end of the tax year their income flows through to their owners and they pay the taxes.[24] If one flow-through entity owns all or part of another flow-through entity, the income continues to flow through to the second entity until it finally reaches an individual, a C corporation, or a fiduciary tax return for payment of the tax.

Example 1.13

The BST partnership is owned one-third by Bob (an individual); one-third by S, an S corporation (owned 100 percent by Jane); and one-third by T (a trust fiduciary). The partnership reports $300 of income at the end of the current tax year. One hundred dollars of income flows through to each of the owners: Bob, S, and T, but T distributes only $40 of its $100 income to Sarah, the beneficiary. Bob includes all $100 of income along with his other income and pays taxes on the total. S does not pay taxes on the $100. This $100 is combined with S's other income; the total then flows through to Jane, the owner of all of the S corporation stock. Jane includes all of this income on her personal tax return. T pays taxes on the $60 retained in the trust; the remaining $40 is taxed to Sarah on her individual tax return, along with her other sources of income.

The income of C corporations is subject to double taxation—once at the corporate level and again at the owner level when the income is distributed as dividends—because dividends are not deductible by the corporation. Flow-through entities avoid double taxation because their income is passed through at the end of the year to their owners and is taxed once only (at that time) at the owner level. The income of a sole proprietorship is reported along with the individual owner's other income and is taxed annually.[25] The advantages and disadvantages of each of these forms of business are explored later in this chapter. At this point, it is not necessary to have a detailed understanding of taxable and flow-through entities. It is, however, important to understand that individuals and C corporations are the primary taxpaying entities. The primary focus of the text is on tax planning for individuals, C corporations, and flow-through entities because of the latter's effects on the taxation of individuals and C corporations.

The fiduciary (trust or estate) has a vastly different role than a business. A trust is established for a specific purpose, such as managing the assets for beneficiaries who are unable or unwilling to manage the assets themselves. The fiduciary has the responsibility to insure that the wishes of the person establishing the trust are followed. An estate is created at the death of an individual, and its primary purpose is to manage the decedent's assets until they can be distributed to his or her heirs. Income tax planning opportunities are limited for estates and trusts.

[23] An estate is a legal entity which comes into existence only upon the death of the individual whose assets are held by the estate. The estate must file a tax return until all assets can be distributed to the heirs or beneficiaries. Any individual may create a trust by transferring assets to the trust. A trustee administers the trust property for the benefit of the beneficiary.

[24] LLCs are usually taxed as partnerships (unless owned by a single individual and then it is taxed as a sole proprietorship); however, an LLC can elect to be taxed as a corporation and would then file a corporate tax return. An S corporation that was previously a C corporation may be subject to tax on specific types of income (as discussed in Chapter 11).

[25] Sole proprietorships are technically disregarded entities; however, they are usually grouped with pass-through businesses. There is no separate entity-level tax return for a disregarded entity. All income is reported on a Schedule C as part of the individual's personal tax return, aggregated with the individual's other income, and taxed using the individual's tax rates.

The final chapter of this text addresses the basics of estate and trust taxation, along with the estate and gift transfer tax. The first eleven chapters are devoted to the two primary tax-paying entities (individuals and C corporations) and their related flow-through businesses, although the basic principles of income, deduction, gain, and loss discussed throughout this text also apply to fiduciary entities.

1.4.1 THE BASIC TAX MODEL

It is important to have an overall sense of the components of the basic tax model before studying the details of the tax laws. This aids in understanding how the terms and concepts referred to throughout our study of tax fit into the scheme of the basic tax model. This basic model (Figure 1.1) is expanded in later chapters as details are introduced for individuals and corporations.

	Gross income
Less	Deductions
Equals	Taxable income (loss)
Times	Applicable tax rate
Equals	Gross income tax liability
Less	Tax credits
Less	Tax prepayments
Equals	Tax liability owed or refund due

FIGURE 1.1 The basic income tax model

Gross Income

The term **gross income** is an all-inclusive term that includes income from all sources that are not specifically excluded.[26] Not all "income" items are positive, however, as losses reduce other positive income items in determining corporate total income or individual gross income. For example, the capital gain on a stock sale increases income while the sale of business assets at a loss reduces income. In general, losses from business or investment transactions are recognized (included in income) only when they are realized through an exchange transaction that determines the amount of the loss. Thus, a decline in stock value cannot be deducted until the stock is actually sold at a loss. Figure 1.2 provides examples of the types of income and loss items included in gross income.

Income item	Discussed in chapter
Gross income from the sale of goods and services	3
Taxable interest income	3
Dividend income	3
Prizes and awards	3
Unemployment compensation	3
Taxable portion of Social Security benefits	3
Wages and salary	4
Taxable retirement plan distributions	4
Income (less loss) from rental real estate	6
Gains (less losses) from sale of capital assets	8
Income (less loss) from sole proprietorships, partnerships, and S corporations	11

FIGURE 1.2 Partial listing of items included in gross income

[26] An individual reports his or her gross income to the Internal Revenue Service on Form 1040: *U.S. Individual Income Tax Return*. A sample filled-in Form 1040 is included at the end of Chapter 5 and complete sample filled-in tax returns are posted on the companion website for this textbook.

Example 1.14

Brogan Corporation has gross income from sales of $4,500,000, taxable interest income of $50,000, and a loss of $400,000 from a partnership that is deducted from its positive income. As a result, Brogan Corporation has total income of $4,150,000 ($4,500,000 + $50,000 – $400,000).

Losses (negative income) can be grouped into three broad categories: business losses, investment losses, and personal losses.[27] Losses are normally deducted from positive income items, except that most personal losses of individuals are not deductible.[28]

Operating losses incurred as part of an active business are deductible in full against ordinary income. Capital losses from the sale of investment assets are subject to limitations on their deductibility; for example, individuals can deduct only $3,000 of capital losses in excess of capital gains annually. Capital losses that are not deductible in the current year may be carried forward indefinitely by individuals. Corporations can only offset capital losses against capital gains; they are not deductible against other income. Corporate capital losses in excess of capital gains are carried back three years and then forward five years to offset capital gains realized in carryover years.

Example 1.15

John has $80,000 of salary income, a $5,000 operating loss from his sole proprietorship, a $4,000 capital gain on the sale of ABC stock, and a $13,000 capital loss on the sale of XYZ stock in the current year. The $4,000 capital gain offsets $4,000 of the $13,000 capital loss on the stocks resulting in a net $9,000 capital loss for the year. The $5,000 operating loss is deductible in full against John's salary income, but only $3,000 of the $9,000 net capital loss is deductible against other income; his net taxable income is $72,000. The remaining $6,000 capital loss is carried forward (but not back) and can be deducted in future years subject to the $3,000 annual limitation.

Example 1.16

Classic Corporation has $120,000 income from operations and a $5,000 net capital loss on the sale of stocks held as an investment in 2018. The loss is not deductible currently; instead, the corporation carries it back first to 2015, then to 2016 and 2017. Classic Corporation offsets the capital loss against any capital gains in those prior years, recomputes its tax liability, and files a claim for a refund. If the capital gain is not offset completely by the prior years' capital gains, the remainder is carried forward sequentially to years 2019 through 2023. (If this had been an individual, $3,000 of the loss could be deducted currently with the remaining $2,000 carried forward to the next year as illustrated in the previous example.)

Over the years, certain items have been excluded from gross income. These excluded items may not even be reported on the tax return. Only if an excluded item could affect some other reporting provision is reporting required along with the taxable items. For example, interest on tax-exempt municipal bonds is excluded from income, but an individual taxpayer must report it because it could affect the determination of the taxability of a taxpayer's Social Security benefits. On the other hand, an individual who is the beneficiary of the proceeds of a life insurance policy excludes them from income and does not report them on the tax return. Figure 1.3 provides examples of the types of items excluded from income.

[27] Losses are distinguished from deductions for which there must be a specific provision in the Code that allows a reduction in corporate or individual taxable income.

[28] Casualty and theft losses of personal property are deductible as itemized deductions to the extent that they exceed 10 percent of the individual's adjusted gross income. These losses are discussed in Chapter 9.

Exclusion item	Discussed in chapter
Tax-exempt interest income from state and local bonds	3
Proceeds of life insurance policies	3
Gifts and inheritances	3
Welfare benefits including food stamps	3
Nontaxable portion of Social Security benefits	3
Scholarships	3
Damages awarded for physical injury	3
Qualified employee fringe benefits	4
Nontaxable portion of retirement plan distributions	4
Up to $250,000 gain on the sale of a personal residence ($500,000 if married filing joint return)	8
Gains and losses on property transactions subject to disallowance or nonrecognition provisions	8 and 9
Unrealized gains and losses	9

FIGURE 1.3 Partial listing of exclusions from gross income

Example 1.17

Brogan Corporation (example 1.14) had $4,150,000 of total income. It also received $100,000 of tax-exempt interest, collected $1,000,000 from the life insurance policy on the life of its now-deceased controller, and had unrealized[29] appreciation on assets of $300,000. Its total income remains $4,150,000 as each of these items is excluded from income.

Deductions

After a corporation determines its total income, or an individual determines gross income, certain deductions are permitted. For an item to be deductible by an individual or a business, there must be either a specific provision or a general category in the Internal Revenue Code that permits the deduction. If there is no provision that allows an item (or class of items) as a deduction, then it cannot be deducted. In addition, deductions for certain items or categories of deductions have been specifically disallowed.

Corporations A corporation's allowable expenses are simply deductions from total income. In general, all businesses, regardless of their form of operation, are allowed deductions for business expenses that are ordinary, reasonable, and necessary. There is a general presumption that all business expenses are deductible unless there is a gross violation of the ordinary, necessary, and reasonable criteria. The tax laws do, however, include several disallowance provisions that disallow deductions for certain items; for example, fines, bribes, and expenses related to tax-exempt income are not deductible.[30]

Example 1.18

After determining its $4,150,000 of total income, Brogan Corporation (example 1.14) calculates $2,300,000 of ordinary and necessary business expenses. Its taxable income is $1,850,000 ($4,150,000 – $2,300,000).

Individuals Each individual taxpayer is permitted two types of deductions in determining taxable income.[31] The first, called deductions *for* adjusted gross income, consists of specific expenses that Congress has singled out for more favorable treatment than other individual deductions. These

[29] Income is taxed (recognized) only when realized. Thus, if securities have appreciated in value from $5,000 to $9,000, the $4,000 in appreciation will not be taxed until the securities are sold.

[30] The latter is an example of the matching principle. These expenses are discussed in Chapter 6.

[31] The qualified business income deduction, a third type of deduction, was added by the Tax Cuts and Jobs Act for 2018–2025 to address the difference between the tax rates for C corporations and pass-through businesses (sole proprietorships, partnerships, S corporations, and LLCs). This deduction is 20 percent of qualified business income and is discussed in Chapter 5.

deductions reduce an intermediate subtotal between gross income and taxable income called *adjusted gross income (AGI)*, a subtotal unique to individual taxpayers. Figure 1.4 lists some of these special deductions. If an individual does not have any of these special deductions, then his or her gross income and AGI will be the same.

Deductions *for* AGI	Discussed in chapter
Contributions to certain pension or retirement plans (including IRAs)	4
One-half of self-employment taxes	4
Self-employed health insurance premiums	4
Qualified student loan interest expense	5

FIGURE 1.4 Partial listing of deductions for AGI

The second type of deduction is the greater of the taxpayer's standard deduction (based on the taxpayer's filing status as discussed later) *or* the taxpayer's allowable itemized deductions (based on actual expenditures for such items as medical expenses, taxes, and interest). Figure 1.5 lists a few of an individual's more common itemized deductions.

Itemized deductions	Discussed in chapter
Taxes (state and local income and property taxes)	5
Interest expense (mortgage interest and investment interest)	5
Medical expenses	5
Charitable contributions	5
Casualty losses	9

FIGURE 1.5 Partial listing of itemized deductions

For those deductions subject to limitations, only amounts that are in excess of a minimum or do not exceed a maximum are deductible. If the taxpayer itemizes deductions, they are reported on Schedule A of an individual's Form 1040 as illustrated in Chapter 5.

Individuals who do not choose to itemize their deductions (and retain the required supporting documentation for their actual expenditures), can instead claim the *standard deduction* set by Congress regardless of actual expenditures. Individuals normally only itemize their deductions if their total deductions exceed their standard deduction allowance. This standard deduction varies by the **filing status** of the taxpayer; for example, a single taxpayer's standard deduction is one-half the standard deduction allowed a married couple filing a joint return as shown in Table 1.4. Thus, an individual may always deduct some amount from income—either the standard deduction *or* his or her itemized deductions—*but not both*.

Table 1.4 Standard Deduction by Filing Status

Filing status	2018	2017
Married filing jointly	$24,000	$12,700
Married filing separately	12,000	6,350
Head of household	18,000	9,350
Single	12,000	6,350
Dependent	1,050*	1,050*

*If larger, a dependent's standard deduction is earned income plus $350 up to their otherwise allowable standard deduction.

The standard deduction varies by filing status because single persons are assumed to have fewer personal expenses than married couples or those who qualify as heads of household.[32] Similarly, individuals who are dependents of another taxpayer (but whose income requires them to

[32] A head of household is a single individual who pays more than half the cost of maintaining a home in which a qualifying child or other dependent relatives lives.

file their own return) are not viewed as needing a large standard deduction because they are not self-supporting.[33]

Example 1.19

Jessica, a single parent who qualifies as head of household in 2018, has $49,000 of salary income but only $3,000 of itemized deductions. Jessica has taxable income of $31,000 ($49,000 AGI – $18,000 standard deduction).

Example 1.20

In 2018, James, who is single, was paid a salary of $62,000. His itemized deductions (including mortgage interest, property taxes, and charitable deductions) total $15,000, which is greater than his allowable standard deduction of $12,000 as a single individual. James has taxable income of $62,000 – $15,000 = $47,000.

Prior to 2018, individuals had another deduction based on the taxpayer's number of personal and dependency exemptions allowing a deduction of $4,050 for each in 2017. If the individual was self-supporting, he or she claimed a personal exemption; married persons filing a joint tax return claimed two personal exemptions (one for the husband and one for the wife). Taxpayers also deducted a dependency exemption for each person they supported who could be claimed as a dependent. A person claimed as a dependent on another taxpayer's return, however, could not take a personal exemption deduction for him- or herself even if he or she filed a tax return. For 2018, Congress has repealed the deduction for personal and dependency exemptions because it chose instead to increase the standard deduction.

Example 1.21

Jason and Jennifer are married with two small children. They have gross income from their salaries of $125,000 and claim the standard deduction. For 2017, their taxable income after deducting their two personal exemptions and two dependency exemptions was $96,100 [$125,000 – $12,700 standard deduction – $16,200 ($4,050 × 4 exemptions)]. For 2018, their standard deduction increases to $24,000 but the deduction for personal and dependency exemptions has been eliminated resulting in taxable income of $101,000 ($125,000 – $24,000). Although their taxable income is higher in 2018, the tax rates have declined slightly compared to 2017.

The standard deduction allows a taxpayer to receive a significant amount of income tax free, exempting a substantial number of low-income taxpayers from filing annual tax returns. For example, a married couple's taxable income would have to exceed the $24,000 standard deduction before they would be required to file an income tax return for 2018. Corporations, on the other hand, must file returns annually regardless of whether they report net income or loss for the tax year.

When the corporation has taken all of its allowable deductions from total income or an individual filer has reduced his or her gross income for the allowable deductions, the taxpayer's taxable income is determined. The taxpayer's next step is to determine the gross tax liability on that income.

Determining the Gross Tax Liability

In 2018, a corporation is subject to a 21 percent flat corporate tax rate on its taxable income.

[33] If a dependent is employed and has earned income exceeding $1,050, the standard deduction is increased to the total of the dependent's earned income *plus* $350 but cannot exceed the standard deduction based on filing status ($12,000 if single).

Example 1.22

Waldo Corporation has $125,000 of taxable income for 2018. Its gross tax is $26,250 ($125,000 × 21%). Molokai Corporation has $20,000,000 of taxable income for 2018. Its gross tax is $4,200,000 ($20,000,000 × 21%).

Individuals determine their tax liability using the appropriate individual tax rate schedule. The tax rate schedule an individual uses corresponds to the taxpayer's filing status; therefore, there are schedules for single individuals, married couples filing jointly, married couples filing separately, and heads of household (e.g., a single parent). Upper income individuals continue to receive the full benefit from the progressive tax rates (that is, there is no phase-out of the lower tax rates). As a result, a single individual with $20,000,000 of taxable income still receives the benefit of the first $9,525 of income taxed at a 10 percent rate. Although the actual tax rates are the same for each filing status, they do not apply at the same level of income—that is, the income level at which each higher rate applies varies by the taxpayer's filing status as shown in Table 1.5.

Table 1.5 2018 Tax Rates for Individual Taxpayers by Filing Status

Schedule X Single Individuals

If taxable income is:	*The tax is:*
Not over $9,525	10% of taxable income
Over $9,525 but not over $38,700	$952.50 plus 12% of the excess over $9,525
Over $38,700 but not over $82,500	$4,453.50 plus 22% of the excess over $38,700
Over $82,500 but not over $157,500	$14,089.50 plus 24% of the excess over $82,500
Over $157,500 but not over $200,000	$32,089.50 plus 32% of the excess over $157,500
Over $200,000 but not over $500,000	$45,689.50 plus 35% of the excess over $200,000
Over $500,000	$150,689.50 plus 37% of the excess over $500,000

Schedule Y-1 Married Individuals Filing Joint Returns

If taxable income is:	*The tax is:*
Not over $19,050	10% of taxable income
Over $19,050 but not over $77,400	$1,905 plus 12% of the excess over $19,050
Over $77,400 but not over $165,000	$8,907 plus 22% of the excess over $77,400
Over $165,000 but not over $315,000	$28,179 plus 24% of the excess over $165,000
Over $315,000 but not over $400,000	$64,179 plus 32% of the excess over $315,000
Over $400,000 but not over $600,000	$91,379 plus 35% of the excess over $400,000
Over $600,000	$161,379 plus 37% of the excess over $600,000

Schedule Y-2 Married Individuals Filing Separate Returns

If taxable income is:	*The tax is:*
Not over $9,525	10% of taxable income
Over $9,525 but not over $38,700	$952.50 plus 12% of the excess over $9,525
Over $38,700 but not over $82,500	$4,453.50 plus 22% of the excess over $38,700
Over $82,500 but not over $157,500	$14,089.50 plus 24% of the excess over $82,500
Over $157,500 but not over $200,000	$32,089.50 plus 32% of the excess over $157,500
Over $200,000 but not over $300,000	$45,689.50 plus 35% of the excess over $200,000
Over $300,000	$80,689.50 plus 37% of the excess over $300,000

Schedule Z Heads of Households

If taxable income is:	*The tax is:*
Not over $13,600	10% of taxable income
Over $13,600 but not over $51,800	$1,360 plus 12% of the excess over $13,600
Over $51,800 but not over $82,500	$5,944 plus 22% of the excess over $51,800
Over $82,500 but not over $157,500	$12,698 plus 24% of the excess over $82,500
Over $157,500 but not over $200,000	$30,698 plus 32% of the excess over $157,500
Over $200,000 but not over $500,000	$44,298 plus 35% of the excess over $200,000
Over $500,000	$149,298 plus 37% of the excess over $500,000

Example 1.23

Patricia is single with taxable income of $40,000 in 2018. Her tax liability is $4,739.50 [$4,453.50 + 22% ($40,000 – $38,700)].

The tax rate schedules illustrate the progressive nature of the federal income tax; that is, as a taxpayer's taxable income increases, his or her marginal tax rate also increases. For example, a single taxpayer with $100,000 of taxable income uses Schedule X, and is in the 24 percent marginal tax bracket (the next dollar of income is taxed at 24 percent). If income had been $250,000, the marginal tax bracket would have been 35 percent.

Example 1.24

Jennie is single and has 2018 taxable income of $58,000. Using Schedule X, her gross income tax liability is $8,699.50 [$4,453.50 + 22%($58,000 – $38,700)].

If Jennie is married and files a joint return with her husband, Peter, they would use Schedule Y-1 for joint return filers. If they had combined taxable income of $58,000, their tax liability would be only $6,579 [$1,905 + 12%($58,000 – $19,050)].

The married filing a joint return schedule normally provides the lowest tax liability for any given amount of taxable income. When higher income spouses each earn approximately the same income, however, their combined incomes are taxed at higher rates on a joint return than if they had remained single and filed separate returns as single individuals. This *marriage penalty* occurs because the bracket width for the 35 percent bracket on joint returns is smaller than twice the bracket width for that tax rate for single returns.

Example 1.25

Barbara is single and has taxable income of $400,000 in 2018. Her income tax is $115,689.50 [$45,689.50 + 35% ($400,000 – $200,000)] using Schedule X.

Shelly and John are married and have $800,000 in taxable income, one-half earned equally by each of them. Their income tax is $235,379 [$161,379 + 37%($800,000 – $600,000)] using Schedule Y-1. This is $4,000 [$235,379 – (2 × $115,689.50)] more than they would have to pay if they were not married and were taxed separately as single individuals. The $4,000 is their marriage penalty. If they file married filing separately, they would each pay $117,689.50 [$80,689.50 + 37%($400,000 – $300,000)] in income tax using Schedule Y-2, a total of $235,379 (2 × $117,689.50) (Note that because they are married, they cannot choose to file as single individuals.)

The previous tax calculations implicitly assumed that the taxpayer had no dividends or net long-term capital gains as part of taxable income for the year. As explained in Chapter 8, an individual with a net long-term capital gain from sales of capital assets, files a Schedule D: *Capital Gains and Losses* to report these gains and losses. The instructions for this schedule include a worksheet to determine total tax liability when long-term capital gains are included in the taxpayer's taxable income. Similarly, a worksheet is available to help determine the tax due on dividend income. The tax rates for long-term capital gains and dividends for 2018 are shown in Table 1.6.[34]

[34] Since 2013, the Affordable Care Act requires high-income taxpayers to pay the Medicare surtax on net investment income (NII), including net capital gains (whether long-term or short-term), taxable interest income, dividends, and rental income. This 3.8% NII tax is assessed on the lesser of net investment income or modified adjusted gross income in excess of thresholds based on filing status. Combining this 3.8% NII tax with the 20% capital gains rate results in an effective tax rate of 23.8% for capital gains and dividend income of high-income taxpayers. The NII tax is discussed in Chapter 5.

Table 1.6 Tax Rates for Dividend Income and Long-term Capital Gains

Long-term capital gains and dividend tax rate*	Taxable income for single individuals	Taxable income for married filing a joint return**	Taxable income for head of household
0%	$0–$38,600	$0–$77,200	$0–$51,700
15%	$38,601–$425,800	$77,201–$479,000	$51,701–$452,400
20%	Over $425,800	Over $479,000	Over $452,400

*Rate can be as high as 28% for collectibles and 25% for unrecaptured §1250 gain (see Chapter 8).
**Amounts if married filing separately are half the amount for filing a joint return.

Example 1.26

George is single and has $45,000 of taxable income, excluding an $8,000 long-term capital gain and $2,000 in dividends eligible for the 15 percent tax rate. George's tax on his $45,000 of ordinary income is $5,839.50 [$4,453.50 + 22%($45,000 – $38,700)]; his tax on the capital gain is $1,200 ($8,000 × 15%); his tax on his dividend income is $300 ($2,000 × 15%) for a total tax liability of $7,339.50 ($5,839.50 + $1,200 + $300). The favorable dividend and capital gain rates save George $700 [$10,000 × (22% – 15%)] in taxes.

There are no favorable income tax rates for long-term capital gains or dividend income included in the taxable income of corporate taxpayers. They are included in and taxed as ordinary income at the 21 percent corporate tax rate.

Tax Credits

Both individual and corporate taxpayers are entitled to certain credits that also reduce the tax liability. A business may benefit from the investment tax credit for investing in business equipment and working parents may benefit from the child care credit. A credit reduces the income tax liability in a different way than a deduction because a credit is a direct reduction in the taxpayer's tax liability.

Example 1.27

Carmen is single and has taxable income of $90,000 in 2018 and her income tax is $15,889.50 [$14,089.50 + 24%($90,000 – $82,500)]. If she is entitled to claim a tax credit of $500, her tax liability is reduced by $500 to $15,389.50. If she can claim a deduction for $500, the deduction reduces her taxable income by $500 to $89,500 which only reduces her tax liability by $120 to $15,769.50. A $500 tax credit is much more valuable than a $500 tax deduction.

A taxpayer must pay the additional tax if the taxpayer's tax liability exceeds allowable credits. If the taxpayer's credits exceed the tax liability, only a limited number of tax credits are refundable after the tax is reduced to zero.[35] If nonrefundable tax credits exceed the tax liability, certain credits (for example, the general business credit) may be carried to other years to offset a tax liability in the carryover year. Other credits that exceed that tax liability are lost entirely (for example, the dependent care credit). Figure 1.6 includes a few of the more common credits.

[35] There are several refundable credits—that is, credits that will result in a payment to the taxpayer even if there is no tax liability. One such refundable credit is the earned income credit applicable to low-income taxpayers. This credit acts like a negative income tax.

Type of credit	Discussed in chapter
Foreign tax credit	4
Child tax credit	5
Dependent care credit	5
Earned income credit	5
Education credits	5
Credit for excess payroll tax withheld	5
General business credits	10

FIGURE 1.6 Partial listing of tax credits

Tax Prepayments

After an individual or corporation reduces its total tax liability for allowable tax credits, its tax prepayments are deducted. Most taxpayers are required to make some form of prepayment for the anticipated tax liability. Most employers deduct a certain percentage of employees' salary and wage income in the form of tax withholdings. The employer then forwards the income tax withheld to the government for the employee. If, however, the taxpayer has a significant amount of income not covered by withholding, such as self-employment income or transactions on which there is no withholding (such as gains on the sale of investment assets), the individual is required to make quarterly estimated tax payments during the year. Corporations also make estimated tax payments based on anticipated taxable income. Estimated payments are so named because taxpayers must estimate how much income they will earn and the related tax they expect to owe for the year. Failure to make the minimum required tax prepayment may subject the taxpayer to penalties and interest. Individuals who owe less than $1,000 and corporations less than $500 when their returns are filed avoid penalties.

Example 1.28

Z Corporation's tax liability was $68,000 and it made $67,600 in estimated tax payments. It now owes only $400 for its $68,000 tax liability because of its $67,600 in estimated tax payments.

1.4.2 TRUSTS AND ESTATES

Trusts and estates are the third type of taxable entity called fiduciary entities—nonbusiness legal entities that hold assets and may have income. An estate is created when any person with asset ownership dies. An executor or personal representative manages the estate assets until they are distributed to the heirs or beneficiaries. A trust is created by a person (the grantor) who places control of trust assets in the hands of a trustee for the benefit of a third party (the beneficiary). Because trusts and estates may hold assets that earn income, they are subject to income taxes. Their tax formula has the same characteristics as the basic tax model. The entity is generally taxed on income to the extent the income remains within the entity. Income that is paid out to a beneficiary is taxed only to the beneficiary. Table 1.7 contains the tax rates for estates and trusts for 2018.

The tax brackets for estates and trusts are much more compact than the individual tax brackets. The highest tax rate begins when taxable income exceeds $12,500 and there are no 12, 22, or 32 percent tax brackets. Distributing income annually to the beneficiaries usually results in lower overall taxes as beneficiaries are usually in lower marginal tax brackets. The taxation of trusts and estates is discussed in detail in Chapter 12.

Table 1.7 2018 Income Tax Rates for Trusts and Estates

Income Tax Rates for Trusts and Estates	
If taxable income is:	*The tax is:*
Not over $2,550	10% of taxable income
Over $2,550 but not over $9,150	$255.00 plus 24% of the excess over $2,550
Over $9,150 but not over $12,500	$1,839.00 plus 35% of the excess over $9,150
Over $12,500	$3,011.50 plus 37% of the excess over $12,500
Tax Rates for Long-term Capital Gains and Dividend Income	
If taxable income is:	*The tax rate is:*
Not over $2,600	0%
Over $2,600 but not over $12,700	15%
Over $12,700	20%

Example 1.29

A trust has $5,000 of taxable income in the current year. It can retain the income or distribute it to Craig, the beneficiary. He is a 24-year-old college student in the 10% marginal tax bracket. If the trust retains the income, it will pay a tax of $843 [$255 + (24% × $5,000 – 2,550)]. If the trust distributes the $5,000 to Craig, he will pay $500 in tax (10% × $5,000). Distributing the income to Craig saves $343 in taxes ($843 – $500).

1.5 CHOICE OF BUSINESS ENTITY

One important consideration when starting your business is determining the best legal and operational structure. This affects its efficiency, transferability, control, reporting of income, taxes paid, and the owners' personal liability. Business entities differ in their legal and tax classification. They are legal structures regulated by state governments and it or its owners are subject to tax at the federal level. It may be difficult to change a legal structure after operations begin, so making the right decision as to its form of operation before the business is opened is important.

A business can be classified as a sole proprietorship, a partnership (general or limited), a corporation, or a limited liability company (LLC). A sole proprietorship is the simplest legal structure for any business. For state law purposes, a sole proprietorship is a single owner business that is not required to formally register with the state, although some states and municipalities may require licenses or permits. Many sole proprietorships do not obtain a separate identification number, but simply use the owner's Social Security number for identification. By default, the legal business name is the same as the owner's name but the business may establish a separate name by creating a "doing business as" (DBA) name. Most states require DBAs to register with the county clerk or Secretary of State.

The ease of forming the sole proprietorship is matched by the ease of closing the business. Any business property reverts to the sole proprietor. The primary disadvantage of the sole proprietorship is that the owner is fully liable for all the debts of the business and could lose all of his or her personal assets to satisfy a judgment against the business. A sole proprietorship is simply not considered an entity separate from its owner.

Example 1.30

Jason operates a small bicycle shop as a sole proprietorship. He recently assembled and sold a bicycle to a new customer. Unfortunately, Jason failed to tighten the nuts securing the front tire. The customer fell off the bike and was severely injured on her first ride. She filed a lawsuit against the bicycle shop for negligence. If Jason loses this lawsuit, he would have to use his personal assets to cover any judgment unless his insurance is sufficient to cover his liability for damages. Jason could lose more than his investment in his business.

Partnerships are formed under state partnership statutes and must have at least two owners (partners). A partnership can be formed as a general partnership, a limited partnership, a limited liability partnership (LLP), or a professional limited liability partnership (PLLP). The difference in these special forms involves the liability protection afforded the owners. One advantage of the partnership form is the absence of restrictions on a partner's identity. A partner can be an individual or any type of entity, including another partnership, a corporation, an estate, or a trust. A partnership can have two types of partners—general and limited. All partnerships must have at least one general partner who not only provides capital to the partnership, but is involved in partnership management. Limited partners only provide capital and generally do not participate in management. All partners have equal ownership of all business assets unless the partnership agreement specifies other ownership arrangements. Ownership percentages can vary based on the specifications included in the written partnership agreement. General partners are fully liable for all liabilities of the partnership while the liability of limited partners is limited to their investment. A partnership usually dissolves if a general partner dies or leaves the partnership (unless the partnership agreement provides for continuation of the business by the remaining partners).

Corporations must file articles of incorporation with the state in which their principal office is located. A corporation can issue different classes of stock and bonds, subject to state and federal securities laws. When a business decides to "go public" with an **initial public offering (IPO)** on one of the public securities exchanges, it will usually solicit a large pool of potential investors to become shareholders. Shareholders are only at risk for their capital investment; if the corporation fails, the shareholders are not liable for the outstanding debts of the corporation. If a shareholder desires to withdraw from the corporation, only a buyer for the stock is necessary. Shareholders do not participate directly in management; instead they only have the right to vote for corporate directors or officers. This facilitates centralized management so that day-to-day operations do not require the input of all the owners. Additionally, the corporation's life is not restricted. The death of an owner or a transfer of stock ownership does not affect the corporation's legal existence.

The limited liability company is a hybrid type of legal business form that provides the limited liability features of a corporation and the operational flexibility of a partnership. The owners are referred to as members. Depending on the state, the members can consist of a single individual (one owner), two or more individuals, corporations, or other LLCs. To form an LLC, you usually must file articles of organization with the state in which the business is organized.

For tax *return* purposes, however, there are only four types of business entities:[36]

1. Sole proprietorships
2. Partnerships
3. C corporations (regular corporations)
4. S corporations (corporations electing S status)

Regardless of their form, all businesses must report their results of operations following the tax rules for one of these four entities. Limited liability companies with two or more owners default to being taxed as partnerships unless they elect to be taxed as corporations. Of these entities, only C corporations (and limited liability companies electing C corporation status) actually pay income taxes. A sole proprietorship passes its income directly to the sole proprietor using a Schedule C included in the sole proprietor's individual tax return. Partnerships, limited liability companies taxed as partnerships, and S corporations also pass their income through to their owners for taxation at the owner level. These businesses, however, must file *information*

[36] There is no separate tax return for an LLC. Most multi-owner LLCs file partnership tax returns but could elect to file as corporations. An LLC choosing to file as an S corporation would have to comply with all of the S corporation rules. A single-owner LLC would usually file as a sole proprietorship.

tax returns (Form 1065 for partnerships and limited liability companies taxed as partnerships and Form 1120S for S corporations) with the IRS. The entity must provide the owners with the information required for filing their tax returns.[37]

1.5.1 SOLE PROPRIETORSHIPS

A **sole proprietorship** may be very small with no employees or a large business with thousands of employees. It can operate any type of business—manufacturing, distribution, retail, or service. The owner of the sole proprietorship is not an employee but is considered self-employed. This means that Social Security and Medicare taxes are not withheld from any payments received by the sole proprietor; instead self-employment taxes[38] must be paid on the net profit of the business. Because the sole proprietor cannot be an employee, he or she is not eligible for the tax-free employee fringe benefits for which a corporate shareholder-employee would be eligible.[39]

There is no separate business tax return for a sole proprietorship; income and expenses from operations are reported on Schedule C: *Profit or Loss from Business (Sole Proprietorship)*. Self-employment tax is computed on Schedule SE: *Self-Employment Tax* based on the business profits. These forms are then included with the individual's completed Form 1040: *Individual Tax Return*. The sole proprietor is taxed on all of the net profits from the business as ordinary income regardless of how much he or she withdrew from the business during the year.

Example 1.31

Gary is the sole proprietor of Gary's Garage. Gross income is $100,000, operating expenses are $40,000 for the year, and Gary withdrew $50,000 from the business for his living expenses. Gary reports these operating income and expenses on Schedule C and shows a net profit of $60,000 ($100,000 – $40,000). Gary includes all $60,000 of net profit from his business and computes taxable income for the year on his Form 1040. The $50,000 he withdrew has no effect on profit reported or taxes owing. Gary pays self-employment tax on the $60,000 net business profits and income taxes on his taxable income (after allowable deductions).

A tax advantage for a sole proprietorship is that a business loss can reduce or *shelter* the individual's other income when calculating taxable income.[40]

Example 1.32

Christina's sole proprietorship reports a net loss of $10,000 for the year. Christina is also an employee of another business with annual salary of $30,000. Christina uses her $10,000 loss from the sole proprietorship to shelter part of her salary from taxation, reducing her adjusted gross income to $20,000.

[37] An information return is a tax return that reports each owner's share of profits or losses to the IRS. No tax is paid with this return; instead any tax owed is paid by the owners with their tax returns.

[38] Self-employed individuals pay both the employer's and employee's share of Social Security and Medicare taxes resulting in a combined rate of 15.3% on the first $128,400 of self-employment income and 2.9% on the excess. If a business has a loss, no self-employment tax is owed that year. See Chapter 4 for a detailed discussion of employment taxes. Additionally, because income tax is not withheld for self-employed individuals, they must make their own quarterly estimated payment to the government. See Chapter 5 for a discussion of estimated payments.

[39] Employee fringe benefits are discussed in Chapter 4. Examples include health insurance, life insurance, and parking benefits.

[40] The Tax Cuts and Jobs Act introduced two new provisions, effective for the 2018 tax year, that affect the deduction for net business losses and taxation of income from sole proprietorships, partnerships, and S corporations. The maximum amount of net business losses from a sole proprietorship, partnership or S corporation that can be deducted on an owner's return is generally limited to $250,000 ($500,000 if married filing jointly); the disallowed excess loss is treated as a NOL and carried forward. Also beginning in 2018, a new deduction addresses the difference between the tax rates for C corporations and flow-through businesses that are taxed at their owners' individual rates. This deduction equals 20 percent of qualified business income. Both of these new provisions are discussed further in Chapters 5 and 11.

The tax savings realized from the flow through of a business loss depends on the marginal tax rate of the individual. The individual's marginal tax rate is dependent on his or her other taxable income.

Example 1.33

Joshua, a single individual, owns a sole proprietorship that has a $20,000 net loss. Joshua's $550,000 of other taxable income before deducting this loss places him in the 37 percent marginal tax bracket (from the tax rate schedule for a single individual). He has tax savings of $7,400 ($20,000 × 37%) from the $20,000 loss deduction. If, instead, Joshua's taxable income is only $35,000 before deducting the loss, he would be in the 12 percent marginal tax bracket and he would have only $2,400 ($20,000 × 12%) in tax savings from the loss.

1.5.2 PARTNERSHIPS

A **partnership** consists of two or more individuals (or other entities) who agree to carry on a business jointly. Similar to sole proprietors, partners cannot be employees of the partnership or participate in most fringe benefits on a tax-free basis. For example, if a partnership provides health insurance for its partners, the partnership can deduct the health insurance premiums as business expenses, but the partners must include them in their taxable income.

A partnership is referred to as a "conduit" or flow-through entity because the income and losses are allocated to and flow through to its owners to be taxed on their individual returns. The partnership itself pays no income tax, but it must file a separate tax return (Form 1065: *U.S. Partnership Return of Income*). This is only an information return that reports each partner's share of the profits or losses to the IRS to inform the IRS how much each partner should be reporting on his or her individual tax return. Most items of income that flow through to the partners retain their individual character. For example, a partnership's operating income is taxed at the partner's ordinary income tax rate while a long-term capital gain is taxed at the partner's rate for long-term capital gains.

One disadvantage of conduit taxation is that owners are taxed on their share of the profits, even if they receive no cash distributions from the business. They can, however, receive distributions of those previously taxed profits at a later date without incurring a second tax. In addition, similar to a sole proprietor, an individual general partner must pay self-employment taxes on his or her share of partnership profits.

Example 1.34

Ginny owns a one-third interest in the PEP Partnership. It reports $21,000 of operating income for the current tax year but makes no distributions to the partners. Ginny must include $7,000 ($21,000 × 1/3) of partnership income in her gross income for the tax year. The $7,000 is subject to self-employment taxes and if she is in the 24 percent marginal tax bracket she will also pay $1,680 income tax on her $7,000 share of the partnership profits this year. In the future, however, Ginny can withdraw $7,000 from the partnership without being subject to additional tax.

If a partnership incurs a loss, the loss also flows through to the partners and may be deductible from the partner's other income effectively *sheltering* that other income from tax. The total loss that an owner may deduct from an investment in a partnership is limited to the partner's basis in the partnership interest.[41]

[41] The passive income and at-risk rules may also prevent the deduction unless the partner materially participates in the partnership and his or her investment is at risk. These rules are discussed in Chapter 11.

Partner's Basis Account

A partner's basis account is a measure of the partner's investment in the partnership at any given time. It ensures that partnership income is taxed only once. It is the upper limit on the amount a partner may receive as a tax-free distribution, as well as the limit on the amount of loss that can be deducted. A partner's beginning basis is determined by the cash and the basis of property contributed to the partnership in exchange for a partnership interest. Basis increases by any income or gains that flow through to the partner and decreases for any losses and distributions. The deduction for losses that flow through is limited to the partner's basis in the partnership interest (after all adjustments for gains, income, and distributions) because a partner's basis can never be negative. Once a partner's basis is reduced to zero, no additional loss can be deducted. This excess loss is carried forward until the partner again has positive basis against which it can then be deducted.

Example 1.35

Jennifer is a 40 percent general partner in ABC partnership. Her partnership basis is $200 at the beginning of year 1. The partnership has $2,000 of ordinary income and distributes $450 in cash to Jennifer at the end of year 1. Jennifer has $800 (40% × $2,000) of income, her share that flows through to her. She increases her basis to $1,000 ($200 beginning basis + $800 income passed through), and then reduces it to $550 by the $450 distribution ($1,000 – $450). Jennifer is in the 32% tax bracket and pays $256 ($800 × 32%) in income taxes on her share of the partnership profits.

At the end of year 2, the partnership reports a $2,500 loss, $1,000 ($2,500 × 40%) of which flows through to Jennifer. Her loss deduction, however, is limited to her $550 basis; Jennifer carries the remaining $450 loss ($1,000 loss – $550 deducted) forward because her partnership interest basis cannot be negative.[42] Jennifer's tax savings from the $550 deductible loss are $176 ($550 × 32%).

The partnership's year 3 income is $5,000 and $2,000 ($5,000 × 40%) flows through to Jennifer. Jennifer reports the $2,000 as income, increases her basis to $2,000, and can now deduct the $450 loss carried over from the prior year. Her basis at the end of the third year is $1,550 ($0 + $2,000 – $450). Jennifer pays only $496 ($1,550 × 32%) in income taxes on her $2,000 share of the profit that is reduced for the deductible loss carried forward from the prior year.

A unique feature of the partnership form is the increase in the partners' bases for their share of partnership liabilities. When the partnership repays the debt, the partners' bases are reduced for their share of the repayment. A partnership with liabilities allows its partners to deduct a greater share of losses as a result of this increased basis. If a partner's share of losses exceeds his or her remaining basis, the partner can only reduce basis to zero. The excess losses (after reducing basis to zero) cannot cause a negative basis and cannot be used until there are future increases in bases (from a share of income, contributions to capital or increase in liabilities) against which to deduct these excess losses.

When liabilities are repaid, partners must also reduce their bases for their share of discharged debt. If the partner's share of the repaid liability exceeds his or her remaining basis, the partner views the excess over basis similar to a "sale" of the partnership interest to avoid a negative basis.

[42] Jennifer can increase her basis by contributing cash or other property to the partnership. Her basis will also be increased when the partnership earns a profit and allocates Jennifer's share of that profit to her basis account.

Example 1.36

The partnership in the previous example borrows $5,000 at the beginning of year 2, increasing Jennifer's partnership basis to $2,550 [$550 beginning basis + (40% × $5,000 liability)]. Jennifer can now deduct her $1,000 second-year loss reducing her basis to $1,550 ($2,550 – $1,000 loss). When the partnership repays $2,000 of the loan at the beginning of year 3, Jennifer's basis decreases by $800 (40% × $2,000) to $750 ($1,550 – $800). If the partnership has a $2,400 loss in year 3, Jennifer's deduction is limited to her $750 remaining partnership basis and her remaining $210 loss [(40% × $2,400) – $750] cannot be deducted until she again has basis.

Alternatively, if the partnership had paid off the entire $5,000 loan at the beginning of year 3, her $1,550 basis would be reduced to zero and Jennifer would be taxed on the $450 share of liability that was repaid and exceeds her basis. Her loss cannot be deducted until basis is restored.

Most multi-member limited liability companies are partnerships for tax purposes, filing the Form 1065: *U.S. Return of Partnership Income*. Like partnerships, they are conduits that have their income or loss flow through to their members. This income or loss retains its character when it flows through to the members. Active members in an LLC also pay self-employment tax on their share of profits in the same manner as general partners or sole proprietors.

1.5.3 C CORPORATIONS

Regular corporations are usually referred to as C corporations to distinguish them from S corporations. Corporate shareholders can be employees subject to the same payroll taxes as all other employees. Shareholder-employees can participate in company fringe benefits that are denied tax-free treatment to the working-owners of other business forms (for example, employee health insurance premiums paid by the corporation are fully deductible by the corporation and are a tax-free benefit to shareholder/employees). In addition, the corporate tax rate is lower than individual tax rates, allowing owners to have increased capital for reinvestment and business expansion. A C corporation computes its taxable income and tax on Form 1120: *U.S. Corporate Income Tax Return*.

The main disadvantage of the corporate form is double taxation of corporate income because dividends are not deductible by a corporation. The corporation first pays a tax on its net income when earned; then the after-tax income distributed to most shareholders is taxed as dividend income. (Generally, the other forms of business avoid this double level of tax.) The impact of this double taxation on individual shareholders is somewhat mitigated by the lower tax rates on dividend income.

Example 1.37

Tom, a taxpayer with dividend income in the 15 percent tax bracket, owns the Big Creek Corporation. Big Creek paid $10,500 in tax on its $50,000 of taxable income and distributes the $39,500 in after-tax earnings to Tom as a dividend. He pays $5,925 ($39,500 × 15%) in federal income taxes on the distribution. Total taxes of $16,425 ($10,500 + $5,925) are paid on the $50,000 earned by the corporation, or almost 33 percent of the pretax earnings.

Another disadvantage of a C corporation is that losses do not flow through to the shareholders and there is no tax benefit to shareholders in the year the corporation experiences the loss. Corporate losses can offset corporate profits in future years, as net operating losses can be carried forward an unlimited number of years. Until there are future corporate profits, however, there are no tax savings from corporate losses. If a new C corporation experiences losses in its early years, those losses are trapped at the corporate level until a future profitable year.[43]

Example 1.38

Newborn Corporation, a new C corporation, has a $40,000 loss in its first tax year, a $30,000 loss in its second year, a $20,000 loss in its third year, and finally a $100,000 profit in its fourth year. Newborn Corporation receives no tax benefit from its losses until its fourth year when it can offset its three years of accumulated losses of $90,000 against its $100,000 profit, reducing its taxable income in the fourth year to $10,000. Its tax savings in the fourth year are $18,900 ($90,000 × 21%), the difference between the corporate tax on $100,000 and the corporate tax on $10,000. The shareholders could not deduct any of Newborn Corporation's losses on their individual tax returns.

1.5.4 S CORPORATIONS

S corporations are formed in the same manner as C corporations but they avoid double taxation of corporate income by making a valid S corporation election. To elect S corporation status, the corporation must qualify as a "small business corporation" as defined under Internal Revenue Code Section 1361. The corporation files Form 2553: *Election by a Small Business Corporation*, along with consent statements signed by all shareholders of record at the time the election is made. The election can be made at any time during the preceding year or before the 15th day of the third month of the tax year for which the corporation wishes to have S corporation status.

An S corporation must be a domestic corporation with no more than 100 shareholders who, with limited exception, must be individuals who are not nonresident aliens. It can have only one class of common stock outstanding. If a corporation violates any one of these requirements at any time, the S corporation status is revoked and it will be taxed as a regular C corporation from that time.

Qualifying S corporations use the conduit concept of taxation, passing profits and losses through to their shareholders (similar to partnerships) for taxation at the shareholder level, avoiding the double tax on corporate profits. S corporation shareholders have the same limited liability protection that C corporation shareholders possess but avoid the principal disadvantage of C corporations—double taxation of income.

S corporations file an information tax return, Form 1120S: *U.S. Income Tax Return for an S Corporation*. The shareholders are taxed on their share of profits, whether they are actually distributed to them or retained in the corporation. A conduit entity is usually appropriate if the profits are distributed to the owners rather than reinvested in the business. These profits can then be distributed without the owners incurring any additional tax. Personal-service business activities (such as accounting or engineering) usually fall into this category.

S corporation shareholders can be employees of an S corporation for employment tax purposes, paying the same payroll taxes as other employees on their salary or wages. Similar to partners, however, shareholders who own more than 2 percent of the corporation's stock cannot participate in most employee fringe benefit programs on a tax-free basis. For example, the payment of health insurance premiums by the corporation for shareholders owning more than a 2-percent interest in the corporation, results in additional salary rather than a tax-free benefit.[44]

[43] Prior to 2018, net operating losses (NOLs) could be carried back two years but forward only 20 years.

[44] Some of the benefits that greater-than-2-percent S corporation shareholders and partners cannot receive on a tax-free basis include health and accident insurance, group term life insurance, on-premises lodging, employee achievement awards, transit passes, and parking benefits. To mitigate the difference in this treatment of employer-provided health insurance for employees and the self-employed, sole proprietors, S corporation shareholders, and general partners may deduct the cost of health insurance for AGI. See Chapter 4.

A shareholder's basis is a measure of the shareholder's investment in the corporation's stock. A shareholder's beginning basis is the cash and adjusted basis of any property contributed to the corporation (or the price paid for the corporate stock). The shareholder's basis increases for the shareholder's share of the corporation's income or gain and decreases for any distributions or losses. The shareholder's deduction for losses is limited to the shareholder's stock basis (similar to a partner's basis limit for a loss deduction). Unlike a partnership, however, S corporation shareholders do not increase basis for debts undertaken by the corporation because S corporation shareholders have no personal liability for corporate debts. Thus, if the entity in examples 1.35 and 1.36 had been an S corporation, Jennifer could not have increased her basis for the corporation's debt.

Example 1.39

Assume the facts in examples 1.35 and 1.36 except that the business is an S corporation. Jennifer's basis adjustments are the same for the S corporation as shown in example 1.35. When the S corporation borrows $5,000 (example 1.36), Jennifer cannot increase her basis and it remains $550. Jennifer's second-year deduction is limited to her $550 basis, reducing it to zero. Her remaining $450 loss is carried forward until she again has basis in her S corporation stock. The loan repayment has no effect on Jennifer's stock basis.

S corporations and partnerships also differ in that shareholder-employees are not subject to self-employment taxes on the profits of an S corporation as are general partners' shares of the partnership profits. This provides an incentive for S corporation shareholders to take lower salaries (subject to employment taxes) but larger distributions of profits (not subject to self-employment taxes). If the IRS deems the salary paid to a shareholder-employee is unreasonably low on audit, it may reclassify some or all of a cash distribution of profits as salary and assess additional employment taxes on both the shareholder and the corporation (as discussed in Chapter 4).

As conduit entities, partnerships, limited liability companies, and S corporations are especially attractive in the early years of a business activity when operating losses are likely to occur. The early losses of a C corporation are locked inside the corporation and provide no tax benefit until the corporation becomes profitable. Losses from a conduit entity flow through to the owners and benefit the owners in the same year that the loss occurs (assuming the owners are able to deduct the losses). When conduit entity owners have high marginal tax rates, the benefit of loss flow-through is especially attractive.

At first glance, conduit entities may appear to be superior to C corporations from a purely tax perspective. Such a conclusion is shortsighted, however. C corporations have some favorable tax characteristics that are not available to any conduit entity. Exploiting these characteristics (such as the ability of owners to be treated as employees and to benefit from tax-free employee fringe benefits), can more than compensate for double taxation.

1.5.5 COMPARING BUSINESS ENTITY ATTRIBUTES

Choosing the best legal entity for the operation of a business activity is an extremely difficult decision. The future needs of both the business and its owners must be estimated and evaluated as part of this decision. Once a decision is implemented it will have long-lasting effects. Changing from one entity type to another can be difficult and expensive. Federal and state income taxes are an important component of the legal entity decision; however, taxes alone are an insufficient criterion for making a decision. Figure 1.7 presents a basic comparison of partnerships, S corporations, and C corporations as operating businesses across some of the tax and nontax attributes that should be considered when evaluating the choice of entity. These various attributes are explored in more detail in later chapters of this text.

Attribute	Partnership	S corporation	C corporation
Limited liability protection	Limited partners have limited liability protection. General partners have unlimited liability with respect to partnership debts.	Yes	Yes
Owner identity restrictions	None; any person or entity may be an owner.	Substantial restrictions: corporations, partnerships, certain trusts, and non-resident aliens not permitted.	None; any person or entity may be an owner.
Number of permitted owners	Minimum 2; maximum unlimited	Minimum 1; maximum 100 (family members treated as one)	Minimum 1; maximum unlimited
Differences in ownership rights permitted between owners	Flexible; economic and management rights can vary between general and limited partners.	Generally fixed; only common stock is permitted, but voting rights may vary.	Flexible; no limit on different classes of stock that may be created.
Excludible employee fringe benefits for employee owners	Generally not available.	Generally not available for greater than 2% owners.	Available to all employees.
Tax treatment of capital gains and losses	Gains flow through to partners and are taxed at partner's capital gains tax rate. Losses deductible by partner subject to capital loss limits.	Gains flow through to shareholders and are taxed at owner's capital gains tax rate. Losses deductible by shareholder subject to capital loss limits.	Gains taxed to corporation at the flat 21% rate applicable to ordinary income. Capital losses are carried back 3 years and forward 5 years.
Marginal tax rate structure applied to ordinary income	Flow through to owner and taxed at owner's marginal tax rate.	Flow through to owner and taxed at owner's marginal tax rate.	Taxed at a flat 21% rate.
Allocation of entity income and loss	Allocations made under partnership agreement.	Fixed; all allocations based on ownership of stock.	N/A; not a conduit entity.
Self-employment taxes	Imposed on ordinary income share of general partners.	Not imposed.	N/A; not a conduit entity.
Overall capacity of owner to derive tax benefit from entity losses	Very good for partners who participate in management and can increase basis for entity debts.	Good for shareholders who are material participants in the business; however, it may be limited because shareholder basis not increased for entity debts.	Not a conduit entity. Corporate net operating losses remain within corporation and are carried forward for eventual corporate tax benefit.

FIGURE 1.7
Comparison of business entity attributes

REVISITING THE INTRODUCTORY CASE

Wing Hue is a resident of the United States and is subject to its income tax laws. As an employee of the consulting firm, Hue is required to pay employment taxes (his share of FICA taxes) through withholding by his employer. His employer also must withhold a certain percentage of his gross income for his income tax liability based on his estimated income. He is subject to income tax rates ranging from 10 to 37 percent of his taxable income.

To obtain backing from venture capitalists, Hue may have to agree to the type of entity that will be used for his manufacturing business. The venture capitalists could require Hue to establish a regular corporation to provide flexible ownership and limit their liability. If so, Hue could own a certain percentage of the corporation while also being an employee, fully participating in the corporation's fringe benefits. (If the venture is successful, he will most likely leave his consulting position.) As an owner-employee, Hue can take profits out of the corporation as a salary, subject to FICA taxes and income tax withholding. It will, however, be paid with the before-tax income of the corporation due to the corporation's salary deduction. Corporate profits taken out as dividends will be paid with the after-tax income of the corporation and will be subject to additional taxes when received by Hue and his backers.

The manufacturing business could be established in several other entity forms, if his financial backers allow. It is unlikely the backers would sanction operations as a sole proprietorship (the lenders would have to lend the money directly to Hue). If they did, however, Hue would have to pay self-employment taxes on all profits as well as income taxes. He will, however, be able to deduct losses against his other income.

The backers could permit the business to operate as either a partnership or an S corporation as an alternative to the C corporation. They can limit their liability through the S corporation or a limited liability company electing partnership taxation. These entities pass income directly through to the owners for taxation, eliminating the double taxation of earnings. As a general partner, Hue would be responsible for self-employment taxes on his share of partnership income, in addition to income taxes. Hue cannot be an employee of the partnership nor participate in tax-free employee fringe benefits. Although he can be an employee of an S corporation (with FICA taxes and income tax withholding on his salary), ownership of more than 2 percent of the stock limits his ability to benefit from tax-free employee fringe benefits.

SUMMARY

Taxes are required payments to a governmental unit unrelated to the benefits received. In addition to funding government operations, taxes are used to redistribute wealth, foster price stability and economic growth, and meet social goals.

A major source of revenue for many jurisdictions is an income tax, but there are many other bases for levying taxes. Various governmental units levy consumption taxes (sales and use taxes), wealth taxes (property taxes), and wealth transfer taxes (estate and gift taxes). These taxes may be proportional, progressive, or regressive. Adam Smith's four canons of taxation of equity, economy, certainty, and convenience can be used to evaluate a tax.

The income tax is the primary source of revenue for the federal government, but only individuals, corporations, and fiduciaries pay income taxes. Other business entities, such as sole proprietorships, partnerships, and S corporations pass their incomes through to their owners until they reach one of the three types of income tax-paying persons. This income is then included with the other types of income subject to income taxes by an individual, corporation, or fiduciary for taxation by the appropriate jurisdiction(s).

The impact of income taxes is just one of many things that must be considered when deciding in which form to operate a business. S corporations and limited liability companies can limit the owner's liability for corporate acts. Sole proprietors and partners may have to surrender personal assets to satisfy judgments against the business. Other variations include, but are not limited to, the treatment of employment taxes, participation in fringe benefit programs, and the ability to sell an interest in the business. These and more must be considered when determining in which form to operate a business.

KEY TERMS

Ad valorem 8
Average tax rate 14
Canons of taxation 15
C corporation 18
Estate tax 9
FICA tax 7
Fiduciary 19
Filing status 23
Franchise tax 6
Gift tax 9
Gross income 20
Horizontal equity 16
Initial public offering (IPO) 30
Internal Revenue Code 4
Losses 21
Marginal tax rate 14
Nexus 6
Partnership 32
Progressive tax system 12
Proportional tax system 14
Real property tax 8
Regressive tax system 15
S corporations 35
Sales tax 10
Sole proprietorship 31
Tax expenditures 5
Use tax 10
Value-added tax (VAT) 11
Vertical equity 17

TEST YOURSELF

Answers Appear after the Problem Assignments

1. Which of the following is correctly categorized as a tax?
   a. The dog license fee
   b. The annual property tax on your home
   c. An assessment for putting streetlights in front of your home that increases the home's value
   d. The bond a person must post to get out of jail

2. What type of tax is a sales tax?
   a. Income tax
   b. Consumption tax
   c. Wealth transfer tax
   d. Turnover tax

3. What characteristic of a tax states that taxpayers with equal incomes should pay equivalent amounts of taxes?
   a. Horizontal equity
   b. Vertical equity
   c. Certainty
   d. Convenience

4. Which of the following applies only to individual taxpayers and not to corporations?
   a. Taxable income
   b. Estimated tax payments
   c. Gross income
   d. Lower tax rates for long-term capital gains

5. Which of the following entities does not pass its income directly through to its owners?
   a. Sole proprietorship
   b. Partnership
   c. C corporation
   d. S corporation

PROBLEM ASSIGNMENTS

Check Your Understanding

1. [LO 1.1] What is a tax? How does a tax differ from a fine?
2. [LO 1.1] What Constitutional Amendment allowed implementation of an income tax? In what year was it ratified?
3. [LO 1.1] Which version of the tax code is applicable today?
4. [LO 1.1] Define tax expenditure.
5. [LO 1.1] What is a SALT practice?
6. [LO 1.1] What is nexus?
7. [LO 1.1] Suntan Corporation sells its products nationwide over the Internet. It has production facilities, warehouses, and offices only in the state of Florida. It has sales in excess of $600,000 for the year to customers in Arizona. It has no physical presence in Arizona. Can Arizona assess state income tax on Suntan Corporation for the sales made to Arizona customers?
8. [LO 1.1] How does a franchise tax differ from an income tax?
9. [LO 1.1] What three factors are generally used to determine the percentage of corporate income allocated to a particular state?
10. [LO 1.1] What employment taxes are imposed on an employee and an employer?
11. [LO 1.1] What is the most common wealth tax and how is it levied?
12. [LO 1.1] What property is subject to the intangible tax?
13. [LO 1.1] Explain the integration of the gift and estate taxes.
14. [LO 1.1] Differentiate a consumption-based tax from an income tax and illustrate with an example.
15. [LO 1.1] Differentiate a wealth tax from a wealth transfer tax and give examples of each.
16. [LO 1.1] What is a use tax?
17. [LO 1.2] Over what ranges of taxable income in 2018 will the total income tax liability for two persons with equal incomes who file as single individuals equal their income tax liability if they file jointly as a married couple?
18. [LO 1.2] Differentiate a progressive tax system from a proportional and a regressive system and give examples of each.
19. [LO 1.2] What basic tax rates apply to the ordinary income, dividend income, and interest income of an individual? What are they for a corporation?
20. [LO 1.2] What tax rates apply to an individual's capital gains?
21. [LO 1.3] Briefly explain Adam Smith's four canons of taxation.
22. [LO 1.3] Differentiate horizontal from vertical equity.
23. [LO 1.4] Which three taxable persons pay all of the income taxes?
24. [LO 1.4] Define gross income.
25. [LO 1.4] Briefly describe the basic elements of the tax model.
26. [LO 1.4] Differentiate the tax treatment of an individual's capital losses from the tax treatment of corporate capital losses.
27. [LO 1.4] What are the basic tax rates for an individual and a corporation?

28. [LO 1.4] What are two fiduciary entities and how are they created? Differentiate the grantor, trustee, and beneficiary of a trust.

29. [LO 1.5] What are three characteristics of a sole proprietorship? Do these characteristics differ from those of a partnership? What are three characteristics of a limited liability company that differ from those of a partnership?

30. [LO 1.5] Compare a C corporation to an S corporation.

Crunch the Numbers

31. [LO 1.1] Dane City's total assessed valuation for all of the property in its jurisdiction is $4,000,000,000. It needs $20,000,000 in revenue for the services it provides its citizens. Joe owns property that is assessed at $150,000. How much will he pay in property taxes?

32. [LO 1.1] If a taxpayer has $40,000 of employee salary in 2018, how much will be withheld for the Social Security and Medicare taxes?

33. [LO 1.1] If a taxpayer has $140,000 of employee salary, how much will be withheld for the Social Security and Medicare taxes in 2018?

34. [LO 1.4] Determine Amy's taxable income for 2018 if she has $40,000 of salary income, is single, and claims the standard deduction.

35. [LO 1.4] Marlee, a single parent of one dependent child, has $19,000 in itemized deductions and files as head of household for 2018. Determine her taxable income if she has a salary of $71,000 and interest income of $1,500.

36. [LO 1.4] Determine a corporation's taxable income if it has $450,000 of gross receipts, $145,000 cost of goods sold, $276,000 of deductible business expenses, $20,000 of gain on the sale of machinery, and $500 of interest income from State of New York bonds.

37. [LO 1.4] The Warner Corporation has gross income of $560,000. It has business expenses of $325,000, a capital loss of $20,000, and $2,500 of interest income on temporary investments. What is the corporation's taxable income?

38. [LO 1.4] Determine George and Mary's taxable income and tax liability for 2018 if George has $65,000 and Mary has $45,000 of salary income, they have $20,000 of allowable itemized deductions, no dependents, and file a joint tax return.

39. [LO 1.4] Refer to the information in problem 34. Determine Amy's income tax liability for 2018.

40. [LO 1.4] Refer to the information in problem 36. Determine the corporation's income tax liability.

41. [LO 1.4] Refer to the information in problem 37. Determine Warner Corporation's income tax liability.

42. [LO 1.4] Sally and Jim are married and have taxable income in 2018 of $700,000. If they could file their income tax as single individuals, each of them would have taxable income of $350,000. Do they have a marriage penalty when they file their joint return? If so, what is the amount of the penalty?

43. [LO 1.4] Conrad, who has $220,000 of taxable income, plans to marry Anita, a college student with no taxable income. If they marry on December 21, 2018, they will file jointly and have $220,000 of taxable income for the year. If they wait until January of 2019 to marry, Conrad will have to file as a single person and report the $220,000 of taxable income on his individual return.
    - **a.** Will it be to their advantage to marry before the end of 2018 or should they wait until 2019?
    - **b.** How much in tax will they save or have to pay extra if they marry in 2019?
    - **c.** How would your answers change if Conrad and Anita marry and each expects $110,000 of taxable income in 2018?

44. [LO 1.4] Carrie and Stephen have gross salary and wages of $76,000 in 2018, file a joint return, and have a seven year old dependent child. They have $15,000 of allowable itemized deductions and a $240 child care credit. Determine their taxable income.

45. [LO 1.4] An estate has $20,000 of taxable income in 2018. What amount of tax will the estate pay if it fails to distribute the income to the beneficiaries?

46. [LO 1.5] John has taxable income of $30,000. William has taxable income of $60,000. Determine their 2018 income taxes if they are both single individuals and claim the standard deduction. Compare their incomes and their income taxes. What does this illustrate?

47. [LO 1.5] Hunter Corporation has $250,000 in gross income, $125,000 in deductible business expenses, and a $12,000 business tax credit. Determine the corporation's net tax liability.

48. [LO 1.5] Carolyn has a 50 percent interest in a general partnership that has a $14,000 loss for the year. She materially participates in the partnership. Her basis in the partnership is $10,000. She also has salary from other employment of $46,000. If she is single, has no dependents, and claims the standard deduction, what are her taxable income and tax liability in 2018?

49. [LO 1.4 & 1.5] June and John decide to form a business. They each plan to contribute $20,000 in exchange for a 50 percent interest in the business. They will then take out a bank loan for $30,000 to cover the balance of their working capital needs. They expect that the business will make a profit of $64,000 in the first year and that it will not make any cash distributions that year. Excluding the business income, June, who files as head of household, has $600,000 of other ordinary taxable income. John is married and files a joint return; he and his wife have $240,000 of other ordinary taxable income. They want to know how much tax the business will pay and how much additional tax they will personally pay in 2018 if they form the business as a partnership, S corporation, or C corporation. Consider only income taxes.

50. [LO 1.4 & 1.5] Assume the same facts as problem 49, except that the business expects to make a cash distribution of $28,000 each to June and John the first year. Determine how much tax the business will pay and how much additional tax they will personally pay if they form the business as a partnership, S corporation, or C corporation. Consider only income taxes.

51. [LO 1.4 & 1.5] Assume the same facts as problem 49, except that John and June expect the business will have a $44,000 loss in the first year (instead of a $64,000 profit) and will not make any cash distributions. Determine the income tax savings in the current year for the business and for them personally if they form the business as a partnership, S corporation, or C corporation. (They both materially participate in the business and their marginal tax bracket will not change because of the business loss.)

52. [LO 1.4 & 1.5] Clara and Charles decide to form a business. They each plan to contribute $15,000 in exchange for a 50 percent interest. The business will borrow $20,000 to cover the balance of its working capital needs. In their business plan, Clara and Charles show that the business will have a loss of $54,000 in its first year. In the second year, however, the business will have a profit of $60,000 and they will each be able to withdraw $5,000 from the business. Clara is in the 35 percent marginal tax bracket and Charles is in the 24 percent marginal tax bracket; both are in the 15 percent tax bracket for dividend income.

a. Determine the taxes paid by the business (if any) in the first and second year if they organize the business as (1) a partnership, (2) an S corporation and (3) a C corporation.

b. Determine Clara's and Charles's income tax savings in the first year and their bases in the business at year-end if they organize the business as (1) a partnership, (2) an S corporation, and (3) a C corporation.

c. Determine the income tax Clara and Charles will pay in the second year from business operations and their bases in the business at year-end if they organize the business as (1) a partnership, (2) an S corporation, and (3) a C corporation.

53. [LO 1.5] Carl is a 30 percent partner in the CCF Partnership. At the beginning of the year, his basis in the partnership is $4,000. The partnership reports $7,000 of ordinary income and distributes $3,000 to the partners. What is Carl's basis at the end of the year?

Develop Planning Skills

54. [LO 1.4] John and Martha are planning to be married. Both are professionals each with taxable incomes of $360,000 annually. They are deciding on a wedding date. They have two dates to choose from: December 14, 2018, or January 11, 2019. If they marry on December 14, 2018, they will have to choose between married filing separately and married filing jointly. Is there an advantage to either method of filing? If they postpone their wedding until the January date and file as single persons, will they reduce their tax bill for 2018?

55. [LO 1.4 & 1.5] Jeremy is setting up a service business. He can either operate the business as a sole proprietorship or he can incorporate as a regular C corporation. He expects that the business will have gross income of $80,000 in the first year with expenses of $12,000 excluding the following. He plans to take $30,000 from the business for living expenses as a salary. Compare his tax costs for 2018 considering only income taxes if he is single, has no dependents or other income, and claims the standard deduction. Which option do you recommend based solely on these tax costs?

56. [LO 1.1, 1.4 & 1.5] Carol has recently incorporated her sole proprietorship and is considering making an S election. The corporation has $200,000 of gross revenue and expenses of $75,000 before Carol's salary. She plans to take a gross salary of $60,000 from the business and this will be her only income for the year. Compare the total tax burden for Carol and the corporation with and without the S election. Consider both income and employment taxes. Carol is single, has no dependents, and uses the standard deduction. She plans to reinvest all of the corporation's net income after taxes into the business. Based on tax burden alone for 2018, should Carol make the S election?

Think Outside the Text

These questions require answers that are beyond the material that is covered in this chapter.

57. [LO 1.2] What is the maximum income tax rate that applies to the employee salary, the employment tax rate(s) on the salary, and the capital gain rate(s) on the long-term capital gains, for these four single individual taxpayers in 2018 (excluding Medicare surtaxes)?
a. Employee Salary = $27,000; Capital Gain = $9,000
b. Employee Salary = $132,000; Capital Gain = $24,000
c. Employee Salary = $176,000; Capital Gain = $139,000
d. Employee Salary = $285,000; Capital Gain = $248,000

58. [LO 1.2] Do you believe that a progressive, proportional, or regressive tax is the most fair? Explain your answer.

59. [LO 1.2] Is a property tax generally a progressive, proportional, or a regressive tax? Explain.

60. [LO 1.2] If the Congress were to enact a flat tax for individual taxpayers, do you believe that there should be any exclusions or deductions from income before the single tax rate is applied? Explain.

61. [LO 1.3] Evaluate the sales tax and the income tax using Adam Smith's four canons of taxation.

62. [LO 1.4] Evaluate allowing married individuals with dual incomes to choose to file a joint tax return or to file as two single individuals as a remedy for the marriage penalty.

63. [LO 1.4] What is the after-tax interest rate that a corporation pays on a loan of $100,000 at 7 percent interest?

64. [LO 1.4] Compare the benefits of a $4,000 deduction and a $4,000 tax credit for two single taxpayers, one with taxable income of $50,000 and the other with taxable income of $200,000.

Search the Internet

For the following four problems, consult the IRS website (www.irs.gov).

65. [LO 1.1] Briefly describe the statistical information available when you search the IRS website for statistics.

66. [LO 1.1] What subheadings appear under the "Statistics of Income"?

67. [LO 1.1] Search the IRS website for VITA. Briefly describe this program.

68. [LO 1.1] Search the IRS website for LEAP. Briefly describe this program.

69. [LO 1.1] Go to www.taxfoundation.org (the website for the Tax Foundation).
a. What is Tax Freedom Day?
b. When were Tax Freedom Days in 2016 and 2017?

Identify the Issues

Identify the issues or problems suggested by the following situations. State each issue as a question.

70. [LO 1.4] John and Mary filed for divorce in November of the current year. The divorce will not become final until May of the following year.

71. [LO 1.5] DEE is an S corporation with 100 shareholders. John, one of these shareholders, gives half of his shares of stock to his new wife as a wedding gift.

72. [LO 1.5] Clifford owns 75 percent of AFK, a C corporation. He spends little time in the business, but takes a salary of $750,000.

ANSWERS TO TEST YOURSELF

1. **b.** The annual property tax on your home

2. **b.** Consumption tax

3. **a.** Horizontal equity

4. **d.** Lower tax rates for long-term capital gains

5. **c.** C corporations

The Tax Practice Environment

CHAPTER 2

LEARNING OBJECTIVES

After completing this chapter, you should be able to:

2.1 Discuss the basic elements of tax compliance including filing requirements, the audit and appeal process, and noncompliance penalties.

2.2 Understand the multiple sources impacting a tax preparer's professional responsibilities and ethical standards and the effects of failure to adhere to them.

2.3 Explain the importance of cash flow, present value, and marginal tax rate when making tax decisions and how they affect tax planning strategies.

2.4 Explain the steps in the tax research process and demonstrate the ability to evaluate primary sources of authority, reach reasonable conclusions, and communicate the results.

CHAPTER OUTLINE

Tax practice involves tax compliance, tax planning, and tax research. A practitioner involved in compliance must understand the laws regulating how and when to file a client's tax return, as well as those governing how and what items are reported on the return. Practitioners who fail to meet acceptable levels of competence or fulfill their responsibilities to their clients and the tax system may be subject to severe penalties. Tax professionals need a well-developed sense of personal and professional ethics to carry out their responsibilities in spite of client pressures.

Although much of the work done by tax practitioners is compliance oriented, the most challenging assignments often involve tax planning. Tax professionals must determine all the relevant facts, completely analyze all possible issues and outcomes (including the present values of net cash flows), and using their knowledge and experience, present their clients with the best alternative.

Taxpayers and the Internal Revenue Service may disagree on the tax treatment of a specific transaction because the Internal Revenue Code does not address every possible variation or tax consequence of every type of transaction. The application of the tax law to a specific set of facts is subject to differing interpretations. Tax research plays a vital role in identifying and interpreting the various sources of tax authority in two commonly encountered situations. First, tax practitioners defend clients' completed transactions so that the client receives the best possible tax outcome. Second, they assist clients contemplating a potential tax transaction to understand the possible outcomes.

Tax professionals must use all of the tools available to solve tax problems. They should consult both the actual tax laws and the interpretations of the Treasury Department and judiciary before communicating their recommendations to their clients, detailing their reasoning and conclusions in acceptable form.

SETTING THE STAGE—AN INTRODUCTORY CASE

Your friend, Kevin, has asked for your advice. He was recently audited by the IRS and received a notice stating that they were reclassifying his part-time dog training business as a hobby. They disallowed many of his deductions related to the business resulting in a tax deficiency of $3,000. Kevin does not believe he owes the additional tax (and really cannot afford to pay it). He would like your advice regarding his appeal options. We will return to this case at the end of this chapter.

2.1 TAX COMPLIANCE

Accountants have many opportunities to specialize in tax compliance, tax planning, or a combination of both. More than 50 percent of all taxpayers pay someone else to prepare their tax returns. Tax preparation is generally referred to as tax compliance. **Tax compliance** consists of gathering relevant information, evaluating and classifying the information, and filing the tax returns. Tax compliance also includes representing clients at an Internal Revenue Service (IRS) audit.

Commercial tax return preparers, attorneys, and certified public accountants (CPAs) all perform tax compliance to some extent. Commercial tax return preparers (such as H&R Block) often complete only the more basic individual and business tax returns. CPAs and attorneys usually prepare more complex tax returns, represent their clients before the IRS, and provide extensive tax planning services. Many businesses employ their own internal tax advisers. The largest U.S. corporate tax departments employ up to 400 tax professionals on a full-time basis who spend much of their time complying with local, state and federal tax provisions. The top tax executive in these corporations typically has a title such as Vice President of Taxation and usually reports to the Chief Financial Officer (CFO). Individuals working for large corporations frequently develop industry specializations, and many accountants hired by private industry have prior tax experience in either public practice or government.

The largest single employer of tax professionals is the Treasury Department, of which the IRS is a part. The Justice Department, the Tax Court, the Office of Management and Budget, and various congressional committees, as well as state and local governments, employ numerous tax professionals.

2.1.1 FILING A TAX RETURN

Returns for individuals, C corporations, estates, and trusts must be filed on or before the fifteenth day of the fourth month following the close of the taxpayer's tax year (April 15 for calendar-year taxpayers).[1] Partnership and S corporate tax returns are due on or before the fifteenth day of the third month following the close of the tax year (March 15 for calendar-year taxpayers). When the legal due date for a return falls on a weekend or legal holiday, the due date is the next weekday.[2] For example, if April 15 is a Saturday, the due date for individual tax returns is Monday, April 17. If the taxpayer cannot file the return by its due date, the taxpayer can file a request by the due date for a six-month extension to file the return. This is normally granted automatically by the IRS.[3] Filing an extension does not extend the time for paying the tax, however. Applications for automatic extensions must include payment of any tax owed based on the taxpayer's reasonable estimate of his or her final tax liability.

---

[1] Prior to 2016, all C corporation returns were due the fifteenth day of the third month following the close of the tax year and partnership returns were due the fifteenth day of the fourth month. C corporations with a June 30 year end will continue to be due September 15th until 2025.

[2] §7503.

[3] Reg. §1.6081-4T. Individuals must file Form 4868 no later than the original due date of the return to obtain an automatic six-month extension. Corporations and partnerships receive an automatic six-month extension by filing Form 7004. Trusts can receive a maximum 5½-month extension.

Taxpayers who overpay their income tax through excess withholding or large quarterly estimated payments effectively loan money to the federal government. The government is not required to pay interest on any tax overpayment that is refunded within 45 days after the due date for the return.[4] This is why the IRS tries to process refund requests quickly. Interest is owed the taxpayer only if the refund is mailed after the 45-day grace period.[5]

Late Filing and Late Payment Penalties

The IRS may impose a *failure-to-file penalty* on taxpayers who fail to file an income tax return on a timely basis, and a *failure-to-pay penalty*, in addition to charging interest, on taxpayers who fail to pay the tax on time.[6] The failure-to-pay penalty is 0.5 percent of the tax liability for each month (or part of a month) that the payment is late. The maximum penalty is 25 percent of the tax liability.

Example 2.1

Kyle's tax return filed on April 15 showed he owed $5,000 in taxes. Due to some bad planning, Kyle could not pay his taxes with his return. Kyle finally made his payment in full on June 6. Kyle's penalty is 1 percent, 0.5 percent for two months—one full month and one partial month. Kyle's late payment penalty is $50 (1% × $5,000).

The failure-to-pay penalty will not be applied during the six-month automatic extension of the filing period if at least 90 percent of the actual tax liability is paid by the original due date and any balance due is paid when the return is filed by the end of the extension period.

The failure-to-file penalty is 5 percent per month (or partial month) that the return is late, with a maximum of 25 percent, also based on the taxpayer's tax liability. If the 0.5 percent failure-to-pay penalty and the failure-to-file penalty both apply, the failure-to-file penalty drops to 4.5 percent per month (or part month), and the total combined penalty remains 5 percent of the tax liability. The maximum combined penalty for the first five months is 25 percent. Thereafter, the 0.5 percent per month failure to pay penalty continues for 45 more months (an additional 22.5 percent). The combined penalties can reach a total of 47.5 percent of the tax liability over time. In abusive situations involving a fraudulent failure-to-file, the late-filing penalty can increase to 15 percent a month, up to a maximum 75 percent of the tax liability.

Example 2.2

Kyle did not to file his return on April 15 because he could not pay the balance due. He files his return on June 5 and pays the full $5,000 balance at that time. He can expect a notice from the IRS charging an additional $500 in late-payment/late-filing penalties ($5,000 × 10%), 5 percent for each of two months. Kyle could have saved $450 in penalties by filing the forms on April 15 even if he could not pay the tax.

If a taxpayer files a return more than 60 days late, the minimum failure-to-file penalty equals the smaller of $210 or 100 percent of the tax due on the return. If no tax is owed on an individual's return, however, there is no penalty. Because flow-through entities, such as partnerships and S corporations normally pay no tax on which to base a penalty, their late filing penalty is based on the number of owners. The penalty is $200 for each month or partial month (up to

[4] §6611(e)(1).

[5] The interest rate for individuals is the federal short-term interest rate plus three percentage points. The interest rate for corporations is generally the short-term rate plus two percentage points. §6611(a) and §6621(a)(1).

[6] The interest rate for tax underpayments is determined by adding three percentage points to the short-term federal rate that is calculated each quarter. §7206.

12 months) the return is late multiplied by the total number of partners or shareholders during the year.

A taxpayer who cannot pay the full tax with the return can request an installment agreement with the IRS.[7] Generally, the IRS will accept an installment agreement if the tax owed is less than $10,000 and the balance due will be paid within three years. The taxpayer must pay a user fee to obtain the installment agreement and is charged interest and late payment penalties.

Statute of Limitations

Some taxpayers feel a sense of relief when they receive their refund check for an overpayment of tax, erroneously assuming that once their refund is processed they will not be audited. Although the IRS usually does not audit an individual's return more than two years after the date a return is filed, the general statute of limitations allows up to three years. The **statute of limitations** is the period of time beyond which legal actions or changes to the tax return cannot be made by either the taxpayer or the government. The general statute of limitations is three years from the date a return is filed or its due date, whichever is later.[8] Filing a return early does not start the clock on the statute of limitations.

Example 2.3

Maureen, a calendar-year individual, files her income tax return for 2018 on March 31, 2019. The return is treated as filed on April 15, 2019, its due date. The statute of limitations expires on April 15, 2022.

If instead of filing her return in March, Maureen requests an automatic six-month extension of time and files her return on October 15, 2019, the statute of limitations for Maureen's 2018 return now expires on October 15, 2022.

The general three-year statute of limitations is extended to six-years if a taxpayer omits gross income in excess of 25 percent of the gross income reported on the tax return. The six-year statute of limitations only applies to omitted income, not excess deductions; therefore, claiming excess deductions does not extend the statute of limitations to six years.

Example 2.4

John filed his 2017 tax return on April 2, 2018. His return showed $30,000 of salary income only. John failed to include an $8,000 capital gain on an early January stock transaction. The omitted gain exceeds 25 percent of the gross income shown on his return (25% × $30,000 = $7,500) and extends the statute of limitations to April 15, 2024.

As part of the government's war on tax shelters, the Treasury instituted disclosure rules that require participants in tax shelters to disclose these transactions (referred to as listed transactions) on their tax returns or face significant penalties. Congress extended the statute of limitations for tax returns not complying with these disclosure requirements until one year after the date the required information is provided to the IRS.

A fraudulent return triggers an unlimited assessment period, as there is no statute of limitations for fraud. Although the government can bring fraud charges at any time, the burden of proof is on the IRS to show that the return was fraudulent.[9] If a fraudulent return is filed, a later

[7] Form 9465: Installment Agreement Request can be filed separately or can be attached to the tax return.

[8] §6501(a) and (b)(1).

[9] Burden of proof is a legal concept requiring the party who is subject to carrying the burden of proof to demonstrate, by appropriate evidence, that the particular requirement has been met.

non-fraudulent amended return does not start the three-year or six-year limitation period. When a taxpayer files an incomplete return or no return at all, the statute of limitations does not begin to run until a complete return is filed.

Refund claims can be initiated by a taxpayer within three years of the filing date for the return or two years from the date the tax is paid, whichever is later. If a taxpayer did not file a return because no tax was due, the claim for refund must be filed within two years of the date the tax was paid. A taxpayer files a claim for refund by amending the return using Form 1040X for an individual or Form 1120X for a corporation.

Example 2.5

Joyce filed her 2015 return on April 15, 2016 paying the $3,000 tax owed. An audit in May 2018 asserted a deficiency of $400 that Joyce paid May 18. Upon reviewing the return, Joyce discovers an unclaimed $700 tax credit. If Joyce files a claim for a refund by April 15, 2019, she can recover $700. If she fails to file a refund claim until after April 15, 2019 (but before May 19, 2020), she can only recover the $400 deficiency payment. If Joyce fails to file her claim before May 19, 2020, she will not be entitled to any refund.

2.1.2 SELECTING RETURNS FOR AUDIT

Over one million individual returns are audited annually, an audit rate of less than one percent of the returns filed. Because only a small number of tax returns can be audited each year, the IRS relies upon a sophisticated computer model to identify returns that possess the greatest potential revenue for the IRS's investment of audit resources. In addition to this computer selection process, a number of returns are manually selected for examination at an examiner's discretion.

All individual and business tax returns are routinely reviewed by the IRS for obvious errors, such as the omission of Social Security or taxpayer identification numbers. After this initial review, tax returns are processed through the IRS computer program. One of the most important functions performed by this program is the matching of information recorded on a return with corresponding data received from third parties (for example, a Form W-2 from an employer). This document matching program uncovers millions of cases of discrepancies between the income that recipients report on their tax returns and the corresponding payments reported by the payers.

This computer program also checks for math errors to uncover relatively simple and readily identifiable problems that can be resolved easily through the mail. When a mathematical or clerical error is identified, the IRS mails a corrected tax computation to the taxpayer and requests that he or she pay the additional tax within ten days of the date of the notice. If the deficiency is paid within this period, no interest is charged on the underpayment. When an error results in a taxpayer overpayment, the IRS usually sends a corrected computation of the tax, together with a brief explanation of the error, and refunds the excess payment.

The IRS also conducts an unallowable item program. If a return includes an unallowable item, the IRS computes the adjustment in taxes and notifies the taxpayer by mail. If the taxpayer is able to adequately explain the questioned item, the assessment is abated. However, the case continues as a correspondence or office audit if the taxpayer's response is deemed unsatisfactory.

After a return is processed through the various programs, it is rated for its audit potential by computer scoring using the discriminant inventory function (DIF) formula. When the computer calculates a high DIF score, the potential that an examination of that return will result in a change to the income tax liability is also high. Attempts have been made by several taxpayers to obtain the actual DIF formula under the Freedom of Information Act, but the courts have refused to require the IRS to disclose detailed information, stating that it would undermine the program.

In addition to the computerized identification methods used to select returns for IRS examination, returns may be selected manually for a variety of reasons. Information provided by an informant may initiate an examination. The IRS Whistleblower Office processes tips it receives from individuals. A reward of between 15 and 30 percent of the total proceeds that the IRS collects can be paid if the IRS moves ahead based on the information provided.[10] All rewards, of course, are fully taxable.[11]

Example 2.6 The highest whistleblower award ever paid was $104 million to a former employee of Swiss bank UBS for revealing schemes used by the bank to help American citizens dodge taxes. UBS paid more than $780 million to avoid criminal prosecution and turned over account information for more than 4,500 American clients.[12]

The government also conducts undercover operations. Each district performs criminal investigations by special agents who look for fraud. Revenue agents suspend work whenever fraud is detected and refer the case to special agents in IRS Criminal Investigation.

KEY CASE *The courts have upheld the legality of evidence that the IRS obtained through a special agent who posed as an investor interested in businesses with substantial cash flow subject to skimming. The owner and his wife disclosed their skimmed invoices to the undercover agent who noted the location of the records in their home. A few days later the IRS agents executed a search warrant and seized the records.*[13]

2.1.3 TYPES OF AUDITS

Frequently, IRS personnel question only one or two items on a selected return, such as charitable contributions. In these cases, an examination is typically conducted as a **correspondence examination**. The IRS auditor requests that the taxpayer verify the questioned item by mailing copies of receipts, canceled checks, or other documentation to the IRS.[14] If the taxpayer requests an interview or the issues become too complex, the case is referred to an office or field examination for resolution.

Office examinations usually involve one or more issues that require some analysis and the exercise of the IRS auditor's judgment, rather than a mere verification of an item. The taxpayer is asked to come to the district office for an interview and bring any records and documents that support the questioned items. Taxpayers may attend this examination alone, with a tax advisor or attorney, or let their tax advisor attend on their behalf.

Field examinations are more comprehensive than office audits and are the least common type of audit. Field examinations are usually conducted on the taxpayer's premises and generally involve a complete review of the entire financial operations of the business. This type of audit can last from months to years and is usually limited to business returns and the most complex individual returns.

When the IRS has audited a taxpayer's return for the same item in either of the two previous years with no change to the tax liability, the taxpayer can request a suspension of the current year's audit and a review of whether the audit should proceed.

[10] §7623. The reward may be limited to 10% if the whistleblower's contribution is not considered substantial. The IRS Whistleblower's Office will determine the extent to which the whistleblower's information contributed to the administrative or judicial action and the amount of the reward.

[11] To claim a reward, Form 211: *Application for Reward for Original Information* is used.

[12] David Kocieniewski, "Whistle-Blower Awarded $104 Million by I.R.S." *New York Times*, 9/11/12.

[13] *Jones v. Berry*, 722 F.2d 443; 83-2 USTC ¶9653; 52 AFTR 2d 6188 (9th Cir., 1983), cert. denied, 466 US 971 (1984).

[14] The *Internal Revenue Manual* suggests that this type of audit is limited to certain types of issues, such as minor business expenses, interest deductions, and charitable contributions.

Example 2.7

In August 2018, the IRS notified Diana that it plans to audit her 2016 interest expense deduction. Two years earlier, the IRS audited Diana's 2014 interest expense deduction but assessed no additional tax. Diana may request that the IRS suspend the audit of her 2016 interest expense deduction.

If, instead of interest expense, the IRS had audited Diana's 2014 charitable contributions, Diana could not request a suspension of her 2016 audit because the previous audit was for a different deduction.

2.1.4 THE APPEALS PROCEDURE

When an audit is complete, there are three possible outcomes. First, the agent may find that the return is correct as filed. If, however, the agent proposes adjustments to either increase or decrease the tax, the taxpayer may agree or disagree. If the taxpayer agrees, the taxpayer signs an agreement and pays the additional taxes owed or receives the proposed refund. Any interest owed is generally determined from the due date of the return to the date of payment. If the taxpayer is owed a refund, interest is paid on the refund.

If the taxpayer disagrees with the agent's proposed adjustments, the agent submits a report of the findings to the review staff. After review, the revenue agent's report is mailed to the taxpayer. The cover letter, called the **30-day letter**, notifies the taxpayer of the proposed deficiency and normally gives the taxpayer 30 days to request a conference with an agent from the **IRS Appeals Division**, which is separate from the IRS division of the examining agent.[15]

The Appeals Division's purpose is to resolve tax controversies without litigation, on a basis that is fair to both the government and the taxpayer. The appeals officer has full authority to consider the hazards of litigation. The term "hazards of litigation" refers to factors that may affect the outcome of the case if it is litigated. This includes ambiguous facts, uncertain application of the law to known facts, credibility of witnesses, and ability to meet the required burden of proof. The great majority of cases are settled at the appellate conference.

If the taxpayer still disagrees with the IRS after an appeals conference or fails to request a conference, a **90-day letter** (statutory notice of deficiency) is mailed to the taxpayer by certified or registered mail. Once this formal assessment has been made, the IRS is entitled to collect the tax. This notice gives the taxpayer three options:

1. File a petition with the U.S. Tax Court within 90 days of receiving the notice.
2. Pay the tax and any penalties; the taxpayer may then go to a U.S. District Court or the U.S. Court of Federal Claims to sue for refund (payment of the tax and penalties stops interest from continuing to accrue if the taxpayer ultimately loses the appeal).
3. Take no action and be subject to IRS-enforced collection procedures.

All litigation begins in one of three trial courts: the U.S. Tax Court, the U.S. District Courts, or the U.S. Court of Federal Claims. The Tax Court is the only court that does not require the taxpayer to pay the tax and then sue for refund. The District Court and Court of Federal Claims cannot hear the taxpayer's case unless he or she is suing for a refund.[16] Consequently, the taxpayer first must pay the disputed tax and then file an unsuccessful claim for refund to obtain a judicial review in either of these latter two courts.

[15] If the additional tax due is more than $10,000, the taxpayer must include a written response to the agent's finding, called a protest letter. For an office audit, an oral request is acceptable if the total proposed additional tax and penalties is $2,500 or less. If the amount is between $2,500 and $10,000, then a brief written statement of disputed issues is required. Reg. §601.106(a)(1)(iii).

[16] The District Court is the only court in which a jury trial can be obtained.

If the amount in dispute (including interest and penalties) does not exceed $50,000 for a tax year, the taxpayer may use the Small Case Division of the Tax Court.[17] Its procedures are less formal than regular Tax Court procedures and the taxpayer may appear without an attorney. This alternative is not available in other courts, and the decision cannot be appealed.

An important consideration is the trial courts' interpretations of the law may differ on the same basic tax issues. Thus, taxpayers usually prefer the court most likely to rule favorably on their issues. Regardless of the judicial route chosen, the unsuccessful party has the right to appeal the decision (except for decisions of the Small Case Division of the Tax Court). Cases decided in the Tax Court and District Court are appealed to the appropriate Circuit Court of Appeals. Appeals from the Court of Federal Claims are decided by the Court of Appeals for the Federal Circuit. Decisions from either appellate court can be appealed to the U.S. Supreme Court. The Supreme Court chooses the cases it will hear on the basis of their significance or because of a conflict in the lower courts. Therefore, the Supreme Court accepts very few tax cases for review.

A taxpayer should not consider tax litigation lightly. The costs for attorney and accountant fees, the filing and processing fees, and the time involved in gathering supporting documentation for the taxpayer's position, make litigation a costly prospect.

2.1.5 TAXPAYER NONCOMPLIANCE PENALTIES

Our self-assessment system requires all individuals filing a tax return to accurately report their income and deductions. Taxpayers who fail to meet their self-assessment obligations are subject to a variety of penalties. Many new penalties have been imposed in response to taxpayers who play the audit lottery; that is, taxpayers take very aggressive positions on their tax returns, gambling that their returns will not be audited. Some view the potential penalties for an unfavorable audit as small enough to be worth the risk. In reaction to this, many penalties were enacted to address this problem.

The most important taxpayer penalties are for negligence and fraud. The negligence penalty is 20 percent of any tax underpayment caused by the taxpayer's intentional disregard of rules and regulations or failure to make a reasonable attempt to comply with the law.[18] The most severe administrative penalty is for civil fraud. This penalty is 75 percent of the tax underpayment attributable to the fraud.[19] Fraud involves deliberately understating the tax owed the government. Due to the severity of the penalty, the burden of proof rests with the IRS to establish by *clear and convincing evidence* that the taxpayer committed fraud.[20] An even more severe penalty applies to criminal fraud, otherwise known as tax evasion. Tax evasion is punishable by imprisonment in addition to significant fines.[21] The IRS has the burden of proof to establish, *beyond a reasonable doubt*, that the taxpayer committed criminal fraud.

KEY CASES *In 2006, Richard Hatch was sentenced to 51 months in federal prison for failing to report $1 million in income won from the first "Survivor" television series along with income from some other sources. He was also ordered to pay almost $475,000 in taxes, interest and penalties.*[22]

---

[17] §7463.

[18] §6662(a) and (b)(1). §6662A increases the penalty to 30% for listed and other nondisclosed avoidance transactions and §6707A imposes a penalty of up to $200,000 for failure to report information on "listed" tax shelter transactions.

[19] §6663.

[20] §7454(a).

[21] §7201. Penalties of up to $100,000 ($500,000 for corporations) and/or up to five years in prison may be assessed.

[22] "Tax Report," *Wall Street Journal*, May 17, 2006, Section D, Column 5, page 2 and "FY2006 Examples of General Tax Fraud Investigations," IRS website, *www.irs.gov*.

In 2008, actor Wesley Snipes was sentenced to 3 years in prison for willfully failing to file tax returns from 1999–2004, a period in which he earned more than $38 million. Following an unsuccessful appeal, he served his sentence in a medium-security prison in Pennsylvania.[23]

In December 2014, Representative Michael Grimm, who had just been re-elected to his third term in Congress, resigned after agreeing to plead guilty to felony tax fraud. The indictment alleged that he kept two sets of records for a restaurant he previously owned, concealing more than $1 million in gross receipts and underreporting his employees' wages to avoid federal and state taxes. He faced up to 30 months in prison.[24]

2.1.6 COLLECTION PROCEDURES

The IRS begins the collection of an unpaid tax liability when it mails a bill to the taxpayer requesting payment. If the taxpayer does not respond, the IRS sends a letter demanding payment within 10 days. If the taxpayer still does not respond, the IRS can impose a lien on the taxpayer's property or seize other assets.[25]

All taxes must be collected within 10 years of an assessment. If a taxpayer has not filed a return (or filed a fraudulent return), the tax must be collected within 10 years of the assessment date, regardless of when that assessment is made.[26]

Offer in Compromise

If the IRS believes that collection of the full tax liability is doubtful, it may accept a payment less than the assessment. Such compromises are made if there is either doubt about the liability or its collectability. The IRS is more inclined to settle a delinquent account if no criminal proceedings are pending or contemplated. A taxpayer files Form 656 to make an offer in compromise. It must include a detailed financial statement specifying the hardship the taxpayer would suffer if the entire tax must be paid. Any offer in compromise with five or fewer installment payments must be accompanied by an initial payment of 20 percent of the total amount offered the IRS. All other offers must include the first proposed installment. If the offer is not rejected within 24 months of submission, it is deemed accepted.[27]

Innocent Spouse Relief

When a married couple files a joint tax return, they become joint and severally liable for any tax deficiency related to that return; that is, the IRS can assess either spouse for the entire deficiency if the return is audited.[28] In some situations (such as a now-divorced couple), the IRS assesses whichever spouse it can locate, even though that person may know nothing about the disputed income. Section 6015(b)(1) provides that the innocent spouse can be relieved of any tax liability if all of the following requirements are met:

1. The return contains an understatement of tax attributable to erroneous items of only one of the individuals filing the return.
2. Considering all facts and circumstances, it is unfair to hold the other individual liable for the deficiency attributable to this understatement. It is critical that the other individual did not know, and had no reason to know, that there was the understatement.
3. The individual elects innocent spouse relief within the time period that the statute of limitations is open for collection activities.

[23] Dave Itzkoff, "Wesley Snipes Surrenders to Begin Sentence on Tax Convictions," *New York Times*, 12/9/10.

[24] William K. Rashbaum, "Rep. Michael Grimm Is Said to Agree to Tax Fraud Guilty Plea," *New York Times*, 12/22/14 and Jason Horowitz, "Michael Grimm, in a Reversal, Will Resign from Congress," *New York Times*, 12/30/14.

[25] §§6621 and 6331.

[26] §6502(a)(1).

[27] §7122.

[28] §6013(d)(3).

Example 2.8

Gillian and Steven filed a joint tax return three years ago but have since divorced. Gillian has no contact with Steven and does not know where he lives. At the time the return was filed, Gillian knew that Steven failed to report $5,000 of gambling winnings as they used the $5,000 won for their vacation trip. On audit, Steven's actual unreported gambling winnings were found to be $25,000. Steven cannot be located and Gillian is assessed the full tax due. If Gillian establishes that she did not know, nor had any reason to know, about the additional $20,000 of gambling winnings, the understatement of tax for the additional $20,000 of winnings qualifies for innocent spouse relief. The $5,000 of winnings that Gillian knew about fails to qualify for relief.

2.2 PROFESSIONAL RESPONSIBILITIES AND ETHICS

2.2.1 AVOIDANCE VERSUS EVASION

Any discussion of a tax professional's responsibilities must include the difference between tax avoidance and tax evasion. There is nothing illegal or immoral in the avoidance of tax according to the tax system's rules. Judge Learned Hand best expressed this doctrine in *Commissioner v. Newman*:

> *Over and over again, courts have said that there is nothing sinister in so arranging one's affairs as to keep taxes as low as possible. Everybody does so, rich or poor; and all do right, for nobody owes any public duty to pay more than the law demands: taxes are enforced extractions, not voluntary contributions. To demand more in the name of morals is mere cant.*[29]

Tax avoidance is the minimization of the tax burden by acceptable, legal alternatives. *Tax evasion*, however, describes illegal means of reducing taxes and is not acceptable. Any practitioner contemplating participation in some form of tax evasion should first study the penalties assessed for civil and criminal tax fraud.

2.2.2 TAX PREPARER REGISTRATION

Since 2011, the IRS has required all tax return preparers to obtain a **preparer tax identification number (PTIN)**. Section 7701(a)(36)(A) defines a tax return preparer as any person who is paid for, or who employs one or more persons who are paid for, the preparation of all or a substantial portion of a federal tax return or claim for refund. Preparers obtain a PTIN by submitting Form W-12 *IRS Paid Preparer Tax Identification Number (PTIN) Application* to the IRS.

2.2.3 TAX PREPARER PENALTIES

Code Section 6694 imposes penalties on preparers when clients' tax deficiencies appear to be the result of an "unreasonable position" on a return that the preparer knew or should have known was a departure from the rules or regulations. The penalty, the greater of $1,000 or 50 percent of the fees for the work, is imposed if the position was not properly disclosed. A reasonable position requires the preparer to have substantial authority upholding a "realistic possibility of success" for nonabusive, undisclosed tax return positions. **Substantial authority** exists if the weight of authorities (discussed later) supporting the reported tax treatment is substantial in relation to the weight of those authorities taking a contrary position. A return

[29] *Commissioner v. Newman*, 159 F.2d 848, 850–851; 47-1 USTC ¶9175; 35 AFTR 857 (CA-2, 1947).

preparer without substantial authority for a tax return position is subject to a penalty unless there is adequate disclosure. Form 8275 is typically used for disclosure—but that would generally raise a red flag with the IRS.

If the tax return position involves a tax shelter (or similar abusive transaction termed a "listed transaction"), a higher "more-likely-than-not" (greater than 50 percent) standard applies. Under current law, a tax return preparer avoids this penalty if the position:

1. Is supported by substantial authority and does not involve a tax shelter
2. Has a reasonable basis and is adequately disclosed or
3. Involves a tax shelter, as defined in Code Section 6662(d)(2)(C)(ii), but the preparer reasonably believes the position is more likely than not correct.

If a preparer takes an unreasonable position in a "willful" attempt to understate the taxpayer's liability or if the preparer is guilty of "reckless or intentional disregard" of rules or regulations, the penalty increases to the greater of $5,000 or 75 percent of the preparer's fees. This type of penalty frequently results in an investigation that may end with the withdrawal of the right to practice.

Preparer penalties are of special importance because of the following:

1. Penalties on the preparer may not be covered by malpractice insurance.
2. Penalties are not deductible.
3. Preparer penalties may result in an IRS review of the preparer's entire practice.

A preparer convicted of criminal tax evasion is subject to a fine of up to $100,000 ($500,000 in the case of a corporation) and imprisonment.

KEY CASES *Raymond Scott Stevenson, the former Vice President of Taxation for Tyco, was sentenced to 3 years in federal prison for failing to report $170 million in company income. Prosecutors claimed that he backdated documents to reduce the company's tax liability. If the correct amount had been reported, Tyco would have faced an additional tax liability of up to $60 million.*[30]

Adrian Dicker, a former BDO Seidman LLP manager, pleaded guilty to tax evasion. He admitted assisting clients engage in tax-shelter transactions that created more than $1 billion in fraudulent tax losses. He faced up to five years in prison for each count of tax evasion.[31]

2.2.4 TAX PROFESSIONALS' DUAL RESPONSIBILITIES

Tax professionals have duties to two parties: the tax system and their clients. In many situations, the duties to these two parties are in conflict. The conflict is most apparent in areas in which the law is not clear or in situations in which the facts are subject to more than one legitimate interpretation. In those cases, the tax professional must decide which party will benefit at the expense of the other. The question then arises to whom the tax professional owes his or her primary responsibility.

Tax practitioners and the IRS view the role of tax practitioners differently. Tax practitioners, especially CPAs and attorneys, see themselves as client advocates. The IRS, however, wants tax practitioners to take an active enforcement role by checking client documentation and probing for other sources of income.

---

[30] "Former Tyco VP gets three years in prison," The *Miami Herald*, November 30, 2006, page 3C.

[31] Chad Bray, "Guilty Plea in Bogus Tax Shelters," The *Wall Street Journal*, March 18, 2009, Section D, Column 1, page 3.

The IRS's position is that the tax practitioner's primary responsibility is to the tax system. The IRS Director of Practice stated the following:

> *While it is generally agreed that a tax practitioner owes a client competence, loyalty and confidentiality, it also is recognized that the practitioner has responsibilities to the tax system as well. The latter responsibility is of pervasive importance . . . . In the normal practitioner–client relationship, both duties are recognized and carried out. However, there are situations in which this is difficult. In those situations, the practitioner is required to decide which obligation prevails and, in so doing, may correctly conclude that the obligation to the tax system is paramount . . . . The IRS relies on tax practitioners to assist it in administering the tax laws by being fair and honest in their dealings with the Service and by fostering confidence by their clients in the integrity of the tax system and in complying with it.*[32]

The position of the American Institute of Certified Public Accountants (AICPA) is that a taxpayer has no obligation to pay more taxes than are legally due, and the CPA has a duty to the client to assist in achieving that result. Thus, the tax system is best served by professionals who act with honesty and who are not swayed by client pressure to do otherwise. At the same time, they best serve the public good by helping their clients determine their minimum tax liability under the law. To resolve honest differences in interpretation in favor of one's client does not, by itself, impair the CPA's integrity.

2.2.5 SOURCES OF PROFESSIONAL GUIDANCE

Literature dealing with the ethical responsibilities of a tax practitioner can be found in various publications. All tax practitioners are regulated by *Treasury Circular 230: Regulations Governing Practice before the Internal Revenue Service*. The ethical conduct of a CPA who is a member of the AICPA must follow its *Code of Professional Conduct* and any other rules generated by state boards of accountancy. The AICPA has also developed the *Statements on Standards for Tax Services (SSTS)* that contain guidelines for CPAs who prepare tax returns.

Circular 230

To effectively serve a client's tax needs, the tax practitioner must maintain the privilege to appear before the IRS on behalf of clients. The regulations governing such representation are found in *Circular 230* that protects the IRS and taxpayers by requiring tax preparers to be technically competent and to adhere to ethical standards. *Circular 230* identifies who may practice before the IRS, including representing clients during audit procedures. Tax return preparation or furnishing information in response to an IRS request is not considered practice before the IRS.

A tax practitioner who violates the rules contained within *Circular 230* may be suspended or disbarred from practice before the IRS for incompetence, disreputable conduct, refusal to comply with the rules and regulations of *Circular 230*, or willfully and knowingly deceiving, misleading, or threatening the IRS.

In June 2014, the Treasury issued final regulations amending *Circular 230* by adding new rules applicable to all written tax advice in client communications. These rules also state that members who oversee a firm's practice must ensure that all employees of the firm comply with *Circular 230*.

[32] Leslie Shapiro, "Professional Responsibilities in the Eyes of the IRS," *The Tax Adviser* (March 1986) p. 139.

AICPA Code of Professional Conduct

In addition to the regulations imposed by the Treasury Department, CPAs in tax practice must adhere to pronouncements of the accounting profession. AICPA members are subject to the *AICPA Code of Professional Conduct* that discusses the CPA's responsibilities to the public, clients, and colleagues. It states that a CPA should strive for behavior above the minimal level of acceptable conduct required by the law and regulations. Members are expected to perform professional services with integrity, objectivity, and independence. Integrity is measured in terms of what is right and just. Integrity requires a professional to observe both the form and spirit of technical and ethical standards. Objectivity and independence require the professional to be impartial, intellectually honest, and have no conflict of interest.

In December 2014, the AICPA updated its *Code of Professional Conduct* to simplify its application. The updated version retains the substance of the existing ethical standards while incorporating two conceptual frameworks, one for members in public practice and one for members in business. These conceptual frameworks would be used for areas in which the code lacks guidance as a means of identifying, evaluating, and addressing threats that may exist and safeguards that may be applied to eliminate or reduce those threats to an acceptable level.

Statements on Standards for Tax Services (SSTS)

To help delineate the extent of the tax practitioner's responsibility to his or her client, the public, the government, and his or her profession, the AICPA Federal Taxation Executive Committee issued a series of statements defining the appropriate standards applying to tax practice.[33] These statements are intended to address specific problems inherent in the tax practitioner's dual role of serving both the client and the public.

SSTS No. 1—Tax Return Positions The CPA should recommend a tax return position to his or her client only if there is a "realistic possibility" of success if challenged either on appeal with the IRS or in court. A CPA should not prepare or sign as preparer a return that he or she knows takes a position that does not meet the realistic possibility standard. A CPA may recommend a specific return position if there is a reasonable basis for that position, and the position is adequately disclosed on the tax return.

SSTS No. 2—Answers to Questions on Returns This statement requires a CPA, before signing as a preparer, to make a reasonable effort to obtain and provide appropriate answers from the client to all questions on a tax return. The fact that an answer might prove disadvantageous is not a valid reason for omitting a response.

SSTS No. 3—Procedural Aspects of Preparing Returns This statement examines the CPA's responsibility regarding examination of supporting data, use of prior years' returns, and consideration of relevant information known to the CPA from tax returns of other clients. It sets forth guidelines as to the extent CPAs may rely on information furnished by clients and other third parties; for example, it specifies that although a CPA may in good faith rely upon information furnished by the client or other third parties without verification, blind reliance is unacceptable. If the information furnished appears to be incorrect, incomplete, or inconsistent either on its face or on the basis of other facts known to the CPA, the CPA should make additional inquiries.

SSTS No. 4—Use of Estimates This statement defines those situations in which the use of estimates is acceptable on a taxpayer's return (for example, a fire or computer failure destroyed relevant records) and discusses whether disclosure is appropriate. Estimates

[33] The *Statements on Responsibilities in Tax Practice (SRTP)* were issued between 1964 and 1977. The *SSTS* replaced the *SRTP* as of October 31, 2000. The revised *SSTS* that became effective on January 1, 2010 combined *SSTS 6* and *SSTS 7*, reducing the total number of statements from eight to seven.

also may be necessary when records are missing or precise information is not available at the time of filing. If a CPA uses a taxpayer's estimates, however, the estimates should not imply greater accuracy than exists or present misleading facts.

SSTS No. 5—Departure from a Previous Position An administrative proceeding or court decision does not bind the CPA to use the same treatment of an item in a later year's return unless there is a binding contract. The CPA may recommend a more advantageous tax treatment for a later year's tax return, however, as subsequent court decisions and revenue rulings may place the taxpayer in a more favorable position. The recommendation for the tax treatment of an item in a tax return should be based on the facts and the law as they are evaluated at the time the return is prepared.

SSTS No. 6—Knowledge of Error: Return Preparation and Administrative Proceedings If a CPA discovers an error in a client's previously filed tax return, an error in a return that is the subject of an administrative proceeding (such as an examination), or a taxpayer's failure to file a return, the CPA is obligated to inform the client of the problem and to recommend appropriate action. Once the taxpayer has been adequately informed, the course of action is the client's decision. The CPA cannot inform the IRS without the client's permission, except if required by law. If the CPA is preparing the current year's return and the client refuses to correct an error in a prior year's return, *SSTS No. 6* indicates that the CPA should consider withdrawing from the preparation of the taxpayer's current year return or from representing the client in the administrative proceeding and should consider severing any professional relationship with the client. If the CPA does prepare the current year's return, the CPA should take reasonable steps to ensure that the error is not repeated.

SSTS No. 7—Form and Content of Advice to Clients This statement recognizes that changes in the tax laws and the development of new interpretations may affect past tax advice. It addresses the circumstances under which a CPA has a responsibility to update a client when subsequent developments affect previously provided advice. *SSTS No. 7* indicates that the CPA has no duty to update the advice unless the CPA is implementing it or the obligation is specifically provided for in the client's contract. CPAs should state that their advice is based on authorities that are subject to change and that subsequent developments could affect previous professional advice. Thus, the communication of significant developments affecting previous advice is an additional service, rather than an implied obligation in the normal client relationship.

Other Moral Standards

There is more to ethical behavior than simply following the AICPA rules of conduct. The tax professional must deal with different standards of personal morality. All individuals do not use the same level of moral standards in determining whether something is morally right or wrong. Some people feel that cheating on their tax return is morally acceptable because "Everyone does it." Professional fees generated from a client who gets too aggressive seldom justify the cost (in dollars or mental anguish) of defending violations of professional standards or Treasury Department rules.

If a tax professional does not agree with the client's views on what is morally acceptable, the practitioner risks losing the client. Alternatively, they both could face fines and penalties (or even risk going to jail) for failure to follow acceptable moral standards. A tax professional must be ready to deal with clients with varying views on acceptable moral behavior and be willing to accept the consequences for the decisions made.

To be prepared to make these ethical decisions, a tax professional must develop two skills:

1. The ability to recognize ethical dilemmas when confronted by them.
2. The ability to evaluate the alternatives.

A CPA must develop awareness to the level that he or she can easily spot a potential ethical problem arising from business situations. In evaluating the alternatives, most practitioners find that real-world problems usually do not involve a clear choice between right and wrong. Instead, a decision frequently must be made between what appears to be two rights or two evils. The true professional must evaluate all the alternatives in light of the competing interests of all parties involved and attempt to predict the consequences of each alternative before making a decision.

2.3 TAX PLANNING

Although much of the work done by tax professionals can be described as compliance oriented, the most challenging assignments often involve tax planning. **Tax planning** is the process of evaluating the tax consequences associated with a transaction and making recommendations that will achieve the desired objective at a minimal tax cost. Tax planning allows a practitioner to exercise a higher degree of creativity than possible in any other area of practice.

Every business generates transactions designed to produce profit for its owners. Some transactions result in cash inflows, others in cash outflows, but many involve both inflows and outflows. Net cash flow is cash inflows less cash outflows. When faced with alternatives, managers should choose the alternative that maximizes positive net cash flow or minimizes cash outflows (when only considering costs).

Net cash flow includes any tax cost or tax savings from the transaction. The **tax cost**, an increase in tax for the period, is a cash outflow. The profit generated from a product sale is a cash inflow, but the income tax paid is a cash outflow that reduces the net cash flow. **Tax savings** are a decrease in taxes for a period, a cash inflow. When a deductible expense is incurred, there is a cash outflow but the expense generates a tax reduction—a tax saving that increases the net cash flow.

Example 2.9

Widget Corporation sells merchandise for $5,000. Its cost for the merchandise is $3,000 and it has $2,000 of taxable income. If Widget is subject to a 21 percent income tax, the tax cost of this sale is $420 ($2,000 × 21%), a cash outflow. This sale results in a positive net cash flow of $1,580 ($5,000 – $3,000 – $420).

Widget also paid $3,000 in wages to its employees that Widget deducts in computing taxable income and result in a tax savings of $630 ($3,000 × 21%). The after-tax cost of the wages is $2,370 ($3,000 – $630).

The federal income tax's impact on cash flow is very different from most other business expenses. There is *no* deduction for federal income taxes in the determination of taxable income. If there is a reduction in income taxes (tax savings), it is a pure cash inflow that does not trigger any additional increase in tax. Tax savings do not create taxable income. The exemption from income tax for tax savings differentiates tax planning from most other profit-motivated activities.

Example 2.10

A corporation with a 21 percent tax rate can pay $10,000 to a marketing consultant who claims he can generate $50,000 in new revenue. Alternatively, the corporation can pay $10,000 to a tax consultant who claims he can save the corporation $50,000 in taxes through tax planning. The corporation can deduct the $10,000 paid to either consultant, and the after-tax cost is $7,900 [$10,000 – ($10,000 × 21%)]. The after-tax cash inflow from the marketing plan is $39,500 [$50,000 – ($50,000 × 21%)] and its net after-tax cash flow is $31,600 ($39,500 – $7,900). The tax savings from the alternate plan are not subject to income tax, however; its after-tax cash inflow is $50,000, resulting in a net after-tax cash flow of $42,100 ($50,000 – $7,900).

2.3.1 CASH FLOWS AND PRESENT VALUE

When cash inflows or outflows continue beyond the current year, it is important to reduce these future net cash flows to their net present value by discounting them to current-year comparable dollars.[34] Present value concepts dictate that a dollar received in a future year is worth less than a dollar received in the current year. Table 2.1 shows how much $1 to be paid at a future date is worth today at the discount rate indicated.[35]

For cash inflows, higher present values are preferred; for cash outflows, lower present values are preferred.

Table 2.1 Present Value of a Single Payment

Year	5%	6%	7%	8%	9%	10%	12%
1	0.952	0.943	0.935	0.926	0.917	0.909	0.893
2	0.907	0.890	0.873	0.857	0.842	0.826	0.797
3	0.864	0.840	0.816	0.794	0.772	0.751	0.712
4	0.823	0.792	0.763	0.735	0.708	0.683	0.636
5	0.784	0.747	0.713	0.681	0.650	0.621	0.567
6	0.746	0.705	0.666	0.630	0.596	0.564	0.507
7	0.711	0.665	0.623	0.583	0.547	0.513	0.452
8	0.677	0.627	0.582	0.540	0.502	0.467	0.404
9	0.645	0.592	0.544	0.500	0.460	0.424	0.361
10	0.614	0.558	0.508	0.463	0.422	0.386	0.322

Example 2.11

HomeBuild Construction must decide between two mutually exclusive construction projects. Each project will take two years to complete, but the company can only complete one of them. The first project will generate $510,000 in revenues in the current year and $130,000 in the next year. HomeBuild estimates expenses of $310,000 in the current year and $80,000 in the next year. The second project will generate $320,000 in revenues and $195,000 of expenses in each of the two years. Assuming an 8 percent discount rate and a 21 percent tax rate, the net present value of each project is calculated as follows:

	JOB 1		JOB 2	
Current year				
Revenues		$510,000		$320,000
Expenses		(310,000)		(195,000)
Before-tax cash flow		$200,000		$125,000
Income tax @ 21%		(42,000)		(26,250)
After-tax cash flow		$158,000		$98,750
Next year				
Revenues	$130,000		$320,000	
Expenses	(80,000)		(195,000)	
Before-tax cash flow	$50,000		$125,000	
Income tax @ 21%	(10,500)		(26,250)	
After-tax cash flow	$39,500		$98,750	
Present value (after-tax cash flow × 0.926)		36,577		91,443
Net present value		$194,577		$190,193

HomeBuild should select Job 1 because it has a greater net present value of $4,384 ($194,577 – $190,193).

[34] Present value = future value/(1 + interest [discount] rate). If you will receive $1,000 in one year, it is only worth $926 to you currently at an interest rate (expected rate of return) of 8 percent ($1,000/1.08 = $926). Alternatively, future value = present value × (1 + interest rate). If you invest $926 in a bond that pays 8 percent interest, after one year the value of the investment has grown to $1,000 ($926 × 1.08 = $1,000).

[35] Additional present value tables are included in the Appendix at the end of this textbook.

2.3.2 SIGNIFICANCE OF THE MARGINAL TAX RATE

The marginal tax rate is the rate that applies to the next dollar of income. This rate should be used when evaluating transactions that increase or decrease taxable income. If a business's marginal tax rate changes from one year to the next, the company's tax costs and savings also fluctuate. The previous example assumed a fixed corporate tax rate of 21 percent. If we change the business in the previous example to a sole proprietorship, the marginal tax rate is determined by the tax rate of the owner (sole proprietor).[36]

Example 2.12

Assume the facts of the previous example except that HomeBuild Construction is a sole proprietorship owned by Arnold. Arnold's marginal tax bracket is 37 percent in year 1 and 24 percent in year 2 due to a decrease in other taxable income. The revised net present value calculation using the sole proprietor's marginal tax rates is as follows:

	JOB 1		JOB 2	
Current year				
Revenues		$510,000		$320,000
Expenses		(310,000)		(195,000)
Before-tax cash flow		$200,000		$125,000
Income tax @ 37%		(74,000)		(46,250)
After-tax cash flow		$126,000		$78,750
Next year				
Revenues	$130,000		$320,000	
Expenses	(80,000)		(195,000)	
Before-tax cash flow	$50,000		$125,000	
Income tax @ 24%	(12,000)		(30,000)	
After-tax cash flow	$38,000		$95,000	
Present value (after-tax cash flow × 0.926)		35,188		87,970
Net present value		$161,188		$166,720

Job 2 now has a $5,532 ($166,720 – $161,188) higher net present value because so much of Job 1's first year income is taxed at 37 percent.

When marginal tax rates are expected to change from one year to the next, the timing of the transaction should be controlled to the extent possible to minimize tax costs and maximize tax savings.

2.3.3 TIMING INCOME AND DEDUCTIONS

Timing involves the question of when income and deductions should be claimed. The traditional technique defers the recognition of income and accelerates the recognition of deductions. This technique relies on savings achieved due to the time value of money by deferring income (and delaying tax payments) or accelerating deductions into an earlier period (reducing current taxes). Changing marginal tax rates also impacts the year that income or deductions should be taken. Good tax plans recognize income in the years with the lowest anticipated marginal tax rates and deduct expenses in years with the highest marginal tax rates.

[36] The tax rates for individuals were introduced in Chapter 1. Also refer to Chapter 1 for a discussion of how sole proprietorships and other businesses are taxed.

Example 2.13

Ronco Company, a cash-basis calendar-year sole proprietorship, is owned by Ron who is in the 32 percent marginal tax bracket. Depending on when Ronco bills its customers, it will receive $10,000 of income in December of year 1 or in January of year 2. If Ron's marginal tax bracket is 32 percent in both years, the only factor to consider is the time value of money; its after-tax cash inflow is $6,800 [$10,000 – ($10,000 × 32%)] in both years. If, however, Ron expects his marginal tax rates to change, Ronco should try to report the income in the year with the lowest expected marginal tax rate. What are the tax effects if Ronco defers income to year 2 when its marginal tax rate is 22 percent, 32 percent, or 37 percent in that year, using an 8 percent discount factor?

	Year 2 Marginal Tax Rates		
	22%	32%	37%
Tax paid in year 2 ($10,000 × tax rate)	$2,200	$3,200	$3,700
Present value factor	×0.926	×0.926	×0.926
Present value if tax paid in year 2	$2,037	$2,963	$3,426
Present value if tax paid in year 1	3,200	3,200	3,200
Net tax savings by deferring income	$1,163	$237	
Net tax cost of deferring income			$226

If Ron expects a marginal tax rate of either 22 or 32 percent in year 2, Ronco should defer recognition of the income. If the marginal tax rate could increase to 37 percent in year 2, Ronco should recognize the income in year 1 because the cost to defer income to year 2 is $226.

The same approach can be used to determine the optimal year in which to take a deduction to maximize the after-tax savings from taxes paid.

Example 2.14

Carbonnaire Company, a cash-basis sole proprietorship, incurs a $20,000 expense that may be paid and deducted in either year 1 or year 2. Carl, the sole proprietor, has a marginal tax rate of 32 percent. If Carbonnaire pays the expense in year 1, its after-tax cost is $13,600 [$20,000 – ($20,000 × 32%)]. What happens if the deduction is deferred to year 2 when Carl's marginal tax rate is 22 percent, 32 percent, or 37 percent using his 8 percent discount factor?

	Year 2 Marginal Tax Rates		
	22%	32%	37%
Tax savings from deduction ($20,000 × tax rate)	$4,400	$6,400	$7,400
Present value factor	×0.926	×0.926	×0.926
Present value of tax savings if deducted in year 2	$4,074	$5,926	$6,852
Present value of tax savings if deducted in year 1	6,400	6,400	6,400
Net tax savings by deducting in year 1	$2,326	$474	
Net tax cost of deducting in year 1			$452

Carbonnaire should claim the deduction in year 1 if the marginal tax rate is expected to decrease to 22 percent or remain at 32 percent to maximize tax savings. If the marginal rate is expected to increase to 37 percent, it should defer the deduction to year 2.

The intent of this timing strategy is to accelerate the tax deduction while delaying the actual cash outflow generating the expense. This strategy is most effective for cash-method taxpayers who have control over the year in which they pay their expenses. Good tax planners spend a considerable amount of time evaluating the optimum period in which to recognize expenses and identifying opportunities to accelerate deductions.

Depreciation deductions, unlike many other expenses, do not require a cash outflow, nor are they intended to represent true reductions in the fair market value of an asset. The tax savings from annual depreciation deductions, however, reduce the effective after-tax cost of an asset. The annual tax savings equal the deduction multiplied by the marginal tax rate. (Note that tax basis is similar to financial accounting book value as explained in Chapter 7.)

Example 2.15

Gamma Corporation purchased an asset for $100,000. For simplicity, assume that it recovers its cost over five years using the straight-line method for tax purposes. Gamma deducts $20,000 each year and reduces the asset's cost basis by this deduction. At the end of the five years, the asset's adjusted basis is zero. If Gamma's tax rate is 21 percent, the depreciation deductions result in a $4,200 annual tax savings. Using a 6 percent discount rate, the net present value of the tax savings is $17,690. Gamma's after-tax cost of the $100,000 asset is $82,310 ($100,000 – $17,690).

Year	Depreciation deductions	Tax rate	Tax savings	Discount factor	Present value
1	$20,000	21%	$4,200	.943	$3,961
2	20,000	21%	4,200	.890	3,738
3	20,000	21%	4,200	.840	3,528
4	20,000	21%	4,200	.792	3,326
5	20,000	21%	4,200	.747	3,137
			$21,000		$17,690

The cost basis of an asset is the same regardless of whether it is purchased for cash or is financed. The use of borrowed funds to create basis reduces the after-tax cost of acquiring an asset because the interest expense is deductible and is referred to as leverage.

Example 2.16

Refer to the facts in the previous example, except Gamma Corporation pays only $20,000 cash for the asset and finances the $80,000 balance at a 6 percent interest rate. Interest payments of $4,800 are due at the end of each year, and the $80,000 principal balance is due at the end of the fifth year. The annual tax savings from deductions for both the interest payments and cost recovery are now $5,208 [($4,800 interest expense deduction + $20,000 cost recovery deduction) × 21% tax rate]. The after-tax cost of the $100,000 asset is reduced to $78,041.

Year	Initial cash payment	Principal repayment	Interest payments	Tax savings	Net cash flow	Discount factor	Net present value
0	$(20,000)				$(20,000)		$(20,000)
1			$(4,800)	$5,208	408	.943	385
2			(4,800)	5,208	408	.890	363
3			(4,800)	5,208	408	.840	343
4			(4,800)	5,208	408	.792	323
5		$(80,000)	(4,800)	5,208	(79,592)	.747	(59,455)
							$(78,041)

Even though Gamma incurred additional net annual interest cost of $3,792 [$4,800 interest payment – ($4,800 × 21% = $1,008 tax savings)], it was able to save an additional $4,269 ($82,310 – $78,041) through leverage.

Recovering an asset's cost over a shorter time period also reduces the after-tax cost of the asset. The Tax Cuts and Jobs Act included a provision for 100 percent bonus depreciation allowing the full cost of assets, such as machinery and equipment (but not buildings), to be deducted as depreciation expense in the first year.

Example 2.17

Use the same facts as example 2.15, except that Gamma elects to recover the cost of the asset in the first year through 100 percent bonus depreciation. Gamma's after-tax cost for the asset is now only $80,197.

Year	Initial cash payment	Tax savings	Net cash flow	Discount factor	Net present value
0	$(100,000)		$(100,000)		$(100,000)
1		$21,000	21,000	.943	19,803
					$(80,197)

Gamma saves an additional $2,113 ($82,310 – $80,197) through accelerated depreciation. Taxpayers usually prefer to write off assets over the shortest time for tax purposes; the choices are limited, however, because the IRS predetermines the life for most assets (as discussed in Chapter 7). For financial purposes, taxpayers can choose the appropriate useful life for their assets.

2.3.4 INCOME SHIFTING

The purpose of income shifting is to lower taxes by splitting income between two or more taxpayers in the same family or between different entities owned by the same individual. The total tax paid is lower because of the progressive tax rate system.

Example 2.18

Vivian and Troy, married taxpayers filing a joint return, have $175,800 in taxable income in 2018. They have 3 children (ages 2 to 12) who have no income that is taxable. If they legally shift $3,600 in taxable interest income to each child, they can save $1,827 in taxes for the family as follows:

Tax on $175,800 for a married couple filing a joint return	$30,771
Tax on $165,000 ($175,800 – $10,800 shifted to children)	(28,179)
Tax savings to parents	$2,592
Tax paid by children ($255 × 3)[37]	(765)
Net tax savings to family from income shifting	$1,827

Tax planners should seek only legitimate methods of shifting income that will withstand IRS scrutiny. This is particularly true for related-party transactions (between family members or owners and their businesses). Unlike arm's-length transactions, in which each party negotiates for his or her own benefit, related-party transactions involve taxpayers who are more willing to negotiate for their common good to the detriment of the IRS. To legally shift income to family members, the parents must transfer ownership of income-producing

[37] Each child is allowed a $1,050 standard deduction, reducing taxable income to $1,050. This is then subject to tax at a 10 percent rate, resulting in a tax liability of $155 per child. The standard deduction was introduced in Chapter 1. See Chapter 5 for more details.

property (such as bonds) to children; a mere assignment of income will not result in the desired tax shifting.[38]

A popular income-shifting technique used by owner-employees of a corporation is to split income between themselves and the corporation through their salaries. They can take advantage of the progressive tax rates for individuals and corporations because salaries are deductible by the corporation.

Example 2.19

Vivian and Troy have $165,800 in taxable income from his sole proprietorship. In a typical year, Troy withdraws half of the profits from the business, leaving the other half in the business for expansion. If Troy incorporates and receives a salary of $82,900, he is taxed on only his $82,900 salary, with the other $82,900 taxed at the corporation's 21 percent rate (Troy's salary is a deductible business expense). Splitting the income between the taxpayer and a corporation in 2018 results in a tax savings of $3,245.

Tax on $165,800 for a married couple	$30,771
Tax on $82,900 for a married couple	(10,117)
Tax saving on the couple's tax return	$20,654
Tax on $82,900 for a corporation	(17,409)
Net tax savings	$3,245[39]

When an owner rents property or loans money to the corporation, income is effectively shifted from the corporation to the owner. Both transactions generate tax deductions (rent expense or interest expense) for the business and income to the owner. Taxpayers should maintain proper documentation for IRS scrutiny of these related-party transactions. If the salary, rent, or other expense is considered excessive, the IRS may reclassify any excessive payments as nondeductible corporate dividends. Other strategies that shift expenses and income between a corporation and the owner include employing children and maximizing the use of tax-free employee fringe benefits (discussed in Chapter 4).

2.3.5 CHANGING THE CHARACTER OF INCOME

To take advantage of these income-shifting strategies, the tax planner must be aware of the differences in tax treatments across various types of income and have both the knowledge and flexibility to change the nature of the income to receive a more advantageous tax treatment. The character of income is determined by tax law and is ultimately taxable using either ordinary income or capital gains rates. Income from merchandise sales to customers is ordinary income and subject to tax using the regular tax rates. Capital assets enjoy favorable tax treatment with most gains on capital assets held (the time from acquisition to disposition) for more than 12 months taxed to individuals at a maximum 20 percent rate, rather than the top current individual tax rate of 37 percent.

[38] On an otherwise valid transfer of property to a child younger than nineteen (twenty-four, if a full-time student), the kiddie tax rules reduce much of the marginal rate advantage by taxing the child's unearned income (such as interest and dividend income) in excess of $2,100 at tax rates used for estates and trusts. See Chapter 12.

[39] This example does not consider the impact of employment taxes. Employment taxes are discussed in Chapter 4. The computation of income tax liability for individuals (including married couples) is discussed in detail in Chapter 5. This example assumes that they have other income that offsets their deductions so the income from the business is their taxable income. The income tax rates were introduced in Chapter 1.

Example 2.20

John owns 10,000 shares of XYZ stock purchased 11 months ago at a cost of $10 per share that is now trading at $18 per share. John's marginal tax rate for ordinary income is 32 percent and 15 percent for long-term capital gains. If John sells the stock now, the gain does not qualify for the 15 percent long-term capital gain tax rate and the ordinary income rate applies. If John waits another month to sell the stock, he changes the character from income taxed at his ordinary rate to a long-term capital gain taxed at the favorable 15 percent rate, significantly increasing his after-tax cash flow:

	32% Tax rate	15% Tax rate
Sales proceeds ($18 × $10,000)	$180,000	$180,000
Cost ($10 × 10,000)	(100,000)	(100,000)
Net before-tax cash flow	$80,000	$80,000
Tax cost ($80,000 × tax rate)	(25,600)	(12,000)
Net after-tax cash flow	$54,400	$68,000

John saves $13,600 ($25,600 – $12,000) in taxes, increasing his cash flow by the same amount, by changing the character of the income to long-term capital gain.

There are several tax policy reasons for the preferential tax rates for long-term capital gains. First, individuals do not pay taxes on their unrealized gains as earned; instead, they are taxed in the year gain is realized. Recognizing several years' gains in one year can result in the taxing of these gains at higher marginal rates than if taxed annually. Second, a lower rate mitigates the effects of inflation as it is likely that some or all of the gain realized is due to inflation. Finally, the preferential rate partially compensates for the risks associated with long-term investments. By offering a preferential rate for gains on capital assets held for more than one year, the government uses tax policy to encourage investors to invest for the long-term rather than churning their investments.

2.3.6 OTHER FACTORS AFFECTING TAX PLANNING

A number of factors affect the estimates of net cash flow used in evaluating projects, such as the discount rate, inflation, and uncertainty.[40] Good tax planning requires nontax factors to be considered as well.

Cash Flow and Discount Rates

The discount rate used for project evaluation is an after-tax rate of interest that must be earned on invested funds over the period. The discount rate used by a firm in evaluating a project is normally its cost of capital (the required return on the firm's invested funds), a composite based on the cost of retained earnings, other equity, and the after-tax cost of debt financing. Financing of a specific project is not traced to any specific financing source. Thus, the actual after-tax interest costs are not separately considered in cash flow evaluations as that would double count after-tax interest costs.

To avoid changing discount rates, many firms use an ideal cost of capital as their discount rate. They may, however, calculate discount rates based on changes in the cost of debt and equity financing from year to year, leading to different problem solutions than a static rate. Moreover, two firms may have differing discount rates. Thus, one firm may accept a project another firm

[40] Most introductory finance texts provide a complete discussion of cost of capital, inflation, and uncertainty in determining cash flows for any project.

would reject. The firm with the lower discount rate (relative to another firm) will have a higher net present value of future cash flows. Conversely, the higher a firm's discount rate, the lower its present value of future cash flows.

Example 2.21

Wilson and Meyers, two competing firms, are each considering taking on a project costing $10,500. The expected net cash inflows from the project are $6,000 at the end of both years 1 and 2. Wilson uses a 6 percent discount rate to evaluate projects and Meyers uses a 12 percent rate.

	Wilson	Meyers
Year 1	$6,000 × .943 = $5,658	$6,000 × .893 = $5,358
Year 2	$6,000 × .890 = $5,340	$6,000 × .797 = $4,782
Total	$10,998	$10,140
Cost	(10,500)	(10,500)
Net cash inflow (outflow)	$498	$(360)

Wilson would accept the project, but Meyers would reject it because of their differing discount rates.

Inflation can be factored into present value calculations in one of two ways: either by increasing the discount rate for expected inflation or by actually factoring inflation-adjusted cash flows into the present value calculations. Although neither method usually produces a completely satisfactory result, ignoring inflation may skew cash flow and lead to poor decisions.

Example 2.22

Using the information in the previous example except that Meyers uses a 12 percent discount rate because of an expected increase in the costs factored into its net cash flow ($6,000) in years 1 and 2 of at least 6 percent. Alternatively, Wilson reduces its estimates of net cash flows to $5,640 in year 1 and $5,302 in year 2. Its net present value is now a negative $462 [($5,640 × .943 = $5,319) + (5,302 × .890 = $4,719) − $10,500 = ($462)] and it, too, would reject the project.

All project evaluations presented previously have been based on projections or estimates of the future cash inflows and outflows. Thus, every evaluation has uncertainty built in. When net present value is calculated on uncertain cash flows, it is worth less than the present value of a guaranteed cash flow (such as U.S. government bond interest). Thus, a higher discount rate is used to evaluate risky cash flows than that used for guaranteed cash flows. As shown previously, the higher the discount rate used for analysis, the greater the required net cash flows in future years for project acceptance. Alternatively, probabilities can be assigned to the cash flows or, if there are several estimates of each cash flow, each estimate can be assigned a probability and an expected value determined.

Example 2.23

Assume that Meyers in the previous examples had estimates of the net cash flow from its project manager of $7,000 with a 40 percent probability and $5,350 with a 60 percent probability for each of the two years. The expected value is $6,010 [(.4 × $7,000 = $2,800) + (.6 × $5,350 = $3,210)]. It would then use the $6,010 expected value of the cash flow in both years to determine if it should accept the project.

Nontax Considerations and Judicial Doctrines

The goal of tax planning is to minimize the tax costs of a transaction while meeting the nontax objectives of the client. Saving taxes is not always the most important consideration for a client. For example, a tax planner may come up with an excellent tax plan for a wealthy grandmother to avoid estate taxes upon her death by transferring title to her assets to her grandchildren while she is alive. She, however, will not give up control of her property to ensure that her grandchildren will visit her in a nursing home. In this case, the taxes saved by the plan are irrelevant because continued control over the property (a nontax factor) outweighs any tax savings. Effective tax planning must consider both tax and nontax factors.

The cost of implementation of any plan is another factor that must be considered. A sophisticated plan may require excessive annual fees that exceed the potential tax savings. Thus, it is imperative to consider all plan costs before beginning implementation.

Tax planners must consider three legal doctrines that the IRS can invoke when it appears that a taxpayer is taking excessive advantage of the tax law. The federal courts and the IRS require taxpayers to adhere not only to the letter of the law but the spirit of the law as well.

The **business purpose doctrine** does not allow recognition of a transaction for tax purposes unless there is a business or economic purpose other than tax avoidance.[41] This allows the IRS to challenge and disallow business expenses or losses for transactions with no underlying business (profit) motivation.

Example 2.24

Mega Corporation has $10,000,000 in taxable income and wants to avoid paying taxes. Loser Corporation has $9,000,000 of tax losses it cannot use because it has no expected profits. Mega Corporation acquires Loser Corporation in a tax-free merger. If Mega Corporation has no business purpose for the merger other than acquiring Loser's tax losses, the IRS can prevent Mega from using them.

In 2010, Section 7701(o) codified the economic substance doctrine in the Internal Revenue Code. This code section specifically requires taxpayers to establish the presence of both economic substance (measured objectively in terms of pre-tax profit potential) and business purpose. This law includes a minimum penalty of 20 percent of the underpayment related to any disallowed tax benefit for a transaction lacking economic substance and increases that penalty to 40 percent if the disallowed benefits were not adequately disclosed in the tax return.

Taxpayers attempting to avoid taxation sometimes craft transactions that are completely unrealistic. Although the courts have consistently held that taxpayers have no legal obligation to pay more tax than the law prescribes, the courts have also held that the form of the transaction cannot disguise its actual substance. This judicially created concept is referred to as the **substance-over-form doctrine** and requires the reality of a transaction, rather than its appearance, to determine its taxability.[42] This allows the IRS to reclassify the transaction according to its underlying substance.

Example 2.25

A profitable corporation that has never paid dividends pays a huge bonus to its sole owner-manager who already earned a more-than-generous salary. The IRS can recharacterize all or part of the bonus as a dividend if, under the circumstances, the substance of the payment is actually a dividend disguised as a bonus. Recharacterizing the bonus as a nondeductible dividend increases both the corporation's taxable income and tax liability.

[41] *Gregory v. Helvering*, 293 US 465 (1935) held that the transaction in question had no business purpose and therefore the applicable tax law did not apply, establishing the business purpose doctrine.

[42] *U.S. v. Phellis*, 257 US 156 (1921) made the first application of the substance-over-form doctrine when it held that the substance of a transaction should be considered and the form of a transaction can be disregarded in applying the provision of the tax law.

The IRS has successfully used the substance-over-form doctrine to attack tax shelters.

KEY CASE *One significant tax shelter case involved Long Term Capital Management, a well-known hedge fund run by Myron Scholes (Nobel laureate and co-author of the Black-Scholes pricing model). The U.S. District Court found that structured partnership transactions resulting in a $106 million capital loss deduction on the sale of preferred stock lacked economic substance. It disallowed the loss and assessed a $40 million tax deficiency along with up to $16 million in penalties.*[43]

Under the **step transaction doctrine**, the IRS collapses a series of intermediate transactions into a single transaction to determine the tax consequences.[44] This doctrine is usually applied to transactions that are so interdependent that the first transaction would not have been completed without anticipating the completion of the entire series of transactions. The IRS most frequently invokes this doctrine for a series of transactions within a short period of time. The taxpayer should have a bona fide business purpose for each individual step to prevent the IRS from disallowing the result of what seems to be a good tax plan.

Example 2.26

Jim, the sole shareholder of a corporation, needs money for another investment. To obtain the funds, Jim sells a large block of his corporation's stock to a friend at a huge profit. Jim's corporation then redeems the stock from his friend for its purchase price. The IRS can collapse the steps and treat this as a redemption of Jim's stock by the corporation, ignoring the friend's involvement. Jim can be taxed on the entire sale proceeds as if they were a dividend distribution by the corporation.

Tax planners need to be aware of these doctrines when crafting a creative tax plan, making sure it complies not just with the letter of the law but also with its spirit or intent.

2.4 TAX RESEARCH

Effective tax planning generally requires extensive tax research. The purpose of tax research is to find solutions to tax problems. Tax research can be divided into two major categories: closed-fact transactions and open-fact transactions. In a closed-fact transaction, all of the relevant transactions have been completed; therefore, research usually consists of finding support for the action that the client has already taken. Issues in a closed-fact tax research problem often arise from a conflict with the IRS. In an open-fact transaction, however, the tax practitioner maintains some degree of control over the tax liability because the transaction is not yet complete. If all the facts have not been established, there is an opportunity to plan anticipated facts carefully. Good tax planning establishes an optimal set of facts from the standpoint of tax results. The procedures followed in making such a determination differ significantly from the procedures used in compliance work.

Typically federal tax research is required in the following instances:

1. During the preparation of a client's return if the tax consequences of a transaction are not clear.
2. When the IRS raises a question during an audit of a client's tax return.

[43] *Long Term Capital Holdings v. U.S.*, 330 F.Supp.2d 122; 94 AFTR2d 2004-5666; 2004-2 USTC 50351 (DC Conn. 2004), aff'd. 96 AFTR2d 2005-6344, 2005-2 USTC 50575 (CA-2, 2005).

[44] *Helvering v. Alabama Asphaltic Limestone Co.*, 316 US 179 (1942).

3. In preparation of a claim for refund if it appears that a client may have overpaid his or her taxes.
4. When recommending whether or not a client should consider litigation.
5. If the government raises issues after a client starts litigation.
6. When a client wants to know the tax consequences of a proposed transaction.

Each time a taxpayer consults a tax practitioner, the practitioner is presented with a new problem. Although many basic questions may be nearly identical, each case may involve a slightly different set of facts. Despite the uniqueness of each case, tax research always involves the same key steps:

1. Gather the facts and identify the issues.
2. Locate the sources of authority
3. Evaluate the relevant authorities.
4. Communicate the recommendations.

Section 2.4.6 provides a basic model for solving and communicating the solution to a sample tax research problem addressing each of the key steps in the form of a memorandum to file followed by a client letter.

2.4.1 GATHER THE FACTS AND IDENTIFY THE ISSUES

To begin the research process, the researcher must gather all the relevant facts. Obtaining facts can include interviewing clients, speaking with third parties such as attorneys or brokers, and reviewing client documents such as prior tax returns, contracts, deeds, and corporate minutes.

After determining the relevant facts, the tax issues or questions need to be identified. Researchers combine their understanding of the facts with their knowledge of the tax law to identify and phrase the critical tax questions implicit in the facts. A combination of training and experience enables the researcher to successfully identify all of the issues in a tax problem. Inexperienced tax researchers find this step to be the most difficult element of the research process because the most important issues may not be obvious.

Good tax planning requires a considerable amount of time simply considering various alternatives to achieve the client's objectives. A common tendency of new tax students is to search too quickly for authority, resulting in their overlooking the best alternative plan.

Frequently, tax professionals are called upon to provide quick solutions to their clients' problems. The average client may feel that the tax adviser is a walking encyclopedia of facts on taxation. The answer may be obvious to the trained observer; but if not, (or when a wrong answer may be costly to a client) research is necessary. Reliance on memory for even the most obvious answer can often be a mistake. The importance of the ability to locate the applicable tax authority cannot be overemphasized.

2.4.2 LOCATE RELEVANT AUTHORITY

The tax treatment of any particular transaction normally must be based on supporting authority; thus, mastery of taxation requires an understanding of how and where the rules of taxation originate. The tax rules contained in each of the chapters in this textbook all have their origin in some source of authority.

Tax authority is generally classified as primary or secondary authority. **Primary authority** comes from statutory, administrative, and judicial sources. Although government publications are available for statutory laws, regulations, rulings, and court decisions, these references are found in a variety of places. The number and complexity of the tax statutes make it impossible for any individual to understand all of the rules and regulations relevant to tax practice. Fortunately, tax practitioners have a variety of secondary authorities at their disposal to help locate the official answers to tax questions in the ever-changing primary authorities. **Secondary authority** consists of tax services, books, journals, and newsletters.

Figure 2.1 lists websites for locating primary sources of authority that can be accessed free of charge. Unfortunately, free materials available on the internet do not have the same search features and indexes that are included in subscription-based tax services commonly used by tax practitioners. Historically, these professional tax services were comprehensive, multivolume, loose-leaf sets of reference information relating to tax problems. The loose-leaf feature permitted frequent updating. Most tax services are now internet-based and available only through paid subscriptions.[45]

Source	Internet address (URL)
Internal Revenue Code	http://uscode.house.gov/
Treasury Regulations	http://www.gpo.gov/fdsys/
Revenue Rulings	http://www.legalbitstream.com
Revenue Procedures	http://www.legalbitstream.com
IRS Announcements and Notices	http://www.legalbitstream.com
Internal Revenue Bulletins	http://www.irs.gov/irb/
Court Decisions	http://www.legalbitstream.com
Tax Court Decisions	http://www.ustaxcourt.gov
Internal Revenue Service	http://www.irs.gov
Tax and Accounting Site Directory	http://www.taxsites.com

FIGURE 2.1 Tax sources on the internet

Tax services provide two major tools for researchers: (1) explanations and (2) citations to primary sources of authority. Explanations may include discussions of the key issues of an Internal Revenue Code section and provide summaries of recent cases or rulings. Anything included in an explanation section of a tax service is a secondary authority because it is only another person's opinion about the tax law. Even though that person may be an expert about that area of tax law, a good researcher does not rely on another person's opinion, but consults the underlying source of authority. Thus, providing citations to primary sources of authority is the principal purpose of a tax service.

Although many of these tax services do contain a topical index, most researchers search by keyword. Identifying the best keywords is an important skill that develops with experience; if the researcher fails to identify the relevant keywords, the most critical tax authority may never be located. Keywords that are too broad or too narrow should be avoided. Good keywords usually identify the relevant area of the law and critical facts that describe the transaction. These keywords are then strung together with connectors to form a search query. The types of connectors vary with the particular tax research service and these systems are continually updated; therefore, users should check the appropriate help menu to determine how best to construct a query for that service.

A researcher wants to locate authorities with similar facts that specifically address the client's issues. Research usually starts with the relevant statutory sources (primarily the Internal Revenue Code and the appropriate congressional committee reports), followed by administrative sources and judicial sources.

[45] Examples of subscription-based tax services include Thomson Reuters Checkpoint® and Wolters Kluwer CCH IntelliConnect.®

Statutory Sources of Authority

Statutory sources of authority include the U.S. Constitution, tax treaties, and tax laws passed by Congress and are the basis for all tax provisions. The Constitution is the source of all federal laws, both tax and nontax; however, it is the 16th Amendment (ratified in 1913) that specifically gives Congress the power to impose a federal income tax.

Tax treaties (sometimes referred to as tax conventions) are agreements negotiated between countries concerning the treatment of individuals and other entities subject to tax in both countries. The purpose of these treaties is to eliminate the double taxation that taxpayers would face if their income were subject to tax in both countries.

The source most tax practitioners are concerned with is the result of the legislative process—the **Internal Revenue Code**. Unfortunately, Congress enacts tax legislation that amends the Code every year, possibly rendering prior research invalid. To develop an understanding of how the primary sources of authority clarify the way a transaction should be treated for tax purposes, one needs to understand the legislative process (how tax bills are enacted), and be able to determine the legislative intent of Congress.

Tax legislation arises from various sources. The president's economic report and budget message, studies made by the IRS, and bills introduced by individual representatives, acting on their own or reacting to pressures exerted by various special interest groups, all give rise to the legislation.

Before there can be a federal law on any subject, there must be general agreement on the matter both in the House of Representatives and in the Senate. Congress operates through committees that act both as drafters and gatekeepers, however, for legislative proposals. Each house has its own committees, and each committee is concerned only with its own legislative proposals that fall into certain categories. The two standing committees concerned with federal tax legislation are the Ways and Means Committee of the House of Representatives and the Finance Committee of the Senate.

Each new bill introduced in Congress is given a number that it retains throughout its congressional journey. A House bill number has the prefix *H.R.* and a Senate bill number has the prefix *S.* A new series of numbers starts in each house with each new Congress.[46]

Example 2.27

The Tax Cuts and Jobs Act is numbered H.R. 1. After passage by Congress, H.R. 1 became P.L. 115-97 and was signed into law by the President on December 22, 2017. The prefix of the public law number (115) refers to the session of Congress that passed the law. The suffix of the public law number (97) indicates that this was the 97th bill adopted during this congressional session.

The Constitution vests the House of Representatives of the U.S. Congress with the basic responsibility for initiating revenue bills. After a tax bill introduced in the House is assigned a number, it is ordinarily referred to the House Ways and Means Committee. This committee usually holds public hearings on the bill, after which it decides either to kill the bill by tabling it (postponing action on it indefinitely) or to submit the bill to the full House for its consideration, usually with amendments made by the committee. The committee sends a report containing a general and technical discussion of the bill's provisions to the floor of the House. This **committee report**, which may provide important authoritative support by indicating the legislative intent of the bill, is often considered in court cases to help resolve disputes between taxpayers and the IRS.

[46] Each session of Congress lasts for two years to coincide with the biannual elections of the congressional representatives. The 114th congressional session extended from 2015 through 2016; the 115th congressional session extends from 2017 through 2018.

The bill is then debated on the floor of the House, typically under *closed rule*, which limits debate and allows no amendments. If the bill fails on the floor of the House, it may go back to the committee; if it passes, the bill is sent to the Senate, where it is referred to the Senate Finance Committee.

The Senate Finance Committee, like its counterpart in the House, also provides an analysis of the bill in its report. After public hearings, the Senate Finance Committee sends its report, along with proposed amendments to the House bill, to the Senate floor. The bill is debated on the Senate floor under *open rule* with unlimited debate and amendments, and often under intense lobbying pressure. Any Senator can filibuster or stall legislation by unlimited debate. It usually takes a three-fifth majority (60 votes) to invoke "cloture" and end the debate.

When the majority party lacks the 60 votes necessary to be "filibuster-proof," it can use special budget "reconciliation" rules. Budget reconciliation is a procedure that allows spending and revenue legislation (including tax bills) to be passed by a simple majority vote of the Senate and avoid a potential filibuster. Only a limited number of reconciliation bills are allowed in any year, however.

Legislation under reconciliation cannot create a deficit beyond the 10-year budget window. If reconciliation is used to pass tax reform, phase-outs or other mechanisms may be necessary to meet this budget requirement. The "Bush tax cuts" in 2001 and 2003, for example, were enacted through reconciliation for only a 10-year period and would "sunset" (end) unless Congress found the revenue to pay for any extension. A phase-out after 10 years, however, usually reduces the estimated positive effect of tax reform on the economy.

Example 2.28

Reconciliation rules were used in 2017 when the Republican-controlled House and Senate agreed to a budget resolution permitting the tax bill to increase the federal deficit by up to $1.5 trillion over the 10-year budget window. The primary focus of the Tax Cuts and Jobs Act was to permanently reduce the tax rates for corporations while providing some relief for other taxpayers. To stay within its budget target (adding $1.456 trillion to the deficit over 10 years), the individual tax provisions were made temporary, by "sunsetting" after 2025, and causing the individual changes to revert to 2017 law in 2026.

Amendments made during consideration of a bill by the full House or Senate are commonly called floor amendments to distinguish them from committee amendments. Thus, the bill passed by the Senate is usually different from the version passed by the House. The bills are then referred to a Joint Conference Committee to work out the differences between the two versions.

The Joint Conference Committee is established to settle the differences between the House and the Senate on a particular bill. The committee members are ordinarily members of the House Ways and Means Committee and of the Senate Finance Committee, though other members of the two houses also can participate in the Joint Conference Committee.

The Joint Conference Committee reviews each provision of the bill on which the two houses disagree. In most instances, the Joint Conference Committee agrees with either the Senate version or the House version. In other instances it may agree with the Senate version but add amendments or propose a compromise version. The Joint Conference Committee also prepares a report explaining its proposed amendments and compromise provisions; it also indicates which house defers to the other if there are any conflicting provisions remaining in the House and Senate versions of the bill. The report is sent back to the House and then to the Senate for a vote on the Joint Conference Committee's compromise bill. Once members of the Joint Conference Committee reach a compromise, the rest of the process may move very quickly. Upon approval of both houses, the bill is sent to the president for signature or veto.

Example 2.29

H.R. 3771, which allowed an income tax deduction on 2013 income tax returns for charitable contributions of cash made in 2014 for the relief of typhoon victims in the Philippines (P.L. 113–92), sailed through Congress in less than 24 hours. It was passed by the House on March 24, 2014 and passed by the Senate on March 25. President Obama then signed it into law on March 25, 2014.

A tax bill passed by Congress is usually enacted as a revenue act that amends the existing Internal Revenue Code. The most recent exception to this practice occurred in 1986, when the Tax Reform Act of 1986 also created the Internal Revenue Code of 1986. From 1954 to 1986, tax legislation simply amended the Internal Revenue Code of 1954.

Shortly after each new revenue act, the major tax services issue explanations of the new tax law that cite or quote the relevant congressional committee reports. Debates and other statements made on the floor of the House or Senate are published in the *Congressional Record* for each day that Congress is in session. The reports from the various committees are published by the subscription-based tax services.

Administrative Sources of Authority

Laws are usually written in general language, as it is impossible to anticipate all the situations to which a particular provision of the law may apply. The general rules of most laws are usually clear. It is the application of those rules to particular facts that is often uncertain.

Example 2.30

It is clear that, under the Internal Revenue Code, business expenses are deductible from gross income. However, it is not always clear whether a particular item incurred at a given time in a particular factual setting is a qualified business expense. In example 2.25, the bonus is really a disguised dividend and is not deductible.

Treasury Regulations The Treasury Department is responsible for implementing the tax statutes passed by Congress. It is authorized to explain and interpret the law as part of its duties. The Internal Revenue Service division of the Treasury Department specifically carries out this function. Regulations provide explanations, definitions, examples, and rules that explain the language in the Code. Frequently, there is a considerable delay between the addition to or amendment of a particular Code section and the issuance of Treasury Regulations. In this situation, taxpayers must rely on the committee reports for guidance until regulations are released.

Other IRS Rulings The IRS issues several types of rulings. These rulings are issued for three reasons: (1) to inform taxpayers how the Code and the regulations have been applied to a particular set of facts; (2) to indicate the government's interpretation of a certain point of tax law and thus establish guidelines that the Treasury will follow; and (3) to outline those procedures that affect the taxpayer's rights or duties.

Taxpayers who are uncertain about the correct tax treatment of a prospective transaction can ask the IRS for a **letter ruling** (also called a private letter ruling) that provides guidance on how the transaction will be taxed. The IRS charges a fee for these rulings. Many taxpayers feel that obtaining a ruling is well worth its cost as a favorable ruling reduces the risk of an IRS challenge to their tax treatment in a subsequent audit.

Each year the IRS publishes **revenue rulings** that clarify ambiguous tax situations for which the public needs administrative guidance. The facts of published revenue rulings are highly individualized, but other taxpayers with similar situations may rely on these rulings. The IRS also issues **revenue procedures**, which explain procedures and the duties of the taxpayer. Revenue rulings and procedures are published in the weekly *Internal Revenue Bulletin* (IRB).

Judicial Sources of Authority

Judicial interpretations are the result of litigation. If the IRS and the taxpayer cannot settle the controversy regarding a tax liability between them, either of them may ask a court to decide.

When a tax controversy is litigated, it is first heard and decided by a trial court. That court decides the question according to its interpretation and understanding of the law. If either party is dissatisfied with the trial court's decision, that party may ask an appellate court to review that decision. Ultimately, the controversy may be appealed to and decided by the U.S. Supreme Court. The judicial decision of each court reflects that particular court's interpretation of the law. Although Congress sets forth the words of law and the administrative branch of government is charged with enforcing those words, it is the judiciary that has the final say with respect to what the words really mean. Under our legal system, every word in the law means whatever the Supreme Court says it means. Thus, one can seldom determine the practical impact of any area of law on a given set of facts without investigating what those words of law have been held to mean under similar factual circumstances. The court's role as the final interpreter of language cannot be overemphasized.

KEY CASE *Shortly after the 16th Amendment to the Constitution was passed, giving Congress the power to tax income, Congress declared stock dividends (a distribution of a corporation's own stock) to be taxable income. In the landmark case of Eisner v. Macomber the U.S. Supreme Court held that stock dividends are not taxable on the grounds that they do not fall within the meaning of the word income as used in the 16th Amendment.*[47]

Although the Constitution contains no definition of the term income, Congress declared that the term includes stock dividends, but the Court held to the contrary. Under current law, stock dividends are generally not taxed.

Under the doctrine of *stare decisis*, each case has precedential value for future cases with the same fact pattern.[48] By consistently treating similar cases in a similar way, the courts establish their interpretations of the statutes as laws in themselves. It is through this use of precedent that the courts build stability and order into the judicial system. Decisions concerning prior similar cases are used as guides when deciding current cases. The process of finding analogous cases from the past and convincing the tax authorities of the precedential value of those cases is a principal focus of research in the judicial area.

Tax services and other secondary authorities provide citations for the court decisions they cite as supporting authorities. Figure 2.2 presents sample citations for decisions from several different courts. In each of these, the name of the case appears first, followed by the volume number and name of reporter service in which the case is located, and then the page or paragraph number where the case begins. The date may appear at the end, in parenthesis, along with the district in which it was heard.

---

[47] *Eisner v. Macomber*, 252 US 189, 3 AFTR 3020; 1 USTC 32 (1920).

[48] The judicial doctrine of *stare decisis* means to let the decision stand on settled points of law so that a court views its own prior decision as precedents to be followed.

Internal Revenue Code	§213(d)(9)
Treasury Regulation	Reg. §1.166-1(e)
Revenue Ruling	Rev. Rul. 2003-102, 2003-2 C.B. 559
Letter Ruling	Ltr. Rul. 200517024
Revenue Procedure	Rev. Proc. 2006-1, 2006-1 IRB 1
IRS Announcement	Ann. 99-77, 199-2 C.B. 243
Tax Court Regular Case	Golsen, 54 T.C. 742 (1970)
Tax Court Memorandum Case	McIntosh, TC Memo 2001-144; RIA TC Memo ¶2001-144; 81 TCM 1772 (2001)
District Court Case	Long Term Capital Holdings v. U.S., 330 F. Supp.2d 122; 94 AFTR2d 2004-5666; 2004-2 USTC ¶50351 (D. Conn, 2004)
Appeals Court Case	Long Term Capital Holdings v. U.S., 96 AFTR2d 2005-6344; 2005-2 USTC ¶50575 (CA-2, 2005)
Supreme Court Case	Comm. v. Groetzinger, 480 U.S. 23; 107 S.Ct. 980; 59 AFTR2d 532; 87 USTC ¶9191 (1987)

FIGURE 2.2 Citation examples

Example 2.31

Golsen, 54 TC 742, means that a decision involving a taxpayer named Golsen is reported in volume 54 of the *Tax Court of the United States Reports* starting on page 742.

Figure 2.3 shows the primary sources of tax authority. Note that the inner circle (Internal Revenue Code, Regulations, and Supreme Court) represents the highest level of authority for each branch of government.

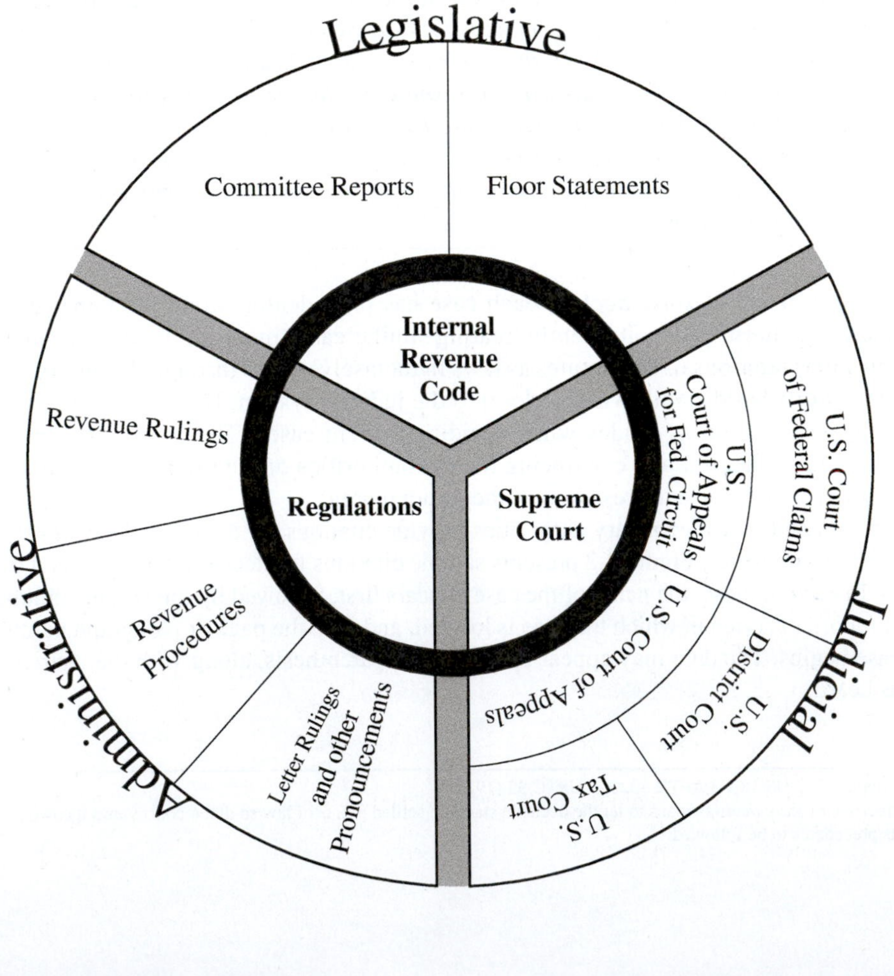

FIGURE 2.3 Primary sources of tax authority

2.4.3 EVALUATE THE SOURCES OF AUTHORITY

After the authorities applicable to the client's facts have been located, the researcher must determine if the authorities apply to the client's case and analyze their inherent strengths or weaknesses as precedents. The researcher compares the facts of the case to the authorities located, evaluates each authority by applying the reasoning of the authority to the client's facts, and draws a conclusion.

Research usually starts with the relevant Code section, followed by reading the appropriate congressional committee reports and regulations, and finally expanding to include relevant rulings and court cases. Reading the text of each applicable authority carefully is necessary to complete this step.

Reading the Code

The Internal Revenue Code is considered the most important source of tax law. The Internal Revenue Code is usually cited simply as Code or IRC. The latter distinguishes the Internal Revenue Code from other Codes, such as the United States Code and the Code of Federal Regulations. The Code is divided into subtitles and related chapters:

Subtitles		Chapters
A	Income Taxes	1–6
B	Estate and Gift Taxes	11–15
C	Employment Taxes and Collection of Income Tax	21–25
D	Miscellaneous Excise Taxes	31–50
E	Alcohol, Tobacco, and Certain Other Excise Taxes	51–55
F	Procedure and Administration	61–80
G	The Joint Committee on Taxation	91–92

The majority of the income tax provisions are included in the first chapter. Subchapters then divide the Code by income tax topics, and each subchapter is further divided into sections. The first chapter of Subtitle A includes the following:

SUBTITLE A. INCOME TAXES

Chapter 1. Normal Taxes and Surtaxes

Subchapter		Sections
A	Determination of Tax Liability	1–59B
B	Computation of Taxable Income	61–291
C	Corporate Distributions and Adjustments	301–385
D	Deferred Compensation, etc.	401–436
E	Accounting Periods and Methods of Accounting	441–483
F	Exempt Organizations	501–530
G	Corporations Used to Avoid Income Tax on Shareholders	531–565
H	Banking Institutions	581–597
I	Natural Resources	611–638
J	Estates, Trusts, Beneficiaries, and Decedents	641–692
K	Partners and Partnerships	701–777
L	Insurance Companies	801–848
M	Regulated Investment Companies and Real Estate Investment Trusts	851–860L
N	Tax Based on Income from Sources from Within or Without the U.S.	861–999
O	Gain or Loss on Disposition of Property	1001–1111
P	Capital Gains and Losses	1201–1298
Q	Readjustment of Tax Between Years and Special Limitations	1301–1351
R	Election to Determine Corporate Tax on Certain International Shipping Activities Using Per Ton Rate	1352–1359
S	Tax Treatment of S Corporations and Their Shareholders	1361–1379

When a tax practitioner wants to refer to a corporate tax matter, the practitioner often identifies it as a "Subchapter C" issue, a partnership tax provision as a "Subchapter K" issue and an S corporation provision as a "Subchapter S" issue.

Other key chapters of the Internal Revenue Code include Chapter 2 Tax on Self-Employment, Chapter 11 Estate Tax, Chapter 12 Gift Tax, and Chapter 79 Definitions.

Citations to provisions of the Internal Revenue Code usually are to sections (often abbreviated as Sec. or §) of the Code. This is the most convenient designation because sections are uniquely numbered in a consecutive manner. In other words, each section number is used only once, although not all numbers are used. If a section has several subdivisions, the citation is usually to the lowest subdivision that supports the point for which the section is cited.

The provisions of the Internal Revenue Code frequently are long and consist of many subdivisions. In researching a tax question, it is important to read every Code section that may be applicable to the client's case in its entirety. A mere sentence or phrase at the very end of a section may include or exclude the client's case from the application of that section.

Language that indicates quantities or time periods must be carefully noted and accurately stated. Carelessness in reading such language may lead to incorrect conclusions. For example, "50 percent or more" is not the same as "over 50 percent," and "not more than 50 percent" is not the same as "less than 50 percent."

Committee Reports

The congressional committee reports and debates contain statements indicating the intent of Congress with respect to some provision of the law. They apply, however, only if that provision was enacted into law in the same form as when the particular committee wrote its report or when it was debated on the floor of the House or Senate. For example, a statement in the House Ways and Means Committee report does not indicate the intent of Congress if the Senate's or the Joint Conference Committee's version of the particular provision was finally enacted.

When examining committee reports for congressional intent, it is generally best to start with the Joint Conference Committee report. This will indicate whether the provision enacted is the conference version or the Senate or House version as amended in conference. If the Senate version was enacted, the explanation will be in the Senate Finance Committee report unless the Senate version was introduced through a floor amendment. In this latter case, the only committee explanation will be in the Joint Conference Committee report.

Regulations

Treasury Regulations, published as Treasury Decisions, are the highest level of administrative interpretations of the Internal Revenue Code. The publication date of the latest Treasury Decision amending a regulation should be compared to the date of the latest amendment of the corresponding provision of the Internal Revenue Code. Regulations often do not reflect Code amendments until a year or more after the Code was amended. The old regulations continue to apply to any part of the Code provision not affected by the amendment. The publication date of the latest amending Treasury Decision is usually indicated at the end or the beginning of each regulation provision in the major tax services. Some tax services also note when a regulation provision does not reflect the latest amendments to the corresponding Code provision.

Most income tax regulations (or *regs*) are interpretative regulations that provide examples and detailed explanations to help interpret the Code. A Code section may, however, specifically authorize regulations to provide the details of the meaning and rules for that particular Code section. Regulations issued under this authority are called *legislative regulations*. These regulations are considered to have the same level of authority as the Code.

Treasury Regulations relating to all federal taxes are printed in Title 26 of the Code of Federal Regulations, which is divided into major subdivisions called *parts*. Part 1 contains the regulations dealing with the income tax provisions of the Internal Revenue Code; part 20 contains the regulations dealing with the estate tax provisions; part 25 contains the regulations dealing with the gift tax provisions; and part 301 contains administrative and procedural rules. Other parts contain temporary regulations and other regulations dealing with employment and excise taxes.

The regulations are arranged in the same sequence as the Code. Each part of the regulations is divided into sections with the same root number as the corresponding section of the Internal Revenue Code. Each section number consists of the following three elements:

1. *A prefix number to the left of the decimal point* indicates the part of Title 26 of the Code of Federal Regulations in which the section will be found. Thus, an income tax section of the regulations has the prefix number 1.

2. *A root number to the right of the decimal* (and before the hyphen) indicates the Code section the regulation is interpreting.

3. *A suffix number (and letter) to the right of the hyphen following the root number* indicates the subdivision of the section of the regulations. It is not, however, the same as the number of any related subdivision of the Internal Revenue Code.

Example 2.32

Reg. Section 1.61–7(a) is an income tax regulation that deals with interest income addressed in Section 61(a)(4) of the Internal Revenue Code.

Because the root elements of the regulation section numbers correspond to the related sections of the Internal Revenue Code, regulations pertaining to a particular section of the Internal Revenue Code are readily ascertainable.

There are three classes of regulations: (1) proposed, (2) temporary, and (3) final. The proposed regulations provide taxpayers with an advance indication of the likely IRS position and signal areas of potential disagreement. Comments and criticisms by interested parties can then be made either in writing or at hearings. Proposed regulations are just proposals and cannot be relied upon. Consequently, when a major tax law is enacted, the Treasury Department may skip the proposal step and issue temporary regulations to provide operating rules in the interim before the issuance of final regulations. The current practice is to issue regulations that are both proposed and temporary. The final regulations are issued after the public comments on the proposed regulations are evaluated; they then supersede the temporary regulations.

Even though proposed regulations do not have the same weight of authority as final regulations, they should not be ignored in researching a tax question that deals with a prospective transaction to which the proposals could apply. If they would have an adverse tax effect on the client's transaction, the tax advisor may wish to recommend completion of the transaction before the proposed regulations are finalized. If this is not practical, the advisor may wish to recommend postponing the transaction until final regulations are adopted, as they may clarify their effect on the taxpayer.

Revenue Rulings and Letter Rulings

A revenue ruling is an application of the law or regulations to a particular set of facts stated in the ruling. It usually discusses other rulings and court decisions as well as the Code and regulations pertinent to the legal questions raised by the facts. The significance of revenue rulings lies in the fact that they reflect current IRS policy. IRS agents are usually reluctant to vary from that policy, so revenue rulings carry considerable weight.

Soon after a revenue ruling is issued, it appears in the weekly *Internal Revenue Bulletin* (cited as IRB), published by the U.S. Government Printing Office (GPO). (Revenue rulings were previously published semiannually by the GPO in bound volumes called the *Cumulative Bulletin* (cited as CB).) Revenue rulings have hyphenated numbers. The number to the left of the hyphen indicates the year in which the ruling was published and the number to the right is the number of the ruling for that year.

Revenue procedures are issued in the same manner as revenue rulings but deal with internal practice and procedures of the IRS in the administration of the tax laws. They provide a way for the IRS to release information to taxpayers. Revenue procedures are cited in the same manner as revenue rulings except that Rev. Proc. is substituted for Rev. Rul.

Example 2.33

Revenue Procedure 2018-18 contains the inflation adjustments for 2018. It is cited as Rev. Proc. 2018-18, 2018-10 IRB 392. This is the 18th Revenue Procedure issued in 2018. It is in the 2018-10 issue of the *Internal Revenue Bulletin* (the 18th week of 2018) on page number 392.

Letter rulings, also called private letter rulings, are interpretations of the Internal Revenue Code and Regulations by the National Office of the Internal Revenue Service. They are similar to revenue rulings except that each letter ruling is issued to a particular taxpayer in response to his or her specific question. Although a letter ruling applies only to the particular taxpayer to whom it was issued, such a ruling could prove helpful to any other taxpayer faced with a substantially identical fact pattern. Letter rulings are not officially published by the government, but are published by several major tax services (after confidential information is deleted).

Acquiescence Policy

In some instances, the Commissioner of Internal Revenue will publicly *acquiesce* or *nonacquiesce* to a court decision in which the court has disallowed a deficiency asserted by the IRS. The acquiescence or nonacquiescence relates only to the issues decided against the government. In announcing an acquiescence, the commissioner publicly declares agreement with a conclusion reached by the court. This does not necessarily mean that the commissioner agrees with the reasoning used by the court in reaching the conclusion. It only indicates that the IRS will dispose of similar disputes in a manner consistent with that established in the acquiesced case. Nonacquiescence is a clear signal that the IRS will not follow the decision, even though it may choose not to appeal it.

An acquiescence or nonacquiescence is issued as an *action on decision* (AOD) and Announcement published in the *Internal Revenue Bulletin*. Their citations are usually shown next to the citations of the related court decision in the tax services and citators.

Other Pronouncements

The IRS also issues information releases for issues that it thinks are of interest to the general public. For example, an information release is used to announce the standard mileage rate allowed for business use of an automobile.

Announcements are information releases that are more technical in nature and are generally aimed at tax practitioners instead of the general public. They are used to summarize new tax law or procedural matters and can be considered equivalent to revenue rulings and revenue procedures.

The IRS also publishes tax return instructions and other materials for the guidance of taxpayers, such as *Pub. 17: Your Federal Income Tax.* None of the statements in these publications are ordinarily supported by citations to the Code, regulations, or any other authority. Additionally, these publications are generally revised only once a year and are not always up-to-date. For these reasons, the IRS does not consider itself bound by the information in these publications.

Court Decisions

The parties in a tax case are generally the taxpayer and the Internal Revenue Service. Cases of a taxpayer contesting a tax deficiency claimed by the IRS are identified as *Taxpayer v. Commissioner of Internal Revenue*, while those in which a taxpayer sues to recover an overpayment of tax, are indicated as *Taxpayer v. United States*.[49]

A case between a taxpayer and the IRS may involve a single question, called an issue, or a number of questions or issues. When several issues are involved in a case, the court decides each issue separately. Although it renders a single decision in the case, that decision indicates how each separate issue was decided. A court's decision on an issue is its determination of who wins that issue. In a two-issue case, for example, one issue may be decided for the taxpayer and the other for the government or both may be decided for the taxpayer or both for the government.

The party who raises an issue generally has the burden of convincing the court that his or her interpretation of that issue is correct. Thus, a taxpayer who contests a deficiency or claims a refund must convince the court that he or she is entitled to the relief asked for in the petition. If the court consists of more than one judge, a majority of them must be convinced.

The burden of convincing the court is usually, but not always, on the taxpayer. The Internal Revenue Code places the burden of proof on the government in a few special instances, such as proof of fraud with intent to evade taxes.[50]

The *opinion*, the court's statement of the reasons for its decision, is generally the largest part of the published case report. It usually consists of a discussion and explanation of the applicable law and of prior court decisions on the same point of law. In contrast to the opinion, the decision may consist of only a few lines at the end of the court's statement.

There are two types of courts: courts of original jurisdiction or trial courts in which cases are first heard, and courts of appeal in which the decisions of the trial courts are reviewed. Courts of original jurisdiction include the U.S. Tax Court, U.S. District Courts, and the U.S. Court of Federal Claims. The Tax Court hears only tax cases and the presiding judge is more familiar with the tax law than is the typical judge presiding in the other courts. Jury trials are available only in district courts.

If either the taxpayer or the government is dissatisfied with the decision of the trial court on any issue, it can appeal to or ask a higher court to review that decision. Sometimes both parties appeal. The taxpayer appeals on those issues decided against him or her, and the government appeals on those issues decided against it. Figure 2.4 lists the 13 Circuit Courts of Appeal (numbered 1 through 11 plus the District of Columbia and the Federal Circuit Court).

Circuit	Circuit court jurisdiction
First	Maine, Massachusetts, New Hampshire, Puerto Rico, Rhode Island
Second	Connecticut, New York, Vermont
Third	Delaware, New Jersey, Pennsylvania, Virgin Islands
Fourth	Maryland, North Carolina, South Carolina, Virginia, West Virginia
Fifth	Louisiana, Mississippi, Texas
Sixth	Kentucky, Michigan, Ohio, Tennessee
Seventh	Illinois, Indiana, Wisconsin
Eighth	Arkansas, Iowa, Minnesota, Missouri, Nebraska, North Dakota, South Dakota
Ninth	Alaska, Arizona, California, Guam, Hawaii, Idaho, Montana, Nevada, Oregon, Washington
Tenth	Colorado, Kansas, New Mexico, Oklahoma, Utah, Wyoming
Eleventh	Alabama, Florida, Georgia
DC	Washington, DC
Federal	US Court of Federal Claims

FIGURE 2.4 Federal circuit courts of appeal

[49] Before 1954, a taxpayer suing to recover an overpayment usually brought the suit against the particular Collector of Internal Revenue (an office since abolished) into whose office the payment had been made. In that event the case was denominated Taxpayer v. the particular collector by name.

[50] The IRS Restructuring and Reform Act of 1998 shifts the burden of proof for factual issues to the IRS only for court proceedings if the taxpayer introduces credible evidence regarding the facts that apply to a tax liability. Note that the burden of proof still falls to the taxpayer at the audit level.

Appellate courts frequently issue decisions without opinions. This ordinarily means that the appellate court is satisfied with the decision and opinion of the lower court. If it is not satisfied, the appellate court may simply refer to its opinion in a prior decision, or it may write its opinion to accompany its decision.

The appellate court separately decides only those questions of fact or of law raised on appeal by either party. It may affirm the decision of the lower court on certain issues and reverse it on other issues. A reversal means that the party who won in the lower court now loses and the other party becomes the winner on that particular issue. The lower court's decisions on issues that neither party appeals are not disturbed because the appellate court has no jurisdiction over those issues.

Example 2.34 Jane wins in the Tax Court and the IRS appeals. The Court of Appeals reverses the Tax Court's decision. This means that the IRS has now won at the appellate level. Jane then appeals the appellate court's decision to the U.S. Supreme Court. The Supreme Court reverses the decision of the appellate court. This means that the case is now finally settled in favor of Jane (the same result as the original Tax Court decision).

Sometimes reversal by an appellate court does not resolve the controversy between the parties without further proceedings. In such instances, the appellate court reverses and remands (returns) the case to the lower court for further consideration in accordance with the appellate court's opinion. The lower court then renders a new decision.

A party who is dissatisfied with a decision of any of the appellate courts may ask the U.S. Supreme Court to review that decision by filing a petition for a *writ of certiorari*. If the Supreme Court denies the writ, its refusal does not mean that the Supreme Court agrees with the decision of the lower court; it merely means that it does not feel the case warrants its attention. The Supreme Court rarely agrees to hear tax cases; as a result, appeals seldom go higher than the Circuit Court of Appeals or the Court of Appeals for the Federal Circuit.

Legal Precedents When a court decides a particular issue, a legal precedent is set for future cases involving the same issue. Legal precedents, however, are circuit-specific; that is, different circuits can hand down different decisions based on identical facts. Cases in which there is disagreement between the different circuit courts of appeal are the types of tax cases the Supreme Court will usually agree to hear to provide uniformity of treatment throughout the country.

The doctrine of *stare decisis* applies in a special way in the Tax Court because the appeal goes to the circuit court based on the taxpayer's residence. After the Tax Court decided the *Golsen* case, it agreed to follow the Court of Appeals that has direct jurisdiction over the taxpayer in question.[51] If the applicable appellate court has not ruled on that issue, the Tax Court can decide the case based of its own interpretation of the issue. This **Golsen rule** allows the Tax Court to reach opposite decisions for taxpayers in different geographical areas of the country, even though their cases have identical facts. Thus, the Tax Court is not required to follow a decision of a prior Tax Court case in the same circuit if it was reversed by the Court of Appeals. The Tax Court may follow the prior Tax Court decision in any circuit in which the Court of Appeals has not considered the issue or a circuit in which the Court of Appeals sustained the Tax Court's position. In judging the precedential value of a Tax Court decision, the researcher must always note whether the Tax Court reached its decision independently or merely followed the Court of Appeals to which its decision would have been appealed, without necessarily agreeing with it.

[51] *Jack E. Golsen*, 54 TC 742 (1970).

Some Tax Court transcripts disclose that a "decision has been entered under Rule 155" (prior to 1974, known as Rule 50). This notation signifies that the court has reached a conclusion regarding the facts and issues of the case but leaves the computational aspects of the decision to the opposing parties. Both parties subsequently submit to the court their versions of the refund or deficiency computation. If both parties agree on the computation, no further argument is necessary. In the event of disagreement, the court will reach its decision based on the data presented by each party.

If there are differences between facts in the research problem and the facts of a case the researcher has located, the researcher needs to determine whether the court would rule differently regarding the client's facts. If there is more than one case on point, the researcher needs to decide which one is the most authoritative. A researcher must citate every case and ruling to ensure that the authority located has not been overruled, modified, or otherwise lost its authoritative validity.

Using a Citator

A citator contains an alphabetical list of tax cases and a numerical list of revenue rulings and some other IRS rulings. A citator allows a researcher to find out two things about a court case: the decision's history and what the other courts may have said about it. There is a list of other decisions that cite or refer to the same court decision after the name of each case. The validity of a particular decision may be assessed by examining how subsequent cases viewed the cited decision. By reading the authorities listed, a researcher can learn whether other courts and the IRS agree or disagree with the decision. Moreover, a case located by the citator that disagrees with an earlier case, but provides a higher level of authority, may provide a more appropriate answer to your question.

For revenue rulings, historical citations consist of related rulings. There may be later revenue rulings that modify, supersede, or revoke the cited revenue ruling or earlier rulings that were modified or revoked by the cited ruling.

When to Stop Searching

An area many researchers wrestle with is deciding when to stop researching. Ideally, the tax researcher would like to find a favorable authority *on all fours* with the client's situation. The term *on all fours* refers to finding a situation in relevant tax authority that is factually similar in all legally pertinent ways to the situation being researched. Such perfect results are seldom achieved. Thus, the researcher must look for a tax authority in which the critical facts are similar to those of the client.

The researcher should consider several items if deciding whether or not to continue searching, First, what is the level of the relevant authority located? The higher the level of authority, the better. Next, has the IRS said anything about the issue? Some degree of comfort is provided when the client's position is supported in IRS rulings. However, an adverse IRS position may prompt the researcher to continue the search for additional authority. Third, do different sources of authority cite the same tax authority? If several different tax services and primary authorities cite the same authority in reaching their answer, this may help the researcher feel more comfortable that the best possible results have been obtained.

After evaluating the authorities, the researcher should be able to reach a conclusion on each issue. The conclusions sum up the state of the law on the issue as indicated by the primary authorities. Occasionally, the research will not offer a clear solution to the client's tax problems. There may be unresolved issues of law. If unresolved issues exist, the researcher might inform the client of alternative possible outcomes for each disputed issue, and provide the best recommendation for each.

2.4.4 COMMUNICATE THE RECOMMENDATIONS

The final step in the research process is to communicate the results and recommendations of the research. The results of the research usually are summarized in a memorandum to the client file and in a letter to the client. Both the memo and the client letter usually contain a restatement of the relevant facts, any assumptions the researcher made, the issues addressed, the applicable authority, and the researcher's recommendations. The memo to the file usually contains more detail than does the letter to the client.

The memo to the file can take different forms. One simple format contains the following four sections:

1. *Facts:* a statement of the relevant facts
2. *Issues:* the tax questions or issues involved
3. *Conclusions:* the researcher's conclusions to the issues
4. *Discussion:* a discussion of the reasoning and authorities upon which the conclusions are based

The *facts* section should include all facts necessary to answer the tax questions or issues raised, with events stated in chronological order and dates given for each event.

Following the facts, the *issues* should be numbered as separate questions. The issues should be arranged in logical order, particularly when the answer to one question raises another question. Tax questions should be as specific as possible, including dates, amounts, and any other relevant information. Over-generalization should be avoided.

The *conclusions* are short answers to each issue. A separate conclusion should be stated for each numbered issue, ensuring that conclusion number 2 answers the question raised in issue number 2.

The *discussion* section is the longest. The reasoning and authorities underlying each conclusion should be presented separately, along with a concise summary of the facts and findings, plus a complete citation for each authority mentioned. Also noted should be the relative strength of each authority, such as whether the IRS expressed acquiescence, nonacquiescence, or neither, and whether the cited authority has been upheld in subsequent decisions. A detailed, logical analysis should be provided to support each of the conclusions using the primary authorities cited.

The client letter typically is structured as follows, allowing approximately one paragraph for each topic:

1. Salutations and general conclusions
2. Summary of the facts
3. Summary of the most important sources of law that lead to the results
4. Implications of the results

2.4.5 KEEPING UP-TO-DATE

Every accountant engaged in tax practice needs to keep up-to-date with the ever-changing federal tax law. Keeping up-to-date does not require the same exhaustive research as a specific tax problem. Numerous tax newsletters cover the more significant tax law developments such as *Tax Notes* published by Tax Analysts and *Daily Tax Report* published by Bloomberg.

Tax magazines or journals contain a variety of articles that may be helpful in researching new or developing areas of tax law. These articles might provide an in-depth review of a recent court decision or an analysis of the impact of a recent change in a tax law on the overall economy. A researcher can use these articles to optimize research time by using the author's expert judgment and bibliography of a relevant topic to quickly identify pertinent primary sources of authority.

2.4.6 SAMPLE RESEARCH PROBLEM

Gather the Facts and Identify the Issues

Royal Hotels, Inc. plans to open a new hotel and casino in Atlantic City. It plans to require its employees to stay on the business premises during their working hours and has decided to provide free meals to those employees in an on-premises employee cafeteria for two reasons. First, if employees ate off-premises, they would have to go through two security checks a day (one when they went to lunch and another when their shifts end). Second, the number of fast-food eating establishments is insufficient to accommodate the large number of employees that would go for meals at one time. Royal would like your advice regarding the correct tax treatment of these meals.

Royal's situation appears to have two separate issues: (1) are the meals tax free to employees and (2) are the costs of the employee cafeteria deductible by Royal Hotels?

Research Results

A summary of relevant authorities follows. The text of IRC Section 119, Section 132(e), Regulation Section 1.119-1, *Boyd Gaming Corp. v. Commissioner*, Announcement 99-77 and IRC Sections 274(n) and (o) as revised by the Tax Cuts and Jobs Act are in the appendix at the end of this chapter.

§119 Meals or lodging furnished for the convenience of the employer.
Meals furnished to employees are excluded from gross income of an employee if furnished by or on behalf of his employer for the convenience of the employer, but only if furnished on the business premises of the employer. All meals furnished on the business premises of an employer to these employees will be treated as furnished for the convenience of the employer if more than half of the employees to whom the meals are furnished are considered for the convenience of the employer.

§132 Certain fringe benefits.
(e)(2) The operation by an employer of any eating facility for employees shall be treated as a de minimis fringe benefit if the facility is located on or near the business premises of the employer, and revenue derived from such facility normally equals or exceeds the direct operating costs of such facility. An employee entitled under Section 119 to exclude the value of a meal provided at such facility shall be treated as having paid an amount for such meal equal to the direct operating costs of the facility attributable to the meal.

Reg. §1.119-1. Meals and lodging furnished for the convenience of the employer.
(a)(2) Meals furnished by an employer without charge to the employee will be regarded as furnished for the convenience of the employer if the meals are furnished for a substantial noncompensatory business reason of the employer. Meals will be regarded as furnished for a substantial noncompensatory business reason of the employer when the meals are furnished to the employee during his working hours because the employer's business is such that the employee must be restricted to a short meal period, such as 30 or 45 minutes, and because the employee could not be expected to eat elsewhere in such a short meal period. Meals will be regarded as furnished for a substantial noncompensatory business reason of the employer when the employee could not otherwise secure proper meals within a reasonable meal period. For example, meals may qualify under this when there are insufficient eating facilities in the vicinity of the employer's premises.

(c)(1) For purposes of this section, the term "business premises of the employer" generally means the place of employment of the employee.

Boyd Gaming Corp. v. Comm., 177 F.3d 1096, 99-1 USTC ¶50,530, 83 AFTR 2d 99-2354, (CA9), 05/12/1999
Meal expense deductions for free meals provided to employees on employer's premises are de minimus fringe benefits with substantial noncompensatory business reasons. Tax Court improperly found that free meals taxpayer/gaming corporation provided shift employees at on-site cafeterias weren't 100% deductible as de minimis fringe benefits; meals were provided for taxpayer's convenience where it required employees to stay on premises during shifts. Court erred in concluding that stay-on-premises policy didn't sufficiently connect meals to business purpose where policy was supported by security, efficiency, and other legitimate business reasons. The Tax Court's decision is reversed.

Announcement 99-77, IRB 199-32
The IRS announced it acquiesced in the Boyd Gaming decision.

Internal Revenue Code Sections 274(n) and (o) as revised by the Tax Cuts and Jobs Act
Section 274(n)(2) as amended by the Tax Cuts and Jobs Act provides that the 50% limit on deducting food or beverage expenses applies to an employer's expenses of providing food and beverages to employees at an eating facility that qualifies as a de minimis fringe benefit.

Section 274(o) as amended by the Tax Cuts and Jobs Act provides that, for amounts incurred or paid after December 31, 2026, no deduction will be allowed for:

- any expense for the operation of an employer-operated eating facility described in Code Section 132(e)(2);
- any expenses for food or beverages, including under Code Section 132(e)(1), associated with an employer-operated eating facility or,
- any expense for meals described in Code Section 119(a)

Sample Memo to File and Client Letter

Memo to File

Client:	Royal Hotels, Inc.
Subject:	Employee Cafeteria Meals
For:	Pam Partner
Researched by:	Steven Staff
Date:	October 1, 2018

Facts

Royal Hotels, Inc. plans to open a new hotel and casino in Atlantic City. It plans to require its employees to stay on the business premises during their working hours for security and logistic reasons and to provide free meals to those employees in an on-premises employee cafeteria. If employees ate off-premises, they would have to go through two security checks a day (one when they went to lunch and another when their shifts ended). Additionally, the number of fast-food eating establishments is insufficient to accommodate the large number of employees that would go for meals at one time.

Issues

1. Are the meals tax free to employees?
2. Are the costs of the employee cafeteria deductible?

Conclusions

1. Meals provided for the convenience of the employer where employees are confined to the premises during mealtimes are tax free under Section 119.
2. The cafeteria will qualify as a de minimis fringe benefit under Section 132, permitting a 50 percent deduction for its costs through 2025. After 2025, these expenses will no longer be deductible.

Discussion of Reasoning and Authorities

1. Section 119 provides that the value of meals is excludible from an employee's income if the meals are furnished on the business premises for the convenience of the employer. Under Regulation Section 1.119-1, a meal is considered furnished "for the convenience of the employer" if it is furnished for a "substantial noncompensatory business reason." A substantial noncompensatory business reason includes meals furnished because the employee could not otherwise secure proper meals within a reasonable meal period because there are insufficient eating facilities in the vicinity. Reg. Section 1.119-1 also defines business premises of the employer as the place of employment of the employee. Under Section 119(b)(4), if more than half the employees satisfy the "for the convenience of the employer" test, then all employees will be considered as satisfying the test.
2. As a general rule, Section 274(n) permits a taxpayer to deduct only 50 percent of the otherwise allowable cost of business meals. However, meals provided to employees were 100 percent deductible in certain circumstances. The two most important are (1) meals treated as compensation and (2) meals that are tax-free de minimis fringe benefits under Section 132(e). Section 132(e) provides an exclusion for de minimis fringe benefits for which accounting would be an unnecessary hassle. Included within these de minimis benefits are subsidized cafeterias for employees. To qualify under Section 132(e)(2), a cafeteria must be located on or near the business premises, must not favor executives, and must generate revenue that normally equals or exceeds its direct operating costs. However, if all employees' meals are excluded under Section 119, the employees are treated under Section 132(e)(2) as having paid an amount equal to the direct operating costs of the facility attributable to meals. This in turn causes the employer-operated cafeteria to qualify as a de minimis fringe benefit under Section 132(e)(2). Under Section 274(n)(2)(B), an employer may fully deduct the cost of meals that are tax-free de minimis fringe benefits under Section 132(e)(2).

   In Boyd Gaming Corp., et al. v. Commissioner (177 F. 3d 1096; 99-1 USTC ¶50,530; 83 AFTR 2d 99-2354), the Ninth Circuit reversed the Tax Court by ruling that a casino with a stay-on-premises policy was permitted to deduct 100 percent of the meals furnished to employees. The court held that once the stay-on-premises policy was adopted, the affected employees had no choice but to eat on the premises and that the furnished meals thus were indispensable to the proper discharge of their duties. The IRS has since acquiesced (Ann. 99-77, 1999-32 IRB 1) to this decision, indicating that it will not challenge similar businesses that have valid business reasons for a stay-on-premises policy. The security concerns of Boyd Gaming appear to be the same as the security concerns of Royal Hotels, so this should meet the valid business reason test.

   Unfortunately, the Tax Cuts and Jobs Act amended Section 274(n)(2) by applying the 50% limit to an employer's expenses incurred after 2018 for providing food and beverages to employees at an eating facility that qualifies as a de minimis fringe benefit. Additionally, Section 274(o) now provides that, for amounts incurred or paid after December 31, 2026, no deduction will be allowed for: (a) any expense for the operation of an employer-operated eating facility described in Code Section 132(e)(2); (b) any expenses for food or beverages, including under Code Section 132(e)(1), associated with an employer-operated eating facility or, (c) any expense for meals described in Code Section 119(a).

Client Letter

October 1, 2018
Royal Hotels, Inc.
123 Park Place
Atlantic City, New Jersey

Dear Mr. Royal:

Thanks again for requesting my advice concerning the tax treatment of your proposed employee cafeteria. I have good news for you. The meals will be tax free to your employees, and you will be able to deduct 50 percent of the costs of the cafeteria.

The facts as I understand them are as follows:

Royal Hotels plans to require its casino employees to stay on the business premises during their working hours for security and logistic reasons and has decided to provide free meals to those employees in an on-premises employee cafeteria.

Generally, a taxpayer was permitted to deduct only 50 percent of the otherwise allowable cost of business meals, but meals provided to employees had been 100 percent deductible when they qualified as tax-free de minimis fringe benefits under Section 132(e) through 2017. However, from 2018–2025, the Tax Cuts and Jobs Act limits the deduction to 50 percent and after 2025, the deduction for any employer operated eating facility is eliminated. To qualify for the deduction until 2025, the cafeteria must be located on or near your business premises and must not favor executives. You must also have valid business reasons for a stay-on-premises policy for the cafeteria to qualify.

Section 119 provided that the value of meals was excludible from an employee's income if the meals were furnished on the business premises for the convenience of the employer. The convenience-of-employer test was met if the meals were provided for a "substantial noncompensatory business reason." Your business reasons were due to security and logistical concerns. First, if employees ate off-premises, they would have to go through two security checks a day (one when they went to lunch and another at the end of their shifts). Additionally, the number of fast-food eating establishments within a reasonable distance of the casino was insufficient to accommodate the employees when going out for meals.

My research had uncovered a case similar to yours that allowed a casino to deduct its costs while employees were permitted tax-free treatment because it required its employees to remain on-premises during their shifts for security and logistic reasons. The IRS had acquiesced to the decision and had indicated that it would not challenge other businesses in similar situations with valid business reasons for a stay-on-premises policy. Unfortunately, recent law changes reduce the deduction and then eliminate it completely after 2025. The good news in that you will have a limited deduction for 50 percent of the costs through 2025, after which time the deduction will be completely eliminated. You should consider some long-term planning as soon as possible to discuss the recent reduction in the deduction and the eventual elimination of the deduction.

Please call me at 661-1234 so that we may discuss any questions you have as well as both short-term and long-term planning.

Sincerely,

Pam Partner

Pam Partner

REVISITING THE INTRODUCTORY CASE

Kevin should request an appeals conference with the IRS during which he can present the reasons why he believes his part-time dog training operation is a business and not a hobby. Most disputes with the IRS are settled at this level. If he cannot reach a satisfactory agreement with the IRS, then he could take the case to the Small Case Division of the Tax Court where he can represent himself. (There is no appeal from this court, however.) If he wants to take his case to any other court, he will probably need to hire an attorney. This expense may not be warranted, however, given the size of the tax deficiency. If he wants to take his case to Tax Court, he must file within 90 days of receiving a Notice of Deficiency. To take his case to either District Court or the U.S. Court of Federal Claims, he will have to first pay the tax and then sue for refund. His final option would be to do nothing and wait for the IRS to begin collection procedures, but this is not advisable.

SUMMARY

Tax practice involves compliance, research, and planning. Tax return preparation and client representation at audit are the primary compliance activities. Taxpayers must file their annual tax returns by specific due dates, with allowable extensions, or numerous penalties along with interest charges can be levied. Extensions of time to file do not permit the taxpayer to extend payment of taxes. Failure to pay the tax due on time can also subject the taxpayer to penalties and interest.

To maintain the integrity of the tax system, the Internal Revenue Service first makes a computerized mathematical check of all tax returns and checks for unallowable items. Many discrepancies are settled through correspondence with the taxpayer. The IRS also selects numerous tax returns for more extensive office and field audits. The latter, however, are usually reserved for business audits. Taxpayers who owe additional taxes after an audit can pay the tax, appeal to an appeals officer, or initiate court action to settle the dispute. The Tax Court is the only court in which the taxpayer can file suit without paying the disputed tax. The Small Case Division of the Tax Court handles disputes that do not exceed $50,000 but its decisions cannot be appealed to a higher court.

Tax professionals have a responsibility to both their clients and the tax system; at times, these responsibilities may appear to be in conflict. All tax preparers are subject to the government's regulations in *Circular 230*; they may be subject to penalties if they recommend unrealistic positions to their clients. CPAs are subject to both the *Code of Professional Conduct* and the *Statements on Standards for Tax Services*, both products of the AICPA. The tax service standards provide guidance specific to the problems faced by tax practitioners. Practitioners who fail in their responsibilities face serious consequences.

Tax planning situations most often involve two or more alternatives that can be evaluated using net present value concepts to find the optimum strategy. Tax planning strategies include timing, income shifting, and changing the character of income. Good tax planning requires consideration of nontax factors as well as the legal doctrines that the IRS can invoke when a taxpayer takes excessive advantage of the tax law.

Tax research involves gathering the relevant facts, identifying issues, locating and evaluating relevant authorities, and communicating recommendations to the client. Both education and experience are necessary to identify the issues in a complex planning situation. The practitioner has both primary sources and secondary sources to aid in solving a tax research problem, but only primary sources should be cited. Primary sources include the Internal Revenue Code, Treasury Regulations, revenue rulings, and judicial opinions. Additional information can be found in congressional committee reports and the *Congressional Record*. Secondary sources include tax services, journal articles, and tax newsletters.

Tax practitioners must maintain an acceptable level of competence by keeping up with the ever-changing tax laws. There are many sources for studying new developments in both print and electronic media.

KEY TERMS

Business purpose doctrine 68
Committee report 72
Correspondence examination 50
Field examinations 50
Golsen rule 82
Internal Revenue Code 72
IRS Appeals Division 51
Letter ruling 74
90-day letter 51
Office examinations 50
Preparer tax identification number (PTIN) 54
Primary authority 70
Revenue procedures 75
Revenue rulings 75
Secondary authority 71
Statute of limitations 48
Step transaction doctrine 69
Substance-over-form doctrine 68
Substantial authority 54
Tax compliance 46
Tax cost 59
Tax planning 59
Tax savings 59
30-day letter 51
Treasury Regulations 78

TEST YOURSELF

Answers Appear after the Problem Assignments

1. George owns 1,000 shares of ABC stock that he purchased a little more than 11 months ago at a cost of $5 per share. The stock is now trading for $40 per share. George's tax advisor suggested that he wait another month before selling the stock. This is an example of which tax planning strategy?
   a. Avoiding income recognition
   b. Deferring income recognition
   c. Shifting income
   d. Changing the character of income

2. While preparing this year's tax return, a CPA discovers that the client has underpaid his income taxes due to an omission on last year's tax return, which was prepared by another accountant. According to the *Statement on Standards for Tax Services*, the CPA preparing this year's tax return:
   a. Must report it immediately to the IRS.
   b. Must advise the client of the omission and recommend appropriate action.
   c. Should refuse to sign the current tax return.
   d. Is not expected to address issues that relate to previous tax returns.

3. The primary purpose of effective tax planning is:
   a. Minimizing tax liability
   b. Repealing all federal taxes
   c. Converting capital gain into ordinary income
   d. Deferring deductions and accelerating income

4. Primary sources of authority include all of the following except:
   a. Treasury Regulations
   b. Tax Court decisions
   c. Internal Revenue Code
   d. Tax journals

5. Regarding the Small Case Division of the Tax Court, which of the following statements is correct?
   a. The IRS (but not the taxpayer) can appeal an adverse judgment.
   b. The taxpayer (but not the IRS) can appeal an adverse judgment.
   c. Either the IRS or the taxpayer can appeal an adverse judgment.
   d. Neither the IRS nor the taxpayer can appeal an adverse judgment.

PROBLEM ASSIGNMENTS

Check Your Understanding

1. [LO 2.1] What is the purpose of the DIF formula? What happens if someone has a high DIF score?

2. [LO 2.1] Describe the various types of audits.

3. [LO 2.1] If the taxpayer does not agree with proposed adjustments, what are the alternatives available to a taxpayer who receives a 30-day letter?

4. [LO 2.1] What alternatives are available when a taxpayer receives a 90-day letter?

5. [LO 2.1] Explain the meaning of hazards of litigation.

6. [LO 2.1] What are the three courts in which a taxpayer initiates tax litigation to settle a dispute with the IRS? To which courts can adverse decisions from these courts be appealed?

7. [LO 2.1] Your client, Teresa, claimed a deduction that the IRS agent disallowed upon audit. Teresa received a 30-day letter notifying her of the proposed additional tax liability of $1,050. Teresa is very upset by this assessment and tells you that she refuses to pay "another dime" and she wants to take this "all the way to the Supreme Court, if necessary." What advice should you give Teresa?

8. [LO 2.1] Do taxpayers face only monetary fines or can they be sentenced to jail?

9. [LO 2.1] What is a statute of limitations? What is its significance to taxpayers?

10. [LO 2.2] What is the difference between tax avoidance and tax evasion?

11. [LO 2.2] Can tax return preparers be assessed penalties?

12. [LO 2.2] Name three sources of guidance for tax professionals.

13. [LO 2.2] What are the *Statements on Standards for Tax Services*? Who issues them?

14. [LO 2.2] What guidelines are provided by the *Statement on Standards for Tax Services No. 3* regarding a CPA's reliance on information supplied by the client for use in preparing the client's tax return?

15. [LO 2.2] *Statement on Standards for Tax Services No. 4* states that a CPA may use estimates in completing a tax return. When would using estimates be appropriate in tax return preparation?

16. [LO 2.3] Distinguish tax planning from tax compliance.

17. [LO 2.3] For each of the following independent situations, identify whether the item would be primarily a tax or a nontax factor in tax planning.
   a. The taxpayer lost a quarter of her net worth when the dot-com bubble burst and does not want to own any investments with risk such as stocks.
   b. The taxpayer hates to pay any federal income taxes and would rather pay an equal amount of money to an accountant or attorney than pay taxes to the federal government.
   c. The taxpayer has a large capital loss carryforward from last year.

18. [LO 2.3] Beta Company, a sole proprietorship, anticipates $800,000 of taxable income for the year before considering additional projects. What marginal tax rate should it use in evaluating a project that may generate $200,000 of additional income?

19. [LO 2.3] Maria is a single individual with taxable income of $75,000 in 2018. What marginal tax rate should she use to determine the tax savings from a $2,000 deductible expense?

20. [LO 2.3] Identify three tax planning strategies.

21. [LO 2.3] Explain the business purpose doctrine.

22. [LO 2.4] What is the difference between primary authority and secondary authority?

23. [LO 2.4] Describe the basic steps in performing tax research.

24. [LO 2.4] What is a tax service?

25. [LO 2.4] As a bill proceeds through Congress, various committee reports are generated. What three committee reports typically are generated as a result of this process?

26. [LO 2.4] Why are committee reports useful to a tax researcher?

27. [LO 2.4] What uniquely numbered part of the Internal Revenue Code does a tax researcher usually cite?

28. [LO 2.4] In the citation Reg. §1.247-3, what do the 1 and the 247 indicate?

29. [LO 2.4] What is the difference between a legislative regulation and an interpretative regulation?

30. [LO 2.4] What is the difference between proposed and temporary regulations? What weight do they carry?

31. [LO 2.4] What is the difference between a letter ruling and a revenue ruling?

32. [LO 2.4] What signal does the IRS give taxpayers to indicate that a court decision will not be followed?

33. [LO 2.4] Explain the Golsen rule.

34. [LO 2.4] What information is found in a citator?

35. [LO 2.4] What does it mean when a Tax Court decision says that the decision has been entered under Rule 155?

36. [LO 2.4] What are the two documents that practitioners use to communicate the results of their tax research?

37. [LO 2.4] What are the four sections of a memo to the file? Explain what each section should include.

Crunch the Numbers

38. [LO 2.1] Adam files his tax return on April 15 and his tax return shows that he owes $3,000. Due to some bad planning, Adam could not pay his taxes when filing his tax return. Adam finally made his payment in full on July 10. What is the late-payment penalty that Adam will be assessed?

39. [LO 2.1] Robert decided not to file his return on April 15 because he knew that he could not pay the balance due. He files his return on August 3, paying the full $4,000 balance. What are Robert's expected late-payment/late-filing penalties?

40. [LO 2.1] Denise files her 2018 tax return on February 4, 2019. If there is no material understatement of income on her return and the return is properly signed and filed, when does the statute of limitations expire for Denise's 2018 tax return?

41. [LO 2.1] Kevin deliberately omitted $40,000 of gross income from his restaurant on his 2018 tax return. The return indicated gross income of $200,000 when filed on April 14, 2019. When can the IRS no longer pursue Kevin with the threat of collection of the related tax, interest, and penalties?

42. [LO 2.1] Alison accidentally omitted $40,000 of gross income from the restaurant she owned on her 2017 tax return. The return showed gross income of $150,000 when filed on October 15, 2018. When can the IRS no longer pursue Alison with the threat of collection of the related tax, interest, and penalties (assuming there was no fraud)?

43. [LO 2.1] Thomas received $30,000 in a legal settlement in 2018. The tax treatment of the item is not certain. Thomas's research results were ambiguous and he is not sure if the income is taxable. Because some doubt remained and because he did not think he would be audited, Thomas decided the income was not taxable and did not include it on his tax return filed on April 14, 2019. His gross income, excluding the $30,000 in question, was $50,000.
    a. When does the statute of limitations expire for Thomas's 2018 tax return?
    b. Would your answer change if the IRS can prove fraud?

44. [LO 2.3] Cynthia and Howard, married taxpayers filing a joint return, have $100,000 in taxable income in 2018. They have 4 children (ages 4 through 12) who have no income that is taxable. If they can legally shift $2,000 in taxable income to each child, how much does the family save in taxes?

45. [LO 2.3] The 4,000 shares of Medco stock that Diana purchased 11½ months ago for $12 per share are now trading at $19 per share. Diana's regular marginal tax rate is 32 percent and her tax rate for long-term capital gains is 15 percent.
    a. What is Diana's after-tax net cash flow from the sale if she sells the stock now?

b. What is Diana's after-tax net cash flow from the sale if she waits one month before selling the stock for $19 per share?
c. What do you recommend?

46. [LO 2.3] Monico Company is a cash-basis, calendar-year sole proprietorship. The owner, Rob, is in the 32 percent marginal tax bracket this year. If Monico bills its customers at the beginning of December, it will receive $5,000 of income prior to year-end. If it bills its customers at the end of December, it will not receive the $5,000 until January of next year.
a. If Rob expects his marginal tax rate to remain 32 percent next year, when should the company bill its customers? Use a 6 percent discount factor to explain your answer.
b. How would your answer change if Rob's expected marginal tax rate next year is only 24 percent? Explain.
c. How would your answer change if Rob's expected marginal tax rate next year is 35 percent? Explain.

47. [LO 2.3] Kimo Company is a cash-basis, calendar-year sole proprietorship. The owner, Karina, is in the 24 percent marginal tax bracket this year. Kimo owes a $15,000 expense that it may pay before the end of this year or in January of next year.
a. If Karina expects her marginal tax rate to be 24 percent next year, should Kimo pay the expense this year or next? Use a 7 percent discount factor to explain your answer.
b. How would your answer change if Karina's expected marginal tax rate next year is only 22 percent? Explain.
c. How would your answer change if Karina's expected marginal tax rate next year is 32 percent? Explain.

Develop Planning Skills

48. [LO 2.3] Jessica plans to invest $150,000 in a second business. She expects to generate a 12 percent before-tax return on her investment the first year. Her marginal tax rate is 32 percent due to the income from her other business. She needs to decide whether to establish this second business as a sole proprietorship or a C corporation.
a. Compute the after-tax cash flow from a sole proprietorship if she withdraws 50 percent of the profits from the business the first year. (Ignore employment taxes.)
b. Compute the after-tax cash flow from a C corporation if she receives a dividend equal to 50 percent of the before-tax profits from the business the first year.
c. What nontax factors should Jessica consider in making this decision?
d. What do you recommend?

49. [LO 2.3] Richard plans to invest $100,000 for a 50 percent interest in a small business. His friend, Jack, will also invest $100,000 for the remaining 50 percent interest. They expect to generate a 10 percent before-tax return on their investment the first year. Richard's marginal tax rate is 24 percent, and Jack's marginal tax rate is 32 percent. Their tax rate for capital gains and dividend income is 15 percent. They need to decide whether to establish the business as a partnership or a C corporation.
a. If they establish a partnership, compute the after-tax cash flow for each partner if each of them withdraws $4,000 of the profits from the business the first year. What is the amount of cash that remains in the partnership?
b. If they establish a C corporation, compute the after-tax cash flow for each shareholder if each of them receives a dividend of $4,000 from the profits of the business the first year. What is the amount of cash that remains in the C corporation?
c. What nontax factors should Richard and Jack consider in making this decision?
d. What you do recommend?

50. [LO 2.3] Norman considers the purchase of some investment land from his neighbor, Robin, a high school math teacher. Robin purchased the land 10 years ago for $6,000. They have agreed on payments of $800 every month for the next three years for a total of $28,800. They have not agreed on how much of each payment is interest and how much is principal. Norman thought that a fair interest

rate would be 8 percent, with the rest of each payment allocated to principal. Robin, however, said that he wanted to "give his neighbor a break" and have only 4 percent designated as interest with the rest of each payment allocated to principal. What difference does it make to Norman and to Robin how much is allocated to interest versus principal if the total of the cash payments will not change? Which interest rate would be better for Norman?

51. [LO 2.3] Debbie owns investment land that she purchased 10 years ago for $12,000. The land consists of two adjoining lots recently appraised at $80,000. She needs $40,000 cash for another investment opportunity and considers two alternatives: (1) sell half of the land for $40,000 or (2) borrow the $40,000 by taking out a mortgage on the land. Discuss the advantages and disadvantages of each alternative. What do you think Debbie should do?

52. [LO 2.3] The manager at Striker Corporation can hire either Ken, a marketing student, who will do research on a marketing plan, or Lisa, a tax student, who will research tax strategies to reduce corporate taxes. If she hires Ken, his wages and benefits will total $5,600 (all tax-deductible expenses). Ken's marketing plan is expected to generate $6,000 in new revenues with a probability of success estimated at 80 percent. If she hires Lisa, her wages and benefits will be $5,600 (also fully tax-deductible). Lisa's tax plan is expected to save Striker $6,000 in federal income taxes. The probability of success for this plan is estimated to be 75 percent. Striker's tax rate is 21 percent. Who should the manager hire?

53. [LO 2.3] Marlin Company, a sole proprietorship owned by Miguel, must decide between two mutually exclusive projects because it lacks sufficient personnel to complete both projects. Each project takes two years to complete and the project selected will be Marlin Company's only source of taxable income for the two years. Miguel is single and expects to have ordinary taxable income from other sources each year of $50,000 (after subtracting his standard deduction). The first job would generate $360,000 of revenues in the first year and $80,000 in the second year. Marlin estimates that this job will incur $200,000 of expenses in the first year and $40,000 of expenses in the second year. The second job will generate $220,000 of revenues and $120,000 of expenses in each of the two years. Assuming a 7 percent discount rate, which project should Marlin accept?

Think Outside the Text

These questions require answers that are beyond the material that is covered in this chapter.

54. [LO 2.1] From the perspective of both the taxpayer and the IRS, what are the advantages and disadvantages of the statute of limitations?

55. [LO 2.1] What type of penalty or incentive provision do you think would significantly improve compliance with the Internal Revenue Code? Do you think such a provision could be passed?

56. [LO 2.3] When Keith created a new corporation as the sole shareholder, he was advised by his accountant to treat 50 percent of the amount invested as a loan and 50 percent as a purchase of stock. Explain the advantages and disadvantages of this structure rather than a 100 percent stock purchase?

57. [LO 2.1, 2.3 & 2.4] Tax law provisions change over time. Explain how this affects tax planning and tax research.

58. [LO 2.4] Revenue-raising bills (such as tax bills) are supposed to originate in the House of Representatives. How could a senator initiate a tax bill?

59. [LO 2.4] How do rulings issued by the IRS benefit both the IRS and taxpayers?

Search the Internet

60. [LO 2.1] Go to *www.irs.gov* (the IRS website) and click on Careers under Work at IRS. Look under Resources, then under Job Descriptions, and finally look under Accounting, Budget & Finance to learn more about Internal Revenue Agent positions.

a. If you are a recent college graduate, how many hours of accounting are required to work for the IRS as an Internal Revenue Agent at the entry level?
b. Click on Learn the GS Schedule. What are the education requirements for GS-7 and GS-9?

61. [LO 2.1] Go to *www.irs.gov* (the IRS website) and locate Publication 971: Innocent Spouse Relief. What form must be filed to request innocent spouse relief?

62. [LO 2.1] Go to *www.irs.gov/irb/* (the IRS site containing Internal Revenue Bulletins). Locate and read IRS Notice 2008-14, 2008-4 IRB 310 and answer the following questions.
a. What is the penalty for filing a frivolous tax return?
b. What are the first three broad categories cited in this notice as examples of frivolous positions?

63. [LO 2.2] Go to the IRS site (*www.irs.gov*) and search for "Circular No. 230." Download a copy of *Treasury Circular 230: Regulations Governing Practice before the Internal Revenue Service*.
a. Read §10.33 and then list four best practices for tax advisors.
b. Read §10.37 regarding requirements for written advice. What six guidelines must a practitioner follow when giving written advice? Under what circumstances can a practitioner rely on the advice of others?

64. [LO 2.2] Go to *www.aicpa.org* (the AICPA's website) and search for Statements on Standards for Tax Services. Read the history section of the most recent version of the Statements on Standards for Tax Services. What reasons were provided for revising the SSTS?

65. [LO 2.4] Go to *www.irs.gov/irb/* (the IRS site containing Internal Revenue Bulletins). Locate the Definition of Terms section in a recent IRB. Differentiate between the following terms as used by the IRS in its rulings: amplified, modified, clarified, and distinguished.

66. [LO 2.4] Go to *www.ustaxcourt.gov* (the Tax Court site). What is the fee to file a small tax case?

Identify the Issues

Identify the tax issues or problems suggested by the following situations. State each issue as a question.

67. [LO 2.4] Your client, Barry Backache, suffers from a pain in the neck caused by arthritis. He installed a hot tub in his backyard. His doctor advised him that daily periods in the hot tub would relieve his pain in the neck.

68. [LO 2.4] Two months before the due date for his tax return, Simon provides his accountant with all the information necessary for filing his return. The accountant was overworked during tax season and filed the return after its due date.

69. [LO 2.4] Jennifer did not file a tax return for 2007 because she honestly believed that no tax was due. In 2018, the IRS audits Jennifer and the agent proposes a deficiency of $500.

70. [LO 2.4] On his 2013 tax return, Stewart inadvertently overstates deductions in excess of 25 percent of the adjusted gross income on his return. In 2018, the IRS audits Stewart and the agent proposes a deficiency of $1,000.

71. [LO 2.4] Georgia researched a major tax plan for a client. She discovered a case in a circuit that is not in the client's circuit that is unfavorable to the client. She has also found a revenue ruling that appears to have facts similar to her client's that sanctions the preferred alternative.

72. [LO 2.4] Bert has developed a position for a client on a potential tax transaction that he believes has approximately a 25 percent chance of surviving in a judicial proceeding.

73. [LO 2.4] In preparing the client's tax return, Verne must use a number of estimates supplied by his client because the client's computer records were corrupted and the client has not been able to retrieve the correct numbers in time to file the return by its due date. The client's tax returns have always included cents as well as dollars.

74. [LO 2.4] Jim was reviewing several of a client's prior tax returns in preparation for completing the current year's return. Jim discovered a serious error on the return filed almost three years earlier that would subject the client to $40,000 in additional taxes.

75. [LO 2.4] Last year, the IRS disallowed a deduction on a client's tax return when it was audited. The client wants you to deduct a similar item on this year's tax return.

Develop Research Skills

76. [LO 2.4] Your client, Ms. I. M. Gorgeous, is an aspiring actress. She has managed to earn a living doing television commercials but was unable to get the acting parts she really wanted. She decided to have botox injections in her forehead and collagen enhancements to her lips. After these procedures, her career improved dramatically and she received several movie offers. Ms. Gorgeous is sure that she should be able to deduct the cost of the cosmetic enhancements because she read about another actress having a face lift in 1988 and deducting the cost on her tax return as a medical expense. Can Ms. Gorgeous deduct the cost of these procedures? [Research Aid: Section 213(d)(9)]

77. [LO 2.4] Last year your client, Barney Bumluck, worked part-time for Timely Tax Return Preparation Service. Barney was promised an hourly wage plus a commission. He worked under this arrangement from early February until April 15. His accrued pay amounted to $900 plus $120 of commissions. When he went to collect his pay, however, he found only a vacant office with a sign on the door reading "Nothing is sure but death and taxes." Can Barney take a bad debt deduction for the wages and commission he was unable to collect? [Research Aid: Reg. Section 1.166–1(e)]

78. [LO 2.4] Your clients, Sonny and his wife, Honey, believe in worshiping Ta-Ra, the Sun God. To practice their religious beliefs, they take a weeklong trip to Hawaii to worship Ta-Ra. The cost of this pilgrimage (including airfare, hotel, and meals) is $2,800. Sonny wants to know if he can deduct the cost of this trip as a charitable contribution to his religion.

79. [LO 2.4] Fred Fisher is a licensed scuba diver who lives in Key Largo. He is employed full-time as an engineer. Five years ago he had been employed as a professional diver for a salvage company. While working for the salvage company, he became interested in marine archaeology and treasure hunting. Until last year he gave diving lessons on weekends and trained individuals in the sport of treasure hunting under the name of "Fred's Diving School." Three of the diving students he taught subsequently found shipwrecks. Fred generally did not engage in recreational diving.

Last year, Fred began a treasure-hunting business named "Treasure Seekers Company." He bought a boat specifically designed for treasure hunting and did extensive research on potential locations of shipwrecks. Fred located several shipwrecks, but none were of substantial value. He did retrieve several artifacts but has not sold any yet. Although these artifacts may have some historical significance, they have a limited marketability. Thus, Fred has not yet had any gross income from his treasure hunting activities.

Other than retaining check stubs and receipts for his expenses and an encoded log, Fred did not maintain formal records for Treasure Seekers Company. Fred maintains as few written records as possible because he fears for his safety. He took steps to keep his boat and equipment from public view and took precautionary measures to maintain the secrecy of his search areas. Fred incurred $5,000 of expenses relating to his treasure-hunting activities last year. Can Fred deduct the expenses of his treasure-hunting business, or will the IRS claim it is a hobby and disallow the expenses?

80. [LO 2.4] Locate and read *Greg McIntosh*, TC Memo 2001-144, 81 TCM 1772, RIA TC Memo 2001-144 (6/19/2001). Answer the following questions.

a. What requirements must be met for a taxpayer to recover litigation costs from the IRS?

b. Was the taxpayer in this case able to recover his attorney fees from the IRS? Why or why not?

81. [LO 2.4] Locate and read the following two cases:

J.B.S. Enterprises, Inc., TC Memo 1991-254, 61 TCM 2829, 1991 PH TC Memo 91,254

Summit Publishing Company, Inc., TC Memo 1990-288, 59 TCM 833, 1990 PH TC Memo 90,288

List those facts that you feel most influenced the judges to reach different conclusions in these two cases.

ANSWERS TO TEST YOURSELF

1. **d.** Changing the character of income
2. **b.** Must advise the client of the omission and recommend appropriate action.
3. **a.** Minimizing tax liability
4. **d.** Tax journals
5. **d.** Neither the IRS nor the taxpayer can appeal an adverse judgment.

APPENDIX: AUTHORITIES FOR SAMPLE RESEARCH PROBLEM

CURRENT INTERNAL REVENUE CODE

119(a) Meals and Lodging Furnished to Employee, his Spouse, and his Dependents, Pursuant To Employment.

There shall be excluded from gross income of an employee the value of any meals or lodging furnished to him, his spouse, or any of his dependents by or on behalf of his employer for the convenience of the employer, but only if—

119(a)(1) in the case of meals, the meals are furnished on the business premises of the employer, or . . .

119(b)(4) Meals Furnished to Employees on Business Premises Where Meals of Most Employees are Otherwise Excludable.

All meals furnished on the business premises of an employer to such employer's employees shall be treated as furnished for the convenience of the employer if, without regard to this paragraph, more than half of the employees to whom such meals are furnished on such premises are furnished such meals for the convenience of the employer . . .

132(e)De Minimis Fringe Defined.

For purposes of this section—

132(e)(1) IN GENERAL.—The term "de minimis fringe" means any property or service the value of which is (after taking into account the frequency with which similar fringes are provided by the employer to the employer's employees) so small as to make accounting for it unreasonable or administratively impracticable.

132(e)(2) TREATMENT OF CERTAIN EATING FACILITIES.—The operation by an employer of any eating facility for employees shall be treated as a de minimis fringe if—

132(e)(2)(A) such facility is located on or near the business premises of the employer, and

132(e)(2)(B) revenue derived from such facility normally equals or exceeds the direct operating costs of such facility.

The preceding sentence shall apply with respect to any highly compensated employee only if access to the facility is available on substantially the same terms to each member of a group of employees which is defined under a reasonable classification set up by the employer which does not discriminate in favor of highly compensated employees. For purposes of subparagraph (B), an employee entitled under section 119 to exclude the value of a meal provided at such facility shall be treated as having paid an amount for such meal equal to the direct operating costs of the facility attributable to such meal.

274(n) Only 50 Percent of Meal Expenses Allowed as Deduction (as amended by the Tax Cuts and Jobs Act)

274(n)(1) In general. The amount allowable as a deduction under this chapter for any expense for food or beverages shall not exceed 50 percent of the amount of such expense which would (but for this paragraph) be allowable as a deduction under this chapter . . .

274(o) Meals Provided at Convenience of Employer

No deduction shall be allowed under this chapter for

(1) any expense for the operation of a facility described in section 132(e)(2), and any expense for food or beverages, including under section 132(e)(1), associated with such facility, or

(2) any expense for meals described in section 119(a) . . .

effective for amounts incurred or paid after December 31, 2025.

Prior to the Tax Cuts and Jobs Act of 2017, Section 274(n) read as follows:

274(n)(1) IN GENERAL.—The amount allowable as a deduction under this chapter for—

274(n)(1)(A) any expense for food or beverages, and

274(n)(1)(B) any item with respect to an activity which is of a type generally considered to constitute entertainment, amusement, or recreation, or with respect to a facility used in connection with such activity, shall not exceed 50 percent of the amount of such expense or item which would (but for this paragraph) be allowable as a deduction under this chapter.

274(n)(2) EXCEPTIONS.—Paragraph (1) shall not apply to any expense if—

274(n)(2)(A) such expense is described in paragraph (2), (3), (4), (7), (8), or (9) of subsection (e).

274(n)(2)(B) in the case of an expense for food or beverages, such expense is excludable from the gross income of the recipient under section 132 by reason of subsection (e) thereof (relating to de minimis fringes) . . .

Current Internal Revenue Code, History Notes, Section 274 (n) 1993, Omnibus Budget Reconciliation Act of 1993 (P.L. 103-66)

P.L. 103-66, §13209(a): Amended Code Sec. 274(n)(1) by striking "80 percent" and inserting "50 percent". Effective for tax years beginning after 12-31-93.

P.L. 103-66, §13209(b): Amended Code Sec. 274(n) by striking "80" in the subsection heading and inserting "50". Effective for tax years beginning after 12-31-93.

FEDERAL TAX REGULATIONS

Regulation 1.119-1., Internal Revenue Service, Meals and lodging furnished for the convenience of the employer

(a) *Meals*

(1) ***In general.***—The value of meals furnished to an employee by his employer shall be excluded from the employee's gross income if two tests are met: (i) The meals are furnished on the business premises of the employer, and (ii) the meals are furnished for the convenience of the employer. The question of whether meals are furnished for the convenience of the employer is one of fact to be determined by analysis of all the facts and circumstances in each case. If the tests described in subdivisions (i) and (ii) of this subparagraph are met, the exclusion shall apply irrespective of whether under an employment contract or a statute fixing the terms of employment such meals are furnished as compensation.

(2) ***Meals furnished without a charge***

(i) Meals furnished by an employer without charge to the employee will be regarded as furnished for the convenience of the employer if such meals are furnished for a substantial noncompensatory business reason of the employer. If an employer furnishes meals as a means of providing additional compensation to his employee (and not for a substantial noncompensatory business reason of the employer), the meals so furnished will not be regarded as furnished for the convenience of the employer. Conversely, if the employer furnishes meals to his employee for a substantial noncompensatory business reason, the meals so furnished will be regarded as furnished for the convenience of the employer, even though such meals are also furnished for a compensatory reason. In determining the reason of an employer for furnishing meals, the mere declaration that meals are furnished for a noncompensatory business reason is not sufficient to prove that meals are furnished for the convenience of the employer, but such determination will be based upon an examination of all the surrounding facts and circumstances. In subdivision (ii) of this subparagraph, there are set forth some of the substantial noncompensatory business reasons which occur frequently and which justify the conclusion that meals furnished for such a reason are furnished for the convenience of the employer. In subdivision (iii) of this subparagraph, there are set forth some of the business reasons which are considered to be compensatory and which, in the absence of a substantial noncompensatory business reason, justify the conclusion that meals furnished for such a reason are not furnished for the convenience of the employer. Generally, meals furnished before or after the working hours of the employee will not be regarded as furnished for the convenience of the employer, but see subdivision (ii) (*d*) and (*f*) of this subparagraph for some exceptions to this general rule. Meals furnished on nonworking days do not qualify for the exclusion under section 119. If the employee is required to occupy living quarters on the business premises of his employer as a condition of his employment (as defined in paragraph (b) of this section), the exclusion applies to the value of any meal furnished without charge to the employee on such premises.

(ii)

(a) Meals will be regarded as furnished for a substantial noncompensatory business reason of the employer when the meals are furnished to the employee during his working hours to have the employee available for emergency call during his meal period. In order to demonstrate that meals are furnished to the employee to have the employee available for emergency call during the meal period, it must be shown that emergencies have actually occurred, or can reasonably be expected to occur, in the employer's business which have resulted, or will result, in the employer calling on the employee to perform his job during his meal period.

(b) Meals will be regarded as furnished for a substantial noncompensatory business reason of the employer when the meals are furnished to the employee during his working hours because the employer's business is such that the employee must be restricted to a short meal period, such as 30 or 45 minutes, and because the employee could not be expected to eat elsewhere in such a short meal period. For example, meals may qualify under this subdivision when the employer is engaged in a business in which the peak workload occurs during the normal lunch hours. However, meals cannot qualify under this subdivision (b) when the reason for restricting the time of the meal period is so that the employee can be let off earlier in the day.

(c) Meals will be regarded as furnished for a substantial noncompensatory business reason of the employer when the meals are furnished to the employee during his working hours because the employee could not otherwise secure proper meals within a reasonable meal period. For example, meals may qualify under this subdivision (c) when there are insufficient eating facilities in the vicinity of the employer's premises.

(d) A meal furnished to a restaurant employee or other food service employee for each meal period in which the employee works will be regarded as furnished for a substantial noncompensatory business reason of the employer, irrespective of whether the meal is furnished during, immediately before, or immediately after the working hours of the employee.

(e) If the employer furnishes meals to employees at a place of business and the reason for furnishing the meals to each of substantially all of the employees who are furnished the meals is a substantial noncompensatory business reason of the employer, the meals furnished to each other employee will also be regarded as furnished for a substantial noncompensatory business reason of the employer . . .

(c) ***Business premises of the employer.***

(1) *In general.* For purposes of this section, the term "business premises of the employer" generally means the place of employment of the employee.

BOYD GAMING CORPORATION

Boyd Gaming Corporation, f.k.a the Boyd Group and Subsidiaries, Petitioner-Appellant v. Commissioner of Internal Revenue, Respondent-Appellee, U.S. Court of Appeals, Ninth Circuit (May 12, 1999)

U.S. Court of Appeals, 9th Circuit, 177 F3d 1096, 99-1 USTC ¶50,530, 83 AFTR 2d 99-2354, reversing the Tax Court, 74 TCM 759, TC Memo. 1997-445, 1997 RIA TC Memo ¶97,445.

Charles L. Almond and Marie R. Yeates, Vinson & Elkins, Houston, Texas, for the petitioners-appellants. Annette M. Wietecha, United States Department of Justice, Tax Division, Washington, D.C., for the respondent-appellee. Gregory R. Smith, Irell & Manella, Los Angeles, California, for the amicus curiae.

Before: FERNANDEZ and MCKEOWN and WEINER.

OPINION

MCKEOWN, Circuit Judge:

This case involves the question whether there really is a "free lunch." In 1986, concerned that the tax laws unfairly allowed high-income taxpayers to structure their business affairs in a manner that generated deductions for personal living expenses, Congress imposed, with certain exceptions, an 80% cap on the amount of deductions for business meals and entertainment. This change, in turn, affected employers who provide "free lunches" to their employees. At issue in this case is whether, under the circumstances here, the employer qualifies for an exception to the 80% cap on deductions associated with "free lunches" furnished to its employees.

Petitioners, California Hotel & Casino, Boyd Gaming Corporation, and their subsidiaries (collectively, "Boyd"), are hotel and casino operators that, for reasons of security and logistics, require their employees to stay on the business premises throughout the work shift. As a consequence of the policy, the employees receive free meals at on-site cafeterias. Boyd contends that it is exempt from the 80% cap on deductions because the meals are provided as a "de minimis fringe" benefit. 26 U.S.C. §274(n)(2); *see* 26 U.S.C. §132(e). Boyd argues that the meals at issue meet the statutory test for "*de minimis* fringe" benefits because they were furnished to "more than half" the employees for the "convenience of the employer." 26 U.S.C. §132(e); *see* 26 U.S.C. §119(a) & (b)(4).

The Tax Court rejected Boyd's "convenience of the employer" argument and held that Boyd's deductions for employee meals were limited to 80% of the related expenses under the general rule of section 274(n). *Boyd Gaming Corp. v.* Commissioner, T.C. Memo. 1997-445 at 3, 79, 74 T.C.M. 759, RIA TC Memo 97,445 (1997). We disagree. Boyd's "stay-on-premises" requirement rendered the employee meals furnished for the "convenience of the employer," and the meals therefore constituted "*de minimis* fringe" benefits. We have jurisdiction pursuant to 26 U.S.C. §7482, and we reverse.

I. BACKGROUND

A. The "Stay-On-Premises" Policy

During the 1987 and 1988 taxable years, Boyd operated four casino and hotel properties in Las Vegas, Nevada: (i) the Stardust Resort & Casino; (ii) the California Hotel & Casino; (iii) the Fremont Hotel & Casino; and (iv) Sam's Town Hotel & Gambling Hall. These properties are open to the public 24 hours a day, seven days a week. Each property operates an on-site cafeteria facility, separate from the public restaurants, where employees can obtain free meals during their work shifts. In addition, approximately 10% of Boyd's employees (primarily managerial and supervisory personnel) are permitted to eat in the on-site public restaurants at no charge.

In a Stipulation of Facts before the Tax Court, the Commissioner of Internal Revenue conceded that Boyd imposed on its employees a "stay-on-premises" requirement, except when overridden by union contract:

During the years at issue, petitioners required their employees to stay on the Properties' premises during their entire shift, except where overridden by union contract or absent permission from a supervisor/manager. An employee who left during his or her shift, without authorization, was subject to disciplinary action, up to and including discharge.

Boyd offers multiple reasons for imposition of the "stay-on-premises" policy, including addressing security and efficiency concerns, maintaining work force control, handling business emergencies and continuous customer demands, and the impracticality of obtaining meals within a reasonable proximity. In response, the Commissioner argues that the evidence did not support these reasons and, in any event, that there was no business nexus between the "stay-on-premises" requirement and the meals furnished to employees.

B. Tax Court's Treatment of Meal Expense Deductions

Boyd claims that it is entitled to deduct 100% of the expenses associated with the meals provided to its employees for the 1987 and 1988 taxable years. The Commissioner sent Boyd notices of deficiency resulting from disagreement over the appropriate level of deduction. Boyd petitioned for redetermination of the deficiencies pursuant to 26 U.S.C. §6213(a).

The Tax Court issued two rulings that set the stage for this appeal. Upon cross-motions for partial summary judgment, the Tax Court held that Boyd would qualify for the exception to the 80% cap if it could establish factually that the meals furnished to its employees constituted a "*de minimis* fringe" benefit. *Boyd Gaming Corp. v.* Commissioner, 106 T.C. 343, 344, 353 (1996). As a result of this ruling, which has not been appealed, the Tax Court set the case for trial to determine whether Boyd fell within the exception.

Following trial, the Tax Court held, pursuant to certain Internal Revenue Service ("IRS") regulations, that Boyd did not furnish meals to "substantially all" of its employees for the "convenience of the employer," and thus, could not deduct more than 80% of the meal expenses. *Boyd Gaming*, T.C. Memo. 1997-445 at 3, 79. This latter ruling is the subject of this appeal. As discussed below, the landscape for the Tax Court's decision was altered when Congress substituted a statutory threshold of "more than half" for the prior regulatory requirement of "substantially all."

II. STANDARD OF REVIEW

The taxpayer bears the burden of showing entitlement to a particular deduction . . .

III. ANALYSIS

This case turns on whether Boyd provided the employee meals for its own "convenience." Before analyzing the issue of "convenience," we first outline the statutes that lead to this test of deductibility.

A. The 80% Cap

The "convenience" test, which Boyd must satisfy to be exempt from the 80% cap on food and beverage expenses, stems from the statutory exception to the cap. During the taxable years at issue, 26 U.S.C. §274(n) limited the amount of a deduction for food or beverages to 80% of the associated expenses. The 80% cap, however, did not apply if the food or beverage expense was "excludable from the gross income of the recipient" under 26 U.S.C. §132(e). 26 U.S.C. §274(n)(2). In general, section 132 excludes "*de minimis* fringe" benefits from an employee's gross income. *See* 26 U.S.C. §132(a)(4). Section 132 further defines as a "de minimis fringe" an employer's operation of an eating facility for employees if the facility meets the following criteria:

(a) such facility is located on or near the business premises of the employer, and
(b) revenue derived from such facility normally equals or exceeds the direct operating costs of such facility.

26 U.S.C. §132(e)(2).

Boyd's facilities were located on the business premises and therefore satisfied subsection (A). For the taxable years at issue, however, Boyd did not charge for the meals and hence could not establish by direct evidence that it met the revenue/operating cost test of subsection (B). Thus, Boyd must rely on a statutory presumption, which treats revenue as equal to operating costs for meals furnished to employees who are entitled to exclude the value of the meals from their gross income pursuant to 26 U.S.C. §119. 26 U.S.C. §132(e). Under section 119, an employee may exclude meals furnished on the business premises of the employer for the "convenience of the employer." 26 U.S.C. §119(a). The applicability of the 80% cap therefore turns on whether Boyd provided the meals at issue for its own convenience.

B. For the Convenience of the Employer

The term "convenience of the employer" is not defined by statute. IRS regulations, however, consider meals as furnished for the "convenience of the employer" if they are provided for a "substantial noncompensatory business reason. "26 C.F.R. §1.119-1(a)(2)(i). The regulations outline a number of circumstances under which meals are treated as furnished for a "substantial noncompensatory business reason." In addition, the regulations define a catch-all provision, which allows an employer to impute a "substantial noncompensatory business reason" for provision of the meals.

Two questions arise: What business reasons meet the test and how many employees must be covered? We address the latter issue first because a recent statute provides a conclusive answer.

1. The Catch-All Provision

Before the Tax Court, Boyd sought to invoke the regulatory catch-all provision, which provides:

If the employer furnishes meals to employees at a place of business and the reason for furnishing the meals to each of substantially all of the employees who are furnished the meals is a substantial noncompensatory business reason of the employer, the meals furnished to each other employee will also be regarded as furnished for a substantial noncompensatory business reason of the employer.

26 C.F.R. §1.119-1(a)(2)(ii)(e) (emphasis added). IRS regulations provide no precise numerical definition for the term "substantially all." The meaning of the phrase, however, is no longer relevant here. In 1998, Congress adopted a statutory catch-all provision, changing the threshold requirement from "substantially all" to "more than half" of the employees:

All meals furnished on the business premises of an employer to such employer's employees shall be treated as furnished for the convenience of the employer if, without regard to this paragraph, more than half of the employees to whom such meals are furnished on such premises are furnished such meals for the convenience of the employer.

26 U.S.C. §119(b)(4) (emphasis added). Section 119(b)(4) was explicitly given retroactive effect. Pub. L. No. 105-206, §5002(b), 112 Stat. 685, 788 (1998).

On appeal, Boyd relies on the more favorable statutory catch-all mechanism. Based just on the parties' stipulations, Boyd comes close, but does not quite trigger the catch-all provision. The Commissioner conceded that, depending on the property, between roughly 41% and 48% of Boyd's employees received meals during the 1987 and 1988 taxable years for the "convenience of the employer." Finding Boyd a few percentage points short of the "more than half" threshold, we must move beyond the stipulations and examine whether Boyd can satisfy the "convenience of the employer" standard for the requisite number of employees.

2. Substantial Noncompensatory Business Reasons

Boyd argued to the Tax Court that it provided employee meals for one or more of the generally accepted business reasons outlined in the regulations, including employee availability for emergencies, short meal periods, and coverage as a food service employee. *See* 26 C.F.R. §1.119-1(a)(2)(ii). Boyd also contended that its "stay-on-premises" policy constituted a "substantial non-compensatory business reason" for furnishing meals. The Tax Court rejected Boyd's arguments. We hold that the Tax Court erred with respect to Boyd's "stay-on-premises" requirement.

For guidance, we look to the Supreme Court's decision in *Commissioner v. Kowalski* [77-2 USTC 9748], 434 U.S. 77 (1977). The Court examined the history of section 119 and concluded that the "convenience of the employer" should be measured according to a "business-necessity" theory. *Id.* at 93 (citing *Van Rosen v. Commissioner* [CCH Dec. 18,635], 17 T.C. 834, 838-40 (1951)). Under that theory, the exclusion from gross income applies only when the employee must accept the meals "in order properly to perform his duties." *Id.* (quoting S. Rep. No. 1622, 83d Cong., 2d Sess. at 190 (1954)). The Tax Court here seized on this language to support its conclusion that "[s]ection 119 requires a closer and better documented connection between the necessities of the employer's business and the furnishing of free meals." T.C. Memo. 1997-445 at 77. We view the Tax Court as both misreading Kowalski and attempting to second guess Boyd's business judgment.

Kowalski is consistent with our earlier decision, *Caratan v. Commissioner*, 442 F.2d 606, 71-1 USTC 9353, 40 AFTR 2d 77-6128 (9th Cir. 1971), in which we held that the Tax Court may not substitute a business judgment that is contrary to the unimpeached and uncontradicted evidence presented by the taxpayer. *Id.* at 609-10 . . .

We find *Caratan* analogous to the case now before us. Boyd has adopted a "stay-on-premises" requirement and, as a consequence, furnishes meals to its employees because they cannot leave the casino properties during their shifts. Common sense dictates that once the policy was embraced, the "captive" employees had no choice but to eat on the premises. As with the lodging in *Caratan*, the furnished meals here were, in effect, "indispensable to the proper discharge" of the employees' duties.

Contrary to the Tax Court's conclusion, no nexus other than the "stay-on-premises" policy was required for the meals to satisfy the Kowalski test. Indeed, the Commissioner's argument that the meals must be linked to an employee's specific duties would render the test virtually impossible to satisfy; only restaurant critics and dieticians could meet such a test. The Commissioner's position is also inconsistent with the IRS regulations themselves, which envision that meals furnished to employees who are similarly confined to the business premises during meal times, but for different reasons (*i.e.*, remote location, insufficient eating facilities in the vicinity), are provided for the "convenience of the employer" and satisfy the *Kowalski* test. *See* 26 C.F.R. §1.119-1(a)(2)(ii)(c) & (f)(7). For these purposes, we can discern no logical distinction between workers isolated by geography and those isolated by employer policy.

We caution that it would not have been enough for Boyd simply to wave a "magic wand" and say it had a policy in order to be entitled to a deduction. Instead, Boyd was required to and did support its closed campus policy with adequate evidence of legitimate business reasons. While reasonable minds might differ regarding whether a "stay-on-premises" policy is necessary for security and logistics, the fact remains that the casinos here operate under this policy. Given the credible and uncontradicted evidence regarding the reasons underlying the "stay-on-premises" policy, we find it inappropriate to second guess these reasons or to substitute a different business judgment for that of Boyd.

As a result of the "stay-on-premises" requirement, "more than half" of Boyd's employees received the free meals for the "convenience of the employer," and thus Boyd is entitled to invoke the catch-all provision of section 119(b)(4). We hold that, for the taxable years at issue, Boyd may deduct 100% of the expenses associated with its employee cafeterias.

REVERSED.

IRS Announcement 99-77, I.R.B. 1999-32, July 21, 1999.

Employer-employee relationship: Casino: Fringe benefits: On-site employee meals: Convenience of employer: IRS position: Action on Decision: Acquiescence.

The IRS is taking three actions in response to the opinion issued by the U.S. Court of Appeals for the Ninth Circuit in Boyd Gaming Corp. Pursuant to that ruling, free meals provided by a casino operator to its employees at on-site cafeterias were de minimis fringe benefits furnished for the employer's convenience . . .

First, the Solicitor General has decided not to file a petition for a writ of certiorari with the United States Supreme Court with respect to the Ninth Circuit's opinion. Accordingly, the Service announces today that it acquiesces in the Ninth Circuit's opinion in Boyd Gaming Corporation. The acquiescence will appear in 1999-32 I.R.B. (August 9, 1999), and a copy of the Action on Decision memorandum in support of that acquiescence accompanies this announcement . . .

Action on Decision

Subject: Boyd Gaming Corporation v. Commissioner,—F.3d—(9th Cir. 1999), rev'g T.C. Memo. 1997-445 T.C. Dkt. Nos. 3433-95, 3434-95

Issue: Whether a meal furnished by the taxpayer/employer on its business premises to an employee is furnished for "the convenience of the employer" within the meaning of that phrase in section 119 of the Internal Revenue Code.

Discussion: Section 119 of the Internal Revenue Code provides that an employee's gross income does not include the value of any meal furnished to him in kind by or on behalf of his employer for the convenience of the employer if the meal is furnished on the employer's business premises. Treas. Reg. §1.119-1(a)(2) provides that a meal is furnished for "the convenience of the employer" if it is furnished for a substantial noncompensatory business reason of the employer. Whether an employer-provided meal is furnished for "the convenience of the employer" is important to the employer for federal tax purposes because the interplay of sections 119, 132, and 274 of the Internal Revenue Code determines whether the employer can fully deduct the cost of the meal.

During the years in issue, the taxpayer furnished free meals on its business premises to all of its employees, most of whom were required to stay on the taxpayer's business premises during their working hours primarily because of the particular security concerns of the casino industry. The taxpayer argued that, because its employees were required to remain on its business premises during their working hours, the meals it provided to its employees were provided for a substantial noncompensatory business reason.

The Tax Court held that the taxpayer's stay-on-the-business-premises requirement did not satisfy the convenience-of-the-employer requirement of section 119, determining that there must be a "closer and better documented connection between the necessities of the employer's business and the furnishing of free meals."

The Ninth Circuit reversed the Tax Court decision. The Ninth Circuit found that the taxpayer's particular security and other business-related concerns provided sufficient justification for its policy of requiring employees to stay on the employer's business premises to satisfy "the convenience of the employer" test of section 119. Specifically, the Ninth Circuit stated that—

Boyd was required to and did support its closed campus policy with adequate evidence of legitimate business reasons. While reasonable minds might differ regarding whether a "stay-on-the-premises" policy is necessary for security and logistics, the fact remains that the casinos here operate under this policy. Given the credible and uncontradicted evidence regarding the [business] reasons underlying the "stay-on-the-premises" policy, it is inappropriate to second guess these reasons or to substitute a different business judgment for that of Boyd.

In light of the Ninth Circuit's opinion, the Service will not challenge whether meals provided to employees of casino businesses similar to that operated by Boyd Gaming meet the section 119 "convenience of the employer" test where the employer's business policies and practices would otherwise preclude employees from obtaining a proper meal within a reasonable meal period. A bona fide and enforced policy that requires employees to stay on the employer's business premises during their normal meal period is only one example of the type of business practice that could justify the employer's providing of meals that would qualify for section 119 treatment. Another example could be a practice requiring "check-out" procedures for employees leaving the premises in order to address the same type of security concerns that were relevant in Boyd Gaming where these procedures have the same practical effect.

More generally, in applying section 119 and Treas. Reg. §1.119-1, the Service will not attempt to substitute its judgment for the business decisions of an employer as to what specific business policies and practices are best suited to addressing the employer's business concerns. By the same token, to paraphrase the Ninth Circuit, "it would not [be] enough for [an employer] to wave a 'magic wand' and say it had a policy in order [for meals to qualify under section 119]." Thus, the Service will consider whether the policies decided upon by the employer are reasonably related to the needs of the employer's business (apart from a desire to provide additional compensation to its employees) and whether these policies are in fact followed in the actual conduct of the business. If such reasonable procedures are adopted and applied, and they preclude employees from obtaining a proper meal off the employer's business premises during a reasonable meal period, section 119 will apply.

Recommendation: Acquiescence

Income, Expenses, and Individual Taxes

PART II

CHAPTER 3 Determining Gross Income

CHAPTER OUTLINE

LEARNING OBJECTIVES

After completing this chapter, you should be able to:

3.1 Explain the differences between income concepts applicable to financial and tax accounting.

3.2 Explain how the tax year and accounting methods affect the recognition of taxable income.

3.3 Describe the effect that the assignment of income doctrine and community property laws have on income recognition.

3.4 Identify how different sources of unearned income are taxed.

3.5 List the most common income exclusions and explain the rationale for excluding them from taxation.

3.6 Describe the framework for multijurisdictional taxation and identify basic issues in international taxation.

The term gross income includes income from all sources unless a specific provision in the tax law excludes it. Certain types of income are excluded from gross income for social, economic, or political reasons. Taxes, however, are levied on taxable income rather than gross income. Taxable income is defined as gross income, net of exclusions, less allowable deductions. This chapter focuses on determining those items included in gross income and identifying the period in which they are included (recognized).

Income for tax purposes differs from financial statement income, because the objectives of tax policy are different than those of generally accepted accounting principles. Basic tax principles affect the determination of gross income, including the realization principle, the return of capital principle, the doctrine of constructive receipt, and the claim of right. In addition, the taxpayer's method of accounting determines the period in which income is recognized. Identifying the period in which income is recognized is important because a taxpayer's marginal tax rate may change, the tax laws may change, and the affect the time value of money has on the value of a dollar paid in taxes.

This chapter discusses the taxability of interest, dividends, annuities, government transfer payments, legal settlements, and prizes. These items normally result in taxable income to the recipient, but exceptions may render some or all of the amount received as nontaxable. The most common income exclusions are discussed along with several provisions that postpone income recognition to a later period. Most exclusions result from congressional action designed to achieve specific policy objectives such as subsidizing certain activities or minimizing the impact of double taxation.

Which taxing authority has the jurisdiction or legal right to tax income earned by an individual or business? The criteria used by a government to assert its right to tax income may be based on the geographical source of the income, the taxpayer's citizenship, or the taxpayer's residence. Multijurisdictional taxpayers must determine how to allocate income to each affected tax jurisdiction. There is only a single U.S. Internal Revenue Code, but there are different tax codes for each country in which taxpayers may be required to pay taxes. As a result, tax practice in the multijurisdictional arena can be extremely challenging.

SETTING THE STAGE—AN INTRODUCTORY CASE

Steven, an individual taxpayer, is subject to a 37 percent marginal tax rate on his ordinary income and a maximum 20 percent tax rate on his long-term capital gains. He has $50,000 to invest for the next five years, after which he plans to liquidate his investment and start his own consulting business. He has identified three investment alternatives: (1) corporate bonds yielding 6 percent before tax with the interest reinvested at 6 percent before tax; (2) general revenue bonds issued by his municipality yielding 4 percent, with the interest reinvested at 4 percent; (3) land that is expected to increase in value by 6 percent each year. Which investment alternative should Steven choose? We will return to this case at the end of this chapter.

3.1 WHAT IS INCOME?

The Internal Revenue Code's definition of *income* is extremely broad. The opening phrase of Section 61(a) provides a general all-inclusive definition of **gross income** by stating "[e]xcept as otherwise provided in this subtitle, gross income means all income from whatever source derived. . . ." Although it lists a number of included items, such as rents, interest, and dividends, two things provide a more definitive explanation of those items that must be included in income. First, courts adopted the accounting concept that income is measured only when a realization event occurs for tax purposes. This is known as the **realization principle**, which states income cannot be recognized (included in gross income) until the taxpayer has realization. Realization usually takes place when there is an arm's-length transaction, such as the sale of goods or the rendering of services.[1] Fluctuations in value are not recognized in income unless that change is realized through a transaction.[2]

Example 3.1

Ambler Company purchased 500 shares of XYZ Company stock at $5 per share. At the end of the year, XYZ stock is trading at $12 per share. Although Ambler's wealth has increased by $3,500 ($7 per share), it has no taxable income from this increase in wealth until the stock is sold and the income is realized.

Second, the tax laws themselves have been refined and amended to either include or exclude a number of other specific items from income. For example, Section 61 specifically mentions interest as taxable, but Section 103 excludes interest earned on bonds issued by a state or a local municipality from gross income.

[1] An arm's-length transaction is one in which both the buyer and seller have bargained in good faith and for their own benefit.
[2] *Eisner v. Macomber*, 252 US 189 (1920).

3.1.1 TAXABLE VERSUS GROSS INCOME

Taxable income is the base against which tax rates are applied to compute the taxpayer's tax liability. Taxable income is gross income less allowable deductions.[3] The determination of items included in gross income does not vary by taxpayer. The Internal Revenue Code applies uniformly, regardless of whether the taxpayer is a business or an individual.[4] Deductions from gross income differ for individuals and businesses, however. Businesses are generally allowed to deduct all ordinary and necessary expenses of operating the business. Individuals are also allowed to deduct their business expenses (but their deductions may be limited). Additionally, individuals are allowed a deduction for a limited amount of personal expenses or the standard deduction. Regardless of the taxpayer, the starting point is always gross income. Unless a specific provision in tax law excludes an income item from gross income, it is taxable. This chapter presents not only an explanation of the most commonly encountered items included in income but discusses several specific exclusions, such as municipal bond interest income, gifts, inheritances, and life insurance proceeds.

3.1.2 TAX VERSUS FINANCIAL ACCOUNTING

There are many similarities between financial accounting income and income included on a tax return, but there are also many differences. The U.S. Supreme Court has indicated three reasons for disallowing generally accepted accounting principles (GAAP) for tax purposes. First, the goals of financial accounting and tax reporting are very different. Financial accounting provides information useful to its shareholders and creditors. The goal of tax accounting, however, is to collect revenue equitably. Second, financial accounting often relies on the principle of conservatism, which tends to understate income when uncertainty exists. In contrast, the income tax system would have great difficulty collecting revenue if taxpayers were allowed the freedom to report income conservatively. Third, financial accounting often relies on estimates and probabilities. The tax system could not function efficiently or equitably if taxpayers were allowed to estimate income or base their reported income on probabilities.

Example 3.2

For tax purposes, a corporation wrote down its excess inventory to net realizable value in accordance with GAAP. The Supreme Court indicated that this treatment was inappropriate because it did not clearly reflect taxable income.[5]

The differences between financial accounting income and taxable income fall into two general categories:

1. Income is taxed in a different period than it is accrued for accounting purposes. For example, prepaid rent generally is taxable when received but is included in financial accounting income only as it is earned. This is a temporary or timing difference.
2. Income is not taxed but is included in financial accounting income. For example, municipal bond interest generally is not taxed but it is recorded as income on the financial statements. This is a permanent difference.

Financial statements prepared in accordance with GAAP report income tax expense based on current-year financial statement income, not current-year taxable income. Thus, the tax

[3] §63(a).
[4] The few special provisions that apply only to corporations are discussed in Chapter 10.
[5] *Thor Power Tool Co. v. Comm.*, 439 US 522 (1979), 43 AFTR 2d 79-362, 79-1 USTC 9139.

expense reported in the financial statements matches the transactions reported in that period on the financial statements, regardless of when the tax is actually paid. As a result, there is a timing difference between income tax expense shown on the books and the actual tax shown on the tax return. These differences are accounted for on financial statements as *deferred tax assets* or *deferred tax liabilities*.[6]

Most businesses do not maintain separate books and records for financial and tax reporting. They simply make the appropriate adjustments to the financial statements and income tax returns to allow preparation from the same basic data with the different concepts of income reconciled.

3.1.3 RETURN OF CAPITAL PRINCIPLE

One of the basic tax principles is that gross income excludes the return of capital, referred to as cost recovery.[7] A **return of capital** is the recovery of a prior investment. The amount invested in an asset is its **basis**. If a taxpayer's return is more than an asset's basis, gain results; if less than basis, the taxpayer has a loss.

Example 3.3

Ambler sells 500 shares of XYZ stock, purchased for $5 per share, for $11 per share. Ambler has a taxable gain of $3,000 [($11 selling price – $5 basis) × 500 shares] after recovering its $2,500 basis. Alternatively, if Ambler sells the stock for only $4 per share, it has a $500 loss [($4 selling price – $5 basis) × 500 shares]. It did not recover $500 of its invested capital.

TAX PLANNING

Two key characteristics that affect an investment's after-tax return are (1) the timing of the income or gain and (2) the rate at which the income or gain is taxed. These variables are directly related to the timing and tax planning strategies introduced in Chapter 2.

Tax law favors investments that yield appreciation rather than annual income (for example, interest). The tax on appreciation (gain) is deferred until gain is recognized and may be taxed at lower long-term capital gains rates.[8] The marginal tax rates on ordinary income (including interest income) are as high as 37 percent while the tax rates for long-term capital gains are usually no more than 20 percent.[9] The long-term capital gains tax rates for single individuals and married couples filing a joint return are presented in Table 3.1.

Table 3.1 Long-Term Capital Gains Tax Rates for 2018

Long-term capital gains tax rate	Taxable income for single individuals	Taxable income for married couples filing a joint return
0%	$0–$38,600	$0–$77,200
15%	$36,601–$425,800	$77,201–$479,000
20%	Over $425,800	Over $479,000

[6] Differences in expense recognition can also result in timing and permanent differences. See Chapter 6 for a discussion of accounting for book/tax differences.

[7] *Doyle v. Mitchell Bros. Co.*, 247 US 179 (1918).

[8] Individuals qualify for lower long-term capital gains rates when an investment has been held for more than a year. If the investment has been held for one year or less, it is a short-term capital gain and ordinary income tax rates apply.

[9] Rates can be as high as 28% for collectibles and 25% for unrecaptured §1250 gain as discussed in Chapter 8. These rates exclude the Medicare surtaxes discussed in Chapter 5. Corporations do not have special tax rates for long-term capital gains.

Example 3.4

Anne's marginal tax bracket is 35 percent for ordinary income and 15 percent for long-term capital gains. She has $20,000 to invest for eight years before she liquidates her investment. She has two investment alternatives: (1) corporate bonds yielding 5 percent before tax with the interest reinvested at 5 percent before tax or (2) land that will increase in value by 5 percent each year. The tax deferral that is a result of investing in the land rather than the bonds is $1,902 ($8,109 − $6,207), determined as follows:

	Corporate bonds	Investment land
Annual interest income $20,000 × 5%	$1,000	
Income tax @ 35%	(350)	
After-tax cash flow	$650	
Reinvested @ 5% for 8 years*	×9.549	
After-tax cash flow from interest for 8 years	$6,207	
Original investment in land		$20,000
5% factor		×1.477
Land value in 8 years		$29,540
Return of capital		(20,000)
Pretax gain		$9,540
Tax on gain @ 15%		(1,431)
After-tax value		$8,109

*Future value tables are in the Appendix at the end of this textbook.

Under the return of capital principle, a taxpayer who takes out a loan or other form of indebtedness does not have income because the amount received must be paid back. This type of transaction increases both the recipient's assets and liabilities, resulting in no net change in equity or wealth—and no income.

3.2 WHEN IS INCOME RECOGNIZED?

Taxable income is measured and reported based on the tax year. Determining the period in which income is taxed is important for several reasons:

1. The taxpayer's marginal tax rate may differ from one year to the next. Changes in marginal rates can result from fluctuations in the taxpayer's taxable income, legislative changes to the tax rate structure, or a combination of both.

2. The tax law may change the treatment of some items. For example, if certain taxable income is no longer taxable, the taxpayer would prefer to postpone the income and report it in the later year.

3. The time value of money affects value; for example, a dollar of tax paid in year 1 actually costs more than a dollar of tax paid in year 2. Thus, taxpayers generally prefer to postpone paying taxes to a later tax year but deduct expenses in the earliest tax year allowed.

Deferring taxable income from one year to the next produces tax savings as discussed in the previous chapter. Taxpayers can reduce tax cost or increase tax savings by controlling the timing of a transaction. Thus, determining the end of a tax year is critical for decision makers. Tax laws restrict the selection of accounting periods and methods to prevent taxpayers from abusing the tax system. Without these restrictions, taxpayers could manipulate income, allowing it to fall into whichever tax year minimized the tax liability.

3.2.1 THE TAX YEAR

A business's tax year corresponds to its annual accounting period for financial statement purposes. If a business keeps its financial records on a **calendar year**, it measures income from January 1 through December 31. Alternatively, a taxpayer can use a **fiscal year**, a 12-month period ending the last day of any month other than December (an allowable annual period), for which adequate books and records are maintained to measure taxable income. The choice of a calendar year or fiscal year is usually determined by the organization's operating cycle. For example, a ski resort may select an April 30 fiscal year-end so it can close its books and calculate its profit at the end of its natural business cycle.

TAX PLANNING

Businesses can also choose a 52-to-53-week fiscal year that ends in any calendar month (including December) but ends on the same day of the week each year. The ending day selected must be either the last time that day occurs in the month or the day closest to the end of the month.[10] For example, a fiscal year that ends on either the last Friday in January or the Friday closest to January 31 is an acceptable 52-to-53-week year. Companies closed for business on weekends often select a Friday for their fiscal year-end because this permits inventory to be taken during the weekend without disrupting regular business operations.

Most individual taxpayers use the calendar year as their taxable year because they do not keep adequate books and records and the publicity surrounding the April 15 tax deadline for filing calendar-year individual tax returns.[11] The calendar year is also more convenient for individuals because most information reporting (W-2 wage statements and 1099 forms for interest and dividends) is based on the calendar year.

Corporations generally maintain extensive financial records and often adopt fiscal years. Flow-through entities (S corporations and partnerships) and personal service corporations (PSCs) face restrictions that usually force them to adopt tax years ending September 30 through December 31, with most adopting a calendar year.[12] These restrictions prevent their owners from enjoying significant tax deferrals.

A new business usually chooses its tax year when it files its initial tax return. This return reports its first-year operating results from the date the business begins operations until the end the tax year selected, usually less than 12 months.[13] Once a tax year is established, a taxpayer (including an individual) cannot change its tax year unless it receives permission to do so from the IRS.[14]

Example 3.5

Jim begins a new business as a sole proprietorship. Jim wants to use a fiscal year, but a sole proprietorship reports its operating results on Jim's tax return, which has always been filed on a calendar-year basis. Although the sole proprietorship is new, Jim is a calendar-year taxpayer. He must request IRS permission to change to a fiscal year to accommodate his sole proprietorship's accounting records.

The IRS usually grants permission for the business to change its taxable year if the taxpayer has a valid business reason for changing its annual accounting period.[15] When the IRS does grant permission to change, the taxpayer has a **short tax year** and files a short-year tax return that reports less than 12 months of operating results.

[10] §441(f).

[11] When an individual taxpayer files his or her first return on a calendar year, the calendar year automatically becomes the taxpayer's tax year.

[12] A PSC is a service corporation whose employees own substantially all of the stock. Examples include engineering, law, accounting, and consulting corporations.

[13] Reg. §1.441-1T(b)(2).

[14] §442.

[15] One valid purpose is to change to a tax year that coincides with the natural business year. To have a natural business year, at least 25 percent of the company's gross receipts for the 12-month period must be realized in the final 2 months of the 12-month period for 3 consecutive years. Usually only seasonal businesses qualify under this test.

3.2.2 ACCOUNTING METHODS

The method of accounting determines the year within which income falls for tax purposes. Taxpayers can use the cash, accrual, or hybrid (a combination of cash and accrual) accounting methods for tax purposes as long as the method chosen clearly reflects income.[16] Many, taxpayers use the same accounting method for both tax and financial accounting purposes. In this case, they must keep a separate set of records that allows them to convert financial accounting data into the information necessary for the tax return. Taxpayers must use the same accounting method from one year to the next unless they receive permission from the IRS to change accounting methods.

A taxpayer can use different tax accounting methods for different activities, however. For example, a taxpayer with two separate sole proprietorships can use the accrual method for one and the cash method for the other or the accrual method for a business and the cash method for personal activities.[17]

Cash Method

Cash method taxpayers recognize income during the tax year in which cash or cash equivalents are received and claim expense deductions during the tax year in which cash or its equivalent are paid.[18] A cash equivalent is defined broadly as anything with a market value, including most non-cash property and services.[19] Cash equivalents are included in income at their fair market value.

Example 3.6

Ted, a cash-basis, calendar-year sole proprietor, prepares a tax return for his dentist, sending a bill for $400 in year 1. The bill was not paid, and on December 31, year 1, Ted shows a $400 account receivable in his ledger. In year 2, Ted accepts dental work worth $350 in full settlement of the bill. Ted has $350 of gross income in year 2. This exchange of services is a barter transaction.

The **constructive receipt doctrine** modifies the requirement that cash-basis taxpayers must actually receive cash (or cash equivalents) before income is recognized. This doctrine requires the cash-basis taxpayer to recognize income when it is credited to the taxpayer's account, set apart for the taxpayer, or made available in some other way to the taxpayer even though they may not have physical possession. In effect, the constructive receipt doctrine prevents cash-basis taxpayers from turning their backs on income and, as a result, arbitrarily shifting gross income between tax years.

Income is not constructively received in three situations: (1) The taxpayer is not yet entitled to the income; the fact that the taxpayer could have contracted to receive the income earlier is irrelevant.[20] (2) The payer has insufficient funds from which to make payment (such as a bounced check). (3) There are substantial limitations or restrictions placed on actual receipt.[21]

Example 3.7

Bongo Company, a cash-basis, calendar-year taxpayer, received a check at noon on December 31, year 1, too late to deposit the check in the bank that day. It was not deposited until January 2, year 2. Bongo recognizes the $12,000 in income in year 1 because it was made available and is considered constructively received in year 1. If, however, the check is postdated to January 3, year 2, because sufficient funds to cover the check will not be deposited until January 2, year 2, Bongo does not recognize the income until year 2.

[16] §446(b), (c).
[17] Reg. §1.446-1(c)(1)(iv)(b).
[18] Reg. §1.446-1(c)(1)(i).
[19] The mere recording of an account receivable, however, is not considered a cash equivalent.
[20] *Amend,* 13 T.C. 178 (1949).
[21] Reg. §1.451-2.

TAX PLANNING

Professional athletes and other highly compensated individuals can avoid application of the constructive receipt doctrine through careful wording of their employment contracts. If the contract language legally defers their right to some portion of their compensation until a later tax year, compensation is not gross income until that time (or until actually received, if earlier).[22]

Example 3.8

Carl's Construction Company is a cash-basis sole proprietorship. Big Developers offers to pay Carl $15,000 in advance for building a retaining wall during December, year 1. Carl expects to be in a lower tax bracket in year 2 and offers to build the wall for $15,100 in December, year 1, if payment is made in January, year 2. The final written contract reflects this counteroffer, and the payment is made according to the contract. Carl does not have constructive receipt in year 1 because it was not entitled to the income until year 2. It does not matter that the company could have contracted for the money earlier. Carl reports the $15,100 of gross income year 2.

Limits on Use of Cash Method

Congress was concerned that taxpayers could manipulate their taxable income under the cash method by deferring income and accelerating payment of expenses. (Cash-basis taxpayers can easily defer income by delaying billing their customers at year-end.) Therefore, it put some restrictions on the use of the cash method. Businesses that carry inventory and sell merchandise to their customers were required to use the accrual method to account for sales and purchases.[23] Also C corporations with average annual gross receipts of more than $5 million were prohibited from using the cash method for tax purposes.[24] Beginning in 2018, the cash method may be used by all taxpayers whose average annual gross receipts for the three prior years do not exceed $25 million. Taxpayers who meet the $25 million gross receipts test are not required to account for inventories; instead they may treat inventories as non-incidental materials and supplies or use a method that conforms to their financial accounting treatment. Personal service corporations, no matter how large, can always use the cash method.

Example 3.9

Appliance Depot Corporation, a C corporation selling appliances, wants to determine if it can use the cash method under the $25 million gross receipts test for 2018. Its gross receipts were $26 million for 2017, $25 million (2016) and $21 million (2015). Its average annual gross receipts for the three-prior-year period are $24 million [($26 million + $25 million + $21 million) / 3]. The corporation meets the gross receipts test for 2018 and can use the cash method.

Accrual Method

Generally accepted accounting principles require the use of the accrual method. Under the **accrual method**, gross income is recognized in the tax year in which it is earned rather than the year in which it is received. Income is earned when all events have occurred that establish the right to the income and the income amount can be determined with reasonable accuracy. These criteria are known as the **all events test** and are generally satisfied when goods are delivered or

[22] Deferred compensation is discussed in Chapter 4.

[23] Reg. §1.446-1 and §1.471-1.

[24] §448. This prohibition of the cash method extended to partnerships with corporate partners.

services performed. For taxpayers with an applicable financial statement, the all events test is considered met no later than the time the item is included in revenue on the taxpayer's financial statements.[25]

Example 3.10

Hightec Computers (a calendar-year, accrual-basis corporation) sold a computer system for $18,000 on account on December 18, year 1, and delivered the computer system on December 22. Hightec billed the customer on January 3, year 2 and the customer paid the bill on February 1, year 2. Hightec has $18,000 of gross income in year 1. All events have occurred that establish the corporation's right to the $18,000 as of December 31, year 1, and the amount is known with reasonable accuracy.

If the liability for payment is in dispute, the all events test is not satisfied; resolution of the dispute is a relevant event in establishing the taxpayer's right to the income. If the taxpayer has received payment, however, the claim of right doctrine modifies the normal rules for accrual-basis taxpayers. The **claim of right doctrine** requires the taxpayer to recognize income when payment is received as long as the taxpayer's use of the money is unrestricted, even if the money may have to be repaid later.[26] If the taxpayer must return all or part of the income, a deduction is allowed in the repayment year.[27] If the repayment exceeds $3,000, the taxpayer can either (1) deduct the repayment in the year repaid or (2) reduce the current year's tax by the prior-year tax paid on the disputed income.[28]

Example 3.11

In November, year 1, Lowtech Company hired Computer Training Services (CTS), an accrual-basis, calendar-year taxpayer, to provide a five-week computer training program for its employees. CTS received its full training fee of $20,000 on the first day of training. After four weeks of training sessions, Lowtech cancelled the last week of training and demanded a $4,000 refund because its employees felt they were not learning anything useful. In January, year 2, CTS refunded $4,000 to Lowtech. CTS's tax rate is 21 percent.

Because the repayment exceeds $3,000, CTS can either deduct the $4,000 repayment in year 2 or reduce its year-2 tax liability by $840 ($4,000 × 21%), the tax reduction in year 1 had the $4,000 refund had been excluded from gross income.

The rationale behind the claim of right doctrine is the concept of **wherewithal to pay**, which asserts that a taxpayer should be taxed on income at the time the taxpayer is best able to pay the tax.[29] The government does not wait for the settlement of a dispute before taxing income. Instead, it taxes the income when the taxpayer receives the income with which to pay the tax. A delay in taxing income increases the risk that the taxes will be uncollectible later. The claim of right doctrine does not apply to contested amounts that the taxpayer has not yet received.

[25] An applicable financial statement is one certified as prepared according to generally accepted accounting principles and is (1) prepared for the Securities and Exchange Commission, (2) an audited financial statement used for credit purposes, reporting to shareholders or any other substantial non-tax purpose, or (3) a financial statement filed with any federal agency for other than federal tax purposes.

[26] *North American Oil Consolidated v. Burnet*, 286 US 417 (1932), 11 AFTR 16, 3 USTC 943.

[27] *U.S. v. Lewis*, 340 US 590 (1951), 40 AFTR 258, 51-1 USTC 9211.

[28] §1341.

[29] One reason for reliance on the cash method for income tax purposes, in addition to its simplicity, is that it imposes the tax at the same time that the taxpayer receives the resources with which to pay the tax.

Accrual-basis taxpayers are often treated as cash-basis taxpayers if they receive prepaid income. Once again, the wherewithal to pay concept is the reason for taxing prepaid income. Prepaid income items taxed when received include rent, royalties, and interest.[30]

Landlords often require tenants to pay the last month's rent in advance. As prepaid rent, it is taxable when received. Instead of prepaid rent, landlords can require a refundable security deposit in the same amount. The tax on a deposit is deferred because the landlord is obligated to return it if all rent is paid and no damage is done to the property.

TAX PLANNING

Special exceptions allow accrual-basis taxpayers to defer recognition of some prepaid items. Income recognition for deposits on the purchase of goods can be deferred if the taxpayer's method used to account for the completed purchase is the same for both accounting and tax purposes.[31] Similarly, prepayments for services to be performed beyond the current year can be deferred until the tax year following the prepayment year. Generally, deferral to a tax year later than the next succeeding year is not allowed.[32]

Example 3.12

On November 1, 2018, Flamingo Dance Studios, a calendar-year, accrual-basis taxpayer, receives advance payment for a two-year contract for 96 one-hour lessons. Flamingo provides 8 lessons in 2018, 48 lessons in 2019, and 40 lessons in 2020. On its financial statement, Flamingo recognizes 1/12 of the revenue in 2018, 6/12 in 2019, and 5/12 in 2020. On its tax return, Flamingo must include 1/12 of the payment in 2018 and 11/12 in gross income for 2019.

Special Methods

Two special methods apply to long-term contracts for the manufacture, building, installation, or construction of property that will not be completed in the year the contract is executed.[33] Under the **completed contract method**, no income is recognized (and no deductions taken) until the contract is complete. Costs simply accumulate until contract completion. At that time, the gross contract price is recognized as income, all related costs are deducted, and the contract's net income is determined.[34] Under the **percentage-of-completion method**, income is recognized annually as the contract progresses,[35] based on estimates of actual costs incurred to total projected costs for the contract. In the final year of the contract, a final calculation is made and any remaining income is recognized.[36]

Given the choice, taxpayers would prefer to use the completed contract method because it defers taxes and is simpler. It can, however, lead to the bunching of income into a single tax year that may be detrimental due to the progressive tax rates. The use of the completed contract method is restricted, however, to certain construction contracts.[37]

The installment method of reporting gain is a taxpayer-friendly application of the wherewithal to pay concept applicable to certain property transactions. Gain is recognized as proceeds

---

[30] Reg. §1.61-8(b).

[31] Reg. §1.451-5(b).

[32] Rev. Proc. 2004-34, 2004-22 IRB 991 and §451(c)(1).

[33] §460(f)(1). A manufacturing contract is considered long term if it is for an item that takes more than 12 months to complete or is a unique item not usually included in the taxpayer's finished goods inventory. §460(f)(2).

[34] Reg. §1.451-4(d)(1).

[35] Under a de minimis rule, if less than 10 percent of the estimated contract costs are incurred by the end of the taxable year, a taxpayer using the percentage-of-completion method can elect to defer the recognition of income and the related costs until the tax year in which cumulative contract costs are at least 10 percent of estimated contract costs. §460(b)(5).

[36] Reg. §1.451-3(c).

[37] §460(e). The completed contract method can only be used for certain home construction contracts and construction contracts that will be completed within a two-year period by a taxpayer whose average annual gross receipts do not exceed $25 million (increased from $10 million in 2018).

from the installment sale are received rather than recognizing the entire gain in the year of sale.[38] A transaction must include one or more payments in any tax year other than the year of sale to be eligible for installment sale treatment.[39] (See Chapter 9 for further discussion.)

3.3 WHO RECOGNIZES THE INCOME?

3.3.1 ASSIGNMENT OF INCOME DOCTRINE

Congress recognized that significant tax revenue could be lost by the shifting of income between taxpayers and has restricted income-shifting techniques through the **assignment of income doctrine**. An assignment involves the transfer of rights from one party to another and this doctrine prevents a taxpayer from shifting personal service income to another.[40]

Example 3.13

Karim is a professional basketball player earning more than $1 million in annual compensation. Karim requests payment of $200,000 of his salary to his girlfriend, Crystal. Karim's employer pays the $200,000 directly to Crystal. Under the assignment of income doctrine, the $200,000 is gross income to Karim because he is the taxpayer who earned it. For tax purposes, Karim earns the income and makes a gift to Crystal.

The doctrine also applies to the assignment of income from property, unless the ownership of the underlying property is transferred.[41]

Example 3.14

Samuel gives his son, Harry, corporate bonds. Interest accrued to the date of the gift is taxed to Samuel. Interest accrued after the gift is taxed to Harry because bond ownership was transferred to him not just the bond interest.

3.3.2 COMMUNITY PROPERTY LAWS

Community property laws affect the allocation of income between spouses. The states that follow a community property system are Arizona, California, Idaho, Louisiana, Nevada, New Mexico, Texas, Washington, and Wisconsin.[42] All other states are common law states. Under common law, income is usually taxed to the individual who earns the income. In most community property states, community income is the sum of personal service income and income from community property. However, in Idaho, Louisiana, Texas, and Wisconsin, community income also includes income from separate property. In other words, all income in these four states is considered community income.[43]

For tax purposes, community income is split evenly between spouses who file separate returns. Separated spouses must still report half of the community income on their separate

[38] The installment method is not available for a transaction in which a loss rather than a gain results.

[39] §453(b)(1).

[40] *Lucas v. Earl*, 281 US 111 (1930), 2 USTC 496, 8 AFTR 10,287. In its now-famous fruit-and-tree analogy, the court explained that fruit (personal service income) must be attributed to (taxed to) the tree on which it grew (the individual who earned it).

[41] *Helvering v. Horst*, 311 US 112 (1940), 40-2 USTC ¶9787, 24 AFTR 1058.

[42] In Alaska, spouses can choose to have community property rules apply.

[43] Personal service income is not considered community income in any of the nine states if the couple lives apart the entire year, does not file a joint return, and does not transfer earned income (such as alimony) between them. §66(a).

returns until such time as their divorce becomes final. (A joint return filed by a married couple effectively taxes them as if each earned half of their combined income.)

3.4 SOURCES OF INCOME

The two most common sources of business gross income are the sale of goods and performance of services. Corporations report gross income on their corporate income tax return and pay tax based on their taxable income. A flow-through business entity (such as a partnership or S corporation), reports its gross income on the entity's information tax return, but does not pay the tax on the income. Instead, income is allocated to and included on the owners' tax returns, where it is subject to income tax.

Service income is usually referred to as **earned income** because it is generated by the taxpayer's efforts. Common sources of earned income include salaries, wages, commissions, bonuses, and tips and are discussed in the next chapter along with other types of employee compensation. Income from property is usually referred to as **unearned income** and includes interest, dividends, rents, royalties, and annuities. The remainder of this chapter focuses on the tax treatment of these and other sources of income. The sample filled-in tax returns on the companion website for this text illustrate the reporting of various sources of income.

3.4.1 INTEREST INCOME

Taxpayers who want current cash flow may choose investments that generate interest income. Individuals and businesses receiving interest income from savings accounts, certificates of deposit (CDs), corporate bonds, and Treasury bills include it in gross income. The primary exception is interest received on municipal bonds.

Interest on Municipal Bonds

The term **municipal bonds** (or munis) describes all tax-exempt bonds issued by any city, county, state, or other governmental entity to raise money for projects such as building schools, highways, hospitals, and sewer systems. The gross income exclusion for municipal bond interest used to finance government operations has existed since 1913. It is a federal subsidy for state and local governments that allows them to issue bonds with a lower interest rate than required by investors if the interest was taxable.[44] The authority for this exclusion is believed to be rooted in the U.S. Constitution's intergovernmental tax immunity doctrine and that taxing such interest impairs the ability of state and municipal governments to finance their basic operations.[45] Although the Supreme Court has since determined there is no constitutional prohibition,[46] the law is unchanged and continues to provide state and local governments with low-interest financing.

This exclusion does not extend to the investor's realized gain on the disposition of municipal bonds, however. Gain on the sale of a municipal bond is taxable; if sold at a loss, the loss is deductible. Only the interest income is tax free. Interest is included in financial accounting income, however, causing a permanent difference between tax and accounting income.

Example 3.15

Bill bought $20,000 of City of Miami general revenue bonds. During the year, he received $600 interest from the bonds. When market interest rates drop, the value of the bonds increases, and Bill sells the bonds for $22,000. Bill reports the $2,000 ($22,000 – $20,000) gain as gross income, but excludes the $600 interest.

---

[44] §103(a). Interest income may be subject to state income taxes if the taxpayer has municipal bonds from a state that is not the taxpayer's state of primary residence.

[45] *Pollack v. Farmer's Loan & Trust Co.*, 3 AFTR 2602, 158 US 601 (1895).

[46] *South Carolina v. Baker III*, 61 AFTR 2d 88–995, 88-1 USTC 9284, 485 US 505 (1988).

TAX PLANNING

It is often advantageous for taxpayers in high tax brackets to invest in tax-exempt state or local bonds. Although offering a lower interest rate than taxable bonds, the after-tax investment yield may be greater.

Example 3.16

Two taxpayers plan to invest $50,000 each. Taxpayer A is in the 32 percent marginal tax bracket and taxpayer B is in the 12 percent bracket. They consider two alternative investments: corporate bonds with a stated interest rate of 6 percent or tax-exempt municipal bonds issued for governmental activities with a stated interest of 4.5 percent.

Taxpayer A	Corporate bonds	Tax-exempt bonds
Interest income		
$50,000 × 6%	$3,000	
$50,000 × 4.5%		$2,250
Income tax @ 32%	(960)	0
After-tax cash flow	$2,040	$2,250
Taxpayer B		
Interest income	$3,000	$2,250
Income tax @ 12%	(360)	0
After-tax cash flow	$2,640	$2,250

Taxpayer A has $210 ($2,250 – $2,040) more in after-tax cash flow by investing in tax-exempt municipal bonds, while taxpayer B has $390 ($2,640 – $2,250) more in after-tax cash flow by investing in the taxable corporate bonds.

A taxpayer in the 32 percent marginal tax bracket requires only a 6.8 percent yield on a tax-exempt bond to obtain the same after-tax income as a taxable bond paying 10 percent interest [6.8%/(1 – .32)].

To maximize these benefits, cash-basis taxpayers may purchase zero-coupon bonds that pay interest only at maturity. Zero-coupon bonds are particularly attractive for taxpayers who want to reinvest the interest each year. Zero-coupon bonds save on broker fees and the hassle of finding a suitable investment for the annual interest earned.

Over the years, the use of municipal bonds has expanded to include bonds issued to finance certain private activities (such as construction of sport facilities) that do not meet essential public needs. These bonds are not completely tax exempt.[47] The interest from bonds issued for qualified private activities (usually called AMT bonds) is exempt from regular income tax but is subject to the federal alternative minimum tax (AMT).[48] The yield on AMT bonds is typically higher than fully tax-exempt municipal bonds. Investors not subject to the AMT can achieve higher returns by investing in AMT bonds rather than fully tax-exempt municipal bonds.

Original Issue Discount

Federal tax law generally does not permit investors to defer the recognition of interest income. Debt instruments issued at a price below their stated maturity value, are said to be issued at a

[47] §103(b). Interest exclusions are also not allowed for unregistered bonds, bonds guaranteed by the federal government, and arbitrage bonds.

[48] §57(a)(5). AMT income is broader than ordinary taxable income. It differs from taxable income in its treatment of certain deductions and also in its inclusion of income from preference items such as interest from private activity bonds. Taxpayers compute their tax under both the regular tax rules and the AMT rules and then pay whichever tax is higher. Refer to Chapter 5 for a more complete discussion.

discount. **Original issue discount (OID)** is the excess of a debt instrument's stated redemption price at maturity over its issue price.[49] OID is essentially interest paid at maturity rather than periodically over the life of the debt instrument. All debt instruments paying no interest before maturity are presumed to be issued at a discount, for example, zero coupon bonds. With some exceptions, Section 1272 requires cash-basis taxpayers to recognize OID as if they were accrual-basis taxpayers. As a result, the debt's adjusted basis increases each year by the amount of the amortized OID. Without this provision, cash-basis taxpayers could defer interest income (OID) until the debt matures.

Upon disposition of an OID debt instrument, the realized taxable gain or loss is the sale price of the debt instrument (or a bond's redemption price if redeemed) minus the instrument's adjusted tax basis. Recognizing OID annually increases its adjusted basis to its face value at maturity.

Example 3.17

Xenon Corporation, a small cash-basis corporation, issued $1,000,000 of 10-year bonds with a stated interest rate of 4 percent for $920,000. Under normal cash-basis rules, Xenon would recognize the entire $80,000 discount as a loss in year 10 when the bonds mature. OID rules, however, require accrual of the discount as part of annual interest expense.

Frederico purchased $20,000 of Xenon Corporation bonds for $18,400. Frederico's return on this investment consists of an $800 ($20,000 × 4%) annual interest payment plus the $1,600 ($20,000 − $18,400) OID that he collects at maturity. Each year Frederico receives a Form 1099 from Xenon Corporation that reports (to him and to the IRS) the $800 interest payment and the portion of the discount Frederico must recognize annually as additional interest income.[50] Frederico increases his basis for the bonds by the OID reported as income each year. When the bonds mature, Frederico's basis will be $20,000 and he receives the $20,000 maturity value as tax-free return of capital.

The OID is considered de minimis and treated as zero if the discount is less than ¼ percent times the number of full years to maturity.[51] In addition, the OID rules do not apply in two situations. First, OID can be deferred if its maturity date is one year or less from the date of issue. Second, government savings bonds (Series EE and I bonds) are generally issued as OID bonds with all interest paid at maturity.[52] The taxpayer does not report the interest until the bonds mature (or are cashed in prior to maturity). The taxpayer may elect to report interest income on an annual basis, but if this election is made, the OID on similar government bonds acquired later must also be amortized.

TAX PLANNING

Parents frequently give their children U.S. government savings bonds to save for college or other future expenses. If a child is in a low tax bracket or has sufficient income to pay taxes currently, it may be preferable to elect to recognize the bond's OID as it accrues each year, rather than later when the child's annual income is greater and he or she is in a higher tax bracket.[53]

The education savings bond program is another favorable provision that allows an interest exclusion if the parents redeem Series EE or Series I bonds to pay for qualified higher education

[49] §1273(a)(1).

[50] The amortization of the discount is calculated using the constant interest rate method. Total interest is calculated by multiplying the interest yield to maturity by the adjusted issue price. Under this method, the amount of OID amortization increases each year the bond is held. If an original issue debt instrument is issued at a premium, the holder may elect to amortize the premium under Reg. §1.171-1(a) on an effective-yield basis as an offset to interest income over the term of the debt.

[51] §1273(a)(3).

[52] Series EE bonds issued at a discount provide a constant rate of return. Series I bonds provide a return that is indexed for inflation.

[53] §454(a).

expenses. Qualified expenses include tuition and fees for the taxpayer, spouse, and dependents but this exclusion is phased out for higher-income taxpayers.[54]

Market Discount

TAX PLANNING

Market discount is the result of a decrease in the value of a debt obligation after the issue date, usually due to an increase in interest rates. Investors who purchase bonds later in the open or secondary market at a price lower than the bond's stated maturity value are not required to accrue the discount as interest income over the life of the bond, although they may elect to do so.[55] If this election is not made, the investor recognizes the excess of the redemption proceeds over the bond's cost as interest income in the year redeemed.[56] Most taxpayers prefer to defer the recognition of the discount until redemption due to the time value of money.

Example 3.18

Sandra purchased $50,000 of corporate bonds from her broker for $46,000. The bonds trade at a discount because their interest rate is below the market rate. Sandra includes only the cash interest payments in income each year. When she redeems the bonds at maturity, Sandra recognizes the $4,000 discount ($50,000 – $46,000) as interest income in that year.

A taxpayer may also elect to amortize the premium on a bond purchased in the secondary market, reducing the annual interest income recognized on the bond. If the premium is not amortized, it remains part of the bond's tax basis and reduces the gain recognized when the bond is sold or redeemed.

Below-Market-Rate and Interest-Free Loans

Interest-free or below-market-rate loans are frequently made between related parties. In these cases, interest income is imputed (treated as received or accrued) at a predefined federal rate of interest though not actually received or accrued. Otherwise, a taxpayer with excess cash could shift investment income to another taxpayer through these low or no-interest loans.

Example 3.19

Gary (in the 35 percent marginal tax bracket) loans $50,000 to his oldest son, Mark (in the 12 percent marginal tax bracket). The loan is interest-free for a term of one year. Mark invests the $50,000 in corporate bonds that yield 8 percent. By foregoing the investment earnings on his $50,000 for this year, Gary, in effect, has shifted $4,000 of income to Mark. If Gary invested $50,000 at the 8 percent interest rate, he would have had to pay $1,400 in tax ($4,000 × 35%), while Mark pays only $480 in tax ($4,000 × 12%), resulting in a tax savings of $920 ($1,400 – $480).

Congress curtailed some advantages of interest-free loans by enacting provisions that turn such loans into multi-step transactions. Section 7872 recharacterizes an interest-free or below-market-rate loan as an arm's-length loan requiring the payment of interest at a predefined federal rate. No actual payments are made, but the lender is deemed to receive imputed interest income at the current applicable federal interest rate.[57] The lender is then assumed to return the imputed

[54] §135. The exclusion begins to phase out when modified adjusted gross income is $79,550 ($119,300 for a married couple filing jointly) in 2018 and is completely phased out over the next $15,000 ($30,000, if married). To be eligible for exclusion, the taxpayer must be at least age 24 when the bonds are issued. This exclusion is computed on Form 8815.

[55] §1278(a) and (b).

[56] §1276.

[57] The applicable federal rate (AFR) changes on a monthly basis and is tied to the yield on Treasury securities. The IRS publishes AFRs each month on its website.

interest to the borrower. Thus, below-market-rate and interest-free loans are redefined as arm's length transactions in which the lender loans money to the borrower; the borrower pays the lender hypothetical interest at the applicable federal rate; the lender then returns the hypothetical payment (equal to the forgone interest) to the borrower. The forgone interest is equal to the interest that is imputed at the applicable federal rate less any interest actually paid on the loan. This hypothetical payment to the borrower is treated as a gift, payment of compensation, or dividend depending on the relationship between the lender and the borrower and loan circumstances.

Regardless of how an interest-free or below-market-rate loan is categorized (as a gift loan, employment-related loan, or shareholder loan), the lender has interest income. It is the characterization of the return of the hypothetical interest to the borrower that differs, as summarized in Table 3.2.

Table 3.2 Below-Market-Rate Loans

Type of loan	Effect on lender	Effect on borrower	Exceptions
Gift	Interest income followed by gift to borrower	Interest expense followed by gift from lender	(1) $10,000 exception (2) Interest limited to net investment income for loans of $100,000 or less (zero if net investment income $1,000 or less)
Employee	Interest income followed by compensation expense	Interest expense followed by compensation income	$10,000 exception if no tax avoidance purpose
Shareholder	Interest income followed by dividend paid	Interest expense followed by dividend income	$10,000 exception if no tax avoidance purpose

A loan made between family members or friends is a gift loan. The return of the imputed interest on these loans is deemed a gift from the lender to the borrower.

Example 3.20

Michael loans his daughter Sarah $200,000 interest-free for one year. The applicable federal rate of interest is 5 percent. Sarah is deemed to pay Michael imputed interest of $10,000 ($200,000 × 5%); Michael is deemed to earn $10,000 interest on the loan and Sarah has $10,000 of imputed interest expense. Michael is then assumed to give the $10,000 back to Sarah (most likely treated as a gift). Michael includes the $10,000 interest in his gross income. Sarah has interest expense of $10,000 that may or may not be deductible, depending on how the money is used.

TAX PLANNING

There are two exceptions to the imputed interest rules on interest-free loans between individuals. First, interest is not imputed if the total outstanding amount of loans between the borrower and lender is $10,000 or less.[58] This exception is for administrative convenience to relieve the potential cost of tracking all small loans between friends and relatives. Therefore, a small amount of income can still be shifted with interest-free loans not exceeding $10,000. Second, the imputed interest on gift loans of $100,000 or less cannot exceed the borrower's net investment income for the year.[59] If the borrower's net investment income for the year is $1,000 or less, imputed interest is deemed zero and the loan has no tax effect.[60] Therefore, small gift loans that produce little income for the borrower or that are used for personal expenses escape the imputed interest rules.

[58] §7872(c)(2).

[59] Net investment income includes interest, dividends, and short-term capital gains, less any deductible investment expenses.

[60] §7872(d)(1)(E)(ii).

Example 3.21

Justin made interest-free loans to his four children: Ben, Dave, Holly, and Joshua. Ben borrowed \$8,500 to buy a new car; his net investment income for the year is \$900. Dave borrowed \$35,000 to invest in land; his net investment income is \$800 for the year. Holly borrowed \$30,000 to invest in stock; she has net investment income of \$1,200 for the year. Joshua borrowed \$150,000 to purchase a new home. Joshua's unrelated net investment income is \$500 for the year.

Ben's loan is exempt because it is for less than \$10,000. The loan to Dave is exempt because he has less than \$1,000 of net investment income. If the applicable federal rate is 5 percent, the imputed interest on Holly's \$30,000 loan is \$1,500 (\$30,000 × 5%), but is limited to her \$1,200 net investment income. There is \$7,500 (\$150,000 × 5%) of interest income imputed on Joshua's loan; it is not limited to his net investment income because the loan is for more than \$100,000. Justin reports imputed interest income of \$8,700 (\$1,200 + \$7,500) for the year.

When an employer makes an interest-free or below-market-rate loan to an employee, the return of the imputed interest is treated as compensation, taxable to the employee and deductible by the employer. Interest on an interest-free loan to a corporate shareholder is a taxable dividend, but the corporation has no deduction for the assumed dividend.

Example 3.22

Rodriguez Corporation loans \$50,000 interest-free for one year to Carl, an employee. If the applicable federal rate of interest is 4 percent. Carl is assumed to pay the corporation \$2,000 (\$50,000 × 4%) in interest. The corporation has assumed interest income of \$2,000 and the imputed interest payment is returned to Carl as compensation, deductible by the corporation. The net effect of this arrangement is zero for the corporation; it has an increase in income of \$2,000 from the imputed interest that is offset by a compensation deduction of \$2,000. If Carl cannot deduct the interest, he has an increase in taxable income for the \$2,000 imputed compensation.

If Carl is a shareholder (not an employee) of Rodriguez Corporation, Carl's \$2,000 hypothetical interest payment is still income to the corporation, but it is now deemed returned to Carl as a dividend. It is taxable to Carl as dividend income, but the corporation cannot deduct the dividend payment.

For employee and shareholder loans, the \$10,000 exception does not apply if tax avoidance is one of the principal purposes of the loan.[61] Few shareholder-employee loans, other than for employee-relocation expenses, qualify for the \$10,000 exception.

3.4.2 DIVIDEND INCOME

Investors who purchase stocks become shareholders of a corporation and are entitled to receive dividends declared by the corporation. Unlike debt holders, shareholders are not legally entitled to receive dividend payments nor is there a guarantee that stockholders will recover their original investments. Thus, from an investor's perspective, stock is riskier than debt.

A shareholder distribution from corporate earnings and profits is an ordinary **dividend** and is included in the recipient's gross income. Dividends can be received as cash, property, or stock. Distributions in excess of corporate earnings and profits are nontaxable dividends that reduce the shareholder's stock basis.[62]

[61] §7872(c)(3).

[62] If the distribution is in excess of the shareholder's stock basis, the excess is taxed as a capital gain.

Historically, dividends were taxed using the taxpayer's ordinary marginal tax rates. The 2003 Tax Act reduced the tax rates for most corporate dividends to those applicable to long-term capital gains (0, 15, or 20 percent as shown in Table 3.1 earlier in the chapter).[63] Qualified dividends are ordinary dividends eligible for the reduced tax rates; they include most dividends received from domestic corporations and qualified foreign corporations.[64] Dividends from most tax-exempt organizations are not eligible for these lower rates.[65] Day traders are also ineligible for the reduced rates. To prevent the purchase of stock immediately prior to the ex-dividend date, collecting the low-tax-rate dividends, then quickly selling the stock to generate a short-term capital loss, the lower dividend tax rates are not applicable unless the stock is held more than 60 days during the 121-day period that begins 60 days before the ex-dividend date.[66]

Investors in stock and mutual funds[67] are frequently offered a dividend reinvestment option in which dividend income is used to purchase additional shares. Taxpayers choosing shares receive no cash payment, but have constructive receipt of the reinvested dividends and have taxable income. They are assumed to receive a cash dividend, using the cash to purchase additional shares.

Some payments called "dividends" may actually be another type of income. Dividends on deposits paid by credit unions and savings-and-loan associations are actually interest. Similarly, dividends paid by mutual funds from gains realized on the sale of investment assets, are actually net long-term capital gains called *capital gains distributions*. Shareholders do not report these distributions as dividend income but report them with their other capital gains.[68]

Example 3.23

Carol owns 10,000 shares of XYZ common stock and 5,000 shares of Leadership mutual fund. Carol participates in Leadership's dividend reinvestment plan, reinvesting her annual dividends and capital gains distributions in additional Leadership shares. Carol receives an $11,000 distribution from XYZ. Her statement (Form 1099-DIV) indicates that $10,000 of the distribution is a dividend and $1,000 is a nontaxable distribution. She receives another statement (Form 1099-DIV) from Leadership mutual fund indicating a $5,000 dividend and a $2,000 capital gains distribution, a $7,000 total gross distribution. Her reinvestment plan used the $7,000 distribution to purchase 140 additional shares of Leadership mutual fund, increasing her total shares of Leadership to 5,140.

Carol includes $15,000 ($10,000 from XYZ and $5,000 from Leadership) in gross income as dividend income and $2,000 as a long-term capital gain (from Leadership). If Carol is in the 32 percent marginal income tax bracket, both the dividend income and long-term capital gains distribution are eligible for the 15 percent tax rate. Carol reduces the basis of her XYZ shares by $1,000 for the nontaxable portion of the distribution.

[63] The zero rate that applies to individuals in the lower tax brackets appears to provide a perfect planning opportunity for parents to transfer stock to their children if the children's tax rates fall within the two lowest tax brackets. The kiddie tax, however, uses the tax rates for estates and trusts instead of the child's rate to tax unearned income in excess of $2,100. The kiddie tax rules apply to all children under age 19 and most fulltime students under age 24. Chapter 12 has a detailed discussion of the kiddie tax.

[64] Qualified foreign corporations include U.S. possessions corporations, foreign corporations whose stock is traded on an established U.S. securities market, and foreign corporations eligible for income tax treaty benefits. Corporations report the amount of dividends and indicate if they are potentially eligible for the preferential tax rate when they send Form 1099-DIV to shareholders after each year.

[65] Dividends are not eligible if they are payments in lieu of dividends (payments received by a person who lends stock in a short sale), distributions on trust-preferred stock (as this really represents interest income), and many distributions by a real estate investment trust (REIT).

[66] The ex-dividend date is the first day on which the purchase of the stock would not be entitled to receive a declared dividend.

[67] Mutual funds are portfolios of investment assets managed by professional managers. The income earned by mutual funds generally flows through to the owners of mutual fund shares who pay the taxes on this income. The nature of the assets held by the mutual fund determines the character of the income.

[68] Some mutual funds and real estate investment trusts (REITs) keep their long-term capital gains and pay tax on them. These gains are reported on Form 2439 *Notice to Shareholder of Undistributed Long-Term Capital Gains* and are currently taxable to the individual investors even though not actually distributed to them. The investors get credit for the tax paid and then increase their basis in the mutual fund or REIT by the difference between the taxable gain they report and the tax credit they claim. See Chapter 8 for a discussion of the tax treatment of capital gains and losses.

TAX PLANNING

The reduced tax rates for dividend income make stock a more attractive investment than corporate bonds with interest taxed at an individual's ordinary marginal tax rate. Dividends taxed at the reduced rates, however, are not treated as investment income when computing the investment interest expense deduction limit (discussed in Chapter 5). Taxpayers may elect to forgo the reduced tax rates and have their dividends taxed as ordinary income; then it is considered investment income when computing this deduction limit. Before making this election, taxpayers should calculate the tax savings from the investment interest expense deduction to ensure that this will provide a greater after-tax benefit than the reduced tax rates for dividend income.

Stock Dividends

A simple common **stock dividend** (shares of the company's own stock) that is issued on a common stock investment is generally nontaxable. A stock dividend is treated the same as a *stock split* for tax purposes. The recipient shareholder realizes no increase in wealth from a stock split or a stock dividend.[69] He or she simply has more shares of stock indicating the same ownership percentage. Shareholders who receive a nontaxable stock dividend reallocate their capital investment in pre-dividend shares to all shares they own after the stock dividend.

Example 3.24

The Board of Directors of ABC Corporation declares a stock dividend of one share of stock for each share of stock owned by a shareholder (commonly known as a *2-for-1 stock split*). Just prior to the dividend, Susan owned 1,000 shares of ABC stock purchased for $30 per share ($30 × 1,000 = $30,000 total basis). Susan receives 1,000 new shares increasing her ownership to 2,000 shares of ABC. The additional 1,000 shares received are not income; her basis in each share after the dividend is $15 ($30,000 original cost of 1,000 shares/2,000 shares).

More complex stock dividends may or may not be taxable.[70] For example, if the corporation declares a stock dividend on one class of common stock but declares a cash dividend on another class of common stock, both the stock and cash dividends are taxable. The shareholders who receive the stock dividend have increased their percentage ownership in the corporation relative to those shareholders receiving cash. They have an increase in their wealth (their share of company assets) and have income equal to the value of the stock received.

3.4.3 ANNUITY INCOME

People usually purchase annuity contracts to provide a fixed stream of income in future years, often for retirement. The purchase amount is invested and returned as an **annuity**, a series of periodic payments consisting of two components—a nontaxable recovery of cost and the interest earned that must be included in gross income. The tax on the interest is deferred until the owner begins receiving the periodic payments. The following formula is used to calculate the nontaxable portion of each payment that represents the annuitant's return of capital;[71] the residual portion of each payment is the interest that is included in gross income.

$$\frac{\text{Investment in Annuity Contract}}{\text{Expected Return from the Contract}} \times \text{Annuity Received} = \text{Nontaxable Portion}$$

[69] *Eisner v. Macomber*, 252 US 189 (1920). The shareholder must sell the shares to realize income.
[70] See Chapter 10 for a discussion of dividends.
[71] §72(b)(1).

The fraction's denominator (expected return from the contract) depends on the term of the annuity, that is, the number of payments and the amount of each payment. If the annuity is payable over a specific period of time, such as 10 years, the annual receipts under the contract are multiplied by 10 to obtain the expected return. If the annuity is payable over the lives of one or more annuitants, an *expected return multiple*, obtained from Treasury Department tables, is multiplied by the annual amount received.[72] For a single-life annuity, the expected return multiple is the estimate of the individual's remaining life.[73]

The amount an annuitant ultimately receives may be more or less than the expected return; that is, the annuitant's actual life may be more or less than his or her expected life. If the annuitant lives longer than expected, the full investment is recovered before death and the additional payments (exceeding the cost) are all gross income. If the annuitant dies prematurely, the unrecovered cost is deducted on the annuitant's final tax return.[74]

Example 3.25

Cindy pays $150,000 for a single-life annuity paying $10,000 a year for life. Treasury Department tables estimate her remaining life to be 20 years. Thus, the expected return under the contract is $200,000 ($10,000 payments × 20 years). Of each $10,000 payment, Cindy reports $2,500 as gross income; $7,500 is a nontaxable return of investment determined as follows:

$$\frac{\$150{,}000 \text{ Investment}}{\$200{,}000 \text{ Expected Return}} \times \$10{,}000 \text{ Receipt} = \$7{,}500 \text{ Nontaxable Portion}$$

If Cindy lives for 25 years and receives total annuity payments of $250,000, she will be taxed fully on each $10,000 payment received in the last five years as her investment was fully recovered. If Cindy dies after receiving annuity payments of $150,000 over 15 years, three-fourths of these payments, or only $112,500 were recoveries of cost. Thus, $37,500 remains unrecovered when Cindy dies; this amount can be deducted on her final tax return.

Any portion of a retirement benefit annuity that represents a return of the employee's *after-tax* investment, is included in the numerator of the annuity formula, ensuring that this amount is not taxed a second time. If, however, the employer made all of the contributions to the retirement plan or the employee made the contributions on a *pretax* basis, the after-tax investment is zero and all amounts collected are taxable.[75]

3.4.4 TRANSFERS FROM OTHERS

Prizes and Awards

Cash and the fair market value of noncash prizes and awards (such as cars or vacations) are included in a recipient's gross income[76] and cannot be excluded as gifts. Thus, the value of prizes received from lotteries, game shows, contests, sweepstakes, raffles, and gambling activities must be included in gross income.[77] Similarly, treasure that a taxpayer finds or discovers is included in gross income once the taxpayer establishes undisputed ownership in the property.[78]

---

[72] The tables are found in Reg. §1.72-9.

[73] If the annuity is paid over lives of more than one annuitant, the denominator is based on the expected return for all annuitants. Since 2010, a nonqualified annuity (an annuity not part of a qualified retirement plan or an IRA) can pay out part over 10 or more years as a separate annuity while the remainder continues to earn interest.

[74] §72(b)(2) and (3).

[75] Retirement plans are discussed in Chapter 4.

[76] §74.

[77] A limited exception for employee length of service and safety awards is discussed in Chapter 4.

[78] Regulation §1.61-14(a).

Example 3.26

Michael wins his state's $9 million lottery, payable over 20 years. In years 1 through 5 he receives annual installments of $450,000. At the beginning of year 6, Michael receives $3,950,000 from a third party for the right to the remaining 15 payments. As a cash-basis taxpayer, Michael includes $450,000 in income each year for years 1 through 5. In year 6, Michael must include $3,950,000 in gross income.[79]

TAX PLANNING

Taxpayers who share winnings with others may have to pay tax on the entire amount, unless there is an pre-existing win-sharing arrangement. If the taxpayer wins and simply gives away part of the winnings, the taxpayer is taxed on the full amount and is treated as making separate gifts (which could be subject to gift tax). If a sharing agreement is made prior to determining the ticket is a winner, each individual reports only his or her share in gross income. The key is when the sharing arrangement (assignment) of the lottery ticket took place, before or after the taxpayer won the lottery.

A limited exclusion was added in 2016 for medals awarded to participants in the Olympic Games (including the Paralympic Games). This exclusion applies only to the value of medals awarded the Olympian or prize money received from the U.S. Olympic Committee. However, the exclusion does not apply to a taxpayer whose adjusted gross income exceeds $1 million ($500,000 if married filing separately).

Government Transfer Payments

Need-Based Payments Individuals who receive need-based payments from a federal, state, or local government agency exclude the payments from gross income.[80] Therefore, welfare payments, school lunches, and food stamps are nontaxable.

Unemployment Compensation Unemployment compensation is a payment from either a government or employer-financed program to provide for an individual's basic living costs during a period of unemployment. At one time, all or part of such income was excluded from income. Since 1987, all unemployment compensation has been included in gross income, as it is a substitute for taxable salary or wages.[81]

Social Security Benefits The Social Security system is a federal program that imposes a tax on employees, employers, and self-employed persons. The tax revenue is pooled in a trust fund to provide monthly Social Security benefits to retirees, disabled individuals, and surviving family members of deceased workers.

Before 1984, Social Security benefits were excluded from gross income as they provided for a person's general welfare. From 1984 through 1993, a maximum of one-half of the benefits could be included in income.[82] Since 1993, however, up to 85 percent of an individual's Social Security benefits may be included in income as this amount represents untaxed employer contributions and income on those contributions. The untaxed 15 percent represents employee contributions that were previously taxed.[83]

---

[79] *Maginnis,* 89 AFTR 2d 2002-3028. The sale of the right to receive future payments of ordinary income is taxed as ordinary income, not as capital gain.

[80] Rev. Rul. 71-425, 1971-2 CB 76.

[81] §85. The American Recovery and Reinvestment Tax Act of 2009 had an exception that excluded the first $2,400 of unemployment benefits received in 2009 only.

[82] Because the employer's half of the contributions has never been subject to federal income tax, beneficiaries should pay a federal income tax on up to that half of the Social Security benefits received.

[83] The 85 percent and 15 percent were actuarially determined.

The government taxes no more than 85 percent of the benefits of taxpayers with significant other income but leaves Social Security benefits completely tax free for taxpayers who have little or no other income. To determine an individual's ability to pay tax on Social Security benefits, tax-exempt interest income along with one-half of the Social Security benefits are included with the taxpayer's other adjusted gross income (for this test only).[84] This modified income is then compared to fixed base amounts established by Congress as follows:

	Tier 1 base	Tier 2 amount
Single	$25,000	$34,000
Married filing jointly	$32,000	$44,000

1. Single individuals with less than $25,000 and married couples with less than $32,000 of modified income are not taxed on their Social Security benefits.[85]
2. Single individuals with modified income between $25,000 and $34,000 and married couples with between $32,000 and $44,000 are taxed on the lesser of 50 percent of their benefits or 50 percent of the excess of modified income over their tier 1 base amount.
3. Single individuals with more than $34,000 and married couples with more than $44,000 of modified income are taxed on the lesser of 85 percent of their benefits or a computed amount.[86]
4. For single individuals, the computed amount is 85 percent of modified income over $34,000, plus the lesser of (a) $4,500 or (b) 50 percent of their benefits.
5. For married couples, the computed amount is 85 percent of modified income over $44,000, plus the lesser of (a) $5,000 or (b) 50 percent of their benefits.

Example 3.27

Silvia, a single individual, received $17,000 of dividend income, $40,000 of interest income from tax-exempt bonds, and $15,000 in Social Security benefits in the current year. Because she has $64,500 of modified income [$17,000 + $40,000 + ($15,000 × 50%)], 85 percent of Silvia's benefits are taxed. The first amount she computes for comparison is $30,425 [85% ($64,500 modified income − $34,000 tier 2 amount) + $4,500]. She adds only the $4,500 because this is less 50% of her benefits ($15,000 benefits × 50% = $7,500). Silvia now compares $12,750 (85% × $15,000 benefits) with the previously calculated $30,425 and includes the smaller of the two amounts in her income. Thus, $12,750 ($15,000 × 85%) of Silvia's Social Security benefits are included in gross income along with her dividend income resulting in gross income of $29,750($12,750 + $17,000).

Silvia's single sister, Sarah, receives $8,000 in Social Security benefits but her modified income is only $33,500. Sarah includes $4,000 ($8,000 × 50%) of her benefits in her gross income because this is less than 50 percent of her modified income in excess of her tier 1 base [($33,500 − $25,000) × 50% = $4,250].

Silvia's brother, John, receives $15,000 in Social Security benefits, but he has no additional income. John excludes all of his Social Security benefits from gross income and pays no income tax.

[84] §86. Modified income also includes any foreign earned income exclusion (discussed in Chapter 4) and interest from qualified U.S. savings bonds.

[85] The base amount is also $25,000 for heads of household, surviving spouses (qualifying widows or widowers), and married persons filing separately if they did not live with their spouse during the year. The base amount is zero if they file separately and lived with their spouse at any time during the year. The base amounts are not indexed for inflation.

[86] IRS Publication 915 contains filled-in worksheets showing the details of the complex calculations and can be downloaded from the IRS website at *www.irs.gov*.

Military Benefits Members of the Armed Forces receive many different types of pay and allowances. Basic pay, most bonuses, and incentive pay must be included in gross income. Many allowances, however, are excluded. The following is a list of the most common exclusions:

1. Combat zone pay
2. Living allowances (such as a basic allowance for housing, basic allowance for subsistence, and overseas housing allowance)
3. Moving allowances (such as military base realignment and closure benefits, storage, and temporary lodging)
4. Travel allowances (such as an annual round trip for dependent students, leave between consecutive overseas tours, and per diems)
5. Family allowances (such as educational expenses for dependents, for emergencies, and evacuation to a place of safety)
6. Death allowances (including burial services and travel of dependents to burial site)
7. Uniform allowances
8. Disability payments

Legal Settlements

The taxability of legal settlements depends on the nature of the underlying claim. Awards for loss of income are included in taxable income, unless a provision in the tax law specifically excludes them because they are substitutes for other taxable income. Similarly, awards for injury to reputation are taxable. Recoveries for property damage are included in income only to the extent they exceed the property's cost basis; these recoveries are treated as if the property had been sold.

Damage Payments for Physical Injuries Compensatory damages paid for an individual's physical injuries are excluded from gross income.[87] The underlying theory is that this type of damage recovery is a tax-free return of human capital under the cost recovery principle. Punitive damages can also be awarded to an individual victim to punish the party who caused the harm. Punitive damages are included in income because they may improve the victim's pre-injury economic situation. Damages awarded for emotional distress are not considered received for physical injury and are included in gross income (excluding expenses paid for medical care).

Example 3.28

Albert, an attorney operating as a sole proprietor, represented Eddie's ex-wife in a dispute that resulted in a $1,000,000 award against Eddie. Eddie then slandered Albert at his office in front of several of Albert's important clients. Then he threw an ashtray at Albert, hitting him in the head. Albert sustained a large gash on his forehead that required treatment at the hospital emergency room. In an out-of-court settlement, Albert received $4,000 for his physical injury, $1,800 for emotional distress, and $4,800 for lost income due to damage to his business reputation. Albert paid $3,100 in medical expenses for the treatment of the wound but was able to recover from his emotional distress without medical care. The $4,000 for physical injury is excluded from gross income, but the $1,800 is included as it relates to a nonphysical injury. The $4,800 is taxable because it is a substitute for business income.

Workers' compensation benefits paid to individuals unable to work because of an occupational injury are exempt from tax if received from a state-sponsored workers' compensation plan.[88]

[87] §104(a)(2).
[88] §104(a)(1).

In 2015, the PATH Act added an income exclusion for damages received by an individual wrongly incarcerated for any criminal offense under federal or state law. This applies to an individual who was convicted, served all or part of a sentence of imprisonment, and was pardoned or had the conviction reversed.

Divorce Married couples who divorce or separate usually enter into legal agreements affecting the financial aspects of breaking up the family unit. A divorce decree is issued to dissolve a marriage. A separate maintenance decree is issued when a couple legally separates and lives apart. Under either of these decrees, a couple is no longer considered married for federal tax purposes. A separation agreement often precedes the divorce or separate maintenance decree to settle the terms of their marital rights. The parties to a separation agreement are usually considered married for tax purposes.

Common financial arrangements include property settlements, alimony, and child support payments. The tax implications for each arrangement differ. A property settlement divides the divorcing spouses' assets between them. The division of marital property is generally a nontaxable event;[89] neither party recognizes gross income nor is entitled to a deduction. The property maintains the same tax basis it had before the settlement.[90]

TAX PLANNING

Property settlements should take into consideration the after-tax value of an asset, not just fair market value. Assume a taxpayer can choose between receiving \$100,000 cash or \$110,000 in stock with a cost basis of \$10,000. At a 15 percent capital gains rate, the \$110,000 in stock has an inherent tax cost of \$15,000 [(\$110,000 – \$10,000) × 15%]; thus, its after-tax value is only \$95,000 (\$110,000 – \$15,000 tax due upon sale).

Alimony is a cash transfer from one former spouse to the other for support.[91] For divorce agreements finalized before 2019, alimony is included in the recipient's gross income and the individual paying alimony excludes the amount from gross income to prevent double taxation.[92] In essence, alimony legally shifts taxable income between former spouses. To qualify as alimony, the payment must be made in cash, according to a divorce or written separation agreement, and terminates when the recipient dies.[93] For divorce agreements finalized after December 31, 2018, alimony is excluded from gross income and is not deductible by the payor.[94]

Child support is paid for the support of the children of divorced or separated parents. Generally, the noncustodial parent pays child support to the custodial parent. Child support is not included in the recipient's gross income because the funds are intended to provide for the

Example 3.29

In 2018, Kathy and Mark divorce after 12 years of marriage. Under the divorce decree, Kathy receives investment land that had been held jointly during the marriage. The land, acquired 9 years ago for \$100,000, is worth \$180,000 today. Kathy also receives \$18,000 cash in return for her half-interest in stock owned jointly. The stock was purchased 8 years ago for \$50,000. Additionally, Mark must pay Kathy \$1,800 per month; \$1,000 is alimony and \$800 is child support for their five-year-old daughter who lives with Kathy.

Mark recognizes no gross income from transferring his half-interest in the land to Kathy. If Kathy later sells the land for \$180,000, she will recognize the entire \$80,000 gain in her gross income at that time. Kathy is not allowed to deduct any loss on the transfer of stock to Mark. If Mark later sells the stock for \$40,000, he will be entitled to deduct the entire \$10,000 loss. Kathy includes \$1,000 per month in her gross income for the alimony and Mark deducts the same amount in determining his adjusted gross income. The child support is neither taxable nor deductible.

[89] For income tax purposes, this is treated as a nontaxable gift. In addition, this transfer is not subject to gift tax.
[90] §1041.
[91] §71(b)(1).
[92] §71 and §215.
[93] §71(b). Additionally, payments are classified as alimony only if the payor and recipient are not members of the same household and the payments are not identified in the divorce decree as payments other than alimony.
[94] The tax treatment of alimony for divorce agreements finalized before 2019 does not change unless a modification expressly provides that the new law applies.

children's support. Similarly, the parent paying child support has no deduction as that parent is fulfilling a legal obligation to care for his or her children.

TAX PLANNING

The person paying child support or alimony would prefer having them both classified as alimony so they are deductible; the recipient, however, prefers payments classified as tax-free child support or property settlement. If the person paying the alimony is in a higher marginal tax bracket than the recipient, both parties may benefit by negotiating an increased payment that qualifies as alimony.

Example 3.30

Roberto and Miriam are negotiating a divorce settlement in 2018. Roberto is in the 37 percent marginal tax bracket and Miriam is in the 12 percent marginal tax bracket. Roberto offered to pay Miriam $11,000 each year for 10 years, with payments ceasing if Miriam dies before the end of the 10-year period. Miriam will accept that amount only if the payments are a tax-free property settlement because she needs at least $11,000 after tax to meet expenses. Roberto's accountant suggests an alternative in which Roberto pays Miriam $13,500 alimony each year, a compromise that improves the after-tax cash flow for both parties.

	Roberto	Miriam
Original property settlement offer	($11,000)	$11,000
Revised alimony payment	($13,500)	$13,500
Tax savings @ 37%	4,995	
Tax @ 12%		(1,620)
After-tax cash flow	($8,505)	$11,880
Benefit from alimony alternative	$2,495	$880

TAX PLANNING

Some divorce agreements provide for larger payments in the early post-separation years that level off in later years. Large up-front payments resemble property settlements even though the agreement might refer to them as alimony. The tax law treats the excess portion of larger payments in the first two years as property settlements, regardless of what they are called. To prevent this reclassification as nondeductible property settlements, alimony payments during the first three years should not decrease by more than $15,000 between years.

3.4.5 DISCHARGE OF INDEBTEDNESS

There is no gross income when a taxpayer borrows money. The taxpayer's increase in cash is offset by an increased liability. Similarly, there is no income when the debt is repaid. If a taxpayer uses appreciated property to pay the debt, however, the taxpayer is taxed on the realized gain as if the property had been sold for its fair market value, repaying the debt with the sale proceeds.[95]

Example 3.31

Davila Corporation owes a creditor $70,000. Davila transfers investment land to the creditor to satisfy the debt. Davila purchased the land five years ago for $50,000, but it is currently worth $70,000. Davila must report a taxable gain of $20,000 ($70,000 – $50,000). It is treated as if Davila sold the land for $70,000 and used the proceeds to repay the debt.

Creditors sometimes forgive debt for many different reasons. Foreclosing could leave the creditor with property it cannot manage or sell; collecting amounts owed is difficult or expensive;

[95] *Kenan v. Comm.*, 25 AFTR 607, 40-2 USTC 9635, 114 F.2d 217 (CA-2, 1940). Generally, loss is also recognized on depreciated property unless it is a personal-use asset or the transfer is between related parties.

and demanding payment may create a negative public image. If a taxpayer satisfies a legal obligation for less than the outstanding debt, the amount the creditor forgives represents an increase in the taxpayer's wealth and is included in gross income.[96]

Example 3.32

Jessica borrowed $100,000 from her bank at 5 percent interest to begin a business, agreeing to make monthly payments for 12 years. Several years later, when her monthly payments reduced the loan principal to $60,000, the bank offers to settle the debt for $58,000 because loan interest rates have increased to 10%. If Jessica accepts the bank's offer, she recognizes $2,000 ($60,000 – $58,000) of gross income.

Exceptions are provided for debtors in certain situations, particularly if hardship is involved. For example, bankrupt and insolvent taxpayers whose debts are forgiven do not recognize gross income. Instead, they reduce tax attributes, including basis in the property, for the debt forgiven.[97] The reduction in tax attributes defers the tax liability for the forgiven debt to some future tax year.

To address the subprime lending crisis, the Mortgage Forgiveness Debt Relief Act of 2007 provided forgiveness of up to $2 million of qualified debt on a homeowner's principal residence through 2017. The basis of the residence was reduced (but not below zero) by the amount excluded under this provision. This provision also applied to mortgage debt reduced through restructuring (a mortgage workout) as well as a short sale or deed-in-lieu-of foreclosure as long as the debt qualified as acquisition debt on the taxpayer's principal residence. A taxpayer who sells property *not* his or her principal residence normally receives a Form 1099-C, *Cancellation of Debt* for the unpaid debt discharged as part of the sale.

Some student loans have a provision that provides forgiveness if the student works in a certain profession upon completion of his or her education. The amount of the student loan forgiven under these conditions is excluded from gross income.[98]

3.4.6 TAX BENEFIT RULE

If a taxpayer claims a deduction in one year and in a later year recovers all or part of the previously deducted amount, the recovery is included in income in the year received. Under Section 111, the amount included in income is limited to the extent that there was a tax benefit received from the tax deduction.

Example 3.33

Mayor Corporation, an accrual-basis, calendar-year taxpayer, sold $8,000 of its product on account to Ted in December, year 1. In year 2, Ted declared bankruptcy, so Mayor took a bad-debt deduction in year 2 for the $8,000. In year 3, Ted won a lottery and repaid some of his previous debts, including $5,000 to Mayor. Because Mayor took a bad-debt deduction in year 2, it includes $5,000 in income in year 3 due to the tax benefit rule. Mayor does not amend its prior year's tax return.

3.4.7 SYSTEM FOR REPORTING INCOME

Employers, banks, and other entities that make income payments (for example, salaries, interest, and dividends) are required to report payments made to the recipients to the IRS along with the

[96] §108.

[97] §§108(a) and (b). The Katrina Emergency Tax Relief Act of 2005 allowed individuals who suffered damage due to Hurricane Katrina to reduce tax attributes instead of recognizing income from a discharge of nonbusiness bad debt.

[98] §108(f). Student loans discharged because of the death or disability of the obligor are excluded from gross income.

Table 3.3 Forms Reporting Payments

Form	Type of payment
W-2	Salaries and wages
W-2G	Gambling winnings
1099-B	Sale of a security
1099-C	Cancellation of debt
1099-DIV	Dividends
1099-G	Government payments including unemployment compensation and tax refunds
1099-INT	Interest
1099-MISC	Miscellaneous income including nonemployee compensation and royalties
1099-OID	Original issue discount
1099-R	Distributions from retirement plans
SSA-1099	Social Security benefits

payee's identification number (Social Security number for individuals). The IRS then matches the reported information with that reported on the payees' tax returns to ensure that income is properly reported. Some of the principal reporting forms are listed in Table 3.3.

3.5 EXCLUSIONS

For various social, economic, and political reasons certain income items are excluded from gross income and are not subject to federal income tax; for example, gifts and inheritances are excluded to eliminate potential double taxation.

3.5.1 GIFTS AND INHERITANCES

Since its inception in 1913, the tax law has excluded gifts of property from the donee's (recipient's) gross income.[99] A **gift** is a voluntary property transfer from one party to another without full and adequate consideration received in return. Whether a transfer of property is intended to be a gift or compensation by the donor depends on all the facts and circumstances. The absence of legal or moral obligation or the fact that the donee does not expect to receive anything do not necessarily mean that the property received is a gift.

Example 3.34

John owns a plumbing business. Stan is an electrical contractor. John knows Stan does excellent electrical work, and when any of his customers needs an electrician, John always refers them to Stan. John believes he only enhances his own reputation by referring his clients to another reputable service person. During last year, almost one-quarter of Stan's business came from John's referrals. As a result, he sent John a Rolex watch valued at $4,000. John must include the value of the watch in income. The watch does not meet the gift requirement of proceeding from "detached and disinterested generosity" made "out of affection, respect, admiration, charity, or like impulses."[100]

Cash and other property that an employer gives to an employee are usually considered compensation, not a gift.[101] However, a transfer that clearly has no direct connection to the employment relationship, such as a wedding gift, may be treated as a gift.[102]

[99] §102(a). If a U.S. person receives a gift from a nonresident alien or foreign estate exceeding $100,000 (or $16,076 from a foreign corporation or partnership in 2018), the U.S. person must report each foreign gift to the IRS. §6039F(a).

[100] *Comm. v. Duberstein*, 363 US 278 (1960), 60-2 USTC 9515, 5 AFTR 2d 1626.

[101] §102(c).

[102] Prop. Reg. §1.102-1(f)(2).

Stocks, bonds, and other investment instruments given to family members in lower tax brackets allow future earnings, such as dividends and interest, to be taxed at lower rates. Additionally, any taxable gain on sale or other disposition of such properties is taxed to the donee, even if all or a portion of the gain accumulated during the donor's possession.

TAX PLANNING

Example 3.35

Joseph gives his 24-year-old daughter, Sara, 400 shares of RapidGrowth stock, purchased nine months ago at $30 per share. On the gift date, the stock is worth $40 per share. Joseph and Sara are in the 37 and 12 percent marginal tax brackets, respectively. After the gift, RapidGrowth declares and pays a $100 cash dividend to Sara because she now owns the stock. One month later, Sara sells her 400 shares for $45 per share. The entire $6,000 short-term capital gain [400 × ($45 – $30)] is added to Sara's gross income and taxed at her ordinary income rate. Thus, $6,100 of income is shifted from Joseph to Sara. The family tax savings from shifting the income is $1,520 {[$6,000 gain × (37% – 12%)] + [$100 dividend × (20% – 0%)]}.

Inheritances are gifts taking place at a donor's death and are excluded from gross income.[103] As with gifts, any income an heir derives from the property after its receipt is gross income.[104] A bequest that is actually compensation for past or future services, however, is included in gross income.[105]

Example 3.36

Miguel dies and bequeaths $100,000 to his son, Mike. Miguel's will also specifies a payment of $9,000 to his attorney, Simon, as the executor of his estate. If Simon fails to serve as executor, he forfeits all rights to the $9,000. Mike's $100,000 inheritance is not income but Simon must include the $9,000 he receives in gross income because it represents compensation for services.

Although the recipient of a gift or inheritance is not subject to income tax on the receipt of the gift, the person making these transfers could be subject to transfer taxes. Gift donors may be subject to the federal gift tax and a decedent's estate may be subject to the estate tax (discussed in Chapter 12).[106] The exclusion of gifts and inheritances from income taxation avoids potential double taxation (income *and* transfer taxes) on these transfers.

3.5.2 INSURANCE PROCEEDS

Life Insurance

Since 1913, life insurance proceeds paid because of the insured's death have been excluded from the beneficiary's gross income.[107] The proceeds of a life insurance policy owned by the decedent, however, generally are included in the gross estate and are subject to the estate tax. To avoid

[103] §102(a). Inherited property is not subject to income tax, but the receipt of income in respect of a decedent (IRD) is taxable. IRD is gross income that the decedent earned before death but was not includible in the decedent's final tax return, such as salary or interest earned but not received before death, and deferred retirement income. Income tax on IRD is paid by the estate or the beneficiary receiving it. See Chapter 12 for details.

[104] §102(b)(1).

[105] *Wolder v. Comm.*, 493 F.2d 608 (CA-2, 1974), 74-1 USTC 9266, 33 AFTR 2d 74-813.

[106] An annual gift exclusion of $15,000 per donee per year prevents small gifts from being subject to the gift tax. Unlimited transfers to a spouse or qualified charities (during lifetime or at death) escape the transfer tax entirely. A unified gift and estate tax credit allows up to $11.18 million of wealth to be transferred to others (including children, grandchildren, other relatives and friends) without tax.

[107] §101(a).

potential double taxation (income and estate taxes), life insurance proceeds a beneficiary receives are excluded from gross income.[108] This exclusion applies to the beneficiary's gross income, even if the decedent's employer paid for the policy rather than having been purchased with the decedent's funds.[109]

If a beneficiary receives life insurance proceeds over time in installments, the interest element in each installment is taxable.[110] The amount excluded (nontaxable) from each installment is calculated by dividing the policy's face value by the number of installments over which the payments will be received. The amount in excess of each installment's exclusion is interest income and is fully taxable.

Example 3.37

Peggy's husband died this year and she is the sole beneficiary of a $200,000 life insurance policy. She has two options: (1) receive the entire $200,000 in one lump-sum payment or (2) receive annual installments of $24,000 for 10 years. If Peggy takes the lump-sum option, the entire $200,000 is excludable. If she elects the installment option, she must include $4,000 [$24,000 – ($200,000/10)] interest in gross income each year.

Many businesses purchase life insurance on their officers and managers naming the business as beneficiary to protect against business disruption if an essential person dies. When an insured employee dies, the business receives the life insurance proceeds. The payment is not taxable income but is recorded as revenue for financial statement purposes.[111]

Some life insurance (whole life) policies provide not only the death benefit but also have an investment element called *cash surrender value*. The premiums paid for whole life policies, less the insurer's costs, are invested by the insurance company in stocks, bonds, and other securities. The cash surrender value increases each year the policy remains in effect; the annual increase in value is called the *inside buildup*. This inside buildup is not considered taxable income unless the taxpayer liquidates the policy for its cash surrender value. The excess of the cash surrender value over the total premiums paid is taxed as ordinary income.[112]

Example 3.38

Gary purchased an insurance policy on his own life that provided a $500,000 death benefit payable to his wife. After divorcing his wife, Gary liquidates the policy for its $56,000 cash surrender value. He paid $40,000 in policy premiums. Gary has $16,000 ($56,000 – $40,000) of ordinary income from surrendering the policy.

TAX PLANNING

Many taxpayers view life insurance as a good investment due to the dual benefits of tax deferral on the inside buildup while providing funds for beneficiaries in the event of premature death. By borrowing against the policy's cash surrender value, the owner can receive the policy's increase in value in cash without recognizing income.

[108] The owner of the insurance policy must have an insurable interest in the insured either through a personal or business relationship.
[109] §101(a).
[110] §101(d). Beneficiaries generally may choose to receive the proceeds as annuities. The annuity rules determine the taxable amount with the face value of the policy considered the invested capital.
[111] Premiums paid on life insurance policies for which the company is the beneficiary are not deductible because the proceeds are not taxable as discussed in Chapter 6. Life insurance proceeds and premium payments result in permanent differences between tax and financial accounting income.
[112] §72(e)(2). Certain terminally ill patients who receive accelerated death benefits from a life insurance policy are an exception, if the death benefits are received from a viatical settlement provider (a company licensed to be in the business of purchasing life insurance from the terminally ill). §101(g).

Owners of closely held businesses often enter into **buy–sell agreements** to buy the shares (or the partnership interest) of another owner who dies. Without such advance planning, the surviving owners could find themselves doing business with the deceased owner's heirs, who may be undesirable business associates. Even if the owners agree that surviving owners (or the business itself) have the first opportunity to buy a deceased owner's interest, funds may not be available to make the purchase. A popular means of financing such buy–sell agreements is through life insurance. The swap of life insurance policies between shareholders or partners or the transfer of life insurance policies to a controlled corporation or a partnership are nontaxable exchanges.[113]

Example 3.39

Maria and Martin each own half of a business worth $500,000. Each would prefer to run the entire business in the event of the other's death, but neither would have sufficient funds to buy the other's share. One possible solution for Maria and Martin is to enter into a buy–sell agreement funded through life insurance. Each purchases a $250,000 policy on his or her own life, transfers the policy to the corporation with the agreement that the corporation will redeem the decedent's shares. The receipt of insurance proceeds upon either Maria's or Martin's death is not taxable.

Accident and Health Insurance

Health and accident insurance benefits individuals receive for themselves, their spouses, or their dependents are excluded from gross income to the extent they only reimburse or pay for qualified medical or dental expenses.[114] Congress encourages this type of insurance coverage so individuals do not need government assistance when they are sick or injured. It is irrelevant whether an employer or employee pays the cost of this coverage.[115] If the employee, however, receives benefits in excess of qualified medical or dental expenses from a policy paid for by the employer, excess benefits are taxable to the employee. If the employee pays part of the cost of the insurance, a ratable portion of the excess payments equivalent to the employee contribution is excluded from income.[116]

Disability insurance (sometimes called wage replacement insurance) provides income for an individual who cannot work because of a serious illness or injury. If an individual purchases disability insurance directly, the cost of the policy is not deductible but disability benefits received are excluded from income. If the employer pays the premiums for disability insurance, the payments are fully taxable as a substitute for income normally paid by the employer. If the employer and employee share the cost, a ratable portion equivalent to the employer contribution is included in the employee's gross income.

Example 3.40

Jessica's employer pays 60 percent of the premium for her disability insurance policy and Jessica pays the other 40 percent. The policy pays Jessica 70 percent of her normal salary in the event she is injured and cannot return to work for an extended period. Jessica severely injures her back and is unable to work for several months. During the current year, Jessica collects $20,000 under her disability policy. Jessica includes $12,000 ($20,000 × 60%) in gross income for the percentage of the premium paid for by her employer; she excludes the other $8,000 ($20,000 × 40%) for the portion of the premium that she paid.

[113] The transfer of a life insurance policy for valuable consideration (such as the payment for a loan) makes life insurance proceeds in excess of basis taxable upon the death of the insured.

[114] Medical expenses are discussed in Chapter 5.

[115] Excluded benefits from long-term care insurance are limited to the greater of $360 for 2017 and 2018 ($340 in 2016) per day or the actual cost of care, whether the employer or employee pays the premiums.

[116] Reg. §§1.105-1(c), (d), (e).

Benefits paid for the permanent loss (or loss of use) of a bodily function or body part by an individual are excluded. Similarly, benefits collected by an individual because of injury or sickness that result in permanent disfigurement are excluded.[117]

3.5.3 SCHOLARSHIPS

Scholarships provide funding for individuals to pursue research or study. Congress encourages education by making these funds tax free. Scholarships, fellowships, and need-based grants, such as Pell grants, are usually excluded from gross income when (1) the recipient is a candidate for a degree, (2) the amount received is not a payment for services, and (3) the amount received is used to pay for tuition, books, and other similar educational expenses.[118] Personal living expenses (such as lodging, meals, and laundry), paid with any portion of the scholarship funds, even if permitted by the scholarship, must be included in gross income. This limitation provides equity with nonstudents who are effectively taxed on income they spend for personal living expenses. Similarly, excess scholarship funds used to pay other nonqualified expenses must be included in gross income.[119]

Any grant received in return for past, present, or future services is included in gross income.[120] Funds received by graduate assistants in return for teaching or research activities are taxable, even if all degree candidates are required to render similar services.[121]

Example 3.41

Laura received an $8,000 per year scholarship to attend the state university. During the current year, Laura spent $7,000 on tuition and required textbooks and $1,000 for room and board. Laura also worked part-time on campus and earned $6,000 to cover her remaining room and board and other expenses. Laura includes $1,000 in gross income for the scholarship funds spent on room and board and the $6,000 she earned from her part-time job.

Sometimes academic year scholarship payments are received in one taxable year, even though some of the expenses are not incurred until the following taxable year. When this happens, the nontaxable portion of the scholarship is not known until the academic year ends. This timing difficulty is resolved by keeping the transaction open and any taxable portion of the scholarship is included in gross income for the taxable year in which the academic year ends.[122]

Example 3.42

Marah receives a scholarship to attend the local university. The scholarship provides $10,000 for tuition, books, and related expenses for the academic year. Marah only spends $4,900 for tuition, books, and qualifying supplies from September through December of year 1 and $4,600 from January through April of year 2. She includes the $500 in excess of her qualified expenses in her gross income on her year-2 tax return.

[117] §105(c).
[118] §117. Payments for books, supplies, and equipment are tax free only if they are required for all students in the course.
[119] Funds included in gross income are treated as earned income, and may increase a student's standard deduction. Prop. Reg. §1.117-6(h).
[120] Students receiving athletic scholarships are usually viewed as "voluntarily" participating in sports without participation being a "requirement" for their scholarships; for this reason, athletic scholarships are usually viewed as tax free if they continue even if the student can no longer participate. See IRS Publication 970: *Tax Benefits for Education* for more details.
[121] Prop. Reg. §1.117-6(d)(2).
[122] Prop. Reg. §1.117-6(b)(2).

Employees of nonprofit educational institutions are allowed to exclude tuition waivers from gross income.[123] This exclusion applies to the employee, the employee's spouse, and dependent children, but is usually limited to undergraduate tuition.[124] This and many other fringe benefits provided by employers are very important components of employee compensations packages and are discussed in Chapter 4.

3.5.4 OTHER EXCLUSIONS

When a lease expires, the landlord regains control of the property, including any improvements made to the property by the tenant. The value of tenant improvements to leased property is excluded from a landlord's gross income unless they are made in lieu of rent.[125] Effectively, any tax on the value of the improvements is deferred until the property is sold.

As a matter of public policy, Congress favors home ownership, and promotes home ownership with an exclusion of up to $250,000 for gain realized on the sale of a principal residence. If the taxpayers are married and file a joint return, the exclusion increases to $500,000. Taxpayers must have owned and occupied the home as their principal residence for at least two years to qualify. This provision is discussed in Chapter 8.

3.6 EXPANDED TOPICS—JURISDICTIONAL ISSUES

Two principles normally guide the determination who will be taxed by a specific jurisdiction: the residency of the earning party (the residency principle) and the jurisdiction in which the income is earned (the source principle). Under the residency principle, individuals or corporations meeting a jurisdiction's residency rules are subject to that jurisdiction's tax rules, and for example, may tax its residents on income earned in other jurisdictions. Under the source principle, a jurisdiction claims the right to tax nonresident individuals and corporations on income earned in that jurisdiction, regardless of residency.

3.6.1 INTERNATIONAL ISSUES

Most countries follow the source principle of taxation of foreign persons and foreign corporations by taxing income earned within their borders but excluding income from activities taking place (sourced) in other countries. The residency principle, however, is applied to resident citizens and corporations by claiming the right to tax their worldwide income. Individuals and corporations that are residents of one country, but earn income in another country, face the prospect of double taxation.

Example 3.43

Corporation A has its home office and a manufacturing facility in Country X. It has a second manufacturing facility in Country Y and sells many of its products in Country Y. Under the residency principle, Country X claims the right to tax all of the profits from A's sales in both Countries X and Y. Under the source principle, Country Y claims the right to tax all the profits from the sales in Country Y.

Most countries address this issue of double taxation through **tax treaties**, agreements between two countries that explain how a taxpayer of one country is taxed when conducting business

---

[123] §117(d).
[124] Graduate teaching and research assistants may qualify for exclusion of graduate tuition waivers. §117(d)(5).
[125] §109.

in the second country. The objective of the treaty is to minimize double taxation. Under a typical treaty, only a corporation's country of residence taxes its income unless the business maintains a permanent establishment (such as an office or factory) in the second country. If such a permanent establishment exists, the treaty allows the source country to tax income earned within its boundaries. The citizens and corporations of the resident country offset the domestic tax on this foreign income with a foreign tax credit up to the amount of tax paid to the source country. As a result, the taxpayer that earned the income pays only one level of tax. The net tax paid is usually the larger tax imposed by the two countries claiming jurisdiction over the income.

Example 3.44

Continuing the previous example, Corporation A also sells its products in Country Z by mail or over the Internet, but has no offices or manufacturing facilities there. Country X has typical tax treaties with Countries Y and Z. Country Y taxes the profits from sales in Country Y only. Country Z does not tax any profits from sales in Country Z. Country X taxes the profits from A's sales in Countries X, Y, and Z, but Corporation A has a maximum tax credit equal to the actual taxes paid to Country Y or for the taxes paid to Country X on that income, if smaller.

3.6.2 TAXPAYERS SUBJECT TO U.S. TAXATION

United States citizens and resident aliens are subject to U.S. tax on their worldwide income.[126] A **resident alien** is not a U.S. citizen, but is an individual who has established a legal residence in the United States by obtaining a permanent resident card (called a green card) or meeting the substantial presence test for residency of 183 days.[127] An individual who is neither a U.S. citizen nor satisfies the alien residency test is a **nonresident alien**.

Income earned by nonresident aliens and foreign corporations is divided into three categories: U.S. business income (called effectively connected income), non-U.S. business income, and U.S. investment income. Nonresident aliens and foreign corporations are taxed similar to U.S. citizens on their effectively connected business income (from sales of goods manufactured in the United States or personal services performed in the United States). A nonresident corporation reports this income and related deductions on Form 1120F, and an individual reports it on Form 1040NR. Business income that is not effectively connected with the United States is usually not subject to U.S. tax. U.S. investment income (fixed and determinable, annual or periodic income) includes interest, dividends, and royalties. Whoever pays this investment income withholds tax at a flat 30 percent rate (or treaty rate if lower) and remits it to the government. There are usually no deductions for this type of income, so the recipient usually does not have to file a tax return.[128]

TAX PLANNING

When a nonresident alien is married to a U.S. citizen or resident alien, and both have taxable income, they normally must file their tax returns as married persons filing separately. The nonresident alien can elect to be taxed as a resident alien, allowing the couple to file a joint return, if both individuals agree to be taxed on their worldwide income. They must provide all information necessary to determine their tax liability, but this allows them to take advantage of the lower tax rates for joint returns.[129]

[126] Until 2018, U.S. corporations were also subject to tax on their worldwide income.

[127] §7701(b). The substantial presence test requires presence in the United States for 31 or more days during the current calendar year and presence in the United States for a total of 183 or more days during the current tax year and the two preceding tax years when using a weighted-average calculation. Some individuals are exempt from this substantial presence test including diplomats, teachers, students, and certain professional athletes.

[128] Nonresident aliens are not subject to the net investment income (NII) tax.

[129] §6013(g). A Social Security number (SSN) must be furnished on all tax returns. If an individual is not eligible to get a SSN, then he or she must apply for an individual taxpayer identification number.

A U.S. corporation may operate its foreign business through a foreign subsidiary. A corporation incorporated outside the United States with more than 50 percent of its shares owned by U.S. shareholders is a **controlled foreign corporation (CFC)**. Until 2018, the U.S. parent corporation was usually not taxed on the earnings of the foreign subsidiary until the earnings were repatriated (brought back) as dividends to the parent. When received, the dividends were included in the parent's income, and the parent was entitled to a foreign tax credit based on the income tax paid by the foreign corporation.[130] If the U.S. parent did not need cash from its overseas operations, it could direct its subsidiary to forgo paying dividends, allowing the parent to postpone paying U.S. taxes.

Certain foreign source income earned by a CFC was subject to tax even if retained in the business and not repatriated to its U.S. shareholders. This income, called **Subpart F income**, was taxed as a constructive dividend even if it was not paid to the parent. Subpart F income consisted of interest, dividends, rents, royalties, and certain other types of income taxed in a manner similar to the earnings of a flow-through entity (a partnership or S corporation). Because the parent was taxed on the Subpart F income when earned, it was not taxed a second time when paid as a dividend by the subsidiary.

In 2018, the U.S. moved from a system of worldwide taxation with deferral to a hybrid territorial system featuring a 100 percent dividend received deduction, current taxation of certain foreign income, a minimum tax on low-taxed foreign earnings, and a base erosion anti-abuse tax (BEAT) to promote production in the U.S.[131] Now a U.S. corporation that owns at least 10 percent of a foreign corporation will get a 100 percent dividend received deduction (DRD) for the foreign-source portion of dividends received from that foreign corporation.[132] To avoid a potential windfall for corporations with undistributed accumulated foreign earnings that will now be eligible for the 100 percent DRD, a transition tax is imposed on accumulated earnings of a foreign corporation without requiring any actual distribution. For the last tax year beginning before January 1, 2018, Subpart F income is increased by a U.S. shareholder's pro rata share of post-1986 deferred foreign income (deferral income) of a CFC. The effective net tax rate is 15.5 percent to the extent the shareholder's foreign earnings are held in cash or cash equivalents or 8 percent for illiquid assets (such as equipment). The tax can be paid over a period of up to 8 years and corporations can use their existing foreign tax credits to settle this tax.

To address concerns that moving to a territorial system could allow shifted profits to be permanently exempt from U.S. tax, new rules on intangible income effectively repeal deferral for multinational corporations with low-tax offshore structures by introducing a new category of Subpart F income that imposes a tax on the shareholder's net CFC income that is **global intangible low-taxed income (GILTI)**. Similar to other amounts included under Subpart F, GILTI is included in a U.S. shareholder's income each year without regard to whether that amount was distributed by the CFC to the U.S. shareholder that year. The inclusion of GILTI ensures that CFC earnings exceeding a certain return on its tangible assets are subject to some U.S. tax (at a nominal rate of 10.5 percent through 2025). In conjunction with the new minimum tax on excess returns earned by a CFC, the law provides a 13.125 percent effective tax rate on excess returns earned directly by a U.S. corporation from foreign sales (including licenses and leases) or services. The new law contains complex rules for determining the amount of a U.S. corporation's foreign-derived intangible income (FDII). All of these new laws added by the Tax Cuts and Jobs Act significantly change the way that foreign income is taxed for U.S. corporations.

---

[130] The foreign tax credit is discussed at the end of Chapter 4.

[131] BEAT works as a type of minimum tax affecting companies with large amounts of deductible payments to related parties.

[132] A foreign tax credit or deduction for foreign taxes paid cannot be claimed for any dividend allowed a 100 percent dividend received deduction.

REVISITING THE INTRODUCTORY CASE

Municipal bonds yield a higher after-tax return than corporate bonds because the interest earned on the municipal bonds is tax free while interest on the corporate bonds is taxable. Steven is subject to income tax rates of 37% for interest income and 20% for long-term capital gains. The investment land yields an even better return because the increase in value avoids taxation for five years until the land is sold. Additionally, the gain on the land sale is taxed at the lower capital gains rate rather than the ordinary rate applied to interest income. Steven should invest in the land.

	Corporate bonds	Tax-exempt bonds	Investment land
Annual interest income			
$50,000 × 6%	$3,000		
$50,000 × 4%		$2,000	
Income tax @ 37%	(1,110)	0	
After-tax cash flow	$1,890	$2,000	
Reinvested for 5 years			
6% annuity factor	× 5.637		
4% annuity factor		× 5.416	
After-tax cash flow from interest for 5 years	$10,654	$10,832	
Original investment in land			$50,000
6% factor			× 1.338
Land value in 5 years			$66,900
Return of capital			(50,000)
Pre-tax gain			$16,900
Tax on gain @ 20%			(3,380)
After tax-value	$10,654	$10,832	$13,520

SUMMARY

The Internal Revenue Code states that all forms of income are taxable unless specifically excluded. Congress excludes certain items from income due to social, economic, and political reasons. A taxpayer can also use certain provisions to defer income recognition. The difference is that excluded income is never taxed, while deferred income is taxed in some future period.

Several key principles govern the determination of gross income. The realization principle prevents income recognition until it is realized by the taxpayer through a sale or other transaction. Under the return of capital principle, a taxpayer's basis in an investment is excluded from gross income and recovered tax free. The assignment of income doctrine prevents taxpayers from shifting income they earn or from property they own to a lower-income individual for taxation.

The method of accounting determines the period in which income is recognized. Cash-basis taxpayers generally recognize income when cash or a cash equivalent is received. Accrual-basis taxpayers generally recognize income when the earnings process is complete and the all events test has been met. The constructive receipt doctrine modifies the cash method by requiring taxpayers to recognize income when it is set aside for them or otherwise made available to them. The claim of right doctrine requires accrual-basis taxpayers to recognize income when it is received, even if some or all of the income may have to be repaid at a later date, unless the taxpayer's use of the income is restricted. Generally accepted accounting principles have different objectives than those of tax reporting and can result in income recognition in different periods for tax and financial accounting.

Two of the most common sources of unearned income are interest and dividends. Although interest and dividends are usually taxable, exceptions exist for state and local bond interest and stock dividends.

The most common income exclusions were discussed as well as several other income items with recognition postponed to a later period. Exclusions are the result of congressional action to achieve specific policy objectives of subsidizing certain activities or minimizing the impact of double taxation. Common exclusions include gifts, inheritances, certain insurance proceeds, and scholarships. Government welfare payments escape taxation, but federal unemployment insurance is fully taxable. Higher-income individuals can have as much as 85 percent of their Social Security benefits taxed, while lower-income individuals' Social Security payments are tax free. As a matter of law, all income is taxed unless a specific provision excludes an item from income taxation.

Multijurisdictional taxpayers face more complex issues. Most countries follow the source principle with regard to foreign persons and foreign corporations by taxing income earned within their borders while excluding income from activities in other countries. Most countries, however, apply the residency principle to their own residents by claiming the right to tax their worldwide income. Many individuals face the prospect of double taxation. Tax treaties between two countries address this potential for double taxation. Typically one country allows a foreign tax credit to offset taxes paid to a second country.

KEY TERMS

Accrual method 115
Alimony 131
All events test 115
Annuity 126
Assignment of income doctrine 118
Basis 111
Buy–sell agreements 137
Calendar year 113
Cash method 114
Child support 131
Claim of right doctrine 116
Completed contract method 117
Constructive receipt doctrine 114
Controlled foreign corporation (CFC) 141
Dividend 124
Earned income 119
Fiscal year 113
Gift 134
Global intangible low-taxed income (GILTI) 141
Gross income 109
Inheritances 135
Municipal bonds 119
Nonresident alien 140
Original issue discount (OID) 121
Percentage-of-completion method 117
Realization principle 109
Resident alien 140
Return of capital 111
Scholarships 138
Short tax year 113
Stock dividend 126
Subpart F income 141
Taxable income 110
Tax treaties 139
Unearned income 119
Wherewithal to pay 116

TEST YOURSELF

Answers Appear after the Problem Assignments

1. Jason receives semiannual annuity checks of $4,500. Jason purchased the annuity five years ago for $110,000 when his expected return under the annuity was $200,000. How much of Jason's total annual payment is a nontaxable return of capital?

a. $9,000
b. $4,950
c. $4,050
d. Zero

2. Kevin owes his gardener $100. After several unsuccessful attempts to collect the debt, the gardener notifies Kevin that the debt is forgiven and that he will continue as gardener only if he is paid cash in advance. How much of the $100 forgiveness should Kevin report as gross income?

a. $100
b. $50
c. $20
d. $0

3. Elio (age 66) is retired. His wife, Mary (age 64) works part-time. They have income from the following sources and plan to file a joint tax return.

Mary's salary	$10,000
Elio's retirement annuity (all contributions made by his employer)	15,000
Elio's Social Security benefits	5,000
Interest income from their municipality's general revenue bonds	1,000
Cash dividend from Ford Motor Company	500
Lottery prize	50

What is their gross income?

a. $31,550
b. $30,500
c. $25,550
d. $10,000

4. Marilyn received the following in the current year:

Alimony (from a divorce decree finalized in 2017)	$12,000
Child support	8,000
Interest income from corporate bonds	800
Dividend income	400
Gift from her sister	200
Jury duty pay	50

What is her gross income?

a. $13,200
b. $13,250
c. $21,200
d. $21,450

5. Cindy was awarded a $6,000 scholarship to attend the state university. She spent $4,000 for tuition, $500 for required textbooks, and $1,500 for room and board. She works part-time on campus earning $5,000, which covers the balance of her room and board and other expenses. How much must Cindy include in her gross income?

a. $0
b. $5,000
c. $6,500
d. $7,000

PROBLEM ASSIGNMENTS

Check Your Understanding

1. [LO 3.1] Explain the realization principle.

2. [LO 3.1] Provide three reasons why generally accepted accounting principles are not allowed for tax purposes.

3. [LO 3.1] What are two major categories of differences between financial accounting income and taxable income?

4. [LO 3.1] What types of investments are favored by tax law and why?

5. [LO 3.2] Michelle (a calendar-year individual) begins a new business as a sole proprietorship. She would like to use an October 31 fiscal year-end for her business because the calendar year ends during her busy season. What must Michelle do to use a fiscal tax year?

6. [LO 3.2] Jabba Company uses the cash method of accounting. Jabba received a computer from a customer as payment for a $2,000 bill. Can Jabba avoid recognizing income because it received payment in a noncash form? Explain.

7. [LO 3.2] Murphy Company, a cash-basis, calendar-year taxpayer, received a call on December 28, year 1, from a client stating that a check for $9,000 as payment in full for their services can be picked up at their offices, two blocks away, any weekday between 1:00 and 6:00 P.M. Murphy does not pick up the check until January 3, year 2. In which year does Murphy recognize the income?

8. [LO 3.2] Are there any restrictions on business use of the cash method of accounting? Explain.

9. [LO 3.2] Explain why accrual-method taxpayers treat prepaid income differently for GAAP and tax purposes.

10. [LO 3.2] What is a long-term contract? Briefly describe the two possible accounting treatments for long-term contracts.

11. [LO 3.3] Ryan's annual salary is $120,000 per year. He asked his employer to pay $20,000 of his salary to his elderly grandmother who is in a nursing home. The employer pays $20,000 directly to the grandmother and the balance to Ryan. What is Ryan's gross income?

12. [LO 3.3] Explain how community property laws can affect the allocation of income between spouses.

13. [LO 3.4] Virginia gave her 14-year-old grandson, Tommy, $10,000 in common stock. One month later, Tommy receives a $100 dividend on the stock. How much income is taxed to Tommy and how much to Virginia?

14. [LO 3.4] Why is interest income on state and local bonds tax exempt?

15. [LO 3.4] At the beginning of the current year, Martha, a cash-basis taxpayer, purchased a $10,000 three-year bond from Lauderhill Corporation at its issue price of $7,000. At the end of the year, $840 of interest had accrued. How much income does Martha report for the current year?

16. [LO 3.4] While walking through the park, Jane finds a $100 bill. No one is around to claim it, so she keeps it. Does Jane have any gross income as a result of this?

17. [LO 3.4] What is the rationale for taxing unemployment compensation?

18. [LO 3.5] Are the recipients of gifts and inheritances subject to double taxation? Explain.

19. [LO 3.5] What is a buy–sell agreement, and how does life insurance facilitate it?

20. [LO 3.6] Compare how the United States taxes a U.S. citizen and a nonresident alien.

21. [LO 3.6] What is the purpose of the United States establishing a tax treaty with a foreign country?

22. [LO 3.6] What is the purpose of the foreign tax credit?

Crunch the Numbers

23. [LO 3.2] Chet, a cash-basis, calendar-year sole proprietor, repairs the computer system in his dentist's office. On December 10, 2018, he sends the dentist a bill for $600 and records the account receivable. In January 2019, Chet accepts dental work worth $575 in full payment of the bill. How much and in which year does Chet report gross income?

24. [LO 3.2] At the end of October, year 1, Dunbar Corporation hired Specialty Training, an accrual-basis, calendar-year S corporation, to provide a six-week training program for its employees. Dunbar paid Specialty its full training fee of $30,000 on the first day of training. After five weeks of training sessions, Dunbar cancelled the last week of training and demanded a refund of $5,000, because its employees felt the training was misrepresented and failed to provide the in-depth coverage of the topics they had specified. In January, year 2, Specialty refunded $5,000 to Dunbar. Specialty owners' marginal tax rate for year 1 is 32 percent.
   a. What choices does Specialty Training have to account for the $5,000 refund?
   b. If Specialty owners' marginal tax rate in year 2 is 37 percent, how should the company account for the refund for tax purposes?
   c. If Specialty owners' marginal tax rate in year 2 is 24 percent, how should the company account for the refund for tax purposes?

25. [LO 3.2] Realty Corporation, an accrual-basis, calendar-year corporation, agrees to rent office space to Tenant Company for $3,000 per month beginning on January 1, year 2. On December 15, year 1, Tenant gives Realty Corporation a $3,000 deposit in addition to rent for the months of January and

February. In year 2, Tenant pays rent for the months of March and April. On May 15 Tenant closes its business and vacates the office. Realty withholds $1,500 from the deposit for unpaid rent and $1,000 for damages. Realty Corporation refunds the balance of the deposit to Tenant on May 20, year 2.

a. How much income should Realty Corporation report in year 1 from the above transactions for tax and financial accounting?

b. How much income should Realty Corporation report in year 2?

26. [LO 3.2] On December 1, year 1, Peak Advertising (a calendar-year, accrual-basis taxpayer) received a $24,000 retainer fee for a two-year service contract.

a. How much income should Peak report in year 1 for tax and financial accounting?

b. How much income should Peak report in year 2 for tax and financial accounting?

c. How much income should Peak report in year 3 for tax and financial accounting?

27. [LO 3.2] In year 1, Highrise Company contracts to manufacture a piece of customized equipment for a customer. The contract will take two years to complete. The contract price is $250,000 and the company estimates total costs of $220,000. Actual costs incurred are:

Year 1	$121,000
Year 2	105,000
	$226,000

What are the company's gross income and deductions recognized in each of the two years, assuming the company uses (1) the completed contract method and (2) the percentage-of-completion method of accounting for long-term contracts?

28. [LO 3.3] Mac's 24-year-old daughter, Alana, is a full-time student. In 2018, Mac gives Alana 600 shares of Highgrowth stock. Mac purchased the stock 10 months ago at $20 per share. On the gift date, the stock is worth $35 per share. After the gift, Highgrowth declares and pays a $170 dividend to Alana. The next month, Alana sells her 600 shares for $38 per share. Mac and Alana are in the 32 and 12 percent marginal tax brackets for ordinary income and in the 15 and 0 percent tax brackets for dividend income, respectively.

a. How much must Alana and Mac include in gross income in 2018?

b. What family tax savings are achieved through this gift?

29. [LO 3.4] Carl paid $40,000 to the City of Hollywood for general revenue bonds. During the current year, he received $2,300 interest income from the bonds. Market interest rates drop, causing the value of the bonds to increase so Carl sells the bonds for $43,000. How much gross income must Carl report for the year?

30. [LO 3.4] Jessica has $10,000 invested in corporate bonds with a stated interest rate of 7 percent and $10,000 in tax-exempt municipal bonds issued for governmental activities with a stated interest rate of 5.5 percent. Calculate her after-tax cash flow from each investment if:

a. her marginal tax rate is 12 percent.

b. her marginal tax rate is 32 percent.

31. [LO 3.4] Joshua loans his son, Seth, $100,000 interest free for five years. Seth uses the money for a down payment on his home. Assume that the applicable federal interest rate is 4 percent.

a. What are the tax consequences of this loan to Joshua and to Seth?

b. How would your answer change if Seth uses the money to invest in corporate bonds paying 8 percent annual interest?

32. [LO 3.4] Sheldon Corporation loans $80,000 interest free for one year to Lynn, an employee. Assume that the applicable federal interest rate is 4 percent. Lynn uses the loan to pay for personal debts. What are the loan's tax consequences for Sheldon and Lynn? How would your answer change if Lynn is a shareholder of Sheldon Corporation?

33. [LO 3.4] George owns 1,000 shares of ABC common stock and 3,000 shares of Brightstar mutual fund. George elects to participate in Brightstar's dividend reinvestment plan, reinvesting his annual dividends and capital gains distributions in additional Brightstar shares. George receives a $5,000 distribution from ABC and a Form 1099-DIV indicating that $4,000 of the distribution is a dividend and $1,000 is a nontaxable distribution. He also receives a Form 1099-DIV from Brightstar mutual fund indicating that he has a dividend of $6,500 and a capital gains distribution of $1,300 for a gross distribution of $7,800 that is reinvested in 90 additional shares of Brightstar mutual fund. How much does George include in his gross income for the year?

34. [LO 3.4] The Board of Directors of CYZ Corporation votes to issue two shares of stock for each share held as a stock dividend to shareholders. Just prior to the dividend, Cheryl owns 100 shares of CYZ Corporation stock that she purchased for $10 per share. She receives 200 new shares as a result of the dividend. How much gross income must Cheryl report as a result of the dividend and what is her stock basis after the dividend?

35. [LO 3.4] Charles pays $120,000 for a single-life annuity that will pay him $11,000 a year for life. Treasury Department tables estimate his expected remaining life at 15 years.

a. How much of each $11,000 payment must Charles report as gross income?

b. If Charles dies after receiving annuity payments totaling $77,000 over seven years, what happens to the unrecovered cost?

36. [LO 3.4] Barney retired from the Marlin Corporation where he worked for 25 years. Barney elects to receive his retirement benefits as an annuity over his remaining life, resulting in annual payments of $15,000. His plan balance consists of $70,000 employer contributions, $20,000 after-tax employee contributions, $10,000 pretax employee contributions, and $22,000 investment earnings. Based on Barney's life expectancy, his expected return is $240,000. Of each $15,000 payment, how much must Barney report as gross income?

37. [LO 3.4] Julie wins $15 million in the lottery payable over 30 years. In years 1 through 4, she receives annual installments of $500,000. At the beginning of year 5, Julie sells her right to receive the remaining 26 payments to a third party for a lump-sum payment of $8,900,000. How much does Julie include in income each year?

38. [LO 3.4] Vera, a single individual, receives $18,000 of dividend income and $38,000 of interest income from tax-exempt bonds. Vera also receives Social Security benefits of $16,000. What is Vera's gross income?

39. [LO 3.4] Jeff, a single individual, receives $5,000 interest income from Treasury bills and $18,000 in Social Security benefits. What is Jeff's gross income?

40. [LO 3.4] Mike was shopping in Produce Market when it was robbed. Mike suffered some injuries during the robbery and filed suit against Produce Market for not maintaining a secure environment for its customers. In an out-of-court settlement, Mike received $12,000 for his physical injuries, $2,000 for emotional distress, and $3,000 for lost wages while he recovered from his injuries. Mike paid $11,000 in medical expenses attributable to treatment for his injuries but was able to recover from his emotional distress without medical care. How much gross income does Mike have as a result of this settlement?

41. [LO 3.4] Stu and Harriett divorce on January 2, 2018 after eight years of marriage. Under the divorce decree, Harriett receives a vacation home that was held jointly with Stu while they were married. The vacation home was acquired seven years ago for $90,000, but is worth $170,000 today. Additionally, Stu is required to pay Harriett $2,000 per month beginning in January; $1,300 is for alimony and $700 is for child support for their six-year-old son who lives with Harriett.

a. How much gross income does Harriett recognize in 2018?

b. Will Stu have a tax deduction for any of these payments?

42. [LO 3.4] Markum Corporation owes a creditor $60,000. Markum transfers property purchased four years ago for $45,000 to the creditor to satisfy the debt. The property is currently worth $60,000. Does Markum have any gross income as a result of this transaction?

43. [LO 3.4] Sandle Corporation, an accrual-basis, calendar-year taxpayer, sold $15,000 of its products on account to Jim in November, year 1. In year 2, Jim declares bankruptcy and Sandle writes off the account as a bad debt. In year 3, Jim unexpectedly inherits a large sum of money and uses part of it to repay his creditors, including a $12,000 payment to Sandle Corporation.
   a. What does Sandle Corporation report on its tax returns for years 1, 2, and 3?
   b. How would your answers change if Sandle is a cash-basis taxpayer?

44. [LO 3.4] Krystyna, a single individual, invested $20,000 in corporate bonds with a stated interest rate of 5 percent and another $20,000 in tax-exempt municipal bonds issued for governmental activities with a stated interest rate of 4.75 percent. Calculate her after-tax cash flow from each investment if:
   a. her marginal tax rate is 12 percent.
   b. her marginal tax rate is 32 percent.

45. [LO 3.3 & 3.4] Justin's 24-year-old son, Carlos, is a full-time student. In April 2018, Justin gave Carlos 450 shares of Striker Oil stock. Justin purchased the stock 8 months earlier at $18 per share. On the gift date, the stock was worth $31 per share. After the gift, Striker Oil declared and paid a $200 dividend to Carlos. Then three months later, Carlos sold his 450 shares for $38 per share. Justin and Carlos are in the 37 and 12 percent marginal tax brackets, respectively.
   a. How much must Carlos and Justin include in gross income in 2018?
   b. What family tax savings were achieved through this gift?
   c. How would your answer to (b) change if Carlos held the stock for 5 months before selling for $38 per share?

46. [LO 3.5] Myra received a $20,000 gift from her cousin and inherited $80,000 in corporate bonds from her aunt at the beginning of the current year. Myra received $7,000 in interest income from the bonds at the end of the current year. How much does Myra include in gross income?

47. [LO 3.5] Linda's husband dies, naming her the sole beneficiary of a $500,000 life insurance policy. The insurance company informs her that she has two options: (1) she can receive the entire $500,000 in one lump-sum payment or (2) she can receive annual installments of $58,000 for 10 years.
   a. How much does Linda include in gross income if she takes the lump-sum payment?
   b. How much does Linda include in gross income each year if she elects the installment payments?

48. [LO 3.5] Mark's employer pays 55 percent of the premiums for a disability insurance policy and Mark pays for the other 45 percent. The policy pays Mark 65 percent of his normal salary in the event he is injured and cannot return to work for an extended period. Mark was hit by a truck and was unable to work for several months. During the current year, Mark collected $30,000 under his disability policy. How much does Mark include in his gross income?

49. [LO 3.5] Sara has a $5,500 per year scholarship to attend the state university. Sara spent $4,000 for tuition, $500 for required textbooks and $1,000 for room and board. Sara also had a part-time job on campus earning $3,000 that covered the balance of her room and board and supply expenses. How much does Sara include in her gross income?

50. [LO 3.5] Larry has a scholarship to attend the local college. The scholarship provides $7,000 for tuition, books, and related expenses for the academic year. Larry only spent $3,200 for tuition, books, and related supplies from August through December of year 1 and $3,400 from January through April of year 2. Does Larry have any income from this scholarship and if so, in which year is it recognized?

Develop Planning Skills

51. [LO 3.2] Robert plans to start a new business that he believes will have steady growth in profits for the next 15 years. He needs to select a method of accounting to use: cash or accrual. He would like to select the method that will provide the higher net present value for the company's cash flows. Which method should he choose and why?

52. [LO 3.2] Palace Company (an accrual-basis taxpayer) is writing the lease agreements for its new apartment complex, Palace Apartments, which will rent for a minimum of $2,000 per month. Palace wants tenants to pay $6,000 when they sign the lease and is considering two alternatives. Under the first alternative, $4,000 would be rent for the final two months of the lease, with $2,000 for the damage deposit. Under the second alternative, $2,000 would be for the last month's rent and $4,000 would be for the damage deposit. Discuss the tax implication of each alternative and recommend one.

53. [LO 3.4] Sandra, a single taxpayer in the 37 percent marginal tax bracket, has $60,000 she can invest in either corporate bonds with a stated interest rate of 9 percent or general revenue bonds issued by her municipality with a stated interest rate of 6 percent. What do you recommend she do? Would your answer change if her marginal tax rate is only 22 percent?

54. [LO 3.4] Kevin and Elizabeth are negotiating a divorce settlement. Kevin is in the 35 percent marginal tax bracket and Elizabeth is in the 12 percent marginal tax bracket. Kevin has offered to pay Elizabeth $15,000 each year for 10 years; payments would cease if Elizabeth dies before the end of the 10-year period. Elizabeth is willing to settle for that amount only if the payments qualify as a tax-free property settlement because she needs at least $15,000 after tax to meet her expenses.
   a. How much would Elizabeth have to receive in taxable alimony payments from Kevin to have the equivalent of a $15,000 tax-free payment?
   b. If Kevin agrees to an $18,500 alimony payment, what is the after-tax cash flow for Kevin and Elizabeth? By how much does their cash flow improve over the proposed $15,000 property settlement payment?

Think Outside the Text

These questions require answers that are beyond the material that is covered in this chapter.

55. [LO 3.2] Walter used the cash method to account for income from his cattle ranch. During an audit in year 3, the IRS auditor discovered a document from a customer indicating that Walter sold 115 head of cattle to the customer two years earlier for $77,000. The document appeared to be a tear slip, the top half of a document that normally includes a business check. Walter's bank records for year 1 showed no such deposit, and a conversation with the customer revealed that its check for $77,000 had never been cashed. A new check was issued in year 3. Walter included the $77,000 as income on his year 3 tax return. The IRS then issued an audit report contending that the income was taxable in year 1 under the doctrine of constructive receipt. If you were a tax court judge hearing this case, how would you rule?

56. [LO 3.4] Some politicians have proposed changing the way Social Security benefits are taxed. One proposal would increase the amount of Social Security benefits included in gross income to 100 percent. A tax rate of 100 percent would then apply for some high-income individuals, effectively preventing them from receiving benefits. What do you think about this proposal?

57. [LO 3.4] Congress has the power to tax income "from whatever source derived." Do you believe that this allows Congress the discretion to tax municipal bond interest (or other tax-exempt income) earned throughout a tax year retroactively if the law to make this income taxable is not enacted until the very end of the tax year? (Note: The Tax Relief Act of 2010 retroactively reinstated the estate tax for decedents dying in 2010 late in the year after it originally had been repealed for 2010.)

58. [LO 3.4] John and Mary are divorcing. John demands that Mary pay him $75,000 alimony in the first year after the divorce, $50,000 in the second year, and $25,000 in the third and all subsequent years until he dies or remarries. What are the income tax ramifications of alimony structured in this manner?

59. [LO 3.5] Joe owes Willy $5,000 from an old gambling debt. Joe knows that there is no way he can repay the debt in the near future. He asks Joe if he will take a $25,000 life insurance policy that has a cash surrender value of $4,200 and release him from the debt. Willy agrees to take the insurance

policy and cancels Joe's debt. Willy makes only one premium payment on the insurance policy of $50 when Joe is killed in an auto accident. Willy collects the $25,000. Explain all the tax consequences of these events for both Joe and Willy.

60. [LO 3.2, 3.4 &3.5] On O's Favorite Giveaway Show, the host gave 100 audience members debit cards, each one for $16,000, with the stipulation that the audience members donate the money to their favorite charitable cause (they cannot keep the money for themselves or give it to their relatives). The debit cards are sponsored by the Bank of America. Each audience member was also given a DVD recorder to record their stories for a future show. Identify all of the possible tax implications of this giveaway and explain what you think the tax treatment is for each.

Search the Internet

61. [LO 3.4] Go to the IRS website (*www.irs.gov*) and locate Publication 915: *Social Security and Equivalent Railroad Retirement Benefits*. Determine how much of the Social Security benefits must be included in income for a single individual who had $20,000 in dividend income and $5,000 in interest from tax-exempt bonds, in addition to receiving $10,000 in Social Security benefits.

62. [LO 3.4] U.S. citizens residing in certain countries are exempt from U.S. tax on their Social Security benefits. Go to the IRS website (*www.irs.gov*) and locate Publication 915: *Social Security and Equivalent Railroad Retirement Benefits* to determine which countries are covered under this special provision.

63. [LO 3.4] Go to *www.legalbitstream.com* (or *www.irs.gov/irb/*and start with IRB 2011–37) and locate Notice 2011–64. Read the appendix of Notice 2011–64 and determine if dividend income received from foreign corporations located in the following four jurisdictions is a qualified dividend eligible for the reduced dividend (i.e., 0, 15, or 20 percent) tax rates: Bermuda, China, Jamaica, and the Netherland Antilles.

64. [LO 3.5] Go to *www.legalbitstream.com* and locate Announcement 2002–18. What is the IRS's policy on taxing frequent flyer miles?

Identify the Issues

Identify the issues or problems suggested by the following situations. State each issue as a question.

65. [LO 3.2] Jason owns a computer repair shop. Jason needs some repair work done on his company car, so he agrees to repair the computer at Bob's Auto Repairs in exchange for fixing the car.

66. [LO 3.2] A landlord requires tenants to pay 3 months' rent in advance at the beginning of a lease. He informs the tenants that this is for the first month's rent, the last month's rent, and a refundable security deposit equal to one month's rent.

67. [LO 3.2] In December, year 1, Sid's Body Shop (an accrual-basis taxpayer) repaired Lisa's car and was to be paid $2,000 by her insurance company. Lisa was not satisfied with the repair job but finally agreed that her insurance company should pay $1,700 for the repair work, subject to approval by the insurance company adjuster. In March, year 2, the insurance company paid $1,700 to Sid's Body Shop.

68. [LO 3.4] While diving in the Florida Keys on vacation, Gillian finds a gold bar from a sunken ship.

69. [LO 3.4] Bill and Susan are planning to divorce. Their daughter, Melissa, will live with Susan. Bill has offered to pay Susan $1,000 per month for eight years.

70. [LO 3.4] Sharp Corporation has $250,000 in assets and $300,000 in liabilities. Sharp negotiates a deal with one of its creditors to write off $20,000 of the $60,000 owed to the creditor.

71. [LO 3.6] Ken receives interest income from Province of Ontario (Canada) bonds.

Develop Research Skills

72. [LO 3.2] Gamma Corporation, a calendar-year accrual-basis taxpayer, operates department stores. Alpha Corporation and Beta Corporation are wholly-owned domestic subsidiaries of Gamma Corporation and file a consolidated federal tax return under Gamma Corporation's consolidated group. Gamma, Alpha, and Beta enter into a gift card service agreement under which Gamma is primarily liable for the value of the gift cards until redemption while Alpha and Beta are obligated to accept the gift cards as payment for goods and services. Gamma issues the gift cards and reimburses Alpha and Beta for the sale price of the goods and services purchased with the gift cards. The group recognizes revenue in its applicable financial statement when the gift cards are redeemed. In year 1, Gamma Corporation makes $2 million in gift card sales. Gamma tracks redemptions of gift cards electronically and determined that $1,800,000 was redeemed in year 1. How much revenue does Gamma Corporation recognize from the gift card sales for tax purposes and in which year(s)?

73. [LO 3.4] Thomas ran for Congress, raising $2 million for his campaign. Six months after losing the election, auditors discovered that Thomas kept $160,000 of the campaign funds and used the money to purchase a vacation home. What are the tax consequences for this use of campaign funds?

74. [LO 3.4] Samantha has been unemployed for some time and is very short of money. She learned that the local blood bank has a severe shortage of her type of blood and is therefore willing to pay $120 for each blood donation. Samantha gives blood twice a week for 12 weeks and receives $120 for each donation. Are these funds includable in Samantha's gross income?

75. [LO 3.4] Alice and Manny agree to divorce. Alice proposes that Manny purchase and assign to her a life insurance policy on his life as part of the divorce agreement. She wants Manny to continue paying the premiums on this policy for the next 10 years. Manny wants to know if the premium payments will be treated as alimony.

76. [LO 3.4 & 3.5] A minister receives an annual salary of $16,000 in addition to the use of a church parsonage that has an annual rental value of $6,000. The minister accepted this minimal salary because he felt that was all the church could afford to pay. He plans to report these amounts on his income tax return but he is uncertain how to treat the cash gifts received from the members of his congregation. These gifts are made out of love and admiration for him. During the year the congregation developed a regular procedure for making gifts on special occasions. Approximately two weeks before each special occasion when the minister was not present, the associate pastor announced before the service that those who wished to contribute to the special occasion gifts could place cash in envelopes, give them to the associate, who then would give them to the minister. Only cash was accepted to preserve anonymity. The church did not keep a record of the amounts given nor the contributors, but the minister estimates that these gifts were about $10,000 in the current year. How should he treat these gifts?

Fill-in the Forms

77. [LO 3.4] Go to the IRS website (*www.irs.gov*). Print the first page of Form 1040 and compute Pierre Lappin's adjusted gross income by entering the following information: $60,000 salary, $5,000 qualified dividend income, $3,000 interest income from corporate bonds, $2,000 interest income from municipal general revenue bonds, $4,000 in long-term capital gains, and $10,000 income from an S corporation. In addition, Pierre paid his ex-wife $5,000 for alimony and $6,000 for child support. Pierre remarried prior to the end of the year and files a joint return with his new wife, Jeanie Lappin. Jeanie earned $10,000 from her part-time job for the year. The Lappins live at 123 Cottontail Lane, Houston, TX and have no dependents. Pierre's Social Security number is 123-45-6789 and Jeannie's Social Security number is 445-67-9876. Pierre's ex-wife's Social Security number is 345-67-8899.

ANSWERS TO TEST YOURSELF

1. **b. $4,950**. ($110,000/$200,000)($4,500 × 2 payments) = $4,950.
2. **a. $100**.
3. **c. $25,550**. ($10,000 salary + $15,000 employer's provided retirement annuity + $500 dividend + $50 lottery prize). The interest is not taxable because it is from municipal bonds, and the Social Security benefits are not taxable because their modified adjusted gross income is less than $32,000.
4. **b. $13,250**. ($12,000 alimony + $800 interest income + $400 dividend income + $50 jury duty pay). The child support and gift are not taxable.
5. **c. $6,500**. The $4,500 portion of the scholarship that is used for tuition and required textbooks is tax exempt. The $1,500 of remaining scholarship used for room and board and the entire $5,000 salary from the part-time job are taxable.

Employee Compensation

CHAPTER 4

LEARNING OBJECTIVES

After completing this chapter, you should be able to:

4.1 Explain the tax implications of compensation from both employer and employee perspectives and identify the differences encountered by independent contractors.

4.2 Identify common employee fringe benefits, both taxable and nontaxable, and explain their tax effects on employers and employees.

4.3 Explore the tax implications of various forms of equity-based compensation for employers and employees.

4.4 Describe the tax ramifications of deferred compensation and retirement plans for employers and employees.

4.5 Understand the impact of employment taxes, fringe benefit rules, and retirement plan provisions on self-employed individuals.

4.6 Identify the favorable tax provisions that affect U.S. citizens working in foreign countries.

CHAPTER OUTLINE

This chapter focuses on compensation from both the employee's and employer's perspectives. It provides the basic information to design a compensation package that offers tax savings to both parties.

Employees can significantly increase the after-tax value of their compensation by accepting tax-exempt fringe benefits as part of their compensation package. The cost of tax-exempt fringe benefits is deductible by the employer, even though these benefits are nontaxable income to the employee—a win-win situation for both employer and employee. To prevent abuse, however, most tax-free benefits have significant limitations. Knowledge of these benefits and their limitations allows maximization of tax savings available by the careful use of tax-free fringe benefits.

Stock and stock options are popular compensation tools used as incentives to both recruit and retain employees, but require no cash outlay by the employer. Stock options allow employees to acquire stock at a bargain price. They can provide the advantage of deferring income to a future year and the conversion of otherwise ordinary compensation income into long-term capital gains taxed at favorable rates.

Deferred compensation plans are key to retirement planning and are important components of most compensation packages. Qualified plans provide an immediate deduction for the employer but defer employee taxation of benefits until retirement. The amount of compensation that can be offered on a tax-deferred basis under qualified plans is limited; as a result, many employers have established nonqualified plans that can provide unlimited deferred compensation to key or highly compensated executives.

Many U.S. businesses have operations in foreign jurisdictions. There are tax benefits available to employees who relocate to other countries that make these relocations quite attractive, including exclusions or credits for foreign earned income. These and other benefits are introduced here.

Employers want to attract and retain talented employees, while employees seek to maximize the value of their compensation. Knowledge of the tax impact on compensation is critical for employees in making the decision to accept or reject a foreign assignment.

SETTING THE STAGE—AN INTRODUCTORY CASE

Bob has received two job offers. Alpha Corporation's offer to hire him as an employee includes an annual salary of $73,000 along with a package of fringe benefits. Beta Corporation would hire Bob as an independent contractor. Bob would earn $89,000 annually in consulting fees but Beta would provide no fringe benefits.

Bob's wife, Julie, works part-time at a company that provides no benefits for its part-time employees. Bob is concerned that he and his family have no medical insurance. Alpha Corporation pays the premium for comprehensive medical insurance for all its employees and their immediate families. Alpha Corporation would pay $9,000 per year for Bob's family medical coverage under its group plan. If Bob accepts Beta Corporation's offer, it would cost $11,000 annually to purchase a similar health insurance plan for himself and his family. Bob asks you to evaluate the after-tax cash flow for each job offered. If Bob is in the 22 percent marginal tax bracket, determine the after-tax cost of each compensation package offered by Alpha and Beta Corporations, assuming each of them is in the 21 percent marginal tax bracket. Is it possible to provide a compensation package that maximizes the after-tax value to the individual while minimizing the after-tax cost to the employer? We will return to this case at the end of this chapter.

4.1 EMPLOYEE COMPENSATION

Compensation includes not only base salaries and wages but also bonuses, vacation pay, employer-provided sick pay, and other fringe and economic benefits provided to employees. The cost of all types of compensation benefits is deductible by employers. Regardless of its form, however, compensation is taxable income to an employee unless excluded by a specific provision of the Internal Revenue Code.

4.1.1 PAYROLL TAXES

Employee wages are subject to several payroll taxes. Both the wages and taxes paid by the employer on these wages are deductible business expenses. Taxes include those under the Federal Insurance Contributions Act (FICA) along with federal and state unemployment taxes. The **FICA tax** has two components: old age, survivors and disability insurance (OASDI), commonly referred to as Social Security, and the Medicare hospital insurance (HI). The employer's tax rate for Social Security, is 6.2 percent of wages up to a maximum of $128,400 for 2018.[1] The Medicare portion is 1.45 percent of total compensation. Thus, an employer pays 7.65 percent FICA tax on each employee's wages up to $128,400 and 1.45 percent on compensation above $128,400.

In addition to the FICA tax on the employer, employees also pay a matching, but nondeductible, FICA tax. Employers withhold the employee portion of the FICA tax from their compensation, along with the employees' federal income tax.

In states that levy an income tax, employers also withhold the state income tax. Withholding is based on marital status and number of exemption allowances the employee provides the employer on **Form W-4**: *Employee's Withholding Allowance Certificate*.[2] Self-employed

[1] The ceiling was $127,200 for 2017 and $118,500 for 2015 and 2016.

[2] Supplemental payments (such as bonuses) may be subject to an alternative 22% withholding rate on up to $1 million (25% before 2018) and 37% on excess over $1 million. See IRS Publication 15 (Circular E) Employer's Tax Guide.

individuals and independent contractors pay their own Social Security and Medicare taxes (discussed in detail later) and make quarterly estimated tax payments for their employment and income taxes.

Example 4.1

Jennifer is an employee of Moneybags Corporation. In 2018, Jennifer received total taxable compensation of $130,000 ($110,000 in salary and a $20,000 bonus). Moneybags Corporation paid a Social Security tax of $7,961 ($128,400 limit × 6.2%) plus a Medicare tax of $1,885 ($130,000 × 1.45%) for a total FICA tax of $9,846. Jennifer also pays FICA tax of $9,846. Moneybags Corporation withholds $23,250 of federal income tax (determined from IRS-issued tables based on information provided on Jennifer's Form W-4) and $9,846 FICA tax from Jennifer's $130,000 compensation. Therefore, Jennifer's net pay is $96,904 ($130,000 – $23,250 withholding – $9,846 employee's FICA taxes) for 2018.

Moneybags deducts $130,000 as employee compensation expense and $9,846 as payroll tax expense for 2018.

Since 2013, taxpayers are required to pay an additional Medicare tax if certain income thresholds are exceeded. The thresholds are $200,000 for single individuals and $250,000 for married taxpayers filing a joint return. Employers are required to withhold the additional Medicare tax from salary, wages, or other compensation (including commissions, bonuses, tips, and any benefits subject to the regular Medicare tax) in excess of $200,000 in a calendar year, regardless of the employee's filing status. The additional tax rate is 0.9 percent on taxable compensation income and is imposed on the employee only—*not* on the employer. The combined employer/employee Medicare rate is 3.8 percent (2.9 percent + 0.9 percent) on compensation above the income threshold. This additional Medicare tax is discussed in Chapter 5.[3]

Employers are required to pay both federal unemployment taxes (FUTA) and state unemployment taxes. The current **FUTA tax** rate is 6 percent on the first $7,000 of covered wages paid per employee during the year; however, employers are allowed to claim a credit against FUTA for their state unemployment taxes. The FUTA tax is paid entirely by the employer.[4]

Example 4.2

Marco is an employee of Moneybags Corporation. In 2018, Marco's salary was $180,000 and he earned a bonus of $40,000 (total taxable compensation of $220,000). Moneybags Corporation paid a Social Security tax of $7,961 ($128,400 limit × 6.2%) plus a Medicare tax of $3,190 ($220,000 × 1.45%) for a total FICA tax of $11,151 on Marco. Marco also paid $7,961 plus $3,190 for Social Security and Medicare taxes, but he also is subject to an additional Medicare surtax of $180 ($220,000 total compensation – $200,000 threshold) × 0.9% for total employee payroll taxes of $11,331 for 2018. Moneybags Corporation withholds $42,300 of federal income tax (determined from IRS-issued tables based on Marco's Form W-4) and $11,331 ($7,961 + $3,190 + $180) payroll tax from Marco's $220,000 compensation. Therefore, Marco's net pay is $166,369 ($220,000 – $42,300 withholding – $11,331 employee's payroll taxes) for 2018.

Moneybags Corporation also pays unemployment tax of $420 ($7,000 × 6%) in 2018 on Marco. Moneybags deducts $220,000 as employee compensation expense and $11,751 ($11,331 + $420) as payroll tax expense for Marco for 2018.

[3] Another Medicare tax of 3.8 percent is levied on net investment income (including taxable interest, dividends, capital gains, annuities, royalties, and certain rents) of individuals with AGI in excess of the $200,000 ($250,000 if married filing a joint return) threshold. This tax is discussed in Chapter 5.

[4] Employers can claim a credit against FUTA tax for state unemployment taxes up to a maximum rate of 5.4% effectively reducing the FUTA rate to 0.6%. Employees in several states pay a special unemployment tax to provide for supplemental unemployment compensation or disability benefits.

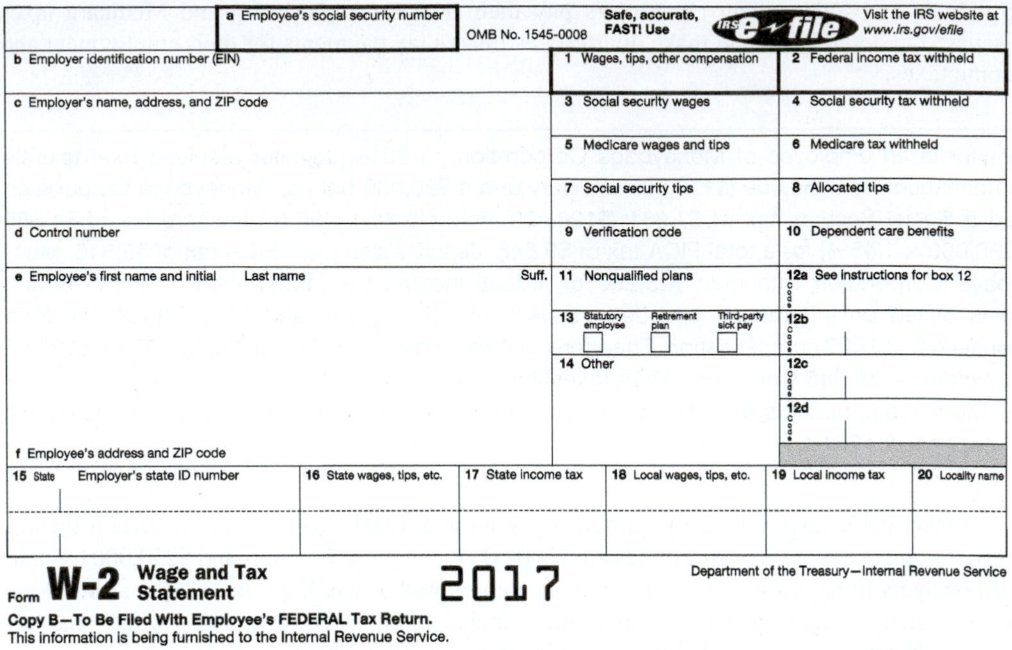

a Employee's social security number		Safe, accurate, FAST! Use	Visit the IRS website at www.irs.gov/efile

OMB No. 1545-0008

b Employer identification number (EIN)	1 Wages, tips, other compensation	2 Federal income tax withheld

c Employer's name, address, and ZIP code	3 Social security wages	4 Social security tax withheld
	5 Medicare wages and tips	6 Medicare tax withheld
	7 Social security tips	8 Allocated tips

d Control number	9 Verification code	10 Dependent care benefits

e Employee's first name and initial Last name Suff.	11 Nonqualified plans	12a See instructions for box 12
	13 Statutory employee □ Retirement plan □ Third-party sick pay □	12b
	14 Other	12c
		12d

f Employee's address and ZIP code

15 State Employer's state ID number	16 State wages, tips, etc.	17 State income tax	18 Local wages, tips, etc.	19 Local income tax	20 Locality name

Form **W-2** Wage and Tax Statement **2017** Department of the Treasury—Internal Revenue Service

Copy B—To Be Filed With Employee's FEDERAL Tax Return.
This information is being furnished to the Internal Revenue Service.

FIGURE 4.1
W-2: Wage and Tax
Statement

Within 31 days following the end of the year, the employer reports the taxable compensation paid and the taxes withheld for the year to the employee on **Form W-2**: *Wage and Tax Statement* as shown in Figure 4.1. A copy is also sent to the government to verify the income the employee reports on his or her individual tax return.

Employers only pay payroll taxes for employees, not for independent contractors. Instead, independent contractors (as self-employed individuals) pay their own Social Security and Medicare taxes as both employee and employer. Therefore, the distinction between employee and independent contractor has significant payroll tax consequences.

4.1.2 EMPLOYEE VERSUS INDEPENDENT CONTRACTOR

Working individuals are either self-employed or employees. Self-employed individuals include partners, sole proprietors, and independent contractors. An **independent contractor** (also known as a freelancer) is an individual who is subject to the direction of another only for the end product of their work, not the means to accomplish it.[5] Most independent contractors will receive a **Form 1099-MISC**: *Miscellaneous Income* from each client who paid them at least $600 for the year. Figure 4.2 shows Form 1099-MISC in which nonemployee compensation is reported in box 7.

The determination of employee or self-employed status is a very controversial area. Businesses try to increase the use of self-employed individuals to avoid paying FICA and FUTA taxes and to exclude them from most employee fringe benefit programs.

Workers who incur significant unreimbursed business expenses have an incentive to be treated as independent contractors, rather than employees. Independent contractors can deduct their business expenses directly from gross self-employment income and pay self-employment taxes only on their net self-employment income.

[5] Revenue Ruling 87-41, 1987-1 CB 296 provides a 20-factor test that is frequently used to determine whether a person is an independent contractor or an employee.

☐ CORRECTED (if checked)

PAYER'S name, street address, city or town, state or province, country, ZIP or foreign postal code, and telephone no.	1 Rents $ 2 Royalties $	OMB No. 1545-0115 2017 Form 1099-MISC	Miscellaneous Income
	3 Other income $	4 Federal income tax withheld $	Copy B For Recipient
PAYER'S federal identification number / RECIPIENT'S identification number	5 Fishing boat proceeds $	6 Medical and health care payments $	
RECIPIENT'S name Street address (including apt. no.)	7 Nonemployee compensation $	8 Substitute payments in lieu of dividends or interest $	This is important tax information and is being furnished to the Internal Revenue Service. If you are required to file a return, a negligence penalty or other sanction may be imposed on you if this income is taxable and the IRS determines that it has not been reported.
City or town, state or province, country, and ZIP or foreign postal code	9 Payer made direct sales of $5,000 or more of consumer products to a buyer (recipient) for resale ► ☐	10 Crop insurance proceeds $	
	11	12	
Account number (see instructions) / FATCA filing requirement ☐	13 Excess golden parachute payments $	14 Gross proceeds paid to an attorney $	
15a Section 409A deferrals $ / 15b Section 409A income $	16 State tax withheld $ $	17 State/Payer's state no.	18 State income $ $

Form 1099-MISC (keep for your records) www.irs.gov/form1099misc Department of the Treasury - Internal Revenue Service

FIGURE 4.2 Form 1099-MISC: Miscellaneous Income

Employees pay FICA taxes on their gross earnings before any deduction for their unreimbursed business expenses.[6] Unlike independent contractors, however, employees have access to unemployment insurance if they lose their jobs, workers' compensation insurance if they are injured at work, and they are protected by workplace antidiscrimination laws. These protections and the minimum wage and overtime laws generally do not apply to contractors.

An employer may try to avoid the payment of employment taxes and fringe benefits to persons working for them by deliberately misclassifying them as independent contractors instead of employees. A person who is anxious to be employed may accept independent contractor status simply to obtain the work. The IRS is aware of this and audits businesses looking for such misclassifications, billing businesses for back taxes and penalties.

KEY CASE *Microsoft hired software testers, production editors, proofreaders, formatters, and indexers as independent contractors. Microsoft employees supervised them, they performed functions also performed by Microsoft employees, and they worked the same hours. Rather than being paid through the Microsoft payroll department, these workers submitted invoices for their services to the accounts payable department. The IRS determined that they were misclassified and were in fact employees. Microsoft agreed to pay back employment taxes and issue retroactive W-2 forms to allow these employees to recover Microsoft's share of FICA taxes, which they had been required to pay. These reclassified employees then sued Microsoft for fringe benefits paid to other employees, including the right to participate in the company's stock purchase and 401(k) plans. The Ninth Circuit ruled against Microsoft and in favor of the workers.*[7]

Incorrectly classifying an employee as an independent contractor can not only result in additional taxes, interest, and penalties, but in some cases, it can also affect careers.

---

[6] Before 2018, they were deductible as miscellaneous itemized deductions to the extent they exceeded 2 percent of adjusted gross income; for 2018–2025 they are not deductible. Itemized deductions are discussed in Chapter 5.

[7] *Vizcaino et al. v. Microsoft Corp.*, 97 F.3d 1187; 96-2 USTC ¶50,533; 78 AFTR 2d. 96-6690, aff'd. 120 F.3d 1006; 80 AFTR 2d 97-5594 (CA-9, 1997).

Example 4.3

The nanny tax affected the careers of three individuals whom President Clinton nominated to his cabinet.[8] Zoe Baird and Kimba Wood (both Attorney General nominees) and retired Admiral Bobby Inman (Secretary of Defense nominee) withdrew from consideration when the press revealed that they had failed to pay employment taxes on the wages of household employees by improperly treating them as independent contractors. Bernard Kerik, President Bush's nominee to head Homeland Security, had a similar problem and also withdrew his name from consideration.

Individuals reclassified as employees may have significant additional taxes assessed, even if they reported their incomes and paid self-employment taxes as required. For example, the home office expense deduction can be lost.[9] Frequently, the refund due for self-employment taxes is less than the now-employee's FICA taxes plus the additional income taxes from lost deductions, leaving the worker with a net tax liability.[10]

Determining whether an individual is self-employed or an employee can be very difficult because there is no unequivocal definition of an independent contractor. Revenue Ruling 87-41 provides a 20-factor test that is used to determine an individual's work status under common law rules.[11] No one factor is decisive, but five of these factors have been found to be most important.[12]

1. **Instructions.** Employers usually have the right to specify how, when, and where their employees are to perform their jobs. Independent contractors decide how to achieve the end result.
2. **Payment.** Employees are usually paid on a regular schedule (by the hour, week, or month). Independent contractors are usually paid by the job.
3. **Tools and Materials.** Employers usually furnish employees with any necessary materials, tools, and supplies. Independent contractors generally supply their own.
4. **Significant Investment.** Employees usually use the employer's office space. Independent contractors frequently invest in their own office facilities.
5. **Realization of Profit or Loss.** An independent contractor bears the risk of realizing a profit or loss.

Example 4.4

Jamie is hired to perform laboratory tests for a medical doctor. Jamie works at the doctor's office, uses the doctor's equipment, and performs the tests by the methods prescribed by the doctor, entering the results in the patients' charts. Marie has a small laboratory in her home. She receives samples forwarded from doctors' offices and performs tests with her own equipment, using methods she determines to be appropriate for the desired analyses. She provides the doctor with a written report of the test results only. Jamie is an employee while Marie is self-employed.

4.1.3 TIMING OF COMPENSATION DEDUCTION

The method of accounting a business uses affects the timing of a compensation deduction.[13] A cash-basis business takes the deduction in the year the compensation is paid. An accrual-basis business usually takes the deduction in the year the liability is incurred. An accrual-basis corporation that

[8] The nanny tax refers to employment taxes that individual taxpayers must pay for household employees, including nannies, babysitters, health aides, maids, yard workers, and other domestic workers, if their wages exceed a threshold of $2,100 in 2018 ($2,000 or more in 2017 and 2016).

[9] The limitations on home office expense deductions are discussed in Chapter 6.

[10] The IRS can assess the employer for the individual's share of FICA taxes if they cannot be collected from the individual.

[11] Rev. Rul. 87-41, 1987-1 CB 296.

[12] Reg. §31.3401(c)-1(b). Jane O. Burns and Tracy A. Freeman, "Avoiding IRS Reclassification of Workers as Employees," The *Tax Adviser*, February 1996, p. 105.

[13] Although most salaries and wages are currently deductible, some compensation is capitalized, for example, direct labor costs that are part of finished goods inventory.

accrues an obligation for compensation must make the payment within 2½ months after the close of the corporation's tax year or it cannot be deducted until the year of payment.

A more restrictive provision prevents a related taxpayer and a business in which the taxpayer owns more than a 50 percent interest from engaging in tax avoidance schemes in which one party uses the accrual method of accounting and the other uses the cash method.[14] An accrual-basis corporation that accrues a payment to a related cash-basis taxpayer (such as an employee-shareholder who owns more than 50 percent of the corporation) must defer the deduction until the year in which the related party recognizes the income payment.

Example 4.5

Black Inc., an accrual-basis, calendar-year corporation, is owned 100 percent by its president, Bill Black, a cash-basis, calendar-year individual. On December 15, year 1, Black Inc. accrues a $90,000 bonus to Bill and a $60,000 bonus to its top sales representative, Steve. It does not pay the bonuses until January, year 2. Black Inc. can deduct Steve's $60,000 bonus on its year 1 tax return but cannot deduct Bill's $90,000 bonus until year 2. Bill and Steve include the income on their year 2 tax returns. The bonuses must be paid by March 15, year 2, or Black cannot deduct either bonus until the year paid.

To preserve the deduction for bonuses to related taxpayers in the year accrued, the corporation should ensure they are paid before year-end. Note that this deferral provision does not apply if the related taxpayers both use either the cash method or the accrual method or if the bonus recipient uses the accrual method but the related party taking the deduction uses the cash method. (There is no tax deferral benefit in these situations.)

4.1.4 REASONABLE COMPENSATION

Employee compensation must be reasonable to be deductible. **Reasonable compensation** is the amount a similar business would pay for the services under similar circumstances. Reasonableness is applied on a per employee basis and frequently arises in closely-held corporations with shareholder-employees. The business has an incentive to inflate shareholder-employees' salaries in lieu of paying dividends as the corporation cannot deduct dividends. If a shareholder-employee's salary is unreasonable, the reasonable portion remains deductible but the IRS classifies the excess as a nondeductible dividend.

Example 4.6

Lynn owns 100 percent of Lowry Corporation, a very profitable business that has not paid dividends for several years. Lynn's salary is $700,000, but similar businesses ordinarily pay $400,000 for services comparable to Lynn's. If the $300,000 excess compensation is reclassified as a dividend, Lynn is still taxed on the $700,000 ($400,000 as salary and $300,000 as dividend income). The $300,000 dividend is taxed at a 20 percent rate rather than the ordinary income rate of 37 percent applied to the salary, saving $51,000 [$300,000 × (37% – 20%)] in income taxes. Lynn also saves $4,350 ($300,000 × 1.45%) for the Medicare portion of FICA taxes (not imposed on dividend income) resulting in total tax savings to Lynn of $55,350 ($51,000 + $4,350). Lowry Corporation can only deduct $400,000 as salary. If Lowry is in the 21 percent tax bracket, the salary reclassified as dividend costs the corporation an additional $63,000 ($300,000 nondeductible dividend × 21%) in corporate income taxes. Lowry saves $4,350 in Medicare taxes but then loses its tax savings of $914 ($4,350 × 21%) from the deduction, resulting in a net corporate tax increase of $59,564 ($63,000 – $4,350 + $914). The net effect is an increase in overall taxes of $4,214 ($59,564 – $55,350).[15]

[14] Related taxpayers include family members (spouse, parents, grandparents, children, brothers, and sisters), as well as a corporation owned more than 50 percent (either directly or indirectly) by the taxpayer. The attribution rules for indirect ownership are discussed in Chapter 10.

[15] Lynn's tax savings will be $8,700 [(3.8% NII – 0.9%) × $300,000] less once the Medicare surtaxes are considered as discussed in Chapter 5.

The IRS can also reclassify any excessive salary paid to someone related to the shareholder (for example, a child or parent) as a nondeductible dividend.

In response to public criticism that the government was subsidizing excessive compensation paid executives of publicly-traded corporations, Congress enacted Code Section 162(m). This provision limits the deductible compensation paid to top executives of publicly traded companies to $1 million annually. Employees covered by the provision include the chief executive officer and the next four most highly compensated officers. Several exceptions, however, allow corporations to deduct pay in excess of this $1 million limit including employer contributions to a qualified retirement plan and tax-free employee benefits (described later).[16]

Example 4.7

Star Corporation's stock is traded on the New York Stock Exchange. During the current year, Jane, the chief executive officer, receives the following compensation: $1,500,000 salary, $24,000 employer contributions to a qualified pension plan, and $9,000 tax-free fringe benefits. Only $1,000,000 of the $1,500,000 salary is deductible by Star Corporation. The retirement plan contributions and fringe benefits are not subject to the $1 million annual deduction limit (and are deductible by the corporation in full). Jane is still taxed on the entire $1,500,000 salary. (As explained later, there is no current tax on the contribution to Jane's pension plan or the tax-free fringe benefits.)

TAX PLANNING

Some corporations protect themselves by having highly compensated employees agree to repay any compensation for which a deduction is disallowed. The employee can deduct the repayment from taxable income in the year repaid if the payback agreement meets two conditions. First, the parties must have entered into the agreement before the compensation is paid. Second, the employee must be legally obligated to repay the excess amount.[17]

S Corporations and Unreasonably Low Salaries

When an individual is the controlling shareholder-employee of an S corporation, IRS auditors look for an unreasonably low salary. Salaries are subject to employment taxes but distributions of profits are not. An S corporation can minimize its payroll tax costs by paying a low salary and distributing income instead.[18] If an employee-shareholder's salary is unreasonably low, however, the IRS can reclassify some of the S corporation's distribution as salary, requiring the payment of additional employment taxes (and possibly penalties).

KEY CASE *David Watson, a CPA with 20 years' experience, formed an S corporation that was a partner in his accounting firm. Watson was an employee of his S corporation. In each of the two years involved in the case, Watson received a salary of $24,000 from the S corporation. Watson also received distributions of $203,651 in one year and $175,470 in the other year from the S corporation that were not subject to payroll taxes. The IRS determined that his $24,000*

[16] Prior to 2018, exceptions to this limit were also available for compensation based on individual performance goals and compensation paid on a commission basis.

[17] See Rev. Rul. 69-115, 1969-1 CB 50 and *Oswald*, 49 TC 645.

[18] An S corporation's income is taxed to the shareholders when earned, even if not distributed. Thus, a distribution incurs no additional tax.

salary was not reasonable compensation and that his salary should have been $91,044. The District Court agreed and an additional $67,044 was subject to FICA tax. The decision was affirmed by the Eighth Circuit Court of Appeals.[19]

Employing Children

TAX PLANNING

Closely-held businesses frequently hire family members as employees. Owners who employ their children can effectively shift income to their children (and have that income taxed on the children's tax returns) if the compensation paid to the children is reasonable for the services performed. The income is usually taxed at the child's lower income tax rates, and the owners benefit from savings in payroll taxes as wages paid an employer's child under age 18 are subject to employment taxes only if the business is incorporated.[20]

Example 4.8

Harry, an individual in the 32 percent tax bracket, owns a sole proprietorship and employs his 16-year-old daughter, Sarah, after school. Harry pays Sarah a reasonable wage of $8,000 for the work performed. Harry deducts the $8,000 for wages paid to Sarah, a tax saving of $2,560 ($8,000 × 32%).[21] This also reduces Harry's net earnings subject to the self-employment tax, resulting in additional tax savings.

4.2 EMPLOYEE FRINGE BENEFITS

Employees usually receive most of their compensation as cash salary or wages but may also receive noncash **fringe benefits**. Congress encourages employers to offer employee fringe benefits by allowing deductions for their cost. Unlike wages, however, the value of certain fringe benefits is excluded from the employee's income. Some benefits, such as insurance, are less expensive if purchased on a group basis by the employer (rather than individual policies purchased directly by employees). The use of qualified fringe benefits can greatly increase the employee's effective after-tax pay while providing a tax deduction to the employer.

Example 4.9

Alistar Corporation employees may opt to participate in the company's health insurance plan (a tax-exempt fringe benefit) or take $2,000 per year in cash. An employee who takes the cash is taxed on the receipt of $2,000. Assuming a 32 percent marginal tax rate, the employee has only $1,360 [$2,000 − (32% × $2,000)] after taxes to purchase alternative insurance. In most situations, an employee cannot purchase a comparable insurance plan for this amount, leaving the employee with fewer after-tax dollars.

[19] *Watson v. U.S.*, 757 F. Supp. 2d 877; 107 AFTR 2d 2011-311; 2011-1 USTC 50,443 (DC IA, 2010), aff'd. No. 11-1589 (8th Cir. 2/21/12). Also see *Spicer Accounting, Inc. v. U.S.* 66 AFTR 2d 90-5806, 918 F.2d 90, 91-1 USTC 50,103 (CA-9, 1990).

[20] §3121(b)(3)(A). Wages paid to a child under age 18 who works in a sole proprietorship or partnership owned solely by one or both parents are not subject to Social Security and Medicare taxes. Wages paid a child under age 21 who works for his or her parents are not subject to FUTA tax. Wages of all children working in a corporation are subject to Social Security, Medicare, and FUTA taxes regardless of the child's age or corporate ownership.

[21] Sarah pays no income taxes because her taxable income does not exceed the standard deduction of $12,000 in 2018. Chapter 5 has a discussion of the standard deduction. Sarah is not subject to any payroll taxes as the owner's child under age 18.

TAX PLANNING

Tax-exempt fringe benefits increase employees' real after-tax compensation without increasing the employer's cash outflow. The employer's income tax savings are the same for the payment of a tax-free benefit as for payment of wages, but tax-free fringe benefits generally are not subject to FICA or FUTA taxes, further reducing the cost of employee compensation.

Example 4.10

Sam is negotiating an employment contract with Friendly Corporation. Sam's tax rate is 22 percent and Friendly's tax rate is 21 percent. Friendly offers Sam a salary of $80,000. The after-tax value to Sam and after-tax cost to Friendly are:

	Sam	Friendly Corp.
Salary	$80,000	($80,000)
FICA ($80,000 × 7.65%)	(6,120)	(6,120)
FUTA ($7,000 × 6%)		(420)
Income tax ($80,000 × 22%)	(17.600)	
Tax Savings:		
Salary deduction ($80,000 × 21%)		16.800
Payroll tax deduction ($6,540 × 21%)		1,374
After-tax value (cost)	$56,280	($68,366)

Sam would prefer to take $20,000 of his compensation in tax-free fringe benefits and be paid a salary of $61,000. The after-tax value to Sam and after-tax cost to Friendly of this $81,000 compensation package is as follows:

	Sam	Friendly Corp.
Salary	$61,000	($61,000)
Fringe benefit value (cost)	20,000	(20,000)
FICA ($61,000 × 7.65%)	(4,667)	(4,667)
FUTA ($7,000 × 6%)		(420)
Income tax ($61,000 × 22%)	(13,420)	
Tax Savings:		
Salary deduction ($61,000 × 21%)		12,810
Fringe benefit deduction ($20,000 × 21%)		4,200
Payroll tax deduction ($5,087 × 21%)		1,068
After-tax value (cost)	$62,913	($68,009)

By trading a significant portion of his salary for tax-free fringe benefits, Sam is $6,633 ($62,913 – $56,280) better off than just the salary. Friendly Corporation saves $357 ($68,366 – $68,009) by providing the compensation package with tax-free fringe benefits.

To prevent abuse of tax-free benefits, significant limitations are built in to prevent the conversion of excess taxable compensation into tax-free income. If an employer provides nonqualifying employee benefits or benefits in excess of the allowable limits, the employee has additional taxable income (reported on Form W-2). The employer can still deduct the excess benefits. The most common employee fringe benefits are summarized in Table 4.1.

To encourage providing all employees (not just top executives) with fringe benefits, many of these benefit programs cannot discriminate in favor of highly compensated employees.[22]

[22] A highly compensated employee is any of the following employees: (1) an officer, (2) a greater than 5% shareholder, (3) an employee who is highly compensated based on the facts and circumstances, and (4) a spouse or dependent of any of the above. Additionally, many benefits are not tax free to employee/owners of S corporations with greater than 2% ownership.

Table 4.1 Employee Fringe Benefits

Benefit	Excluded amount
Group Term Life Insurance	Employer-paid premiums for up to $50,000 coverage
Health and Accident Insurance	Employer-paid premiums and most benefits received
Child and Dependent Care	Annual exclusion of $5,000 ($2,500 if married and filing separately) for cost of dependents under age 13 or disabled
No-Additional-Cost Services	Value of excess capacity services
Employee Discounts	Bargain element on property up to normal gross profit; up to 20% of value for services
De Minimis Fringes	Employer-provided items of small value
Working Condition Fringes	Employer-provided items related to job that would be deductible if paid by employee rather than employer
Educational Assistance	Annual exclusion of $5,250. No dollar limit if job related.

Source: IRS Publication 15B: Employer's Tax Guide to Fringe Benefits

The details of the limitations on employee fringe benefits change frequently from inflation adjustments or by congressional action. Their specifics can be researched by a tax practitioner when needed at any point in time.[23]

4.2.1 GROUP TERM LIFE INSURANCE PREMIUMS

Premiums on employer-provided life insurance are included in the employee's gross income, except for limited coverage under a group term life insurance policy. **Term life insurance** has no cash surrender value and covers the insured individual for a specific period of time. The annual premium for up to $50,000 of group term life insurance coverage provided by the employer is excluded from employee gross income. Employer-paid life insurance premiums in excess of $50,000 coverage are taxed as income to the employee. To simplify the income computations, the IRS provides a table with the taxable amount in excess of the $50,000 exclusion for employer-paid premiums based on the employee's age. Table 4.2 provides the monthly premium for each $1,000 of taxable coverage.[24]

Table 4.2 Uniform Monthly Premiums for Each $1,000 of Group Term Life Insurance Coverage

Employee's age	Monthly premium
Under 25	$.05
25 to 29	.06
30 to 34	.08
35 to 39	.09
40 to 44	.10
45 to 49	.15
50 to 54	.23
55 to 59	.43
60 to 64	.66
65 to 69	1.27
70 and above	2.06

If the employer's group term life insurance plan discriminates in favor of key employees, each key employee must report gross income equal to the greater of (1) the employer's actual

[23] This is one of the reasons why it is important to be able to do tax research. Tax research is addressed in Chapter 2.

[24] Reg. §1.79-3(d)(2).

premiums paid or (2) the benefit determined from the table without excluding the first $50,000 of coverage.[25] If the plan is nondiscriminatory, key employees use the table to determine their gross income from excess coverage but can exclude the cost of the first $50,000 in coverage.

Example 4.11

Gloria, a 46-year-old employee, has an $80,000 group term life insurance policy provided by her employer for which the employer pays $300 annually. Gloria includes $54 in her gross income (30 increments of $1,000 above the $50,000 threshold × $.15 × 12 months). If Gloria is a key employee and the insurance plan is discriminatory, Gloria must include $300 in her gross income, the greater of the actual premiums paid ($300) or the $144 computed from the table without excluding the first $50,000 of coverage (80 × $.15 × 12 months). If Gloria is a key employee but the plan is not discriminatory, she includes only $54 in gross income.

The group term life insurance exclusion applies only to coverage for an employee or former employee. The cost of covering the employee's spouse or other dependents paid by the employer is included in income. No other types of life insurance (such as whole life) qualify for the exclusion.

4.2.2 HEALTH AND ACCIDENT INSURANCE PREMIUMS

To encourage employers to provide health insurance for employees and their families, the cost of health and accident insurance plan premiums paid by an employer is a tax-free fringe benefit. Many employees rely on their employers for insurance protection and this fringe benefit has a significant impact on the U.S. labor force. Employees can exclude the value of both employer-paid premiums and benefits received from their health and accident plans from income, even if the plans discriminate in favor of key employees.[26] This exclusion also applies to employer-provided benefits for the employee's dependent children and spouse.

Example 4.12

Kenneth is the president of Sterling Corporation, which pays the premiums on a group health insurance policy for all its employees. The annual premiums for Kenneth and his family are $25,000. Kenneth excludes this benefit from gross income.

Some businesses choose to self-insure their health plans and reimburse their employees directly from the business rather than using insurance or other prepaid plans such as a health maintenance organization (HMO). Under health reimbursement arrangements (HRAs), the employer makes payments to the plan and the plan reimburses the employees for qualified medical expenses. The reimbursements are usually excluded from income. Highly compensated employees, however, can exclude all reimbursements for medical care only if the self-insured medical plan is nondiscriminatory. If the plan is discriminatory, highly compensated employees must recognize gross income for any medical reimbursement unavailable to all other participants.[27] Employees who are not highly compensated, however, exclude all reimbursements for medical care, even if the plan is discriminatory.[28]

[25] §79(d)(1). A key employee is an employee who is (1) an officer with annual pay of more than $175,000, (2) a 1% owner whose annual pay is more than $150,000, or (3) a 5% owner.

[26] §106. Payments received for medical benefits that do not qualify as tax-deductible medical expenses will result in taxable income (Chapter 5 includes the discussion of deductible medical expenses).

[27] §105(h)(1), (7).

[28] Reg. §1.105-11(a).

Example 4.13

Wayne is chief financial officer of Sonesta Corporation, which has a self-insured health plan that covers only its executive officers. Wayne incurs $11,000 in medical expenses that are all reimbursed by the plan. Wayne must include the $11,000 reimbursement in his gross income because the plan discriminates in favor of highly compensated employees (only executive officers are covered).

4.2.3 CHILD AND DEPENDENT CARE PROGRAMS

An employee can exclude up to $5,000 ($2,500 if the taxpayer is married filing separately) annually for the value of an employer-financed program for child or dependent care at either an on-site or off-site facility.[29] Excluded benefits cannot exceed the employee's earned income for the year or, if less, the earned income of a spouse.[30] Any excess benefits are included in gross income.[31]

The program must benefit employees exclusively and be nondiscriminatory. Highly compensated employees cannot exclude the value of services received if the plan discriminates in their favor. All other employees continue their eligibility for the exclusion, however.[32]

4.2.4 CAFETERIA PLANS AND FLEXIBLE SPENDING ARRANGEMENTS

One reason fringe benefit plans are so popular is that the employer's cost of providing a benefit is usually less than the benefit's value to the employee. Employers can usually provide health insurance or on-site child care for less cost than an employee would pay for comparable services. The value of these benefits varies by employee, however. For example, a single individual with no dependents derives no benefit from employer-provided child care. Other employees could prefer cash to fringe benefits. If an employee is offered a choice of a fringe benefit or cash, the doctrine of constructive receipt would cause the fringe benefit to be taxed.

Fringe benefits offered under a cafeteria plan are an exception to the doctrine of constructive receipt. A **cafeteria plan** is a nondiscriminatory, written agreement that allows employees to choose cash or select their benefits from an available menu of options up to a certain dollar amount. The menu may include both qualified nontaxable benefits (including health insurance, dependent care assistance, adoption assistance, and group-term life insurance) as well as taxable cash.[33] Participants exclude the value of nontaxable benefits chosen, but are taxed on cash or any taxable benefits selected. The cafeteria plan allows employees to combine both taxable and nontaxable benefits to obtain optimum after-tax compensation based on the employee's individual needs.

Example 4.14

Marco Corporation employees can choose from a variety of their cafeteria plan benefits up to an amount equal to six percent of their annual salary. Sara selects $8,000 of health insurance coverage for herself and her family, $3,000 of child care assistance, $500 for a health club membership, and $600 in cash for the current year. The $500 health club membership and the $600 cash are taxable while the health insurance and child care assistance are tax free.

[29] §129(e)(8).

[30] §129(a). Generally, the type of assistance that qualifies for the dependent care credit (as discussed in Chapter 5) when paid by an employee can be excluded when provided by an employer.

[31] §129(b).

[32] §129(d)(1)-(3)

[33] §137. Only the cost of up to $50,000 of group term life insurance is tax free.

To qualify for this favorable treatment, the plan must be available to all employees on a nondiscriminatory basis. If the plan discriminates in favor of highly compensated employees, those employees include all benefits received in their gross income.[34]

One of the most useful plan options offered is a flexible spending arrangement (FSA). A **flexible spending arrangement** allows employees to reduce their salaries for the cost of certain nontaxable fringe benefits not employer-provided, such as dental expenses or co-payments required by their medical insurance. FSAs can be offered for medical and dependent care. Under an FSA, a participant decides how much to set aside for future costs not covered by the employer or insurance. For 2018 the maximum amount is $2,650 ($2,600 in 2017) for a health FSA. The employer withholds the designated amount from the employee's salary and deposits it with the employer's FSA plan administrator. The amount withheld is excluded from the employee's taxable compensation. The participant then receives nontaxable reimbursements from the plan administrator for qualified expenses incurred. Any amount withheld in excess of employee reimbursements is lost. Employees should carefully estimate their anticipated expenses and set aside only an amount they are certain they will spend for qualified expenses during that year.[35]

TAX PLANNING

Example 4.15

Carl's employer pays $7,000 of the $8,500 cost of health insurance for him and his family. Carl reduces his $50,000 salary to $48,500, using the $1,500 reduction to pay for his cost for the health insurance. Carl also sets aside $1,000 in an FSA for unreimbursed dental expenses, further reducing his salary to $47,500. During the year, Carl incurs $970 of unreimbursed dental expenses and receives $970 from the funds in his FSA. Although he lost the remaining $30, he was able to pay for $2,470 of medical insurance and dental expenses with the pretax $2,500 that reduced his taxable salary to $47,500.

4.2.5 NO-ADDITIONAL-COST SERVICES

When an employer provides free "excess capacity" services to employees without incurring substantial additional costs, the employees can exclude the value of the services from gross income; for example, the value of unsold seats on an airplane or train is excluded.[36] Only services (not property) offered in the ordinary course of business qualify for this exclusion. Employees of a business providing similar services or of an affiliated corporation also qualify for the exclusion.[37] An employee of the company handling the airline's baggage is considered to be in the same business as the airline and qualifies for the exclusion, for example.[38]

Example 4.16

Gary, an employee of the Empty Arms hotel chain, may stay in unreserved rooms at any of its hotels for 10 nights a year without charge. Gary uses the chain's rooms for six nights during the year and can exclude the value of the rooms. The value of any rooms reserved by Gary that would have been sold to paying guests cannot be excluded as a no-additional-cost service. (As discussed below, a portion of the cost might be excludable as an employee discount.)

[34] A highly compensated employee includes: (1) an officer, (2) a more than 5% shareholder (3) a highly compensated employee based on the facts and circumstances, and (4) a spouse or dependent of (1), (2), or (3). Small employers (100 or fewer employees) can establish a Simple Cafeteria Plan with a safe harbor exception from the nondiscrimination requirements to encourage more small employers to offer tax-free benefits to their employees. This plan also includes self-employed individuals as qualified employees.

[35] The IRS has eased this rule by permitting employers to allow a grace period of up to 2½ months following the end of the year. Notice 2005-42, 2005-23 IRB 1204. In 2013, the IRS issued Notice 2013-71, 2013-47 IRB 532 that allows employers to amend their plans to offer employees a $500 carryover of unused funds per year instead of the 2½-month grace period; however, a plan cannot offer both.

[36] §132(b)(2) and Reg. §1.132-2(a)(2). To determine if substantial additional costs are incurred, lost revenues count as a cost; however, any employee payments for services are ignored and do not reduce the costs incurred. Reg. §1.132-2(a)(5)(i).

[37] §132(b)(1).

[38] §132(j)(5).

In addition to current employees, a spouse and dependent children of current employees, retired employees, and parents of airline employees may benefit from this exclusion.[39] Highly compensated employees and their families, however, cannot exclude the value of these benefits if they are received on a discriminatory basis.[40] Partners who perform services for the partnership are eligible for this exclusion.[41]

4.2.6 EMPLOYEE PURCHASE DISCOUNTS

Sales of property or services to employees at below fair market value result in taxable income unless qualifying as an employee discount. The discounted service or property (excluding real estate and investment property) must be offered to customers in the ordinary course of business to qualify.[42]

A merchandise discount is excluded from income if it is limited to the gross profit percentage times the price charged customers. This effectively prevents employees from purchasing property below employer cost without recognizing taxable income. The gross profit percentage is based on sales data from the preceding tax year computed by dividing total sales in excess of the merchandise cost by total sales. The discount for services (other than no-additional-cost services) cannot exceed 20 percent of the price normally charged customers to be excluded.[43] Any additional discount is taxable income.

Example 4.17

Fine Furnishings Corporation's gross profit percentage was 25 percent last year allowing employees to buy its products at a 25 percent discount without recognizing income. Mack, an employee, paid $450 for furniture that normally retails for $600 and excluded the $150 discount from income. Mack also paid $600 for some used office equipment valued at $1,000; Mack includes in income and is taxed on the $400 discount, as this equipment is not normally sold by Fine's business.

Example 4.18

Linda works for Speedy Carwash Company. Its normal charge is $10 for car washes, but employees pay only $5. During the current year, Linda washed her car 12 times, paying a total of $60 ($5 × 12). The maximum discount allowed for services is 20 percent and Linda must report $36 as income ($5 discount – $2 maximum discount allowed = $3 excess × 12 car washes).

Only employees, who work in the same line of business selling property or rendering services to nonemployee customers, can exclude their discounts.[44] Highly compensated employees can exclude their discounts only if such discounts are nondiscriminatory.[45]

Bargain purchases are essentially employee discounts that are made available only to select employees and are taxable.

4.2.7 EMPLOYEE ACHIEVEMENT AWARDS

The value of most awards and prizes is included in gross income, except for employee awards for length of service or safety achievement. To qualify for exclusion, the award must be in the form

---

[39] §132(h).
[40] §132(j)(1).
[41] Reg. §1.132-2(b)(1).
[42] §132(c)(4).
[43] §132(c)(2).
[44] §132(c)(4). The employee discount exclusion also is available to certain individuals other than employees who qualify for no-additional-cost exclusions. §132(h).
[45] §132(j)(1).

of tangible personal property (such as a watch) rather than as cash or a gift certificate.[46] Under a nondiscriminatory qualified plan, a single award can be valued up to $1,600 in any year, if the average value for all achievement awards does not exceed $400. If the award is not made under a qualified plan, exclusions are limited to $400 per employee per year.[47]

4.2.8 DE MINIMIS FRINGE BENEFITS

Employees can exclude from income the value of **de minimis benefits** (small in value) provided by their employers. Property and services are de minimis when their value is so small that accounting for them would be unreasonable or impractical.[48] Examples of de minimis fringe benefits include coffee and doughnuts, limited personal use of photocopy machines or computers, use of business phones for local personal calls, occasional tickets to sporting or cultural events, noncash holiday gifts with minimal value such as turkeys, nominal birthday gifts, occasional company picnics or cocktail parties, and flowers sent to an employee because of illness.[49] If an employee receives cash or an item easily exchanged for cash, the employee has taxable compensation.

KEY RULING *In prior years, an employer often gave employees a ham, turkey, or gift basket as an annual holiday gift. These items qualified as excludable de minimis benefits. To satisfy employees with religious or dietary limitations, the employer began distributing gift certificates. The gift certificates had a face value of $35 (equal to the value of holiday gifts previously provided) and were redeemable for groceries at several local markets during a 2½-month period. They could not, however, be exchanged for cash. The IRS determined that the coupons were not excludable as de minimis benefits because the certificates had a value that was readily ascertainable and, therefore, accounting for them was not impractical.*[50]

Food service employees can exclude meals furnished by their employer during, immediately before, or immediately after their working hours. An employer can also provide subsidized meals for employees as a de minimis fringe benefit if the dining facility is on or near the employer's business premises and employees are charged an amount equal to or exceeding the facility's direct operating costs.[51] De minimis fringe benefits, except subsidized meals, can be provided on a discriminatory basis.[52]

4.2.9 WORKING CONDITION FRINGE BENEFITS

If an employer pays ordinary and necessary business expenses on behalf of its employees, the employees can exclude their value from gross income as **working condition fringe benefits.**[53]

---

[46] This exclusion does not apply to awards of cash, cash equivalents, gift certificates, or other intangible property such as vacations, meals, lodging, tickets to theater or sporting events, stock, bonds, and other securities. §274(j).

[47] §74(c).

[48] The frequency with which similar benefits are provided to employees is one factor in determining whether property or services are de minimis. §132(e)(1). If an employer provides a benefit that is not de minimis because of either its value or its frequency, no portion of the benefit can be considered de minimis. Reg. §1.132-6(d)(4).

[49] De minimis fringes do not include season tickets to sporting or cultural events, commuting use of employer vehicles more than one day a month, memberships in social or athletic clubs, and weekend use of an employer's boat or hunting lodge. Reg. §1.132-6(e). Fringe benefits that are not considered de minimis might be excludable under other provisions, such as no-additional-cost services or working condition fringe benefits.

[50] TAM 200437030 (9/10/2004).

[51] Prior to 2018, employers could deduct 100 percent of the cost of employer-provided cafeterias. For 2018–2025, employers can deduct only 50 percent of the cost of these employee dining facilities. After 2025, no deduction will be allowed. §274(n) and (o).

[52] Reg. §1.132-6(f) and §1.132-7.

[53] §132(d). The key is whether the expense would qualify as a valid business expense if the employee had paid for the expense and was entitled to deduct business expenses. If an employee is reimbursed for a nonqualified expense, it is income and it is subject to payroll taxes as wages.

Excludable working condition fringes include job-related education, professional membership dues, subscriptions to professional journals, bodyguards, use of an employer-provided cellphone, and use of the company car or plane for business.[54] Highly compensated employees can exclude working condition fringes, even if made on a discriminatory basis.[55]

Example 4.19

Alan is a CPA employed by a public accounting firm. The firm pays Alan's annual professional dues to the AICPA. Alan excludes the payment from gross income.

The business use of a company-owned car is a tax-free working condition fringe benefit; the value of an employee's personal use of a company car, however, is taxable as compensation. The employer may use one of three methods to value an employee's personal use of an employer's vehicle: the lease-value, the cents-per-mile, or the commuting method. The annual lease value is determined from a table in the regulations and this is multiplied by the ratio of the employee's annual personal mileage to the total annual mileage.[56] A portion of this table is reproduced as Table 4.3.[57]

Table 4.3 Partial Table of Annual Lease-Value Amounts for Personal Use of Employer-Provided Automobiles

Fair market value of auto	Annual lease value
$0–$999	$600
1,000–1,999	850
10,000–10,999	3,100
15,000–15,999	4,350
20,000–20,999	5,600
30,000–31,999	8,250
40,000–41,999	10,750
50,000–51,999	13,250

Under the vehicle cents-per-mile method, the employer taxes the employee at the rate of 54.5 cents per mile for personal use in 2018.[58] The special unsafe conditions commuting valuation method only requires the employer to include a value of $1.50 per one-way commute in the employee's income.[59]

Example 4.20

LMN Corporation purchased three cars for its president and two employees, Will and Sara. The president's car has a fair market value of $40,000. Fifty percent of the miles the president drives are for personal trips. The president has $5,375 of taxable compensation for his personal use of the car ($10,750 table value × 50% personal use) under the lease-value method.

[54] Business expense deductions are discussed in Chapter 6.

[55] Reg. §1.132-1(b)(2). Independent contractors, partners, and corporate directors can receive qualifying working condition fringe benefits tax free.

[56] See Reg. § 1.61-21(d)(2)(iii) for a list of the five specific requirements that must be met to use this method.

[57] The complete table can be found at Reg. §1.61-21(d)(2)(iii). For vehicles valued at $60,000 or more, the annual lease value = [(25% × fair market value) + $500].

[58] Notice 2018-3, 2018-21 IRB. The rate was 53.5 center per miles in 2017 and 54 cents per mile for 2016.

[59] Reg. §1.61-21(f)(1). To qualify, (1) the employee would ordinarily walk or use public transportation for commuting; (2) the employer has a written policy that transportation for personal purposes is not allowed other than commuting because of unsafe conditions; and (3) the employee does not use the vehicle for personal purposes other than commuting because of unsafe conditions. To qualify, the employee must be paid on an hourly basis for services and receive pay of not more than $115,000 during the year.

Will drives 12,000 personal miles in his company-owned car that cost $15,000. Using the standard mileage rate, LMN Corporation includes $6,540 (12,000 miles × 54.5¢) in Will's taxable compensation for 2018 for his personal use of the car.

Sara uses a company-owned car for commuting that is provided by LMN Corporation when she works the night shift because commuting via public transit and walking in her neighborhood late at night is not safe. The LMN Corporation prohibits Sara from using the auto for personal purposes other than commuting. Sara used the car 220 days to commute to work during the year. Sara has $660 in taxable fringe benefit compensation (220 days × $1.50 each way × 2 one-way trips each day).

The employer cannot deduct the noncash compensation for vehicle use, however. Instead, the employer deducts depreciation (or lease payments), gasoline, insurance, repairs, and other expenses of operating the vehicle.[60]

All of an employee's use of an identifiable police, fire, or public safety vehicle (a qualified business vehicle) is considered a working condition fringe benefit because an employee is unlikely to use this type of vehicle for personal use more than a de minimis amount.

Normally, the cost of commuting to and from work is not a deductible expense and does not qualify as a tax-free benefit. Employees can exclude a limited amount of employer-provided qualified transportation benefits from gross income, however.[61] These benefits include a ride in an employer-provided commuting van, a transit pass, or free parking. Mass transit passes and free or discounted parking on or near the employer's business premises valued up to $260 per month can be excluded in 2018.[62] Benefits in excess of these amounts must be included in income.

4.2.10 EDUCATION EXPENSES

An employer can reimburse employees for their job-related education expenses or establish a qualified educational assistance plan. An educational assistance program is a separate written plan that provides educational assistance only to employees, but the education does not have to relate directly to employment.[63] Employees can exclude up to $5,250 in education plan reimbursements annually for tuition, fees, books, supplies, and equipment. The plan cannot favor highly-compensated employees and cannot provide more than 5 percent of its benefits for the year to shareholders or owners of more than 5 percent of the business.

Employers can make nontaxable reimbursements or direct payments to schools for qualified job related educational expenses to maintain or improve skills required in the taxpayer's business. Qualified educational expenses include books, tuition, fees, and transportation from the workplace to school. Expenses for education that (1) meet the minimum educational requirements for the taxpayer's job or (2) qualify the taxpayer for a new trade or profession do not qualify for this exclusion.

Continuing professional education (CPE) requirements imposed by states on professionals (such as CPAs, attorneys, and physicians) as a condition for retaining a license to practice are considered qualifying education expenses. Fees incurred for professional qualification exams

[60] As long as the value of all personal use is taxed as employee income, the auto is considered used 100 percent for business, regardless of the actual business use. Employer depreciation deductions are discussed in Chapter 7.

[61] After 2017, employers can no longer deduct employee transportation fringe benefits; however, the exclusion from income for employees still continues. Prior to 2018, employees who commuted to work by bicycle could receive up to $20 per month from their employers to cover the cost of the bicycle purchase, improvements, repairs, and storage. The benefits for bicycle commuting were suspended for 2018–2025.

[62] §132(f)(2) and Rev. Proc. 2017-58, 2017-45 IRB 489. The parking exclusion and transit pass exclusions were $255 for 2016 and 2017. Partners and greater than 2% owners of S corporation are ineligible for tax-free treatment of these benefits and must include the value of free parking and similar benefits in gross income.

[63] §127(c)(1). The value of instruction for sports, games, or hobbies (unless part of the required course of instruction) and the value of meals, lodging, transportation or supplies that the employee can retain (other than textbooks) are included in income.

(such as the bar exam or CPA exam) and fees for review courses (such as a CPA review course) do not qualify.[64]

Example 4.21

Cherie, an accountant with a bachelor's degree in accounting, was hired when a bachelor's degree was her employer's minimum educational requirement. Recently, her employer changed the minimum educational requirements for all current and newly hired accountants to a master's degree, and Cherie must now take graduate classes to keep her job. Because Cherie satisfied the minimum requirements at the date she was hired, the expenses related to completing a master's degree qualify as job related and reimbursements for these expenses are not taxable. Tom, a newly hired accountant, has not completed a master's degree. Any reimbursement by the employer for expenses related to his completion of the master's degree is taxable income to him because the master's degree is now needed to satisfy the minimum educational requirements for his position.

Figure 4.3 illustrates the steps necessary to determine if education expenses qualify as work related. Prior to 2018, employees who paid for their own job-related education and were not reimbursed could deduct these expenses as miscellaneous itemized deductions. This deduction has been eliminated for 2018–2025.

Educational institutions frequently provide qualified tuition reduction plans to employees and their family members. These benefits are excluded from income if the tuition is for education below the graduate level; graduate tuition waivers are taxable.[65]

Employees who pay for their own tuition, but are not eligible to deduct it as job-related education, may be eligible for the American opportunity or lifetime learning tax credit for eligible expenses.[66] Education expenses cannot create a double tax benefit; that is, if a taxpayer excludes them from income, the taxpayer cannot also claim a tax credit for the same expenses. Table 4.4 summarizes the possible tax benefits that may be derived from education expenses.

4.2.11 EMPLOYEE RELOCATION EXPENSES

Prior to 2018, an employee did not have income for employer reimbursement of qualified relocation expenses incurred in connection with a move to a new principal place of work. If the employee paid for qualified moving costs directly and was not reimbursed, the employee could take a deduction for adjusted gross income. For 2018–2025, the Tax Cuts and Jobs Act suspends the exclusion of reimbursements for moving expenses except for members of the U.S. Armed Forces on active duty who move because of a permanent change in station. The deduction for nonreimbursed moving expenses is also suspended until 2026.

Qualified moving expenses include reasonable costs for the following:

1. Packing, crating, and transporting household goods and personal belongings (including personal vehicles and household pets) from the old home to the new home
2. 30 days of storage and insurance while in transit and before delivery to the new home
3. Travel expenses for all family members from the old home to the new home

---

[64] Reg. §1.212-1(f) and Rev. Rul. 69-292, 1969-1 CB 84.

[65] §117(d). A special provision excludes tuition reduction benefits paid to graduate teaching and research assistants employed by education institutions from gross income, but the exclusion is limited to the value of the tuition benefit in excess of reasonable compensation for services. Prop. Reg. §1.117-6(d). Free or discounted tuition provided to employees of an educational institution cannot qualify as a no-additional-cost benefit or working condition fringe benefit.

[66] The lifetime learning credit and the American opportunity tax credit are phased out over specified income levels as discussed in Chapter 5. Prior to 2018, a deduction for AGI of up to $4,000 of qualified education expenses was allowed, as discussed in Chapter 5.

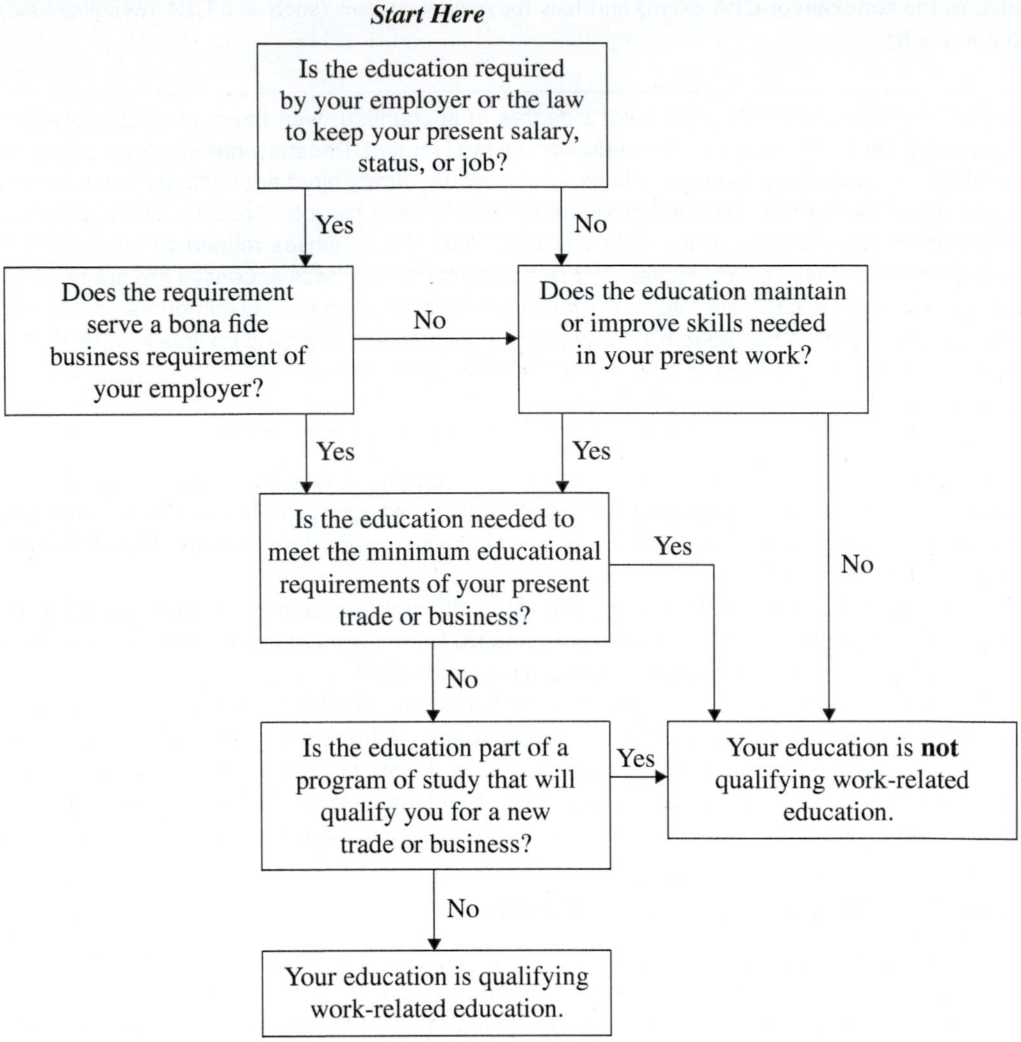

FIGURE 4.3 When do education expenses qualify as work related? *Source:* IRS Publication 970: *Tax Benefits for Education.*

Table 4.4 Tax Benefits From Education Expenses

Provision	Type of benefit	Must be work related?	Type of qualifying expenses
Working Condition Fringe Benefit	No dollar limit on exclusion from income	Yes	Tuition, fees, books, supplies, equipment, transportation, meals, and lodging
Educational Assistance Program	Maximum exclusion from income of $5,250 per year	No	Tuition, fees, books, supplies, and equipment
Qualified Tuition Reduction	No dollar limit on exclusion from income of employee	No	Tuition for undergraduate courses only
Qualified Scholarship	No dollar limit on exclusion from income	No, but will not qualify if for past, present or future services	Tuition, fees, books, supplies, and equipment
American Opportunity Credit	Maximum credit of $2,500 per year per student	No	Tuition, fees, and books for only first four years
Lifetime Learning Credit	Maximum credit of $2,000 per year per taxpayer	No	Tuition and fees

Indirect expenses, such as pre-move house-hunting trips and temporary living expenses do not qualify and will result in taxable income if paid or reimbursed by the employer. A qualified move includes a transfer by a current employer, hiring by a new employer, and obtaining employment after the move. A move in any of these situations qualifies, as long as the distance and time requirements are met.

To meet the distance test, the distance between the old residence and the new principal place of work (the new commuting distance if the taxpayer does not move) must be at least 50 miles greater than the distance between the old place of work and the old residence (the old commuting distance).

To meet the time test, a taxpayer must have full-time employment for any 39 weeks during the 12 months following the move.[67] A self-employed individual must work full-time at the new location for at least 78 weeks during the 24 months following the move. The individual must work 39 of the 78 weeks within the first 12 months.[68] Semi-retired persons, part-time students, and other individuals who work only a few hours each week do not meet this test.[69]

No moving expense deductions are allowed for relocation to a temporary place of employment. An assignment is considered temporary unless it is for more than one year. If the employment is temporary, there is no change in tax home and expenses for travel away from home are deductible.[70]

4.2.12 SUBSTANTIATING BUSINESS EXPENSES

Most employers require some form of accounting for business expenses to support reimbursement requests. If the employer has an **accountable plan**, the employee must provide a record of the amount, date, place of expenditure, and business purpose, along with all appropriate receipts.[71] Receipts are required to support any expenditure for lodging (regardless of cost) while traveling away from home and for any other expenditure of $75 or more.

With an accountable plan:

1. If the reimbursement equals the business expenses, the employee excludes the reimbursement from income and the employer deducts the expenses.
2. If the reimbursement exceeds the expenses, the excess reimbursement is income.[72]
3. If the expenses exceed the reimbursement, the unreimbursed expenses are not deductible.[73]

If an employee does not make an adequate accounting, the employer has a **nonaccountable plan** and the employee includes reimbursements in income.

Some employers reduce their paperwork by using a **per diem allowance**. This is a flat dollar allowance per day of business travel. When a per diem allowance is used, expenses are deemed substantiated to the extent of the lesser of the per diem allowance or the federal per diem rate.[74] The per diem method only substantiates the amount of expense; the other substantiation requirements must still be met, including the place, date, and business purpose for the expense.

---

[67] Reg. §1.217-2(c)(4)(iii).

[68] Reg. §1.217-2(c)(4)(i)(b).

[69] Reg. §1.217-2(f)(1).

[70] Deductible travel expenses are discussed in Chapter 6.

[71] Effectively, the employee should maintain a diary or account book in which this information is recorded at the time the expense is incurred.

[72] If the reimbursement equals or exceeds the expenses and is included in the employee's income, the employee takes an offsetting deduction for the expenses.

[73] Prior to 2018, unreimbursed employee business expenses could be deducted as miscellaneous itemized deductions if they were in excess of 2 percent of AGI, as discussed in Chapter 5.

[74] The federal per diem rates differ by location. These amounts may be found at http://www.gsa.gov and searching for per diem rates.

4.3 EMPLOYEE STOCK AND STOCK OPTIONS

Stock and stock options can provide employees with potentially valuable rewards if the employer's stock value increases after the employee is granted stock options or restricted stock. There is, however, an element of risk. If the employer's stock price fails to increase, the employee's options may become worthless and expire without exercise. The underlying stock may also be of limited value.

From the employer's perspective, the use of its stock as compensation is attractive. It requires no cash outflow and encourages employees to work for the success of the company as stockholders who are able to share in that success. To avoid diluting existing shareholders' control, however, employers frequently issue nonvoting stock to employees.[75] If a corporation uses stock as payment for services, the employee recognizes ordinary income equal to the stock's fair market value when received. The employer takes a corresponding compensation deduction, but recognizes no gain or loss on the transaction.

Example 4.22

Todd Corporation paid Randy $80,000 salary plus 2,500 shares of Todd stock valued at $25,000. Todd deducts $105,000 as compensation expense and Randy pays taxes on $105,000 of ordinary income. When Randy sells the stock, he will recognize a capital gain or loss equal to the difference between his $25,000 basis in the stock and the sales price.

4.3.1 RESTRICTED STOCK

Stock transferred to an employee as compensation for services that vests according to a schedule is referred to as restricted stock. Normally, the employee does not pay for the stock. Restricted stock plans are usually established to retain key employees who otherwise might leave the company. Employees cannot sell the restricted stock until some future date because the employee's right to the stock is either nontransferable or subject to substantial risk of forfeiture when received. Employees are required to forfeit their shares (return them) if they leave the company before the stock vests (becomes unrestricted), typically a two- to five-year period. In some cases, the shares are tied to the company's financial performance and are forfeited if certain targets are not met. Thus, the stock is not treated as owned by the employees until it vests.

The value of restricted stock usually is not taxed until it vests. That is the date the employee is considered to own the stock and the holding period begins. At that time, the employee recognizes ordinary income equal to the stock's fair market value and the employer has a corresponding compensation deduction.[76] The income recognized is ordinary income because the stock was transferred in return for services. Restricted stock shares have value when granted but that value can vary between the grant and vesting dates. This differs from stock options (discussed later) that generally have no value to the employee (the option price is usually equal to or greater than current market price) unless the stock appreciates in value after the option is granted. As a result, a share of restricted stock has some current value while an option to acquire a share of stock may have none. Thus, employers are able to use fewer shares of restricted stock relative to stock options to provide the same value to employees.

Shareholders holding restricted stock are normally entitled to receive any dividend payments on their shares, even before the stock vests. These dividends are taxed as ordinary income, however, and are deductible by the employer as compensation expense. After vesting, the dividends are eligible for the reduced dividend tax rates (0/15/20 percent based on the taxpayer's taxable income).

---

[75] When employers issue new shares the earnings per share of existing stockholders are diluted. A company can use its cash reserves to purchase its own shares in the market. From a cash-flow perspective, this is the same as paying cash compensation.
[76] §83(a). The amount of income taxed to the employee becomes the basis for the stock.

Example 4.23

On July 1, year 1, Maria received a bonus of 300 shares of her employer's stock. If she leaves the company before July 1, year 5, she must return the stock to the company, but after that date, the risk of forfeiture lapses and the stock vests (she has an unrestricted right to the shares). If the shares are worth $60,000 when the stock vests, Maria has $60,000 of ordinary income at that time and this becomes her basis (cost) for the stock. The employer also has a $60,000 compensation deduction in year 5. Dividends received prior to vesting are taxable as ordinary income; after vesting they are eligible for reduced dividend tax rates.

Employees may accelerate the income recognition on restricted stock by electing to recognize its fair market value as income on the grant date.[77] If this election is made, then the dividends received are immediately eligible for the reduced dividend rate. The income recognized is the stock basis and the holding period starts as of the grant date; appreciation after that date will be taxed at long-term capital gains rates as long as the stock is held for at least one year. There is a significant risk associated with this election, however. If the employee forfeits the stock prior to vesting, there is no deduction allowed for the loss on the stock forfeited, nor are any taxes paid from the prior income recognition refunded.[78] The employer, however, recognizes income equal to the prior compensation deduction.

Example 4.24

Continuing the previous example, the fair market value of the stock was $12,000 when issued. If Maria elects income acceleration, she recognizes only $12,000 ordinary income in year 1, but no additional income in year 5 when the restrictions lapse. (The employer has a $12,000 matching compensation deduction in year 1 but has no additional deduction when the restrictions lapse.) Her basis in the shares is $12,000. Any dividends received are eligible for the reduced dividend tax rate based on her other taxable income. When she sells the shares, the difference between the selling price and her $12,000 basis is taxable at capital gains rates.

If Maria recognized the $12,000 of ordinary income in year 1 but quits her job in year 3, she cannot deduct her $12,000 basis in the forfeited stock and she would have paid tax on income never realized. Her employer also must repay any taxes saved by the compensation deduction in year 1.[79] If she had not made the election, she would have recognized no income and had no basis in the forfeited stock.

TAX PLANNING

Few employees make the income acceleration election because it results in immediate recognition of ordinary income (no stock can be sold so there is no cash flow to pay the tax) and other potential adverse consequences from forfeiture. The election could be considered, however, if the value of the stock is initially low, substantial appreciation is expected, there is a very high probability that the stock will vest, and the tax on the current fair market value is less than the expected discounted present value of the tax on the stock's fair market value in the year it vests.

Deferral Election for Private Company Stock

Employees of private companies who receive restricted stock units or stock options often have taxable income when the stock option is exercised or the restricted stock unit is settled. Some private companies permit employees to sell back a number of the shares to the company sufficient to pay the tax. If, however, the company does not offer this option, the employees may not have

[77] §83(b). The employee has only 30 days after the grant date to make the election by filing a statement with the IRS indicating the employee is making a §83(b) election.

[78] A capital loss would only be allowed for any amount the employee paid for the stock.

[79] Reg. §§1.83-6(c) and 2(a).

sufficient cash for the taxes owed. To address this problem, the Tax Cuts and Jobs Act added a new deferral election for private company stock attributable to restricted stock units settled or stock options exercised after 2017. This elective provision allows qualified employees to defer the recognition of income attributable to restricted stock or stock options, received from an eligible corporation and connected to the performance of services, for up to five years. Instead of including income at the delivery of fully vested stock or at the exercise date of a nonqualified stock option, the employee will be subject to income tax at the earliest of the following dates:

- Five years after the employee's right to the stock is substantially vested,
- The date the qualified stock is transferrable or publicly traded,
- The date the employee becomes an excluded employee, or
- The date the employee revokes the election.

When a qualified employee makes this deferral election, the employer's deduction is also deferred until the tax year in which the employee includes the deferred amount in income.

A qualified employee is an individual who is not an excluded employee. The following are considered excluded employees (and thus not eligible):

- An individual who becomes a one percent owner during the taxable year or has been a one percent owner at any time during the 10 preceding calendar years.
- The current or former chief executive officer or chief financial officer of the corporation (or an individual acting in either capacity).
- A family member of an individual described above.
- One of the four highest compensated officers of the corporation during the taxable year or the four highest-compensated officers for any of the 10 preceding taxable years.

An eligible corporation is one whose stock has never been publicly held (including any predecessor corporations). The corporation must also have a written plan under which at least 80 percent of all U.S. employees are granted stock options or restricted stock units with the same rights and privileges to receive qualified stock. Only stock options or restricted stock units awarded in connection with services qualify.[80]

The employee must make the deferral election no later than 30 days after the first date the employee's right to the stock is substantially vested or is transferable, whichever is earlier.[81] If the share value increases, employees receive capital gains treatment on any increase in value after the exercise of the option or issuance of the restricted stock. If share value declines, the employee owes ordinary income tax based on the original value of the stock at the time the employee's right to the stock first became substantially vested.

4.3.2 STOCK OPTIONS

A corporate **stock option** is a right to purchase a certain number of shares of the corporation's stock for a stated price (called the *strike price* or exercise price) for a specified period of time. The grant date is the date on which the option is first offered to the individual. An employee *exercises* an option when he or she purchases the stock from the company. Stock options are often granted to corporate employees as part of a compensation package or as an incentive to forgo seeking employment elsewhere. The option allows an employee the opportunity to benefit

[80] Qualified stock includes incentive stock options (ISO), but an election would disqualify the ISO. Qualified stock cannot be eligible to be cashed out at vesting.

[81] §83(i)(4)(A).

from any increase in the stock value without having to risk any funds. An employee has no obligation to exercise an option and would normally do so only when it is beneficial; that is, when the stock has appreciated beyond the strike price between the grant date and the exercise date. Unlike actual stock ownership, if the stock value declines, the employee has no direct loss and can simply allow the option to lapse. The employee usually recognizes no income when an option is granted; instead, income is deferred until the option is exercised. Employees also like the inherent leverage in options because the increase in an option's value is proportionately greater than any increase in the value of the company stock.

Example 4.25

Adam receives 3,000 shares of restricted stock worth $20 per share. If the price increases to $50, the shares are worth $150,000. Alternatively, assume Adam receives 10,000 stock options with a strike price of $20. When the stock price reaches $50, the options are worth $300,000 [($50 – $20) × 10,000].

Employers favor stock options because there are no cash outlays when options are granted, but there is a cash inflow when employees exercise their options. Employers may also receive a tax benefit from the compensation deduction equal to the employee's compensation income when that income is recognized.

Nonqualified Stock Options

A majority of stock options issued to employees are nonqualified stock options. A **nonqualified stock option (NQSO)** allows an employee to purchase employer stock at a strike price that is usually at or above its current selling price.[82] If the employee exercises the option when fair market value exceeds the strike price (the cost to the employee), the employee recognizes income equal to this unrealized gain. (The difference between the strike price and stock's fair market value on the exercise date is called the *bargain element*.) The employer has a matching compensation deduction for the employee's recognized income. If the fair market value of the stock is less than the strike price (referred to as *out-of-the-money*), the option should not be exercised. When the employee sells the stock acquired through options, the gain or loss is recognized on the difference between the employee's basis (the strike price plus the bargain element) and the selling price of the stock.

Example 4.26

In year 1, Kam Corporation grants Janis an option to buy 1,000 shares of Kam stock for $32 per share (current selling price of $30 per share) at any time during the next seven years. The option has no ascertainable value and Janis has no income from the option grant because the strike price exceeds the market price. If the stock price stays at or below $32 per share over the seven-year term of the option, Janis will let the option lapse. Janis has no income and Kam Corporation has no deduction.

In year 7, Kam Corporation stock is selling for $82 per share. Janis pays the corporation $32,000 ($32 strike price × 1,000 shares) and exercises her option for the 1,000 shares of stock that now have a fair market value of $82,000 ($82 FMV × 1,000 shares). Janis recognizes the $50,000 bargain element ($82,000 FMV – $32,000 cost) as ordinary income in year 7 and Kam Corporation deducts the $50,000 bargain element as compensation paid to Janis. Janis has to pay $32,000 for the stock purchase along with the tax on her $50,000 of additional compensation. If she needs to generate cash by selling some of her shares of stock, Janis will recognize no additional gain unless she sells the stock for more than her $82 per share basis.

[82] If an employee receives a stock option currently exercisable at a strike price below the current market value, the option has an ascertainable value and is taxable compensation at the grant date.

Some employers allow employees to exercise their stock options under a cashless program. This program allows an employee to exercise stock options and immediately sell some or all of the shares at the prevailing market price (referred to as a *same-day sale*). The employee receives the proceeds of the sale after deducting the strike price, withholding taxes, and any brokerage commissions.

For financial statement purposes, a corporation records the estimated value of the options as a compensation expense in the year the option is granted,[83] but it is allowed no tax deduction until the year the options are exercised. This causes a book/tax difference for the year the options are granted that reverses in the year they are exercised. Employers favor NQSOs because they can get a tax deduction without incurring any cash outflow.

Incentive Stock Options

Incentive stock options (ISO), also known as qualified or statutory stock options, have a more favorable tax treatment from the perspective of the employee because there is no income recognition at either the grant date or at exercise. Instead, employee income recognition is postponed until the stock is sold, with the employee recognizing long-term capital gain rather than ordinary income. To qualify for this favorable tax treatment, the employee cannot sell the stock for one year after exercising the option or two years after the grant date, whichever is later. Failure to hold the stock for the required time disqualifies the ISO changing the tax treatment for the employer and employee so that it is taxed like an NQSO.

The significant negative feature of ISOs is that the employer receives no compensation deduction at any time for the option. The lack of a tax deduction, however, may not be as important to startup firms or corporations with net operating losses that can use ISOs to attract and retain employees. Similar to the NQSO, the corporation still records the estimated value of qualified stock options as compensation expense for financial statement purposes in the year the options are granted. This also causes a book/tax difference, but it is a *permanent* book/tax difference because the corporation never gets a tax deduction for this expense. In addition, an ISO also has more requirements and restrictions than an NQSO.[84]

Example 4.27

Assume the facts of the previous example except that Janis's option qualifies as an ISO. Janis recognizes no income when she purchases the 1,000 shares of stock worth $82,000 for $32,000 in year 7. Janis holds these shares until year 13, when she sells them for $200,000. Her capital gain on the sale is $168,000 ($200,000 selling price – $32,000 cost basis), $50,000 of which represents the untaxed bargain element on exercise of the option. Thus, Janis's ISO has two advantages over an NQSO: (1) the taxes are deferred until the year of sale and (2) the option's bargain element ($50,000) is converted from ordinary income to capital gain. Because this option is an ISO, Kam Corporation receives no tax deduction from the option. Kam's only benefit is the $32,000 cash from Janis when she exercised her option and the shares were issued.

TAX PLANNING

Individuals who are planning to exercise ISOs should consider that the untaxed bargain element is an individual alternative minimum tax (AMT) adjustment. Individuals may wish to plan the exercise of their ISOs in years in which they are not likely to be subject to the AMT.[85]

[83] FASB ASC 718 Stock Compensation. Since 2006, the FASB has required expensing of stock options for financial accounting purposes. Businesses must measure the economic value of options on the grant date and then amortize this cost over the vesting period of the options.

[84] The option price cannot be less than the stock's fair market value at grant date; the option cannot be exercised more than 10 years after the grant date; the individual granted the option must own less than 10% of the employer; and the option is not transferable. Employees can purchase no more than $100,000 through ISOs annually. §422(d).

[85] §56(b)(3). See Chapter 5 for a discussion of the AMT.

4.3.3 PHANTOM STOCK AND STOCK APPRECIATION RIGHTS

A drawback of stock options is the need for employees to have cash available when they exercise their options. To address this, corporations have developed alternative forms of deferred compensation that allow the employee to benefit from the appreciation in company stock without having to actually buy the stock. In a **phantom stock plan**, an employee's deferred compensation is hypothetically invested in company stock. At the end of the deferral period (typically when employment ends), the employer pays the employee the full fair market value of the phantom shares in cash or in stock, which is taxable as ordinary income.

In a **stock appreciation right (SAR)** plan, employees receive a cash payment equal to the appreciation only in their assumed shares of the employer's stock over a certain period of time. The employees recognize ordinary income for these payments when they exercise their SARs. In a SARs plan only the stock appreciation over a period of time is received. In contrast, under a phantom stock plan the full value of the stock is usually received.

Example 4.28

Horizon Corporation granted 400 SARs to Lillian in year 1, when its stock was selling for $10 per share. Lillian can exercise the rights at any time during the next eight years. In year 7, when the stock is selling for $40 per share, Lillian exercises the 400 SARs. She receives $12,000 [400 SARs × ($40 − $10)] from Horizon Corporation and has $12,000 income. Horizon has a corresponding $12,000 compensation deduction in year 7. If this had been a phantom stock plan, Lillian would have received $16,000 (400 hypothetical shares × $40).

TAX PLANNING

Plans that provide the advantages of stock options without the employees owning stock can be particularly useful to S corporations that are limited to 100 shareholders and closely-held corporations that do not want their employees to become shareholders.

4.4 DEFERRED COMPENSATION AND RETIREMENT PLANNING

Deferred compensation plans are agreements under which an employer makes a promise to pay benefits to its employees in future years. These deferred compensation plans also allow the deferral of the taxes on this income. When the funds are withdrawn from the plan, they are taxed at ordinary income rates. The most common deferred compensation plan is the retirement plan. Retirement plans may be qualified or nonqualified.

4.4.1 QUALIFIED RETIREMENT PLANS

Deferred compensation plans that meet the requirements of the Internal Revenue Code and the Employee Retirement Income Security Act of 1974 (ERISA) are referred to as **qualified deferred compensation plans**; those not meeting the requirements are referred to as *nonqualified plans*. Qualified deferred compensation plans are funded arrangements that receive the following favorable tax treatment:

1. The employer deducts contributions as they are paid into a trust administered by an independent trustee.
2. The earnings on these contributions accumulate tax free.
3. The employee is not taxed on the benefits until they are actually received.[86]

Thus, the employer gets an immediate tax deduction while the employee's tax is deferred until income is received in a future year. Employees may also make contributions to a qualified

[86] In many cases, employees can further delay taxation by transferring these amounts into another tax-deferred plan, such as an IRA.

retirement plan and defer taxation of these contributions until they are withdrawn. This deferral is in addition to the tax deferral for employer contributions.

Example 4.29

Cindy is an employee of Xtra Corporation. Xtra contributes 7 percent of each employee's salary annually to a qualified pension plan. Cindy's current year salary of $50,000 results in a retirement plan contribution of $3,500 (7% × $50,000). Because Xtra Corporation's plan is qualified, the corporation can deduct the $3,500 payment but Cindy has no current tax liability. Xtra Corporation's employees can also contribute up to 7 percent of their annual salary to the pension plan. Cindy also contributes the maximum $3,500 (7% × $50,000) to the plan, reducing her gross salary from $50,000 to $46,500. Cindy is not taxed on her contribution (or on her employer's contribution) until she withdraws the funds from the plan.

Nondiscrimination rules ensure that qualified deferred compensation plans provide benefits in an equitable manner to all participating employees. Additional rules require that employees vest fully (have a nonforfeitable right to the retirement benefits) after they have worked for the employer for a certain number of years. Gradual vesting allows an employee to vest a specified percentage for each year of employment; for example, 20 percent vesting per year starting in the second year with full vesting at the end of the sixth year. An alternate method is cliff vesting in which an employee is fully (100%) vested at the end of a fixed number of full years of employment, but the employee is not vested in any employer contribution until that point. In all cases, employee contributions vest immediately. Vesting requirements encourage employees to continue working at the business. Once employees are fully vested, they can take the employer's contributions with them if they terminate employment with that employer.

The IRS imposes a 10 percent penalty (in addition to the regular income tax) on **premature withdrawals** (generally a withdrawal before age 59½) to discourage employees from withdrawing funds before retirement. Exceptions exist, however, for the disability or death of the employee.[87] To ensure that the income in a retirement plan is eventually taxed, the IRS requires participants to begin minimum distributions from their plan after they reach age 70½.[88] These distributions are taxed in the year received as ordinary income.

A taxpayer who receives a premature lump-sum distribution must roll over (deposit) all or part of the distribution into another qualified plan or an individual retirement account within 60 days or pay a tax and penalty on all or part of the distribution. The plan trustee withholds 20 percent of any lump-sum distribution, however, unless the distribution is transferred directly into another plan (a trustee-to-trustee rollover). Thus, if the taxpayer receives a lump-sum distribution, the withheld 20 percent is a tax prepayment that is not available for rollover into the new plan, and is subject to a premature withdrawal penalty and income taxes.

Example 4.30

Ellen, age 35, has $50,000 in her employer-sponsored retirement plan. She takes the maximum distribution of $40,000 ($50,000 less 20 percent withheld in taxes) when she changes jobs. If she fails to roll over the entire $50,000 into another qualified plan, she must pay a $5,000 (10% × $50,000) penalty on the premature withdrawal. If she rolls over only $40,000 into a new plan within the required 60 days, her penalty tax on the premature distribution is $1,000 (10% × $10,000) for the withheld taxes and $10,000 is also included in income. Ellen should have requested a direct rollover (trustee-to-trustee transfer); no withholding would be required and no taxes would be due. It may, however, be possible for her to borrow money to replace the withheld taxes until she receives her tax refund. The interest expense on the borrowed funds should be far less than the penalty and taxes on the premature distribution.

[87] The penalty is also waived if the employee is age 55 or over and has terminated employment with the plan sponsor.

[88] §401(a)(9) and §408(a)(6). A 50 percent excise tax is assessed on the undistributed amount if a participant does not receive the minimum required distribution by April 1 of the year following the year in which he or she reaches age 70½. Employees who continue to work after age 70½ may postpone distributions from their employer-sponsored plans until they retire.

4.4.2 TYPES OF RETIREMENT PLANS

There are two basic types of qualified retirement plans: defined benefit plans and defined contribution plans. A **defined benefit plan** provides a fixed benefit at retirement based on the employee's years of service and compensation. These plans are funded entirely by the employer. Contributions are actuarially calculated to provide the promised benefits. For example, a defined benefit plan might provide a retirement benefit equal to 40 percent of an employee's average salary for the five years before retirement. The employer has a compensation expense deduction for the contributions, even though employees do not recognize income until benefits are received. Companies must meet the minimum funding standards that may require contributions even in years when there are operating losses.[89]

A **defined contribution plan** is a qualified plan in which the contribution is specified (such as a fixed percentage of compensation) but the future benefit to be paid is not. Each plan participant has an individual account with benefits based solely on contributions to the participant's account and any allocated investment income, gains, and losses. The employer receives a deduction when it makes a contribution into the employee trust account, but the employee does not recognize income until benefits are received.

Example 4.31

Sara, a manager for Soho Corporation earning $100,000 annual salary, is a participant in Soho's qualified defined contribution plan. Soho contributes $25,000 to its defined contribution plan for Sara. Soho Corporation deducts Sara's $100,000 salary and the $25,000 retirement plan contribution as compensation expense for the year. Sara is taxed only on the $100,000 currently. The $25,000 retirement plan contribution remains untaxed until she withdraws the funds.

The two most common defined contribution plans are the *money purchase plan* and the *profit sharing plan*. In a money purchase plan, the company (and the employee if it is a contributory plan) contributes a fixed percentage of the employee's salary to the plan. Because the employer's annual contribution is fixed, this may not be an attractive plan for a new or growing business.

TAX PLANNING

Profit-sharing plans are very popular with start-up companies because employer contributions are based on earnings. In profitable years, the business contributes a percentage of the profits to an employee trust account. In unprofitable years, no contributions are required.

One difference between defined benefit and defined contribution plans is which party bears the risk of investment losses. In a defined benefit plan, investment gains or losses do not affect the ultimate benefits promised employees. Rather, gains and losses affect the employer's contributions and the employer bears the risk of investment losses. In a defined contribution plan, investment gains or losses increase or decrease the value of the employee's account. Thus, the employee bears the risk of investment losses.

A **401(k) plan**, also called a *cash or deferred arrangement (CODA)* or a salary reduction plan, is a defined contribution plan that permits an employee to defer a certain amount of pay that is then contributed to the 401(k) plan by the employer on his or her behalf. The employees' salaries are reduced by the deduction for their contributions.[90] These contributions effectively are made on a pretax basis. The contributions and the plan earnings remain untaxed until the employee withdraws them.[91] The employer is still entitled to a current deduction for the funds it puts into the plan. For this type of plan, the employer has little cost beyond the costs of administering the plan.[92]

---

[89] §412.

[90] This compensation is subject to FICA tax in the year contributed.

[91] Funds usually cannot be withdrawn until the employee reaches age 59½, retires, becomes disabled, leaves the employer, or dies (loans and hardship withdrawals may be permitted). Plans can elect to have all or part of their contributions treated as non-deductible Roth contributions. The Roth 401(k) has no income limitations. A Roth 401(k) account can only consist of employee contributions and the earnings on those contributions but can be withdrawn at a later date tax free.

[92] Employees of tax-exempt educational, charitable, and religious organizations can qualify for similar benefits under a 403(b) plan also known as a tax-sheltered or tax-deferred annuity program.

The popularity of 401(k) plans is due primarily to their flexibility.[93] Each year an employee can contribute a different amount, or no amount, from his or her salary to the plan, within plan limits. Nondiscrimination rules make the contributions of highly compensated employees depend on the level of nonhighly compensated employee participation and contributions. Some employers match all or part of an employee's contribution to provide an incentive for lower-paid employees to join the plan.[94]

Example 4.32

Under the Boulder Company 401(k) plan, employees may direct Boulder to contribute up to 10 percent of their salaries to the plan rather than receiving it in cash. Boulder matches 50 percent of the employee's contribution up to a maximum of 5 percent of compensation. Charlie, whose salary is $45,000, elects to contribute the maximum allowable $4,500 (10% × $45,000), and Boulder makes a matching contribution of $2,250 (5% × $45,000). Charlie's current taxable salary is only $40,500 ($45,000 – $4,500), but Boulder deducts the entire $45,000 salary plus its matching contribution of $2,250.

Other plans within these general categories include the following:

1. *Employee stock ownership plans (ESOPs)*—shares of employer stock are purchased to fund the plan.[95]
2. *Simplified employee pension (SEP) plans*—small businesses make contributions to SEP individual retirement accounts on behalf of employees and receive tax advantages similar to other qualified plans.
3. *Savings incentive match plan for employees (SIMPLE) retirement plans*—an employer with 100 or fewer employees establishes an individual retirement account for each employee and makes matching contributions based on contributions elected by participating employees under a qualified salary reduction arrangement. It is not subject to complex nondiscrimination requirements so administrative and legal costs are minimized.
4. *SIMPLE 401(k) plans*—these plans are similar to SIMPLE plans but are deemed to meet the complex nondiscrimination tests for 401(k) plans.

TAX PLANNING

Employers should consider the demographics and incomes of their workforce when selecting a particular type of pension plan. If most workers earn at or near minimum wage, it is highly unlikely that they would make contributions to any type of contributory plan. The more highly educated and older the workforce, the more likely they are to welcome a contributory plan that allows them to make significant contributions to their accounts in addition to the employer's contributions.

4.4.3 CONTRIBUTION LIMITS

All qualified plans limit the amount of employee compensation that can be tax deferred through an employer-sponsored retirement plan. For defined benefit plans, the maximum pension benefit that a plan can fund is 100 percent of a participating employee's average compensation for the three highest-paid years, subject to a $220,000 cap.[96]

[93] Participants can direct their contributions to a broad range of investment options, including self-directed brokerage accounts.
[94] Even with employer matching, few low-income wage earners contribute to retirement plans because they spend almost all their disposable income. To encourage greater participation, a tax credit was added for low-income employees, as discussed in Chapter 5.
[95] Employees who participate in ESOPs become shareholders. When employees retire, they receive distributions of stock held in the ESOP accounts so the value of their retirement benefits is dependent upon the market value of the stock. Distributions are taxable to the extent of the ESOP's aggregate stock basis with gain on unrealized appreciation deferred until the shares are sold.
[96] §415(b). The maximum dollar amount is indexed for inflation.

Two important annual limits affect defined contribution plans. One limits the maximum sum of employer and employee contributions to each participant's account to 100 percent of compensation up to a maximum of $55,000.[97] The other restricts the maximum deductible contribution to 25 percent of compensation paid to all employees covered by the plan.[98]

Example 4.33

Tom, a 35-year-old engineer, owns an incorporated engineering practice that maintains a profit-sharing plan. Tom is the only employee and his annual compensation is $120,000. The business may contribute up to $55,000 to Tom's account, but its deduction is limited to $30,000 (25% × $120,000).

For 401(k) plans, the maximum pretax compensation that an employee can defer is $18,500 in 2018.[99] If an employer matches an employee's contribution, the maximum deduction is 25 percent of covered employee compensation.

TAX PLANNING

Catch-up contributions allow employees age 50 or older at year-end to make additional contributions to certain pension plans as they approach their retirement years. The maximum catch-up contribution for 401(k) plans is $6,000.[100] This means that the maximum contribution in 2018 by an employee age 50 or older is $24,500 ($18,500 + $6,000) and a maximum overall limit of $61,000 ($55,000 + $6,000) applies to the sum of employee and employer contributions. These catch-up contributions provide a significant tax-deferral opportunity for highly compensated employees age 50 and over because catch-up contributions are not subject to the plan's nondiscrimination rules. However, the limit on employer contributions may mean that highly compensated employees may not be able to receive the full employer match available to other employees.

Example 4.34

Baker Corporation matches employee contributions to its 401(k) account on a two-for-one basis up to 4% of the employee's salary. Bill, a 52-year-old employee of Baker Corporation, earns $480,000 annually. In 2018, Bill contributes the maximum $24,500 ($18,500 plus an additional elective catch-up contribution of $6,000) to his 401(k) plan. If there was no limit on the employer contribution, Baker would be allowed to make a matching contribution of up to $38,400 ($480,000 × 4% × 2). The $61,000 limit on employer and employee contributions prevents Baker from contributing more than $36,500 ($61,000 – $24,500 Bill's contribution). Bill's taxable income is $455,500 ($480,000 – $24,500) while Baker deducts Bill's entire $480,000 salary plus its $36,500 matching employer contribution.

Bill would be better off if he reduced his contribution to $22,600. Baker could then contribute $38,400. Bill's taxable income would be $457,400 ($480,000 – $22,600). Baker deducts Bill's entire $480,000 salary plus its $38,400 matching employer contribution. Bill receives an additional $1,235 ($1,900 less 35% tax) in take-home pay while the same $61,000 is contributed to his 401(k) account.

4.4.4 NONQUALIFIED DEFERRED COMPENSATION PLANS

A **nonqualified deferred compensation plan** is one that does not meet the requirements of the Internal Revenue Code or ERISA. Under a nonqualified plan, an employer can defer an unlimited

[97] §415(c). The maximum dollar amount will increase for inflation in future years in $1,000 increments and was $54,000 in 2017 ($53,000 in 2016).

[98] Since 2002, elective deferrals as well as employees' elective set-asides in cafeteria plans are treated as compensation.

[99] The maximum compensation deferral was $18,000 in 2017 and 2016. This limit also applies to 403(b) annuities and salary reduction SEPs. The maximum annual elective deferral that may be made to a SIMPLE plan is $12,500 for 2016 to 2018.

[100] These catch-up limits also apply to 403(b) annuities and salary reduction SEPs.

amount of compensation for highly compensated executives without extending the plan benefits to other employees. The employer and the employee usually have a contract that defers payment of part of the employee's compensation for the present employment until sometime in the future (for example, after a specified number of years, at retirement, or on the occurrence of a specific event, such as a corporate take-over). The employer accrues its liability but sets aside no assets to secure the liability. The employer has no tax deduction until the year in which the deferred compensation is actually paid to the employee and the employee is taxed when the funds are received. If the employer's business fails and is unable to pay its liabilities for deferred compensation, the employee becomes an unsecured creditor.

Example 4.35

In year 1, David, the chief executive officer of Arco, Inc. receives a bonus of $280,000 to be paid in four annual installments, beginning when David retires in three years. Arco accrues a $280,000 liability for the deferred compensation on its financial statements but sets aside no cash or other property to fund David's deferred compensation. In year 1, David recognizes no income and Arco takes no tax deduction for the bonus. When David receives the first $70,000 installment in year 4, he recognizes $70,000 as income and Arco deducts $70,000 as compensation. David recognizes income and Arco takes a deduction over the remaining years as the compensation is actually paid. If Arco declares bankruptcy prior to paying the entire $280,000, David may collect little or none of the remaining compensation. He is merely another unsecured Arco creditor.

TAX PLANNING

The employee's risk can be somewhat reduced by using an arrangement called a *rabbi trust*.[101] The employer funds this deferred compensation arrangement by transferring property or cash into a trust. Although the employer is legally prohibited from reclaiming the trust assets, they are subject to claim by the employer's creditors. The employee has no interest in the assets and does not recognize income until the trust pays the compensation.

4.4.5 INDIVIDUAL RETIREMENT ACCOUNTS

An **individual retirement account (IRA)** is a personal retirement plan available to anyone with earned income during the year.[102] The maximum each individual may contribute is the lesser of $5,500 ($6,500 if age 50 or older) or earned income.[103] A married taxpayer can also contribute up to an additional $5,500 ($6,500 if age 50 or older) to a spousal IRA for a nonworking spouse or a spouse whose earned income is less than $5,500, as long as the total contribution to all of their IRAs does not exceed their combined earned income. Contributions are not required each year allowing individuals to contribute a lesser amount or nothing at all in a particular year. All earnings accumulate tax free until withdrawn. The earnings and contributions will be taxed as ordinary income as they are withdrawn.

Example 4.36

Sharon (single and age 28) earned a salary of $34,000. She can contribute up to $5,500 to her IRA.

Jim (age 51) and Olga (age 48) are married and file a joint return. Jim earned a salary of $50,000 and Olga earned $2,000 working at a part-time job. Jim may contribute up to $6,500 to his IRA and up to $5,500 to Olga's IRA.

[101] This is referred to as a rabbi trust because one of the first plans that received IRS approval involved a rabbi.

[102] Earned income includes all wages, salaries, commissions, tips, bonuses, and self-employment income. Alimony is also included for this provision.

[103] The maximum annual IRA contribution limit was $5,000 for 2008–2012. The additional catch-up contributions by individuals age 50 has been $1,000 from 2006 to the present.

If the taxpayer is not an active participant in any other qualified retirement plan, the contribution to a traditional IRA is fully deductible *for* AGI (contributions are made pretax). Employees who are active participants in employer-sponsored qualified retirement plans may have their deductions limited. Table 4.5 shows the adjusted gross income (AGI) ranges over which the deductibility of contributions to traditional IRAs are reduced to zero. For example, a taxpayer who is an active participant in an employer-sponsored retirement plan, is married, and files a joint return in 2018, must have AGI in excess of $101,000 before the deduction begins to decrease; the deduction is completely eliminated when AGI equals or exceeds $121,000.[104]

Table 4.5 AGI Phase-Out Ranges for Deductible IRAs

	Phase-out range	
Tax years	**Single**	**Married filing jointly**
2018	$63,000–$73,000	$101,000–$121,000
2017	$62,000–$72,000	$99,000–$119,000
2016	$61,000–$71,000	$98,000–$118,000

The nondeductible portion of the contribution is determined as follows:

$$\frac{(\text{AGI} - \text{Beginning of phase-out range})}{\text{Amount in phase-out range}} = \text{Percentage phased out}$$

$$\text{Maximum contribution} \times (1 - \text{Percentage phased out}) = \text{Maximum IRA deduction}$$

A taxpayer who is not covered by an employer's retirement plan but whose spouse is an active participant in an employer's plan may make a fully deductible contribution to an IRA if their AGI is no more than $189,000. The deduction phases out, however, over an AGI range of $189,000 to $199,000.[105] High-income individuals who do not get a deduction for their IRA contributions, can still benefit from the tax deferral on the earnings in their IRA. When they make withdrawals, only the earnings portion is taxed because the rest of the withdrawal is a return of their after-tax contribution.

Example 4.37

In 2018, Cindy and David (both age 38), a married couple with AGI of $112,000, file a joint tax return. Both are active participants in qualified retirement plans and they each contribute the $5,500 maximum to their IRAs. Due to the phase-out rules, they cannot deduct 55 percent [($112,000 – $101,000)/$20,000 = 55%] or $3,025 of the contribution, and their deductions are limited to $2,475 ($5,500 – $3,025) by each of them.

If Cindy is not an active participant in a qualified retirement plan, she can deduct her entire $5,500 contribution, while David would still be limited to a $2,475 deduction.

If their AGI is $199,000 or more, neither spouse's contribution would be deductible, as their AGI now exceeds the income limit.

Taxpayers must set up their IRA and make the contribution by the *unextended* due date of the tax return. Thus, a calendar-year taxpayer has until April 15, 2019, to establish and make a contribution into an IRA and deduct the contribution on his or her 2018 tax return. Care should

[104] The AGI phase-out threshold for a married person filing separately remains at zero for all years so that otherwise deductible contributions phase out ratably between zero and $10,000.

[105] These deductions phased out in 2017 over an AGI range of $186,000 to $196,000 ($184,000 to $194,000 for 2016).

be taken that the contribution limit is not exceeded because a 6 percent nondeductible excise tax penalty applies to any excess contributions to an IRA during the year (including any contributions after age 70½).

Earnings on IRA contributions accumulate tax free, but taxes must be paid on the earnings and all pretax (deductible) contributions when the funds are withdrawn. On funds withdrawn before age 59½, taxpayers must pay a 10 percent penalty in addition to the regular tax.[106] Taxpayers must begin taking minimum distributions from IRAs no later than age 70½.[107]

TAX PLANNING

An individual's traditional IRA may also accept a rollover distribution from a qualified retirement plan, as discussed previously. Distributions rolled over into a traditional IRA are not subject to any contribution limits.

Roth IRAs

An individual may make a nondeductible contribution of up to $5,500 ($6,500 if age 50 or over) per year to a **Roth IRA**, but the total contribution to both the traditional and Roth IRAs cannot exceed $5,500 ($6,500 if 50 or over).[108] With a traditional IRA, the money is contributed on a pretax basis (the contribution is deductible), but both contributions and earnings are taxed when withdrawn. Although taxpayers make contributions to a Roth IRA with after-tax dollars (there is no deduction), they withdraw earnings tax free along with the contributions that were already taxed. Qualified distributions generally cannot begin until five tax years after the year for which the first contribution is made and the taxpayer must be at least age 59½.[109]

Contributions to Roth IRAs phase out for single individuals with AGIs between $120,000 and $135,000 and for joint filers with AGIs between $189,000 and $199,000.[110] These phase-out limits apply whether or not the individual is an active participant in an employer-sponsored plan.

TAX PLANNING

Individuals still working after age 70½ may continue to make contributions to their Roth IRAs. There are no minimum distribution requirements during the owner's lifetime, so funds can be left in the account to continue to grow tax free. This can be used as an estate-planning tool for passing funds to beneficiaries.[111]

Individuals who can make either nondeductible contributions to a traditional IRA or a nondeductible contribution to a Roth IRA should contribute to the Roth IRA to take advantage of the tax-exempt treatment of earnings upon withdrawal.[112]

Example 4.38

Martha (single and age 51) is an active participant in her employer's qualified retirement plan. Her AGI is $40,000 and she would like to contribute the maximum to an IRA for 2018. Martha can make a $6,500 fully deductible contribution to a traditional IRA or a $6,500 nondeductible contribution to a Roth IRA.

If Martha's AGI is $90,000, she can make a $6,500 *nondeductible* contribution to a traditional IRA or a $6,500 nondeductible contribution to a Roth IRA.

If Martha's AGI is $140,000, she can only make a nondeductible contribution to a traditional IRA.

[106] There are exceptions to the 10 percent penalty for certain qualified distributions, such as the death or disability of the taxpayer and payment of medical expenses, education expenses, and limited first-time home purchases.

[107] Taxpayers who do not take minimum distributions are subject to a penalty tax of 50 percent of the amount by which the minimum required distribution exceeds the actual distribution.

[108] The Roth IRA is named after Senator William Roth, who was its primary advocate. Annual contribution limits (including catch-up provisions) are the same for both traditional and Roth IRAs.

[109] Exceptions apply for death, disability, and for first-time home buyers (subject to a $10,000 maximum).

[110] For 2017, contributions to a Roth IRA for single individuals were phased out at AGIs between $118,000 and $133,000 ($117,000 and $132,000 for 2016). For joint return filers the contributions phased out at AGIs between $186,000 and $196,000 for 2017 ($184,000–$194,000 for 2016).

[111] See Chapter 12 for a discussion of wealth transfer planning.

[112] Deciding between a deductible contribution to a traditional IRA and a nondeductible Roth IRA is complex and depends upon the individual's current and retirement tax rates and other investment issues.

TAX PLANNING

Taxpayers can rollover (transfer) all or part of the funds in a traditional IRA to a Roth IRA. There is a tax cost to do this, however. The earnings and deductible contributions transferred from a traditional IRA to a Roth IRA are taxed as ordinary income, but no penalty tax is assessed. The tax cost when converted may be small if there are substantial losses on IRA investments; this is one of the few ways to benefit from such losses. Additionally, for high-income individuals who cannot make a direct contribution to a Roth IRA due to the income limits, a rollover of funds from a traditional IRA provides a "back door" way to contribute to a Roth IRA.

4.5 SELF-EMPLOYED INDIVIDUALS

Self-employed individuals include independent contractors, sole proprietors, partners, and LLC managing members. Income and expenses for a sole proprietorship (including an independent contractor) are reported on Schedule C: *Profit or Loss from Business (Sole Proprietorship).* A partner's share of income from a partnership (including an LLC taxed as a partnership) is reported on Schedule E: *Supplemental Income and Loss.*[113]

4.5.1 EMPLOYMENT TAX CONSEQUENCES

Similar to the FICA tax on employers and employees, self-employed individuals are subject to the Self-Employment Contributions Act (SECA) tax. They are responsible for paying **self-employment taxes** on their self-employment net income at a rate that is equal to the combined employer and employee FICA tax rates for Social Security and Medicare. Thus, self-employed persons pay Social Security and Medicare taxes as if they are both the employer and employee. For 2018, the SECA tax rate is 15.3 percent, 12.4 percent for the Social Security portion up to a maximum income of $128,400 and 2.9 percent (the sum of the 1.45 percent rate for the employee and employer) for the Medicare portion with no maximum.[114]

To provide tax relief for self-employed individuals (similar to the deduction for the employer's 7.65 percent share of FICA taxes they pay), Congress enacted two deductions, one that reduces the self-employment income subject to tax and the other that allows a deduction from adjusted gross income similar to the deduction an employer has for FICA taxes.

To compute self-employment income subject to self-employment taxes, a deduction is first allowed for the employer's 7.65 percent share of the tax. This effectively taxes only 92.35 percent (100% − 7.65%) of net income from self-employment.[115] This reduced net income is multiplied by the 2.9 percent Medicare rate to compute the Medicare portion of the SECA tax. (There is no limit on income subject to the Medicare portion of the tax). The Social Security portion of the tax however, is imposed on no more than $128,400 of the taxpayer's income (after the 7.65% reduction). Thus, the Social Security tax rate (12.4%) applies to the lesser of (a) net earnings from self-employment (self-employment income × 92.35 percent) or (b) $128,400.[116] Once total SECA tax is computed, the individual deducts the employer's half of the total tax *for* AGI on his or her individual income tax return, reducing the taxpayer's income subject to the federal income tax.[117] Self-employment taxes are calculated on Schedule SE: *Self-Employment Tax* and are paid along with the individual's regular income tax.

Self-employment tax rates are summarized in Table 4.6.

---

[113] Sample filled-in forms are on the companion website for this text.

[114] When the additional 0.9 percent Medicare tax on salaries, wages, and other compensation of higher-income individuals is added to the 2.9 percent employee/employer rates, the combined rate increases to 3.8 percent if certain income thresholds are exceeded. The thresholds are $200,000 for single individuals (and heads of household), $250,000 for married taxpayers filing a joint return, and $125,000 for married taxpayers filing separately. The additional Medicare tax is discussed in Chapter 5.

[115] To simplify this computation, the deduction is allowed for the full 7.65% even when the income exceeds the Social Security ceiling limit. The instructions on Schedule SE state that the self-employment income should be multiplied by 92.35% before the tax is computed.

[116] The ceiling for the Social Security portion was $127,200 in 2017, $118,500 in 2015 and 2016.

[117] Deductions for AGI are discussed in depth in Chapter 5.

Table 4.6 FICA and SECA Tax Rates and Limits

6.2% FICA Social Security tax rate for employees
12.4% SECA Social Security tax rate for self-employed individuals
1.45% FICA Medicare tax rate for employees
2.9% SECA Medicare tax rate for self-employed individuals
$128,400 Social Security income limit for employees and self-employed individuals
No Medicare income limit
15.3% Total SECA rate below Social Security income limit (employer plus employee or self-employed individuals)
7.65% Deductible SECA rate below Social Security income limit (employer or self-employed individual)

Example 4.39

Steven, a single individual, has $130,000 of net income from his sole proprietorship in 2018. His self-employment taxes are $18,369 as computed on Schedule SE: *Self-Employment Tax*. He reports $130,000 in income from his sole proprietorship on Schedule C: *Profit or Loss from Business (Sole Proprietorship)*[118] and takes a $9,185 deduction *for* AGI.

Determining self-employment tax	
Sole-proprietorship income	$130,000
Less SECA deduction (7.65% × $130,000)	(9,945)
Net earnings from self-employment ($130,000 × 92.35%)	$120,055
Medicare tax ($120,055 × 2.9%)	$ 3,482
Social Security tax [12.4% x $120,055 (the lesser of $120,055 net earnings from self-employment or $128,400 income limit)]	14,887
Self-employment tax liability	$18,369

Determining adjusted gross income	
Sole-proprietorship income	$130,000
Deduction for employer's portion of self-employment tax ($18,369 × 50% employer's share)	(9,185)
Adjusted gross income	$120,815

An individual with income both as an employee and as a self-employed individual first considers employment taxes paid as an employee. Employee compensation on which FICA taxes are paid reduces the $128,400 ceiling for Social Security taxes imposed on self-employment earnings.

Example 4.40

Juan earned $50,000 of income as an employee and $90,000 of self-employment income in 2018. Juan's employer withheld $3,825 ($50,000 × 7.65%) from his salary for Social Security and Medicare taxes and also paid the employer's $3,825 ($50,000 × 7.65%) share of these taxes. To determine his self-employment tax, Juan first multiplies his $90,000 self-employment income by 92.35% ($90,000 × 92.35% = $83,115) to determine net earnings from self-employment. Juan then reduces the $128,400 ceiling by the $50,000 of employee earnings on which Social Security tax has already been paid. Only $78,400 ($128,400 – $50,000) of his self-employment income is subject to the Social Security tax; however, his entire $83,115 net earnings from self-employment are subject to the Medicare tax. Juan's self-employment taxes are $12,132 [($78,400 × 12.4%) = $9,722 + ($83,115 × 2.9% = $2,410)].

[118] Schedule C or C-EZ is the form on which an individual's sole-proprietorship income and expenses are reported. It is attached to the individual's income tax return as is Schedule SE. Sample filled-in tax returns are included on the website for this text.

Unlike employees whose employers withhold tax throughout the year on their behalf, self-employed individuals pay their self-employment and income taxes through quarterly estimated tax payments (due April 15, June 15, September 15 of the current year and January 15 of the following year).[119] Individuals who are both employees and self-employed may have their employers withhold additional tax to cover both the added income tax and self-employment tax obligations. If self-employment taxes paid through quarterly estimated payments or withholding are insufficient, the balance must be paid with the individual's tax return.

4.5.2 FRINGE BENEFITS LIMITED

Self-employed individuals cannot participate in many of the fringe benefits provided on a tax-free basis to employees and must use after-tax dollars for many of the benefits that employees can obtain with before-tax dollars.[120] Benefits that self-employed individuals cannot receive on a tax-free basis include health and accident insurance, group term life insurance, employee achievement awards, transit passes, and parking benefits.

To mitigate the difference in the before-tax cost a self-employed person pays with the cost of employer-provided health insurance, self-employed individuals may deduct the cost of health insurance *for* AGI. This health insurance deduction is limited in two ways, however. First, the deduction cannot exceed net earnings from self-employment (92.35 percent of self-employment income). Second, if the self-employed individual is entitled to participate in any subsidized health plan maintained by the taxpayer's employer or the taxpayer's spouse, a deduction is not allowed.[121] A subsidized health plan is one in which someone other than the employee pays for part or all of the cost of the plan.

Example 4.41

Jordan, a single individual, operates an electrical contracting business as a sole proprietorship in which his net earnings from self-employment are $290,000. He employs three electricians who participate in the company-sponsored health insurance plan in which Jordan also participates. The premium for each employee is $2,100 per year. Jordan deducts $6,300 from business revenue for the cost of the health insurance for the three employees on Schedule C. Jordan deducts $2,100 for his own health insurance as a deduction *for* AGI.

Rachel has $80,000 in self-employment net income from her consulting business. She has an individual-only health insurance policy through her business for which she pays $2,000 per year. Her husband, Adam, works for an employer that provides health insurance coverage for all employees with the employer paying 40 percent of the premium cost. Although Adam can cover Rachel under his policy, they decide not to do this because the cost is higher than Rachel's current policy. Rachel cannot deduct her health insurance premiums for AGI (but could as an itemized deduction) because she could have participated in a subsidized plan. The fact that she chose not to be covered through Adam's plan does not matter.

Self-employed individuals can participate on a tax-favored basis in certain benefits including educational assistance plans, no-additional-cost benefits, dependent care assistance, employee discounts, and de minimis benefits.

---

[119] If net earnings from self-employment are less than $400, no self-employment tax is owed.

[120] For this rule, self-employed individuals also include shareholders of S corporations who own more than 2 percent of the S corporation's outstanding stock. When a partnership pays a partner's health insurance premiums, it is treated as a guaranteed payment (salary). When an S corporation pays a greater-than-2 percent shareholder's health insurance premiums, it is treated as wages subject to withholding but is not subject to employment taxes.

[121] §162(l)(2).

4.5.3 RETIREMENT PLANS

Self-employed individuals can provide for their retirement on a tax-deferred basis by establishing a **Keogh plan** (or HR 10) or a simplified employee pension (SEP) plan administered through an IRA called a SEP IRA.[122] These plans are subject to the same basic plan qualifications, contribution limits, and nondiscrimination rules that apply to qualified corporate retirement plans. Thus, a sole proprietor who establishes a Keogh plan or SEP IRA for himself or herself must provide similar retirement benefits for all eligible employees. Due to this requirement, these plans offer the greatest tax savings when used by a self-employed person with no employees.

The business deducts contributions to the employees' retirement accounts in determining its net income. The limit on contributions to the sole proprietor's retirement account is determined after the deduction for contributions to the employees' accounts and is a deduction *for* AGI.

For 2018, the maximum contribution under a defined contribution Keogh plan or SEP IRA is the lesser of $55,000 or 20 percent of net earnings from self-employment, calculated after subtracting the deduction for self-employment taxes.[123]

Example 4.42

Mac's sole proprietorship has a net profit of $57,000 in 2018. He pays self-employment tax of $8,054 ($57,000 × 92.35% × 15.3%). He deducts $4,027 ($57,000 × 92.35% × 7.65% employer's portion of tax) *for* AGI. His eligible self-employment income is $52,973 ($57,000 – $4,027). Mac can contribute a maximum of $10,595 to his SEP IRA. His contribution is limited to the lesser of $55,000 or 20 percent of his eligible self-employment income ($52,973 × 20% = $10,595).

TAX PLANNING

A sole proprietor must establish a Keogh plan before the end of the tax year to deduct the current year's contribution, but the contribution is not due until the extended due date for his or her tax return. SEP IRAs must be established and funded by the due date for the return, including extensions. If a taxpayer cannot fund a contribution by April 15, he or she can request an automatic extension of time to file the individual tax return, and this extends the due date for making the contribution, as well as to the date for filing the tax return.

A sole proprietor's contributions to these plans are made with before-tax dollars; thus, they are fully taxed as ordinary income when withdrawn. With limited exceptions, contributions may not be withdrawn before age 59½ without a penalty for premature withdrawal.[124]

A sole business owner who does not have any employees can also establish an individual 401(k) plan. For 2018, the maximum contribution is the lesser of $55,000 or 20 percent of net earnings from self-employment (after subtracting the deduction for self-employment taxes) for the employer's portion of the contribution *plus* an additional $18,500 employee's contribution. If the sole proprietor is at least age 50 or older, he or she can contribution an additional $6,000 catch-up contribution. Total contributions, however, cannot exceed the net earnings from self-employment (after subtracting the deduction for self-employment taxes).

---

[122] The Keogh plan is named after the congressman who sponsored the legislation that created this plan.

[123] The limit for 2017 was $54,000 ($53,000 for 2016). The contribution percentage is actually 25% for a profit-sharing or stock bonus plan but it is based on earned income after the contribution effectively reducing the percentage to 20% as follows: 25%/(100% + 25%) = 20%.

[124] The exceptions and the 10 percent penalty for premature withdrawals are similar to those for employer-sponsored qualified retirement plans.

Example 4.43

Justin, age 55, earned $48,000 net income from his sole proprietorship. His self-employment tax is $6,782 ($48,000 × 92.35% × 15.3%); his net earnings after subtracting the deduction for the self-employment tax are $44,609 [$48,000 – ($6,782 × 50%)]. The employer's contribution is limited to $8,922 (20% × $44,609). The employee's maximum contribution is $18,500 plus an additional $6,000 catch-up contribution. Justin can make a total contribution of $33,422 ($8,922 + $18,500 + $6,000).

A self-employed individual may also contribute to an IRA. If the sole proprietorship has a net loss, however, the taxpayer must have earned income from another source to make an IRA contribution. The net loss does not reduce this other earned income in determining the amount eligible to be contributed to the IRA.

Example 4.44

Jorge is an architect in a small firm that provides no retirement benefits. His salary is $42,000. Additionally, Jorge operates a small cleaning service as a sole proprietorship that lost $2,100 this past year. He has $600 of net income from a rental property and $1,340 in interest income. Jorge has $42,000 of earned income that determines the amount he is eligible to contribute to an IRA. He does not reduce his salary for the loss from his sole proprietorship. If Jorge has no salary income, he could not make any IRA contribution for the year because the cleaning business had a loss and neither the rental nor the interest income is earned income.

4.6 EXPANDED TOPICS—FOREIGN ASSIGNMENTS

All income of United States citizens is subject to federal income taxation regardless of how or where that income is earned. As a result, individuals who work in foreign countries (referred to as **expatriates**) may be subject to double taxation when those foreign countries also tax the income earned within their borders. To lessen the burden of potential double taxation, qualifying individuals may (1) elect to exclude up to $103,900 for 2018 ($102,100 in 2017 and $101,300 for 2016) of their foreign earned income or (2) include the foreign income when computing U.S. taxable income and then claim a credit for foreign taxes paid.[125] Expatriates working in foreign countries that either impose no income tax or have effective rates lower than those in the United States should elect the foreign earned income exclusion, if eligible, instead of the credit.

TAX PLANNING

4.6.1 FOREIGN EARNED INCOME EXCLUSION

The **foreign earned income** exclusion applies to salaries, bonuses, allowances, and noncash benefits earned in a foreign country for the individual's personal services (other than as an employee of the United States government).[126] Earned income is excludable only if it is considered foreign source income, with income normally sourced according to where the services are performed.[127]

To be eligible for the foreign earned income exclusion, an individual must have a tax home in a foreign country[128] and meet either the bona fide foreign resident test or physical presence

[125] Taxpayers may deduct the foreign taxes paid instead, but the credit usually results in greater tax savings.

[126] The denial of the foreign earned income exclusion to government employees, including diplomats and members of the U.S. armed forces, is justified on the basis that they are typically exempt from tax by a host country. Additionally, members of the armed services are entitled to many other tax benefits as discussed in Chapter 3.

[127] Reg. §1.911-3(a). The location where the money is received is irrelevant as long as the services for which the income is earned are performed in a foreign country.

[128] Reg. §1.911-2(g). The term foreign country does not include United States possessions and territories such as Puerto Rico, Guam, the Northern Mariana Islands, the Virgin Islands, American Samoa, Wake, and the Midways Islands.

test. The bona fide resident test requires a U.S. citizen to be a bona fide resident of one or more foreign countries for an uninterrupted period of at least one tax year.[129] The physical presence test requires that a U.S. citizen or resident be physically present in a foreign country (or countries) for 330 full days during a period of 12 consecutive months.

Some factors used to decide if an individual is a bona fide resident of a foreign country include:[130]

1. Intention of the taxpayer with regard to the length and nature of the stay;
2. Establishment of the taxpayer's home in the foreign country for an indefinite period;
3. Status of resident and payment of taxes to the foreign country;
4. Marital status and residence of his or her family; and
5. Reason and length of temporary absences from his or her foreign home.

Once a taxpayer establishes bona fide residency in a foreign country, this status can extend backward to a prior partial year beginning with the date that the residency actually began and forward to any subsequent partial year ending with the date of return to the United States. The exclusion, however, must be prorated based on the actual number of residency days in the partial period. When both spouses work in a foreign country, the exclusion limit applies separately to each spouse.[131]

Example 4.45

Jim and Christina, husband and wife, became bona fide residents and worked in New Zealand for the last 78 days of 2017 and all of 2018. Jim has foreign earned income of $17,000 for 2017 and $84,000 for 2018. Christina has foreign earned income of $25,000 for 2017 and $109,000 for 2018. Because they are bona fide residents of New Zealand for all of 2018, they are each eligible to exclude up to $103,900 of their foreign earned income for that year. They also qualify for a partial exclusion in 2017 for the 78 days that they were bona fide residents of up to $21,819 (78/365 × $102,100). Jim can exclude all $17,000 of his 2017 income and all $84,000 of his 2018 income. Christina can exclude only $21,819 of her 2017 income and $103,900 of her 2018 income. Unused exclusions of one spouse cannot be applied to the other spouse's income.

The tax on income in excess of the exclusion is computed using the marginal tax rate that would apply as if the foreign income is still included (that is, at the taxpayer's highest marginal rate).

TAX PLANNING

If doubt exists about a taxpayer's ability to satisfy the bona fide foreign resident test, detailed records should be kept to establish that the 330-day physical presence test was met. The days do not need to be consecutive[132] and this rule only requires physical *presence* in a foreign country, whether that day is a work or nonwork day.[133] If the 330-day physical presence requirement is met, but the taxpayer is in the foreign country for less than one full tax year, the exclusion must be prorated for the number of qualifying days present that tax year.

Persons working abroad for less than 330 days should consider the tax advantages of extending their assignments (if the option is available), particularly if the foreign country does not tax the individual's compensation.

[129] §911(d)(1)(A).
[130] *Sochurek v. Comm.*, 300 F.2d 34 (CA-7, 1962), 9 AFTR 2d 883, 62-1 USTC 9293, rev'g 36 T.C. 131 (1961).
[131] Reg. §1.911-5(a).
[132] Reg. §1.911-2(d)(2) requires 330 full days with full days defined as beginning at midnight of one day and ending the following midnight. Partial days (such as the day of departure or arrival) are excluded.
[133] Rev. Rul. 57-570, 1957-2 CB 458.

4.6.2 EXCESS HOUSING COST EXCLUSION

When working in foreign countries, many expatriates incur additional costs to maintain the same standard of living they enjoyed in the United States. Normally, personal housing costs paid or reimbursed by an employer must be included in taxable income. Section 911(c)(1)(B), however, allows an individual who qualifies for the foreign earned income exclusion to exclude housing costs paid or reimbursed by an employer in *excess* of a base amount equal to 16 percent of the foreign earned income exclusion, or $16,624 ($103,900 × 16%) for 2018. Reimbursements equal to or less than the base amount are subject to tax as the minimum costs taxpayers would incur for housing regardless of where they lived.

The exclusion for excess foreign housing cost reimbursements is capped at 30 percent of the foreign earned income exclusion less the base amount resulting in a maximum excess housing exclusion for 2018 of $14,546.[134] This amount is also prorated for the number of days in the tax year that the individual's tax home is in a foreign country. The sum of the foreign earned income exclusion and the housing cost exclusion cannot exceed the individual's foreign earned income for the tax year. The foreign earned income and housing cost exclusion elections are made separately on Form 2555.[135]

4.6.3 CREDIT FOR FOREIGN TAXES

Individuals who do not qualify for the foreign earned income exclusion (or who choose to forego it) are allowed a **foreign tax credit** for the taxes paid to the foreign government. To prevent taxpayers from using the foreign tax credit to reduce taxes on income earned in the United States, the foreign tax credit cannot exceed the tax on the foreign income as if earned in the United States.[136] To compute this limit, the taxpayer's total U.S. tax liability is multiplied by the ratio of the taxpayer's taxable income from all foreign countries divided by his or her total worldwide taxable income. The foreign tax credit equals the lesser of the computed foreign tax credit limit or the taxes paid to all foreign countries. Taxpayers who qualify for the income exclusion and the credit should calculate both, selecting the option with the lower net tax payable.

Example 4.46

Roger, who is single, works in Europe for all of 2018. His salary is $102,000 and he pays $20,500 in tax to the foreign government. His other taxable income (from U.S. sources) after allowable deductions is $20,000. If he claims the foreign earned income exclusion, Roger excludes the $102,000 salary, leaving only the $20,000 of taxable income on which he will pay a U.S. tax of $4,800 using the 24 percent rate that applies to income from $102,000 to $122,000. If he does not claim the foreign earned income exclusion, Roger's taxable income is $122,000 ($102,000 foreign salary plus $20,000 other taxable income). The U.S. tax on income of $122,000 is $23,570.[137] Roger's foreign tax credit is limited to the equivalent U.S. tax on his foreign income of $19,706 [$23,570 × ($102,000/$122,000)], as this is less than the $20,500 of foreign taxes paid. Roger's tax is reduced to $3,864 ($23,570 – $19,706). Roger's remaining $794 ($20,500 – $19,706) foreign tax credit may be carried over subject to the foreign credit limitation. Taking the tax credit instead of the income exclusion results in tax savings of $936 ($4,800 – $3,864).

[134] §911(c)(2)(A). The maximum exclusion is $14,546 calculated as 30% of the foreign earned income exclusion ($31,170) less the 16% base amount ($16,624). §911(c)(2)(B) allows the Treasury Secretary to increase the 30 percent limit for locations with very high housing costs. See Notice 2018-33, 2018-17 IRB 508. Self-employed individuals can elect to deduct these expenses in computing adjusted gross income. §911(c)(4)(A).

[135] A taxpayer may use Form 2555-EZ if no housing exclusion (or deduction) is claimed, foreign earned income does not exceed the maximum earned income exclusion, and the taxpayer has no self-employment income or business expenses, for the year. If a husband and wife each qualify for the exclusion, each must file a separate form. Once made, an election remains in effect for all subsequent years unless the taxpayer revokes it. Once revoked, the election cannot be made for the next five years without IRS approval. §911(e) and Reg. §1.911-7.

[136] §904(a).

[137] The tax on $122,000 is calculated using the tax rate schedule for a single individual in Chapter 5 (and in the Appendix at the end of this text) as follows: [($122,000 – $82,500) × 24%] + $14,089.50 = $23,569.50.

TAX PLANNING

A key factor in whether to elect the exclusion or the foreign tax credit is the foreign tax rate on the foreign earned income compared to the U.S. tax rate. In a country with a low tax rate (or no income tax), taxpayers will usually benefit by electing the exclusion. In foreign countries with rates higher than those of the United States, taxpayers are usually better off claiming the foreign tax credit instead of the exclusion. Taxpayers with foreign earned income in excess of the exclusion may also qualify for a partial foreign tax credit, but only for the taxes on income in excess of the excluded foreign income.

4.6.4 TAX REIMBURSEMENT PLANS

To encourage employees' acceptance of foreign assignments, some companies agree to include payment of the employees' taxes as part of their compensation packages in addition to housing allowances. If an employer pays an employee's taxes, the employee has additional taxable compensation. The two most common types of tax reimbursement arrangements are tax protection and tax equalization plans.

A **tax protection plan** reimburses an individual for any U.S. or foreign taxes paid in excess of the liability he or she would have incurred for U.S. tax if the individual had remained in the United States. If actual taxes are lower than the assumed tax liability, the employee benefits from the foreign assignment because only the actual U.S. and foreign taxes are paid; the employee keeps any tax savings. Thus, under a tax protection plan, an employee may realize significant tax savings in a move to a low-tax country. From an employer's perspective, however, employees may be reluctant to accept assignments in high-tax countries in which actual taxes exceed the assumed U.S. tax.

TAX PLANNING

Under a **tax equalization plan**, an employee working in a foreign country has the same net tax liability he or she would have paid had the employee remained in the United States. To achieve this balance, the employee's salary is reduced by the hypothetical U.S. tax, but the employee is then reimbursed for the actual U.S. and foreign taxes on the covered income. Under this plan, the employer pays any excess tax but keeps any tax benefit from having employees in low-tax countries. This helps offset the tax costs of having employees in high-tax countries and also prevents employees from preferring one foreign assignment over another merely due to tax differences. Although the objectives of tax protection and equalization plans are similar, a tax equalization plan is usually considered less costly for the employer. Any amounts excluded under foreign earned income or housing cost exclusions reduce the cost of protection or equalization plans to employers because the company does not have to reimburse the employee for U.S. tax on those amounts.

4.6.5 TAX TREATIES

The United States has income tax treaties with many countries. Although no two treaties are exactly alike, they generally provide tax exemptions to residents of one treaty country on short-term assignments to the other country. If an American employer maintains its employee on the U.S. payroll, physical presence in the other treaty country for a short period usually exempts that personal service income from foreign income tax. A typical treaty allows no more than 183 days presence in a year. Thus, an assignment for the last 183 days in one year and the first 183 days in the next year may comply with the typical treaty. Some treaties, however, use a shorter period of time and others have monetary limits. Treaties also frequently exempt teachers and students from foreign income tax. Thus, it is important to know the specific provisions of the treaty for any country where the taxpayer plans to conduct business.

REVISITING THE INTRODUCTORY CASE

If Bob accepts the position with Alpha Corporation, he will be taxed on his $73,000 salary. Alpha Corporation will deduct FICA of 7.65 percent from his gross pay and the corporation will pay a matching amount. Alpha will also pay unemployment tax on the first $7,000 of wages at a rate of 6 percent. The benefits of medical insurance will be tax free to Bob and deductible by Alpha Corporation.

If Bob works as an independent contractor for Beta Corporation, he will receive $89,000 in consulting fees on which he will have to pay self-employment taxes of 15.3 percent. He can, however, deduct half his self-employment tax. He will also have to pay $11,000 for his own medical insurance, but he can deduct the health insurance premiums. The after-tax values of Bob's alternatives are computed as follows:

	Employee	Independent contractor
Salary	$73,000	
Consulting fees		$89,000
Income tax on salary ($73,000 × 22%)	(16,060)	
Income tax on consulting fees ($89,000 × 22%)		(19,580)
Employee FICA tax ($73,000 × 7.65%)	(5,585)	
Self-employment tax ($89,000 × 92.35% × 15.3%)		(12,575)
Tax savings from self-employment tax deduction ($12,575 × 50% × 22% tax rate)		1,383
Medical insurance cost		(11,000)
Tax savings from medical insurance deduction ($11,000 × 22% tax rate)		2,420
After-tax value	$51,355	$49,648

Accepting the job with Alpha Corporation results in a $1,707 ($51,355 – $49,648) higher after-tax value for Bob. Note that Alpha Corporation can provide this higher value to Bob at approximately the same cost as Beta Corporation would spend for its compensation package. Thus, it is possible to develop a compensation package that maximizes the value to the employee at almost no additional cost to the employer—a win-win situation. The after-tax costs to Alpha and Beta Corporations are computed as follows:

	Alpha Corporation	Beta Corporation
Salary payment	$(73,000)	
Consulting fees paid		$(89,000)
Employer FICA tax ($73,000 × 7.65%)	(5,585)	
Unemployment tax ($7,000 × 6%)	(420)	
Medical insurance cost	(9,000)	
Income Tax Savings:		
Salary deduction ($73,000 × 21%)	15,330	
Consulting fee deduction ($89,000 × 21%)		18,690
Unemployment tax deduction ($420 × 21%)	88	
Medical insurance deduction ($9,000 × 21%)	1,890	
After-tax cost	$(70,697)	$(70,310)

SUMMARY

Businesses deduct employees' gross compensation paid for the services performed, including base salaries and wages, bonuses, vacation pay, fringe benefits, and any other economic benefits received in the course of their employment. All these forms of compensation are taxable income to the employee unless a specific provision of the Internal Revenue Code excludes them.

Employee fringe benefits are taxable income unless the benefits fit one of the tax-exempt categories. The cost of tax-exempt fringe benefits is deductible by the employer even though their values are not taxable income to the employee. To prevent abuse of tax-free benefits and attempts to convert excess taxable compensation into tax-free benefits, most have significant limitations. Benefits in excess of these limits remain deductible by the corporation but are now taxable compensation to the employee.

Public corporations frequently offer their executives some form of stock or stock options as part of their total compensation package. Stock-based incentive plans offer employees an opportunity to acquire stock at a bargain price and can provide the dual tax advantages of deferring income to a future year and converting what would otherwise be ordinary compensation income into long-term capital gain. Employers view stock options as a form of compensation with no cash outlay. They may also receive cash if the options are exercised.

Employees may lack the cash required to exercise their options. In response, corporations have developed alternative forms of deferred compensation tied to the stock's fair market value at a future date, but do not require the employee to actually buy the stock. Both phantom stock plans and stock appreciation rights capture appreciation in a company's stock and can be used to compensate employees without any cash payment.

Under a deferred compensation plan, an employer promises to pay benefits to the employee in a future year. The most common deferred compensation plan is the retirement plan. Contributions to qualified plans are deductible by the employer, but the benefits paid to employees are not taxable until received. The employer's contributions, any taxpayer contributions made with before-tax dollars, and all income earned on the contributions, are fully taxed when withdrawn. Any distributions from the taxpayer's after-tax contributions are exempt from tax when withdrawn (including distributions from Roth IRAs, which are completely excluded).

There are limitations on the amount of compensation that can be offered on a tax-deferred basis with qualified plans, and such plans are subject to complex nondiscrimination requirements. As a result, many employers have established nonqualified plans. These plans, allow employers to offer unlimited deferred compensation to key or highly compensated executives without extending the benefits to other employees. Similar to qualified plans, the employee has no income until retirement payments are received and the employer has no deduction until the employer makes actual payments into the plan.

Americans who work outside the United States may be eligible for the foreign earned income exclusion or a credit for their foreign income taxes. They may also be eligible to exclude excess foreign housing costs.

KEY TERMS

401(k) plan 181
Accountable plan 173
Bargain purchases 167
Cafeteria plan 165
Catch-up contributions 183
Compensation 154
Defined benefit plan 181
Defined contribution plan 181
De minimis benefits 168
Expatriates 191
FICA tax 154
Flexible spending arrangement 166
Foreign earned income 191
Foreign tax credit 193
Form 1099-MISC 156
Form W-2 156
Form W-4 154
Fringe benefits 161
FUTA tax 155
Incentive stock options (ISO) 178
Independent contractor 156
Individual retirement account (IRA) 184
Keogh plan 190
Nonaccountable plan 173
Nondiscrimination rules 180
Nonqualified deferred compensation plan 183
Nonqualified stock option (NQSO) 177
Per diem allowance 173
Phantom stock 179
Premature withdrawals 180
Qualified deferred compensation plans 179
Reasonable compensation 159
Roth IRA 186
Self-employment taxes 187
Stock appreciation right (SAR) 179
Stock option 176
Tax equalization plan 194
Tax protection plan 194
Term life insurance 163
Working condition fringe benefits 168

Answers Appear after the Problem Assignments

TEST YOURSELF

1. Sarah, a cash-basis, calendar-year individual, is the president of SRS Corporation and owns 80 percent of its stock. SRS is an accrual-basis, calendar-year C corporation. In December year 1, SRS Corporation accrued a $50,000 bonus payable to Sarah and $120,000 in bonuses payable to other employees. The bonuses were all paid on March 1, year 2. How much of the bonuses can SRS deduct in year 1?
   a. 0
   b. $50,000
   c. $120,000
   d. $170,000

2. Martha, an employee of Beneficial Corporation, receives annual salary of $60,000. Beneficial has a cafeteria plan that allows all employees to select an amount equal to 7 percent of their annual salary from a menu of nontaxable fringe benefits or receive the cash. Martha selects $45,000 of group term life insurance that costs the company $400 and also selects health insurance that costs the company $1,600; she takes the remaining $2,200 in cash. How much income does Martha recognize from Beneficial Corporation?
   a. $60,000
   b. $62,200
   c. $63,800
   d. $64,200

3. Mike received two job offers. Friendly Corporation would like to hire him as an employee at a salary of $50,000 and would pay the premiums for comprehensive medical insurance. Micro Corporation would like to hire him as an independent contractor. Mike would earn $55,000 annually in consulting fees working for Micro but would have to pay for his own medical insurance coverage at an annual cost of $5,000. Assume Mike is in the 24 percent tax bracket. Calculate the after-tax cash flow generated by each job.
   a. $34,175 from Friendly and $31,162 from Micro
   b. $35,000 from Friendly and $36,250 from Micro
   c. $37,500 from Friendly and $31,950 from Micro
   d. $42,350 from Friendly and $33,479 from Micro

4. In year 1, Incentive Corporation grants Jessica, an employee, an ISO to buy 1,000 shares of Incentive stock for $28 per share at any time during the next seven years. On the grant date, Incentive stock is selling for $26 per share. In year 5, when the stock is selling for $38 per share, Jessica exercises the option and pays $28,000 ($28 strike price × 1,000 shares) to the corporation for the 1,000 shares of stock. Jessica holds these shares until year 8, when she sells them for $128,000. How much income or gain does Jessica recognize and how much can Incentive Corporation deduct, respectively?
   a. No income and no deduction
   b. $26,000 ordinary income at date of grant and $26,000 deduction at date of grant
   c. $10,000 ordinary income when options are exercised and $10,000 deduction when options are exercised
   d. $100,000 capital gain when options are sold and no deduction

5. During 2018, Robin has net income from his sole proprietorship of $25,000. He also earned $109,900 as an employee in 2018. How much must Robin pay for self-employment tax?
   a. $2,137
   b. $2,788
   c. $2,964
   d. $3,825

PROBLEM ASSIGNMENTS

Check Your Understanding

1. [LO 4.1] Gaudy Gift Gallery Corporation (owned 100 percent by Barbara) operates a gift shop. Barbara employs her daughter, Jenny, after school and on weekends. Other employees with similar responsibilities are paid $7 per hour while Jenny earns $15 per hour. Jenny earned $15,000 in the current year from the store. Is Jenny's salary fully deductible by the corporation? Explain.

2. [LO 4.2] Anne is an employee of Marvel Corporation that has an educational assistance plan that pays for up to $5,000 in tuition for any work-related courses. Marvel Corporation also provides free on-premises parking (valued at $50 per month) and free child care (valued at $300 per month). Does Anne have any taxable income as a result of these benefits?

3. [LO 4.2] What is the difference between a qualified employee discount and a bargain purchase by an employee?

4. [LO 4.2] In which of the following cases should the employees report income?
   a. The employer provides an annual picnic for employees and their families to celebrate Independence Day.
   b. Employees can use the company photocopier for small amounts of personal copying as long as the privilege is not abused.
   c. Employees receive a free ticket to watch the Dolphins play the Raiders.
   d. Each employee receives a $50 check on his or her birthday.

5. [LO 4.3] What is the difference between an NQSO and an ISO?

6. [LO 4.3] Gabor Family Enterprises, a closely-held family corporation, plans to offer a stock option plan as an incentive to its employees, but it does not want its stock owned by anyone who is not a member of the Gabor family. What type of plan should Gabor consider?

7. [LO 4.3] High-Tec Corporation offers a stock option plan as an incentive to its employees. Few employees participate in the plan because they do not have the cash necessary to exercise the options. What alternative type of incentive plan can High-Tec offer these employees?

8. [LO 4.4] What are the advantages of a qualified retirement plan?

9. [LO 4.4] Discuss why corporations frequently offer both qualified and nonqualified retirement plans to their employees.

10. [LO 4.4] Ricardo is a professional football player. In negotiating his contract for the upcoming season, Ricardo is given two options. He can receive (1) 12 monthly checks of $325,000 with no deferred payments or (2) $250,000 monthly with the $900,000 balance placed in escrow and payable to him (with interest) after he retires from professional sports. What are the tax implications of these two alternatives?

11. [LO 4.4] Your friend Mark suggested that you should open an Individual Retirement Account. He said that an IRA is a great way to save because you do not have to pay tax on the income from the investment and you get a tax deduction for your contribution. Is Mark correct? Explain.

12. [LO 4.4] Identify the type of IRA (Roth or traditional) that would be best for a taxpayer in each of the following circumstances:
    a. Sharon believes she will be in a higher tax bracket when she withdraws the money in retirement.
    b. Ken believes he will be in the same or a lower tax bracket in retirement.
    c. Susan wants to use her retirement savings to build her estate to pass to her children.

13. [LO 4.2 & 4.5] James and Dean plan to start a new business but have not decided whether to organize as a partnership, an S corporation, or a C corporation. They are interested in taking advantage of any

tax-free fringe benefits that may be available to them. Discuss the advantages and disadvantages from a fringe-benefit perspective of each form of business entity.

14. [LO 4.6] John is a single individual who works for Auto Rental Cars in Japan during the entire calendar year. His salary is $140,000. How much of this salary can he exclude?

15. [LO 4.6] Explain the difference between a tax protection plan and a tax equalization plan. Which one is usually less costly to the employer?

Crunch the Numbers

16. [LO 4.1] Helen is an employee of Keys Corporation. In 2018 Helen earned a salary of $100,000.

a. How much in Social Security and Medicare taxes must be paid by Keys Corporation and how much of these taxes can it deduct?

b. How much Social Security and Medicare taxes are paid by Helen?

17. [LO 4.1] Melissa is an employee of Largo Corporation. In 2018 Melissa's salary was $120,000 and she earned a bonus of $24,000.

a. How much in Social Security and Medicare taxes must be paid by Largo Corporation and how much of these taxes can it deduct?

b. How much Social Security and Medicare taxes are paid by Melissa?

18. [LO 4.1] Rebecca is single and an employee of Grand Corporation. In 2018 Rebecca's salary was $190,000 and she earned a bonus of $45,000.

a. How much in Social Security and Medicare taxes must be paid by Grand Corporation and how much of these taxes can it deduct?

b. How much Social Security and Medicare taxes are paid by Rebecca?

19. [LO 4.1] Charlie, who is in the 37 percent marginal tax bracket, is the president and sole owner of Charlie Corporation (a C corporation in the 21 percent tax bracket). His current salary is $700,000 per year. What are the income and FICA tax consequences if the IRS determines that $200,000 of his salary is unreasonable compensation?

20. [LO 4.1] Amy, a cash-basis taxpayer, received a salary of $100,000 during years 1, 2, and 3. Amy also was awarded a $30,000 bonus that was accrued by her employer, Vargus Corporation (an accrual-basis, calendar-year C corporation), in December of year 1 but which was not paid until March 31 of year 2. In December of year 2, Vargus accrued an additional $32,000 bonus that was paid to Amy in January of year 3.

a. How much income does Amy recognize in year 1, year 2, and year 3?

b. How much can Vargus Corporation take as a compensation deduction in year 1, year 2, and year 3?

21. [LO 4.2] Tom is 68 years old. His employer pays the premiums for group term life insurance coverage of $110,000. The cost for Tom's coverage is $3,000.

a. If the plan providing this coverage is nondiscriminatory and Tom is not a key employee, how much gross income does Tom have?

b. How does your answer to (a) change if Tom is a key employee?

c. If the plan is discriminatory, but Tom is not a key employee, what is Tom's gross income?

d. How does your answer to (c) change if Tom is a key employee?

22. [LO 4.2] Priscilla, an employee of Choice Corporation, has an annual salary of $70,000. Choice has a cafeteria plan that allows all employees to choose an amount equal to 8 percent of their annual salary from a menu of nontaxable fringe benefits or to take cash. Priscilla selects $50,000 of group term life insurance that costs the company $900 and also selects health insurance that costs the company $2,000; she takes the remaining $2,700 in cash. How much compensation income does Priscilla recognize from Choice Corporation?

23. [LO 4.2] Jennifer elects to reduce her salary by $2,500 so she can participate in her employer's flexible spending arrangement. Her salary reduction is allocated as follows: $1,700 for medical and dental expenses and $800 for child care expenses. During the year, Jennifer uses $1,500 of her salary reduction for medical and dental care and $700 for child care assistance.

a. How much of the $2,500 set aside in the FSA is included in Jennifer's gross income?

b. How much of the $2,200 reimbursed from the FSA is included in Jennifer's gross income?

c. What happens to the remaining $300?

24. [LO 4.2] Kevin is an employee of One Hour Dry Cleaners, Inc. All employees of One Hour are eligible for a 40 percent discount on their dry cleaning. During the year, Kevin paid $300 for cleaning that normally would have cost $500. Does Kevin have any taxable income as a result of this discount?

25. [LO 4.2] Betsy receives a salary of $50,000 from her employer (a retail clothing store) and several fringe benefits. Her employer pays premiums of $300 for her $40,000 group term life insurance coverage and pays $3,200 for medical insurance premiums. Her employer provides dependent care facilities (where she places her young children while she is at work) valued at $4,500 per year. Her employer also allows employees to purchase clothing (the employer's inventory) at 50 percent off the retail sales price (which is 5 percent more than the employer's cost). During the year, Betsy purchases clothing with a retail value of $10,000 for $5,000. In addition to her salary, how much must Betsy include in gross income?

26. [LO 4.3] Luis received 400 shares of his employer's stock as a bonus. He must return the stock to the company if he leaves before the 5-year vesting period ends. The fair market value of the stock at the time it was issued was $20,000. After five years, the stock vests when it has a fair market value of $75,000. Two years after vesting, Luis sells the stock for $100,000.

a. If Luis makes no election, how much income or gain does he recognize (1) when the stock is issued, (2) when the stock vests, and (3) when the stock is sold?

b. If Luis makes an election to accelerate the recognition of income, how much income or gain does he recognize (1) when the stock is issued, (2) when the stock vests, and (3) when the stock is sold?

c. If Luis makes an election to accelerate the recognition of income but he leaves the company after three years, is he eligible for a refund of taxes paid?

27. [LO 4.3] Five years ago, Cargo Corporation granted Mark a nonqualified stock option to buy 3,000 shares of Cargo common stock at $10 per share exercisable for five years. At the date of the grant, Cargo stock was selling for $9 per share. This year, Mark exercises the option when the price is $50 per share.

a. How much income should Mark have recognized in the year the option was granted?

b. How much income does Mark recognize when he exercises the option?

c. What are the tax consequences for Cargo from the NQSO in the year of grant and in the year of exercise?

28. [LO 4.3] Three years ago, Netcom granted an ISO to Karen to buy 2,000 shares of Netcom stock at $6 per share exercisable for five years. At the date of the grant, Netcom stock was selling for $5 per share. This year, Karen exercises the ISO when the price is $30 per share.

a. How much income should Karen have recognized in the year the ISO was granted?

b. How much income does Karen recognize when she exercises the ISO?

c. What are the tax consequences for Netcom from the ISO in the year of grant and in the year of exercise?

d. What are the tax consequences to Karen and Netcom if Karen sells all of the stock for $50 per share two years after exercising the options?

29. [LO 4.3] Four years ago, Handcock Corporation granted 300 SARs to Maria as a bonus. Handcock's stock was worth $20 a share on the date of grant. Maria exercises her SARs this year when the stock is worth $60 a share.

a. How much income should Maria have recognized in the year she received the SARs?

b. How much income does Maria recognize when she exercises the SARs?

c. If Maria is in the 24 percent marginal tax bracket, what is her after-tax cash flow from the exercise of the SARs?

d. Does Handcock Corporation get a tax deduction for the SARs and if yes, when and in what amount?

30. [LO 4.2 & 4.4] Larry, age 32, works for Horizon Corporation. His annual salary is $60,000 and he is not a key employee. Horizon provides the following benefits to all employees:

- Group term life insurance (each employee is provided with $80,000 worth of coverage that costs Horizon $120 per employee)
- Medical insurance (the cost of Larry's policy is $3,900)
- Qualified pension plan (Horizon matches employee contributions up to $2,500. Larry contributes 7 percent of his salary to the plan.)
- Qualified award program (Larry received a watch Horizon purchased for $100 to recognize his 5 years of service with Horizon.)

How much income must Larry recognize and how much can Horizon Corporation deduct in the current year?

31. [LO 4.4] Nick, age 53, is single and has AGI of $67,000. He contributes $5,000 to his IRA in 2018.

a. How much can Nick deduct if he is not covered by an employer-sponsored qualified retirement plan?

b. How much can Nick deduct if he is covered by an employer-sponsored qualified retirement plan?

32. [LO 4.4] In 2018, Elizabeth and Daniel (both age 40), a married couple with AGI of $118,000, file a joint tax return. They each contributed $5,500 to their IRAs.

a. How much can they deduct if they are both active participants in qualified retirement plans?

b. How much can they deduct if Elizabeth is not an active participant in a qualified retirement plan, but Daniel is an active participant in his qualified retirement plan?

c. How would your answer change if they are both active participants in qualified retirement plans but their AGI is $200,000?

33. [LO 4.4] Jennifer, age 35, is single and an active participant in her employer's qualified retirement plan. Compute the maximum Roth IRA contribution that she can make in 2018 if

a. her adjusted gross income is $140,000.

b. her adjusted gross income is $59,000.

c. her adjusted gross income is $38,000 and she makes a $2,000 contribution to a traditional IRA.

34. [LO 4.5] Carrie owns a business that she operates as a sole proprietorship. The business had a net profit of $25,000 in 2018. This is Carrie's only earned income.

a. How much must she pay for self-employment taxes?

b. How much can she deduct on her tax return?

c. If the business had a net loss of $10,000 (instead of a $25,000 profit), how much in self-employment taxes must Carrie pay?

35. [LO 4.5] Sarah owns a business that she operates as a sole proprietorship. The business had a net profit of $130,000 in 2018. This is Sarah's only earned income.

a. How much must she pay for self-employment taxes?

b. How much can she deduct on her tax return?

36. [LO 4.5] George has $91,700 in salary from his full-time position and $43,000 in net income in 2018 from his sole proprietorship. What is his self-employment tax? What portion of this can he deduct?

37. [LO 4.5] Melissa has $90,000 in salary from her full-time position and $40,000 in net income in 2018 from consulting as an independent contractor. What is her self-employment tax? What portion of this can she deduct?

38. [LO 4.5] Luis operates a bakery as a sole proprietorship which generated $280,000 in net income. He has four bakers whom he employs on a full-time basis and who participate in a company-paid health insurance plan. Luis is also covered by this same plan. The annual premiums are $2,300 per person. The business paid $11,500 for health insurance premiums for 2018. Are these insurance premiums deductible? If they are, where does Luis deduct them on his tax return?

39. [LO 4.5] Alexander works as an electrician at a small company that provides no retirement benefits. He receives a salary of $45,000. In addition, Alexander operates a small roof repair service as a sole proprietorship; this business has a net loss of $2,500. In addition, Alexander realizes $800 of net income from rental property and $1,500 in interest income. What is Alexander's earned income for determining the amount he is eligible to contribute to an IRA?

40. [LO 4.6] Wendy is a single individual who works for MTP, Inc. During the entire calendar year, she works in France and pays French taxes of $8,000 on her $95,000 salary. Her taxable income without considering her salary from MTP is $10,000. Should Wendy claim the income exclusion or tax credit and how much tax does she save using the alternative selected?

Develop Planning Skills

41. [LO 4.1] Melinda has been offered two competing employment contracts for the next two years. Argus Corporation will pay her a $75,000 salary in both years 1 and 2. Dynamic Corporation will pay Melinda a $100,000 salary in year 1 and a $49,000 salary in year 2. Melinda expects to be in the 24 percent marginal tax bracket in year 1 and in the 35 percent marginal tax bracket in year 2 (due to a significant amount of income from new rental properties). She does not expect either offer to change her marginal tax bracket for either year. Both Argus Corporation and Dynamic Corporation expect their tax brackets to remain at 21 percent over the two-year period and expect that employment tax rates will remain the same.

a. Compute the net present value of the after-tax cash flow for Melinda and after-tax cost for Argus and Dynamic for each of the proposed employment contracts using a 6 percent discount rate.

b. Which alternative is better for Melinda and which is better from the corporation's perspective?

42. [LO 4.2 & 4.4] Sherry just received a big promotion at Barcardo Corporation. Last year her salary was $100,000, but due to her promotion she expects to earn $180,000 this year. She expects that she will be able to save about $60,000 of her pay raise and is interested in exploring ways to minimize her federal tax liability. List some of the tax-planning opportunities with respect to her salary.

43. [LO 4.4] Maria, age 42, just resigned from Bygone Corporation to accept a new job with Future, Inc. Bygone informed Maria that she has a $38,000 balance in its qualified retirement plan and wants to know if she plans to roll over this balance into another plan or prefers to receive a lump-sum payment. Maria is in the 24 percent marginal tax bracket and would like to buy a new car with the funds although the local car dealer is currently offering very attractive low-interest financing. Determine the amount of after-tax funds Maria would have available to pay for the car if she takes a lump-sum distribution, and make a recommendation regarding what you think she should do.

44. [LO 4.4] William, an employee for Williamson Corporation, receives an annual salary of $120,000 and is in the 24 percent marginal tax bracket. He is eligible to contribute to Williamson's 401(k) plan and could contribute the pretax amount of $12,000. Alternatively, he could contribute only $6,000 to the plan and use the remaining $6,000 to purchase municipal bonds paying 6 percent interest. Evaluate the tax savings and after-tax cash-flow effect of each of these investment choices. State which option you recommend for William and explain why.

45. [LO 4.4] Robert, age 55, plans to retire when he reaches age 65. He is not currently an active participant in any qualified retirement plan. His budget will allow him to contribute no more than $3,000 of his income before taxes to either a traditional IRA or a Roth IRA to provide retirement income. His marginal tax rate will be 24 percent until he retires, at which time it will drop to 12 percent. He anticipates a rate of return on either type of IRA of 7 percent before considering any tax effects. Prepare an analysis for Robert comparing the tax effects of investing in a traditional IRA and in a Roth IRA.

46. [LO 4.6] Jorge, a single individual, agrees to accept an assignment in Saudi Arabia, a country that imposes no income tax on compensation, beginning on January 1. Jorge will be paid his normal monthly salary of $5,000, plus an additional $1,400 per month for each month he works in Saudi Arabia. His employer requires him to remain in Saudi Arabia for at least six months; however, he can elect to continue working there for up to six additional months if he wishes or return to work in the U.S. office. Advise Jorge of the tax ramifications if he stays in Saudi Arabia only six months and if he stays there an additional six months.

Think Outside the Text

These questions require answers that are beyond the material that is covered in this chapter.

47. [LO 4.1] Cindy is president and sole shareholder of Chipsmart Corporation. Through her hard work (frequently putting in 70 hours per week), she has managed to triple the number of clients and revenue in the past year. Chipsmart has never paid a dividend to Cindy, although it does have retained earnings. Last year, Cindy's salary was $200,000; this year, due to her success, she would like to pay herself a $600,000 salary. As Chipsmart's tax adviser, prepare a list of questions you would like to ask Cindy when you meet her to discuss the salary increase.

48. [LO 4.3] What tax planning should be done before exercising incentive stock options?

49. [LO 4.3] Construct a scenario in which the tax treatment of stock options is very unfavorable for the employee.

50. [LO 4.4] The scandal on backdating stock options introduced new terminology to describe these controversial practices. Describe what you think each of these terms means.
    a. Backdating
    b. Repricing
    c. Reloading
    d. Spring-loading
    e. Bullet-dodging

51. [LO 4.4] Would an employee who first becomes a participant in a pension plan at age 52 generally prefer to have a defined benefit plan or a defined contribution plan? Explain.

52. [LO 4.4] What do you think the effect would be if Congress changes the law so that retirement plan contributions are included in taxable income at the time they are made rather than taxing the payment when received in retirement?

53. [LO 4.1 & 4.5] Evan is setting up a new business. He can operate the business as a sole proprietorship or he can incorporate as a regular C corporation or as an S corporation. He expects that the business will have gross income of $130,000 in the first year with expenses of $25,000 excluding the following. He plans to take $35,000 from the business for living expenses as a salary and will have the business pay $3,000 annually for his health insurance premiums.
    a. Compute the total tax cost in 2018 for each alternative if Evan is single, this is his only source of income, and he claims the standard deduction.
    b. Which alternative business form do you recommend based solely on the first year tax costs?
    c. What are some of the other factors Evan should consider in deciding between a C corporation and an S corporation for his business?

Search the Internet

54. [LO 4.2] Go to *www.legalbitstream.com.* Locate and read Regulation Section 1.62–2(j), example 6. If an employer has an otherwise accountable plan but reimburses employees at 60 cents per mile, how is the reimbursement treated?

55. [LO 4.2] Go to *www.legalbitstream.com.* Locate and read Revenue Ruling 2003–102. What type of medicines and drugs can be reimbursed through a flexible spending arrangement (FSA) according to this ruling? What change took effect in 2011?

56. [LO 4.4] Find an article on the Internet that describes how a traditional IRA can be converted into a Roth IRA. Summarize the process explaining any tax costs associated with the conversion. Include the URL for the article.

Identify the Issues

Identify the issues or problems suggested by the following situations. State each issue as a question.

57. [LO 4.1] Susan is the second-highest-paid executive for Sanibel Corporation, a publicly traded corporation. Her salary is $1,600,000.

58. [LO 4.1] Virginia is the president and founder of VT Corporation. She is extremely devoted to the business, frequently working 70-hour weeks. She did not take any salary from the business for its first two years of operations. She is now receiving a salary that is 150 percent of what comparable businesses pay their presidents.

59. [LO 4.2] Victor has full-time use of a company-owned Jaguar automobile. This year Victor drove 24,000 miles for business and 10,000 personal miles. His employer does not require him to report his personal mileage but, instead, includes the lease value of the full-time use of the automobile as additional compensation on his Form W-2.

60. [LO 4.4] Sarah is single and earns $60,000 in salary. She wants to invest $2,500 per year in an IRA but is not sure which type she qualifies for and whether this would be a better investment than putting her money in preferred stock paying a 6 percent annual dividend.

61. [LO 4.4] Ken is single and earns a salary of $60,000 per year. He also receives $4,000 a year in taxable interest and dividend income. Ken would like to contribute the maximum allowable to his company's qualified pension plan.

Develop Research Skills

62. [LO 4.1] Martin Martindale, the 40-year-old founder and president of Martindale Corporation (an accrual-basis, calendar-year C corporation), owns 60 percent of the stock and receives a salary of $600,000. Four unrelated shareholders own the rest of the stock equally. The corporation has paid dividends regularly to the shareholders and plans to continue to do so in the future. Martin plans to recommend that the board of directors authorize the payment of a bonus to himself and two other employees (all cash-basis, calendar-year individuals). The first employee is the vice president, who owns 10 percent of the corporation and receives a salary of $400,000. The other employee is the controller, who is not currently a shareholder in the corporation and receives a salary of $200,000. Martin would like the bonus to equal 75 percent of each recipient's current salary. Martin believes that the total compensation is probably a little high when compared to the corporation's competitors but Martindale is much more profitable. Martindale's profits have increased by more than 20 percent in the last two years due to the efforts of the individuals who will receive the bonuses, while other businesses in the same industry showed an increase in profits of less than 10 percent. Martin asks you, as the corporation's tax advisor, to recommend what the corporation needs to do so that it gets a deduction for the planned bonuses. Martin would prefer to pay the bonuses next year but deduct them this year.
   - **a.** Locate and read *Mayson Manufacturing Co.,* 178 F.2d 115, 38 AFTR 1028, 49–2 USTC 9467 (CA6, 1949) and *Elliotts Inc.* 716 F.2d 1241, 52 AFTR 2d 83-5976, 83-2 USTC ¶9610 (CA9, 1985). Summarize the important points of these cases as they relate to Martindale.
   - **b.** Prepare a summary of the relevant Code and regulation sections as they apply to Martindale.
   - **c.** Prepare a one-paragraph summary for Martin on what the corporation needs to do to qualify for a deduction for the planned bonuses.

63. [LO 4.2] McGuire Corporation is planning to acquire a corporate jet to increase the efficiency and security of its executives who will use the jet for both business trips and personal vacations. McGuire Corporation wants to know how it should determine the amount that is taxed to its employees when they use the corporate jet for personal travel.

64. [LO 4.4] Robert, age 35, has accumulated $36,000 in his traditional IRA. He recently married and would like to withdraw $25,000 from his IRA for a down payment on his first house. Write a letter to Robert stating the tax implications of his proposed withdrawal.

65. [LO 4.4] Jennifer, age 40, has accumulated $40,000 in her traditional IRA. She would like to withdraw $22,000 from her IRA to pay for her daughter's college expenses. She plans to use $15,000 for tuition and $7,000 for room and board. Write a letter to Jennifer stating the tax implications of her proposed withdrawal.

Fill-in the Forms

66. [LO 4.5] Go to *www.irs.gov* and print Form 1040 and Schedule SE. Complete the first page of Form 1040 and Schedule SE for Angelina Carlyle who is single. She reports $195,000 of net profit on her Schedule C from her sole proprietorship and $2,000 of taxable interest income. Her SSN is 167-88-5544 and her address is 1234 Main Street, Dayton, Ohio.

ANSWERS TO TEST YOURSELF

1. **c. $120,000**. Compensation accrued to employees must be paid within 2½ months after the close of the corporation's tax year or the payment is considered deferred compensation and cannot be deducted until the year of payment (so the $120,000 accrued for employee bonuses is deductible in year 1). A more restrictive provision applies to related taxpayers who own more than 50 percent of the corporation; the deduction for the president's bonus is deferred until the year the president recognizes the income (so the $50,000 bonus will not be deductible until year 2).

2. **b. $62,200**. The $60,000 salary and the $2,200 cash are taxable. The noncash benefits of life insurance premiums (not in excess of $50,000 insurance value) and health insurance premiums are tax free.

3. **a. $34,175 from Friendly and $31,162 from Micro.**

	Friendly	Micro
Salary	$50,000	
Consulting fees		$55,000
Income tax on salary ($50,000 × 24%)	(12,000)	
Income tax on consulting fees ($55,000 × 24%)		(13,200)
Employee FICA tax ($50,000 × 7.65%)	(3,825)	
Self-employment tax ($55,000 × 92.35% × 15.3%)		(7,771)
Tax savings from self-employment tax deduction ($7,771 × 50% × 24% tax rate)		933
Medical insurance cost		(5,000)
Tax savings from medical insurance deduction ($5,000 × 24% tax rate)		1,200
After-tax value	$34,175	$31,162

4. **d. $100,000 capital gain when options are sold and no deduction**. Jessica recognizes a $100,000 ($128,000 selling price − $28,000 basis) capital gain when the stock is sold. However, because this option is an ISO, Incentive Corporation receives no tax deduction and thus derives no tax benefit from the option.

5. **c. $2,964**. Robin first multiplies his $25,000 self-employment income by 92.35% ($25,000 × 92.35% = $23,087.50). Robin then reduces the $128,400 ceiling by the $109,900 of employee earnings on which Social Security tax has already been paid. Only $18,500 ($128,400 – $109,900) of his self-employment earnings is subject to the Social Security tax; however, his entire $23,087.50 of self-employment earnings is subject to the Medicare tax. Robin's self-employment taxes are $2,963.54 [($18,500 × 12.4% = $2,294) + ($23,087.50 × 2.9% = $669.54)].

CHAPTER 5

Deductions for Individuals and Tax Determination

CHAPTER OUTLINE

LEARNING OBJECTIVES

After completing this chapter, you should be able to:

5.1 Understand the components of the individual tax model.

5.2 Identify the deductions for AGI and apply the appropriate limitations.

5.3 Determine the specific standard deduction that applies to each taxpayer and explain the characteristics that identify each of the filing statuses.

5.4 Explain the different types of itemized deductions and determine any specific limitation for each deduction.

5.5 Explain the reason for the new qualified business income deduction and how it is calculated.

5.6 Determine who qualifies as a dependent.

5.7 Identify tax credits available to an individual taxpayer and demonstrate the difference in their effect from that of deductions.

5.8 Apply the correct tax rate(s) to a taxpayer's taxable income and compute any additional taxes paid with an individual's tax return.

5.9 Determine the individuals who must file an individual tax return and understand the payment provisions for taxes owed.

This chapter focuses on the determination of an individual taxpayer's income tax liability. It begins with an expanded version of the basic tax model introduced in Chapter 1. The deductions unique to individuals are examined in detail including deductions for adjusted gross income, the standard deduction, and itemized deductions. Taxpayers are allowed certain deductions for personal expenses, but Congress only partially subsidizes them. Some deductions are limited to amounts exceeding specific minimums while others cannot exceed certain maximums.

The latter part of this chapter focuses on an individual's allowable tax credits and the computation of special taxes paid with an individual's tax return. Individuals are required to make prepayments of their tax liability through estimated tax payments or withholding on wages and salaries. If the tax prepayments exceed the tax liability after all credits and additions, the taxpayer has a refund due. If the prepayments are less than the net tax liability, the taxpayer owes additional taxes.

SETTING THE STAGE—AN INTRODUCTORY CASE

Amy and Steve, a married couple who file a joint tax return, just signed a contract to purchase their first home. They have never itemized their deductions and are looking forward to all the tax savings their real estate agent told them they would realize from their home mortgage interest and real property tax deductions. The interest on their home acquisition mortgage (principal amount of $350,000) is estimated to be $14,000 per year, and their real property taxes about $5,500. Friends told them their tax savings would be even greater for expenses they have not been able to deduct due to claiming the standard deduction. These other expenses include $4,500 of unreimbursed medical expenses and $8,400 in charitable contributions. Their adjusted gross income is $190,000, and they are in the 24 percent marginal tax bracket. They expect to deduct an additional $32,400 due to these expenses and save $7,776 ($32,400 × 24%) in taxes. Their mortgage company told them that they will be required to pay $3,000 in points at the closing but they have the option of closing in either the fourth week of December or the first week of January. Assuming their other expenses remain the same for both the current and the next tax year, when should they schedule the closing? At the end of this chapter we will return to this case.

5.1 THE INDIVIDUAL TAX MODEL

The tax model is the formula individuals follow to report their tax liability. Figure 5.1 presents an expanded version of the basic tax model introduced in Chapter 1. It begins with the concept of gross income and ends with the taxpayer's net tax due.

	Gross income
Less	Deductions for adjusted gross income
Equals	Adjusted gross income (AGI)
Less	Itemized deductions or standard deduction
Less	Personal and dependency exemptions (before 2018 and after 2025)
Less	Qualified business income deduction (2018–2025)
Equals	Taxable income
Times	Applicable tax rates
Equals	Gross income tax liability
Less	Tax credits
Plus	Additional taxes
Less	Tax prepayments
Equals	Net tax due or tax refund

FIGURE 5.1 The individual tax model

Chapters 3 and 4 discussed the items included in and exclusions from gross income, respectively. Figure 5.2 shows the income section of Form 1040: *U.S. Individual Tax Return.*[1] Salary and wages, interest, dividends, tax refunds, and alimony received are reported on lines 7 through 11. Gains and losses from investment transactions are reported on line 13, and retirement plan distributions are reported on lines 15 and 16.

A sole proprietorship first reports its income and expenses on a Schedule C (or C-EZ) with its net income (or loss) included on line 12. An individual with ownership interests in partnerships or S corporations aggregates their profits and losses (reported on Schedule E) with income from rental real estate, royalties, and trusts for reporting on line 17 of Form 1040. Other income,

[1] A sample filled-in Form 1040 is included at the end of this chapter and sample filled-in sets of tax forms are included on the website for this textbook.

Income	7	Wages, salaries, tips, etc. Attach Form(s) W-2	7
	8a	**Taxable** interest. Attach Schedule B if required	8a
	b	**Tax-exempt** interest. **Do not** include on line 8a . . . 8b	
Attach Form(s) W-2 here. Also attach Forms W-2G and 1099-R if tax was withheld.	9a	Ordinary dividends. Attach Schedule B if required	9a
	b	Qualified dividends . . . 9b	
	10	Taxable refunds, credits, or offsets of state and local income taxes	10
	11	Alimony received	11
	12	Business income or (loss). Attach Schedule C or C-EZ	12
	13	Capital gain or (loss). Attach Schedule D if required. If not required, check here ▶ ☐	13
If you did not get a W-2, see instructions.	14	Other gains or (losses). Attach Form 4797	14
	15a	IRA distributions . 15a ; b Taxable amount	15b
	16a	Pensions and annuities 16a ; b Taxable amount	16b
	17	Rental real estate, royalties, partnerships, S corporations, trusts, etc. Attach Schedule E	17
	18	Farm income or (loss). Attach Schedule F	18
	19	Unemployment compensation	19
	20a	Social security benefits 20a ; b Taxable amount	20b
	21	Other income. List type and amount	21
	22	Combine the amounts in the far right column for lines 7 through 21. This is your **total income** ▶	22

FIGURE 5.2 Income section of Form 1040

reported on line 21, includes income from a hobby, prizes, awards, gambling winnings, jury duty fees, and reimbursements for prior-year expense deductions to the extent any tax benefit was received.

Most excluded income items are not reported on an individual's tax return, except for tax-exempt interest (used to determine the taxable portion of Social Security) and the nontaxable portions of retirement plan distributions and Social Security benefits.

After an individual determines his or her gross income, two sets of deductions are permitted: deductions *for* adjusted gross income (or above-the-line deductions) and deductions *from* adjusted gross income (below-the-line deductions). The "line" refers to adjusted gross income which is the last line on page 1 of Form 1040.

Deductions *for* adjusted gross income include several expenses that Congress has singled out for more favorable treatment than other individual deductions, discussed in detail in the next section. Subtracting these deductions results in an intermediate subtotal between gross income and taxable income called **adjusted gross income (AGI)**, a subtotal unique to individual taxpayers. AGI is an important reference point that limits some deductions.

Once AGI is determined, individuals have additional deductions *from* adjusted gross income to determine taxable income: (1) the greater of the taxpayer's itemized deductions or standard deduction, (2) the deduction for personal and dependency exemptions (before 2018 and after 2025), and (3) the qualified business income deduction for income from flow-through businesses (for 2018–2025). The taxpayer first compares the automatic standard deduction determined by the taxpayer's filing status (currently $12,000 for a single individual) to the itemized deduction total and deducts the greater of the two (but not both). Itemized deductions are those personal expenses that a provision of the Internal Revenue Code allows as a deduction, such as medical expenses, home mortgage interest, property taxes, and charitable contributions. The second deduction from AGI, the taxpayer's personal exemption and dependency exemptions for each of the taxpayer's dependents, was available before 2018 and will be reinstated in 2026. The third deduction, equal to 20 percent of income from sole proprietorships, partnerships, and S corporations, addresses the difference between the tax rates for C corporations and pass-through businesses and is available for tax years 2018–2025. These deductions from AGI are discussed in greater detail later.

After reduction of an individual's gross income by the allowable deductions *for* and *from* adjusted gross income, he or she can determine taxable income. The appropriate tax rates are then applied to taxable income to calculate the gross income tax liability.

Individuals next use their allowable tax credits to reduce the gross tax liability. Tax credits reduce a taxpayer's gross tax liability dollar-for-dollar; in contrast, a tax deduction only reduces taxable income by the marginal tax rate times the deduction. Taxpayers are also subject to additional taxes including the self-employment tax, Medicare surtaxes, and the alternative minimum tax that are added to the gross tax liability.

After adjusting the gross tax liability for tax credits and additional taxes, taxpayers subtract their prepayments to determine their net tax liability or refund due. The most common prepayment results from income tax withholding on salaries and wages. If, however, the taxpayer has self-employment income or transactions on which there is no withholding (such as asset sales), then the individual must make estimated tax payments directly to the IRS. If these prepayments exceed the net tax liability, the taxpayer has a refund due; if the payments are less than the net tax liability, the taxpayer must pay the difference. A Form 1040 is included later in this chapter in Figure 5.5.

5.2 DEDUCTIONS FOR ADJUSTED GROSS INCOME

Congress subsidizes specific activities to achieve its policy objectives by allowing a special category of deductions for individuals aptly called **deductions for adjusted gross income**. These items are deducted *before* arriving at the subtotal of adjusted gross income, and they reduce an individual's AGI and taxable income regardless of whether the individual chooses to itemize or take the standard deduction. In addition, deductions for AGI are not subject to the ceiling and floor limits that are based on a percentage of AGI imposed on itemized deductions.

5.2.1 STUDENT LOAN INTEREST DEDUCTION

Congress created several benefits to encourage higher education. Although most personal loan interest is not deductible, taxpayers can deduct up to $2,500 of interest paid annually on qualified student loans. As the taxpayer's modified AGI increases from $65,000 to $80,000 ($135,000 to $165,000 for married persons filing jointly), the deduction is reduced (phases out) proportionately over the phaseout range.[2]

Example 5.1

Laura is single, has $2,300 of qualifying student loan interest, and modified AGI of $74,000 in 2018. Her AGI exceeds $65,000 by $9,000 and 60 percent ($9,000/$15,000 phaseout range) of her allowable deduction is phased out. She can only deduct $920 [$2,300 × (1 – .60)] of her $2,300 interest expense.

Mike and Monica, a married couple, file a joint tax return that shows AGI of $147,000 and $3,300 of student loan interest paid in 2018. Their AGI exceeds $135,000 by $12,000 and they lose 40 percent ($12,000/$30,000 phaseout range) of their allowable deduction. They can deduct only $1,500 [$2,500 maximum × (1 – .40)] of their $3,300 interest expense.

The loans must have been incurred to pay for eligible education expenses (tuition, fees, room, board, and other necessary education expenses) at postsecondary educational institutions or certain vocational schools for the education of the taxpayer and/or the taxpayer's spouse and dependents. Eligible education expenses must be reduced for tax-exempt scholarships, fellowships or grants, and costs for which education tax credits are claimed.[3]

[2] §221(b)(2)(C) defines modified AGI as adjusted gross income before deducting any student loan interest and before any tuition and fees deduction but after adding back excluded foreign income. Married taxpayers filing separately are ineligible for this deduction.

[3] These education credits are discussed later in this chapter.

Example 5.2

John incurred $20,000 of qualifying educational expenses but obtained a $25,000 student loan. He begins payments on the loan on July 1, 2018 and makes $1,300 of payments by the end of 2018; $1,000 is interest expense and $300 principal. John's modified AGI is $50,000. John can deduct only $800 of this interest *for* AGI [($20,000/$25,000) × $1,000].

TAX PLANNING

To claim the student loan interest deduction, a taxpayer may not be claimed as a dependent by another taxpayer and must have a legal obligation to make the interest payments under the terms of the loan. When a student is no longer a dependent, he or she can deduct interest on a student loan in his or her name even if someone else makes the payments; for example, a parent or grandparent makes interest payments for the student although not legally obligated to do so. The payment is treated as a gift to the student who then makes the deductible interest payment.

Prior to 2018, there was another education-related deduction for qualified higher-education tuition and fees.[4] Single individuals could deduct up to $4,000 of qualifying expenses if their modified adjusted gross income was below $65,000 (below $130,000 if married filing jointly) or deduct up to $2,000 if their income was between $65,000 and $80,000 (between $130,000 and $160,000 if married filing jointly).[5] This deduction expired at the end of 2017.[6]

5.2.2 EDUCATOR EXPENSES

In 2002, Congress added a deduction for teachers who spend their personal funds for classroom supplies. Kindergarten through 12th-grade teachers can deduct up to $250 of unreimbursed expenses for books, supplies, computer equipment, software, and other supplementary materials used in the classroom or for professional development expenses.[7]

5.2.3 HEALTH SAVINGS ACCOUNTS

Taxpayers covered only by high-deductible medical insurance plans may put aside a specific amount of money in a health savings account (HSA) on a tax-deferred basis (that is, they are allowed a deduction for AGI). Earnings on these savings grow tax free and neither contributions nor earnings are taxed when withdrawn to pay for qualified medical expenses. Distributions for other than qualifying medical expenses are included in gross income and are subject to a 20 percent penalty.

To qualify as a high-deductible medical policy for 2018, the insurance must have an annual deductible of at least $1,350 for individual coverage or at least $2,700 for family coverage. Additionally, the 2018 maximum annual out-of-pocket expenses (other than for premiums) for covered benefits cannot exceed $6,650 for individual coverage and $13,300 for family coverage.

Contributions to HSAs are deductible if total contributions do not exceed $3,450 for individual coverage or $6,850 for family coverage in 2018.[8] Premiums on other medical

---

[4] §222(d)(4). If a tuition waiver granted an employee of an educational institution is included in the employee's income, the employee is deemed to have paid the tuition and the payment may be eligible for the tuition deduction.

[5] Modified adjusted gross income is adjusted gross income before taking into account the tuition and fees deduction but after adding back any foreign earned income excluded and after deducting any student loan interest expense.

[6] This deduction expired at the end of the 2016 tax year and was retroactively extended by Congress through 2017.

[7] The amount of this deduction is indexed for inflation in future years.

[8] Similar to the catch-up contributions allowed for IRAs, individuals who are at least age 55 are allowed additional contributions of $1,000 to an HSA. If an employer contributes to an HSA, the contribution is excluded from the employee's income. Once individuals are enrolled in Medicare, they are no longer eligible to make HSA contributions. An alternative to the HSA is the more restrictive Archer medical savings account (MSA) that has higher deductibles.

insurance policies are deductible as a medical expense by employees who itemize their deductions. A self-employed individual is allowed to deduct this medical insurance premium *for* AGI (as discussed in Chapter 4).

Example 5.3

Ellen, who is single and employed by ABC Corporation, has a high-deductible medical insurance policy with a $3,000 deductible. Ellen contributes $3,450 to an HSA. Ellen can deduct the HSA contribution *for* AGI but can only deduct the medical insurance premiums if she itemizes.

Jonah is married and owns a sole proprietorship. He has a high-deductible medical policy for himself and his family with a $4,500 deductible. Jonah contributes $6,650 to an HSA. Because he is self-employed, he can deduct both the HSA contribution and the premium paid for the medical insurance *for* AGI.

TAX PLANNING

HSAs may attract individuals who want to switch from a low-deductible health plan to a less expensive high-deductible plan. A portion of the savings from the reduced premiums can be contributed to an HSA to accumulate funds on a tax-free basis to pay the medical expenses not covered due to the increased deductible. Additionally, HSAs are portable so employees who change employers can take their HSAs with them.

5.2.4 PENALTY ON EARLY WITHDRAWAL OF SAVINGS

Certificates of deposits (CDs) and time savings accounts usually require holding an investment for a fixed period of time. If the depositor withdraws the funds prior to the end of the fixed period, the depositor normally forfeits part of the interest income that would have been earned. When the taxpayer makes this premature withdrawal, the bank reports the entire amount of interest income earned to the IRS but reduces that amount by the early withdrawal penalty, paying the taxpayer only the net amount. This penalty differs from other nondeductible penalties in that it is a reduction of interest income; without this special provision, the penalty could only be deducted as a miscellaneous itemized deduction (and this miscellaneous category is no longer deductible after 2017). Gross interest is included in income as taxable interest but the penalty is deducted *for* AGI to ensure that only the net interest income received is included in taxable income.

5.2.5 OTHER DEDUCTIONS FOR AGI

Several unrelated deductions for AGI are combined and reported on line 24 due to space limitations. Taxpayers are allowed deductions for unreimbursed travel expenses to attend U.S. Armed Forces Reserve or National Guard meetings (100 miles or more from home), expenses incurred by certain performing artists, and expenses of officials employed by a state or local government, such as court reporters, who are compensated on a fee basis (rather than a salary) for their services.

Congress provides deductions for certain other less frequently claimed expenses for AGI but with no specific line on Form 1040 on which to report them. For example, the American Jobs Creation Act of 2004 created a deduction for AGI for legal fees paid from court awards or settlements from discrimination suits. The total for this and other deductions for AGI for which no line is provided are simply included on line 36 with an appropriate schedule providing the details.[9]

[9] Repayments of items previously included in income are also deducted here, such as the repayment of excess supplemental unemployment insurance benefits or jury duty fees remitted to an employer.

Table 5.1 lists additional deductions for AGI and the chapters where they are discussed.

Table 5.1 Additional Deductions for Adjusted Gross Income

Deduction	Discussed in chapter
Alimony paid (for divorce agreements executed before 2019)	3
Contributions to IRAs	4
Contributions to self-employed retirement plans	4
One-half of self-employment taxes	4
Self-employed health insurance premiums	4

5.3 STANDARD DEDUCTION

Taxpayers are allowed to deduct the greater of their standard deduction or their itemized deductions in determining taxable income.

5.3.1 STANDARD DEDUCTION AMOUNTS

The standard deductions usually are adjusted annually for inflation. Table 5.2 shows the standard deductions for 2017 and 2018.

Table 5.2 Standard Deductions

	2018	2017
Filing status		
Single (Unmarried) Individual	$12,000	$6,350
Head of Household	18,000	9,350
Married Filing a Joint Return	24,000	12,700
Surviving Spouse (Qualifying Widow or Widower)	24,000	12,700
Married Filing a Separate Return	12,000	6,350
Additional Amount if Single, Head of Household or Surviving Spouse*	1,600	1,550
Additional Amount if Married*	1,300	1,250

*Additional amount for each instance of blindness or age (65 or older) of the taxpayer (or taxpayer and spouse if a joint return is filed).

Taxpayers compare the standard deduction to their itemized deductions to determine the greater benefit. If their standard deduction equals or exceeds their itemized deductions, they take their standard deduction.[10]

Example 5.4

Jerry and Elaine, married filing jointly, have AGI of $75,000. Their itemized deductions are only $9,870. They should claim their standard deduction of $24,000, as it exceeds their itemized deduction total.

Taxpayers age 65 or older at the end of the year or who are blind, are allowed additional standard deductions.[11] Taxpayers who file as single or as heads of household are allowed additional

[10] A nonresident alien or a married individual filing a separate return is not permitted to use the standard deduction if his or her spouse itemized deductions. For 2016 and 2017, the net casualty loss from a federally declared disaster could be added to the standard deduction for taxpayers who did not itemize.

[11] §63(c)(3). Blindness is defined in §63(f)(4) as vision not exceeding 20/200 in the better eye with correcting lenses or a field of vision of 20 degrees or less.

standard deductions for age or blindness of $1,600 each. They may add a total of $3,200 to their basic standard deduction if they are both blind and age 65 or older. The additional standard deduction for married taxpayers for age or blindness is $1,300 each. The maximum additional standard deduction on a joint return if both the taxpayer and spouse are at least age 65 and blind would be $5,200 (4 × $1,300). The additional standard deductions are adjusted periodically (in $50 or $100 increments) for inflation.

There is no additional standard deduction allowed for dependents who are blind or age 65 or older. These additional deductions can only be claimed on the taxpayer's own return. For example, a taxpayer who claims her 68-year-old grandmother as her dependent is allowed no additional standard deduction because of her grandmother's age.

The additional standard deduction(s) are added to the basic standard deduction, after which the taxpayer compares this total to the total of his or her itemized deductions and deducts the greater of these two amounts from AGI to determine taxable income.

Example 5.5

Newton and Betsy, a married couple, are both 68 years old. Newton is legally blind. The couple's total standard deduction is $27,900: the sum of their basic standard deduction of $24,000 plus three additional standard deductions of $1,300 each. If their itemized deductions are less than $27,900, they will use their standard deduction in computing taxable income. If their itemized deductions exceed $27,900, they will claim their itemized deductions instead.

The standard deduction for an individual who is a dependent of another person is limited to the *greater* of $1,050 or their earned income for the year plus $350. Earned income includes salaries, wages, tips, and net business income, but it does not include net rental income, interest, dividends, or capital gains.

Example 5.6

Johnny, age 12, has $3,000 of dividend income for the year from inherited stock and this is his only income. He is a dependent of his parents and has neither itemized deductions nor earned income. Thus, his standard deduction is limited to $1,050. Johnny has $1,950 of taxable income: his $3,000 dividend income less his standard deduction of $1,050.

If Johnny has $1,200 income from a newspaper route in addition to his $3,000 dividend income, his gross income is $4,200. His standard deduction is now $1,550 ($1,200 earned income + $350) and his taxable income is $2,650 ($4,200 − $1,550).

The standard deduction for a dependent cannot exceed the standard deduction allowed a taxpayer in that filing status.[12] Most dependents are single, so their basic standard deduction is limited to $12,000 if their earned income exceeds $11,650.

Example 5.7

Susie, age 17, is a dependent of her parents. She earns $12,850 from modeling and has no itemized deductions. Her standard deduction is limited to $12,000 (the basic standard deduction for a single individual). Susie's taxable income is $850: her earned income of $12,850 less her standard deduction of $12,000.

[12] The limit on the standard deduction for dependents applies only to their basic standard deduction. Any additional standard deductions for age and blindness are added in full to the limited basic standard deduction on their own tax returns.

TAX PLANNING

Taxpayers can maximize the use of their standard deductions and itemized deductions by timing certain deductible payments. This involves shifting payments for qualifying itemized deductions into one year so that their total exceeds the standard deduction for the year, and then deducting the standard deduction the next year, or vice versa.

Example 5.8

Trudy is single; assume a $12,000 standard deduction in years 1 and 2. In late December, year 1, she receives a $20,000 cash gift from her grandparents. Trudy plans to donate the entire sum to her church—her only potential itemized deduction. If she donates $10,000 in December, year 1, and $10,000 in January, year 2, she obtains no tax benefit from either of the donations as neither exceeds her standard deduction. If, however, she donates the entire $20,000 in year 1, she has a $20,000 itemized deduction from AGI in computing her taxable income. She can then deduct her $12,000 standard deduction in year 2. Trudy has total deductions from AGI over the two years of $32,000 ($20,000 + $12,000), an increase of $8,000 ($32,000 – $12,000 – $12,000) over her standard deductions for the two years. By timing her deductible expenditures, Trudy generated deductions over two years greater than the sum of her standard deductions.

The taxpayer's standard deduction depends on the filing status for which he or she qualifies. Taxpayers must select their filing status from the five available categories: married filing jointly, married filing separately, surviving spouse (a qualifying widow or widower), head of household, and single.

5.3.2 MARRIED FILING JOINTLY

Couples who are legally married on the last day of the tax year are married for the entire year for federal tax purposes. A married taxpayer who is granted a divorce in December is single for the entire year. An individual is considered married, even though living apart from his or her spouse, unless the individual is legally separated under a decree of divorce or separate maintenance.[13]

In addition to being married at the end of the year, both spouses must be U.S. citizens or residents of the United States to file a joint return.[14] If one spouse is a nonresident alien, a joint return can be filed only if the nonresident spouse agrees to include his or her worldwide income in the joint U.S. tax return. If a joint return is not filed, each must file the married filing separately return. In this case, however, the nonresident spouse is taxed on U.S. source income only.

TAX PLANNING

If the nonresident spouse has little U.S. source income but a significant amount of foreign-source income, it may be advantageous for the couple to file separate returns.

If one spouse dies during the year, marital status is determined on the date of death of the decedent. As long as the surviving spouse has not remarried prior to the end of the year, the surviving spouse is still considered married to the decedent spouse and may file a joint return for the year of death. The widow or widower may also qualify for relief as a surviving spouse for two subsequent years, if certain conditions are met.

5.3.3 SURVIVING SPOUSE

A **surviving spouse**, a widow or widower who has not remarried and has at least one dependent child in the home (for whom he or she pays more than one-half the cost of maintaining the home

[13] The determination of whether a couple is legally married is a question of state law. If a state recognizes common law marriages, then the couple is recognized as husband and wife under federal tax law as well. For federal tax purposes, the term marriage includes a marriage between same sex individuals if they were legally married in a state with laws authorizing the marriage, even if the couple lives in a state that does not recognize the validity of same-sex marriage—the "state of celebration rule." Rev. Rul. 2013-17, 2013-38 IRB 201.

[14] §6013(a)(1).

for the entire year), may claim the standard deduction for married filing jointly and may use the joint tax rate schedule for two years after the year of the spouse's death. Congress recognized that the death of a spouse can cause a particular hardship for a surviving spouse when a dependent child still lives at home. At the end of this two-year period, the surviving spouse may qualify as head of household.

Example 5.9

Mark and Mindy are married and have two dependent children living with them. Mark dies in year 1. Mindy remains unmarried and the two children continue to live with her. Mindy files a joint return for year 1. For years 2 and 3, Mindy files as a surviving spouse (qualifying widow) but is allowed to claim the same standard deduction for a joint tax return. Beginning in year 4 she can file as head of household.

A widow or widower without a dependent child living with him or her does not qualify as a surviving spouse, but must file as a single individual or, if qualified, as head of household.

5.3.4 MARRIED FILING SEPARATELY

Married taxpayers who do not file a joint return generally must file returns as married filing separately. They are not allowed to file as "single" individuals. A nonresident alien and his or her U.S. citizen or resident alien spouse, who both have taxable income, must normally file as married persons filing separately (unless both spouses agree to be taxed on their worldwide income).[15]

Married persons filing separately face a number of limiting factors on separate tax returns. For example, married persons cannot claim either the earned income credit or the child and dependent care credit if they file separately. In spite of the disadvantages, filing separately may have some benefits. First, if the married couple is contemplating a separation or divorce, filing separately relieves one spouse of any liability for taxes, penalties, and interest arising from the other spouse's return. (Both are fully liable for the taxes, penalties, and interest on a return filed jointly.) Although it may cost the couple extra tax dollars, lack of trust or animosity between them may warrant separate returns. If problems are resolved, the couple may file an amended joint return within the time allowed for amending returns. If, however, the due date has passed for filing a joint return, separate amended returns may not be filed.

TAX PLANNING

In some unusual situations, the couple can save tax dollars by filing separately. If the spouse with the lower AGI claims the majority of itemized deductions, a greater percentage of these may be deductible due to the lower threshold based on AGI. Their combined AGI may exceed the required thresholds based on AGI and could wipe out many of their itemized deductions. If the couple does file separately and one spouse itemizes, then both must itemize deductions.

Example 5.10

Jill has $7,900 of qualified medical expenses. Jill's AGI is $15,000 and her husband's AGI is $60,000. Medical expenses are deductible only to the extent they exceed 7.5 percent of AGI. On a joint return, only $2,275 of the medical expenses [$7,900 – ($75,000 joint AGI × 7.5%)] is deductible. If they file separately, Jill can deduct $6,775 for medical expenses [$7,900 – ($15,000 × 7.5%)]. If Jill itemizes, Jack must also itemize his deductions; he cannot claim the standard deduction on his separate return.

[15] §6013(g).

5.3.5 HEAD OF HOUSEHOLD

To file as **head of household**, an individual must meet two tests:

1. He or she must be single at the end of the year (unless qualifying as an *abandoned spouse* defined later).
2. He or she must pay more than half the costs of maintaining a home in which a *qualifying child* or other relative who is a dependent lives for more than half the tax year.[16]

A qualifying child does not have to be a dependent of the taxpayer.[17] This exception was intended to protect a parent who had custody of a child claimed as a dependent by the noncustodial spouse. The parent with custody can still claim head of household filing status, if he or she provides more than one-half the cost of maintaining the household. Temporary absences for school, vacation, or medical care count as time lived in the home.

Generally, a dependent relative, except a dependent parent, must live in the home with the taxpayer. This exception allows a single taxpayer to claim head of household status if he or she pays more than one-half the costs of a dependent parent's home (for example, a separate apartment or a nursing home).

Example 5.11

Phillip is single and supports his elderly father, who lives in another city. Phillip pays more than one-half of the costs of maintaining the apartment and his father qualifies as his dependent. Phillip can file as head of household because he pays more than one-half the cost of his father's support.

Table 5.3 summarizes the types of qualifying relatives that enable a taxpayer to claim head of household status.

Table 5.3 Relatives Qualifying Taxpayer for Head of Household Status

Type of relative	Dependency status	Household requirements
Qualifying child who lives with taxpayer for more than half the year	Child does not need to be dependent of taxpayer	Taxpayer must pay more than half of the costs of maintaining a home in which the qualifying child lives for more than half the tax year
Taxpayer's mother or father	Mother or father must be a dependent of the taxpayer	Taxpayer must pay more than half of the costs of maintaining the home in which the mother or father lives for more than half the tax year (but can live apart from the taxpayer)
Qualifying relative (other than mother or father) who lives with the taxpayer for more than half the year	Qualifying relative must be a dependent of the taxpayer	Taxpayer must pay more than half of the costs of maintaining the home in which the qualifying relative lives for more than half the tax year.

[16] Qualifying household costs include real property taxes, mortgage interest, rent, utility bills, repairs and maintenance, property insurance, and the cost of food consumed in the household. They do not include clothing, education, or medical expenses. Reg. §1.2-2(d).

[17] To be a qualifying child, four tests must be met: (1) residency, (2) relationship, (3) age, and (4) support. These tests are discussed in detail later in this chapter in section 5.6.1.

The classification as an **abandoned spouse** is an exception to the rule that a taxpayer claiming the head of household status must be single at the end of the year. An abandoned spouse is a person married at year-end but who has

1. lived apart from his or her spouse at all times during the *last six months* of the tax year *and*
2. paid more than one-half the cost of maintaining a home in which he or she lived with a dependent child for more than half the tax year.[18]

Without this provision, a married, but abandoned, taxpayer would have to file as married filing separately, unless a joint return is filed. More likely, the spouse cannot be found or refuses to file a joint return. If the taxpayer does not meet these specific requirements for abandoned spouse relief and does not file a joint return, the taxpayer must file as married filing separately.

Example 5.12

Kelly and Kyle are married. Kyle left town and has not been heard from in two years. Their two dependent children live full-time with Kelly and she provides more than half the cost of maintaining the home. Based on these facts, Kelly can file as head of household under the abandoned spouse provision.

5.3.6 SINGLE (UNMARRIED) INDIVIDUAL

Taxpayers who do not qualify for one of the other filing statuses must file as single individuals. Thus, a single (unmarried) taxpayer who cannot file as head of household or as a surviving spouse must use the single filing status. A taxpayer is single if he or she is unmarried on the last day of the tax year.[19]

5.4 ITEMIZED DEDUCTIONS

Itemizing deductions is the alternative to claiming the standard deduction. Under the guise of tax simplification, Congress imposed limitations on itemized deductions, reducing the number of taxpayers who benefit from this option. The amount spent for certain **itemized deductions** (medical expenses and casualty losses) must exceed a specified "floor" (or minimum) based on the taxpayer's AGI before the excess can be included as an itemized deduction.[20] Other deductions (charitable contributions) are limited by a "ceiling" (or maximum) based on various percentages of adjusted gross income.[21]

Table 5.4 summarizes the various statutory provisions that limit itemized deductions.

Table 5.4 Limitations Applied to Itemized Deductions

Deduction	Limitation type	Limit described
Medical expenses	Floor	7.5% of AGI
Taxes	Ceiling	$10,000
Home acquisition mortgage interest	Ceiling	Interest on up to $750,000 of debt principal
Investment interest	Ceiling	Interest up to amount of net investment income
Cash charitable contributions	Ceiling	60% of AGI
Charitable contributions of long-term capital gain property	Ceiling	30% of AGI
Casualty loss from a disaster	Floor	10% of AGI

[18] §2(c).
[19] §6013.
[20] The floor, or threshold, is the minimum expense a taxpayer must incur before the excess can be deducted.
[21] A ceiling is the maximum deduction that can be claimed in any one year.

5.4.1 MEDICAL EXPENSES

Section 213 allows taxpayers to deduct expenditures paid for medical care for the following:

1. Diagnosis, cure, mitigation, treatment, or prevention of disease or for the purpose of affecting any structure or function of the body.
2. Transportation primarily for and essential to medical care.[22]
3. Insurance for medical care.

Medical and dental expenses qualify as itemized deductions when incurred for the benefit of taxpayers and their dependents, including costs incurred for cosmetic surgery to correct a deformity resulting from a congenital abnormality, personal injury, or disease. Amounts incurred for elective cosmetic surgery (for example, hair transplants, facelifts, liposuction, and other medical procedures dictated by vanity) are not deductible.[23]

The costs for prescription drugs and insulin are deductible, but nonprescription drugs (except insulin) are not deductible even if recommended by a doctor. Other specialized medical products, such as wheelchairs, eyeglasses, contact lenses, crutches, false teeth, hearing aids, and artificial limbs, are deductible. Their cost is deducted when purchased, even though the item may have an extended life. The cost of meals is deductible if provided by a hospital or similar care facility as a necessary part of a patient's medical care.

Health insurance premiums for taxpayers and their dependents are a deductible medical expense only if paid from the taxpayer's after-tax income. Thus, health insurance premiums paid with pre-tax income through an employer-sponsored cafeteria plan (flexible spending account) are not deductible.[24]

TAX PLANNING

Taxpayers should use their employer's cafeteria plans to purchase medical insurance and to pay for medical expenses not covered by insurance, if available. The tax savings from the exclusion are normally greater than a deduction as a medical expense.

Health insurance premiums paid by the taxpayer's employer are excluded from the employee's gross income and cannot be deducted by the employee. As previously discussed, self-employed individuals can deduct their health insurance premiums *for* AGI.

Premiums for disability insurance and insurance for the loss of life, limb, or income are not deductible insurance premiums. Premiums for long-term-care insurance qualify for the medical expense deduction, subject to limits based on the taxpayer's age. The limits are adjusted annually for inflation.[25]

The taxpayer's qualifying unreimbursed medical expenses are deductible to the extent the total exceeds 7.5 percent of the taxpayer's AGI. In 2019, the 7.5 percent floor will increase to 10 percent of AGI.[26]

Example 5.13

Mario, age 50, has AGI of $75,000. During the year, he incurred $12,000 of medical expenses and was reimbursed $4,000 for these expenses. Mario's allowable deduction for medical expenses is $2,375, computed as follows:

Medical expenses	$12,000
Less: reimbursements	(4,000)
Unreimbursed expenses	8,000
Less: $75,000 AGI × 7.5%	(5,625)
Allowed deduction	$2,375

[22] The mileage rate for using a car to get medical care is 18 cents per mile for 2018 and was 17 cents per miles for 2017. Notice 2018-3, 2018-2 IRB. The cost of parking and tolls can be deducted in addition to the mileage rate.

[23] §213(d)(9)(A) and (B).

[24] Cafeteria plans and flexible spending accounts are discussed in Chapter 4.

[25] §213(d)(1)(D). For 2018, deductible premiums are limited by age as follows: not more than age 40, $420 ($410 for 2017); more than age 40 but not more than age 50, $780 ($770 for 2017); more than age 50 but not more than age 60, $1,560 ($1,530 for 2017); more than age 60 but not more than age 70, $4,160 ($4,090 for 2017); over age 70, $5,200 ($5,110 for 2017).

[26] §213(d).

Medical expenses charged on a credit card are deemed paid when charged, not when the credit card bill is paid.[27] Medical expenses paid in advance are not deductible until the year treatment is received unless prepayment is required as a condition of receiving medical care.[28] When medical expenses are paid in one tax year and reimbursed in a subsequent year, the tax benefit rule requires including the reimbursement in the taxpayer's income to the extent the prior deduction resulted in a tax benefit.

5.4.2 TAXES

Deductions are allowed for up to $10,000 ($5,000 if married filing separately) in income and property taxes paid to state and local governments; however, no deduction is allowed for most taxes paid to the federal government.[29] Deductible taxes include:

- State, local, and foreign income taxes.
- State and local real property taxes.
- State and local personal property taxes.
- Other state, local, and foreign taxes that are incurred in the context of a trade or business or other income-producing activity.

Common, but *nondeductible* taxes, incurred by individuals (other than federal income taxes) include federal and state excise taxes on the purchase of tires, motor fuels, tobacco, and alcohol; federal excise taxes on commercial airline tickets; and the employee's share of federal payroll taxes.

A taxpayer must be careful to differentiate between taxes and fines imposed by a governmental unit. Section 162(f) specifically prohibits the deduction of a fine.

Income Taxes

Most state, local, and foreign income taxes are deductible as itemized deductions in the year they are paid or accrued. Cash-basis taxpayers deduct taxes in the year actually paid. A refund of a cash-basis taxpayer's overpayment of income taxes from a prior year is income only to the extent that the prior tax payment produced a tax benefit.

Example 5.14

Nick, a single taxpayer, reported AGI of $60,000 in 2018 and allowable itemized deductions of $12,150, including $3,500 for state income taxes. Nick receives a $1,100 state income tax refund in 2019. Nick includes only $150 of the $1,100 refund in his 2019 gross income. His $1,100 overpayment of 2018 state income taxes reduced his tax base by only $150. He was entitled to a $12,000 standard deduction in 2018 if he did not itemize. He effectively saved only $150 by itemizing ($12,150 total itemized deductions – $12,000 standard deduction = $150 benefit).

If Nick's refund had been only $100, he would have had to include the entire $100 refund in 2019 income.

TAX PLANNING

Foreign income taxes are deductible as an itemized deduction only if the taxpayer forgoes the foreign tax credit for the amount of tax paid. In most circumstances, the taxpayer receives a greater tax benefit by electing the foreign tax credit than by deducting foreign income taxes.

[27] Rev. Rul. 78-38, 1978-1 CB 67.

[28] Rev. Rul. 75-303, 1975-2 CB 87.

[29] §164. Prior to 2018 there was no dollar limit for deductible state and local taxes. The $10,000 limit applies only through 2025.

Sales Taxes

In 2004, Congress added a provision intended to benefit states with tax revenues dependent on sales taxes rather than income taxes (such as Florida and Texas), at the state and local levels. Taxpayers can elect to deduct state and local general sales taxes *instead* of state and local income taxes as itemized deductions. Taxpayers subject to state income taxes should compare both deductions and deduct the higher of the two.

To determine the allowable sales tax deduction, taxpayers can use actual sales taxes paid (documented by accumulating receipts) or IRS-published tables based on average consumption (determined by taxpayer income and sales tax rates). Taxpayers who elect to use these tables can add actual sales taxes paid for major purchases, such as a car or boat, to the table amount.

Real and Personal Property Taxes

State and local personal property taxes and real property taxes are deductible when paid for property that the taxpayer owns. It is important for taxpayers to distinguish between the payment of real property taxes and the payment of assessments that fund improvements specifically benefiting the taxpayer's property. Property assessments generally are not deductible as they usually are levied for improvements to the taxpayer's property, increasing its value, and are added to the property's basis instead. If, however, the assessments are for maintenance, repairs, or current interest due to financing improvements, they are deductible.

A personal property tax must be an *ad valorem* tax (that is, it is based on the value of the property) to be deductible. For example, a fee levied by a state for vehicle registrations based on the value of the vehicle is deductible as a personal property tax. A flat registration fee on a per-vehicle basis is not deductible.

5.4.3 INTEREST EXPENSE

The deductibility of any interest paid or incurred by an individual taxpayer is determined by the nature of the underlying debt; that is, taxpayers trace the use of borrowed funds to their end use to determine their deductibility.[30] Interest paid on individual taxpayer's nonbusiness indebtedness falls into one of four general categories: interest on student loans (deductible *for* AGI as discussed earlier); investment interest; qualified residence interest; and nondeductible personal interest. This last category includes nondeductible interest on credit cards, automobile loans, and other personal debts. Investment interest and qualified residence interest are itemized deductions.

Investment Interest

Investment interest expense includes interest paid on loans to acquire or hold investment property (such as stocks, bonds, and land) and margin interest paid to a broker to borrow against a brokerage account. The deductibility of investment interest expense is limited to a taxpayer's net investment income for the year.[31] Without this limitation, taxpayers could deduct interest paid to carry investments that produce little or no current income and whose income could be deferred at the discretion of the taxpayer. Interest expense incurred to acquire investments that produce nontaxable income (for example, interest on municipal bonds) is nondeductible investment interest.[32]

Net investment income is the excess of gross investment income over deductible investment expenses (excluding interest) directly connected with the production of investment income.

---

[30] Temp. Reg. §1.163-8T.

[31] §163(d)(1). Net investment income is gross investment income less deductible investment expenses (deductible as a miscellaneous itemized deduction prior to 2018) excluding investment interest expense (an interest deduction).

[32] §163(h).

Income from investment sources taxed as ordinary income such as interest, annuity payments, and net short-term capital gains from the sale of investment property are included in investment income. Prior to 2018, investment-related expenses such safe deposit box rental fees, investment counseling fees, brokerage account maintenance fees, and investment advisory publication subscriptions were deductible as miscellaneous itemized deductions. To the extent that these investment expenses were deductible, they reduced net investment income. Investment interest not currently deductible because of this limitation is carried forward indefinitely.

Example 5.15

Craig incurs interest expense of $9,400 for loans taken out to invest in stocks and bonds. His $7,400 of investment income consists of a $5,000 short-term capital gain and $2,400 interest income. Craig deducts his investment interest to the extent of his $7,400 net investment income and carries forward the $2,000 ($9,400 − $7,400) of remaining investment interest expense, treating it as paid in the next tax year. Craig deducts the $7.400 of investment interest expense in the interest section of Schedule A: *Itemized Deductions*.

TAX PLANNING

Investment income excludes net long-term capital gains from the sale of investment property or dividend income that is taxed at lower favorable tax rates unless the taxpayer elects to forgo these rates.[33] Before electing to forgo the favorable rates for long-term capital gains and dividend income, taxpayers should calculate the tax savings from the investment interest expense deduction to ensure that this provides a greater after-tax benefit than the reduced tax rate on the dividend income and capital gains. In making this comparison, individuals should take into account the time value of money and the marginal tax brackets for the current year and any future year to which the investment interest could be carried forward and deducted.

Qualified Residence Interest

Home mortgage interest expense on a personal residence is not considered investment interest because ownership of a personal residence (a personal-use asset) does not qualify as an investment. Congress, however, decided it was important to encourage home ownership with a deduction for home mortgage interest for acquisition debt.

Acquisition debt includes a mortgage secured by the taxpayer's residence to acquire, construct, or substantially improve the residence. For mortgages obtained before December 15, 2017, interest expense paid on acquisition debt principal of up to $1,000,000 is deductible as an itemized deduction. There is no carry forward of any amount in excess of the $1,000,000 limit.[34] The acquisition debt on the taxpayer's principal residence can be combined with the acquisition debt on one additional residence, however, to reach the $1,000,000 principal limit. If the second residence is rented out for part of the year, then the taxpayer's personal use of it must exceed the greater of 14 days or 10 percent of the rental days for any of the interest expense to qualify as acquisition debt.

For 2018–2025, the Tax Cuts and Jobs Act reduced the qualifying debt principal to $750,000 ($375,000 if married filing separately) for loans made after December 15, 2017. The principal limit of $1,000,000 continues to apply for mortgages obtained before December 16, 2017 and does not decrease as a result of refinancing. In 2026, the $1,000,000 debt limit will be restored and apply to all qualifying mortgages regardless of when the debt was incurred.

[33] §163(d)(4)(B). Investment income and expenses from economic activities that are passive activities under Section 469 are also excluded from the determination of net investment income.

[34] The deduction for interest paid on acquisition indebtedness incurred prior to October 13, 1987, is not limited. The $1,000,000 debt principal limitation for liabilities incurred after October 13, 1987, is reduced, however, for any preexisting acquisition indebtedness. The $1,000,000 is a per taxpayer limit except taxpayers who are married filing separately are limited to $500,000.

Example 5.16

Donna and Carl own three homes, all acquired before 2017. The principal amounts of the acquisition mortgages are $800,000 on their principal residence and $150,000 on their vacation home in the Florida Keys. They also own a condo in Breckenridge, Colorado that they used for 10 days and rented out for 6 months during the year; the principal amount of this mortgage is $200,000. In the current year, they paid $30,000 for mortgage interest on their principal residence, $6,750 mortgage interest on their Florida vacation home, and $9,800 mortgage interest on their Colorado condo. They do not meet the minimum personal-use requirement for the Colorado rental home to qualify as a personal residence. Only total interest on their $950,000 for acquisition debt for their principal residence and Florida vacation home is deductible. They can deduct $36,750 ($30,000 + $6,750) mortgage interest expense as an itemized deduction.[35]

Kevin and Kaylee purchased a new principle residence on January 1, 2018. The mortgage principal on their acquisition debt is $1,250,000 and the interest paid on this mortgage is $46,875. They can deduct only $28,125 of the interest expense [($750,000/$1,250,000) × $46,875] for this mortgage.

Prior to 2018, a taxpayer could also deduct up to $100,000 mortgage interest based on the equity in a taxpayer's personal residence as loan security (a home equity loan). Home equity loans were popular because the loan proceeds did not have to be spent on the home but could instead be used to purchase an automobile, take a vacation, or anything else the homeowner wished. This provision was repealed and has not been reinstated; thus, this type of home equity loan interest expense is no longer deductible after 2017 regardless of when the mortgage was incurred.[36]

Mortgage companies typically charge fees to borrowers for finding, placing, or processing their loans. These fees, called points or loan origination fees, are usually expressed as a percentage of the amount borrowed; each point equals one percent of the loan principal. The payment of points is treated as the equivalent of prepaying interest to the extent that such fees do not represent service charges for real estate appraisals, title searches, or other legal work. When points are paid in connection with loans to purchase or improve a taxpayer's primary personal residence, they are deductible as interest expense in the year paid.[37] If incurred to refinance an existing home mortgage, points and other prepaid interest must be capitalized and amortized over the duration of the loan.

Example 5.17

Richard and Helen purchased a $100,000 home with a $20,000 down payment and an $80,000 acquisition mortgage. The mortgage company charged two points ($1,600) for originating the loan that they paid at closing. Richard and Helen deduct the points as an interest expense in the tax year in which they are paid.

Three years later Richard and Helen refinance their mortgage to obtain a lower interest rate. They pay points of $1,500 to refinance their original mortgage with a new 30-year fixed-rate mortgage. Richard and Helen cannot immediately deduct the points but must amortize them over the 30-year life of the mortgage ($50 per year). If Richard and Helen pay off their mortgage early, the can deduct the balance of unamortized points at that time.

[35] As discussed in Chapter 6, their Colorado condo qualifies as rental property with rental income and expenses reported on Schedule E.

[36] Interest on home equity loans is now deductible only if all of the proceeds are used on the home and the principal (when combined with other acquisition debt) is within the total allowable limitation.

[37] §461(g)(2). For 2007 through 2017, the cost of mortgage insurance premiums paid on the purchase of a qualified residence was also allowed as deductible interest expense. (There is no deduction for any part of the homeowner's insurance.) Taxpayers qualified for this deduction if they purchased a home with a low or no down payment and were required by the lender to buy mortgage insurance (such as PMI). The premiums were deductible mortgage interest if they were paid in connection with qualified acquisition debt. The deduction was gradually phased out at the rate of 10% for each $1,000 (or fraction thereof) of AGI over $100,000 so that no deduction was permitted if AGI exceeded $109,000. For married taxpayers filing separately, the phase-out rate was 10% for each $500 in excess of $50,000 AGI.

5.4.4 CHARITABLE CONTRIBUTIONS

Section 170 allows taxpayers to deduct gifts made to qualified charitable organizations operated for religious, charitable, scientific, literary, or educational purposes based in the United States, as well as for gifts to U.S. federal, state, or local governments.[38] Contributions must be made through qualified organizations (such as the Red Cross or United Way) and not directly to individuals, regardless of the person's financial needs. In addition, contributions to organizations are not deductible to the extent any part of the donation is used for political lobbying purposes.[39]

If a taxpayer receives goods or services in return for a contribution, only the portion of the contribution in excess of the value of the goods or services received is deductible.[40]

Example 5.18

Lynn and Dave, a married couple who file a joint tax return, contributed $3,000 to the Zoological Society, a qualified charity, in return for a one-year membership at the sponsor level. Sponsors receive free admission to all zoo exhibits, free cocktail party receptions for all exhibit openings, and a 10 percent discount at the zoo gift shop. The collective value of all sponsor member benefits is $1,000. Lynn and Dave have made a $2,000 contribution to the zoo. They are considered to have purchased member benefits valued at $1,000.

Contributors to universities who receive preferred rights to purchase tickets for seating at university athletic events may not deduct their contribution.[41]

Example 5.19

Jim donated $4,500 to become a Hurricane Club contributor to the athletic department at the University of Miami. His membership allows him to purchase preferred seats to all home games. Jim also contributed $4,000 to the scholarship fund for the business school. Jim may deduct the $4,000 contributed to the scholarship fund but he cannot deduct the $4,500 contribution to the Hurricane Club because he received preferred seating rights for this contribution.

Deductible charitable contributions may be made in cash or property. No deduction is allowed, however, for a contribution of services or rent-free use of a taxpayer's property, as the owner simply has forgone income—income not subject to tax. Unreimbursed expenses related to charitable services, such as transportation and supplies, are deductible.[42]

Prior to 2018, total charitable contributions were deductible up to a limit of 50 percent of adjusted gross income (AGI). This 50 percent of AGI limit applied to contributions of cash and ordinary income property as well as serving as an overall limit. To encourage more gifts of cash to charitable organizations, Congress increased the AGI percentage ceiling on cash contribution to 60 percent (from 50 percent) for 2018 through 2025. The increase in the limit for cash contributions was the only change and all of the other limits continue to apply. Excess contributions can be carried forward for up to five years.

[38] §170(c). Cash-basis taxpayers must usually deduct a contribution in the year the contribution is made; however, Congress has created exceptions to encourage relief for certain disaster and unique situations. For example, under the Slain Officer Family Support Act of 2015, cash contributions made between January 1 and April 15, 2015 for the relief of the families of slain police officers could be deducted on the taxpayer's 2014 tax return.

[39] §170(c)(2)(D).

[40] Under de minimis rules, contributions will be fully deductible in 2018 if the donor makes a minimum payment of $54 ($53.50 in 2017) and receives benefits that cost no more than $10.80 ($10.70 in 2017). Additionally, the contribution is fully deductible if the benefit is no more than the lesser of $108 ($107 in 2017) or 2% of the amount contributed.

[41] §170(l). Prior to 2018, up to 80 percent of the contribution to a university's athletic booster club could be deducted.

[42] A statutory standard mileage rate deduction of 14 cents per mile is provided in §170(i) for an automobile used in a charitable activity.

Contributions of Property

Property contributions are subject to different limitations and valuations depending on the type of property donated and the type of qualifying organization receiving the property. For tax purposes, the value of donated property (excluding capital assets) is the lesser of the property's fair market value or cost. The value of appreciated property that, if sold, would produce a long-term capital gain, is its fair market value; thus, the capital gain element in the property escapes income taxation.[43] The ceiling limit is reduced, however, in exchange for this favorable valuation. Long-term capital gain property valued at fair market value is deductible up to a reduced ceiling limit of 30 percent of adjusted gross income; in addition, the deduction for property contributions subject to the 50 percent limitation are considered before the value of this property is deducted.[44]

Example 5.20

Jason contributes $25,000 to his favorite charity—$10,000 in cash and XYZ stock with a fair market value of $15,000. Jason acquired the XYZ stock four years ago for $4,000. Jason's adjusted gross income is $40,000. His cash contribution deduction limit this year is $24,000 (60 percent of his $40,000 AGI) but he has an overall limit of $20,000 (50 percent of AGI) for noncash contributions. The stock (long-term capital gain property) is subject to the 30 percent of AGI limit, limiting his current deduction for the stock to no more than $12,000 ($40,000 × 30%). The cash contribution is deducted from the 50 percent overall limit before the long-term capital gain property. This limits the stock contribution deduction to $10,000 ($20,000 overall AGI limit – $10,000 cash = $10,000 remaining current deduction). The remaining $5,000 stock deduction ($15,000 FMV – $10,000 current deduction) is carried forward to the next year, subject to the 30 percent limitation in the future year.

The value of a contribution of *tangible personalty* that qualifies as long-term capital gain property is reduced to the donor's basis (but the 50 percent of AGI limit now applies) if it is sold rather than *used* by the organization in its tax-exempt activity (unrelated-use property).[45] This reduction does not apply to contributions of real estate (land and buildings) or *intangible* long-term capital gain property (marketable securities). A contributor of property should verify that the charitable organization plans to *use* tangible personalty before such a gift is made to ensure the maximum tax deduction is allowed.

Example 5.21

Noah, whose current-year AGI is $100,000, owns a painting purchased 10 years ago for $5,000 that is now worth $20,000. He wants to donate the painting to one of two charities: the metropolitan art museum or the local humane society. If he donates the painting to the museum, they will display it in their art collection and Noah will be entitled to a $20,000 charitable contribution deduction. If he donates the painting to the humane society, they will sell it at their next fundraising auction and Noah's deduction will be limited to $5,000. This tax policy encourages donating art to a charity where it can be on display to the public rather than in the hands of a private collection.

The charitable deduction for capital assets other than long-term capital gain property—short-term capital gain property, capital loss property, and ordinary income property—is limited to the lesser of fair market value or the donor's adjusted basis.

---

[43] Capital assets are discussed in Chapter 8 and include investment assets (such as stock) and personal-use assets. Assets must be owned for more than one year to be considered long-term capital assets. §170(b)(1)(C)(iv) expands the definition of donated long-term capital gain property to include Section 1231 gain property used by a taxpayer in a trade or business activity. The value of long-term capital gain property that is donated to a private nonoperating foundation generally is its adjusted basis, except for marketable securities held more than 12 months. §170(e).

[44] The 30% of AGI limit also applies to contributions of cash and ordinary income property given to a private nonoperating foundation (a privately sponsored foundation that disburses funds to other charities). The deduction for contributions of capital gain property to these private charities is limited to 20% of AGI.

[45] Tangible personalty is any property, other than land or buildings, that can be seen or touched. Examples include paintings, jewelry, cars, furniture, and books (stocks and bonds are intangible property). Long-term capital assets include investment and personal-use assets owned for more than one year.

Maximizing the Tax Benefit from Contributions

TAX PLANNING

Long-term capital gain property makes an excellent charitable gift. The owner not only gets a charitable deduction but avoids income tax on the element of appreciation in the property. Appreciated stock makes an even better contribution because the charity may be readily able to sell the stock if it does not wish to hold it without the sale affecting the donor's contribution deduction.

The deduction for appreciated stock is limited to 30 percent of AGI, however. Any contribution in excess of 30 percent of AGI can be carried forward for five years, but the longer the deduction is deferred, the lower the present value of the deduction. Therefore, donors should try to limit contributions of appreciated stock to no more than 30 percent of their AGI in any one year.

A taxpayer can elect to value long-term capital gain property under alternate valuation rules (its value equal to the lesser of cost basis or fair market value) and avoid the 30 percent contribution limit.[46] If this election is made, the contribution is subject only to the 50 percent contribution limit. This election can prove beneficial if there is only a small amount of appreciation and the additional deduction at fair market value is not worth the cost of deferring a portion of the contribution to a future tax year. It can also be advantageous if the 30 percent limitation greatly reduces the taxpayer's allowable contribution deduction and little tax benefit is expected to be derived from carrying the unused contribution forward.

Example 5.22

Walter, a single taxpayer, donated his collection of Mexican primitive art to the Metropolitan Museum last year. The value of Walter's gift was $800,000, and his basis was $500,000. Walter died unexpectedly after making this charitable contribution. His adjusted gross income was $1,000,000 in the year of his death. Walter's contribution deduction on his final income tax return normally would be limited to $300,000 (30 percent of $1,000,000). The $500,000 ($800,000 − $300,000) unused portion of his contribution would be lost because there are no future tax years for the contribution carryforward. Electing to value the contribution at $500,000 (the lesser of fair market value or adjusted basis), allows all $500,000 to fall within the 50 percent ceiling limit ($1,000,000 AGI × 50%).

Stocks that have declined in value should be sold so that the loss can be claimed; the proceeds from the sale can be donated, preserving the loss deduction. No loss can be claimed on donated depreciated property.

The burden of proof is always on the taxpayer to substantiate the value of property donated to charity. To deduct *any* charitable donation of money, the individual must have a bank record (a canceled check, bank statement, or credit card statement) or a written communication from the charity showing the name of the charity and the date and amount of the contribution.[47] These requirements effectively make taxpayers write checks to preserve the tax deduction rather than dropping cash in a church collection plate or the Salvation Army Christmas buckets.

Donations of clothing and household items (furniture, appliances, and electronics) to qualified charities must be in no less than "good used condition" to claim a deduction for their value. The IRS has not defined "good used condition" but taking a photo might help substantiate that the items were in good condition when donated. Any single donation valued at $250 or more requires written substantiation from the charitable organization. If the value of the donation is between $500 and $5,000, the donor is required to furnish additional information on Form 8283. If a noncash donation exceeds $5,000, the taxpayer must obtain a qualified appraisal for

[46] §170(b)(1)(C)(iii).

[47] Bank statements should show the name of the charity and the date and amount paid; credit card statements should show the name of the charity and the transaction posting date. For contributions by phone or text message, a phone bill showing the name of the charity, the date, and amount contributed will satisfy this requirement. For payroll deductions, retain a pay stub, Form W-2 wage statement or other document furnished by an employer showing the total amount withheld for charity, along with the pledge card showing the name of the charity.

the property.[48] Failure to follow these requirements may result in the loss of the charitable contribution deduction. Fees incurred for professional third-party appraisals of donated property may be deducted as a miscellaneous itemized deduction as part of the cost of determining the tax liability.

5.4.5 CASUALTY LOSSES

Although individuals are not allowed to deduct a loss on the sale of a personal-use asset, a deduction may be allowed for casualty and theft losses on personal-use property.[49] A casualty loss results from a sudden and unexpected event such as a fire, flood, or hurricane. The value of the loss is the lesser of the asset's cost or its decline in fair market value from the casualty, less any insurance proceeds. The deduction is limited by two provisions. First, the potential deduction for each separate casualty is limited to an amount in excess of a $100 floor.[50] Then the total for all casualties (after application of the floor to each casualty) is limited to an amount that exceeds 10 percent of the taxpayer's AGI for the year. The loss remaining, after applying these limitations, is an itemized deduction. The $100 loss reduction per event removes an individual's small losses from deductibility, and the 10 percent threshold for all losses requires the net loss to be fairly large relative to income to provide a deduction.

For 2018–2025, Congress suspended the deduction for personal casualty and theft losses except for personal casualty losses incurred in a federally declared disaster. If, however, a taxpayer has personal casualty gains (if, for example, insurance proceeds exceed the property's cost), then nondisaster losses are deductible to the extent of the casualty gains. (Casualty losses are discussed in more detail in Chapter 9.)

Example 5.23

Melissa's home was damaged in a flood occurring in a federally declared disaster area. The home's fair market value before and after the storm was $200,000 and $120,000, respectively. She received only $60,000 from her flood insurance due to the large deductible applying to flood-related losses. She purchased the home 8 years earlier for $155,000. Melissa's adjusted gross income of $50,000 limits her deductible casualty loss to $14,900, computed as follows. Melissa first determines the lesser of the home's decline in value ($200,000 – $120,000 = $80,000) or her basis ($155,000 cost). She then subtracts her insurance recovery ($60,000) resulting in a net $20,000 loss. She must reduce the $20,000 loss first by the $100 floor and then by 10 percent of her $50,000 AGI ($5,000) resulting in a deductible loss of only $14,900.

5.4.6 MISCELLANEOUS ITEMIZED DEDUCTIONS

Prior to 2018, miscellaneous itemized deductions (for example, unreimbursed employee business expenses and investment expenses) were deductible to the extent they exceeded a 2 percent of AGI floor limitation. For 2018–2025, no deduction is allowed for expenses in this miscellaneous category. Employee business expenses included costs for professional dues, union dues, uniforms, subscriptions to employment-related publications and business travel.[51] Previously deductible investment expenses included safe deposit box rental to store stock certificates, investment advisor fees, subscriptions to investment publications, software to track investment portfolios, and depreciation on a computer used to monitor personal investments. Other deductible

[48] More stringent rules apply to donated vehicles (cars, boats, and airplanes) to close a loophole that allowed charities to sell the items for only a fraction of the value that the contributors claimed as a charitable contribution deduction. Taxpayers must obtain a qualified appraisal for any vehicle valued at more than $500 (excluding inventory). If the charity sells the vehicle rather than using it in its regular charitable activities, the charitable contribution deduction cannot exceed the gross sales proceeds.

[49] §165(h).

[50] For losses in federal disaster areas in 2009, 2016, and 2017, the floor was $500 and the 10 percent threshold did not apply.

[51] Although these business expenses cannot be deducted by employees as itemized deductions, they are deductible on a Schedule C if incurred by a self-employed sole proprietor. See Chapter 6 for the details on deductible business travel expenses.

miscellaneous expenses included hobby expenses (to the extent of income as discussed in Chapter 6) and expenses related to the determination, collection, or refund of any tax. The last category included tax return preparation fees, appraisal fees to document the value of property donated to a charity, accounting and legal fees for representation in a tax audit, and accounting fees for tax planning advice.

One type of miscellaneous itemized deduction not subject to the 2 percent of AGI floor that remains deductible is gambling losses.[52] All gambling winnings must be included in gross income but gambling losses cannot directly reduce gambling winnings; instead, gambling losses are deductible as itemized deductions.

Example 5.24

Miguel has AGI of $70,000 in 2017 and 2018 which includes $1,500 of gambling winnings. Miguel's expenses for each year are: $700 unreimbursed employee business expense ($300 for professional dues and $400 for subscriptions to employment-related publications), $550 for investment expenses ($50 safe deposit box to store stock certificates and $500 investment advisor fees), and $275 for tax return preparation fees—a total of $1,525. Miguel also has $1,800 of gambling losses each year. Because the $1,525 exceeded 2 percent of his AGI ($70,000 × 2% = $1,400) in 2017, he could deduct the $125 excess ($1,525 – $1,400). None of these business or investment expenses are deductible in 2018, however. Although the gambling losses are not subject to the 2 percent floor, they are deductible only to the extent of his gambling winnings of $1,500 in each year.

Prior to 2018, high-income taxpayers lost some of their itemized deductions if their AGI exceeded a specific threshold.[53] For example, the thresholds were $313,800 for married filing a joint return and $261,500 if single for 2017. The affected itemized deductions (such as charitable contributions, home mortgage interest, and taxes) were reduced by three percent of the taxpayer's AGI over the threshold AGI with taxpayers losing up to 80 percent of affected itemized deductions. Medical expenses, casualty losses, investment interest, and gambling losses were not reduced by this phaseout.

Example 5.25

Carlos and Angela Sanchez had AGI of $313,228 (including $4,650 of investment interest income) for 2017 with itemized deductions (before AGI limits) as follows:

Medical expenses (unreimbursed)	$18,000
State income taxes	14,500
State and local sales taxes	2,800
Real property taxes on their home	9,000
Home mortgage interest reported on Form 1098 (acquisition debt with principal of $700,000)	28,000
Investment interest expense	13,000
Charitable contributions in cash	7,000
Charitable contributions of stock	25,000

The medical expenses are not deductible because they are less than 7.5 percent of AGI. State income taxes of $14,500 are deducted (as they exceed state sales and only sales or income tax is deductible). Real property taxes are also deductible resulting in a $23,500 deduction for taxes paid. Investment interest expense is limited to $4,650 net investment income. Their $88,150 in itemized deductions are reported on Schedule A for 2017 as shown in Figure 5.3. Their Form 1040 is shown later in this chapter in Figure 5.5.

[52] Other expenses that are not subject to the 2 percent of AGI floor such as impairment-related work expenses incurred by a disabled person (for example, a reader for a blind person) are still deductible.

[53] Prior to 2018, personal and dependency exemptions were also phased out for individuals with AGI above a certain threshold similar to the phase out for itemized deductions.

SCHEDULE A (Form 1040) Department of the Treasury Internal Revenue Service (99)	**Itemized Deductions** ▶ Go to *www.irs.gov/ScheduleA* for instructions and the latest information. ▶ Attach to Form 1040. **Caution:** If you are claiming a net qualified disaster loss on Form 4684, see the instructions for line 28.	OMB No. 1545-0074 20**17** Attachment Sequence No. **07**

Name(s) shown on Form 1040

Carlos and Angela Sanchez

Your social security number: 150-66-5432

Medical and Dental Expenses		**Caution:** Do not include expenses reimbursed or paid by others.			
	1	Medical and dental expenses (see instructions)	**1**	18,000	
	2	Enter amount from Form 1040, line 38 **2** 313,228			
	3	Multiply line 2 by 7.5% (0.075).	**3**	23,492	
	4	Subtract line 3 from line 1. If line 3 is more than line 1, enter -0-		**4**	0
Taxes You Paid	5	State and local **(check only one box):**			
		a ☑ Income taxes, **or** }	**5**	14,500	
		b ☐ General sales taxes			
	6	Real estate taxes (see instructions)	**6**	9,000	
	7	Personal property taxes	**7**		
	8	Other taxes. List type and amount ▶ _____			
			8		
	9	Add lines 5 through 8		**9**	23,500
Interest You Paid **Note:** Your mortgage interest deduction may be limited (see instructions).	10	Home mortgage interest and points reported to you on Form 1098	**10**	28,000	
	11	Home mortgage interest not reported to you on Form 1098. If paid to the person from whom you bought the home, see instructions and show that person's name, identifying no., and address ▶ _____	**11**		
	12	Points not reported to you on Form 1098. See instructions for special rules	**12**		
	13	Mortgage insurance premiums (see instructions)	**13**		
	14	Investment interest. Attach Form 4952 if required. See instructions	**14**	4,650	
	15	Add lines 10 through 14		**15**	32,650
Gifts to Charity If you made a gift and got a benefit for it, see instructions.	16	Gifts by cash or check. If you made any gift of $250 or more, see instructions.	**16**	7,000	
	17	Other than by cash or check. If any gift of $250 or more, see instructions. You **must** attach Form 8283 if over $500 . . .	**17**	25,000	
	18	Carryover from prior year	**18**		
	19	Add lines 16 through 18		**19**	32,000
Casualty and Theft Losses	20	Casualty or theft loss(es) other than net qualified disaster losses. Attach Form 4684 and enter the amount from line 18 of that form. See instructions		**20**	
Job Expenses and Certain Miscellaneous Deductions	21	Unreimbursed employee expenses—job travel, union dues, job education, etc. Attach Form 2106 or 2106-EZ if required. See instructions. ▶ _____	**21**		
	22	Tax preparation fees	**22**		
	23	Other expenses—investment, safe deposit box, etc. List type and amount ▶ _____	**23**		
	24	Add lines 21 through 23	**24**		
	25	Enter amount from Form 1040, line 38 **25**			
	26	Multiply line 25 by 2% (0.02)	**26**		
	27	Subtract line 26 from line 24. If line 26 is more than line 24, enter -0-		**27**	
Other Miscellaneous Deductions	28	Other—from list in instructions. List type and amount ▶ _____ _____		**28**	
Total Itemized Deductions	29	Is Form 1040, line 38, over $156,900? ☐ **No.** Your deduction is not limited. Add the amounts in the far right column for lines 4 through 28. Also, enter this amount on Form 1040, line 40. ☑ **Yes.** Your deduction may be limited. See the Itemized Deductions Worksheet in the instructions to figure the amount to enter. } . .		**29**	88,150
	30	If you elect to itemize deductions even though they are less than your standard deduction, check here ▶ ☐			

For Paperwork Reduction Act Notice, see the Instructions for Form 1040. Cat. No. 17145C Schedule A (Form 1040) 2017

FIGURE 5.3 Schedule A itemized deductions

If they have the same income and expenses in 2018, they can deduct only $74,650 as itemized deductions, because their total deduction for taxes is now limited to $10,000.

5.5 QUALIFIED BUSINESS INCOME DEDUCTION

A new deduction was added for 2018–2025 to address the difference between the tax rates for C corporation and pass-through businesses (including sole proprietorships, partnerships, S corporations, and LLCs) that are taxed at their owners' individual rates. Under new Section 199A, this deduction is 20 percent of qualified business income (QBI). QBI is defined as the net amount of items of income, gain, deduction, and loss from an eligible business conducted in the U.S.

It excludes investment-related items (capital gains, capital losses, dividends, and nonbusiness interest income), reasonable compensation paid to the individual, and guaranteed payments from a partnership.

This deduction cannot exceed 20 percent of the excess of the taxpayer's income over net capital gain, however. If QBI is negative (less than zero), it is treated as a loss from a qualified business in the next year.

Example 5.26

Tim and Sara, a married couple filing a joint return in 2018, have $190,000 in taxable income computed as follows: $200,000 income from an S corporation plus $30,000 in net capital gains less $40,000 in itemized deductions. Their Section 199A deduction is limited to the lesser of: (a) 20% of $200,000 qualified business income = $40,000 or (b) 20% of $190,000 taxable income less $30,000 net capital gains = $32,000, resulting in a maximum deduction of $32,000.

Several rules may limit the amount of the deduction for high-income taxpayers with taxable income in excess of $157,000 ($315,000 for married couples filing a joint return). These limitations are based on the W-2 wages and the adjusted basis of qualified property acquired by the business. Specifically, the deduction cannot exceed the greater of (1) 50 percent of the taxpayer's share of the W-2 wages paid by the business or (2) the sum of 25 percent of such W-2 wages plus 2.5 percent of the unadjusted basis of tangible depreciable business property acquired.

Example 5.27

Marco is single and has taxable income of $500,000. As a 25% partner in a partnership that produces ordinary income of $800,000, his share of partnership income is $200,000. The partnership paid $144,000 of W-2 wages and the total unadjusted basis of tangible depreciable business property is $150,000; his 25% share of W-2 wages is $36,000 ($144,000 × 25%) and his 25% share of property is $30,000 ($120,000 × 25%). The greater of the two limits is $18,000 computed as follows:

1. $36,000 share of W-2 wages × 50% = $18,000 or
2. $36,000 shares of W-2 wages × 25% = $9,000 plus $30,000 share of property × 2.5% = $750 for a total of $9,750.

Although 20% of Marco's $200,000 partnership QBI is $40,000, his deduction is limited to $18,000 by the W-2 wage limitation.

There are also rules to prevent taxpayers with taxable income above the $157,000 (or $315,000) threshold from converting compensation for personal services into income eligible for this deduction. This deduction phases out for high-incomes taxpayers that are in a service business, including accounting, law, health, consulting, financial services, performing arts, actuarial science, athletics, brokerage services, investing, trading in securities, or any business where the principal asset is the reputation or skill of its employees (except for engineering and architecture which are specifically excluded). The deduction gradually phases out for taxpayers in these service businesses for incomes between $157,500 and $207,500 ($315,000 and $415,000 if married filing jointly). If a taxpayer is in one of the affected service business and taxable income exceeds $207,500 ($415,000 if married filing a joint return), the QBI deduction is zero for that business.

Example 5.28

Daniel's taxable income is $187,500 of which $138,000 is attributable to his consulting sole proprietorship. He paid W-2 wages of $70,000 to his employees. Because his taxable income exceeds the $157,500 threshold by $30,000, 60% will be phase out ($30,000 excess above threshold/$50,000 phase out range = 60%) so he can take into account only 40% of his $138,000 consulting income of $55,200 in determining his QBI. He then takes into account 40% of $70,000 wages or $28,000. Daniel computes his deduction by taking the lesser of: (a) 20% × $55,200 eligible QBI = $11,040 or (b) 50% × $28,000 eligible wages = $14,000. Daniel can take a Section 199A deduction of $11,040.

This new deduction is discussed in more detail in Chapter 11.

5.6 DEPENDENTS

Prior to 2018, a taxpayer was allowed to claim a deduction for each qualifying dependent and an additional personal exemption deduction for himself or herself of ($4,050 in 2017, scheduled to increase for inflation to $4,150 for 2018); married taxpayers filing a joint return were allowed to claim one personal exemption for the taxpayer and one for the spouse.[54]

Taxpayers could only claim a dependency exemption deduction for an individual who was either a qualifying child or other qualifying relative. A qualifying child had to meet four tests and other qualifying relatives had to meet three similar tests. In addition, a dependent could not file a joint return with a spouse and had be a citizen or national of the United States or a resident of the United States.[55]

For 2018–2025, the deduction is suspended while preserving all of the rules for determining who is a dependent for use in other provisions (such as determining head of household status and the child tax credit). This essentially makes the deduction for personal and dependency exemptions zero for 2018–2025.

5.6.1 QUALIFYING CHILD

A qualifying child must satisfy each of these four tests to qualify as a **dependent**:[56]

1. a residency test,
2. a relationship test,
3. an age test, and
4. a support test.

To satisfy the residency test, the child must have the same principal place of abode as the taxpayer for more than one-half of the year. Temporary absences for educational purposes, vacations, illness, business, or military service, are ignored for purposes of this test.

To meet the relationship test, the child must be the taxpayer's son, daughter, brother, sister, or descendant of any of these individuals (for example, a grandchild).[57]

[54] If one spouse died during the year, the surviving spouse could file a joint return for the year and claim two personal exemptions.

[55] An adopted child who is a nonresident alien will qualify as a dependent as long as the taxpayer is a citizen or national of the United States, the taxpayer and the child have the same principal residence, and the child is a member of the taxpayer's household for the taxable year. §152(b)(c).

[56] §152(c). The definition of qualifying child also applies to the child tax credit (if the child is under age 17), the earned income credit, the dependent care credit (if the child is under age 13 or disabled), and for the head-of-household filing status.

[57] A child includes a legally adopted child or stepchild and a stepbrother or stepsister; a foster child must live in the home the entire year. §152(c) and (f).

To satisfy the age test, the child must be under age 19 (or under age 24 if a full-time student during at least 5 calendar months of the tax year). Additionally, the child must be younger than the taxpayer. There is no age limit for individuals who are totally and permanently disabled.

If a child provides more than one-half of his or her own support during the year the support test cannot be met. Additionally, a child cannot be a qualifying child if he or she files a joint return, unless the return was filed only to claim a refund.

Special tie-breaking rules apply if the child could be a qualifying child of more than one individual (for example, a child who lives with his or her mother and grandmother in the same home). In this case, a parent takes precedence over other relatives. If both parents want to claim the child but do not file a joint return, the child is deemed a qualifying child of the parent with whom the child resides for the longer period of time. If the child resides with both parents for an equal amount of time, then the child is a qualifying child of the parent with the higher adjusted gross income. If neither parent claims the child, the child can be claimed by another qualifying relative with the highest adjusted gross income (if it is higher than the highest adjusted gross income of either of the child's parents).[58]

5.6.2 QUALIFYING RELATIVES

If the individual is not a qualifying child, then he or she must pass three tests to be a dependent:

1. a relationship test,
2. a support test, and
3. a gross income test.

Under the relationship test, the dependent must either be a qualifying relative of the taxpayer *or* a resident in the taxpayer's household for the entire year.[59]

Qualifying relatives include the following.[60]

- Parents, grandparents, and other direct ancestors.
- Children, grandchildren, and other lineal descendants. Children include stepchildren, adopted children, and foster children who live with the taxpayer for the entire year.
- Sisters and brothers, including stepbrothers and stepsisters.
- Sisters and brothers of the taxpayer's parents.
- Children of brothers and sisters.
- In-laws including brothers and sisters-in-law, sons-in-law, daughters-in-law, mothers-in-law, and fathers-in-law.

A cousin is not a qualifying relative, but could be claimed as a dependent if he or she meets the member of household test. In addition, only nieces, nephews, aunts, and uncles by blood are qualifying relatives. Relationships established by marriage do not end with divorce or death, however.

[58] For divorced parents, the exemption could be transferred to the noncustodial parent if the custodial parent completed Form 8332: *Release of Claim to Exemption for Child of Divorced or Separated Parents*.

[59] The relationship cannot be in violation of local or state law. If a man and woman live together in violation of local or state law, no dependency relationship exists. If the state declares them common law husband and wife, they could file a joint tax return.

[60] Qualifying relatives do not have to live in the taxpayer's household. In most cases, however, a dependent's failure to live in the taxpayer's household for more than half the year prevents the taxpayer from claiming head of household status, unless otherwise qualified.

Example 5.29

Mary and John are married and have two children who live with them. In addition, Mary's cousin lived with them the entire year and they also supported John's aged father who is in a nursing home. Assuming the other dependency tests are met, Mary and John have four dependents: their two children, Mary's cousin, and John's father. The cousin qualifies as a member of the household (lived with them the entire year) and John's father is a qualifying relative and does not need to live in the same household.

Support Test

The taxpayer must provide more than half the support for an individual to be considered a dependent and that support must exceed support provided by anyone else, including the potential dependent.[61] Support includes amounts spent for food, clothing, shelter, medical and dental care, recreational items, summer camp, and education.[62] Support also includes capital expenditures made solely on behalf of the dependent, such as a car purchased by the taxpayer for the dependent. Support excludes the value of services provided for the individual and scholarships.[63] The source of the funds is irrelevant; thus, nontaxable income used for support must be included in the support determination.

Example 5.30

John and Martha provide $15,000 support to their 25-year-old daughter, Ann, a full-time student at the state university, and help support John's mother, who lives in a separate apartment. His mother spent $10,000 of her Social Security payments for clothes, utilities, and groceries. John and Martha only paid the $700 monthly rent on the apartment ($8,400 in total). Ann has a swimming scholarship that pays her annual tuition of $15,000. John and Martha can treat Ann as a dependent because the scholarship does not count as support, assuming the other dependency tests are met. His mother, however, does not qualify as a dependent because she provided more than half of her support. It is irrelevant that it came from tax-exempt Social Security income.

Gross Income Test

A potential dependent's taxable gross income must be less than the exemption amount for the year ($4,050 for 2017 and $4,150 for 2018).[64]

Example 5.31

Jack provides more than half the support for his elderly mother, whose only income is $12,000 of Social Security and $3,000 from interest on state and local bonds. Jack's mother has no taxable gross income (her income is from sources that are excluded from gross income) and can qualify as Jack's dependent if all other tests are met.

Jack also provides more than half the support of his 26-year-old brother, whose income for the year consists of $4,200 from a part-time job. The income earned from the part-time job is included in the brother's taxable gross income and exceeds the exemption amount for the year. Thus, Jack's brother will not qualify as a dependent.

---

[61] A multiple support agreement allowed one member of a group providing more than half of the dependent's support to claim the dependency exemption.
[62] Reg. §1.152-1(a)(2).
[63] §152(d).
[64] For 2018, $4,150 is to be used when a dollar amount is needed for the exemption amount.

Table 5.5 compares the dependency requirements for a qualifying child with the requirements for a qualifying relative.

Table 5.5 Dependency Requirements

Test	Qualifying child	Qualifying relative
Residence	Lives with taxpayer for more than half of the year (temporary absences for education, vacation, illness, business, or military service are ignored for this test).	Not applicable.
Relationship	Taxpayer's child, stepchild, foster child, brother, sister, half-brother, half-sister, or a descendant of any of these relatives.	Taxpayer's descendant or ancestor, brother or sister, stepmother or stepfather, stepbrother or stepsister, niece, nephew, aunt, uncle, in-law, or any individual (except a spouse) who lives with the taxpayer for the entire year.
Age	Child must be under age 19 or a full-time student under age 24 and younger than the taxpayer claiming the child. No age limit for individuals who are totally and permanently disabled.	Not applicable.
Support	Child must not provide more than half of his or her own support.	Taxpayer must provide more than half of the support for the qualifying relative (except if claiming under a multiple support agreement).
Gross income	Not applicable.	Gross income must be less than exemption amount ($4,050 for 2017 and $4,150 for 2018).

5.7 TAX CREDITS

5.7.1 CREDITS VERSUS DEDUCTIONS

Deductions reduce a taxpayer's taxable income, but the actual tax savings depend on the taxpayer's marginal tax rate. In contrast, credits reduce the tax liability dollar-for-dollar. When considering tax policy, a tax credit has the advantage of providing equal tax relief for all taxpayers regardless of their marginal tax bracket. The benefit of a tax deduction depends on the taxpayer's marginal tax rate. A $1,300 tax credit provides the same tax savings to a person in the 12 percent marginal tax bracket as it does a taxpayer in the 37 percent marginal tax bracket.

Tax credits can be refundable or nonrefundable. A nonrefundable credit can reduce the gross tax liability to zero, but any excess credit is lost. Refundable credits in excess of the tax liability are refunded to the taxpayer. Most credits are listed in the credits section of Form 1040 on page 2, just below the income tax liability calculation. Refundable credits, however, are part of the payments section of Form 1040, along with taxes withheld and estimated tax payments. They receive the same treatment as excess taxes withheld and can create a refund. Most of the common credits available to individual taxpayers are summarized in the following sections.

5.7.2 CHILD TAX CREDIT

A taxpayer can claim a tax credit for each of the taxpayer's qualifying children under age 17; the amount of the credit for each child is $2,000 for 2018 ($1,000 for 2017).[65] A credit of up to $1,400 is refundable in 2018; if the taxpayer owes no taxes, he or she can still receive a refund

[65] The definition of a "qualifying child" is the same as previously discussed under dependents.

of up to $1,400 per child. To claim the credit, the child's social security number must be reported on the tax return.

In addition to the credit for a qualifying child, a new nonrefundable $500 credit is allowed for each of the taxpayer's dependents other than a qualifying child (such as a grandmother who lives with the taxpayer). A dependent for this credit is a qualifying relative (as defined in section 5.6.2. of this chapter on dependents) who is a U.S. citizen, national, or resident of the United States.

The total child tax credit is phased out at the rate of $50 for every $1,000 (or part thereof) of modified AGI in excess of $400,000 for married taxpayers filing jointly and $200,000 for all other taxpayers for 2018.[66]

Example 5.32

Carol and John, married with three dependent children ages 8, 12, and 17, have AGI of $414,000. They are eligible for the child tax credit for the two children under age 17 but must reduce their $4,000 child tax credit by $700 {[($414,000 – $400,000)/1,000] × $50} to $3,300.

All or part of this tax credit may be treated as a refundable credit to the extent of 15 percent of the taxpayer's earned income in excess of $2,500 for 2018 ($3,000 for 2017).[67] The refundable portion is referred to as an additional child tax credit and is reported on a separate line in the tax payments section of the tax return.

Example 5.33

Joseph is a single parent with two young children for whom he claims a $4,000 child tax credit in 2018. His income is only $16,000, which does not exceed his standard deduction. Thus, he owes no income tax. Without the refund provision, he would have no benefit from the credit. This provision allows him to receive a refund of $2,025 [($16,000 – $2,500) × 15%] for the child tax credit.

If Joseph's income had been only $8,500, then only $900 [($8,500 – $2,500) × 15%] would have been refundable.

5.7.3 EDUCATION CREDITS

There are two elective tax credits that apply to a taxpayers' cost of undergraduate or graduate education or vocational training. The American opportunity tax credit equals 100 percent of the first $2,000 and 25 percent of the next $2,000 for qualifying expenses for each year of postsecondary education pursued on at least a half-time basis.[68] This $2,500 credit is limited to four years for each student.

The lifetime learning credit equals 20 percent of qualifying expenses up to a $10,000 annual maximum for part-time or full-time undergraduate, graduate, or professional degree programs. This $2,000 annual lifetime learning credit limit does not vary with the number of students in the taxpayer's family;[69] however, it is available for an unlimited number of years.[70]

---

[66] Modified AGI is adjusted gross income plus any excluded foreign earned income.

[67] For taxpayers with 3 or more qualifying children, the credit is refundable to the extent of the greater of (1) the excess of the taxpayer's Social Security taxes over earned income or (2) 15% of earned income in excess of $3,000.

[68] For 2016 and 2017, the maximum American opportunity credit was also $2,500 per student. The previous Hope scholarship credit (that the American opportunity credit replaced) could be claimed for only the first two years of higher education for each student.

[69] For 2016 and 2017, the maximum lifetime learning credit was also $2,000 per taxpayer.

[70] §25A(c)(1).

The taxpayer, the taxpayer's spouse, and the taxpayer's dependents may be eligible for both of these credits. A student claimed as a dependent on a parent's or another's return cannot claim either credit on his or her own return. Any qualified tuition or related expenses paid by the child during the year, however, are treated as paid by the parent and are deductible on the parent's return.[71]

Qualifying expenses for the American opportunity credit include the tuition and fees paid by an individual to attend an eligible institution. They include the required course materials (textbooks, supplies, and equipment) purchased at the institution or elsewhere. Qualifying lifetime learning credit expenses include tuition and fees but exclude textbooks and other course-related materials (unless the institution requires the payment). Costs and fees associated with room, board, student activities, athletics, insurance, transportation, and similar personal, living, or family expenses do not qualify for either credit. Non-credit courses involving sports, games, or hobbies are not eligible for any credit, unless part of the student's degree program.[72]

Calculating these credits only takes into account the student's out-of-pocket expenses. Expenses paid with a Pell grant, a tax-free scholarship, or a tax-free employer-provided educational assistance plan are not out-of-pocket expenses.[73] The student's expenses must be paid with income, loans, gifts, inheritances, or personal savings. Any qualifying expenses for which the American opportunity credit is claimed for a particular student, prevent the student's claiming the lifetime learning credit for any of the student's other qualifying expenses for the year. In addition, expenses paid with distributions from a Coverdell educational savings account (educational IRA) are not eligible for either the American opportunity or lifetime learning credit (although excess expenses may qualify). A taxpayer who claims either the American opportunity or lifetime learning credit is allowed no deduction for any of that student's other education expenses.

The American opportunity and lifetime learning credits are both targeted to low and middle-income taxpayers and are subject to income-based phaseouts.[74] The American opportunity credit phases out over a modified adjusted gross income range of $80,000 to $90,000 for single taxpayers ($160,000 to $180,000 for married taxpayers filing a joint return). Modified adjusted gross income is adjusted gross income increased by any excluded foreign earned income. A percentage determined by dividing modified AGI in excess of the $80,000 ($160,000 for joint return filers) threshold by the $10,000 ($20,000 for joint return filers) reduces the phaseout range. Thus, single taxpayers with $90,000 and joint filers with $180,000 of modified adjusted gross income exceed the income limit and cannot claim the American opportunity credit.

Example 5.34

Ricardo and Lucy's joint return shows AGI of $175,000 for 2018. Their two sons, Ricky and Billy are full-time students at State University. Ricky is a freshman and Billy is a junior. Ricardo and Lucy pay $4,000 in qualified tuition annually for each son. Because their AGI is greater than $160,000, they are not allowed to claim the full $5,000 ($2,500 for each son) American opportunity credit. Their tentative credit of $2,500 per student is partially phased out and Ricardo and Lucy can only claim an American opportunity credit of $1,250 ($625 for each son) computed as follows:

$$(\$175,000 - \$160,000)/\$20,000 = 75\%$$
$$75\% \times \$2,500 \text{ tentative credit} = \$1,875 \text{ phaseout}$$
$$\$2,500 \text{ tentative credit} - \$1,875 \text{ phaseout} = \$625 \text{ allowable credit for each student}$$

[71] §25A(g)(3). If a third party pays the education expenses for a student who is claimed as a dependent by another taxpayer, the dependent will be considered to have paid the expenses and the taxpayer claiming the students as a dependent can claim the education credit.

[72] §25A(f).

[73] §25A(g)(2).

[74] §25A(d). The American opportunity credit is partially refundable (up to 40 percent); if, however, the taxpayer is subject to the kiddie tax (see Chapter 12), the credit is not refundable. The American opportunity credit may also offset a taxpayer's alternative minimum tax liability. The lifetime learning credit is neither refundable nor can it offset an alternative minimum tax liability.

The lifetime learning credit also phases out proportionately, but over a modified AGI range of $57,000 to $67,000 for single taxpayers ($114,000 to $134,000 for joint return filers).[75] Similar to the American opportunity credit, a reduction in the taxpayer's lifetime learning credit is determined by dividing modified AGI in excess of the $57,000 ($114,000 for joint filers) threshold by the $10,000 ($20,000 for joint returns) phaseout range. Taxpayers with modified adjusted gross incomes exceeding $67,000 ($134,000 for joint filers) may not claim the lifetime learning credit.

Example 5.35

Mason, a single taxpayer with modified AGI of $61,000, pays $7,000 tuition for MBA courses in management in 2018. Mason's tentative lifetime learning credit is $1,400 ($7,000 × 20%). His modified AGI exceeds the threshold for single taxpayers by $4,000 or 40 percent of the phaseout range [($61,000 AGI − $57,000 threshold AGI)/$10,000]; his $1,400 tentative lifetime learning credit is reduced by $560 ($1,400 × 40%) to $840.

Table 5.6 compares the American opportunity and the lifetime learning credits. For both credits, qualified tuition and fees generally include only out-of-pocket expenses and exclude expenses covered by employer-provided educational assistance programs (see Chapter 4) or scholarships unless the payments are included in gross income.

Table 5.6 Comparison of Education Credits

	American opportunity credit	Lifetime learning credit
Maximum benefit	Maximum $2,500 credit per year per student	Maximum $2,000 credit per year per taxpayer
Phase-out range	Phase-out range $80,000 to $90,000 AGI ($160,000 to $180,000 if MFJ)	Phase-out range $57,000 to $67,000 AGI ($114,000 to $134,000 if MFJ)
Refundable or nonrefundable	40% of credit is refundable	Nonrefundable
Qualifying expenses	Tuition, fees and course materials (course-related books, supplies and equipment do not need to be purchased from the institution to qualify)	Tuition and fees (only includes course-related books, supplies and equipment if required to be paid to the institution)
Number of years credit available	4 years per student	Unlimited
Minimum enrollment	Must be enrolled at least half-time	Available for one or more courses
Type of program	Program must lead to degree or other recognized credential	No requirement

TAX PLANNING

When an educational institution reduces tuition for an employee (or the spouse or dependent child of an employee) and includes the tuition reduction in the employee's gross income, the tuition reduction may qualify for an education credit. The employee is treated as receiving taxable income equal to the tuition reduction followed by payment of that amount to the educational institution.

5.7.4 DEPENDENT CARE CREDIT

Taxpayers who are employed and pay for child or dependent care are eligible for a dependent care credit. The credit percentage, however, varies from 20 to 35 percent of qualifying expenditures

[75] The phaseout range for the lifetime learning credit for 2017 was $56,000 to $66,000 for single taxpayers and $112,000 to $132,000 for joint return filers.

based on the taxpayer's AGI. The credit is 35 percent of qualifying expenses for taxpayers with AGI not exceeding $15,000. The rate is gradually reduced to 20 percent at the rate of 1 percent for each $2,000 (or fraction thereof) that AGI exceeds $15,000. Any taxpayer with AGI exceeding $43,000 is allowed the 20 percent credit for qualifying expenses. Qualifying expenses include costs incurred for babysitting, cooking, and housekeeping, but exclude expenses for a gardener, chauffeur, or an overnight camp. The credit is limited to $3,000 of qualifying expenses for one eligible child or $6,000 for two or more eligible children (however divided between them) under the age of 13.[76]

Example 5.36

Celina, a single attorney, has AGI of $50,000. Celina spent $6,000 for child-care during the year for her four-year-old daughter while she worked. Only $3,000 qualifies for the credit. Celina's child care credit is $600 ($3,000 × 20%). If she spent only $2,000 on child care, her credit would be $400 ($2,000 × 20%). If Celine also has both eleven and four-year-old daughters for whom she paid $400 and $6,000, respectively, for childcare, she could base her credit on the maximum $6,000 even though she only spent $400 for the older child's care.

The child care credit is a nonrefundable credit; that is, there is no refund or carryover if the credit exceeds the tax liability—the excess credit is simply lost.

5.7.5 EARNED INCOME CREDIT

The standard deduction shelters many low-income individuals from paying income tax, but does nothing to minimize the effect of payroll taxes. The earned income credit reduces the impact of payroll taxes through a refundable credit. This credit, available to lower-income taxpayers, equals a certain percentage of the taxpayer's earned income below a creditable maximum.[77] The credit percentages vary depending on whether the taxpayer has one, two, or three or more, or no qualifying children in the home. Earned income includes salary, wages, tips, and net self-employment income.

In 2018, the maximum earned income credit for a taxpayer with one qualifying child is $3,461 ($10,180 × 34%), $5,716 ($14,290 × 40%) for a taxpayer with two qualifying children, and $6,431 ($14,290 × 45%) for three or more qualifying children. If the greater of AGI or earned income exceeds $24,350 for married taxpayers filing a joint return ($18,660 for others), the credit gradually phases out.

A small credit is available to taxpayers with no qualifying children, but only applies to working taxpayers ages 25 through 64 who cannot be claimed as a dependent of another taxpayer. For 2018, this credit is 7.65 percent of earned income up to $6,780 ($519 credit). It gradually phases out at incomes exceeding $14,170 for married taxpayers filing a joint return and $8,490 for others.

Taxpayers do not have to calculate the earned income credit. The IRS provides simplified tables that show the credit for all qualifying income levels and family sizes.[78] The earned income credit is refundable; thus, any part of the credit greater than the taxpayer's income tax liability is refunded to the taxpayer. If the taxpayer has $3,500 or more of investment income (unearned income), no credit can be claimed.

---

[76] §21. There is no age limit for disabled dependents. The maximum qualifying expense cannot exceed the individual's earned income. For married couples, the limitation applies to the earned income of the spouse with the lower income. A spouse who is a full-time student or is incapacitated is considered to have earned income of $250 per month for purposes of claiming the credit for one qualifying person or $500 a month for a couple claiming the credit for more than one qualifying person. §21(d)(2).

[77] §32. In 2017, the maximum amount of earned income on which the earned income tax credit was computed was $6,670 for taxpayers with no qualifying children, $10,000 for taxpayers with one qualifying child, and $14,040 for taxpayers with two or more qualifying children.

[78] Refer to the instructions for Schedule EIC for the table.

Example 5.37

Emily has a gross income tax liability of $600. She has an earned income credit of $1,000. The credit completely eliminates her tax liability and creates a $400 refund for her.

5.7.6 EXCESS PAYROLL TAX WITHHELD

If an individual works for more than one employer during the year and earnings exceed the Social Security ceiling of $128,400 in 2018 ($127,200 in 2017), excess Social Security tax will be withheld.[79] Each employer performs payroll tax calculations independent of any other employer the taxpayer may have had during the year. The employee has a credit for any excess Social Security taxes withheld that can create or increase a refund.

Example 5.38

Tim worked for Alpha Company the first seven months of 2018, earning $80,000 from which Alpha withheld $6,120 ($80,000 × 7.65%) for payroll taxes. In August, Tim accepted a job with Baker Company. During the last five months of the year he earned $60,000 and Baker withheld $4,590 ($60,000 × 7.65%) for payroll taxes. The 1.45 percent Medicare portion of the tax is owed on Tim's entire $140,000 ($80,000 + $60,000) earned in 2018, but the 6.2 percent Social Security portion of the tax is due on only the first $128,400 of salary. Baker Company withheld $719 excess payroll taxes computed as follows:

Payroll taxes withheld:		
Alpha Company ($80,000 × 7.65%)		$6,120
Baker Company ($60,000 × 7.65%)		4,590
Total payroll taxes withheld		$10,710
Tim's 2018 payroll tax:		
$140,000 total wages × 1.45% Medicare tax	$2,030	
$128,400 Social Security ceiling × 6.2%	7,961	
Total payroll taxes		9,991
Excess withheld		$ 719

Tim claims a $719 refundable tax credit for the excess payroll tax withheld. This credit has no effect on his employers, however, as they are not entitled to a refund of any excess employer payroll tax.

5.7.7 OTHER CREDITS

Table 5.7 lists other common tax credits available to individual taxpayers.

Table 5.7 Other Credits

Type of tax credit	Description
Adoption Credit	A nonrefundable credit of $13,810 in 2018 is allowed for expenses incurred to adopt an eligible child. Credit phases out for taxpayers with AGIs exceeding $207,140.
Elderly or Disabled Credit	A nonrefundable credit for low-income individuals who are age 65 or older or who retired because of a permanent disability. The maximum credit is 15% of the $5,000 base amount ($7,500 MFJ) less reductions for Social Security and other nontaxable benefits and one-half of AGI in excess of $7,500 ($10,000 MFJ).
Retirement Savings Contributions Credit	A nonrefundable credit of up to 50 percent of contributions to employer retirement plans or IRAs (maximum credit is $1,000). Credit rate (50, 20 or 10 percent) depends on filing status and AGI. No credit is available once AGI exceeds $31,500 if single ($63,000 if married filing a joint return). An individual who is a dependent, a full-time student, or is not at least age 18, is not eligible for this credit.
Foreign Tax Credit	Individuals with foreign income can choose to take a deduction for foreign taxes paid or claim a foreign tax credit (discussed in Chapter 4).

[79] Social Security and other payroll taxes are discussed in Chapter 4.

5.8 COMPUTING THE TAX

After determining taxable income, individuals compute their gross income tax liability. The complete tax rate schedules for individual taxpayers for 2018 are shown in Table 5.8. Individuals use the appropriate schedule based on filing status to determine their tax liability.

Table 5.8 Tax Rate Schedules for 2018

Schedule X Single Individuals

If taxable income is:	*The tax is:*
Not over $9,525	10% of taxable income
Over $9,525 but not over $38,700	$952.50 plus 12% of the excess over $9,525
Over $38,700 but not over $82,500	$4,453.50 plus 22% of the excess over $38,700
Over $82,500 but not over $157,500	$14,089.50 plus 24% of the excess over $82,500
Over $157,500 but not over $200,000	$32,089.50 plus 32% of the excess over $157,500
Over $200,000 but not over $500,000	$45,689.50 plus 35% of the excess over $200,000
Over $500,000	$150,689.50 plus 37% of the excess over $500,000

Schedule Y-1 Married Individuals Filing Joint Returns

If taxable income is:	*The tax is:*
Not over $19,050	10% of taxable income
Over $19,050 but not over $77,400	$1,905 plus 12% of the excess over $19,050
Over $77,400 but not over $165,000	$8,907 plus 22% of the excess over $77,400
Over $165,000 but not over $315,000	$28,179 plus 24% of the excess over $165,000
Over $315,000 but not over $400,000	$64,179 plus 32% of the excess over $315,000
Over $400,000 but not over $600,000	$91,379 plus 35% of the excess over $400,000
Over $600,000	$161,379 plus 37% of the excess over $600,000

Schedule Y-2 Married Individuals Filing Separate Returns

If taxable income is:	*The tax is:*
Not over $9,525	10% of taxable income
Over $9,525 but not over $38,700	$952.50 plus 12% of the excess over $9,525
Over $38,700 but not over $82,500	$4,453.50 plus 22% of the excess over $38,700
Over $82,500 but not over $157,500	$14,089.50 plus 24% of the excess over $82,500
Over $157,500 but not over $200,000	$32,089.50 plus 32% of the excess over $157,500
Over $200,000 but not over $300,000	$45,689.50 plus 35% of the excess over $200,000
Over $300,000	$80,689.50 plus 37% of the excess over $300,000

Schedule Z Heads of Households

If taxable income is:	*The tax is:*
Not over $13,600	10% of taxable income
Over $13,600 but not over $51,800	$1,360 plus 12% of the excess over $13,600
Over $51,800 but not over $82,500	$5,944 plus 22% of the excess over $51,800
Over $82,500 but not over $157,500	$12,698 plus 24% of the excess over $82,500
Over $157,500 but not over $200,000	$30,698 plus 32% of the excess over $157,500
Over $200,000 but not over $500,000	$44,298 plus 35% of the excess over $200,000
Over $500,000	$149,298 plus 37% of the excess over $500,000

Example 5.39

Jennie, single with a dependent child in her home, files as head of household. Her 2018 taxable income is $58,000. Using Schedule Z, her gross income tax liability is $7,308 [$5,944 + 22%($58,000 – $51,800)].

If Jennie were a recent widow and qualified as a surviving spouse, she would use Schedule Y-1 for joint return filers and her tax liability would be only $6,579 [$1,905 + 12%($58,000 – $19,050)].

As a surviving spouse, Jennie's tax liability is lower than filing as head of household, because she did not reach the 22 percent tax bracket. The married filing a joint return schedule (used by a surviving spouse) provides the lowest tax liability for any given amount of taxable income.

Qualifying dividend income and long-term capital gains are taxed at lower favorable rates as summarized in Table 5.9 (note that the break points are not the same as the break points for the ordinary income rates). When an individual has a net long-term capital gain from sales of capital assets, he or she files a Schedule D: *Capital Gains and Losses* to separately report these gains and losses (see Chapter 8 for more details). The instructions for this schedule include a worksheet to determine total tax liability when long-term capital gains are included in the taxpayer's taxable income. Similarly, there is a worksheet to determine the tax due on dividend income.

Table 5.9 Tax Rates for Dividend Income and Long-term Capital Gains

Long-term capital gains and dividend tax rate*	Taxable income for single individuals	Taxable income for married filing a joint return**	Taxable income for head of household
0%	$0–$38,600	$0–$77,200	$0–$51,700
15%	$38,601–$425,800	$77,201–$479,000	$51,701–$452,400
20%	Over $425,800	Over $479,000	Over $452,400

*Rate can be as high as 28% for collectibles and 25% for unrecaptured §1250 gain (see Chapter 8).
**Amounts if married filing separately are half the amount for filing a joint return.

Example 5.40

George is single and has $55,000 of taxable income, including $2,000 in qualified dividend income and an $8,000 long-term capital gain, both taxed at the 15 percent rate in 2018. George's tax on his $45,000 of ordinary income is $5,839.50 [$4,453.50 + 22% ($45,000 – $38,700)]. His tax on the dividend income and capital gains is $1,500 ($10,000 × 15%). His total tax liability is $7,339.50. The favorable dividend and capital gains rate saves George $700 [$10,000 × (22% – 15%)].

Congress limits the tax savings from asset transfers to children by taxing unearned income (dividend, interest, and net capital gains) of certain children at the rates that apply to estates and trusts, as presented in Table 5.10. This tax is generally referred to as the *kiddie tax* because it applies to children under age 19 and full-time students under age 24. A special tax calculation applies only to the child's net unearned income that exceeds $2,100, but does not apply to earned income (such as salaries and wages) or to children whose net unearned income is $2,100 or less.

Table 5.10 Tax Rates for Kiddie Tax

Income Tax Rates for Trusts and Estates and Kiddie Tax	
If taxable income is:	***The tax is:***
Not over $2,550	10% of taxable income
Over $2,550 but not over $9,150	$255.00 plus 24% of the excess over $2,550
Over $9,150 but not over $12,500	$1,839.00 plus 35% of the excess over $9,150
Over $12,500	$3,011.50 plus 37% of the excess over $12,500
Tax Rates for Long-term Capital Gains and Dividend Income	
If taxable income is:	***The tax rate is:***
Not over $2,600	0%
Over $2,600 but not over $12,700	15%
Over $12,700	20%

The tax calculation is a four-step process:

1. Determine the child's taxable income; if the child is a dependent, the child's standard deduction is limited to the greater of $1,050 or earned income plus $350.

2. Calculate the tax on the child's net unearned income in excess of $2,100 using the tax rates for estates and trusts.

3. The child's remaining taxable income is taxed at the child's normal tax rates (for a single individual).

4. Add the taxes determined in (2) and (3) to determine the child's gross income tax liability.

The tax calculated is then compared to the tax that would be paid if all of the child's income were taxed at the child's normal rates. The greater of these two amounts is the tax that must be paid. It is unlikely that the child's tax would exceed that determined under the kiddie tax rules, as that would require the child's income to fall into a higher tax bracket than the trust tax rate.

Example 5.41

Monica, age 13, has $12,100 interest income from bonds given to her by her parents; this is her only source of income for the year. She has no itemized deductions. Monica's net unearned income is $10,000, the interest income in excess of $2,100. Her taxable income is $11,050 ($12,100 – $1,050 standard deduction). Monica's tax on her unearned income at the tax rates used for estates and trusts is $2,137 [$1,839 + ($850 × 35%)]. The remaining $1,050 income ($11,050 taxable income – $10,000 taxed at rates for estates and trusts) is taxed at the child's regular rates resulting in $105 of tax ($1,050 × 10%). The total tax owed is $2,242 ($2,137 + $105).

The kiddie tax does not apply to a child age 19 or older, unless that child is a full-time student; it will not apply to any child age 24 or older regardless of student status. Age is determined at the end of the year under current law. The kiddie tax is discussed in more detail in Chapter 12.

5.8.1 MEDICARE SURTAXES

As discussed in Chapter 4, employees and employers pay 6.2 percent Social Security and 1.45 percent Medicare (FICA) taxes on salaries and wages. Self-employed individuals must pay both the employer's and employee's portion of these taxes for a combined 15.3 percent tax called self-employment tax. Self-employed individuals compute this tax on Schedule SE and pay it along with their regular income tax on Form 1040.

Since 2013, taxpayers pay an additional Medicare tax if certain income thresholds are exceeded. The thresholds are $200,000 for single individuals (and heads of household), $250,000 for married taxpayers filing a joint return, and $125,000 for married taxpayers filing separately. The Medicare surtax rate is 0.9 percent on taxable compensation income and is imposed on the employee (or self-employed person) only and not on the employer. Employers are required to withhold the additional Medicare surtax from salary, wages, or other compensation they pay to employees in excess of $200,000. Any additional tax owed is paid by the employee (or self-employed individual) on their individual tax return.

If a taxpayer has both wage income and self-employment income, the additional Medicare surtax is calculated in four steps:

1. Calculate net earnings from self-employment by multiplying self-employment income by 92.35 percent.[80]

2. Add salary and wages to the net earnings from self-employment determined in (1).

[80] To compute net income from self-employment income, a deduction is allowed for the employer's 7.65 percent share of tax. Note that this is effectively the same as taxing only 92.35 percent (100% – 7.65%) of net income from self-employment. (See Chapter 4.)

3. Subtract the appropriate threshold from the amount determined in (2).
4. Multiply the amount in (3) by 0.9 percent for the tax owed.

This tax is computed on Form 8959 and paid along with the regular income tax on the individual's tax return. The following examples illustrate computation of this 0.9 percent Medicare surtax.

Example 5.42

Maria and Jose are married and file a joint tax return. Maria has $150,000 in salary and Jose has $189,497 in self-employment income from his medical practice. Before calculating the additional Medicare tax on Jose's self-employment income, his $189,497 in self-employment income is multiplied by 92.35% to determine the $175,000 net earnings from self-employment subject to Medicare tax. This $175,000 is added to Maria's $150,000 salary and the $250,000 threshold is subtracted resulting in $75,000 subject to the additional tax. Maria and Jose must pay a $675 (0.9% × $75,000) additional Medicare tax on $75,000 of self-employment income on their individual tax return.

Example 5.43

John, a single individual, has $225,000 in salary and $54,142 in self-employment income. John's employer withheld the additional Medicare tax on $25,000 ($225,000 salary minus the $200,000 withholding threshold) with his FICA taxes. John net income from self-employment is $50,000 ($54,142 × 92.35%). He adds this to his $225,000 salary which is then reduced by the $200,000 threshold. John is liable for an additional Medicare tax of $675 [($25,000 of his salary + $50,000 self-employment income) × 0.9%]. John's employer already withheld the additional Medicare tax of $225 on his salary in excess of $25,000. He only owes the remaining $450 ($50,000 × 0.9) when he files his tax return.

If John's $225,000 salary had been from two different employers, neither of which paid him over $200,000, there would have had no additional Medicare tax withheld and he would have to pay the entire $675 when he files his tax return.

Prior to 2013, the Medicare part of the employment tax was assessed only on salaries, wages, self-employment income, and similar types of taxable compensation. Since 2013, the Affordable Care Act requires high-income taxpayers to pay the Medicare surtax on net investment income (NII). This tax, computed on Form 8960: *Net Investment Income Tax*, is added to the regular income tax on the individual's tax return.

Investment income is very broadly defined and includes not only net capital gains (long- and short-term), taxable interest income, dividends, royalties, and certain annuities, but also includes rental income and profits from passive investments, such as a limited partnership interests. Investment income does not include business income from a partnership or S corporation in which the taxpayer is actively involved, but the owners could be affected if they are considered passive investors such as limited partners.[81]

Some common types of income *not* considered investment income for the NII tax include: unemployment compensation, Social Security benefits, alimony, income from qualified retirement plan distributions, and tax-exempt interest income. Additionally, earned income, such as wages, salaries, self-employment income, and other taxable compensation are not subject to the NII tax because they are subject to the additional 0.9 percent Medicare surtax instead.

[81] Chapter 11 includes a discussion of limited partnerships and other passive income concepts. Passive income excludes rental income received by a qualified real estate professional and income from an annuity based on the taxpayer's employment.

The 3.8 percent NII tax rate is assessed on the *lesser* of (1) net investment income or (2) modified adjusted gross income[82] in excess of a threshold based on filing status. The thresholds are $200,000 for single individuals (and heads of household), $250,000 for married taxpayers filing a joint return, and $125,000 for married taxpayers filing separately.

Example 5.44

Jules, a single individual, has adjusted gross income of $232,000 from his $192,000 salary and $40,000 of taxable interest income. His NII tax is assessed on the lesser of his $40,000 investment income or the $32,000 excess over the income threshold ($232,000 – $200,000). His NII tax is $1,216 (3.8% × $32,000); it is reported on his individual tax return and is added to his regular income tax liability.

Alternatively, if Jules's $232,000 adjusted gross income consists of $212,000 in salary and $20,000 of taxable interest income, only $20,000 is subject to the NII tax and his tax is only $760 (3.8% × $20,000 investment income).

If his adjusted gross income did not exceed $200,000, none of his interest income would be subject to the NII tax.

To determine the *net* investment income subject to the NII tax, gross investment income is reduced by related investment expenses. Common investment expenses include investment interest expense, investment advisory and brokerage fees, expenses related to rental and royalty income, and state and local income taxes allocated to investment income.[83]

Example 5.45

Lenora, a single individual, has $190,000 of salary income, $5,000 in dividends, $20,000 interest from corporate bonds, $10,000 interest income from tax-exempt municipal bonds, and $60,000 in net long-term capital gains in 2017. She had $4,500 of brokerage fees related to her dividends and interest from corporate bonds, and $600 of fees related to the municipal bonds. Lenora's modified adjusted gross income is $275,000 ($190,000 + $5,000 + $20,000 + $60,000), which exceeds the $200,000 NII threshold by $75,000. Lenora's NII tax is based on the lesser of $75,000 (her excess income over the $200,000 threshold) or $80,500 ($5,000 dividends + $20,000 interest from corporate bonds + $60,000 capital gains – $4,500 brokerage fees related to taxable investment income) net investment income. The tax-exempt income from municipal bonds and the related expenses are excluded from net investment income. Lenora owes a NII tax of $2,850 ($75,000 × 3.8%).

When the NII tax is added to the highest capital gains and regular income tax rates, the effective tax rate for many higher-income taxpayers can be 23.8 percent for long-term capital gains and dividend income, and 43.4 percent for short-term capital gains and interest income.

5.8.2 ALTERNATIVE MINIMUM TAX

High-income taxpayers are required to compute an alternative taxable income subject to the alternative minimum tax to ensure they pay their "fair share" of taxes. In computing alternative taxable income, certain deductions are reduced or excluded and certain exempt income items are

[82] Modified adjusted gross income for this purpose is adjusted gross income with the foreign earned income exclusion (discussed in Chapter 4) added back.

[83] Refer to Figure 5.5 later in this chapter and the related footnote for computation of the NII tax.

included. This alternative income is called **alternative minimum taxable income (AMTI)**, and the tax is the **alternative minimum tax (AMT)**. If the AMT is greater than the regular tax, taxpayers pay the larger amount.[84]

The AMT is intended to affect those taxpayers whose true economic income diverges significantly from taxable income, due to their "excessive use" of tax reduction provisions; unfortunately, it can also apply to middle-income taxpayers who fail to plan wisely. The AMT is paid only if it exceeds the regular tax liability.

The characteristics most likely to cause AMT liability for individuals include:

- Nontaxable interest income from private activity bonds[85]
- Large amounts of state and local tax deductions
- The bargain element of incentive stock options

To compute the AMT, taxpayers generally start with regular taxable income, add/subtract certain adjustments, add tax preferences, and subtract exempt amounts. The tentative minimum tax (TMT) is then calculated using the following AMT schedule for individuals:

AMTI	Tentative minimum tax
0–$191,100	26% × AMTI
Over $191,100	$49,686 + 28% (AMTI – $191,100)[86]

The TMT is then compared to the regular tax. If the TMT exceeds the regular tax, only this difference is the alternative minimum tax (AMT) that is added to the regular tax on page 2 of Form 1040. An AMT can only be positive. If the TMT is less than the regular tax, the AMT is simply zero. Figure 5.4 illustrates the AMT model.

	Taxable Income
Plus/Minus	Adjustments to Taxable Income
Plus	Tax Preferences
Less	Allowable Exemption
Equals	Alternative Minimum Taxable Income (AMTI)
Times	AMT Tax Rates
Equals	Tentative Minimum Tax (TMT)
Less	Regular Income Tax
Equals	AMT

FIGURE 5.4 The AMT model

Example 5.46

An individual taxpayer has AMTI of $775,000. His TMT is $213,178, computed as follows:

$$\$49,686 + 28\%(\$775,000 - \$191,100) = \$213,178$$

If the taxpayer's regular income tax is $100,000, the AMT is $113,178 ($213,178 – $100,000), and total income tax is $213,178 (equal to the TMT). If the taxpayer's regular tax is $220,000, there is no AMT liability because the TMT ($213,178) is less than this regular tax. The taxpayer's total income tax remains $220,000. The AMT does not change the amount of the tax, just its technical designation.

[84] §55.

[85] Private activity bonds are state or local bonds that are issued to help finance a private business. Interest income on these bonds is exempt from regular income tax but is considered a tax preference item.

[86] For 2017, the 28 percent rate started at $187,800. For the married persons filing separately, the 28 percent rate starts at $95,550 for 2018 ($93,900 for 2017). Individuals who qualify for the 15 percent capital gains rate for regular income tax can also use the 15 percent rate for AMT. §55(b)(3).

If the taxpayer's AMTI is below a certain level, a portion of the income may be exempt from the alternative tax. The exemption, based on the individual's filing status, is indexed for inflation. If the taxpayer's AMTI before the exemption exceeds the phaseout threshold, the exemption phases out at a rate of 25 cents for each dollar AMTI exceeds the exemption threshold. The exemption is completely phased at the point where the threshold plus four times the exemption amount is reached. Table 5.11 shows the exemptions for 2018 along with the phaseout ranges.[87]

Table 5.11 AMT Exemptions for 2018

Filing status	Exemption	Phaseout begins at	Phaseout complete at
Married filing a joint return	$109,400	$1,000,000	$1,437,600
Married filing separately	54,700	500,000	718,800
Single and Head of household	70,300	500,000	781,200

Adjustments can be positive or negative, but most result in a reduction or disallowance of an item that was deducted in computing the regular income tax. For example, the standard deduction and personal and dependency exemptions are disallowed in computing AMTI. Additionally, many itemized deductions are limited or disallowed. Medical expenses, interest on home acquisition mortgages, investment interest expense, charitable contributions, and casualty losses are the same for both regular taxable income and AMTI. No deduction is allowed for any taxes or miscellaneous itemized deductions.

Example 5.47

Samantha, single and age 45, has 2018 adjusted gross income of $280,000 and the following itemized deductions before any limitations:

Medical expenses	$19,200
Interest on home acquisition mortgage ($720,000 principal amount)	27,000
State and local income and real property taxes	15,000
Charitable contributions	5,000
Total	$66,200

To compute regular taxable income, Samantha cannot deduct any medical expenses because they do not exceed 7.5% of AGI (7.5% × $280,000 = $21,000). She can deduct a maximum $10,000 for taxes, reducing her total itemized deductions to $42,000 from $66,200.

To determine Samantha's alternative minimum tax liability, her itemized deductions are reduced even further. She cannot deduct any of the taxes for the AMT, only her $27,000 mortgage interest and $5,000 charitable contributions are deductible for a combined total of $32,000.

TAX PLANNING

Taxpayers who expect to be subject to the alternative minimum tax in a given tax year should attempt to shift their itemized deductions to a future tax year in which the AMT may not applicable. If, however, the taxpayer is in the 32 percent or above regular tax bracket in a year when the alternative minimum tax applies, accelerating income into that year can save taxes. Additional income will be subject to the 28 percent alternative minimum tax until the point at which the recalculated regular tax with the additional income equals the tentative minimum tax (also including this income).

Tax preferences are positive additions to AMTI—but most preferences are somewhat obscure. Only the nontaxable interest on private activity bonds and the bargain element of stock options are considered here as examples.[88]

[87] §55(d). For 2017, the exemption amounts were $84,500 for married couples filing a joint return, $42,250 for married filing separately, and $54,300 for head of household and single individuals.

[88] A portion of the excluded gain on the sale of small business stock is another preference item. §57(a)(7).

Interest on private activity bonds issued by a state or local government is fully taxable to the bond holders if the proceeds are used for private business operations rather than for certain qualified exempt activities. The interest on proceeds used to construct exempt facilities such as airports, hazardous waste facilities, or water and sewage treatment facilities, is exempt from the regular income tax. The tax-exempt interest on private activity bonds is a tax preference item, however. This interest is added to regular taxable income to determine alternative minimum taxable income.

Example 5.48

Samir has taxable income of $175,000 and tax-exempt private activity bond interest of $800,000. Although this interest is exempt from regular taxation, his regular taxable income increases by $800,000 to determine AMTI.

Taxpayers who receive incentive stock options (ISOs) from their employers pay no regular income tax when the options are exercised but may be subject to the AMT. The difference between the exercise price and the stock's higher fair market value on the exercise date (the bargain element) is a tax preference item subject to the AMT. Exercising the stock option when the fair market value of the stock is low can minimize the employee's AMT.

Example 5.49

In January year 1, RapidGrowth Corporation granted its employee, Ken, 25,000 ISOs with an exercise price of $10 per share. On January 5, year 3, Ken exercises all of the ISOs when the stock's fair market value is $30 per share. Ken recognizes no gain on the stock appreciation for regular tax purposes until the year the stock acquired with the ISO is sold. At that time, he will have long-term capital gain. For AMT purposes, however, Ken's year-3 income tax return shows a positive AMT adjustment of $500,000 [($30 fair market value at exercise date – $10 exercise price) × 25,000 shares] that is included in and taxed as part of his AMTI. When Ken sells the stock, Ken's long-term capital gain for AMTI will be measured from $30. If Ken waits until December to exercise his options when the fair market value of the stock is $50 per share, his year-3 income tax return AMT adjustment will be $1,000,000 [($50 fair market value at exercise date – $10 exercise price) × 25,000 shares].

The basis for regular tax purposes is the exercise price, whereas the basis for AMT purposes is the fair market value of the stock on the exercise date. A difference in the capital gain recognized for regular tax and AMT purposes is the result of this difference.

Example 5.50

Refer to the previous example. Ken sells his stock for $70 per share in November of year 5. He has a $1.5 million long-term capital gain [($70 – $10) × 25,000] for regular tax determination. If Ken had exercised the option at the $30 per share value, his AMT long term capital gain would be $1 million [($70 – $30) × 25,000]. If he exercised the option when the value was $50, his AMT long-term capital gain would be only $500,000 [($70 – $50) × 25,000].

TAX PLANNING

Ken's AMTI and AMT are significantly lower when the ISOs are exercised at the lower fair market value. The lower stock value decreases both the AMT adjustment and the corresponding AMT. Ken trades AMT ordinary income taxed at 26 to 28 percent for AMT long-term capital gain income, generally taxed at 15 percent (maximum 20 percent excluding the net investment income Medicare surtax). Ken also deferred payment of the tax because AMT ordinary income is a year-3 income tax liability, while the AMT long-term capital gain tax from the subsequent sale of the stock is deferred until year 5.

5.8.3 OTHER TAXES

Table 5.12 lists other taxes paid on individual taxpayer returns.

Table 5.12 Other Taxes

Type of tax	Description
Early Distributions from Retirement Plans	A 10 percent penalty is assessed on premature (usually before age 59½) withdrawals from IRAs and other retirement plans (see Chapter 4).
Household Employment Taxes	If you pay any household employee (e.g., nanny, babysitter, or yard worker) $2,100 or more in 2018, you determine their Social Security and Medicare taxes on Schedule H and pay these taxes on your Form 1040.

5.9 PAYMENT OF TAX AND FILING THE RETURN

5.9.1 PAYMENT OF TAX

To determine the net tax due or expected refund, an individual subtracts income tax prepayments (withholding on salaries and other income plus estimated tax payments) from the tax liability adjusted for credits and additions. Estimated payments are tax prepayments by persons with more than minimal income from sources for which the taxpayer has no withholding (for example, self-employed individuals). It is a form of self-withholding. Generally, taxpayers pay estimated taxes in equal quarterly installments, unless sufficient taxes are withheld from earned income sources (primarily wages and salary). The required quarterly payments are based on total estimated taxes for the current year. Some taxpayers, however, may base their current year's estimates on their prior year's tax liability. A calendar-year individual's quarterly estimated tax payments are due on April 15, June 15, and September 15 of the current year, and January 15 of the following year. Each estimated payment is expected to cover 25 percent of the required annual payment (less taxes paid through withholding on wages).

If no installment payments are made, or total payments are less than 90 percent of the tax liability, a penalty may be imposed on the difference between the tax due and the prepayment.[89] This penalty is not imposed if the tax due for the year is less than $1,000 or the taxpayer had no tax liability in the prior year. The penalty rate is determined quarterly by the IRS and is computed as simple interest based on each quarter's underpayment. Thus, a different penalty rate could apply to each quarter's underpayment. An individual who underpays an estimated tax installment cannot avoid the penalty by increasing a later estimated tax payment (although payment in a later period reduces the period for which the penalty applies). One way to minimize any exposure for underpayment is to increase withholding on salary or other income (even if there is additional withholding near the end of the year). The penalty may also be reduced or eliminated by using a special annualization method that essentially matches the required quarterly payments to the pattern in which income is received.

After subtracting prepayments, the taxpayer has completed the determination of his or her net tax due or the tax refund expected. After signing and dating, the taxpayer is ready to file the tax return.

[89] The penalty is not assessed if the tax prepayment is equal to at least 100 percent of the previous year's tax liability if AGI is $150,000 or less, or 110 percent if AGI is over $150,000. §6654(d)(1). The required annual payment for individuals with small businesses is the lesser of 90 percent of the tax for the current year or 90 percent of the previous year's tax liability, if the prior year's AGI was less than $500,000 ($250,000 if married filing separately), and 50 percent or more of gross income was from a business employing an average of no more than 500 people.

TAX PLANNING

It is usually better to underpay taxes (assuming an underpayment of less than $1,000) rather than deliberately overpaying to receive a refund. The IRS pays no interest on a refund issued within 45 days from the later of the filing date or due date of the return.[90] An overpayment is an interest-free loan to the government. If a taxpayer has unusually large deductions, additional withholding allowances may be claimed on Form W-4 to avoid an overpayment of taxes.

5.9.2 NOL

Although a corporation has a **net operating loss (NOL)** when its expenses exceed its operating income, an individual whose expenses exceed his or her income, does not necessarily have a NOL. Individuals must make adjustments to negative income to determine any potential NOL because an individual's NOL can only be the result of business losses (for example, S corporations, partnerships, or sole proprietorships). Employee wages and salary, however, are considered business income and effectively reduce any business losses in determining the NOL.

To compute the NOL, an individual cannot take the standard deduction; nonbusiness capital losses only offset nonbusiness capital gains (excess capital losses cannot increase an NOL); and nonbusiness deductions (most itemized deductions) only offset nonbusiness income (interest and dividends).

Example 5.51

In 2018 Jim has a $25,000 loss from his sole proprietorship, $10,000 in wages from a part-time job, and $500 of interest income. His AGI is a negative $14,500. After $13,050 of itemized deductions, he has negative income of $27,550.

To determine his NOL, Jim adds back the $12,550 excess nonbusiness deduction ($13,050 of itemized deductions less his $500 nonbusiness interest income). His NOL is reduced to $15,000—the same number reached by offsetting his $25,000 sole proprietorship loss with his $10,000 in wages. Jim can carry this $15,000 NOL forward to offset up to 80 percent of his taxable income in future years.

A new limitation applies to the deduction for net business losses of a sole proprietorship, partnership, or S corporation that can be claimed on an owner's return for 2018–2025. The deductible amount is generally limited to $250,000 ($500,000 if married filing jointly); the disallowed excess loss is treated as a net operating loss (NOL) and carried forward. This new limit on deductible net business losses is discussed in Chapter 11.

Example 5.52

Justin is single and has $670,000 of gross income and $980,000 of deductions from his sole proprietorship resulting in a $310,000 loss for 2018. His excess business loss is $60,000 ($980,000 − ($670,000 + $250,000)). Justin can deduct a loss of $250,000 in 2018 but can carry the $60,000 excess business loss to 2019 as an NOL.

5.9.3 WHO MUST FILE A RETURN?

A taxpayer with gross income exceeding the applicable basic standard deduction (plus the addition for age and blindness), must file a tax return on or before April 15 following the end of the tax year.[91] If the taxpayer's gross income is less than this standard deduction, no tax liability

---

[90] §6611(e).

[91] §6012(a)(1). Taxpayers can file a Form 1040 (long form), a Form 1040A (short form), or an even shorter form, 1040EZ. Taxpayers may qualify for an automatic extension of time to file of 6 months, as discussed in Chapter 2.

is owed even if the taxpayer has no deductions. Filing a return only creates an unnecessary administrative and compliance burden on both the taxpayer and the IRS. Regardless, the taxpayer must file a tax return to obtain any expected tax refund because the IRS must receive a tax return before it will send a taxpayer's tax refund due.

Example 5.53

Bill is single and age 32. In 2018 his employer withheld $400 for income taxes on his $9,000 of gross income. Bill's gross income is less than the $12,000 standard deduction. He is not required to file a tax return for 2018 because both his taxable income and gross income tax liability are zero. Although not required, Bill would have to file a return to claim his $400 tax refund from employer withholding.

There are certain exceptions to the normal gross income thresholds that may require a taxpayer to file a return. The four principal exceptions are:

1. Self-employed individuals must file a tax return, regardless of their gross income, if their net earnings from self-employment are $400 or more for the year.
2. Taxpayers who are age 65 or older or blind may add their additional standard deduction of $1,300 (married taxpayers) or $1,600 (single or head of household) to determine their gross income filing requirements. Taxpayers who are dependents are subject to a complex set of filing rules. The most often encountered are for children who are dependents of their parents. The gross income threshold for them is the greater of $1,050 or their earned income plus $350. Thus, a child with *only* investment income must file a return if that investment income exceeds $1,050.
3. A married person filing a separate return must file if gross income equals or exceeds $12,000.

Penalties for not filing a timely return (if one is required) and for underpayment of tax are discussed in Chapter 2.

Example 5.54

Figure 5.5 shows the first two pages of Form 1040 based on the following information. Carlos and Angela Sanchez are married and file a joint tax return. They have one child, Victoria (age 15) who lives with them. Their income for 2017 was as follows:

Salary for Carlos	$200,000
Taxable interest income	4,650
Tax-exempt interest income	4,000
Dividend income	8,300
Net income from Angela's sole proprietorship	110,000
Long-term capital gains	10,000
Loss from an S corporation	(6,000)
Income from jury duty	50

Angela and Carlos each contributed $3,000 to their traditional IRA accounts; these contributions are deductible *for* AGI. Their other deduction for AGI is 50 percent of the $15,543 self-employment tax that Angela pays on the income from her sole proprietorship. Subtracting these deductions results in AGI of $313,228. Their itemized deductions are $88,150 as shown earlier in this chapter in Example 5.25 and their Schedule A in Figure 5.3.

They are allowed to deduct $12,150 ($4,050 × 3) for their three exemptions, resulting in taxable income of $212,928.

Their regular income tax is $44,125 consisting of $41,380 tax on ordinary income of $194,628 plus $2,745 tax at the 15% rate on long-term capital gains and dividend income. (Note that this 15% rate saved them $2,379 compared to being taxed as ordinary income).

They now have several additional taxes to pay. Their alternative minimum tax is $2,221 ($46,346 tentative minimum tax[92] – $44,125 regular tax). Angela's self-employment tax on her $110,000 of net income from her sole proprietorship is $15,543 ($110,000 × 92.35% × 15.3%). Their addition Medicare tax on salary and self-employment income is $464 [($110,000 × 92.35%) + $200,000 salary – $250,000 threshold × 0.9%] which is computed on Form 8959. Their NII tax is computed on Form 8960 as $655. This is a 3.8% tax computed on net investment income of $17,237 ($4,650 taxable interest income + $8,300 dividend income + $10,000 long-term capital gains – $5,713 investment expenses allocated to investment income).[93] Carlos had $43,000 in income tax withheld from his salary by his employer and they also made $21,000 in estimated tax payments during the year. They are owed a refund of $992. They are not allowed a child tax credit because it is completely phased out.

REVISITING THE INTRODUCTORY CASE

Amy and Steve should schedule the closing for January. They failed to consider that there is no standard deduction when they itemize, and floors apply to some categories of itemized deductions. Medical expenses are only deductible to the extent they exceed 7.5 percent of AGI ($190,000 × 7.5% = $14,250), so none of their medical expenses are deductible. Amy and Steve must wait until 2019 to deduct a full year's mortgage interest ($14,000), property taxes ($5,500), and charitable contributions ($8,400), resulting in total itemized deductions of $27,900. If they close the last week of December in 2018, the deductible mortgage interest and property taxes for that year are reduced to $269 (1/52 × $14,000) for mortgage interest and $106 (1/52 × $5,500) for taxes. Thus, their itemized deductions for 2018 are $269 mortgage interest, $106 taxes, $8,400 charitable contributions, and $3,000 for points (interest) on the mortgage, a total of $11,775. This is less than their $24,000 standard deduction and they would get no benefit from itemizing in 2018. In 2019, they should benefit from itemizing because their itemized deductions are $27,900 ($14,000 for a full year's mortgage interest plus $5,500 for taxes and $8,400 for their charitable contributions), which is significantly more than their standard deduction. If the wait until 2019 to close, they can deduct the $3,000 points on the purchase, increasing their itemized deductions to $30,900 ($27,900 + $3,000 for points).

In estimating their potential tax savings of $7,776 from itemizing their deductions, they forgot to consider that their tax benefit is determined by the incremental increase in deductions over their standard deduction. Based on the 2018 standard deduction, the $30,900 itemized deductions are only $6,900 greater than their $24,000 standard deduction. Their maximum additional tax savings are only $1,656 ($6,900 × 24%). They may still be slightly better off itemizing their deductions in future years, but certainly they will not save as much in taxes as they had hoped.

[92] Alternative minimum taxable income of $248,578 is computed by adding back the $12,150 personal and dependency exemptions and certain itemized deductions ($23,500 taxes) to $212,928 taxable income. They are allowed an AMT exemption of $62,580. Their $18,300 of dividends and capital gains are taxed at 15% and their remaining $167,698 is taxed at 26% resulting in a tentative AMT of $46,346.

[93] Investment expenses include $4,650 investment interest expense plus $1,063 of the state income taxes ($22,950 investment income/$313,228 AGI = 7.33% × $14,500 state income taxes).

Form **1040** Department of the Treasury—Internal Revenue Service (99)
U.S. Individual Income Tax Return **2017** OMB No. 1545-0074 IRS Use Only—Do not write or staple in this space.

For the year Jan. 1–Dec. 31, 2017, or other tax year beginning , 2017, ending , 20 See separate instructions.

Your first name and initial	Last name	Your social security number
Carlos	**Sanchez**	**150 66 5432**
If a joint return, spouse's first name and initial	Last name	Spouse's social security number
Angela	**Sanchez**	**150 65 4321**

Home address (number and street). If you have a P.O. box, see instructions. Apt. no.
1234 Fountaingrove Road
▲ Make sure the SSN(s) above and on line 6c are correct.

City, town or post office, state, and ZIP code. If you have a foreign address, also complete spaces below (see instructions).
Santa Rosa, CA 95404

Foreign country name | Foreign province/state/county | Foreign postal code

Presidential Election Campaign
Check here if you, or your spouse if filing jointly, want $3 to go to this fund. Checking a box below will not change your tax or refund. ☐ You ☐ Spouse

Filing Status

Check only one box.

1 ☐ Single
2 ☑ Married filing jointly (even if only one had income)
3 ☐ Married filing separately. Enter spouse's SSN above and full name here. ▶
4 ☐ Head of household (with qualifying person). (See instructions.) If the qualifying person is a child but not your dependent, enter this child's name here. ▶
5 ☐ Qualifying widow(er) (see instructions)

Exemptions

6a ☑ **Yourself.** If someone can claim you as a dependent, **do not** check box 6a . . . . .
b ☑ **Spouse** . . . . .
Boxes checked on 6a and 6b: **2**

c **Dependents:**

(1) First name	Last name	(2) Dependent's social security number	(3) Dependent's relationship to you	(4) ✓ if child under age 17 qualifying for child tax credit (see instructions)
Victoria	**Sanchez**	**150 67 1234**	**Daughter**	☑
				☐
				☐
				☐

If more than four dependents, see instructions and check here ▶ ☐

No. of children on 6c who:
• lived with you: **1**
• did not live with you due to divorce or separation (see instructions)
Dependents on 6c not entered above

d Total number of exemptions claimed . . . . . Add numbers on lines above ▶ **3**

Income

Attach Form(s) W-2 here. Also attach Forms W-2G and 1099-R if tax was withheld.

If you did not get a W-2, see instructions.

Line	Description	Inner box	Amount
7	Wages, salaries, tips, etc. Attach Form(s) W-2		200,000
8a	**Taxable** interest. Attach Schedule B if required		4,650
b	**Tax-exempt** interest. **Do not** include on line 8a	8b 4,000	
9a	Ordinary dividends. Attach Schedule B if required		8,300
b	Qualified dividends	9b 8,300	
10	Taxable refunds, credits, or offsets of state and local income taxes		
11	Alimony received		
12	Business income or (loss). Attach Schedule C or C-EZ		110,000
13	Capital gain or (loss). Attach Schedule D if required. If not required, check here ▶ ☐		10,000
14	Other gains or (losses). Attach Form 4797		
15a	IRA distributions 15a	b Taxable amount (15b)	
16a	Pensions and annuities 16a	b Taxable amount (16b)	
17	Rental real estate, royalties, partnerships, S corporations, trusts, etc. Attach Schedule E		(6,000)
18	Farm income or (loss). Attach Schedule F		
19	Unemployment compensation		
20a	Social security benefits 20a	b Taxable amount (20b)	
21	Other income. List type and amount **jury duty pay**		50
22	Combine the amounts in the far right column for lines 7 through 21. This is your **total income** ▶		327,000

Adjusted Gross Income

Line	Description	Inner box	Amount
23	Educator expenses	23	
24	Certain business expenses of reservists, performing artists, and fee-basis government officials. Attach Form 2106 or 2106-EZ	24	
25	Health savings account deduction. Attach Form 8889	25	
26	Moving expenses. Attach Form 3903	26	
27	Deductible part of self-employment tax. Attach Schedule SE	27 7,772	
28	Self-employed SEP, SIMPLE, and qualified plans	28	
29	Self-employed health insurance deduction	29	
30	Penalty on early withdrawal of savings	30	
31a	Alimony paid b Recipient's SSN ▶	31a	
32	IRA deduction	32 6,000	
33	Student loan interest deduction	33	
34	Tuition and fees. Attach Form 8917	34	
35	Domestic production activities deduction. Attach Form 8903	35	
36	Add lines 23 through 35		13,772
37	Subtract line 36 from line 22. This is your **adjusted gross income** ▶		313,228

For Disclosure, Privacy Act, and Paperwork Reduction Act Notice, see separate instructions. Cat. No. 11320B Form **1040** (2017)

FIGURE 5.5 Form 1040 pages 1 and 2

Form 1040 (2017) Page **2**

Section	Line	Description	Line	Amount
Tax and Credits	38	Amount from line 37 (adjusted gross income)	38	313,228
	39a	Check if: ☐ **You** were born before January 2, 1953, ☐ Blind. ☐ **Spouse** was born before January 2, 1953, ☐ Blind. } **Total boxes checked ▶ 39a** ☐		
	b	If your spouse itemizes on a separate return or you were a dual-status alien, check here ▶ 39b☐		
Standard Deduction for— • People who check any box on line 39a or 39b **or** who can be claimed as a dependent, see instructions. • All others: Single or Married filing separately, $6,350; Married filing jointly or Qualifying widow(er), $12,700; Head of household, $9,350	40	**Itemized deductions** (from Schedule A) **or** your **standard deduction** (see left margin)	40	88,150
	41	Subtract line 40 from line 38	41	225,078
	42	**Exemptions.** If line 38 is $156,900 or less, multiply $4,050 by the number on line 6d. Otherwise, see instructions	42	12,150
	43	**Taxable income.** Subtract line 42 from line 41. If line 42 is more than line 41, enter -0-	43	212,928
	44	**Tax** (see instructions). Check if any from: a ☐ Form(s) 8814 b ☐ Form 4972 c ☐	44	44,125
	45	**Alternative minimum tax** (see instructions). Attach Form 6251	45	2,221
	46	Excess advance premium tax credit repayment. Attach Form 8962	46	
	47	Add lines 44, 45, and 46 ▶	47	46,346
	48	Foreign tax credit. Attach Form 1116 if required — 48		
	49	Credit for child and dependent care expenses. Attach Form 2441 — 49		
	50	Education credits from Form 8863, line 19 — 50		
	51	Retirement savings contributions credit. Attach Form 8880 — 51		
	52	Child tax credit. Attach Schedule 8812, if required — 52		
	53	Residential energy credits. Attach Form 5695 — 53		
	54	Other credits from Form: a ☐ 3800 b ☐ 8801 c ☐ — 54		
	55	Add lines 48 through 54. These are your **total credits**	55	
	56	Subtract line 55 from line 47. If line 55 is more than line 47, enter -0- ▶	56	46,346
Other Taxes	57	Self-employment tax. Attach Schedule SE	57	15,543
	58	Unreported social security and Medicare tax from Form: a ☐ 4137 b ☐ 8919	58	
	59	Additional tax on IRAs, other qualified retirement plans, etc. Attach Form 5329 if required	59	
	60a	Household employment taxes from Schedule H	60a	
	b	First-time homebuyer credit repayment. Attach Form 5405 if required	60b	
	61	Health care: individual responsibility (see instructions) Full-year coverage ☑	61	
	62	Taxes from: a ☑ Form 8959 b ☑ Form 8960 c ☐ Instructions; enter code(s)	62	1,119
	63	Add lines 56 through 62. This is your **total tax** ▶	63	63,008
Payments	64	Federal income tax withheld from Forms W-2 and 1099 — 64 — 43,000		
	65	2017 estimated tax payments and amount applied from 2016 return — 65 — 21,000		
If you have a qualifying child, attach Schedule EIC.	66a	**Earned income credit (EIC)** — 66a		
	b	Nontaxable combat pay election — 66b		
	67	Additional child tax credit. Attach Schedule 8812 — 67		
	68	American opportunity credit from Form 8863, line 8 — 68		
	69	Net premium tax credit. Attach Form 8962 — 69		
	70	Amount paid with request for extension to file — 70		
	71	Excess social security and tier 1 RRTA tax withheld — 71		
	72	Credit for federal tax on fuels. Attach Form 4136 — 72		
	73	Credits from Form: a ☐ 2439 b ☐ Reserved c ☐ 8885 d ☐ — 73		
	74	Add lines 64, 65, 66a, and 67 through 73. These are your **total payments** ▶	74	64,000
Refund	75	If line 74 is more than line 63, subtract line 63 from line 74. This is the amount you **overpaid**	75	992
	76a	Amount of line 75 you want **refunded to you.** If Form 8888 is attached, check here ▶☐	76a	992
Direct deposit? See instructions.	▶ b	Routing number ▶ c Type: ☐ Checking ☐ Savings		
	▶ d	Account number		
	77	Amount of line 75 you want **applied to your 2018 estimated tax** ▶ 77		
Amount You Owe	78	**Amount you owe.** Subtract line 74 from line 63. For details on how to pay, see instructions ▶	78	
	79	Estimated tax penalty (see instructions) — 79		

Third Party Designee Do you want to allow another person to discuss this return with the IRS (see instructions)? ☐ **Yes.** Complete below. ☑ **No**
Designee's name ▶ Phone no. ▶ Personal identification number (PIN) ▶

Sign Here Under penalties of perjury, I declare that I have examined this return and accompanying schedules and statements, and to the best of my knowledge and belief, they are true, correct, and accurately list all amounts and sources of income I received during the tax year. Declaration of preparer (other than taxpayer) is based on all information of which preparer has any knowledge.
Joint return? See instructions. Keep a copy for your records.
Your signature | Date | Your occupation | Daytime phone number
Spouse's signature. If a joint return, **both** must sign. | Date | Spouse's occupation | If the IRS sent you an Identity Protection PIN, enter it here (see inst.)

Paid Preparer Use Only Print/Type preparer's name | Preparer's signature | Date | Check ☐ if self-employed | PTIN
Firm's name ▶ | Firm's EIN ▶
Firm's address ▶ | Phone no.

Go to *www.irs.gov/Form1040* for instructions and the latest information. Form **1040** (2017)

FIGURE 5.5 *(Continued)*

SUMMARY

Individuals have two sets of personal deductions: deductions *for* adjusted gross income and deductions *from* adjusted gross income. Adjusted gross income, an intermediate income subtotal, limits most of the taxpayer's deductions from adjusted gross income except taxes and interest, although other limits may apply to interest deductions. Deductions for adjusted gross income are not subject to limits based on a percentage of AGI.

Filing status determines the taxpayer's basic standard deduction and the tax rate schedule. The five filing statuses are married filing jointly, married filing separately, surviving spouse, head of household, and single. The determination of filing status is based on marital status, the year a spouse dies, if deceased, and whether or not the taxpayer provides a home for a qualifying relative. The taxpayer subtracts the standard deduction (based on filing status) or their itemized deductions, if greater, from adjusted gross income.

After calculating the regular income tax on taxable income, taxpayers subtract their allowable credits (such as the child tax credit, the earned income credit for low-income taxpayers, and the dependent care credit). A tax credit is more valuable than an equal deduction because the value of a deduction is dependent on the taxpayer's tax rate.

Taxpayers may also be required to pay additional taxes such as the Medicare surtaxes and the alternative minimum tax, which increase the tax due. After these adjustments to the tax liability, the taxpayer subtracts tax withholding and any prepayments of tax to determine the tax due or the refund expected.

KEY TERMS

Abandoned spouse 217
Adjusted gross income (AGI) 208
Alternative minimum tax (AMT) 244
Alternative minimum taxable income (AMTI) 244
Deductions for adjusted gross income 209
Dependent 230
Head of household 216
Itemized deductions 217
Net operating loss (NOL) 248
Surviving spouse 214

TEST YOURSELF

Answers Appear after the Problem Assignments

1. Tony and Anita are married and file a joint tax return. They provide more than half the support for their daughter (age 16) who had gross income of $4,100 and their nephew (Tony's deceased brother's child) who is 17 and lives with them. He had gross income of $3,400. Both the daughter and the nephew are full-time students. Who qualifies as a dependent of Tony and Anita?
   a. Daughter only
   b. Nephew only
   c. Both daughter and nephew
   d. Neither the daughter nor the nephew

2. Maria, age 12, is a dependent of her parents. Her gross income consists solely of $2,800 in taxable dividends. What is Maria's taxable income?
   a. $2,800
   b. $1,800
   c. $1,750
   d. $0

3. George and Laura, a married couple with an adjusted gross income of $100,000, made the following contributions to qualified charitable organizations:
   - $8,000 cash given to State University.
   - Used personal clothing, acquired within the last two years for $6,000, donated to Goodwill. Its current fair market value is $2,000.
   - Apex stock donated to their church. The stock cost $30,000 when acquired in 1990. Its current fair market value is $15,000.

- Microsoft stock donated to the Red Cross. The stock acquired in 1993 cost $4,000. Its current fair market value is $11,000.
- Laura volunteers at the local charity that feeds homeless persons. The fair value of her volunteer service was $7,000.

How much can George and Laura deduct for these charitable contributions on their current year's tax return?

a. $8,000
b. $10,000
c. $25,000
d. $36,000
e. $50,000

4. Lynn and Dave, a married couple, have AGI of $300,000 in 2018 and report the following itemized deductions before deducting any floors that may apply:

Interest on their home acquisition mortgage ($750,000 principal amount)	$32,000
Taxes	13,000
Charitable contributions	15,000
Medical expenses	12,000

What is their taxable income for 2018?

a. $228,000
b. $230,000
c. $240,000
d. $243,000

5. Donna, a single individual with no dependents, reports AGI of $100,000. She also reports the following itemized deductions:

Medical expenses ($11,000 total – 7.5% of AGI)	$3,500
Interest on her home acquisition mortgage ($250,000 principal amount)	10,000
Property taxes on her principal residence	3,000
State income taxes	6,000
Qualified charitable contributions	5,000

What are Donna's allowable deductions for her alternative minimum taxable income (AMTI)?

a. $10,000
b. $16,000
c. $18,000
d. $28,000

PROBLEM ASSIGNMENTS

Check Your Understanding

1. [LO 5.1] What changes were made to the individual tax model for 2018; that is, what was added and what was eliminated?

2. [LO 5.1] Briefly explain two deductions that an individual has for adjusted gross income.

3. [LO 5.1] What is the purpose of adjusted gross income?

4. [LO 5.2] Explain why Congress allows taxpayers to deduct the penalty for a premature withdrawal from a certificate of deposit?

5. [LO 5.3] What are the filing statuses available to unmarried taxpayers? Which statuses are available only to married taxpayers?

6. [LO 5.3] What are the requirements to file as head of household?

7. [LO 5.3] What is the purpose of the abandoned spouse provision?

8. [LO 5.3] Differentiate between an abandoned spouse and a surviving spouse.

9. [LO 5.3] When would a taxpayer claim the standard deduction rather than itemizing deductions?

10. [LO 5.4] Which itemized deductions must exceed a basic minimum (floor) before the taxpayer's taxable income is reduced for the excess?

11. [LO 5.4] Contrast ceiling and floor limitations for itemized deductions. Provide an example of each.

12. [LO 5.4] Which types of taxes qualify as itemized deductions?

13. [LO 5.4] Why is investment interest expense limited to net investment income?

14. [LO 5.4] Lynn paid $12,000 of investment interest expense in a year in which she has the following investment income: $3,000 taxable dividend income, $4,000 taxable interest income, $1,000 from a short-term capital gain, and $4,000 from a long-term capital gain. Explain the election Lynn should make to maximize her deduction for her investment interest expense this year.

15. [LO 5.4] What is qualified residence interest?

16. [LO 5.4] What are "points" paid on a home mortgage and when are they deductible?

17. [LO 5.4] What is the overall charitable contribution deduction limitation? How are charitable contributions in excess of the current year's limit treated?

18. [LO 5.4] Collin pledged a $5,000 gift to his church's building fund. He has 125 shares of stock that he purchased six years ago for $100 per share. They are currently worth $40 per share. Collin plans to give the stock to the church to satisfy his pledge. What advice do you have for Collin?

19. [LO 5.4] Describe the types of expenses that were allowed as miscellaneous itemized deductions for 2017. What limitation was imposed on these expenses? When will this expense category be reinstated?

20. [LO 5.4] Briefly explain how itemized deductions were phased out for 2017. Could a taxpayer lose the benefit of all of his or her itemized deductions?

21. [LO 5.5] What is the purpose of the qualified business income deduction? Explain how it is calculated.

22. [LO 5.6] Explain the deduction that was allowed prior to 2018 if a taxpayer claimed someone as a dependent. Which relatives could qualify for this deduction and which relatives did not qualify? When will this deduction be reinstated?

23. [LO 5.6] If the dependency exemption deduction for claiming children as dependents on their parents' tax return has been eliminated, then what is the purpose of preserving the rules for determining who is a dependent?

24. [LO 5.6] Compare the requirements to be considered a dependent for a qualifying child and a qualifying relative.

25. [LO 5.6] Explain the gross income test to qualify as a dependent.

26. [LO 5.7] Explain the difference between a tax credit and a tax deduction?

27. [LO 5.7] Explain the difference between a refundable and a nonrefundable credit? Provide examples of each.

28. [LO 5.7] Compare similarities and differences of the American opportunity tax credit and the lifetime learning credit.

29. [LO 5.8] What is the kiddie tax and when does it apply?

30. [LO 5.8] Describe the two types of Medicare surtaxes and explain how they are computed.

31. [LO 5.8] What is the purpose of the alternative minimum tax for an individual?

32. [LO 5.8] How do alternative minimum tax rates compare to the regular income tax rates?

33. [LO 5.8] How do alternative minimum tax itemized deductions differ from the regular income tax itemized deductions?

34. [LO 5.9] If an individual has a negative taxable income does that mean that he or she has an NOL? Explain.

35. [LO 5.9] Explain how a taxpayer determines if he or she is required to file a tax return?

Crunch the Numbers

36. [LO 5.2] Cecilia is married and files a joint return with her husband, Steve. They have modified adjusted gross income of $145,000 for 2018. Cecilia paid $2,700 in student loan interest this year. How much of this interest is deductible?

37. [LO 5.2] Ashley is single and owns a sole proprietorship. Her annual premium is $2,600 for her high-deductible medical policy with a $2,300 deductible. How much can Ashley set aside in an HSA? How much can she deduct for AGI?

38. [LO 5.3] Harry and Silvia, a married couple, are both age 67 and legally blind. What is their standard deduction for 2018?

39. [LO 5.3] Lynn, age 66, is an unmarried individual who has a dependent grandchild who lives with her. What is Lynn's standard deduction for 2018?

40. [LO 5.4] Daniel's adjusted gross income is $90,000. During the year he incurred $18,000 of medical expenses and was reimbursed for $3,000 of these expenses. What is his allowable medical expense deduction if he is age 45, single, and itemizes? If this is Daniel's only itemized deduction, should he itemize or claim the standard deduction for 2018?

41. [LO 5.1 & 5.4] Rebecca and Gregory, a married couple filing a joint return, reported adjusted gross income of $70,000 and total allowable itemized deductions of $24,900, including $3,100 for state income taxes, in 2018. They received a $1,000 refund of state income taxes in April 2019. How much of the state income tax refund must be included in their income and in which year do they include it?

42. [LO 5.4] Edward is single with income that places him in the 35 percent marginal tax bracket for ordinary income and 15 percent for long-term capital gains. He incurs interest expense of $10,000 attributable to his investment in stocks and bonds. His gross investment income is $6,200 ($1,000 of which is from long-term capital gains and dividends) in 2018.
   a. What are Edward's options in determining his deduction for investment interest expense? Explain.
   b. What happens if he cannot deduct all of the investment interest expense in the current year?

43. [LO 5.4] Pablo and Adriana, a married couple who file a joint return, purchased a $190,000 home making a $38,000 cash down payment and taking out a mortgage for the balance of the purchase price. They also paid the mortgage company $3,000 in points for originating the loan at closing. They paid $7,000 in interest on the mortgage this year. They also purchased a new car for $28,000 with a car loan from their credit union, paying $975 in interest for the year. What is their deduction for interest expense if they itemize their deductions?

44. [LO 5.4] Arnold is a single individual and has adjusted gross income of $65,000 in the current year. Arnold donates the following items to his favorite qualified charities:
   a. $5,000 cash to the athletic department booster club at State University. This contribution gives him the right to purchase preferred seats to all home games.
   b. ABC stock acquired six years ago for $6,000. Its fair market value at the date of contribution was $22,000.
   c. Personal clothing items purchased two years ago for $1,000. Their fair market value at the date of contribution was $400.

   What is Arnold's charitable contribution deduction for the current year?

45. [LO 5.4] Mario and Kaitlin are married and file a joint tax return. They have adjusted gross income of $385,000 that includes $4,700 of investment income ($3,000 short-term capital gains and $1,700 of corporate bond interest). They paid the following expenses for the year:

Unreimbursed medical expenses	$26,000
Home mortgage interest on acquisition debt of $1,200,000 (the purchase price was $1,800,000 in 2016)	36,000
Investment interest expense	5,000
Other investment expenses	1,800
State income taxes	4,900
Real property taxes	13,000
Cash contribution to the State University athletic department booster club (for preferred seating at games)	3,000
Cash contribution to the State University Business School student scholarship fund	2,000
Unreimbursed employee business expenses	6,600
Tax return preparation fee	500

What are their itemized deductions for 2018 after applying all limitations?

46. [LO 5.3] Michael's adjusted gross income for 2018 is $90,000. He is age 30 and single. What is Michael's taxable income?

47. [LO 5.3] Scott is 15 years old and qualifies as a dependent of his parents. During 2018 he earns $2,500 from a part-time job and also receives $800 of dividend income on stock given to him by his aunt. What is Scott's taxable income?

48. [LO 5.5] Rich is single and has taxable income of $510,000. As a 30% partner in a partnership that produces $850,000 ordinary income from manufacturing a product, his share of partnership income is $255,000. The partnership paid $250,000 of W-2 wages and the total unadjusted basis of tangible depreciable business property is $400,000. What is Rich's qualified business income deduction?

49. [LO 5.5] Justin is single and has taxable income of $190,000 of which $140,000 is attributable to his consulting sole proprietorship. He paid W-2 wages to his employees of $60,000.
   a. What is Justin's qualified business income deduction?
   b. How would your answer change if Justin's taxable income was instead $300,000?
   c. How would your answer change if Justin's taxable income was instead only $155,000?

50. [LO 5.3 & 5.7] Elena has AGI of $150,000 and is single but her mother, Maria, lives with her. Maria's sole income is $7,000 in Social Security (which she saves for unexpected medical expenses) and $500 of interest income on that account. Elena provided a room in her home for Maria that could have been rented for $5,500 and Elena spent $5,200 on groceries for them to share and another $1,800 on clothing for Maria.
   a. What is the total amount of support Elena provided for her mother?
   b. Is Maria a dependent of Elena?
   c. What is Elena's filing status?
   d. Is Elena eligible to claim a tax credit in 2018 and, if yes, how much?

51. [LO 5.4 & 5.7] Mark and Patricia report adjusted gross income of $410,000 and itemized deductions of $31,000 for the interest on their home acquisition mortgage (principal amount of $890,000 acquired in 2015), $14,000 in state and local taxes, and $38,000 in charitable contributions. They file a joint income tax return and have four dependent children under age 16. What is their taxable income for 2018 and allowable tax credits?

52. [LO 5.7] Cindy files as head of household and has three dependent children ages 12, 14, and 16. Her AGI is $205,000 for 2018. How much can Cindy claim for the child tax credit?

53. [LO 5.7] Maria and Roberto are married with two dependent children ages 9 and 11. Their AGI for 2018 is $418,000. How much can they claim for the child tax credit?

54. [LO 5.7] Greg and Barbara, a married couple with an AGI of $80,000, have three children who are full-time college students. They pay $6,000 for tuition annually for each child. One son is a sophomore in college and the other son is a senior. Their daughter is a graduate student. How much can Greg and Barbara claim for education credits for 2018?

55. [LO 5.7] Doris is a single individual with modified AGI of $58,000. During the year, she paid $11,000 tuition for a master's in taxation program. How much can Doris claim for the lifetime learning credit for 2018?

56. [LO 5.7] June is a single individual with AGI of $45,000 for the year. June has a five-year-old son in day care while she works.

a. What is her dependent care credit if she spends $5,000 for child care during the year?

b. What is her dependent care credit if she spends $2,000 for child care during the year?

57. [LO 5.7] Roland worked for Sorbonne Company for the first four months of 2018 and earned $40,000 from which his employer withheld $3,060 for payroll taxes. In May, Roland accepted a job with Lyon Company. During the last eight months of the year, Roland earned $94,000 from which Lyon withheld $7,191 for payroll taxes. What is Roland's credit for excess payroll taxes withheld?

58. [LO 5.8] Linda received $90,000 in salary income for 2018. She has no dependents. Determine her income tax liability under each of the following independent situations:

a. She files as a single individual.

b. She is married and files a joint return with her spouse. Their only income is her $90,000 salary.

c. She is married but files a separate return.

59. [LO 5.8] Andrew, a single individual, has $220,000 in salary and $60,000 in self-employment income in 2018. How much must he pay for his additional Medicare surtax?

60. [LO 5.8] Lenora and Sam are married and file a joint tax return. Lenora has $180,000 in salary and Sam has $190,000 in self-employment income in 2018. How much must they pay for their additional Medicare surtax?

61. [LO 5.8] Marco and Lisa are married and file a joint tax return. Lisa has salary income of $260,000 and Marco has salary income of $400,000. They also have the following items of investment income: $60,000 net long-term capital gain on sale of stock, $8,000 dividend income, $6,000 interest income from corporate bonds, and $5,000 interest income from tax-exempt municipal bonds. Compute their net investment income (NII) tax.

62. [LO 5.8] During 2018, Raymond, a single individual, earned a salary of $196,000. He also had the following items of investment income: $40,000 net short-term capital gain on sale of stock, $7,000 dividend income, $5,000 interest income from corporate bonds, and $4,000 interest income from tax-exempt municipal bonds. Compute Raymond's net investment income (NII) tax.

63. [LO 5.8] Diana, a single individual, has regular taxable income of $220,000 and alternative minimum taxable income of $350,000.

a. What is Diana's tentative minimum tax?

b. What is Diana's AMT?

64. [LO 5.8] Michelle, a single individual, reports 2018 adjusted gross income of $210,000 and has paid for the following expenses:

Medical expenses	$18,000
Interest on home acquisition mortgage with a principal amount of $650,000	25,000
Taxes	18,000
Charitable contributions	15,800

a. What are Michelle's itemized deductions for regular tax purposes?

b. What are Michelle's itemized deductions for AMT purposes?

65. [LO 5.9] Jennifer, a single individual, has a $20,000 loss from an S corporation, $11,000 salary from a part-time job, and $2,000 of interest income. Her itemized deductions include $8,000 interest on the $200,000 principal on her home acquisition mortgage, $2,800 in taxes, and $2,500 in charitable contributions. Compute Jennifer's net operating loss.

66. [LO 5.9] Noah, a single parent, has a gross income tax liability of $8,000. He made estimated tax payments of $5,900 during the year. Noah also determined that he is entitled to claim a child tax credit of $2,000. What is Noah's tax due?

67. [LO 5.9] Which of the following individuals must file a tax return in 2018?

a. Carolyn is single and age 66. She receives $2,000 of interest income, $3,000 of dividend income, and $6,000 in Social Security benefits.

b. Tim is single, age 18, and a full-time student. He is a dependent of his parents. Tim earned $2,000 from a part-time job and $400 in interest income.

c. Justin is single, age 25, and a full-time graduate student. He earned $11,750 from a part-time job.

68. **Comprehensive Problem:** Kelly Martin is divorced; her child, Barbara, lives with her and is her dependent. Kelly has the following items of income and expense:

Income:	
Salary	$58,000
Cash dividends	3,000
Interest income on City of New York bonds	5,000
Interest income on U.S. Treasury bills	4,000
Net rental income	3,500
Alimony received from ex-husband	2,500
Child support received from ex-husband	3,500
Life insurance proceeds received on the death of her mother	100,000
Sales of Capital Assets:	
Stock held for 3 months (basis is $12,000) sold for	18,000
Investment land held 5 years (basis is $30,000) sold for	14,000
Expenses:	
Interest on the $150,000 principal from her home acquisition mortgage	6,000
Real property taxes on the home	2,000
Charitable contributions	7,000
Qualifying child care expense	3,700
Federal income tax withheld	6,000

Compute Kelly's taxable income and her net tax due or refund expected for 2018.

69. **Comprehensive Problem:** Jennifer and Jason Greco are married and file a joint tax return. Their two dependent children (Jim, age 14 and Jessica, age 16); both live at home. The Grecos have the following income and expenses:

Income:	
Jennifer's salary	$120,000
Jason's net profit from his consulting sole proprietorship (which paid $30,000 in W-2 wages)	148,000
Interest income on State of Texas bonds	10,000
Interest income on corporate bonds	12,000
Cash dividends	19,000
Long-term capital gain from sale of stock	70,000
Expenses:	
Interest on the $850,000 principal from their home acquisition mortgage (acquired in 2018)	48,000
Real property taxes on their home	11,000
Charitable contributions to their church	49,000
Federal income tax withheld from Jennifer's salary	35,000
Estimated federal tax payments for this year	20,000

a. What is their adjusted gross income and taxable income for 2018?
b. What is their net tax due or refund expected for 2018?

Develop Planning Skills

70. [LO 5.3 & 5.8] Lauren is single, age 60, and has an annual salary of $120,000. She paid off her mortgage in December 2017 but expects that her annual real estate taxes will continue to be approximately $10,000. Lauren contributes $3,000 each year to her favorite qualified charities but she has no other itemized deductions. For your answer, assume that the 2018 tax rates and standard deduction are the same for 2019.

a. If Lauren contributes $3,000 to the charity each year, what will be her income tax liabilities for 2018 and 2019?
b. If Lauren contributes $6,000 to the charity at the end of 2018 but makes no contribution in 2019, what will be her income tax liability for each year?
c. How should Lauren time of her charitable contributions so that she can minimize her total tax liability over the two years?

71. [LO 5.4] Manuel plans to make a significant contribution to his favorite charity with one of the following assets. Which asset would you recommend Manuel contribute and why?

a. Stock acquired five years ago at a cost of $16,000. The current fair market value is $13,000.
b. Stock acquired six months ago at a cost of $7,000. The current fair market value is $13,000.
c. Inventory items acquired last year for Manuel's sole proprietorship. Their cost was $15,000, and their current fair market value is $13,000.
d. $13,000 in cash.

72. [LO 5.4] Martin, a single man, contributes a painting to an art museum in the current year. The museum is thrilled to get the painting because it fits its Impressionist collection. Martin purchased the painting 10 years ago for $50,000. The painting is currently appraised at $60,000. Martin's adjusted gross income this year is $100,000 and his only other itemized deduction is his annual $5,000 for property taxes. Martin plans to retire next year. A significant portion of his income will be from tax-exempt bonds so his expected AGI in future years is only $15,000. Martin asks you to explain his options regarding his charitable contribution deduction and what he could claim as a deduction this year. Assuming his allowable standard deduction remains unchanged, what do you recommend?

73. [LO 5.7] Laura and Bryan's daughter, Lillian, starts college in a few months. What tax issues should they consider when they pay for Lillian's college tuition and related expenses.

74. [LO 5.7] Sharon has not worked outside the home since her first child was born five years ago and the younger of her two children is now three. She thinks they are old enough to go to a day care center so she can return to work. Sharon received two job offers. Mahalo Company offered her a salary of $19,000 and also provides free on-site child care facilities as an employee fringe benefit. Ohana Company offered to pay her $26,000 but offers no employee fringe benefits. The day care facility across the street from Ohana Company would cost $525 per month. Sharon files a joint tax return with her husband, Tom. Their current taxable income, without Sharon's salary, is $86,000. Sharon and Tom would like to know which job provides the greater after-tax cash flow.

75. [LO 5.7] Eileen files as head of household and earns a salary of $75,000. She has a 4-year-old dependent daughter for whom she pays $5,000 in annual day care expenses so that she can work. Eileen's employer offers a dependent care flexible spending arrangement in which she could contribute up to $5,000 (before income and FICA taxes). If she does not participate in the FSA, Eileen can claim a dependent care credit for this expense. Eileen has no other income or deductions. Compare the tax savings of these two alternatives and make a recommendation.

76. [LO 5.8] Two years ago, Micro Corporation granted Alisa, their General Manager, 20,000 incentive stock options with an exercise price of $15 per share. The stock currently trades at $40 per share, but Alisa expects its price to continue to increase. She wants to exercise her options this year, either now or later in the year when she believes the stock will be trading at $55 per share. Regardless of when she exercises the options, she expects to hold onto the stock for at least a year before selling it at an expected price of $100 per share. Alisa wants to know if it makes any difference when she exercises the options. She also wants to know what the tax implications are for each stock sale alternative.

Think Outside the Text

These questions require answers that are beyond the material that is covered in this chapter.

77. [LO 5.2] Select one of the expenses that is deductible *for* adjusted gross income. Present an argument about why you think that expense is misclassified and should be reclassified as a deduction *from* adjusted gross income.

78. [LO 5.4] Select one of the expenses that is deductible *from* adjusted gross income. Present an argument about why you think that expense is misclassified and should be reclassified as a deduction *for* adjusted gross income.

79. [LO 5.4] Prior to 1986, all consumer interest expense was deductible. In 1986, Congress eliminated the deduction for consumer interest expense, including interest paid on car loans and credit card balances. Why do you think Congress made this change?

80. [LO 5.7] Discuss the factors to consider when choosing between taking the child and dependent care credit and participating in an employer-sponsored qualified dependent care assistance program.

Search the Internet

81. [LO 5.3] Go to the IRS website (*www.irs.gov*) and locate the publication on the standard deduction. What documentation is necessary for a taxpayer with impaired vision to qualify for the additional standard deduction for blindness?

82. [LO 5.4] Go to the IRS website (*www.irs.gov*) and locate Publication 502: *Medical and Dental Expenses*. What expenses qualify for impairment-related work expenses? How do self-employed individuals deduct these expenses?

Identify the Issues

Identify the issues or problems suggested by the following situations. State each issue as a question.

83. [LO 5.3] Last year, after a very bad argument, Holly's husband moved out and has not been seen since. Holly's eight-year-old daughter lives with her.

84. [LO 5.4] Liza pays $5,000 for extensive liposuction surgery. Her medical insurance does not cover this expense.

85. [LO 5.4] Barry has a chronic back problem that requires that he receive regular therapy in a swimming pool. He purchased a new home with a larger backyard so that he could install a swimming pool. The purchase price of the home was $180,000. The cost of installing the pool was $12,000, and the real estate appraiser said that it increased the value of the home by $7,000. The pool is used only for Barry's therapy workouts.

86. [LO 5.4] Megan and Sam have a 10-year-old daughter, who is autistic. Megan and Sam pay $16,000 annual tuition for their daughter to attend a special school for autistic children.

87. [LO 5.4] In March, Helen purchased a new home for $140,000. She paid $28,000 cash down and financed the balance with a mortgage for which she also paid $1,800 in closing costs and $1,100 in points. Her interest on the mortgage for the year is $5,300.

88. [LO 5.4] Sabrina pays most of the cost for her Aunt Betty to live in a nursing home. Betty receives Social Security benefits of $8,200 a year (all paid to the nursing home). Betty has no other income so Sabrina pays the remaining nursing home cost of $36,800 a year. Sabrina regularly visits Betty and meets with her doctors regarding Betty's medical care. Sabrina also pays any of Betty's additional medical costs not provided by the nursing home.

89. [LO 5.6 & 5.7] Carla is single and provides more than 50 percent of the support for her mother who lives in a nursing home. Her mother received $2,000 interest on her State of Florida bonds, $3,000 in dividend income, and $8,000 in Social Security benefits.

90. [LO 5.7] Gillian and Paul are married and have a son who is a sophomore at the local university. In the current year, they paid $5,000 for tuition and $3,000 for room and board for him. Their adjusted gross income is $95,000, and they are in the 22 percent marginal tax bracket.

Develop Research Skills

91. [LO 5.4] Don has a very painful terminal disease and has learned that marijuana may mitigate his pain. Don lives in a state in which it is legal to use the drug if under the direction of a medical doctor. Can Don deduct the cost of the marijuana as a medical expense?

92. [LO 5.4] Charlene provides 100 percent of the support for her elderly handicapped mother, Amanda. Amanda insists on living alone in her own apartment even though she has a severe hearing impairment. Amanda has always liked cats, so Charlene purchased a cat that is registered as a hearing assistance animal with the county animal control division. The cat is trained to respond to unusual sounds in an instantaneous and directional manner, alerting Amanda to possible dangers. Charlene paid $800 for the cat and an additional $1,000 for special training. The maintenance costs for the cat are $15 a week. Charlene would like to know if any of these costs qualify as deductible expenses.

93. [LO 5.7] Howard is a single parent with an 11-year-old dependent son. The son currently attends sixth grade at public school. Howard accepts a temporary foreign assignment from his employer, which is expected to last from August through December. Because of the unstable political environment in the foreign country, Howard is uncomfortable taking his son with him. Therefore, Howard sends his son to a boarding school for the fall term at a cost of $5,000 ($3,000 for tuition and $2,000 for room and board). Will the $5,000 qualify for the dependent care credit?

94. [LO 5.7] Sarah pays $800 per month for her five-year-old daughter to attend a private kindergarten from 8:30 A.M. until 2:30 P.M. and after-school care until 5:30 P.M. The price of the kindergarten without the after-school care is $300 per month. Assuming Sarah pays the $800 each month of the year, how much qualifies for the dependent care credit?

Fill-in the Forms

95. [LO 5.4] Go to the IRS website (*www.irs.gov*) and print Schedule A: Itemized Deductions. Using the following information, complete this form for Simon and Ellen, both age 48 and married filing jointly, who have adjusted gross income of $60,000. They paid the following unreimbursed expenses during the year:

Prescription drugs	$ 600
Doctor bills	4,600
Contact lenses	300
Dentist bills	900
State income tax withheld from salary	1,800
Real property taxes	3,000
Interest on a home acquisition mortgage with a principal amount of $160,000 (reported on Form 1098)	6,000
Cash charitable contributions	1,400

96. **Tax Return Problem.** Go to the IRS website (*www.irs.gov*) and print Form 1040 and Schedule A. Using the information in problem 68, complete these forms to the extent possible.

97. **Tax Return Problem.** Janice Morgan is 17 and in her senior year of high school. She lives with her parents at 7829 Dowry Lane, Boston, MA 02112, and they are her primary source of support and claim her as a dependent. She is covered under their health insurance plan. Her Social Security number is 988-77-6543. She elects to contribute to the Presidential Election Campaign fund. From January through May of the current tax year, Janice took care of two children on weekends and earned $1,600. Her employer did not withhold any federal income tax but did withhold the proper amount of FICA taxes. During the summer, she then worked full-time at a fast-food restaurant and during the remainder of the year she worked part-time. Her earnings totaled $5,580 from which the employer withheld $255 for federal income taxes along with her FICA taxes. Janice's only other income was $210 in interest on her savings account. She had no foreign accounts. Complete a Form 1040EZ for Janice using the latest year form available on the IRS website at *www.irs.gov*.

98. **Comprehensive Tax Return Problem.** Jose (SSN 150-45-6789) and Rosanna (SSN 123-45-7890) Martinez are a married couple who reside at 1234 University Drive in Coral Gables, FL 33146. They have two children: Carmen, age 19 (SSN 234-65-4321), and Greg, age 10 (SSN 234-65-5432). Carmen is a full-time student at the local university; she lives at home and commutes to school. Jose is an architect for Deco Design Architects and is covered by his employer's defined benefit pension plan. His Form W-2 reported the following information:

Wages	$65,000	Federal income tax withheld	$6,100.00
Social Security wages	65,000	Social Security tax withheld	4,030.00
Medicare wages	65,000	Medicare tax withheld	942.50

Rosanna was a loan officer at BankOne until October. Her Form W-2 reported the following information:

Wages	$43,000	Federal income tax withheld	$3,000.00
Social Security wages	43,000	Social Security tax withheld	2,666.00
Medicare wages	43,000	Medicare tax withheld	623.50

Rosanna's employer does not provide any retirement plan for its employees.

Jose and Rosanna received $3,500 of interest income from BankOne and $130 of qualified dividend income on Microserf stock (reported in boxes 1a and 1b on Form 1099-DIV). Rosanna received $45 in jury duty pay in May.

The Martinez family has medical insurance that they purchase through the cafeteria plan offered by Jose's employer (on a pre-tax basis). The annual cost of this medical insurance for the entire family was $3,600. Martinez family also paid $12,300 for qualified medical expenses for which they received no insurance reimbursements.

The Martinez family paid $9,400 in interest on their home mortgage acquired in 2015 with a principle balance of $300,000 (which Overnight Mortgage Company reported to them on Form 1098). The Martinez family also owns a vacation home in Breckenridge, Colorado, for which they paid $4,100 of mortgage interest (acquired in 2016 with a principal balance of $82,000). Other interest paid by Jose and Rosanna includes $1,100 for a loan on their personal automobile and $400 on credit cards.

The Martinez family paid real estate taxes on their principal residence of $3,500, $2,000 of real estate taxes on their vacation home and $3,200 of sales taxes during the year.

The Martinez family has the necessary documentation for the following contributions made to qualified charitable organizations: (1) Cash of $2,500 given to their church. (2) Ford stock purchased 6 years ago on March 16, at a cost of $750 was given to United Way (a qualified charitable organization located at 1 Flagler St. Miami, FL 33156) on February 22 when it had a fair market value of $1,650 (the average stock price on the date of donation).

Jose and Rosanna received a Form 1098-T reporting in box 1 the $8,000 they paid for Carmen's tuition at Florida University (59-11223344; 111 College Road, Miami, FL 33134) where she is a sophomore. Box 8 was checked to indicate she was at least a half-time student. They also paid $750 for textbooks she needed for her classes. They want to maximize any tax benefits they can receive from the expenses they paid for Carmen's education.

In October, Rosanna quit her job with the bank and began a consulting business. The business code is 541990. She is operating the business under her own name and rented a small office at 1234 Coral Way, Coral Gables, FL 33146. Since Rosanna began her business so late in the year, her consulting income was only $7,000. She incurred the following expenses: $475 supplies, $210 telephone, $2,200 office rent, and $325 advertising.

Rosanna contributed $2,000 to a traditional individual retirement account on December 5. This is the first time she has contributed to an IRA.

Other information: They have no foreign accounts and no one in the family was ever convicted of a felony. Jose was born on April 1, 1977; Rosanna was born May 1, 1978.

Based on the information presented above, prepare a Form 1040 (married filing jointly) and any required related forms and schedules using the forms for 2017 available on the IRS website at *www.irs.gov*.

ANSWERS TO TEST YOURSELF

1. **c. Both daughter and nephew.** Under the dependency definition, the nephew is a qualifying child and the gross income test is waived for qualifying children under age 19 or full-time students under the age of 24. The gross income test is waived for the daughter and would be for the nephew if his income was $4,150 or more.

2. **c. $1,750.** Because the child is a dependent of her parents, her standard deduction is limited to $1,050. Her taxable income is $1,750 ($2,800 – $1,050).

3. **d. $36,000.** They can deduct the $8,000 cash, $2,000 FMV of clothing, $15,000 FMV of Apex stock, and $11,000 FMV of Microsoft stock. No deduction is allowed for the value of the donated services.

4. **d. $243,000.** $300,000 less $32,000 mortgage interest less $10,000 taxes less $15,000 charitable contributions = $243,000. Medical expenses do not exceed the 7.5% of AGI floor and the deduction for taxes is limited to $10,000.

5. **b. $16,000.** Only the medical expenses in excess of 10% of AGI, mortgage interest, and charitable contribution deductions are allowed for AMT purposes. Taxes are not deductible.

Business and Property Concepts

PART III

CHAPTER 6 Business Expenses

CHAPTER OUTLINE

LEARNING OBJECTIVES

After completing this chapter, you should be able to:

6.1 Describe the general provisions that apply to trade or business expenses.

6.2 Explain how accrual and cash methods affect the timing of business expense deductions.

6.3 Discuss provisions applicable to a start-up business differentiating them from those affecting a fully operational business.

6.4 Identify common operating expenses and describe the provisions limiting their deductibility for tax purposes.

6.5 Describe the expense deduction limitations applicable to residential rental property, home offices, and hobbies.

6.6 Explain why financial accounting tax expense reported on financial statements differs from actual taxes paid; identify and explain how temporary and permanent tax differences are reported.

The tax treatment of many business expenses differs from their treatment for financial accounting. Tax deductions for business expenses are allowed only if there is a specific provision in the Internal Revenue Code granting it. Other restrictions may limit the amount of a current year's expense deduction. For example, business start-up costs may have to be amortized over several years, business meal expenses are only partially deductible, and fines are not deductible at all.

The taxpayer's method of accounting determines the year in which a tax deduction is taken. Accrual-basis taxpayers deduct expenses when the all events test is met and economic performance has occurred. Cash-basis taxpayers usually deduct expenses in the year paid but may be able to make early payments for expenses at year-end to accelerate the tax deduction. Before making early payments, however, taxpayers should consider their tax rates for each year. Usually the time value of money dictates taking the deduction as soon as possible. If the tax rate is higher in the later year, however, the time value of money may not offset the tax savings achieved by deferring the expense.

Taxpayers should avoid the trap of making unnecessary expenditures solely to obtain a tax deduction. They should avoid expenses whenever possible to maximize after-tax income. If an expense is desirable or necessary, however, then every possibility should be explored to make it deductible. That is the essence of good tax planning.

SETTING THE STAGE—AN INTRODUCTORY CASE

Mark has a great idea for a new business. He spends $2,000 for a market survey and $2,200 for a feasibility study, investigating the potential for success prior to formation. After positive results from this investigative work, Mark forms the business as a sole proprietorship. He plans to use one room in his home as an office, and live off his substantial savings until the business becomes profitable.

Mark spends $1,500 for pre-opening advertising prior to beginning operations on July 1. For the balance of the current year he anticipates incurring the following expenses: $3,300 for business travel ($1,300 for meals, $900 for hotels, and $1,100 for airfare), $5,000 for supplies, and $1,800 for advertising. He joins the local country club as a place to entertain potential customers, paying annual dues of $2,400. Mark estimates that he will drive his Toyota Camry approximately 4,500 miles on business travel and approximately 8,000 miles for personal travel this year. This morning he received a speeding ticket while rushing to meet a potential customer and paid a $60 fine.

Mark will use one room in his home exclusively and regularly as his office. The room occupies 400 of the 2,000 square feet in his house. Annual expenses for his home include $8,000 for mortgage interest, $3,000 for real property taxes, $1,600 in utility bills, and $600 for homeowner's insurance. Allocated depreciation for the exclusive use of the room as a home office is $500.

Mark estimates first-year gross receipts of only $19,700, but anticipates a much better second year. He expects to be in the 24 percent marginal tax bracket this first year because of his other income. Mark assumes that all expenses incurred this year for his new business are fully deductible. Is he correct? We will return to this case at the end of the chapter.

6.1 CRITERIA FOR DEDUCTIBILITY

The previous chapters explained that all income is taxable unless there is a specific provision in the Internal Revenue Code excluding it. In contrast, no deductions are allowed for expenses unless a specific provision in the Internal Revenue Code grants them. Although this may not seem fair, the tax laws define income very broadly while deductions are defined narrowly. Tax deductions have been described as a matter of "legislative grace," meaning that Congress can decide from year to year which expenses are deductible.[1]

6.1.1 GENERAL PROVISIONS FOR TRADE OR BUSINESS EXPENSES

Section 162 governs the deductibility of expenses by corporations, partnerships, sole proprietorships, and all other forms of business organizations, and reads as follows:

> *There shall be allowed as a deduction all the ordinary and necessary expenses paid or incurred during the taxable year in carrying on any trade or business . . .*

Although this appears to suggest that every business expense is deductible, problems arise from differing interpretations of the terms *ordinary, necessary*, and *trade or business*. The term **trade or business** is used many times throughout the Internal Revenue Code but is never precisely defined. As a result, determining trade or business status depends on the facts and circumstances surrounding each business activity. Several criteria have been developed as a result of hundreds of cases litigated over the years. The first, profit motive, requires the activity be entered into with the expectation of revenues exceeding expenses. This issue is critical in determining whether a particular activity is a trade or business rather than a hobby. When a taxpayer consistently reports losses, the IRS may assert that the real motivation is personal enjoyment rather than the conduct of a profitable business. If the taxpayer cannot establish that an activity is a profit-motivated trade or business, many deductions may be lost. Until 2018, the tax law limited

[1] *New Colonial Ice Co. v. Helvering*, 13 AFTR 1180, 292 US 435, 4 USTC 1292 (1934).

deductions attributable to hobbies to the income from the hobby. From 2018 through 2025 *no* hobby deductions are allowed as discussed later.

The second criterion for recognizing a trade or business is the taxpayer's involvement on a regular and continuous basis. If a taxpayer enters into an activity with the intention of making a profit but does not spend the necessary time and effort required to elevate it to trade or business status, it may be considered an investment only. **Production of income** or **investment activities** consist of the ownership of income-producing assets or assets held for long-term appreciation in value. Generally, owners have a passive role in their investment activities, and it is this passivity that distinguishes an investment activity from a business activity.

Example 6.1

Kay and Larry are partners in the Office Supply Company. When they started the business three years ago, Larry provided start-up capital and set up the accounting system. Since then, however, he has not been involved. Instead he works full-time in his accounting practice. Kay invested some of her own money in the business and also serves as manager for the company. She spends 45 hours per week overseeing daily operations and has no other employment. Kay's unreimbursed expenses are business expenses; Larry's unreimbursed expenses are investment related.

Section 212 authorizes deductions for expenses paid or incurred (1) for the production or collection of income; (2) for the management, conservation, or maintenance of the property held for the production of income; and (3) in connection with the determination, collection, or refund of any tax, even though these expenses are not incurred in a trade or business.

Example 6.2

Jill invests in marketable securities. She subscribes to the *Wall Street Journal* to monitor the performance of specific stocks. She also rents a safe deposit box in which she keeps stock certificates and other investment-related documents, and pays a fee to an investment counselor for advice. All these expenses would qualify as deductible under Section 212 because they relate to her activity as an investor in marketable securities.

Although Section 212 authorizes a deduction for investment expenses, the deduction may be limited. Prior to 2018, investment expenses of individuals were deductible only as miscellaneous itemized deductions (deductible to the extent they exceed 2 percent of adjusted gross income).[2] The Tax Cuts and Jobs Act completely eliminated this deduction for years 2018 through 2025; as a result many individuals will have no tax benefit from their investment expenses (as discussed in Chapter 5).

Example 6.3

In 2017, Roger had an adjusted gross income (AGI) of $60,000 and incurred $1,500 of investment expenses, his only *miscellaneous* itemized deductions during the year. Roger can deduct only $300 of the investment expenses on his 2017 tax return because the $1,500 is less than his 2 percent of AGI threshold of $1,200 ($60,000 × 2%). As of 2018, his investment expenses will no longer be deductible.

6.1.2 ORDINARY AND NECESSARY

A deductible expense must be ordinary, necessary, and reasonable. An **ordinary** expense is one that is common and accepted in that type of business, but it does not have to occur on a regular

[2] This limitation does not apply to investment interest expense. Individuals' itemized deductions are discussed in Chapter 5.

basis. A **necessary** expense is one that is appropriate and helpful to the production of revenues. The expense does not have to be indispensable to be necessary. The courts generally do not second-guess taxpayers on the necessity of making expenditures. The expense merely needs to appear necessary when incurred.

In addition to being ordinary and necessary, the amount of a deductible expense must also be **reasonable**. Technically, this requirement is included in Section 162(a)(1) as it relates to compensation only. The courts, however, have found that the element of reasonableness was inherent in the ordinary and necessary tests.[3] There is no limit on the amount of a deduction if it is reasonable. An expense is considered reasonable if it is an amount that would typically be charged in the market by unrelated parties. If the deductions are large enough to create a net loss, however, the expense deduction may be limited.[4] For example, the deductions for home office expenses are subject to limitation as discussed later in this chapter.

In addition to the above criteria, certain expenditures cannot be deducted as an expense if they are

- contrary to public policy
- related to tax-exempt income
- accrued to a related party
- the obligation of another taxpayer

6.1.3 CONTRARY TO PUBLIC POLICY

Section 162 disallows deductions for several types of expenses considered contrary to public policy to avoid subsidizing the taxpayer's undesirable activity. Examples include fines and penalties imposed by a governmental unit for such items as speeding, violations of city housing codes, and violations of federal laws regulating safety standards.[5]

Example 6.4

Heavy Freight, Inc. is a trucking company that moves freight cross country. Because certain states have more stringent weight restrictions than others, the company is regularly fined for overweight trucks. To follow the strictest weight limitations would cost the company more than the overweight penalties. Although the fines are a necessary business expense, they are not deductible because the violations are considered contrary to public policy.

The same code section disallows a deduction for expenses incurred for political contributions and lobbying to avoid the perception that the government subsidizes political influence. Contributions to a political party or candidate, or by extension to a political action group or committee, as well as expenditures to influence public opinion about legislation or how to vote in an election, are not deductible.[6] The nondeductible contributions include direct or indirect payments of cash, payments for attending a convention or admission to a dinner, and gifts of any other property.[7]

---

3 *Comm. v. Lincoln Electric Co.*, 38 AFTR 411, 176 F.2d 815, 49-2 USTC 9388 (CA-6, 1949).

4 Deductions can also be limited by the at-risk and passive loss rules discussed in Chapter 11.

5 Additionally, bribes and kickbacks (payments for referring customers) are not deductible if they are made directly or indirectly to an official or employee of any government in violation of the law.

6 §162(e).

7 §276. Prior to December 22, 2017, direct lobbying expenses at the local level (such as city and county governments) were deductible.

6.1.4 RELATED TO TAX-EXEMPT INCOME

The taxpayer cannot deduct interest or any other expense incurred in earning tax-exempt income.[8] Absent this provision, a taxpayer in an upper marginal tax bracket might be able to "game the system" and obtain a positive cash flow by borrowing higher-interest money and investing it in lower-interest tax-exempt municipal bonds.

Example 6.5

Tim, a taxpayer in the 37 percent marginal tax bracket, borrows $1 million at 10 percent and invests the proceeds in 7 percent tax-exempt municipal bonds. Annual interest expense is $100,000. Without Section 265, Tim could reduce his tax liability by $37,000 (37% × $100,000). The tax-exempt interest earned on the bonds is $70,000, producing a net positive cash flow of $7,000 per year ($70,000 income + $37,000 tax savings − $100,000 interest expense). Section 265 prevents this by disallowing a deduction for the interest expense.

Similarly, no deduction is allowed for premiums paid on life insurance policies for which the business is the beneficiary as the proceeds are tax exempt.

Example 6.6

Mega Corporation takes out a $1 million insurance policy on its president for which Mega Corporation is the beneficiary. If the president dies, the $1 million in insurance proceeds are not taxable to Mega Corporation. Therefore, Mega Corporation is not permitted to deduct the premiums it pays for this insurance policy.

6.1.5 ACCRUED TO RELATED PARTY

If two taxpayers are related but one uses the accrual basis of accounting and the other the cash basis, expenses cannot be deducted by the accrual-basis taxpayer until the related revenues are recognized by the cash-basis taxpayer.[9] This provision prevents the accrual-basis taxpayer from recognizing an expense prior to the related party's recognition of income. The government tolerates this type of mismatch only when it involves unrelated parties.

Example 6.7

Bigcom, an accrual-basis, calendar-year corporation, hires Littlecom, a cash-basis, calendar-year corporation, to provide services for it. Bigcom receives the bill in December of year 1 and pays it in January of year 2. If Littlecom and Bigcom are not related, then Bigcom can deduct the expense on its year 1 tax return. If, however, Bigcom owns more than 50 percent of Littlecom, they are related taxpayers and Bigcom cannot deduct the expense until year 2 when Littlecom includes it in income.

6.1.6 OBLIGATION OF ANOTHER TAXPAYER

An expense must be incurred for the taxpayer's benefit or arise from the taxpayer's obligation to be deductible. If one taxpayer pays the obligation of another taxpayer, the payment is usually not deductible.

[8] §265.

[9] §267. Related parties include brothers, sisters, spouse, parents, grandparents, children, and grandchildren of the taxpayer; a corporation owned more than 50 percent by the taxpayer; and several other relationships. See Chapters 9 and 10 for discussions of related party transactions.

Example 6.8

Ted does not have the money to make his monthly interest payment on a business loan. If his mother, Sara, makes the payment for him, neither of them can take the deduction for the loan interest expense. Sara is not entitled to a deduction because the loan is not her obligation. Ted is not entitled to a deduction because he did not make the payment.

TAX PLANNING

The tax result would have changed if Sara made either a cash gift or loan to Ted. Ted then makes the loan payment and can deduct the interest. This would have preserved the deduction with no cash difference to the family.

6.1.7 SUBSTANTIATION

All taxpayers must maintain records that substantiate their expense deductions. Without adequate records, the IRS will usually prevail over the taxpayer if a dispute arises. It seems reasonable to require the taxpayer to properly document a transaction to obtain a deduction, as the taxpayer usually controls the transaction.

Substantiation can take the form of receipts, canceled checks, and paid bills.[10] Taxpayers must be prepared to retain these records for a reasonable time period because it is frequently several years after the expenditure has been made before the IRS conducts an audit.[11] If substantiation is not available at the time of an audit, the courts have sometimes allowed an unsubstantiated deduction if it is clear that the taxpayer made the expenditure. In this case, the taxpayer estimates the expense based on facts and circumstances.[12]

Stringent substantiation requirements must be followed for travel, gifts, and automobile expenses.[13] The substantiation may consist of diaries, trip sheets, travel logs, paid bills and receipts, account books, expense reports, and statements of witnesses.[14] Items that need to be documented for these expenses include:

- Amount of expenditure
- Time and place of expenditure, or date and description of gift
- Business purpose of expenditure
- Business relationship to person receiving a gift[15]

6.2 TIMING OF DEDUCTIONS

The taxpayer's method of accounting determines when an expense is deductible. The Internal Revenue Code frequently uses the phrase "paid or incurred" in determining when an expense is deductible. A cash-basis taxpayer is allowed to deduct an expense only when the expense is paid. An accrual-basis taxpayer can take the deduction when the liability for the expense is incurred (the amount and liability are certain) whether or not it is paid for in the same period.

6.2.1 ACCRUAL METHOD

Taxpayers who use the accrual method deduct their business expenses when both of the following conditions are met:

1. The **all events test** is met—that is, when all events have occurred that fix the fact of liability and the liability can be determined with reasonable accuracy.
2. There is economic performance.

[10] Rev. Proc. 92-71, 1992-2 CB 437 discusses procedures to use when a bank does not return checks to a taxpayer.
[11] See Chapter 2 for a discussion of the statute of limitations.
[12] *Cohan v. Comm.*, 8 AFTR 10552, 39 F.2d 540, 2 USTC 489 (CA-2, 1930).
[13] §274(d) and §280F(d)(4).
[14] Temp. Reg. §1.274-5T(b).
[15] §274(d).

Economic performance occurs when the property or services are provided or the property is used.[16]

Example 6.9

Elizabeth, a sole proprietor, had some repairs made at her business in late November of year 1. She received the bill in December of year 1 and paid it in January of year 2. If Elizabeth uses the accrual method, she deducts the expense on her year 1 tax return. All events have occurred establishing the liability and there was economic performance in that year. If Elizabeth uses the cash method, she deducts the expense on her year 2 tax return when she actually pays the bill.

Generally accepted accounting principles frequently require establishing reserves for estimated future expenses. These reserves normally are not deductible for tax purposes because the economic performance test is not satisfied. This is one of many examples of differences between financial statement (book) income and taxable income. The details of accounting for these differences are at the end of this chapter.

6.2.2 CASH METHOD

Taxpayers using the cash method of accounting are allowed to deduct an expense when the expense is paid. An expense paid by check is deductible when the check is mailed, not at the time the check is received by the intended recipient. If a check is not honored because the taxpayer has insufficient funds to pay the check (the check bounces), the deduction is not allowed until there are sufficient funds for the check to clear. When a taxpayer pays an expense with a credit card (or borrows from another source), the expenditure and the borrowing of funds occur simultaneously. Therefore, an expense charged on a credit card is deductible in the year charged, even if the credit card payment is made in another tax year.[17] Simply promising to pay or issuing a promissory note does not constitute payment, however.[18]

Example 6.10

Stu, a cash-basis sole proprietor, purchased $500 of office supplies for his business on December 12 of year 1 by using his business credit card. The charge for these office supplies appeared on the January statement in year 2, and Stu paid the credit card bill on February 1 of year 2. The purchase is deductible in year 1.

If an expense is paid with property or services, payment occurs when the taxpayer surrenders the property or renders the services. The deduction is generally the fair market value of the property or services provided. When appreciated property is used to pay an expense, the taxpayer usually must recognize gain on the excess of the property's fair market value over its cost basis.[19] When a cash-basis taxpayer pays an expense by providing services, he or she can deduct the expense but must recognize the fair market value of the services as income.

[16] The recurring item exception allows a current deduction even if economic performance has not yet occurred. To qualify, economic performance must occur within 8½ months after the close of the year and the expense either is not material or the accrual of the expense results in a better matching of income and expenses. Reg. §1.461-4.

[17] Rev. Rul. 78-39, 1978-1 CB 73.

[18] *Page v. Rhode Island Trust Co.*, 19 AFTR 105, 88 F.2d 192, 37-1 USTC 9138 (CA-1, 1937).

[19] Effectively the transaction is treated as if the taxpayer sold the property for its fair market value, recognized the gain (resulting in a tax liability on the gain), and then used the cash proceeds from the sale to pay for the expense.

Example 6.11

Ken does computer programming for a local newspaper in exchange for weekly ads for his computer programming business. During the year, Ken receives $2,800 worth of newspaper advertising for his services. Ken reports $2,800 as business income and deducts $2,800 as advertising expense.

Not all payments by a cash-basis taxpayer result in a current deduction. The regulations require capitalizing the cost of assets with useful lives extending substantially beyond the end of the year. Their cost is then recovered through depreciation, amortization, or depletion, regardless of the taxpayer's method of accounting.[20] Cost recovery methods for these assets are discussed in the next chapter.

TAX PLANNING

Cash-basis taxpayers sometimes have the ability to make early payments for their expenses at year-end. Examples of business expenses that are candidates for acceleration include purchasing supplies normally not part of inventory, advertising, and travel expenses. A tax deduction in the current year may be worth more than the same deduction in the next year due to the time value of money. Before taxpayers pay their expenses early, they should consider their tax rates for both years. Additionally, an early payment may not be wise if it causes a cash-flow problem.

Example 6.12

Hugo, a cash-basis, sole proprietor, is considering paying $20,000 of expenses at the end of this year rather than waiting until their January 10 due date next year. Hugo's marginal tax rate for the current year is 35 percent, and expects it to be the same next year. Hugo will save $7,000 ($20,000 × 35%) in taxes when it deducts the expenses on its tax return. If Hugo uses a 6 percent discount rate and waits until next year to pay the expenses, the present value of the $7,000 tax savings is $6,601 ($7,000 × .943). Hugo saves $399 ($7,000 – $6,601) more in taxes by paying the expenses this year due to the time value of money. If Hugo's current-year tax rate is only 24 percent but is expected to increase to 35 percent next year, postponing the expense deduction until next year produces greater tax savings [($20,000 × 35% × .943 = $6,601) – ($20,000 × 24% = $4,800) = $1,801 additional tax savings].

Businesses that sell merchandise to their customers must use the accrual method to account for purchases and sales of inventory because the cash method is easily manipulated to accelerate deductions (and defer income).[21] Small businesses with average annual gross receipts of $25 million or less can deduct the cost of merchandise inventory as materials and supplies expense in the year they are consumed or used.[22] Large corporations, defined as those with average annual gross receipts of more than $25 million, are prohibited from using the cash method for tax purposes.[23] This prohibition does not extend to personal service corporations; no matter their size, they may use the cash method.[24]

---

[20] Reg. §1.461-1(a).

[21] Reg. §1.446-1(a)(4)(i) and §1.471-1.

[22] §471(c).

[23] §448. This prohibition of the cash method extends to partnerships with corporate partners. Prior to 2018, the average annual gross receipts limit was $5 million.

[24] A personal service corporation is a corporation that provides services in the field of accounting, actuarial science, architecture, consulting, engineering, health, law, or the performing arts and whose employees own substantially all of the corporation. §448(d)(2).

6.2.3 RESTRICTIONS ON PREPAID EXPENSES

A **prepaid expense** is the current period payment for future benefits. Generally, an expenditure that benefits a future period should be capitalized. Payments for assets to be consumed by the close of the following year are fully deductible in the year of payment, however.[25]

Example 6.13

On December 20, Lowkey Corporation (a calendar-year, cash-basis corporation) spent $3,000 for office supplies for the next five months and $6,000 for an insurance policy covering its office building for the next three calendar years. Lowkey Corporation can deduct the $3,000 payment for office supplies because the supplies will be used by the end of the next year. Lowkey must capitalize the $6,000 insurance premium and deduct one-third ($2,000) of the cost in each of the next three taxable years.

Prepaid rents are deductible in the period paid only if the prepayment period does not exceed one year and the taxpayer has a contractual obligation to prepay rent beyond the current tax year.[26] Prepaid rents not meeting both of these requirements, must be capitalized as if the taxpayer was on the accrual method of accounting.

Example 6.14

Carlton Company (a cash-basis, calendar-year taxpayer) signs a lease with Realty Corporation to rent office space for 36 months on November 1. Carlton obtains monthly rent of $700 by agreeing to prepay the rent for the entire 36-month period. Only $1,400 ($700 × 2 months) of the total payment is deductible in the current year. The balance must be capitalized and amortized over the life of the lease. If the lease terms require Carlton to prepay $8,400 for each 12-month rental period on November 1, it could deduct $8,400 annually because each prepayment does not exceed one year.

Section 461(g) requires prepaid interest to be allocated to the time period over which the interest accrues. Thus, both cash- and accrual-basis taxpayers deduct prepaid interest in the same period.

Example 6.15

Taxatron (a cash-basis, calendar-year corporation) borrows $100,000 from the bank at 12 percent annual interest on November 1. Taxatron pays the bank $12,000 on December 29 for the first year's loan interest. Even though Taxatron is a cash-basis taxpayer, it can deduct only $2,000 interest expense (the interest for November and December). The $10,000 interest charged for the period from January 1 through October 31 of the following year cannot be deducted by Taxatron until the following year.

Original issue discount (OID) is a form of prepaid interest. The original issue discount is the difference between the stated redemption price at maturity (principal) and the issue price (proceeds) of the loan. OID must be amortized over the term of the loan.[27]

[25] Reg. §1.263(a)-4(f) provides a 12-month rule stating if an expenditure has a benefit lasting 12 months or less and that benefit does not extend beyond the end of the taxable year following the year of payment, the expense is deductible in the year of payment. An expenditure with benefits lasting more than 12 months must be capitalized.

[26] *Zaninovich v. Comm.*, 45 AFTR 2d 80-1442, 616 F.2d 429, 80-1 USTC 9342 (CA9-1980).

[27] The OID can be deducted on a straight-line basis if it is de minimis. OID is considered de minimis if it is less than one-fourth of 1 percent of the stated redemption price of the loan at maturity multiplied by the number of full years from the date of original issue to maturity. If the OID is not de minimis, the constant-yield method must be used.

Example 6.16

RiteMart Corporation borrowed $100,000 on January 1, year 1, and received $98,500 in proceeds. The loan matures in 10 years, and the $100,000 principal is due on that date. Interest of $10,000 is payable on January 1 of each year beginning January 1, year 2. The $1,500 OID ($100,000 – $98,500) is deductible at the rate of $150 each year for 10 years. The $10,000 interest is also deductible each year as it is paid.

The term *points* refers to the interest prepaid when a borrower takes out a loan or mortgage. Points are also called *loan origination fees*. Points are usually treated in the same manner as OID, as described above.[28] Individuals' deductions for interest expense on personal loans are limited to home mortgage interest or student loan interest, as discussed in Chapter 5.

6.2.4 DISPUTED LIABILITIES

TAX PLANNING

If a taxpayer contests a liability, the deduction usually cannot be taken until the dispute is settled by compromise or court decision. A taxpayer may, however, claim an immediate deduction for a contested liability by paying the disputed amount or placing that amount in escrow until the dispute is settled. When the dispute is finally settled, any adjustment to the deduction is made to income in the year of settlement.

6.3 COSTS OF STARTING A BUSINESS

Once a business actually begins operations, its ordinary and necessary expenses are deductible under Section 162. Expenses incurred *before* operations cannot be deducted as ongoing business expenses but are capital expenditures. Even if the taxpayer has an existing business, these costs may still have to be amortized rather than deducted currently. Examples include expenses of investigating a new business, start-up costs, and organization costs.

6.3.1 BUSINESS INVESTIGATION AND START-UP EXPENSES

Business investigation expenses are expenses incurred prior to the actual decision to enter into a new business operation. These include expenses for travel, market surveys, feasibility studies, and engineering reports. The deductibility of business investigation expenses depends on the nature of the taxpayer's current business activities, if any, and the nature of the business being investigated.

For taxpayers investigating a new business similar in nature to one of the taxpayer's *existing* businesses, all business investigation expenses are deductible in the current period, whether or not the new business is actually acquired. These expenses are treated as the expansion of the taxpayer's ongoing business activities.[29]

For taxpayers with no current business, or who are investigating a new business unrelated to any existing taxpayer business, one of the following applies:

1. If the new business is not acquired, the investigation expenses are not deductible.[30]
2. If the new business is acquired, all investigation expenses are included as part of start-up expenses.[31]

[28] An exemption exists for points paid on a home mortgage. See Chapter 5.
[29] *York v. Comm.*, 2 AFTR 2d 6178, 261 F.2d 421, 58-2 USTC 9952 (CA4-1958).
[30] Rev. Rul. 57-418, 1957-2 CB 143.
[31] §195(b).

Example 6.17

Pam, president and sole shareholder of Southbay Construction, Inc., spends $3,000 to travel to New York to investigate the feasibility of Southbay purchasing a restaurant there. Southbay Construction builds only townhouses. If the new business is not acquired, Southbay may not deduct any of the expenses. If the restaurant is acquired, the $3,000 is included with any start-up expenses incurred. If Southbay currently operates a chain of restaurants, expenses of adding the New York restaurant to its chain are deductible in the current year, even if it does not acquire the restaurant.

Start-up expenses are costs incurred before the beginning of actual operations and include employee training, advertising, professional services, and development of distributors and customers. Start-up costs include business investigation expenses and qualifying taxpayers can elect to deduct up to $5,000 of these combined costs with the balance amortized over 15 years (180 months).[32] If these total costs exceed $50,000, however, the $5,000 expensing allowance is reduced for each dollar total start-up expenses exceed $50,000. Thus, a company with $55,000 or more in investigation and start-up costs must amortize all of these costs over 15 years. Start-up costs to expand an existing business, however, are deductible as a cost of continuing operations.[33]

Example 6.18

Continuing the previous example, Pam directs Southbay to invest in the New York restaurant, a new business for the construction company. Southbay incurs $5,600 of start-up expenses for advertising and training of the staff. The $3,000 of business investigation expenses are included with the start-up expenses, a total of $8,600. Southbay can expense $5,000 of these expenses with the remaining $3,600 ($8,600 – $5,000) amortized at $20 per month ($3,600/180), beginning with the first month of actual operations. If this had not been a new business for Southbay, it could have expensed the entire $8,600 immediately as a cost of continuing an existing business.

6.3.2 ORGANIZATION COSTS

When a corporation is formed, its **organization costs** include fees for legal and accounting services incident to the formation process, fees paid to the state of incorporation for the corporate charter, and expenses for organization meetings of directors and stockholders. These expenditures create an intangible asset (the corporate form) that lasts for the life of the entity and are capitalized rather than deducted currently. Similar to start-up expenses, however, taxpayers can elect to deduct up to $5,000 of organizational costs, amortizing the balance over 15 years (180 months). If organizational costs exceed $50,000, the $5,000 expensing allowance is reduced ratably and phases out completely when organizational costs reach $55,000.[34]

Example 6.19

Newborn Corporation, a calendar-year taxpayer, incorporates and begins operations on July 1. It incurred $54,000 of organization costs and $20,000 of start-up expenses. Newborn can expense $1,000 of the organization costs and $5,000 of its start-up costs. It amortizes the remaining $53,000 of organizational costs and $15,000 of its start-up costs over 15 years [($53,000 + $15,000)/180 months = $377.78 per month] resulting in a first year deduction of $8,267 [$6,000 + ($377.78 × 6 months)].

[32] Prior to October 2004, start-up expenses were capitalized and amortized over 60 or more months with amortization beginning the month operations actually began.

[33] §195(c)(1)(B).

[34] §248. An election to expense or amortize start-up or organization costs is made by attaching Form 4562: *Depreciation and Amortization* to the business's first tax return.

6.4 OPERATING EXPENSES

Most operating expenses shown on income statements prepared under generally accepted accounting principles (GAAP) are also deductible on a business tax return. Examples include advertising, bank charges, commissions, depletion, depreciation, employee benefit programs, insurance, legal fees, licenses, pension and profit sharing plans, rent or lease payments, repairs and maintenance, salaries and wages, supplies, taxes, travel, and utilities. Nevertheless, some current financial expenses are not deductible in computing taxable income, and not all tax-deductible expenses can be expensed under GAAP. In dealing with these inconsistencies, the general rule is that tax deductions are more narrowly defined than accounting expenses.

6.4.1 BUSINESS MEALS AND ENTERTAINMENT

In 1986, Congress first tightened the rules on deductions for business meals and entertainment by imposing an 80 percent limit on the deductible amount. Among the principal targets of this tax reform were extravagant business luncheons where little business was discussed. In 1993, Congress further reduced the deductible portion of business meals and entertainment to only 50 percent. Since then, Section 274(n)(1) has limited the deduction for business meals to 50 percent of qualified expenses.[35] This limit applies to the cost of food, beverages, taxes, and tips associated with the business meal.[36]

This 50 percent limit applies to either the employer or the employee, whoever ultimately pays the cost of the meal. If the employer pays the expense directly or reimburses the employee, the 50 percent limit applies to the employer. If the employee is not reimbursed, the employee's deduction is limited to 50 percent of the expense. The 50 percent disallowance rule does not apply to any meal that is considered compensation to the recipient.[37]

Prior to 2018, expenses to entertain current and potential clients or customers were 50 percent deductible if they were either directly related to or associated with the active conduct of the taxpayer's trade or business. To be directly related to the taxpayer's business, an active discussion related to that business had to take place in a clear business setting.[38] Thus, entertainment at certain events at which the noise level prevented a meaningful discussion did not meet this requirement.

Events that did not meet the directly related standard could meet the associated with test if the event preceded or followed a meaningful business discussion. There had to be a clear business purpose for the discussion, it had to be substantial in relation to the entertainment, and the taxpayer had to expect a clear business benefit.[39] If entertainment tickets were involved, not only were they subject to the 50 percent limit, but the 50 percent limit applied to the face value of the tickets.

Example 6.20

In 2017, Mark took a customer to see a new Broadway show. The face value of each ticket was $100, but he paid a scalper $500 for each ticket. After leaving the theater, they discussed a new product that Mark would like to sell the customer. As it is unlikely that the two discussed business during the show, the ticket cost does not qualify as directly related entertainment. A deduction could be allowed for the tickets if the business discussion following the show qualified as "associated with" the conduct of Mark's business. Mark's deduction is limited to $50 for each ticket ($100 face value × 50%) for 2017. If, however, there was no business discussion, the costs are not deductible as entertainment. If Mark incurs this expense in 2018, no entertainment deduction will be allowed.

[35] Under §274(n)(3)(B), an 80% deduction limit applies to individuals subject to the hours of service limitations of the Department of Transportation, including airline personnel, interstate truck and bus drivers, and railroad employees.

[36] §274(n)(1)(B). Transportation expenses, such as taxi fares for getting to and from a restaurant, are 100 percent deductible.

[37] §274(n)(2). Samples and promotional activities available to the general public as advertising are not affected by this limit.

[38] Reg. §1.274-2(c)(3).

[39] Costs of including the customer's or the taxpayer's spouse were normally considered part of the active conduct of business and were deductible. Reg. §1.274-2(d)(4).

This is no deduction allowed for the costs of owning and maintaining recreation facilities, such as hunting lodges and yachts, nor for membership dues and fees (including initiation fees) paid to social, athletic, or sporting clubs. This prohibition does not apply to dues for professional organizations (such as bar associations and medical associations), public service organizations (such as Rotary, Kiwanis, and Lions), or trade associations (including business leagues and chambers of commerce).

Example 6.21

Jack, a CPA, pays $5,000 annual membership dues to the local country club where he entertains his clients playing golf while they discuss business. Jack also pays $250 per year for dues to the American Institute of Certified Public Accountants (AICPA). Jack can deduct the $250 AICPA dues, but he cannot deduct the country club dues.

The deduction for business gifts is limited to $25 per donee per year.[40] Gifts costing $4 or less with the company's name on them or other promotional materials are not included in the $25 limit. Samples given to customers or potential customers to elicit business are not treated as business gifts subject to the $25 limitation.

Example 6.22

Chandon Corporation gives each of its best 100 customers a $70 bottle of champagne. It also distributes 500 pens (costing $2 each) with the company's name on them. Chandon can deduct the first $25 of each champagne gift for a total of $2,500 ($25 × 100) and can also deduct the full $1,000 (500 × $2) cost of the pens.

6.4.2 TRAVEL AND TRANSPORTATION EXPENSES

Congress imposes numerous restrictions and limitations on the deductibility of travel expenses because of the potential for taxpayer abuse. Taxpayers can easily bend the rules, so IRS agents pay particular attention to these deductions, scrutinizing a taxpayer's records for any unsubstantiated or suspicious expenses.[41]

Travel Away from Home

Travel expenses include amounts spent for lodging and meals while temporarily away from home on business, the cost of transportation to the destination and back, and incidental expenses. The expenses must be reasonable, necessary, and directly attributable to the taxpayer's business.[42] To qualify as travel, taxpayers must be away from home overnight or for substantially longer than an ordinary workday so that sleep or rest is required.

Example 6.23

Dan is a truck driver who leaves his home terminal on a regularly scheduled round-trip run between two cities and returns home 18 hours later. During the run, he has 6 hours off at the turnaround point where he eats two meals and rents a hotel room to sleep before starting the return trip. He is away from home and can deduct his travel expenses. If his trip took only 9 hours, with only 1 hour for a meal, Dan would not be away from home and could not deduct the meal.

[40] §274(b)(1). Incidental costs such as engraving or nominal charges for gift wrapping are not included in the cost of the gift in applying this limitation.

[41] An employer's reimbursement of an employee's personal travel expenses does not convert them to business travel expenses. The payment is income to the employee.

[42] Reg. §1.162-2(a).

To determine if a taxpayer is away from home, home must be defined. A **tax home** is identified by the IRS as the location of the taxpayer's principal place of employment, regardless of where the family residence is maintained.

Example 6.24

Linda and her husband maintain a home in Red Bank, New Jersey. Linda teaches at a university in New York City, where she rents a room and eats in restaurants four days during the week. She returns to New Jersey the other days. New York City, where she works, is her tax home. She cannot deduct any expenses for lodging or meals in New York City, as she is not away from home. Her transportation between New Jersey and New York is also a personal nondeductible expense.

Local Lodging Exception

Lodging expenses when not traveling away from home are normally considered nondeductible personal expenses. In 2014, the IRS finalized regulations that provide a limited exception when circumstances show that the local lodging expenses are necessary for an employee to participate fully in a bona fide business meeting, conference, or other business function.[43] Qualifying examples include employees required to stay at a local hotel during a work-related training session and professional athletes required to stay at a local hotel before a home game. If the lodging is primarily for the employee's convenience, it does not qualify. Local lodging because the employee must work overtime, lodging to avoid a long-distance commute, temporary housing for a recently-relocated employee, and a weekend at a luxury hotel provided for the employee's benefit, are examples that do not qualify as business related expenses.

Temporary Assignments

The away-from-home test requires a **temporary absence** from the home. If the employment away from home in a single location is expected to last (and does in fact last) for no more than one year, it is temporary.[44] Assignments of more than one year are not temporary; the individual's tax home shifts to the new location and travel expenses and living costs there are not deductible.[45] If the expected length of temporary employment later increases to more than one year, the employment is temporary *until* the date the taxpayer's expectation changes.

Example 6.25

Alan is employed in Fort Pierce, Florida, but accepts an assignment in Jacksonville, 250 miles away. Alan expects to work in Jacksonville less than six months, but is actually employed for 10 months before returning to Fort Pierce. His employment in Jacksonville is still temporary and his travel expenses are deductible.[46] If after six months, however, Alan agrees to stay an additional 7 more months (a total of 13 months), his employment ceases to be temporary. His travel expenses for the additional 7-month period are not deductible.[47]

Transportation Expenses

Transportation expenses are the costs of traveling from one place to another when the taxpayer is *not* away from home, and include automobile expenses, tolls, parking, and taxi fares. When

---

[43] Reg. §1.132-32.
[44] Rev. Rul. 93-86, 1993-2 CB 71.
[45] §162(a).
[46] Rev. Rul. 93-86, Situation 1, 1993-2 CB 71.
[47] Rev. Rul. 93-86, Situation 3, 1993-2 CB 71.

the taxpayer uses a personal automobile for business transportation, either the actual expenses for the business-use portion or a standard mileage allowance may be deducted. Actual expenses include depreciation or lease payments, gas and oil, tires, repairs, insurance, registration fees, parking, and tolls.[48] The standard mileage allowance is 54.5 cents per mile in 2018.[49] Parking and tolls are deductible in addition to the mileage allowance.[50] The actual cost method for automobile expenses usually results in a larger deduction than the standard mileage allowance. The principal disadvantage of using the actual cost method is the additional record keeping necessary to substantiate them.

TAX PLANNING

Qualifying transportation expenses include travel between home and a *temporary* work location (temporary is defined as one year or less) if the taxpayer has a regular place of business,[51] or travels from one job to another on the same day. Transportation expenses do not include the cost of commuting to and from work as this is considered a nondeductible personal expense.[52]

Example 6.26

Carl, an accountant employed by a Houston CPA firm, travels 60 miles round-trip from his home to an audit client located in the Houston metropolitan area. Carl eats lunch on his own at a restaurant near the client's office and returns home in time for dinner. Carl's employer reimburses him $32.70 (60 miles × 54.5 cents per mile). The employer deducts the $32.70 as a business expense on its tax return. If Carl was a self-employed CPA, he could deduct the $32.70 with his other business expenses on his Schedule C. However, no deduction is allowed for Carl's lunch because he is not traveling away from home. Carl cannot deduct the cost of commuting to his office.

6.4.3 COMBINING BUSINESS WITH PLEASURE TRAVEL

If the primary purpose of combined business and pleasure travel within the United States is business, transportation costs to and from the destination are deductible. The primary purpose is business if the number of days on business exceeds those on pleasure. If the number of days on pleasure exceeds those on business, the primary purpose is pleasure and none of the transportation expense is deductible. Travel days, however, are considered business days along with any days on which business is conducted. Meals and lodging are deductible only for business days.

Example 6.27

Carol flies from Atlanta to San Diego for business. She conducts business on four days while in San Diego, then stays an additional day for sightseeing. The primary purpose of her trip is business and she can deduct her entire round-trip airfare between Atlanta and San Diego, along with her lodging and meals for the four business days. She cannot deduct her lodging or meals on the sightseeing day, as they are considered nondeductible personal expenses. If she spends more than four days on pleasure, her airfare would not be deductible.

[48] Depreciation limits are discussed in the next chapter.

[49] Notice 2018-3, 2018-2 IRB. The standard mileage allowance was 53.5 cents per mile in 2017, 54 cents per mile in 2016, and 57.5 cents per mile in 2015.

[50] A self-employed individual may also deduct the business part of interest on the car loan.

[51] Rev. Rul. 90-23, 1990-1 CB 29. It is not necessary for the individual to report to his or her office first before going to the temporary work site to deduct these transportation expenses.

[52] Reg. §1.162-1(e).

Bryan takes a one-week vacation trip to San Diego. While there, he meets a client for six hours on one day. The rest of the week is spent sightseeing and relaxing. The primary purpose of Bryan's trip is a vacation and none of his airfare to San Diego is deductible. Bryan can deduct his travel expenses associated with his one business day (meals and lodging). His other travel expenses are considered nondeductible personal expenses.

The IRS has accepted Saturday meal and lodging expenses as qualified business travel expenses when an employer requests that an employee extend the business trip to take advantage of a low-priced airfare requiring a Saturday night stay. The savings in airfare must be greater than the cost of the weekend meals and lodging.[53]

TAX PLANNING

If a taxpayer's presence is required for business both on a Friday and the following Monday, the intervening weekend expenses are deductible if staying for the weekend is cheaper than returning home. Thus, scheduling business on both a Friday and the following Monday turns the weekend into business days for allocation purposes.

No deduction is permitted for travel expenses of a spouse, dependent, or other person accompanying the taxpayer unless that person is also an employee (or owner) of the business, the travel is for a bona fide business purpose, and the expenses otherwise would be deductible.[54] Expenses incurred to attend a convention, seminar, or meeting related to the taxpayer's business are allowable travel expenses; however, attendance at the convention or other meeting must be for the benefit of the taxpayer's trade or business, rather than for social, political, or similar purposes unrelated to the business.[55] No deductions are allowed if the travel is for general education only.[56]

There are somewhat different rules for travel outside the United States.[57] If the entire time outside the United States is spent on business activities, all allowable travel expenses are deductible as if the travel had been entirely in the United States. If personal activities are combined with foreign business travel, transportation expenses must be allocated between business and personal days unless (1) the travel does not exceed one week or (2) less than 25 percent of the total time is spent for personal purposes.[58] If a foreign trip is primarily personal, the travel expenses to and from the destination are not deductible (even if the traveler engages in limited business activities at the destination).[59]

Example 6.28

Joan flies to Paris from Cincinnati. She spends three days in Paris on business, stays over in Paris for a two-day vacation, and returns to Cincinnati. The full cost of transportation and 50 percent of meals while traveling to and from Paris are deductible. No allocation of the transportation cost to personal activities is required because the travel does not exceed one week. The cost of meals and lodging for the two vacation days are nondeductible, however.

If Joan spends seven days in Paris on business and four days on vacation, she is gone for more than one week and spends more than 25 percent of the time on vacation. She must allocate 4/11 of her transportation costs to nondeductible personal expenses. If Joan spent only four days on business and seven were spent on vacation, none of the transportation would be deductible.

[53] LTR 9237014.
[54] §274(m)(3).
[55] Reg. §1.162-2(d). Travel to attend investment seminars is generally disallowed if the travel relates only to an income-producing activity (under Section 212) instead of the taxpayer's trade or business. §274(h)(7).
[56] §274(m)(2).
[57] Foreign travel is travel outside the geographical United States, defined as the 50 states and the District of Columbia only. Reg. §1.274-4(a).
[58] §274(c)(2).
[59] Reg. §1.274-4(f)(5)(ii).

Expenses of attending conventions, seminars, or other meetings aboard cruise ships are not deductible unless the cruise ship is a vessel registered in the United States and all ports of call are in the United States or its possessions. Because most cruise ships are registered in foreign countries, this requirement effectively prevents most cruises from qualifying.[60]

6.4.4 BAD DEBT EXPENSES

According to generally accepted accounting principles, businesses should use the allowance method to account for bad debts.[61] Congress, however, does not allow businesses to base a tax deduction on the expectation of a future event. Thus, businesses must use the **specific charge-off method** for tax purposes, under which they deduct accounts receivable or other business debts only when actually written off as uncollectible during the year.

Example 6.29

Marlin, Inc. (an accrual-basis corporation) began the year with a $50,000 balance in its allowance for bad debts. During the year, the controller writes off $40,000 of Marlin's accounts receivable as worthless against this allowance. Based on Marlin's year-end accounts receivable, the independent auditor determines that a $48,000 addition to the bad debt reserve is necessary. As a result, the year-end reserve balance increases to $58,000 ($50,000 + $48,000 − $40,000). Although Marlin's financial statement shows bad debt expense of $48,000, Marlin can deduct only $40,000 on its tax return.

No deduction is allowed for a bad debt unless the receivable was included in income. So cash-basis taxpayers are not allowed a bad debt deduction because they have not recognized the revenue and the inability to collect income is a nondeductible loss.

Example 6.30

Bob (a cash-basis individual) did some consulting for FlyByNight Company. He sent a bill to FlyByNight for $2,000 for work he had done, but received no response. He went to the office to collect his $2,000 and found that FlyByNight had moved and left no forwarding address. Thus, Bob is unable to collect the $2,000 he is owed. Because Bob is a cash-basis taxpayer, he had not included the $2,000 in taxable income and is not allowed a bad debt deduction.

Substantial restrictions apply to the deductibility of nonbusiness bad debts.[62] First, the taxpayer must be able to substantiate that the loan is, in fact, a valid debt. This may present a problem for a loan between friends or related parties because it often resembles a gift rather than a loan. For these loans, the taxpayer needs to provide evidence that *both parties* intended the transaction to be a loan. If at all possible, taxpayers should obtain written documentation, signed by both parties, that provides for a specific due date for repayment of the debt, and for payment of interest at a reasonable rate. If the taxpayer can substantiate the debt, a nonbusiness bad debt is deductible only as a capital loss.[63]

[60] Even when all the requirements are met, the maximum deduction allowed is $2,000 per individual per year. §274(h)(2).

[61] Under this method, businesses estimate the portion of their accounts receivable that are uncollectible. An annual addition is made to the allowance account to bring the total up to the amount of the current year's receivables expected to be uncollectible.

[62] Investment and personal loans made by taxpayers are considered nonbusiness loans.

[63] §166(d)(1)(B). Nonbusiness bad debts are always treated as short-term capital losses. The capital loss deduction for individuals is limited to $3,000 in excess of capital gains. Losses not deductible due to the $3,000 limit are carried forward to future years.

Example 6.31

Jerry loaned $1,000 to his brother, Gary, to invest in the stock market. Jerry did not establish a specific due date for repayment of the debt, nor did he charge Gary interest on the loan. There is no documentation of any sort indicating that the transaction was a loan rather than a gift. Gary never repaid the money. Accordingly, Jerry is not allowed a bad debt deduction.

6.4.5 INSURANCE PREMIUMS

Insurance premiums for fire, casualty, and theft coverage on business property are deductible as business expenses. If a business self-insures, however, payments into the self-insurance reserve are not deductible for tax purposes; only actual losses are deductible. Life insurance premiums paid by a business as employee fringe benefits are deductible, but premiums paid on key-person life insurance policies are not deductible if the business is the beneficiary.[64]

6.4.6 INTEREST EXPENSE

Prior to 2018, business-related interest expense was usually fully deductible.[65] Beginning in 2018, the Tax Cuts and Jobs Act introduced a new limitation on the deductibility of business interest expense for all large businesses (including corporations, partnerships, and sole proprietorships). Small businesses, defined as those with average annual gross receipts for the three prior years not exceeding $25 million, are not subject to this limit.

The deduction for business interest expense cannot exceed the sum of the taxpayer's business interest income for the year plus 30 percent of its adjusted taxable income.[66] Until 2022, adjusted taxable income is the business's taxable income before business interest expense, business interest income, and the deductions for depreciation, amortization or depletion. After 2021, adjusted taxable income is computed *after* deducting depreciation, amortization and depletion. Any business interest that is not deductible due to this limitation is treated as if paid in the next year and can be carried forward indefinitely.

Example 6.32

In 2018, Gamma Corporation has $10,000,000 of adjusted taxable income, $200,000 of business interest income, and $600,000 of business interest expense. Gamma can deduct all $600,000 of its interest on its 2018 tax return because this is less than its $3,200,000 limit [($10,000,000 × 30% = $3,000,000) + $200,000].

In 2019, Gamma Corporation has only $1,000,000 of adjusted taxable income but still has $200,000 of business interest income, and $600,000 of business interest expense. Gamma can deduct only $500,000 [($1,000,000 × 30% = $300,000) + $200,000] of its interest on its 2019 tax return. The excess $100,000 will be treated as if paid in 2020 and can be carried forward indefinitely.

If the taxpayer's taxable income is negative, it is treated as zero for this calculation so that deductible interest expense is limited to interest income.

Real property businesses can elect to be exempt from this business interest limit if they are willing to use the alternative depreciation system (discussed in Chapter 7). Real property

[64] §165. See example 6.6.

[65] §163(j) limited the ability of certain corporations to deduct interest paid when no U.S. tax was imposed on their interest income. For a taxpayer (other than a corporation), investment interest expense is limited to net investment income (see Chapter 5).

[66] §163(j)(1). Motor vehicle businesses using floor plan financing can increase this limit by their floor plan financial interest so that it is fully deductible. Public utilities are also exempt from this limit.

businesses include property development, redevelopment, construction, reconstruction, acquisition, conversion, rental, operating, management, leasing, or brokerage.

6.4.7 LEGAL EXPENSES

Legal expenses are deductible only if the taxpayer can show that the origin and character of the claim are directly related to a trade or business, such as legal fees to protect an existing business or its reputation. Personal legal expenses (such as the preparation of a will) are not deductible. Legal fees incurred for the determination, collection or refund of taxes are deductible after 2017 only if business related. Legal fees incurred in the acquisition of property or to defend title to property are added to the asset's basis. If a taxpayer incurs legal fees in connection with the defense of a criminal charge, these fees are deductible only if the legal action has a direct relationship to a profit-seeking activity.

Example 6.33

Miguel owns a tabloid newspaper. A famous talk show host featured in his paper sued Miguel for libel. Miguel paid $50,000 in legal fees for his defense but was found guilty. Miguel also paid his attorney $500 to prepare his personal will. Because the $50,000 in legal fees is related to Miguel's business, it is deductible. The $500 for preparation of the will is a nondeductible personal expense.

The Tax Cuts and Jobs Act added a provision denying a deduction for any settlement, payout, or attorney fees related to sexual harassment or sexual abuse if payments are subject to a nondisclosure agreement. This is effective for amounts paid or incurred after December 22, 2017.

6.4.8 TAXES

Taxes paid by most businesses are deductible with one exception—federal income taxes. Deductible taxes include the following:

1. State, local, and foreign real property taxes
2. State and local personal property taxes
3. State, local, and foreign income taxes[67]
4. Employer's payroll taxes (employer's share of FICA and unemployment taxes)
5. Other federal, state, local, and foreign taxes that are incurred in a business or other income-producing activity

When state income taxes are deducted in computing federal taxable income, the tax savings from this deduction reduce the cost of the state tax.

Example 6.34

Carson Corporation paid $20,000 in state income tax this year. If its federal tax rate is 21 percent, the after-tax cost of its state income tax payment is only $15,800 [$20,000 − ($20,000 × 21%)].

When a taxpayer pays income tax at both the federal and state level, it increases its total effective tax rate and decreases the after-tax cash flow.

[67] Either a deduction may be taken for foreign income taxes or a foreign tax credit may be claimed, but not both.

Example 6.35

Yanney Corporation has before-tax income of $500,000 and is subject to a state income tax of 6 percent. Yanney's total effective tax rate for the current year is 25.74 percent, computed as follows:

State income tax ($500,000 × 6%)	$30,000
Federal income tax [($500,000 – $30,000) × 21%]	98,700
Total income tax	$128,700

$128,700/$500,000 income = 25.74%

Yanney's after-tax cash flow = $371,300 ($500,000 – $128,700).

Sales taxes paid on services or for the purchase or use of property are included in the cost of the service or property. If the property is depreciable, the sales tax is added to the cost of the depreciable property.

When real estate is sold, the real estate taxes for the entire year are apportioned between the buyer and seller based on the number of days the property is held by each. The seller's portion of the taxes begins on the first day of the year and ends on the day before the date of sale. A taxpayer must distinguish between the payment of real property taxes and assessments that fund improvements specifically benefiting the taxpayer's property. Assessments include construction of or improvements to streets, sidewalks, water mains, sewer lines, and public parking facilities. Assessments generally are not deductible but instead increase the cost basis of the property by the amount of the assessment.[68]

6.5 LIMITED EXPENSE DEDUCTIONS

Expenses for the rental of residential property, the use of part of the home as an office, or for an activity classified as a hobby are limited to prevent taxpayers from generating tax losses from activities with little or no gross income.

6.5.1 RESIDENTIAL RENTAL PROPERTY

The rental of real estate is usually treated as a trade or business. All income is included and all expenses are deducted, even if they exceed income.[69] Expenses typically include advertising, cleaning, maintenance, utilities, insurance, taxes, interest, commissions for collecting rent, and travel to collect rental income or to manage or maintain the rental property.

Most expenses for the personal use of residential property are not deductible except for property taxes and mortgage interest, which are deductible as itemized deductions. This provision encourages home ownership but limits the taxpayer's deduction for mortgage interest to the interest incurred for a principal residence and one other residence.[70] There are two situations in which a taxpayer must allocate expenses between the personal and rental use of residential property: when the personal residence is converted from (to) personal use to (from) rental real estate, and when the real estate is used for both rental and personal purposes.

[68] Assessments for maintenance, repairs, or current interest on financed improvements are deductible.

[69] The deductibility of these losses may be limited by the at-risk and passive loss rules. The passive loss rules are discussed in more detail in Chapter 11.

[70] The interest deduction is generally limited to mortgages with a principal balance of $750,000 or less ($1 million or less if acquired before December 15, 2017) as discussed in Chapter 5.

Example 6.36 Ken moves out of his home in May and rents it starting on June 1. He deducts 7/12 of the annual expenses, such as mortgage interest, property taxes, and insurance, against the rental income. Starting in June, he also deducts the monthly expenses, such as utilities and maintenance. Ken deducts the mortgage interest and property taxes for the first five months of the year as itemized deductions, but cannot deduct the insurance during his personal-use of the home.

When a home is rented to others for part of the year but is not converted to or from rental property (for example, a vacation home) the expenses must be allocated between rental use and the owner's personal use. Expenses directly related to the rental of the property are fully deductible against rental income. The rental portion of mixed-use expenses is deductible against rental income, subject to limitations based on the classification of the property as primarily a residence with some rental use or primarily rental property.

De Minimis Exception

Rental payments are usually included in gross income, but for administrative convenience a de minimis exception applies if a taxpayer's home is rented for less than 15 days during the year. Under this exception, the home is not considered rental property. The rental income is excluded from gross income but no deduction is allowed for expenses related to the rental of the property, except for the mortgage interest and property taxes otherwise allowed as itemized deductions. This provision allows taxpayers to rent their home for a short period of time (such as a major sporting event) without paying tax on the rental income.

TAX PLANNING

Residence with Some Rental Use

When property is rented for more than 14 days, the property is still considered a residence if personal use is more than the greater of 14 days or 10 percent of the number of rental days during the year. Days when the property is available for rent, but not actually rented, do not count as either personal or rental days. Personal use includes:

- Days the taxpayer or any other owner stays in the property
- Days a family member of an owner stays in the property (even if full fair market value rent is paid)[71]
- Days used under a home-exchange arrangement
- Days when rented for less than fair market value

Rental use includes days when the property is rented at fair market value and days spent repairing or maintaining the property for rental use.

Expenses directly related to the rental of the property, such as advertising and real estate fees to obtain tenants, are fully deductible against rental income. Other expenses must be allocated between personal-use and rental days, however, using the following allocation formula:[72]

$$\frac{\text{Number of rental days}}{\text{Total number of days used}} \times \text{Total expense} = \text{Rental use expense}$$

[71] Family members include brothers, sisters, spouse, ancestors, and lineal descendants. §267(c)(4).

[72] An alternative to this formula substitutes the total number of days in the year for the total number of days used and is sanctioned by several courts, but not the IRS. See *Bolton v. Comm.*, 51 AFTR2d 82-305, 82 USTC ¶9699 (9th Cir., 1982) and *McKinney v. Comm.*, 52 AFTR 2d 83-6281, 83-2 USTC ¶9655 (10th Cir., 1983). This method allocates a smaller portion of the taxes and interest to the rental use and allows a greater portion of other expenses to be deducted against the income. This method only applies to taxes and interest, not to other expenses.

A residence with some rental use is subject to special rules to prevent a loss deduction; that is, the deductible expenses for the rental portion are limited to the rental income.[73] Both rental income and rental expenses are reported on Schedule E: *Supplemental Income and Loss*. Any net rental profit is combined with the taxpayer's other income. The mortgage interest and taxes related to personal-use, and any portion of these expenses disallowed due to the rental income limitations, are deductible as itemized deductions.[74]

Rental Property with Limited Personal Use

When personal use of property subject to rental *does not exceed* the greater of 14 days or 10 percent of the rental days, the property is no longer a residence but is treated as rental property. All rents are included in income and all expenses related to the rental use are deductible even if they exceed rental income (subject to passive activity loss limitation rules discussed below). Property taxes allocated to personal use remain deductible as itemized deductions, but not the personal use part of mortgage interest expense; only the rental portion is deductible.

Figure 6.1 summarizes the tax treatment of residential rental property.

Rental period	Personal use	Tax treatment
All occupied days	None	Report all rental income and deduct all expenses for the property.
Less than 15 days	Balance of year	No rental income reported and no rental expenses deducted. Mortgage interest and property taxes are deducted as itemized deductions.
More than 14 days	Does not exceed the greater of 14 days or 10% of rental days	Rental income reported and all rental expenses deducted on rental schedule. Property taxes for personal use are deducted as itemized deductions.
More than 14 days	Exceeds the greater of 14 days or 10% of rental days	Rental income reported and rental expenses deducted on rental schedule but expenses are limited to rental income (cannot create a rental loss). Mortgage interest and property taxes for personal use are deducted as itemized deductions.

FIGURE 6.1 Tax treatment of residential rental property

Example 6.37

John rents his vacation home in Maui to some friends for 12 days for $1,200. Although John does not use the home himself this year, the $1,200 is not income under the de minimis exception and he does not deduct any of the related expenses. He can, however, deduct his mortgage interest and property taxes that would be deductible as if the home had not been rented.

The next year John takes a leave from his job and uses the Maui home for 100 days and rents it for 100 days. The home is now treated as a personal residence with limited rental use. John apportions expenses between his personal and rental use. The apportioned rental expenses are deductible only to the extent of the income from the property. He can, however, deduct both the personal portion of the mortgage interest and property taxes and any portion of these expenses disallowed as an expense deduction due to the rental income limitation as itemized deductions.

In the next year John uses the Maui home for 10 days and rents it for 190 days during the year. John apportions 95 percent (190/200) of the expenses to the rental of the home. All rental income and the rental portion of all the expenses are reported on Schedule E: *Supplemental Income and Loss*. He deducts all rental expenses even if they exceed rental income (subject to the passive loss limitation exception) as the property is considered *primarily* rental property. He can deduct the personal portion of property taxes as an itemized deduction.

[73] There are specific provisions in §280A that prevent the temporary rental of the taxpayer's primary residence from being subject to these rules.

[74] As discussed in Chapter 5, individuals are allowed to deduct the mortgage interest expense for their principal residence plus only one additional home as an itemized deduction. For any of the mortgage interest on a property that has been rented to qualify as an itemized deduction, the taxpayer must have personally used the home more than the greater of 14 days or 10 percent of the rental days during the year. §280A(d)(1).

TAX PLANNING

Although the term *vacation home* is usually used, the term is broader than what is normally considered a home because Section 280A refers to dwelling units. A dwelling unit is one that provides shelter for living and sleeping and cooking facilities.[75] Thus, campers, motor homes, trailers, and houseboats that provide these facilities qualify as vacation homes.

Losses on Rental Property

Congress enacted the **passive activity loss rules** (discussed in Chapter 11) in an attempt to discourage investment in tax shelters. Investors used their losses from tax shelters (many of them operated as rental activities) to offset income from sources such as salaries, interest, dividends, and capital gains. The passive activity rules separate income or loss into one of three categories: active (salaries, wages, and profit or loss from a business in which the taxpayer materially participates), portfolio (interest, dividends and capital gains), and passive (rental activities and limited partnerships). Losses from passive activities can only offset profits from another passive activity (not income from the other two categories). Disallowed passive rental losses are carried forward to offset profits in a future year from this property or another rental or passive activity.

In an effort to provide relief to lower-to-middle-income taxpayers, Congress added a limited exception to the passive loss rules that allows a deduction for losses from rental real estate by taxpayers with adjusted gross incomes of $150,000 or less. To be eligible for this relief, the taxpayer must own at least 10 percent of the rental activity, must not be a limited partner, and must "actively" participate in the activity. **Active participation** requires the taxpayer to participate in the management of the property, such as setting rents, qualifying renters, and approving repairs (a lower level of activity than material participation by the taxpayer in a business, as explained in Chapter 11).

Section 469 permits a deduction of up to $25,000 loss from rental properties by qualified individuals. To deduct the full $25,000, the taxpayer's AGI must not exceed $100,000. For every dollar the taxpayer's AGI exceeds $100,000, the taxpayer loses 50 cents of the deduction. The entire deduction is completely phased out when the taxpayer's AGI reaches $150,000.

Example 6.38

Barbara owns a townhouse in Key West that is rented through a local real estate agent. Barbara participates in management decisions by approving new tenants, deciding on rental terms, and approves repairs and capital expenditures. Barbara's AGI is $120,000. This year the rental expenses were $16,000 greater than the rental income resulting in a rental loss. Barbara can deduct $15,000 of the $16,000 loss from the townhouse. The $25,000 special deduction is reduced by $10,000 (50% of the $20,000 her AGI exceeds $100,000). She carries the remaining $1,000 loss forward to a future year.

The next year, Barbara's rental income from the townhouse is $4,000 more than the rental expenses. Barbara uses the $1,000 loss from the previous year to reduce taxable net rental income to $3,000.

6.5.2 HOME OFFICE EXPENSES

A home office of a sole proprietor or independent contractor must be used exclusively and on a regular basis and meet *one of the following three tests* for its costs to be deductible:[76]

1. It is the principal place of business for any business of the taxpayer.
2. It is used as a place to meet clients or customers regularly in the normal course of business.
3. It is located in a structure separate from the home.

[75] Reg. §1.163-10T(p)(3)(ii).

[76] There are two exceptions: (1) if a part of the home is used on a regular basis to store inventory or product samples, a deduction is permitted for that part of the home; (2) if the home is used on a regular basis as a daycare facility, the allocation of expenses must be made both on space and amount of time used.

The term **principal place of business** includes the place used by the taxpayer for administrative or management activities of the business, if there is no other fixed location at which the taxpayer can conduct these activities. Costs of a home office that is not the taxpayer's principal place of business may still be deductible if he or she meets patients, clients, or customers there on a regular and continuous basis.[77]

Example 6.39

Dr. George, a dentist, has an office in a nearby city. He also maintains an office in his home as he lives in an area that does not have another dentist. He sees patients at his home one and one-half days per week and four days per week at his city office. The costs of the office in the home are deductible because he regularly meets patients there, even though it is not the principal location of his business.

TAX PLANNING

If the home office occupies a separate structure (such as a detached garage), only one of the taxpayer's businesses must use the structure exclusively and regularly. A sole proprietor whose home office does not meet the principal-place-of-business requirement (or the seeing of clients, patients, and customers) should consider moving the office to a detached garage or building a small separate structure to house the office.

Exclusive use does not require that the office occupy a separate room; however, the room(s) or portion of a room used for business purposes must be used only for those business activities. Any personal use of the home office space by the taxpayer makes the home office expenses nondeductible.

In addition, an employee cannot deduct costs of a home office unless the office meets the requirements applicable to all home offices (discussed above) *and* it is *for the convenience of the employer*. If the employer provides an adequate workplace outside the home for the employee, no home office deduction is allowed, even if the employee uses the area exclusively and on a regular basis.

Deductible home office expenses include allocated rent or mortgage interest, property taxes, insurance, utilities, and repairs related to the office space.[78] Depreciation is allowed on the part of the home used as the office. The IRS and courts prefer an allocation of household expenses based on relative square footage.

Home office expenses are deductible only to the extent of income generated by the business use of the home and are deductible in the following order:

1. Expenses directly related to the business other than home office expenses (such as supplies)
2. The allocated portion of expenses that would otherwise be deductible as itemized deductions (mortgage interest and property taxes)[79]
3. Operating expenses including utilities, insurance, and maintenance
4. Depreciation

This income limitation prevents a tax loss from home office deductions if the business does not produce sufficient gross income.

If income is insufficient to deduct all of the expenses, the mortgage interest and property taxes are still deductible as itemized deductions by the individual. Other expenses exceeding the

[77] Occasional meetings in the home office are not sufficient. The physical presence of a client is also necessary; thus, the mere phoning of clients from the home office is not sufficient.

[78] If a home office qualifies as the individual's principal place of business, daily transportation expenses incurred in traveling between the taxpayer's residence and other work sites are deductible.

[79] Home mortgage interest, property taxes, and other itemized deductions are discussed in Chapter 5.

income limitation can be carried forward and deducted in future years, subject to the same limitations. Nondeductible depreciation expense does not reduce the basis of the property.

Example 6.40

Holly, a self-employed artist, uses two rooms in her home exclusively and regularly for her home office. This office space consists of 400 square feet of the home's total 2,000 square feet or 20 percent of the floor space. Her gross income from the business is $7,000 and her expenses (other than home office expenses) are $4,500. Holly has the following household expenses:

Mortgage interest on her home	$5,000
Real property taxes on her home	2,400
Utility bills for her home	1,900
Homeowner's insurance	1,800
Depreciation (for the 20 percent used as an office)	600

Holly first deducts the $4,500 nonhome office expenses, reducing available income to $2,500. Next she deducts $1,000 of her mortgage interest ($5,000 × 20%) and $480 of property taxes ($2,400 × 20%), a total of $1,480 otherwise allowable as itemized deductions. This leaves only $1,020 of income against which to deduct the remaining expenses. She deducts $380 ($1,900 × 20%) for utilities, and $360 ($1,800 × 20%) for insurance, and $280 of depreciation. The remaining $320 of depreciation expense is carried to the next year; Holly does not reduce her basis in the home for this disallowed amount.

Since 2013, the IRS has allowed a simplified option that taxpayers may elect to use to determine deductible home office expenses. This alternative permits the taxpayer to simply deduct $5 per square foot for up to 300 square feet of qualified use, a maximum of $1,500 for a full year home office deduction, excluding any allocation of mortgage interest or property taxes.[80] Thus, taxpayers can deduct 100 percent of mortgage interest and 100 percent of property taxes as itemized deductions in addition to deducting up to $1,500 for other home office expenses. The home office must still be used regularly and exclusively for business to qualify for this simplified provision. Taxpayers with higher home office expenses can use the regular provision.

If the home office is used for only part of the year (or if the business square footage changes) the deduction is limited to the average monthly allowable square footage. This is calculated by adding the amount of allowable square feet (not to exceed 300) per month and dividing the total by 12. If the qualified business use is less than 15 days in a month, then zero is used for that month.

Example 6.41

On May 18, 2017, Justin began qualified business use of 400 square feet of his home that continued through the end of the year. Justin's average monthly allowable square footage is 175 computed using the maximum 300 square feet per month from June through December divided by 12 months [(7 months × 300)/12 = 175]. Under the simplified method, Justin can claim a deduction of $875 ($5 × 175) for 2017. If Justin continues to use at least 300 square feet for business use for each month during 2018, he can deduct $1,500 (300 × $5) for 2018.

A self-employed individual files Form 8829: *Expenses for Business Use of Your Home* to claim a home office deduction. Form 8829 is not required when the simplified method is used; instead the expenses are reported directly on Schedule C. Prior to 2018, an employee's home

[80] Rev. Proc. 2013-13, 2013-6 IRB 478.

office expenses were deductible as miscellaneous itemized deductions. For 2018–2025, no deduction is allowed for unreimbursed employee expenses.

6.5.3 HOBBY EXPENSES

Some individuals engage in activities primarily for personal enjoyment but they also generate revenue. Taxpayer activities that earn income and incur expenses but do not meet the requirements of a business or investment are classified as personal hobbies. If the activity is classified as a **hobby**, expenses are deducted up to the revenue generated from the hobby; some or all of the expenses exceeding the revenue from the activity may be disallowed.

The regulations list a number of factors to consider in determining whether an activity should be classified as a hobby, including the following:[81]

1. The manner in which the taxpayer carries on the activity
2. The expertise of the taxpayer and/or the taxpayer's consultants
3. The time and effort spent by the taxpayer in the activity
4. The taxpayer's history of profits or losses for this activity
5. The success of the taxpayer in similar activities
6. The overall financial status of the taxpayer
7. The elements of pleasure or recreation that are part of the activity

All the facts and circumstances surrounding the activity are considered in determining if the taxpayer's activity is a hobby or if it has the requisite profit motive.

The burden of proof normally rests upon the taxpayer to establish that the activity meets the requirements of a trade or business. If, however, the activity shows a profit in at least three out of five years of operation (two out of seven for activities involving breeding or racing horses), the burden of proof shifts to the IRS.[82] The IRS must then prove that the activity is a hobby.

If the activity does not have a profit in three out of five consecutive tax years, the burden of proof remains with the taxpayer to show that the activity is a legitimate business. The taxpayer can do this by showing that the activity was run in a businesslike manner, good business records were maintained, and there was intent to make a profit.[83]

If the activity is a hobby, all income from the hobby is included in gross income, but expenses are deductible to the extent of the gross profit from the hobby, but only as miscellaneous itemized deductions before 2018 and after 2025. They are deducted in the following order:[84]

1. Expenses otherwise deductible as itemized deductions (home mortgage interest, property taxes, and casualty losses)
2. Other business-type expenses (advertising, insurance, utilities, and maintenance)
3. Depreciation and amortization expense

Expenses in categories 2 and 3 in excess of income are simply lost because there are no carryover provisions for any nondeductible expense. (The asset bases are not reduced for disallowed cost recovery deductions, however.)[85]

---

[81] Reg. §1.183-(2)(b)(1)-(9).
[82] §183(d).
[83] Reg. §1.183-2(b).
[84] Reg. §1.183-1(b). Hobby expenses are not deducible in 2018–2025.
[85] If only a portion of the depreciation expense can be deducted, the allowable depreciation should be apportioned across all the depreciable assets, based on the ratio of allowed depreciation to total depreciation for all the assets. Reg. §1.183-1(b). Depreciation is discussed in Chapter 7.

Example 6.42

Chet is an orthodontist whose hobby is making cabinetry in his spare time. He uses a workshop that occupies 10 percent of his home for the woodworking. Chet has the following expenses from the activity in 2017:

Solid woods and veneers	$4,000
Other supplies	600
Workshop expenses:	
Property taxes and interest on home	10,000
Utilities and maintenance on home	4,000
Depreciation (10% of home)	500

Chet sold four pieces of cabinetry for $6,200. He is able to deduct expenses from the $1,600 gross profit ($6,200 revenue – $4,600 for wood and other supplies) as follows:

Taxes and interest (10%)	$1,000
Utilities and maintenance (10%)	400
Depreciation	200
Total	$1,600

Chet cannot deduct the remaining $300 of depreciation, but he does not have to reduce the basis of the home for the nondeductible amount.

For years 2018 through 2025, Chet would be required to include the income from his hobby but would not be allowed any offsetting expense deductions.

6.6 EXPANDED TOPICS—BOOK/TAX DIFFERENCES

6.6.1 ACCOUNTING FOR INCOME TAX EXPENSE

A corporation's income tax expense is frequently the largest expense item on its income statement. Thus, understanding how tax expense is determined is critical for all readers of financial statements. In addition, a company's chief executive officer and chief financial officer must certify that financial reports filed with the Securities and Exchange Commission fairly present the company's financial position (including the adequacy of the tax-related accounts), since the passage of the *Sarbanes-Oxley Act* in 2002. These corporate executives as well as tax professionals must understand how tax expense and deferred taxes (commonly termed the tax provision) are determined. Failure of this required executive oversight can lead to significant personal penalties.

Financial statements prepared in accordance with generally accepted accounting principles (GAAP) must follow the provisions of Accounting Standards Codification (ASC) Section 740.[86] According to **ASC 740**, the income tax expense reported on the current-year financial statements must be based on financial statement income rather than taxable income. As a result, income tax expense reported on the income statement matches financial accounting income, even though the actual taxes paid differ substantially from recognized tax expense. Taxes paid are determined on taxable income, which can differ dramatically from accounting income due to the differences in the rules followed in their determination.

Differences in underlying principles lead to differences between taxable income and financial income and are divided into permanent differences and temporary differences. A **permanent difference** results from an expense that is never deducted on the tax return (fines and political

[86] The Financial Accounting Standards Board issued FAS 109: Accounting for Income Taxes in February 1992. The accounting standards were codified in 2009 with FAS 109 included under ASC 740. FAS 109 was preceded by FAS 96, which replaced Accounting Principles Board Opinion No. 11.

contributions), expenses with limited deductibility (the nondeductible portion of meals), or income that is not subject to tax (tax-exempt bond interest). A **temporary difference** is the result of reporting an income or expense item in one year for accounting income but in a different year for taxable income. Temporary differences include depreciation on fixed assets (accelerated depreciation used for tax, straight-line used for book purposes), accrued expenses (warranty expenses and bad debt expenses accrued for book purposes but not deductible for tax purposes until incurred), and accrued income (sales reported under the percentage-of-completion method for book purposes but reported under the completed contract method for tax purposes). These items are fully recognized in both types of income statements, but the timing of their recognition differs. Timing differences between statements in one period (for example, tax depreciation that exceeds financial depreciation) *reverse* when recognized in a later period (when financial depreciation exceeds tax depreciation). Figure 6.2 provides examples of temporary and permanent book/tax differences.

Temporary differences	Permanent differences
Amortization of organization & start-up costs	Fines and penalties
Bad debts	Interest on state & local bonds
Depreciation	Life insurance proceeds
Installment sales	Meal expenses
Inventory costs capitalized under UNICAP	Premiums on key-person life insurance
Net operating loss carryovers	Political contributions & lobbying expenses
Prepaid income	Dividend received deduction (see Chapter 10)
Related party transactions	
Warranty expenses	

FIGURE 6.2 Examples of book/tax differences

Schedule M-1 of Form 1120: *U.S. Corporate Income Tax Return* reconciles accounting (book) income to the taxable income reported on the tax return by accounting for the permanent and temporary differences occurring in that tax year.

Example 6.43

Targo Corporation has income per books before tax of $4,000,000. Permanent differences are: $10,000 interest income from tax-exempt municipal bonds and $500,000 of life insurance proceeds from the death of a corporate officer included in book income; the $30,000 nondeductible portion for meal expenses and $5,000 for premiums on officers' life insurance policies (the corporation is the beneficiary of these policies) are deductible for book income. Temporary differences include the straight-line depreciation of $80,000 on its financial statements, the $120,000 of accelerated depreciation claimed on its tax return, and the $30,000 accrued for bad debt expense (using the allowance method) on its financial statements, while it only wrote off $10,000 in bad debts. Targo reconciles its book income to taxable income as follows:

Income per books before tax	$4,000,000
Interest income from tax-exempt municipal bonds	(10,000)
Life insurance proceeds	(500,000)
Nondeductible portion of meals	30,000
Nondeductible premiums on officers' life insurance policies	5,000
Excess of tax accelerated depreciation over book straight-line	(40,000)
Increase in the bad debt allowance exceeding its direct write off	20,000
Taxable income	$3,505,000

Targo computes its income tax liability (the actual amount paid) on its tax return as $736,050 ($3,505,000 × 21%). It calculates its tax expense, however, based on its financial accounting income, following the principles of ASC 740.

Corporations with assets of $10 million or more on the last day of the tax year file Schedule M-3 instead of Schedule M-1. Corporations are required to separately disclose each item of income, gain, loss, deduction, or credit for book-tax differences greater than $10 million with temporary differences reported separately from permanent differences on Schedule M-3. The IRS is particularly interested in the disclosure of permanent differences because many abusive tax shelters are structured either to reduce taxes paid without reporting a corresponding decrease in book income or to increase book income without a corresponding increase in tax liability.

Calculating Tax Expense

If a corporation has permanent tax differences, it modifies its book income by adding back nondeductible tax expenses and subtracting tax exempt income. If it has only permanent differences (that is, there are no temporary differences to consider), it determines its book tax expense based on this modified book income at its current tax rates.

Example 6.44

Refer to the information in the previous example excluding temporary differences. Targo Corporation subtracts the $10,000 tax-exempt interest and $500,000 life insurance proceeds and adds $30,000 for one-half of the meal expenses and $5,000 for the life insurance premiums. Targo's modified income is $3,525,000. At a 21 percent tax rate, its book tax expense is $740,250 ($3,525,000 × 21%). Due to these adjustments, its effective tax rate is only 18.5 percent ($740,250/$4,000,000).

Permanent differences have no effect on deferred taxes; however, they cause the effective tax rate for the period to differ from the statutory tax rate. As a consequence, the firm's notes to its financial statements must reconcile the statutory rate to the effective rate so that the reader can determine the significance of any permanent differences.

If a corporation has both permanent and temporary differences, the permanent differences are accounted for first as described. Accounting for temporary differences is more complex because temporary differences cause income tax expense per books to differ from the tax expense shown on the tax return. This difference in tax expenses is accounted for using deferred tax accounts.

ASC 740 prescribes a balance sheet approach to account for the deferred taxes from temporary differences by using a deferred tax asset or deferred tax liability account. A deferred tax asset account represents future tax savings while a deferred tax liability account represents future tax costs. Although it is normal to think of assets as good news and liabilities as bad news, the reverse is true for the deferred tax asset and liability accounts. A deferred tax liability is essentially an interest-free loan from the government, allowing the business to invest the savings until the taxes are paid at a later date. The longer the taxes are deferred, the greater the value of the tax savings. Deferred tax assets, however, are prepayments of taxes, the benefit of which may not be realized until many years in the future.

A **deferred tax liability** is a current tax savings that will be paid in a future year when temporary differences reverse. It is created when (1) an expense is deducted for tax in the current period but not deducted on the books until some future period or (2) income is included in book income currently but not included in taxable income until a future period. If the deferred tax expense is not accrued, a corporation's current-year financial statement income and retained earnings are overstated to the extent that taxes will have to be paid when the differences reverse.

Example 6.45

Cargo, a corporation with a 21 percent tax rate, recognizes tax depreciation expense of $60,000 in year 1 and $20,000 in year 2. On its financial statements, Cargo reports depreciation expense of $40,000 in both year 1 and year 2. In year 1, the tax depreciation is $20,000 greater than the book depreciation and the adjusted basis of the assets is $20,000 greater for book purposes than for tax purposes. The deferred tax liability is credited (increased) for $4,200 ($20,000 × 21%) accounting for the favorable temporary difference between the provision for income tax expense in the financial statements and the income tax payable per the tax return. In year 2, the difference reverses and the book depreciation is $20,000 greater than the tax depreciation. The deferred tax liability account is debited (reduced) for the $4,200 ($20,000 × 21%) that the income tax payable exceeds the provision for income tax expense in the financial statements, eliminating the deferred tax liability account.

A **deferred tax asset** is a prepayment of tax that will be refunded in a future year when temporary differences reverse. It is created when (1) an expense is deducted on the books in the current year but not deducted for tax until some future period or (2) income is included in taxable income currently but not included in income per books until a future period. Book tax expense is based only on the reported financial statement net income; it excludes any tax prepayments related to these nondeductible expenses or includible income for tax purposes. Instead, the prepayment is a deferred tax asset (a receivable).

Example 6.46

Warwick, a corporation with a 21 percent tax rate, accrues $40,000 in warranty expense on its year 1 financial statements for expected warranty repairs. Repairs are not deductible for tax purposes until actually performed, however. If the $40,000 of warranty expense is not actually incurred until year 2, a temporary difference is created in year 1. A deferred tax asset is debited (increased) for $8,400 ($40,000 × 21%) accounting for the difference between the provision for income tax expense on the financial statements and the income tax payable per the tax return. In year 2, when the warranty expense is incurred, the book tax warranty difference reverses and the deferred tax asset is credited (reduced) for $8,400, eliminating that account.

Figure 6.3 shows when temporary differences are reported as deferred tax assets or deferred tax liabilities.

	Revenues	Expenses
Reported on tax return before books	Deferred tax asset	Deferred tax liability
Reported on books before tax return	Deferred tax liability	Deferred tax asset

FIGURE 6.3 Reporting temporary differences

Deferred tax assets and liabilities were previously classified as current or noncurrent. For simplification, the Financial Accounting Standards Board (FASB) Accounting Standards Update 2015–17 announced that all deferred tax assets and liabilities will be classified as noncurrent.

Effects of NOL Carryovers

When a corporation's deductible expenses exceed its gross income, it has a net operating loss (NOL).[87] Because there is no taxable income, there is no income tax liability for that year. For losses incurred prior to 2018, corporations were allowed to carry these NOLs back two years (filing a claim for refund of the previous years' taxes) and forward up to 20 years. For financial statement purposes, the corporation reported the tax benefit of a NOL carryback by debiting a tax refund receivable on its balance sheet and crediting a benefit due to loss carryback (negative tax expense) on its income statement.

Example 6.47

Milor Corporation, a calendar-year, accrual-basis corporation, had a $20,000 NOL for both book and tax purposes for 2017. Milor carried the loss back to 2015 when its taxable income was $75,000 and is entitled to a $5,000 refund ($20,000 × 25% tax rate) of 2015 taxes. Milor accounted for the tax effect of the NOL on its financial statements by debiting a tax refund receivable (an asset) on its 2017 balance sheet for $5,000 and crediting a tax benefit due to loss carryback (negative tax expense) on its 2017 income statement for the same amount.

If the corporation does not elect to carry the NOL back, the tax benefit can only be realized in a future year or years to which the corporation carries the NOL forward. For financial accounting purposes, the future tax savings *expected* from the loss carryforward is reported as a deferred tax asset in the year the loss occurs.

Example 6.48

Assume the facts in the previous example except that Milor elected to carry the 2017 NOL forward to 2018 when its expected tax rate is 21%. For 2017 financial accounting, however, Milor debits a deferred tax asset account for $4,200 for the *expected* tax effect of the NOL on its 2017 balance sheet and credits a tax benefit due to loss carryforward (negative tax expense) for the same amount on its 2017 income statement. In 2018, Milor has $400,000 of taxable income before deducting the NOL carried forward; when it deducts the $20,000 NOL, it realizes tax savings of $4,200 ($20,000 × 21%). Milor recognizes tax expense on its income statement of $84,000 ($400,000 × 21%) and its income tax payable is $79,800 [($400,000 – $20,000) × 21%]. In 2018 Milor accounts for the difference between the two amounts by crediting (reducing) the deferred tax asset created in 2017.

For NOLs incurred after 2017, the NOL carryforward can offset only 80 percent of taxable income. In addition, NOLs arising after 2017 can be carried forward indefinitely, but carrybacks are prohibited.

Realizing Deferred Tax Assets

A business must have future income (and related taxes) to realize the benefit of a deferred tax asset (tax prepayment). Determining whether the tax benefit should be recognized currently or modified using a valuation allowance is based on a more-likely-than-not test (greater than 50 percent probability). If it is determined to be more likely than not that the benefits can be realized, the adjustment is included in the current tax provision. If not, the adjustment is deferred by use of a valuation allowance to reflect only the amount the company expects to realize in the future. The valuation allowance is a contra-asset account that offsets all or a portion of the deferred tax

[87] This discussion is based solely on corporate businesses as they are not flow-through entities. The owners of flow-through entities with NOLs would also be allowed carryovers of these losses subject to possible adjustments based on the type of owner.

asset. The existence of net operating loss carryforwards[88] and excess foreign tax credits[89] most often give rise to problems surrounding the realization of a deferred tax benefit.

Example 6.49

Carson Corporation reports income per books and taxable income of $1 million. Its current income tax liability is $210,000 ($1 million × 21%). During the current year it paid $50,000 in foreign income taxes that cannot be used as a credit against its current tax liability due to the foreign tax credit limitation. If its auditors believe that Carson will only be able to use $30,000 of the foreign tax credit before it expires, the $50,000 future tax benefit recorded in the deferred tax asset account should be reduced to $30,000 by use of a valuation allowance. The net income tax expense should be recorded at $180,000 ($210,000 – $30,000 expected benefit from foreign tax credit). This is recorded on Carson's books through the following journal entry:

Income tax expense	210,000	
Deferred tax asset	50,000	
Valuation allowance		20,000
Income tax expense (benefit)		30,000
Income tax payable		210,000

The valuation allowance increases Carson's current effective book tax rate from 16 percent [($210,000 tax payable – $50,000 deferred tax asset)/$1 million] to 18 percent ($180,000/$1 million). If Carson can satisfy its auditors in a later year that the adoption of a new tax planning strategy will allow use of the entire foreign tax credit carryforward, the valuation account will be released and the company can recognize the expected tax benefit. The release eliminates the valuation allowance, reduces the provision for income tax expense, and reduces the effective tax rate for the release year.

The determination of whether the more-likely-than-not test is met can have a significant impact on book tax expense and the reported book net income. Without a careful review of the allowance by the auditors, it is possible for companies to smooth their earnings by adjusting the valuation allowance up or down as needed, possibly misleading readers of the financial statements.

Accounting for Uncertainty in Income Taxes

In an attempt to improve transparency and accountability of companies and restore investor confidence after the Enron and WorldCom scandals, the Financial Accounting Standards Board (FASB) issued an interpretation of FAS 109 called FASB Interpretation No. 48, *Accounting for Uncertainty in Income Taxes* (FIN 48) which was incorporated into ASC 740-10-55. It applies to flow-through and nontaxable entities, as well as taxable corporations.

ACS 740 does not provide any specific guidance on accounting for deferred taxes when a business takes an uncertain tax position. The term tax position refers to the manner of recognition of a transaction in a current or previously filed tax return that results in a current or deferred income tax asset or liability. Examples of **uncertain tax positions (UTPs)** include: a deduction taken on a tax return for a current expenditure that the IRS may assert should be capitalized and amortized over future periods, the determination of the amount of taxable income to report on

[88] Although NOLs can be carried forward indefinitely, they can only offset up to 80 percent of taxable income after 2017; a valuation allowance may be necessary for the remaining 20 percent.

[89] The allowable foreign tax credit in any year is limited to the U.S. tax imposed on the foreign source income included on the U.S. tax return. The foreign tax credit limitation can prevent the total amount of foreign taxes paid in high-tax jurisdictions from being credited, thereby reducing the value of the related deferred tax asset.

intercompany transfers between subsidiaries in different tax jurisdictions, or a decision to classify a particular transaction as tax exempt.

Prior to the issuance of FIN 48, businesses used diverse criteria to determine whether tax return benefits should be recognized in their financial statements. Many companies simply assumed that amounts reported on their tax returns would be allowed, except for a few very aggressive and material positions that were considered so uncertain that the IRS could successfully challenge them on audit and increase the company's tax liability. ASC 740 (FIN 48) no longer allows this approach. Instead, any tax benefit from an uncertain tax position that reduces a business's current or future income tax liability can only be reported in its financial statements to the extent each benefit is recognized and measured under a two-step approach.

Step 1: The business must evaluate each tax position to assess whether it is more likely than not (greater than 50 percent) that the position will be sustained upon examination (including the administrative appeals and litigation process). The business must base its assessment on an analysis of the relevant tax authorities (such as the Code, regulations, rulings, and court cases) and it must assume that the tax authorities have full knowledge of all relevant information (including access to work papers and legal opinions from outside tax advisors). This requirement must be met even if the business believes the possibility of audit or discovery of the matter is remote. Additionally, each tax position must stand on its own technical merits so a business may not consider one position as a bargaining chip against another tax position.

Step 2: If a tax position satisfies the first step, the business can then proceed to measure the tax benefit it can recognized in the financial statements from its uncertain position. If no single amount is more likely than not to be realized, then a cumulative probability analysis of the possible outcomes is required. The business records the largest tax benefit that meets a greater than 50 percent cumulative probability of realization upon ultimate settlement.

Example 6.50

Solaris Corporation claims a $10,000 deduction in its current year tax return and this tax position meets the recognition threshold of more likely than not. Having met the requirements of the first step, Solaris measures the benefit. As there is no single amount that can be recognized, Solaris determines the benefit using the possible range of outcomes from $10,000 (complete success in litigation or settlement with the IRS) to zero (total loss) and the cumulative probability. The possible outcomes and their probabilities are as follows:

Possible outcome	Probability of occurring	Cumulative probability of occurring
$10,000	25%	25%
$7,500	20%	45%
$5,000	25%	70%
$2,500	20%	90%
0	10%	100%
	100%	

Solaris will recognize a $5,000 deduction in its financial statements because that is the largest amount of benefit that is more than 50 percent likely to be sustained based on the outcome's cumulative probability.

After the initial two-step evaluation, there is a review of the information available at each subsequent financial reporting date to determine if there should be a reassessment of its prior uncertain tax positions. This reassessment is based on new information rather than a new evaluation or interpretation of information that was available at the earlier reporting date. If a tax position that previously failed to meet the more-likely-than-not threshold subsequently meets that threshold, the business may recognize a tax benefit in its financial statements in the first interim period in which it meets the more-likely-than-not standard, is settled through negotiation or litigation, or upon the expiration of the statute of limitations. If a business subsequently determines that a tax position no longer meets the more-likely-than-not threshold of being sustained, then the business must derecognize all or a portion of the tax benefit previously recognized for that tax position. FIN 48 prohibited the use of a valuation allowance as a substitute for derecognition of the tax benefit.

One of the more controversial aspects of financial reporting for uncertain tax positions is an expanded disclosure requirement. Companies must include a table that identifies their beginning and ending unrecognized tax benefits, along with the details related to tax uncertainties that have a reasonable possibility that unrecognized tax benefits will significantly increase or decrease within the next year. Previously, many companies bundled together their various uncertain positions and provided one general reserve to account for the possibility of losing some of the tax positions upon audit. Now, companies must disclose the nature of the uncertainty and the nature of the event that could cause a change in the next twelve months.

Some managers expressed concern that IRS will use these disclosures as a roadmap for identifying tax positions to audit. It appears that this concern is well founded. In 2010, the IRS announced that it would require any corporation with total assets in excess of $10 million that has any uncertain tax positions to file a Schedule UTP: *Uncertain Tax Position Statement* with its tax return.[90] The IRS agreed to phase-in this reporting requirement based on a corporation's asset size to reduce the burden on businesses, but since 2014 corporations that have total assets equal to or exceeding $10 million have been required to file Schedule UTP.[91]

Example 6.51

Beta, a U.S. corporation with more than $100 million in assets, claims a deduction for the entire amount of an expenditure on its 2018 tax return. In reviewing its tax positions for its 2018 audited financial statements, Beta determines that it is uncertain if the expenditure should have been amortized over 5 years or expensed and records a reserve on its financial statements. The tax position taken on the return (that the expenditure could be fully deducted in 2018 rather than amortized) must be reported on Schedule UTP filed with its 2018 tax return.

Schedule UTP requires a corporation to describe each uncertain tax position for which the corporation has recorded a reserve in its audited financial statements and then rank all of these tax positions based on the U.S. federal income tax reserve recorded for them. Although the actual amount of reserve for each position does not need to be reported, the corporation must identify the positions for which the reserve exceeds 10 percent of the aggregate amount of the reserves for all of the reported positions. This information can assist the IRS in identifying those uncertain tax positions that are large enough to warrant IRS inquiry so that its audit can be focused on those areas.

Traditionally, understanding the complex provisions of accounting for income taxes typically was left to corporate accountants and their independent auditors. Now it is essential that tax professionals, in both private industry and public practice, have a good understanding of how uncertain tax positions are recognized, measured, and disclosed.

[90] Ann. 2010-9, 2010-7 IRB 408.

[91] Ann. 2010-75, 2010-41 IRB 428. The asset threshold was reduced from $100 million to $50 million in 2012 and to $10 million in 2014.

6.6.2 UNICAP RULES AND INVENTORY

The cost of merchandise purchased is its invoice price, less discounts, plus incidental costs such as shipping and handling.[92] Under the **uniform capitalization (UNICAP) rules**, indirect costs are also capitalized as part of inventory by businesses with average annual gross receipts exceeding $25 million in the three preceding three years.[93] The UNICAP rules require the value of inventory to include all direct costs of manufacturing, purchasing, and storage, along with the following overhead items:

- Factory repairs, maintenance, utilities, insurance, rent, and depreciation (including the excess of tax depreciation over financial depreciation)
- Rework, scrap, and spoilage
- Factory administration and officers' salaries related to production
- Taxes (other than income tax)
- Quality control and inspection
- Profit sharing and pension plans, for both current and past service costs
- Service support such as payroll, purchasing, and warehousing

Nonmanufacturing costs (such as research, selling, advertising, and distribution expenses) are not required to be included in inventory. The UNICAP rules include indirect costs typically not part of the traditional full absorption costing used for financial accounting, creating temporary differences. For example, personnel and data processing costs are usually excluded from manufacturing overhead. UNICAP rules, however, require the allocation of costs associated with these departments between manufacturing and nonmanufacturing functions.[94]

Example 6.52

Leather Works Corporation manufactures leather furniture in a factory with 50 employees. The office staff has 5 employees who handle personnel, accounting, and other office responsibilities. The sales staff includes 7 employees who travel extensively selling the furniture to retail outlets. The remaining 38 employees work in the factory. Under the UNICAP rules, manufacturing costs include the wages of the 38 factory workers and all other factory costs, plus a portion of the salaries for the 5 office employees. The costs for the sales staff are not manufacturing costs and are deducted with selling expenses. Any reasonable method can be used to allocate the cost of the office staff between manufacturing overhead and deductible expenses. If the allocation is made based on the number of employees, 84 percent (38/45) of the office costs are treated as manufacturing overhead and allocated to inventory, while 16 percent (7/45) are expensed.

The allocation of costs between ending inventory and cost of goods sold is determined by the method of accounting selected. A number of methods are acceptable, including specific identification, FIFO (first-in-first-out), LIFO (last-in-first-out), or the average cost methods. The choice of method has significant effect on taxable income and the resulting income tax liability. As defined in financial accounting, the FIFO method assumes that most recently acquired items remain in ending inventory. LIFO assumes the opposite—that ending inventory consists of the oldest items. The weighted average (average cost) method yields inventory valuation somewhere

---

[92] Reg. §1.471-3.

[93] §263A.

[94] Wholesalers and retailers must also capitalize certain storage costs, purchasing costs, and handling, processing, assembly, and repackaging costs.

between FIFO and LIFO. In periods of rising prices, LIFO results in higher cost for goods sold and a smaller ending inventory valuation than FIFO.

TAX PLANNING

An incentive exists to value inventory as low as possible for tax purposes. The low valuation results in tax savings through the higher cost of goods sold deduction.[95] Although the tax benefit is from a deferral, the deferral is of indefinite duration. As inventories increase with business expansion, more taxable income is deferred.

Example 6.53

Adams Corporation, a new business, uses the FIFO method for valuing its inventory because this method reflects the physical flow of goods. At the end of its first year, its ending inventory using FIFO is $200,000. If Adams used LIFO, its ending inventory would be $150,000. Adams has a 21 percent tax rate. Using LIFO would increase its cost of goods sold by $50,000, decrease taxable income by $50,000 ($200,000 – $150,000), and produce a tax savings of $10,500 ($50,000 × 21%).[96]

In general, there is no requirement to use the same accounting method for both financial accounting and tax purposes, with one exception: a taxpayer who uses the LIFO method for tax purposes must also use it for any report or statement to owners or to obtain credit—the **LIFO conformity rule**.[97] A taxpayer can use an alternative inventory method as a supplement to or in an explanation of the financial statements, but the supplemental information cannot be presented on the face of the income statement.[98] The use of LIFO may affect the perceived performance of the company and compensation (or even job security) of management if the compensation level of managers of the business is tied to net income. The use of LIFO can be a two-edged sword.

The potential adoption of International Financial Reporting Standards (IFRS) is a major issue for businesses using LIFO as LIFO is not permitted under IFRS. Unless the LIFO conformity rule is changed, businesses currently using LIFO face a tax cost when they change their inventory valuation method to meet financial reporting IFRS. Under current law, the impact on income of a change from LIFO to FIFO may be spread over four years; however, Congress could repeal the use of the LIFO method of inventory valuation for tax purposes. If it does, it may allow a longer period (one proposal would allow up to 8 years) over which to spread the income and resulting tax effect. Businesses using LIFO should monitor progress on the adoption of IFRS as well as pending tax legislation.

REVISITING THE INTRODUCTORY CASE

The $2,000 for the market survey and $2,200 for the feasibility study are investigation expenses; they are combined with the $1,500 for pre-opening advertising for a total of $5,700 of start-up expenses. The first $5,000 is expensed and the remaining $700 is amortized over 180 months beginning July 1. Club dues are not deductible and only 50 percent of Mark's meals are deductible. Mark uses the standard mileage rate of 54.5 cents per mile (and also deducts any parking and tolls) but cannot deduct the speeding ticket. Mark allocates his home expenses based on the square footage (400/2,000 = 20%) of his home office. The home office expenses are only deductible to the extent of income and are deducted in a specific order (interest and taxes first, utilities and insurance next, and depreciation last). Only $134 of his $500 depreciation expense can be

[95] A lower ending inventory cost means a smaller reduction in cost of goods sold.

[96] A taxpayer can change to the LIFO method by attaching Form 970: *Application to Use LIFO Inventory Method* with the tax return for the year of change. A change from LIFO to any other method requires IRS approval.

[97] §472(c), (e)(2).

[98] Presentation in the footnotes, appendixes, or supplements to the financial statements is acceptable. Reg.§1.472-2(e).

deducted this year due to the income limit (his home office expenses are deducted last but cannot create a loss). Mark's cash outflow and deductible expenses are:

Cash outflow	Deductible expenses	
$2,000	$2,000	Market survey
2,200	2,200	Feasibility study
1,500	823	Pre-opening advertising [$800 + ($700/180 months × 6)]
2,400	0	Club dues (nondeductible)
1,300	650	Meals ($1,300 × 50%)
900	900	Hotels
1,100	1,100	Airfare
5,000	5,000	Supplies
1,800	1,800	Advertising
2,453	2,453	Automobile mileage (4,500 miles @ 54.5 cents per mile)*
60	0	Speeding ticket (fines are not deductible)
1,600	1,600	Mortgage interest for home office ($8,000 × 20%)
600	600	Real property taxes for home office ($3,000 × 20%)
320	320	Utilities for home office ($1,600 × 20%)
120	120	Insurance for home office ($600 × 20%)
0	134	Depreciation for home office ($500 but limited to remaining income)
$23,353	$19,700	Total deductible expenses

*This example assumes the standard mileage expense is the same as the cash outflow.

Mark can carry forward the $366 unused depreciation expense and deduct it in a future year when he has sufficient net income from his business. Figure 6.4 shows parts I and II of Mark's Schedule C: *Profit or Loss From Business (Sole Proprietorship).*

Part I Income

1	Gross receipts or sales. See instructions for line 1 and check the box if this income was reported to you on Form W-2 and the "Statutory employee" box on that form was checked . . . . ▶ ☐	1	19,700
2	Returns and allowances	2	
3	Subtract line 2 from line 1	3	19,700
4	Cost of goods sold (from line 42)	4	
5	**Gross profit.** Subtract line 4 from line 3	5	19,700
6	Other income, including federal and state gasoline or fuel tax credit or refund (see instructions)	6	
7	**Gross income.** Add lines 5 and 6 . . . . . ▶	7	19,700

Part II Expenses. Enter expenses for business use of your home **only** on line 30.

8	Advertising	8	1,800	18	Office expense (see instructions)	18	
9	Car and truck expenses (see instructions)	9	2,453	19	Pension and profit-sharing plans .	19	
				20	Rent or lease (see instructions):		
10	Commissions and fees .	10		a	Vehicles, machinery, and equipment	20a	
11	Contract labor (see instructions)	11		b	Other business property . . .	20b	
12	Depletion	12		21	Repairs and maintenance . . .	21	
13	Depreciation and section 179 expense deduction (not included in Part III) (see instructions)	13		22	Supplies (not included in Part III) .	22	5,000
				23	Taxes and licenses	23	
				24	Travel, meals, and entertainment:		
14	Employee benefit programs (other than on line 19) . .	14		a	Travel	24a	2,000
				b	Deductible meals and entertainment (see instructions) .	24b	650
15	Insurance (other than health)	15					
16	Interest:			25	Utilities	25	
a	Mortgage (paid to banks, etc.)	16a		26	Wages (less employment credits) .	26	
b	Other	16b		27a	Other expenses (from line 48) . .	27a	5,023
17	Legal and professional services	17		b	**Reserved for future use** . . .	27b	

28	**Total expenses** before expenses for business use of home. Add lines 8 through 27a . . . . . . ▶	28	16,926
29	Tentative profit or (loss). Subtract line 28 from line 7	29	2,774
30	Expenses for business use of your home. Do not report these expenses elsewhere. Attach Form 8829 unless using the simplified method (see instructions). **Simplified method filers only:** enter the total square footage of: (a) your home: ________ and (b) the part of your home used for business: ________ . Use the Simplified Method Worksheet in the instructions to figure the amount to enter on line 30	30	2,774
31	**Net profit or (loss).** Subtract line 30 from line 29. • If a profit, enter on both **Form 1040, line 12** (or **Form 1040NR, line 13**) and on **Schedule SE, line 2.** (If you checked the box on line 1, see instructions). Estates and trusts, enter on **Form 1041, line 3.**	31	0

FIGURE 6.4 Schedule C: *Profit or Loss From Business (Sole Proprietorship)*

Alternatively, Mark could elect the simplified method (on line 30 of Schedule C) and deduct $750 (6/12 months × 300 sq. ft. × $5) instead of $574 ($320 + $120 + $134) for utilities, insurance, and depreciation. He could then deduct 100% of the mortgage interest and real property taxes as itemized deductions. If he does, however, his deductible expenses decrease to $17,676 ($19,700 + $750 − $574 − $1,600 mortgage interest − $600 property taxes) and his self-employment income increases to $2,024 ($19,700 − $17,676). He is now liable for $286 ($2,024 × .9235 × .153) self-employment tax on this $2,024 net income and his adjusted gross income increases by $1,881 ($2,024 less the $143 deduction for one-half his self-employment tax). His itemized deductions for mortgage interest and property tax are $2,200 greater and his taxable income decreases by a net $319 ($2,200 − $1,881). The reduction in income tax at 24% is $77 but this does not offset his $286 of self-employment taxes. Thus, Mark would be worse off if he used the simplified method unless his total itemized deductions do not exceed his standard deduction.

Mark should rethink his plans to join the country club, as these dues are not deductible. Unless he feels that club membership is essential to his business, these dollars may be better spent elsewhere. Additionally, Mark should keep track of all of his automobile expenses so he has the information to deduct the greater of his actual expense or the standard mileage allowance.

If Mark would change his mind and decide not to continue with the business, none of his pre-opening or investigation expenses would be deductible.

SUMMARY

Expenses incurred in a trade or business can be deducted from gross income if they are ordinary, necessary, and reasonable in amount. An activity is a trade or business if the taxpayer is regularly involved and intends to make a profit. Expenses incurred in activities that are contrary to public policy or related to tax-exempt income are not deductible.

The method of accounting determines the year in which a taxpayer takes a deduction. An accrual-basis taxpayer deducts expenses when the all events test is met and economic performance has occurred. A cash-basis taxpayer usually deducts expenses in the year paid; however, prepaid expenses that benefit future years may have to be capitalized.

After applying the limited expensing provisions, start-up and organizational costs associated with a new business are capitalized and amortized over a period of 180 months. If a taxpayer is in a similar business, business investigation expenses can be deducted currently. If the taxpayer has no similar business and abandons starting the new business after investigation, the expenses are nondeductible.

Deductions for business expenses, particularly for travel or gifts, require proper documentation. Taxpayers who lack adequate substantiation may lose the expense deduction.

The taxpayer must be away from home to deduct travel expenses. When combining business and personal travel, careful planning can maintain the deductibility of the costs of getting to and from the destination. If the taxpayer is not away from home, only business-related transportation can be deducted but the cost of meals is nondeductible. The actual cost of the business use of the car or a standard mileage rate can be used to compute automobile expenses. The cost of commuting to and from work is a personal, nondeductible expense.

Limits apply to the deductions for expenses incurred in hobby activities, the renting of vacation homes, and home offices. In general, deductible expenses cannot exceed the income earned from the activity, and they must be deducted in a specific order, if deductible at all.

Both temporary and permanent differences between financial accounting (book) income and taxable income are the result of the differences in income and expense recognition for book and tax purposes. Temporary differences reverse and require a deferred tax account. Permanent differences do not reverse and require an adjustment to tax expense in the financial statements.

The UNICAP rules for inventory valuation require larger companies to include additional costs in ending inventory beyond those normally required for full absorption costing.

KEY TERMS

TEST YOURSELF

Answers Appear after the Problem Assignments

1. On October 1, Pembroke Inc. (a cash-basis, calendar-year corporation) borrowed $60,000 from the bank at 12 percent annual interest. On December 30, Pembroke pays $7,200 to the bank for the first year's interest on the loan. What is Pembroke's interest expense deduction in the current year?
   a. 0
   b. $600
   c. $1,800
   d. $5,400
   e. $7,200

2. Which of the following items is *not* deductible?
   a. Dues for club used solely for business meetings
   b. Business meals while traveling
   c. Fire insurance premiums for office building
   d. Dues for professional association

3. Howard, a self-employed consultant, uses one room in his home exclusively and regularly for his home office. The office occupies 360 square feet of floor space in the 2,400 square foot home. Howard's gross income from his business is $10,000. Expenses of his business (other than home office expenses) are $7,400. Howard has the following home-use expenses:

Total mortgage interest on the home	$8,000
Total real property taxes on the home	3,000
Utility bills for the home	2,000
Homeowner's insurance	2,000
Depreciation (15% for the office)	400

   How much of these home-use expenses can Howard deduct as home office expenses if he does not elect the simplified method?
   a. $15,400
   b. $10,000
   c. $3,080
   d. $2,600

4. Esslinger Corporation has income per books before tax of $300,000. Included in the income per books is $4,000 interest income from tax-exempt municipal bonds. Esslinger also deducted $20,000 for business meal expenses, $3,000 for premiums on officers' life insurance policies (the corporation

is the beneficiary for these policies), and $100 for fines. What is Esslinger Corporation's taxable income?
a. $296,100
b. $299,100
c. $306,100
d. $309,100
e. $313,100

5. Stadler Corporation's federal income tax rate is 21 percent. It reports $100,000 depreciation expense on its financial statements and deducts $140,000 depreciation expense on its tax return. How should Stadler account for the difference between its federal tax liability and its book tax expense on its financial statements?
a. $8,400 deferred tax liability
b. $8,400 deferred tax asset
c. $40,000 deferred tax liability
d. $40,000 deferred tax asset

PROBLEM ASSIGNMENTS

Check Your Understanding

1. [LO 6.1] What are the characteristics of a qualified trade or business?

2. [LO 6.1] What is an investment activity and are its expenses deductible?

3. [LO 6.1] What records should a taxpayer be able to provide the IRS to substantiate a tax deduction?

4. [LO 6.2] Marvin, an attorney, is a cash-basis, calendar-year taxpayer. Marvin's two daughters each own 50 percent of the stock of Marvil Corporation, a calendar-year, accrual-basis corporation. During year 1, Marvin completes some legal work for Marvil Corporation on December 18 and earns a $20,000 fee. In which year should Marvil Corporation deduct the legal expense if
a. payment is made to Marvin on December 30, year 1?
b. payment is made to Marvin on January 6, year 2?

5. [LO 6.2] Aloha Airlines is required by law to have its aircraft engines tested and recertified after 5,000 flight hours. Molokai Maintenance performs the engine tests and recertification for $2,200 per aircraft. For financial accounting purposes, Aloha accrues maintenance expenses of 44 cents per flight hour in a reserve account. When the maintenance is done, the amount paid is deducted from the reserve account. For tax purposes, when is the maintenance expense deducted?

6. [LO 6.3] Diane owns and manages a successful clothing store in Dallas. She and her brother, Cameron, investigated the possibility of opening another store in Atlanta for Cameron to manage. Diane and Cameron each paid $1,600 in travel costs while looking for sites for the store. Each paid $300 in legal fees for a lawyer to compile a list of zoning regulations and other relevant city ordinances. They decide that it is not feasible to open a new store at the present time. Can Diane and Cameron deduct their business investigation expenses? Explain.

7. [LO 6.3] In its first year of operations, Bell Corporation paid its attorney $4,000 and its accountant $2,000 for services related to the organization of the corporation. In its second year of operations, Bell paid the attorney $700 to handle contract negotiations with a new customer. Which expenses are immediately deductible and which ones must Bell Corporation amortize?

8. [LO 6.4] Randy gave one of his best customers a $150 bottle of wine. How much can he deduct for this business gift?

9. [LO 6.4] Explain the differences between the rules governing travel within the United States and those governing travel outside the United States.

10. [LO 6.5] How are deductions for expenses of rental property limited if the taxpayer also uses the property as a vacation home?

11. [LO 6.5] What are the passive activity loss rules and how do they affect the deductibility of losses from rental property?

12. [LO 6.5] What are the requirements for a self-employed person to claim a deduction for an office in the home?

13. [LO 6.5] What factors differentiate a hobby from an active business?

14. [LO 6.6] Differentiate permanent differences and temporary differences. Provide examples of each.

15. [LO 6.6] Which corporations are required to file Schedule M-3? What is the purpose of this schedule?

16. [LO 6.6] Explain the two-step evaluation process of FIN 48.

17. [LO 6.6] What are the UNICAP rules, and which businesses do they affect?

18. [LO 6.6] Which of the following costs must be included in inventory by a manufacturer under the UNICAP rules?
a. Factory insurance
b. Advertising
c. Payroll taxes for factory employees
d. Research and experimentation costs
e. Repairs to factory equipment

19. [LO 6.6] Explain the advantages and disadvantages of a publicly held company using LIFO for inventory valuation.

Crunch the Numbers

20. [LO 6.1] Mary, a taxpayer in the 35 percent marginal tax bracket, borrows $500,000 at 10 percent interest to invest in 7 percent tax-exempt municipal bonds. The annual interest expense on the loan is $50,000. Mary earns $35,000 interest income on the bonds. What is Mary's interest expense deduction?

21. [LO 6.1] When Kelley couldn't make several monthly payments on a business loan, her brother Mike made three of the monthly payments of $700 each, a total of $2,100 ($1,950 for interest expense and $150 for principal) for Kelley's loan. Kelley made the other nine monthly payments herself ($5,850 for interest expense and $450 for principal).
a. What is Mike's deduction for interest expense?
b. What is Kelley's deduction for interest expense?
c. What could they have done to preserve the tax deductions? Explain.

22. [LO 6.2] On October 1, Bender Company (a calendar-year, cash-basis taxpayer) signs a lease with Realco Corporation to rent office space for 36 months. Bender obtains favorable monthly payments of $600 by agreeing to prepay the rent for the entire 36-month period.
a. If Bender Company pays the entire $21,600 on October 1, how much can it deduct in the current year?
b. Assume the same facts except the lease requires that Bender Company make three annual payments of $7,200 each on October 1 of each year for the next 12 months rent. Bender Company pays $7,200 for the first 12-month rental period on October 1 of the current year. How much can Bender Company deduct in the current year?

23. [LO 6.2] On December 15, Simon Corporation (a cash-basis, calendar-year corporation) paid $5,000 for five months of supplies and $9,000 for an insurance policy covering its office building for the next three calendar years. How much can Simon deduct this year for these expenses?

24. [LO 6.2] Foster Corporation, a cash-basis taxpayer, borrowed $100,000 on January 1, year 1, but received only $98,000. The loan matures in 10 years with the $100,000 principal due on that date.

Interest of $10,000 is payable on January 1 of each year beginning January 1, year 2. How much interest is deductible in year 1 and in year 2?

25. [LO 6.3] In January, Marco incurs $2,800 in expenses traveling to San Diego to investigate the feasibility of acquiring a new business. He acquires the business and on March 1 forms a new corporation, Marco Enterprises, Inc. and pays $6,000 for organization costs. In April he begins operations and incurs $4,600 of start-up expenses. How much is deductible in the first year for these expenses?

26. [LO 6.4] Elisa spends $1,000 to entertain her customers at the local country club. The club charges an annual membership fee of $800. Elisa uses the facility 80 percent of the time for business. Her employer does not reimburse her for any of these expenses.

a. What are her deductible expenses if incurred in 2017?

b. What are her deductible expenses if incurred in 2018?

27. [LO 6.4] Jim, a self-employed individual, takes an important customer to the hockey playoffs. Although the face value of a ticket is only $70, he pays a scalper $400 for each ticket. How much can Jim deduct for the two tickets in 2018?

28. [LO 6.4] Martha lives with her husband in Los Angeles but works in San Diego. During the week she stays in a hotel in San Diego and eats in nearby restaurants. On weekends, she flies home to Los Angeles. During the year, Martha spent $5,000 for the hotel, and $2,000 for meals while in San Diego. Her airfare for travel between San Diego and Los Angeles was $2,500. What is Martha's deduction for travel expenses?

29. [LO 6.4] Mark flew from Baltimore to Phoenix on business. He spent four days on business and visited friends for two days before returning home. He stayed at a hotel for the four business days but he stayed at his friend's home the last two days. He paid the following expenses:

Airfare	$420
Hotel	500
Meals for 4 business days	200
Meals for 2 days visiting friends	80
Rental car for 6 days at $20 per day	120

How much qualifies as deductible travel expenses?

30. [LO 6.4] Tim accepts a temporary assignment that is 500 miles away from his office. The assignment is expected to last 7 months. Tim spends $7,000 for lodging and transportation and $3,000 for meals during these 7 months. At the end of the 7 months, Tim is notified that the assignment is extended for another 10 months. Tim incurs $13,000 in travel expenses ($4,000 of which is for meals) during months 8 through 17. What qualifies as deductible travel expenses?

31. [LO 6.4] Dan's employer assigned him to the New York office for 18 months. During this 18-month assignment, Dan spent $18,000 for apartment rent and $8,500 for meals, because his family remained in St. Louis. At the end of the 18-month assignment, Dan returns to St. Louis. Dan's employer paid his airfare between St. Louis and New York, but did not reimburse him for his other temporary living expenses. What expenses can Dan deduct for travel away from home?

32. [LO 6.4] John is a teacher at a local high school. During 2017 and 2018, he travels three days per week to a school in the next county to work with gifted children in an after-school program that does not end until 6:30 p.m. He normally eats dinner before driving home. If he drives 75 miles each way on 90 days each year to the gifted program, his annual meal expense is $900, and he maintains adequate records, how much may John deduct for these trips in 2017 and 2018?

33. [LO 6.4] Luis, a self-employed individual, flies from New York to Rome. He spends seven days in Rome on business and stays in Rome for an additional three days to vacation. Transportation costs incurred were $1,400; his hotel cost $200 per day for a total of $2,000; and his meals cost $100 per day for a total of $1,000. What expenses can Luis deduct?

34. [LO 6.4] Maria earns $50,000 from consulting contracts during the year. She collects only $48,000 from her clients and expects the $2,000 will remain uncollectible.

a. If Maria's business uses accrual basis, what is her gross income for the year and how much can she deduct for bad debt expense?

b. If Maria's business uses cash basis, what is her gross income for the year and how much can she deduct for bad debt expense?

35. [LO 6.4] In the current year, Melbourne Corporation pays the $2,000 annual premium for a life insurance policy on its president, for which Melbourne Corporation is the beneficiary. Melbourne also pays $20,000 in annual premiums for group term life insurance for its employees as an employee benefit; the employees designate the beneficiaries. Additionally, Melbourne pays $16,000 in annual premiums for business fire, casualty, and theft insurance. How much can Melbourne deduct as business expenses?

36. [LO 6.4] Jim, the owner of a tabloid magazine, is sued by an actor for libel and pays $15,000 in legal fees. Jim is found guilty. Jim also received many parking tickets while attending various business meetings in areas where legal parking spaces are extremely difficult to find. The tickets totaled $1,000. How much qualifies as deductible?

37. [LO 6.5] Maureen operates a cosmetics sales business from her home. She uses 400 of 1,600 square feet of the home as an office for the entire year. Her income before her home office deduction is $3,400 and unapportioned expenses for the home are as follows:

Mortgage interest	$5,000
Property taxes	1,400
Utilities	1,200
Repairs and maintenance	600
Depreciation for entire home	6,000

a. How much can Maureen deduct for her home office if she uses the actual expense method?

b. How much can Maureen deduct for her home office if she uses the simplified method?

c. If any of the expenses are not deductible currently, how are they treated for tax purposes?

38. [LO 6.5] Teresa is an accomplished actress. During the summer, she rented a vacant store to stage productions of four plays, using the local townspeople as actors and stagehands. She sold $24,000 of tickets to the various plays. Her expenses included $10,000 for copyright fees, $3,000 for store rental, $8,000 for costume purchases and rentals, $2,000 for props and other supplies, and $4,000 for all other miscellaneous expenses related to producing the series of plays.

a. How does Teresa treat the revenue and expenses if the activity is deemed a business?

b. How does Teresa treat the revenue and expenses if the activity is considered a hobby?

c. What are some of the factors that should be considered in deciding if this constitutes a business or a hobby?

39. [LO 6.5] Neil owns a ski lodge in Aspen. His use of this lodge varies from year to year. The annual expenses for the lodge are as follows:

Mortgage interest	$24,000
Property taxes	10,000
Snow removal	1,000
Yard maintenance	800
Utilities	2,000
Repairs and other maintenance	1,200
Annual depreciation	12,000

How does Neil treat the income and expenses if

a. he uses the lodge for 100 days and rents it out for 10 days at a rate of $150 per day?

b. he uses the lodge for 10 days and rents it out for 100 days at $150 per day?

c. he uses the lodge for 50 days and rents it out for 60 days at $150 per day?

40. [LO 6.6] Maxwell Corporation has income per books before tax of $400,000. Included in the income per books is $8,000 interest income from tax-exempt municipal bonds. In computing income per books, Maxwell deducted $22,000 for meal expenses, $3,300 for premiums on officers' life insurance policies (the corporation is the beneficiary for these policies), and $200 for fines.

a. What is Maxwell Corporation's taxable income?

b. What should Maxwell Corporation report as its income tax expense on its financial statements, assuming it uses a 21 percent tax rate?

41. [LO 6.6] Sorbon Corporation pays federal income tax at a 21 percent rate. In year 1, Sorbon deducts $80,000 as bad debt expense in computing its book income but deducts only $70,000 for bad debt expense on its tax return.

a. What is the difference between Sorbon's book tax expense and its federal tax liability?

b. How does Sorbon account for this difference on its financial statements?

c. In year 2, Sorbon reports $50,000 for bad debt expense on its books and $60,000 bad debt expense in computing taxable income. How does Sorbon account for this difference on its financial statements?

42. [LO 6.6] Arnold Corporation (a calendar-year, accrual-basis taxpayer) reported $500,000 pre-tax income on its financial statements for the year. In examining its records, you find the following:

- $3,000 of interest income from municipal bonds
- $200 of expenses incurred in earning the interest income from the municipal bonds
- Arnold wrote off $900 of accounts receivable as uncollectible and added $3,000 to its allowance for bad debts this year
- Arnold deducted $4,000 for business meal expenses on its financial statements
- Straight-line depreciation for financial reporting is $7,000; MACRS tax depreciation is $11,000
- Arnold paid $2,800 in premiums on key officer life insurance policies for which it is the beneficiary
- Arnold collected $50,000 from a life insurance policy due to the death of a key officer
- Arnold paid $2,500 in fines for violating Environmental Protection Agency anti-pollution regulations.

a. Identify Arnold's permanent and temporary book/tax differences.

b. Compute Arnold's taxable income and income tax payable.

43. [LO 6.6] Refer to the information in problem 42 for Arnold Corporation.

a. Identify which of Arnold Corporation's book/tax differences result in a deferred tax asset or a deferred tax liability.

b. Prepare the journal entry to record the federal tax expense and federal tax liability for Arnold Corporation.

44. [LO 6.6] Makai Corporation has a potential deduction of up to $1,000 that it would like to claim on its current-year tax return. Its tax position meets the recognition threshold of more likely than not, but the deduction cannot be measured by a single amount. The possible outcomes and their probabilities determined by Makai are as follows:

Possible outcome	Probability of occurring	Cumulative probability of occurring
$1,000	10%	10%
$750	30%	40%
$600	25%	65%
$500	15%	80%
$200	10%	90%
$100	5%	95%
0	5%	100%

What amount should Makai deduct on its financial statements according to ASC 740?

45. [LO 6.6] Tropical Patios Corporation manufactures patio furniture in a factory with 24 employees. The office staff consists of 4 employees who handle personnel, accounting, and other office responsibilities. The sales staff includes 6 employees who travel extensively selling the furniture to retail outlets. The remaining 14 employees work in the factory. If the allocation for UNICAP purposes is based on the number of employees, what percentage of the office costs would be allocated to inventory?

46. [LO 6.6] Barley Corporation used the FIFO method for inventory valuation when it began operations because this reflected the true physical flow of inventory. Its inventory under FIFO is valued at $375,000 at the end of its first year of operations. If Barley instead used LIFO, its ending inventory would be valued at $75,000. Barley Corporation's tax rate is 21 percent. For the next several years, Barley expects to see a steady increase in the cost of its products. Barley expects that its inventory will remain at about the same quantity for the next several years.

a. Is Barley Corporation required to use the inventory method that matches its actual physical flow?

b. If Barley Corporation used LIFO instead of FIFO, how much income tax could it have saved in the current year?

c. If Barley changes from FIFO to LIFO for tax purposes, does this have any impact on what it reports on its financial statements?

47. **Comprehensive Problem for Chapters 4 and 6.** Martin Galloway, the sole proprietor of a consulting business, has gross receipts of $45,000. His address is: 1223 Fairfield Street, Westfield, New Jersey and his SSN is 158-68-7799. Expenses paid by his business are

Advertising	$ 500
Supplies	2,900
Taxes and licenses	500
Travel (other than meals)	600
Business meals	400
Health insurance premiums (for Martin)	1,400
Individual retirement account contribution	2,500

During the year, Martin drives his car a total of 15,000 miles (700 business miles and 550 personal miles per month). He paid $100 for business-related parking and tolls. He paid $120 in fines for speeding tickets when he was late for appointments with clients. Martin's office is located in his home. His office occupies 500 of the 2,000 square feet in his home. His total (unallocated) expenses for his home are

Mortgage interest	$6,000
Property taxes	1,700
Insurance	700
Repairs and maintenance	300
Utilities	1,600

Depreciation for the business portion of his home is $1,364.

a. What is Martin's net income (loss) from his business for 2018?

b. How much self-employment tax must Martin pay?

c. Based on this information, are there any other deductions that Martin can claim on his individual tax return other than those reported on his Schedule C?

d. How would your answers to the above items change if Martin elects to use the simplified method for home office expenses?

Develop Planning Skills

48. [LO 6.2] Kondex, a cash-basis sole proprietorsip, is considering paying $50,000 of expenses at the end of this year rather than waiting until next year. The owner of Kondex has a marginal tax rate for the current year of 35 percent but expects to be in the 24 percent marginal tax bracket next year. Kondex uses a 7 percent discount rate for evaluation purposes. Should Kondex pay the expenses at the end of the current year?

49. [LO 6.4] Bob lives in Atlanta and needs to set up three days of business meetings with customers in San Francisco. While he is in California, he would like to spend two days sightseeing in the wine country. Bob's customers are willing to meet any weekday with him, so the scheduling is totally up to him. Bob wants to maximize the deductible portion of his travel expenses. What should he consider in scheduling his business meetings?

50. [LO 6.4] Ken, owner of Kendrick Corporation, needs to send an employee on a temporary assignment at a plant in another state. He can either send one employee for 18-months or two employees for 9-months each. Kendrick Corporation will pay for all the meal and lodging expenses while the employees are on their out-of-town assignments. Does it make any difference from a tax perspective to Kendrick and to the employees which option Ken chooses?

51. [LO 6.5] John has a vacation condo in the Florida Keys that he rented out for two weeks in December for $250 a day. John has used this vacation home himself for a total of three weeks during the year. His total (unallocated) expenses for the condo are

Taxes	$1,500
Insurance	2,000
Repairs and maintenance	1,100
Interest	4,500
Depreciation for year	1,000

John received a call from his tenants and they want to extend their rental of the condo for another week. John is in the 35 percent marginal tax bracket. What tax factors should John consider in making the decision to extend the rental of the condo?

Think Outside the Text

These questions require answers that are beyond the material that is covered in this chapter.

52. [LO 6.5] Orlando purchased a time-share property in Hawaii that he can use for five weeks each year. If Orlando uses this property for his vacations during the year and rents the property to others when he chooses not to use it, can he deduct any expenses related to this property? Explain.

53. [LO 6.5] Michael's friend suggests that he file Form 5213: *Election to Postpone Determination to Whether the Presumption Applies That an Activity Is Engaged in for Profit* if he expects to incur losses in his new activity. If he files this form within the first three years, the IRS cannot question whether it is a hobby for 5 years after beginning operations. What do you think are the possible advantages and disadvantages of filing this form with the IRS?

54. [LO 6.6] List three types of expenses or allowances that can cause temporary differences between book and taxable income and explain how their financial accounting treatment differs from their tax treatment. Why do you think the treatments differ?

55. [LO 6.6] Your friend recently read a newspaper article that said the largest of the Fortune 500 companies do not pay the federal income tax expense reported on their financial statements. The tax they pay is frequently a lower number. Your friend asks you to explain how this is possible. Do you believe this is good public policy?

56. [LO 6.6] Effective 2018, Congress reduced the progressive corporate income tax rates to a flat rate of 21 percent. How do you think this affects deferred tax liabilities and deferred tax assets?

57. [LO 6.6] AAA Airlines, an accrual-basis taxpayer, frequently issues travel vouchers to customers who voluntarily surrender their reserved seats on overbooked flights. The vouchers are for a specific dollar amount that customers can use to reduce the purchase price of future tickets. The vouchers are valid for one year and many expire unused. Explain how AAA Airlines should account for these vouchers for both financial accounting and tax purposes.

Search the Internet

58. [LO 6.4] Go to the IRS website (*www.irs.gov*) and locate the publication on travel. Julie plans to attend a business convention in Costa Rica. Her friend told her that she cannot deduct expenses for attending a convention outside of North America. Does Costa Rica qualify as part of North America?

Identify the Issues

Identify the issues or problems suggested by the following situations. State each issue as a question.

59. [LO 6.1] Ace Builders begins construction on a building in January. Its contract specifies that the building must be completed by July 1 or it must pay a penalty of $100 for each day the building is delayed. Ace Builders completes the building on July 31 and pays a penalty of $3,000.

60. [LO 6.1 & 6.4] Carl is the president of Carlton Corporation. He spends three days testifying before Congress on the impact that proposed legislation has on his industry. In his testimony he states that if the legislation passes, he will have to lay off 20 percent of his workforce. He spent $1,000 for airfare, $700 for the hotel, and $310 for meals.

61. [LO 6.4] Ken is a high school history teacher. Each summer he travels to a different location to further his knowledge of American history. This summer he plans to attend a four-day conference for high school history teachers in Philadelphia. Immediately following the conference he plans to spend a week exploring the battlefield area at Gettysburg. He plans to incorporate the information he learns from his trip into the classes he teaches.

62. [LO 6.4] In year 1, Sharon loaned her friend Christina $10,000 to start a new business. The loan was documented by a signed note, at market interest rate, and required repayment in two years. Christina appeared successful at first but her office manager embezzled a large amount of money, causing Christina to declare bankruptcy in year 2. In year 3 Sharon recovers only $1,000 of the $10,000 she loaned to Christina.

63. [LO 6.5] You rent your beach house to your friend, Sarah. Sarah rents her condo in Aspen to you. You each pay a fair rental price.

64. [LO 6.5] Scott is the CEO of a large corporation in Chicago. He spends the month of August in Wisconsin at his vacation home, where he has a separate structure furnished as an office. Scott uses the office each August for long-range corporate planning because he can avoid the interruptions that occur in Chicago and he finds the isolation he needs to concentrate. The rest of the year the office is not used.

65. [LO 6.5] Anne operates a dog-training business out of her home. She started the business four years ago but has not yet made a profit. She gets all of her business by word-of-mouth and thinks that she might try running some ads in the newspaper to increase her business.

Develop Research Skills

66. [LO 6.1 & 6.4] Gary Sanders owns his own real estate business. He has a reputation within the community for honesty and integrity and believes that this is one of the reasons his firm has been so successful. Gary was a 30 percent shareholder in an unsuccessful fast-food restaurant, Escargot-to-Go. Although he personally thought the business had great food and was well run, escargot never appealed to the local community. Early this year the corporation filed for bankruptcy.

Many of the creditors of Escargot-to-Go were also clients of Gary's real estate business. After Escargot declared bankruptcy, Gary's real estate business began to suffer. Gary felt that the decline in his real estate business was related to the bankruptcy of Escargot, so Gary used income from his real estate business to repay all the creditors of Escargot-to-Go. Within a few months, Gary's real estate business began to pick up. Gary has asked you to determine if his real estate business can deduct the expenses of repaying Escargot-to-Go's creditors.

67. [LO 6.4] Ben is the chief executive officer of a restaurant chain based in Maine. Ben began the business 15 years ago and it has grown into a multimillion-dollar company, franchising restaurants all over the country. Ben has a new interest, however, in horse breeding. He previously raised horses with some success over the years but has only recently decided to pursue this new business with the same intensity with which he originally pursued the restaurant business. Ben likes South Florida and sets up his new horse breeding business there. He purchased a fully operational breeding farm and leased a nearby condominium for six months so he can oversee the business. Ben plans to spend about six months each year in Florida for the next three years overseeing his horse business, which should provide about 30 percent of his total income. Ultimately, Ben wants to sell his interest in his restaurant business and retire to Florida to devote all of his time to his horses. Ben wants to know if he can deduct any of the costs associated with his travel to Florida.

68. [LO 6.4] Marino Corporation paid $6,500 to rent a 10-seat skybox for three football games in 2017 to use for business entertainment at each game and paid an additional $6,500 for three additional games in 2018. The price for a regular nonluxury box seat at each game is $45. How much can Marino Corporation deduct for this entertainment expense?

69. [LO 6.5] Suzanne owns a vacation home at the beach in which she lived for 30 days and rented out for 61 days during the current year. Her gross rental income is $2,600. Her total expenses for the vacation home are as follows:

Mortgage interest	$1,500
Property taxes	900
Utilities	700
Maintenance	300
Depreciation for entire house	1,100

a. Compute Suzanne's net rental income using the IRS method for allocating expenses.
b. Compute Suzanne's net rental income using the Tax Court method (also known as the Bolton method) for allocating expenses.
c. Which method results in less taxable income? Explain.

Fill-in the Forms

70. [LO 6.4] Go to the IRS website (*www.irs.gov*) and print Form 2106: *Employee Business Expenses* for 2017. Use the following information to complete this form.

Carl is an employee of Intelligent Devices, Inc. in San Jose. In a typical week in 2017, Carl spent the majority of his time on the road showing products to prospective customers. He also frequently took customers to lunch to discuss new products. Carl purchased his car on January 1, 2015. Carl's wife has her own automobile used for most of their personal driving. Carl uses the standard mileage rate for his automobile expenses. He keeps a written log of his mileage that shows he drove a total of 30,000 miles during the year of which 24,000 (2,000 miles per month) were for business. His records also show that he spent $300 for business parking and tolls, $2,800 for business meals, $1,200 for business entertainment, and $1,100 for hotel expenses while traveling away from home on business. He also paid $250 for a business-related seminar. He was not reimbursed for any of these expenses.

71. [LO 6.5] Go to the IRS website (*www.irs.gov*) and print Schedule E: *Supplemental Income and Loss*. Use the following information to complete this form.

Gillian Martin rented her vacation home in Telluride, Colorado for 60 days during the year receiving $6,900 in rental income. She used the property herself for 15 days. Her total expenses were: $4,000 mortgage interest, $2,000 property taxes, $500 utilities, $400 insurance, $200 cleaning, $700 annual depreciation, and a $600 rental commission paid to the real estate agent who found the tenant.

72. [LO 6.6] Go to the IRS website (*www.irs.gov*) and print the page of Form 1120: *U.S. Corporate Income Tax Return* that includes Schedule M-1. Use the information in example 6.43 to complete Schedule M-1.

73. **Comprehensive Problem for Chapters 4 and 6.** Go to the IRS website (*www.irs.gov*) and print Schedule C: *Profit or Loss for Business (Sole Proprietorship)*, Schedule SE: *Self-Employment Tax*, and Form 8829: *Expenses for Business Use of Your Home* for 2017. Use the information in problem 47 to complete these forms for 2017 and assume Martin does not elect the simplified method. He uses the cash method of accounting and materially participated in the business. He began his business two years ago and he did not make any payments that would require filing Form 1099.

74. **Comprehensive Problem for Chapters 4, 5, and 6.** Jordan (SSN 150-66-7788) and Diana (SSN 150-67-4321) Diego are a married couple who reside at 111 Coral Drive in Miami, FL 33156. They have one dependent daughter, Emily (SSN 155-88-4321), age 18, who lives at home.

 Jordan is a manager at Big Box Corporation. His Form W-2 wages are $68,000 and federal income tax withheld is $8,300. The correct payroll taxes were withheld.

 Diana worked at a local department store for the first half of the year. Her Form W-2 wages are $40,000 and federal income tax is $3,300. The correct payroll taxes were also withheld.

 The Diego family paid $9,200 interest on their home mortgage (reported to them by the mortgage company on Form 1098). The Diego family also owns a vacation home in Breckenridge, Colorado, for which they paid $4,100 of mortgage interest. (This is qualified mortgage interest for a second home.)

 The Diego family paid real estate taxes on their principal residence of $3,400, $2,000 of real estate taxes on their vacation home and $3,200 of sales taxes during the year.

 The vacation home in Breckenridge was rented out for 120 days during the year for which they received $12,000 in rental income. Jordan and Diana made significant decisions such as approving new tenants while a local management company handled the day-to-day needs. The Diego family used it for 30 days for a personal vacation during the year. Other expenses for the year for this vacation home (excluding interest and taxes mentioned above) were: $700 for real estate management fees paid to a local agent who handles the rental of the property, insurance expense $2,200, repairs expense $500, and utilities expense $1,800. Their depreciation expense for the rental use of this property for the year is $1,455. They use the IRS formula for allocating interest and taxes.

 The Diego family contributed $3,000 cash to their church and they have the necessary documentation for this contribution.

 In August, Diana quit her job and began a consulting business. The business code is 541990. She is operating the business under her own name and rented a small office at 1234 Coral Way, Coral Gables, FL 33146. Since Diana began her business so late in the year, her consulting income was only $8,000. She incurred the following expenses: $475 supplies, $210 telephone, $3,200 office rent, and $325 advertising. In addition, Diana drove her two-year old Lexus on business 750 miles to visit prospective and current clients. This car was also driven 7,000 miles for personal use. She materially participated in the business and did not make any payments that would require filing Form 1099.

 Jordan was born on April 1, 1976; Diana was born May 1, 1977. They have health insurance for the entire family through Jordan's employer. They have no foreign accounts.

 Based on the information presented above, prepare a Form 1040 (married filing jointly), Schedule A, Schedule C (or C-EZ), Schedule E, and Schedule SE using the forms for 2017 available on the IRS website at *www.irs.gov*.

ANSWERS TO TEST YOURSELF

1. **c. $1,800.** $7,200/12 months = $600 per month × 3 months = $1,800.
2. **a. Dues for club used solely for business meetings.** All of the other items are deductible.
3. **d. $2,600.** Home office expenses are only deductible to the extent of the income from the business after first deducting the other expenses ($10,000 – $7,400 = $2,600). Howard first deducts 15 percent of his

mortgage interest ($8,000 × 15% = $1,200) and property taxes ($3,000 × 15% = $450) for a total of $1,650 otherwise allowable itemized deductions. This leaves only $950 ($2,600 – $1,650) of income against which the remaining expenses can be deducted. He deducts $300 ($2,000 × 15%) for utilities $300 ($2,000 × 15%) for insurance, and $350 for depreciation. The remaining $50 of depreciation expense is carried forward to the next year; Howard does not reduce his basis in the home for this disallowed amount.

4. **d. $309,100.** $300,000 income per books – $4,000 tax-exempt interest + $10,000 disallowed 50% of meals + $3,000 insurance premiums + $100 fines.

5. **a. $8,400 deferred tax liability.** ($140,000 – $100,000) × 21% = $8,400.

CHAPTER 7

Property Acquisitions and Cost Recovery Deductions

CHAPTER OUTLINE

LEARNING OBJECTIVES

After completing this chapter, you should be able to:

7.1 Differentiate capital expenditures from deductible expenses and understand the difference between basis and adjusted basis.

7.2 Calculate MACRS depreciation deductions based on the allowable depreciable lives, conventions, and methods for personalty and realty.

7.3 Explain the special Section 179 expensing and bonus depreciation rules and calculate the allowable deductions.

7.4 Apply the special provisions limiting cost recovery deductions for mixed-use assets and passenger vehicles.

7.5 Understand cost recovery of natural resources and determine the allowable deductions under cost and percentage depletion.

7.6 Explain cost recovery for intangible assets and calculate amortization expense.

The cost of a long-lived asset is recovered over the accounting periods in which it produces income through depreciation (for most tangible property), depletion (for natural resources), or amortization (for intangible assets). The method and timing of the cost recovery deductions for tax reporting affect the after-tax cost of the asset. The earlier a taxpayer recovers the cost of an asset through depreciation deductions, the greater the present value of the tax savings and the lower the net after-tax cost of the asset (as discussed in Chapter 2).

The tax laws, however, restrict the choice of method and useful life allowed for cost recovery. The current Modified Accelerated Cost Recovery System (MACRS) restricts the allowable recovery life and averaging convention to a predetermined accelerated or alternative straight-line method.

Significant limits apply to the tax depreciation deductions for certain assets often used for both business and personal purposes, such as automobiles. Incentive tax provisions, including Section 179 expensing and bonus depreciation, allow an immediate write off in the first year, encouraging investment in long-lived assets. Understanding these incentive and limitation provisions and their interplay with regular MACRS depreciation deductions allows the taxpayer to maximize the value of tax savings from cost recovery deductions.

SETTING THE STAGE—AN INTRODUCTORY CASE

Windom Corporation, a calendar-year taxpayer, purchased and placed the following business assets in service in 2017:

Asset	Date placed in service	Initial cost
New automobile	March 10	$48,000
New computer equipment	June 12	300,000
Used office furniture	July 18	550,000
New general purpose equipment	September 15	800,000
Warehouse	November 28	2,400,000

The land was allocated $400,000 of the $2,400,000 total cost of the warehouse. The president of Windom Corporation read that the tax law allows a business to write off 100 percent of all purchased assets in the year of acquisition. Is he correct? Does it make a difference whether these assets were placed in service in 2017 or 2018? We will return to this case at the end of the chapter.

7.1 CAPITAL EXPENDITURES

Many business capital expenditures are for the acquisition of long-lived assets or to significantly improve the efficiency or useful lives of existing assets. These costs are treated in one of three ways: (1) expensed (deducted) currently, (2) capitalized until disposal, or (3) capitalized with the cost allocated to the years the asset's use is expected to benefit the taxpayer (the cost recovery period).[1]

Bonus depreciation and Section 179 expensing allow taxpayers to deduct the cost of qualifying depreciable business property (discussed later) upon acquisition. The cost of nonwasting assets such as land and works of art (the second category), cannot be recovered until the assets are sold. The majority of capital expenditures, however, fall into the third category in which costs are capitalized and then recovered over multiple years through depreciation, amortization, or depletion deductions. This method applies to both cash and accrual basis taxpayers.

Example 7.1

Kilgo Corporation made the following capital expenditures: $10,000 for new computer equipment, $100,000 for a mineral interest in a coal mine, and $300,000 for a new office building ($100,000 for the land and $200,000 for the building). The computer equipment can be expensed immediately (under bonus depreciation or Section 179) or depreciated. The interest in the coal mine is recovered through annual depletion allowances. The cost allocated to the office building is recovered through annual depreciation allowances, but the cost of the land on which the office building is located is capitalized and will remain on the company's books until recovered in the year of disposition.

Before 1981, tax depreciation was based on an estimate of the useful life of the property, similar to financial accounting depreciation. As part of the Economic Recovery Tax Act of 1981, Congress enacted the Accelerated Cost Recovery System (ACRS) to replace the existing depreciation rules. ACRS allowed very short lives for depreciation, greatly accelerating depreciation deductions, to stimulate capital investment. ACRS also simplified the law by establishing only a few class lives, standardizing averaging conventions, and eliminating estimated salvage value in determining an asset's depreciable basis.

[1] The cost of personal-use assets cannot be recovered until they are sold. When a cost is capitalized, it is added to an asset account rather than an expense account.

In 1986, the **Modified Accelerated Cost Recovery System (MACRS,** pronounced "makers"), replaced ACRS, lengthening the recovery periods over which depreciation deductions were taken. Congress made this change when focused more on raising tax revenue than stimulating the economy. Neither ACRS nor MACRS require a business to estimate actual useful lives, as required for financial accounting. As a result, the depreciation deductions on the business's tax return are very different than those on its financial statements, creating deferred tax accounts.

Example 7.2

Biltmore Corporation's federal income tax rate is 21 percent. It reports $100,000 depreciation expense on its financial statements and deducts $150,000 depreciation expense on its tax return, resulting in a favorable temporary difference. Biltmore's book income is $50,000 more than its taxable income, and its book tax expense is $10,500 ($50,000 × 21%) more than its federal tax payable. Biltmore records this $10,500 tax expense as a deferred tax liability. In future years when the depreciation expense difference reverses, the corporation's taxable income will be $50,000 more than its book income, its tax payable will be $10,500 more than its tax expense, and the $10,500 deferred tax liability will be eliminated.

Cost recovery deductions begin the year an asset is placed in service; that is, when it is set up and ready to be used for its intended business purpose.[2] This may not always be the same year in which an asset is purchased.

Example 7.3

Ratronic Corporation (a calendar-year taxpayer) purchased $90,000 of equipment on December 28, year 1. The equipment is installed and ready for use on January 4, year 2. Ratronic begins depreciating the equipment in year 2.

The tax rules that apply when an asset is placed in service are used over the asset's entire life until its basis is fully recovered, the asset is disposed of, or it is no longer used in the business. As a result, a business that places two identical assets into service in two different tax years may be required to use different methods to compute the tax depreciation. This is particularly important after the Tax Cuts and Jobs Act temporarily introduced 100 percent bonus depreciation in late 2017. Although this provision (discussed later in 7.3.2.) allows an immediate write off for many types of property, it does not change the depreciation method and rules for assets acquired before this provision took effect. Thus, the basic MACRS depreciation rules continue to apply to property acquired before and after the temporary increase in bonus depreciation phases out.

7.1.1 CAPITALIZE OR EXPENSE

Incidental materials and supplies with an acquisition cost of $200 or less can be deducted at the time of purchase. Other, more costly, materials and supplies are usually expensed to the extent they are expected to be consumed in the operation of the business during the current year or have an expected useful life of not more than 12 months. The purchase price of assets with useful lives of more than 12 months, however, are usually capitalized with their costs recovered through depreciation, depletion, or amortization.

The treatment of expenditures for repairs or maintenance is more complicated. Section 162(a) states that expenditures are currently deductible if they are incidental repair expenses; Section 263(a) states that expenditures are required to be capitalized, however, if they are for permanent

[2] Reg. §1.167(a)-2.

improvements or betterments that increase the value of the property, restore its value or use, substantially prolong its useful life, or adapt it to a new or different use. Thus, it is up to a business to determine if the costs of repairs or refurbishing of existing equipment are simply "incidental," merely maintaining its current function. If so, they should be treated as ordinary repair expenses. If, however, the costs incurred are sufficiently significant that they meet the criteria in Section 263(a), they effectively create a new depreciable asset (for cost recovery purposes).[3]

7.1.2 BASIS OF PROPERTY

Basis is the taxpayer's unrecovered investment in an asset that can be recovered through a sale or other disposition without tax cost. Basis is reduced as the taxpayer deducts depreciation, amortization, or depletion expense on the asset; this reduced basis is called **adjusted basis**.

The original basis of an asset (cost basis) includes the following:[4]

- The cash and the fair market value of the property given up by the purchaser;
- Money borrowed to pay for the property acquired;[5]
- Liabilities of the seller assumed or taken "subject to" by the purchaser; and
- Purchase expenses, such as attorney fees and brokerage commissions.

Example 7.4

Katleen Corporation purchased a storage building for $18,000 cash and a $22,000 mortgage. It also assumed the seller's property tax liability of $2,000 and paid attorney's fees of $1,800 to complete the purchase. The corporation's original basis is $43,800, because all were part of the cost of the purchased property.

If more than one asset is acquired in a single transaction (such as land, buildings, and equipment), the cost is apportioned to each of the individual items to determine their original bases using their relative fair market values (FMV).[6] The original basis of each asset is equal to its FMV divided by the FMV of all of the assets acquired multiplied by the cost of all of the assets, as summarized in the following formula:

$$\text{Total Purchase Price} \times \frac{\text{FMV of Specific Asset}}{\text{FMV of All Assets Acquired}} = \text{Original Basis of Specific Asset}$$

If the purchase price exceeds the sum of the value of the individual assets, the excess price is considered goodwill (an intangible asset discussed later).

TAX PLANNING

The buyer and seller can agree to a written allocation of the purchase price for individual assets, instead of this allocation method.[7] Buyers should allocate as much of the purchase price as possible to assets that are subject to some form of cost recovery and as little as possible to those assets for which bases cannot be recovered until sold.

[3] Reg. §1.263(a)-1(f) and Notice 2015-82, 2015-50 IRB. For businesses that have a policy of immediately deducting the cost of small purchases for financial accounting purposes, the IRS provides a de minimis safe harbor provision that allows businesses to immediately deduct up to $5,000 per item if the business has an applicable financial statement (AFS) or $2,500 if no AFS. An AFS is an audited financial statement or one required to be filed with the Securities and Exchange Commission. If the cost of an item exceeds the $5,000 or $2,500 limit, then no portion of it qualifies for this de minimis provision; the full cost must be capitalized and follow the usual depreciation rules for tax purposes.

[4] See §1012, Reg. §1.1012-1 and *Crane v. Comm.*, 35 AFTR 776, 331 US 1, 47-1 USTC 9217, (USSC, 1947).

[5] Payments on debt used to finance the acquisition of property do not affect the basis because these payments affect only the liability and cash accounts.

[6] Reg. §1.61-6(a).

[7] §1060.

Example 7.5

Maryco Corporation purchases land, an office building, and furniture for $400,000. The appraised values are: land: $200,000; building: $270,000; and furniture: $30,000. Maryco's original basis for each asset under the relative FMV method is

$$\$400,000 \times \frac{\$200,000}{\$500,000} = \$160,000 \text{ for the land}$$

$$\$400,000 \times \frac{\$270,000}{\$500,000} = \$216,000 \text{ for the building}$$

$$\$400,000 \times \frac{\$30,000}{\$500,000} = \$24,000 \text{ for the furniture}$$

If Maryco had paid $550,000, the bases would be $200,000 for the land, $270,000 for the building, $30,000 for the furniture, and $50,000 for goodwill.

After acquisition, a taxpayer increases an asset's basis for nondeductible capital expenditures that prolong its useful life or enhance its usefulness. Cost recoveries (such as depreciation expense) reduce the property's basis to avoid a double tax benefit. Without a basis reduction for cost recoveries, gains would be smaller or losses larger on the subsequent sale or other disposition of the property. Other recoveries, such as casualty losses, also reduce original basis for similar reasons (as discussed in Chapter 9).

Example 7.6

At the beginning of year 1, Marino Corporation bought equipment for $80,000 cash and a $30,000 loan. Later that year it spent $25,000 to make a major improvement to the equipment. In years 1 through 3, it deducted annual depreciation of $18,000 on the equipment and paid $14,000 on the debt. Marino's adjusted basis at the end of year 3 is $81,000 ($80,000 + $30,000 + $25,000 − $18,000 − $18,000 − $18,000). The debt payment has no effect on the asset's adjusted basis.

Cost recovery deductions are allowed only on property that is used in a trade or business or in an income-producing activity. If an asset is used for both business and personal purposes, generally depreciation is based on the relative amount of time that the asset is used for business.

Example 7.7

Mark purchased a computer for $3,000 that he uses 80 percent for business and 20 percent for personal use. Mark's basis for depreciation is $2,400 ($3,000 × 80%). He cannot depreciate the personal-use portion.

If the property is converted from personal use to business use, the basis for depreciation is the lesser of the property's adjusted basis or fair market value at the date of conversion, preventing taxpayers from depreciating a loss in value during the time it was personal-use property.

Example 7.8

Prior to October 4 of year 3, Roger used his computer entirely for personal use. The computer cost Roger $2,700 in year 1 and has a fair market value of $1,000 when converted to business use. The computer's basis for depreciation is limited to $1,000.

If a taxpayer fails to claim a depreciation deduction on an asset in any year, the basis of the asset is still reduced by the allowable depreciation (depreciation based on the applicable depreciation method the taxpayer should have claimed).[8]

[8] §167(a) and Reg. §1.167(a)-1.

Example 7.9

Last year, Ray paid $4,800 for a computer with an estimated useful life of five years for use in his consulting business. Ray forgot to claim any depreciation deduction last year. He must still reduce the computer's basis for the unclaimed depreciation to which he was entitled. Ray may not claim a double depreciation deduction in a later year.[9]

Acquisition in a Taxable Exchange

Assets are occasionally acquired in exchange for services or property other than cash. In these situations, the basis of the acquired asset equals the fair market value of the property given up or the services performed. Unless an exchange of properties qualifies as a tax-deferred exchange, the parties recognize gain or loss as if cash had been exchanged, and the basis of the property acquired is its fair market value.[10]

Example 7.10

Gilpin Corporation exchanged $50,000 in equipment for DVP Corporation's tract of undeveloped land in a taxable exchange. Gilpin has a $50,000 basis in the land, the fair market value of the equipment Gilpin gave up to acquire the land.

John, an attorney, performed legal services for New Corporation and billed the corporation $20,000 for these services. New Corporation issued John 2,000 shares of its own common stock to pay the bill. John recognizes $20,000 income and has a basis of $20,000 in the stock.

Acquisition by Gift

Section 1015 provides that a donee (gift recipient) takes the donor's adjusted basis in appreciated property as his or her basis. If the donor pays a gift tax on appreciated property, the donee increases the donor's adjusted basis by the gift tax attributable to the net increase in value of the gift property up to the date of the gift.[11] This net increase is calculated as follows:

$$\text{Gift tax paid by donor} \times \frac{\text{FMV at date of gift} - \text{donor's adjusted basis}}{\text{FMV at date of gift}}$$

Example 7.11

Larry receives appreciated property worth $24,000 as a gift from Gene. Gene's basis is $18,000, and he pays $2,000 in gift taxes on the transfer. Larry's basis is $18,500 (Gene's $18,000 basis plus a $500 basis increase for part of the gift tax), determined as follows:

$$\$18,000 + \left[\$2,000 \times \left(\frac{\$24,000 - \$18,000}{\$24,000}\right)\right] = \$18,500$$

If a gift property's value has depreciated (fair market value is now less than the donor's basis), no gift tax is added to the basis. The donee normally uses this lower fair market value as basis to determine loss on a subsequent disposition. This prevents donors from shifting losses to other taxpayers through gifts. If, however, the property regains its original value and the donee then sells it at a price equal to or greater than the donor's original basis, the donee uses the donor's higher basis to determine gain. The donee recognizes no gain or loss on a disposition at a price between the donee's reduced basis and the donor's original basis. Thus, a donee who receives a gift of loss property must keep track of its dual basis until the property is sold.

[9] Ray should amend the previous year's tax return to claim the depreciation deduction.

[10] Tax-deferred exchanges are discussed in Chapter 9.

[11] For gifts before 1977, the entire gift tax was added to basis. Gift taxes are discussed in Chapter 12.

Example 7.12

Helen gave Sherry stock worth $18,000 that she purchased three years ago for $20,000. Helen paid $1,000 in gift taxes on the transfer to Sherry. If Sherry sells the stock for $14,000, she uses the $18,000 fair market value as basis for determining loss and she has a $4,000 loss. [Sherry cannot claim Helen's $2,000 loss ($18,000 – $20,000).] If Sherry sells the stock for $23,000, she uses Helen's $20,000 basis to determine her gain of $3,000. If her selling price is between $18,000 and $20,000, she has neither gain nor loss. No gift tax was added to the stock's basis because its fair market value was lower than the donor's basis. If Helen had sold the stock (an investment asset) for its fair market value and gifted the sale proceeds to Sherry, Helen could have claimed the tax loss.

Acquisition by Inheritance

Beneficiaries use fair market value for their basis in inherited property.[12] This favorable treatment of inherited property may be due to administrative convenience because in many cases it is difficult to determine the decedent's basis due to lack of records. Congress briefly created a carryover basis rule for inherited property that was repealed very quickly due to its complexity.[13]

Example 7.13

Sam inherited two assets from his mother this year. The first asset, purchased five years ago for $40,000, was worth $50,000 when she died, and the second asset purchased last year for $47,000 was worth $45,000. Sam's basis for the first asset is $50,000, and $45,000 for the second asset, their fair market values when she died.

TAX PLANNING

The differences in bases between appreciated property that is inherited and property received as a gift during the donor's lifetime, form one of the major considerations for persons wishing to reduce the total tax burden on property passing to younger generations. If appreciated property is gifted, the donee pays income tax on *all* the appreciation (while owned by both the donor and the donee) if sold. The property, however, is removed from the donor's estate, reducing potential estate taxes. If appreciated property is inherited, the heir's basis is the higher fair market value, reducing taxable gain on a future sale. Potential estate taxes are higher, however, because the asset's fair market value is included in the decedent's estate.[14]

7.2 MACRS

Assets are divided into two broad categories: realty (real property) and personalty (personal property). **Realty** includes land and buildings (although the cost of land cannot be depreciated). **Personalty** is defined as any tangible asset that is not realty and includes machinery, equipment, furniture, and many other types of assets. It is important distinguish personalty (or personal property) from personal-use property. **Personal-use property** is any property (personalty or realty) that is used for personal purposes rather than in a trade, business, or in an income-producing activity. Depreciation is not allowed for personal-use assets.

[12] §1014. Usually, fair market value is determined as of the date of death, or, if elected, the alternate valuation date (six months after the date of death).

[13] The Tax Relief Act of 2010 allowed executors of estates for decedents dying in 2010 to elect to pay no estate tax and use the carryover basis rules instead of receiving a stepped-up basis for inherited property. President Obama's State of the Union address again proposed taxing gains on certain investment property held by estates closing what he termed the "trust fund loophole."

[14] See Chapter 12 for a discussion of wealth transfer planning.

Assets eligible for depreciation under MACRS are assigned to a class with a predetermined recovery period. Table 7.1 lists the recovery periods, averaging conventions, and examples of assets assigned to each recovery period for assets most commonly encountered in business.[15]

Table 7.1 MACRS Recovery Periods and Averaging Conventions

Recovery period	Averaging convention	Examples of assets
5 years	Half-year or mid-quarter	Automobiles, taxis, trucks, buses, computers and peripheral equipment, typewriters, calculators, and duplicating equipment.
7 years	Half-year or mid-quarter	Office furniture and fixtures (such as files and safes) and most other machinery.
27½ years	Mid-month	Residential rental property that includes buildings or other structures if 80 percent or more of the gross rental income is from dwelling units. This does not include a unit in a hotel, motel, or similar establishment where more than 50 percent of the units are used on a transient basis.
39 years[a]	Mid-month	Commercial and industrial buildings and other realty that is not residential rental property.

[a]Nonresidential realty placed in service after December 31, 1986, but before May 13, 1993, was subject to a 31½-year MACRS recovery period.

There are two depreciation methods for MACRS properties: the 200 percent declining-balance method with a switch to straight line to maximize deductions and the straight-line method. The 200 percent declining-balance method applies to MACRS property in the 5-year and 7-year classes of personalty. The straight-line method must be used for all property in the 27½-year and 39-year classes of realty.

Taxpayers who acquire property to which the accelerated depreciation method applies, can elect the straight-line method, but must use the recovery period and averaging convention for its class. The election to use the straight-line method is made annually on a class-by-class basis.[16] For example, if the taxpayer elects to depreciate 5-year class property on a straight-line basis in the current year, all 5-year class property acquired in this year must be depreciated using the straight-line method. Taxpayers can choose different methods for different classes, however; therefore, the taxpayer can depreciate 7-year class property on an accelerated basis and 5-year property on the straight-line basis, even though purchased in the same year.

7.2.1 AVERAGING CONVENTIONS

To minimize the difficulty of computing depreciation for a fraction of a year, Congress adopted three averaging conventions: half-year, mid-quarter, and mid-month. All the IRS depreciation tables incorporate the appropriate averaging convention. Providing these conventions means that an exact acquisition date is unnecessary to compute depreciation.

Half-Year Averaging Convention

Under MACRS, property in the 5-year and 7-year classes is treated as placed in service exactly halfway through the year. The **half-year averaging convention** allows one half-year of depreciation in the first year of an asset's recovery period, regardless of when the asset is actually placed in service. This half-year rule also applies to the year in which an asset is sold.

[15] Examples of other classes include 3 years for certain horses, 10 years for barges, 15 years for land improvements, and 20 years for water utilities. A special 15-year, straight-line class applies to qualified improvements made to the interior of nonresidential property. §168(e)(6).

[16] §167(j)(2)(B).

The IRS tables incorporate these averaging rules and consist of a series of annual percentages multiplied by the original cost basis of the asset to determine the depreciation deduction for the year. Most business assets are in the 5-year or 7-year classes; only the MACRS rates for 5-year and 7-year personalty are included here in Table 7.2.[17] These rates are computed using the 200 percent declining-balance method with a switch to straight-line depreciation when the latter yields a larger depreciation deduction.

Table 7.2 MACRS Rates for 5-Year and 7-Year Personalty Using the Half-Year Averaging Convention

Recovery year	5-year	7-year
1	20.00%	14.29%
2	32.00	24.49
3	19.20	17.49
4	11.52[a]	12.49
5	11.52	8.93[a]
6	5.76	8.92
7		8.93
8		4.46

[a]Switchover to straight line.

Example 7.14

Funco Corporation (a calendar-year taxpayer) purchases a $4,000 computer (5-year personalty) on January 15 and $20,000 of office furniture (7-year personalty) on July 30. Funco's first-year depreciation expense is $800 ($4,000 × 20%) for the computer and $2,858 ($20,000 × 14.29%) for the office furniture, a total of $3,658. Funco's second-year depreciation expense is $1,280 ($4,000 × 32%) for the computer and $4,898 ($20,000 × 24.49%) for the office furniture, a total of $6,178.

The half-year averaging convention[18] causes the write-off to extend an additional year to recover the last half-year depreciation.[19] Thus, 5-year property is really depreciated over six years and 7-year property is depreciated over eight years.

Example 7.15

Juan purchases 5-year class equipment for $10,000 on April 2 in year 1. Juan has a depreciation deduction of $2,000 for year 1, $3,200 for year 2, $1,920 for year 3, $1,152 for year 4, $1,152 for year 5, and $576 for year 6. The half-year averaging convention extends the recovery period one year longer than the class-life for the property.

Mid-Quarter Averaging Convention

To discourage taxpayers from waiting until the end of the year to make their purchases, Congress introduced a generally less beneficial averaging convention, the **mid-quarter convention**, under which depreciation is computed from the midpoint of the quarter in which property is placed in service. If more than 40 percent of all personalty purchased during the year is placed in service

[17] Complete tables for all recovery periods are included in Rev. Proc. 87-57, 1987-2 CB 687 and in IRS Publication 946: *How to Depreciate Property*. IRS publications can be downloaded from the IRS website at *www.irs.gov*.

[18] The 200 percent declining-balance rate is double the straight-line rate or 40 percent for five-year property. When the half-year averaging convention is applied to the 40 percent rate, it results in a 20 percent rate for the first year, extending depreciation into the sixth year.

[19] The sixth-year deduction (5.76%) for five-year personalty is one-half of the previous year's deduction (11.52%).

in the last quarter (three months) of the tax year, the mid-quarter convention method must be used; it is not an elective provision. Personalty expensed under Section 179 (discussed later in this chapter) and all realty are excluded from the more-than-40 percent test calculation.[20] If the taxpayer must use the mid-quarter convention, *all* personalty placed in service during the year (except expensed personalty) is subject to the mid-quarter convention rules. Property acquisitions are grouped into the quarter acquired, based on the taxpayer's taxable year. The mid-quarter convention tables must then be used throughout the life of these assets.

The mid-quarter convention divides the tax year into four quarters. An asset acquired in any quarter is depreciated from the midpoint of that quarter. Thus, an asset acquired anytime during the first quarter of the tax year is allowed 10½ months/12 months times a full year's depreciation. The IRS provides tables with this averaging convention already built in, so the principal problem is identifying when the mid-quarter convention must be used. Table 7.3 shows the mid-quarter depreciation rates for 5-year and 7-year property.

Table 7.3 MACRS Rates for 5-Year and 7-Year Personalty Using the Mid-Quarter Averaging Convention

5-year property				
Recovery year	**First quarter**	**Second quarter**	**Third quarter**	**Fourth quarter**
1	35.00%	25.00%	15.00%	5.00%
2	26.00	30.00	34.00	38.00
3	15.60	18.00	20.40	22.80
4	11.01	11.37	12.24	13.68
5	11.01	11.37	11.30	10.94
6	1.38	4.26	7.06	9.58
7-year property				
Recovery year	**First quarter**	**Second quarter**	**Third quarter**	**Fourth quarter**
1	25.00%	17.85%	10.71%	3.57%
2	21.43	23.47	25.51	27.55
3	15.31	16.76	18.22	19.68
4	10.93	11.97	13.02	14.06
5	8.75	8.87	9.30	10.04
6	8.74	8.87	8.85	8.73
7	8.75	8.87	8.86	8.73
8	1.09	3.33	5.53	7.64

Example 7.16

Bigbucks Corporation, a June 30 fiscal year-end taxpayer, purchased a small machine (7-year property) for its business for $30,000 on November 15 . On May 2, Bigbucks purchased a larger machine for $50,000. These are the only two personalty purchases in the current year. (The company claims no Section 179 expensing or bonus depreciation.) Because more than 40 percent [$50,000/($30,000 + $50,000) = 62.5%] of total purchases occur in the last quarter of Bigbucks's tax year, the mid-quarter convention must be used. Depreciation on the smaller machine (purchased in the second quarter) is $5,355 ($30,000 × 17.85%), and the depreciation on the larger machine (purchased in the fourth quarter) is only $1,785 ($50,000 × 3.57%). Second-year depreciation is $7,041 ($30,000 × 23.47%) for the smaller machine and $13,775 ($50,000 × 27.55%) for the larger machine.

[20] Reg. §1.168(d)-1(b)(4). Property expensed under §179 is not included in the numerator or denominator of this test. This computation is done after subtracting any §179 expensing but before basis is reduced for any bonus depreciation claimed.

Taxpayers must understand that they cannot *choose* between averaging conventions; they must use the convention that applies to the type of asset and date of acquisition. As a rule, the total depreciation deduction using the mid-quarter convention is smaller than the half-year convention when acquisitions are spaced throughout the year, due to the small first-year depreciation allowed for fourth-quarter acquisitions. To maximize their depreciation deductions, most taxpayers should plan place in service no more than 40 percent of their personalty acquisitions during the last three months of the tax year.[21] There are, however, situations in which the mid-quarter convention can result in a larger depreciation deduction. If most assets are acquired in the first and fourth quarters, the mid-quarter convention may be beneficial.

TAX PLANNING

Example 7.17

ABC, a calendar-year corporation, acquires $50,000 of 5-year property in the first quarter and $40,000 of 7-year property in the fourth quarter. ABC uses the mid-quarter convention because over 40 percent ($40,000/$90,000 = 44%) of the property is placed in service in the fourth quarter. Using the mid-quarter convention, total depreciation is $18,928 [($40,000 × 3.57%) + ($50,000 × 35%)]. The half-year convention depreciation deduction would have been only $15,716 [($40,000 × 14.29%) + ($50,000 × 20%)]. The mid-quarter convention increases the depreciation deduction by $3,212.

Careful planning of asset acquisitions allows taxpayers to use the conventions to their advantage.

Mid-Month Averaging Convention for Realty

Realty (buildings) are always depreciated using the straight-line method based on the month in which the property is placed in service.[22] Depreciation is calculated from the midpoint of the month in which the property is placed in service (one-half month depreciation is allowed for the first month of use) under the **mid-month convention**. Table 7.4 shows the MACRS table for residential rental property. The rates are selected based on the month in the taxpayer's tax year in which the property is placed in service.

Table 7.4 MACRS Rates for 27½-Year Residential Rental Property[a]

Month	Year 1	Years 2–18	Years 19–27	Year 28	Year 29
1	3.485%	3.636%	3.637%	1.970%	0
2	3.182	3.636	3.637	2.273	0
3	2.879	3.636	3.637	2.576	0
4	2.576	3.636	3.637	2.879	0
5	2.273	3.636	3.637	3.182	0
6	1.970	3.636	3.637	3.485	0
7	1.667	3.636	3.637	3.636	0.152%
8	1.364	3.636	3.637	3.636	0.455
9	1.061	3.636	3.637	3.636	0.758
10	0.758	3.636	3.637	3.636	1.061
11	0.455	3.636	3.637	3.636	1.364
12	0.152	3.636	3.637	3.636	1.667

[a]This table groups years 2–18 and 19–27 for simplicity in presentation. In some cases, this produces a rounding difference of .001 when compared with the official table. See Appendix at the end of this text for complete table or Revenue Procedure 87-57.

[21] Property expensed under Section 179 is excluded from this test.

[22] §168(b)(3). Realty placed in service prior to 1987 could use accelerated depreciation.

Example 7.18

Construction Corporation (a calendar-year taxpayer) purchased a rental apartment building on July 10 for $1,200,000, with $200,000 allocated to the land. The remaining $1,000,000 for the building will be depreciated over 27½ years. The first-year depreciation rate is 1.667 percent since July is the seventh month of the taxpayer's year. The depreciation deduction for the first year is $16,670 ($1,000,000 × 1.667%) and $36,360 ($1,000,000 × 3.636%) in the second year. The building will be completely depreciated in year 29 after the final year's depreciation of $1,520 ($1,000,000 × 0.152%) is claimed.

Table 7.5 presents the MACRS table for nonresidential real property.[23]

Table 7.5 MACRS Rates for 39-Year Nonresidential Real Property

Month	Year 1	Years 2–39	Year 40
1	2.461%	2.564%	0.107%
2	2.247	2.564	0.321
3	2.033	2.564	0.535
4	1.819	2.564	0.749
5	1.605	2.564	0.963
6	1.391	2.564	1.177
7	1.177	2.564	1.391
8	0.963	2.564	1.605
9	0.749	2.564	1.819
10	0.535	2.564	2.033
11	0.321	2.564	2.247
12	0.107	2.564	2.461

Example 7.19

Crane Corporation (a calendar-year taxpayer) purchased a warehouse on December 6 for $250,000 (allocating $50,000 to land). The remaining $200,000 for the building is depreciated over 39 years. December is the twelfth month of the taxpayer's year and the first-year depreciation rate is 0.107 percent. First-year depreciation is $214 ($200,000 × 0.107%) and the second-year depreciation deduction is $5,128 ($200,000 × 2.564%).

Similar to the half-year convention, the depreciation deduction for realty under the mid-month convention extends beyond 27½ and 39 tax years.

7.2.2 YEAR OF DISPOSITION

Taxpayers must use the same averaging convention that applied at acquisition if the asset is not fully depreciated under MACRS at the time of sale or other disposition. For the half-year convention, the cost recovery rate is one-half the annual rate at disposition. For the mid-quarter convention, depreciation is only allowed from the beginning of the year to the midpoint of the quarter in which asset disposition takes place. For example, a corporation that disposes of mid-quarter property during its first quarter calculates depreciation from the beginning of the year to the midpoint of the first quarter only (1½ months/12 months times the normal annual depreciation for the year). For assets disposed of in the second, third, or fourth quarter, only 4½/12, 7½/12 or 10½/12 months' depreciation is allowed, respectively.

[23] Nonresidential real property placed in service before May 13, 1993, was depreciated over a 31½-year life.

Example 7.20

Ryan Corporation (a calendar-year taxpayer) purchased a computer, on June 1, year 1, for $20,000. Ryan claims $4,000 ($20,000 × 20%) depreciation in year 1 and $6,400 ($20,000 × 32%) depreciation in year 2 using the MACRS half-year convention. If Ryan sells the computer in year 3, its year-3 depreciation deduction is only $1,920 ($20,000 cost × 19.2% × ½), one-half year's depreciation. Alternatively, if Ryan Corporation purchased the computer on December 7, year 1, it must use the mid-quarter convention. If Ryan sells the computer on July 17, year 3, its year-3 depreciation deduction is $2,850 ($20,000 cost × 22.8% mid-quarter rate × 7½ months/12 months). Depreciation is computed from the beginning of the tax year (January 1) to the midpoint of the quarter of disposition (August 15).

Similarly, for the mid-month convention for realty, the month in which a building is sold determines the percentage of the annual depreciation rate. Depreciation is allowed from the beginning of the year to the midpoint of the month in which the disposition takes place.

Example 7.21

Dylan Corporation (a calendar-year taxpayer) purchased an office building on April 25, year 1, for $1,200,000 of which $200,000 is for the cost of the land. It sells the building on March 2, year 3. It claims a depreciation deduction in year 3 of $5,342 ($1,000,000 building cost × 2.564% mid-month rate × 2½ months/12 months). Depreciation is computed from the beginning of the tax year (January 1) to the midpoint of the month of disposition (March 15).

7.2.3 ALTERNATIVE DEPRECIATION SYSTEM (ADS)

The **alternative depreciation system (ADS)** uses the straight-line method along with the appropriate averaging convention. Although the recovery period for computers and automobiles is the same under ADS as under MACRS (5 years), the ADS recovery periods for many other assets are longer. For example, buses are assigned a 9-year life and nonresidential realty is assigned a 40-year life. Table 7.6 provides the straight-line depreciation percentages under ADS for 5- and 7-year property using the half-year convention.

Table 7.6 ADS Straight-Line (Half-Year Convention) for 5-Year and 7-Year Personalty

Recovery year	5-year	7-year
1	10.00%	7.14%
2	20.00	14.29
3	20.00	14.29
4	20.00	14.28
5	20.00	14.29
6	10.00	14.28
7		14.29
8		7.14

The alternative depreciation system must be used for the following:[24]

- For certain *listed* property (listed property is discussed later in this chapter)
- To compute earnings and profits[25]

[24] §168(g).

[25] If the ADS straight-line method is elected, separate depreciation records are not required for earnings and profits calculations. Refer to Chapter 10 for a discussion of earnings and profits.

- For property financed with tax-exempt bonds
- For property used outside the United States
- For property used by a tax-exempt entity
- For property used by certain businesses electing to forgo bonus depreciation to be exempt from the limitation on business interest expense.[26]

Taxpayers with net operating losses may prefer using the straight-line method with a longer recovery period to reduce their losses by electing to use ADS.

TAX PLANNING

7.3 SPECIAL EXPENSING PROVISIONS

7.3.1 SECTION 179 EXPENSING ELECTION

Section 179 immediate expensing has a long history as an incentive specifically targeting small businesses. Expensing is the most accelerated form of depreciation for tax purposes. Expensing has the potential to encourage increased business investment in qualified assets in the short run by reducing the company's cost of capital and increasing its cash flow. It also simplifies depreciation accounting when a business makes the expensing election.

Prior to 2003, $25,000 was the maximum annual amount that could be expensed by a taxpayer. To stimulate a sluggish U.S. economy, the annual expensing limit was increased incrementally to $500,000 in 2012, where it remained until adjusted for inflation in 2017 to $510,000. The Tax Cuts and Jobs Act increased this limit to $1,000,000 in 2018, indexing it for inflation in future years.

Property eligible for immediate expensing includes both new and used tangible personalty but *not* real property.[27] Each year, the taxpayer can elect to expense all or part of the acquisition cost of eligible property placed in service during that year up to the allowable limit. Basis remaining after reduction for the Section 179 expensing deduction is subject to regular MACRS depreciation.

Example 7.22

Sampson Corporation, a calendar-year taxpayer, purchased $548,000 of used 5-year equipment on September 15, 2017. Sampson elects to expense $510,000 under Section 179. It claims $7,600 [($548,000 − $510,000 expensed) × 20% regular MACRS rate] of MACRS depreciation on the $38,000 balance, resulting in total depreciation for 2017 of $517,600. Sampson's 2018 depreciation expense is $12,160 [($548,000 − $510,000 expensed) × 32% regular MACRS rate]; $7,296 [($548,000 − $510,000 expensed) × 19.2% regular MACRS rate] for 2019; $4,378 [($548,000 − $510,000 expensed) × 11.52% regular MACRS rate] for 2020; $4,378 [($548,000 − $510,000 expensed) × 11.52% regular MACRS rate] for 2021; and $2,189 [($548,000 − $510,000 expensed) × 5.76% regular MACRS rate] for 2022.

If Sampson Corporation purchased the equipment in January 2018, it could deduct the entire $548,000 in 2018. It could claim no depreciation in future years because its adjusted basis is reduced to zero at the end of 2018.

[26] Real property businesses can make an irrevocable election to forgo bonus depreciation and be exempt from the interest expense limit. The definition of real property businesses is broad and includes property development, redevelopment, construction, reconstruction, acquisition, conversion, rental, operation, management, leasing, or brokerage. If a real property business elects out of the limits on the business interest deduction, the taxpayer must depreciate all buildings and qualified improvement property using the ADS. The ADS period for qualified improvement property is 20 years, 30 years for residential rental realty, and 40 years for nonresidential realty.

[27] Also eligible are qualified leasehold improvements (described in §168(e)(6)), qualified restaurant property (described in §168(e)(7)), and qualified retail improvement property §168(e)(8) acquired before 2018. As of 2018, this category was renamed improvement property and §179(f)(2) further expands property eligible for expensing to "qualified real property" for the following nonresidential property components: roofs; heating, ventilation and air conditioning property; fire protection and alarm systems; and security systems. Expensing is not available for assets used in investment activities, nor is it available for property acquired by gift, inheritance, or from a related party as defined in §267. §179(d)(1) and (2).

Two other limitations, one based on the total amount invested in qualifying assets and the other on taxable income, may restrict the amount expensed under Section 179 beyond the basic limit. First, the expensing provision is intended to benefit only small businesses. Taxpayers that acquire *qualifying* assets in excess of $2,030,000 in 2017 ($2,500,000 in 2018) must reduce the maximum annual limitation on a dollar-for-dollar basis for each dollar in excess of the threshold. Taxpayers that acquire and place in service $2,540,000 ($2,030,000 threshold + $510,000 Section 179 limit) or more of eligible assets in 2017 or $3,500,000 ($2,500,000 threshold + $1,000,000 Section 179 limit) or more in eligible assets in 2018 are allowed no Section 179 expense deduction. Only assets eligible for Section 179 expensing are included in this limit; thus, buildings are ignored in the computation. There is no carryover to a future year for the acquisition cost of an asset disallowed by this cost limitation. The cost is simply subject to regular MACRS depreciation in the acquisition and future years.

Example 7.23

Barnard Corporation purchased $2,310,000 equipment during the first eight months of 2017 reducing its Section 179 expensing limitation to $230,000 [$510,000 – ($2,310,000 – $2,030,000)]. The $280,000 disallowed by the limitation cannot be carried over to a future year. If Barnard had purchased equipment for $2,540,000 or more, it could not claim any Section 179 expensing in 2017. All $2,540,000 would simply be depreciated under MACRS.

The Section 179 expense claimed is also limited to the taxable income from the taxpayer's business, determined before the Section 179 expensing deduction (but after all regular depreciation).[28] If the taxpayer's Section 179 deduction is limited by its taxable income, the currently nondeductible portion may be carried to future taxable years; however, any carryforward is subject to the dollar expensing limit in the carryover year.

Example 7.24

Rocko Company's income is $10,000 before the Section 179 deduction. It purchased $25,000 of equipment (7-year class) and claims a $25,000 Section 179 deduction. Rocko can deduct only $10,000 due to the income limit and carries the excess $15,000 to the next year. The $15,000 carryover and any additional Section 179 expense are subject to the overall expensing limit next year, however.

A taxpayer may choose to use all, part, or none of the annual Section 179 deduction. By electing to expense less than the maximum for a tax year, the taxpayer can avoid a Section 179 carryforward.

Example 7.25

In August 2017, Makai Corporation purchased $25,000 of computer equipment (5-year class property). Makai's income is only $20,000 before the Section 179 deduction. If Makai expenses $18,750 under Section 179, it can depreciate the remaining $6,250 ($25,000 – $18,750) using regular MACRS depreciation ($6,250 × 20% = $1,250). Makai's total depreciation deduction is $20,000 ($18,750 under Section 179 + $1,250 regular MACRS depreciation) and equals taxable income prior to the deduction. Next year, Makai can claim regular MACRS depreciation of $2,000 ($6,250 × 32%) and it will be allowed the full expensing deduction for other equipment acquired that year.

[28] §179(b)(3). A self-employed individual's taxable income is computed without regard to the deduction for one-half of self-employment taxes paid; if he or she is also an employee, wages and salary may be included in determining taxable income for purposes of this limitation. §280F(d)(2); Temp. Regs. §1.280F-4T(a)(1).

The expensing limit applies separately to each business entity (C corporation, S corporation, partnership) and to individual taxpayers. As flow-through entities, a portion of any Section 179 expensing deduction elected by an S corporation or partnership flows through to its owners and is deducted on the owner's tax return. This Section 179 deduction plus the individual's Section 179 deductions from all other sources cannot exceed the annual taxpayer limit. Any excess Section 179 deduction is carried forward and can be deducted in future years (subject to the annual limits).

TAX PLANNING

How to maximize the benefits from Section 179 expensing when multiple qualifying Section 179 assets are placed in service during the year is an important consideration. Generally, taxpayers should maximize current deductions based on the time value of money. Using Section 179 to expense assets with the longest class lives generally maximizes the value of this deduction.

The application of the mid-quarter convention can be altered by use of Section 179 expensing. Amounts expensed under Section 179 are excluded from both the numerator and denominator in determining if more than 40 percent of assets placed in service were acquired in the last quarter of the year. Preference usually should be given to avoiding the mid-quarter convention when compared with accelerating depreciation of assets with longer lives.

7.3.2 BONUS DEPRECIATION

First-year **bonus depreciation** was introduced as an incentive for businesses to purchase new equipment to stimulate the economy after September 11, 2001. Initially, the bonus depreciation only applied to new (not used) property; the initial 30 percent rate was subsequently increased to 50 percent. The Tax Cuts and Jobs Act temporarily increased bonus depreciation to 100 percent for assets acquired after September 27, 2017 and extended it to used property. The 100 percent rate begins phasing out in 2023 and expires at the end of 2026.[29]

The 100 percent rate only applies to property purchased and placed in service after September 27, 2017. If a written binding contract to acquire property existed prior to September 28, 2017, the property is not considered acquired after the contract date and is not eligible for 100 percent bonus depreciation; instead, the 50 percent rate applies, with only new property eligible.

Bonus depreciation is limited to tangible personalty, software, and certain improvements.[30] Basis remaining after reduction for the bonus depreciation is subject to regular MACRS depreciation. Realty and other assets with recovery periods greater than 20 years are not eligible for bonus depreciation.[31] Unlike Section 179 expensing, bonus depreciation is not limited to small businesses and has no phase-out provision (or taxable income limitation).

If Section 179 expensing is elected, the amount expensed is deducted first before computing bonus depreciation; thus, bonus depreciation is sandwiched between the Section 179 expensing and regular MACRS depreciation deductions.

---

[29] Bonus depreciation will be gradually phased out in future years and will no longer be available after 2026. The rate will be reduced from 100% to 80% in 2023, 60% in 2024, 40% in 2025 and 20% in 2026.

[30] Qualified improvement property for the interior portion of nonresidential property that is placed in service after the date the building was first placed in service is eligible. Qualified improvement property does not include expenditures attributable to the enlargement of a building, elevator, escalator, or the internal structural framework of a building. §168(e)(6).

[31] Property required to be depreciated using ADS is ineligible, but property for which ADS was elected could be eligible.

Example 7.26

On September 1, 2017, Molokai Corporation, a calendar-year corporation, purchased $1,810,000 of new 5-year equipment, expensing $510,000 under Section 179. Its maximum allowable depreciation expense deduction for 2017 is $1,290,000, consisting of $510,000 Section 179 expense, $650,000 [($1,810,000 – $510,000) × 50%] bonus depreciation and $130,000 [($1,810,000 – $510,000 – $650,000) × 20%] regular MACRS depreciation. Its 2018 depreciation for this equipment would be $208,000 [($1,810,000 – $510,000 – $650,000) × 32%].

If this was used equipment, the maximum allowable depreciation for the first year would have been $770,000: $510,000 Section 179 expensing and $260,000 [($1,810,000 – $510,000) × 20%] regular MACRS depreciation. Its second-year depreciation would be $416,000 [($1,810,000 – $510,000) × 32%].

If Molokai had instead purchased the equipment after September 27, 2017, it could have deducted the entire $1,810,000 in the first year.

Bonus depreciation can still be claimed even if the mid-quarter averaging convention is required for depreciation (because more than 40 percent of personalty is placed in service in the last quarter of the year). Bonus depreciation has no income limits and can be claimed even in years when businesses have losses (similar to regular MACRS depreciation).

Bonus depreciation applies to all eligible property unless the taxpayer elects to forgo the deduction. A real property business might elect to forgo bonus depreciation to be exempt from the interest expense limit imposed by the Tax Cuts and Jobs Act.[32]

Figure 7.1 presents the first page of a filled-in Form 4562: *Depreciation and Amortization* using the 2017 limits and the following information for Milano Corporation:

Asset	Date acquired	Original basis	Section 179 expense	Bonus depreciation	MACRS depreciation
Used office furniture	1/28/17	$810,000	$510,000	N/A	$42,870
New computer equipment	2/26/17	548,000	0	274,000	54,800
Warehouse building	3/2/17	400,000	N/A	N/A	8,132
Warehouse land	3/2/17	100,000	N/A	N/A	N/A

In completing Form 4562, the amount of the Section 179 expensing election is shown in part I. Bonus depreciation is shown in part II on line 14 as a special depreciation allowance for qualified property. Regular MACRS depreciation is reported in part III. It includes the $300,000 of office furniture that exceeds the amount expensed and is subject to MACRS depreciation, along with the computer equipment and the warehouse building. Parts I, II, and III are then totaled and shown in the part IV summary on line 22. The total on line 22 is then reported as depreciation expense on the first page of the corporate tax return (Form 1120).

[32] Real property businesses include property development, redevelopment, construction, reconstruction, acquisition, conversion, rental, operation, management, leasing, or brokerage.

Form **4562**

Department of the Treasury
Internal Revenue Service (99)

Depreciation and Amortization
(Including Information on Listed Property)
▶ **Attach to your tax return.**
▶ **Go to *www.irs.gov/Form4562* for instructions and the latest information.**

OMB No. 1545-0172
2017
Attachment Sequence No. **179**

Name(s) shown on return	Business or activity to which this form relates	Identifying number
Milano Corporation		

Part I **Election To Expense Certain Property Under Section 179**
Note: If you have any listed property, complete Part V before you complete Part I.

1	Maximum amount (see instructions)	1	**510,000**
2	Total cost of section 179 property placed in service (see instructions)	2	**1,358,000**
3	Threshold cost of section 179 property before reduction in limitation (see instructions)	3	**2,030,000**
4	Reduction in limitation. Subtract line 3 from line 2. If zero or less, enter -0-	4	**0**
5	Dollar limitation for tax year. Subtract line 4 from line 1. If zero or less, enter -0-. If married filing separately, see instructions	5	**510,000**

6	(a) Description of property	(b) Cost (business use only)	(c) Elected cost
	Office furniture	**810,000**	**510,000**
7	Listed property. Enter the amount from line 29	7	

8	Total elected cost of section 179 property. Add amounts in column (c), lines 6 and 7	8	**510,000**
9	Tentative deduction. Enter the **smaller** of line 5 or line 8	9	**510,000**
10	Carryover of disallowed deduction from line 13 of your 2016 Form 4562	10	
11	Business income limitation. Enter the smaller of business income (not less than zero) or line 5 (see instructions)	11	**510,000**
12	Section 179 expense deduction. Add lines 9 and 10, but don't enter more than line 11	12	**510,000**
13	Carryover of disallowed deduction to 2018. Add lines 9 and 10, less line 12 ▶ 13		

Note: Don't use Part II or Part III below for listed property. Instead, use Part V.

Part II **Special Depreciation Allowance and Other Depreciation (Don't** include listed property.) (See instructions.)

14	Special depreciation allowance for qualified property (other than listed property) placed in service during the tax year (see instructions)	14	**274,000**
15	Property subject to section 168(f)(1) election	15	
16	Other depreciation (including ACRS)	16	

Part III **MACRS Depreciation (Don't** include listed property.) (See instructions.)

Section A

17	MACRS deductions for assets placed in service in tax years beginning before 2017	17	
18	If you are electing to group any assets placed in service during the tax year into one or more general asset accounts, check here ▶ ☐		

Section B—Assets Placed in Service During 2017 Tax Year Using the General Depreciation System

(a) Classification of property	(b) Month and year placed in service	(c) Basis for depreciation (business/investment use only—see instructions)	(d) Recovery period	(e) Convention	(f) Method	(g) Depreciation deduction
19a 3-year property						
b 5-year property		**274,000**	**5 years**	**HY**	**200 DB**	**54,800**
c 7-year property		**300,000**	**7 years**	**HY**	**200 DB**	**42,870**
d 10-year property						
e 15-year property						
f 20-year property						
g 25-year property			25 yrs.		S/L	
h Residential rental property			27.5 yrs.	MM	S/L	
			27.5 yrs.	MM	S/L	
i Nonresidential real property	**March 2017**	**400,000**	39 yrs.	MM	S/L	**8,132**
				MM	S/L	

Section C—Assets Placed in Service During 2017 Tax Year Using the Alternative Depreciation System

(a) Classification of property	(b)	(c)	(d)	(e)	(f)	(g)
20a Class life					S/L	
b 12-year			12 yrs.		S/L	
c 40-year			40 yrs.	MM	S/L	

Part IV **Summary** (See instructions.)

21	Listed property. Enter amount from line 28	21	
22	**Total.** Add amounts from line 12, lines 14 through 17, lines 19 and 20 in column (g), and line 21. Enter here and on the appropriate lines of your return. Partnerships and S corporations—see instructions	22	**889,802**
23	For assets shown above and placed in service during the current year, enter the portion of the basis attributable to section 263A costs	23	

For Paperwork Reduction Act Notice, see separate instructions. Cat. No. 12906N Form **4562** (2017)

FIGURE 7.1 Sample filled-in form 4562

7.4 PROVISIONS LIMITING DEPRECIATION

7.4.1 MIXED-USE ASSETS

If an asset is used for both business and personal purposes, depreciation is permitted for the business-use only.

Example 7.27

Julio purchases a computer for $5,000 on March 1. He uses the computer 70 percent for business and 30 percent for personal use. Julio's basis is $3,500 ($5,000 × 70%) for business-use depreciation. No depreciation is allowed for the $1,500 ($5,000 × 30%) personal-use portion.

No depreciation deductions are permitted beyond the end of the cost recovery period even though there is unrecovered basis related to the personal use of the asset. The asset is considered fully depreciated for business-use.[33]

Limitations are imposed on MACRS deductions for **listed properties** readily used for both business and personal purposes, including passenger automobiles, computers and peripheral equipment, and other personal and business-use property used for entertainment, amusement, or recreation.[34]

The listed property rules require the taxpayer to substantiate the percentage of time an asset is used for business. If the property is used predominantly for business (more than 50 percent is business use), the taxpayer uses the MACRS tables to determine depreciation expense for the business portion of the property's use. If, however, business use is 50 percent or less, the ADS straight-line depreciation method is required and Section 179 expensing may not be claimed. The time that property is used for investment purposes rather than in a trade or business does not count toward meeting the more-than-50 percent threshold, and the actual depreciation claimed must reflect a reduction for nonbusiness use. Once a taxpayer is required to use ADS depreciation because business use does not exceed 50 percent, ADS depreciation must continue to be used in all future years, even if business use subsequently exceeds 50 percent.

Example 7.28

Elisa purchased a computer for $8,000 on July 24, 2017. Elisa uses the computer 40 percent for business and 60 percent for personal use. She must use the ADS straight-line method to calculate her depreciation because her business use does not exceed 50 percent. Elisa's 2017 depreciation deduction is $320 ($8,000 × 10% ADS rate × 40%) for business use. If Elisa increases her business use of the computer to 90 percent in 2018, she must continue using the ADS straight-line method to calculate depreciation for that asset. Elisa's 2018 depreciation deduction is $1,440 ($8,000 × 20% ADS rate × 90% business use).

Prior to 2018, computers or peripheral equipment used exclusively at a regular business and owned or leased by the person or entity operating the establishment were exempt from classification as listed property. Computers and peripheral equipment purchased in 2018 or later years will not be considered listed property due to a change made by the Tax Cuts and Jobs Act; however, computers purchased before 2018 that did not meet this exception continue to be subject to these listed property rules.

---

33 §280F(d)(4).

34 §280F(d)(2).

Reduction in Business Use

Previously-claimed depreciation must be *recaptured* (included in ordinary income) if business use decreases to 50 percent or less. The amount that must be recaptured is the excess of depreciation deducted (including any Section 179 expensing) over the alternative straight-line depreciation deduction.[35] In a year when business use decreases to 50 or less, the following steps should be taken:

1. Compute total depreciation expense actually claimed on the asset for all prior years.
2. Compute total depreciation expense that would have been deducted if the taxpayer had used the ADS straight-line method for all prior years.
3. Subtract step 2 depreciation from step 1 depreciation to determine the excess over straight-line depreciation that must be recaptured (included in ordinary income) in the current year.
4. Compute the depreciation expense for the current year (and all subsequent years) using the ADS straight-line method.

Example 7.29

Martina purchased a computer on April 29, 2017, for $10,000. She used the computer 90 percent of the time for business in 2017 and 2018 and claimed only regular MACRS depreciation. In 2019, she uses the computer only 45 percent for business. Martina adds (recaptures) $1,980 to ordinary income in 2019 because her business-use no longer exceeds 50 percent in 2019. The $1,980 is the difference between the $4,680 MACRS depreciation she claimed [$1,800 in 2017 ($10,000 × 90% × 20%) and $2,880 in 2018 ($10,000 × 90% × 32%)] and the alternative straight-line depreciation of $2,700 [$900 for 2017 ($10,000 × 90% × 10%) and $1,800 for 2018 ($10,000 × 90% × 20%)] for those years. She deducts straight-line depreciation of $900 (10,000 × 45% × 20%) in 2019 and continues straight-line depreciation in 2020, 2021 and 2022, even if her business use exceeds 50 percent.

If Martina had expensed the computer under Section 179 in 2017, she would have to recapture the $6,300 ($9,000 Section 179 expensing for the 90% business use less the $2,700 ADS depreciation), the excess expensed over alternative straight-line depreciation for the first two years. She then claims ADS straight-line depreciation each year it continues to be used for business.

7.4.2 LIMITS FOR PASSENGER VEHICLES

Automobiles are subject to more restrictive rules than those applicable to other depreciable assets.[36] Regular depreciation is computed for the vehicle and compared to the ceiling limit; the allowable deduction is the lesser of the two. Bonus depreciation can be claimed on an eligible vehicle of up to $8,000.[37] The ceiling limits in Table 7.7 apply to total depreciation (including Section 179 expensing and bonus depreciation) that can be claimed on passenger vehicles. Taxpayers cannot circumvent these automobile ceiling limits through Section 179 expensing.

[35] §280F(b)(3).

[36] A passenger automobile is any four-wheeled vehicle that is manufactured primarily for use on public streets, roads, and highways, and which is rated at 6,000 pounds unloaded gross vehicle weight or less. §280F(d)(5).

[37] The $8,000 bonus depreciation limit for vehicles is not indexed for inflation and will remain $8,000 until it expires after 2026.

Table 7.7 Ceiling Limits for Automobiles

	2017		2018	
Year	Without bonus depreciation	With bonus depreciation	Without bonus depreciation	With bonus depreciation
1	$3,160	$11,160	$10,000	$18,000
2	5,100	5,100	16,000	16,000
3	3,050	3,050	9,600	9,600
4 and thereafter	1,875	1,875	5,760	5,760

Example 7.30

Kendrick Corporation, a calendar-year corporation, purchased two automobiles on June 1, 2017: one is a used car costing $14,500 and the other a new car costing $60,000. Both cars are used exclusively for business. The first year's depreciation for the used car is $2,900, the lesser of the regular MACRS depreciation of $2,900 ($14,500 × 20%) and the ceiling limit of $3,160 (used vehicles were not eligible for bonus depreciation). The 2017 depreciation for the new car is the $11,160 limit including bonus depreciation because this is less than the $36,000 regular depreciation [($60,000 × 50% bonus) + 20%($60,000 – $30,000 bonus)]. Electing Section 179 expensing would increase the first year's depreciation by $260 (from $2,900 to the $3,160 ceiling) for the used car, but would not increase depreciation for the new car. If Kendrick has other assets that qualify for Section 179 expensing, it should expense those other assets up to the allowable limit rather than waste it on the automobiles. In future years, automobile depreciation continues to be determined using the lesser of regular MACRS depreciation and the ceiling limit. At the end of 6 years, the $14,500 car will be fully depreciated while it will take an additional 19 years (at the rate of $1,875 per year) to fully depreciate the $60,000 car.

If Kendrick Corporation purchases both vehicles in 2018, it could deduct $32,500 ($14,500 for the used vehicle and $18,000 for the new vehicle) as both new and used vehicles are now eligible for bonus depreciation in 2018.

TAX PLANNING

Separate, but slightly higher, ceiling limits apply to trucks and vans that weigh no more than 6,000 pounds for 2017: $3,560 ($11,560 with bonus depreciation) for the first year, $5,700 for the second year, $3,450 for the third year, and $2,075 for each year thereafter. For 2018, the limits for trucks and vans are as the same as for automobiles. Vehicles, such as heavy sport utility vehicles (SUVs) weighing more than 6,000 pounds, however, are excluded from the ceiling limits.[38] Congress partially closed this loophole by limiting Section 179 expensing to $25,000 for SUVs weighing up to 14,000 pounds with any excess depreciated using the regular MACRS rates. SUVs weighing 6,000 pounds or less continue to be subject to the vehicle ceiling limits.

Example 7.31

On August 28, 2017, Beta Corporation purchased a new heavy SUV for $40,000. Beta expensed the first $25,000 under Section 179 and claimed $7,500 [($40,000 – $25,000) × 50%] for bonus depreciation and $1,500 [($40,000 – $25,000 – $7,500) × 20%] for regular MACRS depreciation, a total depreciation deduction of $34,000 for 2017. If Beta Corporation instead purchases the SUV in 2018, it could deduct the entire $40,000 as bonus depreciation in the first year.

If the car is used less than 100 percent in a trade or business, the annual limitations must be reduced accordingly.

[38] Other vehicles excluded from the §280F restrictions include taxicabs, rental trucks, ambulances, and hearses used in a trade or business.

Example 7.32

In 2018, Julie purchases a new automobile for $58,000 primarily for use in her sole proprietorship. She drove 70 percent of the miles for business in 2019 and 90 percent for business in 2019. Julie's depreciation deduction is $12,600 ($18,000 limit × 70%) for 2018 and $14,400 ($16,000 × 90%) for 2019. The personal-use portion of the car's cost is never depreciated.

If an employee uses an employer's auto for personal use and the employee is taxed on the value of that use as income, the employer's qualified business use is considered 100 percent and the employer is entitled to claim 100 percent of the allowable depreciation deduction.[39]

Example 7.33

Sara, a salesperson for Monitor Corporation, purchased a used car for $22,000 in August 2017, She used the car 80 percent for business and 20 percent for personal purposes. Her 2017 depreciation is limited to $2,528, the lesser of regular MACRS depreciation [($22,000 × 80% business use × 20% = $3,520 regular MACRS depreciation) or the ceiling limit ($3,160 × 80% business use = $2,528)]. If Monitor purchased the car for Sara, treating her personal use as taxable fringe benefit income, Monitor's qualified business use of the car is 100 percent and it can claim a full depreciation allowance of $3,160 for 2017.

The steps for computing the basis on which the depreciation is claimed are as follows:

1. Determine asset basis (total cost).
2. Multiply basis by business-use percentage to determine depreciable basis.
3. Subtract Section 179 expensing (if elected) from depreciable basis.
4. Determine if mid-quarter averaging convention must be used.
5. Calculate bonus depreciation on adjusted basis (after Section 179 expensing) and subtract from adjusted basis.
6. Calculate regular MACRS depreciation on any remaining basis.
7. If a passenger vehicle, compare to applicable ceiling limit (adjusted for any personal use) and deduct the lesser of depreciation or ceiling limit.

Automobile Leasing

Taxpayers who lease autos can deduct the business portion of their lease payments. To prevent taxpayers from taking advantage of the difference between lease payments and the limit on depreciation deductions for automobiles, taxpayers must add a **lease inclusion** amount determined

Example 7.34

On April 12, Carrie leased an automobile for five years. During the first year, Carrie used the automobile 70 percent for business and 30 percent for personal use. Assume that the IRS lease inclusion table amount is $70 for the first year and $150 for the second year. Carrie includes $35 [$70 × (263 days leased/365 days in year) × 70% business use] in income for the first year and deducts 70 percent of the lease payments. If Carrie continues to use the automobile 70 percent for business, she includes $105 ($150 × 70% business use) in income for the second year and deducts 70 percent of the lease payments.

[39] Personal use of a company car by a more-than-5 percent owner of a business or someone related to the owner is never qualified business use for MACRS depreciation.

from IRS tables to their income.[40] The dollar amount of the inclusion is based on the fair market value of the automobile and is prorated for the number of days the automobile is leased. This lease inclusion factor effectively replaces the depreciation ceiling limits that apply to car buyers.

7.5 DEPLETION

The cost of minerals, other natural resources, and timber are recovered through **depletion**. Depletion deductions on certain natural resources are calculated using either cost depletion or percentage depletion, and taxpayers claim the greater of the two amounts for qualifying property. The choice between cost and percentage depletion is an annual election. Thus, cost depletion may be used in one year and percentage depletion used in the following year.

Cost depletion is similar to the units-of-production method of depreciation. Depletion per unit is calculated by dividing the adjusted basis of the asset by the estimated recoverable units of the asset (such as tons or barrels). Cost depletion is determined by multiplying the depletion per unit by the number of units sold (not the units produced) during the year.[41] Under cost depletion, total deductions cannot exceed the taxpayer's cost basis in the property.

Example 7.35

On January 1, year 1, Striker Oil Company purchases the mineral rights to an oil well for $100,000. At that date, the well is expected to produce 20,000 barrels of oil. The depletion per unit is $5/barrel ($100,000 cost/20,000 estimated recoverable barrels). During the first year, 6,000 barrels of oil are produced and sold. The cost depletion deduction for the first year is $30,000 (6,000 barrels sold × $5 per barrel). The adjusted basis is now $70,000 ($100,000 – $30,000) and the estimated remaining oil is 14,000 barrels. During the second year, 6,000 barrels of oil are produced, but only 4,000 are sold. The cost depletion for the second year is $20,000 (4,000 barrels sold × $5 per barrel) and the adjusted basis is now reduced to $50,000.

Percentage depletion is calculated as a specified percentage of gross income from the property and is unrelated to the property's cost. Percentage depletion uses percentage rates specified in Section 613. These rates vary from 5 to 22 percent, depending on the type of resource being mined or refined. Following are some examples:

Platinum, uranium, and sulfur	22%
Copper, gold, silver, oil, and gas	15%
China clay, rock asphalt, and vermiculite	14%
Coal, lignite, and perlite	10%
Gravel, sand, and pumice	5%

TAX PLANNING

Percentage depletion continues as long as revenue is generated, even if the costs of acquiring and developing the property have been fully recovered. Thus, when percentage depletion is used, it is possible to deduct more than the original cost of the property, but the adjusted basis of the property can go no lower than zero. The percentage depletion deduction cannot exceed the net income from the property in any year prior to this deduction.[42] By permitting deductions far in excess of their actual investment, the government provides an incentive for companies to continue to make the investment necessary to extract essential natural resources.

[40] Reg. §1.280T(a). The complete lease inclusion tables for leases commencing in 2017 are included in Rev. Proc. 2017-29, 2017-14 IRB and apply to vehicles with a value exceeding $19,000. The lease inclusion tables have not yet been released for 2018.
[41] §611.
[42] The percentage depletion deduction cannot be more than 50 percent (100 percent for oil and gas property) of taxable income from the property computed without the depletion deductions.

Example 7.36

Kevin purchased a royalty interest in an oil well for $112,000. Kevin's share of the gross income from the sale of oil for the year is $35,000. His share of the expenses related to the production of the oil is $10,000. His share of taxable income before considering the depletion deduction is $25,000 ($35,000 gross income – $10,000 expenses). The percentage depletion deduction is $5,250 (15% × $35,000), which is less than his taxable income. The adjusted basis of Kevin's investment is reduced to $106,750 ($112,000 cost – $5,250 depletion expense).

Intangible drilling and development costs (IDCs) are incurred to develop oil and gas properties and include costs for labor to clear the property, erect derricks, and drill the well. These costs generally have no salvage value and are lost if the well is dry. At the taxpayer's option, IDCs can be expensed fully in the year incurred, or capitalized and deducted through depletion.

TAX PLANNING

If the percentage depletion deduction exceeds cost depletion, capitalizing the IDC has no benefit for the taxpayer. Percentage depletion is not calculated on the property's basis and a deduction for the IDCs could be lost if they are capitalized. Expensing IDCs permits the taxpayer to deduct them entirely in the current year plus claim percentage depletion.[43] By allowing an immediate deduction for IDCs, the government in effect reduces the cost of dry holes and provides an incentive for oil producers to drill for new oil wells.

7.6 AMORTIZATION

The cost of intangible assets generally is recovered through **amortization** if the intangible asset has a determinable life that can be established with reasonable accuracy.[44] As a result of the determinable life requirement, intangible assets are grouped into three categories: (1) intangibles with a perpetual life that cannot be amortized, (2) 15-year intangibles acquired as part of a business purchase (called Section 197 assets), and (3) intangibles amortizable over a life other than 15 years. Assets in the first category include equity investments such as stock and partnership interests, and they are not amortizable. Basis is recovered only upon disposition of the asset. The rest of this discussion focuses on the other two categories.

When an ongoing business is purchased, the purchase price frequently exceeds the value of the separate assets. Fair market value is allocated to and becomes the basis for each asset. The purchase price in excess of value allocated to the tangible assets is an intangible asset, most often classified as goodwill. Disputes frequently arose between the IRS and taxpayers over whether an intangible asset such as a covenant-not-to-compete[45] (an amortizable asset) was separate and distinct from goodwill or going-concern value (at that time a nonamortizable asset). To address this problem, Congress added Section 197, requiring amortization of most intangible assets (including franchise rights) acquired when purchasing a business over a 15-year period using the straight-line method. The 15-year recovery period applies regardless of the actual useful life of the Section 197 intangible asset. Taxpayers are allowed a full month's amortization in the month of purchase and a full month in the month of disposition.

Example 7.37

ABC Company acquires all the assets of XYZ Company for $3 million. On the purchase date, the appraisal values of the assets acquired by ABC were:

Asset	Appraised value
Supplies	$ 50,000
Inventory	950,000
Furniture and fixtures	1,400,000
Covenant-not-to-compete for 5 years	200,000
	$2,600,000

[43] The taxpayer makes the election in the first year the expenditures are incurred by either taking a deduction on the tax return or by adding them to the basis for depletion. Whichever option the taxpayer chooses, it is binding on the taxpayer for similar future expenditures.

[44] Reg. §1.167(a)-3.

[45] A covenant-not-to-compete is a contract between the seller of a business and its buyer that the seller will not operate a similar business that would compete with the previous business for a specific period of time.

ABC will use the appraised value as its basis for each asset. The $400,000 difference between the purchase price and the fair market value of the appraised assets is considered goodwill. ABC will recover its basis in these assets as follows:

Asset	Basis recovery
Supplies	Deducted as consumed
Inventory	Deducted through cost of goods sold
Furniture and fixtures	Deducted through MACRS depreciation
Covenant-not-to-compete	Deducted through amortization over 15 years
Goodwill	Deducted through amortization over 15 years

Note that the covenant-not-to-compete, which prohibits the former owner from establishing a similar business in the same area for 5 years, must be amortized over 15 years (not the 5-year duration of the agreement not to compete).

Patents and copyrights acquired separately, rather than as part of the purchase of an entire business, are amortized over the expected legal life of the asset instead of the 15-year statutory amortization period. Costs of "self-created" patents or copyrights are amortized over their legal lives of up to 17 years for patents and 28 years for copyrights. Other intangibles, acquired independently of the purchase of a complete trade or business (for example, a customer list), can be amortized if a definite and limited life can be established.

Example 7.38

Blazing Computers Corporation purchases the new patent on a computer chip from Smartchip Corporation. Blazing pays $600,000 for the patent. No other assets of Smartchip Corporation are included in the purchase. Because the patent has a remaining legal life of 17 years, the annual amortization deduction for the patent is $35,294 ($600,000/17 years).

7.6.1 RESEARCH AND EXPERIMENTATION EXPENDITURES

Regulation Section 1.174–2(a) defines research and experimentation expenditures as costs incident to obtaining a patent, and costs for development of an experimental or pilot model, formula, invention, or similar property. Research and experimentation (R&E) expenditures do not include the expenses incurred for the ordinary testing or inspection of products for quality control or those for efficiency surveys, management studies, consumer surveys, advertising, or promotions.

Three alternatives are available for handling research and experimentation expenditures until 2022:

1. Expense them in full in the year paid or incurred.
2. Amortize them over a period of not less than 60 months.
3. Capitalize them.

TAX PLANNING

If costs are capitalized, a deduction is not allowed until the research project becomes worthless or is abandoned. Either of the first two choices is usually preferable to capitalization because many products resulting from research projects do not have a definite useful life. Usually a taxpayer elects to immediately expense the research expenditures because of the time value of money. By allowing an immediate deduction, the government provides an incentive for businesses to conduct basic research.

Beginning in 2022, the Tax Cuts and Jobs Act requires that R&E expenditures (including software development costs) must be capitalized and amortized over a 5-year period, beginning with the midpoint of the tax year in which the expenditures are paid or incurred. Research expenditures that are attributable to research conducted outside the United States will be capitalized and amortized over a period of 15 years.

7.6.2 SOFTWARE

The cost of acquiring off-the-shelf software is deducted on a straight-line basis over 36 months, beginning in the month the software is placed in service.[46]

Example 7.39

In June, JM Corporation, a calendar-year taxpayer, purchased $130,000 of off-the-shelf software. Assuming none of its cost was expensed, the deduction for the first year is $25,278 [($130,000/36 months) x 7 months] and is $43,333 for the second year. Alternatively, the entire amount could have been expensed under Section 179 in the first year.

TAX PLANNING

If software is purchased with hardware (bundled software), the cost of the software is depreciated as part of the hardware cost unless the software cost is separately stated.[47] Thus, making sure that the cost of bundled software is separately stated can provide a faster write off.

If software is leased, the lessee can deduct the lease payment as a business expense. If the cost of developing computer software is considered research and development, then it can either be expensed in the year the costs are incurred (until 2022) or amortized over 60 months.

REVISITING THE INTRODUCTORY CASE

If the assets were acquired in 2017, the first-year total depreciation deduction is $1,170,456, computed as follows:

New automobile	limited to $3,160 base + $8,000 bonus	$ 11,160
New computer equipment	($300,000 x 50% bonus depreciation = $150,000) + [($300,000 – $150,000 bonus) x 20% = $30,000] =	180,000
Used office furniture	$510,000 Sec. 179 expense + [($550,000 – $510,000) x 14.29% = $5,716] =	515,716
New general purpose equipment	($800,000 x 50% bonus depreciation = $400,000) + [($800,000 – $400,000 bonus) x 14.29% = $57,160] =	457,160
Warehouse	$2,000,000 x 0.321% = $6,420	6,420
Total depreciation		$1,170,456

The land is not eligible for depreciation; 50 percent bonus depreciation applies to new property acquired before September 27, 2017. The Section 179 expensing should be claimed on the used property because it is not eligible for bonus depreciation.

[46] Off-the-shelf software is software that is readily available to the general public, subject to a nonexclusive license, and not substantially modified. Software is also eligible for Section 179 expensing and bonus depreciation.

[47] Rev. Proc. 2000-50, 2000-2 CB 601.

If the assets are not purchased until 2018, they are eligible for 100 percent bonus depreciation (except for the building) but ceiling limits still apply to the automobile. Depreciation for 2018 is $1,674,420 computed as follows:

New automobile	limited to $10,000 base for Sec. 179 + $8,000 bonus	$ 18,000
New computer equipment	$300,000 × 100% bonus depreciation	300,000
Used office furniture	$550,000 × 100% bonus depreciation	550,000
New general purpose equipment	$800,000 × 100% bonus depreciation	800,000
Warehouse	$2,000,000 × 0.321% = $6,420	6,420
Total depreciation		$1,674,420

Although the corporation can write off $503,964 more due to 100 percent bonus depreciation, it cannot completely write off the automobile or the building in the first year.

SUMMARY

The method and timing of the cost recovery deductions used for tax reporting affect the after-tax cost of an asset. As a general rule, the earlier the taxpayer can recover the cost of an asset through depreciation deductions, the greater the present value of the tax savings and the lower the net after-tax cost of the asset.

MACRS assigns assets to a class with a predetermined recovery period. The 5-year and 7-year classes are the most common for personalty, and the 27½-year and 39-year classes are the most common for realty. Most personalty is depreciated using the 200 percent declining-balance method, while realty is depreciated using the straight-line method. A half-year convention applies to personalty; however, if more than 40 percent of all personalty placed in service occurs during the last quarter of the tax year, the mid-quarter convention must be used. A mid-month convention applies to depreciable realty.

The Section 179 incentive tax provision allows immediate expensing of a limited amount of qualified new or used personalty (subject to annual dollar limits) with the remaining basis deductible using regular MACRS depreciation. The increase for bonus depreciation from 50 percent to 100 percent for personalty placed in service after September 27, 2017 provides a significant tax savings because there are no dollar limits. It is important to understand the limitations of any incentive provisions and their interplay with regular MACRS depreciation deductions to maximize the value of tax savings from cost recovery deductions.

Significant limits apply to tax depreciation deductions for certain assets that are most likely to be used for both business and personal purposes, such as automobiles. Depreciation deductions for passenger vehicles are subject to annual ceiling limits that cannot be circumvented through expensing provisions.

The cost of intangible assets is recovered through amortization deductions using the straight-line method over 15 years for most intangibles acquired in connection with the purchase of a business. The cost of natural resources is recovered through depletion. Taxpayers can claim the greater of cost depletion or percentage depletion; the choice is an annual election. Percentage depletion, under which it is possible to deduct more than the original investment, is one way the government provides an incentive for companies to continue to make the investment necessary to extract essential natural resources.

Businesses must routinely make choices that affect the timing and amount of cost recovery expenses. Understanding these important concepts helps businesses determine how to compute and characterize gain and loss when they sell or dispose of these assets. The relationship between cost recovery deductions and gain or loss on property disposition is explored in the next chapter.

KEY TERMS

Adjusted basis 319
Alternative depreciation system (ADS) 328
Amortization 339
Basis 319
Bonus depreciation 331
Cost depletion 338
Depletion 338
Half-year averaging convention 323
Lease inclusion 337
Listed property 334
Mid-month convention 326
Mid-quarter convention 324
Modified Accelerated Cost Recovery System (MACRS) 318
Percentage depletion 338
Personalty 322
Personal-use property 322
Realty 322
Section 179 329

Answers Appear after the Problem Assignments

TEST YOURSELF

1. Maria received Mega Corporation stock as a gift from her Uncle Glen two years ago when its fair market value was $90,000. Glen paid $60,000 for the stock five years ago, and he paid $3,000 in gift taxes when he made the gift to Maria. What is Maria's basis for the stock?
   a. $60,000
   b. $61,000
   c. $63,000
   d. $90,000
   e. $93,000

2. Ricardo purchased a personal computer for $3,000 two years ago that is currently worth $1,000. He used the computer exclusively for personal use until the current year, when he began using it exclusively in his sole proprietorship. What basis must Ricardo use in calculating his depreciation on the computer?
   a. $3,000
   b. $2,000
   c. $1,000
   d. $0

3. Probest Corporation (a calendar-year corporation) purchased and placed the following assets in service during 2018:

Date	Asset	Cost
March 4	Automobile	$39,000
May 23	Warehouse	900,000
October 1	Office furniture	535,000

   All assets are used 100 percent for business. $100,000 of the cost of the warehouse property is allocated to the cost of the land. The corporation has $1,000,000 in income from operations before calculating depreciation deductions. What is Probest's maximum cost recovery deduction for the year?
   a. $163,793
   b. $529,573
   c. $565,840
   d. $1,353,000

4. On October 2, 2018 Bedrock Corporation (a calendar-year corporation) acquired and placed into service 7-year used business equipment costing $5,900,000. It made no other acquisitions during the year. What is the maximum depreciation expense Bedrock can claim for 2018?
   a. $510,000
   b. $555,366
   c. $843,110
   d. $5,900,000

5. In May 2017, Jose purchased a used automobile for $12,000 and used it 75 percent for business. No Section 179 election was made for this asset. In 2018, Jose's business use of the automobile decreased to 45 percent. As a result of this change in business use
   a. there is no change in the way Jose computes his 2018 depreciation.
   b. Jose's depreciation in 2018 is $2,250.
   c. Jose must recapture $900 as ordinary income in 2018.
   d. Jose must amend the 2017 tax return and recompute depreciation.

PROBLEM ASSIGNMENTS

Check Your Understanding

1. [LO 7.1] Linda inherited a car from her Uncle Ted, who had purchased the car two years ago for $38,000. The car's value was $30,000 at the date of Ted's death. What is Linda's basis for the car?

2. [LO 7.1] Cynthia, a sole proprietor has a loss this year and would like to claim no depreciation this year and then take double depreciation next year. Can she elect to do this?

3. [LO 7.2] What averaging conventions exist under MACRS? How does a taxpayer determine which averaging convention should be used?

4. [LO 7.2] Is a depreciation deduction allowed for a warehouse used in business in the year it is sold? If yes, explain how it is calculated.

5. [LO 7.2] Why would a business elect to use the ADS straight-line method to compute regular income tax depreciation rather than the 200 percent declining-balance method allowed under MACRS?

6. [LO 7.3] What limits are placed on the amount and type of property that can be expensed under Section 179?

7. [LO 7.3] Delta Corporation purchased three assets during 2017: a new automobile costing $60,000 acquired in April, used office furniture costing $600,000 acquired in July, and a warehouse costing $850,000 (of which $100,000 is for the land) acquired in October. For which asset(s) should Delta Corporation elect Section 179 expensing to maximize its depreciation expense for 2017 and why?

8. [LO 7.3] Why is the Section 179 expensing election more valuable to a small business than to a large business?

9. [LO 7.4] What is listed property? Explain how the change to listed property affects computers purchased in 2018.

10. [LO 7.4] Carl purchased a Jaguar automobile for $90,000 to use exclusively in his business. He boasts that he can recover his cost through MACRS depreciation deductions over five years. What restrictions reduce the tax benefits of purchasing a luxury automobile for business use? Explain these restrictions. Will he be able to circumvent these restrictions by leasing the vehicle?

11. [LO 7.4] Mark wants to purchase a new luxury sedan for $70,000 for use exclusively in his business. The car salesman told Mark that he could expense the entire cost in the first-year. Is he correct? Explain your answer.

12. [LO 7.4] An employee uses her employer's auto 75 percent for business and 25 percent for personal use. The personal use is taxed to her as income. What percentage of the auto can the employer consider business use and depreciate? Will your answer change if the employee's business use decreases to only 35 percent?

13. [LO 7.5] Explain the difference between cost depletion and percentage depletion.

14. [LO 7.5] What are IDCs and how are they treated for tax purposes?

15. [LO 7.1, 7.4 & 7.6] Indicate whether a taxpayer can claim deductions for depreciation or amortization for the following:
    - **a.** Land used in the taxpayer's ranching business.
    - **b.** An automobile used in business. The taxpayer accounts for the deductible car expenses using the standard mileage rate.
    - **c.** The costs attributable to goodwill and a covenant-not-to-compete.

16. [LO 7.6] RCL Corporation is negotiating with Royal Corporation to acquire a patent that has nine years remaining on its legal life. RCL can either purchase the patent for $50,000 or purchase all of the assets for Royal Corporation for $500,000, including the patent. Discuss how amortization of the patent will be handled under each alternative.

17. [LO 7.6] What activities are deductible as research and experimentation expenditures? How are they usually treated for tax purposes?

Crunch the Numbers

18. [LO 7.1] Two years ago, Warren purchased a computer for $4,000 that was used exclusively for personal purposes until this year. At the beginning of the current year, Warren opened a consulting business as a sole proprietorship and began using the computer solely for business; it is now worth only $900. What basis must Warren use in calculating his depreciation on the computer?

19. [LO 7.1] Last year, Anne purchased a condo unit for $125,000 as her personal residence. In the current year, the condo unit appraises at $132,000, and Anne moves out and converts the condo to rental property. What basis can Anne use when computing her depreciation on the rental condo unit?

20. [LO 7.1] Six years ago, Sharon purchased her principal residence for $500,000. In the current year, she converts the property to rental use because she has been unable to sell it due to the depressed real estate market. The property's current fair market value is $400,000 (of which $100,000 is for the land). What basis does Sharon use when computing depreciation on her rental property?

21. [LO 7.1] David received a gift of stock from Ted this year when it was worth $24,000. Ted purchased the stock for $18,000 five years ago and paid $2,000 of gift taxes on the gift. What is David's basis for the stock?

22. [LO 7.1] Gisela gave Ellen stock worth $50,000 this year. Gisela purchased the stock for $60,000 four years ago. Calculate Ellen's basis for the stock if she sells it
    a. for $65,000.
    b. for $45,000.
    c. for $55,000.

23. [LO 7.2] Blanco Corporation (a calendar-year taxpayer) purchased $2,200,000 of used manufacturing equipment in July, $400,000 of used computer equipment in August, and an office building for $850,000 (of which $170,000 was for the land) in November. Compute Blanco's depreciation deduction for 2017.

24. [LO 7.1 & 7.2] In 2015, Chris purchased a machine (7-year property) that cost $20,000 for use in his sole proprietorship. He claimed only regular MACRS depreciation (no Section 179 expensing or bonus depreciation) due to his low income that year. In 2016 and 2017 his business had operating losses and he claimed no depreciation in those years. On April 1, 2018 he sold the machine for $21,000. What is his adjusted basis for determining his gain on sale of the machine in 2018?

25. [LO 7.1 & 7.2] On April 1, Radcliff Corporation, a calendar year taxpayer, purchased land, a warehouse, and used equipment (7-year property) for a total price of $500,000. An appraiser determined that the land has a value of $220,000, the warehouse a value of $264,000, and the equipment a value of $66,000. If Radcliff does not elect Section 179 expensing or bonus depreciation, what is its depreciation expense for this first year?

26. [LO 7.2] Azona Corporation (a calendar-year taxpayer) purchased only one business asset during the year, 7-year used property that cost $2,600,000. Compute Azona's depreciation for 2017 assuming that bonus depreciation was not elected and
    a. the asset was purchased and placed in service on September 25, 2017.
    b. the asset was purchased and placed in service on October 1, 2017.

27. [LO 7.2] Tatum Corporation (a calendar-year corporation) purchased a building on June 6 of the current year for $300,000, of which $60,000 is for the land. What is the depreciation for the first year if the building is
    a. a warehouse?
    b. a rental apartment building?

28. [LO 7.2] At the beginning of 2018, AB Corporation (a calendar-year corporation) owned the following assets:

	Office furniture	Computer equipment
Date placed in service	11/15/15	4/15/14
Initial cost	$20,000	$10,000
Accumulated depreciation	$10,160	$8,272
Recovery period	7 years	5 years
Averaging convention	Mid-quarter	Half-year

On February 1, 2018, AB sold its office furniture. On March 15, 2018, AB sold its computer equipment. Compute AB Corporation's 2018 depreciation deduction for these two assets.

29. [LO 7.2] Craig Corporation (a calendar-year corporation) purchased $3,000,000 of office furniture in April. It would like to know what is its reduction in depreciation expense for the first three years if it elects to use ADS to compute its depreciation instead of regular MACRS accelerated depreciation.

30. [LO 7.2 & 7.3] Willis Corporation (a calendar-year corporation) purchased $550,000 of machinery (7-year property) on August 1, 2018. No other property was acquired in 2018. What is the maximum depreciation expense Willis Corporation can claim for 2018?

31. [LO 7.3] In July 2017, Lenux Corporation (a calendar-year taxpayer) purchased $2,140,000 of new office furniture. Lenux claimed the maximum allowable Section 179 expensing and regular MACRS depreciation (but no bonus depreciation). Calculate Lenux's total depreciation deduction for 2017 and 2018 for this office furniture.

32. [LO 7.3] Kondar Corporation (a calendar-year taxpayer) spent $2,090,000 to purchase used machinery in February 2017. It elected to expense the maximum under Section 179. What is Kondar's total depreciation deduction for 2017 and 2018?

33. [LO 7.3] Corando Corporation (a calendar-year taxpayer) purchased $850,000 of factory equipment in April 2018. Determine the maximum depreciation deduction for the equipment for 2018.

34. [LO 7.3] On March 1, 2017 Harry Corporation (a calendar-year taxpayer) purchased and placed in service office furniture costing $550,000. Compute the maximum amount Harry Corporation could elect to expense under Section 179 for this furniture if

a. this is the only asset placed in service this year by Harry Corporation.

b. in addition to the $550,000 of office furniture, Harry Corporation also acquired and placed in service $980,000 of factory equipment during the year.

c. in addition to the $550,000 of office furniture, Harry Corporation also acquired and placed in service $1,890,000 factory equipment during the year.

35. [LO 7.3] David operates his business as a sole proprietorship. In 2017, he spends $20,000 for a used machine (7-year property). His business income, before consideration of any Section 179 deduction, is $17,000. David elects to expense $20,000 under Section 179. Calculate his total depreciation deduction for 2017.

36. [LO 7.3] In August, 2017 Jimbo Corporation (a calendar-year corporation) purchased used computer equipment for $665,000, the only assets Jimbo purchased this year. Jimbo Corporation was in the 34 percent marginal tax bracket for 2017 and used a discount rate of 6 percent for evaluation. Assuming that Jimbo made any necessary elections to maximize the depreciation deduction, what was the after-tax cost of the computer equipment?

37. [LO 7.3] Nicko Corporation (a calendar-year corporation) purchased a new machine (7-year property) in July 2015 for $20,000. Nicko did not elect Section 179 for this asset but did claim 50 percent bonus depreciation. In November 2018, Nicko sells the machine. What is the machine's adjusted basis at the date of sale?

38. [LO 7.3 & 7.4] McDowell Corporation (a calendar-year corporation) purchased and placed in service in 2017 a $25,000 new automobile on August 15, $300,000 of new furniture on September 1, and a $680,000 warehouse (of which $100,000 was for the land) on November 8. Compute the maximum depreciation deductions for the first two years of these assets' lives.

39. [LO 7.4] Karen is an employee of KF Corporation (a calendar-year taxpayer). In February 2017, KF purchased a new $40,000 car for Karen's use. During 2017, 2018, and 2019, 60 percent of Karen's mileage on the car was business related and 40 percent was for her personal driving. Her personal use was properly treated as taxable fringe benefit income.
   a. Compute KF Corporation's depreciation deductions for 2017, 2018, and 2019 if the maximum depreciation was claimed.
   b. How would your answers change if Karen had used the car for only 45 percent business use and 55 percent personal use?

40. [LO 7.4] On June 26, 2016, Elaine purchased and placed into service a new computer system costing $8,000. The computer system was used 80 percent for business and 20 percent for personal use in both 2016 and 2017 and Elaine claimed only regular MACRS depreciation. In 2018, the computer system was used 45 percent for business and 55 percent for personal use.
   a. Compute the depreciation deduction for the computer system in 2018 and the cost recovery recapture.
   b. Assume that Elaine had instead expensed the cost of the computer system under Section 179 in 2016. Compute the cost recovery recapture in 2018.

41. [LO 7.4] Jillian is an employee of Monrow Corporation (a calendar-year corporation). In February 2018, Monrow purchased a new $50,000 car for Jillian's use. During 2018 and 2019, 60 percent of Jillian's mileage on the car was business related and 40 percent was for her personal driving. Her personal use is properly treated as taxable fringe benefit income. Compute Monrow Corporation's depreciation deductions for this car for 2018.

42. [LO 7.4] Trish entered into a 36-month lease of an automobile on January 1. She uses it 90 percent for business and 10 percent for personal use. The fair market value of the automobile at the inception of the lease is $50,000. She made 12 monthly lease payments of $650 during the year. The IRS lease inclusion table amount is $61.
   a. What is Trish's deduction for the lease payments made during the year?
   b. What is the lease inclusion amount that Trish must include in her gross income this year?

43. [LO 7.4] Byron entered into a 36-month lease of an automobile on March 1, year 1. He used it 80 percent for business and 20 percent for personal use. In year 2 he used it 90 percent for business and 10 percent for personal use. The fair market value of the automobile at the inception of the lease was $60,000. Byron made 10 monthly lease payments of $660 in year 1 and 12 monthly payments in year 2. The IRS lease inclusion table amounts are $80 for the first year and $174 for the second year.
   a. What is Byron's deduction for lease payments made during year 1? What is his deduction for year 2?
   b. What is the lease inclusion amount that Byron must include in his gross income for year 1? What amount must he include in income for year 2?

44. [LO 7.5] Goldrush Corporation bought a mine in year 1 for $90,000 and estimated there were 100,000 tons of extractable ore. In year 1, it mined 8,000 tons and sold 7,000 tons. In year 2, it mined 7,000 and sold the remaining 1,000 tons from year 1 and 6,500 of the ore mined in year 2. At the end of year 2, Goldrush Corporation estimated that, including the ore extracted but unsold, there were 160,000 tons of ore remaining. Compute the allowable cost depletion for year 1 and year 2.

45. [LO 7.5] Striker Corporation bought a mine in year 1 for $100,000 and estimated that there were 100,000 tons of extractable ore. In year 1, it mined 10,000 tons and sold 8,000 tons. In year 2, it mined 9,000 and sold the remaining 2,000 tons from year 1 and 6,000 of the ore mined in year 2. At the end of year 2, Striker Corporation estimated that, including the ore extracted but unsold, there were 150,000 tons of ore remaining. Compute the allowable cost depletion for year 1 and year 2.

46. [LO 7.5] Paul purchased a royalty interest in an oil well for $125,000. Paul's share of gross income from oil sales for the year is $40,000 and his share of expenses for the oil production is $13,000. What is Paul's percentage depletion deduction for the year? What is the adjusted basis of Paul's investment after deducting the depletion allowed?

47. [LO 7.6] Orange Corporation acquired all of the assets of Lemon Company for $10,000,000. The fair market value of the tangible assets totaled $8,000,000. The $2,000,000 difference is considered goodwill. Orange Corporation expects to continue its business operations for at least 40 years. What is its annual amortization deduction for the goodwill?

48. [LO 7.6] Zenon Corporation (a calendar-year corporation) began work on a new experimental project in year 1. It incurred $8,000 in qualifying research expenses in year 1 and $11,000 in year 2. The benefits from the project will be realized beginning in February year 3.

a. If Zenon elects a 60-month amortization period, how much will it deduct in years 1, 2, and 3?

b. If Zenon elects to expense the research expenditures, how much will it deduct in years 1, 2, and 3?

49. **Comprehensive Problem for Chapters 4, 6, and 7.** Robert Lento, the sole proprietor of a consulting business, has gross receipts of $600,000 in 2018. Expenses paid by his business are

Advertising	$ 2,500
Employee salaries	150,000
Office rent	24,000
Supplies	18,000
Taxes and licenses	17,000
Travel (other than meals)	3,800
Business Meals	2,400
Utilities	3,800
Employee health insurance premiums	6,600
Health insurance premiums for Robert	2,200

Robert purchased a new car for his business on May 15 for $50,000. He also purchased $50,000 of new 5-year equipment and $238,000 of 7-year fixtures on August 1. Robert drove the car 10,000 miles (8,000 for business and 2,000 personal miles). He paid $200 for business-related parking and tolls. He also paid $1,000 for insurance and $1,200 for gasoline and oil for the new car. He would like to maximize his deductions.

a. What is Robert's net income (loss) from his business?

b. How much self-employment tax must Robert pay?

c. If this is Robert's only source of income, what is his adjusted gross income?

Develop Planning Skills

50. [LO 7.1 & 7.2] Arco Corporation acquired some heavy equipment mid-year (in addition to the $2,600,000 in equipment purchased in January of this year). The new equipment is 7-year class property, but Arco expects to use the equipment for 8 years. It could purchase the equipment for $120,000 cash, and at the end of 8 years it would have no salvage value. Alternatively, Arco could lease the equipment for 8 years for $22,000 annually. Arco is in the 21 percent marginal tax bracket and uses a 6 percent discount rate for evaluation. Should Arco purchase or lease the equipment? Prepare a schedule showing your calculations to support your recommendation.

51. [LO 7.2, 7.3 & 7.4] Roman Corporation (a calendar-year corporation) purchased and placed in service the following assets in 2017:

Date placed in service	Asset description	Cost
May 8	Used automobile	$ 30,000
May 15	Used equipment	700,000
October 1	Used office furniture	800,000
November 3	Warehouse	260,000

$60,000 of the cost of the warehouse property is for the land.

a. What is Roman Corporation's depreciation deduction for 2017 if it only claims regular MACRS depreciation?

b. What is Roman's depreciation deduction for 2017 assuming it takes maximum advantage of Section 179 expensing and bonus depreciation?

c. What is Roman's depreciation deduction for 2018 if it instead placed all of these assets in service in 2018 instead of 2017?

52. [LO 7.2 & 7.3] Herald Corporation, a calendar-year taxpayer, purchased the following business assets:

Asset	Date placed in service	Initial cost
Used computer equipment	April 3	$ 50,000
Used office furniture	July 14	940,000
Used office fixtures	October 29	1,090,000
New office furniture	December 15	460,000
Office building (building only)	December 18	2,000,000
Land for office building	December 18	300,000

a. If these assets were placed in service in 2017, what is Herald Corporation's depreciation deduction for 2017 if it makes any elections that will maximize its deduction?

b. If these assets were instead placed in service in 2018, what is Herald Corporation's depreciation deduction for 2018 if it makes any elections that will maximize its deduction?

53. [LO 7.3] Bing Corporation can buy a new car for business use for $40,000 (including tax, license, and title fees) or it can lease an identical car for $450 per month, paying $2,100 up front for tax, license, and title fees. The corporation normally keeps its cars for three years and, if the car is purchased, expects that it will be able to sell the car at the end of three years for $18,000. The corporation is in the 21 percent tax bracket and uses a 6 percent discount rate for evaluation purposes. (For simplicity, the monthly rental fees are assumed to be paid at the end of years 1, 2, and 3.) Should Bing purchase or lease the automobile? Prepare a schedule showing your calculations to support your recommendation if the lease inclusion amounts are $43 for year 1, $95 for year 2, and $140 for year 3.

Think Outside the Text

These questions require answers that are beyond the material that is covered in this chapter.

54. [LO 7.1] How do you think assets that are acquired and disposed of in the same tax year are handled for depreciation purposes?

55. [LO 7.1] When a business rents tangible property for use in its business, it may incur up-front costs to acquire the lease on the property. How do you think these leasehold costs are treated for tax purposes?

56. [LO 7.4] You are a self-employed individual thinking about buying or leasing a car to use in your business. What information is needed to properly evaluate this lease versus purchase decision?

57. [LO 7.6] Your friend is thinking about starting up a new Internet business and would like to know how website development costs are treated for tax purposes. What are some of the costs involved in website development, and what are the issues involved in determining their tax treatment?

58. [LO 7.6] Is the treatment of purchased goodwill the same for tax and for GAAP? Explain.

Search the Internet

59. [LO 7.2] Go to the IRS website at *www.irs.gov* and locate Publication 946: How to Depreciate Property. Locate the depreciation tables at the end of the publication and calculate the first-year depreciation for a $60,000 bus using ADS.

60. [LO 7.6] Go to the IRS website at *www.irs.gov* and locate Publication 946: *How to Depreciate Property*. Locate the section on where amortization is reported. On what form is amortization reported? On which part of that form is amortization reported if this is the first year of amortization?

Identify the Issues

Identify the issues or problems suggested by the following situations. State each issue as a question.

61. [LO 7.1] James Corporation had a net operating loss of $30,000 before claiming any depreciation deductions. James purchased $26,000 in equipment in 2018 but claimed no depreciation on its 2018 tax return.

62. [LO 7.1] Demark Corporation took delivery of a new machine on December 31, 2018. Due to the high number of employees out for the holidays, the machine was not set up for use until January 3, 2019.

63. [LO 7.1] Marble Corporation purchased 300-year-old marble statutes that it displays in the entrance hall of its main office building.

64. [LO 7.3] Monicon Corporation purchased a $24,000 computer in 2015 and elected to expense it under Section 179. In 2018, the IRS audited Monicon and determined that its taxable income was incorrectly calculated and was only $20,000 before considering Section 179 expensing instead of the $24,000 reported on its 2015 tax return.

Develop Research Skills

65. [LO 7.1] Robert owns some investment land that has a basis of $1,000 and a fair market value of $22,000. He expects that it will continue to appreciate in value. Robert's uncle, Mike, has a terminal illness and is expected to survive no more than six months. Robert would like to increase the basis of the land and has devised a scheme in which he gifts the land to Mike. When Mike dies, Robert will inherit the land. Mike has agreed to participate in the plan; however, Robert wants you to confirm what his basis will be when he inherits the land from Mike.

66. [LO 7.1] Jessica, a professional violinist with the Lincoln Symphony Orchestra, purchased a 100-year-old antique violin at a cost of $180,000. She thinks that it is a good investment because she knows that it will continue to appreciate in value as a treasured work of art. She plays this violin in concerts and wants to know if she can depreciate it as a business-use asset.

67. [LO 7.6] Juan owns 40 percent and Mario owns 60 percent of Crispy Donuts, Inc. (CDI). Juan wants to buy out Mario's interest in CDI, so he arranges a stock sale agreement under which CDI will redeem (purchase) all of Mario's shares for $900,000. This will then make Juan the sole shareholder of CDI. Juan wants to ensure that Mario does not open a competing donut business nearby so he also has a covenant-not-to-compete drawn up at the same time as the stock sale agreement. Under the terms of the covenant-not-to-compete, Mario cannot open another donut business within a 10-mile radius for a period of five years. During this 60-month period, CDI will pay Mario $9,000 per month in return for his agreement not to compete. CDI wants to know over what time period it should amortize the covenant-not-to-compete.

Fill-in the Forms

68. [LO 7.2, 7.3 & 7.4] Go to the IRS website at *www.irs.gov* and print Form 4562. Using the following information, complete this form to the extent possible. Barclays Corporation, a calendar-year taxpayer, had taxable income of $2,000,000 for 2017 before computing its depreciation deduction. It purchased and placed the following business assets in service:

Asset	Date placed in service	Initial cost
New automobile	February 15	$42,000
New computer equipment	May 17	400,000
Used office furniture	August 25	752,000
Used office fixtures	September 15	1,100,000

69. Comprehensive Problem for Chapters 4, 5, 6 and 7. Maria Sanchez, the sole proprietor of a consulting business, has gross receipts of $720,000 for 2017. Expenses paid by her business are:

Advertising	$4,500
Employee salaries	150,000
Office rent	24,000
Supplies	18,000
Taxes and licenses	15,000
Travel (other than meals)	4,800
Business meals	3,400
Utilities	3,800
Employee health insurance premiums	7,600
Health insurance premiums for Maria	2,400

Maria purchased a new car for her business on June 18 for $39,000. She also purchased $90,000 of new computer equipment and $128,000 of used 7-year fixtures on August 1, and $200,000 of new 7-year equipment on September 15. Maria drove the car 20,000 miles (16,000 for business and 4,000 personal miles). She paid $250 for business-related parking and tolls. She also paid $1,200 for insurance and $1,400 for gasoline and oil for the new car. She would like to maximize her deductions.

She operates her consulting business at 111 Sand Lake Road, Orlando, Florida as Maria Sanchez Consulting. Her SSN is 155-46-6789 and her home address is 1234 Universal Avenue, Orlando, Florida 32819. She is a single individual with no dependents, claims the standard deduction, and has no other income. She paid $16,000 in estimated federal income taxes.

a. Go to the IRS website at *www.irs.gov* and print Form 4562. Complete this form using the information above.

b. Print Form 1040, Schedule C, and Schedule SE. Complete these forms for 2017 to the extent possible.

ANSWERS TO TEST YOURSELF

1. **b. $61,000.** Maria adds $1,000 of the gift tax onto her uncle's cost of $60,000 to get a basis of $61,000. The portion of the gift tax added is the portion due to appreciation [($90,000 − $60,000)/$90,000 × $3,000 = $1,000].

2. **c. $1,000.** When property is converted from personal use to business use, the lower of basis or fair market value at the date of conversion is used as basis for depreciation.

3. **c. $565,840.** Depreciation on the automobile is limited to the ceiling limit of $18,000. Depreciation for the warehouse (39-year property) is $12,840 ($800,000 × 1.605%). The warehouse is not eligible for Section 179 expensing or bonus depreciation. The entire $535,000 of office furniture can be expensed under either Section 179 expensing or 100 percent bonus depreciation.

4. **d. $5,900,000.** The entire $5,900,000 can be expensed under 100 percent bonus depreciation.

5. **c. Jose must recapture $900 as ordinary income in 2018.** MACRS depreciation was $12,000 × 20% × 75% = $1,800. Straight-line depreciation would have been $12,000 × 10% × 75% = $900. The $900 difference ($1,800 − $900) must be recaptured. The 2018 depreciation will be $1,080 ($12,000 × 45% × 20%).

Property Dispositions

PART IV

CHAPTER 8 Property Dispositions

CHAPTER OUTLINE

LEARNING OBJECTIVES

After completing this chapter, you should be able to:

8.1 Differentiate and classify realized and recognized gains and losses on asset dispositions and calculate their value accurately.

8.2 Apply the netting provisions to short- and long-term capital gains and losses to determine the effect on taxable income and specify the capital gains tax rates to which individual and corporate taxpayers are subject.

8.3 Understand the effect of the recapture provisions on gains and complete the netting process applicable to gains and losses on Section 1231 asset sales.

8.4 Identify mixed-use property and adjust gain/loss recognition as required.

8.5 Explain the specific provisions of Section 1244 stock transactions and investments in qualified small business stock.

8.6 Apply the Section 121 provisions to sales of personal residences.

8.7 Apply the correct capital gains tax rates to sales by taxpayers subject to the modified capital gains tax rates.

The tax treatment of gains and losses on property dispositions requires navigating a complex set of definitions, netting procedures, and potential alternative tax rates. It starts with determining the character or type of gain (income) or loss recognized on the property disposition. All gains and losses are ultimately characterized as either ordinary or capital. Businesses, however, also have gains and losses identified as Section 1231 gains and losses that require several additional steps before they can be characterized as ordinary or capital. This characterization is important because different tax rates may apply. For example, long-term capital gains are taxed at preferential (lower) tax rates for individuals but the deductibility of capital losses is limited for all taxpayers.

Income or losses from the sale of inventory or services are classified as ordinary and are included in determining ordinary income. Section 1231 gains and losses are the result of dispositions of operating assets (machinery, equipment and buildings) used in business for more than one year. Section 1231 gains and losses are subject to a netting process to determine their disposition. A net loss is deducted directly from ordinary income, but a net Section 1231 gain is treated as a net capital gain and is included and taxed with other capital gains.

A taxpayer must know the length of time a capital asset has been owned (the holding period) before beginning the capital gain and loss netting process. The holding period may be long-term (more than one year) or short-term (one year or less). After all of the capital gains and losses are netted, the remaining long-term capital gains may be taxed at more favorable tax rates, depending on the type of taxpayer. If the final result is net capital loss, the loss deductible from current income, if any, also depends on the taxpayer. Carryover features may allow all or part of these losses to be deducted against gains in other years, however.

Careful planning of property dispositions may allow taxpayers to reduce taxes. To take full advantage of the opportunities to time asset dispositions, the taxpayer must first understand gain and loss classification; then be able to identify whether the gains and/or losses are included directly in income or are subject to a netting process; finally, the appropriate tax rates must be applied to net gains and the deductibility of net losses determined, based upon whether the taxpayer is a corporation or an individual.

Several provisions encourage taxpayers to invest in specific assets by either changing the character of the loss (Section 1244 stock) or excluding gain from income (sales of qualified small business stock and personal residences). These provisions do not apply to all taxpayers, and they are subject to limitations. The details of these provisions must be understood to plan for and take advantage of their benefits or avoid unexpected results.

SETTING THE STAGE—AN INTRODUCTORY CASE

Albert Hoffman retired from his business (a sole proprietorship) as an electrical contractor at the beginning of 2018. He sold the business assets to a new owner but remained a consultant for six months during a transition period, earning a salary of $200,000. All of the assets (except for the inventory) were purchased more than two years ago. Albert is single and has no dependents.

Albert and the new owners of the business agreed on the following selling prices for the assets that were purchased.

Asset	Original cost	Selling price	Prior depreciation
Inventory of electrical supplies	$50,000	$70,000	N/A
Office furniture	15,000	3,000	$7,000
Electrical equipment	67,000	35,000	16,000
Office & warehouse building	200,000	200,000	45,000
Land for above building	50,000	50,000	N/A

Albert also sold the following personal assets (none purchased within the last two years) so that he would have the funds to purchase a luxury condominium in Florida.

Asset	Original cost	Selling price
Salvador Dali drawing	$137,500	$175,000
Mermaid sculpture	60,000	40,000
20,000 shares ABCD stock	175,000	145,000
7,500 shares XYZ stock	224,000	240,000

Albert was told by a friend that he would have to pay a maximum of 15 percent capital gains tax on the items that he sold. He wants to have a good estimate of what his tax expense will be for 2018. He plans to purchase a new residence with the cash from these various sales after he pays his taxes. He has asked you to determine if the capital gains tax rate his friend told him is correct and what his tax liability will be using his standard deduction. Albert's retirement funds are all in tax-deferred accounts, so income from sales and salary constitute his entire income for the year. He will not start drawing from the retirement accounts until next year. We will return to this case at the end of this chapter.

8.1 DETERMINING GAIN OR LOSS ON DISPOSITIONS

The previous chapter examined the tax consequences of asset acquisitions, their cost recovery through depreciation, amortization, or depletion, and a determination of adjusted basis. This chapter continues the discussion of property transactions by focusing on taxable dispositions of assets. To accurately determine the realized gain or loss on an asset sale, two attributes must be identified: the amount realized (net value received) on the disposition and the adjusted basis of the property. To determine the character of the realized gain or loss on an asset disposition, the taxpayer must (1) identify the asset as a business, investment, or personal-use asset, (2) determine the owner's holding period, and (3) using this information, determine if the gain or loss recognized generates ordinary, capital, or Section 1231 gain or loss. Finally, after consulting the applicable tax laws, the taxpayer either recognizes the gain or loss currently or defers recognition to a future period. Prior to examining these details, it is important to understand the tax impact of dispositions on cash flow.

8.1.1 PROPERTY DISPOSITIONS AND CASH FLOW

When property is disposed of in a taxable transaction, the gain or loss realized is the difference between the amount realized on the sale and the adjusted basis of the property sold. Cash flow equals the cash received on the sale net of the tax effect of any gain or loss recognized.[1] The taxpayer's cash flow is reduced for taxes on a recognized gain, while the cash flow increases for the tax savings generated by a recognized loss. The tax cost of a gain or tax reduction of a loss on a sale impacts the cash flow on the asset dispositions.

Example 8.1

Mega Corporation sells an asset (adjusted basis of $150,000) for $180,000 cash. Mega's tax rate is 21 percent. It pays $6,300 [($180,000 – $150,000) × 21%] in taxes and its net cash inflow is $173,700 ($180,000 cash received – $6,300 tax). If, however, Mega sells the asset for only $125,000, its $25,000 loss ($125,000 – $150,000 adjusted basis) reduces its taxes by $5,250 ($25,000 × 21%). Its net cash inflow is $130,250 ($125,000 cash received + $5,250 tax savings). If Mega Corporation sells the asset for $150,000, it recognizes neither gain nor loss, and its cash inflow is $150,000.

The type of taxpayer (corporation or individual), the taxpayer's marginal tax rate, and the type of asset all affect the taxpayer's cash flow. Gains on sales of assets by individuals are potentially subject to taxes at statutory rates ranging from zero to 37 percent. Long-term capital gains of individuals have basic tax rates of zero, 15 percent or 20 percent with short-term capital gains taxed at ordinary income tax rates.[2] Determining which tax rate to use is explained later in this chapter.

Individuals' losses may be deductible in full, limited, or completely disallowed based on the character of the loss. Ordinary and net Section 1231 losses are fully deductible against ordinary income, but individuals' net capital loss deduction is limited to $3,000 annually. Losses from most personal-use assets, however, are not deductible at all.

Corporate taxpayers apply the same tax rates to ordinary income, Section 1231, and capital gains. (They have no favorable tax rates for Section 1231 or capital gains.) Corporations can

[1] For simplicity, our cash flow examples assume only cash is received. If property other than cash is received, the cash flow analysis requires assuming the property is sold for cash; its net realizable value would then be included as cash received.

[2] The basic maximum long-term capital gains tax rate had been 15 percent since 2002 but returned to the previous 20 percent rate for individuals in the top marginal tax bracket in 2013. Certain capital gains are subject to 25% or 28% tax rates. Higher-income taxpayers are also subject to the 3.8% Medicare surtax on net investment income (see Chapter 5).

deduct ordinary and Section 1231 losses in full against ordinary income but their capital losses can only be deducted against capital gains.[3]

Example 8.2

Jim has income from many different sources and is in the 24 percent marginal tax bracket and 15 percent for capital gains. During the year, he realizes a $25,000 long-term capital gain on a stock sale and earns $25,000 of ordinary income from his sole proprietorship. Jim pays $3,750 ($25,000 × 15%) tax on the long-term capital gain and $6,000 ($25,000 × 24%) tax on the ordinary income.

If this was a corporation, both the ordinary income and long-term capital gain would be taxed at the corporation's 21 percent rate.

Example 8.3

Refer to the previous example except Jim has a $25,000 capital loss on his stock sale and a $25,000 ordinary loss from his sole proprietorship. Jim can deduct the entire $25,000 ordinary loss against his other income, resulting in immediate tax savings of $6,000 ($25,000 × 24%), but his capital loss deduction is limited to $3,000 and provides only an additional tax savings of $720 ($3,000 × 24%). Although Jim can carry the remaining $22,000 capital loss forward, the time value of money reduces its value.

If this was a corporation, only the ordinary loss would be deductible from its other income. The capital loss could only be carried back to offset capital gains from an allowable prior year or carried forward to offset future capital gains.

These examples illustrate the importance of understanding the basic requirements of property dispositions. Analyzing and classifying asset dispositions for tax purposes are addressed in the following sections. Misapplication can result in unfavorable tax consequences and reduced cash flows.

8.1.2 TYPES OF DISPOSITIONS

Asset dispositions may take several forms: sale, exchange, involuntary conversion, or abandonment. By far the most common disposition, however, is the simple sale. A sale is a transaction in which the seller receives cash or cash equivalents in return for one or more of his or her properties or assets.[4] A buyer's assumption of a seller's liability is considered a cash equivalent. An **exchange** is a transaction in which the taxpayer receives property other than cash or cash equivalents in return for property (other than money) transferred to the other party.[5]

Involuntary conversions include "destruction in whole or in part, theft or seizure, or requisition or condemnation."[6] Involuntary conversions are events that are not under the control of the taxpayer and, as a result, gains and losses may receive favorable tax treatment.[7]

Abandonments are not sales or exchanges. Nevertheless, an abandonment can result in a recognized loss on business or investment property (but not on personal-use property). A taxpayer abandons property by permanently withdrawing it from use in the taxpayer's trade or business or activity operated for profit.

---

[3] Corporations carry capital losses back three years and forward five years to offset capital gains in those years.
[4] Reg. §1.1002-1(d).
[5] Reg. §1.1002-1(d). An exchange can also involve money paid or received, and either the property exchanged or the property received may be subject to a mortgage or other liability.
[6] §1231(a)(4)(B).
[7] Involuntary conversions are discussed in the next chapter.

Example 8.4

Tom's sole proprietorship has $2,400 of ordinary income from the sale of its inventory of 4,000 screen printed T-shirts above cost. The business also sold an old screen printer for $1,000 less than its adjusted basis resulting in a loss deductible from ordinary income. Tom sold his personal auto to Jerry for $1,000 cash and Jerry assumed Tom's $6,000 balance on the car loan; Tom received cash and cash equivalents of $7,000 on this sale. Tom will have a taxable gain if his basis for the auto is less than $7,000 and a nondeductible personal loss if his basis is more than $7,000. Next, Tom exchanged a pool table valued at $1,200 for Lenny's motorcycle valued at $1,100 and $100 cash. Depending on their bases in these properties, Tom and Lenny will have either a taxable gain or nondeductible personal loss on this exchange transaction. Next, Tom had an investment painting destroyed in a fire at a museum where it was displayed and computers stolen from his business. These events qualify as involuntary conversions; part of the losses may be deductible after the loss limitations are applied. Finally, the business discards an old machine that was producing defective goods. The abandonment loss is equal to the machine's adjusted basis and is deductible from ordinary income.

The steps required to determine the tax impact of a property disposition are: (1) determine the amount realized on the disposition and the property's adjusted basis, (2) calculate the gain or loss realized, (3) determine the character of the gain or loss, and (4) analyze the applicable tax laws to determine if all, part, or none of the realized gain or loss is recognized currently and the amount of any gain or loss that is deferred.

Realized gains on sales and exchanges are generally recognized and taxable unless a specific provision provides for nonrecognition or postpones recognition to a later time. Realized losses on sales, exchanges, and abandonments are recognized and deducted only if the property involved is used in a trade or business or held for investment. The character of a recognized gain or loss refers to how a gain or loss is classified for tax purposes. Gains and losses are characterized as (1) ordinary gains and losses, (2) capital gains and losses, and (3) Section 1231 gains and losses, as explained later.

8.1.3 AMOUNT REALIZED

The **amount realized** on a transaction equals the sum of the following:[8]

1. The amount of money received
2. The fair market value of property received
3. Seller's liabilities that are assumed by the buyer

Minus the sum of the following:

1. The selling or exchange expenses
2. Buyer's liabilities assumed by the seller

The **fair market value** of property received is the price at which the property changes hands between a willing buyer and a willing seller.[9] In some cases, valuation by a qualified appraiser may be necessary to determine fair market value. Market quotations for property sold on established markets (for example, stock) can be used to determine value. If the property's fair market value is not readily determinable, the fair market value of the property given up in

[8] §1001(b) and Reg. §§1.1001 and 1.1002.

[9] See *Comm. vs. Marshman*, 60-2 USTC ¶9484, 5 AFTR 2d 1528 (CA-6, 1960).

the exchange can be used.[10] Liabilities assumed by the buyer are equivalent to giving cash to the seller to pay off the liability. Property taxes owed by the seller are a liability assumed by the buyer if the seller does not pay them.

Example 8.5

Charlie received $5,000 cash and gold coins with a fair market value of $10,000 on a land sale. The buyer also assumed Charlie's $40,000 mortgage on the land. Charlie paid attorney's fees of $2,000 and broker's fees of $3,000 on the sale. Charlie's realized $50,000 ($5,000 cash + $10,000 gold coins + $40,000 mortgage assumed by the buyer − $2,000 attorney's fees − $3,000 broker's fees) on the sale.

8.1.4 REALIZED VERSUS RECOGNIZED GAIN OR LOSS

The realized gain or loss on an asset disposition is the mathematical difference between the amount realized on the transaction and the asset's adjusted basis.[11] A **realized gain** occurs when the amount realized is larger than the asset's adjusted basis. There is a **realized loss** if the asset's adjusted basis is greater than the amount realized.[12]

Example 8.6

Cart Corporation exchanged a truck with an adjusted basis of $5,000 for a machine worth $3,000 and cash of $500. Cart has a realized loss of $1,500 (the $3,500 amount realized is less than the $5,000 adjusted basis of the truck). If Cart had received $3,000 cash (instead of $500), it would have had a gain of $1,000 ($6,000 − $5,000).

After determining the realized gain or loss, the taxpayer can determine the recognized gain or loss. A **recognized gain** is the amount of a realized gain includible in the taxpayer's gross income,[13] while a **recognized loss** is the amount of a realized loss deductible by the taxpayer.[14]

All realized gains are recognized, unless a special nonrecognition provision applies (such as the like-kind exchange provision discussed in the next chapter). Recognition of losses, however, is generally limited to business, investment, and casualty losses. With limited exceptions, taxpayers cannot deduct realized losses on personal-use property.[15]

8.1.5 HOLDING PERIOD

For certain types of assets, it is important to know the holding period (the period of time the property was owned) to determine how a gain or loss is taxed. For example, both capital assets and Section 1231 assets (defined later) must be held for "more than one year" to receive tax-favored treatment.[16]

[10] *U.S. vs. Davis*, 82 S Ct. 1190, 62-2 USTC 9509, 9 AFTR 2d 1625 (USSC, 1962).

[11] The asset's adjusted basis is its original basis increased by any capital expenditures and reduced by any capital recoveries, as discussed in Chapter 7.

[12] §1001(a).

[13] See §61(a)(3) and Reg. §1.61-6(a).

[14] See §165(a) and Reg. §1.165-1(a).

[15] §165(c)(3) permits deductions for losses arising from disasters (such as hurricanes or floods) on personal-use property as discussed in the next chapter.

[16] A worthless security (a capital asset) is deemed to be sold on the last day of the tax year. Its holding period is determined by the date acquired and the date of deemed sale. §165(g)(1).

Example 8.7

Gilpin Corporation, an equipment manufacturer, purchased land for $50,000 (a Section 1231 asset) from Goodwin Corporation on July 15, year 1, for store expansion. Gilpin's holding period for the land begins on the date of the purchase. Gilpin later decides against the expansion and must hold the land until July 16, year 2, to meet the more-than-one-year holding period required for tax-favored treatment.

An asset's holding period normally begins on the date acquired. If, however, an asset's basis carries over from another asset (a carryover basis) or takes its basis by reference to another asset (a substituted basis), then the holding period normally carries over (adds to) the holding period of the acquired asset.

Example 8.8

The Venus Corporation acquires land for a warehouse in a qualified like-kind exchange on which no gain or loss is recognized. The land acquired has the same basis as the warehouse exchanged (a substituted basis) under the like-kind exchange provisions[17] and its holding period includes the time it owned the warehouse. If, however, Venus acquires the land for cash or nonlike-kind property, it is a purchase; the land's basis is the purchase price and its holding period begins on the date of acquisition.

The holding period of a gift is determined by the basis used by the donee on a subsequent sale of the gift property. When the donee uses the donor's basis on a subsequent sale (fair market value is greater than the donor's basis), the holding period carries over as well. If fair market value is lower than the donor's basis, however, the donee uses the gift's lower fair market value at the time of the gift as basis, and the holding period begins on the date the donee receives the gift.[18]

Example 8.9

Sherry received a gift of stock from Helen that she had purchased eight months earlier for $20,000. If Sherry sells the stock for $23,000 five months later, she uses Helen's $20,000 basis to determine gain and adds Helen's holding period to hers; thus, Sherry's gain is $3,000 and her holding period is 13 months (8 months + 5 months). If however, the stock's fair market value is only $18,000 on the gift date and Sherry sells the stock for $14,000 after five months, she must use this value as her basis for loss. Sherry has a $4,000 loss ($14,000 – $18,000 basis), and her holding period is only five months.

The holding period of any asset acquired by inheritance is always long term (more than one year) regardless of the amount of time the decedent held the asset before it passed to the heir.

TAX PLANNING

The basis rules for gifts and inheritances that require the recipient's use of a fair market value when that is lower than basis effectively prevent recognition of any loss in value accrued during the time the donor or decedent held the property. Thus, property with fair market value below basis (on which the owner can recognize a realized loss) should be sold rather than given away or kept as part of a future estate; otherwise, neither the donee nor heir will be able to realize a tax benefit from the loss in value.[19]

[17] The like-kind provisions are discussed in Chapter 9.

[18] See Chapter 7 for a discussion of gift basis.

[19] Gifts and inheritances are discussed in Chapter 12. Their holding periods are included here to complete the discussion of holding period.

8.1.6 CHARACTER OF GAINS AND LOSSES

The character of the gain or loss recognized depends on the type of property sold. There are only three types of property that determine this character: ordinary, capital, and Section 1231 assets. Briefly, ordinary assets (inventory and stock in trade) are those assets that yield ordinary income through their sale in the ordinary course of business operations. Capital assets include personal use assets and assets in which an individual or a business invests (stocks and bonds) but excludes operating assets. Section 1231 assets (machinery and equipment used in the business for more than one year) comprise the bulk of business assets by which the business carries on its operations. Taxpayers must classify their property into one of these three categories to determine how the gain or loss on asset dispositions will be taxed.

Ordinary Income Assets

Ordinary income assets form an integral part of the income-generation process from normal business operations and include assets created by the taxpayer or sold in the ordinary course of business. Inventory held for sale to customers and accounts receivable from the sale of business services or inventory are ordinary income assets. Assets used in the business but not held for more than one year are also ordinary assets.[20] When ordinary income assets are sold at a gain, the gain is included with operating income and taxed at ordinary income rates. When ordinary assets are sold at a loss, the loss is deductible from ordinary operating income.

Example 8.10

The Marywood Corporation, an accrual-basis taxpayer, manufactures household linens. Its total revenue from linen sales is $5,200,000, its cost of goods sold is $2,800,000, and its other deductible expenses are $1,700,000. Marywood has net income of $700,000 for the year from the sale of its linens. The entire amount is ordinary income because it results from the sale of goods (inventory) in the course of its normal operations.

Marywood sold a truck that it used in the business for only three months. The truck cost $14,000 and was sold for $12,500. The company has a $1,500 ordinary loss on the sale of the truck because it was not used for more than one year when sold.

Lastly, Marywood sold $500,000 of linens on account during the last week of December. Due to a year-end cash shortage, it factors the receivables at 80 cents on the dollar. Marywood recognizes $500,000 of sales revenue, but it has a $100,000 ordinary loss when it factors the receivables for $400,000. Assuming no other taxable transactions, Marywood's operating/ordinary income is $598,500 ($700,000 – $100,000 – $1,500).

Capital Assets

Capital assets are assets usually held for investment or for personal use. Section 1221 states that **capital assets** are any assets *other* than the following:

1. Inventory or stock in trade held for sale in the ordinary course of business to customers
2. Accounts and notes receivable from the performance of services or sale of inventory in the ordinary course of business
3. Patents, copyrights and artistic and literary compositions created by the taxpayer or acquired by gift or nontaxable exchange from the creator[21]
4. Real and depreciable property used in a trade or business

[20] In addition to the ordinary income or loss on the disposition of the ordinary assets mentioned above, part or all of the gain on the sale of Section 1231 assets that is subject to depreciation recapture is ordinary income as discussed later in this chapter.

[21] The creator or gift recipient of a musical composition or copyright for a musical work can elect to treat its sale as the sale of a capital asset.

Categories 1, 2, and 3 assets normally are ordinary income assets and category 4 assets constitute the bulk of Section 1231 assets.

Although the definition of capital assets defines which assets are *not* capital assets, in general, capital assets are readily identifiable. Capital assets held for investment by businesses and individuals include securities, investment real estate, and collectibles. Personal-use assets include jewelry, clothing, personal autos, furniture, and personal residences. The sale or exchange of a capital asset results in capital gain or loss. While capital gains from personal-use assets are usually taxable, losses from personal-use assets are usually not deductible.

Section 1231 Assets

The complex tax treatment of Section 1231 assets evolved before and during World War II. Initially, all business assets were afforded capital asset treatment with limited deductibility of capital losses on disposal. This discouraged businesses from investing in new assets. To stimulate investment, business assets became ordinary income assets with gains and losses taxed as ordinary income or loss. During World War II, the government acquired business property through condemnation but businesses could not use the nonrecognition provisions for involuntary conversions as no qualified replacement property was available.[22] As a result, capital gain treatment was reinstated for the gains on business property but ordinary loss treatment for losses remained—today's Section 1231 asset treatment. To ensure this treatment, however, the gains and losses on the disposal of Section 1231 assets must go through a complex netting process explained later.

The principal **Section 1231 assets** are depreciable realty and personalty used in a business and nondepreciable business realty.[23] To qualify as Section 1231 assets, however, these assets must be held for *more than one year*.

Example 8.11

Wilma owns a painting acquired at an auction two years ago and land purchased three months ago as investments. She also owns a rental apartment building purchased five years ago. The painting and the land are capital assets (investments), but the apartment building is Section 1231 rental property. She also owns two automobiles—a minivan used solely for her accounting business and a convertible used for pleasure. Both autos have been owned for more than one year. The minivan is a Section 1231 business asset and the convertible is a capital asset because it is a personal-use asset.

Example 8.12

Meghan owns a business manufacturing children's toys. The manufactured toys are inventory and their sales produce ordinary income. She sold a machine (purchased 13 months ago) used to manufacture toys at a loss. The asset was used in Meghan's business so it is not a capital asset. She owned it for more than one year and it was depreciable, so it is a Section 1231 asset. If she had not owned it for more than 12 months, it could not be a Section 1231 asset. It could only be an ordinary income asset and the loss would be an ordinary loss rather than a Section 1231 loss.

Example 8.13

Forge Company owns the land and the buildings used in its cement product manufacturing operations and all its necessary machinery and equipment. As long as these assets have been owned for more than one year, they are Section 1231 assets because they are used in a business. Forge also owns the gravel pit from which materials for making cement are extracted and a patent on a special cement curing process that will not expire for eight more years. Both of these assets are subject to cost recovery allowances—depletion and amortization, respectively—similar to depreciation and are Section 1231 assets.

[22] To avoid recognition of gain, qualified replacement property must be acquired. These rules are discussed in the next chapter.

[23] Additional Section 1231 assets include (a) long-term capital gain property held for the production of income that is involuntarily converted by theft, casualty, seizure, or condemnation; (b) land from which wasting assets are taken and (c) some patents and franchises under specific circumstances.

It is important to correctly identify trade or business and investment assets because Section 165 specifically *disallows* the recognition of losses on personal-use property, except for losses resulting from casualties.[24]

Table 8.1 presents the character of assets as determined by the property's use and holding period.

Table 8.1 Character of Assets Determined by Property Use and Holding Period

	Property use		
Holding period	**Used in business**	**Inventory and accounts receivable**	**Investment or personal-use***
Long-term (more than one year)	Section 1231**	Ordinary	Long-term capital
Short-term (one year or less)	Ordinary	Ordinary	Short-term capital

*Gains on the sale of personal-use assets are taxable capital gains but losses on the sale of personal-use assets are not deductible.

**Through a netting process (explained later), gain or loss on Section 1231 assets is eventually characterized as long-term capital or ordinary.

8.1.7 MIXED-USE ASSETS

Properties used both for business and personal purposes are mixed-use assets. Any transactions affecting these assets must be partitioned into the business and personal-use portions.

Example 8.14

Alma owns a beauty salon that occupies 40 percent of her home. She depreciates only 40 percent of the home's basis. If she sells the home, 40 percent of the home qualifies as the sale of property used in a trade or business (Section 1231 property); the other 60 percent qualifies as a sale of a personal-use asset.

8.2 DISPOSITION OF CAPITAL ASSETS

The majority of all assets held by individual taxpayers are capital assets. The majority of these are their personal-use assets such as personal residences, personal automobiles, clothing, and home furnishings, and their investment assets such as stocks, bonds, land held for appreciation, and collectibles such as coins, works of art, and other rare objects. Businesses, however, may also hold assets as investments rather than for business use; these are also capital assets. The majority of capital assets held by businesses are stocks or securities, although investment in other types of assets is possible.

If a taxpayer disposes of a capital asset, the taxpayer's holding period at the time of disposition is important. Subject to certain exceptions, capital assets held for more than one year are **long-term capital assets** and capital assets held one year or less are **short-term capital assets**.[25]

8.2.1 THE CAPITAL GAIN AND LOSS NETTING PROCESS

A taxpayer with both capital gains and capital losses in the same year completes a multi-step netting process. During this netting process, the taxpayer continues to subtract losses from gains until the final result is only gains or only losses.

[24] §165(h) limits the deductibility of personal casualty losses, however, as discussed in the next chapter.

[25] §1222.

This netting process consists of the following steps:

1. Determine the recognized gain or loss on each short-term and each long-term capital asset, separating the long term from the short term.
2. Subtract all long-term losses (including any long-term losses carried forward from a prior year) from all long-term gains. If the net amount is positive, it is a net long-term capital gain; if the net amount is negative, it is a net long-term capital loss.
3. Subtract all short-term losses (including any short-term losses carried forward from a prior year) from short-term gains. If the net amount is positive, it is a net short-term capital gain; if the net amount is negative, it is a net short-term capital loss.
4. If step 2 and step 3 both end in gains only or losses only, no further netting is required. If there is both a remaining gain and a remaining loss, net the remaining loss (gain) (either short- or long-term) with the remaining gain (loss)(either short- or long term); the result will be just a single short- or long-term net gain or net short- or long-term loss.

The resulting net gain(s) and/or net loss(es) are taxed based on the final gains/losses and type of taxpayer, as explained later. Figure 8.1 illustrates this netting process.

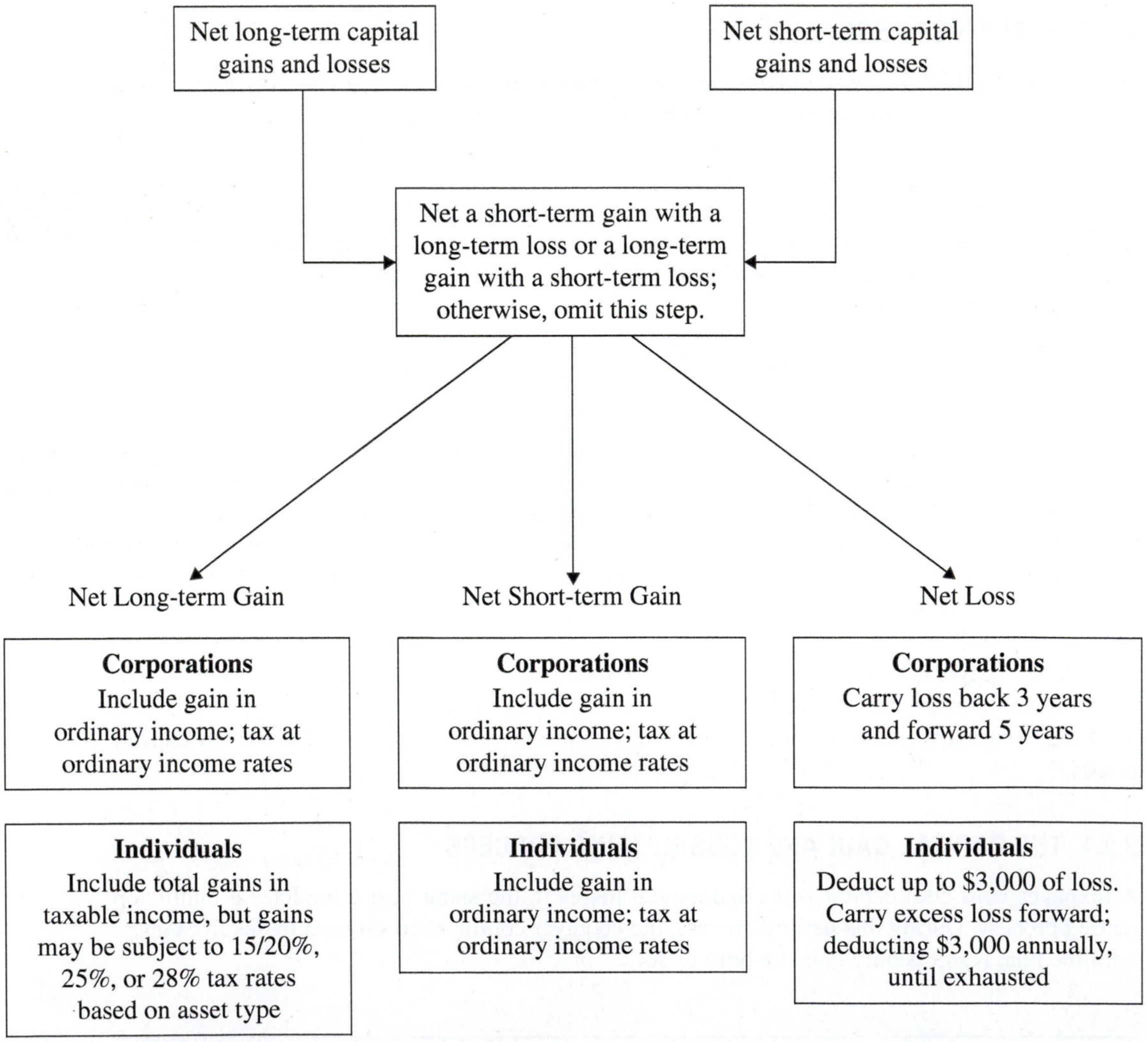

FIGURE 8.1 Capital gain and loss netting procedure

Example 8.15

The Buck Company disposed of securities as follows:

Asset	Date acquired	Date of disposition	Gain or loss
100 shares A	2/2/year 1	5/5/year 5	$200
200 shares B	2/6/year 2	5/5/year 5	(800)
400 bonds	8/8/year 5	11/1/year 5	(200)
200 shares C	5/4/year 5	11/1/year 5	500

Stocks A and B, held more than one year, are long term. Stock C and the bonds, held less than one year, are short term. Following the above procedure, Buck first nets the short-term gains and losses and the long-term gains and losses.

- The $200 long-term capital gain is netted with the $800 long-term capital loss; the result is a net $600 long-term capital loss.
- The $200 short-term capital loss is netted with the $500 short-term capital gain; the result is a net $300 short-term capital gain.

As there is both a net loss and a net gain, further netting is required.

- The $600 long-term capital loss offsets the $300 short-term capital gain; the final result is a net $300 long-term capital loss.
- If the result had been either net gains or net losses only, there would have been no further netting. The net gains would be included in income as required and the net losses would be treated appropriately based on the type of taxpayer as explained in the following section.

8.2.2 TAX TREATMENT OF NET CAPITAL GAINS AND LOSSES

The treatment of net capital gains (their taxation) and net capital losses (their deductibility) depends on whether it is a corporate or individual taxpayer reporting the results of the capital asset netting process. Corporate taxpayers follow one set of rules and individual taxpayers follow another set. Flow-through entities, such as partnerships and S corporations, report their capital gains and losses to their partners and shareholders for inclusion in their respective tax returns.

Corporate Taxpayers

After completing the netting process, corporations include their net short-term and/or long-term capital gains in ordinary income for taxation at their regular corporate tax rate. There are no special tax rates for corporate capital gains.[26]

A corporation with net capital losses (whether short term or long term) cannot deduct these losses in the year incurred. Instead, corporations carry net losses to other tax years to offset capital gains realized in those years. Corporations first carry capital losses back to the three prior tax years, beginning with the third prior tax year (if there is one) or earliest of the three prior years for which there were capital gains. The corporation offsets the capital loss against any capital gains in the carryback year, recomputes the tax, and files a claim for refund. If any unrecognized losses remain after the carryback period, the corporation must wait and carry the remaining losses forward in turn to the next five consecutive tax years after the current year.[27] Regardless of whether the current year's net capital losses are short term or long term, they are all considered short-term capital losses when carried to another year within the netting process.[28]

---

[26] §1201(a).

[27] §1212(a).

[28] For all practical purposes, it is irrelevant whether they are carried over as long term or short term under current law; under prior law, however, it was an important distinction.

The longer it takes to use a loss carryover, the less valuable that carryover is to the taxpayer; any losses remaining after the five-year carry-forward period are permanently lost. Figure 8.2 illustrates this carryover provision.

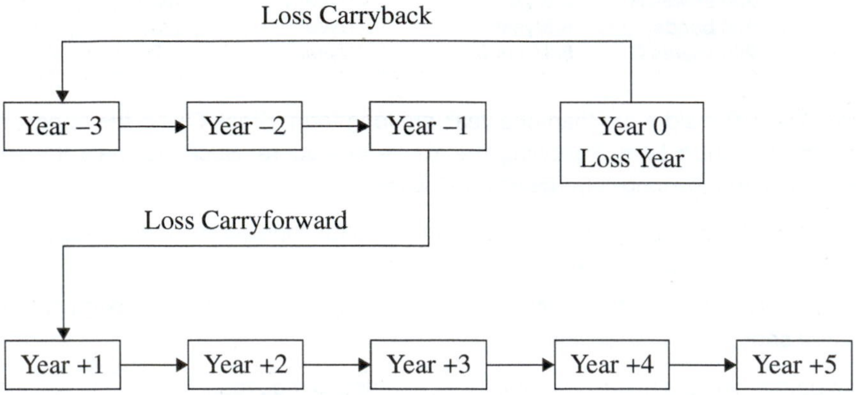

FIGURE 8.2 Corporate capital loss carryovers

Example 8.16

Corporation C has a capital loss in the current tax year of $450,000. Its only prior capital gain was $50,000 recognized in the immediately preceding year. It carries back $50,000 of the current year's capital loss, offsetting the gain recognized in the prior year. It files a claim for refund of taxes paid relative to this gain. The remaining $400,000 capital loss can be carried forward to each of the next five succeeding tax years in turn. Corporation C, however, does not expect to have any capital gains against which to offset its remaining $400,000 loss for four years. Thus, it cannot realize the $84,000 potential tax savings ($400,000 × 21%) from the remaining loss in the current year. The deferral of the loss deduction reduces its value. If the corporation uses a 6 percent discount rate for present value evaluations and cannot use the $400,000 loss until year 4, the present value of the tax effect of the deferred loss for four years is only $66,528 ($84,000 × .792).

TAX PLANNING

If there are capital losses about to expire after the five-year carryforward period, a corporation should accelerate disposing of any unwanted capital assets that could yield net capital gains as this will incur little or no tax cost.

Example 8.17

Masten Corporation has a net short-term capital loss of $18,000 and a net long-term capital loss of $15,000 in year 4. None of the losses are deductible in year 4. The $33,000 total loss is carried back as a short-term capital loss to year 1, in which Masten reported a net short-term capital gain of $12,000 and a net long-term capital gain of $8,000, both taxed at a 21 percent tax rate. Masten claims a tax refund of $4,200 [($12,000 + $8,000) × 21%]. Masten has no capital gains in years 2 and 3 and must now wait and carry the remaining $13,000 ($33,000 – $12,000 – $8,000) short-term capital loss to years 5 through 9. Masten has no capital gains in years 5, 6, 7, or 8, but has a $2,000 long-term capital gain in year 9. Masten can use $2,000 of the $13,000 loss in year 9, but permanently loses a deduction for the remaining $11,000 balance of the loss.

The treatment of capital gains and losses is not as favorable for corporations as it is for individuals. This significantly limits corporate tax savings generated by a capital loss and tax planning opportunities.

Individual Taxpayers

Taxation of an individual's net capital gains and losses begins with the identical basic multi-step netting process outlined previously but the treatment of the resulting net capital gains and losses differs significantly and is more complex than that of a corporation. At the end of the netting process, an individual will have only gain(s) or only loss(es) which would consist of one of the following:

- a single net long-term capital gain,
- a single net short-term capital gain,
- a single net long-term capital loss,
- a single net short-term capital loss,
- a combination of short- and long-term capital gains or
- a combination of short- and long-term capital losses.

An individual's net short-term capital gain is included in income and is taxed at ordinary income tax rates. A net long-term capital gain is also included in income, but it is taxed at the favorable capital gains tax rates. Unlike corporations, individuals are not allowed to carry back any current-year capital losses to offset prior year's capital gains. Individuals are instead allowed to deduct up to $3,000 of capital losses from current ordinary income. Short-term losses are deducted before long-term losses. Any remaining losses can be carried forward an unlimited number of years.

The losses carried forward maintain their character as short term or long term when they enter the netting process in a carryover year. The $3,000 limit on the deduction for net capital losses from ordinary income applies to all capital losses in a year, whether arising from transactions in that year or as carryovers from a prior year.

Example 8.18

Betty has a $12,000 long-term capital loss, an $8,000 short-term capital loss, a $9,000 long-term capital gain, and a $6,000 short-term capital gain in year 1. Netting the long-term capital loss and long-term capital gain results in a $3,000 net long-term capital loss. Netting the short-term capital loss and the short-term capital gain yields a $2,000 net short-term capital loss. Betty deducts the $2,000 net short-term capital loss first and then $1,000 of the net long-term capital loss. The remaining $2,000 net long-term capital loss retains its character and is carried forward to the next year.

In year 2, Betty has the following gains and losses exclusive of her $2,000 long-term capital loss carryover:

Long-term capital gain	$1,000
Long-term capital loss	900
Short-term capital gain	900
Short-term capital loss	700

The long-term capital loss carryover is treated as if it were incurred in year 2 and Betty has total long-term capital losses of $2,900 ($900 + $2,000 carryover). Netting the year-2 short-term and long-term capital gains and losses yields a $1,900 net long-term capital loss ($2,900 – $1,000) and a $200 ($900 – $700) net short-term capital gain. Betty now nets the $1,900 net long-term loss with the $200 short-term capital gain and deducts the $1,700 ($1,900 loss + $200 gain) remaining net long-term capital loss. No carryover remains.

The majority of long-term capital gains of individuals are subject to three basic tax rates—0 percent, 15 percent, and 20 percent—based on the individual's taxable income.[29] The 2018 breakpoints between the zero and 15-percent rates (15-percent breakpoint) and the 15 and 20-percent rates (20-percent breakpoint) are based on the 2017 breakpoints except they are indexed for inflation.[30] Table 8.2 presents these rates and the 2018 breakpoints.

Table 8.2 2018 Long-Term Capital Gains Tax Rates

Long-term capital gains tax rate	Taxable income for single individuals	Taxable income for married filing a joint return*	Taxable income for head of household
0%	$0–$38,600	$0–$77,200	$0–$51,700
15%	$38,601–$425,800	$77,201–$479,000	$51,701–$452,400
20%	Over $425,800	Over $479,000	Over $452,400

*Amounts if married filing separately are half the amount for filing a joint return.

The applicable long-term capital gains tax rates cannot be determined until total taxable income is computed. Net short-term capital gains are added to an individual's *ordinary* taxable income before adding an individual's *net long-term capital gains* to determine the individual's *total taxable income*.

Taxpayers whose total taxable income does not exceed the 15-percent breakpoints are subject to a 0 percent tax rate on their long-term capital gains. The net long-term capital gains of taxpayers with total taxable income exceeding the 15-percent breakpoint but not exceeding the 20-percent breakpoint are taxed at the 15 percent rate on the long-term capital gains part of total taxable income. The long-term capital gains of taxpayers with total taxable income exceeding the 20-percent breakpoint are taxed at the 20 percent rate on those gains. Long-term capital gains below this breakpoint remain subject to the 15 percent tax rate.

Example 8.19

In 2018, John, who is single, has $21,000 of ordinary income and a $6,000 long-term capital gain. John's $27,000 of total taxable income is less than the maximum income at the 15-percent breakpoint for single individuals; thus, his capital gains escape taxation due to the 0% tax rate.

Example 8.20

In 2018, Mary and Steven file a joint return and report $168,000 of total taxable income that includes $40,000 of long-term capital gains. Their taxable income exceeds the 15-percent breakpoint but does not exceed the 20-percent breakpoint; as a result, their long-term capital gains are taxed at 15 percent.

Although the majority of long-term gains are taxed at the maximum capital gains rates of 15 or 20 percent, two other special rates may apply: 25 percent and 28 percent. When individuals sell depreciable real property, some or all of the gain (called unrecaptured Section 1250 gain) may be subject to a 25 percent tax rate, as explained later in this chapter. Additionally,

[29] As discussed in Chapter 5, a 3.8 percent Medicare surtax on net investment income (including capital gains) increases the effective tax rate when modified adjusted gross income exceeds a specific threshold based on the taxpayer's filing status ($200,000 single, $225,000 head of household, and $250,000 married filing jointly).

[30] The breakpoint between the zero and 15 percent capital gains rates differs slightly from the breakpoints that apply to ordinary income. For example, for single individuals the 15 percent breakpoint for capital gains is $38,600 but the breakpoint for the 22 percent rate for ordinary income is $38,700. The ordinary income tax rates are provided in the Appendix to this text.

a 28 percent rate applies to gains on collectibles such as antiques, art objects and rare coins and to the gain on Section 1202 small business stock, also discussed later in this chapter.[31]

The *adjusted net capital gain* of an individual is the net long-term capital gain reduced (but not below zero) by the sum of the 25 percent rate gain and the 28 percent rate gain.[32] The adjusted net capital gain is then increased by the amount of qualified dividend income subject to the same rates as long-term capital gains. The tax on all long-term capital gains (and qualified dividends) is determined before the tax on the remaining ordinary income.

Example 8.21

Cletus, who is single, has $340,000 taxable income including $145,000 of capital gains. He has a $25,000 long-term capital gain on the sale of stock (a 15% asset) and a $120,000 long-term capital gain on the sale of a Salvador Dale sketch (a 28 percent collectible). These are his only capital transactions for the year. The tax on the collectible is $33,600 ($120,000 × 28%). The tax on the stock is $3,750 ($25,000 × 15%). His remaining $195,000 of ordinary taxable income is taxed using the regular tax rate schedule resulting in $44,090, tax for a total tax liability of $81,440.

The last section of the chapter provides additional information on the complex taxation of the different classes of assets when the taxpayer has both capital gains and losses along with the modification of the rates for taxpayers subject to ordinary income tax rates that are less than the capital gains tax rates.

Tax Planning Strategies

TAX PLANNING

Individuals should look for opportunities to take advantage of the capital asset disposal provisions. Although an individual can carry a capital loss forward for an unlimited number of years, the value of the $3,000 annual capital loss deduction becomes smaller and smaller the further into the future the loss is carried. Thus, an individual should consider accelerating disposal of assets on which gains are realized, as effectively there is no current tax cost to the extent they offset losses. Similarly, accelerating the disposal of loss assets into years in which gains are realized can reduce or eliminate the tax cost. The individual may also be able to plan dispositions to use the tax rates on capital gains to his or her advantage by estimating ordinary income prior to the end of the year. Accelerating capital gains into years in which ordinary income is expected to be low may avoid the 20 percent capital gains tax rate. If income is expected to be high, postponing dispositions of capital gain assets to a lower tax rate year may be possible. Additionally, a capital loss on a 15 percent taxed asset offsets a gain on a 28 percent taxed asset. Thus, accelerating gains on 25 and 28 percent assets to offset losses is more advantageous than accelerating a 15 percent gain asset. Assets should not be disposed of simply for the tax effect, however, if the dispositions do not make economic sense.

Example 8.22

Jason plans expensive dental work before he begins a new job at a much higher salary in January. He needs to sell a capital asset with a $6,000 gain to pay for it. He does not think his current year's taxable income will exceed the 0% tax bracket for long-term capital gains but expects to be in a much higher bracket next year. He should sell his capital asset before the end of year so that his $6,000 gain escapes capital gain taxation. If he waits until next year, his gain may be subject to a 15% capital gains tax. He saves $900 by selling before the end of the year.

[31] The 28 percent rate was the previous long-term capital gain rate before it was reduced to the current level. When Congress reduced the rates for most other capital gains, it chose to maintain the 28 percent rate for collectibles because of the inherent personal enjoyment factor not present with other types of capital assets. The taxable portion of Section 1202 stock is also subject to the 28 percent rate because part of the gain is excluded as explained later in this chapter.

[32] The adjusted net capital gain is also reduced by the amount of gain that is treated as investment income for purposes of determining the investment interest expense deduction as discussed in Chapter 5.

Example 8.23

Greg is in the 15 percent tax bracket for long-term capital gains and recently sold a collectible at a $10,000 long-term capital gain taxed at the 28 percent capital gains tax rate. He has two stocks that he plans to sell next year. He expects a $10,000 long-term capital gain (taxed at 15%) on one and a $10,000 capital loss on the other. Unless Greg does some planning, he will pay a tax of $2,800 on the gain in this year but have no taxable gain next year. If he accelerates the sale of the loss stock to the current year, his $10,000 loss offsets this year's 28% gain. He will have no taxable gain this year and his tax on the $10,000 gain next year will be only $1,500. By accelerating the loss to the current year, he reduces his total tax by $1,300. (Deferring the tax for one year provides additional savings due to the time value of money.)

Example 8.24

Davis, who is in the 35 percent marginal tax bracket for ordinary income and 15 percent for long-term capital gains, sold stock in January resulting in a $40,000 short-term capital gain on which he will have to pay $14,000 in taxes ($40,000 × 35%). He holds some other stock that has declined in value by $48,000. Davis should consider selling enough of the loss stock this year to realize a $43,000 capital loss, which will offset the $40,000 short-term capital gain and $3,000 of ordinary income. As a result, Davis can save $15,050 in taxes ($43,000 × 35%). If he sells the stock at the $48,000 loss next year, assuming no future capital gains, he will deduct a $3,000 capital loss and save $1,050 of taxes per year ($3,000 × 35%) over the next 16 years. By timing the loss sale with the gains, Davis's tax savings in the current year are far greater due to the time value of money.

Example 8.25

Ted is single and in the 35 percent marginal tax bracket for ordinary income and 15 percent for long-term capital gains. As of June 1, he has some Marco stock that if sold would result in a $10,000 short-term capital gain. If he holds the stock until September 30, he will meet the more-than-one-year holding period and have the gain treated as a long-term capital gain. If the price of the stock is expected to hold steady or increase, the stock should be held at least until September 30. Holding the stock until then increases his after-tax profit by at least $2,000 [$10,000 × (35% − 15%)]. If Ted needs cash immediately, he could borrow the needed money using the stock as collateral, selling the stock on September 30 to pay off the loan. His net gain would be the tax savings less the interest on the loan. If the stock's price is declining, however, a current sale may be warranted as the tax savings of holding the stock until September 30 may not offset the potential reduced selling price.

TAX PLANNING

If an individual has already realized net short-term or long-term capital losses during a given year of less than $3,000, additional loss property could be sold up to $3,000 in total to take advantage of this offset against ordinary income. If capital losses already exceed $3,000, the taxpayer may find it advantageous to sell appreciated assets to generate gains to offset the excess capital losses.

Example 8.26

Shelli sold capital assets in the current year, generating a $4,000 short-term capital loss and a $5,000 long-term capital loss. If she sells no more capital assets during the current year, she can deduct $3,000 of the short-term capital loss only and carry over the remaining $1,000 short-term and $5,000 long-term losses to next year. If she has other disposable capital assets that would generate capital gains, she should consider selling enough to generate short-term or long-term capital gains to offset her remaining $6,000 of capital losses. In making this decision, however, she should consider the expected future price for these assets and her investment potential for the proceeds.

In planning for asset dispositions, individuals must also consider gains and losses that flow through to them from partnerships and S corporations.[33] Their net long-term and/or short-term capital gains and losses are included in the determination of the individual's taxable income. These gains and losses are combined with the individual's own gains and losses that must be recognized. The results of the netting processes are taxed or deducted on the individual owners' returns.

Example 8.27

Jim is a shareholder in an S corporation. The corporation sold a long-term capital asset and Jim's share of the gain is $20,000. Jim is in the 35 percent tax bracket for ordinary income and 15 percent for long-term capital gains. If Jim does nothing, he will pay $3,000 in taxes ($20,000 × 15%) on the long-term capital gain. If, however, Jim has stock that he can sell and that has declined in value sufficiently to generate a $20,000 capital loss, he can offset this gain with the $20,000 loss and save $3,000 in taxes. In addition, he has the cash flow from the sale of the loss asset that he can now invest in a more profitable asset.

If, instead of selling the asset at a gain, the S corporation sells the asset at a loss and passes through the $20,000 capital loss to Jim, Jim can only deduct $3,000 of the capital loss this year against his ordinary income, resulting in tax savings of only $1,050 ($3,000 × 35%). If Jim has a short-term stock investment that he can sell that will generate at least a $17,000 short-term capital gain, he can get an immediate tax benefit from the corporation's capital loss of $7,000 that is made up of the $1,050 tax savings from $3,000 of the loss that is deductible and the $5,950 ($17,000 × 35%) tax saved by offsetting the $17,000 gain.

These examples show why taxpayers receive maximum benefit from their capital losses in years in which they have sufficient capital gains to offset against them. This is even more critical for corporate taxpayers because they are permitted no deduction for capital losses and their capital gains are taxed at ordinary income rates.

Both individuals and corporations file a Schedule D to report their current capital transactions along with any capital loss carryovers and capital gains and losses passed through from partnerships or S corporations. To encourage accurate reporting of property transactions, brokers must by law report the gross proceeds on sales and exchanges of stocks and securities on Form 1099-B and real estate transactions on Form 1099-S to the government and to taxpayers.[34]

8.3 DISPOSITION OF SECTION 1231 PROPERTY

Section 1231 property includes all depreciable realty and personalty, and all nondepreciable realty (land) used in a trade or business, as long as the property has been held for more than one year.[35] The disposition of Section 1231 property can be the most complex of all property dispositions because of the potential treatment of losses as ordinary losses while gains may be afforded capital gain treatment. Taxpayers must complete a number of steps to determine the correct tax treatment for gains and losses on Section 1231 asset dispositions as explained in detail in the following sections:

1. Determine the gains and losses on individual Section 1231 assets.
2. Reduce the gain on depreciable assets with realized gain for depreciation recapture (explained below). Include depreciation recapture in ordinary income.

[33] The flow-through nature of partnerships and S corporations is discussed in Chapter 11.
[34] §6045(a)-(c).
[35] In addition, capital assets held by a trade or business or for the production of income (for more than one year) and are *involuntarily converted* are considered Section 1231 property.

3. Offset (net) the remaining gains (after reduction for depreciation recapture) and losses.[36] If the result is a net loss, it is deducted directly from ordinary income. If the result is a net gain, a five-year look-back procedure (explained later) is applied. Gains subject to the look-back rule are deducted from the net gains and included in ordinary income.
4. The remaining balance of the Section 1231 net gain is included in the capital asset netting process as a long-term capital gain (explained in the preceding section).

A corporation with no capital gains or losses to offset the remaining net Section 1231 gain (step 4), includes the net Section 1231 gain in ordinary income. An individual with no capital gains or losses treats the net Section 1231 gain as a long-term capital gain, generally taxed at the basic zero, 15, or 20 percent capital gains tax rate based on taxable income. Depreciation recapture and the look-back rules are all explained in sequence below.

8.3.1 DEPRECIATION RECAPTURE

Depreciation deductions on rental realty and related personalty, and on trade or business realty and personalty, offset ordinary income. These deductions result in tax savings based on the taxpayer's marginal tax rate. The deductions also reduce an asset's basis. When the taxpayer disposes of the asset, some or all of the gain realized may be a result of this reduced basis. The net tax savings could be significant if this gain is then taxed at reduced capital gains rates. As a result, the recapture rules limit this tax-favored Section 1231 gain treatment for the gain realized on subsequent dispositions of depreciable assets by converting all or part of the Section 1231 gain to ordinary income.[37]

Example 8.28

Jack is single and owns Sims Appliances, a sole proprietorship. He is in the 35% percent marginal tax bracket for ordinary income and 15 percent for long-term capital gains. Two-and-a-half years ago, Sims purchased depreciable equipment at a cost of $100,000. Sims claimed $61,600 in depreciation deductions, reducing the asset's adjusted basis to $38,400. Jack deducted these expenses from the sole proprietorship income, resulting in a $21,560 ($61,600 × 35%) tax savings. Because of a shortage of this equipment, Sims is able to resell the asset for $100,000. The gain on the sale of this equipment is $61,600 ($100,000 sales price – $38,400 adjusted basis), all of which is attributable to the depreciation claimed. In the absence of recapture rules, Jack would be taxed on the gain at the 15 percent long-term capital gain rate, resulting in $9,240 ($61,600 × 15%) tax. Jack would have saved $12,320 ($21,560 – $9,240) in taxes due to the rate differential between ordinary income and capital gains. The recapture provisions change this result. Jack must include the depreciation recapture in ordinary income and pay tax on the gain at his 35 percent ordinary income tax rate, resulting in $21,560 ($61,600 × 35%) in taxes—the same amount that he saved over the past two-and-a-half years because of the depreciation deductions. Thus, there is no net tax savings generated by the equipment when depreciation is recaptured at ordinary income tax rates (except for the time value of the deductions relative to the gain).

The two most important points to remember about property subject to recapture are:

1. The property's basis must have been reduced through depreciation deductions.
2. Gain must be realized on the disposition.

[36] The next chapter describes the additional steps when there is an involuntary conversion.

[37] The recapture provisions under §1245 and §1250 are the ones most commonly encountered by taxpayers. Other recapture provisions exist (see, for instance, §1252 and §1254); they apply to other specialized property and their treatment is beyond the scope of this text, but the same principles apply to other types of recapture provisions.

If the property is sold at a loss, there can be *no* recapture. The recapture provisions have no effect on the determination of the *amount* of gain or loss realized on an asset's disposition. Total gain recognized remains the amount realized less the adjusted basis. The recapture rules operate solely to *recharacterize all or part* of the Section 1231 gain that represents depreciation recapture as ordinary income.

A good time to dispose of Section 1231 assets on which there will be depreciation recapture is a year in which other operating income is very low (or there is a loss) to take advantage of lower income tax brackets.

TAX PLANNING

Table 8.3 illustrates the different types of Section 1231 assets.

Table 8.3 Section 1231 Assets and Potential Recapture

Section 1231 only (no recapture)	Section 1231 subject to Sec. 1245 recapture	Section 1231 subject to Sec. 1250 recapture
Business-use land	Depreciable personalty	Depreciable realty

Section 1245 Full Recapture

The **Section 1245 full recapture** provision requires ordinary income tax treatment for the gain realized on the disposition of specific Section 1231 assets up to the total of *all* previously allowed depreciation deductions. Although depreciation methods have changed over the years, the provisions for determining Section 1245 recapture have changed very little. Depreciable property subject to the Section 1245 recapture rules includes[38]

1. Machinery, equipment, furniture, and fixtures
2. Property (except buildings and their structural components) used as an integral part of manufacturing, production, or extraction or to furnish transportation, communications, electrical energy, gas, water, or sewage disposal services.[39]

Buildings and their structural components are generally excluded from Section 1245 recapture.[40]

The method of depreciation used by the taxpayer to depreciate the property subject to Section 1245 recapture (as well as immediate expensing) is irrelevant.[41] The taxpayer recognizes ordinary income in an amount equal to the *lesser* of the gain realized or prior depreciation deductions.[42] Any realized gain in excess of prior depreciation deductions is Section 1231 gain.

Example 8.29

Harmon Corporation sells a machine tool with a $3,000 adjusted basis for $6,000; it originally cost $10,000. All of the $3,000 gain on the sale is Section 1245 recapture taxed as ordinary income because it is less than the $7,000 prior depreciation deductions. There is no Section 1231 gain.

If, however, Harmon Corporation sells the machine tool for $11,000; the resulting $8,000 gain is made up of $7,000 of Section 1245 recapture income (limited to prior depreciation deductions) and $1,000 of Section 1231 gain. Harmon reports this sale on Part III of Form 4797 as illustrated in Figure 8.3. The $7,000 recapture is included with Harmon's other ordinary income. If Harmon has no other Section 1231 gains or losses, the $1,000 Section 1231 gain would be reported as a long-term capital gain.

[38] §1245(a)(3).

[39] Certain other specialized equipment and facilities also are subject to Section 1245 recapture.

[40] Nonresidential realty put into service during 1981 through 1986 on which accelerated ACRS depreciation was taken is subject to Section 1245 recapture.

[41] Depreciation subject to recapture includes any amounts expensed under Section 179 (see Chapter 7).

[42] §1245(a).

Part III **Gain From Disposition of Property Under Sections 1245** (see instructions)

19 **(a)** Description of section 1245, 1250, 1252, 1254, or 1255 property:

A **Machine tool**
B
C
D

	These columns relate to the properties on lines 19A through 19D. ▶		**Property A**
20	Gross sales price (**Note:** *See line 1 before completing.*)	20	11,000
21	Cost or other basis plus expense of sale	21	10,000
22	Depreciation (or depletion) allowed or allowable	22	7,000
23	Adjusted basis. Subtract line 22 from line 21	23	3,000
24	Total gain. Subtract line 23 from line 20	24	8,000
25	**If section 1245 property:**		
	a Depreciation allowed or allowable from line 22	25a	7,000
	b Enter the **smaller** of line 24 or 25a	25b	7,000

FIGURE 8.3 Reporting depreciation recapture on Form 4797

Example 8.30

Moldov, Inc. purchased a new machine for $16,000, expensing the entire purchase price under Section 179. Two years later, Moldov sells the machine for $11,500 and recognizes a gain of $11,500, all of which is Section 1245 recapture. If Moldov sold the machine for an $18,000 gain, its Section 1245 recapture would be limited to its $16,000 purchase price (the amount expensed under Section 179). Its remaining $2,000 gain would be Section 1231 gain.

Section 1250 Partial Recapture

Section 1250 recapture of Section 1231 gains differs from Section 1245 recapture because it *only* applies to realty and only *part* of the gain realized from prior depreciation deductions is recaptured. Originally, **Section 1250 recapture** applied only to the excess of the accelerated depreciation deduction over the depreciation determined using the alternative straight-line depreciation method.[43] Since 1986, however, realty has been depreciated only on a straight-line basis,[44] and there is no excess depreciation. Instead of repealing Section 1250, Congress added Section 291 that subjects corporations to an additional amount of recapture under Section 291 as an alternative to the original Section 1250 recapture.

Additional Section 291 Corporate Recapture

Corporate taxpayers that dispose of realty must convert a percentage of their Section 1231 gain to ordinary income under the Section 291 recapture rules. This additional recapture is 20 percent of the excess of the Section 1245 recapture (as if Section 1245 recapture applied) over Section 1250 recapture. As Section 1250 recapture is zero for acquisitions after 1986 under MACRS, the corporate recapture increment is simply 20 percent of the Section 1245 recapture.[45]

---

[43] §1250(a).
[44] MACRS depreciation for realty is discussed in the preceding chapter.
[45] §291(a)(1). On a pre-1987 asset subject to Section 1250 recapture, the corporation adds the actual Section 1250 recapture to 20 percent of the excess of Section 1245 recapture over the actual Section 1250 recapture to determine the total Section 291 recapture.

Example 8.31

The Wanyu Corporation sells a factory building for $1,025,000. The building cost $1,010,000 when purchased eleven years ago. The corporation claimed $260,000 of MACRS depreciation, and the building has an adjusted basis of $750,000. The total recapture is determined as follows:

Step 1. Determine the Section 1250 recapture.
There is no Section 1250 recapture as the building was depreciated using the straight-line method under MACRS.

Step 2. Determine the Section 1245 recapture.

Amount realized	$1,025,000
Less adjusted basis	(750,000)
Total gain	$275,000

Section 1245 recapture is $260,000, the lesser of the total gain realized ($275,000) and the prior depreciation deductions ($260,000).

Step 3. Determine the additional recapture.

Section 1245 recapture	$260,000
Less Section 1250 recapture	(0)
	$260,000
Step 4. Multiply by 20 percent	× 20%
Additional recapture	$52,000

Step 5. The $52,000 of depreciation recapture is taxed as ordinary income.
The remaining $223,000 ($275,000 – $52,000) gain is Section 1231 gain.

This provision applies only to corporate taxpayers and creates depreciation recapture on real property dispositions that otherwise would have no recapture. This corporate recapture rule eliminates some of the capital gains that would otherwise be available to offset capital losses, as corporations can only offset capital losses with capital gains.

8.3.2 UNRECAPTURED SECTION 1250 GAINS FOR INDIVIDUALS

Individuals who have realized and recognized gains on depreciable real property (that previously would have been classified as Section 1250 gain) do not have to recapture any of the gain as ordinary income. Instead they may be subject to a higher capital gains tax rate on gain up to the amount of the straight-line depreciation deductions taken.[46] As these gains are no longer subject to recapture, they are called the unrecaptured Section 1250 gain, and individuals are subject to a maximum 25 percent tax rate on this gain.

Example 8.32

Judy sold an apartment building for $1,400,000. She had purchased the building 12 years ago for $1,200,000 and had taken $300,000 of MACRS straight-line depreciation deductions on the building. Judy has a $500,000 realized gain ($1,400,000 – $900,000) on the apartment building, $300,000 of which is classified as unrecaptured Section 1250 gain (the lesser of the gain realized or the prior depreciation deductions) and is subject to the maximum 25 percent tax rate. The remaining $200,000 of Section 1231 gain is subject to the lower 15 or 20 percent basic capital gains tax rates, based on filing status and other income (excluding any potential NII surtax.)

[46] If the real estate was acquired prior to 1987, the unrecaptured Section 1250 gain would be the lesser of the gain realized or depreciation deductions reduced by the actual Section 1250 recapture.

Table 8.4 summarizes the tax treatment of gains and losses by asset type.

Table 8.4 Tax Treatment of Gains and Losses

Asset type	Example	Treatment of gain	Treatment of loss
Nondepreciable Section 1231 asset	Business-use land	Section 1231 gain	Ordinary loss
Depreciable personalty	Equipment	Prior depreciation (not exceeding realized gain) recaptured under Section 1245 as ordinary income; excess is Section 1231 gain	Ordinary loss
Depreciable realty	Office building	Corporations: 20% of prior depreciation (not exceeding realized gain) recaptured under Section 291 as ordinary income; excess is Section 1231 gain Individuals: 25% maximum tax rate applies to Section 1250 unrecaptured gain equal to or less than prior depreciation; excess is Section 1231 gain	Ordinary loss
Capital asset	Investment land	Capital gain	Capital loss
Ordinary asset	Inventory	Ordinary income	Ordinary loss

8.3.3 SECTION 1231 LOOK-BACK RULES

The Section 1231 look-back rules prevent taxpayers from generating tax savings by bunching their Section 1231 gains into one year (to receive the tax-favored long-term capital gain treatment for gains) and losses into alternate years (deducting the Section 1231 losses against ordinary income).[47]

Example 8.33

Dave, who is in the 35 percent marginal tax bracket for ordinary income and 15 percent for long-term capital gains, deducted a $50,000 net Section 1231 loss last year. In the current year, Dave has a $50,000 net Section 1231 gain. Dave's tax savings from the loss deduction last year were $17,500 ($50,000 × 35%). Without the Section 1231 look-back rules, the current gain would be taxed at 15 percent ($50,000 × 15% = $7,500). Dave would have a net tax savings of $10,000 ($17,500 – $7,500) due to the taxing of his net Section 1231 gains at favorable capital gains tax rates.

To limit this maneuver, Section 1231(c) requires taxpayers to recapture any of the current year's net Section 1231 gains as ordinary income to the extent of any net Section 1231 losses deducted in any of the previous five tax years.

To determine the Section 1231 gain that must be recognized as ordinary income in the current year:

1. Total all Section 1231 losses deducted in the previous five years.
2. Total all Section 1231 gains already recaptured as ordinary income due to losses deducted in the previous five years.
3. Subtract the previously recaptured Section 1231 gains from the total Section 1231 losses recognized in the five previous years. These are the current year's unrecaptured Section 1231 losses [(1) – (2)].

[47] Although a corporation has no tax-favored capital gains rates, the look-back rules reduce the amount of Section 1231 gain that can be treated as capital gain; this, in turn, reduces the amount of capital gain available to offset capital losses. Excess capital losses cannot be deducted in the current year but instead must be carried back 3 years and forward 5 years.

4. The look-back recapture is the lesser of the current year's unrecaptured Section 1231 losses (3) and the current year's net Section 1231 gain; this is included in and taxed as ordinary income.
5. If the current year's net Section 1231 gain exceeds the amount recaptured as ordinary income (4), the excess is treated as a long-term capital gain and is included in the capital asset netting process explained previously.

Figure 8.4 is a diagram of the Section 1231 look-back process.

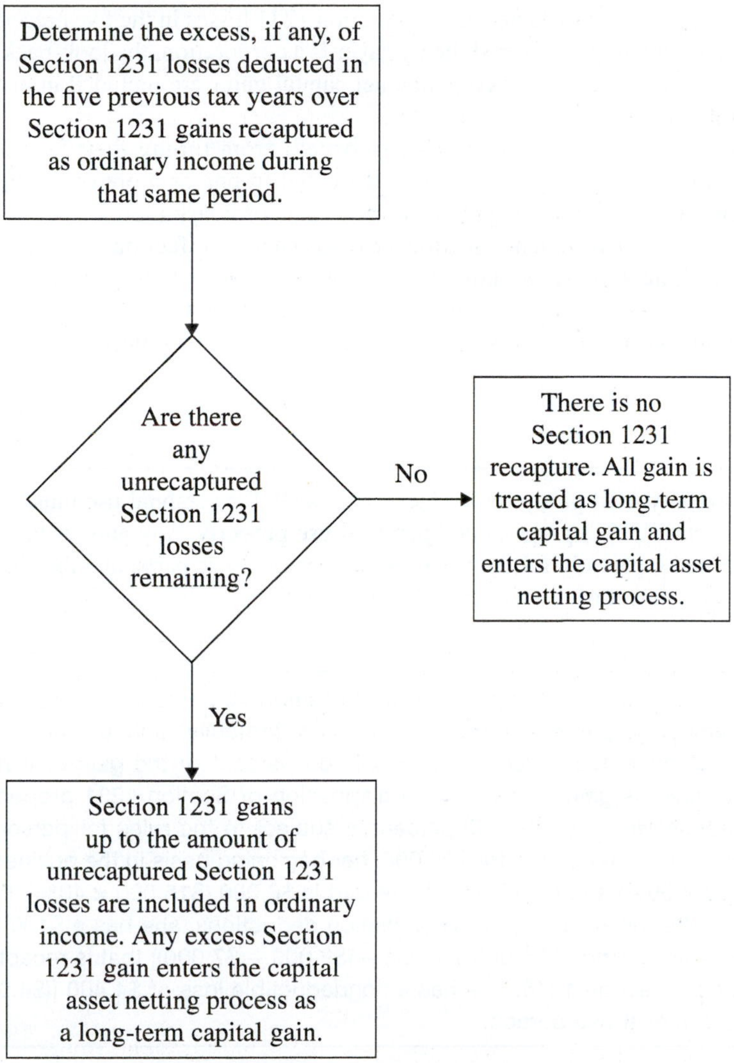

FIGURE 8.4 The Section 1231 look-back rules

Example 8.34

George has a recognized Section 1231 loss of $22,000 remaining from two years ago. In 2018, George sells several business properties with the following results:

Property A	$10,000	Section 1231 loss
Property B	25,000	Section 1231 gain
Property C	5,000	Section 1231 loss

George nets the Section 1231 gain on Property B with the Section 1231 losses on Properties A and C resulting in a net Section 1231 gain of $10,000 (– $10,000 + $25,000 – $5,000). He treats this entire gain as ordinary income due to the Section 1231 look-back rules, and he has $12,000 ($22,000 – $10,000) of unrecaptured Section 1231 losses remaining.

If George has a net Section 1231 gain of $16,000 in 2019, he only recaptures $12,000 (2018's remaining unrecaptured Section 1231 loss) of this gain. The remaining $4,000 ($16,000 – $12,000) receives long-term capital gain treatment.

If the taxpayer has not deducted any net Section 1231 losses in the five preceding tax years, the look-back rules are inoperative.[48] If the taxpayer is a corporation, the look-back rules have no effect on the taxation of the gain as corporate net capital gains are included in ordinary income and have no preferential capital gains tax rates.

TAX PLANNING

Individual taxpayers still may be able to benefit from timing their Section 1231 gains and losses, however. A net Section 1231 loss deducted in one or more of the five prior years causes a current net Section 1231 gain to be treated as ordinary income. A net Section 1231 gain realized in a year prior to a net Section 1231 loss has no effect on the deductibility of the loss. Thus, to the extent possible, individuals can benefit by realizing net Section 1231 gains in years prior to Section 1231 loss years. The net gain can be taxed at the individual's lower capital gains rate, but the loss is deducted against ordinary income taxed at the taxpayer's marginal tax rate.

8.4 MIXED-USE PROPERTY

Realty and personalty used partly for business and partly for personal use must be divided into business-use (Section 1231) property and personal-use property. Any gain or loss on the disposition is determined separately for the business and personal-use parts, and the character of each part dictates the treatment of the recognized gain or loss.

Example 8.35

Wanda uses her automobile 60 percent for business and 40 percent for personal use. Wanda can only depreciate 60 percent of the cost of the automobile; only 60 percent of the auto is classified as Section 1231 property; and only 60 percent of the gain or loss on the disposition is classified as gain or loss on the disposition of Section 1231 property, subject to Section 1245 recapture. The other 40 percent is subject to the rules for personal-use property. If Wanda purchased the auto for $15,000, her beginning basis in the business-use part is $9,000 ($15,000 × 60%) and the personal-use part is $6,000 ($15,000 × 40%). If she sells the auto for $4,000 after taking $7,000 in depreciation deductions, she has a $400 Section 1231 gain on the business portion [($4,000 × 60%) – ($9,000 – $7,000)] that is recaptured as ordinary income under Section 1245. She has a nondeductible loss of $4,400 [($4,000 × 40%) – $6,000] on the personal-use portion.

Tables 8.5 and 8.6 summarize the tax treatment of gains and losses on ordinary, capital, and Section 1231 assets for individual and corporate taxpayers.

48 §1231(c).

Table 8.5 Summary of Property Transaction Taxation for Individuals

Type of property	Treatment of gains	Treatment of losses
Ordinary	Taxed at ordinary income rates up to 37%.	Deductible against other ordinary income taxed at rates up to 37%.
Short-term capital assets	Net short-term capital gain taxed at ordinary income rates up to 37%.	Maximum $3,000 of net short-term capital losses deductible annually against ordinary income. Excess losses may be carried forward indefinitely.
Long-term capital assets	Most net long-term capital gains taxed at a maximum rate of 20%; Section 1250 unrecaptured gain and collectibles gain taxed at a maximum 25% and 28% rate, respectively.	Maximum $3,000 of net long-term capital losses deductible annually against ordinary income; deduction for net short-term and long-term losses combined cannot exceed $3,000. Excess losses may be carried forward indefinitely.
Section 1231	Net Section 1231 gain taxed as a long-term capital gain at a maximum rate of 20%, except Section 1250 unrecaptured gain taxed at 25%.	Net loss deductible against other ordinary income taxed at rates up to 37%.

Table 8.6 Summary of Property Transaction Taxation for Corporations

Type of property	Treatment of gains	Treatment of losses
Ordinary	Taxed at ordinary income rates.	Deductible against other ordinary income.
Short- and long-term capital assets	Net short-term or long-term gain taxed at ordinary income rates.	Net short-term or long-term loss not deductible in the year realized. May be carried back three and forward five years to offset capital gains in those years.
Section 1231	Net gain taxed at ordinary income rates.	Net losses fully deductible against ordinary income.

8.5 SPECIAL RULES FOR SMALL BUSINESS STOCK

The preferential capital gain tax rates encourage investment in capital assets (including stock and securities). Two additional provisions—Section 1244 (which allows ordinary loss treatment for certain capital losses) and Section 1202—(which allows all or part of a gain on stock to escape taxation) encourage investment in new corporations.

8.5.1 LOSSES ON SECTION 1244 STOCK

The $3,000 limit on the deductibility of capital losses discourages investment in risky capital assets. Individuals who invest in a business whose stock qualifies as Section 1244 stock may be able to deduct losses of up to $50,000 on qualifying Section 1244 stock annually as an ordinary loss.[49] Any loss in excess of the $50,000 is a capital loss subject to all the previously discussed capital loss provisions. This provision applies only to individuals and partnerships that are the original purchasers of the stock.[50] There is no lifetime limit on the total loss a taxpayer may deduct, but the annual limit is $50,000 for losses incurred in one year.[51]

[49] If the taxpayer files a joint return, the eligible ordinary loss is increased to $100,000 whether the stock is owned by one spouse or both spouses. Joint returns are discussed in Chapter 5.

[50] Individuals who are partners when a partnership acquires Section 1244 stock are also eligible for this treatment when the *partnership* sells the stock. If the partnership distributes the stock to the partners, it no longer qualifies as Section 1244 stock.

[51] Because of the $1,000,000 capitalization limit, the Section 1244 losses of all individuals are effectively limited to $1,000,000.

Only stock in a domestic small business corporation issued in exchange for money or property qualifies as **Section 1244 stock.**[52] A small business corporation is one with total capitalization not exceeding $1,000,000. For losses to receive the Section 1244 loss treatment, the corporation must be an operating company at the time the shareholder disposes of the stock. To qualify as an **operating company**, 50 percent or more of the corporation's gross revenues must be from the sales of goods or services (operations) for the five years preceding the year in which the Section 1244 stock is sold. Income from rents, royalties, dividends, interest, annuities, and gains on the sales of securities (generally, investment income) is limited to 50 percent or less in the five years preceding the sale year.

Example 8.36

In 2015, John contributed $120,000 cash for a 40 percent interest in JBC Corporation, an operating company whose stock qualified as Section 1244 at the time it was issued. In 2017, John sold one-half of his 40 percent interest in JBC Corporation for $25,000. He had a $35,000 loss ($25,000 – $60,000) on the sale of the stock, all of which was deductible as an ordinary loss. In the current year, John sells his remaining stock to another shareholder for $5,000. John has a $55,000 loss ($5,000 – $60,000) on the sale. He can deduct only $50,000 as ordinary income. The other $5,000 loss is a capital loss and is included in the capital loss netting process. If John has no other capital gains, he can only deduct $3,000 of the $5,000 capital loss in the current year and must carry the remaining $2,000 loss forward as a capital loss.

8.5.2 SECTION 1202 GAINS ON QUALIFIED SMALL BUSINESS STOCK

The second provision that makes investment in small corporations more attractive is the exclusion of all or part of the recognized gain from a noncorporate shareholder's taxable income on the sale of qualified small business stock (QSBS or Section 1202 stock) held for more than five years. To be a **qualified small business corporation**, a corporation must meet restrictions that are far more extensive than those for a small business corporation under Section 1244:

1. It must be a domestic C corporation (not an S corporation).[53]
2. The gross assets (cash plus adjusted basis of other property) of the corporation cannot exceed $50,000,000 when the stock is issued.
3. The original owner(s) acquired the stock in exchange for money, property, or services.
4. The corporation is an active trade or business engaged in manufacturing, retailing, or wholesaling.[54]

Only the stock sold by an original owner is eligible for this capital gain exclusion.

When qualifying Section 1202 stock held for more than five years is disposed of by its owner, up to 100 percent of the capital gain can be excluded from capital gain taxation based on its *purchase* date as follows:

1. 100 percent for stock acquired after September 27, 2010;
2. 75 percent for stock acquired after February 17, 2009 and before September 28, 2010;
3. 50 percent for stock acquired before February 18, 2009.

[52] A domestic corporation is a corporation incorporated in one of the 50 states.

[53] C and S corporations are discussed in Chapters 10 and 11.

[54] The corporation cannot be a personal service corporation, a banking or other financing-type business, a farm corporation, a mining corporation, or a motel, hotel, or restaurant. It cannot own rental realty or securities that exceed 10 percent of its total assets.

Gain eligible for the exclusion, however, cannot exceed the greater of (1) 10 times the taxpayer's adjusted basis of the qualifying stock sold in the tax year or (2) $10,000,000 less any eligible gain on qualifying stock taken into consideration in the preceding tax years by the taxpayer. The remaining recognized capital gain (if purchased before September 28, 2010) is included in the capital gain netting process and is taxed at the 28 percent capital gains tax rate along with gains on assets characterized as collectibles.

Example 8.37

In 2017, Jonas sold one-quarter of his qualifying Section 1202 stock in Magnum Corporation for $4,000,000. His original purchase price in 2008 was $1,200,000 and his gain on the sale was $3,700,000 [$4,000,000 – ($1,200,000 x 25%)]. He excluded $1,850,000 (50% x $3,700,000) of the gain. The remaining $1,850,000 of gain is included in the capital asset netting process and is taxed at a maximum 28 percent tax rate. (The stock is not eligible for either the 75% or 100% gain reductions as it was purchased before February 18, 2009.)

In 2018, Jonas sells his remaining 75 percent interest (basis of $900,000) in Magnum Corporation for $12,000,000. His total gain on the sale is $11,100,000. His gain exclusion is limited to $4,500,000—50 percent of the greater of $9,000,000 (10 times the $900,000 adjusted basis of the stock) or $6,300,000 (the maximum $10,000,000 eligible gain exclusion less the $3,700,000 eligible gain on the previous sale). His remaining $6,600,000 gain is taxed at the maximum 28% rate.

Prior to 2018, a taxpayer who sold Section 1202 stock held for at least six months and reinvested all the proceeds in another qualified small business corporation's stock could defer all gain recognition.[55] If only a portion of the proceeds were reinvested, only the gain proportionate to the reinvested proceeds could be deferred.

Example 8.38

In 2017, Carolyn sold Section 1202 stock that she held for nine months for $750,000. The stock has a basis of $600,000. She reinvested $500,000 of the proceeds in other qualifying Section 1202 stock. Carolyn has a gain of $150,000 on the sale. Due to her reinvesting in qualifying stock, she could defer two-thirds of her gain on the sale or $100,000. She cannot exclude any of the remaining $50,000 gain, however, as she has not held the stock for more than five years. Carolyn has a $50,000 short-term capital gain in 2017 and her basis in the stock acquired is $400,000 ($500,000 – $100,000 deferred gain).

8.5.3 COMPARISON OF SECTIONS 1244 AND 1202

Both Section 1244 stock and Section 1202 stock provisions are designed to encourage new investment, but with major differences as shown in Table 8.7. Section 1244 applies to potentially far smaller corporations than does Section 1202, but the activities of the QSB are far more limited than the small business corporation. A more important distinction, however, relates to the investor's risk tolerance. An investor who assesses loss on the stock as the more likely possibility, would prefer the Section 1244 stock knowing that up to $50,000 of losses would offset other ordinary income. An investor with confidence in the success of a business would be attracted to the gain exclusion of Section 1202 stock.

TAX PLANNING

[55] The basis of the qualified stock acquired with the proceeds is reduced for the excluded gains. Seven percent of the 50 percent or 75 percent excluded gains (but not the 100 percent) are a preference item for the AMT.

Table 8.7 A Comparison of Sections 1244 and 1202

Section 1244 stock provisions	Section 1202 (QSBS) stock provisions
• Applies only to shareholders that are individuals or partnerships.	• Applies to all noncorporate shareholders that own the stock for five or more years.
• Applies to stock of C and S corporations.	• Applies to C corporation stock only.
• Only stock issued for the first $1,000,000 of capital is eligible.	• Only stock issued when the corporation's gross assets do not exceed $50,000,000 qualifies.
• Allows ordinary loss treatment for a shareholder's losses of up to $50,000 annually ($100,000 if married filing jointly). Excess loss remains capital loss.	• Excludes 50% (on stock acquired before February 18, 2009), 75% (on stock acquired after February 17, 2009 and before September 28, 2010) and 100% (on stock acquired after September 27, 2010) of the capital gain if held more than five years. Total gain eligible for the exclusion is generally $10,000,000 over all years. Eligible gain is limited annually to 10 times the basis of the stock sold if it is greater than the balance of the overall exclusion.
• At least 50 percent of the corporation's income must be from operations for the five years preceding the year of the sale.	• Rental and investment securities are limited to 10 percent of total assets at time of sale. Numerous restrictions apply to the corporation's business activities. Generally, the corporation must be a manufacturer, retailer, or wholesaler.

8.6 SALE OF PRINCIPAL RESIDENCE—SECTION 121

Investing in a personal residence can be one of the best ways to avoid gain recognition and the taxes on the sale of a personal asset. Taxpayers who meet the applicable provision for the sale of a principal residence can elect to exclude up to $250,000 of realized gain ($500,000 if married filing jointly) from income. This elective provision applies to all taxpayers regardless of age and does *not* require the purchase of a new residence.[56] Any gain in excess of the $250,000 ($500,000) allowable exclusion is capital gain and is subject to the capital gain treatment for individuals discussed previously. Losses, however, on the sale of a personal residence are personal and nondeductible.

The taxpayer's realized gain on the sale of the principal residence is the difference between the amount realized on the sale and the home's adjusted basis. The amount realized is the selling price less selling expenses. For many individuals, the current adjusted basis of the home is not the home's original purchase price. Basis of a home begins with the purchase price but is adjusted upwards for capital improvements (for example, room additions, major remodeling of the existing structure, and the addition of landscaping, driveways, and fencing). Normal repairs, however, do not increase a home's basis. Basis must also be reduced for deductible casualty losses or insurance recoveries that are not reinvested in the property.

Calculation of the amount realized on the sale of the home can be complex as selling costs can be significant, depending on the state in which the property is located. In general, any costs that the seller must pay as part of the sale reduces the amount realized. There is an exception, however; if the taxpayer takes a current tax deduction for an allowable selling expense, the deducted expense cannot also reduce the amount realized.[57]

[56] Under the laws in effect for sales prior to May 6, 1997, persons under 55 could only exclude gain to the extent the proceeds of the sale were reinvested in a new residence. Persons age 55 or over could exclude gain of up to $125,000 if certain conditions were met.

[57] States often levy an ad valorem tax on the deed transfer that is paid by the seller; as an ad valorem tax, it is deductible as an itemized deduction.

Example 8.39

William, a bachelor, sold his condominium purchased for $189,000 five years ago for $ 325,000. He had made a number of capital improvements to the home at a cost of $47,000, increasing his basis in the property to $236,000 ($189,000 + $47,000). William paid a realtor's commission of $18,000, a $3,250 tax on the transfer of the deed, and other selling expenses of $400. William's amount realized on the sale is $303,350 ($325,000 –$18,000 – $3,250 – $400). William's realized gain on the sale is $67,350 ($303,350 – $236,000). He recognizes none of the gain because it is less than $250,000. If William instead deducts the transfer taxes as an itemized deduction, the amount realized is $306,600 ($325,000 – $18,000 – $400).

The amount realized on the sale of a home may require an adjustment for the property tax levied in the year of sale. Property taxes must be prorated based on the date of sale. If there is no proration, the selling price must be adjusted to reflect the required split.

Example 8.40

Barton sells his home for $300,000 on July 15 of the current year. Barton agreed to this reduced selling price only after the purchaser agreed to pay the property taxes for the entire year. The property taxes for the year of the sale are $3,650. Barton's apportioned share is $1,960 ($3,650 × 196/365).[58] Barton increases his amount realized on the sale to $301,960. Alternatively, if Barton had paid the property taxes for the entire year without apportionment between him and the buyer, he would have reduced his amount realized by $1,690 ($3,650 × 169/365), the buyer's share for the time after the sale.

A taxpayer must meet ownership and use tests to qualify for nonrecognition of gain on the sale of the principal residence,. The ownership test requires the taxpayer or the taxpayer's spouse to have owned the residence for at least two of the previous five years.[59] The taxpayer must also have occupied the residence as his or her principal residence for two of the last five years prior to the date of sale. For a married couple filing jointly to qualify for the $500,000 exclusion, they both must meet the use test, but only one of them must meet the ownership test.[60] If the home is sold within two years after the year of a spouse's death (when a joint return can no longer be filed), the surviving spouse remains eligible for a maximum exclusion of $500,000 as long the requirements for the $500,000 exclusion were met immediately before the spouse's death.

Under normal circumstances, owners who fail to meet the two-year ownership and use tests (or who have sold another principal residence within two years of the sale of the current principal residence) cannot claim the gain exclusion. If, however, the sale is due to a change in health, employment, or other circumstances beyond the control of the taxpayer, a portion of the gain may be excluded.[61] The allowable exclusion equals the $250,000 exclusion times a ratio that has a denominator of 24 months and a numerator that is the shorter of the following:[62]

1. The time period the ownership and use tests were met in the previous five years
2. The time period since the exclusion was last claimed

[58] The day of the sale is attributed to the seller.

[59] Ownership by a divorced or deceased spouse is included.

[60] §121(a) and (b). Neither of them may have sold or exchanged a personal residence within two years of the sale to claim the $500,000 exclusion.

[61] Reg. §1.121-3T(e). Examples of unforeseen circumstances include death of a spouse or co-owner, divorce, unemployment, disasters, and involuntary conversion of residence.

[62] §121(c).

Example 8.41

Bob bought a new principal residence on June 1 of year 1. In December of year 2, he was laid off from his job and found a new job in a city 200 miles away. He sold his house on February 1, year 3, at a gain of $230,000. Because Bob's move was necessitated by a change of employment, he can exclude a portion of the gain. He owned the house for 20 months and can exclude $208,333 of the gain (20/24 of the $250,000). He is taxed on the remaining $21,667 capital gain that cannot be excluded.

This exclusion increases to $500,000 only if both spouses meet the use test and neither has claimed the exclusion in the previous two years.

Since 2013, the net investment income surtax has applied to the amount of gain from the sale of a residence that is taxable for regular income tax purposes.[63] It does not apply to any gain that is excluded under Section 121.

Example 8.42

Savanah and Kevin are married and file a joint return. They sold the principal residence that they owned and lived in for the last 15 years for $1,200,000. Their basis in the home is $575,000 and their realized gain on the sale is $625,000. Under Section 121, they exclude $500,000 of the gain and recognize a $125,000 gain. They have $70,000 of other net investment income for total net investment income of $195,000. Their modified adjusted gross income is $300,000, which exceeds the $250,000 threshold amount for a married couple filing a joint return by $50,000. They are subject to the NII surtax on the lesser of $195,000 (their NII) or $50,000 (the amount their income exceeds the threshold). The NII tax that they must pay is $1,900 ($50,000 × 3.8%) in addition to their regular income and capital gains taxes.

TAX PLANNING

A taxpayer may have problems determining the principal residence, particularly if the taxpayer owns two or more homes. It is possible for a taxpayer to own two homes used on a regular basis that meet the occupancy requirement of two out of five years on each. Under these circumstances the home that is occupied the greater amount of time is considered the **principal residence**. If a taxpayer contemplates selling one of the homes in the future, careful planning can help establish that home as the permanent residence. Some other relevant factors in determining which home is the principal residence include the taxpayer's place of employment, the principal abode of the taxpayer's family, and the address on the taxpayer's state and federal tax returns, driver's license, car registration, and voter registration.[64]

A vacation home or rental property does not qualify for this exclusion because it is not the taxpayer's principal residence. The Housing Assistance Tax Act of 2008 closed a loophole that allowed taxpayers to convert a vacation home into a principal residence qualifying for the exclusion if it met the two-year ownership and use tests at the time of sale. For sales or exchanges after December 31, 2008, the realized gain eligible for the exclusion must be reduced based on nonqualified use (any period after December 31, 2008 during which the house is not used as the principal residence of the taxpayer or spouse). The reduction is computed as a percentage by dividing the period of nonqualified use after 2008 by the period of ownership.[65]

[63] The net investment income tax rate of 3.8 percent is assessed on the lesser of (1) net investment income or (2) modified adjusted gross income in excess of a threshold based on the taxpayer's filing status ($200,000 single, $225,000 head of household, and $250,000 married filing jointly). See Chapter 5.

[64] Reg. §1.121-1(b)(2) includes factors to be considered in determining if a home is a taxpayer's principal residence.

[65] §121(b)(4).

Example 8.43

Robert and Sarah, a married couple, bought a vacation home on January 1, 2008 for $400,000. They used it as a vacation home until January 1, 2012 when it became their principal residence. It continues to be their principal residence until January 1, 2018 when they sell the home for $700,000, a realized gain of $300,000 ($700,000 – $400,000). Because they did not use the home as their principal residence for 3 years after 2008 (2009 through 2011) of their 10 years of ownership (2008 through 2017) $90,000 (3/10 × $300,000) of the gain is ineligible for the exclusion. They exclude $210,000 ($300,000 – $90,000) of the gain under Section 121 and recognize a gain of $90,000 ($300,000 – $210,000). If Robert and Sarah had used the home as their principal residence for the entire time they owned it, they could have excluded the entire $300,000 gain.

If a taxpayer claims depreciation for a portion of the home used as a home office, any gain related to the depreciated portion of the home is not eligible for this exclusion. Any gain realized on this part must be recognized as gain on the sale of business property.[66]

8.6.1 DEBT REDUCTIONS, SHORT SALES, AND FORECLOSURES

When all or part of a taxpayer's debt is reduced or forgiven, the taxpayer normally has income that must be recognized. Fortunately for taxpayers, the Mortgage Forgiveness Debt Relief Act of 2007 (as extended through 2017) allowed taxpayers to exclude cancellation of up to $2 million of qualified principal residence debt from income. The provision applied to debt cancellation of qualified principal residence debt occurring after 2006 and before 2018 through a modification of mortgage loan terms, disposal of the property in a short sale, abandoning the property, or having the property taken in foreclosure proceedings.[67] Debt forgiveness in excess of $2 million (or forgiven beyond 2017) is income from the cancellation of debt for the owner.

Qualified principal residence indebtedness is acquisition debt[68] on the taxpayers' principal residence of no more than $2 million ($1 million for married individuals filing separately),[69] determined under Section 121 rules for gain exclusion on the sale of the principal residence. Acquisition debt includes debt secured by the residence for the acquisition, construction, or substantial improvement of the residence and applies only to that part of the loan representing qualified principal residence debt. No refinanced debt that exceeds acquisition debt (immediately before refinancing) qualifies as acquisition debt. If the taxpayer continues to own the home after debt cancellation, the basis of that home is reduced by the cancelled debt, but not below zero.

8.7 NAVIGATING INDIVIDUAL CAPITAL GAINS TAX RATES

Determining tax liability and tax planning for individuals (unlike corporations) is complicated by the different long-term capital gains tax rates that apply to individual taxpayers. Though most capital gains are taxed at 0, 15, or 20 percent, a maximum 25 percent rate applies to unrecaptured Section 1250 gains on realty and a 28 percent rate for gains on the disposition of collectibles (for example, antiques and art objects) and Section 1202 stock (qualified small business stock).[70] It is important to note that there are no losses in the 25 percent category when the netting process is discussed.

[66] Reg. §1.121-1(e)(4), Ex. 5. Any gain due to depreciation is unrecaptured Section 1250 gain taxed at a 25 percent rate.
[67] §108(a)(1)(E).
[68] §163(h)(3)(B).
[69] §108(h)(2).
[70] The 25 percent tax rate only applies to gains resulting from depreciation deductions on Section 1231 real property that are not recaptured at ordinary income tax rates.

Because the additional 25 and 28 percent capital gains rates apply to different types of long-term capital gains, a person with more than one type of capital gains includes them in taxable income in a specific order: 25 percent gains are included first, 28 percent gains are included next, and 15 percent gains are included last. If taxable income exceeds the 20-percent breakpoint, the rate on capital gains taxed at 15 percent increases to 20 percent (as discussed previously).

8.7.1 DETERMINING THE LONG-TERM CAPITAL GAINS TAX RATE

With three categories of long-term capital gains tax rates (28%, 25%, and 15%) based on the type of property, there is an extended gain/loss netting procedure required to determine at what rate net gains will ultimately be taxed. If a taxpayer has multiple gains and losses on 28%, 25%, and/or 15% capital gain property, the net gains and losses in the separate 28% and 15% asset categories are netted first to determine if the result is a net gain or net loss in each category. Note, however, that there are no losses in the 25% category, only net gains. If the result is:

A. Net gains in all categories:
The 25%, then 28%, and then 15% gains are simply added to taxable income in that order to determine the total tax as explained below.

B. Net gains in 28% and/or 25% assets; net loss in 15% assets.
The 15% net loss eliminates or reduces 28% net gain first, then reduces or eliminates the 25% net gain. (a) Add any remaining 28% gain and/or 25% gain to taxable income and determine tax as explained below. (b) If a 15% net loss remains, take the allowable $3,000 deduction and carry the remaining loss forward.

C. Net loss in 28% category; net gains in 25% and 15% categories.
The 28% net loss eliminates or reduces the 25% net gain first and then reduces or eliminates the 15% net gain. (a) Add any remaining 25% gain and/or the 15% gain to taxable income, before determining the applicable tax rates as explained below. (b) If a net loss remains, deduct the allowable $3,000 deduction and carry the remaining loss forward.

D. Net loss in 28% and 15% categories; net gain in the 25% category.
The 25% net gain eliminates or reduces the 28% loss first and then reduces or eliminates the 15% loss. (a) If a gain remains add it to taxable income, before determining the applicable tax rate as explained below. (b) If net losses remain, deduct the allowable $3,000 and carry the remaining loss forward.

If the taxpayer has a net gain in one or more categories at the end of the above netting process, the net gains are added to ordinary taxable income in the following order: 25% gains are added first, 28% gains next, with 15% net gains added last. The level of income for specific tax rates vary by filing status. To determine the tax on the gains, taxable income must first be determined and the specific capital gains are added to taxable income to determine the total tax as follows:

1. First add 25% gains and then the 28% gains to ordinary taxable income.
   a. 25% and/or 28% gains *not exceeding* the 10% tax bracket are taxed at a 10 percent tax rate.
   b. 25% and/or 28% gains not exceeding the 20% breakpoint are taxed at the 15 percent capital gains tax rate.
   c. The 25% and/or 28% gains *beyond* the 20% breakpoint are taxed at their 25% and 28% tax brackets, respectively.

2. Add the 15% gains to ordinary taxable income after the 25% and 28% gains have been added.
   a. 15% gains not exceeding the 15% breakpoint are taxed at 0%.
   b. 15% gains exceeding the 15% breakpoint but not exceeding the 20% breakpoint are taxed at 15%.
   c. 15% gains exceeding the 20% breakpoint are taxed at 20%.

The existence of short-term capital losses and capital loss carryovers further complicates the extended capital gain and loss netting procedure and the determination of the tax liability. These losses, however, will reduce the gains that remain after the netting process. While this process is extremely cumbersome, it is necessary only when the net result of the final netting process is a net long-term capital gain.[71] If a taxpayer has no short-term or long-term capital losses or capital loss carryovers included in the netting process, the taxpayer simply separates the gains into their categories and applies the appropriate tax rates.

Example 8.44

Toby's ordinary income places him in the 32 percent income tax bracket before considering a number of transactions involving several types of capital assets held more than one year: a $6,800 long-term capital gain and a $4,300 long-term capital loss on some stock investments; a $2,000 Section 1250 unrecaptured gain on property; a $4,200 gain on the sale of his gun collection, a $3,100 loss on the sale of an antique automobile, and a $1,500 loss on a painting (collectibles).

He first nets all of his long-term gains and losses (regardless of their type or tax rate) to determine if he has a net long-term capital gain or loss. Because he has a net $4,100 long-term capital gain ($6,800 – $4,300 + $2,000 + $4,200 – $3,100 – $1,500), Toby must separate his long-term gains and losses into their proper categories to determine which rates apply to the net gain. He has a $2,500 ($6,800 – $4,300) net long-term gain on his investments (15 percent category), a $2,000 Section 1250 gain (taxed at 25 percent); and a $400 ($4,200 – $3,100 – $1,500) net loss on the collectibles (28 percent assets). The $400 net loss on the 28 percent assets offsets $400 of the $2,000 Section 1250 gain. As a result, Toby has a $1,600 net capital gain taxed at 25 percent and a $2,500 net capital gain taxed at 15 percent.

8.7.2 PLANNING WITH MULTIPLE TAX RATES

The zero long-term capital gains tax rate that applies to individuals below the 15 percent breakpoint may appear to provide a perfect planning opportunity for parents to gift appreciated stock to their children in this tax bracket and then have the children sell the securities tax-free. To close this loophole, Congress increased the age at which the kiddie tax rules apply to all children under age 19 as well as most full time students under age 24. These kiddie tax rules tax unearned income (including capital gains) of a "child" in excess of a minimal fixed amount at the same rates as trusts and estates, effectively preventing all but a small amount of gain to escape taxation.[72]

TAX PLANNING

Individuals can benefit from the difference in the tax rates on gains for specific long-term capital asset dispositions if alternative asset dispositions are available. For example, a loss on a 15 percent long-term capital asset can offset gains on both 25 and 28 percent assets. A long-term capital loss can offset a short-term capital gain and a long-term capital loss carryover offsets gains in the 28 and 25 percent asset categories before a gain taxed at 15 percent. These rate differences and the order in which they are imposed offer planning opportunities for individuals.

[71] If the long-term capital gains are all in one category, any resulting net capital gain is simply taxed at that category's tax rate.

[72] The kiddie tax taxes a child under 19 (under 24 if a full-tine student) at the same rates as estates and trusts on unearned income over $2,100 if higher than the tax the child would otherwise pay. Prior to 2018, the parents' marginal tax rates were used instead of the estate and trust rates. See Chapter 12 for the discussion of the kiddie tax.

Example 8.45

George (who is in the 35 percent marginal tax bracket) has a long-term capital gain of $20,000 on the sale of some artwork. As a collectible, the gain is taxed at 28 percent. He has 100,000 shares of CDC stock that have decreased in value by $22,000 since he bought them five years ago. If George sells the stock before the end of the tax year, he will realize the $22,000 long-term capital loss and he can offset the entire $20,000 gain taxed at 28 percent and an additional $2,000 of ordinary income taxed at 35 percent. Instead of paying an additional $5,600 ($20,000 × 28%) in taxes from the sale, he saves $700 ($2,000 × 35%) on his regular tax bill.

Example 8.46

Christian, who is in the 35 percent marginal tax bracket, has a $12,000 short-term capital loss on ABC stock purchased earlier in the year. He also has an unrealized gain of $18,000 on XYZ stock purchased several years ago. He deals with a discount broker who charges only $20 per transaction. If Christian sells half of his XYZ stock, he realizes a $9,000 gain and reduces his net loss for the year to a fully deductible $3,000. He can then repurchase identical XYZ shares to replace those sold at a cost of $40 for the two trades. (The wash sale rules only affect loss recognition, not gain, as explained in Chapter 9.) By realizing the $9,000 gain, he accelerates an additional $9,000 loss deduction that would normally have to be deducted at a rate of $3,000 per year over the next three years. At a discount rate of 8 percent, he is better off by $404 [($9,000 × 35%) – ($3,000 × 35% × .926) – ($3,000 × 35% × .857) – ($3,000 × 35% × .794) – $40].

REVISITING THE INTRODUCTORY CASE

The tax rate Albert's friend said would apply to the sales of his business and personal assets is incorrect. Although Albert has several 15 percent capital assets, others are subject to a 25 percent rate, 28 percent rate, or are taxed as ordinary income.

The inventory is an ordinary income asset so the $20,000 gain on its sale is added to his salary as ordinary income; thus, $220,000 of his gross income is subject to ordinary income rates. The gains and losses from the rest of the assets are netted and taxed as follows:

	Section 1231 gain (loss)	Capital gain (loss)	Taxed at 28%*	Taxed at 25%**	Taxed at 15%
Business assets					
Furniture	$(5,000)				
Equipment	(16,000)				
Building	45,000				
Land	0				
Net Sec. 1231 gain	$24,000 →	$24,000		$24,000	
Personal assets					
Dali art		37,500	$37,500		
Sculpture		(20,000)	(20,000)		
ABCD stock		(30,000)			$(30,000)
XYZ stock		16,000	____		16,000
Net capital gain		$27,500			
Net 28% gain			$17,500		
Net 15% loss					$(14,000)
Apply 15% loss to 28% gain			(14,000) ←	____	
Final gains			$3,500	$24,000	
Apply tax rates			×28%	×25%	
Tax			$980	$6,000	

*28% rate applies to collectibles.

**25% rate applies to unrecaptured Section 1250 gain.

Section 1231 (Business) Assets: There is a net Section 1231 gain on the office furniture ($5,000 loss), electrical equipment ($16,000 loss), and the office and warehouse ($45,000 gain) building. There is no depreciation recapture on the office furniture, the electrical equipment (both sold at losses), or the office & warehouse building. The remaining Section 1231 gain (after the Section 1231 losses) is an unrecaptured Section 1250 gain. The net gain of $24,000 ($45,000 – ($16,000 + $5,000)) is added to the net capital assets from the capital asset netting process and is subject to the 25 percent capital gains tax rate.

Personal Assets: Albert has a $37,500 capital gain on the Dali art and a $20,000 loss on the sculpture (both collectibles and 28 percent capital assets) and the $30,000 capital loss on the ABCD stock and $16,000 gain on the XYZ stock (both 15 percent capital assets) are all combined with the $24,000 gain from the Section 1231 netting process (above) for a net gain of $27,500 ($24,000 + $37,500 – $20,000 – $30,000 + $16,000). Because there is a net gain and multiple rate assets in the group, gain or loss must be determined for each asset rate-type to determine the final tax rates on the gains and a specific priority followed in offsetting gains by losses.

There is a net $17,500 ($37,500 – $20,000) gain on the collectibles (28 percent assets). The net $14,000 ($16,000 – $30,000) loss on the 15 percent assets offsets all but $3,500 of the $17,500 net gain on the 28 percent assets and the remaining $3,500 is taxed at 28 percent or $980. With this loss completely absorbed, the $24,000 unrecaptured Section 1250 gain is taxed at 25 percent, a tax of $6,000. The total capital gains tax is $6,980 ($980 + $6,000).

Because Albert's AGI exceeds the $200,000 threshold, his $27,500 net capital gains are subject to the 3.8 percent net investment income (NII) surtax. $27,500 × 3.8 percent = $1,045. (The $20,000 gain on the inventory is taxed as ordinary income and is not subject to the NII tax.)

Albert's taxable income is determined as follows:

Income:	Salary		$200,000
	Gain on inventory sale		20,000
	Net capital gain		27,500
	Adjusted gross income		$247,500
Deductions:	Standard deduction		(12,000)
	Taxable income		$235,500
	Regular income tax*	$48,490	
	Capital gains tax	6,980	
	NII tax	1,045	
	Total tax liability		$56,515

*2018 income tax on $208,000 ($235,500 – $27,500 capital gains) = $48,490.

SUMMARY

Two important ways to classify assets for tax purposes are: (1) business, investment, or personal use and (2) ordinary, capital, or Section 1231. Together, these classifications determine the tax treatment of all asset dispositions. The most common asset disposition is a sale; other dispositions include exchanges, abandonments, and involuntary conversions.

The primary ordinary assets are inventory, accounts receivable, and business-use assets that fail to meet the more-than-one-year holding period for Section 1231 status. Gains and losses on ordinary income assets are included directly in the taxpayer's income along with ordinary income from business operations.

Capital assets include personal-use property and most investment assets. Gains and losses on capital assets go through a netting process after they are separated into long term and short term. The treatment of capital gains and losses for individuals and corporations differs widely. Corporations include all net capital gains directly in income and are only allowed to deduct net capital losses against capital gains in the three carryback and five carryforward years.

Individuals may deduct a maximum of $3,000 of net capital losses annually, but they may carry forward remaining net losses indefinitely. A net short-term capital gain is included directly in income. Net long-term capital gains of individuals are subject to multiple tax rates varying from zero to 28 percent based on the specific type of capital gain and the taxpayer's tax rate bracket.

Section 1231 property includes all depreciable property and all nondepreciable realty used in a trade or business and rental realty and related property held for more than one year. Generally, net Section 1231 gains are included in the capital asset netting process as long-term capital gains. Net Section 1231 losses are deducted immediately from ordinary income.

Several provisions impact the treatment of Section 1231 gains, requiring all or part of the gain to be treated as ordinary income. The Sections 1245 and 1250 recapture provisions reduce Section 1231 gains for all or part of the prior depreciation deductions on assets, which are then taxed as ordinary income. Section 291 requires corporations to recapture an extra 20 percent as ordinary income. The Section 1231 look-back rule provisions require Section 1231 gains to be treated as ordinary income to the extent of Section 1231 loss deductions in the prior five years.

Two provisions encourage taxpayers to invest in smaller corporations. The first allows taxpayers to deduct up to a $50,000 loss annually on Section 1244 stock as an ordinary loss, rather than a capital loss. The second excludes up to 50, 75, or 100 percent of the gain on qualified small business stock from taxation based on purchase date.

Section 121 allows individuals who have owned and occupied a home as the principal residence to exclude up to $250,000 ($500,000 if filing jointly) of the gain on its sale from income. This provision is available once every two years to all individuals who meet the ownership and occupancy requirements.

The addition of the 25 percent and 28 percent tax rates for specific types of long-term capital gain assets has added significant complexity to determining the total tax liability. A careful and complete analysis of capital gains and losses is necessary to determine the final tax liability of individual taxpayers with extensive capital asset transactions.

KEY TERMS

TEST YOURSELF

Answers Appear after the Problem Assignments

1. Vera has three assets she plans to sell. The first is her personal automobile that is seven years old; the second is a truck used in her business for 11 months; and the third is some land that she bought four years ago for expansion of her business. What types of assets are they: capital, Section 1231, or ordinary income?
   a. car = capital; truck = Section 1231; land = capital
   b. car = capital; truck = ordinary; land = Section 1231
   c. car = ordinary; truck = ordinary; land = capital
   d. car = ordinary; truck = Section 1231; land = capital

2. A taxpayer has the following gains and losses from property transactions in the current year:

$40,000	Section 1231 gain
$25,000	Section 1231 loss
$12,000	Long-term capital gain
$9,000	Short-term capital loss

   How are these transactions treated for tax purposes if the taxpayer recognized an $8,000 Section 1231 loss in the previous tax year?

a. $18,000 long-term capital gain
b. $15,000 Section 1231 gain; $3,000 short-term capital loss
c. $8,000 ordinary income from look-back; $10,000 long-term capital gain
d. $8,000 ordinary income from look-back; $7,000 Section 1231 gain; $3,000 long-term capital gain

3. Trendy Corporation has a net short-term capital loss of $9,000 and a net long-term capital loss of $14,000 in year 5. Trendy Corporation can
   a. deduct $3,000 of the short-term capital loss from its ordinary income and carry the remaining losses back to year 2.
   b. deduct $3,000 of the long-term capital loss from its ordinary income and carry the remaining losses forward indefinitely.
   c. deduct all $23,000 of the capital losses from its ordinary income.
   d. deduct none of the capital losses. The corporation must carry back the entire net capital loss as a short-term capital loss to year 2.

4. Jonathon sells the computer that he used 75 percent for business and 25 percent for personal purposes for $1,200. The computer cost $4,000 and the allowable depreciation on the computer is $2,200. How much gain or loss does Jonathon recognize?
   a. $800 gain
   b. $400 gain
   c. $100 gain
   d. $800 loss

5. Mason is single and the original shareholder of 1,000 shares of Section 1244 stock in Miles Corporation acquired four years ago. He has a basis of $65,000 in the stock. The stock has significantly declined in value so he sells it in the current year for $5,000. Identify the amount and type of gain or loss that Mason has on this sale.
   a. $50,000 ordinary loss and a $10,000 capital loss
   b. $60,000 capital loss
   c. $53,000 ordinary loss and a $12,000 capital loss
   d. $60,000 ordinary loss

Check Your Understanding

PROBLEM ASSIGNMENTS

1. [LO 8.1] How are assets classified to determine their tax treatment on disposition? What are other ways to classify assets?

2. [LO 8.1] What events qualify as asset dispositions?

3. [LO 8.1] How is the amount realized on a sale or exchange determined?

4. [LO 8.1] Explain the difference between a realized gain and a recognized gain.

5. [LO 8.1] What types of assets are Section 1231 assets? What types of assets are capital assets? What types of assets are ordinary income assets? Give several examples of each type of asset.

6. [LO 8.1] What type of loss would be recognized on the sale of receivables to a factor at 80 percent of the face value?

7. [LO 8.1] Core Carpet Factory purchased a $40,000 binding machine (seven year property) six months ago that they expected to use for at least ten years. They began to use the machine immediately. Unfortunately, the machine kept breaking down and the company finally returned it to the manufacturer. Because Core would not allow them to repair it and purchased an alternative machine, they refunded only $20,000 to Core for the return of the machine. How should Core treat the loss on the machine? How would your answer change it they had used the machine for 18 months before returning it and receiving $20,000?

8. [LO 8.2] How are capital assets classified as short term and long term? How are long-term gains and losses and short-term gains and losses treated in the capital asset netting process?

9. [LO 8.2] How are net short-term capital gains of individuals treated? How are net short-term capital gains of corporations treated?

10. [LO 8.2] How are net capital losses of individuals treated for tax purposes? How are net capital losses of corporations treated for tax purposes?

11. [LO 8.2] Determine the amount of the capital gain or loss in each of the following transactions and state whether the gain or loss is long term or short term.

a. 100 shares of Bilco stock bought for $8,000 on January 22 of year 3 and sold for $10,000 on January 22 of year 4.

b. 20 acres of investment land bought for $8,000 on January 31 of year 3 and sold for $7,000 on February 2 of year 4.

c. 150 shares of Dantron stock bought for $15,000 on April 1 of year 3 and sold for $17,000 on May 28 of year 5.

12. [LO 8.2] In the current year, Serena sold investment land for $105,000 that she purchased six years ago for $61,000; a diamond engagement ring for $1,800 that her ex-fiancée had given her nine months ago (purchased for $2,500 a week before giving it to her); 2,000 shares of stock for $14,000 that had been purchased two years ago for $18,000; and a personal auto for $12,000 purchased two months ago for $10,900. Determine the capital gain or loss on each sale, if it is short or long term, and the result of the capital asset netting process.

13. [LO 8.2] Sharon has salary income of $68,000, a net short-term capital gain of $15,000, and a net long-term capital loss of $24,000. What is Sharon's adjusted gross income if she has no other income items?

14. [LO 8.2] Chester provides you with the following income information for years 1 through 3, exclusive of capital loss carryovers:

	Short-term capital gain	Short-term capital loss	Long-term capital gain	Long-term capital loss
Year 1	0	$2,400	$400	$3,500
Year 2	$500	$1,700	$900	$1,000
Year 3	$2,000	$400	$300	$500

Determine the amount and type of capital loss deduction each year, if any, and identify any carryover to the following year.

15. [LO 8.3] Why do taxpayers have to recapture depreciation on depreciable assets sold at a gain? To which assets do the Section 1245 and 1250 recapture provisions apply?

16. [LO 8.3] Explain the look-back procedure for Section 1231 assets. Why did this particular provision evolve?

17. [LO 8.3] What is Section 291 recapture? Compare this to unrecaptured Section 1250 gains.

18. [LO 8.3] How are net losses treated in the Section 1231 netting process? How is a net Section 1231 gain taxed?

19. [LO 8.4] Wally sells the auto that he used 80 percent for business and 20 percent for personal use annually for $6,000. He purchased the auto four years ago for $20,000. If used 100 percent for business, he could have claimed $16,000 in depreciation. What is his gain or loss on the sale of the auto and how is it classified?

20. [LO 8.5] What is the significance of having stock qualify as Section 1244 stock?

21. [LO 8.5] What is the potential advantage to having a substantial investment in stock in a qualified small business corporation rather than an equal investment in other corporate stock not meeting their provisions?

22. [LO 8.6] What are the ownership and use tests that must be met to exclude the maximum gain on the sale of a personal residence? Under what circumstances may the owner of a personal residence exclude gain if the required ownership and use tests are not met?

Crunch the Numbers

23. [LO 8.1] Charlie sold Whiteacre for $40,000 cash and the buyer assumed Charlie's $19,000 mortgage on the property. Charlie paid a realtor commission of $2,000 on the sale. What is his realized gain or loss if Whiteacre's adjusted basis is
    a. $47,000?
    b. $67,000?

24. [LO 8.1] Allan received $5,000 cash and an auto worth $15,000 in exchange for land encumbered by a $13,000 liability that the buyer assumed.
    a. What is the amount realized on this sale?
    b. If Allan had a basis of $34,000 in the land, what is his realized gain or loss on the sale?
    c. If Allan has owned the land for five years as an investment, what is the character of the recognized gain or loss?
    d. How would your answer to (c) change if the land had been used by Allan's business as a parking lot?

25. [LO 8.1] Corgill Corporation sold land that it used for storing old equipment. Corgill owned the land for seven years and it had a basis of $234,000. Corgill received $50,000 cash and a note for $100,000 and the purchaser assumed Corgill's $150,000 mortgage on the property. Corgill also paid a realtor's fee of $15,000 and other selling expenses of $2,000.
    a. What is Corgill's recognized gain or loss on the sale and what is its character?
    b. If Corgill had held the land as an investment, how would your answer change?

26. [LO 8.1] Bernadette sold her home. She received cash of $40,000, the buyer assumed her mortgage of $180,000, and she paid closing costs of $2,300 and a broker's commission of $7,000.
    a. What is the amount realized on the sale?
    b. If she has a basis in the home of $138,000, what is her realized gain or loss on the sale?
    c. What is the character of the recognized gain or loss?
    d. How would your answer to (c) change if Bernadette sold a building used by her sole proprietorship rather than her personal residence?

27. [LO 8.1] Calahan Corporation regularly factors its receivables when they are short of cash. This spring they not only factored $325,000 of receivables at 80 percent of their value but sold two company automobiles that they had purchased five months earlier for $45,000 for only $38,000. What are Calahan's losses on these sales and how do they affect its income?

28. [LO 8.3] DDF Corporation sold land it had used for parking and storage for 20 years for $575,000. Its basis in the land was $68,000. It also sold some manufacturing equipment for $125,000 that it replaced with more modern equipment. The equipment sold had an adjusted basis of $760,000.
    a. Determine the amount and character of DDF's recognized gains or losses on these sales.
    b. If DDF has no other property transactions, how is the net gain or loss treated?

29. [LO 8.3] Barry Corporation sold a machine used in its business for two years for $27,000. The machine originally cost $24,000 and it had an adjusted basis at the time of the sale of $17,000. Determine the amount and type of gain recognized on the sale.

30. [LO 8.3] The Grid Corporation owns a bank of boring machines. They regularly replace two machines each year. In the current year, the company sold Machine 8 for $12,000. It was purchased six years

earlier for $40,000, and its adjusted basis was $14,000. Machine 6 was sold for $24,000. It was purchased four years ago for $45,000 and had an adjusted basis of $19,000.

a. How much gain or loss is realized on each asset?

b. What is the character of the gain or loss?

c. If the company disposed of no other assets during the year, how are the results of these sales treated for tax purposes?

31. [LO 8.3] Jonas, an individual, acquired a building nine years ago for $650,000. He sold it in the current year for $680,000 when its adjusted basis was $500,000. Determine the amount and type of gain or loss recognized on the sale

a. if the building is a factory.

b. if the building is an apartment complex.

c. if Jonas is a corporation rather than an individual.

32. [LO 8.3] Barbara had the following Section 1231 gains and losses in the previous four years.

Year	Section 1231 gain (loss)
1	$50,000
2	($45,000)
3	$20,000
4	$15,000

a. How will Barbara treat a $25,000 gain in year 5?

b. Is there any unrecaptured Section 1231 loss remaining?

33. [LO 8.3] The Angel Corporation purchased an office building for $600,000 12 years ago. The corporation claimed $80,000 of cost recovery deductions before it sold the building for $700,000.

a. Determine the amount and type of gain or loss that Angel Corporation recognizes on the sale of the building.

b. Would your answer change if Angel was a sole proprietorship?

c. Would your answer change if Angel Corporation incurred $43,000 of Section 1231 losses in the prior year?

34. [LO 8.2 & 8.3] An individual taxpayer has the following gains and losses from property transactions. What is the effect on the taxpayer's taxable income?

$ 4,000	Long-term capital gain
7,000	Long-term capital loss
10,000	Section 1231 gain
6,000	Section 1231 loss
3,000	Short-term capital gain
6,000	Short-term capital loss

35. [LO 8.2 & 8.3] Juno Corporation had ordinary taxable income of $167,000 in the current year before consideration of any of the following property transactions. It sold two blocks of stock held for investment. One yielded a short-term capital gain of $8,000 and the other a long-term capital loss of $14,000. In addition, Juno sold four pieces of machinery for $30,000. It purchased the machines three years ago for $80,000 and claimed $35,000 of depreciation deductions. Juno also sold a building for $400,000 that it had purchased fifteen years ago for $390,000. The depreciation deductions up to the date of sale for the building were $108,000.

a. Determine the amount and character of each gain or loss from the property transactions and Juno Corporation's taxable income for the current year.

b. How would your answers to (a) change if Juno were a single individual with no dependents and $14,000 of itemized deductions instead of a corporation?

c. How would your answers to (b) change if Juno has $550,000 of ordinary taxable income?

36. [LO 8.4] Wilma does secretarial work out of her home. She purchased her own computer and used it 2,250 hours for her work during the year; her children, however, also use the computer for 250 hours to do their homework. She paid $4,000 for the computer and had claimed $2,200 of depreciation on it when she sold it for $1,100. Determine the amount and type of her gain or loss recognized on the sale of the computer.

37. [LO 8.5] In January 2009, Daniel bought some qualified small business stock for $2,000,000. In the current year, he sells that stock for $13,000,000. How much and what kind of gain or loss does he have? How would your answer change if Daniel sold the stock for $25,000,000?

38. [LO 8.5] Vanessa bought 2,000 shares of Barbco stock when the company was formed for $107,000. The company had $900,000 of total capital upon formation; thus, it qualified as Section 1244 stock. Vanessa sold the stock three years later for $3,000. If Vanessa is single, how much and what kind of gain or loss does she recognize?

39. [LO 8.5] Taylor bought 10,000 shares of qualifying Section 1202 stock from a start-up company A on May 1, 2012 for $1,000,000 and 5,000 shares of Section 1202 stock from start-up company B on June 1, 2014 for $200,000. In February 2018, she sold 1,000 shares of A for $500,000; in December she also sold 2,000 shares of B for $300,000.
   a. What are the tax effects on Taylor's income for these sales in 2018?
   b. How would your answers change if Taylor had purchased the stock of start-up company A in 2007?

40. [LO 8.5] George bought 6,000 shares of Section 1244 stock from Dorado Corporation six years ago for $160,000. The company has not done well so this year George sold all of his stock for $45,000.
   a. Determine the amount and type of George's loss if he is single.
   b. How would your answer change if George is married and files a joint return?

41. [LO 8.6] Tina and Tony, a married couple, have owned and lived in their house for 20 years. They want to sell it now and move to a smaller place. They purchased the home for $56,000 and put $30,000 of improvements into the home over the years. If they sell the house for $387,000, what is their realized and recognized gain?

42. [LO 8.6] Carlotta moved into a smaller home ten months ago, after her husband died. She sold the home that they had lived in together for fifteen years and elected Section 121 so she would not have to recognize the $150,000 of gain on that home. She then purchased the smaller home for $210,000. She is unhappy in the neighborhood after living there for 10 months and wants to move again. If she sells the home for $235,000, what is her realized and recognized gain? How would your answer change if Carlotta were forced to move into a nursing home because of her health?

43. [LO 8.1, 8.2 & 8.7] Barbara sold three assets during 2018. How much and what kind of gain or loss does she recognize from each sale? What tax rate applies to the net gain if Barbara is a single individual with $160,000 ordinary income taxed at a 32 percent marginal tax rate?
   a. On February 25 she sold 200 shares of XYZ stock for $19,000. She bought that stock for $16,000 on February 23, 2017.
   b. On July 20 she sold an antique automobile for $30,000 that she purchased for $31,000 on July 21, 2017.
   c. On August 2, she sold qualified small business stock for $28,000 that she had purchased for $20,000 on December 19, 2008.

44. [LO 8.4 & 8.7] Clarice became very ill in August of 2018 and was unable to work the rest of the year. She had only $30,000 of income from her job for the time she worked and was forced to sell the following investments to pay for her living expenses. She sold 10,000 shares of BBC stock purchased two years ago for $34,000 (basis = $16,000) and a coin collection she inherited from her grandfather many years ago for $55,000 (basis = $30,000). If Clarice is single and has no dependents, determine her taxable income and her income tax liability for 2018.

45. [LO 8.7] Al Shalou, a single individual, had $170,000 of salary income in 2018 and also had a number of taxable gains and losses on his property transactions during the year with the following results:

a. $26,000 Section 1202 gain on ABC stock
b. $5,000 short-term capital loss on Zephyr bonds
c. $24,000 long-term capital loss on Magnum stock
d. $13,000 Section 1245 recapture and $3,000 Section 1231 gain on equipment
e. $8,000 long-term capital loss on a coin collection
f. $6,000 Section 1231 loss on a machine
g. $20,000 long-term capital gain on Jobe stock.

Calculate Shalou's taxable income and his income tax liability for 2018.

46. [LO 8.7] Geraldine is single with $165,000 ordinary income that is taxed at a marginal tax rate of 32 percent after a number of transactions involving taxable gains and losses on several types of capital assets held more than one year, including several collectibles: a $10,200 gain on a stamp collection, a $5,000 loss on the sale of antique jewelry, and a $2,500 loss on an original oil painting. She also had a $15,000 long-term capital gain, an $11,300 long-term capital loss on some stock investments, and a $5,000 Section 1250 unrecaptured gain on some real property. Determine the result of the netting process for these transactions and the tax rates that would apply.

47. [LO 8.7] What are the maximum tax rates that apply to a single individual's $20,000 long-term capital gain on corporate stocks if total taxable income in 2018 is

a. $30,000?
b. $230,000?
c. $450,000?
d. How would your answer change for (c), if the $20,000 gain was from the sale of an Egyptian statue from the 1400s?
e. How would your answer change for (c), if the $20,000 was an unrecaptured Section 1250 gain?

48. [LO 8.7] A single taxpayer has $158,000 of ordinary taxable income in 2018 (after his standard deduction but before consideration of the following recognized gains), a $9,000 long-term capital gain on the sale of an antique painting, a $10,000 unrecaptured Section 1250 gain on realty, and a $25,000 gain on the sale of bonds.

a. What is his 2018 tax liability?
b. How would your answer change if his ordinary taxable income was $550,000?

49. [LO 8.7] Bill had the following gains and losses on asset sales: $500 gain on stock held 11 months; a $2,300 gain on land held two years; $1,900 loss on gold coins held two years; $1,200 gain on antique toys held three years; and a $1,300 loss on investment land held six months. Determine Bill's taxable income and income tax for 2018 assuming Bill is married, has no dependents, files a joint return with his wife using the standard deduction, and their only other income is Bill's salary of $240,000.

Develop Planning Skills

50. [LO 8.1] Betty is a real estate dealer and has numerous properties for sale, many of which she owns. Her son is finishing his education and plans to go into the consulting business. Betty has committed at least $25,000 to help him out until the business becomes self-sufficient. Betty plans to dispose of one of the properties but wants to know if there is any way the gain on the property can be taxed at capital gains rates rather than as ordinary income.

51. [LO 8.2] Natalie expects her ordinary income to exceed $600,000 putting her in the 37 marginal percent tax bracket for 2018. So far this year, she has a $5,000 short-term capital loss. As of June 1, she is holding 1,000 shares of Dritco stock purchased on June 15 of last year for $15,000. The market value of the stock as of May 21 is $27,000. Lately the value of the stock has been decreasing and Natalie feels it may go down by $1,000 or so in the next month and probably stabilize thereafter. Advise Natalie as to the various courses of action she might take.

52. [LO 8.2] George has a short-term capital loss of $42,000 this year. His brother wants to buy a piece of land that George has owned as an investment for $60,000. The land's basis is only $20,000. George also knows that the land is appreciating in value every year, and he is not sure he should sell it now. He thinks if he holds on to the land for three more years, he will be able to sell it for $66,000 net of expenses. If George's ordinary income is taxed at 37 percent and he uses a 6 percent discount rate for all decisions, should he sell the land now?

53. [LO 8.2] Wilma had a number of stock transactions during the year that resulted in an $18,000 capital loss. She has one stock remaining in her portfolio and would realize a $16,000 capital gain if she sold it now. She believes this stock is going to continue to increase in value and is reluctant to sell it. What do you suggest that Wilma do?

54. [LO 8.2 & 8.3] Monique is planning to increase the size of the manufacturing business that she operates as a sole proprietorship. She has a number of older assets that she plans to replace as part of the expansion. To finance this expansion she will have to sell some of her personal assets. Because it is close to the end of the tax year, she can time the sales of the assets to take the greatest advantage of the tax laws. Monique's ordinary income of $600,000 currently places her in the 37 percent marginal tax bracket.

Following are the assets that Monique plans to sell; assume that she will realize their fair market value on the sales.

Business assets	Acquisition date	Fair market value	Depreciation method	Adjusted basis	Original cost
Truck	2001	$3,000	MACRS	$0	$20,000
Office building	1996	300,000	MACRS	160,000	285,000
Machine 1	2010	10,000	MACRS	25,000	80,000
Machine 2	2011	60,000	MACRS	55,000	95,000

Personal assets	Acquisition date	Fair market value	Original cost
Sculpture	1998	$400,000	$260,000
Painting	2005	400,000	525,000
100,000 shares ACC	2012	800,000	1,050,000
10,000 shares of BBL	2016	400,000	350,000

In addition to the proceeds from the sales of the business assets, Monique needs a minimum of an additional $800,000 for her planned expansion. Which assets should Monique sell to minimize her tax liability on the sales of the business and personal assets?

55. [LO 8.6] Joy purchased a home in Maine on December 15, 1999 for $250,000 and lived in it full-time until she purchased a second home in Florida on October 1, 2013 for $380,000. In 2013 and 2014 she continued to have her primary residence in Maine. On October 1, 2015, however, she changed her primary residence to Florida. She needs to sell one of these homes before the end of 2018 as she needs cash for an investment opportunity. If she expects a minimum gain of $200,000 on either home, which home do you recommend she sell?

Think Outside the Text

These questions require answers that are beyond the material that is covered in this chapter.

56. [LO 8.1] Beth had been using an automobile for personal purposes. In year 2, when she started a business, she began to use the car exclusively for this business at a time when it was worth $12,000. She had purchased the auto in year 1 for $16,000.

a. Assuming that she takes $3,000 of depreciation on the auto and then sells it, how much gain or loss does she recognize and what is its character if the amount realized is $8,000?

b. How would your answer change if she realizes $14,000?

57. [LO 8.1] Mary had the following transactions involving BMN stock:

Date	Shares purchased	Shares sold	Price per share	Total price
July 2, year 2	150		$5.00	$ 750
April 9, year 3	250		6.00	1,500
May 4, year 3		200	7.00	1,400
November 5, year 3	200		6.50	1,300
April 12, year 4		150	4.00	600

a. Determine Mary's gain or loss on each sale, assuming the shares are not specifically identified.

b. Determine Mary's gain or loss on the second sale if she specifically identifies the shares as coming from the November 5 of year 3 purchase.

58. [LO 8.3] If the netting process for capital gains really has no impact on corporations, why do you think it still remains as part of the tax law?

59. [LO 8.3] In 2018, Gregory, a single person, had $450,000 of ordinary taxable income. He sold Section 1202 stock at a taxable gain of $45,000, his art collection at a taxable gain of $102,000, and stock at a taxable gain of $55,000. Compare the tax result if Congress would simplify the capital gains tax provisions by having a single 20 percent capital gains rate versus the current capital gains tax provisions now in effect for 2018.

60. [LO 8.6] What are the policy reasons for allowing a portion of the gain on a personal residence to escape taxation?

Search the Internet

61. [LO 8.2] Locate the Schedule D and the accompanying instructions for both an individual and a corporation on the IRS website, *www.irs.gov*. Compare the length of the two forms and the instructions as they appear on the website. Summarize your findings.

62. [LO 8.6] Using the IRS website, *www.irs.gov*, locate the information and instructions for reporting the sale of a personal residence. Write a summary of what the taxpayer needs to do to elect Section 121 gain exclusion and how the sale is reported.

Identify the Issues

Identify the issues or problems suggested by the following situations. State each issue as a question.

63. [LO 8.1] Kwan Lu bought 100 shares of Duchco stock on July 25, year 3, for $1,000. The company declared bankruptcy on July 8 of year 5, and his stock became worthless.

64. [LO 8.1] The Gallagher Farms has been in business for a number of years. During the peak planting and harvesting season, it hired a number of temporary workers. To house the temporary workers, it built three buildings that were essentially dormitories that had bathing and sleeping facilities. It provided meals in a central kitchen with an attached dining area. The dormitories were built in 1983 and depreciated under ACRS accelerated methods. Recently, the state declared that the buildings were inadequate for the workers. Gallagher Farms has decided to sell the buildings and the portion of the land on which they sit. It expects to have a $100,000 gain on the land and a $75,000 gain on the sale of the buildings.

65. [LO 8.1 & 8.3] Martco, a manufacturer and seller of eyeglasses and contact lenses, purchased all the stock of Fetco, a manufacturer of hearing aids. Management of Martco quickly had second thoughts about keeping Fetco in business and liquidated the company. Martco was unsuccessful selling the hearing aids to customers, although a few small lots were sold to several retail outlets before the balance was sold to one distributor at $100,000 profit.

66. [LO 8.6] Geralyn and Marco sold their home and moved into a smaller home. They used their Section 121 election to exclude their $20,000 gain on the sale of the larger home. Six months after they moved into the smaller home, Geralyn died. Two months later Marco had a stroke and was in the hospital for one month and in a rehabilitation center for another seven months. At the end of that time, Marco moved back to his home. Three months later, he put the home up for sale and sold it within one month at a gain of $185,000 and moved out.

Develop Research Skills

67. [LO 8.1] A number of specific transactions do not necessarily follow the general tax provisions applicable to property transactions. Following are a group of transactions that are subject to specific tax provisions. For each of the situations, you are to answer the questions and cite the source for your answer.

a. Martin, a securities dealer, bought 100 shares of Datacard stock on April 5 of year 5 for $10,500. Before the end of that day, he identified the stock as being held for investment purposes.

   1. Never having held the stock for sale to customers, he sold the stock on May 22 of year 6 for $11,500. How much and what kind of gain or loss does he have?

   2. Assume that later in year 5 he starts trying to sell the stock to customers and succeeds in selling it on May 1 of year 6 for $9,000. How much and what kind of gain or loss does he have?

b. Ruth subdivided a piece of real estate she had owned for seven years into 12 lots. Each lot was apportioned a $10,000 basis. In year 2, she sold four lots for $15,000 apiece with selling expenses of $500 per lot.

   1. How much and what kind of gain or loss does Ruth have?

   2. If in year 3 she sold two more lots for $20,000 apiece and incurred selling expenses of $500 per lot, how much and what kind of gain or loss does she have?

c. For 60 years, Shakia owned 1,000 acres of land in Kentucky on which coal was being mined under a royalty arrangement. Shakia received $164,000 in the current tax year in royalties. The coal's adjusted basis for depletion was $37,000. Determine the amount and type of gain Shakia realizes on the income.

d. Howard owned a large farm on which he raised a variety of farm animals. Determine the type of gain or loss he would realize on the following sales:

   1. a six-month-old calf

   2. a one-and-one-half-year-old foal

   3. six-week-old chickens

   4. a 6-year-old bull

   5. a 12-year-old mare

   6. six-month-old lambs

   7. a 2-year-old ram

68. [LO 8.1] A subsidiary of Corporation A, an electrical utility located in Springfield, and a subsidiary of Corporation B, a diversified manufacturer also located in Springfield, formed a joint venture under the general partnership laws of their state. The partnership was formed to construct and ultimately operate another electrical generating plant. Sufficient excess space was provided at the plant site to accommodate substantial future additions to the initial generating equipment. Three years after construction of the generating equipment had been started and was 50 percent complete, the partnership on the advice of its financial counselors, began negotiations with a consortium of businessmen for the possible sale and leaseback of the generating equipment. Thirteen months later, when the plant was complete, the deal was finalized with the consortium for the sale and leaseback of the generating equipment. The sale resulted in a gain of $500,000 that the partnership treated as $250,000 of Section 1231 gain and $250,000 as ordinary income. Was the partnership correct in its determination of the type of gain recognized?

69. [LO 8.1] Sheralyn was in the wholesale distribution business for pecans and peanuts grown in Georgia. She and her brother owned and operated several warehouses. Seven years ago, they purchased property for another warehouse in the eastern part of Georgia because the nut crop had been getting progressively larger over the past several years. Early last year, they had plans drawn up for the warehouse and had gotten several bids from contractors. Unfortunately, Sheralyn's brother was killed in an auto accident just days before they were to sign papers to begin the construction. Sheralyn knew that she would not be able to manage their existing warehouses and oversee the construction of this new facility. She abandoned plans to construct the warehouse and put the property up for sale. It was sold early this year at a $125,000 loss. How should Sheralyn treat the loss on the sale?

Fill-in the Forms

70. [LO 8.2] Go to the IRS website (*www.irs.gov*) and print Schedule D for Form 1040 and Form 8949. Compute the net effect of the following asset sales on Gineen Tibeau's taxable income using Form 8949 and Schedule D:

a. 100 shares of ABC stock; original cost = $4,000; selling price = $6,000
b. $5,000 in CDF bonds; original cost = $5,100; selling price = $4,950
c. Original Dali drawing; cost = $23,000; selling price = $31,000
d. 200 shares of GHI stock; original cost = $8,000; selling price = $6,400
e. 5,000 shares of XYZ stock; original cost = $20,000; selling price = $12,000
f. All assets except the CDF bonds have been held for more than one year.

71. [LO 8.3] Go to the IRS website (*www.irs.gov*) and print Form 4797: *Sales of Business Property*. Complete Form 4797 for the following sales of machinery on December 20, year 6:

Machine	Cost	Date acquired	Cost recovery	Selling price
A	$45,000	April 24, year 2	$25,000	$25,000
B	$75,000	March 5, year 1	$67,000	$18,000
C	$63,000	June 18, year 4	$21,000	$51,000
D	$87,000	Nov. 10, year 5	$18,000	$93,000

ANSWERS TO TEST YOURSELF

1. **b. car = capital; truck = ordinary; land = Section 1231.** The car is a personal-use asset; the truck cannot be a Section 1231 asset as it has not been held for more than one year; the land was to be used in the business and is not an investment.

2. **c. $8,000 ordinary income from look-back; $10,000 long-term capital gain.** Only $7,000 of the net Section 1231 gain becomes long-term capital gain. $8,000 must be treated as ordinary income due to the Section 1231 look-back rules.

3. **d. deduct none of the capital losses.** The corporation must carry back the entire net capital loss as a short-term capital loss to year 2.

4. **c. $100 gain.** ($1,200 × 75%) – [($4,000 × 75%) – $2,200] = $100 gain; the depreciation applies to the 75 percent business portion only and only 75 percent of the proceeds apply to that portion.

5. **a. $50,000 ordinary loss and a $10,000 capital loss.** $50,000 of the loss is an ordinary loss under Section 1244. The remaining loss is a long-term capital loss; he can deduct $3,000 of this loss from ordinary income in the current year but that does not change its character.

Tax-Deferred Exchanges

CHAPTER 9

LEARNING OBJECTIVES

After completing this chapter, you should be able to:

9.1 Identify those transactions that affect the recognition of all or part of a realized gain or loss.

9.2 Understand the provisions affecting exchanges of like-kind properties eligible for gain deferral, determine boot's effect on gain recognition, and calculate the basis and holding period of exchanged properties.

9.3 Apply the involuntary conversion provisions, including applicable tax-deferrals, to qualifying casualties, thefts, and condemnations.

9.4 Recognize other exchanges or dispositions qualifying for specific non-recognition or deferral provisions.

9.5 Understand the basic tax consequences of transferring asset ownership to a sole proprietorship, corporation, or partnerships.

9.6 Describe a corporate reorganization and its basic tax consequences.

CHAPTER OUTLINE

This chapter introduces several types of common tax-deferred transactions that taxpayers can use to their advantage when planning asset exchanges or transfers. Taxpayers who sell or exchange property are usually required to recognize gain or loss immediately unless a specific provision in the tax law allows deferral. Taxpayers can defer gain recognition in certain types of exchanges if receipt of some or all of the proceeds are deferred because taxpayers may not have the "wherewithal to pay" taxes due on the realized gain immediately. Two taxpayers who simply exchange qualifying like-kind business assets have not changed their relative economic positions. Neither has received anything with which to pay a tax. Thus, any gain or loss is deferred until disposition of the replacement asset.

Taxpayers suffer involuntary conversions when property is damaged, destroyed, or taken due to a casualty, theft, or condemnation because of circumstances beyond their control. Although taxpayers experience a loss of property, they may realize a gain for tax purposes if their insurance proceeds exceed the property basis. Taxpayers could experience financial hardship if required to recognize and pay taxes on a realized gain in such circumstances. Thus, gain recognition is deferred if all insurance proceeds are used to repair the damaged property or obtain qualified replacement property.

Some transactions, such as like-kind exchanges, defer losses as well as gains. If the taxpayer wants to recognize the loss rather than deferring it, the relevant provisions must be understood so that the transaction qualifies for loss recognition. Other deferral provisions, such as installment sales in which gain is recognized over the time period that sale proceeds are received, apply only to gains and not to losses.

An important set of deferral provisions allows taxpayers to transfer assets to sole proprietorships, partnerships, or controlled corporations in exchange for an ownership interest in the business. These provisions allow the tax laws to remain neutral in relation to the taxpayer's selection of business form.

Complex tax laws affect the reorganization of corporations through mergers and acquisitions. Adherence by all parties to the specific provisions applicable to each type of reorganization is necessary to defer gains. An explanation of the various types of reorganizations is provided in the appendix to this chapter.

SETTING THE STAGE—AN INTRODUCTORY CASE

Perry Winkle Corporation had held a large tract of land adjacent to its manufacturing facility for a number of years for future expansion. November 12 of last year, the state condemned 30 percent of the corporation's total land for a highway and access ramps, taking most of the land held for expansion. Perry Winkle received $500,000, the fair market value of the land, which had a basis of $100,000.

This year, one of Perry Winkle's new products far exceeded its anticipated first-year sales and the corporation needs to expand as soon as possible. The company received an offer from one of its current suppliers to purchase its current facilities at a fair price. The sale, however, would result in a large gain in addition to the gain on the condemned property. The corporation needs to conserve its cash for expansion. What plans can you devise for the corporation so it can defer as much of any realized gains as possible? We will return to this case at the end of this chapter.

9.1 BASICS OF TAX-DEFERRED EXCHANGES

A **tax-deferred exchange** is a transaction in which the recognition of all or part of a realized gain or loss is postponed to a later period. A number of events permit the deferral of gain or loss, such as like-kind exchanges, casualty losses, condemnations, and wash sales. In some cases, both gains and losses are deferred (like-kind exchanges), or in others only gains (condemnations) or losses (wash sales) are deferred. When recognition is deferred, it is excluded from current income. The gain or loss will usually be recognized at some point in the future, however, in a tax-deferred exchange.

The ability to postpone gain recognition has tax advantages due to the time value of money.

Example 9.1

Jordan, a single taxpayer in the 20 percent capital gains tax bracket, plans to dispose of 20 acres of investment land. If he sells the land, he will have a long-term capital gain of $400,000 and owe a tax of $80,000 ($400,000 × 20% capital gains tax rate). If Jordan can arrange a qualifying like-kind exchange and postpone gain recognition for 10 years, the present value of the $80,000 tax paid in 10 years, at a 6 percent discount rate, is $44,640 ($80,000 × .558). At a 10 percent discount rate, the present value is only $30,880 ($80,000 × .386). If he can postpone the gain for 20 years at 6 percent, the present value is $24,960 ($80,000 × .312).[1]

[1] This example excludes the 3.8% net investment income surtax (see Chapter 5) and assumes that tax rates remain constant (see Chapter 2 for present value concepts).

This example demonstrates that (1) postponing gain recognition for a longer period and (2) a higher discount rate provide greater tax savings. By similar reasoning, the longer a loss is postponed and the higher the discount rate, the less valuable a loss.

The previous chapter included explanations of the nonrecognition of gains on the sale of certain property, including gain on the sale of qualified small business stock under Section 1202 and on the sale of a personal residence. Table 9.1 provides a list of some of the more common nonrecognition provisions (discussed previously) and introduces the tax-deferral provisions discussed in this chapter. The Section 1244 provision, discussed in Chapter 8 is neither a deferral nor nonrecognition provision, but changes the character of the loss recognized.

Table 9.1 Common Nonrecognition and Tax-Deferral Provisions

	Tax deferral		Nonrecognition	
Nonrecognition provision	**Gain**	**Loss**	**Gain**	**Loss**
Wash sales		×		
Related-party sales		×*		
Rollover of qualified small business stock into another qualified small business stock	×			
Sales of qualified small business stock			×	
Sales of personal-use assets				×
Like-kind exchanges	×	×		
Involuntary conversions	×			
Sales of personal residence			Limited	×
Installment sales	×			
Exchanges of property between divorcing spouses	×	×		
Exchanges of qualifying insurance policies	×	×		
Exchanges of common stock for common stock in the same corporation	×	×		
Transfers to corporations and partnerships by owners	×	×		
Reorganizations of corporations	×	×		

*The loss may offset gain realized on a subsequent sale of the property by the related party.

The at-risk rules and the passive loss rules may postpone the deductibility of losses by the S corporation shareholders and partners in partnerships. A basic explanation of the at-risk and passive loss deferral rules is included in Chapter 11.

9.1.1 BASIS ADJUSTMENTS

The **basis adjustment** as part of a tax-deferred property transaction provides for the deferral of gains and losses until the subsequent disposition of the assets at later date. If a gain is deferred, the acquired asset's basis is reduced by the deferred gain.[2] This downward basis adjustment increases the gain on a subsequent disposition. Similarly, a deferred loss results in a basis increase for the acquired asset.[3] Later, when the asset is sold this increased basis causes a realized loss or a reduced gain on a subsequent disposition.[4]

[2] §1031(d).

[3] Ibid.

[4] The loss disallowance on related party transactions is an exception to the usual basis adjustment on a deferral transaction as explained later in this chapter.

Example 9.2

Peter exchanges land with a basis of $20,000 for other realty valued at $30,000 in a qualified like-kind exchange. Peter realizes a $10,000 gain ($30,000 – $20,000) on the land that is deferred. The basis of the realty received is $20,000, its purchase price (fair market value) reduced by the deferred gain ($30,000 price paid – $10,000 deferred gain). This basis adjustment builds a $10,000 gain into the basis of the realty that may be recognized on a future transaction. If Peter sells the realty next year for $35,000, Peter will recognize a gain of $15,000 ($35,000 – $20,000 adjusted basis). This $15,000 gain consists of the $10,000 gain that was built in due to the gain deferral, plus the $5,000 gain from additional appreciation.

There are several types of deferral transactions. In some, the basis of the original asset follows the asset to the new owner (the carryover basis); in others, the basis of the original asset is substituted for the basis of the asset acquired (the substituted basis).

Example 9.3

James joins three friends in forming a new corporation. The formation of a corporation is a tax-deferral provision. James contributes an asset valued at $400,000 to the corporation in exchange for stock valued at $400,000. James's basis in the asset is $250,000 at the time of its contribution to the corporation. James does not recognize the $150,000 gain on the asset transfer; instead, he substitutes his $250,000 basis in the asset for his basis in the corporate stock received. The corporation "carries over" James's basis and also has a $250,000 basis in the asset contributed. If James later sells the stock for its $400,000 value, he will recognize a $150,000 ($400,000 – $250,000) gain at the time of sale. If the corporation sells the asset it received for its $400,000 value, it will recognize a $150,000 ($400,000 – $250,000) gain on the sale.

9.1.2 HOLDING PERIOD

When an asset's basis is determined by reference to the basis of another asset (either through carryover, substitution, or basis adjustment), the holding period of the old asset is added to the holding period of the new asset.[5]

9.2 LIKE-KIND EXCHANGES—SECTION 1031

A **like-kind exchange** is an effective planning tool to defer recognition of gain on the disposition of business or investment property. A number of requirements must be met, however, for a transaction to qualify as a like-kind exchange. The most important characteristic is that the exchange consists solely of noncash qualifying properties.[6] If *only* qualifying properties are exchanged, no gain or loss is recognized by any of the parties to the exchange. This is not an elective provision; if the transaction qualifies as a like-kind exchange, no gain or loss can be recognized.

Example 9.4

PRT Corporation exchanges a piece of land for an office building in a qualifying like-kind exchange. If PRT sells the land at its fair market value, it must recognize a $200,000 gain. PRT expects to use the office building for at least 15 years before it would sell it. By arranging a like-kind exchange, PRT postpones recognizing the $200,000 gain for at least 15 years. PRT is in the 21 percent tax bracket and saves $42,000 ($200,000 × 21%) in taxes this year. The present value of a $42,000 tax paid after 15 years (assuming no change in tax rates and a discount rate of 6 percent) is $17,514 ($42,000 × .417). The company saves over $24,000 by deferring the taxes through a qualifying exchange rather than a sale of the land.

[5] There is a more complete discussion of holding period in the preceding chapter.
[6] §1031(a)(1).

The inclusion of cash or other nonqualifying property may not prevent the use of the like-kind exchange provision, but the parties may have to recognize some of the gain realized. Cash and other nonqualifying property received as part of the exchange are considered **boot**—something added to equalize the difference in property values. Gain (but not loss) must be recognized to the extent of the *lesser* of the gain realized on the exchange or the fair market value of the boot received.[7] Boot only affects recognition of a realized gain; it has no effect on a realized loss.

Example 9.5

The Kilgore Corporation owns a small warehouse but needs a larger unit due to recent growth. One of its suppliers will trade a larger warehouse it no longer uses for Kilgore's smaller one plus $200,000 cash to equalize the difference in values. The exchange qualifies as a like-kind exchange, but the $200,000 cash payment by Kilgore is boot. Kilgore recognizes no gain or loss on the exchange because it *gave* boot. The supplier may have to recognize a gain of up to the $200,000 cash for the boot—the lesser of the gain realized or the boot received. If the supplier realizes a loss on the exchange, neither Kilgore nor the supplier would have any current gain or loss recognition as only boot received triggers gain recognition.

TAX PLANNING

A taxpayer who wants to recognize a loss should avoid qualifying for nonrecognition by structuring the exchange so that the properties fail to qualify as like-kind or by engaging in a sale instead of an exchange.

9.2.1 QUALIFYING PROPERTIES

The nonrecognition provisions of Section 1031 apply to business or investment property only, not to personal-use property. In addition, any exchanges after 2017 cannot be of tangible personalty or real property held primarily for sale.[8]

Almost any type of business or investment realty can be exchanged for any other type of business or investment realty as long as both properties are situated in the United States. For example, exchanging a factory building (including land) in Michigan for undeveloped investment land in Hawaii or exchanging a rental apartment building (including land) in Ohio for a shopping mall (including land) in New Jersey would both qualify as like-kind exchanges.[9]

9.2.2 DETERMINING REALIZED GAIN OR LOSS AND THE EFFECT OF BOOT

Realized gain on an exchange is the amount realized less the adjusted basis of the property surrendered. The **amount realized** is the total of the cash, fair market value of the like-kind property and any nonlike-kind property received less fees incurred. If only qualifying like-kind property is received, neither party recognizes gain or loss.

The difference in the fair market values on exchanges of like-kind properties is a practical problem that can arise. The party with the lesser-valued property may have to transfer additional property (boot) to the other party to equalize the values. Although the transaction may still qualify as a like-kind exchange, there is now a sale element embedded in the transaction for the boot received. The taxpayer receiving boot now has the wherewithal with which to pay taxes and, therefore, recognize, some or all of the gain realized.[10] The **recognized gain** is the *lesser* of the realized gain or the value of the boot received. The **deferred gain** equals the difference between realized and recognized gain.

---

[7] §1031(b).

[8] Prior to 2018, exchanges of tangible personalty such as an automobile exchanged for another automobile could qualify for like kind exchanges.

[9] An improvement to land (e.g., a building) cannot be exchanged for land under the like-kind provision unless the land to which the improvement is attached is also exchanged as part of the transaction.

[10] §1031(b).

Example 9.6

Joann exchanges a small apartment building (including land) with an adjusted basis of $46,000 for a piece of undeveloped land valued at $60,000 and $5,000 cash. She paid fees related to the exchange of $7,000. Joann's amount realized is $58,000 ($60,000 + $5,000 – $7,000) and her realized gain is $12,000 ($58,000 – $46,000). Joann recognizes $5,000 gain on the exchange, the lesser of the boot received ($5,000) and the realized gain ($12,000). She defers $7,000 ($12,000 – $5,000) of the gain.

The *giving up of boot does not* affect the gain recognition on the like-kind property exchanged. If, however, the boot given up has a fair market value greater or smaller than its basis, gain or loss is recognized. Boot, by definition, is not part of the like-kind property and does not qualify for nonrecognition of gain or loss.

The assumption of liabilities as part of a like-kind exchange is treated as boot and can lead to gain recognition. Liability relief is treated as cash (boot) received, with the cash then used to satisfy the liability.[11]

Example 9.7

Grunt Corporation exchanges an office building with a $125,000 mortgage for land valued at $325,000 owned by Tug Corporation. Tug assumes Grunt's $125,000 mortgage, relieving Grunt of the debt. The office building has a basis and fair market value of $230,000 and $450,000, respectively. The amount realized by Grunt is $450,000 ($325,000 + $125,000); its gain realized is $220,000 ($450,000 – $230,000). Because the mortgage assumption is considered cash (boot) received, Grunt recognizes $125,000 of gain on the transaction. It defers the remaining $95,000 ($220,000 – $125,000) of gain.

If both parties to an exchange assume the other party's mortgage, the liabilities offset each other and only the net liability is considered boot given or received. Actual cash (or other boot) received, however, cannot offset any part of the mortgage assumed by either party on the exchange.

Example 9.8

Refer to the previous example, but assume the fair market value of the land Grunt Corporation received from Tug Corporation is $400,000 but is encumbered by a $75,000 mortgage that Grunt assumes. The amount realized by Grunt is still $450,000 consisting of $400,000 fair market value of land plus $50,000 ($125,000 – $75,000) net liability relief. Grunt's realized gain remains $220,000 ($450,000 – $230,000), but its net mortgage relief is only $50,000, the limit of its recognized gain. Grunt defers $170,000 ($220,000 – $50,000) of gain.

If there is no mortgage on Grunt's property and Grunt receives $125,000 cash instead of mortgage relief, none of Tug's mortgage assumed can offset any portion of the cash received. The cash received is boot. Grunt recognizes gain of $125,000 and can defer only $95,000 ($220,000 – $125,000) of the gain.

Several points are important to remember with like-kind exchanges:

1. There must be an exchange of qualifying business or investment realty.
2. No gain is recognized unless boot is received.
3. The amount of gain recognized is the *lesser* of the fair market value of the boot received or the gain realized.

[11] §1031(d).

4. The receipt of boot only causes realized gain recognition, not loss recognition.
5. Net liability relief is considered boot.

9.2.3 BASIS AND HOLDING PERIOD OF LIKE-KIND PROPERTY

The basis of the like-kind property received in a qualifying exchange is its fair market value less the unrecognized (deferred) gain or plus the unrecognized loss. If no boot is involved in the exchange, the basis of the property given simply carries over to the basis of the property received.[12] If boot is received, the basis of the like-kind property remains its fair market value, adjusted for deferred gain or loss. Basis of any boot received is always its fair market value.

The **holding period** for like-kind property received in a qualifying exchange includes the holding period of the property surrendered. The holding period for boot always begins on the date of the like-kind exchange.[13]

Example 9.9

Nomad Corporation exchanges a small building acquired on January 4, year 1, for a parking lot that ABC Corporation owned for 20 years and a bond with a fair market value of $20,000. The building has a basis of $50,000 and a fair market value of $75,000. The parking lot has a fair market value of $55,000 and a basis of $40,000. Nomad Corporation realizes a $25,000 ($55,000 + $20,000 – $50,000) gain on the exchange. It recognizes $20,000 of gain equal to the bond (boot) received and $5,000 of the gain is deferred. The parking lot's basis is $50,000 ($55,000 – $5,000 deferred gain) and its holding period begins on January 4, year 1. The bond's basis is its $20,000 fair market value and its holding period begins on the date of the exchange.

ABC has a $15,000 gain realized ($75,000 – $40,000 – $20,000) on the exchange, all of which is deferred because it receives no boot. Its basis in the building is $60,000 ($75,000 – $15,000 deferred gain), and the parking lot's 20-year holding period is added to the building. If the basis of the bond that ABC transferred was more (or less) than its $20,000 fair market value, ABC would recognize the loss (or gain) on its transfer to Nomad.

The Code provides an alternative basis calculation that defines the basis of the property received as the basis of the property surrendered, plus the adjusted basis of boot *given* plus gain recognized less the fair market value of boot received.[14]

Example 9.10

Using the information in the previous example, Nomad's basis in the land is equal to the following:

	$50,000	basis of building surrendered
Plus	0	boot given
Plus	20,000	gain recognized
Minus	20,000	fair market value of the boot received
Equals	$50,000	basis of land received

ABC's basis in the building is as follows:

	$40,000	basis of parking lot surrendered
Plus	20,000	boot given
Plus	0	gain recognized
Minus	0	fair market value of boot received
Equals	$60,000	basis of the building received

These are the same bases calculated by the first formula.

[12] Ibid.

[13] §1223 and Reg. §1.1223-1(a).

[14] §1031(d). The Code also includes a subtraction for loss recognized, but loss is not recognized on a like-kind exchange. This alternative formula is used later in this chapter to determine the basis of stock received when assets are transferred to a corporation.

When loss is deferred, the basis of the new property is its fair market value increased by the deferred loss.[15]

9.2.4 INDIRECT EXCHANGES

A direct exchange of properties may not be possible if there aren't two or more parties willing to exchange properties. Taxpayers do not have to give up on an exchange transaction and the potential gain deferral, however. This dilemma can be solved in two ways, but both involve third parties and some additional costs. In the first, the taxpayer hires a third-party intermediary. The intermediary purchases the desired property from the owner. The taxpayer and the intermediary then exchange properties and the intermediary sells the taxpayer's original property. The taxpayer has a qualifying exchange, but the seller of the property and the intermediary treat the transactions as taxable events. A reverse exchange can also qualify in which replacement property is acquired before the taxpayer transfers the like-kind property.

Example 9.11

Corrine has some investment land recently rezoned residential, which she wants to trade for land on which to build a factory. She locates a suitable piece of land owned by Billie, but Billie refuses to exchange properties because their families were involved in a business dispute years ago. Corrine asks Sam, a licensed real estate broker, to be a third-party intermediary and purchase the property from Billie. After Sam purchases the property, Corrine exchanges her land for the property. Sam then sells Corrine's land. Corrine has a qualifying like-kind exchange because she exchanged investment land for business property, but Billie and Sam have taxable transactions.

The alternate way to structure a like-kind exchange is through use of the nonsimultaneous exchange provisions. In a nonsimultaneous exchange, the taxpayer sells the property to be exchanged, but a third party intermediary holds all proceeds preventing the taxpayer's access to any cash or other property received in the sale. The taxpayer has 45 days from the date the property is sold to identify like-kind property to be exchanged and 180 days to complete acquisition of the identified property using the original proceeds that are now released by the intermediary.[16]

Example 9.12

Fianola's neighbor offered to purchase her entire farm at a very good price, but Fianola did not want to recognize the substantial gain on the sale. Instead, she hires an escrow agent as an intermediary to close the sale and hold all the proceeds until she locates suitable investment land. The sale closes on May 25. Fianola has until July 9 to locate the property she wants and until November 21 for the intermediary to close the purchase of the desired property in Fianola's name, using the escrowed proceeds from the sale of the farm.

In either of these indirect exchanges, the taxpayer must weigh the costs of using a third-party intermediary with the tax savings, but with multimillion-dollar properties and significant gains to defer, these savings normally far outweigh the costs.

TAX PLANNING

Although gain deferral is usually desirable, there are situations in which the immediate recognition of gain may be preferable, for example, when taxpayers have net operating or capital loss carryovers or if they expect to be in significantly higher marginal tax brackets in future years.

[15] The alternative formula can also be used for deferred-loss situations by inserting zero for gain recognized.

[16] A nonsimultaneous exchange is sometimes referred to as a *Starker* exchange named after the landmark court case that first allowed deferred exchanges. *Starker v.* U.S., 602 F2d 1341, 44 AFTR2d 79-5525, 79-2 USTC 9451. The taxpayer may identify up to three alternative like-kind properties but must obtain only one to close the exchange. Reg. §1.1031(d)-1(c)(4).

Example 9.13

Quorum Corporation can sell an office building with a basis of $2,500,000 for $4,000,000 and purchase a replacement building for $4,000,000. Alternatively, it can exchange the building for another building with a fair market value of $3,500,000. Both buildings are equally attractive to Quorum. The owner of this second building is unwilling to pay Quorum anything additional to make up for the difference in appraisals. Should Quorum sell the building at its fair market value and purchase the $4,000,000 property, or should it make the exchange? Assume Quorum has a 21 percent tax rate in all years, depreciates the building evenly over 40 years, and has a 6 percent discount rate.

If Quorum sells the building, it has a recognized gain of $1,500,000 and a tax of $315,000 ($1,500,000 × 21%) on that gain. Its basis in the purchased building will be $4,000,000. If it exchanges the buildings, it has no recognized gain, but its basis in the new building is only $2,500,000 ($3,500,000 – $1,000,000 deferred gain). It has increased depreciation deductions of $37,500 annually on the sale option over the 40 years, which reduce its taxes by $7,875 ($37,500 × 21%), the equivalent of an annuity of $7,875 per year for 40 years. At a 6 percent discount rate the annuity has a value of $118,487 ($7,875 × 15.046). Thus, if Quorum exchanges the building, it has tax savings of $196,513 ($315,000 – $118,487).

Alternatively, assume Quorum Corporation has a $1,200,000 net operating loss. It can offset all but $300,000 of the gain on the sale with this loss. Its tax liability of $63,000 (21% × $300,000) in the current year is $55,487 ($118,487 – $63,000) less than the tax savings over the next 40 years for the increased depreciation deductions.

9.3 INVOLUNTARY CONVERSIONS

Taxpayers can involuntarily "dispose" of property due to circumstances beyond their control. **Involuntary conversions** occur when property is damaged, destroyed or taken due to thefts, casualties, or condemnations. A **theft** loss includes embezzlement, larceny, and robbery but does not include simply losing items. A **casualty** requires some form of sudden, unexpected, and unusual event that affects the taxpayer's property, such as fires, floods, hurricanes, tornadoes, vandalism, and mine disasters. The event must be identifiable, and it must directly affect the taxpayer's property. The erosion or destruction of property that takes place over a period of time, such as damage from mold or termites, does not meet the requirement of suddenness. Events that indirectly affect value, such as an area becoming flood prone due to excessive development, are not casualties. A **condemnation** is the lawful taking of property for its fair market value by a governmental unit under the right of eminent domain (such as for highway expansion).

When insured property is subject to a casualty or theft, the difference between the amount of damage or loss and insurance proceeds (if covered) results in a net gain or loss. Taxpayers could have financial hardships if required to recognize and pay taxes on realized gains in these circumstances. Following the wherewithal-to-pay concept, gain is deferred if all insurance proceeds are used to repair the damaged property or to obtain qualified replacement property. If the property is uninsured, only loss is realized. Casualties and thefts are much more likely than condemnations to result in losses, even if insured, due to insurance policy deductibles.

9.3.1 CASUALTY AND THEFT LOSSES

Gains and losses sustained on casualties and thefts are not under a taxpayer's control and receive special tax treatment. Allowable losses from thefts and casualties are immediately deductible, but realized gains may be deferred if qualifying replacement property is acquired. Business and investment casualty losses and nondeferred gains are included as Section 1231 gains and losses.[17]

[17] Business property includes rental realty and property producing royalties. The basic taxation of Section 1231 gains and losses is discussed in the preceding chapter. The impact of involuntary conversions on the Section 1231 netting process is discussed later in this chapter.

Although most personal losses are not deductible, a limited deduction applies to casualty losses of personal-use property due to a federally declared disaster.

Measuring the Loss

To measure the loss on casualties and thefts, business and investment property are separated from personal-use property. The loss on business or investment property that is stolen or totally destroyed is always its adjusted basis at the time of the loss, regardless of the property's fair market value.[18] If the business or investment property is only partially destroyed, the loss is the *lesser* of its adjusted basis at the time of the loss or the difference in the property's fair market value immediately before and after the loss occurrence.[19]

Example 9.14

A fire destroyed part of the building and all the machinery inside that the Cairn Corporation used for manufacturing. The building had a basis of $450,000 and an estimated fair market value of $750,000 before the fire. Its fair market value after the fire is $400,000. The machinery had a basis of $320,000 and an estimated fair market value of $400,000 before the fire. Cairn has a loss of $350,000 on the partial destruction of the building (the lesser of the $450,000 basis and the $350,000 difference in its fair market value before and after) and a loss of $320,000 (its basis) on the complete destruction of the machinery.

The loss on personal-use property, whether completely or partially destroyed, is always the lesser of its adjusted basis at the time of the loss or the difference in the property's fair market value before and after the casualty. The loss on mixed-use property must be determined separately for the personal-use and business portions. Often, the difference in fair market value before and after a loss is not available.[20] In this case, the costs to restore the property may substitute for the amount of the loss if the repairs do not improve the property beyond its pre-loss condition and the value of the property after repairs does not exceed its pre-loss value.[21]

Example 9.15

Georgette's car was damaged when a tree fell on it during a hurricane. The loss was not insured because Georgette had forgotten to pay her insurance premium. The car cost $23,000; its value before the accident was $15,000 and $6,000 after the accident. Georgette's loss is $9,000, the difference between the car's value before and after the accident ($15,000 – $6,000). If Georgette could not establish the fair market value of the car before and after the accident, she could substitute her repair cost to restore the car to its pre-loss condition as the amount of her loss.

Insurance and Basis Considerations

Insurance proceeds for covered property on which there is a casualty or theft loss reduce the amount of the loss.[22] If the insurance proceeds are less than the loss, the excess of the total loss over the insurance proceeds is the maximum deductible loss. If the insurance proceeds exceed the loss, the taxpayer has a casualty gain.

[18] Taxpayers can recover their investment (basis) in an asset under the capital recovery doctrine.

[19] Reg. §1.165-7(a).

[20] Appraisals are readily available for the after-loss fair market value, but it may not be possible to obtain a valid pre-loss fair market value after the fact.

[21] Reg. §1.165-7(a)(2).

[22] §165(h)(4)(E). If covered, a taxpayer must file an insurance claim for damage to personal-use property.

Example 9.16

GDG Corporation had a computer stolen and a car totally destroyed when a truck hit it. The computer's basis was $1,200 and its fair market value was $800. Insurance paid $600 for this loss. The car's basis was $6,000 and its fair market value was $7,000. GDG received $6,500 from the insurance company for the car. GDG has a $600 loss on the computer ($1,200 basis – $600 insurance recovery) and a $500 gain on the car ($6,500 insurance recovery – $6,000 basis).

Expected insurance recoveries affect the timing of the loss deduction. If the taxpayer expects full payment for the loss, no deduction is allowed in the year of the loss. If the taxpayer expects only partial recovery, only the loss less the expected insurance recovery is deductible in the loss year. If the final settlement is less (more) than the amount expected, the taxpayer has a loss (income) in the settlement year.

Example 9.17

Cordero Corporation had $40,000 of damage to its manufacturing plant from a hurricane last year. It anticipated receiving an insurance settlement of $36,000 because its deductible was 10 percent of the loss. It deducted a $4,000 loss on last year's return for the amount the insurance was not expected to cover. This year Cordero learned that there was a specific provision for hurricanes that stated the first $5,000 loss was not covered at all and a 20 percent deductible applied to the balance. Thus, its insurance reimbursement was only $28,000 [$40,000 – $5,000 – (20% × $35,000)]. It deducts the additional $8,000 loss in the current year.

A taxpayer reduces the basis of property subject to a casualty for a deductible loss. If the insurance recovery covers all or part of the loss, the basis is reduced for the insurance recovery and any remaining deductible loss. If the taxpayer uses the insurance proceeds or other funds to repair the damaged property, the amount spent on repairs increases the property's basis.

Example 9.18

Crup Corporation's office building suffered $600,000 in damages from a fire. It received $500,000 from its insurance company and deducts the remaining $100,000 loss. The building had a $750,000 basis at the time of the loss. Crup reduces the basis of the property to $150,000 ($750,000 – $100,000 deduction – $500,000 insurance proceeds) for its $100,000 casualty loss deduction and the $500,000 of insurance proceeds. If the company spends $800,000 repairing and upgrading the building, its basis after repairs are complete is $950,000 ($150,000 + $800,000). If the building had not been insured, the final basis would be the same except that Crup would deduct the entire $600,000 loss ($750,000 – $600,000 loss + $800,000 repairs = $950,000).

Deductible Amount

To determine the **deductible loss** from casualties and thefts, business and individual taxpayers follow different tax treatments. A business with casualty and theft gains and losses on business and investment property enters these gains and losses in the Section 1231 netting process. The preceding chapter described the basic Section 1231 netting process, but there are several additional details specific to the treatment of involuntary conversions.

After all Section 1231 gains are adjusted for depreciation recapture, the remaining Section 1231 gains and all Section 1231 losses are separated into two baskets. The first basket contains only the gains and losses resulting from involuntary conversions specifically defined as *casualties* or *thefts* of Section 1231 and investment properties held for more than one year.[23]

[23] Section 1231 property includes realty and personalty used in a business and investment property such as properties held for the production of rents and royalties if held for more than one year.

The second basket contains the gains and losses from all *other* involuntary conversions (for example, condemnations) of Section 1231 and investment properties (held for more than one year) and the gains and losses from all other dispositions of Section 1231 properties. The netting procedure involves two steps:

Step 1. Net all gains and losses on assets in the first basket (casualty and theft gains and losses on Section 1231 and investment property held more than one year). If the result is a net loss, the net loss is deducted directly from ordinary income. Only a net *gain* continues to Step 2.

Step 2. Net all the gains and losses from the involuntary conversions of other Section 1231 and investment property (not considered in Step 1) with the net gains and losses from the remaining Section 1231 property dispositions and the *net gain* only from Step 1.

A corporation with a net loss at the end of Step 2 also deducts the net loss directly from ordinary income, providing an immediate deduction (the same as a net loss in Step 1).[24] If Step 2 results in a net gain, the corporation first applies the five-year look-back rule to this gain and then any remaining gain enters the capital asset netting process (discussed in the previous chapter).

The Section 1231 netting process for an individual taxpayer is the same as that for corporate taxpayers *unless* the individual has losses from the involuntary conversion of *investment* assets held for more than one year. Thus, if the individual has no losses from the involuntary conversion of *investment* property, the procedure is identical to that of corporations: net losses at Step 1 and 2 are deducted directly from income and a net gain at Step 2 is subject to the 5-year look-back rule with any remaining gain entering the capital asset netting process. If Bobbitt Corporation (in example 9.19) is a sole proprietorship, the Section 1231 netting process would be the same as there are no involuntary conversions of investment property.

Example 9.19

Bobbitt Corporation has a $400,000 casualty loss on a factory building, a $50,000 casualty gain on machinery (after depreciation recapture), a $200,000 Section 1231 gain on the condemnation of land, a $150,000 Section 1231 loss, a $210,000 Section 1231 loss, and a $120,000 Section 1231 gain.

Step 1. Net the $400,000 casualty loss with the $50,000 casualty gain = $350,000 net casualty loss that is deducted directly from ordinary income.

Step 2. Net the remaining gains and losses ($200,000 – $150,000 – $210,000 + $120,000) = a net $40,000 Section 1231 loss that is deducted directly from ordinary income.

Thus, Bobbitt has a total deduction of $390,000 for net Section 1231 losses. If Step 2 had resulted in a net Section 1231 gain instead of a loss, the corporation would treat the net gain as a long-term capital gain after applying the Section 1231 look-back rule.

If the Section 1231 netting process includes *any* losses from involuntary conversions of investment property (through theft, casualty or other involuntary conversion), the process is altered only for individual taxpayers and only if there is a net loss at the end of Step 1 and/or Step 2. In this case, the *losses* on the involuntarily converted investment assets are removed from the net loss total at the end of either Step 1 or Step 2. These losses are then deducted separately as itemized deductions.[25] The net loss (or a net gain) remaining after deducting the loss on investment assets separately, is included directly in ordinary income.

[24] Technically, the corporation includes all gain items as ordinary income and deducts all loss items from ordinary income.

[25] An individual's loss on the involuntary conversion of an investment asset was not subject to the 2 percent floor as were other miscellaneous itemized deductions. See Chapter 5.

Figure 9.1 illustrates the Section 1231 netting process.

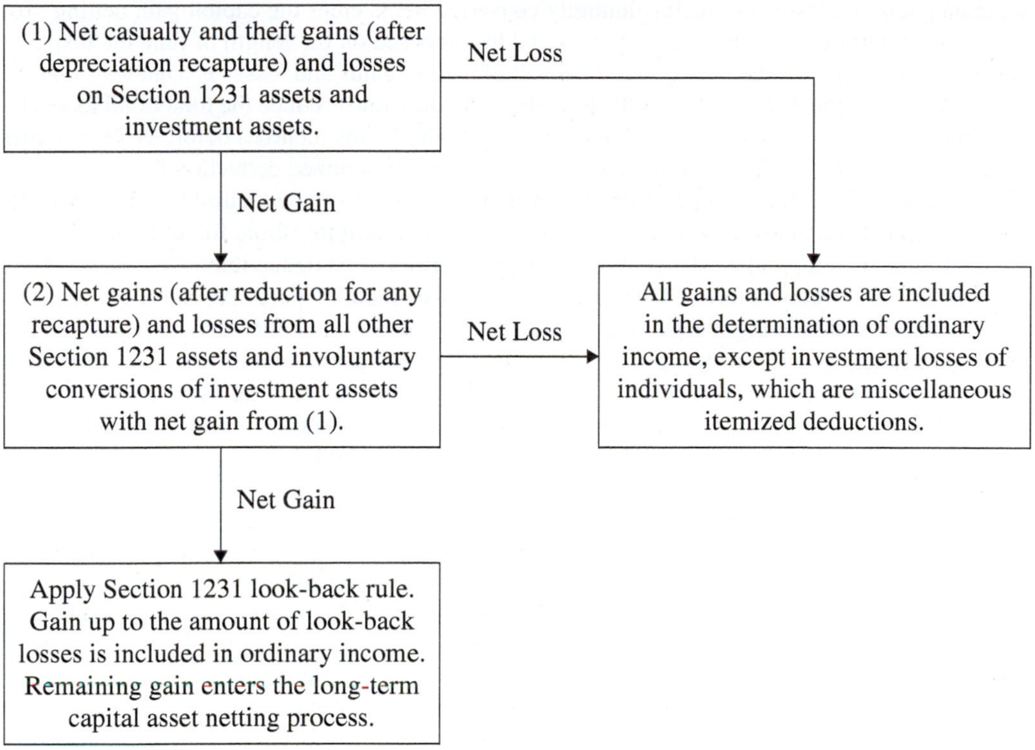

(1) Net casualty and theft gains (after depreciation recapture) and losses on Section 1231 assets and investment assets.
Net Loss
Net Gain
(2) Net gains (after reduction for any recapture) and losses from all other Section 1231 assets and involuntary conversions of investment assets with net gain from (1).
Net Loss
All gains and losses are included in the determination of ordinary income, except investment losses of individuals, which are miscellaneous itemized deductions.
Net Gain
Apply Section 1231 look-back rule. Gain up to the amount of look-back losses is included in ordinary income. Remaining gain enters the long-term capital asset netting process.

FIGURE 9.1
Section 1231 netting process

Example 9.20

Walter owns a sole proprietorship. One of his business computers and some artwork (investment property) were stolen from the business by an employee and were not recovered. The computer cost $2,400, had a basis of $1,100, and a fair market value of $900. The artwork cost $4,800 but was currently valued at $5,200. Walter has a $5,900 total casualty loss for the computer ($1,100) and the artwork ($4,800). He deducts the $1,100 loss directly from income as it is a business loss, but the $4,800 loss on the artwork is an itemized deduction because it is a theft loss of investment property.[26]

If Walter's business had been incorporated, the corporation could have deducted the entire $5,900 loss from ordinary income.

TAX PLANNING

Taxpayers generally have no control over the timing of the realized gains and losses from involuntary conversions, but they can control dispositions of other Section 1231 assets. If gains must be recognized from involuntary conversions in high marginal tax years, the taxpayer should consider disposing of loss assets to offset these gains. If losses occur in high marginal tax years, however, the taxpayer may benefit by postponing planned dispositions of appreciated property so the losses can be recognized.

A separate netting procedure applies to the casualty and theft gains and losses on an individual's personal-use property. Before entering this netting process, however, the value of each casualty or theft loss occurrence is first reduced for a basic $100 floor. This $100 floor applies to *each* loss occurrence (but has no effect on casualty gains) and reduces the loss for each separate event by $100.[27]

[26] Property transactions of a sole proprietorship are treated as incurred by the sole proprietor.

[27] This $100 floor applies only to the casualty losses of individual taxpayers and does not apply to casualty gains.

Next, all of the individual taxpayer's gains and losses (net of the $100 floor) on personal casualties and thefts are netted to yield either a net gain or a net loss. If the result is a net gain, the separate gains and losses on the involuntarily converted items enter the capital gain netting process as short-term or long-term capital gains and losses based on the length of time the taxpayer held the asset subject to the casualty. If the result of netting gains and losses is a net loss, there is a second limit on the deductibility of the loss; the individual must reduce the total of all losses by 10 percent of adjusted gross income. For personal casualty losses incurred before 2018 and after 2025, the loss amount, after applying these limitations, is an itemized deduction.[28]

The $100 loss reduction per event removes small losses from deductibility for individuals (similar to the deductible on an insurance policy). The 10 percent threshold for all losses requires the net loss to be fairly large relative to income for a portion to be deductible.

After 2017 (and before 2026) Congress limits deductible personal casualty losses to those incurred in a federally declared disaster area. An exemption applies to a taxpayer that has personal casualty gains for the year. An individual that has both personal casualty gains and personal casualty losses first reduces the amount of personal casualty gains by the amount of the nondisaster personal casualty losses. Any remaining personal casualty gains then reduce the taxpayer's deductible federal disaster losses. Any remaining federal disaster losses are deductible to the extent they exceed the 10 percent threshold.

Example 9.21

In 2018, Cheryl's adjusted gross income is $200,000. She has $40,000 of nondisaster personal casualty losses, $60,000 of federal disaster losses, and $50,000 of personal casualty gains for the year after applying the $100-per casualty floor to each loss. She first offsets her nondisaster casualty losses against her personal casualty gains, reducing the personal casualty gains to $10,000 ($50,000 gains − $40,000 nondisaster losses). To determine how much of the remaining $50,000 federal disaster losses ($60,000 disaster losses less $10,000 remaining gains) are deductible, she subtracts the 10 percent floor of $20,000 ($200,000 AGI × 10%) leaving $30,000 ($50,000 − $20,000) of deductible disaster losses.

Taxable Year of Deduction

Taxpayers deduct a theft loss in the year the theft is discovered, even if the theft occurred in a different tax year. Casualty losses, however, must be deducted in the year the casualty occurs since a casualty is usually the result of a specific, identifiable event such as a fire or storm. If a casualty is discovered after the taxpayer has filed a tax return for the year of the casualty, an amended return must be filed to claim the loss.

If the casualty occurs in an area that the president declares a disaster area, the taxpayer may elect to deduct the allowable casualty loss in the year prior to the year of occurrence. This allows the taxpayer to file an original or an amended return for the prior year to obtain a quick refund to speed recovery from the casualty. If the election is made, the taxpayer treats the casualty as having occurred in the year the deduction is claimed. A **presidentially declared disaster** occurs in an area that warrants federal assistance under the Disaster Relief and Emergency Assistance Act.[29]

TAX PLANNING

A business taxpayer generally is better off claiming the eligible casualty deduction in the year prior to the casualty for a disaster in a presidentially declared disaster area. An individual, however, should carefully consider which year would be more advantageous due to the reduction

[28] If an individual uses the standard deduction (does not itemize), the casualty or theft loss cannot be deducted. For 2016 and 2017, however, individuals were allowed to add a net disaster loss to their standard deduction if they did not itemize. In computing this loss, a $500 floor applied (instead of $100) but the 10% of AGI threshold did not apply.

[29] Special rules were enacted for disasters in presidentially declared disaster areas that occurred in 2008 and 2009—the 10% of AGI threshold for deducting a casualty loss was not applied and nonitemizing taxpayers could add their deductible casualty loss to their standard deduction.

in the loss (after the deduction for the $100 floor) for 10 percent of adjusted gross income. The year with the lower adjusted gross income would normally provide the greater deduction.

Example 9.22

Jamie's home is severely damaged by a wildfire in a federal disaster area in May, 2019. She sustains a $40,000 loss on the property. If her adjusted gross income for 2019 is $50,000, she can claim an itemized deduction of $34,900 ($40,000 – $100 – $5,000) for the loss on her 2019 tax return. She can, however, deduct the loss on an amended 2018 return (an allowable option) to obtain a refund of taxes already paid, because the loss was in a presidentially declared disaster area. If Jamie's 2018 adjusted gross income was only $24,000, she could claim a casualty loss of $37,500 ($40,000 – $100 – $2,400) due to the lower income reported on that tax return.

9.3.2 GAINS ON INVOLUNTARY CONVERSIONS—SECTION 1033

Section 1033 allows all or part of the gain on an involuntary conversion to be deferred if the taxpayer acquires qualifying property within the prescribed time limits. Gains are most likely to result from condemnations because these proceeds are normally the fair market value of the property. Although it is less likely that insurance recoveries on thefts and casualties will exceed the affected property's basis, gains are deferred on all types of involuntary conversions as long as the taxpayer acquires qualifying property within the required time period.

A governmental unit exercises its power of eminent domain when it takes a person's property involuntarily through condemnation or requisition for the common good (such as highway widening). The benefits of this tax provision even extend to property owners whose property is under threat of condemnation that can be objectively verified. The owners can sell the property to a third party rather than a governmental unit, as long as there is a real threat of condemnation. In addition, the provisions apply even if later the condemnation does not take place.[30]

Tax Deferral on Involuntary Conversions

Involuntary conversions are events that taxpayers cannot avoid by planning. The tax consequences are moderated, however, by specific provisions in the tax law designed to help those persons who are the victims of involuntary conversions. The key word here is *involuntary*. If the taxpayer is deliberately responsible for the conversion (for example, hiring an arsonist to set fire to a property), it is not involuntary and the provisions do not apply.[31]

A taxpayer that realizes a gain on an involuntary conversion of his or her property, may defer the gain if qualifying property is acquired within the required time period for replacement.

- This provision defers gain only; qualifying losses are recognized.[32]
- This provision defers gain on business, investment, and personal-use property subject to an involuntary conversion.[33]
- The taxpayer may receive cash (or nonqualifying replacement property) with which to acquire qualifying replacement property.
- The taxpayer generally has an extended period of time in which to acquire qualifying replacement property.

[30] Rev. Rul. 81-180, 1981-2 CB 161.
[31] Rev. Rul. 69-654, 1969-2 CB 162.
[32] §165(b). For personal-use property, only certain casualty and theft losses are deductible. Losses on condemnations of personal-use property are not deductible.
[33] Like-kind exchange provisions are not applicable to personal-use property.

To defer the entire gain, the cost of the qualifying replacement property must equal or exceed the proceeds realized from the conversion. If the taxpayer does not reinvest the entire amount in qualified property, gain equal to the lesser of the gain realized or the proceeds that were not reinvested must be recognized.[34] Any deferred gain reduces the fair market value of the qualifying replacement property. If gain is recognized, the character of the property determines the character of the gain recognized.

Example 9.23

The city condemned Byron's parking lot for a highway interchange. The property's basis is $290,000 and Byron receives $400,000 on the condemnation. Byron purchases property for $425,000 as a replacement parking lot. Byron's realized gain is $110,000 ($400,000 – $290,000) on the condemnation. Byron defers recognition of the entire gain because the cost of the replacement property exceeds his $400,000 condemnation proceeds. His basis of the new property is $315,000 ($425,000 – $110,000 deferred gain).

If the replacement parking lot cost only $350,000, Bryon must recognize $50,000 of Section 1231 gain, the amount he fails to reinvest. The basis of the replacement property is $290,000 [$350,000 – ($110,000 – $50,000) deferred gain].

If Byron reinvests only $250,000, he must recognize the entire $110,000 gain (the lesser of $110,000 or $150,000 unreinvested proceeds) as Section 1231 gain. The property's basis is its $250,000 cost and there is no deferred gain.

TAX PLANNING

Under most circumstances, the deferral of gain is optional. If, however, in the rare instance in which a taxpayer receives replacement property directly (rather than through a purchase), gain deferral is mandatory.[35] A business might recognize gain in the year of the conversion if its current year tax bracket is lower than that expected in future years. The higher depreciation deductions on replacement property would offset income in those higher tax years. If the taxpayer has capital loss carryovers that are about to expire, recognizing the gain may have little or no tax cost.

Example 9.24

Clyde Corporation has a $30,000 realized loss from the sale of a capital asset. A painting (basis = $20,000) hanging in its corporate offices was stolen. The company received $40,000 from the insurance company for the theft loss. A replacement painting cost $45,000. The company has no other property transactions during the year, but the corporation had a net capital gain two years ago of $10,000. The corporation's tax rate is 21 percent. If Clyde defers the $20,000 gain on the theft of the painting, it can carry the $30,000 capital loss back two years and apply for an immediate refund of $2,100 ($10,000 × 21%). It will have a $20,000 loss carryover for future years.

If Clyde recognizes the $20,000 gain in the current year, it is offset by $20,000 of the loss on its capital asset and Clyde still has a $10,000 capital loss carry back to offset the prior capital loss. It will have a $2,100 refund, and there will be no loss carryover. The corporation now has a basis of $45,000 in the replacement painting for any future disposition.

This latter strategy is sound if there are few asset dispositions planned for future years. If, however, the corporation expects significant gains on assets in future years, it may still decide to defer gain recognition to preserve the loss carryover for those gains; however, this must be balanced against the loss in value due to the time value of money. If it does not expect additional capital gains, however, it must remember that capital loss carryovers expire in five years.

[34] §1033(a)(2)(A).

[35] §1033(a). An insurance company could find a substantially similar automobile to replace one that is totaled rather than paying out cash, or a governmental unit might replace one piece of condemned land with a satisfactory substitute.

Qualifying Replacement Property

Two differing rules determine qualifying replacement property depending on the taxpayer's use of the converted property. The first, the **functional-use test**, requires replacement property to provide the same function as converted property that was owned and used by the taxpayer. This is the most restrictive of all the replacement tests and is narrowly interpreted. Thus, a bowling alley replaced with a billiards center did not meet the functional-use test.[36]

The second test, the **taxpayer-use test**, is far less restrictive but applies only to investment real estate that is rented and not used by the owner. The owner of rental real estate is only obligated to replace it with other property that can be leased. The use that the tenant makes of the replacement property is irrelevant.[37]

Example 9.25

Harvey owns a strip mall with a small out-building, both destroyed by a tornado. The strip mall was entirely leased to others, but Harvey used the building for his offices. Harvey builds a high-rise apartment complex on the land previously occupied by both the strip mall and office building with the insurance proceeds. Harvey realizes a $3,000,000 gain on the conversion of the mall and a $50,000 gain on the office building. Harvey can defer all the gain on the mall (rental property) because he replaces it with an apartment complex (also rental property) that is qualified replacement property under the taxpayer-use test. He cannot defer the $50,000 gain on the office building because the apartment complex does not meet the functional-use test.

An exception to these two rules allows the replacement property for business or investment real property that is condemned to follow the replacement rules for like-kind property.[38] Thus, investment property can replace property used in a business or raw land can replace improved property.

Time Limits for Replacement

The last requirement for gain deferral on involuntarily converted property is the time limit for replacement. Replacement property must be acquired within "two tax years after the close of the first taxable year in which any part of the gain upon the conversion is realized," unless it is business or investment real property that is condemned.[39] For condemned realty, the replacement period is extended one additional year, that is, until three years after the close of the year in which any gain is realized.

Example 9.26

Lotic Corporation, a calendar-year corporation, lost its manufacturing facility due to a hurricane on November 12, year 1. Its insurance company claimed that it had not received the premium payment for November or December and it took until early January to locate their clerical error. They issued a check to Lotic for the damage on February 1, year 2. Lotic has until the end of year 4 to replace the plant because the insurance proceeds were not received and the gain realized until the year following the hurricane. If Lotic Corporation's manufacturing facility had been condemned, it would have until the end of year 5 to find replacement property.

---

[36] Rev. Rul. 76-319, 1976-2 CB 242.

[37] Rev. Rul. 64-237, 1964-2 CB 319.

[38] If converted business or investment property is located in a presidentially declared disaster area, any tangible property that is used in a productive trade or business is qualified replacement property.

[39] §1033(a)(2)(B).

9.3.3 INVOLUNTARY CONVERSION OF A PRINCIPAL RESIDENCE

A taxpayer whose principal residence is involuntarily converted may exclude gain using the sale provisions under Section 121 (discussed in Chapter 8), under the involuntary conversion provisions discussed above, or under a combination of both provisions. A taxpayer whose principal residence is involuntarily converted and uses all the proceeds to acquire a replacement residence, can defer all gain under Section 1033. The involuntary conversion is considered a sale. It may be to the taxpayer's advantage to use both **Section 121** and Section 1033 provisions, if eligible. If the taxpayer does not want to reinvest all of the insurance proceeds to purchase a replacement residence, gain recognition may still be avoided. The taxpayer reduces the required reinvestment amount by the allowable gain exclusion under Section 121 (up to $250,000 or $500,000 if both spouses qualify). If the amount reinvested equals or exceeds this reduced required investment, the taxpayer can avoid gain recognition and have cash remaining.

Example 9.27

Monica and Steve, a married couple filing a joint return, lost their home of 30 years in a wildfire. They had replacement-value insurance on the home and received a $1,200,000 settlement from the insurance company. Their basis in the home was $350,000. The smaller replacement home built on the same land cost $800,000. They have a realized gain of $850,000 ($1,200,000 – $350,000) from the insurance settlement and can exclude $500,000 of the gain under Section 121. As a result, their required investment is only $700,000 ($1,200,000 – $500,000) to exclude the remaining $350,000 ($850,000 – $500,000) gain. Their investment exceeds this amount and they recognize no gain on the conversion. Their basis in the new residence is $450,000 ($800,000 – $350,000 deferred gain). Section 121 is a nonrecognition provision and they do not adjust the basis of the new home by this excluded gain. They only reduce the basis by the $350,000 deferred gain under Section 1033.

9.4 OTHER TAX-DEFERRED EXCHANGES OR DISPOSITIONS

9.4.1 WASH SALES

When a taxpayer sells or exchanges stock and then acquires substantially identical stock or securities within 30 days, either before or after the sale or exchange of stock, the taxpayer has a **wash sale**. A loss realized on a wash sale is not recognized. The sale is treated as a nontaxable exchange and loss recognition is deferred. Wash sale rules do not affect gain recognition, however. The deferred loss increases the basis of the substantially identical stock acquired, and the holding period of the stock includes the holding period of the stock sold.[40] Loss is deferred, even if tax avoidance is not the motive and the taxpayer is unaware that the prohibited sale took place. If more stock is sold than the taxpayer purchased within the 61-day window (the day of sale, 30 days before, and 30 days after), only a portion of the loss representing the repurchased stock is deferred. The wash sale rules also apply to losses on options to acquire or sell stock and short sales.

Example 9.28

Barker purchased 100 shares of ABC stock for $4,000 on June 10 and 200 shares of MNO stock on June 30 for $3,000 through the Internet. Without consulting Barker, his broker sold 100 shares of ABC for $3,800 and 200 shares of MNO stock for $3,300 on June 28. The broker purchased the ABC shares for $4,100 and MNO shares for $3,100 two years ago. He had held them in Barker's account until the sale. Barker's stock purchases were made within 30 days of the sale of identical stock by his broker. Barker has a realized loss on the ABC stock of $300

[40] A "substantially identical stock or security" is open to interpretation. Common and preferred stock of the same company would not be similar nor would common stock and bonds, but preferred stock and bonds could be substantially similar if they are both convertible into common stock. Rev. Rul. 56-496, 1956-2 CB 523.

($4,100 – $3,800) that cannot be recognized but his realized gain on the MNO stock of $200 ($3,300 – $3,100) is recognized. The adjusted basis of the ABC stock acquired on June 10 is $4,300 ($4,000 + $300 deferred loss), and it has a two-year holding period. The basis of the MNO stock is its purchase price of $3,000, and its holding period begins on June 30 purchase date.

If the broker sold 200 shares of ABC stock for $7,600 with a basis of $8,200, Barker would have a $600 realized loss. He would defer only $300 ($600 × 100/200) of the loss because he only purchased 100 shares of ABC; the $300 remaining would be recognized.

9.4.2 INSTALLMENT SALES

The installment method of reporting gain on certain transactions is a taxpayer-friendly application of the wherewithal to pay concept. It allows taxpayers to defer recognition of income and the taxes payable until payments are received. Under the **installment method**, gain is recognized as proceeds from the sale are received rather than recognizing the entire gain in the year of sale.[41] To qualify as an installment sale, one or more payments must be received in any tax year other than the year of sale and involve eligible property.[42] The installment method does not apply to losses, with deductible losses recognized immediately.

To determine how much gain the seller recognizes as each installment payment is received, a gross profit percentage—gross profit divided by contract price—is computed. Gross profit is the sales price less the adjusted basis of the property. The contract price is the sales price reduced by the seller's liability (if any) assumed by the buyer. As each payment is received, it is multiplied by this gross profit percentage to determine the recognized gain portion of the payment. The balance of each payment is a return of capital. Once the gross profit percentage is established, it does not change; the same percentage is used each year as payments are received. The character of the gain recognized is determined by the character of the asset sold; however, any interest income received by the seller is taxed immediately as ordinary income.

Example 9.29

Todd sells a parcel of land for $100,000 purchased 10 years ago for $40,000. Todd's long-term capital gain is $60,000 ($100,000 – $40,000). The buyer agrees to pay Todd the $100,000 at the rate of $25,000 per year for four years, plus interest on the unpaid balance. Sixty percent of the principal payment Todd receives represents gain ($60,000 gain/$100,000 payments) that he recognizes in the year received. Each $25,000 payment triggers recognition of $15,000 ($25,000 × 60%) gain. After Todd receives all four payments, he will have recognized a total gain of $60,000.

If Todd's capital gains tax rate is 15 percent, the present value of his tax savings from using the installment method is $846 assuming a discount rate of 7 percent.

	Year of sale	Year 1	Year 2	Year 3	Total
Regular Sale					
Gain	$60,000				
Tax rate	×15%				
Tax	$9,000				$9,000
Installment Sale					
Gain	$15,000	$15,000	$15,000	$15,000	
Tax rate	×15%	×15%	×15%	×15%	
Tax	$2,250	$2,250	$2,250	$2,250	
Discount factor	×1.0	× .935	× .873	× .816	
Discounted tax cost	$2,250	$2,104	$1,964	$1,836	8,154
Present value of tax savings					$846

[41] The installment method is not available for a transaction in which a loss rather than a gain results.

[42] §453(b)(1).

The use of the installment method is restricted, however, and is generally available only for what might be called a taxpayer's casual sales. It cannot be used for the sale of (1) inventory,[43] (2) personal property regularly sold on the installment plan (revolving charge accounts),[44] (3) depreciable property between a taxpayer and a controlled entity,[45] (4) the sale of stock or securities traded on an established securities market,[46] and certain other transactions. The installment method cannot be used for financial accounting, leading to a temporary difference between financial and taxable income.[47]

There is a significant complication for the use of the installment sales provisions on sales of depreciable property. All depreciation recapture must be recognized in the year of sale; only the remaining Section 1231 gain can be recognized using the installment method. To ensure depreciation recapture is taxed only once, it is added to the adjusted basis of the property sold to determine the gross profit percentage. By increasing basis, the gross profit percentage is reduced, reducing the amount of gain recognized in later years.

Example 9.30

Markum Corporation sells excess equipment for $50,000 down in the year of sale and a $50,000 payment in each of the next two years ($150,000 total), plus interest. Markum purchased this equipment several years ago for $139,200; its accumulated depreciation is $48,000 and it has an adjusted basis of $91,200 at the sale date. Markum's realized gain is $58,800 ($150,000 – $91,200) of which $48,000 is taxed as ordinary income due to the depreciation recapture rules. The remaining $10,800 Section 1231 gain is eligible for the installment method. The gross profit percentage is 7.2% ($10,800 eligible gain divided by $150,000 contract price). Markum recognizes a $3,600 ($50,000 × 7.2%) Section 1231 gain and $48,000 of depreciation recapture in the year of sale. In years 2 and 3, Markum will recognize $3,600 Section 1231 gain. At the end of the third year, Markum will have recognized the entire $58,800 taxable gain. For financial accounting purposes, Markum recognizes the entire gain in the year of sale, creating a temporary book-tax difference.

TAX PLANNING

The taxpayer must report a qualifying transaction under the installment method unless the taxpayer elects not to use it.[48] A taxpayer might elect to report all gain in the year of sale if the taxpayer's marginal tax rate is expected to increase in future years when the payments are received. The election to accelerate the recognition of gain may be advantageous if the taxpayer has unused net operating losses or unused capital losses (if a capital gain). The taxpayer simply reports the entire gain in the year of sale to elect out of installment sale reporting.

9.4.3 RELATED-PARTY SALES

Taxpayers may sell assets to family members or other related buyers (such as family-owned corporations), hoping to trigger a loss for tax purposes without fully relinquishing control of the asset. Though there is no prohibition against selling property to **related parties**, Section 267 disallows loss recognition on a sale or exchange of property between related parties, even if the selling price is fair market value at the time of the sale. This provision only applies to losses; gains on sales to related parties are recognized.

[43] Exceptions exist for the sale of farm property, timeshares, and unimproved residential lots. §453(l)(2)(A), (B).
[44] §453(l)(1)(A).
[45] §453(g).
[46] §453(k)(2)(A).
[47] Financial accounting standards authorize the use of the installment method only for the sale of real property where the collectability of the payments is in doubt or other special conditions exist.
[48] §453(a), d(1).

An individual is directly related to his or her spouse, brothers and sisters, ancestors, and lineal descendants. A taxpayer who owns more than 50 percent of the stock in a corporation is related to a corporation. If an individual owns more than 50 percent in each of two entities (corporate and/or partnership), the entities are considered related parties under the attribution rules.[49]

The related buyer's basis is the price actually paid, even though the seller's loss is not deductible. If the buyer later sells the property at or below its purchase price, the deductible loss is measured from that purchase price. The net effect is that the original seller's loss is never deducted.

If the buyer sells the asset at a gain, however, no gain is recognized unless the purchase price exceeds the related-party's original basis. In effect, the *seller's* unrecognized loss now offsets all or part of the buyer's gain on a subsequent sale.

Example 9.31

Gerry had a $2,000 capital gain on which he did not want to pay taxes. To avoid the tax, he sold 100 shares of stock purchased for $5,000 to his brother, Ben, for $3,000. Gerry has a realized loss of $2,000, but he is unable to recognize the loss to offset the gain because of loss disallowance on related-party sales.

If Ben sells the stock at a price between $3,000 and $5,000, he will recognize no gain. Gerry's $2,000 unrecognized loss offsets the gain. Ben recognizes gain only if he sells the stock for more than $5,000. If Ben sells the stock for $3,000 or less, the tax benefit of Gerry's $2,000 loss is never recognized. Ben recognizes loss only if he sells the stock for less than $3,000.

Under Section 1239, when a taxpayer sells property to a related party at a gain and it is *depreciable property to the buyer,* the seller's entire gain on the sale is characterized as ordinary income. If this provision did not exist, a taxpayer could recognize capital gain on the sale of an appreciated asset to a related party. The buyer could then depreciate the asset and take a depreciation deduction from ordinary income. To prevent the creation of tax savings by the current sale of an appreciated asset to a related party who deducts depreciation expense, Section 1239 requires the seller to recognize ordinary income currently for depreciation deductions the buyer will receive in the future. (This differs from depreciation recapture that requires recognition of ordinary income currently for depreciation deductions received in the past). If both depreciation recapture and the Section 1239 recapture provision apply to the same gain, the depreciation recapture rules apply first.

Example 9.32

Jason sells a piece of personal equipment purchased two years ago for $88,000 to Argon Corporation for $100,000. The equipment will be used by Argon Corporation in its business and Argon will depreciate its $100,000 cost. Jason owns 75 percent of Argon Corporation and is considered a related party. Although the equipment was Jason's personal asset, he recognizes $12,000 ordinary income on this sale. His entire gain is reclassified as ordinary income because the equipment is a depreciable asset to Argon Corporation and this is a related-party transaction.

If Jason owned only 45 percent of Argon Corporation with the other 55 percent owned by unrelated parties, Section 1239 would not apply and Jason would recognize a $12,000 long-term capital gain.

[49] There are also rules covering relationships between controlled corporations and the parties involved in estates and trusts that are beyond the scope of this brief discussion.

9.4.4 OTHER DEFERRALS

Under Section 1035, a life insurance contract can be exchanged for a life insurance contract, an endowment contract, or another annuity contract.[50] In addition, an annuity contract can be exchanged for either an endowment or an annuity contract, and an endowment contract can be converted (exchanged) to an annuity contract. Realized gain or loss, recognized gain on the receipt of boot, and the basis of the policy received are all determined under the like-kind exchange provisions.[51]

TAX PLANNING

A taxpayer recognizes no gain or loss on the transfer of property to an ex-spouse if the transfer is part of a divorce settlement. The actual property transfer must occur no later than one year after the date of the final divorce decree.[52] The property basis carries over to the ex-spouse. The structuring of property settlements as part of divorce proceedings is one reason divorcing parties should both consult separate tax practitioners as well as attorneys to avoid any unpleasant tax surprises.

Exchanges of stock between a corporation and its shareholders and between shareholders of the same corporation are tax-deferred exchanges if common stock is exchanged for substantially similar common stock and preferred stock is exchanged for substantially similar preferred stock.[53]

If stocks of the same class have significant differences, the exchange is taxable. Similarly, common stock exchanged for preferred and preferred stock exchanged for common are normally taxable exchanges (except for the exercise of a preferred stock conversion feature).

9.5 ASSET TRANSFERS TO BUSINESSES

The deferral of gains and losses is the hallmark of transfers of assets to businesses. This effectively removes the tax consequences of formation from consideration when choosing the type of entity in which to operate a business. Thus, an individual can transfer personal assets to his or her sole proprietorship, potential partners can transfer assets to a partnership, and potential shareholders can transfer assets to corporations without gain or loss recognition as long as certain basic requirements are met. Although ignoring the overall effect of taxation on the operation of any business would be a mistake, the tax laws remain relatively neutral to initial formation.

9.5.1 TRANSFERS TO SOLE PROPRIETORSHIPS

Sole proprietors often transfer personal assets other than money to their sole proprietorship as a matter of convenience. Fortunately, there is no gain or loss recognized on these transfers. Instead, the basis of these transferred assets is the lower of adjusted bases or fair market values at the date of conversion, following the general rule that any asset converted from personal to business use has as its basis the lower of fair market value or basis.[54]

It is important to establish a realistic fair market value for converted assets, as the sole proprietorship's depreciation deductions are based on fair market value (or basis, if lower). Some form of appraisal or comparable value should be obtained from a dealer in used furniture and equipment similar to the converted assets. Using original cost is normally not an option unless it can be shown that the type of converted asset is one that maintains its original value or has appreciated.

[50] An endowment contract is a contract with an insurance company that depends in part on the life expectancy of the insured but may be payable in full in a single payment during life. An annuity contract is a contract sold by an insurance company that pays a monthly (quarterly, semiannual, or annual) income benefit for the life of one or more persons or for a specified period of time.
[51] §1035(a) and (d).
[52] The transfer is treated as a gift from the taxpayer to the ex-spouse, but no gift taxes are due.
[53] §1236.
[54] If fair market value is below basis, the basis for depreciation and a loss on a subsequent sale is the lower fair market value; the basis for gain, however, is the carryover basis reduced for any depreciation.

9.5.2 TRANSFERS TO CONTROLLED CORPORATIONS—SECTION 351

The purchase of corporate stock by an individual for cash is not a taxable transaction. If, however, an individual transfers assets from a sole proprietorship to a corporation in exchange for stock, this potentially could be interpreted as a taxable sale of each separate proprietorship asset. There could be taxable gain to the extent the fair market value of an asset exceeds its basis. To prevent this barrier to incorporation, potential and existing shareholders can transfer money and other property to a corporation in exchange for its stock and defer any gain or loss by following the requirements of **Section 351**. Section 351(a) states:

> *No gain or loss shall be recognized if property is transferred to a corporation by one or more persons solely in exchange for stock in such corporation and immediately after the exchange such person or persons are in control of the corporation.*

To be a fully nontaxable event, the transfers must meet three requirements:

- The transfer must be of property (including money) only (not services).
- The transferor(s) must receive only stock in exchange for the property transferred.
- The transferor(s) must be in control of the corporation immediately after the transfer.

If any of these requirements is not met, either the entire transaction is treated as a taxable sale or exchange or one or more of the transferors may be required to recognize gain or income. Generally, only the failure to meet the control requirement renders the entire transaction taxable to all transferors. The transfer of services for stock or the receipt of property other than stock causes gain (income) recognition only to the parties involved, leaving the remaining transferors with a nontaxable event and recognition deferral.

The Control Requirement

Control is defined as owning 80 percent of all outstanding voting stock and 80 percent of each separate type of nonvoting stock, measured immediately after the transfer.[55] Most new corporations issue only one type of stock—voting stock, and may never issue any additional stock unless they are very successful. The shareholders exchange money and other assets for the newly issued stock in the corporation. This exchange should take place according to a predetermined shareholder plan within a reasonable time period. Once the stock transfers are complete, generally the new shareholders can dispose of the stock whenever they choose since control is measured "immediately" after the transfers. Any commitment to sell or otherwise transfer stock prior to the completion of the stock transfers, however, should be avoided.[56]

Example 9.33

Sara transfers property with a fair market value of $30,000 and a basis of $18,000 for 60 shares of SaraDan Corporation stock. Dan transfers property valued at $15,000 and a basis of $18,000 for 30 shares. The transfer qualifies for nonrecognition because Sara and Dan, the transferors, receive 100 percent of the outstanding stock.

The deferral provisions of Section 351 allow existing shareholders to make tax-free transfers of additional property to the corporation in exchange for stock as long as the transferring shareholders meet the provisions of Section 351.

---

[55] §368(c).

[56] Immediate sale of the stock after the transfer may give the appearance of a prearranged plan and should be avoided.

Example 9.34

Continuing the previous example, SaraDan Corporation needs to relocate its operations. Sara is willing to contribute a small building she owns valued at $50,000 (basis $30,000) but wants an additional 60 shares in exchange. After the transaction, Sara will own 120 of the 150 shares outstanding, exactly 80 percent, and her contribution qualifies for nonrecognition.

If another person wants to become a shareholder by contributing assets to the corporation, existing shareholders may have to contribute additional assets to the corporation to meet the 80 percent control requirement. To be included as transferors (guaranteeing the tax-free entry of new shareholders), existing shareholders must contribute cash or property equal to or greater than the value of 10 percent of their existing shares. The shareholders who make a qualifying asset transfer become part of the planned transfer and all of their shares are included in meeting the 80 percent control requirement.[57]

Example 9.35

George, Sara's friend, has machinery he would like to exchange for stock in SaraDan. The machinery has a value of $35,000 and a basis of $10,000. George wants to receive 70 shares of stock but does not want to recognize gain on his contribution. If Sara agrees to contribute $15,000 for an additional 30 shares of stock, George will own 70 shares and Sara will own 150 shares of the outstanding 250 shares. Together they will own 88 percent (220/250) and the transfers qualify as nontaxable under Section 351.

Existing shareholders can make contributions to a corporation's capital account (with no additional shares of stock received) with no gain or loss recognized by the corporation or the shareholder. The corporation takes a carryover basis in the property contributed, and its holding period includes that of the shareholder. The shareholder increases the basis of his or her existing stock for the basis of the property contributed.[58] If an existing or new shareholder has loss property to contribute on which loss could be recognized, the shareholder should either sell the property to the corporation (if not a related party) or a third party, or otherwise fail the requirements of Section 351 in order to recognize the loss.

The transfer provisions discussed above apply equally to C corporations and S corporations. No separate Code provisions cover the transfer of property to an S corporation at formation or at a later time.

Property Other Than Stock Received

If a transferor receives property other than stock (for example, cash, stock rights, stock warrants, and any short-term or long-term corporate debt) in exchange for the property transferred to the corporation, the other property is considered boot. The transferor recognizes gain to the extent of the lesser of gain realized or boot received.[59] If the transferor has a loss on the transfer of depreciated assets (basis greater than fair market value) to a controlled corporation, loss is not recognized even if boot is received.[60] To recognize the loss, either the transaction must fail the Section 351 requirements (usually by failing to meet the 80 percent control test) or the shareholder sells the property to the corporation and then transfers the proceeds.

[57] Reg. §1.351-1(a)(1)(ii) and Rev. Proc. 77-37, Sec. 3.07, 1977-2 C.B. 568.

[58] If loss property is contributed, the shareholder defers the loss by using the property's basis for the stock but the corporation may be required to use the lower fair market value for its basis.

[59] §351(b).

[60] This boot rule is similar to the boot rule for like-kind exchanges.

If the corporation transfers appreciated property as boot to a shareholder in a qualifying Section 351 exchange, the corporation must recognize gain. If the boot is depreciated property, however, the corporation cannot recognize the loss. In this latter case, the corporation would be better off selling the depreciated asset, recognizing the loss, and transferring the proceeds to the shareholder. If an outside sale is not available, the transfer of depreciated property allows the shareholder to extract something of value from the corporation without corporate income tax consequences.

Example 9.36

Gregory receives 1,000 shares of Wolly stock and a $5,000 corporate bond in exchange for machinery valued at $55,000 with a basis of $42,000. The bond is boot. Gregory recognizes gain equal to $5,000 on the transfer, the lesser of the gain realized of $13,000 ($55,000 – $42,000) or the boot (the bond) received.

Sherona receives 1,000 shares of stock and $5,000 of office furniture (basis equal to $2,000) in exchange for a heavy duty truck valued at $55,000 (basis equal to $47,000). The office furniture is boot and Sherona recognizes $5,000 gain on the transfer, but the corporation must also recognize gain of $3,000 on the office furniture.

Example 9.37

Three shareholders of Baby Corporation transfer the following cash and property to the corporation for common stock and other property in a qualifying Section 351 transaction:

1. *Shareholder A:* Transfers a building; fair market value = $800,000; basis = $850,000. He receives 70 shares of common stock and $100,000 cash.
2. *Shareholder B:* Transfers $800,000 cash. She receives 70 shares of common stock and a machine valued at $100,000 that has a basis of $150,000.
3. *Shareholder C:* Transfers land; fair market value = $700,000; basis = $400,000. He receives 60 shares of common stock and 100 Baby Corporation bonds with a face value of $1,000 each.

Shareholder A has a realized loss of $50,000 ($800,000 – $850,000); the loss is not recognized even though he receives $100,000 cash (boot). Baby Corporation has no gain or loss.

Shareholder B realizes no gain or loss on the transfer of cash. Baby Corporation has a $50,000 ($100,000 – $150,000) realized loss that it cannot recognize on the transfer of the machine to Shareholder B.

Shareholder C has a realized gain of $300,000 ($700,000 – $400,000) on the land; he recognizes only $100,000, however, the lesser of gain realized or boot received. Baby Corporation has no gain or loss.

Shareholder *A and Baby Corporation* could have sold their depreciated assets to outsiders, recognizing their losses, and used the proceeds to complete the transaction.

Transferred Services

In some cases, a person with particular expertise is given stock in exchange for past or future services as part of a corporate formation. If the person receives stock solely for services, the stock is excluded from control determination.[61] To include the stock received to determine control, the person must transfer property in addition to performing services. If the value of the property transferred equals 10 percent or more of the value of the services provided, then all stock received is included in meeting the control requirement. A person who receives stock in exchange for services recognizes income for the value of the services regardless of the tax consequences to the other transferors.

[61] §351(d)(1). If the person receives more than 20 percent of the stock solely for services, the control requirement will not be met.

Example 9.38

Claudia performed $10,000 worth of accounting services in exchange for 1,000 shares of stock when her friends formed FGH Corporation. Claudia must recognize $10,000 income. If she transfers no property, the other owners cannot include her 1,000 shares in determining if they meet the 80 percent control requirement for a qualifying Section 351 corporate formation. If Claudia contributed at least $1,000 in cash or property along with her services, her shares would be included in determining control.

Basis and Holding Period

In most qualifying Section 351 transactions, the transferor's basis in the stock received is:[62]

	Basis of property transferred
Plus	Gain recognized
Less	Fair market value of the boot received
Equals	Basis of stock received

If no boot is received, there is no gain recognized and the stock has the same basis as the property transferred (a substituted basis). If the shareholder receives boot, the shareholder recognizes gain and has a fair market value basis in the boot received.[63] If the shareholder receives more than one class of stock, basis is apportioned using relative fair market values.

The corporation's basis in property received normally equals the shareholder's basis (a carryover basis), unless the transferor recognizes gain. The corporation's basis in the property increases by the shareholder's recognized gain to prevent the corporation from being taxed on the same gain in the future.[64]

These basis provisions may be altered, however, if the aggregate bases of the property transferred to a corporation by a transferor exceeds the property's fair market value. In this unlikely case, the aggregate basis the corporation takes in the transferred property cannot exceed the aggregate fair market value unless the transferor-shareholder agrees to reduce the stock basis by this excess property basis over fair market value.[65]

Example 9.39

Zoar transfers land (basis $200,000 and fair market value $400,000) to Cory Corporation in exchange for 200 shares of common stock. Yara transfers machines (basis $150,000 and fair market value $260,000) to Cory in exchange for 200 shares of stock and $60,000 cash. These are qualified Section 351 transfers. Zoar has a $200,000 ($400,000 – $200,000) realized gain that is deferred and has a $200,000 basis in her stock. The corporation has a $200,000 basis in the land. Yara has a realized gain of $110,000 ($260,000 – $150,000) and recognizes $60,000 gain, the lesser of her realized gain ($110,000) and the boot received ($60,000 cash). The basis in her stock is $150,000 ($150,000 + $60,000 gain recognized – $60,000 boot received). The corporation's basis in the machines is $210,000 ($150,000 basis of the machines + $60,000 gain recognized by Yara).

If Zoar's basis in the land transferred is $450,000 rather than $200,000, the corporation's basis cannot exceed the land's $400,000 fair market value unless Zoar elects to reduce her basis in the stock received to $400,000.

[62] §358(a)(1). If the aggregate basis of property transferred is greater than its aggregate fair market value, the transferor's stock basis cannot exceed the property's fair market value if the corporation takes the carryover basis in the transferred property. §362(e)(2).

[63] §358(a)(2).

[64] §362(a).

[65] §362(e)(2).

The holding period of stock a shareholder receives in exchange for capital or Section 1231 property includes the property's holding period. The holding period for stock exchanged for ordinary income property (such as inventory) begins on the date of the exchange. The holding period for all property received by a corporation in exchange for its stock in a Section 351 transaction includes the shareholder's holding period.[66]

A shareholder who receives stock in exchange for services has a basis in the stock equal to the income recognized. The holding period begins on the date of the exchange. The corporation either expenses or capitalizes the value of the services as appropriate.[67] If capitalized, the asset's holding period begins on the date of the exchange.

Effect of Liabilities

Liabilities encumbering assets transferred to a corporation as part of a Section 351 transfer have no effect on the transferor's nonrecognition of gain and loss or the amount of gain recognized when boot is received. The value of liabilities assumed does reduce the transferor's basis in the stock received, however. The liability assumption has value separate from the stock and cannot become part of the stock basis. Thus, the transferor's stock basis formula is modified to:[68]

	Basis of property transferred
Plus	Gain recognized
Less	Fair market value of the boot received and liabilities assumed by the corporation
Equals	Basis of stock received

There are two situations in which the assumption of liabilities is modified. First, if the liabilities assumed by a corporation in a qualifying Section 351 asset transfer exceed the transferor's bases in the properties transferred, gain must be recognized to the extent of the excess liability to avoid a negative basis in the stock received.[69]

Example 9.40

As part of a qualifying Section 351 transaction, Gene transfers a building with a fair market value of $750,000 (basis = $500,000) for $500,000 in corporate stock and the corporation's assumption of the $250,000 mortgage on the building. Although Gene has a $250,000 realized gain, he recognizes no gain on the transfer. His basis in the stock received is $250,000 ($500,000 basis – $250,000 liability assumed). If Gene receives only $200,000 but the liability assumed is $550,000, Gene recognizes $50,000 gain equal to the excess liability ($550,000 liability – $500,000 basis) to avoid a negative basis in the building and his stock basis is zero.

Assume in the preceding example that Gene needs cash and obtains the $250,000 mortgage on the building just weeks before he contributes it to the corporation. (If he sells the building to the corporation for cash, he would have to pay taxes on the gain.) Section 357(b) steps in, however, and recharacterizes the assumption of a recently-acquired mortgage as boot, and taxable to Gene. This section converts ***all*** liabilities to boot if the principle purpose of undertaking any liability is tax avoidance by looking at the details surrounding the transaction. Gene now must recognize the entire $250,000 gain and his basis in the building increases to $750,000.

---

[66] §§1223(1) and (2). Because the holding periods are combined, the corporation is responsible for any depreciation recapture associated with the disposal of the assets transferred.

[67] Rev. Rul. 74-503, 1974-2 CB 117.

[68] When gain is recognized because liabilities are assumed in excess of basis, the basis of the stock acquired is always zero.

[69] §357(c).

9.5.3 TRANSFERS OF PROPERTY TO A PARTNERSHIP

The transfers of property to a partnership have certain similarities to transfers of property to corporations, but are also unique in other areas. For example, no gain or loss is recognized when a partner transfers property to a partnership in exchange for a partnership interest. A partner takes a basis in the partnership interest equal to the basis of the property transferred, and the partnership has a carryover basis in the property received. Unlike a corporation, however, the transferring partners are not required to have any minimum level of ownership for gain or loss deferral.[70] Additionally, taxes are deferred on any gains and losses from qualifying transfers whether the transfers are at formation or during the life of the partnership, making the partnership provisions more flexible. Transferred property takes a carryover basis thus deferring recognition of any gains or losses on contributed property.

Example 9.41

Corbin transfers $1,000 cash and land with a basis of $44,000 to a partnership in exchange for a 50 percent interest in the partnership. Corbin has a $45,000 substituted basis in his 50 percent partnership interest and the partnership has a $1,000 and $44,000 carryover basis in the cash and land, respectively. Neither Corbin nor the partnership has tax consequences as a result of this transfer of property to the partnership.

Basis and Holding Period of a Partnership Interest

Partner's basis is one of the most important concepts at formation and throughout the life of a partnership. At formation, the basis of a partner's interest in a partnership is determined by the basis of the property (including money) transferred to the partnership. A partner that transfers services in exchange for a partnership interest has taxable income equal to the fair market value of the partnership interest. The definition of property excludes services. The value of a partnership interest received is determined at the time a service provider has unconditional control of the partnership interest and establishes basis in the partnership interest. The partnership recognizes either a deductible expense or a capitalized asset on the transfer of services and establishes a capital account for the partner.

If a partner receives property from the partnership in addition to a partnership interest, the property is *not* considered boot. Instead, the transaction is separated into a *transfer* of part of the assets for a partnership interest and a *sale* of the remaining part of the assets for the property received from the partnership.

Example 9.42

Myron transfers an asset valued at $100,000 (basis equal to $50,000) for a partnership interest valued at $90,000 and $10,000 cash. Myron recognizes the transfer of the $100,000 asset as part nontaxable transfer (for the $90,000 partnership interest) and part sale (for the $10,000 cash received). Myron has a substituted basis of $45,000 [.90 × $50,000 property basis] in his partnership interest from the nontaxable asset transfer and an unrecognized $45,000 ($90,000 FMV – $45,000 basis) deferred gain for the remaining fair market value of the transferred asset. On the sale portion, however, Myron recognizes gain of $5,000 ($10,000 – [.10 × $50,000] apportioned basis) on the sale of the other 10 percent of the property. He has a basis of $45,000 in his partnership interest.

This example illustrates another unique feature of the partnership form—the concepts of inside and outside basis. The partnership has a carryover basis in the contributed property of

[70] Reg. §1.721-1(b)(2).

$45,000 (the inside basis) and Myron has a substituted basis of $45,000 (the outside basis) in his partnership interest, both derived from the $45,000 basis of the transferred asset. Myron's capital account is credited with the full $90,000 fair market value of the asset, however. A partner's outside basis and capital account are equal at formation only if the bases of property contributed and their fair market values are equal.[71] Outside basis generally is the more relevant for tax purposes, and unless otherwise stated, the general term basis refers to the partner's outside basis.

TAX PLANNING

A partner may deal at arm's length with the partnership and may either sell or lease assets to it rather than exchange them for a partnership interest. Leasing allows the partner to avoid gain or loss recognition while allowing the partnership to have use of the assets for the rental period.[72]

If the partner transfers Section 1231 or capital assets to the partnership, his or her holding period for the partnership interest includes the period of time the assets were held prior to contribution. If cash or ordinary income assets are transferred, the holding period for the partnership interest begins on the date of transfer, thus a partnership interest may have more than one holding period based on the contributed assets.[73]

Example 9.43

X, Y, and Z form the XYZ Partnership. X transfers materials and machines with a fair market value of $45,000 (basis equal to $35,000) to the partnership. Y transfers land valued at $35,000 (basis equal to $40,000) and $10,000 cash to the partnership; Z transfers services valued at $5,000 and $5,000 cash to the partnership. X and Y each receive a 45 percent interest in the partnership, and Z receives the other 10 percent. X has a realized gain of $10,000 ($45,000 – $35,000) and Y a realized loss of $5,000 ($35,000 + $10,000 – $50,000) on their transfers; neither, however, recognizes the gain or loss. Z, however, recognizes $5,000 of income when she has unrestricted right to her 10 percent partnership interest. X has a basis of $35,000 in his partnership interest (the adjusted basis of the materials and machines), Y has a basis of $50,000 in her interest (the adjusted basis of the land plus the cash), and Z has a basis of $10,000 ($5,000 cash plus the $5,000 income recognized on the value of services) when she has an unrestricted right to her partnership interest.

Partnership Basis and Holding Period in Contributed Property

The partnership takes a carryover basis in the property acquired in a tax-deferred transfer; that is, the partnership "steps into the shoes" of the partners with respect to the bases of contributed assets. The partnership uses this carryover basis for computing depreciation, if applicable, and for determining gain or loss on subsequent dispositions of the assets.

Example 9.44

Using the facts in the previous example, the XYZ Partnership has a $35,000 basis in the materials and the machines from X, a $40,000 basis in the land and a $10,000 basis in the cash from Y, and a $5,000 basis in the cash from Z. It will either have a $5,000 asset or a $5,000 expense for the services provided by Z.

Because the partnership has a carryover basis in the assets, its holding periods for the materials, machines, and land include the time they were held by the partners. If Z's services are capitalized, its holding period begins when Z recognizes the income.

[71] The built in gain or loss on property contributed to a partnership and then returned to either the contributing or another partner within seven years must be adjusted and reapportioned to the original contributing partner before any excess is allocated to the partners. If the partnership disposes of the asset contributed by Myron immediately after its contribution for $90,000, Myron is allocated the $45,000 built in gain.

[72] The entity theory of partnership allows both the sale and the rental because the partner and the partnership are considered separate taxpayers as discussed in Chapter 11.

[73] The partnership interest's holding period is partitioned to reflect different holding periods for contributed assets.

Effect of Liabilities

Liabilities assumed by a partnership on assets transferred by a partner add complexity to the determination of a partner's basis. Liabilities assumed by the partnership on property transferred by a partner reduce the partner's basis in the assets transferred. If, however, the transferring partner may be held personally responsible for payment of a share of all partnership's liabilities, the partner's basis then also increases for the partner's share. All responsible partners' bases (including the transferring partner's) increase for this potential payment.[74] A 30 percent partner who can be held liable for 30 percent of the $100,000 debt increases his or her partnership interest basis by $30,000 ($100,000 × 30%). When the liability is paid off by the partnership, the partner's basis is reduced by his or her share of the liability.

This provision affects the nonrecognition of gain when a partner transfers assets encumbered by liabilities in excess of the property's basis that the partnership assumes. Gain is recognized when liabilities assumed exceed basis, but the transferring partner's basis is first increased for the partner's share of the liability assumed by the partnership before excess liabilities can be determined. The formula for determining the transferring partner's basis of the partnership interest received is as follows:

	Basis of the property transferred
Less	Liabilities assumed by the partnership
Plus	Partner's share of partnership liabilities
Plus	Gain recognized
Equals	Basis of partnership interest received

Gain is recognized to the extent that the combination of the first three items is a negative number.

Example 9.45

Joe transfers a building to a partnership for a 20 percent interest in the partnership valued at $50,000. The building has a fair market value of $100,000, a basis of $45,000, and a liability of $50,000 that the partnership assumes. Joe's realized gain is $55,000 ($100,000 – $45,000). His basis in the partnership interest after the transfer is $5,000 [$45,000 – $50,000 liability assumed + his $10,000 ($50,000 × 20%) share of the liability]. Joe's gain is deferred because he does not have a liability assumed in excess of basis.

If Joe's basis in the building is only $20,000, his realized gain is $80,000 ($100,000 – $20,000). He must recognize a gain of $20,000 ($20,000 basis – $50,000 liability assumed + his $10,000 share of the liability = negative $20,000) to avoid a negative basis in his partnership interest. His basis in his partnership interest is zero.

The effects of liabilities become even more complicated by the fact that partnerships can have two types of partners, general partners and limited partners. All partnerships must have two or more entities or individuals as partners and one must be a general partner. There can be an unlimited number of other general or limited partners. The partnership agreement determines how income and expenses are allocated to the different types of partners and, more importantly, how losses affect the partners. Limited partners' losses are limited to their investment, but the necessity of at least one general partner stems from the fact that general partners can be held liable for some or all of the partnership losses beyond their investment. Thus, the limited liability afforded corporations gave rise a number of years ago to the remodeled partnership form of a limited liability company.

A comparison of asset transfers by owners to corporations and partnerships is illustrated in Table 9.2.

[74] The effect of liabilities on a partner's basis in the partnership interest is discussed in more detail in Chapter 11.

Table 9.2 Comparison of Asset Transfers by Owners to Corporations and Partnerships

	Partnership	Corporation
Control required by owner	No	Yes; 80 percent by transferors
Loss recognized	No	No
Gain recognized	Liabilities assumed in excess of basis (basis must be adjusted for partner's share of liabilities assumed)	If gain realized and boot received
	Services exchanged for partnership interest	Liabilities assumed in excess of basis of all properties transferred
	Boot not a factor; any property, other than a partnership interest received, treated as a separate sale	Services exchanged for stock
Basis of partnership interest or stock	Basis of property transferred plus gain recognized minus net liabilities assumed	Basis of property transferred plus gain recognized minus liabilities assumed
Holding period in partnership interest or stock	Carries over on Section 1231 and capital assets	Carries over on Section 1231 and capital assets
	Starts at transaction date for ordinary income assets and partnership interest for services rendered	Starts at transaction date for ordinary income assets and stock received for services rendered

9.5.4 FORMATION OF A LIMITED LIABILITY COMPANY

When a limited liability company is formed, for tax purposes, its members may elect to treat the limited liability company as a corporation or it will be treated as a partnership by default. Most limited liability companies are treated as partnerships for tax purposes because it provides its members with limited liability along with the single level of taxation as a conduit or flow-through entity. There are no separate rules for the formation of the limited liability company. If it is a partnership for tax purposes, then the members follow the tax provisions related to the formation of a partnership. If an election is made to treat the limited liability company as a corporation, then the members will follow the tax consequences of corporate formations. In states that allow a single-owner LLC, the LLC is taxed as a sole proprietorship unless it elects to be taxed as a corporation.

9.6 AN INTRODUCTION TO CORPORATE REORGANIZATIONS

Over the past several decades, numerous businesses have restructured to increase their opportunity to grow and survive in an increasingly competitive business environment. They have acquired new businesses, disposed of unwanted enterprises, and merged with other firms to ensure remaining competitive. Legal and accounting firms have specialists who handle these complex mergers and acquisitions. Hollywood has even produced movies that portray the less flattering side of the mega-mergers and their architects. Although the pace of mergers and acquisitions has slowed, corporate reorganizations play a major role in business restructuring because these provisions provide the blueprint for acquiring or disposing of entire corporations or their assets at little or no tax cost.

A tax-deferred **corporate reorganization** involves the transfer of all or part of one corporation's assets or stock to a second corporation over which it has control in a transaction that qualifies as a reorganization under Section 368. A reorganization may be an acquisitive reorganization in which one corporation acquires the assets or stock of another corporation; it can be a divisive reorganization in which one corporation splits into two or more corporations; or it can involve a recapitalization or reincorporation that makes minimal changes in an existing corporation.

Corporations and their shareholders that participate in a qualified reorganization may exchange stock for property and stock for stock on a tax-deferred basis. As with most other tax-deferred transactions, the property or stock received will have a carryover or substituted basis to ensure that gain or loss is built into a future disposition. Boot received will also cause part or all of a realized gain to be recognized.

Example 9.46

Pam owns 1,400 shares of Target Corporation when Target is merged into Giant Corporation. Pam receives 700 shares in Giant Corporation (fair market value $23,000) and $1,000 cash in exchange for her Target Corporation stock. Pam's Target stock had a basis of $20,000 and a $24,000 fair market value. Although Pam has a $4,000 realized gain ($23,000 + $1,000 – $20,000), she recognizes only $1,000 gain. The gain recognized is the lesser of the realized gain ($4,000) or the boot received ($1,000 cash). Pam's basis in the Giant stock is $20,000 ($20,000 basis of Target stock + $1,000 gain recognized – $1,000 boot received).

A more complete discussion of corporate reorganizations is included in the appendix to this chapter.

REVISITING THE INTRODUCTORY CASE

Perry Winkle Corporation's most cost-effective solution would be to combine the like-kind provisions with those applicable to the condemnation of the land. To do so, it may have to use an indirect acquisition, although it might be possible to find suitable property that the owner would be willing to surrender in a direct exchange. Because time is important, and a buyer is waiting for the property, the indirect exchange seems more practical. Perry Winkle needs to engage an escrow agent to hold the proceeds of the sale while it locates suitable property for its business. To avoid all gain, the property purchased should have a price of at least $500,000 in excess of the selling price of its facilities. As they are looking to expand their current facilities, the purchase price will most likely be well in excess of the $500,000 plus sale proceeds. Winkle will trade its land and give boot of $500,000 from the condemnation proceedings to complete the transaction. The corporation needs to pay close attention to the time requirements for a like-kind exchange: 45 days to identify property and 180 days to closing. If the corporation does not use the entire $500,000 from the condemnation, it has more than two years to acquire additional real property and avoid gain recognition. Alternatively, Perry Winkle could contact the supplier and have the supplier purchase a large section of the property that Winkle could then exchange for its property. Winkle could purchase adjacent or other property with the condemnation proceeds.

SUMMARY

In a tax-deferred exchange, the taxpayer postpones recognizing gain or loss until a future event triggers recognition. Deferral is accomplished by decreasing basis for unrecognized gains and increasing it for unrecognized losses. The holding period of the asset received includes the holding period of the asset surrendered in a tax-deferred exchange.

One of the most important deferral provisions is the like-kind exchange that allows business or investment property to be exchanged for other business or investment property under certain conditions. To qualify, any investment or business realty may be exchanged for other investment or business realty. If property other than like-kind property is received as part of a qualifying like-kind exchange, gain is recognized to the extent of the boot received or the gain realized, if smaller. Exchanges may involve more than two parties, and third-party intermediaries may be used to arrange a qualifying exchange.

Asset dispositions include involuntary conversions by theft, casualty, and condemnation. Deductible losses on involuntary conversions are reduced by insurance recoveries. Involuntary conversions of business and investment property are deductible as Section 1231 losses. Casualty losses of individuals' personal-use property can be deducted only to the extent they exceed a $100 floor per occurrence and 10 percent of adjusted gross income and after 2017, must be from a disaster.

Gains on involuntary conversions may be deferred if the taxpayer acquires qualifying replacement property. If the taxpayer owns and uses the property, the replacement property must have the same function as the converted property. If the taxpayer owns and leases the converted property to another, the taxpayer is only required to replace the converted property with other property that can be leased. The installment sales provision postpones gain recognition (but not loss recognition) while wash sales and sales between related parties are loss disallowance provisions.

Individuals may transfer property to a sole proprietorship without tax effects. Gains and losses on transfers of property to a controlled corporation in exchange for stock in the corporation, and gains and losses on transfers of property to a partnership in exchange for a partnership interest, are deferred. Corporations may acquire the stock or property of another corporation in a qualified reorganization without tax consequences.

KEY TERMS

Amount realized 405
Basis adjustment 403
Boot 405
Casualty 409
Condemnation 409
Control 423
Corporate reorganization 431
Deductible loss 411
Deferred gain 405
Functional-use test 417
Holding period 407
Installment method 419
Involuntary conversions 409
Like-kind exchange 404
Partner's basis 428
Presidentially declared disaster 414
Realized gain 405
Recognized gain 405
Related parties 420
Section 121 418
Section 351 423
Tax-deferred exchange 402
Taxpayer-use test 417
Theft 409
Wash sale 418

TEST YOURSELF

Answers Appear after the Problem Assignments

1. JB Manufacturing and BP Company exchange two pieces of land. JB's land has a basis of $800,000 and a fair market value of $750,000. BP's land has a basis of $560,000 and a fair market value of only $700,000 so BP gives JB an additional $50,000 cash. What are JB's and BP's deferred gain or loss on this exchange?

a. JB $50,000 deferred loss; BP $140,000 deferred gain
b. JB $50,000 deferred gain; BP $140,000 deferred gain
c. JB $50,000 deferred loss; BP $90,000 deferred gain
d. JB $50,000 deferred gain; BP $90,000 deferred gain

2. Cragin's manufacturing facility had an adjusted basis of $7,600,000: $2,000,000 for the land and $5,600,000 for the building when destroyed by fire. It received $7,000,000 from its insurance company to replace the building, and it sold the land for $2,800,000. How much must Cragin invest in a new facility to defer all of its gain?

a. $7,000,000
b. $7,600,000
c. $9,000,000
d. $9,800,000

3. The Joneses' home that they had owned and lived in for 12 years was destroyed in a flood. Fortunately, they had flood insurance that paid replacement value of $280,000 for their loss. The home had a basis of $223,000. How much gain must they recognize if they purchase a new home for only $268,000?
   a. 0
   b. $12,000
   c. $45,000
   d. $57,000

4. Marylou transfers $220,000 of equipment (basis = $170,000) to her wholly owned corporation in exchange for all the authorized nonvoting stock and $20,000 cash. How much gain or loss does Marylou recognize on the transfer, and what is her basis in the stock?
   a. gain = 0; basis = $150,000
   b. gain = $20,000; basis = $150,000
   c. gain = $20,000; basis = $170,000
   d. gain = $50,000; basis = $220,000

5. Mark, Nancy, and Carl form a partnership with each partner having an equal share in profits and losses. Mark and Carl each contribute $40,000 in cash to the partnership. Nancy contributes land valued at $100,000. The land has a basis of $90,000 and is encumbered by a $60,000 mortgage that the partnership assumes. What basis does Nancy have in her partnership interest immediately after the contribution of land to the partnership?
   a. $50,000
   b. $90,000
   c. $100,000
   d. $110,000

PROBLEM ASSIGNMENTS

Check Your Understanding

1. [LO 9.1] How is gain or loss deferral usually accomplished? How is holding period affected by gain or loss deferral?

2. [LO 9.2] What types of realty qualify for like-kind exchange treatment?

3. [LO 9.2] What is boot? What effect does boot have on a like-kind exchange?

4. [LO 9.2] What is a nonsimultaneous exchange? What are the critical factors in qualifying a nonsimultaneous exchange for tax deferral?

5. [LO 9.2] What is an indirect exchange? What are the two most common forms of indirect exchanges?

6. [LO 9.3] How is a casualty loss that completely destroys personal-use property measured? How is a casualty loss that partially destroys personal-use property measured?

7. [LO 9.3] How is a casualty loss that completely destroys business or investment property measured? How is a casualty loss that partially destroys business or investment property measured?

8. [LO 9.3] What limits are placed on the deductibility of casualty and theft losses of personal-use property?

9. [LO 9.3] Explain how the deductibility of personal casualty losses changed after 2017.

10. [LO 9.3] Explain the functional-use test. Explain the taxpayer-use test.

11. [LO 9.3] What provisions apply to a personal residence that is subject to an involuntary conversion?

12. [LO 9.4] Charlie exchanged land valued at $450,000 and a sports car valued at $50,000 for a 40 percent interest in a partnership that planned to build an apartment complex on the property. The land has a $325,000 basis and the auto a $40,000 basis. Explain the tax effects of this exchange for Charlie and the partnership.

13. [LO 9.4] Bob and Ray started a tree trimming business that recently became profitable. They each buy a $250,000 life insurance policy on themselves. They then exchange ownership of the policies to provide funds in case of either of their deaths. How is this exchange treated for tax purposes?

14. [LO 9.4] On May 10 of the current year, Claire purchased 1,000 shares of ABCO stock for $10 per share because she believed the price had hit bottom. She did not know that her broker had sold 500 shares that he held in her brokerage account at $18 per share on April 18 when the price dropped from its $22 purchase price. Explain the effect of these transactions on Claire.

15. [LO 9.4] What is an installment sale? If a transaction qualifies for installment sale treatment, when will the taxpayer be taxed on the sale? What does a taxpayer do if the taxpayer does not want to use the installment method?

16. [LO 9.5] What is the critical requirement of a corporate formation to ensure tax-deferred property transfers to all participants?

17. [LO 9.5] How do liabilities assumed by a corporation affect a shareholder transferring property to it in a qualifying Section 351 transfer?

18. [LO 9.5] Explain the general provisions applicable to a partner transferring property to a partnership in exchange for a partnership interest.

19. [LO 9.5] Explain the tax treatment of services transferred to a partnership in exchange for a partnership interest.

20. [LO 9.6] What is a corporate reorganization? Briefly define each of the types of corporate reorganizations.

Crunch the Numbers

21. [LO 9.1] Wilma had a loss of $25,000 on some investment artwork that was stolen and never recovered. She suffered a $20,000 loss when a piece of land she had held as an investment was condemned to make way for a new city park. She also had a Section 1231 gain of $60,000 and a Section 1231 loss of $15,000 from asset sales by her sole proprietorship.

a. Determine the result of both Step 1 and Step 2 of the Section 1231 netting process and explain the treatment of the resulting gains or losses.

b. How would your answer change if Wilma had a Section 1231 loss of $12,000 two years ago?

22. [LO 9.2] Peter exchanges a building valued at $400,000 for land also valued at $400,000 in a qualifying like-kind exchange. The building has a basis of $230,000. What are Peter's realized gain or loss and the basis of the land?

23. [LO 9.2] Shawn exchanges a factory building for an apartment building in a qualifying like-kind exchange. The factory has a basis of $350,000 and the apartment building has a fair market value of $320,000.

a. What is Shawn's realized gain or loss and the basis of the apartment building?

b. What alternative could you suggest to Shawn?

24. [LO 9.2] JR received 10,000 shares of Jones-Redding valued at $50 per share in exchange for a building valued at $1,000,000 and the assumption of the building's $500,000 mortgage. What are the tax consequences for JR if the building has a basis of (a) $1,200,000; (b) $700,000; or (c) $400,000?

25. [LO 9.2] Delta Corporation exchanges a warehouse for an office building from Gamma Corporation. Delta's warehouse has a fair market value of $4,000,000 and a basis of $2,250,000. The office building has a fair market value of $3,750,000, so Delta received $250,000 cash from Gamma to complete the exchange.
   a. What are Delta's realized and recognized gain or loss on the exchange?
   b. What is its deferred gain or loss?
   c. What is its basis in the building acquired?
   d. How would your answers change if Delta's basis in the warehouse was $3,900,000?
   e. How would your answers change if its basis in the warehouse was $4,150,000?

26. [LO 9.2] Lab Kennels, Inc. and Wolman Developers agree to exchange two parcels of land and each assume the other's mortgage on the parcel acquired. Lab owns 500 acres within city limits that has a value of $750,000 and a basis of $300,000. It is encumbered by a $200,000 mortgage. Wolman's property is raw land outside the city that has a value of $900,000, a basis of $400,000, and is encumbered by a $350,000 mortgage.
   a. What are Lab Kennels, Inc. and Wolman Developer's realized and recognized gains or losses on the exchange?
   b. What are their deferred gains or losses?
   c. What are their bases in the land acquired?

27. [LO 9.2] DDD Corporation agrees to exchange $50,000 and some raw land for a building owned by Jason Briggs. DDD Corporation's land has a value of $600,000, a basis of $200,000 and is encumbered by a $200,000 mortgage that Briggs agrees to assume. Briggs's building is valued at $450,000 and has a basis of $125,000.
   a. What are DDD Corporation's and Briggs's realized and recognized gains or losses on the exchange?
   b. What are their deferred gains or losses?
   c. What are their bases in the properties acquired?

28. [LO 9.2] The Clover Corporation wants to exchange land held for expansion for a building that will provide additional office space to avoid gain recognition. The land has a value of $1,200,000 and a basis of $800,000. What alternative can you suggest to Clover to accomplish its goal?

29. [LO 9.2] Bently Corporation wants to dispose of a warehouse valued at $800,000 but with a basis of only $300,000. It has two replacement alternatives. Bently can purchase a replacement warehouse for $800,000 or it can make a direct exchange for another suitable warehouse. Bently located a suitable warehouse that the owner is willing to exchange for her warehouse, but its fair market value is only $725,000. The owner refuses to pay anything additional as part of the exchange for Bently's warehouse. Assume Bently uses a 21 percent tax rate and an 8 percent discount rate for all asset decisions. Also assume either property would be depreciated evenly over 40 years. Should Bently sell the building at its fair market value and purchase the $800,000 property, or should it make the exchange?

30. [LO 9.3] A tornado destroyed part of the offices of Heywood Corporation. The building had a fair market value of $500,000 before and $200,000 after the tornado. The basis of the building is $320,000.
   a. What is Heywood's casualty loss from the tornado?
   b. What is its remaining basis in the property, assuming it deducts its loss?
   c. What is Heywood's gain or loss if it receives $250,000 from its insurance company as compensation for its loss?
   d. What is its basis in the property if it spends $150,000 to repair the property?

31. [LO 9.3] Jewel's home was completely destroyed by a wildfire in 2018 in an area declared a national disaster. The building had an appraised value of $185,000 before the fire. Four years ago Jewel paid $160,000 for the house and the land, with $25,000 of the price allocated to the land.
   a. What is Jewel's loss on the fire, assuming no insurance?
   b. What is her deductible loss if her adjusted gross income is $40,000?

c. What is Jewel's realized gain or loss if she receives $190,000 from the insurance company to rebuild the home?
d. What is her recognized gain if she uses only $130,000 of the insurance proceeds to rebuild a smaller replacement residence on the same land?

32. [LO 9.3] Danny's living room furniture and his flat screen television were damaged in a fire in his home in January. In March, his golf cart was damaged in a flood. He was able to establish the following information to determine his losses on these assets.

Asset	FMV before casualty	FMV after casualty	Insurance recovery	Cost	Date purchased
Television	$4,600	$1,100	$2,000	$5,000	10 months ago
Furniture	5,500	1,500	3,200	3,000	11 years ago
Golf Cart	6,500	2,000	1,500	7,000	8 months ago

Danny's AGI is $37,000 before considering these casualties and he has $12,000 of other itemized deductions.
a. Determine Danny's deductible casualty loss if the events occurred in 2017.
b. How would your answer change if these events happened in 2018?

33. [LO 9.3] Cora was in Europe from Thanksgiving of 2018 until early January of 2019. When she returned, she found her home office had been broken into and equipment with a fair market value of $40,000 and a basis of $54,000 was missing. Her adjusted gross incomes in 2018 and 2019 are $56,000 and $72,000, respectively. If she is a calendar-year sole proprietor, what is her theft deduction, and in which year should she take the deduction?

34. [LO 9.3] Clayton Corporation owns business realty that the county condemns on July 15, year 1. The county pays Clayton $400,000 for the property that has an allocated basis of $235,000.
a. What are Clayton's realized and recognized gains, assuming it does not replace the property?
b. What is its recognized gain, assuming it spends $350,000 on replacement property?
c. What is its basis in the replacement property?
d. What is its recognized gain, assuming it spends $500,000 on replacement property?
e. What is its basis in the replacement property?
f. If the corporation has a June 30 fiscal year-end, what is the last date that it can acquire qualifying replacement property?

35. [LO 9.3] Coronado Corporation owns business realty that was destroyed by fire on March 15, year 1. Its insurance company pays Coronado $325,000 for the property, which has an allocated basis of $275,000.
a. What are Coronado's realized and recognized gains, assuming it does not replace the property?
b. What is its recognized gain, assuming it spends $300,000 on replacement property?
c. What is its basis in the replacement property?
d. What is its recognized gain, assuming it spends $350,000 on replacement property?
e. What is its basis in the replacement property?
f. If the corporation has an April 30 year-end, what is the last date on which it can acquire qualifying replacement property?

36. [LO 9.3] Performance Industries, Inc. sold three pieces of equipment and a small building on March 1, year 6. Data on these disposals are as follows:

Machine	Cost	Date acquired	Depreciation	Selling price
1	$45,000	April 24, year 2	$35,000	$19,000
2	$105,000	May 2, year 1	$90,000	$24,000
3	$63,000	June 4, year 4	$12,000	$66,000
Building	$400,000	April 30, year 1	$45,000	$425,000

a. Determine the amount and character of the gain or loss on each of these assets.
b. Determine the sum of each type of gain or loss and the net effect these gains/losses have on Performance Industries' net income.
c. How would your answers change if Performance Industries had $6,000 of Section 1231 losses in year 3?

37. [LO 9.3] Late in the current year, Bradley Corporation's factory was destroyed by a tornado. Bradley determined that its unreimbursed loss on their building built ten years ago was $200,000. They also had a $75,000 gain on the sale of a ten-year-old machine (cost $100,000). Prior to the tornado, Bradley had a condemnation gain on land of $100,000, a Section 1231 loss of $150,000, and a $25,000 Section 1231 gain.
a. Determine the results of both Step 1 and Step 2 of the Section 1231 netting process and the effect of these occurrences on Bradley's net income.
b. How would your answers change if Bradley was a sole proprietorship instead of a corporation?

38. [LO 9.4] Moore bought 2,000 shares of VBT stock over the Internet on January 2 of year 4 for $50,000. On December 28 of year 3, his broker sold 3,000 shares of VBT for $85,000 that she had been holding in Moore's account. This stock had been purchased in year 1 for $100,000. What is Moore's realized and recognized gain or loss? What is his basis in the stock purchased on January 2?

39. [LO 9.4] Monroe Corporation's chief financial officer sold 2,000 shares of TNC stock the corporation was holding as a temporary investment on July 3 at a $4,000 loss. On July 30, the controller of Monroe purchased 1,000 shares of TNC for the corporation at $8 per share as the stock had received a favorable recommendation from the corporation's financial advisor. What are the tax consequences of these transactions?

40. [LO 9.4] Marilyn owned 500 shares of Ibis stock that she purchased several years ago for $25,000. This year, she sold 200 of the shares to her brother for $7,000, its fair market value, when she wanted money for some plastic surgery. Determine Marilyn's realized and recognized gain or loss on the sale and her basis in the 300 shares remaining. Determine her brother's basis in the purchased stock and his realized and recognized gain or loss if he sells the shares for $12,000 the following year to an unrelated party.

41. [LO 9.4] William bought 1,000 shares of Bevo stock three years ago for $100 per share. This year he has a $20,000 short-term capital gain from the sale of his shares of an initial public offering of GBD Company stock. To offset the gain, William sells his shares of Bevo to his grandfather for $80,000, its current fair market value. The next month, William's grandfather sells the stock for $85,000 to his neighbor. Determine William's realized and recognized gain or loss on the sale of Bevo stock. Determine the grandfather's basis in the stock purchased from William and his realized and recognized gain or loss when he sells the stock to his neighbor.

42. [LO 9.4] Kelly was active in the market, buying and selling stocks for her own account. Below are a series of transactions Kelly initiated during the last quarter of 2018:

Date of transaction	Transaction	Number of shares	Stock	Price per share
10/15	Bought	1,000	ABC	$25
10/29	Bought	500	DEF	$20
11/01	Sold	800	XYZ	$15
11/04	Sold	500	DEF	$22
11/07	Bought	1,000	GHI	$16
11/18	Bought	2,000	XYZ	$12
11/20	Sold	500	ABC	$22
11/22	Bought	500	DEF	$18
12/02	Bought	1,000	ABC	$21

The XYZ stock sold on 11/01 had been purchased two years earlier for $18 per share. What is Kelly's realized and recognized gain or loss on each of the sale transactions? (Use FIFO for determining which stocks were sold.) What is Kelly's basis in each of the stocks remaining in her portfolio?

43. [LO 9.4] On January 2, year 1, Randy sold a parcel of land held as an investment. Randy's basis in the land was $8,500. The buyer made a $6,000 down payment on the date of sale and $7,000 payments on January 2 in both year 2 and year 3. In addition, the buyer paid 8 percent interest on the unpaid balance. How much income should Randy have recognized in years 1, 2, and 3, assuming that he used the installment method? What is the result if Randy elected out of the installment method for this sale?

44. [LO 9.4] Conroy Corporation agrees to sell some of its excess machinery for $190,000 consisting of a $70,000 down payment in year of sale and additional payments of $60,000 in each of the next two years, plus interest. Conroy purchased this machinery several years ago for $156,000 and had claimed accumulated depreciation of $47,000. How much income should Conroy Corporation recognize in each year assuming that it uses the installment method? How does your answer change if Conroy elects out of the installment method for this sale?

45. [LO 9.5] Jim and Cindy form JC Corporation, with each receiving 50 percent of the shares issued. Jim transfers land valued at $50,000 with a $40,000 basis for his stock, and Cindy transfers property valued at $45,000 with a basis of $50,000 for her stock. In addition, Cindy provides $5,000 of legal and accounting services in establishing the corporation. What are the tax consequences of the incorporation? What are Jim and Cindy's bases in their stock?

46. [LO 9.5] Wilbur transfers property valued at $100,000 (basis = $70,000) to the Debold Corporation in exchange for 100 percent of its stock.

a. What is Wilbur's realized gain or loss on the transfer and his recognized gain or loss?
b. What is his basis in the stock received?
c. What is the corporation's basis in the property received?

47. [LO 9.5] Arleta transfers property valued at $210,000 (basis = $190,000) to BCD Corporation in exchange for 70 percent of its stock. Georgia transfers property valued at $85,000 (basis = $75,000) and performs $5,000 in accounting services in exchange for the other 30 percent of BCD's stock.

a. What are Arleta and Georgia's gains/income or losses realized?
b. What are Arleta and Georgia's gains/income or losses recognized?
c. What are their bases in BCD's stock?
d. What is BCD's basis in the property received?

48. [LO 9.5] Carol decides to transfer her rental apartment building to a wholly owned corporation to insulate herself from tenant liabilities. The apartment building is valued at $1,250,000 and has a basis of $1,350,000 due to $400,000 of recent improvements made to the building. The new corporation also assumes the $200,000 remaining on Carol's mortgage on the building.

a. What is the value of the stock Carol receives from the corporation?
b. What is Carol's realized and recognized gain or loss on the transfer?
c. What are Carol's basis in her stock and the corporation's basis in the building? Explain your answer.

49. [LO 9.5] Cornelia transfers property valued at $500 (basis = $350) to Wayside Corporation in exchange for 50 percent of its stock. Ferdinand transfers property valued at $450 (basis = $260) in exchange for 40 percent of Wayside's stock and $50 cash. Cheryl transfers $100 cash in exchange for the remaining 10% of the stock.

a. What are Cornelia's and Ferdinand's realized gains or losses?
b. What are their recognized gains or losses?
c. What are their bases in Wayside's stock?
d. What is Wayside's basis in the property received?
e. Does Wayside have any other tax consequences?

50. [LO 9.5] Tinker incorporates his sole proprietorship by transferring a building, equipment, and inventory to the Tinker Corporation in exchange for all its stock. The building has a value of $750,000 and a basis of $800,000, the equipment has a value of $400,000 and a basis of $375,000, and the inventory has both a value and basis of $50,000.
   a. What is Tinker's gain or loss realized on the transfer?
   b. What is Tinker's gain or loss recognized on the transfer?
   c. What is his basis in the stock received and the corporation's basis in the property received? Explain your answer.

51. [LO 9.5] Jim and Angie form the JAZ Partnership with Zoe by contributing $75,000 each to partnership equity. Zoe, the third partner, contributes property with a basis of $50,000 and fair market value of $75,000. The three are equal partners in the partnership. Determine the tax consequences to Zoe for the contribution of property to the partnership. What are the partnership's tax consequences? What is each partner's basis in the partnership interest? What is the partnership's basis in the property?

52. [LO 9.5] Moe, Larry, and Curly form a partnership with each partner having an equal share in profits and losses. Moe and Curly each contribute $50,000 cash to the partnership. Larry contributes a piece of land valued at $170,000. The land has a basis of $125,000 and is encumbered by a $120,000 mortgage (non-recourse debt). What basis does each of the partners have in their partnership interest immediately after the contribution of money and land to the partnership?

53. [LO 9.5] X, Y, and Z form XYZ Partnership by contributing cash and property as follows: X contributes $40,000 cash for a 20 percent interest. Y contributes property valued at $80,000 for a 40 percent interest. This property has a basis in Y's hands of $50,000. For the remaining 40 percent interest, Z develops the partnership agreement and performs other services that are valued at $5,000. In addition, he contributes property with a fair market value of $100,000 with a $25,000 mortgage that the partnership guarantees. The property has a basis of $70,000 in Z's hands. Determine X, Y, and Z's bases in their partnership interests. Determine the partnership's basis in the assets contributed.

Develop Planning Skills

54. [LO 9.2] The Glades Corporation located a building it would like to have for its new warehouse. The corporation has contacted the owner about making a trade for its existing property. The owner of the desired property is only willing to sell the building for cash as he will have little gain on the sale and has no use for the Glades property. Glades, however, has an extremely low basis in its property and is unwilling to sell it in order to purchase the new property. Is there an alternative that will satisfy Glades and the owner of the warehouse property?

55. [LO 9.2] The Timberlake Corporation has an opportunity to sell its manufacturing facility to Carroll Corporation for $4,500,000. The property has a basis of $2,000,000, and the prospective purchaser is willing to wait up to six months for occupancy to allow Timberlake time to locate and purchase new facilities. Timberlake's tax rate is 21 percent. What alternatives should Timberlake consider, and what are the tax consequences of the alternatives?

56. [LO 9.2] Refer to the material in the preceding problem. Timberlake locates suitable property that the owner would sell for $4,800,000 although the property appraises at only $4,250,000. Carroll Corporation is willing to purchase this property for the $4,800,000 asking price. It would then trade this property to Timberlake for its property, but Timberlake would have to pay it $300,000 in addition to transferring the property. What are the tax consequences?

57. [LO 9.5] William, Wally, and Wilma want to form a corporation. William has cash of $100,000; Wally has property valued at $100,000 with a basis of $80,000; and Wilma has property valued at $50,000 that has a $70,000 basis. Wally doesn't want to recognize his gain, but Wilma wants to recognize her loss because she has capital gains to offset the loss. As their tax advisor, develop several alternatives

from which they can choose that would allow Wally to avoid gain recognition but allow Wilma to recognize her loss.

Think Outside the Text

These questions require answers that are beyond the material that is covered in this chapter.

58. [LO 9.3] What policy reason do you think explains why losses on the personal-use property of individuals are nondeductible except for a limited amount of loss from involuntary conversions?

59. [LO 9.3] Why do you think businesses are allowed an additional year to find qualifying replacement real estate for realty that is condemned?

60. [LO 9.3] What is a possible reason for allowing persons to use the provision that allows the deferral of gain or loss for involuntary conversions on property that is sold under the threat of condemnation only?

61. [LO 9.5] What is the rationale behind a corporation's increasing its basis in property received in a Section 351 transaction for the gain recognized by the transferor shareholder?

62. [LO 9.5] A shareholder receives stock valued at $500,000 and $50,000 cash for two pieces of equipment as part of a Section 351 transaction. He transfers (1) Machine A with a fair market value of $330,000 and a basis of $300,000 and (2) Machine B with a fair market value of $220,000 and a basis of $250,000. How do you think the shareholder should determine if he should recognize any gain on the transfer of the equipment? Comment on the result.

Search the Internet

For the following problems, consult the IRS website (www.irs.gov).

63. [LO 9.2] Locate and read Publication 544: *Sales and Other Disposition of Assets*. How is a like-kind exchange reported? If there is a recognized gain, how is that reported?

64. [LO 9.3] Locate and read Publication 547: *Casualties, Disasters, and Thefts*. Where is a casualty loss on a personal-use asset reported? Where is a casualty gain on personal-use property reported?

65. [LO 9.4] Locate and read Publication 550: *Investment Income and Expenses*. How do you report a wash sale?

Identify the Issues

Identify the issues or problems suggested by the following situations. State each issue as a question.

66. [LO 9.3] The Westlawn Corporation is located in a flood plain. Twelve years ago, its offices were flooded when the nearby river overflowed. Six years ago, the area received 12 inches of rain in a six-hour period, the river overflowed, and the offices flooded again. This year, excessive runoff from melting snow in the nearby mountains caused the river to overflow again and flood the company's offices.

67. [LO 9.3] The Timmins Corporation has three acres of land on which its warehouse and offices are located. The state condemned two acres of the land for an extension of a highway frontage road. The strip that was condemned took the warehouse and parking area, leaving only the small office building. The corporation received $3,000,000 for the property that was condemned and $1,000,000 in severance damages due to the separation of the office property from the rest of the facility. The warehouse and parking area have a basis of $425,000 and the office area a basis of $250,000. Timmins plans to replace the entire warehouse and office facility.

68. [LO 9.3] Claiborne, Inc. has received an offer to purchase its manufacturing facilities for $7,500,000. If sold, it would have a gain of $5,000,000 on the property. Claiborne has found an ideal location for a new facility, but the only available property is three times as large as it needs. It can, however, acquire a one-third interest in the property and move its operations into that area. The purchaser of its property is willing to cooperate in an indirect exchange.

69. [LO 9.3] Barry owned a number of rental properties. One of the rental properties was located next to his personal residence. Both properties were condemned by the state. Barry found a perfect residence to replace the rental property almost immediately but not one to replace the personal residence. As a result, Barry moved into the replacement rental unit for five months until he found a suitable home to replace the residence.

70. [LO 9.3] Carlson Manufacturing's plant was condemned by the federal government to allow for expansion of one of its secured locations for government employees. The government paid the company $6,800,000 for the property that had a basis of $2,500,000 and it moved out in December of year 1. In March of year 2, Carlson contracted with a construction company to build new facilities in West Virginia. The construction was to take two years with occupancy planned for June of year 4. Severe floods followed extraordinary rains in the spring of year 4. The construction company was forced to halt construction for six months until a bridge into the property could be replaced. As a result, construction was not completed until February of year 5. Carlson occupied the building in March of that year.

Develop Research Skills

71. [LO 9.2] Barry is very dedicated to the arts and has made a career of purchasing copyrights to various art forms. Once purchased, he publicizes these works to capitalize on the copyrights and has been very successful. Last year, he acquired a book manuscript that he believes would be better suited to a mainstream publisher. He approaches a publisher about trading the book copyright for the copyright on the words and music for a new musical comedy that he heard the publisher had acquired. Will the exchange qualify as like-kind exchange?

72. [LO 9.3] Cheryl owned six horses that she and her family used for riding and occasionally showing in hunter-jumper competitions. At the beginning of May, one of the horses showed signs of severe illness and was diagnosed with equine encephalitis. She was required to destroy all of her horses, none of which was insured. The horses had been purchased for $23,000 but had a current value of $45,000. What type of a loss does Cheryl have on these horses?

73. [LO 9.5] Joe, June, and Jim—coworkers—decide that they want to start their own business. Joe has $200,000 to contribute, June has equipment valued at $100,000 (basis = $90,000), and Jim has real estate suitable for the business valued at $200,000 (basis = $110,000). Joe and Jim are each to receive 40 percent of the corporate stock, and June is to receive 20 percent. Joe and June transfer title to their property to the corporation immediately. When Jim tries to transfer title to the real estate to the corporation, several legal errors in the title are discovered, and he is unable to transfer title until the errors are corrected. Correcting the errors takes more than 14 months. In the meantime, the corporation begins operating, renting the building from Jim. In the 15th month, Jim is able to transfer title and receive his stock. Is Jim eligible to use the nonrecognition provisions of Section 351 on this transfer?

Fill-in the Forms

74. [LO 9.3] Locate and print Form 4684 (Casualties and Thefts). Enter the following information and complete the form to the extent possible: Howser Corporation, a calendar-year corporation, discovered in January that its bookkeeper (who was fired late last year) had embezzled $45,000 from the company. The theft was not covered by insurance. In October, a hurricane damaged its warehouse building in the Florida Keys. The building's fair market values before and after the hurricane were $425,000 and $150,000, respectively. The basis of the building at the time of the damage was $235,000. Howser received only $200,000 from its insurance company due to its limited hurricane coverage.

75. Comprehensive Individual Return Problem. Cletus and Josepha Mayor have been married for twelve years and currently live at 2907 Seven Oaks Lane, Columbia, SC 29210. Their Social Security numbers are 223-34-4444 and 322-32-2222, respectively. They have two daughters, Sheena, age 10, (SSN 344-44-1234) and Carletta, age 7, (SSN 566-55-6543) who live with them and are fully supported by them.

Cletus is a manager for a local building contractor and earned a salary of $59,800 for the current tax year. He had $5,600 withheld for federal income taxes and $1,300 for state income taxes. Josepha is an elementary school teacher and earned $31,950. She had $2,280 withheld for federal income taxes and $700 for state income taxes.

On July 20 they purchased a new home for $210,000. The last five years they have lived in rented homes or apartments because they moved frequently for Cletus's job before settling in Columbia. They paid total mortgage interest on their new home of $7,250 for the period of time they owned the home, all of which was reported to them on Form 1098. Points incurred on the purchase of the new home were $1,800 (also reported on Form 1098).

Cletus contributed $2,000 to his Roth IRA and Josepha contributed $1,000 to hers.

They paid $1,200 in premiums for medical and dental insurance, had $2,800 in unreimbursed doctor and dentist bills, and paid $300 for an unreimbursed hospital bill.

They paid property taxes of $1,825 on the new home, which was properly allocated between them and the seller on their closing statement.

In June, they renewed the license plates on their two cars paying a total of $265. This amount included a flat fee of $40 per auto plus one percent based on the value of the autos. They also paid a total of $1,100 in state general sales taxes during the year.

They contributed $500 in cash to their church this year.

Josepha spent $1,120 on materials for use in her classroom. She spent $1,400 on tuition for two courses leading to her master's degree in education at State College (59-9812345). She received a Form 1098-T reporting the $1,400 in box 1 and box 9 was checked indicating she was a graduate student. Cletus took two continuing education courses to maintain his general contractor's license. These courses cost $300 and were not reimbursed by his employer.

Just prior to moving to the new home, the Mayor's had a party for the neighbors to say "goodbye." During the party, Josepha took off her diamond ring while she was working in the kitchen. When she went to get the ring later, it was gone. It was established that the ring had been stolen and could not be recovered. The ring cost $3,700 when purchased five years before. Because Josepha had replacement value insurance on the ring, she received $5,000 from the insurance company to acquire a substantially similar ring. She decided not to purchase a replacement.

Josepha paid $2,300 in after-school child care expenses ($1,150 for each daughter) to Dawn-to-Dusk Care, 18 Elk Grove Street, Columbia, SC 29210, EIN 59-12345678.

The couple earned $90 in interest on their savings and checking accounts with the First National Bank of South Carolina and $220 in interest on the Teacher's Union money market fund. They have no foreign accounts and no one in the family was ever convicted of a felony.

a. Complete Form 1040 (married filing jointly) and any required related forms and schedules for the Mayors using the 2017 forms available on the IRS website at *www.irs.gov*.

b. Briefly describe what would change if the tax year was instead 2018.

ANSWERS TO TEST YOURSELF

1. **a. JB $50,000 deferred loss** ($750,000 – $800,000); **BP $140,000 deferred gain** ($750,000 – $610,000).

2. **d. $9,800,000**; even though the proceeds were obtained from two sources, all must be reinvested to defer the entire gain.

3. **a. $0**; they recognize no gain under Section 121 because this is considered a sale.

4. **c. gain = $20,000; basis = $170,000**. Marylou must recognize gain equal to the lesser of gain realized or boot received. Her basis = $170,000 + $20,000 gain – $20,000 boot received.

5. **a. $50,000**. $90,000 carryover basis – $60,000 liability + ($60,000 × 1/3).

APPENDIX: CORPORATE REORGANIZATIONS

LEARNING OBJECTIVES

After completing this appendix, you should be able to:

9A.1 Identify qualifying forms of acquisitive corporate reorganizations and explain the basic tax consequences.

9A.2 Describe the forms of divisive reorganizations.

9A.3 Explain the primary characteristics of Types E, F, and G reorganizations.

9A.4 List tax considerations in planning for a corporate reorganization.

Seven types of reorganizations, commonly referred to as Types A through G, are presented in Section 368(a)(1)(A) to (G). Types A, B, and C are acquisitive reorganizations. Types E and F involve only one corporation making technical changes. Type D reorganizations can be either divisive or acquisitive reorganizations. Type G reorganizations are similar to Type D reorganizations but apply only to corporations in bankruptcy.

9A.1 ACQUISITIVE REORGANIZATIONS

An acquisitive reorganization generally involves (1) the acquisition of one corporation's assets (the target) by a second corporation (the acquirer), after which the target ceases to operate or (2) the acquisition of the target corporation's stock for stock of the acquirer, after which the target becomes a subsidiary of the acquiring corporation. Types A (the statutory merger or consolidation), C (a stock for asset acquisition), and acquisitive D reorganizations follow this asset acquisition pattern, while Type B is the stock for stock acquisition.

Figures 9A.1 and 9A.2 illustrate the asset and stock acquisitive reorganizations.

BASIC TAX CONSEQUENCES

In an asset acquisition, an Acquirer corporation transfers stock and securities to a Target corporation in exchange for Target's assets. If it is a qualifying reorganization, neither Acquirer nor Target recognizes gain or loss on this transfer. Acquirer takes the same basis in the assets as their basis in Target's hands. Target recognizes no gain or loss on the receipt of stock or securities; it recognizes no gain on the receipt of any other property as long as that property is distributed to its

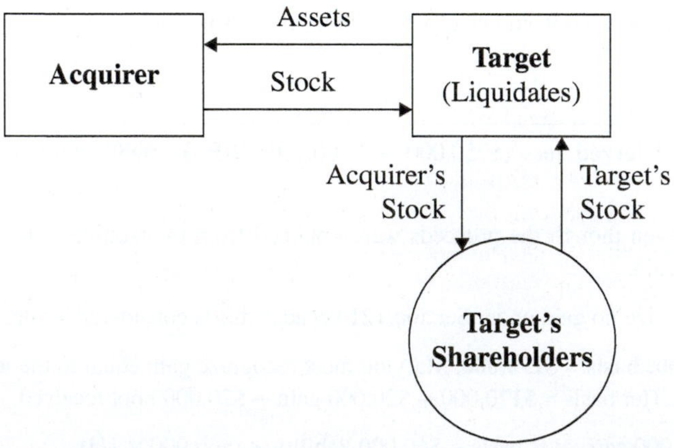

FIGURE 9A.1 Acquisitive reorganization asset acquisition

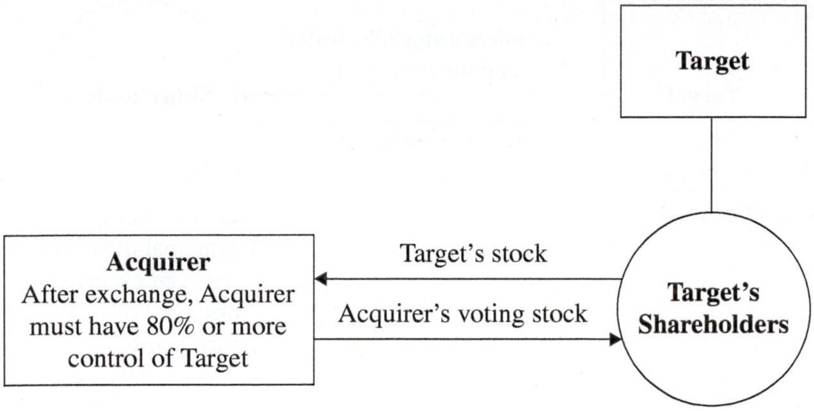

FIGURE 9A.2 Type B acquisitive reorganization stock acquisition

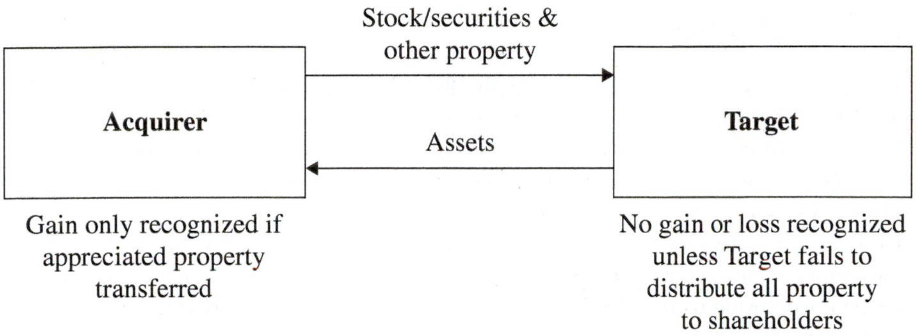

FIGURE 9A.3 General tax consequences for corporations that are part of an asset acquisition reorganization

shareholders. Gain is recognized only by Acquirer if it transfers appreciated property other than stock or securities to Target, in which case Target uses fair market value for its basis in the property retained. (No loss is recognized on depreciated property transferred.) Figure 9A.3 illustrates the asset transfers between the corporations and the tax consequences.

Target's shareholders recognize no gain or loss on the receipt of stock in exchange for their stock in Target; they may be required to recognize gain on the receipt of securities if the principal of the securities received exceeds the principal of the securities surrendered.[75] If Target distributes cash or property other than stock or securities, the shareholders receive boot and recognize gain to the extent of the lesser of the fair market value of the boot received or gain realized. Boot received may be assets that Target did not transfer to Acquirer, or it may be property that Acquirer transferred to Target as part of the acquisition. Target's shareholders have the same basis in the stock and securities received as they had in the stock surrendered, decreased for the boot received and increased by any gain recognized. They use fair market value for the basis of the boot received. Figure 9A.4 illustrates the shareholder's consequences on a Type A reorganization.

In a Type B stock-for-stock reorganization, the acquiring corporation acquires Target's stock from its shareholders in exchange solely for stock of Acquirer. This is an acquisition that involves Target's shareholders and Acquirer only, not Target's management. Acquirer can use nothing but its own voting stock to acquire Target's stock; thus, neither Acquirer nor Target's shareholders recognize gain or loss on this exchange. Figure 9A.2 illustrates the Type B reorganization.

[75] Technically, gain is recognized only if the fair market value of the excess principal on securities received exceeds the fair market value of the excess principal of securities surrendered.

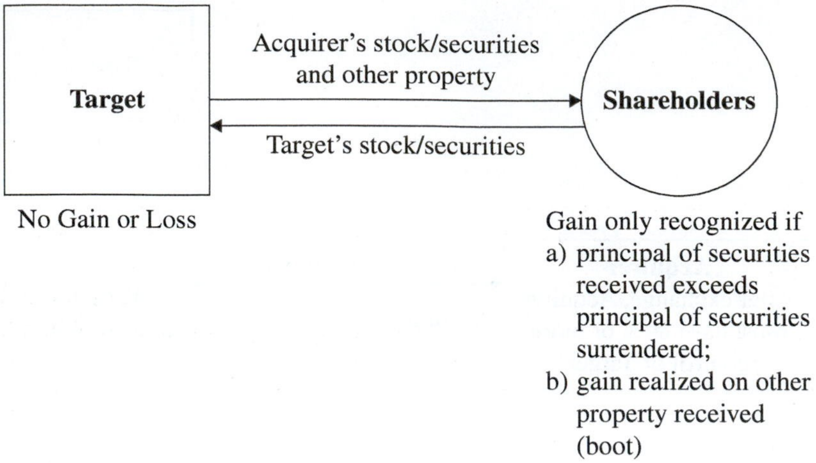

FIGURE 9A.4 Target shareholder's general tax consequences in an asset acquisition reorganization

TYPE A REORGANIZATION

A basic Type A reorganization, a statutory merger or consolidation, is the most flexible of all reorganizations. A merger is the acquisition of the assets of a target corporation; the target liquidates and the acquiring corporation continues. A consolidation is the transfer of assets by two or more corporations to a new corporation; the transferring corporations liquidate and the new corporation survives.

To qualify as a Type A reorganization, the reorganization must follow the provision of law in the state in which the corporation reorganizes. The acquiring corporation can acquire the assets of the target corporation using both its stock and securities, but the reorganization must meet the judicial doctrine of continuity of interest. To meet this doctrine (as interpreted by the IRS), at least 50 percent of the shareholders of the target corporation must become shareholders of the acquired corporation.[76] The basic Type A reorganization has disadvantages, however. In most states, the shareholders of both the acquiring corporation and the target corporation must approve the merger. In addition, the acquiring corporation becomes liable for all the liabilities (including contingent liabilities) of the target.

Example 9A.1

Corporation A exchanges stock valued at $20,000,000 for all the assets of target Corporation T (basis = $12,000,000) in a Type A reorganization. Corporation T distributes Corporation A's stock to its sole shareholder in exchange for all of her stock with a basis of $7,500,000. Corporation T does not recognize its $8,000,000 realized gain; Corporation A takes a carryover basis of $12,000,000 in the transferred assets. The sole shareholder recognizes none of her $12,500,000 realized gain on the exchange of T's stock for A's stock. Her basis in Corporation A's stock is $7,500,000.[77]

Alternatively, Corporation A acquires the assets of Corporation T for $8,000,000 cash and $12,000,000 stock, distributing both the cash and stock to the sole shareholder. Corporation T does not recognize its $8,000,000 realized gain because all of the cash (other property) is distributed its sole shareholder. The sole shareholder recognizes $8,000,000 gain, the lesser of the realized gain of $12,500,000 or the value of other property received, and defers gain recognition of $4,500,000 ($12,500,000 − $8,000,000). The shareholder's basis in the distributed stock is $7,500,000 ($7,500,000 − $8,000,000 boot + $8,000,000 gain recognized).

[76] The IRS will not issue advance rulings on a Type A reorganization unless the 50 percent continuity of interest is met.
[77] This reorganization could also qualify as a C reorganization. In a Type C reorganization, the target corporation must liquidate.

The Type A reorganization has a variety of permissible alternative formulations: (1) the acquiring corporation may transfer the assets of the target to a subsidiary corporation; (2) a subsidiary could be the acquiring corporation with the target shareholders becoming minority shareholders of the target; (3) a subsidiary may acquire the assets of the target corporation using the stock of the parent corporation. These latter two are called forward triangular mergers. Using the subsidiary to acquire Target may avoid the requirement of having parent's shareholders approve the acquisition. It also has the advantage of insulating the parent-acquiring corporation from target corporation's liabilities.

If target cannot liquidate (for example, it has nontransferable licenses or patents), the parent can transfer a subsidiary's assets (which include the parent's stock) to the target, after which the subsidiary liquidates and the target becomes a new subsidiary of the parent. In this form, the parent has effected a reverse triangular merger.[78] The triangular merger using the parent's stock and the reverse triangular merger impose additional requirements to qualify as a tax-free reorganization.[79]

TYPE B REORGANIZATION

The acquisition of a target corporation's stock in exchange for voting stock of the acquiring corporation is a Type B (the stock for voting stock) reorganization. After the reorganization, Target's shareholders are shareholders in the acquiring corporation and the acquiring corporation controls Target. Control is defined as owning 80 percent of the voting stock and 80 percent of all other stock of the acquired corporation. A parent corporation may use a subsidiary as the acquiring corporation using stock solely of the parent, or it may drop the stock of the target corporation into a subsidiary as part of the reorganization.[80]

The Type B reorganization has several advantages. First, if the acquiring corporation has acquired stock in the target for cash in transactions prior to establishing a plan of reorganization, the prior purchases will not taint the acquisition as long as they took place a reasonable time period prior to filing the reorganization plan. Second, the acquiring corporation has a period of up to one year after establishing a plan of reorganization to complete the acquisition of control of the target.[81] Moreover, control does not have to be acquired as part of the reorganization. Thus, a parent already owning 82 percent of the target may acquire 10 percent more in a tax-free reorganization.

Example 9A.2

Three years ago, Corporation B acquired 15 percent of Corporation T's stock for cash. It filed a plan of reorganization on January 3 of the current year that spells out its intention to acquire a controlling interest in T. Corporation B transfers 200,000 shares of its voting stock to the shareholders of Corporation T in exchange for 75 percent of their stock in T, completing the exchange on December 14 of this year. This qualifies as a Type B reorganization. The previous purchase does not taint the stock acquisition because it took place substantially before the corporation filed its plan of reorganization to acquire control of T.

TYPE C REORGANIZATION

The Type C reorganization looks like the basic Type A reorganization, but has specific requirements to qualify as a tax-free reorganization. The acquiring corporation acquires substantially all the assets of Target solely for its voting stock. It distributes any of Target's remaining assets and Acquirer's stock to Target's shareholders and liquidates Target. Generally, the assets acquired

[78] §§368(a)(1)(c) and 368(a)(2)(C), (D), and (E).

[79] In a forward triangular merger, only stock of the parent can be used and substantially all of the target's assets must be acquired. In a reverse triangular merger, only voting stock of the parent can be used to acquire control (80 percent voting and 80 percent of all other stock) of the target; additionally, the target must have substantially all of its assets and the assets of the subsidiary, except for parent stock, after the merger.

[80] §§368(a)(1)(B) and 368(a)(2)(B).

[81] The Type B reorganization is often called a creeping consolidation for this reason.

must permit Acquirer to continue Target's historic business. The acquiring corporation can assume an unlimited amount of Target's liabilities if only the acquirer's voting stock is used in the acquisition. A limited amount of boot is permitted in the acquisition, but the combination of boot and liabilities assumed cannot exceed 20 percent of the value of the consideration used to acquire Target's assets. Only Target's shareholders must approve the merger and liquidation of Target.

The acquiring corporation in a C reorganization may transfer the assets acquired from Target into a subsidiary, or a subsidiary may use the parent stock to acquire the Target in a forward triangular merger. The Type C reorganization does not include a reverse triangular merger, however.

9A.2 TYPE D REORGANIZATIONS

TYPE D ACQUISITIVE REORGANIZATION

In a Type D acquisitive reorganization, the acquiring corporation transfers substantially all of its assets to Target in exchange for the stock of the Target. Target corporation holds its own assets, as well as those of the acquiring corporation. A sufficient amount of Target's stock is distributed to the acquiring corporation's shareholders for control of the target corporation. Control, however, in this type of reorganization is only 50 percent of the voting stock or 50 percent of the value of all stock. The acquiring corporation in a Type D acquisitive reorganization may not transfer the assets to a subsidiary nor may it use a subsidiary to acquire the target corporation.

TYPE D DIVISIVE REORGANIZATION

The Type D divisive reorganization can take three forms commonly known as a *spin off, split off,* and *split up*. In a spin off and a split off, some (but not all) of the original corporation's assets are transferred to a subsidiary and the subsidiary's stock is then distributed to shareholders of the original corporation. If the original shareholders generally receive a pro rata distribution of stock but do not surrender stock of the original corporation, it is a spin off. If the stock of the new corporation is distributed to some of the shareholders in exchange for their stock in the original corporation, it is a split off. Figure 9A.5 illustrates these divisions.

If all of the assets of the original corporation are split between two or more new companies and the stock of each company is distributed to the shareholders in exchange for their stock in the original corporation (with the original corporation going out of business), it is a split up. Both the split off and split up allow a division of shareholder groups when differences among shareholders hamper continued operations.

The transfer of assets to a new corporation normally is not taxable if it meets the requirements of Section 351. As a reorganization, the stock of the transferee corporation can also be distributed to (spin off) or exchanged by (split off and split up) the shareholders tax free.[82]

To qualify for nonrecognition, the divisive D reorganization must meet several requirements. First, the transfer of assets must result in at least two corporations, each of which must conduct an active business immediately after the transfer. These active businesses must have been conducted for at least five years prior to the separation. Second, sufficient stock and securities of the new corporation(s) must be distributed to the shareholders to constitute at least 80 percent control of the corporation(s). Any other property distributed to the shareholders is boot and causes all or part of realized gain to be recognized. Finally, the reorganization may not be a device to distribute a corporation's earnings without tax.

If the division fails to qualify as a reorganization, a spin off will be taxed as a dividend distribution; a split off will be treated as a redemption of the stock of those shareholders surrendering their stock in the old corporation; the split up will be treated as a liquidation of the old corporation in exchange for the stock received in the new corporation. The basic taxation of dividend distributions, redemptions, and liquidations are discussed in the following chapter.

---

[82] §354(a).

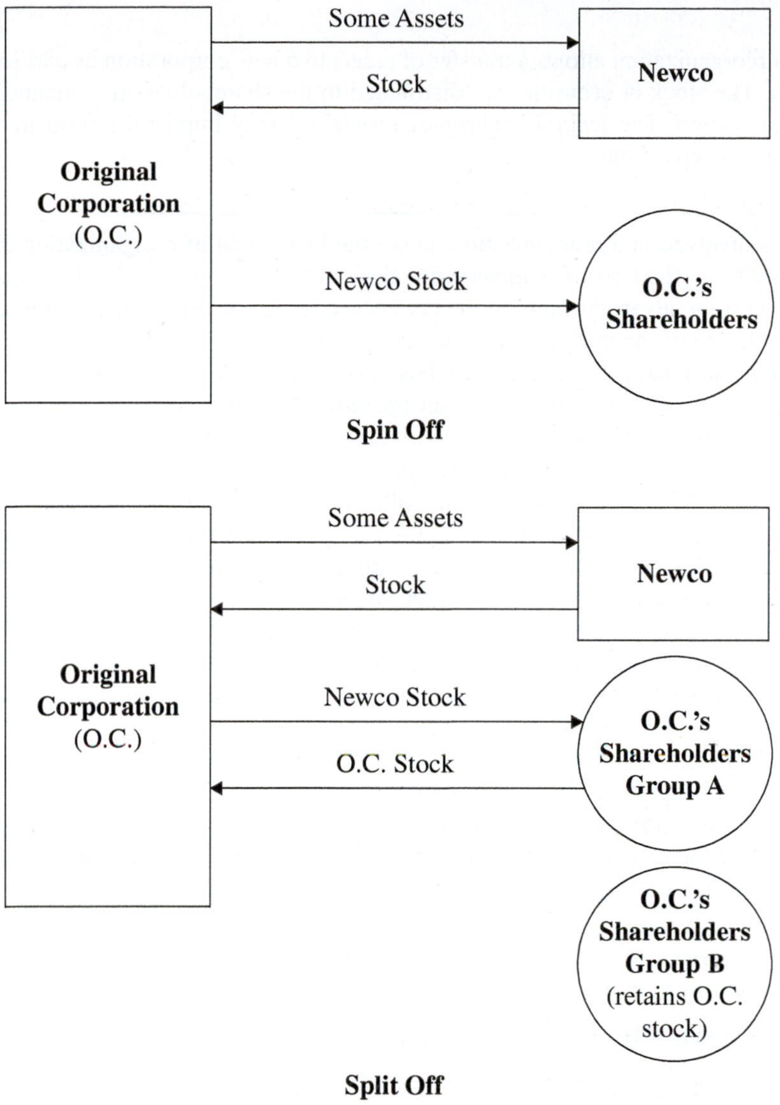

FIGURE 9A.5 Spin off and split off

9A.3 OTHER TYPES OF REORGANIZATIONS

TYPE E

The Type E reorganization is a recapitalization of an existing corporation. This allows the tax-free exchange of common or preferred stock for other common or preferred stock, bonds for other bonds, and bonds for stock. Stock, however, may not be exchanged tax free for bonds as that upgrades a shareholder to the status of a creditor.

TYPE F

A Type F occurs when a corporation simply changes its name, its place of incorporation, or its status from profit to nonprofit or vice versa. The shareholders of the original corporation continue as shareholders of the reorganized corporation for this to qualify as a tax-free reorganization.

TYPE G

The Type G reorganization allows a transfer of assets to a new corporation as part of bankruptcy proceedings. The stock or securities are distributed to the shareholders in a manner resembling the D reorganization. The federal bankruptcy provisions may impact the form in which the G reorganization is carried out.

9A.4 OTHER CONSIDERATIONS

Corporations involved in a reorganization must establish a plan of reorganization following the tax rules specific to the type of reorganization desired.[83] It is advisable for the acquiring corporation to request an advance ruling on the tax consequences of the reorganization to ensure the tax-deferred nature of the transaction if the plan is followed as stated in the ruling request. The reorganization must have a sound nontax business purpose. Acquiring an unprofitable corporation primarily to take advantage of its net operating loss or capital loss carryovers does not meet this requirement.[84] There must be a continuity of ownership that requires a majority of the participating corporations' shareholders to continue to have a financial interest in the reorganized corporation.[85] There must be continuity of business enterprise by the acquiring corporation continuing the historic business of the acquired corporation or using a significant part of the assets acquired.[86] This prevents acquiring a corporation and immediately selling off its assets. Failure to take these factors into consideration can doom the reorganization to failure.

In addition, any reorganization should not be undertaken unless consideration has been given to factors other than the tax consequences of the actual transfers. The acquiring corporation must consider the status of the target corporation's net operating losses and applicable limitations, capital loss carryovers, the earnings and profits of the combined corporations, the other attributes that follow the target corporation, the provisions affecting built-in gains on acquired assets, the change in tax years for the acquired corporation, and other effects of filing a consolidated return. The applicable Code sections, related regulations, and interpretive rulings related to these other factors are much too extensive to include with this introductory material, but they must be consulted to achieve the best tax result for all parties to the reorganization.

PROBLEM ASSIGNMENTS

Check Your Understanding

1. [LO 9A.1] Which reorganizations entail asset acquisitions?
2. [LO 9A.1] Which reorganizations may use a subsidiary to acquire the assets or stock of another corporation?
3. [LO 9A.1] When does an acquiring corporation in a reorganization recognize gain?
4. [LO 9A.1] When does a shareholder recognize gain if he or she participates in a reorganization?
5. [LO 9A.2] Which reorganizations allow the shareholders to divide one corporation into two or more corporations?
6. [LO 9A.2] Describe the three types of divisive reorganizations.
7. [LO 9A.3] If a corporation changes its name, what type of reorganization is it?
8. [LO 9A.3] If a corporation changes its state of incorporation, what type of reorganization is it?
9. [LO 9A.3] Which reorganization is used by a corporation filing for bankruptcy?
10. [LO 9A.4] What does continuity of interest mean?

[83] Reg. §1.368-3(a).
[84] Reg. §1.355-2(b).
[85] The continuity of interest applies primarily to Type A reorganizations. The tax law only requires that the merger or consolidation meet the requirements of the law in the state in which it is effected; if it does not meet the continuity of interest doctrine, however, it will not qualify as a tax-deferred reorganization in spite of meeting state law.
[86] Reg. §368-1(d).

Business Taxation

PART V

CHAPTER 10 Taxation of Corporations

CHAPTER OUTLINE

LEARNING OBJECTIVES

After completing this chapter, you should be able to:

10.1 Explain the advantages and disadvantages of the corporate form of business and understand the elements of a corporate capital structure.

10.2 Discuss the specialized corporate deductions, the computation of the corporate income tax, and the requirements for filing corporate income taxes.

10.3 Understand the differences between cash, property, and stock dividends and determine the effect of cash distributions on both the current and accumulated earnings and profits of a corporation.

10.4 Compare the corporate tax provisions affecting corporate redemptions, partial liquidations, and complete liquidations.

10.5 Explain the tax issues commonly encountered by closely held corporations and differentiate the parent-subsidiary relationship from the brother-sister controlled group.

10.6 Understand the basic provisions for filing a consolidated corporate tax return and the adjustments necessary to determine taxable consolidated corporate net income.

Selecting the type of entity for business operations is one of the most important decisions owners can make. Formation of a sole proprietorship, partnership, or corporation generally is without tax consequences, but that is only a small part of what must be considered when selecting an operating entity. It is far more important to consider day-to-day operations and any applicable legal or tax restrictions on a particular business form. What are permissible tax years and methods of accounting? How will income be taxed? How can the business raise additional capital to grow? How will owners be compensated? Can an owner easily divest himself or herself of the ownership interest? How easily are new owners able to join the business? What are the tax consequences to the business and its owners if the business ceases operations? Who bears the liability if the business fails?

No one entity generally satisfies all characteristics an owner desires. Selecting the entity usually involves determining a priority for the desirable characteristics and determining which form satisfies the most important characteristics. To make these compromises, it is necessary to understand an entity's characteristics from formation through dissolution. This chapter begins to answer these questions for a regular C corporation by exploring its operating characteristics, how profits are distributed, and the process for dissolution. The following chapter addresses these questions for sole proprietorships, partnerships, and S corporations. At the end of these two chapters, there is a basic comparison of the operating characteristics of these entities.

The latter part of this chapter addresses some of the problems that may arise if a corporation is deemed a personal holding company or has accumulated earnings that exceed its operating needs. An explanation of brother-sister or parent-subsidiary controlled groups of corporations is followed by an introduction to corporations permitted to file consolidated returns.

SETTING THE STAGE—AN INTRODUCTORY CASE

John Williams has owned and managed a manufacturing business for seven years. It has grown from a shop in his garage with revenues of $25,000 its first year to a facility on two acres of land with revenues of $2.3 million and profits in excess of $200,000. Three years ago John incorporated the business, which had previously operated as a sole proprietorship.

John manufactures a unique product on which he holds the patent. The demand for his product has grown, and he needs to expand the business. To do this, however, he needs a cash infusion. He has considered "going public," but discussions with investment bankers have indicated that he would have to give up control of the business to have a successful initial public offering (IPO). He has also discussed loans with the local banks, but quoted interest rates are excessive unless John accepts personal liability for the loan, something John is unwilling to do.

John has identified several persons potentially interested in investing in the corporation: (a) John's chief engineer has a minimum amount of money to invest in the corporation, but is willing to work out an arrangement by which a significant portion of his compensation will be paid in company stock and stock options based on profitability. (b) Management of one of his suppliers (another corporation) has proposed investing cash in exchange for a minimum 20 percent of the voting stock to ensure that it remains one of the major suppliers. (c) John's father-in-law has $500,000 that he would invest if he can be guaranteed a return of $30,000 per year for 10 years with his investment repaid at the end of the 10-year period. (d) John's brother recently received a $2,000,000 settlement for injuries received in an auto accident. He is interested in investing $1,000,000 of this in John's company, having worked in the business for 5 years prior to the accident. He believes John is an excellent businessman and manager. He wants a reasonable annual return on this investment but plans to leave the stock to his heirs when he dies.

John plans to continue reinvesting as much of the corporation's income as possible to sustain its growth, but he needs a steady income from the business to support his family—a wife and four children, ages 12 to 19. His wife has recently taken a number of courses in computer operations, database management, and network administration, but is not employed outside the home. His two older sons are both attending college while living at home. They have part-time jobs in the fast-food industry.

John was not fully aware of the double taxation of corporate income when he incorporated. If all of the potential investors receive common stock, he realizes the corporation will have to pay large dividends to satisfy some of them. Suggest ways John could minimize taxes while obtaining the cash infusion that the corporation needs. Can John save on taxes in other ways? We will return to this case at the end of this chapter.

10.1 INTRODUCTION TO CORPORATIONS

A corporation is a business entity created under the laws of the state in which it is incorporated. The corporation owns property in its own name and can be sued directly. The shareholders own a part of the corporation as a whole but do not own an interest in the corporation's individual assets. Except in unusual circumstances, shareholders' liability is limited to their investment in the corporation.[1] This is commonly referred to as *limited liability*.[2] The corporation's charter allows it to carry on business indefinitely. Thus, a corporation has *unlimited life*. Corporate stock is freely traded on the open market or through private sales, and the corporation must have a board of directors that oversees general management and approves the corporate officers. Thus, the corporate form allows *free transferability of interest* and provides for *centralized management*.

These four characteristics, along with associates and a profit motive, defined a corporation for tax purposes prior to 1997.[3] A business entity that possessed three of these four characteristics was taxed as a corporation regardless of its legal form. This led to numerous disagreements with the IRS whether certain unincorporated entities (for example, limited liability companies) would be taxed as corporations or partnerships. Since 1997, most partnerships and limited liability companies can elect taxation as a partnership or a corporation.[4] Any entity with a corporate charter under state law, however, is always taxed as a corporation.

The four characteristics (limited liability, unlimited life, free transfer of interest, and centralized management) apply to both regular corporations (also referred to as C corporations) and S corporations, corporations whose income flows through to its shareholders. General corporate and specific C corporation concepts are discussed here with the specific S corporation characteristics explained in the following chapter.

10.1.1 CORPORATE ADVANTAGES

A C corporation has the flexibility to sell both common and preferred stock with different voting and dividend rights, along with an ability to sell corporate bonds. As a result, corporations generally find it easier to raise capital than other business forms. The major stock exchanges list these corporations, and this facilitates the exchange of their stock in the secondary market.

Prior to the 2013 tax year, the maximum tax rate for individuals (35%) was the same as the maximum tax rate for C corporations (excluding surtaxes). The Taxpayer Relief Act of 2012 increased the maximum individual tax rate to 39.6 percent while leaving the corporate tax rates unchanged. For tax years beginning after 2017, the Tax Cuts and Jobs Act reduced the corporate tax rate to a flat 21 percent and reduced the top individual tax rate to 37 percent. Due to the difference in the rate structures, corporations that reinvest their income rather than pay dividends can have a lower tax bill than flow-through entities with equivalent income taxed at the shareholders' marginal rates. It is possible to lower an overall tax bill (corporation and shareholder) by splitting income. Shareholders can be employees of the corporation, taking income out of the corporation in the form of salary that is deductible by the corporation and taxed only to the shareholders. As a result, both may be able to take advantage of the lower tax rates for incomes under certain levels.

Example 10.1

In 2018, a corporation has taxable income of $75,000 after deducting its sole shareholder-employee's salary of $75,000. The corporation pays a tax of $15,750 ($75,000 × 21%) on this income. The shareholder pays a tax of $9,800 on this income.[5] Their combined tax is $25,550 ($15,750 + $9,800). If the corporation does not pay the salary, it is taxed on $150,000 of income and its tax is $31,500 ($150,000 × 21%). A tax savings of $5,950 ($31,500 – $25,550) is obtained by employing the shareholder.[6]

[1] In certain circumstances, the corporate veil is pierced and a shareholder is held liable for corporate acts. This generally happens when the corporation is a sham; that is, it has no real business purpose but to protect the owner.
[2] The shareholders of new or closely held corporations may have to provide personal guarantees on any loans to the corporation, but their liability is limited to the amount of the loan.
[3] Reg. §301.7701-2, effective prior to January 1, 1997.
[4] A limited partnership, organized after December 17, 1987, that is traded on the securities market is a publicly traded partnership (PTP) and is taxed as a corporation.
[5] $75,000 gross income – $12,000 standard deduction = $63,000 taxable income. The tax on $63,000 for a single individual is $9,800 [([$63,000 – $38,700] × 22%) + $4,453.50].
[6] This example ignores the effect of employment taxes, however.

An often overlooked advantage of the corporate form is the ability of a shareholder-employee to participate in tax-free employee fringe benefits that are a deductible expense of the corporation.[7] Corporations are also the only entities that can offer employees stock options and other stock-based plans designed to share corporate ownership as an employee incentive.[8]

A corporation is free to select either a calendar or fiscal year as its tax year. Thus, it can select the tax year that best fits its natural business cycle. For example, retail department stores often choose a January 31 year-end because inventories are low from post-holiday sales.

10.1.2 DISADVANTAGES OF THE CORPORATE FORM

The corporate disadvantage most often cited is the double taxation of income; that is, income is taxed once as earned by the C corporation and taxed a second time as dividends when after-tax income is distributed to its shareholders.[9] The effective tax rate for this income can far exceed the maximum rate applied to individuals or corporations separately. Shareholders of closely held corporations (corporations with few shareholders) often reduce some of the effects of double taxation by becoming employees of the corporation or renting property to it.[10]

Example 10.2

In 2018, ABC Corporation earned $100,000 and paid a tax of $21,000 ($100,000 × 21%) for the year. It distributed the $79,000 balance to its sole shareholder who has other income of $90,000 placing him in the 15 percent tax bracket for dividend income. The shareholder pays a tax of $11,850 ($79,000 × 15%) on the dividend. Total taxes on the $100,000 of income are $32,850, an effective tax rate of 32.85 percent. As individual income increases, the tax rates increase, and effective rates can approach 40 percent.

DEF Corporation earned $500,000, paid a tax of $105,000 ($500,000 × 21%), and distributed the remaining $395,000 as a dividend to its sole shareholder who has $450,000 of other income. The dividend is now taxed at the highest rate of 20% and is also subject to a 3.8% NII surtax, a tax of $94,010 ($395,000 × .238). Total taxes are $199,010—an effective tax rate of 39.8%.

Unlike flow-through entities, C corporation shareholders cannot deduct losses of the corporation in the year incurred. A corporation can only deduct its operating and net capital losses against its operating income and capital gains, respectively, recognized in other years.

Establishing and maintaining a corporation can be costly in time and money. Normally, a lawyer handles the filing of the articles of incorporation and states charge for issuing corporate charters. In addition, yearly fees must be paid to maintain the corporation's charter and conduct its business. The corporation must maintain a list of all its shareholders, and generally it will conduct at least one shareholder meeting per year, adding to its corporate expenses.

10.1.3 CAPITAL STRUCTURE

A corporation's capital structure may include both **equity** (stock) and **debt** (bonds and other long-term securities). The corporate board of directors determines the types and number of shares of common and preferred stock to be issued as part of the corporate formation. The board can

[7] Greater-than-2-percent S corporation shareholders, partners, and LLC members do not qualify for most tax-free fringe benefits as discussed in Chapter 4.

[8] Chapter 4 contains a more complete discussion of employee compensation and stock option plans.

[9] Lower income taxpayers may have all or a portion of their corporate dividends taxed at a zero percent rate. Stock appreciation due to corporate earnings is also taxed a second time when the shareholder sells the stock, but lower income taxpayers may also have all or a part of their capital gains taxed at a zero percent rate.

[10] Both rents and salaries must be reasonable, or they can be recharacterized as dividends.

also authorize additional shares as the company grows. A corporation may have a single class of common stock only or may have multiple classes of common and preferred stock.

A corporation must have **common stock**. Common shareholders have the last claim on the corporation's income and its assets in liquidation. There is no limit, however, on the income common shareholders may share when a corporation is successful. Consistent with the financial risk-reward relationship, common shareholders take the risk that they could lose everything invested in the corporation for the opportunity to share in its unlimited income potential. When a corporation fails, however, the value of limited liability protection becomes apparent. Although shareholders can lose all their investment in the stock, corporate creditors cannot seize their personal assets.

Preferred stock is preferred because the owners' claims to dividends and assets in liquidation take precedence over the claims of the common stockholders. Preferred stock generally carries a stated dividend rate based on its par value. A corporation cannot pay common stock dividends until it first pays dividends on the preferred stock. If the preferred stock is cumulative, the corporation must also pay all preferred stock dividends in arrears in addition to the current dividend before it can pay any common stock dividends.

Corporations may also issue bonds to obtain funds. From the shareholder's perspective, both interest on debt and dividends on stock are included in taxable income but taxed at differing rates. Taxpayers would prefer dividends that have a maximum tax rate of 20 percent (23.8 percent with the NII surtax) to the maximum tax rate on interest of 37 percent (40.8 percent with the surtax.) Corporations, however, have a significant incentive to issue debt rather than equity. Interest is deductible but dividends are not, making the after-tax cost of debt less than its stated interest rate.

Example 10.3

Crayton Corporation issues $100,000 in bonds at a 7 percent interest rate. Its income tax rate is 21 percent, and its after-tax cost of debt is only 5.53 percent [(100% – 21%) × 7%].

For tax years beginning after December 31, 2017, Congress attempted to level the tax difference between businesses that capitalize through equity and those using debt by limiting the deduction for net interest expense to 30 percent of adjusted taxable income.[11] Any amount exceeding this limit carries over to the next year. Businesses with average annual gross receipts of $25 million or less are not subject to this limit.

Corporate debt must be structured as legitimate debt, with a stated interest rate, interest paid at least annually, and a reasonable maturity date specified. Although bonds can be convertible into stock, the conversion provision cannot be so attractive that most creditors are likely to exercise this feature. These restrictions satisfy the IRS that the debt is legitimate and not stock disguised as debt.

Corporations whose shareholders are also creditors must avoid an excessive debt-to-equity ratio (the corporation is *thinly capitalized*). The IRS can assert that the debt is disguised equity and that the interest and principal payments are dividends (taxable to the shareholder but nondeductible by the corporation). A *safe* debt-to-equity ratio is two or three to one. Debt issued to the shareholders in the same proportion as equity is the most likely to be reclassified as equity.[12]

Example 10.4

Wing Corporation issued $10,000 in common stock and $20,000 in debt securities to its sole shareholder at formation. The stated interest rate on the debt is 5 percent, but no maturity date is specified. For the first seven years, the corporation pays no interest to the shareholder. The IRS could recharacterize the debt as equity and reclassify interest and principal payments as dividends.

[11] Adjusted taxable income is taxable income computed before business interest income and business interest expense. For years beginning before 2022, this income is also computed before any deduction for depreciation, amortization, or depletion. See Chapter 6.

[12] §385 lists factors that may indicate that debt is disguised equity and gives the IRS the authority to make this reclassification.

10.2 TAXATION OF C CORPORATIONS

A corporation calculates **taxable net income** and financial accounting net income by subtracting its relevant expenses from its relevant revenues.[13] There are significant differences between taxable income and expenses and accounting income and expenses.

A corporation's accounting method determines revenues and gains that are included in the current tax year's accounting income. Corporations with more than $25 million in average annual gross receipts must use the accrual method.[14] Corporations that have not passed this threshold may choose between the cash or the accrual method of accounting.

The sale of goods or services is the primary source of revenue for most businesses. They may also have dividend, interest, and rental income, as well as gains and losses on property transactions. Gross income for tax purposes is an all-inclusive concept that applies equally to corporations and individuals. Unless an item is specifically excluded, the corporation must include it in income. Determining a corporation's gross income follows the concepts discussed in Chapter 3. Gains and losses on property transactions are discussed in Chapters 8 and 9.

Example 10.5

A C corporation has $100,000 of service revenue, a $10,000 gain on the sale of property, and $5,000 interest from municipal bonds. The corporation has gross income of $110,000. The $5,000 tax-exempt bond interest is excluded from taxable income but is included in financial accounting income.

The corporation follows the general tax rules for deducting expenses and losses; that is, unless there is a specific provision that allows the deduction, it is nondeductible. Chapters 4, 6 and 7 explain the deductions for employee compensation and other business expenses, including depreciation and amortization. Several deductions are modified for corporations, however.

Example 10.6

TiBo Corporation has gross sales revenues of $200,000, cost of sales of $100,000, a $20,000 Section 179 expense deduction, and $45,000 of other expenses, including a fine of $2,000 for failing to dispose of hazardous waste materials properly. TiBo's taxable income is $37,000 ($200,000 – $100,000 – $20,000 – $43,000). If financial accounting depreciation on the expensed item is $4,000, TiBo's pretax accounting (book) income is $51,000 ($200,000 – $100,000 – $4,000 – $45,000). Immediate expensing of a long-term asset is not permitted for financial accounting, but a deduction is allowed for the fines.

10.2.1 DIVIDEND RECEIVED DEDUCTION

To relieve some of the burden of multiple taxation on corporate income, corporate shareholders are allowed a **dividend received deduction (DRD)** based on the percentage ownership in the distributing corporation.[15]

Corporate shareholder ownership	DRD before 2018	DRD after 2017
80% or more (must be an affiliated corporation)[16]	100%	100%
20% up to 80%	80%	65%
Less than 20%	70%	50%

[13] The following discussion of corporate taxation applies solely to C corporations.
[14] §448. The gross receipts limit was $5 million before 2018.
[15] When a corporate shareholder receives a dividend, it could be taxed at least three times by the time an individual shareholder benefits from it. Dividends from foreign corporations are not eligible for this dividend received deduction.
[16] Affiliated corporations are corporations eligible to file a consolidated return as explained later.

Example 10.7

JF Corporation has operating income of $30,000 and owns 70 percent of JN Corporation in both 2017 and 2018. JF receives a $100,000 dividend each year from JN for total income of $130,000 before its dividend received deduction. In 2017, JF has an $80,000 ($100,000 × 80%) dividend received deduction and effectively includes only $20,000 of the dividend in its income; JF's taxable income for 2017 is $50,000. In 2018 JF's dividend received deduction is only $65,000 ($100,000 × 65%) and it must include $35,000 of the dividend in its income. JF's taxable income for 2018 is $65,000.

There are two other factors that can affect a dividend received deduction: an income limit and an exception when the income limit is waived. First, the dividend received deduction (DRD) may be limited to 50% or 65% (70% or 80% for 2017) of taxable income (before the DRD) if the DRD is less than the percentage multiplied by the dividend income (the normal DRD). Thus, the DRD is limited to the *lesser* of dividend income or taxable income multiplied by the appropriate percentage and is referred to as the income limitation. There is an exception to this limitation: if taking the normal (unlimited) DRD either creates or increases a net operating loss, the income limitation is waived and the corporation may take the normal (unlimited) dividend received deduction.[17]

Example 10.8

Assume the facts in the preceding example, except JF has a $10,000 loss from operations in 2018. Its income including the dividend but before the dividend received deduction is $90,000 ($100,000 – $10,000). Its dividend received deduction is limited now to $58,500 ($90,000 × 65%) by the income limitation, as this is less than its $65,000 normal DRD ($100,000 dividend income × 65%). Its taxable income is $31,500 ($90,000 – $58,500). If, however, JF's loss from operations is $40,000, its income (including the dividend but before the dividend received deduction) is only $60,000 ($100,000 – $40,000). JF may now take the full $65,000 dividend received deduction because it creates a net operating loss of $5,000 ($60,000 – $65,000) after the dividend received deduction; JF now qualifies for the exemption and the income limitation does not apply.[18]

TAX PLANNING

A corporation that may lose part of its dividend received deduction due to the income limitation should accelerate deductions or postpone income if possible to take advantage of the exception for a net operating loss. Alternatively, it could accelerate income or postpone deductions to ensure income exceeds the dividend received deduction. There is no carryover permitted for the part of a dividend received deduction that is lost due to the income limitation.

10.2.2 CHARITABLE CONTRIBUTION DEDUCTION

Corporations may make charitable contributions but they are subject to the **charitable contribution deduction limitation** of 10 percent of taxable income, determined before the charitable contribution and dividend received deductions, but after any net operating or capital loss *carryforwards*.[19] (Loss carrybacks are excluded as they originate in a future year and inclusion would require amending prior years' returns.) Contributions in excess of the limit can be carried forward up to five years.

[17] These provisions do not apply to the 100 percent dividend received deduction.

[18] The income limitation applies if the corporation's net income, including the dividend but before the dividend received deduction, is less than the dividend but more than the dividend received deduction. In the example, if JF's income before the dividend received deduction is between $80,000 and $100,000, the income limitation applies.

[19] §170(b).

Example 10.9

The Bama Corporation has net income of $600,000 before its $55,000 charitable contribution and a $100,000 net operating loss carryover from a prior year. The corporation's charitable contribution deduction is limited to $50,000 [($600,000 − $100,000) × 10%] with a $5,000 contribution carry forward. A capital loss carried *back* to this year from a subsequent year does not cause a recomputation of the charitable contribution deduction limitation and does not change the contribution deduction.

The deduction for ordinary income property is generally limited to its basis, while the deduction for most long-term capital gain property is its fair market value. If a corporation donates inventory to a charitable organization solely for the care of infants, the poor, or the ill, the deduction is increased by 50 percent of the difference between basis and fair market value; the deduction, however, cannot exceed twice the property's basis.[20] A similar exception applies to gifts of scientific property given to universities and certain other research organizations for research purposes.[21]

Example 10.10

Cody Corporation donates a large supply of measles vaccine to the local health department for baby vaccinations as part of their well-baby initiative. The vaccine's fair market value is $25,000, but its basis is only $9,000. The corporation's charitable contribution is $17,000 [$9,000 + ($25,000 − $9,000) × 50%]. If the vaccine's basis was only $3,000, the deduction would be limited to $6,000 (2 × $3,000) as this is less than the alternate deduction of $14,000 [$3,000 + ($25,000 − $3,000) × 50%].

A corporation normally deducts its contributions in the year made, but an accrual-basis corporation may deduct charitable contributions in the year accrued if (1) payment is authorized by the board of directors prior to year-end and (2) payment is actually made by the 15th day of the fourth month following the close of the tax year in which it was accrued.

10.2.3 CAPITAL GAINS AND LOSSES

Corporations also follow the netting process outlined in Chapter 8 for short-term and long-term capital gains and losses, but determining their taxation is relatively straightforward. A net capital gain, whether short-term or long-term, is included in and taxed as ordinary income by corporations. A net capital loss is carried back to the three prior years as a short-term capital loss, starting with the earliest year; if the loss is not completely absorbed in the three carryback years, it is carried forward five years in sequence from the loss year.[22] If the loss is not used within this period, it is lost.

Example 10.11

Jeans Corporation has a $50,000 net capital loss in year 4. It had a $4,000 net capital gain in year 1 and a $20,000 net capital gain in year 3. The corporation first carries the $50,000 loss back to year 1 to offset the $4,000 net capital gain. Next, it carries the $46,000 remaining net capital loss to year 3, offsetting the $20,000 gain. The remaining $26,000 loss is carried in sequence to years 5, 6, 7, 8, and 9 to offset capital gains in those years. Any loss remaining after year 9 is lost.

[20] §170(e)(3). The general rules for the deductibility of property contributions are discussed in Chapter 5.

[21] §170(e)(4).

[22] The short-term loss is netted with the corporation's other capital gains and losses in the carryover year.

TAX PLANNING

Corporations need to keep track of expiring capital losses. They can avoid paying taxes in later years if they accelerate the realization of capital gains to offset any expiring capital losses. Similarly, corporations that have included capital gains in income in prior years can realize losses in a current year and carry the loss back for a refund of taxes paid in previous years.[23]

10.2.4 DEDUCTION FOR QUALIFIED U.S. PRODUCTION ACTIVITIES

In response to the World Trade Organization's ruling that U.S. export subsidies were illegal, Congress eliminated the subsidies and replaced them with a deduction that effectively decreased the corporate tax rate for manufacturers by three percentage points for tax years 2009 through 2017.[24] Corporations were allowed a deduction in computing taxable income equal to 9 percent of the lesser of qualified production activities income or taxable income without consideration of this deduction (an effective tax rate reduction of approximately three percent). Because the principal purpose of this provision was to increase manufacturing jobs, the deduction was limited to a maximum of 50 percent of wages paid during the year.[25]

Qualified production activities income equaled domestic production gross receipts less the sum of (1) cost of goods sold, other deductions, expenses, and losses directly related to these gross receipts and (2) a ratable share of other deductions, expenses, and losses not directly related to this or other income classes.[26] Domestic production gross receipts were broadly defined to include those from most manufacturing, leasing, construction, and architectural or engineering activities that took place within the United States.

Example 10.12

Calabrese Company manufactures shoes in its New Jersey plant. Its 2017 total gross receipts were $4,000,000, $3,250,000 of which were related to sales within the United States. Sales-related expenses were $3,100,000 of which $2,600,000 were for U.S. sales. Total net income was $900,000 with $650,000 attributed solely to U.S sales. Its qualified production activities deduction for 2017 was $58,500, the lesser of nine percent of qualified production activities income ($650,000 × 9% = $58,500) or taxable income ($900,000 × 9% = $81,000).

This deduction was repealed for tax years beginning after 2017 by the Tax Cuts and Jobs Act.

10.2.5 NET OPERATING LOSSES

A corporation reports its taxable income on an annual basis. If it has income in one year and a loss the next, it must pay taxes in the income year. If the corporation could combine the two years, it might have little or no income on which to pay taxes. The **net operating loss (NOL)** carryovers simulate the combining of income in some years with the losses in other years to reduce the corporation's taxes. Prior to 2018, corporations could carry back net operating losses to the two previous tax years. The corporation could then carry any remaining unused NOL forward up to a maximum of 20 years. The corporation first carried the NOL back to the earliest eligible year and then carried any remaining loss forward in sequence. It could not choose the NOL carryover year. The corporation could elect, however, to forgo the two-year carryback and carry the NOL forward only. In making this decision, a corporation had to look at its pattern of income, taxes, and credits in the available carryback years.

---

[23] See examples in Chapter 8 that illustrate the timing of capital gains and losses.

[24] A 9% deduction for a corporation in the 35% tax bracket decreases the corporation's marginal tax rate by about 3% (35% × 9% = 3.15%). The deduction had been 3% for tax years 2005 and 2006 and 6% for tax years 2007 through 2009.

[25] The 50% wage limit was based on wages paid (including elective deferred compensation) in the calendar year that ended in the corporation's tax year.

[26] IRS developed rules for proper allocation similar to §263A uniform capitalization rules (as discussed in Chapter 6).

Example 10.13

Hightec Corporation has an $80,000 operating loss in 2017. In 2015 Hightec Corporation reported taxable income of $50,000 and paid income taxes of $7,500 ($50,000 × 15%). In 2016 it reported taxable income of $20,000 and paid income taxes of $3,000 ($20,000 × 15%). Hightec is entitled to receive a refund of $10,500 ($7,500 + $3,000) from the NOL carryback and has a $10,000 carryforward ($80,000 – $70,000) remaining.

Net operating losses incurred after December 31, 2017 can no longer be carried back but are permitted to be carried forward indefinitely. When carried forward, the NOL can offset no more than 80 percent of taxable income (determined without regard to the NOL deductions). This 80 percent limit only applies to NOLs incurred in years after 2017; NOLs from prior years follow prior year rules.

Example 10.14

Arcadia Corporation has a $90,000 net operating loss in 2018. Its 2019 income is $60,000. Arcadia can offset only $48,000 ($60,000 × 80%) of its 2019 income with the 2018 NOL and its remaining $12,000 income is subject to tax in 2019. Arcadia carries the remaining $42,000 loss forward to use in future years; however, it cannot carry any of the loss back.

10.2.6 COMPUTING THE CORPORATE INCOME TAX

The formula to compute the regular **corporate income tax** is as follows:

	Taxable revenues
Less	Deductible expenses
Equals	Taxable income
Times	Corporate tax rate
Equals	Corporate gross tax liability
Plus	Additions to tax
Less	Tax credits
Equals	Net corporate tax

The relevant tax laws dictate taxable revenues and deductible expenses that are included in this formula, as discussed in earlier chapters. The corporation's gross tax liability is determined by applying the corporate tax rate to the excess of taxable revenues over deductible expenses.

Prior to 2018, the **corporate tax rate** followed a progressive rate schedule, with rates that increased as taxable income increased, as shown in Table 10.1.[27] Technically, the 34 percent

Table 10.1 Corporate Tax Rate Schedule for Years Before 2018

Corporate income		
Over	**But not over**	**Tax rate**
$0	$50,000	15%
$50,000	$75,000	25%
$75,000	$100,000	34%
$100,000	$335,000	39%*
$335,000	$10,000,000	34%
$10,000,000	$15,000,000	35%
$15,000,000	$18,333,333	38%†
$18,333,333		35%

*The 34 percent rate plus a 5 percent surtax.
†The 35 percent rate plus a 3 percent surtax.

[27] §11(b). A single rate of 35% applied to personal service corporations. A qualified personal service corporation (PSC) is a corporation that provides service in the fields of accounting, actuarial science, architecture, consulting, engineering, health, law, or the performing arts and its employees own substantially all of the corporate stock. §448(d) (2).

bracket extended from $75,000 to $10,000,000; and the 35 percent bracket applied to all income over $10,000,000. Surtaxes were added to gradually eliminate the benefit of the lower rates. A surtax of 5 percent was added to the tax rate on incomes of $100,000 to $335,000; a 3 percent surtax was added to the tax rate on incomes of $15,000,000 to $18,333,333. For income of $335,000 to $10,000,000, a flat tax rate of 34 percent applied; for income over $18,333,333, a flat tax rate of 35 percent applied. Beginning in 2018, corporations pay tax at a flat rate of 21 percent.

Example 10.15

Davila Corporation had $225,000 of taxable income in 2017. Davila's income tax for 2017 was $71,000 [($50,000 × 15%) + ($25,000 × 25%) + ($25,000 × 34%) + ($125,000 × 39%)] resulting in an effective tax rate of 31.56% ($71,000/$225,000). Davila Corporation's taxable income is also $225,000 in 2018, but it now pays a flat 21% tax rate resulting in a tax liability of only $47,250.

10.2.7 RECONCILING BOOK AND TAXABLE INCOME

A corporation uses **Form 1120**, the **corporate tax return**, to determine its taxable income. The first page of Form 1120 is presented in Figure 10.1. It must complete a number of schedules including **Schedule L**, the corporation's beginning and ending financial accounting balance sheet, Schedule M-2, and either Schedule M-1 or M-3. **Schedule M-1** is a basic reconciliation of after-tax net income (or loss) on the financial accounting books with taxable income (or loss) before the dividends received deduction and net operating loss carryovers. Corporations with assets of less than $10 million may use the Schedule M-1, but larger corporations must complete the more complex Schedule M-3.

The left column of the M-1 schedule starts with after-tax book income to which the corporation adds its federal income tax liability. Items that are deductible for book purposes but are not deductible for tax are added back to calculate taxable income. The Schedule M-1's right side contains all the reductions in book income in arriving at taxable income (income items excluded from taxable income and expense items excluded from book income). A number of these additions and subtractions are listed in Table 10.2.

Example 10.16

Corporation BDC reports financial accounting income of $250,000 that includes $5,000 of tax-exempt bond interest income. It has federal income tax expense per books of $80,000; tax depreciation is $40,000 but financial depreciation is only $30,000; total meal expense is $30,000; and net capital losses are $20,000. Its book income is reconciled to taxable income on Schedule M-1 as follows:

Schedule M-1 **Reconciliation of Income (Loss) per Books With Income per Return**
Note: Schedule M-3 required instead of Schedule M-1 if total assets are $10 million or more—see instructions

1	Net income (loss) per books	250,000	7	Income recorded on books this year not included on this return (itemize):	
2	Federal income tax per books	80,000		Tax-exempt interest $ 5,000	
3	Excess of capital losses over capital gains	20,000			
4	Income subject to tax not recorded on books this year (itemize):				5,000
5	Expenses recorded on books this year not deducted on this return (itemize):		8	Deductions on this return not charged against book income this year (itemize):	
a	Depreciation $		a	Depreciation $ 10,000	
b	Charitable contributions $		b	Charitable contributions $	
c	Travel and entertainment $ 15,000				10,000
		15,000	9	Add lines 7 and 8	15,000
6	Add lines 1 through 5	365,000	10	Income (page 1, line 28)—line 6 less line 9	350,000

Form **1120**
Department of the Treasury
Internal Revenue Service

U.S. Corporation Income Tax Return

For calendar year 2017 or tax year beginning ________________, 2017, ending ________________, 20 ______

▶ Go to *www.irs.gov/Form1120* for instructions and the latest information.

OMB No. 1545-0123

2017

A Check if:			
1a Consolidated return (attach Form 851) . ☐	**TYPE OR PRINT**	Name	**B Employer identification number**
b Life/nonlife consolidated return . . . ☐		Number, street, and room or suite no. If a P.O. box, see instructions.	**C** Date incorporated
2 Personal holding co. (attach Sch. PH) . . ☐		City or town, state, or province, country, and ZIP or foreign postal code	**D** Total assets (see instructions) $
3 Personal service corp. (see instructions) . . ☐			
4 Schedule M-3 attached ☐	**E** Check if: **(1)** ☐ Initial return **(2)** ☐ Final return	**(3)** ☐ Name change **(4)** ☐ Address change	

Income	**1a**	Gross receipts or sales	**1a**			
	b	Returns and allowances	**1b**			
	c	Balance. Subtract line 1b from line 1a			**1c**	
	2	Cost of goods sold (attach Form 1125-A)			**2**	
	3	Gross profit. Subtract line 2 from line 1c			**3**	
	4	Dividends (Schedule C, line 19)			**4**	
	5	Interest			**5**	
	6	Gross rents			**6**	
	7	Gross royalties			**7**	
	8	Capital gain net income (attach Schedule D (Form 1120))			**8**	
	9	Net gain or (loss) from Form 4797, Part II, line 17 (attach Form 4797)			**9**	
	10	Other income (see instructions—attach statement)			**10**	
	11	**Total income.** Add lines 3 through 10 ▶			**11**	
Deductions (See instructions for limitations on deductions.)	**12**	Compensation of officers (see instructions—attach Form 1125-E) ▶			**12**	
	13	Salaries and wages (less employment credits)			**13**	
	14	Repairs and maintenance			**14**	
	15	Bad debts			**15**	
	16	Rents			**16**	
	17	Taxes and licenses			**17**	
	18	Interest			**18**	
	19	Charitable contributions			**19**	
	20	Depreciation from Form 4562 not claimed on Form 1125-A or elsewhere on return (attach Form 4562)			**20**	
	21	Depletion			**21**	
	22	Advertising			**22**	
	23	Pension, profit-sharing, etc., plans			**23**	
	24	Employee benefit programs			**24**	
	25	Domestic production activities deduction (attach Form 8903)			**25**	
	26	Other deductions (attach statement)			**26**	
	27	**Total deductions.** Add lines 12 through 26 ▶			**27**	
	28	Taxable income before net operating loss deduction and special deductions. Subtract line 27 from line 11.			**28**	
	29a	Net operating loss deduction (see instructions)	**29a**			
	b	Special deductions (Schedule C, line 20)	**29b**			
	c	Add lines 29a and 29b			**29c**	
Tax, Refundable Credits, and Payments	**30**	**Taxable income.** Subtract line 29c from line 28. See instructions			**30**	
	31	Total tax (Schedule J, Part I, line 11)			**31**	
	32	Total payments and refundable credits (Schedule J, Part II, line 21)			**32**	
	33	Estimated tax penalty. See instructions. Check if Form 2220 is attached ▶ ☐			**33**	
	34	**Amount owed.** If line 32 is smaller than the total of lines 31 and 33, enter amount owed			**34**	
	35	**Overpayment.** If line 32 is larger than the total of lines 31 and 33, enter amount overpaid			**35**	
	36	Enter amount from line 35 you want: **Credited to 2018 estimated tax ▶**		**Refunded ▶**	**36**	

Sign Here

Under penalties of perjury, I declare that I have examined this return, including accompanying schedules and statements, and to the best of my knowledge and belief, it is true, correct, and complete. Declaration of preparer (other than taxpayer) is based on all information of which preparer has any knowledge.

▶ Signature of officer | Date | ▶ Title

May the IRS discuss this return with the preparer shown below? See instructions. ☐ **Yes** ☐ **No**

Paid Preparer Use Only	Print/Type preparer's name	Preparer's signature	Date	Check ☐ if self-employed	PTIN
	Firm's name ▶			Firm's EIN ▶	
	Firm's address ▶			Phone no.	

For Paperwork Reduction Act Notice, see separate instructions. Cat. No. 11450Q Form **1120** (2017)

FIGURE 10.1 Form 1120 page 1

Schedule M-2 provides details of the changes in the corporation's unappropriated retained earnings from the beginning to the end of the tax year and should reconcile with the change in unappropriated retained earnings reported in comparative balance sheets. Beginning retained earnings is increased for net income and reduced by dividend payments. Changes in appropriations of retained earnings, as well as other changes from retiring stock and accounting provisions that require a direct addition or reduction to retained earnings (for example, certain changes in value of marketable securities), must be shown here.

Table 10.2 Additions to and Subtractions from Book Income to Calculate Taxable Income on Schedule M-1

Additions to book income	Subtractions from book income
Left Side of Schedule M-1	Right Side of Schedule M-1
Federal income tax	Tax-exempt bond interest
Capital losses that exceed capital gains	Tax depreciation in excess of book depreciation
Excess of book depreciation over tax depreciation	Carryover of contributions from prior tax years
Contributions in excess of the contributions limit	Percentage-of-completion income recognized prior to the year of completion when the completed contract method is used for tax purposes
The excess of completed contract income in this year over income recorded on the books under the percentage-of-completion method	Increase in the cash value of key-person life insurance
Insurance premiums on key-person life insurance policies	Bad debt expense in excess of the addition to bad debt reserves
Bad debt reserve deductions in excess of actual bad debt expense	Life insurance proceeds
The nondeductible portion of meals and entertainment expense	
Fines and bribes	
Expenses related to tax-exempt income	

Example 10.17

The Babco Company had retained earnings of $51,000 at the beginning of the year. Its net income after taxes is $21,000, and it paid $15,000 in dividends to its shareholders. Its end-of-year retained earnings is $57,000 ($51,000 + $21,000 – $15,000).

Schedule M-2 **Analysis of Unappropriated Retained Earnings per Books (Line 25, Schedule L)**

1	Balance at beginning of year	51,000	5	Distributions: a Cash	15,000
2	Net income (loss) per books	21,000		b Stock	
3	Other increases (itemize):			c Property	
			6	Other decreases (itemize):	
			7	Add lines 5 and 6	15,000
4	Add lines 1, 2, and 3	72,000	8	Balance at end of year (line 4 less line 7)	57,000

Corporations with at least $10 million in assets must complete a **Schedule M-3** instead of the M-1. The first part of the Schedule M-3 reconciles the corporation's worldwide book income reported on its consolidated financial statements with book income for entities included in its consolidated tax return.[28] Corporations must then itemize book-tax differences for each item of income, gain, loss, deduction, or credit that is greater than $10 million. This schedule requires much more detailed information on book-tax differences than Schedule M-1 with temporary and permanent differences reported separately.[29] The IRS hopes that this expanded book-tax reconciliation will identify those corporations with large tax shelter transactions as audit targets.

10.2.8 TAX CREDITS

A corporation can reduce its tax liability, but not below zero, by tax credits for which it is eligible. The **general business credit**, a corporation's most useful tax credit, is actually an extensive list

[28] For financial accounting purposes, the consolidated reporting group usually includes the parent corporation and all subsidiaries (both domestic and foreign) in which the parent has a greater-than-50%-ownership interest. For tax purposes, a consolidated group consists of only the domestic parent corporation and its domestic subsidiaries in which it owns at least an 80% interest.

[29] Temporary and permanent book-tax differences are discussed in Chapter 6.

of credits, not just one.[30] Each credit in the group is calculated separately according to its specific provisions. The separate credits are then aggregated into one general business credit to which a specific overall limit applies. The allowable credit cannot exceed $25,000 plus 75 percent of the corporation's tax liability in excess of $25,000.[31]

Example 10.18

Behan Corporation has a regular tax liability of $205,000 and a general business credit of $190,000. The general business credit offsets only $160,000 of the corporation's regular tax [$25,000 + ($205,000 – $25,000) × 75%]. The corporation pays a net tax of $45,000, and it has $30,000 of general business credit remaining.

Unused general business credits are not lost but are carried back one year to reduce taxes in the prior year (subject to the same limitation as above) and then forward 20 years. If a corporation has carryover business credits from more than one year, the credits arising in the earliest years are used first (a FIFO basis). The following is a list of some of the credits that make up the general business credit and their related Code sections:[32]

1. Investment credit, which itself is made up of several credits including the rehabilitation credit, the energy credit, and the reforestation credit (Section 46)
2. Credit for increasing research activities (Section 41)
3. Low-income housing credit (Section 42)
4. Disabled access credit (Section 44)
5. Orphan drug credit (Section 45C)
6. Small-employer pension plan startup credit (Section 45E)
7. Credit for employer-provided child care (Section 45F)
8. Work opportunity credit (Section 51)

The credits contained within the general business credit have not remained static over time. Credits have been added and credits have been allowed to expire. Often credits that have expired are reinstated on a retroactive basis.[33] The addition, expiration, and retroactive reinstatement add significant complexity for the taxpayer; for example, a credit may not be carried back to a year before its addition to the general business credit.

For 2018-2019, employers are allowed a new credit for providing paid family and medical leave that is part of the general business credit. The credit equals 12.5 percent of wages paid for paid family and medical leave (if the rate of payment is 50 percent of wages normally paid to an employee). The credit increases by 0.25 percent (but not above 25 percent) for each percent the payment rate exceeds 50 percent of normal wages. If the leave payment rate is 100 percent of the normal wage rate, the credit is 25 percent of the leave payment. The maximum leave allowed an employee for a tax year is 12 weeks.[34]

---

[30] Corporations are also eligible for the foreign tax credit and the alternative minimum tax credit.

[31] §38(c). As originally enacted, the general business credit could not exceed the corporation's regular tax liability less its gross alternative minimum tax, as the general business credit could not reduce a corporation's alternative minimum tax liability. A number of targeted credits, however, have been allowed to reduce the AMT; for example, eligible small businesses could offset the AMT liability in tax years beginning in 2010. The alternative minimum tax is discussed later.

[32] §§43 and 45 contain a description of other credits that make up the general business credit.

[33] The work opportunity credit expired at the end of 2014 but was retroactively extended through 2019.

[34] §45S(a).

TAX PLANNING

Corporations should recognize and take advantage of all allowable business credits. Credits are far more valuable than deductions of equal amounts as credits are a direct reduction in taxes.

A further discussion of these credits is beyond the scope of this text as each of these credits is calculated under a specific set of guidelines. The relevant Code sections should be consulted.

10.2.9 ALTERNATIVE MINIMUM TAX

Many corporations with significant accounting income substantially reduce taxable income by the judicious use of allowable deductions and income exemptions. To ensure that most corporations paid some taxes, Congress instituted a second parallel tax system aptly named the **alternative minimum tax (AMT)**, which applied to all corporations prior to 2018 except those exempt as *small* corporations. A small corporation had average annual gross receipts of less than $5,000,000 in each of its prior taxable years. Once qualified, a small corporation continued to be exempt from the AMT until its average annual gross receipts for the previous three years exceed $7,500,000.[35] If this threshold was exceeded, a corporation was no longer exempt from AMT, even if its receipts declined in future years.

To determine the AMT, the regular income tax base was broadened by a series of positive and negative adjustments and positive preference items to arrive at alternative minimum taxable income (AMTI). Next the corporation deducted its exemption (subject to limitation) to determine its AMTI base. This base was then multiplied by a flat tax rate of 20 percent to determine gross AMT.[36] Finally, the corporation's regular tax liability and foreign tax credit were deducted from this gross AMT. If the result was a positive number, this net amount was the AMT that the corporation was required to pay. If it was a negative number (the regular tax and foreign tax credit exceeded the gross AMT), the corporation had no AMT. The formula for the AMT was as follows:

	Corporate taxable income
Plus or minus	AMT adjustments
Plus	Preference items
Equals	AMT income
Less	Exemption
Equals	AMTI base
Times	AMT rate
Equals	Gross AMT
Less	Regular corporate tax
Equals	Alternative minimum tax
Less	Credits
Equals	Net AMT

The corporation only paid an AMT if the gross AMT was greater than its regular corporate income tax plus applicable credits.

Example 10.19

In 2017, Corporation LP paid a regular income tax of $136,000 on taxable income of $400,000. Its AMTI base was $800,000, and its gross AMT was $160,000. Its AMT was $24,000 ($160,000 – $136,000). The corporation would pay its AMT with its regular tax by the due date of its income tax return. It would have paid no AMT if its regular tax had exceeded $160,000.

[35] §55.

[36] §§55(a)(2) and (3).

AMT adjustments represented timing differences only; that is, in earlier years any adjustments that increased (decreased) taxable income reversed in later years and reduced (increased) taxable income.[37] Adjustments included the following:[38]

1. The difference between regular tax depreciation and AMT depreciation[39]
2. The difference between gains reported for AMT by the percentage-of-completion method over gains reported on the completed contract method for regular tax
3. 75 percent of the difference between adjusted current earnings (ACE) and AMT income before this adjustment and any allowable exemption[40]

A corporation had a $40,000 exemption if its AMT income was $150,000 or less. The exemption phased out at a rate of $1 for every $4 its AMT income exceeded $150,000. When AMT income reached $310,000 ($310,000 – $150,000 = $160,000; $160,000/4 = $40,000), the exemption was completely phased out and the AMT income equaled the AMTI base.

Example 10.20

Baylor Corporation had $100,000 of taxable income in 2016 on which it paid a regular tax of $22,500. It had $150,000 of net positive adjustments and a $10,000 preference item. Its AMT was:

	$100,000	Taxable income
Plus	150,000	Positive adjustments
Plus	10,000	Preferences
Equals	$260,000	AMT income
Minus	12,500	Exemption(1)
Equals	$247,500	AMTI base
Times	20%	AMT rate
Equals	$49,500	Gross AMT
Minus	22,500	Regular Tax
Equals	$27,000	AMT

	(1)Exemption	
	$260,000	
Minus	150,000	
Equals	$110,000	
Times	25%	
Equals	$27,500	Exemption reduction
	$40,000	Maximum exemption
Minus	27,500	Exemption reduction
Equals	$12,500	Exemption allowed

The corporation had an AMT credit against the regular tax because the adjustments to regular taxable income were the result of timing differences. The AMT credit was equal to the AMT paid in prior years. The AMT credits were carried forward indefinitely, but could only offset regular taxes in excess of the AMT.

[37] This is an example of how the government takes advantage of the time value of money.
[38] §§56(a) and (c) list the adjustment items applicable to corporations.
[39] Applies to property placed in service after 1986.
[40] The ACE adjustment includes tax-exempt bond interest, life insurance proceeds, and 100 percent of the gain on an installment contract. Disallowed deductions include the 70 percent dividend received deduction and the amortization of organization expenses.

Example 10.21

Continuing the previous example, Baylor Corporation paid a regular tax of $230,000 in 2017. If its gross AMT was only $210,000, the corporation could use $20,000 ($230,000 – $210,000) of its previous $27,000 AMT as a credit against its regular tax in 2017. It could continue to carry the remaining $7,000 AMT forward as a credit against its regular tax liability in excess of its AMT until used up.

In 2018, Congress eliminated the corporate AMT. Corporations with unused AMT credits can offset them against their regular tax liability for any year. Excess AMT credits are refundable for tax years after 2017. Until 2021, 50 percent of the excess AMT credit over the amount of credit allowable against regular tax liability is refundable. Beginning in 2021, any remaining AMT credits will be fully refundable.

10.2.10 FILING AND PAYMENT REQUIREMENTS

Corporations file Form 1120: *U.S. Corporate Income Tax Return*. The return is due on the 15th day of the fourth month following the close of its tax year.[41] Corporations may obtain an automatic six-month extension for filing the return by filing Form 7004: *Application for Automatic Extension of Time to File Corporation Income Tax Return* by the unextended due date.[42] **Estimated taxes** due must be paid with this extension request. The IRS can terminate the extension with 10 days' notice, however.

Example 10.22

CBC, a corporation with an April 30 fiscal year-end, has an unextended due date for its 2019 tax return of August 15, 2019; its six-month extended due date is February 15, 2020.

Corporations must make estimated payments throughout the tax year equal to one-quarter of their tax liability for the year on the 15th day of the 4th, 6th, 9th, and 12th months of the corporation's tax year.[43] For a calendar-year corporation, these dates are April 15, June 15, September 15, and December 15.

An underpayment penalty is assessed if a corporation's tax liability is at least $500 more than its estimated payments.[44] Corporations with taxable income of less than $1,000,000 in each of the preceding three years can avoid the underpayment penalty if each of their estimated tax payments equals 25 percent of their prior year's tax liability.[45]

10.3 CORPORATE DIVIDEND DISTRIBUTIONS

Corporate distributions take many forms, but the most common is the corporate **dividend**. Dividends can be distributed in the form of cash or property and are normally taxable to the recipients. The corporation can also distribute stock dividends—but these are usually nontaxable distributions. Corporations can also distribute cash or assets to redeem all or part of a

[41] §6072(b). Corporations are permitted to use calendar or fiscal years for tax purposes. Corporations with a June 30 year end retain their September 15 filing deadline through 2025.

[42] §6081(a) allows a maximum extension of six months. Calendar year corporations will only be allowed a 5 month extension through 2025. Because Form 7004 provides for an automatic extension of six months, no additional extension is normally allowed.

[43] §6655(b). Corporations with $1 billion or more in assets were required to make larger estimated payments in certain months in 2017. For a payment due in July, August, or September 2017, the amount due was 100.25 percent of what they otherwise would be required to pay. For October, November, and December, the amount due was 99.75 percent.

[44] §6655(f).

[45] §§6655(d) and (e). This exception only applies to the first estimated payment for a corporation with taxable income exceeding $1,000,000; otherwise it can only avoid a penalty by annualizing its income.

shareholder's stock. Unless properly structured, however, a redemption could have dividend consequences.

A corporation can also downsize through a partial liquidation or go completely out of business through a complete liquidation, distributing all of its remaining cash and property to its shareholders. These latter distributions are discussed later in this chapter.

10.3.1 TAX EFFECTS OF DIVIDEND DISTRIBUTIONS

Corporations reward their shareholders through dividend distributions—the distribution of corporate earnings and profits (E&P)—taxable income to shareholders but nondeductible by the corporation. Earnings and profits is a corporate level account that determines if a distribution of cash or property is a taxable dividend distribution or a tax-free return of invested capital. The calculation of E&P begins with a corporation's taxable income that is adjusted to reflect more closely its economic income. Most corporate distributions come only from E&P; if it exceeds E&P, however, it is treated as a return of invested capital and reduces shareholders' bases in their stock. As a return of the original corporate investment, it is tax free to the extent it does not exceed stock bases. If basis is reduced to zero, the excess distribution is treated as proceeds from the sale of the stock and is normally taxed as capital gain.

Example 10.23

Alexander receives $5,000 cash as a distribution from his 100 percent owned corporation. The corporation has only $2,000 in earnings and profits; Alexander has only a $2,000 dividend with a $3,000 return of capital. If Alexander's basis in his stock is only $1,000, then only $1,000 of the $3,000 return of capital is tax free. The remaining $2,000 is taxed as gain on sale of stock. Alexander has received $5,000 of which $4,000 is taxable ($2,000 as dividend income and $2,000 as capital gain).

The majority of corporations do not distribute dividends unless they have two things: earnings and profits to distribute to their shareholders and sufficient cash to cover the dividend payment. To determine which distributions are taxable, it is important to calculate and keep track of the corporation's earnings and profits because E&P is not the same as taxable income.

10.3.2 CALCULATING EARNINGS AND PROFITS

Earnings and profits (E&P) is the yardstick by which a corporation measures how much it can distribute as dividends while leaving contributed capital intact. Taxable income includes a number of legislative exclusions and deductions and bears little resemblance to an amount the corporation could distribute without impairing corporate capital. Thus, many of the exclusions and artificial deductions allowed in determining taxable income are disallowed in the E&P calculation.[46] The starting point for determining each year's E&P is taxable income. A number of positive and negative adjustments are then made to determine the current year's E&P. Table 10.3 is a partial list of the adjustments.[47]

[46] Earnings and profits more closely resemble an economic concept of income or the financial accounting concept of retained earnings than it does taxable income.
[47] §312.

Table 10.3 Adjustments to Taxable Income to Calculate Current Earnings and Profits

Positive adjustments	Negative adjustments
Federal income tax refunds	Federal income taxes paid
Dividends received deductions	Capital losses in excess of capital gains
Proceeds of life insurance policies	Premiums on life insurance policies
Excess of a current year's installment gain over portion recognized	Installment sale gain from a prior year's installment sale
Percentage depletion in excess of cost depletion	Nondeductible fines and bribes
Depreciation expense in excess of allowable E&P depreciation	Disallowed losses on sales to related parties
Charitable contribution carryovers	Charitable contributions in excess of 10% limit
NOL carryovers	20% of cost of Section 179 expensed item
Capital loss carryovers	
Section 179 expense in excess of allowable depreciation[48]	

Example 10.24

Judah Corporation has $400,000 of taxable income and pays $84,000 of federal income tax. To arrive at taxable income, the corporation reported the following:

$10,000 dividend received deduction	$4,000 excess capital loss
$2,000 tax-exempt income	$5,000 nondeductible fines
$20,000 Section 179 expense	$6,000 NOL carryover

The corporation's E&P for the current year is determined as follows:

	$400,000	Taxable income
Minus	84,000	Federal income tax
Plus	10,000	Dividend received deduction
Plus	2,000	Tax-exempt income
Minus	5,000	Nondeductible fines
Minus	4,000	Excess capital loss
Plus	16,000	Excess of §179 expense (20% allowed)
Plus	6,000	NOL carryover
Equals	$341,000	Earnings and profits for the current year

10.3.3 APPLYING E&P TO DISTRIBUTIONS

The E&P determined above is more accurately called **current earnings and profits (CE&P)**. Current earnings and profits is the amount calculated from the current year's taxable income with the appropriate adjustments. This is distinguished from **accumulated earnings and profits (AE&P)**, the accumulation of CE&P for all prior years that has not been distributed as dividends.

At the end of each tax year, CE&P is calculated. Dividend distributions made during the tax year reduce CE&P first. If the dividend does not exceed CE&P, the remaining CE&P is added at the beginning of the next year to the balance in AE&P from all prior years.[49]

Example 10.25

Corn Corporation has taxable income of $40,000 for the year, its CE&P prior to dividend distributions is $56,000, and it has a balance of $23,000 in AE&P. It distributes a $27,000 dividend to its shareholders during the year. The dividend distribution reduces Corn's positive CE&P balance to $29,000 ($56,000 – $27,000); this $29,000 then increases its AE&P balance to $52,000 ($23,000 + $29,000) at the beginning of the next year.

[48] For earnings and profits, 20 percent of the expensed amount is deducted in each of the current and four succeeding years.

[49] The calculation of CE&P can result in a negative number. If CE&P is negative, it can cause the balance in AE&P to be negative as well. Dividend distributions cannot cause a negative balance in either current or accumulated E&P.

If the distribution exceeds CE&P, the remaining distribution is applied against AE&P. The distribution is fully taxable as long as both current and accumulated E&P are equal to or greater than the distribution. If the distribution exceeds both CE&P and AE&P, they are allocated to the shareholders to determine the amount of each distribution that is dividend, with any excess identified by the corporation as a return of corporate capital.

If a distribution does not exceed CE&P, determining a shareholder's taxable dividend is straightforward. Whether there is only one dividend distribution or several during the year, CE&P is allocated on a pro rata basis to all distributions regardless of when they were made during the year.

Example 10.26

ABC Corporation has two shareholders, X and Y. Each own 50% of its shares. ABC has $10,000 in CE&P and no AE&P.

a. ABC declared a $6,000 dividend on May 1. Shareholders X and Y each have $3,000 dividend income and CE&P is reduced to $4,000; this $4,000 will be its beginning AE&P on the first day of the next year.

b. ABC instead makes two $6,000 distributions to X and Y, one on February 1 and the second on November 30. The $10,000 in CE&P is allocated ratably to each distribution. X and Y each have a $5,000 dividend ($2,500 from each distribution) from CE&P ($10,000/$12,000 × $6,000) and a $1,000 return of capital [($12,000 – $10,000)/2]. AE&P on the first day of the next year is zero.

c. Assume same facts as (b) except Y sells her stock on May 1 to Z. X and Y each still have the same $2,500 ($5,000/$6,000 × $3,000) dividend and $500 return of capital for the Feb. 1 distribution. For the November distribution, X and Z now each have a $2,500 dividend and $500 return of capital from the distribution. X has a $5,000 dividend and a $1,000 return of capital for the year. Y and Z each have a $2,500 taxable dividend and a $500 return of capital. AE&P on the first day of the next year is zero.

In the above example, the corporation had no AE&P. Few profitable corporations would have CE&P with no AE&P. The corporation first distributes its CE&P as described previously, but then distributes its AE&P by a different procedure—a first-come-first-served basis; that is, all or part of AE&P is allocated to the first dividend distribution (the earliest distribution) of the tax year up to the total distribution; remaining AE&P is allocated to the second distribution and then the third, continuing chronologically until AE&P is exhausted. The allocations of CE&P and AE&P distributions are then reapportioned to each of the shareholders based on their percentage of stock ownership on the date of distribution.

Example 10.27

The facts are the same as the previous example except that ABC Corporation has $1,500 in AE&P.

a. The answer is the same as in (a) of the previous example because CE&P was not exceeded.

b. X and Y each have a $3,000 dividend from the February 1 distribution. Both the February 1 and November 30 distributions are still allocated $5,000 each of CE&P. The February 1 dividend is allocated $1,000 of AE&P and the entire $6,000 distribution is dividend ($3,000 each to X and Y). X and Y each receive another $3,000 from the November 30 distribution but now only $2,750 is dividend—$2,500 each from CE&P and $250 [($1,500 – $1,000 February 1) / 2] from the remaining AE&P. They each have a $250 return of capital. As a result, X and Y each have $5,750 of dividend income for the year and a $250 return of capital.

c. X and Y each still have a $3,000 dividend from the first distribution. X and Z each have a dividend of $2,750 and a $250 return of capital on the second distribution. As a result, X has a $5,750 ($3,000 + $2,750) dividend and a $250 return of capital for the year; Y only has a $3,000 dividend; Z has a $2,750 dividend and a $250 return of capital.

Shareholders who receive a distribution identified as a return of capital must reduce the basis in their stock for this distribution.

Example 10.28

Corporation J has CE&P of $40,000 and AE&P of $20,000. It makes a $70,000 distribution to its shareholders. Only $60,000 is taxed as a dividend, $40,000 from CE&P and $20,000 from AE&P. The remaining $10,000 is a return of capital and reduces shareholders' stock bases.

A shareholder's basis cannot be reduced below zero, however. If the distribution exceeds the shareholder's basis, the shareholder is treated as selling the stock for the excess and generally recognizes capital gain.

Example 10.29

Tango Corporation has $5,000 in CE&P and $1,000 in AE&P when it makes a distribution of $15,000 to its sole shareholder, Tim. Tim has a $7,000 basis in his stock. The first $6,000 of the distribution is a taxable dividend from the corporation's CE&P and AE&P. The next $7,000 is a nontaxable recovery of Tim's $7,000 investment in the corporation and reduces his stock basis to zero. The remaining $2,000 ($15,000 – $6,000 – $7,000) distribution is gain on the sale of his stock, and Tim recognizes a $2,000 capital gain.

If a corporation has had an excess of losses over income in prior years, it could have a negative balance in AE&P, but a positive CE&P from the current year's operations. The corporation can still pay dividends to the extent of CE&P as dividends always are paid first from CE&P. A negative AE&P does not affect this payment of current dividends from CE&P. (The result would be the same as Example 10.26 in which the corporation had no AE&P.) If, however, a corporation has a loss at the end of the year (a negative CE&P) but positive AE&P, it may or may not be able to pay a dividend based on the timing and amount of the dividend. The deficit in CE&P is generally assumed to accrue ratably during the year. The ratable portion of the CE&P deficit is netted at the day before the dividend against positive AE&P. If the result is positive E&P, the distribution is a dividend to the extent of the positive amount. If it is negative, there is no dividend.

Example 10.30

Oregon Corporation has a $2,000 negative CE&P at the end of the current year but $5,000 in its AE&P; it paid a $3,000 dividend at midyear to its sole shareholder. The $2,000 loss is assumed to have been earned ratably during the year with $1,000 accrued at midyear. This reduces mid-year AE&P to $4,000. The entire $3,000 distribution is a dividend and reduces AE&P to $1,000. (AE&P would be zero (–$2,000 + $5,000 – $3,000) at the beginning of the following year, however.)

If, instead, Oregon had a negative $12,000 of CE&P, the $6,000 ratable portion of CE&P at midyear completely offsets the $5,000 of AE&P and AE&P is a net negative $1,000. None of the distribution is a dividend and it is treated entirely as a return of capital. At the beginning of the next tax year, the $12,000 deficit in CE&P offsets the $5,000 of positive AE&P and AE&P is now negative $7,000.

Alternatively, if the $3,000 distribution had been made on the 61st day of the year, only $1,973 (60/365 × $12,000) of negative CE&P would have accrued by the distribution date; AE&P would still be a positive $3,027 ($5,000 – $1,973) and the entire $3,000 distribution would be dividend. (The balance in AE&P at the beginning of the next year is negative $10,000 (–$12,000 CE&P + $2,000 AE&P) after the dividend.)

If a corporation has negative balances in both AE&P and CE&P, then the corporation cannot pay dividends and any distribution is a return of capital. Note, however, a dividend distribution of cash or property can never create a negative balance in either CE&P or AE&P.

They are only the result of negative CE&P. Once both CE&P and AE&P are reduced to zero by all or part of a dividend distribution, any further distribution is not taxed as dividend income, but as a return of capital.

10.3.4 PROPERTY DISTRIBUTIONS

Most corporate distributions are in cash, but a corporation may also make property distributions—distributions of something other than cash or the corporation's own stock. The preceding discussion was based on cash distributions, but the same rules apply to property distributions (except nontaxable stock dividends) in allocating CE&P and/or AE&P to determine a shareholder's taxable income. However, several questions arise:

1. What is the value of a property distribution?
2. What is the property's basis in the recipient's hands?
3. Does the distributing corporation have any tax consequences?

The value of a property distribution is its net fair market value at the date of distribution.[50] If the property is encumbered by a liability, the property's value is reduced by the liability, but the basis the shareholder has in the property received remains its fair market value (unreduced by any liability assumed).

A corporation that distributes appreciated property as a dividend recognizes gain equal to the difference in its basis and its fair market value when distributed.[51] If depreciated property is distributed, however, the corporation is not permitted to recognize the loss.[52] Gain recognized increases the corporation's CE&P but an unrecognized loss on a distribution does not reduce CE&P. Instead, CE&P is reduced for the greater of the property's fair market value or adjusted basis less any liability assumed by the shareholder on the property distribution.

Example 10.31

Howel Corporation has E&P of $100,000. Lynn receives a distribution of a piece of land valued at $50,000 with a $10,000 mortgage (assumed by Lynn) and a basis of $25,000. Howel also distributes machinery to Dave valued at $40,000 with a basis of $45,000. Howel recognizes a $25,000 gain on the distribution of the land but does not recognize the loss on the distribution of the machinery. Lynn and Dave both recognize taxable dividends of $40,000. Lynn's basis for the land is $50,000 and Dave's basis for the machine is $40,000.

The $25,000 gain recognized by Howel increases the land's basis to $50,000 (fair market value and basis are now equal) and its CE&P by the $25,000 gain. Its distribution of the land then reduces CE&P by $40,000, the fair market value less the $10,000 mortgage assumed. Howell did not recognize the loss on the machinery, but it reduces its CE&P by $45,000, the greater of basis or fair market value.

Any "distribution" of cash or property that is reclassified as a constructive dividend (for example, a shareholder has free personal use of a company automobile), will also reduce a corporation's earnings and profits for the fair market value in the manner discussed above. If a corporation has neither current nor accumulated earnings and profits, the reclassification is moot.

---

[50] §301.

[51] §311. If the property is encumbered by a liability in excess of its fair market value, the fair market value is assumed to be no less than the liability.

[52] If the distributed property is appreciated, the corporation first increases its E&P for the gain realized and then reduces it for the fair market value of the property; on depreciated property, however, the corporation only reduces E&P by the property's basis.

10.3.5 STOCK DIVIDENDS

The most common form of **stock dividend**, a distribution of common stock on common stock, does nothing more than give a shareholder a greater number of shares of stock. The shares have a proportionately smaller value per share and the shareholder has no income, but he or she apportions the stock's original basis over all the shares now owned.[53] The net effect is similar to a stock split from the shareholder's perspective

Example 10.32

B has 10 shares of stock that cost $60 per share. The corporation issues a 20 percent stock dividend when the stock's value is $120 per share. After the dividend, the price of a share falls to $100 per share (1 share at $120 now equals 1.2 shares valued at $120 or $100 per share). B received 2 shares of stock and allocates her original $600 basis in the 10 shares between the 12 shares she now owns ($50 per share).

If common shareholders receive a pro rata distribution of stock or **stock rights** on common stock, the distribution is tax free.[54] Basis of the shares of stock on which the stock dividend or stock rights are distributed is apportioned to the property received using relative fair market value. If the value of the rights is less than 15 percent of the value of the stock on which they were issued, the shareholder may ignore the allocation and assign a zero basis to the rights.[55]

Example 10.33

Joanna receives one stock right to purchase one additional share of stock in V Corporation at $20 for each of the 200 shares (basis = $3,000) that she currently owns. V stock is currently selling for $25 per share. The value of the stock rights is $5 ($25 – $20) per right, which is more than 15 percent of the value of the stock (5/25 = 20%). Joanna allocates part of her basis to the rights. The total value of the shares is $5,000. The total value of the rights is $1,000. Her basis in the stock rights is $500 [$1,000/($5,000 + $1,000) × $3,000]. She reduces her stock basis to $2,500 ($3,000 – $500). If she exercises the rights, the basis for the 200 new shares acquired will be $4,500 [$500 basis allocated to the rights + ($20 exercise price × 200)]. If, however, she allows the rights to lapse, the $500 basis allocated to them returns to her original shares; no loss is recognized.

In several instances, however, a shareholder will have tax consequences on a stock dividend. If a shareholder can choose between cash and a stock dividend (the usual stock reinvestment plan), the dividend is taxable under the doctrine of constructive receipt regardless of which alternative is selected. In general, if a distribution of stock or stock rights increases the percentage ownership of some shareholders relative to others, the distribution is taxable.[56] If a distribution of stock or stock rights is taxable, the shareholder recognizes income equal to the property's fair market value. Nontaxable stock dividends have no effect on corporate earnings and profits but a taxable stock dividend would be treated as any other cash or property distribution.

Example 10.34

Shareholders of Class A common stock receive a 10 percent stock dividend while shareholders of Class B common stock receive a cash dividend. As a result, Class A shareholders now own a greater proportion of the stock of the corporation due to the stock dividend and both the stock (valued at fair market value) and the cash dividends are taxable. The basis of the stock received by the shareholders is its fair market value.

[53] §§305(a) and 307(a).

[54] §305. Stock rights are rights to acquire additional shares of stock at a set price (similar to stock options).

[55] §307(b).

[56] Stock dividends can also be taxable if some holders of common stock receive preferred stock and others receive additional common stock.

10.4 CORPORATE REDEMPTIONS AND LIQUIDATIONS

Corporate redemptions and liquidations each involve the return of part or all of shareholders' outstanding stock to the corporation. Redemptions may be initiated by either the corporation or the shareholder. Liquidations may be either partial or complete and are normally initiated by the corporation. In a partial liquidation, a corporation chooses to downsize by distributing all or part of its unneeded assets. If a corporation determines that going out of business is in its best interest, it usually sells it assets and distributes its cash and any remaining property to its shareholders.

10.4.1 REDEMPTION SALE REQUIREMENTS

A corporate **redemption** is the repurchase of the issuing corporation's own stock from one or more of its shareholders. In a qualifying redemption, the shareholder surrenders all or part of his or her stock in exchange for the corporation's cash or property and recognizes capital gain or loss equal to the difference between the amount realized and the basis of the stock surrendered. A shareholder could use a redemption, however, to extract assets from a continuing corporation to avoid dividend income.[57] As a result, Congress enacted a complex set of rules designed to prevent taxpayers from disguising dividends as redemptions.

To qualify for sale treatment, the redemption must result in a significant reduction in the shareholder's equity ownership. This can be achieved by showing the redemption is either (1) substantially disproportionate or (2) a complete termination of a shareholder's interest in the corporation.[58]

The requirement for the redemption to be substantially disproportionate has specific numerical guidelines:[59]

1. The shareholder must own less than 50 percent of the voting power after the redemption.
2. The shareholder's percentage ownership of voting stock and common stock must be less than 80 percent of the ownership percentage before the redemption.

Example 10.35

Al and Barbara each own 30 of the 100 outstanding shares of ABC Corporation's common stock; Carrie owns 40 shares. The corporation redeems 25 shares from Al and 5 shares from Barbara, paying each shareholder $1,000 cash for each share redeemed. The corporation has $100,000 in earnings and profits. The corporation's outstanding stock before and after these transactions is as follows:

	Before redemption			After redemption	
Shareholder	(A) Shares Owned	(A) /100 Percentage Ownership	(B) Ownership Redeemed	(A)–(B) Shares Owned	[(A)–(B)]/70 Percentage Ownership
Al	30	30%	25	5	7.1%
Barbara	30	30%	5	25	35.7%
Carrie	40	40%	0	40	57.2%
Total	100	100%	30	70	100.0%

Al's redemption is substantially disproportionate because he owns less than 50 percent of the stock after the redemption and his post-redemption ownership (7.1 percent) is less than

[57] Although the tax rates for dividend income and long-term capital gains are similar, a shareholder recovers stock basis tax free in a qualifying redemption while the entire dividend distribution is taxed if the corporation has sufficient earnings and profits.

[58] There is a third test, "not essentially equivalent to a dividend," which must result in a "meaningful reduction in the shareholder's interest." *U.S. v. Maclin P. Davis*, 70-1 USTC ¶998, 25 AFTR 2d 70-287, 397 US 301 (USSC, 1970). See *William F. Wright v. U.S.*, 73-2 USTC 9583, 32AFTR 2d 73-5490, 482 F.2d 600 (CA-8, 1973). Also see Rev. Rul. 75-502, 1975-2 CB 111.

[59] §302(b)(2). Such numerical guidelines are often referred to as *bright lines*.

80 percent of his pre-redemption ownership (30% × 80% = 24%). Al receives sale treatment and recognizes capital gain equal to the difference between the $25,000 cash received and his basis for the 25 shares redeemed. Barbara's redemption is not substantially disproportionate. Although she owns less than 50 percent after the redemption, her post-redemption ownership (35.7 percent) is not less than 80 percent of her pre-redemption stock ownership (30% × 80% = 24%). Barbara has a $5,000 dividend.

A complete termination of interest means the shareholder must divest himself or herself of all shares of the stock in the corporation. Under normal circumstances, a complete termination of interest also qualifies as a substantially disproportionate redemption, but the attribution rules may make it difficult to completely terminate all interest in the corporation when the redeeming shareholder is related to continuing shareholders.

Related persons have common interests and can be expected to act for mutual benefit of all related persons. The attribution rules are based on this assumption and the stock owned by one related party is considered to be indirectly owned by the other related party.

Relationships include the following:[60]

1. Family Attribution	An individual owns stock owned by a spouse, parent, child, and grandchild.
2. Entity to Owner	**a.** Stock owned by a partnership is owned proportionately by the partners.
	b. Stock owned by a corporation is attributed proportionately only to a 50 percent or more shareholder.
	c. Stock owned by an estate or trust is attributed proportionately to the beneficiaries.
3. Owner to Entity	**a.** Stock owned by a partner is attributed in full to the partnership.
	b. Stock owned by a 50 percent or more shareholder is attributed in full to the corporation.
	c. Stock owned by a beneficiary is attributed in full to the estate or trust.

The attribution rules are applied when calculating the ownership tests to determine if the redemption is a significant reduction in ownership to qualify for sale treatment. For a complete termination of interest, an individual is allowed to waive only the family attribution rules.[61]

Example 10.36

John and Jackie, husband and wife, own 100 percent of the outstanding stock of J & J Corporation. John has other business interests and leaves the running of the business completely to Jackie. J & J redeems all of John's stock. Because John and Jackie are closely related, John is assumed to have influence over Jackie, and her shares are attributed to him. This influence could deny him redemption as a complete termination of interest. If he waives the family attribution rules, however, the transaction will qualify as a complete termination of interest.

[60] §318(a). These rules differ somewhat from the rules applicable to transactions between related parties.

[61] §302(b)(3). When attribution is waived, a shareholder can have no interest in the corporation for 10 years except that of a creditor (that is, the shareholder may still own corporate bonds). §302(c).

A redemption that meets a third, far more tenuous provision, of "not essentially equivalent to a dividend" may also receive sale rather than dividend treatment, but this provision relies on all the facts and circumstances that are undefined. As a result this provision should be avoided unless neither of the two more quantifiable provisions can be met.

If a sale fails to qualify as a redemption, the proceeds the shareholder receives are dividends to the extent of the corporation's earnings and profits. The shareholder's basis transfers to the other shares still owned. If the shareholder owns no other shares, the basis transfers to the related party's shares.[62]

If the corporation distributes appreciated property to redeem the shareholder's stock, the corporation must recognize gain; it is prohibited from recognizing loss on depreciated property that is distributed, however.[63]

TAX PLANNING

If a corporation has little or no earnings and profits, a nonqualifying stock redemption may result in little or no dividend income before the shareholder begins to recover basis. If the shareholder is a corporation, dividend treatment may be preferable to sale treatment, due to the dividend received deduction.

10.4.2 PARTIAL LIQUIDATION

A partial corporate liquidation resembles a corporate redemption except that qualifying for sale treatment depends on the corporation rather than the shareholder. A distribution of cash or property by a corporation qualifies as a **partial liquidation** if the corporation significantly reduces its operations or terminates one of its qualifying businesses.[64] Treatment of the distributing corporation's corporate and noncorporate shareholders differs, however. Noncorporate shareholders receive sale treatment for the distributions on the surrender of their shares in a partial liquidation, while corporate shareholders usually treat the distributions as dividends.[65] The distributing corporation recognizes gain (but not loss) on the distribution of appreciated (depreciated) property in a partial liquidation.

Example 10.37

Bard Corporation has two divisions, one making women's hats and the other purses. The hat division lost money for the last five years. The company liquidates the assets of that division and distributes the proceeds to its shareholders in exchange for one-third of their outstanding stock in a qualifying partial liquidation. The individual shareholders automatically qualify for sale treatment recognizing capital gain on the difference between the fair market value of property received and basis of stock surrendered. Corporate shareholders receive dividend treatment and are eligible for the dividend received deduction (unless the quantity of stock surrendered qualifies as a sale under the redemption rules).

10.4.3 LIQUIDATING DISTRIBUTIONS

When a corporation adopts a plan of liquidation, ceases operations, distributes its assets to its shareholders in exchange for all of their stock, and cancels the stock, the corporation is liquidated. While the corporation is liquidating, it no longer is a going concern and its activities are directed at the closing of the business. The corporation's treatment in liquidation

---

[62] §302(d).

[63] §311. These gain/loss rules are the same as those that apply to dividend distributions.

[64] The corporation must abandon one of its qualifying businesses and continue to operate another qualifying business; both must be active businesses operated for at least five years and neither of these businesses were acquired in a taxable transaction within the preceding five years. §302(e)(3).

[65] Because of the dividends received deduction, this treatment may be advantageous to a corporation.

differs from that of other distributions, however, because the corporation not only recognizes gain on the distribution of appreciated assets but also recognizes loss on depreciated property distributed.[66]

Example 10.38

BH Corporation is liquidating. It sold most of its assets for cash except it distributes its two remaining business assets to its sole shareholder—a car valued at $3,100 (basis = $2,000) and a machine valued at $6,800 (basis = $9,000)—in exchange for her stock, along with the cash. The corporation recognizes the $1,100 gain on the car and the $2,200 loss on the machine.

All shareholders of a liquidating corporation recognize gain or loss on the distribution of assets in exchange for their stock, based on the cash and fair market value of the property received and the basis of the stock surrendered.[67] If the shareholder receives the liquidation proceeds over several years, loss cannot be recognized until the final distribution is received. The shareholder recognizes gain, however, on any current (and subsequent) distribution after basis is fully recovered.

Example 10.39

Green Corporation distributes $20,000 cash and property having a $12,000 fair market value to Jennifer as part of its plan of liquidation. Jennifer's basis in her Green stock is $16,000. Jennifer recognizes a $16,000 gain ($20,000 + $12,000 – $16,000) on the liquidation. If Jennifer received the $20,000 cash in the first year and the $12,000 of property in a subsequent year, she would recognize $4,000 gain ($20,000 – $16,000) in the first year and the remaining $12,000 gain in the subsequent year. If she received less than $16,000 total on the distributions, she could recognize no loss until the final year of distributions.

A parent corporation that liquidates a subsidiary corporation is subject to separate liquidation provisions.[68] Neither the subsidiary nor the parent recognizes gain or loss on the distribution of property from the subsidiary to the parent. The parent takes a carryover basis in the assets, effectively postponing any gain or loss until the parent disposes of the assets.

10.4.4 DIVIDEND AND REDEMPTION PLANNING ISSUES

In 2013, Congress increased the maximum basic tax rate for dividends and capital gains from 15 percent to 20 percent for individuals with incomes in the top marginal tax bracket. For 2018, the basic tax rates for dividend income and long-term capital gains are:

Tax rate	Taxable income for single individuals	Taxable income for married filing a joint return	Taxable income for head of household
0%	$0 – $38,600	$0 – $77,200	$0 – $51,700
15%	$38,601–$425,800	$77,201–$479,000	$51,701–$452,400
20%	Over $425,800	Over $479,000	Over $452,400

A net investment income (NII) surtax of 3.8 percent is added to the tax rate of individuals with AGI greater than $250,000 married filing a joint return ($200,000 if single). The increase

[66] Losses may not be recognized on certain distributions to controlling shareholders or on recently acquired assets.
[67] Gain and loss are determined separately for different blocks of stock.
[68] The parent corporation must own directly at least 80 percent of the voting power or at least 80 percent of the value of all of the subsidiary's stock.

in the maximum rate for upper income taxpayers, however, makes extracting cash or property from a corporation less attractive. Although distributing dividends to shareholders in higher tax brackets is no longer as attractive as it was prior to 2013, the top effective rate for dividends of 23.8 percent (20 percent + 3.8 percent surtax) remains 17 percent less than the top effective rate of 40.8 percent (37 percent + 3.8 percent surtax) that applies to ordinary interest income.

Example 10.40

A corporation with $1,000,000 taxable income distributes all of its after-tax income as a dividend to its sole shareholder in the top marginal tax bracket. The corporation pays $210,000 tax on the $1,000,000 of income and the shareholder pays an additional $188,020 ($790,000 × 23.8%) on the dividend income; total taxes are $398,020.

The recharacterization of excessive salary or rental payments as dividends poses a threat, but may not be prohibitive at current rates, particularly if the corporation reports a loss or very low income for the year.

Example 10.41

ABC Corporation reports a $100,000 loss for the year while raising its owner's salary from $650,000 to $850,000. If the $200,000 raise is considered excessive compensation and is recharacterized as a dividend, the corporation loses the $200,000 deduction and has $100,000 of taxable income on which it will pay a tax of $21,000. The owner's tax rate on the $200,000, however, decreases from 37.9% (37% + 0.9% surtax) to 23.8% (20% + 3.8% NII surtax) and he saves [$28,200 (37.9% – 23.8%) × $200,000] in taxes. In addition, both ABC and the owner will receive a refund of employment taxes on the $200,000 recharacterized as dividend.

Although the corporation could have made the $200,000 dividend payment directly to the owner with the same result, it would have been required to make similar proportionate dividend payments to the other shareholders holding that same class of stock as the owner.

TAX PLANNING

Shareholders with loans from a corporation should still have the corporation distribute sufficient cash as a dividend to pay off the loan directly even though it could be taxed at a maximum effective rate of 23.8 percent. If the debt had been forgiven, the shareholder would be taxed at ordinary income rates (up to 37 percent) for the discharge of indebtedness income.

With the current dividend rates, shareholders who want some or all of their stock redeemed may still benefit from dividend treatment on the proceeds. Family members who want to redeem only a portion of their stock may still do so generally with less tax cost. Family members can only qualify for sale treatment if they dispose of all of their stock and waive the family attribution rules. This waiver requires the shareholder to cease all interest in the corporation except as a creditor for ten years. This prevents a family member from remaining an employee or consultant of the corporation if they want to receive sale treatment.

Example 10.42

Frank wants to redeem all 10,000 shares of his stock in a family corporation while remaining as a consultant on future projects. Beverly, Frank's sister, wants to redeem only a portion of her shares for her son's college expenses. Neither Frank nor Beverly have sufficient other taxable income that would result in dividend income taxed at more than 15 percent of the total proceeds. Although sale treatment may have resulted in less tax (only the gain would be subject to tax), neither would be able to receive sale treatment due to their circumstances. The entire distribution will be taxed to them as a dividend (assuming there is sufficient E&P).

TAX PLANNING

It may make little difference to shareholders with very low stock basis if they receive long-term capital gain or dividend treatment. For shareholders who have not held their stock for more than one year, however, dividend treatment may be preferable to treatment as a short-term capital gain.

Example 10.43

Shelly has a basis of $20,000 in the 2,000 shares of stock she wants ABC to redeem; Carol has a basis of only $2,000 in her 2,000 shares. Both Shelly and Carol are in the 35% marginal tax bracket for ordinary income (15% dividend and capital gains tax rates). The corporation pays each of them $40,000 for their shares. If Shelly has sale treatment as a long-term capital gain, her tax is $3,000 [($40,000 – $20,000 basis) × 15%] but her tax doubles to $6,000 (15% × $40,000) if it is a dividend. Carol, however, pays $6,000 tax as a dividend but $5,700 [($40,000 – $2,000) × 15%] tax as a long-term capital gain. If Shelly had held her stock for less than one year, however, she would prefer dividend treatment. At ordinary income rates, her $20,000 short-term capital gain would result in a tax of $7,000 ($20,000 × 35%).

There are several other situations in which sale treatment remains preferable to dividend treatment. For example, a shareholder with capital loss carryforwards would prefer a capital gain from sale treatment to offset these capital losses. In addition, sale treatment is preferable for a redemption if the taxpayer is going to receive proceeds over more than one year. The installment method would not be available for sale proceeds recharacterized as dividend.[69]

10.5 ISSUES FOR CLOSELY HELD CORPORATIONS

Section 542(a)(2) defines a **closely held corporation** as one that has five or fewer individuals who own 50 percent or more of the value of a corporation's outstanding stock at any time during the last half of the tax year. A practical definition for tax avoidance purposes is one in which one or several of the shareholders acting together can prevail on the corporation to act in a way that reflects their will. Nothing is intrinsically wrong with this, but closely held corporations come under particular scrutiny by the IRS to ensure that transactions are not designed to avoid taxes.

10.5.1 CONSTRUCTIVE DIVIDENDS

Shareholders of closely held corporations may try to avoid direct dividend payments and receive informal economic benefits with constructive dividends. Examples include rents in excess of a property's fair rental value, the use of corporate property for personal purposes, a sale of property to a shareholder below its fair market value, loans to shareholders at low or no interest, and payment of a shareholder's personal expenses by a corporation. Shareholder-employees may also receive excessive compensation through these or similar strategies.

Example 10.44

ABC Corporation rents office space from its majority shareholder. The office space normally rents for $5,400 per month but the corporation pays the shareholder $7,000 per month. The shareholder recognizes the $7,000 monthly rent as income, and the corporation deducts the full amount as rent expense. If the IRS reclassifies the $1,600 in excess monthly rental payment as a constructive dividend, the corporation loses $1,600 per month in deductible expenses.

[69] See Andrew R. Lee, "New Dividend Planning Strategies for Shareholders and Corporations," *Practical Tax Strategies*, October 2003.

If a party related to the shareholder receives any of the benefits listed above because of the shareholder's relationship to the corporation, the benefit received by the related party can also be reclassified as a constructive dividend to the shareholder.

Example 10.45

Continuing the previous example, the corporation also allows the shareholder's son to use a company vehicle solely for his personal use. The corporation deducts depreciation and other expenses for the vehicle. If the vehicle's rental value is $500 per month, this value can be reclassified as a constructive dividend to the shareholder, and the corporation loses its deductions for expenses related to the vehicle.

A reclassification as a constructive dividend is normally detrimental to the corporation but it may benefit the shareholder. If excess compensation or rental payments have already been included in the individual shareholder's ordinary income, their reclassification as dividends could reduce the tax rate to which they are subject to a maximum 20 percent (23.8 percent with the surtax) rate.[70] The loss of a deduction for an expense reclassified as a dividend, however, can subject the corporation to penalties and interest. If the corporation does not have positive earnings and profits, however, any value received by the shareholder cannot be taxed as a dividend, but would be treated as a return of capital by the shareholder and taxable only if the shareholder's stock basis is reduced to zero.

10.5.2 PENALTY TAXES TO ENCOURAGE DIVIDEND PAYMENTS

When individual tax rates are higher than corporate rates, there is an incentive to leave earnings in a corporation so that the shareholders can profit from share price appreciation rather than from dividends. The personal holding company (PHC) tax and the accumulated earnings tax (AET) are penalty taxes designed to discourage corporations from retaining earnings. The purpose of the penalty tax is to encourage the payment of dividends, so the penalty tax rate equals the individual 20 percent maximum tax rate for dividend income. If a corporation is subject to either penalty tax, the tax is assessed as an addition to the regular corporate income tax. (If a corporation could be subject to both the AET and the PHC tax, only the PHC tax is imposed.) Paying sufficient dividends to shareholders avoids imposition of either of these penalty taxes.

Personal Holding Companies

A **personal holding company** is a corporation that meets both ownership and income tests in any year. If (1) five or fewer individuals own more than 50 percent of the value of the corporation's outstanding stock at any time during the last half of the corporation's taxable year and (2) 60 percent or more of the corporation's adjusted ordinary gross income (AOGI) is personal holding company income (PHCI), the corporation is a personal holding company (PHCI/AOGI is greater than or equal to 60 percent).[71] A corporation whose stock is owned by nine or fewer individuals automatically meets the ownership test. Attribution rules under Section 544 are applied in determining ownership.[72]

Personal holding company income (PHCI) generally is passive income including dividends, interest, royalties, and annuities. Rental income, copyright royalties, software royalties, and royalties

[70] The taxpayer would have to file an amended return to redetermine the tax if the return was filed prior to the reclassification.

[71] S corporations, banks, and other financing companies, insurance companies, and foreign personal holding companies are exempt from this tax.

[72] These attribution rules are similar to those explained earlier for stock redemptions except that family is extended to include brothers, sisters, and all lineal ancestors and descendants.

from mineral, oil, and gas rights are excluded if at least one-half of the corporation's income is from one of these sources and certain other requirements are met.[73]

The PHC can avoid a penalty if sufficient dividends are paid. The corporation self-assesses the 20 percent tax on adjusted taxable income less the dividends paid deduction to determine the PHC tax, paying this along with its regular corporate tax.

Accumulated Earnings Tax

The **accumulated earnings tax (AET)**, which is assessed by the IRS, applies only to corporations that are "formed or availed of for the purpose of avoiding income tax with respect to the shareholders."[74] No mechanical method can prove this intent, but a corporation that accumulates earnings beyond its reasonable needs or is an investment or holding company is deemed to meet the intent requirement.[75] Corporations having a balance in accumulated earnings and profits in excess of $250,000 ($150,000 for a personal service corporation) must prove that the accumulation is reasonable to avoid the 20 percent tax on excess accumulations.

The reasonable needs of a business include all current and reasonably anticipated future needs.[76] To meet reasonably anticipated needs, the corporation must have plans that are "specific, definite, and feasible."[77] A corporation that has reserves for plant expansion approved by the board of directors and for which there is a definite timetable established is not subject to the tax. Other reasonable needs for which the corporation may accumulate earnings include liability losses, replacement of plant and equipment, retiring of debt, and working capital. Factors cited as indicative of unreasonable accumulations include a poor dividend history, investments that are not related to the corporation's ongoing business, and loans to shareholders. Corporations are permitted to accumulate a maximum of $250,000 ($150,000 for a personal service corporation) of earnings as a credit without penalty.[78] Paying sufficient dividends precludes the IRS from imposing the AET.

10.5.3 CONTROLLED CORPORATE GROUPS

To prevent taxpayers from establishing multiple corporations to benefit from the prior progressive corporate tax rates (and other favorable provisions), a controlled group of corporations could take advantage of the lower rates one time only. The lower rate could be apportioned to the controlled corporations in any manner the taxpayer chose, but the corporations must calculate taxes as if they were one corporation.[79]

Example 10.46

James owns 100 percent of the stock in Bee and Cee Corporations. In 2017, Bee Corporation reported $300,000 of income and Cee Corporation reported only $10,000 of income. If Cee Corporation calculated the tax on its $10,000 of income at the 15 percent tax rate, Bee Corporation could use the 15 percent tax rate to calculate its tax only on the first $40,000 ($50,000 – $10,000) of income. The remaining rates applied to Bee in the usual manner.

[73] §543(a)(1). For example, rents are excluded if a large portion of the nonrental income is distributed as dividends.
[74] §532(a). As the law is written, the AET could apply to any corporation not just one that is closely held. Imposing the tax on a widely held corporation with no single person or related group controlling it is impractical because of the intent requirement.
[75] §533.
[76] §532(a)(1).
[77] Reg. §1.537-1(b).
[78] The credit allowed is either the current year's earnings and profits net of capital gains (adjusted for taxes) that the corporation needs to retain to meet its reasonable needs or the minimum credit, whichever is greater.
[79] A controlled group of corporations is permitted only one accumulated earnings tax credit.

Although corporations pay a flat 21 percent tax rate after 2017, the controlled group rules continue to apply to other areas. Parent–subsidiary and brother–sister controlled groups are the two types of controlled corporate groups. A parent–subsidiary controlled group is one that

1. consists of two or more corporations, one of which is a common parent corporation;
2. owns directly 80 percent or more of the voting power *or* 80 percent or more of the total value of all classes of stock of a second corporation (the subsidiary); and
3. includes all other corporations, 80 percent or more of whose stock is owned jointly or separately by the parent and its subsidiary corporations, measured by voting power *or* total value of all classes of stock.

The accumulated earnings credit and the alternative minimum tax exemption amount are apportioned to two or more corporations with five or fewer individual shareholders who (1) own more than 50 percent of the total combined voting power *or* (2) more than 50 percent of the value of all shares of stock of the corporations, the brother-sister controlled group. Either percentage is determined by taking into account only the lowest stock ownership percentage of each shareholder that is identical across each corporation. For all other purposes, the shareholders must own at least 80 percent of the combined voting power or value of the corporations *and* own more than 50 percent (voting or value) of the stock taking into account only the identical ownership by the shareholders across the corporations.[80]

Example 10.47

	Ownership percentage by shareholder			
Corporation	X	Y	Z	Totals
A	20%	40%	25%	85%
B	40	40	15	95
C	60	15	10	85
D	20	20	50	90
Lowest percentage ownership of each shareholder	20	15	10	Total lowest percentage ownership = 45

Although the three shareholders own over 80 percent of each corporation, the sum of the shareholder's lowest percentage ownership in each corporation does not equal more than 50 percent. Therefore, the four corporations are not a brother–sister controlled group. If, however, only Corporations A, B, and D are considered, the total of the lowest common percentage ownership is 55% (A = 20%, B = 15%, D = 20%) and A, B, and D constitute a brother–sister controlled group.

Controlled groups of corporations remain a problem, however, because of the ease by which one corporation can be used to avoid taxes for the owners of another corporation in the group. For example, one or more corporations in the group could pay constructive dividends to the shareholders of a related corporation through excessive salaries or rents or bargain purchases.

Example 10.48

Corporations P and S are a parent and subsidiary. P has only two shareholders, J and K. J works for the subsidiary as an accounts payable manager with a salary of $400,000. Salaries for comparable work are only $50,000. As long as either P or S has earnings and profits, the excess salary is a constructive dividend taxable to J but no longer deductible by S.

[80] §1563.

One of the more common schemes using controlled corporations is using one corporation to purchase the shares of another corporation from a shareholder (a backdoor redemption). The IRS has been aware of these schemes for many years and has developed slightly altered applications of the substantially disproportionate redemption rules to apply to these corporations. Failure to meet these rules results in dividend treatment and the earnings and profits available for the dividend are not limited to the redeeming corporation's earnings and profits.[81]

10.6 CONSOLIDATED RETURNS

The consolidated return regulations recognize that one corporation can exert substantial control over a second corporation in which it has substantial ownership. It allows a controlling corporation to file a consolidated return with an affiliated corporation as if it is a division of the controlling corporation for tax purposes. To form an **affiliated group**, a **parent corporation** (Corporation P) must directly own 80 percent or more of the stock of another corporation—the **subsidiary** (Corporation S)—measured both by voting rights and the value of all outstanding stock. An affiliated group can have more than two corporations if each of the other included corporations meets the ownership requirements. In this case, 80 percent of an affiliated corporation's stock must be owned by one or more of the corporations that are part of the affiliated group, measured both by voting rights and the total value of outstanding stock.

Example 10.49

Corporation P owns 90 percent of Corporation S's voting stock and 85 percent by value of all its outstanding stock. It is a subsidiary of P. Corporation S owns 95 percent of S1's voting stock, the only class of outstanding stock. Corporation P is the common parent; Corporation S is the subsidiary of Corporation P; and Corporation S1 is a subsidiary of Corporation S. The three corporations form an affiliated group.[82]

Tax-exempt corporations, insurance companies,[83] foreign corporations, DISCs (domestic international sales corporations), REITs (real estate investment trusts), and RICs (real estate investment corporations) are not permitted to be part of an affiliated group.[84]

Corporations that are eligible and meet the ownership requirements can join in filing a **consolidated return**. A consolidated return reports the combined results of the operations of all corporations in the group. The parent corporation must elect to file a consolidated return, and all of the subsidiaries must consent to the election. This election is generally binding on the affiliated group as long as there is at least the one parent and one subsidiary at all times during the tax year.[85]

All corporations joining in a consolidated return must either have or change to the parent's tax year. Subsidiaries changing to the parent's tax year must generally file short-period returns for the period before the change by closing their books as of the date of consolidation.

[81] See §304 and the related regulations for a further discussion of redemptions by related corporations.

[82] An affiliated group is also a parent-subsidiary controlled group, but not all parent-subsidiary controlled groups (discussed later) are affiliated groups eligible to file consolidated returns.

[83] Affiliated groups consisting only of insurance companies are permitted.

[84] §1504(b).

[85] The members at the beginning of the year may be completely different than at the end of the year as long as the parent corporation has direct ownership of one subsidiary at all times during the tax year. The affiliated group must show good cause to receive permission from the IRS to discontinue filing consolidated returns unless the IRS grants blanket permission to all affiliated groups to discontinue filing consolidated returns for a change in law or regulation.

10.6.1 CONSOLIDATED NET INCOME

To determine consolidated net income, each corporation first computes separate taxable income, the corporation's taxable income after modification for intercompany transactions, and certain items that must be determined on a consolidated basis.[86] Deferred intercompany transactions and intercompany dividends are two of the transaction that require modifications determined by looking at the affiliated corporations simply as divisions of the parent corporation.

Example 10.50

Corporation P owns 100 percent of Corporation S and files a consolidated return. P sells land to S for $50,000 that has a basis of $25,000. S pays $5,000 of dividends to P. On their separate books, P recognizes a $25,000 gain on the sale of the land and $5,000 of dividend income. S recognizes the dividend paid of $5,000 and records the land at its cost of $50,000. When S is viewed as a division of P, S cannot pay a dividend to itself and P cannot recognize gain on a sale to itself. Thus, separate taxable income excludes both the $25,000 gain on the land sale of land and the dividends received.[87] They are eliminated in the determination of consolidated income.

Items that are subject to limitations and netting must be determined on a consolidated basis because they are subject to limitations and netting for the group as a whole. These items include capital gains and losses, Section 1231 gains and losses, and the charitable contribution deduction. After determining separate taxable income and items subject to limitations or netting on a consolidated basis, the parent can complete the consolidated return based on consolidated net income.

Example 10.51

Corporations P and S file a consolidated return. P has $50 of separate taxable income and a capital gain of $40. S has $25 of separate taxable income, a capital loss of $30, and a charitable contribution of $5. P and S have a combined capital gain of only $10 ($40 – $30) included in their regular income. Consolidated taxable income before the charitable contribution deduction is $85 ($50 + $25 + $10) for the year and $80 ($85 – $5) after the contribution deduction. If S had filed a separate return, it would not have been able to deduct its $30 capital loss, and its charitable contribution deduction would have been limited to $2.50.

From the preceding brief discussion, some of the advantages of filing consolidated returns become apparent:

1. Intercompany dividends are eliminated.
2. Gains on intercompany transactions are eliminated.
3. Deductions that are disallowed on a separate corporation basis due to limitations may be deductible when the limitations are applied to the consolidated group.
4. The losses of one corporation can offset the gains of another corporation.
5. Income from one corporation can offset losses from another corporation.
6. Limitations based on the consolidated return income or taxes may permit greater use of deductions or credits.

---

[86] §1502. Intercompany transactions include deferred intercompany transactions, intercompany distributions, built-in deductions, initial inventory adjustments, recapture of excess loss accounts, and income or loss due to changes in accounting methods. Only deferred intercompany transactions and dividend distributions are discussed here.

[87] The gain on the sale is eliminated by reducing the basis of the land to S by $25,000.

A number of disadvantages also must be considered when electing to file consolidated returns, such as the complex issues that result when corporations enter and leave the consolidated group; the tax-year change of subsidiaries to conform to the tax year of the parent; and that the combining of separate income may not always benefit the consolidated group.[88]

REVISITING THE INTRODUCTORY CASE

The corporation has four potential investors: the chief engineer, the supplier, John's father-in-law, and John's brother. The best case scenario for John would have each of the investors accept bonds instead of stock, as interest payments are deductible, and John's total control of the corporation is preserved—but this is unlikely.

The supplier is the one least likely to accept bonds. As a corporation, dividends are far more desirable due to the dividend received deduction. Owning 20 percent of the voting stock to preserve its status as a supplier also means it will have a 65 percent dividend received deduction. John also maintains control of the corporation, but John might consider issuing a second class of voting common stock so dividends do not have to be paid on all common stock at one time.

John's father-in-law is the ideal candidate for corporate bonds. The corporation can issue bonds with a minimum of 6 percent annual interest that mature in 10 years to meet the father-in-law's income requirements. The interest is deductible by the corporation, reducing its after-tax cost.

John's brother only wants an annual return on his investment as he plans to leave his investment to his heirs (most likely to take advantage of the step up in basis upon his death). Neither bonds nor preferred stock have significant appreciation potential, but John's brother might be agreeable to long-term bonds that have a conversion feature allowing them to be converted to common stock after some extended period of time (for example, 10 to 20 years). Bonds will provide current interest income that is deductible by the corporation. Preferred stock is a second, less desirable alternative as preferred stock dividends are not guaranteed and they are not deductible by the corporation.

It is a distinct advantage for the corporation to pay part of the engineer's compensation in stock. The value of the stock is considered income to the engineer and deductible by the corporation. The corporation conserves cash by paying a part of the engineer's salary in stock while preserving the total compensation deduction. The company could also consider incentive stock options as they normally have no tax consequences. Thus, it may be best for the company to work out a combination of stock and stock options as compensation for the engineer. John may want to set an upper limit on the amount of stock the engineer can receive, however, to ensure that he maintains control. Alternatively, John could use the second class of voting stock. The corporation can declare a dividend on this stock to satisfy the supplier and the engineer without having to pay a dividend to John.

As an employee, John can take a reasonable salary from the corporation, but he can further extract money from the corporation on a before-tax basis by employing his wife and his college-age sons. His wife, with her recent computer education, should be able to command a substantial salary without causing any constructive dividend problems. The two sons can work part-time in suitable positions at appropriate salaries. John should also consider employing the other two children as soon as they are old enough to take on appropriate jobs.

All of the potential investors appear to be viable candidates to invest in the corporation. The engineer is probably the one that John should include as his livelihood is invested in the corporation. John needs to further consider his relationships with his father-in-law and brother to

[88] A discussion of these issues is generally postponed until an advanced course in corporate tax.

insure that he will be allowed to continue to run the company without personal conflict that could impact his family. He should also ensure that there are sufficient safe guards that his supplier will continue to provide the goods that he needs at the market price, and at some point, attempt to take control of the company. John should encourage his sons to come to work at the firm with the idea of their following John into management and ownership.

SUMMARY

A corporation has a number of advantages and disadvantages when compared to other forms in which to operate a business. Its principal advantages are limited liability, unlimited life, free transferability of its stock, the ease of raising additional capital, and the ability of shareholders to enjoy the benefits of employee status. Disadvantages include the double taxation of income and the costs of establishing and maintaining a corporate charter.

Corporations are subject to tax on their income as determined under the rules of tax accounting. These rules have numerous differences from the rules the corporation follows in calculating financial accounting income under GAAP. A corporation's net capital gains are taxed at its regular corporate tax rates. Its net capital losses can only be carried to years in which it had net capital gains. A corporation's shareholders are taxed a second time on corporate income when it is distributed in the form of dividends. Corporate shareholders are permitted a dividends received deduction to alleviate some of the effects of double taxation.

The corporation maintains two accounts that affect distributions to shareholders: current earnings and profits and accumulated earnings and profits. Current earnings and profits is calculated starting with the current year's net income to which specific items are added or subtracted. This calculated current earnings and profits is the amount that a corporation could distribute from its current operations as a dividend. Accumulated earnings and profits is the sum of prior undistributed current earnings and profits less dividends paid. Together, these accounts determine whether a corporate distribution is wholly taxable as a dividend or if all or part of the distribution is a tax-free return of corporate capital.

Corporations can also make distributions to shareholders as part of qualifying redemptions, partial liquidations, or complete liquidations. The shareholders recognize gain or loss on the receipt of cash or property in exchange for their stock. The corporation recognizes gain on the distribution of appreciated property. It can only recognize loss on the distribution of depreciated property if it is distributed as part of a complete liquidation.

If a corporation fails to pay dividends to its shareholders, the IRS can levy one of two penalty taxes in addition to the regular corporate tax. The personal holding company tax is self-assessed if the corporation meets specific numerical guidelines as a personal holding company and fails to distribute sufficient dividends. The IRS asserts the accumulated earnings tax when a corporation accumulates earnings beyond its reasonable needs.

Shareholders who control a corporation or a group of controlled corporations may attempt to extract income from the corporation in such a way as to avoid dividend classification. Excess salary and rents, bargain purchases, low-interest loans, and personal use of corporate property are ways a shareholder could benefit from a constructive dividend. If the IRS reclassifies a benefit as a dividend, the corporation loses the deduction.

KEY TERMS

Accumulated earnings and profits (AE&P) 470
Accumulated earnings tax (AET) 482
Affiliated group 484
Alternative minimum tax (AMT) 466
Charitable contribution deduction limitation 458
Closely held corporation 480
Common stock 456
Consolidated return 484
Corporate income tax 461
Corporate tax rate 461
Corporate tax return 462
Current earnings and profits (CE&P) 470
Debt 455
Disqualified person 499
Dividend 468
Dividend received deduction (DRD) 457
Earnings and profits (E&P) 469
Equity 455
Estimated taxes 468
Exempt organization 497
Form 1120 462
General business credit 464
Net operating loss (NOL) 460
Net unrelated business income 498

TEST YOURSELF

Answers Appear after the Problem Assignments

1. The Glass Corporation has $156,000 of income from operations. It has a $21,000 capital loss and a net operating loss from the prior year of $36,000. What is its taxable income for 2018?
   a. $156,000
   b. $120,000
   c. $99,000
   d. $84,000

2. Refer to the information in the previous problem. What is Glass Corporation's income tax liability for 2018?
   a. $17,640
   b. $20,790
   c. $25,200
   d. $32,760

3. Walter Corporation reports $500,000 of taxable income for 2018. Determine its book income if tax depreciation was $15,000 more than book depreciation, its deductible business meal expenses were $40,000, and it had $10,000 of tax-exempt income.
   a. $500,000
   b. $485,000
   c. $380,000
   d. $285,000

4. Beggin Corporation had $100,000 of regular taxable income in 2017. It had $40,000 of positive adjustments and a $50,000 preference item. What was the corporation's alternative minimum tax liability for 2017?
   a. $38,000
   b. $30,000
   c. $9,750
   d. $0

5. The Little D Corporation has $150 in current earnings and profits and $100 in accumulated earnings and profits. It makes a $400 distribution to its sole shareholder whose stock basis is $100. What are the shareholder's tax consequences?
   a. $250 dividend
   b. $250 dividend; $50 capital gain
   c. $250 dividend; $100 capital gain
   d. $400 dividend

PROBLEM ASSIGNMENTS

Check Your Understanding

1. [LO 10.1] Explain how a corporation's income is subject to double taxation.

2. [LO 10.1] List five desirable characteristics of the corporate form of business.

3. [LO 10.2] What is the dividend received deduction? What are the percentages and when do they apply? When is the dividend received deduction limited to a percentage of taxable income?

4. [LO 10.2] What is a corporation's overall charitable contribution deduction limitation?

5. [LO 10.2] What are the carryover periods for corporate net operating losses?

6. [LO 10.2] List three items that increase book income and three items that reduce book income when reconciling book to taxable income.

7. [LO 10.2] What was the purpose of the alternative minimum tax? What was the alternative minimum tax rate for corporations?

8. [LO 10.2] What is the unextended due date for the income tax return of a corporation whose fiscal year ends on February 28? What is its extended due date? In what months must it make estimated payments for the next tax year?

9. [LO 10.3] What is the purpose of corporate earnings and profits? Why isn't taxable income used to determine if a distribution is a dividend?

10. [LO 10.3] What is the difference between accumulated and current earnings and profits?

11. [LO 10.3] Can a corporation have negative amounts in both its current and accumulated earnings and profits accounts? Explain.

12. [LO 10.3] List five items that are added to a corporation's taxable income to determine earnings and profits. List five items that are deducted from a corporation's taxable income to determine earnings and profits.

13. [LO 10.4] What is a corporate redemption? What are the tax consequences to the shareholder in a qualifying redemption? What are they if it is not a qualifying redemption?

14. [LO 10.4] What is a corporate liquidation? What are the tax consequences for a corporation that distributes property as part of a complete liquidation? What are the tax consequences to the shareholders?

15. [LO 10.4] What is the difference in tax treatment for losses realized in a partial liquidation and a complete liquidation?

16. [LO 10.5] What is the purpose of the personal holding company tax? What is the penalty tax rate that applies to a personal holding company? How does a personal holding company avoid this tax?

17. [LO 10.5] What is the purpose of the accumulated earnings tax? What is the penalty tax rate that applies to excess accumulated earnings? How does a company avoid this tax?

18. [LO 10.5] What are the two types of controlled groups?

19. [LO 10.6] Why are corporations permitted to file consolidated returns?

20. [LO 10.6] What are the ownership requirements for a group of corporations to file a consolidated return? Illustrate.

Crunch the Numbers

21. [LO 10.1] A corporation has operating income of $75,000. What is its taxable income if it receives a $20,000 dividend from another corporation in which it has the following ownership:
    a. 10%
    b. 65%
    c. 90%

22. [LO 10.1] The Crane Corporation issues $1,500,000 in bonds with a 7.5 percent interest rate. If its tax rate is 21 percent, what is its after-tax cost of the debt?

23. [LO 10.2] A corporation has taxable income is $1,500,000. If it distributes its after-tax income to its shareholders whose dividend tax rate is 15 percent, what are the total tax and the combined effective tax rate on corporate income?

24. [LO 10.2] A corporation has gross sales revenue of $289,000, cost of sales of $98,000, a Section 179 deduction of $20,000 (financial depreciation = $5,000), operating expenses of $122,000, and a Section 1231 gain of $21,000 on the sale of some machinery (the gain is only $14,000 for financial accounting).

a. What is the corporation's taxable income?
b. What is the corporation's pretax financial accounting income?

25. [LO 10.2] The Jingle Corporation has income from operations of $459,000. It has dividend income of $68,000 from a corporation in which it owns 5 percent.

a. What is the corporation's taxable income for 2018?
b. How would your answer change if Jingle owns 35 percent of the corporation paying the dividend?

26. [LO 10.2] Velvet Corporation has revenues of $340,000 and deductible expenses of $350,000. It also received a $40,000 dividend from a corporation in which it owns 10 percent. What is the corporation's taxable income for 2018?

27. [LO 10.2] What is a corporation's income tax if its taxable income is $14,000,000:

a. for 2017?
b. for 2018?

28. [LO 10.2] Whitlaw Corporation has $150,000 of gross profit on sales, operating expenses of $60,000 (excluding cost recovery), $4,000 dividend income from a one-percent-owned corporation, a $10,000 capital gain and $15,000 capital loss, tax depreciation of $40,000 (total financial accounting depreciation is $22,000), a $5,000 charitable contribution, and a net operating loss carryover from the prior year of $10,000.

a. What is Whitlaw's taxable income?
b. What is Whitlaw's income tax for 2018?
c. Complete a Schedule M-1 or a facsimile for the corporation.

29. [LO 10.2] Donut Corporation has $400,000 of taxable income for 2018. What is its net tax liability if it has a $120,000 general business credit available?

30. [LO 10.2] Mondial Corporation's financial accounting records show it had gross revenue of $980,000, cost of goods sold of $420,000, operating expenses of $380,000, and $4,000 of dividends received from a 40-percent-owned owned corporation. Its operating expenses included the following:

$6,000 of life insurance premiums on which it was the beneficiary

$22,000 of business meal expenses

$30,000 of charitable contributions

a. Determine Mondial Corporation's taxable income.
b. Determine Mondial Corporation's income tax liability for 2018.
c. Determine Mondial Corporation's income tax liability if book depreciation is $15,000 less than tax depreciation.

31. [LO 10.2] Palmdale Corporation has a regular tax liability of $94,000. It is eligible for a $54,000 general business credit for the current year and has a $30,000 general business credit carryover from the prior year. What is Palmdale's allowable general business credit for the current year? What is its credit carryover, if any, to future years?

32. [LO 10.2] The Falcon Corporation has $68,000 in taxable income for 2017. Its accountant uncovered $87,000 in net positive adjustments and $2,000 of preference items for its alternative minimum taxable income. What are the corporation's AMTI and AMT for 2017?

33. [LO 10.2] Jenkins Corporation had $675,000 of taxable income for 2017 and $575,000 for 2018. What is the minimum amount that it must submit for each estimated quarterly tax payment to avoid any penalty for underpayment?

34. [LO 10.3 & 10.6] General Corporation has $900,000 of service revenue, a $15,000 capital loss, a $20,000 casualty loss, operating expenses of $685,000, and a charitable contribution of $25,000.
    a. Determine General's separate taxable income.
    b. What items must be determined on a consolidated basis?

35. [LO 10.3] Gordon Corporation had $102,000 of retained earnings at the beginning of the year. It had $87,000 of financial accounting income and paid $45,000 in dividends. What is the corporation's ending retained earnings balance?

36. [LO 10.3] The Caribe Corporation has $668,000 of taxable income for the current year. In determining this income the accountant listed the following items:
    $45,000 in dividends from a 30 percent owned corporation
    $40,000 net operating loss carryover from the prior year
    $68,000 disallowed loss on a sale to its sole shareholder
    $40,000 capital loss in excess of capital gains
    $23,000 in excess charitable contributions
    Determine Caribe's current earnings and profits.

37. [LO 10.3] The Amble Corporation has $4,000 in current earnings and profits and $23,000 in accumulated earnings and profits. It makes a $6,000 dividend distribution at the end of the year to its shareholders. How is this distribution taxed, and what is the corporation's balance in CE&P and AE&P at the beginning of the next year?

38. [LO 10.3] Vanguard Corporation has excess land that it distributes to its shareholders as a dividend. Each of the four shareholders gets a portion of the land valued at $23,000 ($92,000 total value). The corporation's basis for the land is $68,000. What are the consequences to the corporation and the shareholders as a result of this distribution?

39. [LO 10.3] Carrie received 10 shares of Collie common stock as a 10 percent dividend on the 100 common shares she currently owns. She paid $4,400 for the original shares. If she sells the 10 shares that she just received for $800, what is her gain or loss on the sale?

40. [LO 10.3] Jo received one stock right for each share of the 10 shares of stock that she owns in Bill Corporation, which she purchased three years ago for $5 a share. Each stock right allows her to purchase one share of stock for $10. The stock is currently selling for $13 per share. What is her basis in the stock rights?

41. [LO 10.3] Clarington Corporation, a calendar year taxpayer, had two shareholders, Adam and Eve. Adam owns 40 percent and Eve 60 percent of the corporation's stock. In each of the following situations, determine how the dividends will be taxed to Adam and Eve and if the corporation has any tax consequences.
    a. Clarington has $20,000 in CE&P and $10,000 in AE&P. It distributed $15,000 cash to Adam and Eve on July 1.
    b. Clarington has $20,000 in CE&P and $10,000 in AE&P. It distributed $25,000 cash to Adam and Eve on July 1.
    c. Clarington has $20,000 in CE&P and $10,000 in AE&P. It distributed $35,000 cash to Adam and Eve on July 1.
    d. Clarington has $20,000 in CE&P and $10,000 in AE&P. It distributed $15,000 cash to Adam and Eve on June1 and $15,000 on December 1.
    e. Clarington has a $5,000 deficit in CE&P and $10,000 in AE&P. It distributed $10,000 cash to Adam and Eve on July 1.
    f. Clarington has $10,000 in CE&P and a $5,000 deficit in AE&P. It distributed $10,000 cash to Adam and Eve on July 1.
    g. Clarington has ABC stock valued at $8,000 with a basis of $4,000 that it distributes pro rata to Adam and Eve on July 1. CE&P is $4,000 and its AE&P is $3,500.
    h. Clarington has XYZ stock valued at $8,000 with a basis of $10,000 that it distributes pro rata to Adam and Eve on July 1. CE&P is $4,000 and its AE&P is $3,000.

42. [LO 10.4] Sheri owns 800 of the 1,500 outstanding shares of Carney Corporation, which she bought a number of years ago for $20 each. She needs money for her daughter's tuition but does not want to sell all of her shares in the corporation. Carney has $200,000 in earnings and profits.
   a. What are the tax consequences if the corporation buys 150 of her shares for $15,000?
   b. What are the tax consequences if the corporation buys 300 of her shares for $30,000?
   c. If Sheri's father owns the other 700 shares of the corporation, what are the tax consequences of each of the sales?

43. [LO 10.4] Beacon Corporation had operated a chain of restaurants for 15 years and owned a small trucking company for 10 years. It decided to sell all the assets of the trucking company (Section 1231 assets) for $1,500,000. The assets had a basis of $900,000 and the corporation is in the 21 percent tax bracket. The company invested half of the after-tax sale proceeds to update some of its restaurants, and distributed the remaining half to its shareholders in exchange for 10,000 shares of their stock in Beacon.
   a. If the shareholders' average bases in their shares are $45 per share, what are the tax consequences to the shareholders and the corporation from this distribution?
   b. How would your answers change if Beacon received only $600,000 for the assets of the trucking business?

44. [LO 10.4] Loser Corporation decides to liquidate and files a plan of liquidation with the IRS. It is unable to sell its assets, so it distributes them to its sole shareholder, Bummer. There are only three assets: inventory (fair market value = $4,000; basis = $3,500), building (fair market value = $56,000; basis = $67,000), and machines (fair market value = $38,000; basis = $29,500). Bummer surrenders all of his stock with a basis of $187,000 in exchange for the property. What are the tax consequences to Loser and to Bummer as a result of this liquidation?

45. [LO 10.5] Identify the brother–sister corporations given the following ownership percentages by four individuals:

Individual/Corporation	A	B	C	D
James	20%	40%	15%	15%
Carol	25%	10%	20%	20%
Joan	20%	40%	40%	20%
Wallace	10%	10%	20%	25%

46. [LO 10.5] A corporation has 10 shareholders. Nine of the shareholders own 9 percent each of the stock. The tenth shareholder owns the remaining stock. Does the corporation meet the shareholder test as a personal holding company? Explain.

47. [LO 10.5] The Green Corporation has only six shareholders. In the current year, it has AOGI of $540,000 and personal holding company income of $390,000. Its adjusted taxable income is $460,000. What is its personal holding company income tax?

48. [LO 10.5] The Prosperity Corporation has accumulated $200,000 of earnings beyond the reasonable needs of the business. The corporation's regular taxable income is $165,000. Its adjusted taxable income for determining the accumulated earnings tax is $178,000. What is the total amount of taxes that the corporation must pay if the IRS assesses the AET?

49. [LO 10.6] P Corporation owns 90 percent of the stock of S1 Corporation. S1 Corporation owns 45 percent of S2 Corporation and 86 percent of S3 Corporation. S3 Corporation owns 40 percent of S2 Corporation and 70 percent of S4. S4 owns 100 percent of S5. Identify the consolidated group of corporations.

Develop Planning Skills

50. [LO 10.1] The Barnard Corporation needs additional cash to improve its facilities. It can borrow $2,000,000 from a bank at 9 percent interest for 10 years, with a balloon payment of the entire principal at the end of the 10-year period. It can issue $2,000,000 in 10-year corporate bonds paying 7.5 percent interest, but it will incur underwriting costs related to issuing the bonds of $200,000. Its third alternative is to issue $2,000,000 in preferred stock that will require annual dividend payments of 5 percent. The stock will be callable at the end of 10 years at 102. The costs of issuing the preferred stock will only be $50,000. Which alternative should the corporation choose? The corporation's effective tax rate is expected to be 21 percent for all relevant years, and the corporation uses a 6 percent discount rate for all of its financial analyses.

51. [LO 10.2] The Overseas Corporation has taxable income of $250,000 before either a deduction for foreign taxes paid or the foreign tax credit. It paid foreign taxes of $45,000 on foreign income of $300,000. Assuming the corporation cannot carry the foreign tax credit back to any prior year, and the availability of carryforwards is uncertain, should the corporation take the deduction or the credit for the foreign taxes paid?

52. [LO 10.4] One of Corbett Corporation's shareholders, Gene, has severe financial problems due to extensive medical expenses. He has approached the company for a loan, but the other shareholders on the board of directors refuse to approve it. Gene owns 25 percent of the corporate stock with a basis of $100,000 and his brother owns 10 percent of the stock. Gene is not related to any of the other shareholders. One percent of the stock is worth $10,000. Gene needs $100,000 to pay off his current medical bills. The corporation has $100,000 in its accumulated earnings and profits account. What alternatives can you suggest to Gene and the corporation that would provide Gene the money he needs while minimizing taxes?

Think Outside the Text

These questions require answers that are beyond the material that is covered in this chapter.

53. [LO 10.2] List at least 10 differences between taxable income and accounting income.

54. [LO 10.3] Waltjohn Corporation has $5,000 in CE&P and $10,000 in AE&P. It has two shareholders, Walter and John. On April 1 of the current year, Walter received a $10,000 distribution from the corporation on his Class A common stock. On July 1, John received a $10,000 distribution on his Class B common stock. How will the corporation identify these distributions on the shareholders' Forms 1099-DIV?

55. [LO 10.3] The Blanton Corporation had a deficit in its current earnings and profits of $36,500 for the current year. It has $75,000 in accumulated earnings and profits. It made two distributions to its shareholders. On April 30, it distributed $40,000, and on November 30, it distributed $20,000. When the corporation sends out its 1099-DIV forms to its shareholders, how much of the distribution will be taxable to the shareholders as dividends?

56. [LO 10.4] Bob and Jane, brother and sister, are equal partners in a family partnership that owns 400 shares of the Sibling Corporation. Their grandfather owns the remaining 100 shares of Sibling Corporation. How many shares of stock are owned directly and indirectly by Bob?

57. [LO 10.3 & LO 10.4] Why do you think Congress requires the recognition of gain on the distribution of appreciated property but does not allow the recognition of loss on depreciated property in a nonliquidating distribution? Why do you think both gain and loss are recognized on liquidating distributions?

58. [LO 10.5] Explain how a parent–subsidiary controlled group differs from an affiliated controlled group. Develop examples of each to illustrate the differences.

Search the Internet

59. [LO 10.2] Go to the IRS website (*www.irs.gov*) and locate instructions for Form 1120. If a corporation has less than $250,000 of total receipts and total assets at the end of the tax year, which schedules included with Form 1120 can it omit?

60. [LO 10.2] Go to the IRS website (*www.irs.gov*) and locate Publication 538: *Accounting Periods and Methods*. How does a corporation make an election to use a 52-53-week tax year?

Identify the Issues

Identify the issues or problems suggested by the following situations. State each issue as a question.

61. [LO 10.4] Seth and Jacob are brothers who own all of Marboro Corporation's 2,000 shares of outstanding common stock. Seth owns 1,100 shares to Jacob's 900 shares, and this has caused many problems over the years. They have not spoken to each other except through their secretaries for more than 10 years, and they have consistently fought over the running of the company. Seth has come upon some hard times, however, and needs cash for some overdue bills. He has the corporation redeem exactly 200 of his shares for $50,000 so that Jacob does not get the controlling interest in the corporation.

62. [LO 10.4] The Cabot Corporation has had financial problems for several years. The two shareholders have discussed liquidating the corporation, but they are concerned that they will have to pay a large tax bill because of the corporation's low basis in its assets and their high fair market value due to their uniqueness. Each shareholder owns some other depreciated business properties that they could give to the corporation as a contribution to capital approximately 20 months before they formally develop their plan of liquidation and liquidate the corporation.

63. [LO 10.4] Seven years ago, the Bonnet Corporation redeemed all of Joe Bonnet's stock as a complete termination of interest. At the time, Joe signed a waiver of family attribution rules because his three sons retained all their stock. As part of this arrangement, Joe agreed to notify the IRS if he acquired a forbidden interest in the corporation. Recently, the corporation acquired a contract with a defense contractor to build a machine to produce specialized instruments for jet planes. Joe had been the company's chief engineer prior to his retirement from the company. The sons asked Joe to come back as a consultant for a short period to get this project up and running.

64. [LO 10.4] Sweeney was the chairman of Sweeney, Inc., a large hardware and lumber store. When Sweeney became ill, his son took over the business but sold the property and all the inventory of lumber valued at $2,000,000 within a year. Shortly thereafter, Sweeney recovered and took control of the corporation. The corporation purchased a new building and started a new hardware store. This store, although slightly larger than the original store, did not carry any lumber. Sweeney changed the name of the corporation, and the board authorized a plan of partial liquidation. Pursuant to that plan, the original shares of the corporation were replaced, and Sweeney distributed almost $2,000,000 to the shareholders as part of the partial liquidation. Each shareholder received $5,000 and one share of stock for every two shares of the old corporation that was owned.

65. [LO 10.5] The owner of a corporation used corporate funds to pay for his home, all the home's expenses, and numerous other personal expenses. This went on for a number of years until the corporation was audited. The IRS asserted that the use of the corporate funds for personal purposes was a constructive dividend. At the time the corporation was audited, the corporation had only $2,000 in earnings and profits.

Develop Research Skills

66. [LO 10.1] Locate and read Section 385 of the Internal Revenue Code and develop a comprehensive list of factors that indicate legitimate debt. What is the status of the regulations that are to expand on this Code section?

67. [LO 10.4] Several years ago, Congress repealed the General Utilities Doctrine. Locate and read General Utilities & Operating Co. v. Helvering, 296 US 200 (1935). Summarize this case. What was the General Utilities Doctrine, and how did its repeal affect current transactions?

68. [LO 10.4] Locate and read Internal Revenue Code Sections 267, 318, and 544. Compare the definition of family in each of these sections.

69. [LO 10.4] June owned all the stock of Corporation A. Over the years, the corporation had been very successful but had never paid any dividends, although it had substantial earnings and profits. June wanted to expand into another line of business as a sole proprietor but did not have the cash to do so. June decided to form B, a new corporation. She contributed all the stock of A to B. B borrowed $100,000 from a bank using A stock as collateral. B then distributed all of its stock and the $100,000 to June. How should June treat the distribution of the stock and the $100,000?

Fill-in the Forms

70. [LO 10.2] Go to the IRS website (*www.irs.gov*), print the first page of Form 1120, and enter the following information. Then determine Chelsea Corporation's tax owed or refund due if it made estimated tax payments of $15,000.

Chelsea Corporation (34 Chelsea Drive, Sarasota, Florida, 33456) is a calendar-year corporation; its EIN is 78–9999999 and it was incorporated on June 15, 2002. It reported the following for the current year:

Sales = $1,450,000	Pension contributions = $28,000
Cost of sales = $625,000	Business meals = $12,000
Officers compensation = $187,000	Utilities = $21,000
Salary and wages = $266,000	Repairs and maintenance = $14,000
Rent expense = $48,000	Vehicle expenses = $34,000
Taxes = $87,000	Insurance = $30,000
Depreciation = $34,000	Employee benefit plans = $17,000

71. Comprehensive Tax Return Problem. The Snap-It-Open Corporation incorporated and began operations on January 15, 2017. Its address is 3701 Commerce Drive, Baltimore, MD 23239. Its employer identification number is 69-7414447. It elects to file its initial tax return as a calendar-year corporation and uses the accrual method of accounting. It elects the FIFO method of inventory valuation.

Jason Sprull (SSN 333-33-3333) and Martin Winsock (SSN 555-55-5555) formed the business. They each contributed $250,000 cash for 50 percent of the 100,000 shares of $1 par value stock issued and outstanding.

The company was formed to assemble and market a unique, compact, snap-open umbrella and its business activity code is 339900. These umbrellas are sold to a variety of organizations as premiums. The company purchases the umbrella frames and several types of waterproof fabric for the umbrella material and covers from various manufacturers. It prints the organizations' advertising logos or other designs on the umbrella material and covers. It then assembles these on the umbrella frames for delivery to the customer along with the covers.

On January 16, the company placed in service two new machines that they had purchased for $250,000 each for printing and cutting the fabric for the umbrellas and two used umbrella assembly machines purchased for $200,000 each. The company obtained a bank loan of $750,000 secured by the machines. Jason and Martin were required to personally guarantee this loan that has an 8 percent annual interest rate on the unpaid balance. The first principal and interest payment of $160,000 is not due until January 16, 2018.

During the year, the company purchased $250,000 of fabric and $310,000 of umbrella frames. It returned one order of frames valued at $5,000 because of a defect in the snap-open mechanism and received a cash refund for that amount.

Both Jason and Martin work full-time in the business. Jason is the salesperson for the company and Martin manages the office and the printing and assembly operations. Each receives a salary of $60,000 per year. They have six employees with the following incomes for the year: $45,000 for an accountant; $21,000 for a receptionist; $28,000 for each of two print machine operators; and $25,000 for each of two assembly machine operators. There are no accrued salaries or taxes as of the end of the current year. FUTA taxes are assessed on the first $7,000 of wages at a rate of 6.0 percent.

By the end of the year, the company had $1,935,000 in umbrella sales, collected $1,430,000 on these sales, and paid the following expenses in cash:

Rent	$190,000
Repairs and maintenance	20,000
Utilities	80,000
Taxes and licenses (excluding FICA and FUTA taxes)	10,000
Health insurance	16,000
Advertising	40,000
Travel (excluding meals)	20,000
Business meals	15,000
Group term life insurance	2,000

As an accrual-basis taxpayer, the company recognized $57,500 in interest expense on the note ($750,000 × .08 × 11.5/12) and established an allowance account for bad debts equal to two percent of sales.

They recognized depreciation expense for financial accounting equal to 10 percent of the purchase price for the new printing machines and 12.5 percent of the purchase price for the used assembly machines.

Their inventory at year-end consisted of $65,000 of fabric and $68,000 of umbrella frames based on the FIFO inventory method. (For simplicity, you are only required to allocate the factory salaries to the calculation of cost of goods sold.)

The company made estimated tax payments of $40,000 for the year.

a. Prepare a financial accounting income statement (before income tax) and balance sheet for Snap-It-Open Corporation for the current year. (Do not forget to compute FICA and FUTA taxes for all employees.)

b. Complete a Form 1120 and Form 4562 for Snap-It-Open Corporation using the following additional information. The corporation wrote off no bad debts for the year and it maximized its cost recovery deductions on the four machines purchased. Use the 2017 tax forms available from the IRS website at *www.irs.gov*.

ANSWERS TO TEST YOURSELF

1. **b. $120,000** Taxable income = $156,000 – $36,000 = $120,000. Capital loss can only offset capital gain.
2. **c. $25,200.** Taxable income of $120,000 × 21% = $25,200 tax.
3. **c. $380,000.** $500,000 taxable income – $105,000 income tax + $15,000 excess tax depreciation – $40,000 additional business meal expense + $10,000 tax-exempt income.
4. **c. $9,750.** AMTI is $160,000 ($190,000 – the exemption of $30,000) for 2017. Regular tax on $100,000 of income = $22,250 for 2017. Tentative AMT = $32,000 ($160,000 × 20%); AMT = $9,750 ($32,000 – $22,250).
5. **b. $250 dividend; $50 capital gain.**

APPENDIX: EXEMPT ORGANIZATIONS

LEARNING OBJECTIVES

After completing this appendix, you should be able to:

10A.1 List types of qualifying tax-exempt organizations.

10A.2 Discuss the provisions affecting application of the unrelated business income tax to tax-exempt organizations.

10A.3 Identify a disqualified person for certain transactions with a tax-exempt organization.

10A.4 Identify which exempt organizations would be classified as private foundations.

Organizations whose purpose is to serve the public are classified as tax-exempt (or simply *exempt*) organizations. An **exempt organization** does not pay tax on its income, and persons who donate to such organizations may be permitted a charitable contribution deduction.[89] To be completely free from tax, the corporation must be an exempt organization as specified in Section 501(c), and it must meet all requirements for tax-exempt status.[90] If it fails to meet these requirements on a continuing basis, it may either lose its status, or it may be assessed an income or excise tax.

10A.1 TYPES OF EXEMPT ORGANIZATIONS

Some of the more common organizations qualifying for exempt status are

1. Organizations operated exclusively for religious, charitable, scientific, literary, educational, and testing-for-public-safety purposes, as well as those operated to facilitate national and international amateur sports competitions (for example, churches, schools, Consumers' Union, and Olympics).
2. Civic leagues operated exclusively to promote social welfare (garden clubs and athletic little leagues).
3. Fraternal associations operating under the lodge system (Elks Club and Moose Lodges).
4. Credit unions and cooperative telephone and electric companies.
5. Trusts established to pay supplemental unemployment benefits.

Exempt organizations normally operate as corporations (incorporated under the laws of one of the states) or as trusts. All but churches must notify the IRS that they are applying for tax-exempt status.[91] The organization's purpose must be to serve the good of the public at large (for example, a tax-exempt hospital) or for the social welfare of a segment of society (an exempt society benefiting AIDs sufferers). The organization must continue its exempt purpose, or it forfeits exempt status.

Example 10A.1

Wilbur formed a tax-exempt organization that solicited grants and public funds to purchase land for a large garden. The organization's volunteers raised vegetables for donation to the various food banks around the city for six years. In the seventh year, Wilbur took over all the gardening and sold the produce to local groceries. Because the organization abandoned its exempt purpose, it loses tax-exempt status.

A tax-exempt organization can be assessed taxes if it engages in prohibited transactions. The two most common are engaging in unrelated businesses and transactions that benefit disqualified persons.[92] If the organization engages in an unrelated business, it can be assessed an unrelated business income tax. Transactions with disqualified persons are subject to punitive excise taxes.

[89] Many tax-exempt organizations are qualified charities, but numerous exclusions apply; for example, the NFL and a city's chamber of commerce do not qualify.

[90] Qualified pension, profit sharing, and stock bonus plans, as well as qualified state tuition programs, are also tax-exempt organizations.

[91] Other exempt organizations with gross receipts not exceeding $5,000 do not have to notify the IRS.

[92] Lobbying expenditures are generally disallowed and may cause loss of exempt status. §504.

10A.2 UNRELATED BUSINESS INCOME TAX

An exempt organization is assessed the **unrelated business income tax (UBIT)** if it regularly carries on a trade or business that is substantially unrelated to the organization's exempt purpose, except for organizations in which

1. volunteers perform substantially all the work (the local literary guild has a retail bookstore open to the general public).
2. the business sells primarily donated merchandise (Goodwill stores).
3. its activities are of a religious, charitable, educational, scientific, or literary nature and the business primarily benefits members, clients, students, or patients (college bookstores, hospital flower shops).

A business is substantially unrelated to an organization's exempt purpose if sales of goods or services do not make a significant contribution to its exempt purpose.[93] Organizations must calculate unrelated business taxable income separately for each business because a loss from one business cannot offset income from a different unrelated business for the same tax year.

Example 10A.2

The local art museum rents out its gallery space for weddings and receptions when it is normally closed. Renting this space does not contribute to the general public's ability to learn about and enjoy art at the museum.

UBIT is assessed when the exempt organization regularly carries on a business that competes with for-profit businesses. If this income is not taxed, its operating costs are lower, putting the for-profit business at an economic disadvantage. Factors considered in determining if an activity is regularly carried on include the frequency and manner in which the activity is pursued.[94] Sales of cookies by Girl Scouts and of candy by baseball teams are examples of occasional sales exempt from the UBIT.

UBIT is assessed on the exempt organization's **net unrelated business income**, the business's gross income reduced for all deductible expenses incurred in operating the business as if it were a regular corporation. Unrelated business income (UBI) is also subject to certain modifications for charitable contributions, certain payments from an 80 percent controlled organization and net passive income (dividends and interest, net of related expenses).[95] The organization is permitted a $1,000 exemption. The tax is assessed on the organization's unrelated business income at the regular corporate tax rates.

	Gross unrelated business income
Less	Deductions
Plus or minus	Modifications
Less	$1,000 exemption
Equals	Unrelated business income
Times	Corporate tax rate
Equals	Unrelated business income tax

Example 10A.3

The Tree Planting Civic Organization, an exempt organization, has $5,500 of gross unrelated business income. It has $3,200 of deductions related to the earning of this income. It has no modifications. Tree Planting has $1,300 of UBI after its $1,000 exemption ($5,500 – $3,200 – $1,000). It pays a tax of $273 ($1,300 × 21%) on this income.

93 §511 and 513. Income from bingo games is not UBIT if the games of exempt entities are legal, even though the games sponsored by for-profit entities are not.

94 §512(a)(1) and Reg. §1.513-1(c).

95 §512.

Exempt organizations normally file Form 990: *Return of Organizations Exempt from Income Tax* (or Form 990-EZ), which is due on the 15th day of the 5th month after the close of the organization's tax year. If it is required to pay UBIT, then it must also file Form 990-T: *Exempt Organization's Business Income Tax Return*.[96]

10A.3 EXCISE TAXES ON CERTAIN TRANSACTIONS

An excise tax is levied on any excess benefit transaction in which a disqualified person participates, such as a bargain purchase or personal use of the organization's assets. A **disqualified person** is anyone who can substantially influence the activities of an exempt organization. The excise tax is levied on the disqualified person and any exempt organization manager who also participates and knows the transaction is tainted.

The excise tax is 25 percent of the excess benefit for the disqualified person and 10 percent for the manager (up to a maximum of $20,000 per act). A 200 percent excise can also be assessed if the disqualified person fails to correct the transaction.[97]

Example 10A.4

John, a friend of the exempt organization's controller, buys some property valued at $2,000 for $500 from the exempt organization. John's excess benefit is $1,500. He can be assessed an excise tax of $375 ($1,500 × 25%), and the controller can be assessed an excise tax of $150 ($1,500 × 10%). If John fails to pay the additional $1,500 or return the property, he could have an additional excise tax of $3,000.

Two new excise taxes were added by the Tax Cuts and Jobs Act for tax years after 2017. A new 21 percent excise tax is imposed on compensation in excess of $1 million paid to a covered employee by an exempt organization. A 1.4 percent excise tax applies to the net investment income of private colleges and university with at least 500 students and assets of at least $500,000 per student beginning with the 2018 tax year.

10A.4 PRIVATE FOUNDATIONS

Exempt organizations are classified as **private foundations** if they are not supported by or operated for the general public as a whole but have a more narrow focus for their activities.

Example 10A.5

The Fletcher family established a corporation in the name of a deceased relative who had been a math educator. The purpose of the corporation was to solicit money primarily from family members to provide scholarships for women studying to become high school math teachers. Fletcher Corporation is a private foundation.

A private foundation excludes 501(c)(3) organizations that receive a major part of their support from the public or governmental units such as churches, schools, hospitals, and related entities. To be excluded from the private foundation category, an exempt organization must meet an external support test and an internal support test. The external support test requires the organization to receive more than one-third of its annual support from the general public, governments, or other exempt organizations. Support includes membership fees, contributions, and grants. The internal support test limits interest, dividends, rent, royalty, and unrelated business income (net of tax) to one-third of the corporation's total support.

[96] Churches and exempt organizations with annual gross receipts not exceeding $50,000 are not required to file Form 990. If they exceed $1,000 in gross UBI, however, they must file the 990-T. Small tax-exempt organizations whose gross receipts are $50,000 or less may be required to electronically file Form 990-N, also known as the e-Postcard.

[97] §4958.

Example 10A.6

Wilton, Incorporated is an exempt organization that has the following revenues:

Interest and dividend income	$50,000
Contributions	20,000
Membership dues	60,000
Total	$130,000

External support = $80,000/$130,000 = 62 percent
Internal support = $50,000/$130,000 = 38 percent
Wilton meets the external support test but fails the internal support test because internal support exceeds one-third of its total revenue. Thus, Wilton is a private foundation.

A private foundation is subject to taxes on its investment income, for failure to distribute its income, for excess business holdings, for investing in speculative assets, and for participating in transactions with disqualified persons. The excise tax on investment income is only 2 percent, but the excise taxes on the other activities are considerably higher. For example, a private foundation that fails to distribute the required minimum amount of investment income is subject to an excise tax of 30 percent of the undistributed income. If corrective actions are not taken, then a second-level tax will be imposed equal to 100 percent of the undistributed income. A third-level tax may also be imposed for flagrant violations.[98]

Example 10A.7

Boone, Inc., a private foundation, failed to distribute $20,000 of unexpected income at the end of the year. Boone is assessed an excise tax of $6,000 ($20,000 × 30%). If it fails to distribute the $20,000 when the excise tax is assessed, it can be assessed an additional investment income excise tax of $20,000 ($20,000 × 100%).

PROBLEM ASSIGNMENTS

Check Your Understanding

1. [LO 10A.1] What can cause an exempt organization to lose its exempt status?
2. [LO 10A.1] What alternatives does the federal government have when an exempt organization engages in a prohibited transaction?
3. [LO 10A.2] Why is an exempt organization taxed on its unrelated business income?
4. [LO 10A.2] Distinguish between an unrelated business and a related business for an exempt organization. Suggest examples.
5. [LO 10A.3] What are at least three examples of prohibited transactions?
6. [LO 10A.4] What distinguishes a private foundation from other tax-exempt organizations?
7. [LO 10A.4] How does a private foundation reduce the excise tax on a prohibited transaction?

[98] §4942, §6684.

Sole Proprietorships and Flow-Through Entities

CHAPTER 11

LEARNING OBJECTIVES

After completing this chapter, you should be able to:

11.1 Define the principal characteristics of a flow-through entity.

11.2 Identify the primary provisions affecting the formation and operation of a sole proprietorship.

11.3 Discuss the types, characteristics, advantages, and disadvantages of business forms taxed as partnerships.

11.4 Explain the specific tax provisions applicable to S Corporation elections, operations, and reporting requirements.

11.5 Understand the basic provisions of the passive activity loss limitations on affected taxpayers.

CHAPTER OUTLINE

The operating characteristics of sole proprietorships, partnerships, and S corporations is the focus of this chapter. Each of these entities has advantages and disadvantages that the taxpayer must sort through to determine which entity best meets the taxpayer's needs.

These entities pass their income through to their owners for taxation rather than being taxed directly, but have other significant differences. The owners' liability exposure, their ability to deduct losses passed through by the entity, and the tax treatment on entity dissolution all differ for these entities.

Variations of the partnership form include general partnerships, limited partnerships, professional limited partnerships, limited liability companies, and professional limited liability companies. Each has its own advantages and disadvantages.

Corporations that meet specific corporate and shareholder restrictions can elect S corporation status. S corporations pass their income through to their shareholders for taxation similar to partnerships. S corporations retain several of the characteristics of regular C corporations but also have their own unique features.

After completing this and the preceding chapter, the basic picture of formation, operation, income distribution, and dissolution should emerge for the sole proprietorship, partnership, S corporation, and C corporation business entities. When this information is fully integrated with the taxation of owners, taxpayers can make decisions that will minimize taxes and maximize wealth.

SETTING THE STAGE—AN INTRODUCTORY CASE

Robert Winesap has operated a dry cleaning business, Sparkling Cleaners, for eight years as a sole proprietorship in St. Paul, Minnesota. All clothes are cleaned at the original store location with two satellite stores used for drop-off and pick-up only. Expansion is not possible as the cleaning capacity at his original store has reached its limit. He would like to build a larger cleaning plant and establish additional store locations, but the recent illness of one of his children has taken all of his available cash and his personal debt is at its maximum.

James Buchman, the controlling shareholder of Crystal Cleaners, Inc. (also in St. Paul), has approached Robert about joining him in a joint business arrangement that would allow Sparkling to build a new plant and add stores in underserved parts of St. Paul. Robert is interested but does not want to become a subsidiary of Crystal Cleaners because of his desire to maintain control of day-to-day operations. Robert learned that Crystal has two shareholders in addition to James—James's brother and a British citizen who resides in London. Robert is concerned that James might sell his controlling interest in the merged corporation to another party who might attempt to undermine Robert's dedication to superior cleaning services.

After weeks of discussion, Robert and James agree to form a new entity that will maintain the Sparkling Cleaners name if the form in which it will continue business operations can meet the following conditions:

1. The formation of the new entity will have no adverse tax consequences to Robert.
2. Robert will control the new entity. He will continue to train the employees in his unique cleaning methods and oversee the general operations to maintain the business's reputation.
3. Robert is worried about potential liability for past operations of Crystal Cleaners and wants to be sure he is insulated from these liabilities.
4. Robert wants to be able to dispose of his controlling interest in the cleaners with the least possible tax cost if he does retire when planned in approximately 12 years.

James is willing to accept Robert's conditions but he also wants to maintain control of his original Crystal Cleaners stores and keep them separate from Sparkling Cleaners. What factors should be considered in selecting the form of business entity for Sparkling Cleaners? At the end of this chapter we will return to this case.

11.1 INTRODUCTION TO FLOW-THROUGH BUSINESS ENTITIES

A **flow-through business entity** is an operating business that passes its income (and certain other items) directly to the owners of the business. Operating income flows through in the year earned and is taxed as ordinary income at the owner's marginal tax rate. Other types of income and gains also maintain their character for taxation at the owner level (for example, long-term capital gains are taxed at long-term capital gain tax rates). Owners then aggregate these items with similar taxable items from other sources to determine the tax on these aggregated items of net income. For example, a 50 percent partner in a partnership that reports $10,000 of net income and a $4,000 long-term capital gain adds $5,000 of ordinary income and $2,000 of long-term capital gain to similar income items from other activities. Taxes are determined on each type of taxable income at the owner's applicable tax rates to determine taxes owed. This single level of tax has great appeal to many taxpayers.

There are a variety of flow-through business forms available, each with its own individual characteristics, from both legal and tax standpoints. These include general partnerships, limited partnerships, limited liability companies (LLCs), limited liability partnerships (LLPs), S corporations, and the most common flow-through business, the sole proprietorship. In addition to the advantage of a single level of tax on net income, each flow-through entity has certain characteristics that may make it more or less desirable than another type for a particular taxpayer.

For example, both a general partnership and a limited liability company pass their income through to their owners in a similar manner for a single level of tax, but the general partners have no protection from personal liability—a benefit the members of an LLC enjoy. State laws related to flow-through entities are not consistent across all 50 states, however. Thus, it is important to consider state tax factors as well as nontax characteristics in selecting the form of entity. In addition, it is important to consider all factors from formation through operation and dissolution in making the choice of entity.

11.2 THE SOLE PROPRIETORSHIP

The simplest flow-through business is the **sole proprietorship**, a business that has only one individual as the owner. Although it may have a name different from that of the sole proprietor and may receive a separate taxpayer identification number (TIN), the sole proprietorship has no identity separate from that of the owner for federal income tax purposes.

A husband and wife who wish to operate a business as a sole proprietorship may have one spouse as the sole proprietor with the other spouse an employee of the sole proprietorship. Alternatively, a husband and wife who jointly own the business may file a joint return but elect to treat the business as two separate sole proprietorships. Each spouse reports 50 percent of the business's income and expenses on their own separate Schedule C: *Profit or Loss From Business (Sole Proprietorship)*. A sample filled-in Schedule C is included in Chapter 6 in Figure 6.4.

The owner (**sole proprietor**) has unlimited liability for the business operations; that is, the owner's personal assets are all at risk for the liabilities of the business. In spite of this, there are many sole proprietorships due to the ease with which they are formed. Legal requirements for formation are minimal, often limited to publishing a fictitious name and obtaining a business occupation license.[1] Many "casual" businesses are formed with no legal requirements at all. The number of businesses in which an individual can be involved is not restricted. Any person who is an employee has a trade or business by virtue of this employment, but many employees also have businesses on the side; for example, a chef employed by a restaurant could also have a separate business catering private parties.

Although usually small, a sole proprietorship is not limited in size. It simply is an unincorporated business owned by one individual. Theoretically, if Bill Gates bought back all the outstanding stock of Microsoft, cancelled the stock, and surrendered the corporate charter, Microsoft could be subject to tax as a sole proprietorship.

11.2.1 FORMING THE SOLE PROPRIETORSHIP

A sole proprietorship is formed whenever an individual, who is the sole owner, starts a business and chooses no other form in which to operate the business. A sole proprietorship cannot be separated from the individual sole proprietor. All of the results of the business operations are included on the individual sole proprietor's income tax return along with any other tax-related personal items.[2] In addition, the business must have the same tax year as the individual owner, which most likely will be a calendar year. If the sole proprietor wants to change the tax year for the proprietorship, he or she must apply to the IRS for permission to change his or her own tax year to the year better suited to the business.

The taxpayer may use either the cash or accrual method of accounting for the business. If, however, there are no separate accounting records, the business must use the cash method. It usually maintains an inventory account if inventory is a material income-producing factor, but

[1] A business uses a fictitious name when it does business under a name other than that of the owner.

[2] A separate schedule, Schedule C: *Profit or Loss from Business (Sole Proprietorship)* (or Schedule C-EZ.), part of Form 1040, includes the results of the sole proprietorship's operations.

it may select its inventory valuation method. The business may select any allowable depreciation method and use the immediate expensing election, but the limit on immediate expensing first applies to the business and then to the sole proprietor (if there is ownership of other businesses). If a person has two or more sole proprietorships, he or she can make separate determinations for the method of accounting, inventory valuation, and other elective provisions for each entity.

Unlike other business forms, a sole proprietor has no capital account or tax basis in the business as a whole. He or she simply has basis in the separate business assets. Many sole proprietors convert some of their personal assets to business use in addition to purchasing additional assets specifically for business use. The conversion of personal-use assets to business use has no tax consequences, but their adjusted bases for cost recovery deductions is the lesser of their bases as personal-use assets or fair market value at the date of conversion.[3]

11.2.2 OPERATING THE SOLE PROPRIETORSHIP

One of the principal stumbling blocks facing a sole proprietor is establishing the business as a legitimate business and not a hobby. To be considered a legitimate business, the owner must have a profit motive.[4] This does not mean that the sole proprietorship *must* show a profit, *but* the business must be carried on in a manner that indicates that profit (not the conversion of personal expenses to deductible "business" expenses) is the primary objective.

Example 11.1

Carrie and Colleen are sisters who grew up riding and showing thoroughbred horses in hunter-jumper competitions. Both are now married with young families. Carrie owns two horses and is teaching her children to ride. She occasionally gives riding lessons to her neighbors' children for a modest fee. She seldom enters competitions at other than the local level. Colleen, on the other hand, owns a small stable in an affluent subdivision. She boards horses along with her own horses that she uses for riding lessons and breeding. Colleen has a regular schedule of lessons for children and adults and trains horses for their owners. Her students regularly enter local and regional competitions for which she earns substantial fees. She runs her own riding competitions for all riders in the area and continues to compete at the national level to enhance her prestige and gain additional clients. Carrie's activities would be considered a hobby while Colleen's rise to the level of a profit-motivated business.

TAX PLANNING

If a business shows a profit in three of five years, (seven years for horse-related businesses), the burden of proof shifts to the IRS to show that the business lacks profit motive and is a hobby. Selection of depreciation and inventory methods that minimize cost of goods sold and cost recovery deductions can help the owner realize a profit in three of five years to ward off an IRS challenge that the business is a hobby.

Once a taxpayer establishes a sole proprietorship as a legitimate business, all reasonable, necessary, and ordinary expenses of the business are deductible from business income unless limited or excluded by a specific tax provision.[5] The sole proprietor uses Schedule C (or C-EZ) of Form 1040 to report proprietorship income and expenses.[6] Business expenses include cost of goods sold, employee wages, depreciation, rent, supplies, and interest expense paid on funds

[3] If fair market value is less than basis (the usual case) two cost recovery schedules should be maintained; on a subsequent sale, gain will be determined on basis less cost recovery, but loss will be determined on fair market value less cost recovery.

[4] Chapter 6 has a more extensive discussion of the requirements to establish a profit motive.

[5] §162. The at-risk and passive loss limitations discussed later also apply to the sole proprietor.

[6] A Schedule C-EZ: *Net Profit from Business* may not be used by a taxpayer if there is more than one sole proprietorship, or if the business has more than $5,000 of expenses, has a net loss, must file a Form 4562: *Depreciation and Amortization*, maintains inventory, has employees, or takes deductions for business use of the home.

borrowed for business activities of the sole proprietorship only. A sole proprietorship cannot be used to deduct personal expenses, nor are results of most property transactions included on Schedule C. Investment income and expenses, charitable contributions, capital gains and losses, and Section 1231 gains and losses[7] are reported on schedules included with the individual's tax return and not on Schedule C.

Example 11.2

Joanna operates a dry cleaners and laundry in a local strip mall. For the current year, she had revenues of $210,000 and the following expenses: employee wages, $54,000; dry cleaning and laundry supplies, $16,000; equipment repairs, $5,000; rent, $18,000; utility and telephone expenses, $8,000; depreciation, $9,000; and insurance expense, $16,000. In addition, Joanna sold an old dry cleaning machine at a $1,000 loss and made a $500 charitable contribution to the United Way from business funds.

Joanna reports $84,000 ($210,000 − $54,000 − $16,000 − $5,000 − $18,000 − $8,000 − $9,000 − $16,000) of net income from the business on Schedule C: *Profit and Loss From Business*. She reports the loss on the equipment on Form 4797 rather than Schedule C; and she includes the $500 charitable contribution as an itemized deduction on Schedule A.

Many sole proprietors use a part of their home as an office from which to operate their business. To take a deduction for space allotted to the home office, the area must be used *exclusively* and on a regular basis as an office. Expenses allocated to a qualifying home office are deductible business expenses, but the deduction is limited to the taxable income from the business after deducting all other business expenses. Thus, expenses of a home office cannot create or increase a loss. The sole proprietor must report these expenses separately on Form 8829: *Expenses for Business Use of Your Home*. Eligible sole proprietors should maintain documentation to substantiate home office expenses and be prepared to justify the need for and exclusive use of the home office space in the event of an audit.

Example 11.3

Carol sells Mary Ray Cosmetics. She uses her den solely to store her inventory of cosmetics, to make phone calls to her customers, and to do all the paperwork necessary for the business. The den occupies one-fifth of the total area of the house. Her mortgage interest is $8,000, taxes $2,500, and insurance $750; her allowable depreciation expense is $400. Her net income this year prior to deducting her home office expenses is only $2,200. Carol's allocated home office expenses are $1,600 interest, $500 taxes, and $150 insurance. She can deduct the interest and the taxes and $100 of the insurance. The remaining expenses can be carried forward and deducted in a year in which there is sufficient income.

TAX PLANNING

If the taxpayer has a computer within the home office space, the computer must be dedicated solely to the business. The use of the computer (or similar asset) for nonbusiness purposes defeats the solely business use requirement for that portion of the home. The taxpayer should keep the computer in another part of the home or have a second computer for personal use. To take a deduction for any use of the computer, the taxpayer should keep a written record of the time spent on business versus personal use.

The proprietor and the sole proprietorship are considered a single taxable entity, and this prevents the proprietor from being an employee of the business. The proprietor cannot receive

[7] When the proprietor disposes of assets used in the business, the gains and losses are reported on Form 4797: *Sale of Business Property*. As discussed in Chapter 8, depreciation recapture on equipment sold at a gain is ordinary income with the balance Section 1231 gain.

a salary or participate in most tax-free employee fringe benefits. The business cannot take a deduction for payments made on behalf of the owner. Paying a salary or the proprietor's personal expenses is treated as a cash withdrawal by the owner. It simply moves cash from the owner's business account to the owner's personal account without any tax consequences to either the owner or the business.

Example 11.4

Barbara's medical transcription business is a sole proprietorship. She has three typists who transcribe on a full-time basis and are eligible for the health insurance plan in which Barbara also participates. Barbara's net profit from the business is $100,000 before the following: health insurance premium for Barbara and her three employees is $1,500 per person per year; stock sold by the business resulted in a $4,000 long-term capital gain; interest income is $1,000; and charitable contributions are $1,500. Barbara withdrew a salary of $40,000 from the business and paid $20,000 of her personal expenses from the business cash account.

The business cannot deduct Barbara's salary, personal expenses, or health insurance premium as business expenses. The business can deduct the health insurance premiums only for employees, reducing the net profit to $95,500 ($100,000 – $4,500). Barbara will be taxed on the $95,500 income from the proprietorship, but can deduct the $1,500 for her own health insurance premiums for AGI. The $4,000 long-term business capital gain is included with her other capital gains; her business interest income is included with her other interest income; her $1,500 charitable contribution is included with her other charitable contributions as an itemized deduction.

TAX PLANNING

A sole proprietor may be able to participate indirectly in some fringe benefits by hiring his or her spouse as an employee of the sole proprietorship. The spouse must meet any requirements set up by the business for employee participation in benefits, however.[8] The sole proprietor may also reduce the taxable income of the business by employing his or her children through the deduction of the child's wages as a business expense. If the child's earned income is less than the standard deduction ($12,000 in 2018), the child pays no income tax, making the transfer completely tax free. An additional benefit of a sole proprietorship is that an owner's child under 18 is not subject to FICA taxes.

A sale of business property is treated as a sale by the sole proprietor. The details of sales are reported on the appropriate schedule (not Schedule C) and the net result is included on the owner's Form 1040. The sole proprietor pays any taxes owing on gains along with the tax on net income reported by the business. A loss on property used solely by the business is recognized and deducted by the sole proprietor. Cash flow from property sales or business operations belongs solely to the sole proprietor. Funds taken from the business by the owner are tax free as he or she is taxed on the business's net income annually regardless of cash withdrawals.

Property distributed to the sole proprietor is treated the same as a cash withdrawal; that is, neither the business nor the owner have any tax consequences. The property basis simply carries over to the owner. If, however, the owner subsequently sells the property, gain or loss is recognized as long as the property has not been converted to personal use. If the property was converted to personal use, the owner cannot recognize any loss on the sale. If the distributed property was used for both business and personal purposes prior to the distribution, loss is recognized on the business portion only.

[8] These fringe benefits would not be available to spouses if this were a partnership owned by both husband and wife but treated as sole proprietorships.

11.2.3 LIMITATION ON EXCESS LOSSES

A sole proprietorship with a net operating loss for the year can use the loss to offset other business income.[9] A new limitation, however, applies to the amount of net businesses losses allowed as a deduction on the tax return(s) by the owner(s) of a sole proprietorship, partnership, or S corporation for 2018–2025. Excess businesses losses are not deductible for the current year but are carried forward and treated as part of the taxpayer's net operating loss (NOL) carryforward in future years. This limitation applies after the passive loss rules (discussed later in this chapter).

An excess business loss is defined in Section 461(l) as the excess of aggregate business deductions attributed to the taxpayer over the sum of aggregate gross income or gain attributable to those businesses plus a threshold amount. The threshold amount for 2018 is $250,000 ($500,000 if married filing jointly) and will be adjusted for inflation in future years.

Example 11.5

In 2018, Miguel is single and is the owner of a proprietorship with $670,000 of gross income and $980,000 of deductions, resulting in a $310,000 loss for the year. His excess business loss is $60,000 [$980,000 – ($670,000 + $250,000)]. Miguel can deduct $250,000 of the loss in 2018 but carries the $60,000 excess business loss forward to 2019 as an NOL.

If Miguel is married and files a joint return. He does not have an excess business loss due to the higher $500,000 threshold and can deduct the entire $310,000 loss on his 2018 tax return.

11.2.4 QUALIFIED BUSINESS INCOME DEDUCTION

A new deduction added for 2018–2025 addresses the difference between the tax rates for C corporations and pass-through businesses (including sole proprietorships, partnerships, S corporations, and LLCs) that are taxed at their owners' individual rates. This new Section 199A deduction is 20 percent of qualified business income (QBI). QBI is the net amount of income, gain, deduction, and loss from an eligible business conducted in the U.S. It excludes investment-related items (capital gains, capital losses, dividends, and nonbusiness interest income), and reasonable compensation paid to the individual.

This deduction is limited to a maximum of 20 percent of the amount the taxpayer's income exceeds net capital gains, however. If QBI is negative (less than zero), it is treated as a loss from a qualified business in the next year.

Example 11.6

Tim and Sara, a married couple filing a joint return in 2018, have $190,000 in taxable income computed as follows: $200,000 income from Tim's sole proprietorship (not a service business) plus $30,000 in net capital gains less $40,000 in itemized deductions. Their Section 199A deduction is limited to the lesser of: (a) 20% of $200,000 qualified business income = $40,000 or (b) 20% of $190,000 taxable income less $30,000 net capital gains = $32,000, resulting in a maximum deduction of $32,000.

Several rules may limit the amount of the deduction for high-income taxpayers with taxable income in excess of $157,500 ($315,000 for married couples filing a joint return). These limitations are based on the W-2 wages and the adjusted basis of qualified property acquired by the business. Specifically, the deduction cannot exceed the greater of (1) 50% of the taxpayer's

[9] The net operating loss (NOL) provisions apply only to business-related losses; certain adjustments must be made for capital losses and nonbusiness deductions. For example, the standard deduction is not a business expense and is added back when computing an individual's NOL. For further discussion, refer to Chapter 5.

share of the W-2 wages paid by the business or (2) the sum of 25% of such W-2 wages plus 2.5% of the unadjusted basis of tangible depreciable business property acquired.

Example 11.7

Marco is single and has taxable income of $500,000 in 2018. His sole proprietorship manufactures custom covers for computers, phones, and tablets. His income from his proprietorship is $200,000 for 2018. He paid $36,000 in W-2 wages to an assistant and he purchased a machine for $30,000 that he used in making the custom covers. The greater of the two wage/property limits is $18,000 computed as follows:

1. $36,000 W-2 wages × 50% = $18,000 or
2. $36,000 W-2 wages × 25% = $9,000 plus $30,000 property × 2.5% = $750 for a total of $9,750.

Although 20% of Marco's $200,000 proprietorship QBI is $40,000, his deduction is limited to $18,000 by the W-2 wage limitation.

There are also rules to prevent taxpayers with taxable income above the $157,500 (or $315,000) threshold from converting compensation for personal services into income eligible for this deduction. This deduction phases out for high-incomes taxpayers that are in a service business, including accounting, law, health, consulting, financial services, performing arts, actuarial science, athletics, brokerage services, investing, trading in securities, or any business where the principal asset is the reputation or skill of its employees (except for engineering and architecture that are specifically excluded). The deduction gradually phases out for taxpayers in these service businesses for incomes between $157,500 and $207,500 ($315,000 and $415,000 if married filing jointly). The QBI deduction is zero, however, for a taxpayer in one of the affected service businesses if taxable income exceeds $207,500 ($415,000 if married filing a joint return).

Example 11.8

Daniel is single with taxable income of $187,500 of which $138,000 is attributable to his consulting sole proprietorship. He paid W-2 wages of $70,000 to his employees. Because his taxable income exceeds the $157,500 threshold by $30,000, 60% ($30,000 excess above threshold/$50,000 phase out range = 60%) of his consulting income is phased out. Only $55,200 (40% of his $138,000) of his consulting income can be considered in determining his QBI. His eligible wages paid are $28,000 (40% of the $70,000 wages). Daniel's deduction is the lesser of: (a) 20% × $55,200 eligible QBI = $11,040 or (b) 50% × $28,000 eligible wages = $14,000. Daniel can take a Section 199A deduction of $11,040.

If Daniel's taxable income had been only $150,000 (instead of $187,500), he would not have had to consider the W-2 wages or property limitation and would simply deduct 20% of his $138,000 QBI resulting in a Section 199A deduction of $27,600. If Daniel's taxable income exceeded $207,500, his Section 199A deduction would be zero.

11.2.5 SELF-EMPLOYMENT TAXES

Self-employed individuals (sole proprietors, general partners, and managing members of LLCs) must pay **self-employment taxes** on their net income from self-employment.[10] Self-employment taxes replace the employee and the employer portions of FICA (Social Security and Medicare)

[10] Guaranteed payments to a partner, net income passed through to a general partner, and income passed through to the managing member of an LLC are generally subject to self-employment taxes.

taxes. A self-employed individual is often surprised by the amount of self-employment taxes that are due. The taxpayer pays these taxes along with his or her income tax and may be required to adjust his or her estimated tax payments or withholding on other sources of income to cover this tax.

There is a separate deduction *for* AGI (a deduction taken before calculating AGI) for the employer portion of the self-employment taxes. This deduction applies not only to sole proprietors but also to partners and LLC members who are individuals and who pay self-employment taxes on income from these flow-through entities.

Example 11.9

Cleo has $15,000 in net income from her sole proprietorship in 2018. Cleo's self-employment taxes are $2,119 ($15,000 × 92.35% × 15.3%).[11] Cleo reports $15,000 in income from her sole proprietorship and deducts $1,060 ($15,000 × 92.35% × 15.3% × 1/2) *for* AGI for the employer's half of self-employment taxes. Cleo's AGI is $13,940. She must pay $2,119 in self-employment taxes in addition to the regular income tax on her taxable income.

11.3 PARTNERSHIPS

Businesses taxed as **partnerships** can take many forms and have a variety of owners. The Code defines a partnership as a "business, financial operation or venture . . . which is not . . . a corporation or a trust or estate."[12] From a legal standpoint, two or more persons who join together to operate a business for profit form a partnership. No formal agreement or legal process is necessary to form a partnership.

Partnerships are one of the more common business forms, partly because of this ease of entry and their flexibility. A partnership can have two or hundreds of partners. No restrictions apply to the individuals or other entities that may be partners in a partnership. Corporations, other partnerships, LLCs, and all individuals (including nonresident aliens) may be partners in a partnership.

Most LLCs are partnerships for tax purposes. Because the Code treats entities that are designated as partnerships uniformly regardless of their appearance, the information that follows regarding the tax treatment of partners and their partnerships applies equally to an LLC and its members if the LLC is taxed as a partnership. Each state, however, may define its own characteristics for partnerships and LLCs. Thus, on legal matters, state statutes should be consulted if particular characteristics are of significance.

11.3.1 TYPES OF PARTNERSHIPS

The two oldest forms of partnerships are general and limited partnerships. A **general partnership** is one that has only general partners. A **limited partnership** is one that has at least one limited partner and at least one general partner. General partners are those who are personally liable for all the debts of the partnership. A limited partner is one whose liability is limited to the full amount of his or her actual or agreed upon invested capital. A general partner has an active role in the management of a partnership and may bind the partnership with respect to third parties. A limited partner is denied these privileges. Limited partnerships are used extensively as investment vehicles, particularly for real estate development, because of their ability to pass deductible losses through to the limited partners while limiting their risk of investment loss.

The **limited liability partnership (LLP)** is a general partnership that conducts a business providing professional services. This entity protects partners from liability for malpractice by other partners, but all partners remain liable for general debts of the partnership.

[11] For a detailed discussion of self-employment taxes, refer to Chapter 4.

[12] §761(a) and §7701(a)(2).

A relatively new and very popular entity that limits owner's liability is the **limited liability company (LLC)**. All 50 states now have provisions for the creation and recognition of these entities. In many respects, the LLC looks like a corporation: it is an entity that is separate and distinct from its owners, and its owners (called *members*) have the same limited liability afforded corporate shareholders. From a tax standpoint, no other business structure provides the flexibility of the LLC. Since 1997, LLCs can choose to be taxed as partnerships or corporations for federal tax purposes. If the LLC fails to elect taxation as a corporation, by default it is taxed as a partnership (if it has two or more members).[13] If the LLC has only one member, it cannot be taxed as a partnership.[14]

An operating agreement that meets the statutes of the state in which it is formed governs an LLC. The members generally can amend the operating agreement at will. The ownership structure is also flexible, allowing different classes of ownership carrying different rights to vote on management questions and to share in the entity's profits and losses. Only a few states, however, allow an LLC to have only one member. Most states also permit professional service organizations to operate as LLCs designated as **professional limited liability companies (PLLCs)**. PLLCs also protect members from liability for malpractice of another member. In addition, the members are protected from the general liabilities of the business similar to the protection afforded corporate shareholders.

11.3.2 ADVANTAGES AND DISADVANTAGES OF PARTNERSHIPS AND LLCs

The primary advantage of electing partnership treatment for an LLC is that the earnings of the entity are taxed only once—at the investor/owner level.[15] This avoids the double taxation of corporations. Partnership and LLC earnings flow through to their owners regardless of any actual distributions received. They have to pay taxes on business income, even if they receive no distributions from the business with which to pay taxes. Losses also flow through to the owners and may offset other income, subject to the at-risk and passive activity loss rules.[16] The rules for the allocation of profits and losses are very flexible, allowing owners to make special allocations, as long as these allocations reflect economic reality.

Forming a partnership is much simpler and less costly than incorporation. No formal agreement is required for partnership formation, although partners should have a clearly written formal agreement that spells out the details of formation, profit and loss sharing, operating policies, distribution treatment, withdrawal of a partner, sale of a partnership interest, and, finally, dissolution of the partnership. The completion of such a document may require the services of both an accountant and an attorney.

The unlimited liability that general partners have for debts of the partnership is a major disadvantage of a partnership. General partners can all participate in the management of the partnership, and this may make it more difficult to carry on business in an orderly manner. The transfer of partnership interests can be very complex and may affect partnership operations long after the transfer dates. Finally, several events may trigger an unexpected termination of the partnership, such as the bankruptcy of a general partner.

Forming an LLC requires a more formal process because it is an entity created under state law. The LLC must file articles of organization and an operating agreement with the state of formation, and the costs associated with this are similar to those incurred to form a corporation.

---

[13] Few LLCs elect to be taxed as corporations; however, if they do make this election they will have the advantage of allowing owners to be treated as employees for fringe benefits.

[14] Unless the corporate election is made, a single member LLC owned by an individual is taxed as a sole proprietorship; if owned by a corporation, it is treated as a corporate branch.

[15] If the investor/owner is a corporation, the earnings flow through to the corporation and are taxed along with the corporation's other taxable income.

[16] The passive activity and at-risk rules are discussed later in this chapter.

Even though an LLC elects tax treatment as a partnership for federal tax purposes, not all states recognize this election, and some states may tax the LLC as a corporation.

A partnership's general partners and the managing and other active members of an LLC must pay self-employment taxes on the net income passed through to them. Limited partners and LLC members who are only investors in the LLC generally do not pay self-employment taxes. All partners and LLC members, however, avoid the payment of self-employment taxes if the partnership or LLC activity is limited solely to investment in rental real estate.

TAX PLANNING

Partners and LLC members cannot be employees of these entities or participate in most tax-free fringe benefits available to employees. Payments by the partnership or LLC for fringe benefits such as medical or life insurance are either guaranteed payments or distributions to the partners, and are not deductible expenses of the entity. If the partner's (or member's) spouse is legitimately employed by the partnership (LLC), the business may pay for some fringe benefits through the spousal relationship (similar to the sole proprietorship).

11.3.3 ENTITY VERSUS AGGREGATE CONCEPTS

Two opposing concepts allow for the flexibility and complexity for which the partnership form is noted. The **entity concept** treats the partnership as separate from its partners and allows a partner to sell property to the partnership and recognize any gain or loss. The **aggregate or conduit concept** treats the partnership as an extension of the partners, however; it is the reason partners are liable for the debts of the partnership and share gains and losses from operations. It is the application of this aggregate concept that contributes additional complexity to the formation, operation, and dissolution of a partnership.

Example 11.10

Edgar and John, equal general partners, each contribute land to their partnership on which to build new homes. Edgar's land has a basis of $40,000 and a fair market value of $70,000. John's land has a basis of $65,000, and a fair market value of $100,000. It is encumbered, however, by a $30,000 mortgage that is assumed by the partnership. John's basis is $50,000 ($65,000 basis of land – $30,000 liability + $15,000 half the liability). He is relieved of the $30,000 mortgage but as a 50 percent partner he is liable for half of that mortgage. Edgar's basis is $55,000 ($40,000 carryover basis + $15,000 half the liability).

It is the aggregate theory that effectively required the transfer of 50 percent of the debt contributed by John to Edgar to determine basis.

11.3.4 PARTNERSHIP OPERATIONS

The general rules for determining the tax effects of operating a partnership apply to general and limited partnerships and to limited liability companies taxed as partnerships.[17] A partnership that is an electing large partnership may aggregate a number of the items that are normally separately stated to simplify the reporting of these partnership operations at the partner level.[18]

Partner's Basis and Capital Account

For tax purposes, a partner has basis in the partnership interest (outside basis) based on tax rules, in addition to a capital account for accounting purposes. Similarly, the partnership maintains separate tax and financial accounting records. When property is contributed to a partnership,

[17] §761(a).

[18] An electing large partnership is one that has at least 100 partners at the end of its preceding tax year and elects to use the simplified reporting procedures.

the tax records and the partner's outside basis in the partnership reflect the basis of the property contributed as discussed in Chapter 9. The partner's capital account and the partnership's financial records, however, are based on the fair market value of the property contributed. Each partner's capital account shows the partner's claim on the net book value of partnership assets. The difference between a partner's capital account and tax basis is due to the unrecognized (deferred) gain or loss on the contributed property.[19]

Example 11.11

Carlton contributes land (basis = $25,000; FMV = $40,000) to ABC partnership for a 20 percent interest as a general partner. The partnership has a carryover basis of $25,000 (inside basis) in the land. Carlton's tax basis is $25,000 (outside basis) but his capital account shows a balance of $40,000, from the $15,000 unrecognized gain on the land.

Partners' Interests

A partner has a proportionate interest in the partnership's assets and a right to share in a percentage of the partnership's profits and losses, as set forth in the partnership agreement. The profit and loss sharing percentages may differ, and neither has to be the same as the partner's interest in the capital (assets) of the partnership. (Profits and losses flow through to the partners for taxation at the partner level; it is the reason partnerships are referred to as "flow-through" entities.) Unless the partners agree otherwise, profit and loss interests are equal, and these interests will be the same as the partners' interests in the capital of the partnership. This is the assumption upon which this discussion of partnership operations is based.

Example 11.12

ABC partnership (in the previous example) has $12,000 of ordinary income and a $3,000 short-term capital loss on an investment in its first year of operations. Carlton includes $2,400 (20% × $12,000) of ordinary income and $600 (20% × $3,000) of short-term capital loss on his own tax return for the year in which the partnership's tax year ends.

Selection of a Partnership Tax Year

Profits and losses flow through to the partners on the last day of the partnership's tax year. The partners report their share of profit or loss on their income tax returns in the year with which or within which the partnership tax year ends. If the partner's tax year is different from the partnership's tax year, the partner's tax on some portion of the partnership's income is deferred. Due to this potential deferral, Section 706(b) requires the partnership to use one of the following:

1. The tax year of its partner(s) who own a majority interest.
2. If the majority-interest partners do not have the same tax year, the tax year of all the principal partners (partners with at least a 5 percent interest in the partnership).

[19] If the contributed property is later sold at fair market value, the gain or loss recognized is allocated to the contributing partner to the extent of the deferred precontribution gain or loss. Gain or loss in excess of the precontribution gain or loss is allocated to all partners in their profit and loss ratio. For accounting purposes, gain or loss will be allocated to the partners' capital accounts only if the selling price differs from the fair market value when contributed.

3. If neither 1 nor 2 applies, the month that provides the least aggregate deferral of income is the tax year-end.[20]

Alternatively, a partnership also may choose a tax year that satisfies the IRS that the tax year selected has a legitimate business purpose, is a natural business tax year, or allows no more than a three-month deferral of flow-through items from the required tax year.[21]

Example 11.13

Bob and J Corporation are partners in BJ Partnership. Bob is a calendar-year individual; both J Corporation and the partnership have January 31 fiscal year-ends that coincide with their natural business years. For the tax year ending January 31, year 2, the partnership reports $20,000 of income. J Corporation includes its share of income on its return for tax year ending January 31, year 2, which is due on May 15. Bob reports his share of income on his year-2 calendar year tax return, which is not due until April 15, year 3.

Partnership Operating Results

A partnership files only an information return, **Form 1065**: *U.S. Return of Partnership Income*.[22] The first page of Form 1065 is presented in Figure 11.1. This return includes **Schedule K**: *Partners' Shares of Income, Credits, Deductions, Etc.*, which shows totals for each of partnership's separately stated items and its aggregate income or loss for the year (a Schedule K is presented in Figure 11.2). A separate **Schedule K-1**: *Partner's Share of Income, Credits, Deductions, Etc.* is prepared for each partner that reflects each partner's share of the separately stated items and aggregate income or loss for the year.[23] A Schedule K-1 is presented in Figure 11.3. The partnership return is due on the 15th day of the third month of the partnerships tax year but the partnership never pays taxes with this return.[24]

Separately stated items are those items that cannot be aggregated into net income because they are subject to special treatment, such as netting, limitation, or restriction at the partner level (for example, charitable contributions are subject to a limit based on a percent of an individual's adjusted gross income). **Partnership net income** or bottom-line income is the aggregate of all items that are *not* separately stated. Separately stated items include the following:

- Capital gains and losses—both short-term and long-term
- Section 1231 gains and losses[25]
- Unrecaptured Section 1250 gain
- Dividends and interest including their related expenses
- Section 179 deductions
- Charitable contributions
- Medical and dental expenses paid by the partnership for partners
- Passive income

[20] This method uses a calculation, weighted by each partner's profits percentage, to determine the year-end that will result in the least deferral of flow-through items to the partners as a whole.

[21] In this latter case, the taxpayer must agree to a prepaid noninterest-bearing deposit of estimated deferred taxes.

[22] Sample filled-in forms are on the companion website for this text.

[23] When a partner contributes appreciated or depreciated property to the partnership, §704(c) requires special allocations of depreciation expense and of gain or loss on disposition to the contributing partner.

[24] A partnership may be assessed certain penalties and interest for failing to file its return on a timely basis.

[25] §1245 depreciation recapture taxed as ordinary income is included with aggregate income, however.

- AMT preferences and adjustment items
- Self-employment income

As a general rule, an item is separately stated if separately stating it could change any partner's income tax liability from the liability determined by including the item in partnership ordinary income.[26]

Form **1065** Department of the Treasury Internal Revenue Service

U.S. Return of Partnership Income

For calendar year 2017, or tax year beginning ________, 2017, ending ________, 20____.

▶ Go to *www.irs.gov/Form1065* for instructions and the latest information.

OMB No. 1545-0123 **2017**

A Principal business activity	Type or Print	Name of partnership	D Employer identification number
B Principal product or service		Number, street, and room or suite no. If a P.O. box, see the instructions.	E Date business started
C Business code number		City or town, state or province, country, and ZIP or foreign postal code	F Total assets (see the instructions) $

G Check applicable boxes: (1) ☐ Initial return (2) ☐ Final return (3) ☐ Name change (4) ☐ Address change (5) ☐ Amended return (6) ☐ Technical termination - also check (1) or (2)

H Check accounting method: (1) ☐ Cash (2) ☐ Accrual (3) ☐ Other (specify) ▶

I Number of Schedules K-1. Attach one for each person who was a partner at any time during the tax year ▶

J Check if Schedules C and M-3 are attached . . . ☐

Caution. *Include **only** trade or business income and expenses on lines 1a through 22 below. See the instructions for more information.*

Income	**1a**	Gross receipts or sales	1a		
	b	Returns and allowances	1b		
	c	Balance. Subtract line 1b from line 1a		1c	
	2	Cost of goods sold (attach Form 1125-A)		2	
	3	Gross profit. Subtract line 2 from line 1c		3	
	4	Ordinary income (loss) from other partnerships, estates, and trusts (attach statement)		4	
	5	Net farm profit (loss) (attach Schedule F (Form 1040))		5	
	6	Net gain (loss) from Form 4797, Part II, line 17 (attach Form 4797)		6	
	7	Other income (loss) (attach statement)		7	
	8	**Total income (loss).** Combine lines 3 through 7		8	
Deductions (see the instructions for limitations)	**9**	Salaries and wages (other than to partners) (less employment credits)		9	
	10	Guaranteed payments to partners		10	
	11	Repairs and maintenance		11	
	12	Bad debts		12	
	13	Rent		13	
	14	Taxes and licenses		14	
	15	Interest		15	
	16a	Depreciation (if required, attach Form 4562)	16a		
	b	Less depreciation reported on Form 1125-A and elsewhere on return	16b	16c	
	17	Depletion **(Do not deduct oil and gas depletion.)**		17	
	18	Retirement plans, etc.		18	
	19	Employee benefit programs		19	
	20	Other deductions (attach statement)		20	
	21	**Total deductions.** Add the amounts shown in the far right column for lines 9 through 20.		21	
	22	**Ordinary business income (loss).** Subtract line 21 from line 8		22	

Sign Here

Under penalties of perjury, I declare that I have examined this return, including accompanying schedules and statements, and to the best of my knowledge and belief, it is true, correct, and complete. Declaration of preparer (other than partner or limited liability company member) is based on all information of which preparer has any knowledge.

Signature of partner or limited liability company member — Date

May the IRS discuss this return with the preparer shown below (see instructions)? ☐ Yes ☐ No

Paid Preparer Use Only

Print/Type preparer's name	Preparer's signature	Date	Check ☐ if self-employed	PTIN
Firm's name ▶			Firm's EIN ▶	
Firm's address ▶			Phone no.	

For Paperwork Reduction Act Notice, see separate instructions. Cat. No. 11390Z Form **1065** (2017)

FIGURE 11.1 Form 1065 first page

[26] Reg. Sec. 1.702-1(a)(8). For a list of separately stated items, refer to the Schedule K for Form 1065.

Form 1065 (2017) Page 4

Schedule K		Partners' Distributive Share Items		Total amount
Income (Loss)	1	Ordinary business income (loss) (page 1, line 22)		1
	2	Net rental real estate income (loss) (attach Form 8825)		2
	3a	Other gross rental income (loss)	3a	
	b	Expenses from other rental activities (attach statement)	3b	
	c	Other net rental income (loss). Subtract line 3b from line 3a		3c
	4	Guaranteed payments		4
	5	Interest income		5
	6	Dividends: a Ordinary dividends		6a
		b Qualified dividends	6b	
	7	Royalties		7
	8	Net short-term capital gain (loss) (attach Schedule D (Form 1065))		8
	9a	Net long-term capital gain (loss) (attach Schedule D (Form 1065))		9a
	b	Collectibles (28%) gain (loss)	9b	
	c	Unrecaptured section 1250 gain (attach statement)	9c	
	10	Net section 1231 gain (loss) (attach Form 4797)		10
	11	Other income (loss) (see instructions) Type ▶		11
Deductions	12	Section 179 deduction (attach Form 4562)		12
	13a	Contributions		13a
	b	Investment interest expense		13b
	c	Section 59(e)(2) expenditures: (1) Type ▶ (2) Amount ▶		13c(2)
	d	Other deductions (see instructions) Type ▶		13d
Self-Employment	14a	Net earnings (loss) from self-employment		14a
	b	Gross farming or fishing income		14b
	c	Gross nonfarm income		14c
Credits	15a	Low-income housing credit (section 42(j)(5))		15a
	b	Low-income housing credit (other)		15b
	c	Qualified rehabilitation expenditures (rental real estate) (attach Form 3468, if applicable)		15c
	d	Other rental real estate credits (see instructions) Type ▶		15d
	e	Other rental credits (see instructions) Type ▶		15e
	f	Other credits (see instructions) Type ▶		15f
Foreign Transactions	16a	Name of country or U.S. possession ▶		
	b	Gross income from all sources		16b
	c	Gross income sourced at partner level		16c
		Foreign gross income sourced at partnership level		
	d	Passive category ▶ e General category ▶ f Other ▶		16f
		Deductions allocated and apportioned at partner level		
	g	Interest expense ▶ h Other ▶		16h
		Deductions allocated and apportioned at partnership level to foreign source income		
	i	Passive category ▶ j General category ▶ k Other ▶		16k
	l	Total foreign taxes (check one): ▶ Paid ☐ Accrued ☐		16l
	m	Reduction in taxes available for credit (attach statement)		16m
	n	Other foreign tax information (attach statement)		
Alternative Minimum Tax (AMT) Items	17a	Post-1986 depreciation adjustment		17a
	b	Adjusted gain or loss		17b
	c	Depletion (other than oil and gas)		17c
	d	Oil, gas, and geothermal properties—gross income		17d
	e	Oil, gas, and geothermal properties—deductions		17e
	f	Other AMT items (attach statement)		17f
Other Information	18a	Tax-exempt interest income		18a
	b	Other tax-exempt income		18b
	c	Nondeductible expenses		18c
	19a	Distributions of cash and marketable securities		19a
	b	Distributions of other property		19b
	20a	Investment income		20a
	b	Investment expenses		20b
	c	Other items and amounts (attach statement)		

Form **1065** (2017)

FIGURE 11.2 Schedule K for Form 1065

Example 11.14

JOED Partnership (owned by equal partners Joe and Ned) reports the following items of income and expense for the current tax year:

Fee income	$40,000
Tax-exempt interest income	3,000
Rent expense	10,000
Depreciation expense	12,000
Section 179 expense	16,000
Charitable contribution	3,000

The tax-exempt interest, Section 179 expense, and the charitable contribution are separately stated items. Net income is $18,000 ($40,000 − $10,000 − $12,000). On their individual tax returns, Joe and Ned each report $9,000 of net income from the partnership, $1,500 of tax-exempt interest, $8,000 of Section 179 expense, and a $1,500 charitable contribution.

651117

☐ Final K-1 ☐ Amended K-1 OMB No. 1545-0123

Schedule K-1 (Form 1065) **2017**

Department of the Treasury
Internal Revenue Service

For calendar year 2017, or tax year

beginning / / 2017 ending / /

Partner's Share of Income, Deductions, Credits, etc. ▶ See back of form and separate instructions.

Part I Information About the Partnership

A Partnership's employer identification number

B Partnership's name, address, city, state, and ZIP code

C IRS Center where partnership filed return

D ☐ Check if this is a publicly traded partnership (PTP)

Part II Information About the Partner

E Partner's identifying number

F Partner's name, address, city, state, and ZIP code

G ☐ General partner or LLC member-manager ☐ Limited partner or other LLC member

H ☐ Domestic partner ☐ Foreign partner

I1 What type of entity is this partner? ____________

I2 If this partner is a retirement plan (IRA/SEP/Keogh/etc.), check here ☐

J Partner's share of profit, loss, and capital (see instructions):

	Beginning	Ending
Profit	%	%
Loss	%	%
Capital	%	%

K Partner's share of liabilities at year end:

Nonrecourse . . . . $ ____________

Qualified nonrecourse financing . $ ____________

Recourse . . . . $ ____________

L Partner's capital account analysis:

Beginning capital account . . . $ ____________

Capital contributed during the year $ ____________

Current year increase (decrease) . $ ____________

Withdrawals & distributions . . . $ ( )

Ending capital account . . . . . $ ____________

☐ Tax basis ☐ GAAP ☐ Section 704(b) book

☐ Other (explain)

M Did the partner contribute property with a built-in gain or loss?

☐ Yes ☐ No

If "Yes," attach statement (see instructions)

Part III Partner's Share of Current Year Income, Deductions, Credits, and Other Items

1	Ordinary business income (loss)	15	Credits
2	Net rental real estate income (loss)		
3	Other net rental income (loss)	16	Foreign transactions
4	Guaranteed payments		
5	Interest income		
6a	Ordinary dividends		
6b	Qualified dividends		
7	Royalties		
8	Net short-term capital gain (loss)		
9a	Net long-term capital gain (loss)	17	Alternative minimum tax (AMT) items
9b	Collectibles (28%) gain (loss)		
9c	Unrecaptured section 1250 gain		
10	Net section 1231 gain (loss)	18	Tax-exempt income and nondeductible expenses
11	Other income (loss)		
		19	Distributions
12	Section 179 deduction		
13	Other deductions	20	Other information
14	Self-employment earnings (loss)		

*See attached statement for additional information.

For IRS Use Only

For Paperwork Reduction Act Notice, see Instructions for Form 1065. www.irs.gov/Form1065 Cat. No. 11394R Schedule K-1 (Form 1065) 2017

FIGURE 11.3 Schedule K-1 for Form 1065

Partners must report their share of partnership items even if they receive no distributions from income with which to pay taxes. Partners who may need money to pay taxes on income passed through should see to it that the partnership agreement permits withdrawals of cash from the partnership to pay the tax liability.

TAX PLANNING

11.3.5 PARTNER'S BASIS ACCOUNT

A partner establishes outside basis at the formation of the partnership or other acquisition of a partnership interest.[27] According to the aggregate concept, however, every transaction that occurs at the partnership level is deemed to occur at the partner level. Their combined effects are summarized and allocated to each partner on the last day of the partnership tax year. The partner increases his or her partnership interest basis for the allocated share of taxable gains and income, and reduces basis by the allocated share of deductible expenses and losses. Partners' bases also increase for their allocated share of tax-exempt income earned by a partnership and decrease for allocated "expenditures of the partnership not deductible in computing its taxable income and not properly chargeable to the capital account."[28]

Example 11.15

Water Corporation is a 40 percent partner of Bath Partnership, both calendar-year entities. Water's partnership interest basis is $100,000 before Bath reported the following items of income and loss.

	Partnership total	Water's 40% share
Ordinary income	$200,000	$80,000
Long-term capital gain	80,000	32,000
Charitable contributions	10,000	4,000
Tax-exempt interest	15,000	6,000

Water's basis in its interest in Bath at the end of the year is $214,000 (beginning basis of $100,000 + $80,000 income + $32,000 long-term capital gain + $6,000 tax-exempt interest – $4,000 charitable contributions).

Effects of Liabilities

The amount and composition of liabilities held by a partnership affect a partner's basis in the partnership interest. The aggregate concept treats partnership liabilities as liabilities of the partners in proportion to their partnership interest. Section 752 recognizes the risk that a partner assumes as a result of these liabilities by increasing a partner's basis for a proportionate share of partnership liabilities or any partnership liabilities assumed by a partner; the partner's basis decreases when these liabilities are discharged.[29] To prevent a negative basis, a partner recognizes gain equal to the amount that any decrease in the partner's share of the liability exceeds basis.

Example 11.16

Ray, a 40 percent partner in the NCCL Partnership, has a basis in his partnership interest of $18,000, when NCCL borrows $50,000 for its business operations. Ray's share of this debt is $20,000 ($50,000 × 40%), and his basis increases to $38,000.

When NCCL retires the $50,000 debt, Ray's basis in his partnership interest is only $14,000. Ray must recognize $6,000 gain because his $20,000 share of the liability discharged exceeds his $14,000 partnership basis interest by $6,000. Ray's basis in his partnership interest is now zero.

[27] Outside basis is a partner's basis in his or her partnership interest. Partnership formation and basis determination at formation are discussed in Chapter 9.

[28] §705(a).

[29] §752(a) and (b). The partner is assumed to contribute money to the partnership equal to a proportionate share of the liability of the partnership or the liability assumed. The partner is assumed to withdraw money from the partnership to pay the liabilities.

The mechanics of basis adjustments are relatively straightforward, but the precise effect of liabilities on a partner's basis depends on two factors: (1) the type of liability the partnership undertakes, whether recourse or nonrecourse, and (2) the type of partner, general or limited.

Recourse debts allow a creditor to take not only all the assets of the partnership for repayment but ultimately to take all the assets of all the general partners if the partnership does not satisfy its obligations. General partners only are responsible for recourse debt and only their partnership interest bases are increased for their proportional share of increased debt, usually based on their loss-sharing ratio.[30] A limited partner's basis neither increases nor decreases for the partnership's recourse liabilities.

Nonrecourse debts restrict the creditor to the collateral only for repayment of debt on default by the debtor; that is, the creditor has no recourse against *any* of the partners for liabilities greater than the value of the property securing the debt. With neither general nor limited partners personally responsible for nonrecourse debts, the partnership must repay these debts with partnership profits. As a result, nonrecourse liabilities increase both general and limited partners' bases using their profit-sharing ratios.[31]

When either the recourse or nonrecourse liabilities are repaid by the partnership, both recourse and nonrecourse liabilities reduce the general partner's basis, but only the repayment of nonrecourse liabilities reduces limited partners' bases.

Example 11.17

The Bad Dog Partnership has one general partner, BD, and two limited partners, AC and EF, who share equally in profits and losses (a one-third profit- and loss-sharing ratio). BD's basis is $13,000. AC and EF have bases of $30,000 each. To develop some land, the partnership obtains a nonrecourse loan of $120,000 secured by the land and a $50,000 recourse loan for working capital needs. Only BD increases basis for the $50,000 recourse loan; limited partners AC and EF cannot be held liable for this debt. Each partner, however, increases basis by $40,000 for the one-third share of the nonrecourse debt that must be paid from partnership profits. Thus, BD has a basis of $103,000 ($13,000 + $50,000 + $40,000), and AC and EF each have bases of $70,000 ($30,000 + $40,000) from these debts.

When the $50,000 recourse loan is repaid only the general partner BD decreases basis; repayment of the $120,000 nonrecourse loan decreases each partner's basis by $40,000.

11.3.6 LOSS LIMITATION RULES

If the partnership's activities generate an operating loss, there are four hurdles partners must clear to deduct the loss. Partner's tax basis, at-risk investment, the passive loss limit, and limit on excess business losses each potentially affect the amount of loss a partner can deduct on his or her individual tax return. No loss can be deducted in excess of the partner's basis in the partnership interest. Next, the at-risk and passive loss rules, enacted to remedy some of the abuses arising from tax shelters, further restrict the deductibility of losses for partners who are individuals or closely held corporations. The Tax Cuts and Jobs Act added in 2017 places additional limits on excess business losses.

General Loss Rules

The **general loss limitation** provisions of Section 704(d) limit the loss that any partner can deduct on his or her tax return to the basis partner has in the partnership interest. A partner

[30] The actual allocation of recourse liabilities uses a hypothetical liquidation scenario under which all liabilities become payable in full and all assets (other than property contributed to secure a liability) are considered worthless. Recourse liabilities are allocated to the partners to the extent they would be required to contribute cash to restore a capital account deficit.

[31] Some nonrecourse debt allocations involve two steps before an allocation according to the profit-sharing ratio. A more detailed discussion of these allocations is beyond the scope of this introductory material.

deducts losses only after all other adjustments are made to the partner's basis for gains, income, and distributions.[32] Losses that are disallowed due to insufficient basis carry forward until such time as the partner has sufficient positive basis resulting from other events, such as contributions to capital or flow through of income. Because debt increases partners' bases, partnerships that finance their operations with substantial amounts of debt allow greater loss deductions by the partners.

Example 11.18

Juan invests $10,000 cash in Risky Ventures Partnership for a 10 percent limited partnership interest. Risky Ventures has $1,000,000 in nonrecourse financing and incurs $400,000 in losses its first year. Juan's share of the partnership liabilities increases his basis to $110,000 [$10,000 cash investment + ($1,000,000 × 10%)]. Juan's share is $40,000 ($400,000 × 10%) and this does not exceed his basis due to the partnership debt. If Juan is in the 37 percent marginal tax bracket, he saves $14,800 ($40,000 × 37%) by deducting this loss, generating a positive cash flow of $4,800 ($14,800 tax savings – $10,000 initial cash investment) the first year. He still has $70,000 basis remaining ($110,000 basis – $40,000 first-year loss) against which he can deduct additional losses. Unfortunately for Juan, having sufficient basis is just the first hurdle to cross to take a current deduction for the loss.

At-Risk Rules

In the late 1960s and early 1970s, many taxpayers invested in tax shelters with losses they deducted against profits from their other income, including salaries and investment income. In 1976, Congress reacted to this abusive use of these tax shelters by instituting a set of **at-risk rules** to limit the deductibility of losses. These rules apply to individuals and closely held corporations that are partners or S corporation shareholders and limit investors' ability to deduct artificial losses using basis from certain types of debt. The loss deductions of these particular entity owners are limited to the amounts for which they are "at risk." For an owner to be at risk, the owner must be responsible for satisfying the debt with his or her personal assets. Thus, regardless of the effect nonrecourse debt has on a partner's basis in his or her partnership interest, the partner is not at risk and does not have to satisfy this type of debt with any personal assets. The at-risk rules limit the deductibility of losses to partners' bases *reduced* by their share of any nonrecourse debt.[33] Similar to the general loss limitation provision, any loss not deductible because of the at-risk provision carries over until the partner is again at risk.

Example 11.19

Refer to the previous example. Although Juan's basis increased to $110,000 for the partnership's $1,000,000 nonrecourse loan and Juan has sufficient basis to deduct the $40,000 loss, the at-risk rules now prevent him from deducting more than $10,000 of his loss. As a limited partner, he is at risk for his initial investment of $10,000 only.

Passive Loss Rules

Neither the basis nor at-risk rules completely eliminated what Congress perceived as abusive deductions from real estate and other tax shelter activities. In response, it enacted Section 469. This provision includes a complex set of limitations affecting the deductibility of **passive losses**, those losses from activities in which the parties have limited participation. These rules, aimed

[32] Reg. §1.704-1(d)(2).

[33] §465(b)(6). The at-risk rules do not apply to nonrecourse debt secured by real property used in the partnership's real estate activity and made by a qualified lender or a government body; that is, the partner is considered at risk for a share of this type of nonrecourse debt.

only at individual taxpayers and closely held corporations,[34] prevent loss deductions by taxpayers who are primarily investors with no management involvement in a business, such as limited partners. The rules prevent the affected taxpayers from deducting losses from passive activities against active income (salaries, wages, and income from businesses in which the taxpayer materially participates) and portfolio income (interest and dividends). They can deduct passive losses only against income from other passive investments.

Example 11.20

Refer to the previous example. As a limited partner, Juan's $10,000 loss is a passive loss and cannot be deducted against either active or portfolio income. He can, however, carry the loss forward to a future year when he has passive income from this limited partnership (or another passive investment) to offset the loss.

Expanded Topics at the end of this chapter provides a more detailed introduction to the passive loss rules primarily affecting individual taxpayers who are owners of flow-through entities.

Limit on Excess Losses

A new limitation applies to the deductible amount of net businesses losses that can be deducted on an owner's return for 2018–2025 from a partnership, S corporation, or sole proprietorship. This excess business loss is defined in Section 461(l) as the excess of aggregate business deductions attributed to the taxpayer over the sum of aggregate gross income or gain attributable to those businesses plus a threshold amount. The threshold amount for 2018 is $250,000 ($500,000 if married filing jointly) and will be adjusted for inflation in future years.

Excess businesses losses are not deductible for the current year but are instead carried forward and treated as part of the taxpayer's net operating loss (NOL) carryforward in future years. This limitation applies after the passive loss rules.

Example 11.21

In 2018, Sarah who is single, is allocated $525,000 of income and $830,000 of deductions from XYZ Partnership resulting in a $305,000 loss for the year. Her excess business loss is $55,000 [$830,000 – ($525,000 + $250,000)]. Sarah can deduct $250,000 of the loss in 2018 and carry the $55,000 excess business loss to 2019 as an NOL.

If Sarah were married and filing a joint return, she would not have an excess business loss (due to the higher $500,000 threshold) and could deduct the entire $305,000 loss on her 2018 tax return.

11.3.7 GUARANTEED AND NONGUARANTEED PAYMENTS

Partners who work in a partnership may require payments similar to a salary for living expenses. Other partners with invested capital in a partnership may also require payment for the use of the capital. **Guaranteed payments** are payments a partnership is obligated to make to a partner for the performance of services or for the use of capital. These payments are required regardless of the partnership results of operations before any other payments are made and are accounted for as if they are salary or interest payments. Payments that depend upon partnership operations are not guaranteed payments. The partnership agreement should include provisions for guaranteed

[34] §469(a)(2). Closely held corporations are allowed to offset net passive losses against portfolio income. For passive loss purposes, a corporation is considered closely held if five or fewer shareholders own 50 percent or more of its stock at any time during the last half of the tax year.

payments, if such payments are expected. A partnership agreement can be amended as necessary, however, to add, change, or delete guaranteed payments.

Example 11.22

June, Jim, and Jerry are equal partners in a partnership. June works full time for the partnership and is guaranteed a payment (salary) of $30,000 annually. Jim invested a significant amount of money in the partnership and is guaranteed a payment equal to 5 percent of his beginning capital balance each year. Jerry, the manager of the partnership, is paid 50 percent of the net accounting profit after all expenses and the payments to June and Jim. Any remaining income is split equally between the partners. In the current year, the partnership has $135,000 of accounting profit prior to June and Jim's payments.

June receives her $30,000 salary, which is a guaranteed payment. Jim's beginning capital balance is $300,000 and he is due a guaranteed payment of $15,000 (5% of $300,000). Partnership accounting net income after guaranteed payments to June and Jim is $90,000 ($135,000 – $30,000 – $15,000). Jerry receives a payment of $45,000 ($90,000 × 50%), and the three partners share the remaining $45,000 equally; each is allocated $15,000 of the remaining income. June has a total of $45,000 in income, Jim a total of $30,000, and Jerry a total of $60,000.

If the partnership had only $15,000 of income, June and Jim would still receive their $30,000 and $15,000 guaranteed payments, respectively. The partnership, however, would show a $30,000 loss ($15,000 – $30,000 – $15,000) and Jerry would have no income because of this loss. The three partners now share equally in the $30,000 loss. June has a net increase of $20,000 ($30,000 – $10,000) in her capital account, Jim has a $5,000 ($15,000 – $10,000) increase in his capital account, and Jerry's capital account decreases by his $10,000 share of the loss. Regardless of other factors, June and Jim each receive their guaranteed payments. Jerry's payment is dependent on partnership income and is not guaranteed.

Although these payments may occur throughout the year, they are all accounted for at year-end and included in the partner's income along with the other results of operations. In the example above, the allocation of a guaranteed payment increases the partner's basis in the partnership. The actual payment of the guaranteed payment then reduces the partner's basis. Thus, the net effect of a guaranteed payment on a partner's basis is zero if the partner receives the guaranteed payment. If, however, the partnership fails to make the actual payment, the partner still recognizes the guaranteed payment as income, increasing basis for this amount. Basis is reduced only when the actual amount is received. (This is alternatively viewed as a full guaranteed payment made to the partner, but any amount that is not paid is considered a contribution to partner's capital.)

11.3.8 PARTNERSHIP DISTRIBUTIONS

The tax effects of partnership distributions (liquidating and nonliquidating) are the most complex area of partnership taxation with their treatment very different from corporate distributions. In the aggregate theory of partnerships, each partner is assumed to own a share of each of the partnership assets. It is this construct that adds a significant amount of complexity to partnership distributions.

Nonliquidating Distributions

A **current** or **nonliquidating distribution** is one in which cash and/or property is distributed to a continuing partner in the partnership (even if the partner's basis has been reduced to zero).[35]

[35] A nonliquidating distribution reduces but does not eliminate a partner's partnership interest.

When a distribution is made, the type of property distributed and the partner's basis are critical factors in determining the tax effect. In a typical current distribution, no gain or loss is recognized. The partnership's basis in the distributed assets (inside basis) carries over to the partner, reducing the partner's basis in the partnership interest (outside basis). Gain or loss is deferred until the partner disposes of the distributed asset. The character (for ordinary income assets) and holding period (for capital and Section 1231 assets) carries over to the partner.

Example 11.23

Maria's basis in her partnership interest is $10,000 (outside basis). She receives a current distribution of $5,000 cash and an asset with a partnership basis of $4,000 and a fair market value of $6,000. Maria has a carryover basis in each asset (cash $5,000 and other asset $4,000). Her partnership interest basis (outside basis) is reduced to $1,000 ($10,000 – $5,000 – $4,000). No gain is recognized.

When a partner's outside basis is less than the basis of the assets received (inside basis) in a partnership distribution, the distribution becomes more complicated. The assets received must be separated into three tiers as follows:[36]

1. Cash—partner's basis is always has the same as the partnership's inside basis.[37]
2. Hot assets—ordinary income property including inventory and unrealized receivables.[38]

   Basis allocated to hot assets can never exceed the partnership's inside basis (that is, this basis allocation must be less than or equal to the partnership's inside basis). This basis limitation for hot assets prevents the conversion of ordinary income into capital gain by simply distributing assets.
3. Other assets—capital and Section 1231 assets. Allocated basis can be greater than, less than, or equal to the partnership's inside basis.

Distributions proceed in the order above until the partner's outside basis is reduced to zero.

On current distributions, partners may recognize gain but not loss. If the partnership distributes cash (with or without any additional distribution of property) and the cash distributed *exceeds* the partner's outside basis in the partnership interest, gain is recognized to the extent this cash distribution exceeds this basis. Any property received in addition to the cash takes a zero basis in the partner's hands.

Example 11.24

George's basis in his partnership interest is $10,000 when he receives a cash distribution of $12,000. George recovers his $10,000 basis and recognizes a $2,000 gain on the distribution. He has a zero basis remaining in his partnership interest.

If George receives only $7,000 cash along with $6,000 FMV of other property (inside basis of $5,500), he still recovers his entire basis, but he does *not* recognize gain. The other property received has a basis of only $3,000 ($10,000 – $7,000 cash), the remaining partnership basis after the cash distribution. Any gain on the other property distributed is deferred until he disposes of that property.

[36] Under Section 737, a property distribution can trigger recognition of previously unrecognized built-in gain or loss if this contributed property is then distributed to any other partner within seven years of contribution. Any Section 737 gain increases the partner's basis before this basis is allocated to the distributed property.
[37] Cash also includes "deemed cash distributions" resulting from a reduction in liabilities.
[38] Unrealized receivables are accounts receivable of cash-basis taxpayers only. Accrual-method taxpayers have already recognized their receivables as ordinary income.

If several properties are distributed but the cash received is *less than* the partner's partnership interest basis, basis is first allocated to cash, then to hot assets, and then finally to any other assets. No gain or loss is recognized.

Example 11.25

Amy receives a proportionate distribution of $5,000 cash, inventory (basis of $15,000), and land (basis of $20,000 and value of $30,000) when her partnership interest basis (outside basis) is $42,000. Amy first reduces her basis in the partnership interest for the $5,000 cash, then for the $15,000 inventory, and finally for the $20,000 land basis. Her remaining basis in the partnership interest (outside basis) is now $2,000 ($42,000 – $5,000 – $15,000 – $20,000). She defers any gain recognition until she disposes of the assets.

If Amy's partnership basis is only $30,000, her basis in the partnership interest is reduced to zero but now the land's basis is only $10,000 ($30,000 – $5,000 – $15,000). Again, gain is deferred until the land is sold. If Amy's basis is only $18,000, only $13,000 ($18,000 – $5,000) basis is available for the inventory after allocating basis to cash, and the land has a zero basis.

When there is a distribution of multiple noncash assets in the same tier but the partnership's inside basis is greater than the partner's outside basis, there is insufficient basis for direct basis allocation. Several steps are required to adjust the basis allocation. The basis shortage is first allocated to any asset with unrealized depreciation in an amount equal to the lesser of the asset's unrealized depreciation or (if more than one depreciated asset) its pro rata share of the basis shortage. Unrealized depreciation is the amount by which an asset's adjusted basis exceeds its current fair market value.

Example 11.26

George's outside basis in his partnership interest is $60,000 when he receives two capital assets as a nonliquidating distribution from the partnership. The first asset has a basis of $70,000 (fair market value = $40,000) and the second asset has a basis of $30,000 (fair market value = $10,000). The partnership's bases for the assets (inside basis) exceed George's partnership basis by $40,000 ($70,000 + $30,000 – $60,000). The basis allocated to each asset is reduced according to the relative amount of unrealized depreciation. The unrealized depreciation for the first asset is $30,000 ($70,000 basis – $40,000 fair market value) and for the second asset is $20,000 ($30,000 basis – $10,000 fair market value). The $40,000 reduction is allocated as follows:

$\$40{,}000 \times [\$30{,}000 / (\$30{,}000 + \$20{,}000)] = \$24{,}000$ reduction allocated *to* the first asset
$\$40{,}000 \times [\$20{,}000 / (\$30{,}000 + \$20{,}000)] = \$16{,}000$ reduction allocated *to* the second asset

George's basis for the first asset is $46,000 ($70,000 partnership's basis – $24,000 decrease) and $14,000 ($30,000 partnership's basis – $16,000 decrease) for the second asset.

The remaining basis in his partnership interest (outside basis) is zero and no gain or loss is recognized.

Liquidating Distributions

Liquidating distributions occur when a partner withdraws from the partnership or when a partnership ceases operations and distributes the assets to the partners, ending the partnership. In a liquidating distribution, the liquidating partner's basis in the partnership (outside basis) must be reduced to zero.

The effects of liquidating distributions are similar to those of nonliquidating distributions, but there is one significant difference—the withdrawing partner or all of the partners (if the entire partnership is liquidating) may recognize loss if the total basis of the cash and ordinary income property received is less than the partner's partnership basis (outside basis) and *no other property* is received.[39] If the basis of cash and ordinary income property is less than the partner's outside basis and the partner receives any capital or Section 1231 property (tier 3 assets), the partner allocates *any* basis remaining in the partnership interest to that property and recognizes no loss.[40] Any loss recognition is postponed until the partner disposes of the tier three properties.[41] In many instances, however, this property is no longer business property when distributed to the partner (it is now personal-use property) and the loss is never recognized.

Example 11.27

Carol liquidates her partnership interest by accepting a proportionate distribution of $10,000 cash and inventory (basis of $12,000 and a fair market value of $15,000) in exchange for her $35,000 basis in the partnership. Carol allocates her first $10,000 basis to cash and the next $12,000 to inventory. She cannot allocate more basis to inventory (or any ordinary income asset) than the partnership's basis (inside basis). She recognizes a $13,000 capital loss ($35,000 partnership basis – $10,000 cash – $12,000 inventory) for her unrecovered basis in her partnership interest. If she sells the inventory for its fair market value, she will recognize $3,000 ordinary income at the time of the sale.

If this had been a nonliquidating distribution instead of a liquidating distribution, Carol could not have recognized the loss. Her remaining basis in her partnership interest would be $13,000. Her basis for the cash and inventory would be $10,000 and $12,000, respectively.

Example 11.28

Walter receives a liquidating distribution from a partnership of $4,000 in cash, inventory valued at $7,000 (basis = $5,000), and land worth $10,000 (basis = $8,000). Walter's basis in his partnership interest is $45,000. Walter allocates the first $4,000 of basis to the cash, the next $5,000 to the inventory (postponing any gain until a future sale), and the remaining $36,000 to the land. He recognizes no gain or loss. If he sells the land without using it for personal use, he will be able to recognize a loss on the difference between this $36,000 basis and its selling price. If he converts the land to personal use, however, the loss cannot be recognized on a personal asset.

TAX PLANNING

Distributions of property, other than money, can effectively postpone gain recognition and may be desirable, but property distributions can also postpone or prevent loss recognition when a partnership liquidates. Partners should carefully plan whether to distribute or sell assets (distributing the cash received) on a partnership liquidation to obtain the optimum tax consequences.

The previous distribution examples have illustrated proportionate distributions in which the partner receives his or her pro rata share of the partnership's ordinary assets and other property. Both current and liquidating distributions become more complex when they are disproportionate. A disproportionate distribution is one in which ordinary income assets and other assets are distributed in other than pro rata proportions to the partners. These complex rules (contained in Section 751) make sure that each partner is responsible for his or her share of ordinary income. These rules do not apply as long as a partner receives a pro rata distribution of ordinary income assets.

[39] A liquidating distribution liquidates a partner's entire partnership interest so he or she ceases to be a partner.
[40] If several properties are received with total basis less than the remaining basis in the partnership interest, the remaining basis is allocated among them based on both their relative fair market values and bases to the partnership. This allocation process (which is similar to the allocation process described for current distributions) can lead to either a decrease or increase in the total basis of these assets. This potential for increasing these assets' bases only occurs in liquidating distributions.
[41] This treatment recognizes the aggregate theory of the partnership.

To determine the tax effect of a disproportionate distribution, the partnership first assumes that it makes a proportionate distribution to the partners. This is followed by a hypothetical sale of assets between partners and the partnership to achieve the disproportion. The complexity arises when partners receive either more of less of their share of "hot assets." Hot assets are broadly defined and extend beyond inventory and unrealized receivables to include the ordinary income on depreciation recapture. Only capital and Section 1231 assets are excluded from the definition of hot assets.[42]

Example 11.29

The Clarose Partnership makes a liquidating distribution of $100,000 cash to Clare, reducing her partnership interest from one-third to zero. Immediately prior to the distribution, the partnership had the following assets: $150,000 cash, unrealized receivables (zero basis, $30,000 fair market value), and inventory ($30,000 basis, $120,000 fair market value). The partnership has no liabilities and Clare's basis in her partnership interest (outside basis) is $60,000.

Clarose Partnership has unrealized receivables and inventory (both hot assets). To prevent Clare from avoiding her share of ordinary income related to these assets, an assumed pro rata distribution is addressed first. Clare is treated as having received her one-third share of each hot asset in a hypothetical current distribution. The partnership's bases in each share (zero for the unrealized receivables and $10,000 for the inventory) carry over to Clare and reduce her basis in her partnership interest (outside basis) from $60,000 to $50,000. Next, Clare hypothetically sells her share of realized receivables (zero basis) and inventory ($10,000 basis) for their fair market values ($10,000 and $40,000 respectively) to the partnership for $50,000 cash, resulting in a $40,000 recognized gain taxed as ordinary income (and increasing her basis to $50,000). The $50,000 cash that Clare receives reduces her outside basis from $50,000 to zero with no additional gain or loss recognized. The net effect is that Clare recognizes $40,000 in ordinary income for her share of the partnership's hot assets.

If Clarose Partnership did not have any hot assets, the liquidation would be treated the same as a proportionate distribution. She would have a $40,000 capital gain for the cash received in excess of her outside basis.

There are situations in which distributions to a withdrawing partner or the liquidation of the partnership become far more complex than the basic examples provided. A withdrawing partner may bargain for a distribution that exceeds his share of partnership assets. For example, a partner receives $25,000 cash for his partnership interest when the withdrawing partner's capital account is only $20,000. The excess $5,000 payment comes from partnership income and not as a part of the sale of his interest. As an additional share of partnership income, these payments are generally taxed as ordinary income.

11.3.9 SELLING A PARTNERSHIP INTEREST

Normally, one might assume that a partnership interest is a capital asset and any gain or loss recognized on the sale of a partnership interest would be a capital gain or loss. The aggregate partnership theory, however, assumes that each partner owns a share of each partnership asset. This causes the tax consequences of the sale of a partnership interest to be far more complex than a simple sale of a capital asset. If the partnership owns ordinary income assets including inventory and unrealized receivables (hot assets), the sale must be partitioned between the hot assets and all other assets to prevent the partner from converting gain on the sale of ordinary income assets to capital gain through the sale of the partnership interest. In this case, unrealized receivables include

[42] §751(d). Inventory is considered a Section 751 asset for distribution purposes only if it is substantially appreciated (its fair market value exceeds 120% of its adjusted basis to the partnership).

the receivables of a cash-basis taxpayer, depreciation recapture, and inventory. Inventory, however, now includes all partnership property except money, capital assets, and Section 1231 assets.[43]

Example 11.30

Helen sells her 25 percent partnership interest to Hal for $20,000 when her basis in her partnership interest is $15,000. The partnership has the following assets: $10,000 cash; inventory with a basis of $30,000 (fair market value = $60,000); investment land with a basis of $20,000 (fair market value = $10,000). Overall, Helen appears to have a $5,000 gain on the sale, but the $20,000 received must be apportioned across Helen's one-quarter interest in each of the assets.

Asset	Adjusted basis	FMV	Amount received	Gain or loss
Cash	$2,500	$2,500	$2,500	-0-
Inventory	7,500	15,000	15,000	$7,500
Land	5,000	2,500	2,500	(2,500)

The apportionment provision causes Helen to recognize ordinary income of $7,500 on the inventory ($15,000 – $7,500) and a capital loss of $2,500 ($2,500 – $5,000) on the sale of the land. Although she still has a net $5,000 gain, the type of gain and loss recognized affect her tax consequences.

There are several other considerations when disposing of a partnership interest. First, when the partner sells an interest, the partnership allocates income up to the date of sale only to the selling partner. The partnership allocates the income from that point on to the purchasing partner. In addition, the partnership's tax year closes with respect to the selling partner; thus, all items pass through to him or her as of the date of sale. To further complicate a sale, the selling partner no longer has a share of liabilities of the partnership. This relief of liabilities is treated as additional cash received on the sale of the partnership interest and must be included in the determination of gain or loss. The purchasing partner then becomes liable for the selling partner's share of liabilities and includes this in his or her basis in the partnership interest purchased.

Example 11.31

The ABC Partnership owns only one asset, a building with a basis of $500,000 and a fair market value of $600,000, which is encumbered by a $300,000 mortgage. Wally sells his one-third interest in the partnership (outside basis = $175,000) for $100,000 in cash. The total amount Wally realizes for his partnership interest is $200,000, consisting of $100,000 cash plus $100,000 (1/3 × $300,000) of liability relief. He recognizes a $25,000 gain on the sale ($200,000 – $175,000). The new owner's basis in the one-third partnership interest is $200,000—the $100,000 cash plus the assumption of the $100,000 one-third interest in the mortgage.

When a partner sells his or her partnership interest to a third party, the partnership's inside basis is usually unaffected by the sale. The new partner simply replaces (steps into the shoes) of the exiting partner to determine his or her share of inside basis. This may create a discrepancy between the new partner's outside basis and his or her share of the partnership's inside basis if the partnership has appreciated assets. The new partner paid full market value for his or her share of appreciation in the partnership's assets. When the partnership sells any of these appreciated assets, the new partner is temporarily overtaxed. To address this, the partnership is allowed to make an election for a special basis adjustment to eliminate discrepancies between the inside and outside bases.[44] Once the partnership makes this election, the partnership is required to make the special basis adjustment for all subsequent sales of a partnership interest and partnership distributions.

[43] §751(a). The definition of Section 751 property is slightly different for sales than for distributions because inventory does not have to substantially appreciated to be Section 751 property.

[44] §754.

11.3.10 QUALIFIED BUSINESS INCOME DEDUCTION

The qualified business income deduction added for 2018–2025 (explained previously at 11.2.4) applies to partnerships as well as other pass-through entities (sole proprietorships, S corporations, and LLCs that are taxed at their owners' tax rates) and addresses these tax rate differences. Briefly, the new Section 199A deduction is 20 percent of qualified business income (QBI), with QBI defined as the net amount of items of income, gain, deduction, and loss from an eligible business conducted in the U.S. Investment-related items (capital gains, capital losses, dividends, and nonbusiness interest income), reasonable compensation paid to the individual, and guaranteed payments from a partnership are excluded from QBI.

This deduction is limited to 20 percent of the amount by which taxpayer income exceeds net capital gains. If QBI is negative (less than zero), it is treated as a loss from a qualified business in the next year.

Example 11.32

In 2018, Michelle has total taxable income of $150,000 including qualified business income of $40,000 from Partnership A and a qualified business loss of $100,000 from Partnership B. Because Michelle's net QBI is negative, she is not allowed a deduction for 2018 and has a $60,000 qualified business loss carried forward to 2019. In 2019, Michelle has qualified business income of $40,000 from Partnership A and qualified business income of $100,000 from Partnership B, a total of $140,000 positive income. Her deduction in 2019 is limited to $16,000 [($140,000 – $60,000 loss carried forward) × 20%].

Several rules may limit the amount of the deduction for high-income taxpayers with taxable income in excess of $157,500 ($315,000 for married couples filing a joint return). These limitations are based on the W-2 wages and the adjusted basis of qualified property acquired by the business. Specifically, the deduction cannot exceed the greater of (1) 50% of the taxpayer's share of the W-2 wages paid by the business or (2) the sum of 25% of such W-2 wages plus 2.5% of the unadjusted basis of tangible depreciable business property acquired.

Example 11.33

Xavier is married filing a joint return and has taxable income of $600,000 in 2018. He is a 40% partner in XYZ Partnership that produces total ordinary income of $1,000,000 in 2018. The partnership paid total W-2 wages of $250,000 and the total adjusted basis of property held by the partnership is $1,200,000. Xavier's 40% share of the income is $400,000, his share of the wages is $100,000, and his share of the property is $480,000. The greater of the two wage/property limits is $50,000 computed as follows:

1. $100,000 W-2 wages × 50% = $50,000 or
2. $100,000 W-2 wages × 25% = $25,000 plus $480,000 property × 2.5% = $12,000 for a total of $37,000.

Although 20% of Xavier's $400,000 partnership QBI is $80,000, his deduction is limited to $50,000 by the W-2 wage limitation.

Tom is a 15% partner in XYZ Partnership but his total taxable income for 2018 is only $155,000. Tom's share of partnership income is $150,000 and he is allocated 15% of the W-2 wages and 15% of the property. Because Tom's total taxable income for 2018 is only $155,000, he does not need to calculate the wage/property limits. Tom can deduct $30,000 ($150,000 QBI x 20%).

There are also rules to prevent taxpayers with taxable income above the $157,500 (or $315,000) threshold from converting compensation for personal services into income eligible for this deduction. This deduction phases out for high-incomes taxpayers that are in a service business, including accounting, law, health, consulting, financial services, performing arts, actuarial science, athletics, brokerage services, investing, trading in securities, or any business where the principal asset is the reputation or skill of its employees (except for engineering and architecture which are specifically excluded). The deduction gradually phases out for taxpayers in these service businesses for incomes between $157,500 and $207,500 ($315,000 and $415,000 if married filing jointly). If a taxpayer is in one of the affected service business and taxable income exceeds $207,500 ($415,000 if married filing a joint return), the QBI deduction is zero for that business.

Example 11.34

Andrew is single with taxable income of $180,000 in 2018. He is a 30% partner in a consulting partnership and he is allocated $158,000 income from this partnership. His share of W-2 wages paid by the partnership is $70,000 but there is no eligible property basis. Because his taxable income exceeds the $157,500 threshold by $22,500, 45% will be phased out ($22,500 excess above threshold/$50,000 phase out range = 45%) and he can take into account only 55% of his $158,000 partnership income of $86,900 in determining his QBI. Andrew's deduction is the lesser of: (a) 20% × $86,900 eligible QBI = $17,380 or (b) 50% × $38,500 eligible wages = $19,250. Andrew can take a deduction of $17,380.

If Andrew was married filing a joint tax return, his taxable income would be below the $315,000 threshold. He would not need to consider the W-2 wages and would simply deduct 20% of his $158,000 QBI, a deduction of $31,600. If Andrew's taxable income had exceeded $415,000, his deduction would be zero.

11.4 S CORPORATION CHARACTERISTICS

An **S corporation** is truly a unique business entity. It is formed under state law in the same manner as a C corporation, and the requirements for a nontaxable formation are identical. A business that meets state filing requirements to become a corporation is a C corporation until its shareholders make a valid S corporation election. When the election is made, the corporation becomes an S corporation—a flow-through entity that passes its income and losses through to its shareholders for taxation at the shareholder level. Thus, an S corporation appears to have the best of all worlds: It is a regular corporation from a legal standpoint with shareholders that enjoy limited liability, but who avoid the double taxation of a C corporation.

Unlike a partnership, an S corporation may have to pay an income tax under certain circumstances. It also continues to have some characteristics of a C corporation because it must follow the Code provisions for C corporations for redemptions and liquidations. The treatment of its cash and property distributions is unique to the S corporation, however.

11.4.1 ELIGIBILITY REQUIREMENTS FOR S STATUS

To elect S status, a corporation must meet a number of restrictions on its operating characteristics and shareholders, and the corporation must continue to meet these restrictions throughout its life; if it fails to do so, the S election terminates.

Corporate Restrictions

An S corporation must be an eligible **domestic corporation**; that is, one that is formed in one of the 50 states of the United States. It cannot be a foreign corporation. Financial institutions using the reserve method for bad debt, insurance companies (taxed under Section L of the Code), and Puerto Rican and possession corporations are not eligible corporations.[45]

[45] §1361(b).

TAX PLANNING

An S corporation can have only one class of stock issued and outstanding, although it can have more than one class of stock authorized.[46] More than one type of common stock may be issued if the only difference is in the voting rights attached to the stock.[47] This difference allows one group of shareholders to retain voting control over the corporation while permitting another shareholder group to benefit on an equal basis from corporate earnings.

An S corporation must pay attention to the terms of any debt instruments, as the reclassification of debt into a second class of stock can cause termination of an S election. Under the safe harbor provision for debt, loans should have a specific maturity date and required interest payments, should not be convertible into stock, and should only be held by an individual.[48] Shareholder debt held in the same proportion as stock and shareholder loans of up to $10,000 are exempt from reclassification as a second class of stock.

Shareholder Restrictions

Only individuals, estates, and certain trusts and not-for-profit organizations may be shareholders of an S corporation.[49] Individuals must be either residents or citizens of the United States.[50] Nonresident aliens are not allowed to own stock in an S corporation.[51]

The corporation can have no more than 100 shareholders, but family members owning stock may elect to be counted as only one shareholder. When a shareholder dies, the deceased shareholder's family members and the estate are still considered one shareholder for meeting the 100-shareholder requirement. Although few S corporations have more than several shareholders, a corporation close to the 100-shareholder limit must closely watch sales to multiple shareholders or unrelated heirs inheriting stock from a deceased shareholder.[52]

TAX PLANNING

To prevent taxpayers from circumventing the 100-shareholder limit, a partnership or C corporation cannot own S corporation stock, but an S corporation can own a partnership interest or own stock in a C corporation. Thus, if two S corporations together own 100 percent of a partnership or a C corporation, more than 100 persons can effectively own an operating business through S corporations.

11.4.2 MAKING THE S ELECTION

An eligible corporation makes the **S election** on Form 2553: *Election by a Small Business Corporation* by the 15th day of the third month of the year for which the election is to be effective. Thus, a calendar-year corporation must file its election by March 15, 2018, to be effective for 2018 (a retroactive election), and it must have been an eligible corporation from the beginning of the year. If the corporation fails to meet that deadline, the election is effective at the beginning of 2019 (a prospective election). A prospective election can be made any time during the current tax year to be effective for the following year. The IRS has authority, however, to accept a late filing of an S election if the corporation can show reasonable cause for the delay in filing the election.[53]

The shareholders of the S corporation must give written consent to the S election. If the corporation has just formed, the forming shareholders sign the consent form. If the corporation

[46] §1361(b)(1)(D).
[47] §1361(c)(4).
[48] §1361(c)(5).
[49] Tax-exempt organizations described in Sections 401(a), 501(c)(3), and 501(a) are eligible shareholders.
[50] 1361(c).
[51] §1361(b)(1)(C). Effective January 1, 2018, a nonresident alien may be a beneficiary of an electing small business trust (ESBT).
[52] For tax years ending prior to 2005, S corporations were allowed to have only 75 shareholders with husband and wife only allowed to be considered one shareholder. The American Jobs Creation Act of 2004 increased the number of permitted shareholders to 100 and allows relatives within 6 generations to elect to be treated as one shareholder. In addition, former spouses may also continue to be counted as one shareholder.
[53] §1362(b). The IRS can also ignore an error in filing of the S election if the error was inadvertent, the corporation acted as an S corporation, and it would have qualified except for the error.

is an existing corporation, a retroactive election requires that all the shareholders who would be affected by the election must consent to it.[54] Persons who become shareholders after the filing of the election do not have to consent. They are presumed to consent to the S election, or they would not have become shareholders.

11.4.3 TERMINATING THE S ELECTION

An S election can terminate by a positive election, or it can terminate by violating one of the S corporation requirements—either deliberately or inadvertently.

Termination Election

To affirmatively revoke an S election, shareholders holding more than 50 percent of the voting rights of the stock must vote to revoke the election. The **revocation** may be retroactive or prospective. To be retroactive, the revocation must be made by the 15th day of the third month of the tax year (March 15 for a calendar-year corporation), and it must not specify a later effective date. If this requirement is met, the revocation is effective from the beginning of the tax year.[55] A prospective revocation request may specify and be effective for any date on or after the date the request is filed.[56] If no date is specified, the revocation is effective as of the first day of the next tax year.

Example 11.35

BH Corporation, a calendar-year S corporation, has three shareholders, each holding one-third of the corporate stock. The corporation's shareholders decide that an S election is no longer advantageous. Only two of the shareholders are required to sign the revocation request that is filed by March 15 for the revocation to be effective as of the first of the current year. If the request is filed after March 15 but no other date is specified, it will be effective at the beginning of the next tax year. If a revocation request is filed on May 31, to be effective July 1, the corporation will no longer be an S corporation as of July 1. It will file a short-year return as an S corporation for the period of January 1 through June 30 and a short-year return as a C corporation from July 1 through December 31.

Terminating Events

If a corporation fails to meet one of the requirements for S corporation status (such as exceeding the 100-shareholder limit), its S election terminates as of the day before the **terminating event**.[57] If the corporation can show that the terminating event was inadvertent and corrects the defect as soon as possible after its discovery, the IRS can allow the S election to continue as if the event never occurred.

An S corporation's election terminates at the beginning of the fourth year if it is assessed a passive income tax for three years in a row and it has earnings and profits from a C corporation tax year.[58] The S corporation passive income tax is addressed later.

11.4.4 S CORPORATION OPERATIONS

When accounting for the operations of an S corporation for tax purposes, there are few differences between S corporations and partnerships. The S corporation separates its income, gain, loss, and

[54] §1362(a)(2).
[55] §1362(d).
[56] §1362(d)(1)(D).
[57] §1362(d)(2).
[58] §1362(d)(3).

expense items into those items that are aggregated to form net income and into separately stated items. The separately stated items are almost identical to those of partnerships. S corporation net income passed through to its shareholders is not subject to self-employment taxes, however. If a shareholder is also an employee of the corporation, the shareholder and the corporation are subject to FICA (Social Security and Medicare) taxes on the shareholder-employee's salary.

The S corporation files a **Form 1120S**: *U.S. Income Tax Return for an S Corporation* to report its operations. Figure 11.4 presents the first page of Form 1120S. It also prepares a Schedule K: *Shareholders' Shares of Income, Credits, Deductions, Etc.* (see Figure 11.5) and

Form **1120S**
Department of the Treasury
Internal Revenue Service

U.S. Income Tax Return for an S Corporation

► **Do not file this form unless the corporation has filed or is attaching Form 2553 to elect to be an S corporation.**
► **Go to *www.irs.gov/Form1120S* for instructions and the latest information.**

OMB No. 1545-0123
2017

For calendar year 2017 or tax year beginning , 2017, ending , 20

A S election effective date	TYPE OR PRINT	Name	**D** Employer identification number
B Business activity code number (see instructions)		Number, street, and room or suite no. If a P.O. box, see instructions.	**E** Date incorporated
C Check if Sch. M-3 attached ☐		City or town, state or province, country, and ZIP or foreign postal code	**F** Total assets (see instructions) $

G Is the corporation electing to be an S corporation beginning with this tax year? ☐ Yes ☐ No If "Yes," attach Form 2553 if not already filed
H Check if: **(1)** ☐ Final return **(2)** ☐ Name change **(3)** ☐ Address change **(4)** ☐ Amended return **(5)** ☐ S election termination or revocation
I Enter the number of shareholders who were shareholders during any part of the tax year ►

Caution: Include **only** trade or business income and expenses on lines 1a through 21. See the instructions for more information.

Income	1a	Gross receipts or sales	1a	
	b	Returns and allowances	1b	
	c	Balance. Subtract line 1b from line 1a		1c
	2	Cost of goods sold (attach Form 1125-A)		2
	3	Gross profit. Subtract line 2 from line 1c		3
	4	Net gain (loss) from Form 4797, line 17 (attach Form 4797)		4
	5	Other income (loss) (see instructions—attach statement)		5
	6	**Total income (loss).** Add lines 3 through 5 ►		6
Deductions (see instructions for limitations)	7	Compensation of officers (see instructions—attach Form 1125-E)		7
	8	Salaries and wages (less employment credits)		8
	9	Repairs and maintenance		9
	10	Bad debts		10
	11	Rents		11
	12	Taxes and licenses		12
	13	Interest		13
	14	Depreciation not claimed on Form 1125-A or elsewhere on return (attach Form 4562)		14
	15	Depletion **(Do not deduct oil and gas depletion.)**		15
	16	Advertising		16
	17	Pension, profit-sharing, etc., plans		17
	18	Employee benefit programs		18
	19	Other deductions (attach statement)		19
	20	**Total deductions.** Add lines 7 through 19 ►		20
	21	**Ordinary business income (loss).** Subtract line 20 from line 6		21
Tax and Payments	22a	Excess net passive income or LIFO recapture tax (see instructions)	22a	
	b	Tax from Schedule D (Form 1120S)	22b	
	c	Add lines 22a and 22b (see instructions for additional taxes)		22c
	23a	2017 estimated tax payments and 2016 overpayment credited to 2017	23a	
	b	Tax deposited with Form 7004	23b	
	c	Credit for federal tax paid on fuels (attach Form 4136)	23c	
	d	Add lines 23a through 23c		23d
	24	Estimated tax penalty (see instructions). Check if Form 2220 is attached ► ☐		24
	25	**Amount owed.** If line 23d is smaller than the total of lines 22c and 24, enter amount owed		25
	26	**Overpayment.** If line 23d is larger than the total of lines 22c and 24, enter amount overpaid		26
	27	Enter amount from line 26 **Credited to 2018 estimated tax** ► **Refunded** ►		27

Sign Here
Under penalties of perjury, I declare that I have examined this return, including accompanying schedules and statements, and to the best of my knowledge and belief, it is true, correct, and complete. Declaration of preparer (other than taxpayer) is based on all information of which preparer has any knowledge.
Signature of officer | Date | Title
May the IRS discuss this return with the preparer shown below (see instructions)? ☐ Yes ☐ No

Paid Preparer Use Only

Print/Type preparer's name	Preparer's signature	Date	Check ☐ if self-employed	PTIN
Firm's name ►			Firm's EIN ►	
Firm's address ►			Phone no.	

For Paperwork Reduction Act Notice, see separate instructions. Cat. No. 11510H Form **1120S** (2017)

FIGURE 11.4 Form 1120S first page

Form 1120S (2017) Page 3

Schedule K Shareholders' Pro Rata Share Items

Section	Line	Description			Total amount
Income (Loss)	1	Ordinary business income (loss) (page 1, line 21)		1	
	2	Net rental real estate income (loss) (attach Form 8825)		2	
	3a	Other gross rental income (loss)	3a		
	b	Expenses from other rental activities (attach statement)	3b		
	c	Other net rental income (loss). Subtract line 3b from line 3a		3c	
	4	Interest income		4	
	5	Dividends: a Ordinary dividends		5a	
		b Qualified dividends	5b		
	6	Royalties		6	
	7	Net short-term capital gain (loss) (attach Schedule D (Form 1120S))		7	
	8a	Net long-term capital gain (loss) (attach Schedule D (Form 1120S))		8a	
	b	Collectibles (28%) gain (loss)	8b		
	c	Unrecaptured section 1250 gain (attach statement)	8c		
	9	Net section 1231 gain (loss) (attach Form 4797)		9	
	10	Other income (loss) (see instructions) . . Type ▶		10	
Deductions	11	Section 179 deduction (attach Form 4562)		11	
	12a	Charitable contributions		12a	
	b	Investment interest expense		12b	
	c	Section 59(e)(2) expenditures (1) Type ▶ (2) Amount ▶		12c(2)	
	d	Other deductions (see instructions) . . . Type ▶		12d	
Credits	13a	Low-income housing credit (section 42(j)(5))		13a	
	b	Low-income housing credit (other)		13b	
	c	Qualified rehabilitation expenditures (rental real estate) (attach Form 3468, if applicable)		13c	
	d	Other rental real estate credits (see instructions) Type ▶		13d	
	e	Other rental credits (see instructions) . . . Type ▶		13e	
	f	Biofuel producer credit (attach Form 6478)		13f	
	g	Other credits (see instructions) . . . . . Type ▶		13g	
Foreign Transactions	14a	Name of country or U.S. possession ▶			
	b	Gross income from all sources		14b	
	c	Gross income sourced at shareholder level		14c	
		Foreign gross income sourced at corporate level			
	d	Passive category		14d	
	e	General category		14e	
	f	Other (attach statement)		14f	
		Deductions allocated and apportioned at shareholder level			
	g	Interest expense		14g	
	h	Other		14h	
		Deductions allocated and apportioned at corporate level to foreign source income			
	i	Passive category		14i	
	j	General category		14j	
	k	Other (attach statement)		14k	
		Other information			
	l	Total foreign taxes (check one): ▶ ☐ Paid ☐ Accrued		14l	
	m	Reduction in taxes available for credit (attach statement)		14m	
	n	Other foreign tax information (attach statement)			
Alternative Minimum Tax (AMT) Items	15a	Post-1986 depreciation adjustment		15a	
	b	Adjusted gain or loss		15b	
	c	Depletion (other than oil and gas)		15c	
	d	Oil, gas, and geothermal properties—gross income		15d	
	e	Oil, gas, and geothermal properties—deductions		15e	
	f	Other AMT items (attach statement)		15f	
Items Affecting Shareholder Basis	16a	Tax-exempt interest income		16a	
	b	Other tax-exempt income		16b	
	c	Nondeductible expenses		16c	
	d	Distributions (attach statement if required) (see instructions)		16d	
	e	Repayment of loans from shareholders		16e	

Form **1120S** (2017)

FIGURE 11.5 Schedule K for Form 1120S

a Schedule K-1: *Shareholder's Share of Income, Credits, Deductions, Etc.* (see Figure 11.6) for each of the shareholders to report net income and separately stated items in total and each shareholder's share, respectively. A comparison of the Form 1120S and Form 1065 and their respective Schedule Ks and K-1s illustrate the similarities of these reports of operations to the taxing authorities.[59]

[59] Sample filled-in tax forms are on the companion Web site for this text.

671117

☐ Final K-1 ☐ Amended K-1 OMB No. 1545-0123

Schedule K-1 (Form 1120S) **2017**

Department of the Treasury
Internal Revenue Service

For calendar year 2017, or tax year

beginning / / 2017 ending / /

Shareholder's Share of Income, Deductions, Credits, etc. ▶ See back of form and separate instructions.

Part I Information About the Corporation

A Corporation's employer identification number

B Corporation's name, address, city, state, and ZIP code

C IRS Center where corporation filed return

Part II Information About the Shareholder

D Shareholder's identifying number

E Shareholder's name, address, city, state, and ZIP code

F Shareholder's percentage of stock ownership for tax year . . . . ______ %

For IRS Use Only

Part III Shareholder's Share of Current Year Income, Deductions, Credits, and Other Items

1 Ordinary business income (loss)
2 Net rental real estate income (loss)
3 Other net rental income (loss)
4 Interest income
5a Ordinary dividends
5b Qualified dividends
6 Royalties
7 Net short-term capital gain (loss)
8a Net long-term capital gain (loss)
8b Collectibles (28%) gain (loss)
8c Unrecaptured section 1250 gain
9 Net section 1231 gain (loss)
10 Other income (loss)
11 Section 179 deduction
12 Other deductions
13 Credits
14 Foreign transactions
15 Alternative minimum tax (AMT) items
16 Items affecting shareholder basis
17 Other information

* See attached statement for additional information.

For Paperwork Reduction Act Notice, see the Instructions for Form 1120S. www.irs.gov/Form1120S Cat. No. 11520D **Schedule K-1 (Form 1120S) 2017**

FIGURE 11.6 Schedule K-1 for Form 1120S

S corporations' tax years are generally restricted to the calendar year to prevent deferral of income by the individual shareholders.[60] S corporation income and loss allocations are based solely on the number of days and the percentage ownership of each shareholder. To make the allocations, the S corporation prorates all income and loss items to each day of the tax year, then multiplies the daily figure by the number of days held and the percentage ownership of the shareholder.[61]

[60] Similar to the partnership, the S corporation can make a Section 444 election that allows up to a three-month deferral of income, but a deposit to cover the taxes on the deferred income is required.

[61] If there is a significant ownership change, the shareholders may elect to use the interim closing of the books method to allocate income and loss.

Example 11.36

At the beginning of the year, John and Amy each own a 50 percent interest in JA Corporation, an S corporation. On January 31, Amy purchased a 10 percent interest from John, so John and Amy are now 40 percent and 60 percent shareholders, respectively. At the end of the tax year of 365 days, the corporation had net income of $36,500 and separately stated Section 1231 gains of $7,300. JA Corporation first allocates $100 of net income and $20 of Section 1231 gain to each of the days of the year. It then allocates $14,910 ([$100 × 31 × 50%] + [$100 × 334 × 40%]) of net income and $2,982 ([$20 × 31 × 50%] + [$20 × 334 × 40%]) of Section 1231 gain to John.[62] It allocates $21,590 ([$100 × 31 × 50%] + [$100 × 334 × 60%]) of net income and $4,318 ([$20 × 31 × 50%] + [$20 × 334 × 60%]) of Section 1231 gain to Amy. Thus, John reports ordinary business income from the S corporation of $14,910 and $2,982 of Section 1231 gain and Amy reports $21,590 of ordinary business income and $4,318 of Section 1231 gain on their individual tax returns.

A shareholder of an S corporation can receive a salary as an employee, and both the employee and the corporation pay their share of FICA taxes on the salary. S corporation shareholders do not pay self-employment taxes on the corporation's net income that flows through to them. Shareholders owning more than 2 percent of the stock may not participate in most tax-free employee fringe benefits, such as medical insurance and group term life insurance.[63] If a greater than 2 percent shareholder receives these fringe benefits from the corporation, the corporation cannot deduct the cost of the fringe benefit unless the shareholder treats the value of the fringe benefit as additional compensation.

An S corporation must pay reasonable compensation to shareholder-employees. Unlike a regular corporation in which shareholder-employees try to receive very large salaries in lieu of dividends, an S corporation's incentive is to pay low salaries and make distributions not subject to payroll taxes to shareholder-employees. It is particularly important in both personal service corporations and family-held corporations for employee-shareholders to receive appropriate salaries because of the risk that the IRS will reclassify these distributions as salary (resulting in additional payroll taxes).

11.4.5 LOSS LIMITATIONS

The same limitations apply to the shareholders of an S corporation that apply to partners in a partnership when determining if the losses flowing through to them are deductible currently:

1. The shareholder must have basis in the corporate interest.
2. He or she must be at risk.
3. If the losses are passive, the shareholder must have other passive income against which to offset the losses, or the activity generating the losses must have been disposed of in the reporting year.[64]
4. Excess business losses are not deductible in the current year but instead are carried forward and treated as part of the taxpayer's net operating loss (NOL) carryforward in future years.

[62] With an S corporation sale, the day of sale is attributed to the seller.

[63] This is the same as the treatment of partners in a partnership.

[64] Like partnerships, the shareholder must first have basis before the at-risk rules are encountered, and both apply before the passive loss limitation rules. The *Expanded Topics* section at the end of the chapter explains the passive loss deduction rules.

There is a striking difference between a partnership and an S corporation, however. An S corporation shareholder is not allocated any basis for any recourse or nonrecourse debt undertaken by the S corporation. To be able to deduct losses in excess of basis in the corporate stock, the shareholder must have loaned money directly to the S corporation. The shareholder can then deduct losses to the extent he or she has basis in this debt.[65] The tax advantage of a current deduction must be weighed against the opportunity cost of lending the money, however. When debt basis has been reduced due to losses, income in a subsequent year first reinstates the basis of the debt before the stock basis is increased. If the corporation pays off the debt before basis has been restored, the shareholder has gain to the extent the payments exceed debt basis.

Example 11.37

Jason owns 50 percent of the Beach Corporation, an S corporation. Due to prior losses, his stock basis is only $4,000. The company forecasts another loss of $24,000, $12,000 of which will be allocated to Jason for the current year. Jason can deduct only $4,000 of the loss unless he lends the company money to create debt basis. If Jason lends $8,000 to the company (creating $8,000 of debt basis), he will be able to deduct the remaining loss, and he will have a zero basis in both his stock and the debt. If Jason is in the 32 percent tax bracket, the additional $8,000 loss deduction reduces his taxes by $2,560. If he borrows the money at 9 percent interest and the corporation pays him only 5 percent interest on the loan, lending the corporation money costs him $320 [$8,000 × (9% – 5%)] annually.[66]

At the end of next year, Beach reports $30,000 income. Jason's $15,000 share first restores his $8,000 basis in the debt before the remaining $7,000 increases stock basis. If the company has only $10,000 income, only $5,000 of Jason's debt basis is restored. If Beach then repays Jason's $8,000 loan, Jason would have to recognize $3,000 gain ($8,000 – $5,000).

TAX PLANNING

If a shareholder expects a lower marginal tax rate in future years, he should consider contributing capital or loaning funds to the corporation before year-end to obtain the tax benefit from the loss now. Conversely, if the shareholder expects a higher marginal tax rate in future years, deferring the tax benefit of the loss to a future year may be beneficial.

11.4.6 TRACKING BASIS

Each shareholder should track his or her stock basis similar to tracking a partnership interest basis by the partner. The shareholder's beginning basis is the original contribution to capital or purchase price of the stock. Any subsequent contributions to capital and all separately and nonseparately stated items of income and gain (including tax-exempt income) increase basis; all nontaxable distributions and all separately and nonseparately stated deductions and losses (including nondeductible items) reduce basis, but never below zero. Also similar to partnerships, stock basis is increased by income items at year-end before it is reduced for distributions and loss items, respectively.

A distribution solely of cash from an S corporation to its shareholders is a nontaxable event as long as the value of the cash does not exceed the shareholder's stock basis. Stock basis represents income on which the shareholder has already been taxed (as well as contributions to capital) and is not income when returned. If the cash distribution exceeds the shareholder's basis, however, the excess is taxed as gain on the sale of the shareholder's stock.

[65] The stock basis and at-risk amount are usually the same for S corporation shareholders.

[66] Additional factors such as the future income potential of the corporation and its ability to pay back the loan must also be considered before a final decision can be made.

Example 11.38

Bob has a basis of $1,300 in his S corporation stock after the increase for his $600 flow through of net income. If he now receives a $400 distribution from the corporation, it is a tax-free return of income that has already been taxed. He simply reduces his stock basis to $900 ($1,300 – $400) for the distribution. If, instead, he receives a $1,500 distribution, only $1,300 of it is tax free because the distribution reduces his basis to zero. The remaining $200 is taxable as gain as if he had sold his stock.

11.4.7 PROPERTY DISTRIBUTIONS

A shareholder who receives a property distribution (with or without additional cash) from an S corporation uses the fair market value of the property received as the basis of the property distributed, similar to regular C corporation dividend distributions. The S corporation recognizes gain on the distribution of appreciated property but cannot deduct any loss on the distribution of depreciated property. Shareholders increase their stock bases for the recognized gains passed through from the distribution of appreciated property. Then they reduce their bases for the fair market value of the property distributed. Thus, this gain is taxed only once at the shareholder level. Because the corporation cannot recognize losses on distributions of depreciated property, it is preferable to sell the property (to an unrelated party) and distribute the proceeds to preserve loss recognition.[67]

Example 11.39

Jim, the sole shareholder of an S corporation, receives a distribution of property valued at $5,000 (basis only $1,000) when his stock basis is $12,000. The corporation recognizes a $4,000 gain on the distribution that is passed through to Jim, increasing his stock basis to $16,000. When Jim receives the tax-free distribution of $5,000, he reduces his stock basis to $11,000 and has a basis of $5,000 in the property received.

If the property's basis had been $8,000, the corporation would have had an unrecognized $3,000 loss, but Jim would still have had a $5,000 basis in the property received.

11.4.8 THE S CORPORATION SCHEDULES M-1, M-2, AND M-3

The S corporation's Schedule M-1: *Reconciliation of Income (Loss) per Books with Income (Loss) per Return*[68] looks quite similar to a C corporation's M-1, except that an S corporation generally pays no taxes and has no contribution carryovers, so those lines are missing. The M-1 reconciles book income to net income adjusted for separately stated items passing through to shareholders. In most cases, an S corporation is not a publicly traded corporation and is not required to prepare financial statements according to generally accepted accounting principles (GAAP). Thus, few reconciling entries may be required. If the statements are prepared according to GAAP, reconciling items are similar to those explained for C corporations.

Schedule M-2: *Analysis of Accumulated Adjustments Account, Other Adjustments Account, and Shareholders' Undistributed Taxable Income Previously Taxed* reconciles the accumulated adjustments account (AAA) at the beginning of the tax year to the balance at the end of the year. Additional columns are provided to reconcile the other adjustments account (OAA) and previously taxed income (PTI) from pre-1983 S corporation years.[69] OAA items are

[67] Property distributions during the post-termination period are taxable as dividends to the extent the now C corporation has earnings and profits; only cash can be distributed tax-free during the post-termination period from income that has been previously taxed.

[68] Sample filled-in forms are on the companion website for this text.

[69] This discussion of S corporations excludes pre-1983 S corporations.

those that do not affect the AAA, such as tax-exempt income and any related expenses. The net adjustments to the AAA and OAA reported on Schedule M-2 generally will equal the change in retained earnings as reported on Schedule L: *Balance Sheets per Books*, the beginning and ending financial accounting balance sheet.[70]

Similar to C corporations, S corporations that have total assets of $10 million or more must file Schedule M-3. Schedule M-3 requires a more detailed reconciliation between financial accounting net income and taxable income than reported on Schedule M-1.

11.4.9 THE ACCUMULATED ADJUSTMENTS ACCOUNT

The **accumulated adjustments account (AAA)** is a corporate-level account that tracks a corporation's undistributed, but previously taxed earnings that are available for distribution to shareholders without additional tax. Adjustments to this account are similar to the adjustments to a shareholder's basis accounts, except that they reflect the aggregate of income and loss items. Each shareholder, however, must track basis individually based on his or her share of income and loss items. Unlike a basis account, an accumulated adjustments account may have a negative value if loss (and expense) items exceed income and gain items. Distributions, however, may neither create nor increase a negative amount in the AAA.

Example 11.40

Carol receives a distribution of $1,000 from her S corporation when her stock basis is $40,000. The corporation's AAA account before the distribution is $2,000. The corporation has $10,000 of ordinary income and $6,000 of charitable contributions for the year. The corporation first increases its AAA to $12,000 for the income items and then reduces it to $5,000 ($2,000 + $10,000 − $6,000 − $1,000) for the contributions and distribution. Carol's $1,000 distribution is tax free.

Schedule M-2 **Analysis of Accumulated Adjustments Account, Other Adjustments Account, and Shareholders' Undistributed Taxable Income Previously Taxed** (see instructions)

		(a) Accumulated adjustments account	(b) Other adjustments account	(c) Shareholders' undistributed taxable income previously taxed
1	Balance at beginning of tax year	2,000		
2	Ordinary income from page 1, line 21 . . .	10,000		
3	Other additions			
4	Loss from page 1, line 21	( )		
5	Other reductions	(6,000)	( )	
6	Combine lines 1 through 5	6,000		
7	Distributions other than dividend distributions	1,000		
8	Balance at end of tax year. Subtract line 7 from line 6	5,000		

The taxability of shareholder distributions for a corporation incorporated after 1982 that never operated as a C corporation is determined solely by the shareholder's basis account. If the shareholder has basis in his or her stock, the distribution is not taxable. If an S corporation has earnings and profits from C corporation years or S corporation years prior to 1983, the AAA determines the extent a distribution is tax free rather than taxable as a distribution of corporate earnings and profits.[71]

TAX PLANNING

An S corporation without earnings and profits still needs to track its AAA. It can be difficult to reconstruct AAA if at some point in the future the S corporation merges with another S corporation that has C corporation E&P. When an S corporation's election terminates (and it reverts to a C corporation), the balance in the AAA at the date of conversion determines the amount of

[70] Only S corporations that have an accumulated E&P balance must provide the AAA reconciliation and OAA balance.

[71] The interplay between AAA, shareholder basis, earnings and profits, and distributions of appreciated property can become quite problematic, particularly where there are multiple shareholders and distributions are nonpro rata. These complications and a complete discussion of AAA are beyond the scope of this introductory material.

cash that the corporation can distribute during the post-termination period[72] as a tax-free return of previously-taxed income. Without AAA to provide this information, cash distributions would be treated as taxable dividends to the extent the corporation now has earnings and profits.

Example 11.41

JJ Corporation, an S corporation, distributes property valued at $10,000 (basis of $5,000) to its sole shareholder. JoJo's stock has a basis of $15,000 and JJ Corporation's AAA is $10,000. The corporation recognizes $5,000 gain ($10,000 fair market value – $5,000 basis) on the distribution. It increases its AAA to $15,000 for the $5,000 gain and then reduces it to $5,000 for the $10,000 fair market value of the property distributed. JoJo's stock basis also increases by the $5,000 gain to $20,000 and is reduced to $10,000 for the property's $10,000 fair market value. (If the property's basis had been greater than the $10,000 fair market value, the corporation would be better off selling the property and distributing the proceeds to JoJo. That would allow it to recognize the loss.)

11.4.10 S CORPORATION TAXES

Under normal circumstances, an S corporation pays no tax. Three special taxes may be imposed on an S corporation, however, if the S corporation converted from a C corporation.[73] The three taxes are the built-in-gains (BIG) tax, the excess passive investment income tax, and the LIFO recapture tax. The tax rate imposed on the taxable amount in all three cases is the maximum regular corporate tax rate (excluding surcharges), currently 21 percent.

The Built-in-Gains Tax

The **built-in-gains** or **BIG tax** is applicable to an S corporation if, at the time of its conversion from a C corporation, the total fair market value of all its assets exceeded the total bases of these assets. The excess of fair market value over total bases is the built-in gain. If the corporation subsequently sells any of those assets at a gain, a BIG tax is assessed unless the actual holding period exceeds a required five-year holding period called the recognition period. Thus, sales in the sixth tax year after conversion to an S corporation avoid the BIG tax.

The corporation applies the current maximum corporate tax rate to the built-in gain to determine the BIG tax. The tax, however, reduces the gain passed through to the corporation's shareholders.

Example 11.42

M Corporation became an S corporation January 1, 2013. It has only one asset with a fair market value different from its basis. This asset has a value of $40,000 but a basis of only $20,000. If the corporation sells the asset for $35,000 in 2018, it is subject to the BIG tax as it does not meet the 5-year holding period. M compares its $20,000 built-in gain on the date of conversion ($40,000 – $20,000) to its realized gain on the sale date of $15,000 ($35,000 – $20,000). Only the $15,000 realized gain is subject to the 21 percent corporate tax rate. The corporation pays a tax of $3,150 on the gain; the gain passed through to the shareholders is $11,850 ($15,000 – $3,150). If M Corporation does not sell the asset for $35,000 until 2019, the sixth tax year after conversion, it is treated as a simple business asset sale at the shareholder level and the BIG tax no longer applies to the S corporation.

[72] The post-termination period is a period of at least one year during which time the corporation can still make cash distributions of income that has already been taxed to the shareholders.

[73] If an S corporation acquires another corporation with C corporation earnings and profits, the excess passive income tax could apply even though the acquiring corporation has always been an S corporation.

The Excess Net Passive Investment Income Tax

The excess net passive investment income tax only applies to an S corporation that has earnings and profits from a prior C corporation year. Passive investment income includes gross receipts from dividends, interest, annuities, passive rents, royalties, and the disposition of stocks and securities, and the net gain only from the sale of capital assets, excluding stocks and securities. The tax applies to excess net passive investment income.[74] The tax rate is the maximum corporate tax rate, currently 21 percent. The tax paid flows through to the shareholders and reduces other income passing through to them.[75]

TAX PLANNING

The S corporation needs to be particularly careful in those years in which the corporation's gross receipts are reduced despite significant asset sales, for example, when a business is contracting. Not only can the corporation be subject to this tax, but its S election terminates if it is subject to this tax three years in a row.[76]

LIFO Recapture Tax

Another potential tax is the LIFO recapture tax. When a C corporation with inventory on the LIFO basis converts to an S corporation it is subject to a LIFO recapture tax on its LIFO recapture amount—the difference between the value of the inventory under FIFO and its value under LIFO at the date of conversion. The rate applied is the highest corporate tax rate (currently 21 percent) and is paid in four installments. The first installment is due with the corporation's final tax return as a C corporation; the next three installments are due with the tax return for each of the corporation's next three S corporation tax years.

11.4.11 REDEMPTIONS AND LIQUIDATIONS BY S CORPORATIONS

The S corporation provisions contain no special rules for stock redemptions by and liquidation of an S corporation. For these provisions, the regular C corporation provisions apply. For example, redemptions are simply treated as sales of stock by shareholders back to the corporation. As the S corporation normally has no potential for dividend income, the complex rules designed to prevent the conversion of dividend income into capital gain are unnecessary. If the S corporation redeems a shareholder's stock for property rather than cash, the S corporation recognizes gain on appreciated property but is not permitted to recognize loss on depreciated property. (These are the same rules that apply to property distributions.) The recognized gain flows through to the shareholders who are taxed on the gain, increasing the bases in their stock.

A liquidation of S corporation stock also follows C corporation liquidation provisions; that is, the S corporation may sell its property and distribute the proceeds to the shareholders in exchange for their stock, or it may distribute its property to the shareholders. In either case, the corporation generally recognizes both gains and losses on the property it sells or distributes to the shareholders. The gains and losses flow through to the shareholders whose stock bases are then increased or decreased for the net gain or loss that flows through. The shareholder recognizes gain or loss on the surrender of his or her stock based on this basis as adjusted for property sales and/or distributions. In this manner, the S corporation shareholders pay only one level of tax on liquidation.

[74] §1362(d)(3). Excess net passive investment income is passive investment income that exceeds 25 percent of the corporation's total gross receipts for the year (excess passive income) adjusted for related expenses by the ratio of net passive income to total passive income for the year (excess net passive investment income); it is limited to an S corporation's taxable income determined as if it were a regular C corporation. §§1374(d)(4) and 1375(a)(b).

[75] Shareholders can elect to treat a distribution first as a taxable distribution of accumulated earnings and profits rather than a nontaxable distribution from AAA to eliminate earnings and profits.

[76] The S election is terminated at the beginning of the fourth year.

Example 11.43

The Regal Corporation's sole shareholder, Peter, decides to liquidate the business due to ill health. Regal has always been an S corporation and Peter's basis in his stock prior to the sale or distribution of any assets is $50,000. The corporation has only two assets: one is a building with a $100,000 fair market value and a basis of $50,000; the other is land valued at $75,000 with a basis of $90,000. The corporation sells the land for $75,000 and distributes the building directly to Peter. The corporation recognizes a $15,000 loss on the sale of the land and a $50,000 gain on the distribution of the building. Both the loss and gain pass through to Peter and increase his stock basis to $85,000 ($50,000 + $50,000 gain − $15,000 loss). Peter includes this gain and loss on his own return, in addition to a gain of $90,000 ($100,000 + $75,000 − $85,000 basis) on the liquidation of his stock. Thus, in total, Peter recognizes a net gain of $125,000 ($50,000 − $15,000 + $90,000) on the liquidation, the same as the difference between the fair market value of the assets ($175,000) and his original $50,000 stock basis.

Table 11.1 summarizes various entity characteristics for C corporations, S corporations, partnerships, and sole proprietorships.

Table 11.1 A Summary of Entity Characteristics

Characteristic	C Corporation	S Corporation	Partnership	Sole proprietorship
Formed under provisions of state law	Yes	Yes	No	No
Tax-free formation (excluding services)	Yes, if 80% control met	Yes, if 80% control met	Yes	Yes
Operating income taxed at entity level	Yes	No, except for certain penalty-type taxes	No	No
Owners receive a salary subject to FICA and Medicare taxes	Yes	Yes	No	No
Owners pay self-employment taxes	No	No	Yes, on all guaranteed payments and residual income except limited partners	Yes
Owners may participate in tax-free employee fringe benefit programs	Yes	No, if over a 2% shareholder	No	No
Distributions of entity income are tax free	No	Yes	Yes	Yes
Gain/loss recognized on nonliquidating property distributions to owners	Gain only	Gain only	Gain only if cash distributed is greater than basis	No
Gain recognized on entity liquidation	Yes	Yes	No, unless cash distributed is greater than basis	No
Loss recognized on entity liquidation	Yes	Yes	Yes, if only money and ordinary income property distributed	No

11.5 EXPANDED TOPICS—THE PASSIVE DEDUCTION LIMITATIONS

Congress enacted the passive loss limitation rules when the basis and at-risk loss limitation rules failed to discourage investments in tax shelters. These rules, which limited the deduction for losses meeting the definition of passive, were enacted to remove the incentive to invest in activities with little economic benefit other than the creation of tax-deductible losses and to refocus investment on profit-making activities. Although the passive loss rules are very complex, a basic understanding of them and their relationship to flow-through entities is important as the majority of owners of flow-through entities are individual taxpayers, at whom these rules are primarily directed.

Under the **passive activity loss rules**, each item of income or loss for the year is categorized as one of the following:

1. Passive—income or loss from an activity in which the taxpayer is not a material participant. These include limited partnership interests and real property businesses that do not qualify for an exception (discussed later).
2. Portfolio—income from investments. These include capital gains and losses, interest, dividends, annuities, and royalties.
3. Active—income or loss from sources in which the taxpayer materially participates. For individuals these include salary and self-employment income as well as the income from flow-through businesses in which the taxpayer materially participates.

Passive losses (category 1) cannot offset income from either portfolio or active income. They can only offset income from its own passive activities or income from other passive activities. Thus, these passive activity loss rules deny taxpayer deductions for allocated losses from real estate activities, S corporations, and partnership operations in which the taxpayer's only participation is as an investor, by defining such investments as passive activities.[77] In addition, Congress defined all limited partnership interests as passive.

Example 11.44

Justin has income from the following sources: $10,000 salary from a part-time job, $60,000 profit from his sole proprietorship in which he materially participates, $12,000 long-term capital gain, $2,000 dividend income, and a $12,000 loss from an investment in a limited partnership. His partnership basis and amount at-risk are $15,000. Justin has $70,000 of active income ($10,000 salary + $60,000 from his sole proprietorship), $14,000 of portfolio income ($12,000 long-term capital gain + $2,000 dividend income) and a $12,000 passive loss. Justin cannot offset any of the $12,000 loss against any of his other income; the loss carries forward to a future year in which he has passive income that he can use to offset his passive losses.

Originally, all rental activities were also included in the definition of passive activities. Congress later modified that definition of rental activities to exempt persons who are in the real property business.

Example 11.45

Dian, the general partner, and two 49 percent limited partners purchased a rental apartment house for $400,000. After spending $100,000 for improvements, they rented out the apartments for a total of $9,000 per month (a cash inflow of $108,000 per year of rental income). The partnership pays Dian $5,000 to manage the building. The partnership also pays $65,000 in mortgage interest, $19,000 in taxes, and $6,000 in insurance. The depreciation deduction is $18,000. Total deductible expenses are $113,000 but cash outflow is only $95,000. Thus, the partnership has a net positive cash inflow of $13,000 but a deductible loss of $5,000. (Mortgage principal payments are ignored.) Each limited partner is allocated 49 percent of the loss or $2,450. As limited partners, the passive loss rules prevent them from deducting the losses against nonpassive income. Dian is allocated the remaining $100 of this loss (2 percent) and may meet the exception for rental property in which a taxpayer actively participates. If so, she could deduct all or part of this loss (as discussed later).

[77] The passive loss rules apply to individual shareholders in an S corporation, partners in a partnership, and sole proprietors who do not meet the participation requirements.

11.5.1 MATERIAL PARTICIPATION

If a taxpayer meets the definition of material participation in an activity (not a passive activity), its losses are currently deductible against other forms of income. The general definition of **material participation** requires involvement that is "regular, continuous and substantial." by a taxpayer (and his or her spouse).[78] Two sets of rules provide bright line tests—one based on current activities and the other based on prior activities. A taxpayer may also qualify under the general standard of regular, continuous, and substantial activity, but this can be a difficult standard to meet. To be exempt from the passive loss limits, individuals and closely held corporations must meet one of the following standards for material participation:

1. Current Activity Level
   - **a.** Taxpayer has 500 hours or more of participation during the tax year.
   - **b.** Taxpayer's participation constitutes substantially all the activity by all persons.
   - **c.** Taxpayer participates at least 100 hours, but no other person's participation exceeds that of the taxpayer.
   - **d.** Taxpayer has at least 100 hours participation in more than one activity such that the aggregate participation in all qualifying activities exceeds 500 hours.
2. Prior Activity Level
   - **a.** Taxpayer participated materially in any 5 of the 10 preceding years.
   - **b.** Taxpayer materially participated in any three prior years, and the business is classified as a personal service activity.

A taxpayer with investments in multiple passive activities generating both profits and losses cannot deduct *net losses* from the passive activities. There are several steps required to determine this nondeductible net loss.[79] The taxpayer first determines the income and losses from all passive activities, netting losses against gains. If total gains exceed total losses, all income is included and all losses are deducted. If total losses exceed gains, only losses equal to gains are deductible. The excess loss is disallowed (unless subject to the rental activities exception as explained later). The disallowed loss is allocated on a pro rata basis to each loss activity, with a portion of the loss carried forward by each loss activity. A taxpayer can only deduct passive losses equal to passive income, unless the activity is disposed of completely.

Example 11.46

JoAnn has $4,000 income from passive activity F and a loss of $6,000 from passive activity B. JoAnn nets the $4,000 income against the $6,000 loss for a net passive loss of $2,000. Although JoAnn includes the $4,000 of passive income on her tax return, her deduction for passive losses is limited to $4,000. (These, in effect, cancel out each other, and the net effect on her income is zero.) JoAnn carries forward the $2,000 passive loss from activity B.

Next year, JoAnn has a $4,000 loss from F and a $5,000 loss from B prior to disposing of B at a $1,000 gain. JoAnn has a net loss of $8,000 [$1,000 – ($4,000 + $5,000)]. JoAnn can deduct a loss of $6,000—B's net $4,000 loss for the current year and its $2,000 loss carryover from the prior year—as she completely disposes of B this year. JoAnn must carry forward F's $4,000 loss until there is passive income or F is disposed of completely.

Disallowed losses may be carried forward indefinitely. The disadvantage to the taxpayer is the timing of the loss deduction. The longer the loss deduction is postponed, the less value it has

[78] §469(h)(1). Both spouses' activities are considered in determining if the requirements for material participation are met.

[79] The loss limitations are applied in a specific order. First, the taxpayer must consider if there is basis against which to deduct the loss. If there is basis, the taxpayer must then consider if he or she is at risk. If the taxpayer is also at risk for the loss, then and only then are the passive loss rules considered.

from a tax reduction standpoint because of the time value of money. There are only two ways to deduct these losses in the current tax year: (1) to have gains from other passive activities or (2) to completely dispose of the activity. If the activity is a continuing loser, it may be difficult to find a buyer for the activity at almost any selling price. It may be possible to invest in a PIG, a passive income generator, but an excessive price may have to be paid for this type of investment because of its income-producing value. (In addition, there may be little guarantee that a current PIG will continue to generate income.)

TAX PLANNING

It is the taxpayer's responsibility to maintain adequate records of the time spent in an activity to establish whether the activity is active or passive. A taxpayer may want a business that is producing income to be passive so that income from that activity can offset losses from other passive activities. A taxpayer must also keep records of basis and at-risk amounts, as any loss disallowed because of these limits cannot be deducted as a passive loss regardless of the amount of passive income.

11.5.2 REAL PROPERTY BUSINESS EXCEPTION

When the passive activity rules were first enacted, passive rental activities included the long-term rental of property that did not require the taxpayer to provide substantial additional services; thus, this definition included most residential and commercial rental properties.[80] Many real estate professionals spend a great amount of time acquiring, renovating, and renting residential and commercial real estate properties, and they have income that often fluctuates between large gains in some years and losses in others. Thus, Congress enacted a mitigating provision for taxpayers in the real property business that allows them to deduct losses currently. To qualify, taxpayers must spend more than half their time in **real property businesses** in which they materially participate, and the time spent must equal or exceed 750 hours. This provision generally (but not always) eliminates persons who hold full-time positions in other occupations but who dabble on the side in real estate.[81]

Example 11.47

Bob retired two years ago as a carpenter. Since then, he has acquired several rundown properties that he has renovated and rented. In his first year following retirement, he spent 400 hours overseeing and working on renovating only one property. In the second year, he bought two more properties and spent 900 hours on renovations. That year the first building was rented out completely, but many units in the other two buildings stood empty. Bob had a $13,500 loss in year 2 on all the rental properties. In year 1, Bob did not qualify as a real estate professional in the real property business. In year 2, however, he meets the real property business exception to the passive loss rules and can deduct his $13,500 loss.

An additional provision is discussed in Chapter 6 that allows taxpayers with adjusted gross income (AGI) of less than $150,000 to qualify for a deduction of up to $25,000 for rental real estate losses if they "actively" participate in the activity. This active participation provision requires less time and effort than material participation under the passive loss rules but the deduction is gradually phased out as AGI increases from $100,000 to $150,000. At taxpayer AGI of $150,000, the entire $25,000 deduction is lost.

[80] See Reg. §1.469-1T(e)(3). Only rental properties for which substantial additional services had to be provided or for which the rental periods were generally short term (for example, hotels, motels, golf courses, and car rentals) were excluded.
[81] Unlike the general material participation requirements, the individual alone must perform the 750 hours for a real property business. A spouse's time is not included.

REVISITING THE INTRODUCTORY CASE

Robert owns all the assets of his cleaning operation because it is a sole proprietorship, To maintain control of the business, Robert should contribute all of these assets to the business in exchange for an ownership interest in the new entity in excess of 50 percent. Crystal Corporation could then contribute cash and/or property for the balance of the contributed capital to the new entity. Together, they could form a regular corporation, a partnership, or an LLC that elects either partnership or corporate treatment, without any tax consequences. They cannot form an S corporation because Crystal Corporation cannot be an S corporation shareholder. (If James joined in the enterprise with Robert instead of Crystal Corporation, an S corporation could be used.) In any of these forms, Robert and his business assets are insulated from Crystal's liabilities, as it is a separate entity. (Unfortunately, any interest in the new entity that is owned by Crystal is an asset and could be seized to satisfy Crystal's debts.)

If Robert and Crystal Corporation form a C corporation or an LLC electing corporate status, they must transfer sufficient cash and property to satisfy the 80 percent control requirement to avoid gain recognition on appreciated assets transferred. As part of the incorporation, Robert could receive all the voting common stock, and Crystal could receive nonvoting common or preferred stock. Either option would ensure Robert's control of the entity.

If they form a partnership, the partnership agreement would have to specify that Robert has the controlling interest. The partnership form, however, cannot insulate Robert from partnership liabilities, as he must be a general partner to control the day-to-day operations of the business. (Crystal could be a limited partner to limit its liability.)

An LLC operating agreement would have to spell out Robert's position as a controlling member. A detailed operating agreement could be written to limit Crystal Corporation's ability to dispose of its interest to someone not approved by Robert. Other than including a right of first refusal, it could be very difficult for Robert to prevent Crystal from selling its interest in the new entity to an undesirable person. Electing either corporate or partnership status for the LLC would limit Robert's liability exposure.

A significant consideration in selecting a regular corporation or an LLC (taxed as a corporation) is the double taxation of income. Although Robert may be able to take out significant entity earnings as salary, any distributions to him or to Crystal would be taxed as dividends. This could be particularly undesirable to Crystal because the new entity would not be a subsidiary eligible for a 100 percent dividend received deduction; thus, part (35 percent or 50 percent) of any dividend distribution to Crystal would be subject to a third round of taxes as part of Crystal's income. If, however, they leave any excess income in the entity beyond Robert's salary, then double taxation is avoided as long as it is retained in the business. Alternatively, a partnership LLC would allow Robert to take tax-free distributions in excess of any guaranteed payments as long as he has basis in the interest. The partnership form of LLC would also allow Crystal to take guaranteed payments for the use of the equity that it is investing in the business. The principal disadvantage of this LLC form is that all income will be taxed to Robert and Crystal as it is earned by the new entity.

When Robert decides to dispose of his controlling interest in the business, he must meet some relatively complex rules on a redemption of his stock to ensure capital gain treatment at minimal tax cost, unless a buyer can be found for all or part of his interest. Any redemption that does not eliminate his entire interest could result in dividend income. As long as the maximum dividend tax rate remains below the ordinary income tax rate, however, this would not be as punitive as ordinary income.

If he liquidates his interest in the LLC, he would be able to take cash distributions from the LLC (partnership). To the extent the LLC has ordinary income assets (also referred to as hot assets), however, he would have ordinary income rather than capital gain. If he takes property other than cash, he would be able to postpone gain recognition until disposition of the property.

As the discussion illustrates, the choice between the corporate form and an LLC operating as a partnership is not simple. As in many tax situations, one option will not satisfy all the desired characteristics of the taxpayer. In this case, we do not have Robert's tax rates, nor do we have information on Crystal's plans for the future. It would be essential in an actual situation like this to become far better acquainted with the relevant parties to make a more informed recommendation. While it may appear that either the LLC (partnership) or the corporate form will meet most needs, it may become clear in talking to the taxpayers that certain traits are far more desirable than others, leading the way to a decision between these two entities.

SUMMARY

There are several forms of business entities available to taxpayers presented in this chapter—the sole proprietorship, the partnership, and the S corporation—all have one level of tax on their income as they are all pass-through entities. (The limited partnership, PLLP, LLC, and PLLC are all variations of the general partnership for tax purposes.) The income and losses that flow through these entities increase and decrease the bases of the equity interest that partners have in partnerships and that shareholders have in S corporations. It is the owners' responsibility to maintain the balances in their bases accounts.

Depending on the type of partner and the type of liability, partners in a partnership increase their bases proportionately for liabilities of the partnership. The bases that owners of both partnerships and S corporations have in their equity interests limit the deduction for losses passed through by the entity.

The at-risk and passive loss rules also apply to partners and shareholders and affect the deductibility of losses. The at-risk rules can prevent partners from deducting losses even if they have bases. Passive losses of individuals or closely held corporations are deductible only to the extent the taxpayer has passive income; however, all passive losses become deductible when the taxpayer completely disposes of an activity.

Nonliquidating distributions of cash or property from partnerships generally have no tax consequences to the partnership or the partner. If the partner receives cash in excess of his or her partnership interest basis, the partner recognizes gain only. There is limited gain or loss recognition on the distribution of assets by a partnership as gain or loss is postponed until the partners dispose of the assets received in the liquidating distribution.

An S corporation must be incorporated in one of the 50 states, have only one class of outstanding stock, and have no more than 100 shareholders. Only individuals, estates, and certain trusts can be S corporation shareholders. Individuals must be either citizens or residents of the United States.

An S corporation recognizes gain on the distribution of appreciated assets to S corporation shareholders if the distribution is either liquidating or nonliquidating. Loss on the distribution of depreciated property is recognized only in a liquidating distribution. These gains and losses flow through to the shareholders and must be taken into account in the shareholders' bases before any shareholder's gain or loss can be determined on the surrender of the stock.

KEY TERMS

Accumulated adjustments account (AAA) 537
Aggregate or conduit concept 511
At-risk rules 519
BIG tax 538
Built-in-gains 538
Current distribution 521
Domestic corporation 528
Entity concept 511
Flow-through business entity 502
Form 1065 513
Form 1120S 531
General loss limitation 518
General partnership 509
Guaranteed payments 520
Limited liability company (LLC) 510
Limited liability partnership (LLP) 509
Limited partnership 509
Liquidating distributions 523
Material participation 542
Nonliquidating distribution 521
Nonrecourse debts 518
Partnership net income 513
Partnerships 509
Passive activity loss rules 541
Passive losses 519
Professional limited liability companies (PLLCs) 510
Real property businesses 543
Recourse debts 518
Revocation 530
Schedule K 513
Schedule K-1 513
S corporation 528
S election 529
Self-employment taxes 508
Separately stated items 513
Sole proprietor 503
Sole proprietorship 503
Terminating event 530

TEST YOURSELF

Answers Appear after the Problem Assignments

1. Lauren Cooper had a beauty shop in the basement of her home. During the current year, she had gross receipts of $32,000. She spent $3,500 for supplies, paid an assistant $4,200, incurred allocated utility expenses of $800, depreciation expense of $1,200, a Section 1231 gain of $800, and a charitable contribution of $500. What is the net income that she will report on her Schedule C?
   a. $22,600
   b. $22,300
   c. $21,800
   d. $21,600

2. Refer to the information in question 1 and assume the entity is an S corporation. What is the corporation's net income excluding separately stated items?
   a. $22,600
   b. $22,300
   c. $21,800
   d. $21,600

3. William and Joan form a partnership with William having a 30 percent interest and Joan the remaining 70 percent. Joan contributed $80,000 cash and services valued at $4,000. William contributed $6,000 cash and property valued at $30,000 that has a basis of $20,000. At the end of the year, the partnership reports the following:

Ordinary income (before guaranteed payments)	$90,000
Tax-exempt bond interest	2,000
Capital loss	4,000
Guaranteed payment to Joan	30,000
Cash distribution to Joan	25,000
New 3-year note on land	15,000

   What is William's basis in his partnership interest at year-end?
   a. $43,400
   b. $45,800
   c. $47,900
   d. $45,900

4. Using the information in question 3, what is Joan's basis in her partnership interest at year-end?
   a. $140,100
   b. $120,600
   c. $110,100
   d. $99,600

5. William and Joan form an S corporation with William owning 30 percent of the stock and Joan the remaining 70 percent. Joan contributed $80,000 cash and services valued at $4,000. William contributed $6,000 cash and property valued at $30,000 that has a basis of $20,000. At the end of the year, the S corporation reports the following:

Ordinary income (before salary expense)	$90,000
Tax-exempt bond interest	2,000
Capital loss	4,000
Salary to Joan	30,000
Cash distribution to Joan	25,000
New 3-year note on land	15,000

   What is Williams's basis in his S corporation interest at year-end?
   a. $43,400
   b. $45,800
   c. $47,900
   d. $45,900

Check Your Understanding

PROBLEM ASSIGNMENTS

1. [LO 11.1] Which entities discussed in this chapter insulate the owners from the general liabilities of the entity?
2. [LO 11.1] Explain the principal difference between an LLP and an LLC.
3. [LO 11.2] The Gem Company, a sole proprietorship, provides health insurance for its owner and two employees. The cost per person is $200 per month. Explain how the Gem Company and its sole proprietor will treat this expense.
4. [LO 11.2] Describe the new limitation for net business losses. What are the threshold amounts for 2018?
5. [LO 11.2] What is the purpose of the qualified business income deduction? Explain how it is calculated.
6. [LO 11.3] Explain how an increase or decrease in partnership liabilities can affect the basis of a general partner and a limited partner.
7. [LO 11.3 & 11.4] Explain the difference between the effects of liabilities of an S corporation on a shareholder's stock basis and the effect of liabilities of a partnership on a partner's partnership interest basis.
8. [LO 11.3] Although partners can generally deduct their share of losses from a partnership, what four things can limit their ability to deduct these losses on their current year's tax return?
9. [LO 11.3] Explain the difference between the entity and aggregate theories applicable to a partnership and give an example of the effect of these theories on partnership transactions.
10. [LO 11.3] Explain the difference between inside and outside basis for partners and the partnership.
11. [LO 11.3] What is the difference between a partner's guaranteed payment and his salary?
12. [LO 11.2, 11.3 & 11.4] Compare an owner's personal liability for debts of a business organized as a sole proprietorship, general partnership, limited partnership, LLP, LLC, and S corporation.
13. [LO 11.3 & 11.4] Why are partnerships and S corporations required to separately state certain items on the Schedule K rather than combining these items with the organization's operating profit or loss? Provide examples of the items that must be separately stated.
14. [LO 11.4] How is income allocated to S corporation shareholders? Develop an example to illustrate this procedure.
15. [LO 11.4] What are the corporate and shareholder restrictions on making an S corporation election?
16. [LO 11.4] What is the difference between a prospective S election and a retroactive S election?
17. [LO 11.4] What is a terminating event in relation to an S corporation?
18. [LO 11.4] Why do the basis and at-risk rules usually prevent the same amount of losses from passing through to shareholders of S corporations?
19. [LO 11.4] What is the purpose of the accumulated adjustments account if the S corporation has always been an S corporation?
20. [LO 11.4] What types of taxes may an S corporation have to pay and under what circumstances?
21. [LO 11.5] What is the income limit for claiming a passive loss deduction under the passive activity real property business exception to material participation?
22. [LO 11.5] What are the three categories into which business losses are separated? What type of business interest is always considered a passive activity?

Crunch the Numbers

23. [LO 11.2] In 2018, John is single and is the owner of a proprietorship with $650,000 of gross income and $970,000 of deductions, resulting in a $320,000 loss for the year. How much of this loss can John deduct in 2018 and what does he do with the excess loss?

24. [LO 11.2] Susanna is single with taxable income in 2018 of $185,000 of which $130,000 is attributable to her consulting sole proprietorship. She paid W-2 wages of $60,000 to her employees. Compute her qualified business income deduction.

25. [LO 11.2] John Mason operates a consulting business, Mason Enterprises, as a sole proprietorship. He had to transfer $100,000 of stocks and securities into Mason Enterprises's name to show financial viability for the business. During the current year, the business had the following income and expenses from operations:

Consulting revenue	$125,000
Travel expenses	40,000
Transportation	3,000
Advertising	7,000
Office expense	3,000
Telephone	1,000
Dividend income	5,000
Interest income	2,000
Charitable contribution	1,000
Political contribution	6,000

Determine the Schedule C net income. How are items not included in the Schedule C net income reported?

26. [LO 11.3] Refer to the information in the preceding problem, except that John and his wife Mary are equal partners in Mason Enterprises, which operates as a partnership. How would they report the income and loss items from partnership operations?

27. [LO 11.4] Refer to the information in problem 25, except that John operates Mason Enterprises as an S corporation. How would John report the income and loss items from S corporation operations?

28. [LO 11.3] Jim and Angie form the JAZ Partnership with Zoe by contributing $75,000 each to partnership equity. Zoe, the third partner, contributes property with a basis of $50,000 and fair market value of $75,000. The three are equal partners in the partnership.
    a. Determine the tax consequences to Zoe for the contribution of property to the partnership.
    b. What are the partnership's tax consequences?
    c. What is each partner's basis in the partnership interest?
    d. What is the partnership's basis in the property?

29. [LO 11.3] George and Georgenne formed the GG Partnership as equal partners. Each partner contributed cash and property with a value of $100,000 for partnership operations. As a result of these contributions, George had a basis of $80,000 and Georgenne a basis of $60,000 in their partnership interests. At the end of their first year of operations, they had the following results:

Gross sales	$150,000
Cost of goods sold	95,000
Rent expense	15,000
Salaries to employees	15,000
Utilities	4,000
Charitable contribution	1,000
Section 1231 gain	2,000

    a. What is the net income, excluding separately stated items, that each partner is required to report at the end of the year?
    b. How is each of the separately stated items treated on the partners' tax returns?
    c. What is each partner's basis at year-end?

30. [LO 11.3] The BDC Partnership has three partners with the following partnership interest percentages and tax-year ends: B has 35 percent ownership and a Dec. 31 year end; D owns 45 percent and has a June 30 year end, and C owns 35 percent and has an Oct. 30 year end. What method must be used to determine the partnership year end and which year end is required?

31. [LO 11.3] John received a proportionate nonliquidating distribution of $10,000 cash and inventory with a $3,000 basis and a fair market value of $12,000 from a partnership in which he has a basis of $8,000.
   a. What are the tax effects of these distributions?
   b. How would your answer change if this was a liquidating distribution?
   c. How would your answers change on the nonliquidating and liquidating distributions if his basis in the partnership was $15,000?

32. [LO 11.3] Quenton received a proportionate nonliquidating distribution of $8,000 cash, inventory with a $5,000 basis and a fair market value of $7,000, and a Section 1231 asset with a $7,000 basis and a fair market value of $15,000.
   a. What are the tax effects of these distributions if his partnership basis is $24,000?
   b. How would your answer change if his partnership basis is $16,000?
   c. How would your answers to a. and b. change if this was a proportionate liquidating distribution?

33. [LO 11.3] The ABC Partnership makes a proportionate nonliquidating distribution to one of its partners of two Section 1231 assets. Asset A has a basis of $40,000 and a fair market value of $15,000; Asset B has a basis of $30,000 and a fair market value of $20,000. If the partner's outside basis in his partnership interest is only $35,000, what basis does he have in the assets that are distributed to him?

34. [LO 11.3] National Partnership makes a proportionate nonliquidating distribution to one of its partners of two Section 1231 assets. Asset X has a basis of $40,000 and a fair market value of $15,000; Asset B has a basis of $20,000 and a fair market value of $10,000. The partner's outside basis in the partnership interest is $30,000. What is the partner's basis in the assets after the distribution?

35. [LO 11.3] Capital Partnership makes a proportionate liquidating distribution to one of its partners of $5,000 cash, $6,000 inventory (FMV = $10,000), and land with a $20,000 basis and an $11,000 fair market value. What are the tax consequences to the partner of this liquidating distribution if his partnership outside basis is $25,000?

36. [LO 11.3] Alexandra received a $40,000 cash liquidating distribution for her 25 percent interest in ABC Partnership that had a $62,500 outside basis. Immediately prior to the distribution, the partnership had the following assets: $30,000 cash, unrealized receivable (zero basis, $60,000 fair market value), inventory ($20,000 basis, $40,000 fair market value), and land ($10,000 basis, $30,000 fair market value). The partnership had no outstanding liabilities. What are the tax effects of this disproportionate distribution on Alexandra's taxable income?

37. [LO 11.3] Walter sells his 40 percent interest in Kennel Kids Playground with a partnership basis interest of $40,000 to George for $60,000. The partnership has the following assets: Cash = $50,000, inventory ($20,000 basis, $60,000 fair market value), and land ($30,000 basis; $40,000 fair market value). What are the tax effects of this sale on Walter's taxable income?

38. [LO 11.3] The Rents-Are-Us Partnership owns a large apartment building with a fair market value of $2,100,000, a basis of $1,600,000, and a mortgage encumbering it of $500,000. Kenneth sells his 20 percent interest in the partnership with an outside basis of $350,000 to Charlie for $450,000 cash and the assumption of his share of the mortgage. What are the tax effects for Kenneth on the sale of his partnership interest to Charlie?

39. [LO 11.3] Alpha, Beta, and Gamma form the ABG partnership by transferring the following to the partnership:

Alpha	$10,000 cash and machinery valued at $20,000 with a basis of $15,000.
Beta	Land valued at $30,000 with a basis of $35,000.
Gamma	Cash of $20,000 and services valued at $10,000.

a. Determine the tax consequences of these transfers to Alpha, Beta, and Gamma.
b. Identify each of their bases in their partnership interests.
c. What basis does the partnership have in each of the properties transferred to it?

40. [LO 11.3] Refer to the information in the preceding problem. If the partnership sells the land for $27,000 after holding it for three years, what are the tax consequences to Alpha, Beta, and Gamma?

41. [LO 11.3] Explain the difference in recourse and nonrecourse liabilities when distinguishing between general and limited partners. Assume the partnership has $100,000 of recourse liabilities and $60,000 of nonrecourse liabilities. It has one general partner, Matt, who has a 20 percent interest in income and loss, and two limited partners, each of whom has a 40 percent interest in income and loss. Illustrate the difference in allocation of liabilities to these three partners.

42. [LO 11.3] CCC Partnership borrowed $100,000 on a five-year recourse note from a local bank. It also purchased land for $60,000, putting $10,000 down and signing a qualified nonrecourse loan secured by the land for the balance. The partners' interests in partnership profits and losses are as follows:

Partner	Loss	Profit
Carol (general partner)	25%	50%
Charles (limited partner)	40%	25%
Charlotte (limited partner)	35%	25%

a. How is the $100,000 recourse note allocated to the partners' bases?
b. How is the $50,000 nonrecourse note allocated to the partners' bases?
c. How would your answers change if Carol, Charles, and Charlotte were all general partners?

43. [LO 11.3] Luis and Jennifer formed the JL Partnership as equal partners. Each partner contributed cash and property with a value of $80,000 for partnership operations. As a result of these contributions, Luis had a basis of $80,000 and Jennifer a basis of $60,000 in their partnership interests. At the end of their first year of operations, they had the following results:

Gross sales	$110,000
Cost of goods sold	75,000
Rent expense	18,000
Employees' salaries	20,000
Utilities	3,000
Charitable contribution	500
Section 1231 gain	1,000
Tax-exempt interest income	2,000

a. What is the net income, excluding separately stated items, that each partner is required to report at the end of the year?
b. How is each of the separately stated items treated on the partners' tax returns?
c. What is each partner's basis at year-end?
d. Explain how Luis and Jennifer's initial bases could differ if they both contributed cash and property valued at $80,000.

44. [LO 11.3 & 11.5] In year 1, Sally invested $45,000 for a 10 percent interest in a limited partnership. This is Sally's only passive investment. The limited partnership has $100,000 of nonrecourse debt. (The debt is not secured by real property.) At the end of years 1 through 5, the partnership passed income and losses through to Sally as follows:

Year	Income (Loss)
1	($31,000)
2	$21,000
3	$4,000
4	$8,000
5	($22,000)

At the beginning of year 6, Sally sells her interest in the partnership for $40,000. For each of the years, determine Sally's deductible and nondeductible (suspended) losses. Explain the reason for the nondeductibility of any losses. What are the results of the sale of her interest?

45. [LO 11.3] Lynn, who is single, is allocated $500,000 of income and $790,000 of deductions in 2018 from ABC Partnership. How much of this loss can Lynn deduct in 2018 and what does she do with the excess loss?

46. [LO 11.3] Roberto is single and has taxable income of $530,000 in 2018. As a 25 percent partner in a partnership that produces $820,000 of ordinary income from manufacturing a product, his share of partnership income is $205,000. The partnership paid $210,000 of W-2 wages and the total unadjusted basis of tangible depreciable business property is $360,000. What is Roberto's qualified business income deduction?

47. [LO 11.3] Partner X, a one-third partner in XYZ Partnership, needs a distribution from the partnership for some unexpected bills. The partnership, however, does not have any extra cash to distribute. It will distribute land to the partner that has a value of $30,000 and a basis of $25,000 to the partnership. X's basis in his partnership interest is $45,000.

a. How will this distribution be treated for tax purposes?

b. Assume alternatively, that the partnership sells the land for its fair market value and distributes the cash to Partner X. What are the tax consequences of the sale and distribution?

c. Which alternative would you recommend to the partnership? Explain.

48. [LO 11.3] Maria, a 25 percent partner in MARS Partnership, needs a distribution from the partnership for some unexpected bills. The partnership, however, does not have any extra cash to distribute. It will distribute land to Maria that has a value of $27,000 and a basis to the partnership of $50,000. Maria's basis in her partnership interest is $55,000.

a. How will this distribution be treated for tax purposes?

b. Assume alternatively, that the partnership sells the land for its fair market value and distributes the cash to Maria. What are the tax consequences of the sale and distribution?

c. Which alternative would you recommend to Maria? Explain.

49. [LO 11.3 & 11.4] Bob is a 50 percent owner of Barco Enterprises. During 2018, Barco earned $80,000 in net income after subtracting Bob's $50,000 salary. Bob also withdrew $20,000 from Barco during the year. Bob would like to know the amount of the FICA taxes and by whom they would be paid if

a. Barco is a general partnership.

b. Barco is an S corporation.

50. [LO 11.4] Refer to the information in problem 29, except that George and Georgenne are equal shareholders in an S corporation.

a. What is the net income, excluding separately stated items, that each shareholder is required to report at the end of the year?

b. How is each of the separately stated items treated on the shareholders' tax returns?

c. What is each shareholder's basis at year-end?

51. [LO 11.4] Charles owns a 25 percent interest in Cal Corporation, an S corporation. The corporation has run into some difficulties recently and Charles loaned it $10,000. At the beginning of the year, Charles's basis in his stock was $16,000.

a. What is Charles's basis in his stock and debt at the end of the year if the corporation reports losses of $60,000?

b. What is Charles's basis in his stock and debt at the end of the year if the corporation reports losses of $90,000?

c. What is Charles's basis in his stock and debt at the end of the year if the corporation reports losses of $120,000?

52. [LO 11.4] Is there any tax advantage to a 100 percent shareholder-employee of an S corporation compared to a shareholder-employee of a C corporation under the following circumstances: shareholder-employee salary is $75,000; the corporate income before the $75,000 salary and any related employment expense is $100,000? The corporation also distributes $15,000 to the shareholder. The shareholder is single, has no dependents, and uses the standard deduction.

53. [LO 11.4] At the beginning of year 1, Lisa and Marie were equal shareholders in LM Corporation, an S corporation. On April 30, year 1, Lisa sold half of her interest to Shelley. On August 8, year 1, Marie sold her entire interest to George. On December 31, year 1, the corporation reported net income of $50,000. How is this income allocated to Lisa, Marie, Shelley, and George? (Year 1 is not a leap year, and the date of sale is allocated to the seller.)

54. [LO 11.4] During the current year, Biggie, Inc., a delivery company operating as an S corporation, reported the following results from operations:

Revenue	$280,000
Salaries	130,000
Truck expense	30,000
Taxes	18,000
Section 1231 loss	8,000
Traffic fines	1,200
Interest expense on truck loans	2,000
Interest income (corporate bonds)	500

What are the corporation's net income and its separately reported items?

55. [LO 11.4] Crow Corporation, an S corporation from the date of its incorporation, is in the process of liquidating. During the current year, it reports gross receipts of only $40,000; it has passive investment income of $25,000 from the money it invested after the sale of a large portion of its operating assets. It has expenses related to this income of $1,000. Is the corporation liable for the passive investment income tax?

56. [LO 11.4] The Jane Corporation, an S corporation, makes several property distributions to its two equal shareholders, A and B, during the year. A received $5,000 cash plus land with a basis of $8,000 and fair market value of $10,000. B received $5,000 cash plus equipment with a basis of $5,000 and a fair market value of $10,000.

At the beginning of the year, the corporation's accumulated adjustments account is $35,000; A's basis in his shares is $24,000; and B's basis is $32,000. The corporation reports net income of $6,000 for the year, excluding any effect of the distributions. Determine the basis in A and B's shares and the balance in the corporation's AAA at the end of the year.

57. [LO 11.4] PA Corporation, an S corporation, has two equal shareholders, P and A. Prior to the end of the current year, PA decides to liquidate and sell its three remaining assets distributing the cash received to P and A. Asset 1 has a basis of $10,000 and is sold for $6,000. Asset 2 has a basis of $4,000 and is sold for $12,000. Asset 3 has a basis of $9,000 and is sold for $10,000. Shareholder P has a basis of $4,000 in her shares, and A has a basis of $20,000. The corporation has a net loss (excluding the sales of the assets) of $2,500. Detail the tax consequences to PA Corporation and its two shareholders on the liquidation of the corporation.

58. [LO 11.5] Alfred has investments in three passive activities: In year 1, PA-1 had a gain of $3,000, PA-2 had a loss of $10,000, and PA-3 had a loss of $5,000. In year 2, PA-1 has a gain of $12,000, PA-2 has a $1,000 loss, and PA-3 has a loss of $2,000. How should Alfred treat the year 1 results from these activities? How should Alfred treat the year 2 results from these activities?

Develop Planning Skills

59. [LO 11.2, 11.3 & 11.4] Clare and Cora have been making wedding cakes in their homes for several years. The Health Department just learned about this and now requires them to shut down or find

a commercial kitchen that can be subject to the proper inspections. Clare and Cora located a suitable small restaurant they can rent for $1,000 per month or purchase for $100,000. Their monthly payments would be $1,000 per month for interest and taxes and $100 per month for the principal on a commercial mortgage if they put $10,000 down. Clara and Cora each have $10,000 in savings they can put into the business. Their husbands are also employed and would be able to provide some support during the start-up period. Both families are in the 24 percent marginal tax bracket. The women know that the first several years will be difficult, as they will need to build the business by more than word of mouth. As a result, their business plan shows losses of $5,000 in the first year, $4,000 in the second year, and $2,000 in the third year, but the fourth year and beyond show profits. These losses do not include either the rent or the mortgage payment. How do you suggest they set up their business? Should they buy or rent the building?

60. [LO 11.2, 11.3 & 11.4] Cynthia needs your advice regarding which form of business entity to choose for her new business. She expects the new business will have losses of approximately $80,000 in each of the first two years but anticipates profits that will grow steadily thereafter. Cynthia has no cash to contribute to the business but plans to work 50 or more hours per week managing the day-to-day operations of the new business. Four individuals will contribute $50,000 each to start the business. To fund growth, Cynthia anticipates that additional funding will be needed in three years. Cynthia wants to meet with you next week to discuss your analysis and preliminary recommendations.

a. Based on this information only, what would you recommend?

b. Before meeting with Cynthia, prepare a list of questions you would like to ask to obtain the additional information you would need to make a more thorough analysis.

61. [LO 11.4] Prior to BJ Corporation's year-end, its sole shareholder comes to you for advice. BJ is an established S corporation that was profitable until two years ago when the economy faltered. Due to distributions and losses passed through in prior years, the shareholder's basis in the S corporation is only $10,000. He anticipates that the corporation will have a loss of $50,000 in the current year. His previous accountant, who retired this year, had mentioned something to him about losses not being deductible if he did not have stock basis. What are the shareholder's alternatives? Make a list of questions you would ask the shareholder to assist you in selecting between alternatives.

62. [LO 11.4 & 11.5] An S corporation shareholder has contacted you for advice. His S corporation is going to pass a very large loss through to him that would otherwise offset other income, except for the fact that he lacks sufficient stock basis to absorb the loss. The shareholder is coming to your office tomorrow to discuss the situation. Make a list of questions you will ask before you will advise him on possible alternatives.

Think Outside the Text

These questions require answers that are beyond the material that is covered in this chapter.

63. [LO 11.2] What do you believe led to the conclusion that a sole proprietorship should report its results on the owner's tax return?

64. [LO 11.3] Why do you think services are excluded from the definition of property when a partner receives a partnership interest in exchange for property?

65. [LO 11.3 & 11.4] Why do you think Congress passed the law that allows an LLC to elect to be treated as a corporation or a partnership?

66. [LO 11.3 & 11.4] Compare the treatment of distributions of depreciated and appreciated property by an S corporation to that of a partnership.

67. [LO 11.4] Why do you think an S corporation is limited to having common stock with no differences other than voting rights?

Search the Internet

68. [LO 11.3] Go to *www.taxsites.com/state-links.html* and locate your state. Find and read your state's filing requirements for forming an LLC and write a one-paragraph summary of these requirements. Does your state recognize a single member LLC?

69. [LO 11.3 & 11.4] In addition to the federal income tax, an entity is subject to the laws of the state in which it is organized. Use the Internet to locate sources of tax law that govern the tax treatment of partnerships, LLCs, and S corporations for your state. Write a brief description regarding how each of those entities is treated for tax purposes in your state.

70. [LO 11.4] Go to the IRS website (*www.irs.gov*) and locate the form that a corporation uses to make an S election and its related instructions. Summarize the information required on the form. Do the instructions include information on how to obtain an extension of time for filing the S election? If so, summarize this information. If not, is this information available elsewhere on this website?

71. [LO 11.2 & 11.4] Walter Williams, a travel writer, has worked for a well-known publication for a number of years as a private contractor. Last year a friend suggested he become an S corporation, but he failed to make the election. During the current year, the business had the following income and expenses from operations:

Publication royalties	$125,000
Travel expenses	40,000
Transportation	3,000
Short-term capital loss	7,000
Office expense	3,000
Section 1231 gain	1,000
Dividend income	5,000
Interest income	2,000
Charitable contribution	1,000
Theft loss	6,000

Determine the Schedule C net income. Where are items not included in the Schedule C net income reported? How would your answers change if he had made the election to become an S corporation?

Identify the Issues

Identify the issues or problems suggested by the following situations. State each issue as a question.

72. [LO 11.3] Shana is a 20 percent limited partner in the STU partnership. Her basis in her partnership interest is $40,000 when she decides to abandon her partnership interest. The partnership's balance sheet reports net assets of $203,000, liabilities of $200,000 and partners' capital accounts as follows:

Shana-Capital	$1,000
Tom-Capital	1,000
Urban-Capital	1,000

73. [LO 11.3] Carol and her husband own 35 percent each of a land development partnership. Carol owns a piece of land purchased six years ago for $60,000 that has been declining in value. The partnership wants to buy the land for development but is only willing to pay $40,000.

74. [LO 11.3] ABCD partnership, a calendar-year partnership, has four owners: A owns a 20 percent interest; B a 25 percent interest; C a 40 percent interest; and D the remaining 15 percent interest. Some of the partners have been having difficulty working with each other; with partnership agreement, D sells his 15 percent interest to F on October 20, year 1; B sells her interest to G on January 15, year 2; and C sells his interest to H on December 1, year 1.

75. [LO 11.4] Craig is a 20 percent shareholder in an S corporation and works an average of 20 hours per week in the business. His wife, Lynn, is a full-time employee of the corporation. The corporation provides fully paid health and life insurance benefits for herself, Craig, and their children.

76. [LO 11.4] The Gemini Corporation, an S corporation, wants to expand its lines of business. To do so quickly, it acquires 85 percent of the stock of Trojan Corporation, a regular C corporation.

Develop Research Skills

77. [LO 11.3] Roberta Wynn has been a partner in the Cato Partnership for a number of years. With the permission of the other partners, she sells her partnership interest to a third party. At the time of sale, her basis in her partnership is only $100. For the portion of the year to the date of sale, she is allocated a partnership loss of $2,100. If she receives $10,000 for her partnership interest, what are the tax consequences of the sale and the results of partnership operations in her final year?

78. [LO 11.3 & 11.4] Locate a recent appellate court case that has reversed a Tax Court decision regarding a partnership or S corporation tax issue.

a. Summarize the facts, issues, and conclusions of the case.

b. Explain why the appellate court reversed the Tax Court.

c. Explain the impact this decision has on tax planning for clients.

79. [LO 11.3 & 11.4] The partners of JPG Partnership want to change the form of entity from a partnership to a corporation. The corporation can be formed in several ways: The partnership can distribute the assets to the partners who then contribute the assets to the corporation. The partnership can transfer the assets directly to the corporation. The partners can transfer their partnership interests to the corporation. Write a memo outlining the tax effects of the various methods of forming the corporation.

Fill-in the Forms

80. [LO 11.2] Go to the IRS website (*www.irs.gov*) and print out copies of Schedule C for Form 1040, Schedule SE, and the first page of Form 1040 for 2017. Using the information in problem 25, complete these schedules and forms to the extent possible from the information given.

81. [LO 11.3 & 11.4] Refer to the information in problems 29 and 50.

a. Go to the IRS website (*www.irs.gov*) and print out the first page and Schedule K for Form 1065. Use the information in problem 29 to complete these two forms to the extent possible with the information given.

b. Go the IRS website (*www.irs.gov*) and print out the first page and Schedule K for Form 1120S. Use the information in problems 29 and 50 to complete these two forms to the extent possible with the information given.

82. [LO 11.4] The operating results for Peep Corporation, an S corporation, for last year were as follows:

Revenues	
Gross sales	$2,000,000
Tax-exempt bond interest	2,000
Dividend income	8,000
Section 1231 gain (land)	10,000
Expenses	
Cost of goods sold	$900,000
Salaries	600,000
Rent	200,000
Utilities	60,000
Depreciation	40,000
Charitable contribution	12,000
Section 179 expense	20,000

a. Determine the corporation's net income and its separately stated items.

b. Determine the corporation's financial accounting income if the gain on the sale of the land is only $6,000 and depreciation is $32,000 under financial accounting rules.

c. Complete a Schedule M-1 of Form 1120S for the corporation. You can obtain forms from the IRS website (*www.irs.gov*).

83. Partnership Tax Return. The Rite-Way Plumbing Company began business March 1, 2014 in Sarasota. Its business address is 124 Division Lane, Sarasota, FL 33645. Its employer identification number is 69-3456789. Its principal business activity is residential plumbing repairs and maintenance; its business code is 238220. It files its income tax returns on the calendar-year basis.

The business was formed as a limited partnership by two brothers, John Henry (SSN 555-55-5555) and James Henry (SSN 666-66-6666), who work full-time in the business, and their father Tom Henry (SSN 888-88-8888), the limited partner. The brothers each have a 25 percent interest in the income, loss, and capital of the business while their father owns a 50 percent interest in income, loss, and capital, but takes no active interest in the business other than as that of an investor.

At the end of 2017, its operations showed cash gross receipts of $1,240,000 and the following cash expenditure items:

Salaries and wages (excluding John and James)	$378,000
Repairs and maintenance	2,000
Rent	28,000
Taxes and licenses	38,000
Advertising	3,000
Pension plans (excluding John and James)	15,000
Health/dental insurance	16,000
Material purchases	220,000
Truck expense	45,000
Insurance (excluding health/dental)	65,000
Legal/professional fees	3,000
Office expenses	6,000
Utilities/telephone	8,000
Business meals	4,000
Draw—John	75,000
Draw—James	60,000
Total cash expenditures	$966,000

John and James each receive a guaranteed payment of $75,000 in addition to the payment of their health and dental insurance premiums, which are $3,000 each for the current year (included in the $16,000 total for health/dental insurance). The other insurance payments include the $1,500 premiums for each of the $200,000 term life insurance policies on John and James that name the partnership as beneficiary.

Although the company maintains a certain level of plumbing supplies for its business, inventory is not a material income producing factor; thus, material purchases are expensed. The partnership uses the cash method of accounting for revenue and expenses.

The company purchased the following items for use solely in the business during the current year: a new truck (weighing over 6,000 pounds) that cost $21,250 (June 21); a new computer system costing $3,200 (August 17); additional new office furniture costing $2,500 (September 4).

At the beginning of 2017, the company owned the following items that were all purchased the month the company began business. In that year, the company claimed only basic MACRS depreciation (that is, it elected no bonus depreciation or Section 179 expensing if available) for any of its trucks, equipment, or furniture purchases:

Asset	Cost basis
Trucks	$78,000
Plumbing equipment (7-year property)	23,000
Office furniture	16,000
Computer system	4,000

On March 12, it sold one of its old trucks for $6,000 that had cost $17,000 originally. It also was able to sell its old computer system on September 12 for $250. It donated two pieces of its old office furniture to Goodwill Industries. This furniture had cost $1,500 and had a current value of $600.

Prepare the first 4 pages of Form 1065 for the Rite-Way Plumbing Company along with the Schedule K-1s for each of the three partners, Form 4562, and Form 4797. The partnership wants to maximize its cost recovery deduction by electing Section 179 this year. Use the 2017 tax forms available from the IRS website at *www.irs.gov*.

84. **S Corporation Tax Return.** John Forsythe (SSN 555-55-5555) began a custom cabinet manufacturing business, John's Cabinets (EIN 86-1122334 and Business Code 321000), July 1, 2013. John incorporated the business, and the corporation made a timely election to be taxed as an S corporation. The business has been highly successful, but to bring in additional capital for expansion, it sold 10,000 shares of previously unissued stock to John's friend, Tom Jones (SSN 666-66-6666), on March 1, 2017 for $80,000. John continues to hold his original 15,000 shares that were issued at incorporation for his contribution of money and property valued at $120,000.

The business used the additional capital to purchase $20,000 of new woodworking machines (7-year property) on September 15 and $60,000 as a down payment on the purchase of a new building for its manufacturing and office operations located at 7620 N. Commerce Place, Beavercreek, OH 45440. The business claimed only the basic MACRS depreciation deductions for these acquisitions. The total cost of the building was $320,000 and the S corporation began using it on October 1.

In the month the business began, the S corporation purchased $60,000 of used woodworking machinery. It elected to use ADS for cost recovery on the 7-year property to reduce any potential losses in the first years of the business. On September 15, 2017, the business sold one of the old machines that had cost $10,000 originally for $5,000. When moving to the new building, a second machine that had cost $5,000 originally fell off the truck used to move it and was a total loss. The loss was not covered by insurance.

John works full-time in the business and takes a salary of $9,000 per month. Wages for his seven employees for the year were $220,000. (None of those employees made less than $7,000 or more than the FICA maximum.)

Additional data for the completion of the S corporation tax return are

Sales revenue	$850,000
Sales returns	12,000
Purchases	335,000
Rent	36,000
Repairs	4,000
Insurance*	21,000
Truck rental	3,000
Taxes and licenses**	14,000
Advertising	2,000
Interest expense	4,000
Charitable contribution	10,000
Business meals	1,000
Fines for improper permitting	2,000
Beginning inventory (at cost)	25,000
Ending inventory (at cost)	30,000

*Includes $500 for John's group term life insurance of $200,000 and $3,000 for medical and dental insurance premiums for him and his family. The balance is for insurance for other employees.
**Excludes FICA and FUTA taxes for John and the other employees. The FUTA rate is 6 percent.

For its books prepared for banks and other creditors, the company shows $2,000 as an addition to its allowance for bad debt for the current year, depreciation of $8,200, a gain on the sale of the machine of $1,500, and a loss of $2,500 on the destruction of the machine.

The corporation is a calendar-year S corporation and uses the hybrid method of accounting, recording all but its sales and cost of goods sold on the cash method of accounting. It has a balance of $35,700 in it accumulated adjustments account at the beginning of the year.

John's home address is 100 Main Street, Kettering, OH 45435 and Tom's home address is 222 Williams Street, Fairborn, OH 45422.

Prepare Form 1120S for this corporation, excluding Schedule L. Complete the schedule K-1s for John and Tom as well as any other required forms. Assume that the Section 263A rules do not apply and that you do not have to apportion any other costs to inventory. Use the 2017 tax forms available from the IRS website at *www.irs.gov*.

ANSWERS TO TEST YOURSELF

1. **b. $22,300.** The Section 1231 gain and the charitable contributions are reported separately.
2. **b. $22,300.** The Section 1231 gain and the charitable contributions are reported separately.
3. **c. $47,900.** $26,000 beginning basis + $18,000 net income + $600 tax-exempt income – $1,200 capital loss + $4,500 share of liability. Guaranteed payments reduce ordinary income.
4. **a. $140,100.** $84,000 beginning basis + $30,000 guaranteed payment + $42,000 net income + $1,400 tax-exempt income – $2,800 capital loss + $10,500 share of liability – $25,000 cash withdrawal.
5. **a. $43,400.** $26,000 beginning basis + $18,000 net income + $600 tax-exempt income – $1,200 capital loss.

Wealth Taxation

PART VI

CHAPTER 12 Estates, Gifts, and Trusts

CHAPTER OUTLINE

LEARNING OBJECTIVES

After completing this chapter, you should be able to:

12.1 Explain the important features of the unified gift and estate (wealth) transfer taxes, explain their basic provisions, and understand why the estate tax is often referred to as the final application of the gift tax.

12.2 Understand the gift tax provisions that differentiate non-taxable gifts from taxable gifts; determine the amount subject to the gift tax.

12.3 Explain the tax implications for a donee who receives a gift; understand the application of the kiddie tax on the incomes of children subject to the tax; explain the tax benefits of education savings plans.

12.4 Determine a taxpayer's gross estate and allowable estate deductions; identify any transfers potentially subject to the generation-skipping transfer tax.

12.5 Evaluate the advantages and disadvantages of lifetime gifts versus testamentary transfers.

12.6 Understand the special issues that affect the preparation of a decedent's final tax return; determine the taxes owing on the taxable income of estates and trusts.

12.7 Compute a donor's gift taxes owing on gifted property; calculate the estate tax on a decedent's taxable estate considering prior gifts subject to taxes; calculate the fiduciary income tax on an estate or a trust.

The federal transfer tax system consists of the gift tax, the estate tax, and a third lesser-known tax called the generation-skipping transfer tax. Transfer taxes are assessed on the transferor of the property. The recipient receives the property free of taxes.

A number of provisions exclude all or a portion of gifts and inheritances from transfer taxation. They include the annual gift exclusion (currently $15,000 per donee), a lifetime exclusion (currently $11.18 million), the charitable contribution deduction, and the unlimited marital deduction. By the wise use of these exclusions, most individuals can transfer their wealth without paying transfer taxes.

One of the major dilemmas facing very wealthy individuals is whether to make lifetime gifts or hold property until their death. Making lifetime gifts removes both income and subsequent appreciation on the transferred assets from the donor's estate and transfers income taxation to the donee. When heirs receive appreciated assets as testamentary transfers, however, the transferred assets normally take fair market values as bases. They will recognize less gain and pay reduced income taxes on any future dispositions. The inclusion of these assets in the taxable estate increases estate taxes, however. Family tax planning involves finding the best solution to this dilemma that both minimizes taxes and meets other family objectives. Through proper planning, both wealth transfer taxes and income taxes can be minimized.

Through the use of trusts, a grantor can transfer the use of an asset to another individual without transferring actual property ownership. Care must be taken in establishing a trust if one of the objectives is to transfer the taxation of trust property income to the trust beneficiaries. Transfers in trust and other transfers to minors and certain adult children need special consideration to avoid having the child's income taxed at the trust's income tax rates.

Trusts and estates are taxable persons, referred to as *fiduciaries*. The income taxation of trusts and estates has many similarities to individual taxation, but there are certain rules that apply specifically to them. These rules must be understood to comply with the requirements for filing a fiduciary income tax return.

SETTING THE STAGE—AN INTRODUCTORY CASE

Sarah, a 70-year-old widow, has a taxable estate valued at over $20 million. Sarah's son, Kevin, has two children, ages 11 and 13. Her daughter, Lisa, also has two children, ages 8 and 12. Sarah has decided that she wants to begin transferring assets to her grandchildren so she can minimize the size of her taxable estate. She specifically wants to provide for her four grandchildren's college educations. What planning opportunities can you suggest to Sarah so that she can provide for her grandchildren's education while minimizing any transfer taxes? At the end of this chapter we will return to this case.

12.1 OVERVIEW OF WEALTH TRANSFER TAXATION

Since 1916, the United States has imposed an **estate tax**, an excise tax based on the value of property transferred at the owner's death. This was enacted as a way to redistribute some of the wealth accumulated by the richest families in the nation. Without some form of transfer tax applicable to gifts during an individual's lifetime, however, individuals could avoid estate taxes by making lifetime gifts. Therefore, the **gift tax** was imposed in 1932 on donors who make lifetime gifts. The recipients of gifts or estates are not subject to income tax on these gifts or inheritances, so there is no second tax assessed on the property transferred.[1] Individuals who have accumulated substantial assets, which they wish to pass to the donees and heirs, need to develop strategies to minimize their transfer taxes and maximize their available wealth.

12.1.1 THE UNIFIED TRANSFER TAX

Prior to 1976, the federal gift tax was imposed separately from the federal estate tax. Gift tax rates were about three-fourths of the estate tax rates for the same dollar value of property transferred. By making lifetime gifts, individuals and families were able to avoid paying substantial estate transfer taxes. This removed the property and any future appreciation value (as well as any gift taxes paid) from the donor's estate. This phenomenon led Congress to enact the unified transfer tax system in 1976 that applies to cumulative transfers made since 1976. Although the gift tax is calculated separately from the estate tax, these two taxes have a significant relationship. They share the lifetime exclusion and a single progressive tax rate schedule, removing the inequity in tax rates prior to the 1976 Act. Essentially, a transfer made through the estate at death (a testamentary transfer) is viewed as a final gift.

[1] It can be argued, however, that double federal taxation is the result of the transferor paying a federal income tax when the assets were acquired and now having to pay a tax on their transfer. Minimizing this second federal tax is the objective of good transfer tax planning.

The next major change to the taxation of gifts and estates came in 2001 when a budget surplus allowed Congress to pay for provisions in the 2001 Act that included a dramatic reduction in the estate taxes over the next several years and its temporary repeal in 2010. First, the unified estate and gift tax rate of 55 percent gradually decreased to 45 percent by 2007. Second, the estate tax exclusion gradually increased from $1 million to $3.5 million in 2009 (the equivalent gift tax exclusion was left at $1 million). Third, the estate tax was to be repealed entirely in 2010 with a modified basis carryover rule and the $1 million gift tax exclusion retained.[2] Gifts would only be taxed at the top individual income tax rate (35 percent in 2010) above the $1 million exclusion. Because the reductions in the estate and gift taxes were not paid for in years beyond 2010, Congress included a sunset provision that automatically reinstated the pre-2001 estate and gift tax provisions in 2011 unless Congress could find the funds to pay for an extension or permanent repeal.[3]

Congress failed to address the repeal of the estate tax until well after the 2010 mid-term elections. They finally enacted legislation that temporarily increased the estate tax lifetime exclusion to $5 million (indexed for inflation) and reduced the maximum estate and gift tax rate to 35 percent. This effectively reinstated the estate tax for decedent's dying in 2010 retroactively. The decedent's executors, however, were given the option of following this new tax law (with the maximum 35 percent tax rate and $5 million exclusion) or electing the earlier provision that repealed the estate tax but imposed a limited basis carryover.[4] In 2012, Congress increased the maximum tax rate to 40 percent and provided a lifetime exclusion of $5.25 million in 2013 that was indexed for inflation and had increased to $5.49 million by 2017. The Tax Cuts and Jobs Act doubled the lifetime exclusion amount to $11.18 million for 2018–2025 and included indexing for inflation.

The 2018 unified rate schedule under Section 2001(c) is reproduced in Table 12.1.[5] Although the rates are progressive in nature, the $11.18 million exclusion is actually applied as a

Table 12.1 Unified Transfer Tax Rates for 2018

Amount of taxable transfer	Tax rate
Up to $10,000	18%
$10,001–$20,000	$1,800 + 20% of excess over $10,000
$20,001–$40,000	$3,800 + 22% of excess over $20,000
$40,001–$60,000	$8,200 + 24% of excess over $40,000
$60,001–$80,000	$13,000 + 26% of excess over $60,000
$80,001–$100,000	$18,200 + 28% of excess over $80,000
$100,001–$150,000	$23,800 + 30% of excess over $100,000
$150,001–$250,000	$38,800 + 32% of excess over $150,000
$250,001–$500,000	$70,800 + 34% of excess over $250,000
$500,001–$750,000	$155,800 + 37% of excess over $500,000
$750,000–$1,000,000	$248,300 + 39% of excess over $750,000
Over $1,000,000	$345,800 + 40% of the excess over $1,000,000

[2] The gift tax was retained to discourage income tax avoidance by taxpayers shifting income-producing property through gifts to family members in lower income tax brackets.

[3] The Congressional Budget Act of 1974 contains a provision that requires any tax cut not paid for by permanent spending cuts to sunset after 10 years unless 60 or more senators vote to waive this requirement. Although the tax bill passed, there was not enough support to waive the sunset rule, which effectively repealed the estate tax after January 1, 2010 and reinstated it on January 1, 2011, with a 55 percent top rate and a $1 million exclusion amount.

[4] If an estate elected the 2010 provision that repealed the estate tax, it would have had to follow modified carryover basis rules, increasing the possibility that the beneficiaries would have had to pay more income tax when they disposed of appreciated inherited property. This carryover basis rule for inherited property was similar to the carryover basis for gifts, but permitted limited basis increases and reduced taxes on subsequent sales of inherited property by adding $1.3 million of basis to certain assets and $3 million of basis could be added to assets transferred to a surviving spouse. The allocated basis increase to a piece of property could not exceed the excess of the property's fair market value over the decedent's basis. Not all property was eligible for a basis increase, however.

[5] For 2010 through 2012, the maximum estate tax rate was 35% on estates in excess of $500,000; the American Taxpayer Relief Act of 2012 increased the rate to 40% for years after 2012. Prior to passage of the 2010 Act, the cumulative nature of gift/estate taxes resulted in higher marginal tax rates applying to taxable gifts given in later years and to taxable estates.

credit (as explained later) and offsets taxes on estates of up to $11.18 million, effectively resulting in a flat tax of 40 percent on transfers in excess of $11.18 million.

Example 12.1

Phyllis gave her first *taxable* gift of $90,000 (after her *annual* exclusion) in 2018. Her tax, before consideration of her *lifetime exclusion*, is $21,000 [$18,200 + 28% ($90,000 – $80,000)]. She owes no tax, however, due to her lifetime exclusion.

12.1.2 FEATURES OF THE UNIFIED TRANSFER TAX

There are many basic features of this unified transfer tax system that distinguish it from the federal income tax system.

- The tax is assessed on the transferor rather than the recipient of the property. The giver of the gift pays the gift tax, not the recipient, and the estate pays the estate tax, not the beneficiaries or heirs. The tax base for levying both gift and estate taxes is the fair market value of property transferred.
- A single transfer tax rate schedule applies to gifts and estates. Since 2013, the maximum tax rate has been 40% for gifts and estates.
- All individuals are permitted to transfer a certain base amount of wealth by lifetime gifts and transfers at death without tax through use of the lifetime exclusion of $11.18 million.
- Although the gift tax is computed on an annual basis, it is cumulative in nature and the tax due in any year is based on the current year's taxable gifts combined with total taxable gifts from prior years. The donor, however, would not owe any tax until the lifetime exclusion is exceeded.
- The gift and estate taxes are also integrated so that all or part of a decedent's estate escapes taxation unless his or her total lifetime taxable gifts and taxable testamentary transfers exceed the lifetime exclusion.

The basic procedures for calculating the estate tax have not changed over the years; only the rates and exclusion amounts have varied. It should also be noted that many states levy a death tax on property owned by a decedent. An understanding of the federal estate tax will aid in understanding death taxes at the state level.

12.1.3 MAJOR EXCLUSIONS

Two exclusions, the annual gift tax exclusion and a lifetime gift and estate exclusion prevent most taxpayers from being subject to transfer taxes.

Annual Gift Tax Exclusion

Theoretically, gifts of any value could be subject to gift taxes, including holiday, wedding, and birthday gifts. To eliminate the reporting and administrative burden for taxpayers and the IRS with respect to small gifts, Congress enacted the Section 2503(b) annual exclusion. This section exempts the value of most gifts up to $15,000 *per donee* (gift recipient) annually from reporting and taxation regardless of the number of donees in any particular year.[6] If the value of property given to any donee in any one year does not exceed the annual exclusion, no gift tax or gift tax return is required. There is no carry over from one year to the next for any unused annual exclusion.

[6] The annual exclusion was $14,000 for 2013–2017; it was $13,000 for 2009–2012. Gifts in excess of the annual exclusion must be reported but may not be taxed due to the lifetime exclusion.

Example 12.2

David gave $15,000 to each of his ten grandchildren this year. Although David gave away a total of $150,000 this year, none of the gifts exceeded the annual exclusion for any donee. No gift tax or gift tax return is required.

Lifetime Transfer Tax Exemption—The Unified Credit

If the value of property transferred during a year exceeds the annual gift exclusion, the excess is a taxable gift. The donor still may not pay any tax on the transfer, however, as the lifetime gift and estate exclusion allows up to $11.18 million in cumulative gifts to escape taxation in 2018.[7] The $15,000 annual gift exclusion does not affect the lifetime exclusion allowance; only gifts in excess of the gift annual exclusion are considered taxable gifts and reduce the lifetime exclusion. Table 12.2 shows the exclusion amounts along with the top marginal transfer tax rates for 2001 through the current year.

Table 12.2 Gift and Estate Tax Exclusion Amounts and Top Marginal Tax Rates by Year

Year of transfer	Top marginal tax rate	Gift tax exclusion amounts	Estate tax exclusion amounts
2001	55%	$675,000	$675,000
2002	50%	$1,000,000	$1,000,000
2003	49%	$1,000,000	$1,000,000
2004	48%	$1,000,000	$1,500,000
2005	47%	$1,000,000	$1,500,000
2006	46%	$1,000,000	$2,000,000
2007 and 2008	45%	$1,000,000	$2,000,000
2009	45%	$1,000,000	$3,500,000
2010	35%	$1,000,000	$5,000,000
2011	35%	$5,000,000	$5,000,000
2012	35%	$5,120,000	$5,120,000
2013	40%	$5,250,000	$5,250,000
2014	40%	$5,340,000	$5,340,000
2015	40%	$5,430,000	$5,430,000
2016	40%	$5,450,000	$5,450,000
2017	40%	$5,490,000	$5,490,000
2018	40%	$11,180,000	$11,180,000

The gift tax is imposed on cumulative gifts; thus, gifts made in prior years increase the total subject to gift taxes in later years. Any lifetime exclusion remaining at death reduces the estate tax liability.

Example 12.3

Clarice gave a taxable gift (after subtracting her annual exclusion) of a home valued at $5 million to her son in 2014. In 2018, she gave her son taxable gifts of stocks valued at $8.15 million (after subtracting her annual exclusion). She paid no tax in 2014 because her $5.34 million lifetime gift exclusion offset the $5 million value of the house. In 2018, she has made cumulative taxable gifts of $13,150,000 and must now pay a gift tax on the $1,970,000 of gifts in excess of her $11.18 million lifetime exclusion ($13,150,000 – $11,180,000).

The taxpayer does not apply the lifetime exclusion directly to taxable gifts to determine the tax on net gifts. In practice, this lifetime exclusion is equated to a lifetime unified credit. Cumulative taxable gifts are first determined; the tax is then determined from the tax rate schedule on cumulative taxable gifts; finally, the unified credit (equal to the tax on the lifetime exclusion) is applied to the tax to determine if any gift tax is due.

[7] The credit equivalent of the $11.18 million exclusion can be determined from Table 12-1 (using the 40% maximum tax rate that applies to gifts and estates exceeding $1,000,000) as follows: $345,800 + (40% × $10,180,000) = $4,417,800.

Example 12.4

Continuing example 12.3, Clarice's tax due on her 2018 taxable gifts (using the rates in Table 12.1) is as follows:

1. Cumulative taxable gifts: $5,000,000 + $8,150,000 = $13,150,000
2. Tax on $13,150,000: $345,800 + .40($13,150,000 – $1,000,000) = $5,205,800
3. Credit equivalent of tax on $11,180,000: $345,800 + .40($11,180,000 – $1,000,000) = $4,417,800 unified credit
4. Net tax after credit applied: $5,205,800 – $4,417,800 credit = $788,000 tax liability

This is the same tax that would be determined by multiplying her $1,970,000 in gifts in excess of her lifetime exclusion by the flat 40 percent tax rate [($13,150,000 – $11,180,000) × .40] = $788,000. A similar procedure is used to determine the estate tax of a decedent that has made prior taxable gifts. Prior taxable gifts are added to the value of the taxable estate. The estate tax is determined from the tax rate schedule and the credit equivalent of the tax on $11,180,000 ($4,417,800 for 2018) is deducted from the tax due. The credit equivalents for years 2009 through 2018 are shown in Table 12.3. These credit equivalents are based on the exclusion amounts in effect in each year shown.

Table 12.3 Credit Equivalents for Exclusion Amounts

Year of transfer	Gift tax exclusion amounts	Gift tax credit equivalent	Estate tax exclusion amounts	Estate tax credit equivalent
2009	$1,000,000	$345,800	$3,500,000	$1,455,800
2010	1,000,000	330,800	5,000,000	1,730,800
2011	5,000,000	1,730,800	5,000,000	1,730,800
2012	5,120,000	1,772,800	5,120,000	1,772,800
2013	5,250,000	2,045,800	5,250,000	2,045,800
2014	5,340,000	2,081,800	5,340,000	2,081,800
2015	5,430,000	2,117,800	5,430,000	2,117,800
2016	5,450,000	2,125,800	5,450,000	2,125,800
2017	5,490,000	2,141,800	5,490,000	2,141,800
2018	11,180,000	4,417,800	11,180,000	4,417,800

Example 12.5

Assume the same facts in example 12.4, but Clarice dies in 2018 leaving a taxable estate of $8,150,000 to her son instead of a taxable gift. The tax result would be the same as in example 12.4. The estate would be liable for an estate tax of $788,000 on the cumulative taxable gifts and taxable estate of $13,150,000.

Exclusion Amount Portability

Prior to 2011, a husband and wife had separate estate tax exemptions that could be used only by that individual. The 2010 Tax Relief Act introduced the concept of portability under which the surviving spouse of a decedent could "inherit" any unused portion of the decedent's lifetime exclusion. Thus, the surviving spouse would not only have available his or her own $5 million exclusion (adjusted for inflation), but the decedent's entire unused exclusion. Only the surviving spouse, no other relative, could "inherit" this exclusion. The surviving spouse, however, could use the "inherited" exclusion to offset gift taxes currently as well as estate taxes upon death. This portability feature was made permanent in 2012.

Example 12.6

Walter died in December 2017 and his estate used only $2 million of his $5.49 million lifetime exclusion for his taxable estate. Wilma, his wife and executor of his estate, elects to add his unused $3.49 million exclusion to her lifetime exclusion. In 2018, Wilma has a $14.67 million exclusion ($3.49 million + $11.18 million assuming that she has not had any prior taxable gifts) to offset any taxes due on current gifts or her estate.

The executor of the estate must make an irrevocable election to pass the unused exclusion to the surviving spouse and show the calculations for the amount transferred. In addition, the surviving spouse can only add the unused portion of the most recently deceased spouse to his or her exclusion. The portable amount is called the **deceased spousal unused exclusion (DSUE)**.

Example 12.7

Refer to example 12.6. Wilma marries Howard three months after Walter's death. In late 2018, Howard dies, but he had used $5.4 million of his lifetime exclusion in 2016 on gifts to his children. Because Howard is the Wilma's most recently deceased spouse, she loses the $3.49 exemption carried over from Walter's estate but now has a $5.78 million DSUE ($11.18 million – $5.4 million used for gifts) from Howard's estate plus her basic $11.18 million exclusion available in 2018.

12.2 THE FEDERAL GIFT TAX

12.2.1 TRANSFERS SUBJECT TO GIFT TAXES

Only gratuitous lifetime transfers of property or property interests are subject to gift taxes. Gift taxes are meant to apply broadly, so they are levied on transfers of property whether real or personal, tangible or intangible, made directly or indirectly, or in trust.[8] Services performed for free are not a taxable gift because of the difficulty in measuring their value.

Example 12.8

John is very wealthy and often shares his good fortune with friends and family. He gave each of his children $1,000,000 in stock, put $6,000,000 in a trust fund for the care of his elderly parents, gave his Saab convertible to a friend who had admired it, and gave his devoted secretary $50,000 for unusual medical expenses. He also took three months off from running his company to head the United Way Campaign. These are all potentially taxable gifts, except for the services to the United Way Campaign.

Transfers for Insufficient Consideration

Sales, exchanges, and other dispositions can be treated as gifts if the transferor receives less than a fair market value payment for the property transferred.[9]

Example 12.9

Eileen sells land worth $180,000 to her son for $60,000. Eileen received less than a fair market value for the land; she has made a gift valued at $120,000 ($180,000 – $60,000) to her son.

[8] The gift tax applies to all gifts made by U.S. citizens or residents and to gifts of tangible property situated within the United States by a nonresident alien. Transfers made during lifetime are called intervivos transfers from Latin meaning "during the life of."

[9] Reg. §25.2512-8.

A sale, exchange, or other transfer of property made in a bona fide business transaction with no donative intent is not a gift.[10] Thus, a business forced to sell inventory items at a substantial discount does not make gifts. Normally, transactions that result from free bargaining between nonrelated parties have no gift implications.

Any item that cannot be valued in money or money's worth (such as love and affection) is excluded from the consideration in an exchange.[11] A transfer of money or property in exchange for something on which a monetary value cannot be determined avoids valuation problems by treating the money or property received as a gift.

Example 12.10

Sam promises his daughter, Sarah, $50,000 if she graduates from college with a nursing degree. When she graduates with this degree, Sam gives her the $50,000. The money is a gift because the act of graduating with the nursing degree cannot be valued in monetary terms.

Joint Property Transfers

When one party places funds into a joint bank account in his or her name and the name of one or more other persons, there is no gift because the donor can withdraw the funds and terminate the joint ownership at will. Instead, a gift is made when one of the other persons withdraws funds, ending the donor's control over the funds withdrawn.[12]

Example 12.11

George places $40,000 into a joint savings account in his and his son's names. Two years later, the son withdraws $20,000. George does not make a gift until the son withdraws the $20,000.

When an individual purchases property (such as stock and realty) with his or her own funds but titles the property (when purchased or at a later date) with one or more other individuals as joint tenants with the right of survivorship, the purchaser makes a gift equal to the value of the other individuals' interests.[13] The donor no longer controls the interests transferred to the other individuals after the transfer.

Example 12.12

Shannet purchases land for $300,000 but enters both her name and Jason's name on the title as joint tenants with right of survivorship. Shannet makes a gift to Jason of $150,000, one-half the value of the property, at the date she puts his name on the title.

Life Insurance Transfers

When an individual irrevocably assigns all rights of ownership in an insurance policy to another, the assignor makes a gift equal to the cost of a comparable policy on the date of the gift.[14] Ownership rights include the right to borrow against the policy, cash in the policy for its cash surrender value, and change the beneficiary. Paying the premium on an insurance policy that is owned by another person is also considered a gift to the policy's owner; the gift is the amount of the premium paid. Naming someone as beneficiary of a life insurance policy is not a gift because the owner of the policy can change the beneficiary at any time in the future.

[10] Ibid.
[11] Ibid.
[12] Reg. §25.2511-1(h)(4).
[13] In a joint tenancy with right of survivorship, if one owner dies, the others automatically receive the decedent's interest. A joint tenancy between husband and wife is a tenancy by entirety.
[14] Reg. §25.2511-1(h)(8).

Example 12.13

On October 12, year 1, Samuel transfers his ownership rights in a $500,000 life insurance policy on his life to his brother, Tony. Samuel makes a gift to Tony equal to the cost of a comparable policy at the date of the gift. In year 2, Samuel pays the $2,000 annual premium on the policy now owned by Tony. The premium payment is also a gift to Tony.

Transfers to a Trust

The creation of a trust may be a gift subject to a gift tax. A **trust** is a legal arrangement involving three parties:

1. **grantor**—transfers assets that become the **corpus** or principal of the trust
2. **trustee**—holds title to the assets, makes investment decisions, files tax returns, and makes distributions according to the trust document[15]
3. **beneficiary**—has the legal right to receive the income or the assets (The beneficiary's rights are defined by state law and by the trust document.)

In some situations, fewer than three persons may be involved in a trust. For example, a parent who wants to transfer assets to a minor child might use a Uniform Transfers to Minors Act (UTMA) account.[16] The grantor parent can also be the trustee and maintain control over the property.

The grantor of a trust gives the beneficiary or beneficiaries rights designed to accomplish the goals of the trust. An **income beneficiary** has the right to receive income generated by the trust assets. A beneficiary who has the right to receive the trust assets upon termination of the trust is the *remainderman*. He or she has a **remainder interest**.

A trust may be established for a specific number of years (a term certain) or until a specific event occurs. For example, the length of a trust might be established as follows:

1. for the life of the income beneficiary (a life tenant)
2. for the life of some other individual
3. until the beneficiary reaches the age of majority
4. until the beneficiary reaches some specified age or marries

Cessation of Donor's Control

A gift must be an unconditional, gratuitous transfer of property, or an interest in property. If the donor retains an interest in the transferred property or control over the use or disposition of the transferred interest, the transfer is not a gift and a gift tax is not assessed.

Example 12.14

Andy transfers property into a trust with the income payable to Sandy for 10 years but retains the right to designate who will receive the remainder interest. Andy has made a gift of the income interest only, as he still controls who will receive the remainder.

---

[15] A trustee can be an individual or a corporation, such as a bank. Many banks have trust departments that manage trust assets for a fee.

[16] Under the Uniform Transfer to Minors Act (also known as Uniform Gifts to Minors Act), parents can give assets to their children and maintain control over the income by retaining custodial authority over the property. If income from property is used to support the minor, it is taxed to the parent.

The transfer of assets into an irrevocable trust is considered a gift by the grantor. A trust is **irrevocable** when the grantor gives up all future control.[17] A trust that the grantor can rescind is a **revocable** trust and is not a gift because the grantor has not given up control of the trust property.[18] Similarly, a trust in which the grantor retains an unlimited right to change trust beneficiaries or to decide how much the beneficiaries of a trust will receive is not a completed gift. When trust income is transferred to the beneficiaries, however, the donor has made a gift of the income transferred (even if the donor retains control or the right to revoke the trust). Transferring income to the beneficiary ends the donor's control and the donor makes a gift at that time.

Example 12.15

Ken transfers property worth $200,000 into a revocable trust for the benefit of David and Mary. The transfer is not a gift. During the current year, however, David is given $18,000 and Mary is given $17,000. Ken has made gifts to David and Mary because the money they received was paid from the trust.

If a donor merely reserves the power to change the manner or timing of a donee's receipt of a property interest, a gift is made when the property is transferred because the donee will ultimately get the property interest free of the donor's control.

Example 12.16

Ray transfers property into a trust for the benefit of his son. Ray can decide whether to transfer the income to his son or to add the income to the trust principal. Ray has made a gift, as he controls only the timing of the payments.

12.2.2 TRANSFERS EXCLUDED FROM GIFT TAXES

Congress has eliminated certain types of transfers from the gift category to limit taxpayer-IRS controversies over their taxability and to recognize that certain transfers represent support of another individual rather than gifts.

Transfers of Marital Property Pursuant to a Divorce

Property transfers from one ex-spouse to the other to satisfy a support obligation or to carry out a court decree are not gifts. Property transferred to an ex-spouse pursuant to a property settlement that is not part of an enforceable court decree could be a gift, however, because agreeing to a divorce does not have a monetary value. To provide relief, Section 2516 provides that any property transferred to an ex-spouse as part of a property settlement agreement entered into within one year before or two years after a divorce is not a taxable gift.

Example 12.17

Michael and Jennifer divorced on November 5, year 1. On January 31, year 2, they entered into an agreement whereby Michael would transfer the Key Largo condo to Jennifer as a condition of the divorce. When he transfers the Key Largo condo to Jennifer, he does not make a taxable gift.

---

[17] Reg. §25.2511-2(c) indicates there is no gift if the donor can revoke the transfer or can otherwise control trust property.
[18] A grantor trust is also ignored for gift and income tax purposes, because the grantor retains the right to dispose of trust income without approval or consent of an adverse party. §§672 and 674.

Other Exclusions

Meeting support obligations is not subject to a gift tax with state law determining what constitutes the obligation for support. The payment of medical expenses and school tuition for minors is normally a support obligation under state law and not a gift. These payments could be treated as gifts if they are made for adults (even elderly parents) and no legal support obligation exists. Yet, many individuals regard these payments as a form of support. To avoid any confusion and inequity surrounding this issue, Section 2503(e) provides an unlimited exclusion for the *direct* payment of qualified medical expenses and tuition and fees of another regardless of the relationship to the donor.[19]

Example 12.18

Alisha paid $15,000 of uninsured medical expenses directly to the hospital and doctors for her Aunt Mary. She also paid $15,000 directly to the university for her grandson's tuition. Neither of these payments is a taxable gift.

Transfers of money and property to political organizations such as national, state, or local political parties for their political purposes are not considered taxable gifts.[20]

12.2.3 VALUATION OF GIFT PROPERTY

The value of a gift is its fair market value at the date of the gift.[21] Fair market value is a price that a willing buyer and willing seller would arrive at in an arm's-length agreement in which neither is under a compulsion to buy or sell and both are aware of the relevant facts.[22] Fair market value is not a distressed sale price or a wholesale value.

Example 12.19

Ken gave his nephew a Toyota Camry. It has a trade-in value of $14,000, but a dealer would normally sell the car for $16,700. The value of the gift is $16,700.

A gift of stock or securities sold on an established securities market has a fair market value equal to the mean of its high and low price on the date of the gift.

Example 12.20

Ken gave 10,000 shares of XYZ stock to Silvia on August 31 when the highest selling price for the stock was $60 per share and the lowest selling price was $50. The stock is valued at $550,000 [10,000 × (($60 + $50)/2)].

If an income interest is given to one individual and a remainder interest is given to a different individual, each gift must be allocated a specific value that in total equals the value of the property given.[23]

12.2.4 SPECIAL RULES AFFECTING THE ANNUAL GIFT TAX EXCLUSION

Certain gifts are not eligible for the annual gift tax exclusion, currently $15,000 per donee per year.

[19] The exclusion is not allowed to the extent medical expenses are reimbursed by the donee's insurance.
[20] §2501(a)(5).
[21] Reg. §25.2512-1.
[22] Reg. §20.2031-1(b).
[23] The value depends on the projected income from the property and the term or life expectancy of the income beneficiary.

Present versus Future Interests

The annual gift tax exclusion only applies to gifts of a present interest—the ability to immediately use the property or the income from it. A **present interest** is an "unrestricted right to the immediate use, possession or enjoyment of property or the income from property."[24] The exclusion is not allowed for gifts of future interests. A future interest is an interest that does not begin immediately or that restricts the use or benefits of the property. The present interest requirement often prevents a gift to a trust from qualifying for the annual gift exclusion if the trust accumulates income and defers the distribution of principal. Outright transfers and transfers of life estates (the right to the income from or enjoyment of property for the donee's life) or term certain interests (the right to income for a specified time period) are present interests. Remainder interests (interests that take effect after termination of a life estate or term-certain interest) or *reversions* (the donor retakes the property) are future interests.

Example 12.21

Darla transfers property into a trust. A life estate worth $28,000 is given to her daughter and the remainder worth $25,000 is given to her grandchildren. The annual exclusion only offsets the life estate, reducing the gift's taxable value to $13,000 ($28,000 – $15,000). The gift of the $25,000 remainder interest does not qualify for the annual gift tax exclusion because it is a gift of a future interest.

Gifts to Minors

Many donors are reluctant to give minors the immediate use of or control over gifted property or the income from it; thus, restricted gifts to minors would not be eligible for the annual exclusion because they are not gifts of present interests. To permit the exclusion, Congress enacted Section 2503(c), which allows an annual exclusion for gifts made into Section 2503(c) minor's trusts. To qualify, two conditions must be met:

1. Before the beneficiary reaches age 21, the trustee may pay the income and/or trust assets to or for the benefit of the beneficiary.
2. Any income and remaining assets must be distributed to the minor once he or she reaches age 21 or to his or her estate or beneficiaries if the minor dies before age 21.

If the trust instrument contains these provisions, the gift is not considered a gift of a future interest. This allows a trustee to accumulate income on behalf of a minor while preserving the annual exclusion. The income, however, is taxed to the trust unless it is distributed (and taxed) to the minor.

A Crummey trust also qualifies for the annual exclusion because it provides for a present interest. A **Crummey trust** is similar to a 2503(c) minor trust, except it is more flexible.[25] It gives the beneficiary a right to withdraw a specified amount from the trust (usually equal to the lesser of the annual exclusion or the amount contributed that year) that expires if not exercised. The donor typically tries to persuade the beneficiary not to exercise his or her right to withdraw current year contributions (such as by tying future contributions to the beneficiary's agreement not to withdraw current contributions). The beneficiary's limited withdrawal right (a Crummey power) causes the gift to the trust to be a gift of a present interest that can be sheltered by the annual gift exclusion. A Crummey trust does not require a distribution of assets when the beneficiary reaches age 21.

[24] Reg. §25.2503-3(b).

[25] Crummey trusts derive their name from the case (Crummey v. Comm, 397 F2d 92, 22 AFTR 2d 6023, 68-2 ¶USTC 12541) that was the first to allow an annual exclusion to apply to this type of trust.

Example 12.22

Simon funds two $500,000 irrevocable trusts and names the local bank as trustee. The first trust is for his 16-year-old son, Sam. The trustee may distribute income or principal to Sam until he reaches age 21. At age 21, all income and assets are to be distributed to Sam. If Sam dies before age 21, the trust assets are payable to whomever Sam appoints in his will or to his estate if he dies without a will. The second trust is for Sarah, Simon's 20-year-old daughter. The trustee may pay income or principal to Sarah until she reaches age 30, at which time she will receive the trust assets. By December 31 of each year Sarah may demand that the trustee pay her the lesser of $15,000 or the amount transferred to the trust that year. Sam's is a 2503(c) trust, and Sarah's is a Crummey trust. Amounts contributed annually to both trusts qualify for the annual exclusion.

TAX PLANNING

Gifts to Coverdell education savings accounts and qualified tuition programs (Section 529 plans) are also considered gifts of a present interest.[26] These plans allow parents to save for their children's education with its earnings exempt from income tax.[27] Gifts to Section 529 plans also qualify for a special election that allows a gift in excess of the annual exclusion to be spread equally over five years for purposes of the annual gift tax exclusion; thus, a lump sum of up to $75,000 can be transferred into a Section 529 account plan at one time free of gift tax consequences.[28] The election may be filed only once every five years for each donee. Any gift in excess of the sum of the annual exclusions for the five-year period is treated as a taxable gift in the year transferred.

Example 12.23

Carolyn contributes $80,000 to a Section 529 plan in year 1 for Barry, her son, as the beneficiary. Carolyn elects to spread the gift over years 1 through 5 and use her annual $15,000 gift tax exclusion each year. The $5,000 excess [$80,000 – ($15,000 × 5 years)] is a taxable gift in year 1.

As part of the Tax Increase and Prevention Act of 2014, Congress passed The Achieving a Better Life Experience (ABLE) Act that allows tax-favored savings accounts for individuals with disabilities similar to Section 529 plans. Annual contributions are limited to the gift tax exclusion (currently $15,000). Distributions from these accounts are tax free (qualified distributions) if they are for housing, transportation, education, and medical expenses. Distributions for nonqualified expenses are taxable and also subject to a 10 percent penalty.

Gift Splitting

When married persons in community property states make gifts of community property, each spouse is treated as giving only his or her one-half share of the gifted property.[29] The gift splitting provision of the gift tax equalizes the treatment of married persons in common law states with those in community property states. The election to split gifts allows married couples to elect to treat the value of any gift made by either spouse as if one-half of each gift's value is made by each spouse, allowing the use of their combined annual exclusions on gifts to each donee.[30] As a result, gift splitting allows two annual exclusions per donee to apply to gifts for which gift splitting is elected.[31]

[26] §530. Education IRAs were renamed for Senator Paul Coverdell, a leading proponent of the improvements made to education IRAs.

[27] The income tax consequences of these plans are discussed later in this chapter.

[28] §529(c)(2)(B). The gift cannot be spread over any period other than for five years.

[29] States with community property rules include Arizona, California, Idaho, Louisiana, Nevada, New Mexico, Texas, Washington, and Wisconsin.

[30] §2513. If gift splitting is elected, it applies to all gifts made by either spouse during the tax year.

[31] In the actual gift tax calculation formula, the spouse making the gift subtracts one-half of the gift from total gifts and the other spouse adds one-half of the gift to total gifts.

Example 12.24

Clem gives $30,000 to each of his 10 grandchildren for $300,000 in total gifts. If gift splitting is not elected, Clem can apply only his $15,000 annual exclusion to each $30,000 gift, leaving a $15,000 taxable gift to each donee, a potential total of $150,000 in taxable gifts. Alternatively, if he and his wife elect gift splitting, Clem and his wife are each treated as having made gifts of $15,000 (1/2 of $30,000) to each of the 10 grandchildren. Each is now allowed to use their $15,000 annual exclusion to reduce taxable gifts to $0. Thus, through the use of gift splitting and the annual exclusion, Clem and his wife can give away $300,000 (10 × $30,000) free of gift tax, rather than having $150,000 of taxable gifts.

Example 12.25

Len and Rita are married. Len gives a cash gift of $32,000 to his nephew to purchase a car. If Len does not elect gift splitting, he has made a taxable gift of $17,000 ($32,000 – $15,000 annual exclusion) to his nephew. If the couple elects to gift split, Len and Rita are each deemed to give a gift of $16,000 (1/2 of $32,000) to the nephew. Each can now take advantage of the $15,000 annual exclusion for this gift. They have $1,000 each in taxable gifts remaining ($16,000 – $15,000). As a family, Len and Rita together have total taxable gifts of $2,000. By gift splitting, the two have each removed $15,000 from transfer taxation.

TAX PLANNING

In most situations, electing gift splitting reduces the overall gift tax. Gift splitting should not be elected, however, if one spouse has used all of his or her unified credit and owes gift taxes on any current gifts as this could increase the gift tax.

12.2.5 GIFT TAX DEDUCTIONS

The Internal Revenue Code allows unlimited deductions for gifts to qualified charitable organizations and for gifts made to the taxpayer's spouse.

Charitable Deduction

To encourage gifts to charitable organizations, Section 2522 provides a deduction for transfers of property or money to a qualified charitable organization. A similar deduction is allowed to estates for charitable transfers. Qualifying charities include U.S. federal, state, and local governments and charities organized for charitable, scientific, literary, or educational purposes or to foster sports competition, foster the encouragement of art, or to prevent cruelty to children. The annual exclusion also applies to charitable gifts; as a result, the actual charitable deduction is calculated as the value of the money or property transferred less the annual exclusion.

Example 12.26

Mary transferred $18,000 of property to United Church, a qualified charity. Her charitable deduction is $2,000 ($18,000 – $15,000 annual exclusion) for gift tax purposes.

Marital Deduction

Before the marital deduction was enacted, one spouse giving part ownership in property to the other spouse (so that they jointly owned the property) would be assessed gift taxes if they lived in a common law state. Couples living in a community property state accomplished this division free of gift taxes, however. This inequity was corrected through the Section 2523 unlimited marital deduction for property transferred to one's spouse (including gifts of community property). The marital deduction is also calculated as the value of the transferred property less the annual exclusion.[32]

[32] For gifts made to noncitizen spouses, only $152,000 can be excluded for 2018 ($149,000 in 2017, $148,000 in 2016, and $147,000 in 2015).

Example 12.27

Bill gave 100 shares of IBM stock worth $25,000 to his wife. The gift tax marital deduction is $10,000 ($25,000 – $15,000 annual exclusion).

A similar unlimited marital deduction is allowed estates as well. Thus, if someone leaves his or her entire estate to the surviving spouse, no estate tax is owed.

12.3 TAX CONSEQUENCES FOR DONEES

The adjusted basis and holding period in property given as a gift carries over from the donor (gift giver) to the donee (gift recipient).[33] This carryover basis shifts unrealized appreciation from the donor to the donee. Income and appreciation on the asset is shifted to and then taxed at the donee's tax rate. Although a dependent's standard deduction is limited to $1,050 (or earned income plus $350, if greater), shifting income-producing assets to dependents can save a significant amount of taxes for the family.

Example 12.28

Larry, (25, single, and an intern at Johns Hopkins) receives stock worth $24,000 as a gift from his parents. They purchased the stock four years ago for $10,000 and elect to gift split, so there is no gift tax on the transfer. Larry's basis and holding period in the stock are $10,000 and four years, respectively, as both carry over from his parents. Later in the year, Larry receives the $1,800 dividend and then sells the stock at year-end for $25,000, and has a $15,000 long-term capital gain ($25,000 – $10,000). Larry's other income for the year is $11,000, which is $1,000 less than his $12,000 standard deduction. Larry's parents are in the 15 percent tax bracket for capital gains and the gift results in a tax savings of $2,520 on the receipt of the dividends and capital gains over the tax cost to his parents if they had not made the gift:

	Larry	Parents
Tax on dividends for Larry [($1,800 – $1,000 remaining deduction/exemption) × 0%]	$0	
Tax on dividends for parents ($1,800 × 15%)		$270
Tax on capital gain for Larry ($15,000 × 0%)	0	
Tax on capital gain for parents ($15,000 × 15%)		2,250
Total tax	$0	$2,520
Tax savings	$2,520	

Additional savings could have been achieved if Larry continued to hold the stock for several more years, collecting additional dividends taxed at his lower tax rate, before selling the stock.

TAX PLANNING

This example demonstrates why many parents want to transfer income-producing assets to their children. Transfers to young children that allow parents to manage the assets have been particularly popular, but do not offer the same level of tax benefit as gifts to adult children due to the kiddie tax. It is still advantageous for parents to transfer assets to adult children who may be self-supporting but in a tax bracket that is lower than theirs. This can significantly lower the overall family tax burden depending on the difference in applicable tax rates and the potential for additional surtaxes on higher levels of investment income.

[33] §1015. See the basis discussion in Chapter 7.

12.3.1 KIDDIE TAX

Congress limits the tax savings that can be achieved on asset transfers to children through the **kiddie tax**, which taxes the unearned income of children up to age 24 using the tax rates for trusts and estates. Prior to 2008, the kiddie tax applied only to children under age 18. With the reduction in dividend and capital gains rates for low-income taxpayers to zero percent, the age at which these provisions apply was raised to children under 19 or, if a full-time student, under age 24.[34] This special tax can apply to net unearned income exceeding $2,100 if the child is under age 19 (or 24 if a full-time student) at year-end.[35] Unearned income includes taxable interest, dividends, and net capital gains on property owned directly by the child, as well as income received as a beneficiary of a trust.[36] The child's earned income (wages, tips, and salaries) and the first $2,100 of unearned income are subject to normal income tax rules. The kiddie tax does not apply to children whose net unearned income is $2,100 or less. This allows a child to earn a small amount of unearned income on wages that were saved or invested.

The tax calculation is a four-step process:

1. Determine the child's taxable income; if the child is a dependent, the child's standard deduction is limited to the greater of $1,050 or earned income plus $350 (but no more than the regular standard deduction).
2. Calculate the tax on the child's net unearned income in excess of $2,100 at the tax rates for trusts and estates.[37] Table 12.4 includes these rates.
3. The child's remaining taxable income is taxed at the child's normal tax rates (for a single individual).
4. Add the taxes determined in (2) and (3) to determine the child's gross income tax liability.[38]

Table 12.4 Tax Rates for Kiddie Tax

Income Tax Rates for Trusts and Estates and Kiddie Tax	
If taxable income is:	***The tax is:***
Not over $2,550	10% of taxable income
Over $2,550 but not over $9,150	$255.00 plus 24% of the excess over $2,550
Over $9,150 but not over $12,500	$1,839.00 plus 35% of the excess over $9,150
Over $12,500	$3,011.50 plus 37% of the excess over $12,500
Tax Rates for Long-term Capital Gains and Dividend Income	
If taxable income is:	***The tax rate is:***
Not over $2,600	0%
Over $2,600 but not over $12,700	15%
Over $12,700	20%

[34] §1(g).
[35] This $2,100 consists of $1,050 offset by the child's standard deduction and $1,050 taxed at the child's regular tax rates; only $1,050 of taxable unearned income is taxed at the child's rates.
[36] The source of the assets is not important. Income from assets transferred from anyone can be taxed at the trust rates.
[37] Prior to 2018, the marginal tax rate of the parents was used instead of the rates for trusts and estates. Parents calculated this tax by adding the child's net unearned income to their taxable income and determining the hypothetical increase in their tax. In certain situations, the parents could elect to include the child's unearned income in their own tax return by filing Form 8814: Parents' Election to Report Child's Interest and Dividends.
[38] The kiddie tax is calculated on Form 8615. The tax is included on page 2 of Form 1040.

Example 12.29

Mary, age 13, has $5,100 interest income from a trust established by her grandparents, her only source of income for the year. She has no itemized deductions. Mary's net unearned income is $3,000, her interest income that exceeds $2,100. Her taxable income is $4,050 ($5,100 – $1,050 standard deduction). Mary's tax on her unearned income at the tax rates for estates and trusts is $363 ($255 + [($3,000 – $2,550) × 24%]). Her remaining $1,050 income ($4,050 taxable income – $3,000 taxed at the rates for estates and trusts) is taxed at 10 percent (her regular tax rate) resulting in a tax of $105 ($1,050 × 10%). The total tax owed is $468 ($363 + $105).

The kiddie tax does not apply to a child age 19 or older, unless that child is a full-time student; it will not apply to *any* child age 24 or older regardless of student status. Age is determined at the end of the year under current law.

Example 12.30

Assume the facts in the preceding example, except that Mary is 24 years old and is no longer subject to the kiddie tax. As a dependent of her parents, her standard deduction is limited to $1,050. Although her taxable income remains $4,050, it is all taxed at 10 percent. Her tax is $405 ($4,050 × 10%).

Example 12.31

Justin, age 17, has $6,800 interest income from a trust. Justin also earned $5,800 working at a part-time job. He is a dependent of his parents. Justin's net unearned income is $4,700, his interest income exceeding $2,100. His standard deduction is $6,150 ($5,800 earned income + $350) and his taxable income is $6,450 ($6,800 + $5,800 – $6,150 standard deduction). Justin's tax on his unearned income taxed at tax rate for estates and trusts is $771 ([$255 + ($4,700 – $2,550) × 24%]). His remaining $1,750 income ($6,450 taxable income – $4,700 taxed at the rates for estates and trusts) is taxed at his 10 percent regular tax rate resulting in a tax of $175 ($1,750 × 10%). The total tax owed is $946 ($771 + $175).

If Justin instead had been age 24, his tax would have been only $645 ($6,450 × 10%).

TAX PLANNING

Families can minimize the impact of the kiddie tax by transferring assets that defer income until the child is age 19 (or 24 for students). For example, taxable income from U.S. government series EE savings bonds can be deferred until they are redeemed. Transferring growth company stock that pays little or no dividends or land expected to appreciate facilitates deferring capital gains until the child reaches the age at which the kiddie tax no longer applies.

12.3.2 SPECIAL EDUCATION SAVINGS PLANS

Parents, whose children are subject to the kiddie tax, may wish to consider two special vehicles to save for their children's education.

- Section 529 qualified tuition programs
- Coverdell education savings accounts (previously known as education IRAs)

Under either plan, income on the funds contributed accumulates tax free. In addition, all distributions from these plans used to pay for a beneficiary's qualified education expenses are never subject to income tax.[39] There is no annual limit on contributions to Section 529 plans.[40] The maximum contribution is $2,000 per year, per child to a Coverdell education savings account.

Another advantage of Section 529 plans is the ability to change the beneficiary.[41] If, for example, a grandchild does not use the entire balance in the Section 529 account for his or her education, the grandparent can change the beneficiary to another grandchild or a great grandchild with no adverse tax consequences as the donor is considered the owner of the plan. Whether the donor can change the beneficiary for a Coverdell account depends on the terms of that particular account.

If distributions are made to the beneficiary for other than qualified education expenses, the investment income is taxed to the beneficiary at the beneficiary's income tax rate and subject to an additional 10 percent penalty tax; distributions in excess of investment income are treated as gifts. Distributions to contributors (e.g., parents or grandparents) in excess of their contributions are included in their income and are also subject to an additional 10 percent penalty tax.

TAX PLANNING

These education accounts may be preferable to a UTMA account because, in addition to kiddie tax issues, the assets from a UTMA account may not be used to pay for college expenses in some states. Moreover, the donor to a Section 529 plan can redirect funds to another beneficiary or cash out the account, pay the income tax (and an additional 10 percent penalty tax), and use the remainder as the donor chooses.

12.4 THE TAXABLE ESTATE

An **estate** is the entity created upon the death of an individual to own and manage the property of the **decedent** (the person who died) until ownership of the property is transferred to the decedent's beneficiaries or heirs.[42] Estate taxes are levied on the value of all property owned by a decedent and transferred to heirs or beneficiaries at the decedent's death.[43] The estate pays the estate taxes. There are three basic steps to compute the decedent's taxable estate:

1. Identify and value the assets included in the gross estate.
2. Identify the deductible claims against the gross estate and deductible expenses of estate administration.
3. Identify any deductible bequests.

[39] Under Section 529 plans, qualified higher education expenses include tuition, fees, books, supplies, and computer equipment at eligible institutions (limited room and board costs may also qualify). Beginning in 2018, Section 529 plans can also be used for tuition at elementary or secondary school. Coverdell funds can also be used for qualified elementary and secondary school expenses.

[40] Contributions are limited to the cost of four years of college at the most expensive institution in some states. If the annual aggregate contributions to a 529 plan exceed the $15,000 gift tax exclusion, electively, the contribution can be taken ratably over a five-year period starting with the year of the contribution. Any excess would be treated as a taxable gift in the year of the actual contribution. §529(c)(3)(B).

[41] §529(c)(3)(C). After 2017, tax-free rollovers can also be made from a 529 plan to an Achieving a Better Life Experience (ABLE) account for the same beneficiary or the beneficiary's family. This is particularly beneficial when the 529 plan beneficiary no longer needs the amounts in the 529 account to pay for qualified education expenses and either the beneficiary or a member of the beneficiary's family is disabled or blind.

[42] Beneficiaries refer to persons named in a will; heirs refer to beneficiaries of property of a decedent who dies intestate (without a will).

[43] The estate tax applies to decedents who were U.S. citizens or residents at death. Nonresident aliens may be taxed on the value of property located in the United States. §2511(a).

12.4.1 IDENTIFYING THE GROSS ESTATE

The **gross estate** includes all property and property interests of the decedent,[44] similar to the all-inclusive definition of gross income contained in Section 61, which states that all income is included in taxable income unless it is specifically excluded.

Probate is the state law process by which a will is declared legally valid and governs the transfer of property by will to the beneficiaries. The probate estate only includes the property governed by the will or by the state's intestacy laws if there is no valid will. It does not include property transferred by operation of law, such as property held in joint tenancy with right of survivorship. The gross estate includes all the decedent's property whether transferred by will and by operation of law. Thus, the decedent's gross estate is usually larger than the decedent's probate estate.

Example 12.32

Gillian owns a car and a bank account in her own name. Her only other asset is a house she owns with her husband as joint tenants with right of survivorship. Upon her death, her gross estate includes the car, the bank account, and half the house. Her probate estate includes only the car and the bank account. The house passes outside of probate directly to her husband, the surviving joint tenant.

TAX PLANNING

One strategy for avoiding probate costs is to use a living trust that holds title to all an individual's assets.[45] The trust document specifies how these assets are transferred when the individual dies. The taxpayer's will only governs the treatment of any assets not included in the trust. Unlike a will, a living trust is not a public document open for inspection. Thus, a living trust has the dual advantages of removing assets from the probate estate and maintaining privacy for the decedent's heirs. Placing property in a living trust does not exclude it from the decedent's gross estate, however.

The estate tax is not a tax on the property owned by the decedent but a tax on the *transfer* of property due to the decedent's death. Thus, the gross estate may include some items not actually owned by the decedent at death. Taxpayers may have given some property away while living, but continued to benefit from or enjoy the property. Such gifts with *strings attached* may have been complete for gift tax purposes but are still included in the gross estate because the transfer did not actually take place until the donor's death. If the decedent retained the right to income from or the right to designate who may possess or enjoy property, the value of the property transferred during life is included in the gross estate.

Example 12.33

Jason transfers a rental apartment building to his daughter, Sarah, but retains the right to collect all the rental income from the building for life (a life estate). When Jason dies, the value of the building is included in his gross estate because he retained an interest in the property.

If prior to death the decedent possessed the right to alter, amend, revoke, or terminate the terms of the transfer, the value of property transferred during life is also included in the gross estate.

[44] §§ 2031, 2033, and 2034.

[45] As the grantor is usually the trustee, the trust is ignored for income tax purposes.

Example 12.34

Robert creates a trust with his local bank as trustee. Robert's four children are to receive the income for their lives. Robert's grandson is to receive a remainder interest upon the death of the children. Robert reserves the right to designate annually the portion of income to be paid to each income beneficiary. Upon Robert's death, the value of the trust assets is included in his gross estate because he kept control over the income flow. If he had *cut the strings* and surrendered his right to designate the income to be paid each year, the property would not be included in his gross estate.

An important part of estate planning involves ensuring that the estate has sufficient funds to pay the estate tax liability. Otherwise, the estate may be forced to sell assets to pay the tax. Life insurance is one of the simplest means to ensure estate liquidity. Life insurance proceeds (which do not come into existence until the decedent's death) are included in the gross estate if (1) the decedent's estate is the beneficiary or (2) the decedent possessed any incidents of ownership at his or her death.[46] Incidents of ownership include the power to change the beneficiary, surrender or cancel the policy, assign the policy, revoke an assignment, pledge the policy for a loan, or obtain a loan from the insurer against the surrender value of the policy. Payment of premiums is not an incident of ownership. If the decedent retains any incidents of ownership or the estate is the beneficiary of the policy, the policy is included in the taxable estate and up to 40 percent of the life insurance proceeds may be wasted on additional taxes.

Example 12.35

James purchased a $2 million life insurance policy on his own life five years ago and named his daughter, Rebecca, as the sole beneficiary. He retained the right to change the beneficiary and to cancel the policy. When James dies, the insurance proceeds are included in his gross estate because he retained incidents of ownership. If James's estate is large enough to be taxed at the 40% flat rate for 2018, the estate will pay an additional $800,000 ($2,000,000 × 40%) in estate taxes from the inclusion of the insurance policy.

TAX PLANNING

If James transferred ownership of the policy to his daughter when it was obtained (retaining no incidents of ownership), the proceeds would not have been included in his estate. James could have made annual cash gifts to Rebecca with which she could pay the policy premiums.

Before the estate and gift taxes were unified, gifts made within three years of a decedent's death, commonly referred to as deathbed gifts, automatically were included in the decedent's gross estate unless it could be shown the gifts were not made in contemplation of death. This rule prevented a decedent from circumventing the then higher estate tax rates by transferring assets as gifts shortly before death. Although gifts within three years of death are no longer automatically pulled back into the estate, a limited version of this provision remains. Any gift tax paid on gifts made within three years of death, and certain property interests transferred within three years of death that would have been included in the gross estate had the gift not occurred, are brought back into the estate.[47] Under these rules, the value of an insurance policy must be included in the gross estate if a decedent gives the policy away within three years of death, as if the transfer had not occurred.

[46] Insurance is deemed payable to the estate if proceeds are required to be used for the payment of the insured's debts.

[47] If a decedent relinquishes the right or control that causes a gift to be included within the estate (§2036 transfers with a retained life estate, §2037 transfers taking effect at death, or §2038 revocable transfers), exercises a general power of appointment (§2041), or gives away an insurance policy (§2042) within three years of death, the property will be brought back into the estate under §2035.

Example 12.36

Two years before his death, Alex gave a whole life insurance policy on his life to his son, Mike. When gifted, the policy had a cash surrender value of $120,000. Upon Alex's death, the policy paid Mike the face amount of $800,000. Alex's gross estate includes the $800,000 value of the insurance policy because it was given away within three years of his death.[48]

12.4.2 VALUATION ISSUES

Normally, the value of the gross estate includes the value of all property, real or personal, tangible or intangible, regardless of location, as of the date of death.[49] Section 2032 allows an **alternative valuation date** of six months after the decedent's date of death. The executor can make this irrevocable election on the estate tax return only if the gross estate and estate tax are both reduced by using this alternate date. If the alternate valuation date is elected, it must be applied to all estate assets. Assets sold prior to the valuation date, are valued at their date of sale.[50] The legislative intent of the alternate valuation date is to protect estates against sudden declines in value.

Example 12.37

When Godfrey died, his assets were valued as follows:

Asset	Date of death valuation	Alternate valuation date
Stocks	$1,100,000	$1,000,000
Bonds	3,000,000	3,100,000
Home	4,000,000	3,800,000
Total	$8,100,000	$7,900,000

If the executor elects the alternate valuation date, all assets are valued as of six months after death. Because the value of the gross estate at the alternate valuation date is $200,000 less than the date of death valuation and the estate taxes will be reduced, the alternative valuation date may be elected.

Three methods of valuation are commonly used: market price, actuarial valuations, and capitalization of earnings. The market price method is used for such items as stocks, bonds, and real estate. Stocks traded on a stock exchange are valued at the average of their high and low selling prices as of the valuation date. Actuarial valuation must be used for annuities, life estates, terms certain, and remainder interests in property. Capitalization of earnings is appropriate when valuing going businesses, particularly those that are closely held.

Example 12.38

At the time of his death, Ken owned 1,000 shares of XYZ stock and a three-bedroom house. On the date of death, the highest selling price for the stock was $60 per share, and the lowest selling price was $50. The stock is valued at $55,000 [1,000 × (($60 + $50)/2)]. The house was appraised at $350,000 on the valuation date. Ken's gross estate is valued at $405,000 ($55,000 + $350,000).

[48] Any gift tax paid would also be included in the gross estate, but the $120,000 value of the policy when gifted would be excluded in the determination of total taxable transfers.

[49] Sec. 2031(a).

[50] If property is distributed to heirs prior to the alternate valuation date, the fair market value on the date of distribution is used.

12.4.3 ESTATE DEDUCTIONS

The gross estate is reduced by outstanding debts of the decedent, the decedent's funeral expenses, and any administrative costs of settling the estate. Casualty and theft losses incurred during the administration of the estate are also deducted for estate tax purposes as well as any state death taxes. The taxable estate is reduced by bequests to charitable organizations and by the property transferred to the decedent's surviving spouse.[51] The unlimited marital deduction allows the estate tax on the wealth accumulated by a married couple to be deferred until both spouses are deceased. The taxable estate is the amount remaining after all deductions are taken.

TAX PLANNING

To maximize the benefits of the marital deduction and the lifetime exclusion, a decedent's will should specify that taxable bequests should be limited to the portion of the $11.18 million lifetime exclusion remaining after prior taxable gifts. The remaining assets can be left tax free to the surviving spouse and the estate can avoid paying any estate taxes.

Example 12.39

Mr. Moneybags died in 2018 and was survived by his wife and their only child, Cherie. Mr. Moneybags made no lifetime gifts that exceeded the annual gift tax exclusion and had used none of his unified credit. Mr. Moneybags's will contained two specific bequests: the Lowe Art Museum received a charitable bequest of his art collection, and Cherie received marketable securities with a value equal to Mr. Moneybags's lifetime transfer tax exclusion of $11,180,000. The remainder of his estate went to Mrs. Moneybags. No transfer tax is owed by Mr. Moneybags's estate.

If the decedent's spouse and children do not have compatible interests (for example, the decedent's children are from a prior marriage), the decedent may be reluctant to maximize the marital deduction. In this case, the decedent can leave the property in trust with all income to be distributed to the surviving spouse for the rest of his or her life with the remainder interest transferred to the decedent's children upon the spouse's death. This type of trust, known as a **qualified terminal interest property (QTIP)** trust, allows the decedent to exclude the value of the property transferred in trust from his or her estate, while still guaranteeing the eventual transfer of property to the designated beneficiaries.[52]

12.4.4 GENERATION-SKIPPING TRANSFER TAXES

The generation-skipping transfer tax, the final transfer tax, is discussed briefly here. Before 1986, many wealthy taxpayers avoided transfer taxes by using generation-skipping trusts. These trusts were set up so that only a life estate was left to each successive generation. When the life estate holder died, the life estate ended and none of the trust's value was included in the decedent's gross estate. The complex generation-skipping transfer tax (GSTT) eliminates this tax benefit by applying a separate flat tax at 40 percent, the highest transfer tax rate in 2018, whenever a transfer skips a generation (whether in trust or otherwise). For example, a direct transfer from a grandparent to a grandchild is a generational skip (unless the grandchild's parent on the transferor's side of the family is deceased).

In 2010, Congress increased the GSTT exclusion to an amount equal to the estate tax exclusion (as indexed for inflation) and increased the GSTT transfer tax rate to the maximum estate tax rate. The GSST is imposed at a 40 percent flat rate on qualifying transfers in excess of $11,180,000 in 2018.[53]

[51] Property passing to a surviving spouse who is not a U.S. citizen is not eligible for the marital deduction unless the surviving spouse becomes a U.S. citizen before the estate tax return is filed. §2056(d)(4).

[52] §2056(b)(7).

[53] The GSTT exclusion amount became the exclusion amount applicable to the federal estate tax in 2004. Because a number of transfers taking place after 2009 and prior to the enactment of the 2010 Tax Relief Act had been made under the assumption that the GSTT had been repealed for 2010, Congress imposed a zero percent tax rate on GSTT transfers in 2010, effectively repealing this tax for the year.

Example 12.40

Grandfather died in 1985 with a taxable estate of $15 million, leaving $12 million to his son, Ronald, and $3 million to his grandson, Bill. This year Ronald died, he left his $12 million estate to his son, Bill. If Grandfather had left the entire $15 million to his son, and Ronald then left the $15 million estate to Bill, Ronald's taxable estate would be $15 million. By skipping Ronald and leaving $3 million directly to grandson Bill, Grandfather allowed the family to avoid estate tax at Ronald's death on this $3 million.

TAX PLANNING

The GSTT would now impose a tax on the $3 million left to the grandson—a generational "skip." This can still be avoided, however, by structuring transactions that take advantage of the GSTT exclusion along with the $15,000 annual gift exclusion.

12.5 TRANSFER TAX PLANNING

12.5.1 SELECTING THE RIGHT PROPERTY TO GIVE

Property gifts (excluding money) can provide income tax benefits, transfer tax benefits, or both. The transfer of investment property such as bonds allows a family to shift the interest income to lower-bracket family members but offers almost no transfer tax benefit due to relatively small differences between the current and future values of the transferred assets. In contrast, a gift of growth stock or appreciating land may provide potentially significant transfer tax savings but may shift little current income to the donee. By comparison, the transfer of an equity interest in a flow-through entity offers both current income tax and future transfer tax benefits. The donor can retain control by giving the donee a minority interest, a nonvoting interest, or a limited partnership interest in the business.

Example 12.41

Elizabeth and Phillip (husband and wife) are the sole shareholders of an S corporation. On January 1 of the current year, when the corporation's net worth is $3,000,000, they give 1 percent of the outstanding stock to each of the children, Harry and Diana, both of whom are married and have modest incomes. The corporation's taxable income for the year is $750,000. The gifts to Harry and Diana are each worth $30,000 ($3,000,000 × 1%) and are offset by the annual gift tax exclusion using gift splitting. Any future appreciation in the gifted stock accrues to the children and is not subject to either gift or estate tax. Each child is taxed on $7,500 ($750,000 × 1%) of income, but at a much lower rate than the parents' rate. Elizabeth and Phillip have successfully shifted $15,000 of income to their children and removed any future appreciation on 2 percent of the stock from their estate. This process can be repeated annually, transferring corporate stock equal to the annual gift tax exclusion to the children and removing it from the parent's estate with no gift tax consequences. The S corporation can distribute sufficient cash to the children to pay the taxes on the income passed through without additional tax consequences to the children.

If the donor is concerned about an unexpected sale of the interest, a buy-sell agreement can guarantee the donor the right to buy the property back if the donee decides to dispose of the asset. The agreement should provide for repurchase at the fair market value to ensure that the original gift is not disregarded and that any income generated by the property is taxed to the donee, not shifted back to the donor.

TAX PLANNING

A gift-leaseback arrangement may be an attractive alternative if a donor wishes to continue using property after giving it away. This arrangement allows the donor to give property to a donee and then lease it back at a fair market value rent. If the donor uses the property for a legitimate business purpose, this arrangement is usually effective at shifting the property's income from the donor to the donee.[54]

Example 12.42

Howard is a dentist. Five years ago, he purchased the building in which his office is located for $400,000. He transfers ownership of the building to his son, Bryan, signing a leaseback agreement stipulating that he would pay annual rent of $40,000 for the use of the building. Assuming that $40,000 is reasonable rent, Howard can deduct the $40,000 payment from the income for his dental practice and Bryan reports the same amount as rental income. This arrangement shifts $40,000 income each year from Howard to Bryan.

12.5.2 ADVANTAGES OF MAKING LIFETIME GIFTS

Although the enactment of the unified transfer tax system reduced some of the advantages of making gifts during one's lifetime, it certainly did not eliminate them. In many cases the advantages of making lifetime gifts still outweigh the disadvantages. A discussion of some of the more common advantages and disadvantages follows.

Shielding of Post-Gift Appreciation from Estate Taxes

TAX PLANNING

Gifts subject to transfer taxes are taxed at their date of gift value. Any later appreciation in value of the gifted property is shielded from any further transfer taxation with respect to the donor. Therefore, everything else being equal, a donor with multiple properties should give away those with the highest appreciation potential during his or her lifetime.

Example 12.43

Maury gave some land near the city limits to his grandchildren many years ago when the land was worth $100,000. Maury, however, expected the city to grow and the value of the land to increase tremendously. The property is now valued at $2,000,000. Because he made a gift of the property when it was worth only $100,000, Maury shielded $1,900,000 ($2,000,000 – $100,000) from estate taxation. If he has at least $11.18 million of other property as part of his taxable estate upon his death, this action saves his estate $760,000 ($1,900,000 × 40%) in transfer taxes (ignoring present value) if he dies in 2018.

The increase in the lifetime exclusion for gifts from $5.49 million in 2017 to $11.18 million in 2018 was an unprecedented increase in this exclusion. It provides an opportunity for persons who have planned to transfer a majority of their wealth through testamentary transfers to take advantage of the increase and make lifetime gifts. This is particularly true for transfers of appreciating property that has a lower transfer value now than its potential future transfer value; thus, using less of the lifetime exclusion currently.

Property that has declined in value should neither be gifted nor held until death. Instead, this property should be sold and any allowable losses deducted for income tax purposes. When a donee or heir receives property that has declined in value, the donor's basis is limited to the fair market value on the date of the gift if sold at a loss. This prevents a donor from shifting a tax loss through a gift or bequest.

[54] Mathews, 61 TC 12 (1973) rev'd 35 AFTR 2d 75-4965 (CA-5, 1975), cert. denied 424 US 957 (1976).

Using the Annual Exclusion and Gift Splitting

A significant amount of an individual's estate can be removed by making gifts qualifying for the annual, per-donee gift tax exclusion. Gifts of $15,000 or less to each of several donees, such as children and grandchildren, repeated annually can remove thousands, if not hundreds of thousands of dollars from the transfer tax base of the donor at no tax cost. Even a terminally ill person can still make a significant reduction in his or her estate. In addition, the income from the gifted properties is shielded from transfer taxes and may even be subject to lower marginal income tax rates in the hands of the donees rather than the donor.

Example 12.44

Charles made seven annual gifts of $13,000 bonds to each of his six grandchildren over the past 7 years. As a result, he transferred $546,000 (6 × 7 × $13,000) of property free of any transfer taxes and removed a like amount from his estate. Additionally, all interest income from the bonds was transferred from Charles to the grandchildren, further reducing his estate and possibly reducing income taxes on the interest.

Through gift splitting, married couples can each take advantage of the annual exclusion on the gifts for each donee. This effectively doubles the transfer tax savings from the annual exclusion and reduces the potential tax applicable to transfers.

Example 12.45

Assume the same facts as the previous example, except that Charles made gifts of $26,000 to each of the six grandchildren but he and his wife elected to split gifts in each of the years. As a result, $1,092,000 of property has been transferred free of any transfer taxes to the grandchildren.

TAX PLANNING

Noncash assets, such as real estate, can be transferred as fractional interests over time using a series of gifts. As an alternative to transferring a fractional interest each year, the taxpayer could sell the real estate under the installment method, making the annual principal and interest installments no more than $15,000 (or $30,000 if gift splitting). The taxpayer then forgives the payments as each annual installment is due. Care must be taken when this sale approach is used so that the IRS does not recharacterize the entire transfer as a gift in the year of sale by arguing substance over form.[55]

The portability of the lifetime exclusion from a deceased spouse to the surviving spouse provides another reason to claim gift splitting on all or at least a major part of taxable gifts. Using gift splitting ensures that the amount of the unused lifetime exclusion "inherited" by the surviving spouse will be relatively equal regardless of which spouse dies first.

Nontax Advantages of Trusts

Trusts can be used for a variety of nontax reasons—to protect property from creditors or others who may bring future claims against the beneficiary (such as a doctor concerned about malpractice claims) or to shield assets of well-known individuals from public scrutiny (such as a politician placing assets in a blind trust). Trusts are commonly formed to hold property for the benefit of a minor child or an adult beneficiary who does not wish to or is unable to manage the property. Trusts are frequently used to transfer property for the benefit of multiple beneficiaries, allowing them to share the benefits of property ownership while management responsibility stays in the

[55] Rev. Rul. 77-299, 1977-2 CB 343.

hands of a single trustee. This minimizes the potential for disputes over the management or division of the trust income. Trusts can also be used to transfer interests sequentially with an income interest going to one beneficiary and a remainder interest to a different beneficiary.

12.5.3 DISADVANTAGES OF LIFETIME GIFTS

A number of disadvantages are associated with the making of lifetime gifts, however. Two of the more common disadvantages are the basis carryover and the acceleration of transfer taxes.

Carryover Basis on Gift Property

In deciding whether to make lifetime gifts of property, donors should recognize that appreciated property has a carryover basis (the donor's adjusted basis plus the applicable gift tax adjustment) if given, but will get a basis stepped up to fair market value if retained until death.

Example 12.46

Dena owns land worth $400,000. She paid $60,000 for the land several years ago. If she gives the land to her son now, the son will have an income tax basis of $60,000 plus any gift tax adjustment. If Dena keeps the property until she dies, the property will have a basis of $400,000 (assuming its value does not change) or more. By keeping the property until her death, $340,000 or more of potentially taxable gain is never recognized, resulting in substantial income tax savings to the family. Dena's gross estate and estate taxes will be higher, however, if her estate now exceeds her lifetime exclusion.

When property is expected to significantly appreciate, the potential income tax savings to the donee (due to the step-up in basis) when the transfer is made at death may be greater than the transfer tax savings from making a current gift (when the tax is assessed on its pre-appreciation value). If the donee expects to keep the property rather than sell it, however, the carryover basis may be of little importance. Thus, a current gift removes the appreciation from the estate.

Early Payment of Transfer Taxes

Any gift taxes paid as a result of making taxable gifts are a form of prepayment or early payment of the transfer taxes due on an estate. If no taxable gifts are made, transfer tax payments may be postponed for many years.

Since 2011, the lifetime exclusions have been identical for gift and estate taxes, currently $11,180,000 as detailed earlier in Table 12.3. The transfer of the decedent spouse's remaining lifetime exclusion to the surviving spouse's remaining lifetime exclusion provides additional transfer opportunities. For example, the surviving spouse could use this increase to make tax-free gifts while preserving her own $11,180,000 lifetime exclusion for her own estate.

12.6 FIDUCIARY INCOME TAX ISSUES

12.6.1 THE DECEDENT'S FINAL TAX RETURN

A federal income tax return is due for the period from the beginning of the tax year up to the date of death for the decedent. The return is due on the decedent's regular income tax due date as if death had not occurred. If the decedent used the cash method of accounting, only income actually or constructively received up to the date of death is included on the final tax return. Income earned by a cash-basis decedent but not received prior to death is called **income in respect of a decedent (IRD)**. Examples of IRD include unpaid salary, interest, dividends, retirement plan income, and unrecognized gains on installment sales.

IRD is included on the income tax return of the estate or beneficiary who is entitled to and actually receives the payment.[56] This has significant income tax consequences to the recipient of IRD and may result in an unexpected income tax liability much greater than any estate tax liability. Unlike other inherited property, there is no step-up in basis; that is, the decedent's basis carries over to the recipient (estate or beneficiary). The income recipient recognizes gain (or loss) on the difference between the amount realized and the adjusted basis of the IRD.[57] The character of the income recognized is the same as it would have been to the decedent.

Deductions in respect of a decedent (DRD) are expenses or liabilities incurred by a cash-basis decedent prior to death, which are not paid until after death (such as property taxes and state individual income taxes). The party legally required to pay these expenses (usually the estate) can deduct them.

Example 12.47

Roland died on September 18 of the current year. On October 1, his estate received a $1,000 check from Roland's former employer for the last pay period of his life. On October 15, Roland's estate received a $50,000 distribution from Roland's 401(k) plan. Both of these amounts are included as IRD taxable as ordinary income. If any deductible items were withheld from the payment, such as state income taxes, they would be deductible as DRD.

12.6.2 INCOME TAX CONSEQUENCES OF INHERITED PROPERTY

Beneficiaries use fair market value for their basis in inherited property, except for property inherited from certain decedents dying in 2010.[58] The result is a stepped-up basis for appreciated property (or a stepped-down basis for property that has depreciated).[59] Using fair market value as bases eliminates income tax gain (and loss) on property at the date of death.[60]

Example 12.48

Sam inherits land from his mother who died in early 2018. When she died, the land was worth $500,000. She purchased the land 15 years ago for $40,000. Sam's basis for the land is $500,000. If Sam sells the land for $500,000, he has no taxable gain and pays no income tax. The $460,000 appreciation is not subject to income tax; instead the $500,000 value is subject to the estate transfer tax.

Appreciated property that is inherited has a higher basis than property received as a gift. The differences in bases between appreciated property that is inherited (fair market value at date of death) and property received by gift (carryover basis from the donor) forms one of the major planning considerations to reduce the total tax burden when passing property to children or grandchildren. If property received as a gift is later sold, the donee will pay income tax on all the appreciation (while owned by both donor and donee); this, however, removes the property from the donor's estate, reducing potential estate taxes. If the property is inherited, the heir's basis is its higher fair market value, reducing taxable gain on a future sale. Potential estate taxes will be higher, however, as the asset's fair market value is included in the decedent's estate.[61]

[56] §691(a) and Reg. §1.691(a)-2.

[57] Typically, as unrecognized income, the decedent's basis in IRD is zero.

[58] §1014. Fiduciaries for decedents dying in 2010 only could elect to apply the law in effect prior to the 2010 Tax Relief Act.

[59] The only property that does not get a basis step-up is IRD, except for the property of decedents dying in 2010 for which the repealed estate provisions were elected.

[60] Or alternate valuation date, if elected by the executor.

[61] The personal representative for decedents dying in 2010 prior to the enactment of the 2010 Relief Act could elect to apply this law that repealed the estate tax in 2010 but with modified carryover basis rules that allowed limited basis increases of $1.3 million for certain assets and $3 million for assets transferred to a surviving spouse.

12.6.3 INCOME TAXATION OF TRUSTS AND ESTATES

Subchapter J of the Internal Revenue Code (Sections 641–692) contains the rules for income taxation of fiduciary entities (estates and trusts). These provisions create a modified conduit approach that taxes an estate or trust only on the income that it retains, not on income distributed to the beneficiaries. The recipient beneficiaries are taxed on any distributed income.[62] The character of all income is determined at the fiduciary level and the income retains this character when distributed to a beneficiary; for example, tax-exempt income received by the estate is tax-exempt income when distributed to the beneficiary.

TAX PLANNING

There is little incentive for a fiduciary to retain income within a trust, as the tax rate structure is highly progressive. The maximum marginal rate of 37 percent is reached at taxable income of only $12,500. The tax rate structure is deliberately designed to ensure that a fiduciary entity distributes its income to the beneficiaries. The tax rates for 2018 are shown in Table 12.5.[63] Distributing income annually usually results in lower overall taxes because the beneficiaries typically are in lower marginal tax brackets.

Table 12.5 Income Tax Rates for Trusts and Estates for 2018

Ordinary Income Tax Rates for Trusts and Estates	
If taxable income is:	***The tax is:***
Not over $2,550	10% of taxable income
Over $2,550 but not over $9,150	$255.00 plus 24% of the excess over $2,550
Over $9,150 but not over $12,500	$1,839.00 plus 35% of the excess over $9,150
Over $12,500	$3,011.50 plus 37% of the excess over $12,500
Tax Rates for Long-term Capital Gains and Dividend Income	
If taxable income is:	***The tax rate is:***
Not over $2,600	0%
Over $2,600 but not over $12,700	15%
Over $12,700	20%

The grantor must be careful in designing the trust to ensure that it is recognized for tax purposes. If the donor retains some incidents of ownership, such as a reversionary interest, the trust will be considered a **grantor trust** with the income taxed to the grantor. It is possible for only a portion of the trust to be treated as a grantor trust, with the remainder treated as a separate trust.

Example 12.49

Dorothy created a trust 10 years ago for the benefit of her children. In the current year, when the value of the trust assets is $800,000, Dorothy transfers additional rental property valued at $400,000 into the trust. Because Dorothy is concerned that she might need some income in a future year if her investments do not perform well, she retains the right to receive the income from this rental property in any year in which her gross income falls below a specified amount. The $400,000 transfer into the trust is not recognized for tax purposes. Dorothy will be taxed on the portion of the trust's income generated by the $400,000 rental property, even if the income is distributed to her children. Income from the trust's original assets continues to be taxed to the trust or the beneficiaries.

[62] An individual taxpayer reports the income that is received as the beneficiary of a trust or estate on Schedule E: *Supplemental Income and Loss* of Form 1040.

[63] If capital gains are allocated to principal, they qualify for the preferential capital gains rates available to individuals.

12.7 EXPANDED TOPICS—THE TAX CALCULATIONS

12.7.1 COMPUTING THE GIFT TAX

Section 2502 provides that the gift tax in any given year is based on the taxable gifts made in that year as well as previous taxable gifts. Thus, the gift tax is determined on a cumulative basis as follows:

	Includible gifts made during the current period
Plus	One-half of gifts made by taxpayer's spouse for which gift splitting is elected
Less	One-half of gifts made by the taxpayer for which gift splitting is elected with the spouse
Less	Annual exclusions
Less	Charitable deduction
Less	Marital deduction
Equals	Taxable gifts for the current period
Plus	Taxable gifts in previous periods
Equals	Cumulative taxable gifts

Determination of gift tax payable:

	Gift tax on cumulative taxable gifts
Less	Current period unified credit
Less	Credit for taxes paid on prior taxable transfers (based on current tax rates but prior year's unified credit)
Equals	Gift taxes payable on current period's gifts

Example 12.50

Charles made a taxable gift of $26,500,000 to his son in 2018 and he and his wife, Emma, elected to split gifts. This is the only gift made by either of them in 2018. In 2009, Charles made an adjusted taxable gift of $2,500,000 paying $660,000 [($500,000 × .45) + $780,800 – $345,800, using the tax rates and credit for 2009] in gift taxes for this gift. The net gift tax liability is $1,222,000 determined as follows:

	Includible gifts made during the current period	$26,500,000
Plus	One-half of gifts made by taxpayer's spouse for which gift splitting is elected	0
Less	One-half of gifts made by the taxpayer for which gift splitting is elected with the spouse	(13,250,000)
Less	Annual exclusions	(15,000)
Less	Charitable deduction	0
Less	Marital deduction	0
Equals	Taxable gifts for the current period	$13,235,000
Plus	Taxable gifts in previous periods	2,500,000
Equals	Cumulative taxable gifts	$15,735,000

Determination of gift tax payable:

	Gift tax on cumulative taxable gifts (1)	$6,239,800
Less	Current period unified credit (2)	(4,417,800)
Less	Credit for taxes paid on prior taxable transfers (based on current tax rates but gift year's unified credit) (3)	(600,000)
Equals	Gift taxes payable on current period's gifts (4)	$1,222,000

1. [($14,735,000 × .40) + $345,800] = $6,239,800
2. [($10,180,000 × .40) + $345,800] = $4,417,800
3. Tax on prior gifts using 2018 rates and 2009 unified credit: [($1,500,000 × .40) + $345,800 – $345,800 unified credit for 2009 = $600,000]
4. This is the same as a 40% tax on total gifts in excess of $11,180,000 ($4,555,000 × .40 = $1,822,000) less credit at current rates for prior gift taxes ($600,000).

The federal gift tax return, Form 709: *United States Gift (and Generation-Skipping Transfer) Tax Return*, must be filed for a calendar year in which the following types of transfers were made:

1. Transfers of present interests in excess of the $15,000 annual exclusion or transfers of future interests.
2. Transfers to charitable organizations in excess of the annual exclusion.
3. Transfers for which married couples elect gift splitting.

The return is due by April 15 of the following year with an additional six-month extension available by filing the same extension form used for the individual income tax return.[64]

12.7.2 COMPUTING THE ESTATE TAX

The taxable estate (the gross estate less allowable deductions) is added to the total amount of the decedent's adjusted taxable gifts (taxable gifts made after 1976). The transfer tax rates are then applied to the sum of the taxable estate plus adjusted taxable gifts. The tentative tax is then reduced by the current unified credit and a credit on prior taxable gifts determined using the current rate structure and the current credit available for taxable gifts. Because of the changing rates and unified credit, this can result in little or no credit for prior taxable gifts on which a tax had actually been paid. This amount is further reduced by any other credits, including the credit for death taxes imposed by a foreign government.

The tax base for the federal estate tax is defined in Section 2501 and is calculated as follows:

	Gross estate
Less	Deductible expenses, debts, taxes, and losses
Less	Charitable deduction
Less	Marital deduction
Equals	Taxable estate
Plus	Adjusted taxable gifts from previous periods
Equals	Tax base

	Gross estate tax
Less	Unified credit
Less	Credit for taxes on prior taxable gifts using current rates and current unified credit
Less	Other allowable credits
Equals	Net estate tax liability

Example 12.51

Charlene died in 2018. In 2009, she had made $2,500,000 in taxable gifts, paying $660,000 [($500,000 × .45) + $780,800 − $345,800 credit] in gift taxes for these gifts (using tax rates and credit in effect in 2009). When she died, she had a gross estate of $9,710,000. Funeral and administrative expenses were $80,000. Under her will, she directed that $100,000 be given to State College, a qualifying charity. Her will also provided the transfer of $400,000 to a QTIP trust

64 The tax must be paid by April 15 to avoid interest and penalties for late payment.

benefiting her husband, with her remaining property left to her son. The net estate tax liability is $180,000, determined as follows:

	Gross estate	$9,710,000
Less	Funeral and administrative expenses	(80,000)
Less	Charitable deduction	(100,000)
Less	Marital deduction	(400,000)
Equals	Taxable estate	$9,130,000
Plus	Adjusted taxable gifts	2,500,000
Equals	Tax base	$11,630,000
	Gross estate tax (1)	$4,597,800
Less	Unified credit	(4,417,800)
Less	Credit for prior transfers (2)	(0)
Equals	Net estate tax liability (3)	$180,000

1. [($10,630,000 × .40) + $345,800]
2. Using the 2018 (date of death) tax rates and credit amount, there will be no credit for prior transfers determined as follows: The tax on $2,500,000 = [($1,500,000 × .40) + $345,800 − $4,417,800] is less than zero, so no credit is allowed.
3. This equals a 40% tax on total transfers in excess of $11,180,000 ($450,000 × .40 = $180,000)

The estate tax return, Form 706, is due nine months after the date of the decedent's death and the tax is due with the return. An extension of up to six months to file the return can be obtained.

12.7.3 COMPUTING THE FIDUCIARY INCOME TAX

Income taxation of fiduciary entities uses a modified conduit approach that taxes the estate or trust on income it retains but taxes the beneficiaries on the income that is distributed to them.

Two types of trusts are defined for tax purposes: simple and complex. A **simple trust** must distribute all of its accounting income annually to its beneficiaries.[65] Normally, the trustee is not required to distribute capital gains, as they are usually allocated to principal and are excluded from accounting income.[66] A **complex trust** is any trust that is not a simple trust. Complex trusts are not required to distribute all their accounting income each year, allowing trust principal to accumulate. They also can make charitable contributions, taking tax deductions for doing so. Estates are taxed as complex trusts.

Fiduciary gross income is computed using rules similar to individual income taxation. For example, if the fiduciary earns tax-exempt income, the income is excluded and no deduction is allowed for expenses related to the exempt income. Deductions are allowed for expenses of producing taxable income, depreciation, administrative expenses, and charitable contributions.[67] Simple trusts are allowed a deduction of $300, complex trusts a $100 deduction, and estates a $600 deduction. Finally, taxable income is reduced by the distribution deduction.

[65] Simple trusts are not allowed to make charitable contributions.

[66] The trust document controls which items of income and expense are trust accounting income and which are allocated to trust principal. If the trust document is silent, state law controls. Most states have adopted the Uniform Principal and Income Act that allocates to principal capital gains and losses, casualty gains and losses, capital improvements, and taxes levied on items allocated to principal.

[67] Administrative expenses for an estate can be claimed on the estate's transfer tax return or its income tax return but not both. The executor can choose to allocate the expenses in whatever way is most beneficial.

Distributable net income (DNI) is the current increase in value available for distribution to income beneficiaries.[68] DNI determines the fiduciary's maximum distribution deduction and the beneficiary's maximum taxable income from the trust. Thus, if the fiduciary distributes more than the current year's taxable income (by distributing prior year's earnings), the excess distributions are not taxable to the beneficiaries. Additionally, if a distribution is made up of both taxable and tax-exempt income, the beneficiaries do not pay tax on tax-exempt income as income retains its character when distributed.

Example 12.52

Simple Trust has two equal income beneficiaries, Steven and Elisa. Simple has trust accounting income of $50,000 for the year and DNI of $48,000. Included in DNI is $12,000 of net tax-exempt income, so the trust distribution deduction is limited to $36,000 (the taxable portion of DNI). Steven and Elisa are each entitled to receive a distribution of $25,000 (50 percent of $50,000 accounting income) of which only $18,000 (50 percent of the $36,000 trust distribution deduction) is taxable. The remaining $7,000 ($25,000 – $18,000) distributed to Steven and Elisa is not taxed. Their share of tax-exempt income is $6,000, which remains tax exempt when distributed; the remaining $1,000 represents income retained and taxed to the trust in a previous year. It is not taxed a second time when distributed to the beneficiaries.

In addition to income tax, an estate or trust may also be subject to the 3.8 percent net investment income (NII) surtax (discussed in Chapter 5). The NII tax is imposed on the lesser of:

- undistributed net investment income (including interest, dividends, annuities, royalties, and capital gains) or
- the excess of adjusted gross income over the threshold of the highest tax bracket for estates and trusts ($12,500 for 2018)

The adjusted gross income for an estate or trust is computed similar to that for an individual except that deductions are only permitted for administrative costs, the standard deduction ($100, $300 or $600), and distributions of income to beneficiaries not in excess of DNI. Distributions to beneficiaries can reduce or eliminate the NII tax.

Example 12.53

A trust pays income and principal to its beneficiary, Glenda, as needed. She is single and her only other income is $45,000 from dividends. The trust's 2018 income consists of $80,000 of interest, $70,000 of dividends, and a $12,000 capital gain. If the trust makes no distributions, its net investment income is $161,700 ($80,000 + $70,000 + $12,000 – $300). If the trust distributes the $150,000 in interest and dividend income to Glenda, the trust will not be subject to the NII tax. Additionally, Glenda will not be subject to the NII tax because her investment income is below the $200,000 threshold for a single individual.

All trusts use a calendar year, eliminating any potential for deferral by adopting a trust tax year that differs from that of the beneficiaries. A trust is required to file a Form 1041: *United States Income Tax Return for Estates and Trusts* by April 15 of the following year if it has gross income of $600 or more or if it has any taxable income. Estates may use either a fiscal or a calendar year. Any estate with gross income of $600 or more is required to file a Form 1041 by the 15th day of the fourth month following the close of the estate's taxable

[68] DNI is calculated by starting with taxable income and adding back the standard deduction, subtracting capital gains and adding capital losses allocated to principal, adding tax-exempt interest, and subtracting expenses allocated to tax-exempt interest. §643.

year.[69] Beneficiaries report their share of income based on the fiduciary's year that ends within the beneficiary's tax year.

Example 12.54

In April of year 1, Samantha, (a calendar-year taxpayer) becomes a beneficiary of both a new calendar-year trust and an estate that elects a January 31 fiscal year-end. During year 1, Samantha receives income distributions of $10,000 from the trust and $15,000 from the estate. Samantha must report the $10,000 distributed in year 1 on her year-1 Form 1040 because the trust's December 31 year-end falls within her tax year. Samantha will not be taxed on the $15,000 distributed from the estate until year 2 because the distribution is not allocated to her until January 31, year 2 (the end of the estate's fiscal year).

When property is distributed to trust beneficiaries, generally no gain or loss is recognized by the trust for any difference between the asset's fair market value and its basis. The beneficiaries take the trust's adjusted basis for the asset acquired. If, however, the property is distributed to satisfy a required income distribution, the distribution deduction is limited to the lesser of the property's basis or its fair market value on the distribution date.[70] The beneficiary still uses the trust's adjusted basis for the property, however.[71]

TAX PLANNING

The trustee can elect to recognize gain on the distribution of appreciated property and may choose to do so if it is capital gain property and the trust has unused capital losses to net against the gain. If this election is made, the beneficiary's basis is the higher fair market value.[72]

REVISITING THE INTRODUCTORY CASE

Sarah can contribute up to $75,000 per grandchild to a Section 529 plan, electing to spread the gift over five years. In this manner, she can give $300,000 ($75,000 × 4 grandchildren) in the current year but cannot claim any additional annual gift exclusions for these grandchildren for five years. When her grandchildren are ready for college, at least a portion of their expenses can be paid by distributions from the Section 529 plan to realize the plans maximum tax benefits. Sarah has removed $300,000 (and the future appreciation on those assets) from her estate (even if she does not live for the full five years). She can then begin to pay tuition for each grandchild as they go to college and add additional amounts to the 529 plan for the other grandchildren not yet college age, to further reduce her estate. Additionally, the funds can be redirected to another beneficiary if the grandchildren do not need all of the funds in the Section 529 account.

Alternatively, Sarah can make $15,000 annual gifts to each of her grandchildren, either in trust or in a UTMA account. Over five years, she can make nontaxable gifts totaling $300,000 (assuming the annual exclusion remains at $15,000). Sarah may then begin paying the tuition expenses for her grandchildren as they attend college and adding to the trust accounts for those not yet in college. This allows her to transfer additional amounts tax free, but she also must live until her grandchildren are in college for them to realize the benefit.

Sarah could also use a portion or all of her unified credit to establish an irrevocable trust for her grandchildren to fund expenses that are not eligible to be paid from a Section 529 plan.

SUMMARY

The transfer tax system consists of the gift tax, the estate tax, and the generation-skipping transfer tax. Transfer taxes are assessed on the transferor of the property, not the recipient. The value of properties transferred by gift and inheritance is measured by their fair market values.

---

[69] §6012(a).
[70] §643(d).
[71] The beneficiary's holding period includes the trust's holding period.
[72] The holding period begins on the date of distribution.

Gifts of a present interest in property are eligible for an annual gift exclusion of $15,000 per donee. An unlimited marital deduction and a charitable contribution deduction make lifetime and testamentary transfers to a spouse or charity tax free. The tax on lifetime gifts and estates is determined on a cumulative basis; thus, taxable gifts cause the estate to be taxed at higher marginal tax rates, and earlier gifts force later gifts into a higher marginal tax bracket. To provide relief for persons with moderate wealth, a unified credit applies to the tax determined on the taxable gifts and estate of an individual.

Trusts provide a method for the transfer of property benefits to one or more persons without transferring outright property ownership to the transferees. Minor and Crummey trusts allow the transferor to circumvent the present interest rule and still claim the annual gift exclusion. Trust beneficiaries or the trust itself are normally taxed on trust income, unless the grantor fails to relinquish all control over the trust property. Transfers of income producing assets to children under age 24 require special consideration to avoid the kiddie tax, which cause most of the child's income to be taxed at the tax rate for estates and trusts.

Trusts and estates are taxable persons and must file income tax returns if more than a minimal amount of income is earned. Income produced by trust or estate properties should be distributed to the beneficiaries each year to avoid the high income tax rates that apply to a fiduciary.

A good family tax plan involves multiple strategies. It allows the family to shift income, and income tax liability, to younger family members. It balances the income tax consequences of property dispositions with the benefits of lifetime gifts or testamentary transfers. Giving appreciating assets to the younger family members eliminates the assets from the donor's taxable estate. As a person ages, the original tax plan should be examined and modified to take advantage of any changes in the tax laws and to ensure the plan continues to meet the person's wealth transfer goals.

KEY TERMS

Alternative valuation date 580
Beneficiary 568
Complex trust 590
Corpus 568
Crummey trust 571
Deceased spousal unused exclusion (DSUE) 566
Decedent 577
Deductions in respect of a decedent (DRD) 586
Distributable net income (DNI) 591
Estate 577
Estate tax 561
Gift tax 561
Grantor 568
Grantor trust 587
Gross estate 578
Income beneficiary 568
Income in respect of a decedent (IRD) 585
Irrevocable 569
Kiddie tax 575
Present interest 571
Probate 578
Qualified terminal interest property (QTIP) 581
Remainder interest 568
Revocable 569
Simple trust 590
Trust 568
Trustee 568

TEST YOURSELF

Answers Appear after the Problem Assignments

1. Marta placed $50,000 into a savings account in her name and the name of her son. Later this year, the son withdraws $17,000 from the account. Marta made no other gifts to her son this year. Marta has made a taxable gift of

a. $2,000
b. $11,000
c. $17,000
d. $25,000
e. $35,000

2. Which of the following transfers is a taxable gift?

a. Alex sold land to an unrelated party for less than its fair market value because he needed cash in a hurry.
b. After a friend's death, Nicole wrote a check to the university to pay the college tuition for the friend's son.
c. Melissa wrote a check to the landlord to pay her aunt's rent for two months when her aunt was unemployed.
d. Howard wrote a check to the doctor to pay a friend's medical bill when he had surgery.

3. Which of the following transactions is a taxable gift?
   a. Mack transfers $5,000 to his favorite political organization.
   b. Sonia gives $25,000 in stocks to her church.
   c. Veronica gives $25,000 to her husband, Jose.
   d. Carla transfers $40,000 into an irrevocable trust for the benefit of her two children.

4. According to the provisions of the decedent's will, the following disbursements were made by the estate's executor:
   1. Payment of the decedent's funeral expenses
   2. Payment of a charitable bequest to a local charity

   What is deductible in determining the decedent's taxable estate?
   a. 1 only
   b. 2 only
   c. Both 1 and 2
   d. Neither 1 nor 2

5. Lorraine created a trust by transferring $500,000 of stock and bonds into it on January 1, year 1. The trust is to provide her mother with income for her lifetime, with the remainder interest going to Lorraine's son. Lorraine retained the power to revoke both the income interest and the remainder interest. Who is taxed on the trust's year 1 income?
   a. Lorraine's son
   b. Lorraine's mother
   c. Lorraine
   d. The trust

PROBLEM ASSIGNMENTS

Check Your Understanding

1. [LO 12.1] What is the lifetime unified credit amount for 2018 and its related exclusion equivalent?

2. [LO 12.1] If the generation-skipping transfer tax did not exist, what type of planning would maximize the preservation of a family's wealth?

3. [LO 12.2] Discount Auto Company sold an automobile at a $2,000 discount to an unrelated customer. Is this a gift?

4. [LO 12.2] Sharon transferred property into an irrevocable trust, but she retained the right to change the beneficiaries. What circumstances are required for this transfer to be a completed gift?

5. [LO 12.2] What is the gift tax annual exclusion and why was it enacted?

6. [LO 12.2] What is a present interest and how is it distinguished from a future interest?

7. [LO 12.2] Under what circumstances will a gift made in trust for a minor child qualify for the annual exclusion?

8. [LO 12.3] Explain why Congress added the kiddie tax provisions and which taxpayers are affected by it.

9. [LO 12.3] Explain the basic provisions of a Section 529 qualified tuition plan.

10. [LO 12.4] Under what circumstances is the face value of life insurance on the decedent's life included in the decedent's gross estate?

11. [LO 12.4] Five years before his death, Troy purchased a $8 million whole life insurance policy on his life and named his son, Don, the beneficiary. Shortly after purchase, Troy transferred the policy to an irrevocable trust, naming his son as trustee. Troy retained no incidents of ownership.
    a. Has Troy made a gift?
    b. Is the $8 million death benefit included in Troy's gross estate?

12. [LO 12.4] How is the value of estate property determined and what is the alternate valuation date?

13. [LO 12.5] Contrast the difference in bases for an appreciated asset that is given as a gift versus one that is inherited.

14. [LO 12.5] Sidney is a psychiatrist. Four years ago, he purchased the building in which his office is located for $375,000. Sidney transfers ownership of the building to his daughter, Nora, and signs a leaseback agreement stipulating that he pay annual rent of $35,000 to Nora for the use of the building for his practice. What family tax-planning goal has this transaction achieved?

15. [LO 12.6] What is income in respect of a decedent, and how is it taxed?

16. [LO 12.6] How do the estate income tax rules encourage a quick distribution of estate assets?

17. [LO 12.7] What are adjusted taxable gifts, and how do they affect the calculation of a decedent's estate tax?

18. [LO 12.7] What distinguishes a simple trust from a complex trust?

19. [LO 12.7] What purpose is served by the distributable net income of a trust or estate?

20. [LO 12.7] How is the net investment income surtax calculated for a trust? Explain how a trust can avoid this tax.

Crunch the Numbers

21. [LO 12.1] Determine the credit for the gift and estate tax exclusion if the indexed exclusion in 2019 is $11,300,000.

22. [LO 12.1 & 12.2] Mary is John's surviving spouse. He used $450,000 of his gift and estate tax exclusion for his lifetime gifts and his estate used $2,300,000 of his estate tax exclusion in closing his estate in 2017. What is Mary's estate tax exclusion when she dies in 2018 if she and John elected to gift split on all taxable gifts.

23. [LO 12.2] Which of the following are completed gifts? How much is the value of each gift before any exclusions?
    - **a.** Hughlene sold stock worth $90,000 to her son for $30,000.
    - **b.** Ken deposits $16,000 into a savings account in his name and his daughter's name as joint owners.
    - **c.** Jim transferred $800,000 into a revocable trust that will pay income to his daughter for her life and the remainder to his granddaughter.

24. [LO 12.2] Determine the taxable gift for each of the following transfers made in 2018.
    - **a.** In February, Cynthia transferred $200,000 into a revocable trust. In October, the trustee distributes $18,000 of income to the beneficiary, Eileen.
    - **b.** Carrie prepared the tax returns at no charge for the elderly in a volunteer program sponsored by a local charity.
    - **c.** Ted gave his cousin $16,000 to pay medical expenses.
    - **d.** Vera paid her nephew's college tuition of $20,000 by writing a check directly to the university.

25. [LO 12.2] Which of the following are completed gifts? Determine the value of each gift before any exclusions?
    - **a.** In March, Stephanie deposits $40,000 cash into a joint checking account for herself and her boyfriend, Michael, who deposits nothing into the account. In July, Michael withdraws $16,000 from the account.
    - **b.** Jennie pays $16,000 of her neighbor's medical expenses directly to the hospital.
    - **c.** Jane pays her sister's $20,000 tuition directly to the university.
    - **d.** Miriam transfers the title of investment land (valued at $85,000) to her son, Kevin.
    - **e.** Miguel deposits $180,000 into a revocable trust in February. In November, the trustee distributes $20,000 of income to the beneficiary, Juan.

26. [LO 12.2] Edward gave 15,000 shares of ABC stock to Valerie on July 15. On July 15, the highest selling price for the stock was $40 per share, and the lowest selling price was $36 per share. What is the value of this gift before any exclusions?

27. [LO 12.2] John gave $32,000 to each of his 10 grandchildren this year. Lisa, his wife, made no gifts during 2018.
  a. How much are John's taxable gifts if gift splitting is not elected?
  b. How much are John's taxable gifts if gift splitting is elected?

28. [LO 12.2] Ginny made the following gifts during 2018. Her husband, Ken, made no gifts during the year.
  - Gift of land valued at $250,000 to her husband
  - Gift of $20,000 in stock to her daughter
  - Gift of $32,000 to her sister to pay for medical expenses

  a. How much are Ginny's taxable gifts if gift splitting is not elected?
  b. How much are Ginny's taxable gifts if gift splitting is elected?

29. [LO 12.2] In 2018, Marah gives $20,000 cash to Sam, $60,000 of stock to Craig, and $100,000 of bonds to Lynn. In the same year, Marah's husband, Bryan, gives land valued at $120,000 to Jerry.
  a. What are Marah and Bryan's taxable gifts if they do not elect gift splitting?
  b. What are the couple's taxable gifts assuming the couple elects gift splitting?

30. [LO 12.2] During 2018, Cherie gives $34,000 cash to her daughter, Helen, and a remainder interest in investment land to her sister, Silvia. The remainder interest is valued at $40,000. In the same year, John, Cherie's husband, gives Dan $18,000 in marketable securities. What is the total dollar amount of the annual gift tax exclusions available to Cherie and John for 2018 if they elect gift splitting?

31. [LO 12.2] Determine whether each of the following situations involves the transfer of a present interest or a future interest.
  a. A trust is established for the donor's 8-year-old daughter. The trustee can decide how much income to pay the daughter each year. At age 21, the daughter will receive all of the accumulated income and principal.
  b. A trust is established by transferring $10,000 each year for each of three beneficiaries who are given 30 days after receiving notice of the transfer to demand payment of the $10,000.
  c. All rights to a life insurance policy are given to the donor's son.

32. [LO 12.2] George transfers investment securities worth $200,000 with a tax basis of $130,000 to a trust, naming himself as trustee. The terms of the trust agreement require the trustee to pay all dividends and interest to George's brother, Mark. George has the right to revoke the trust at any time and take back title to the securities. During the trust's first year, George, as trustee, distributes $20,000 in dividends and $10,000 interest from the securities to Mark. None of the income was tax exempt.
  a. How much gross income does Mark recognize from the payments?
  b. How much gross income does George recognize from the above?

33. [LO 12.3] On January 15, 2018, Eileen, age 24, receives stock worth $30,000 as a gift from her parents. Her parents jointly purchased the stock six years ago for $14,000. During the year, Eileen receives $2,100 dividend income on the stock. In December, she sells the stock for $41,000.
  a. Assuming this is Eileen's only income for the year, and her parents are in the 24 percent marginal tax bracket, how much income tax does the family save as a result of this gift?
  b. Are there any transfer taxes as a result of this gift? Explain.

34. [LO 12.3] Joan is 15 and a dependent of her parents. If she has $4,900 income from her trust fund this year, how much income tax will she pay for 2018 if her parents have $150,000 of taxable income?

35. [LO 12.3] Lenny, age 12, has $5,500 interest income from a trust established by his uncle. This is Lenny's only source of income for 2018.
  a. What is Lenny's taxable income and how much income tax does he owe?
  b. How would your answers change if Lenny were age 24?

36. [LO 12.3] Cindy, an 18-year-old full-time student, has $5,000 interest income from a trust established by her grandparents. Cindy also earned $6,000 working at a part-time job. She lives at home with her parents and has no itemized deductions.

a. What is Cindy's taxable income and how much income tax does she owe for 2018?

b. How would your answers change if Cindy were age 24?

c. How much tax would be saved if she were age 24?

37. [LO 12.4] Which of the following items are included in the decedent's gross estate?

a. A life estate in a trust that pays the decedent $25,000 per year until he dies

b. A remainder interest in a trust worth $60,000 owned by the decedent

c. A one-half interest in investment land valued at $100,000 owned as joint tenants with right of survivorship

38. [LO 12.4] Five years ago, Jason purchased a $400,000 life insurance policy on his life. For each of the following, indicate how much of the $400,000 policy proceeds are included in his gross estate.

a. The proceeds are payable to his estate.

b. The proceeds were paid to his daughter, but Jason retained the right to change beneficiaries.

c. $100,000 of the proceeds are used to pay debts of his estate with the balance paid to his daughter. Jason retained no rights in the policy.

39. [LO 12.2 & 12.4] Laura transferred property valued at $120,000 into an irrevocable trust. Laura is to receive one-half of the income each year for the balance of her life. The other half of the income and the remainder interest are to go to Robert. One year before her death, Laura gave up her right to receive her half of the income, so all the income is payable to Robert. The property is worth $160,000 when Laura dies. How much is includible in Laura's gross estate?

40. [LO 12.4] When Ben died, his executor elected the alternate valuation date. What value is included in the gross estate for each of the following properties?

a. Marketable securities valued at $80,000 at date of death, valued at $89,000 six months after death, and sold for $92,000 by the estate 10 months after death.

b. Investment land, valued at $100,000 at date of death, was valued at $102,000 when it was distributed to a beneficiary four months later, and valued at $110,000 six months after death.

41. [LO 12.4] Samson's gross estate was valued at $3 million when he died. Determine the value of his taxable estate before any credits using the following information:

- The executor's fees were $16,000.
- His funeral expenses were $15,000.
- A cash donation of $110,000 was given to San Jose State University.
- Real estate worth $700,000 was transferred to his surviving spouse, Delilah.
- Samson had promised to give stock worth $24,000 to his nephew, but he never did.

42. [LO 12.3, 12.4 & 12.5] Jessica owns investment land currently worth $8,000,000. She paid $3,000,000 for the land 10 years ago. She expects that the land will probably increase in value to at least $12,000,000 before she dies. She has not previously given any taxable gifts.

a. If Jessica gives the land to her son Mark now, what basis will he use for determining gain when he sells the land?

b. If Jessica dies in 2018 and bequeaths the land to her son, what basis will he use for determining gain when he sells the land?

c. If Jessica's son plans to keep the land instead of selling it, should she give it to him now or bequeath it to him? Explain the reason for your choice.

43. [LO 12.2, 12.3 & 12.5] Cherry's 62-year-old widowed mother, Nancy, had to quit working for health reasons and now her only income is $1,100 per month from Social Security. Cherry recently became partner of a law firm and has moved into the 32% marginal tax bracket. Cherry's mother steadfastly insists on living independently so Cherry gave her mother $200,000 in 9% corporate bonds to supplement her income.

a. How much of her lifetime unified credit and related exclusion must Cherry use to avoid paying a gift tax?

b. How much income taxes are saved by the transfer of the bonds by Cherry to her mother?

44. [LO 12.5 & 12.6] Glen transferred corporate stock worth $300,000 with a tax basis of $160,000 to an irrevocable trust. No gift taxes are paid. The terms of the trust require the independent trustee to distribute the trust income annually to Glen's sister, Barbara. Any capital gain or loss is charged to trust corpus. Upon Barbara's death, the trust corpus is to be distributed to Barbara's children on a pro rata basis. During the first year of the trust, the trustee distributes $23,000 in dividend income to Barbara. The trust also has capital gains of $20,000.

a. What is the trust's tax basis in the securities transferred to it by Glen?

b. Who is taxed on the dividend income?

c. Who is taxed on the capital gains?

45. [LO 12.6] Thomas died on August 15 of the current year. On September 2, his estate received a check for $2,000 from Thomas's former employer for his final pay period. On September 18, Thomas's estate received a $70,000 distribution from his employer's retirement plan. Both Thomas and the estate are cash-basis, calendar-year taxpayers. How much income must the estate report as a result of receiving these items?

46. [LO 12.6] Wayne created a trust six years ago for the benefit of his children. In the current year, when the value of the trust assets is $1,000,000, Wayne transfers additional property valued at $300,000 into the trust. Because Wayne is concerned that he might need some income in a future year if his investments do not perform well, he retains the right to receive the income from this latter property in any year in which his gross income falls below a specified amount. The trust received $100,000 in income this year: $30,000 from the newly transferred assets and $70,000 from the original assets. The entire $100,000 income is distributed directly to Wayne's children before the end of the year. Who is taxed on the income?

47. [LO 12.6] In June of year 1, Angelina (a calendar-year taxpayer) becomes the beneficiary of a new calendar-year trust. At the same time, Angelina also becomes the beneficiary of an estate that elects a March 31 fiscal year-end. In December of year 1, Angelina receives income distributions of $12,000 from the trust and $18,000 from the estate.

a. In which year does Angelina report the income from the trust?

b. In which year does Angelina report the income from the estate?

48. [LO 12.7] Carolyn has made no previous taxable gifts. Determine her potential gift tax before deducting her unified credit if she makes $2,650,000 in taxable gifts in the current year (after each donee's annual exclusion).

49. [LO 12.7] Benjamin has made no previous taxable gifts. Determine his gift tax if he makes $14,000,000 (after annual exclusions) in taxable gifts in 2018.

50. [LO 12.7] Steven had a taxable estate of $14,850,000 when he died in 2018. If he had no prior taxable gifts, what is his net estate tax liability?

51. [LO 12.7] Sondra and Jason, a wealthy married couple, won $96 million in a 2018 Powerball drawing. They decided to share some of this new wealth immediately with some of their friends and family. They paid $4,800,000 on a new home for Sondra's parents, titling the home jointly in the parents' names; bought a condominium on Captiva Island for Jason's widowed mother for $1,950,000; gave $1 million to a local charity that provides homes and job training for homeless families; sent $150,000 to Stanford University to be used for their nephew's college tuition for his next 4 years in school; gave $500,000 each to Sondra's sister and Jason's brother for new homes; gave $750,000 to the best man at their wedding last year to defray the costs of a needed kidney transplant; and finally donated $250,000 to their church to build a wedding chapel. The only taxable gift previously made by either Sondra or Jason was a $200,000 cash gift in 2014 by Jason to the widow of an employee who had been killed in an auto accident. This gift was made prior to their marriage. Sondra and Jason elect gift splitting. Determine their separate total taxable gifts and the gift taxes they will owe after applying each of their lifetime unified credits.

52. [LO 12.7] Julie had a gross estate of $13 million when she died in 2018. Her funeral expenses were $26,000; her administrative expenses were $30,000; her charitable deduction was $350,000; and her marital deduction was $600,000. She made no prior taxable gifts. What is her net estate tax liability?

Develop Planning Skills

53. [LO 12.2 & 12.5] Your client, Ted, would like your assistance in selecting one of the following assets to give to his 16-year-old daughter.

Asset	Fair market value	Adjusted basis
Cash	$15,000	$15,000
Corporate stock	15,000	6,000
10 percent of the outstanding shares of Ted's wholly owned S corporation	15,000	8,000
Limited partnership interest	15,000	3,000

The corporate stock pays only $100 in dividend income each year but has doubled in value since Ted purchased it three years ago. The S corporation has generated a profit of $80,000 each year for the past three years and is expected to perform even better in the future. The limited partnership has generated losses for the past three years and is expected to do so for at least the next several years.

a. Discuss the advantages and disadvantages from both transfer and income tax perspectives for each asset as a potential gift.

b. Which asset do you recommend Ted choose and why?

54. [LO 12.4] When Godfrey died in 2018, his assets were valued as follows:

Asset	Date of death valuation	Valuation six months later
Stocks	$5,220,000	$5,180,000
Bonds	4,600,000	4,620,000
Home	1,800,000	1,780,000
Total	$11,620,000	$11,580,000

The executor sold the stock two months after the decedent's death for $5,200,000. The bonds were sold seven months after the decedent's death for $4,630,000. What valuation should be used for the gross estate?

55. [LO 12.6 & 12.7] You are the trustee for the Steadman Trust. The trust has $50,000 of interest income, all of which it plans to distribute to its beneficiaries in the current year. The trust also has $14,000 in net capital losses for the year that are allocated to corpus. The trust distributes some investment land to one of its beneficiaries. The land was acquired eight years ago and has an adjusted basis of $40,000 and a fair market value of $55,000. The beneficiary plans to sell the land.

a. What would be the impact on the trust and the beneficiary if an election is made to recognize gain on the land?

b. What is the impact on the trust and the beneficiary if the election is not made?

c. What you do recommend?

56. [LO 12.3 & 12.7] Oscar (age 70) and Maggie (age 60) were married and jointly owned a personal residence valued at $3,800,000 when Oscar died in 2018. Oscar also owned stocks valued at $6,700,000; an art collection valued at $4,400,000; a retirement account valued at $900,000 (contributions were entirely from pretax income); $800,000 in cash; and $1,000,000 in other miscellaneous assets. Oscar's will specified that when he died his half of the personal residence would go to Maggie but that all his other assets would pass to his four children because Maggie has sufficient income from a trust fund she inherited from her grandfather. Oscar made no previous taxable gifts.

a. What was Oscar's estate tax liability when he died in 2018?

b. Each of Oscar's four children has three children (total of 12 grandchildren). If Oscar had begun transferring assets to his children and grandchildren in years 2013 through 2018, how much could he have removed in value from his estate over those six years through gift splitting and making annual transfers equal to the gift exclusion?

Think Outside the Text

These questions require answers that are beyond the material that is covered in this chapter.

57. [LO 12.1] In 2010, Congress chose to repeal the estate tax for that year, but retained the gift tax. Why do you think they did that?

58. [LO 12.1] For 2018–2025, Congress increased the lifetime exclusion amount for estate and gift taxes to $11,180,000 with inflation indexing. What (if any) changes do you think Congress might make in this area in the future?

59. [LO 12.2] Mark's father, Michael, loaned Mark $300,000 interest free for five years to invest in securities that yield a 10 percent annual return. At the end of the five years, Mark sells the securities to repay his father. Unfortunately, the market declined and Mark was able to sell the securities for only $280,000. Michael accepted the $280,000 as payment in full on the loan. How do you think this transaction will be treated for tax purposes?

60. [LO 12.3] Why do you think Congress enacted the kiddie tax? Do you think it is achieving its goal? Can you think of a better way to achieve this goal?

Search the Internet

61. [LO 12.4] Go to the IRS website (*www.irs.gov*) and locate the instructions for Form 706-NA for the estate of a nonresident alien.

a. What is the definition of a nonresident alien decedent?

b. Under what circumstances must the executor for a nonresident alien decedent file a Form 706-NA?

62. [LO 12.2 & 12.7] Go to the IRS website (*www.irs.gov*) and locate the instructions for Form 709. Can spouses who elect to gift split file a joint gift tax return? Explain how they must file.

Identify the Issues

Identify the issues or problems suggested by the following situations. State each issue as a question.

63. [LO 12.2] Martha provides the sole support for her son, David, who lives at home while he attends school. Martha gives David a $40,000 automobile for his 18th birthday.

64. [LO 12.2 & 12.4] Ten years ago, Carolyn created a revocable trust using marketable securities valued at $500,000. The trust department at the local bank is the trustee. Under the terms of the trust, Carolyn retained a life estate with a remainder interest for her grandchildren. Last year, when the trust assets were valued at $900,000, Carolyn released her right to revoke the trust, making it irrevocable. Carolyn dies in the current year when the trust assets are valued at $1 million.

65. [LO 12.2 & 12.4] In year 1, Loren and Tim enter into a property settlement agreement under which Tim agrees to pay $600,000 to Loren in return for the release of her marital rights. The payment is to be made in three annual installments of $200,000 each. Loren and Tim divorce in year 2, but Tim dies late in the year before the second and third installments can be paid. In year 3, Tim's executor pays Loren the $400,000 balance due.

66. [LO 12.2 & 12.6] Jennifer plans to establish a trust in which she will place all her income-producing investments. She will be the income beneficiary for the balance of her life, with her son having a remainder interest. She plans to name herself as trustee.

67. [LO 12.4] Jorge is a resident and citizen of Spain. He invests $500,000 in Miami Beach real estate. When Jorge died in 2018, he owned $12,000,000 in assets in Spain in addition to the Miami Beach real estate.

68. [LO 12.4 & 12.7] At the time of Frank's death, he had received $6,000 in credit card bills that had not been paid.

69. [LO 12.6 & 12.7] The Lincoln Trust is a simple trust whose only investments are in corporate bonds producing interest income. The trustee is thinking about moving some of the investments into municipal bonds.

70. [LO 12.4 & 12.7] When Chet died on March 12, 2018, he owned $900,000 in stock of ABC Corporation and $100,000 in City of Omaha bonds. The ABC Corporation declared a cash dividend on March 1 that was payable to shareholders of record on March 15. In early April, the executor of Chet's estate received the following: ABC Corporation dividend of $6,000 and interest of $3,200 ($200 accrued since March 12) on the City of Omaha bonds.

Develop Research Skills

71. [LO 12.4] Two years ago, Herbert, a widower, made a gift of marketable securities to his 35-year-old daughter, Sabrina, on which he paid a federal gift tax of $3 million. When Herbert died in December 2017, his estate had been greatly reduced in value due to his having given away most of his assets over his lifetime. Herbert's executor filed an estate tax return that showed an estate tax liability attributable to the gift to Sabrina. The estate tax was not paid because the estate had no liquid assets. The IRS assesses the portion of the estate tax related to this gift that Sabrina previously received against Sabrina under the rules relating to transferee liability. Is Sabrina liable for the estate tax?

72. [LO 12.6] Samantha is a single parent providing the sole support for her six-year-old daughter, Hillary. They live in an area where the public school is known to have problems with drugs and other crimes. Samantha wants to send Hillary to a private school to avoid these problems and provide a better environment for Hillary's educational development. Eight years ago, Samantha set up two trusts to manage the securities she inherited from her grandfather. Samantha is the sole beneficiary of Trust A from which she receives bimonthly distributions each made after approval by the trustee. Hillary is the sole beneficiary of Trust B and all distributions from this trust must be approved by its trustee. If Samantha convinces the trustee to pay for Hillary's tuition, writing a check out of the Trust B funds to the school, are there any income tax consequences to Samantha?

ANSWERS TO TEST YOURSELF

1. **a. $2,000.** ($17,000 – $15,000 exclusion).
2. **c. Melissa wrote a check to the landlord to pay her aunt's rent for two months when her aunt was unemployed.**
3. **d. Carla transfers $40,000 into an irrevocable trust for the benefit of her two children.**
4. **c. Both 1 and 2.**
5. **c. Lorraine.**

Selected Tax Tables for 2018 and 2017

APPENDIX

CORPORATE TAX RATES FOR 2018 AND 2017

Corporate Tax Rate for 2018 = 21% flat rate

CORPORATE TAX RATES FOR 2017

If taxable income is:	***Tax liability is:***
Not over $50,000	15% of taxable income
Over $50,000 but not over $75,000	$7,500 + 25% of the excess over $50,000
Over $75,000 but not over $100,000	$13,750 + 34% of the excess over $75,000
Over $100,000 but not over $335,000	$22,250 + 39% of the excess over $100,000
Over $335,000 but not over $10,000,000	$113,900 + 34% of the excess over $335,000
Over $10,000,000 but not over $15,000,000	$3,400,000 + 35% of the excess over $10,000,000
Over $15,000,000 but not over $18,333,333	$5,150,000 + 38% of the excess over $15,000,000
Over $18,333,333	$6,416,667 + 35% of the excess over $18,333,333
Corporate alternative minimum tax rate = 20%	

INDIVIDUAL INCOME TAX RATE SCHEDULES FOR 2018 AND 2017

2018 INDIVIDUAL ORDINARY INCOME TAX RATE SCHEDULES

Schedule X Single Individuals

If taxable income is:	***The tax is:***
Not over $9,525	10% of taxable income
Over $9,525 but not over $38,700	$952.50 plus 12% of the excess over $9,525
Over $38,700 but not over $82,500	$4,453.50 plus 22% of the excess over $38,700
Over $82,500 but not over $157,500	$14,089.50 plus 24% of the excess over $82,500
Over $157,500 but not over $200,000	$32,089.50 plus 32% of the excess over $157,500
Over $200,000 but not over $500,000	$45,689.50 plus 35% of the excess over $200,000
Over $500,000	$150,689.50 plus 37% of the excess over $500,000

Schedule Y-1 Married Individuals Filing Joint Returns

If taxable income is:	***The tax is:***
Not over $19,050	10% of taxable income
Over $19,050 but not over $77,400	$1,905 plus 12% of the excess over $19,050
Over $77,400 but not over $165,000	$8,907 plus 22% of the excess over $77,400
Over $165,000 but not over $315,000	$28,179 plus 24% of the excess over $165,000
Over $315,000 but not over $400,000	$64,179 plus 32% of the excess over $315,000
Over $400,000 but not over $600,000	$91,379 plus 35% of the excess over $400,000
Over $600,000	$161,379 plus 37% of the excess over $600,000

2018 INDIVIDUAL ORDINARY INCOME TAX RATE SCHEDULES

Schedule Y-2 Married Individuals Filing Separate Returns

If taxable income is:	*The tax is:*
Not over $9,525	10% of taxable income
Over $9,525 but not over $38,700	$952.50 plus 12% of the excess over $9,525
Over $38,700 but not over $82,500	$4,453.50 plus 22% of the excess over $38,700
Over $82,500 but not over $157,500	$14,089.50 plus 24% of the excess over $82,500
Over $157,500 but not over $200,000	$32,089.50 plus 32% of the excess over $157,500
Over $200,000 but not over $300,000	$45,689.50 plus 35% of the excess over $200,000
Over $300,000	$80,689.50 plus 37% of the excess over $300,000

Schedule Z Heads of Households

If taxable income is:	*The tax is:*
Not over $13,600	10% of taxable income
Over $13,600 but not over $51,800	$1,360 plus 12% of the excess over $13,600
Over $51,800 but not over $82,500	$5,944 plus 22% of the excess over $51,800
Over $82,500 but not over $157,500	$12,698 plus 24% of the excess over $82,500
Over $157,500 but not over $200,000	$30,698 plus 32% of the excess over $157,500
Over $200,000 but not over $500,000	$44,298 plus 35% of the excess over $200,000
Over $500,000	$149,298 plus 37% of the excess over $500,000

2017 INDIVIDUAL ORDINARY INCOME TAX RATE SCHEDULES

Schedule X Single Individuals

If taxable income is:	*The tax is:*
Not over $9,325	10% of the taxable income
Over $9,325 but not over $37,950	$932.50 + 15% of the excess over $9,325
Over $37,950 but not over $91,900	$5,226.25 + 25% of the excess over $37,950
Over $91,900 but not over $191,650	$18,713.75 + 28% of the excess over $91,900
Over $191,650 but not over $416,700	$46,643.75 + 33% of the excess over $191,650
Over $416,700 not over $418,400	$120,910.25 + 35% of the excess over $416,700
Over $418,400	$121,505.25 + 39.6% of the excess over $418,400

Schedule Y-1 Married Individuals Filing Joint Returns

If taxable income is:	*The tax is:*
Not over $18,650	10% of the taxable income
Over $18,650 but not over $75,900	$1,865 + 15% of the excess over $18,650
Over $75,900 but not over $153,100	$10,452.50 + 25% of the excess over $75,900
Over $153,100 but not over $233,350	$29,752.50 + 28% of the excess over $153,100
Over $233,350 but not over $416,700	$52,222.50 + 33% of the excess over $233,350
Over $416,700 but not over $470,700	$112,728 + 35% of the excess over $416,700
Over $470,700	$131,628 + 39.6% of the excess over $470,700

Schedule Y-2 Married Individuals Filing Separate Returns

If taxable income is:	*The tax is:*
Not over $9,325	10% of the taxable income
Over $9,325 but not over $37,950	$932.50 + 15% of the excess over $9,325
Over $37,950 but not over $76,550	$5,226.25 + 25% of the excess over $37,950
Over $76,550 but not over $116,675	$14,876.25 + 28% of the excess over $76,550
Over $116,675 but not over $208,350	$26,111.25 + 33% of the excess over $116,675
Over $208,350 but not over $235,350	$56,364 + 35% of the excess over $208,350
Over $235,350	$65,814 + 39.6% of the excess over $235,350

2017 INDIVIDUAL ORDINARY INCOME TAX RATE SCHEDULES

Schedule Z Heads of Households

If taxable income is:	***The tax is:***
Not over $13,350	10% of the taxable income
Over $13,350 but not over $50,800	$1,335 + 15% of the excess over $13,350
Over $50,800 but not over $131,200	$6,952.50 + 25% of the excess over $50,800
Over $131,200 but not over $212,500	$27,052.50 + 28% of the excess over $131,200
Over $212,500 but not over $416,700	$49,816.50 + 33% of the excess over $212,500
Over $416,700 but not over $444,550	$117,202.50 + 35% of the excess over $416,700
Over $444,550	$126,950 + 39.6% of the excess over $444,550

Individual Tax Rates for Long-term Capital Gains and Dividend Income for 2018 and 2017

2018 Tax Rates for Dividend Income and Long-term Capital Gains

Long-term capital gains and dividend tax rate	Taxable income for single individuals	Taxable income for married filing a joint return*	Taxable income for head of household
0%	$0–$38,600	$0–$77,200	$0–$51,700
15%	$38,601–$425,800	$77,201–$479,000	$51,701–$452,400
20%	Over $425,800	Over $479,000	Over $452,400

*Amounts if married filing separately are half the amount for filing a joint return.

25% on unrecaptured Section 1250 gains
28% on collectibles and Section 1202 gains

2017 Tax Rates for Dividend Income and Long-term Capital Gains

0% for taxpayers in the 10% or 15% tax bracket
15% for taxpayers in 25% to 35% brackets
20% for taxpayers in 39.6% bracket
25% on unrecaptured Section 1250 gains
28% on collectibles and Section 1202 gains
(use 10% or 15% marginal tax rate if gain falls within those tax brackets)

Individual Alternative Minimum Tax Rates

AMT Rate	2018	2017
26%	0–$191,100	0–$187,800
28%	Over $191,100	Over $187,800

SOCIAL SECURITY AND MEDICARE TAXES FOR 2018 AND 2017

	2018	2017
FICA Social Security tax rate	6.2%	6.2%
SECA Social Security tax rate	12.4%	12.4%
FICA Medicare tax rate	1.45%	1.45%
SECA Medicare tax rate	2.9%	2.9%
Social Security income limit	$128,400	$127,200
Medicare tax income limit	None	None
Total SECA rate below SS income limit	15.3%	15.3%
Deductible SECA rate below SS income limit	7.65%	7.65%

Medicare Surtaxes for 2018 and 2017

Filing status	Thresholds	NII rate	Compensation rate
Single (Unmarried) Individual	$200,000	3.8%	0.9%
Head of Household	200,000	3.8%	0.9%
Married Filing a Joint Return	250,000	3.8%	0.9%
Married Filing a Separate Return	125,000	3.8%	0.9%

STANDARD DEDUCTIONS FOR 2018 AND 2017

Filing status	2018	2017
Single (Unmarried) Individual	$12,000	$6,350
Head of Household	18,000	9,350
Married Filing a Joint Return	24,000	12,700
Surviving Spouse (Qualifying Widow or Widower)	24,000	12,700
Married Filing a Separate Return	12,000	6,350
Dependent (if greater, earned income + $350)	1,050	1,050
Additional Amount if Single, Head of Household or Surviving Spouse*	1,600	1,550
Additional Amount if Married*	1,300	1,250

*Additional amount for each instance of blindness or age (65 or older) of the taxpayer (or taxpayer and spouse if a joint return is filed).

Personal and dependency exemption amount for 2017 = $4,050

For 2018, use $4,150 when an amount is needed for dependent.

TAX RATES FOR ESTATES, GIFTS, AND TRUSTS FOR 2018 AND 2017

Estate and Gift Transfer Tax Rates for 2018 and 2017

Amount of taxable transfer	Tax rate
Up to $10,000	18%
$10,001–$20,000	$1,800 + 20% of excess over $10,000
$20,001–$40,000	$3,800 + 22% of excess over $20,000
$40,001–$60,000	$8,200 + 24% of excess over $40,000
$60,001–$80,000	$13,000 + 26% of excess over $60,000
$80,001–$100,000	$18,200 + 28% of excess over $80,000
$100,001–$150,000	$23,800 + 30% of excess over $100,000
$150,001–$250,000	$38,800 + 32% of excess over $150,000
$250,001–$500,000	$70,800 + 34% of excess over $250,000
$500,001–$750,000	$155,800 + 37% of excess over $500,000
$750,001–$1,000,000	$248,300 + 39% of excess over $750,000
Over $1,000,000	$345,800 + 40% of excess over $1,000,000

2018 Lifetime gift tax and estate tax exemption = $11,180,000 (equivalent to credit of $4,417,800)
2017 Lifetime gift tax and estate tax exemption = $5,490,000 (equivalent to credit of $2,141,800)
Annual gift tax exclusion: $15,000 for 2018 and $14,000 for 2017

Trust and Estate Income Tax Rates for 2018 and 2017

Income Tax Rates for Trusts and Estates for 2018

If taxable income is:	*The tax is:*
Not over $2,550	10% of taxable income
Over $2,550 but not over $9,150	$255.00 plus 24% of the excess over $2,550
Over $9,150 but not over $12,500	$1,839.00 plus 35% of the excess over $9,150
Over $12,500	$3,011.50 plus 37% of the excess over $12,500

Tax Rates for Long-term Capital Gains and Dividend Income

If taxable income is:	*The tax rate is:*
Not over $2,600	0%
Over $2,600 but not over $12,700	15%
Over $12,700	20%

Income Tax Rates for Trusts and Estates for 2017		
Taxable income	Ordinary income tax rates	Long-term capital gains and dividend income tax rates
0–$2,550	15%	0%
$2,551–$6,000	25%	15%
$6,001–$9,150	28%	15%
$9,151–$12,500	33%	15%
Over $12,500	39.6%	20%

DEPRECIATION TABLES

MACRS Rates for Tangible Personalty Using the Half-Year Averaging Convention

Recovery year	5-Year	7-Year
1	20.00%	14.29%
2	32.00	24.49
3	19.20	17.49
4	11.52	12.49
5	11.52	8.93
6	5.76	8.92
7		8.93
8		4.46

Section 179 Expensing and Bonus Depreciation

2018 Section 179 Expensing: $1,000,000 limit, phase out begins when more than $2.500,000 in qualifying assets are acquired

2017 Section 179 Expensing: $510,000 limit; phase out begins when more than $2,030,000 in qualifying assets are acquired

Bonus depreciation = 100% for assets acquired after September 27, 2017; 50% for new assets only acquired before September 28, 2017

Limits for Passenger Vehicles

	2017		2018	
Year	Without bonus depreciation	With bonus depreciation	Without bonus depreciation	With bonus depreciation
1	$3,160	$11,160	$10,000	$18,000
2	5,100	5,100	16,000	16,000
3	3,050	3,050	9,600	9,600
4 and thereafter	1,875	1,875	5,760	5,760

Alternatively, the standard mileage rate is 54.5 cents per mile for 2018 and 53.5 cents per mile for 2017.

MACRS Rates for Tangible Personalty Using the Mid-Quarter Averaging Convention

5-Year Property				
Year	First quarter	Second quarter	Third quarter	Fourth quarter
1	35.00%	25.00%	15.00%	5.00%
2	26.00	30.00	34.00	38.00
3	15.60	18.00	20.40	22.80
4	11.01	11.37	12.24	13.68
5	11.01	11.37	11.30	10.94
6	1.38	4.26	7.06	9.58

7-Year Property				
Year	First quarter	Second quarter	Third quarter	Fourth quarter
1	25.00%	17.85%	10.71%	3.57%
2	21.43	23.47	25.51	27.55
3	15.31	16.76	18.22	19.68
4	10.93	11.97	13.02	14.06
5	8.75	8.87	9.30	10.04
6	8.74	8.87	8.85	8.73
7	8.75	8.87	8.86	8.73
8	1.09	3.33	5.53	7.64

Rates for 27½-Year Residential Rental Property Mid-Month Convention

Year	Month property placed in service											
	1	2	3	4	5	6	7	8	9	10	11	12
1	3.485%	3.182%	2.879%	2.576%	2.273%	1.970%	1.667%	1.364%	1.061%	0.758%	0.455%	0.152%
2-9	3.636	3.636	3.636	3.636	3.636	3.636	3.636	3.636	3.636	3.636	3.636	3.636
10	3.637	3.637	3.637	3.637	3.637	3.637	3.636	3.636	3.636	3.636	3.636	3.636
11	3.636	3.636	3.636	3.636	3.636	3.636	3.637	3.637	3.637	3.637	3.637	3.637
12	3.637	3.637	3.637	3.637	3.637	3.637	3.636	3.636	3.636	3.636	3.636	3.636
13	3.636	3.636	3.636	3.636	3.636	3.636	3.637	3.637	3.637	3.637	3.637	3.637
14	3.637	3.637	3.637	3.637	3.637	3.637	3.636	3.636	3.636	3.636	3.636	3.636
15	3.636	3.636	3.636	3.636	3.636	3.636	3.637	3.637	3.637	3.637	3.637	3.637
16	3.637	3.637	3.637	3.637	3.637	3.637	3.636	3.636	3.636	3.636	3.636	3.636
17	3.636	3.636	3.636	3.636	3.636	3.636	3.637	3.637	3.637	3.637	3.637	3.637
18	3.637	3.637	3.637	3.637	3.637	3.637	3.636	3.636	3.636	3.636	3.636	3.636
19	3.636	3.636	3.636	3.636	3.636	3.636	3.637	3.637	3.637	3.637	3.637	3.637
20	3.637	3.637	3.637	3.637	3.637	3.637	3.636	3.636	3.636	3.636	3.636	3.636
21	3.636	3.636	3.636	3.636	3.636	3.636	3.637	3.637	3.637	3.637	3.637	3.637
22	3.637	3.637	3.637	3.637	3.637	3.637	3.636	3.636	3.636	3.636	3.636	3.636
23	3.636	3.636	3.636	3.636	3.636	3.636	3.637	3.637	3.637	3.637	3.637	3.637
24	3.637	3.637	3.673	3.637	3.637	3.637	3.636	3.636	3.636	3.636	3.636	3.636
25	3.636	3.636	3.636	3.636	3.636	3.636	3.637	3.637	3.637	3.637	3.637	3.637
26	3.637	3.637	3.637	3.637	3.637	3.637	3.636	3.636	3.633	3.636	3.636	3.636
27	3.636	3.636	3.636	3.636	3.636	3.636	3.637	3.637	3.637	3.637	3.637	3.637
28	1.970	2.273	2.576	2.879	3.182	3.485	3.636	3.636	3.636	3.636	3.636	3.636
29	0.000	0.000	0.000	0.000	0.000	0.000	0.152	0.455	0.758	1.061	1.364	1.667

Rates for 39-Year Nonresidential Real Property Mid-Month Convention

Month property placed in service	Year 1	Years 2-39	Year 40
1	2.461%	2.564%	0.107%
2	2.247	2.564	0.321
3	2.033	2.564	0.535
4	1.819	2.564	0.749
5	1.605	2.564	0.963
6	1.391	2.564	1.177
7	1.177	2.564	1.391
8	0.963	2.564	1.605
9	0.749	2.564	1.819
10	0.535	2.564	2.033
11	0.321	2.564	2.247
12	0.107	2.564	2.461

Alternative Depreciation System Rates for Tangible Personalty Using Half-Year Averaging Convention

Recovery year	5-Year	7-Year
1	10.00%	7.14%
2	20.00	14.29
3	20.00	14.29
4	20.00	14.28
5	20.00	14.29
6	10.00	14.28
7		14.29
8		7.14

PRESENT VALUE AND FUTURE VALUE TABLES

Present Value of $1

Periods	4%	5%	6%	7%	8%	9%	10%	12%
1	0.962	0.952	0.943	0.935	0.926	0.917	0.909	0.893
2	0.925	0.907	0.890	0.873	0.857	0.842	0.826	0.797
3	0.889	0.864	0.840	0.816	0.794	0.772	0.751	0.712
4	0.855	0.823	0.792	0.763	0.735	0.708	0.683	0.636
5	0.822	0.784	0.747	0.713	0.681	0.650	0.621	0.567
6	0.790	0.746	0.705	0.666	0.630	0.596	0.564	0.507
7	0.760	0.711	0.665	0.623	0.583	0.547	0.513	0.452
8	0.731	0.677	0.627	0.582	0.540	0.502	0.467	0.404
9	0.703	0.645	0.592	0.544	0.500	0.460	0.424	0.361
10	0.676	0.614	0.558	0.508	0.463	0.422	0.386	0.322
11	0.650	0.585	0.527	0.475	0.429	0.388	0.350	0.287
12	0.625	0.557	0.497	0.444	0.397	0.356	0.319	0.257
13	0.601	0.530	0.469	0.415	0.368	0.326	0.290	0.229
14	0.577	0.505	0.442	0.388	0.340	0.299	0.263	0.205
15	0.555	0.481	0.417	0.362	0.315	0.275	0.239	0.183
16	0.534	0.458	0.394	0.339	0.292	0.252	0.218	0.163
17	0.513	0.436	0.371	0.317	0.270	0.231	0.198	0.146
18	0.494	0.416	0.350	0.296	0.250	0.212	0.180	0.130
19	0.475	0.396	0.331	0.277	0.232	0.194	0.164	0.116
20	0.456	0.377	0.312	0.258	0.215	0.178	0.149	0.104
21	0.439	0.359	0.294	0.242	0.199	0.164	0.135	0.093
22	0.422	0.342	0.278	0.226	0.184	0.150	0.123	0.083
23	0.406	0.326	0.262	0.211	0.170	0.138	0.112	0.074
24	0.390	0.310	0.247	0.197	0.158	0.126	0.102	0.066
25	0.375	0.295	0.233	0.184	0.146	0.116	0.092	0.059
30	0.308	0.231	0.174	0.131	0.099	0.075	0.057	0.033
40	0.208	0.142	0.097	0.067	0.046	0.032	0.022	0.011

Present Value of Annuity of $1

Periods	4%	5%	6%	7%	8%	9%	10%	12%
1	0.962	0.952	0.943	0.935	0.926	0.917	0.909	0.893
2	1.886	1.859	1.833	1.808	1.783	1.759	1.736	1.690
3	2.775	2.723	2.673	2.624	2.577	2.531	2.487	2.402
4	3.630	3.546	3.465	3.387	3.312	3.240	3.170	3.037
5	4.452	4.329	4.212	4.100	3.993	3.890	3.791	3.605
6	5.242	5.076	4.917	4.767	4.623	4.486	4.355	4.111
7	6.002	5.786	5.582	5.389	5.206	5.033	4.868	4.564
8	6.733	6.463	6.210	5.971	5.747	5.535	5.335	4.968
9	7.435	7.108	6.802	6.515	6.247	5.995	5.759	5.328
10	8.111	7.722	7.360	7.024	6.710	6.418	6.145	5.650
11	8.760	8.306	7.887	7.499	7.139	6.805	6.495	5.938
12	9.385	8.863	8.384	7.943	7.536	7.161	6.814	6.194
13	9.986	9.394	8.853	8.358	7.904	7.487	7.103	6.424
14	10.563	9.899	9.295	8.745	8.244	7.786	7.367	6.628
15	11.118	10.380	9.712	9.108	8.559	8.061	7.606	6.811
16	11.652	10.838	10.106	9.447	8.851	8.313	7.824	6.974
17	12.166	11.274	10.477	9.763	9.122	8.544	8.022	7.120
18	12.659	11.690	10.828	10.059	9.372	8.756	8.201	7.250
19	13.134	12.085	11.158	10.336	9.604	8.950	8.365	7.366
20	13.590	12.462	11.470	10.594	9.818	9.129	8.514	7.469
21	14.029	12.821	11.764	10.836	10.017	9.292	8.649	7.562
22	14.451	13.163	12.042	11.061	10.201	9.442	8.772	7.645
23	14.857	13.489	12.303	11.272	10.371	9.580	8.883	7.718
24	15.247	13.799	12.550	11.469	10.529	9.707	8.985	7.784
25	15.622	14.094	12.783	11.654	10.675	9.823	9.077	7.843
30	17.292	15.373	13.765	12.409	11.258	10.274	9.427	8.055
40	19.793	17.159	15.046	13.332	11.925	10.757	9.779	8.244

Future Value of $1

Periods	4%	5%	6%	7%	8%	9%	10%	12%
1	1.040	1.050	1.060	1.070	1.080	1.090	1.100	1.120
2	1.082	1.103	1.124	1.145	1.166	1.188	1.210	1.254
3	1.125	1.158	1.191	1.225	1.260	1.295	1.331	1.405
4	1.170	1.216	1.262	1.311	1.360	1.412	1.464	1.574
5	1.217	1.276	1.338	1.403	1.469	1.539	1.611	1.762
6	1.265	1.340	1.419	1.501	1.587	1.677	1.772	1.974
7	1.316	1.407	1.504	1.606	1.714	1.828	1.949	2.211
8	1.369	1.477	1.594	1.718	1.851	1.993	2.144	2.476
9	1.423	1.551	1.689	1.838	1.999	2.172	2.358	2.773
10	1.480	1.629	1.791	1.967	2.159	2.367	2.594	3.106
11	1.539	1.710	1.898	2.105	2.332	2.580	2.853	3.479
12	1.601	1.796	2.012	2.252	2.518	2.813	3.138	3.896
13	1.665	1.886	2.133	2.410	2.720	3.066	3.452	4.363
14	1.732	1.980	2.261	2.579	2.937	3.342	3.798	4.887
15	1.801	2.079	2.397	2.759	3.172	3.642	4.177	5.474
16	1.873	2.183	2.540	2.952	3.426	3.970	4.595	6.130
17	1.948	2.292	2.693	3.159	3.700	4.328	5.054	6.866
18	2.026	2.407	2.854	3.380	3.996	4.717	5.560	7.690
19	2.107	2.527	3.026	3.617	4.316	5.142	6.116	8.613
20	2.191	2.653	3.207	3.870	4.661	5.604	6.728	9.646
21	2.279	2.786	3.400	4.141	5.034	6.109	7.400	10.80
22	2.370	2.925	3.604	4.430	5.437	6.659	8.140	12.10
23	2.465	3.072	3.820	4.741	5.871	7.258	8.954	13.55
24	2.563	3.225	4.049	5.072	6.341	7.911	9.850	15.18
25	2.666	3.386	4.292	5.427	6.848	8.623	10.83	17.00
30	3.243	4.322	5.743	7.612	10.06	13.27	17.45	29.96
40	4.801	7.040	10.29	14.97	21.72	31.41	45.26	93.05

Future Value of Annuity of $1

Periods	4%	5%	6%	7%	8%	9%	10%	12%
1	1.000	1.000	1.000	1.000	1.000	1.000	1.000	1.000
2	2.040	2.050	2.060	2.070	2.080	2.090	2.100	2.120
3	3.122	3.153	3.184	3.215	3.246	3.278	3.310	3.374
4	4.246	4.310	4.375	4.440	4.506	4.573	4.641	4.779
5	5.416	5.526	5.637	5.751	5.867	5.985	6.105	6.353
6	6.633	6.802	6.975	7.153	7.336	7.523	7.716	8.115
7	7.898	8.142	8.394	8.654	8.923	9.200	9.487	10.09
8	9.214	9.549	9.897	10.26	10.64	11.03	11.44	12.30
9	10.58	11.03	11.49	11.98	12.49	13.02	13.58	14.78
10	12.01	12.58	13.18	13.82	14.49	15.19	15.94	17.55
11	13.49	14.21	14.97	15.78	16.65	17.56	18.53	20.65
12	15.03	15.92	16.87	17.89	18.98	20.14	21.38	24.13
13	16.63	17.71	18.88	20.14	21.50	22.95	24.52	28.03
14	18.29	19.60	21.02	22.55	24.21	26.02	27.98	32.39
15	20.02	21.58	23.28	25.13	27.15	29.36	31.77	37.28
16	21.82	23.66	25.67	27.89	30.32	33.00	35.95	42.75
17	23.70	25.84	28.21	30.84	33.75	36.97	40.54	48.88
18	25.65	28.13	30.91	34.00	37.45	41.30	45.60	55.75
19	27.67	30.54	33.76	37.38	41.45	46.02	51.16	63.44
20	29.78	33.07	36.79	41.00	45.76	51.16	57.28	72.05
21	31.97	35.72	39.99	44.87	50.42	56.76	64.00	81.70
22	34.25	38.51	43.39	49.01	55.46	62.87	71.40	92.50
23	36.62	41.43	47.00	53.44	60.89	69.53	79.54	104.6
24	39.08	44.50	50.82	58.18	66.76	76.79	88.50	118.2
25	41.65	47.73	54.86	63.25	73.11	84.70	98.35	133.3
30	56.08	66.44	79.06	94.46	113.3	136.3	164.5	241.3
40	95.03	120.8	154.8	199.6	259.1	337.9	442.6	767.1

Index

U

V

W

Y

Z